Introduction to Forensic and Criminal Psychology

Introduction to Forensic and Criminal Psychology

6th Edition

Dennis Howitt Loughborough University

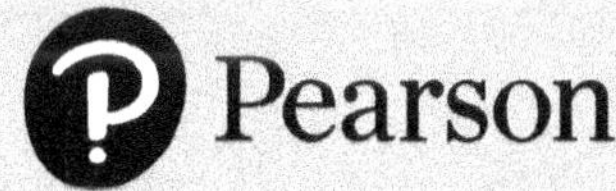

Harlow, England • London • New York • Boston • San Francisco • Toronto • Sydney • Dubai • Singapore • Hong Kong
Tokyo • Seoul • Taipei • New Delhi • Cape Town • São Paulo • Mexico City • Madrid • Amsterdam • Munich • Paris • Milan

Pearson Education Limited
KAO Two
KAO Park
Harlow CM17 9NA
United Kingdom
Tel: +44 (0)1279 623623
Web: www.pearson.com/uk

First published 2002 (print)
Second edition published 2006 (print)
Third edition published 2009 (print)
Fourth edition published 2011 (print)
Fifth edition published 2015 (print and electronic)
Sixth edition published 2018 (print and electronic)

ISBN: 978-1-292-18716-7 (print)
978-1-292-18719-8 (PDF)
978-1-292-18720-4 (ePub)

British Library Cataloguing-in-Publication Data
A catalogue record for the print edition is available from the British Library

Library of Congress Cataloging-in-Publication Data

Names: Howitt, Dennis, author.
Title: Introduction to forensic and criminal psychology / Dennis Howitt, Loughborough University.
Description: 6th Edition. | New York : Pearson, [2018] | Revised edition of the author's Introduction to forensic and criminal psychology, 2015.
Identifiers: LCCN 2017047126| ISBN 9781292187167 (print) | ISBN 9781292187198 (PDF) | ISBN 9781292187204 (epub)
Subjects: LCSH: Criminal psychology. | Forensic psychology.
Classification: LCC HV6080 .H69 2018 | DDC 364.3--dc23
LC record available at https://lccn.loc.gov/2017047126

10 9 8 7 6 5 4 3 2 1
22 21 20 19 18

Image on cover and chapter titles © DigitalVision Vectors/korhankaracan/Getty Images
Print edition typeset in 9.5/12 pt Times LT Pro by iEnergizer Aptara®, Ltd.

NOTE THAT ANY PAGE CROSS REFERENCES REFER TO THE PRINT EDITION

To the continued memory of Professor Marie Jahoda who died in 2001. I have a big personal debt. Not only did she let me study on the psychology degree course she had set up at Brunel University, but also she showed me that some things in life are worth getting angry about.

Brief contents

Contents

List of figures, tables and boxes

Figures

Tables

Boxes

Preface

The sixth edition of *Introduction to Forensic and Criminal Psychology* caused me to revise a lot of the material which had built up through previous editions. The main reason is that forensic and criminal psychology as an area of research is now substantial and well-established. Just what underlies my thinking when preparing a new edition? Most important is my intention to present forensic and criminal psychology as a vigorous, developing discipline. Forensic and criminal psychology is not simply a compendium of settled facts. Despite its still relatively short history, like other disciplines, it gradually develops, building on earlier achievements. It is important to capture this so that the reader can sense this progression. This is not entirely an orderly, even and predictable process. Ideas in some fields of research have changed markedly – even reversing – since the early editions of this book. These developments exemplify not a series of errors but the way in which disciplines advance. We can see this both in the short term and the long term. It should also be possible to spot the unevenness of this progress. In its simplest form, over the various editions once-hot topics have gradually received less attention and Cinderella topics have blossomed markedly. At its most mundane, this means that some chapters have been updated with lots of new material, while a very few have changed little. No doubt there will be a reversal of the fortunes of some of these in future years. Nevertheless, some traditional topics have been retained simply because they were important in the early days of the discipline. This is particularly the case with FBI-style offender profiling.

One big change is that many of the pioneers of the revival of forensic and criminal psychology in the 1970s and 1980s are retiring to be replaced by second- and third-generation researchers. I have tried to anticipate change as far as is possible – the new directions in which research is going. Just what is likely to be of future significance? I have lost count of the number of times that I have been struck by the newness of the ideas of young researchers coming into the field. It is only right that the text highlights as many of these as possible.

I am pernickety about contextualising research. Because legal and criminal justice systems are not the same in different parts of the world, we should acknowledge this fact. It is important to understand just what this variation is. This cannot be done by simply ignoring context – as has so frequently been done in the parent discipline, psychology. On the contrary, I would argue that the context of the research is integral to a full appreciation of the research. So throughout the book it should generally be clear just where in the world the research was carried out. This should be informative but is never an excuse for neglecting the research. That the research was done, say, in Poland or Australia does not mean that it has no relevance to the United Kingdom. But its relevance will always need to be considered. Forensic and criminal psychology is international in its nature and textbooks ought to reflect this.

The question of the amount of detail to include is a complex matter. I firmly believe that sufficient detail should be provided to enable the reader to do something with the material apart from merely citing it. The stimulus to thought lies in the detail provided. There are many textbooks which are structured around a commentary or linking text bolstered by numerous citations of the literature, with no clear relationship between the two. Some academic writing, if not a great deal, is like that. This imposes severe limits on what the student can learn and also constrains the critical thinking which academics cherish. It is impossible to form an opinion on something one has only read a sentence about. My preference is to give the reader something to think about and possibly question. Just how does a particular research study lead to a particular conclusion and is this the only possible conclusion? How did this research develop from previous research? How does this research lead to future research? The questions which the reader should be asking are much more obvious when a text provides material to get one's teeth into. Of course, the text asks critical questions where these need to be addressed – especially because they are part of a debate among professionals in the field. When deciding whether to include a new piece of research, the fundamental criterion is whether it introduces a significant new idea or question. In what way does the research change the way that we look at things? In what way does the new work place established wisdom on the back foot? That I rely heavily on the judgement of others when making my decisions is not only self-evident but also unavoidable. What the social network of forensic and criminal psychologists collectively judge to be important is one way of defining what the discipline is, after all. I also consciously prioritise theory in the text for much the same reason. Theory which synthesises what has gone before helps the text tell a coherent story. Often the theories, in themselves, are not fully testable in the empiricist tradition, but they do have something to say and they have to say it about a substantial chunk of research. Similarly, modern ways of synthesising research findings such as the systematic review and meta-analysis are integral to the presentation of research findings in the text. One reason is the impossibility of incorporating the vast number of research studies into the text without the compact summaries which meta-analysis, for example, provides. Of course, there are problems with systematic reviews and meta-analyses but they point in directions which might otherwise have been obscured by the sheer amount of the evidence. Anyway, they are part and parcel of modern research and need to be included if only for that reason alone. Researchers refer to them and use them a lot. Better get used to them.

All of this is very different from the situation when I was a student. My first real contact with the criminal justice system was the six months I spent at Wakefield Prison, in Yorkshire. My strongest recollection of this period was the emerging realisation that, for the most part, the men there seemed like ordinary men despite the fact that they were incestuous fathers or killers or had committed some other unfathomable crime. Nobody at university, staff or student, shared my interest in the field of crime and I had no idea of how my fumbling research interest could be turned into good psychology. Sex offenders fascinated me and I tried to research incestuous fathers but this was not a serious topic for research in the prevailing ethos of those days. A few years on and the sexual abuse of children became a massive area for research in several disciplines. Perhaps I could have been responsible for that, but I was not. The boat was missed. Others, a little later, had much better ideas of what were the important things to think about, research and practise. But the field of forensic and criminal psychology has, nevertheless, been a stimulus to my own work and its massive development over the years a delight to watch. Psychology students today who study forensic and criminal psychology are exposed to the power of research and theory in creating understanding of one of the fundamental institutions of the state – the criminal justice system.

Dennis Howitt

Author's acknowledgements

A great deal happens before a manuscript is started and after it is finished to turn the typescript into a book. This involves the expertise and effort of a number of people who I would like to express my appreciation to. Not everyone can be named but the following are of particular importance. First of all, Janey Webb as Portfolio Manager was responsible for commissioning this new edition and seeking knowledgeable opinion about its content. It is always stimulating to work with Janey. The production side of the process was the seemingly seamless work of Melanie Carter (Content Producer), Jennifer Sargunar (Managing Content Producer) and for Aptara, Vinay Agnihotri (Project Manager). Not only do they do their work brilliantly but they made life much easier for me.

There are two others to mention. Kelly Miller was responsible for both the cover and the text design. Her work makes the book the attractive thing in your hands but, more importantly, adds greatly to its readability. Finally, Antonia Maxwell was responsible for turning my manuscript into Kelly's text design. But she did far more than that and did me the great service of proof reading the material at the same time. It is difficult to say in words just how reassuring a good copy editor and proof reader are to an author. Antonia more than fulfilled all of my hopes in that regard.

So thank you to all of these and the many unnamed others.

Dennis Howitt

Publisher's acknowledgements

We are grateful to the following for permission to reproduce copyright material:

Figures

Figure 3.1 from *Psychology and Crime: Myths and Reality*, Harlow: Longman (Ainsworth, P.B. 2000) Copyright © Pearson Education Ltd., used by permission.; Figure 3.3 adapted from Fear of crime and criminal victimization, *The British Journal of Criminology*, 38(3), pp. 473–84 (Winkel, F.W. 1998), Oxford University Press (OUP) (UK) (English Hymnal Company).; Figure 5.3 from H.J. Eysenck in Fagin's kitchen: the return to biological theory in 20th-century criminology, *History of the Human Sciences*, 19, pp. 37–56 (Rafter, N.H. 2006), used by permission.; Figure 6.2 from The development of children's orientations toward a moral order: I. Sequence in the development of moral thought, *Vita Humana*, 6, pp. 11–33 (Kohlberg, L. 1963), S. Karger AG, Basel, used by permission.; Figure 6.3 adapted from Physically aggressive boys from ages 6 to 12: family background, parenting behavior, and prediction of delinquency, *Journal of Consulting and Clinical Psychology*, 62(5), pp. 104–52 (Haapasalo, J. and Tremblay, R.E. 1994), Copyright © American Psychological Association. Reprinted with permission.; Figure 6.6 after Bullying and delinquency: The mediating role of anger, *Personality and Individual Differences*, 48, 391–6. (Sigfusdottir, I.D., Gudjonsson, G.H. and Sigurdsson, J.F. 2010); Figure 7.2 after *Diagnostic and Statistical Manual of Mental Disorders* 4th ed., American Psychiatric Association (2000) Washington, DC: APA.; Figure 7.3 after The statistical association between drug misuse and crime: A meta-analysis, *Aggression and Violent Behavior*, 13(2), pp. 107–18 (Bennett, T., Holloway, K. and Farrington, D. 2008); Figure 8.6 from Multiple murder: a review, The British Journal of Criminology, 34(1), pp. 1–14 (Gresswell, D.M. and Hollin. C.R. 1994), Oxford University Press (OUP) (UK) (English Hymnal Company); Figure 9.2 after *A General Theory of Crime Stanford*, Stanford University Press (Gottfredson, M.R. and Hirschi, T. 1990); Figure 12.1 from Differentiation of international terrorism: attack as threat, means, and violence, *Journal of Investigative Psychology and Offender Profiling*, 4, pp. 131–45 (Yokota, K., Watanabe, K., Wachi, T., Hoshino, A., Sato, A. and Fujita, G. 2007), © John Wiley and Sons 2007; Figure 12.2 from Life story accounts of left wing terrorists in India, *Journal of Investigative Psychology and Offender Profiling*, 2, pp. 69–86 (Sarangi, S. and Alison, L. 2005), © John Wiley and Sons 2005; Figure 12.4 from Role playing: applications in hostage and crisis negotiations skills training, *Behaviour Modification*, 32(2), pp. 248–63 (Van Hasselt, V.B., Romano, S.J. and Vecchi, G.M. 2008), Copyright © 2008 by Sage Publications, Author(s), Journal Title (volume number and issue number), pp. xx–xx, copyright © Year by (copyright holder). Reprinted by permission of SAGE Publications.; Figure 12.5 from Introducing the four-phase model of hostage negotiation, *Journal of Police Crisis Negotiations*, 9(2), pp. 119–33 (Madrigal, D.O., Bowman, D.R. and McClain, B.U. 2009), Introducing the four-phase model of hostage negotiation, Journal of Police Crisis Negotiations, 9(2), pp. 119–33 (Madrigal, D.O., Bowman, D.R. and McClain, B.U. 2009); Figure 13.1 after Effective CCTV and the challenge of constructing legitimate suspicion using remote visual images, *Journal of Investigative Psychology and Offender Profiling*, 4, 97–107 (Williams, D. 2007); Figure 13.3 after Eyewitness identification tests, *Legal and Criminological Psychology*, 15, pp. 77–96 (Brewer, N. and Palmer, M.A. 2010), © John Wiley and Sons 2010; Figure 15.6 from What works in offender profiling? A comparison of typological, thematic, and multivariate models, *Behavioral Sciences and the Law*, 27, pp. 507–29

(Goodwill, A.M., Alison, L.J. and Beech, A.R 2009), © John Wiley and Sons 2009; Figure 16.2 after Recovered memories of childhood sexual abuse: Current findings and their legal implications, *Legal and Criminological Psychology*, 13, pp. 165–76 (Geraerts, E., Raymaekers, L. and Merckelbach, H. 2008); Figure 17.2 after The Gudjonsson Confession Questionnaire-Revised (GCQ-R): Factor structure and its relationship with personality, *Personality and Individual Differences*, 27, pp. 953–68 (Gudjonsson, G.H. and Sigurdsson, J.F. 1999), Elsevier; Figure 17.4 from Custodial interrogation: What are the background factors associated with claims of false confession to police?, *Journal of Forensic Psychiatry and Psychology*, 18(2), pp. 266–75 (Gudjonsson, G.H., Sigurdsson, J.F., Asgeirsdottir, B.B. and Sigfusdottir, I.D. 2007), used by permission.; Figure 20.1 after *Forensic interviews of children in A. Memon and R. Bull (Eds), Handbook of the Psychology of Interviewing*, John Wiley & Sons (Lamb, M.E., Sternberg, K.J. and Orbach, Y. 1999) pp. 253–77, John Wiley & Sons; Figure 20.4 from Post-event information affects children's autobiographical memory after one year, *Law and Human Behaviour*, 33(4), pp. 344–55 (London, K., Bruck, M. and Melnyk, L.), Copyright © 2008, American Psychology-Law Society/ Division 41 of the American Psychological Association., used by permission of author.; Figure 23.6 from Dangerous decisions: a theoretical framework for understanding how judges assess credibility in the courtroom, *Legal and Criminological Psychology*, 14, pp. 119–34 (Porter, S. and ten Brinke, L. 2009), Figure 1, p. 126; Figure 24.2 from Juror selection: a comparison of two methods in several criminal cases, *Journal of Applied Social Psychology*, 10(1), pp. 86–99 (Horowitz, I.A. 1980), © John Wiley and Sons 1980.

Tables

Table 2.1 from Technical Report on Revised Population Estimates and NLSY79 Analysis Tables for the Pew Public Safety and Mobility Project, Harvard University (Pettit, B., Sykes, B. and Western, B. 2009), used by permission.; Table 2.3 after data from Kings College London, Department of Law (2010) and from van Dijk, van Kesteren and Smit (2007).; Table 3.1 after data from Van Dijk, J., van Kesteren, J. and Smit, P. (2007) 'Criminal Victimisation in International Perspective: Key findings from the 2004–2005 ICVS and EU ICS' Tilburg University: Wetenschappelijk Onderzoeken Documentatiecentrum. http://www.unicri.it/services/library_documentation/publications/icvs/publications/ICVS2004_05report.pdf; Table 14.1 after *Profiling Violent Crimes: An Investigative Tool*, Sage Publications (Holmes, R.M. and Holmes, S.T. 1996) Copyright © 1996; Table 25.1 after *Offender Rehabilitation and Treatment: Effective Programmes and Policies to Reduce Re-offending*, John Wiley & Sons, Ltd (Redondo, S., Sanchez-Meca, J. and Garrido, V. 2002).

Text

Quote 7. from It takes skills to take a car: perceptual and procedural expertise in carjacking, *Aggression and Violent Behavior*, 20, p. 22 (Topalli, V., Jacques, S., and Wright, R. 2015), http://www.sciencedirect.com/science/article/pii/S1359178914001268; Quote 19. from Statement validity analysis of 'The Jim Ragsdale story': implications for the Roswell incident, *Journal of Scientific Exploration*, 12(1), pp. 57–71 (Houran, J. and Porter, S. 1998), published by the Society for Scientific Exploration, www.scientificexploration.org ., used by permission.

Picture Credits

The publisher would like to thank the following for their kind permission to reproduce their photographs:

(Key: b-bottom; c-centre; l-left; r-right; t-top)

Getty Images: DigitalVision Vectors / korhankaracan 1t, 16t, 28t, 41t, 64t, 83t, 110t, 132t, 159t, 186t, 214t, 245t, 267t, 293t, 310t, 330t, 350t, 369t, 387t, 408t, 433t, 453t, 469t, 490t, 512t, 527t, 549t.

Cover images: *Front:* **Getty Images:** DigitalVision Vectors / korhankaracan

All other images © Pearson Education

Chapter 1

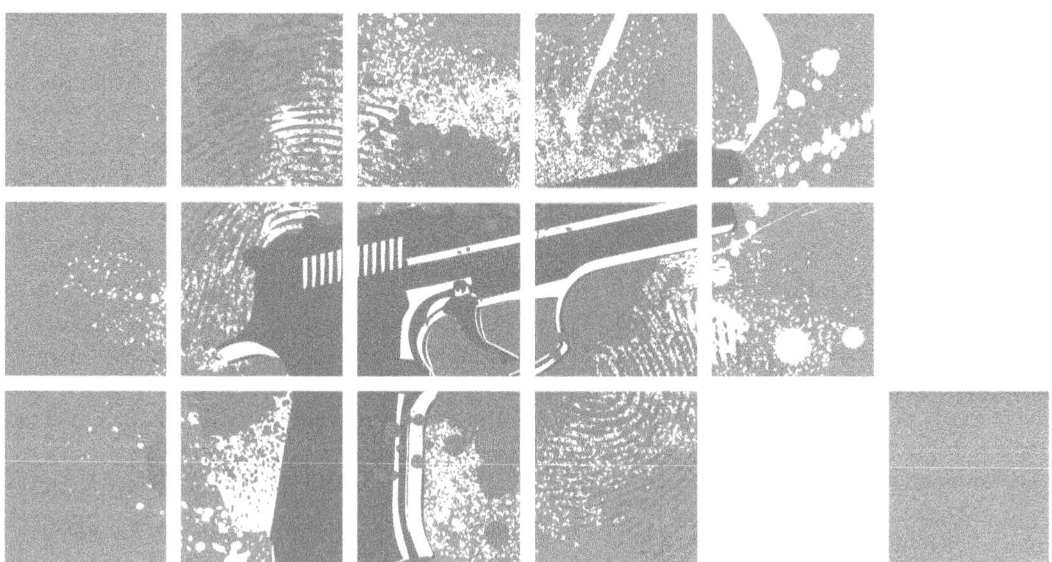

What is forensic and criminal psychology?

Overview

- Strictly speaking, forensic psychology is psychology applied to the work of courts of law. However, nowadays the term is used rather more generally to include all aspects of the criminal justice system.
- The term 'forensic and criminal psychology' is used in this book to encompass the very wide field of psychology applied to the law, legal system, victims and law breakers.
- Although both involve the understanding of human nature, the disciplines of psychology and the law can be incompatible. Even when lawyers and psychologists use identical words, they may intend very different meanings.
- Many practitioner-researchers work in the field of forensic and criminal psychology, and the twin skills of 'practitioner' and 'researcher' contribute substantially to progress in the field.
- Historical interpretations of forensic and criminal psychology depend much more on the finishing point than the starting point. Clinically based practitioners, for example, may see the history more in terms of how concepts of mental illness and other vulnerabilities have developed within the legal system and the need for experts in these fields to advise the court. On the other hand, academic psychologists may see the history as lying in the work of European and US academics around the start of the twentieth century.
- Interest in forensic and criminal psychology was at best spasmodic and minimal until the late twentieth century when growth became rapid. Its history can be traced back several centuries to when crucial legal changes occurred which demanded psychological expertise.
- Forensic and criminal psychology now constitutes an important branch of modern psychology and benefits greatly from developments across the whole world. It unites psychologists from a variety of fields of psychology, though it can now be regarded as a specialism in its own right.

Introduction

As with many aspects of psychology, providing a concise definition of *forensic and criminal psychology* can be problematic. Forensic psychology literally is psychology to do with courts of law. The words 'forensic' and 'forum' have the same Latin origins. A 'forum' is merely a room for public debate, such as a court of law, hence the word 'forensic'. Criminal psychology is easier to define since it is mainly to do with psychological aspects of criminal behaviour, such as the origins and development of criminality. Defining forensic psychology is problematic since it is applied far more widely than courts of law and includes all aspects of the criminal justice system, including prisons and policing. The law deals with virtually every aspect of life and forensic and criminal psychology reflects this diversity. In court it is likely that psychologists, no matter what their specialism, will be asked to provide expert psychological evidence on all sorts of matters. Which begs the question of when is and when is not a psychologist a forensic and criminal psychologist? Currently, many psychologists work primarily in the criminal justice system (i.e. police, criminal courts and prisons). Should they all be classified as forensic psychologists?

Definitions of terms like 'forensic psychology' have changed somewhat over the years. For example, in the 1980s and 1990s when the field was beginning its rapid expansion, some influential psychologists defined forensic psychology in terms of the professional activities of practitioners working primarily or almost exclusively in law courts. Gudjonsson and Haward (1998) were proponents of such a viewpoint when they defined 'forensic psychology' as:

> . . . that branch of applied psychology which is concerned with the collection, examination and presentation of evidence for judicial purposes. (p. 1)

Crucial to this definition is the use of the terms 'evidence' and 'judicial'. Whether or not they intended this, Gudjonsson and Haward appear to limit forensic psychology to legal evidence for the use of lawyers and judges. Moreover, the phrase 'judicial purposes' seems to be conceived no more widely than the purposes of courts of law. Others at the same time also defined forensic psychology as referring to the work of psychologists working in close collaboration with officials of the court:

> [forensic psychology is] the provision of psychological information for the purpose of facilitating a legal decision.
>
> (Blackburn, 1996: 7)

These are narrow and specific definitions – nowadays a broader approach is taken. Such narrow definitions exclude much of the criminal justice system of which the courts are just part – and make no reference to other settings such as prisons and the police service. The work of psychologists in such settings is clearly relevant to courts of law, though they may only rarely, if ever, work directly in courts. Currently, forensic psychology is defined in terms of activities beyond courts of law. For example, the British Psychological Society extends the definition to include much of the criminal justice system beyond courts of law. Indeed, the British Psychological Society does not mention courts of law currently:

> Forensic psychology deals with the psychological aspects of legal processes, including applying theory to criminal investigations, understanding psychological problems associated with criminal behaviour, and the treatment of criminals.
>
> British Psychological Society (2017)

In much the same way, the Australian Psychological Society defines forensic psychology such that the focus is not primarily on courts of law but much wider – for example the areas of prison and other forms of correction, the police, and so forth:

> Forensic psychologists are scientist-practitioners. They apply psychological knowledge, theory and skills to the understanding and functioning of legal and criminal justice systems, and to conducting research in relevant areas. They often work in criminal, civil and family legal contexts and provide services for litigants, perpetrators, victims, and personnel of government and community organisations.
>
> Australian Psychological Society (2017)

Although its language is not quite so direct, the American Psychological Association takes a fairly similar stance:

> . . . forensic psychology refers to professional practice by any psychologist working within any sub-discipline of psychology (e.g., clinical, developmental, social, cognitive) when applying the scientific, technical, or specialized knowledge of psychology to the law to assist in addressing legal, contractual, and administrative matters.
>
> American Psychological Association (2017)

The value of these wider definitions of forensic psychology is obvious when one considers the sorts of work that psychologists do. Wrightsman (2001) mentions the following as some of the things done by psychologists in the context of the law:

- A mediator psychologist employed by a law firm to mediate between parties in an attempt to resolve legal disputes.
- A social psychologist dealing with civil cases such as commercial litigation. The psychologist conducts surveys of roleplaying 'jurors' in order to assess what might work in a real trial.

- A counselling psychologist who works on the assessment of potentially violent behaviours for the US secret service. For example, threats of violence are often made to the national leaders – which ones are to be taken seriously?
- A correctional psychologist who assesses the competence of prisoners to stand trial and makes suggestions about possible treatments for particular offenders.
- A clinical psychologist in private practice. This psychologist works as a consultant to police departments.

The list deals solely with practitioners and does not mention researchers in the field of forensic psychology. In addition, it should be stressed that these examples are not very representative of the work of the majority of psychologists who claim the title.

Once one could find suggestions that the definition of forensic psychology lacked consensus (e.g. McGuire, 1997) or that the use of the term 'forensic' was disorderly and chaotic (Stanik, 1992). Currently, as we have seen, there seems to be much more consensus. Along with this, the organisational infrastructure of forensic psychology has become much more developed. It is important to differentiate between the *field of forensic psychology* and identifying *who should be entitled to call themselves forensic psychologists*. The first (establishing what forensic is) is essentially addressed by all of the definitions discussed so far. The question of who is qualified to call themselves a forensic psychologist needs to be approached in a different way. This involves identifying the nature of the skills and knowledge required by anyone working in the field, apart from a basic training in psychology itself. In the United Kingdom, it has been suggested that forensic psychologists (i.e. all chartered forensic psychologists) should possess the following knowledge and skills (DCLP Training Committee, 1994). The list would probably be much the same elsewhere in the world, though the precise mix of skills would vary according to the area of practice within the field of forensic psychology:

- An understanding of the conceptual basis of their work context in terms of:
  - the psychology relevant to the study of criminal behaviour;
  - the legal framework including the law and structure of the criminal justice system, for example, of the country in which they practise.
- An understanding of the achievements and potential achievements of the application of psychology to:
  - criminal investigation processes;
  - legal processes;
  - custodial processes;
  - treatment processes (for both offenders and victims).
- A sufficiently detailed understanding of the psychology relevant to the following individuals, including adults and children where appropriate:
  - offenders (whether or not mentally disordered);
  - victims;
  - witnesses;
  - investigators.
- An understanding of the practical aspects of forensic psychology in terms of the following:
  - different demands for assessment;
  - processes of investigation, prosecution and defence;
  - decision making in respect of innocence, guilt, sentencing, custody, treatment and rehabilitation;
  - approaches to assessment;
  - professional criteria for report production and giving of testimony.
- This is combined with an additional requirement of having had extensive practical experience in at least one area of forensic psychology (pp. 7–8).

Underlying this list one perhaps can discern the view that the education and training of all psychologists working in the forensic field needs to be broad, encompassing a wide range of knowledge, skills and abilities. The range and depth of the training of a forensic psychologist needs to be comprehensive – it is not enough to know the minimum to function on a day-to-day basis.

Defining *criminal psychology* in contrast is not so problematic. This is partly because it is not a title that is claimed by any significantly large or influential group of psychologists. Nevertheless, like forensic psychology, criminal psychology may be defined relatively narrowly or somewhat broadly. The narrow definition would merely suggest that it concerns all aspects of the psychology of the criminal. A difficulty with this is that it seems to concentrate solely on the offender. Does it or should it also include psychological aspects of the wider experience of the criminal, for example, in courts of law or prison? Criminality, as we shall see, is not a characteristic of individuals that can be separated meaningfully from the social context of crime and the criminal justice system. Thus the field of criminal psychology must be defined in terms of knowledge and skills which substantially overlap those of the forensic psychologist described above. Indeed, one might suggest that the main difference between the two is that forensic psychology may involve the civil law as well as the criminal law. The use of the phrase 'forensic and criminal psychology' in this book tacitly acknowledges problems in the definition of both 'forensic' and 'criminal psychology'. There is no rigid distinction between the two. Forensic psychology and criminal psychology are to be regarded as inseparable rather than a marriage of two distinct aspects of psychology.

Other terms sometimes used for this field of psychology include 'psychology and the law' and 'legal psychology'. These more clearly hint at an interface between the two disciplines and practices – psychology and the law. Again, there is some merit in a designation of this sort. In particular, it stresses the two disciplines in combination. The implication is that both lawyers and psychologists may be interested in similar issues but from their differing perspectives. While the terms suggest that researchers/practitioners should be knowledgeable about both psychology and the law, this is also a weakness. Very few researchers/practitioners are trained in both disciplines in depth. In recent years there has been a movement to define a field known as investigative psychology, which seems to embrace quite a substantial chunk of what forensic psychology covers. So topics such as eyewitness testimony and deception detection are included alongside the more statistical forms of profiling (Granhag and Vrij, 2010). Whether or not this term gains wider acceptance only time will decide.

Terms like 'psychology and the law' imply a comfortable relationship between the two. However, attempts at a marriage between psychology and the law have not been without their difficulties. Both psychologists and lawyers may have problems when engaging with each other's discipline. Psychology is not a compact discipline united by a single theory or approach – it is a broad church which psychologists themselves often find lacking in coherence. Clifford (1995) suggested that lawyers should be excused for regarding psychology as a 'bewildering confederacy' (p. 26). Eastman (2000) wrote of the two disciplines as if they were different countries – Legaland and Mentaland. These differ, as countries do, in terms of their culture, language, history and terrain. When the inhabitants of these two lands mix, things are difficult because they have big differences of purpose. Nevertheless, there are times when the people of Legaland need the help of people from Mentaland but Legaland language is confusing to the people of Mentaland – and vice versa. Legaland people are often more powerful and make it extremely obvious that, in their view, the ideas of Mentaland are secondary to those of Legaland. So, according to them, it is the people of Mentaland who need to make it abundantly clear that Mentaland ideas are sub-servient to those of Legaland and that Mentaland people will have to adjust their language. Mentaland people also sometimes need the people of Legaland to give them the authority for things they do. For example, social and public policy legislation may need to be tested by Legaland, then interpreted for the people of Mentaland. In this way, the people of Mentaland obtain extra tools to get on with their job.

For others, such as Carson (2011), ideas of the incompatibility of psychological thinking and legal thinking can be overstated. Although the two can differ to some extent in how they value different sorts of knowledge and argument, probably these differences are less than the general view of psychologists and lawyers might suggest. Too much emphasis is placed in forensic psychology, the argument goes, on the narrow focus of what happens in courts of law. This is to neglect the wider range of settings in which psychologists may have a lot to offer in collaborations with lawyers. For example, there might be a great deal to gain when psychologists and lawyers work together and promote legal reforms, both in terms of the contents of the law and the legal procedures through which the law is administered. In addition, civil and criminal cases both involve investigations and psychologists may have a lot to offer in terms of improving such investigations. That is, psychology and the law might make better bedfellows away from legal decision making in court.

BOX 1.1 Forensic psychology in action

The expert witness

Given that psychologists are experts in many different aspects of human nature and behaviour, it is not surprising that their knowledge is frequently applicable in court. The extent of their involvement is dependent on a number of factors. According to Groscup *et al.* (2002), a quarter of expert witnesses in American criminal appeal hearings were from the social and behavioural sciences. Different legal jurisdictions have different requirements of expert witnesses and certain expert evidence may not be admissible in all legal systems. An expert witness differs from any other witness in court since they are allowed to express opinions rather than simply report facts. The opinions of forensic and criminal psychologists will normally be supported by scientific evidence and they will be required to establish their scientific credentials. The expert witness should not offer evidence outside the range of their expertise. These matters are normally determined at the stage of the *voir dire* (usually described as a trial within a trial but essentially a preliminary review of matters related to the trial, such as jurors and evidence, before the trial proper begins) in the Anglo-American system. Different legal jurisdictions vary in terms of how the expert witness is employed. In the Anglo-American system, the adversarial system, this is normally the decision of the prosecution or the defence. Inquisitorial legal systems such as those common in Continental Europe (Stephenson, 1992) are likely to use experts employed by the court itself (Nijboer, 1995) and, furthermore, they will be regarded much as any other witness. Guidelines for expert witnesses are available (e.g. British Psychological Society, 2015).

The *Daubert* decision currently influences which 'experts' may be allowed to give evidence in American courts. The *Daubert* case was about a child, Jason Daubert, who was born with missing fingers and bones. His mother had taken an anti-morning-sickness drug and sued the manufacturers. 'Rules' designed to exclude 'junk' science were formulated. What is interesting is that the decision formulated what should be regarded as proper scientific methodology. That is, it should be based on the testing of hypotheses that are refutable. Furthermore, in assessing the admissibility of the expert evidence, attention should be paid to issues such as whether the research had been subject to review by others working in the field (Ainsworth, 1998). Perry (1997) lists *Daubert* criteria as including:

- whether the technique or theory is verifiable;
- whether the technique or theory is generally accepted within the scientific community;
- what the likelihood of error in the research study is.

This obviously causes problems for expertise that is not part of this model of science: for example, therapists giving evidence on the false memory syndrome in which there is a fierce debate between practitioners and academics (see Box 16.1).

In England and Wales, the main guidelines according to Nijboer (1995) are as follows (see also Crown Prosecution Service, 2014):

- Matters that the judge believes are within the capacity of the ordinary person – the juror – in terms of their knowledge and experience are not for comment by the expert witness.
- The expert witness cannot give evidence that 'usurps' the role of the judge and jury in connection with the principal issue with which the trial is concerned.
- Expert opinion is confined to matters that are admissible evidence.

A survey of American lawyers (including judges) investigated how mental health experts were selected to give evidence (Mossman and Kapp, 1998). Their academic writings and national reputation were rarely criteria – nor was the fee that they charged. Apart from knowledge in a specific area, the key criteria for selection were their communicative ability and local reputation. There may be reason to be concerned about the value of some expert testimony since there are many examples of what might be described as pseudo-science. Coles and Veiel (2001) took issue with the willingness of psychologist expert witnesses to reduce complex matters to fixed characteristics of the individual. So the idea of fitness to plead is regarded in the thinking of some psychologists as a characteristic of some individuals – that is, it is a characteristic of their personality. But the legal definition of fitness to plead (see Chapter 22) concerns whether an individual has the intellectual resources to contribute effectively to their own defence. Naturally, this means that fitness to plead evaluations need to take into account the complexity of the trial in question. Someone may be perfectly fit to plead where the trial is simple but unfit to plead in a complex trial. Furthermore, they may appear competent in one area but not in another area. An individual may be perfectly capable of communicating with their lawyer but unable to understand the purpose of the trial.

Researcher-practitioners

The concept of the 'scientist-practitioner' originated in the late 1940s among clinical psychologists seeking to improve both research and practice. Some argue that the synergy resulting from combining research and practice has not been achieved (Douglas, Cox and Webster, 1999), though this may be disputed on the basis of the extensive research contributed currently by forensic psychology practitioners. Historically and traditionally in psychology, researchers and practitioners were seen as at odds with each other – each side being dismissive of the contribution of the other. Academics criticised practitioners for their lack of knowledge of the pertinent research; practitioners criticised academics for their ignorance of clinical needs and practices. Such views seem extremely old-fashioned and inaccurate from a modern perspective. More and more, employers of forensic and criminal psychologists require that practitioners should participate fully in a research-led discipline. Practitioners do not just apply psychological knowledge; they are among those who create it. Appropriately for an applied discipline such as forensic and criminal psychology, the usual and preferred term is researcher-practitioner rather than scientist-practitioner.

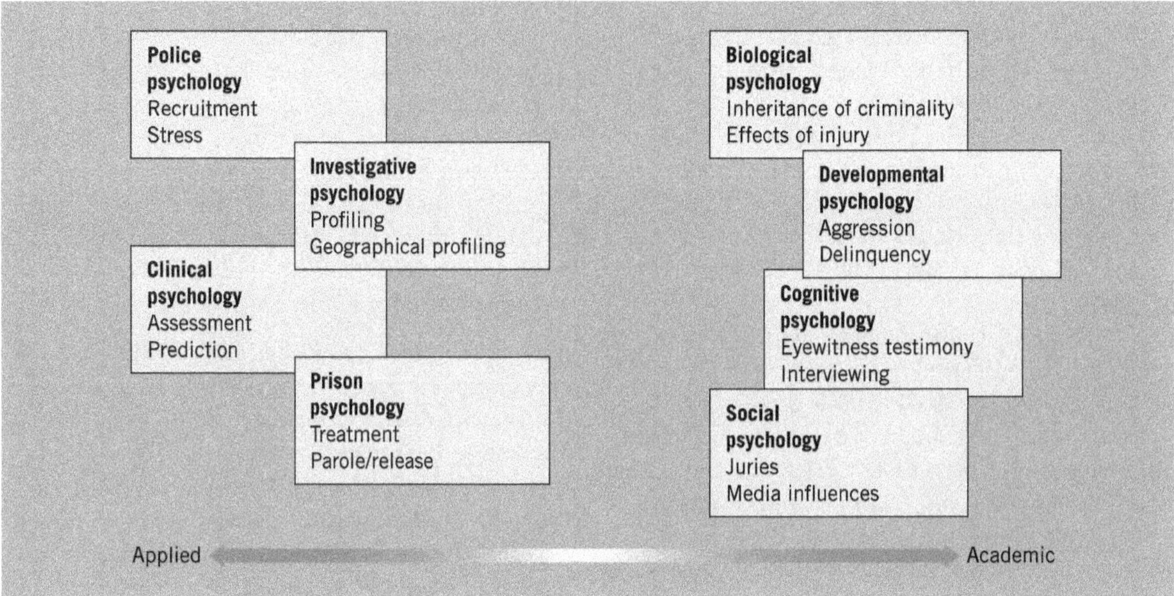

Figure 1.1 Major components of forensic psychology

The latter reflects a view of psychology which many practitioners have difficulty relating to. For some, the purpose of psychology is not to develop scientific laws of human behaviour but to ground the discipline in social reality through the effective use of empirical research. There is another phrase – *evidence-based practice* – which is increasingly used to describe an ideal relationship between practitioners in any discipline and research in that discipline. It means that practice should be based on what research has shown to be effective.

So in forensic and criminal psychology, the division between researcher and practitioner is breached. It is a generally accepted principle that training in both research and practice is crucial to effective practice. Practitioners who understand research methods well are much more likely to be able to incorporate the findings of other researchers into their therapies, assessments and when giving their professional advice to clients and colleagues. Furthermore, practitioners are usually in a good position to know what sorts of research are needed by them compared with academics, whose knowledge of practitioner requirements cannot be so direct. Indeed, academic researchers may have academic and theoretical priorities that are different from those of practitioners. There is nothing wrong with this. Many academic psychologists make important contributions despite lacking the practical experience and training of practitioners.

Figure 1.1 illustrates some of the major components of forensic and criminal psychology. Notice how widely they are drawn from the discipline of psychology. Also note the underlying dimension of applied research/practice as opposed to the academic. The distinction is not rigid but nevertheless must be considered as an essential component of the structure of the field (e.g. British Psychological Society, 2007/8; 2011).

History of forensic and criminal psychology

Many would argue that history is often self-serving in some way. History is written from the viewpoint of the teller and serves a purpose (Quinsey, 2009). It is almost inevitably partial in both meanings of the term. It is made up of accounts which are written through the lens of the present. American and European academics may give rather different versions of forensic and criminal psychology's history – each offering versions that stress the contribution of their traditions to the discipline. The history as written by a psychiatrist will be different from that of a psychologist, since it may ignore the contribution, for example, of cognitive psychology. And the history written by a lawyer will be different again. The self-serving nature of history cannot be escaped. Although the history of forensic and criminal psychology tends to be brief, the history of certain topics which are now considered aspects of forensic psychology is quite extensive. For example the history of fire-setting/pyromania (Umanath, Sarezky and Finger, 2011) and post-traumatic stress disorder (Miller, 2012) is substantial. However, many of the important contributions are by psychiatrists and medical professionals rather than psychologists. It is probably the case that most – if not all – accounts of the history of forensic and criminal psychology are more to do with the experimental/laboratory tradition in psychology than anything else. Perhaps this reflects a bias towards the academic rather than practice.

With caveats such as these, it is nevertheless worthwhile to highlight some of the features that a definitive history of forensic and criminal psychology should incorporate. Some important events are to be found in Figure 1.2. Some important events in the background of forensic and criminal psychology occurred long before psychology emerged in broadly its modern form towards the end of the nineteenth century.

Changes in the law

A number of crucial developments in the law that occurred centuries before modern psychology was founded were vital to the development of forensic and criminal psychology. These, in particular, were to do with legal principles concerning the mentally ill and other vulnerable individuals. The earliest recorded legal principle about the mentally ill was that of Marcus Aurelius in AD 179 (Spruit, 1998; Quinsey, 2009) when dealing with a question posed by a Roman governor. Aurelius suggested that the governor should not be concerned about punishing an offender

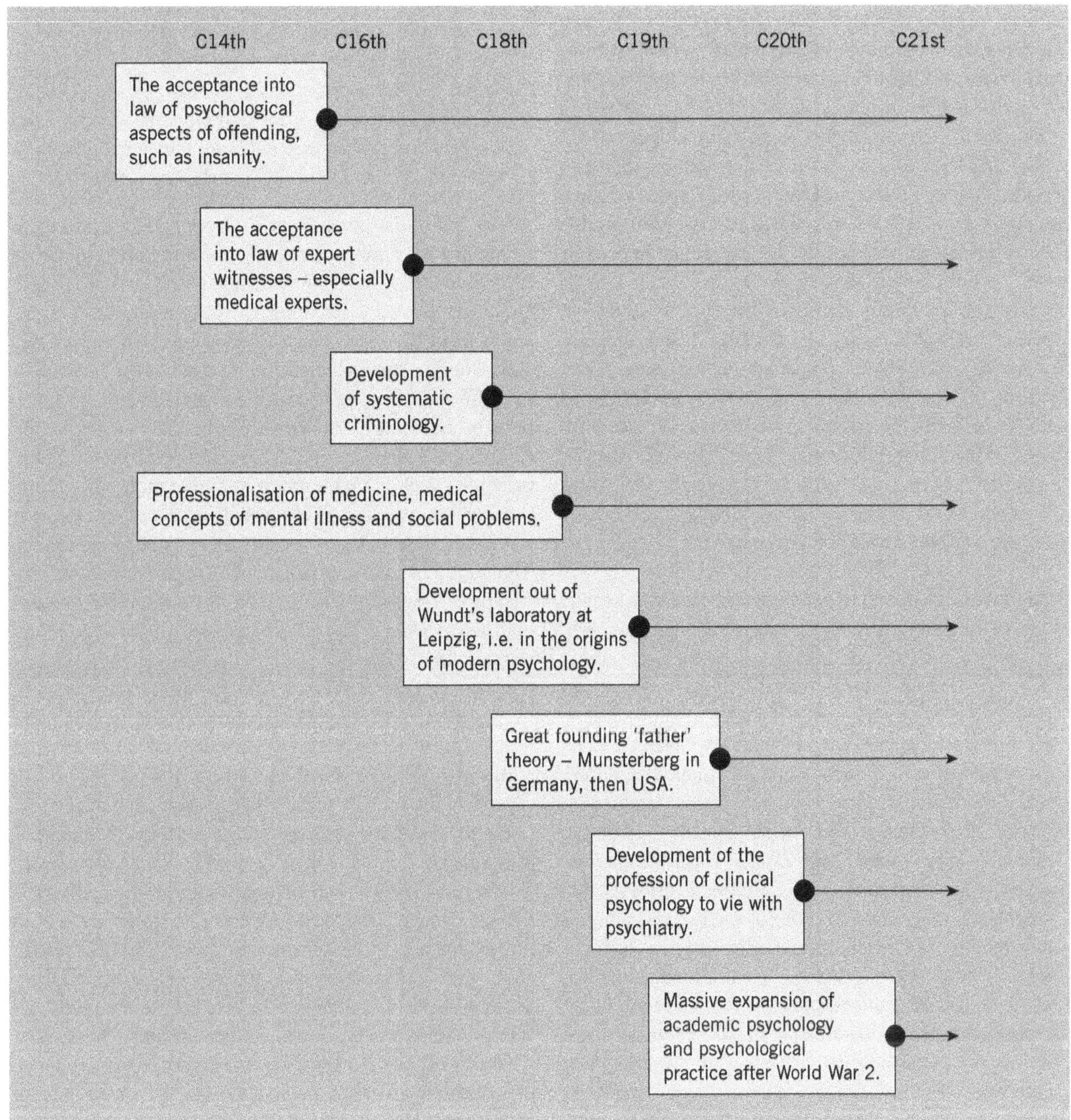

Figure 1.2 Different components in the historical origins of forensic and criminal psychology

who had murdered his own mother. The man was permanently insane and there was no evidence that he was feigning his disturbance. According to Aurelius, insanity itself was sufficient punishment. But there was a need for the man to be kept in custody for his own protection and that of the community. Had the crime occurred during a period of sanity, then the full punishment would have been appropriate.

Madness was not always an issue in law, although it was a consideration as long ago as Roman times, as we have just seen. Before the thirteenth century, in English law, the doing of something evil was sufficient to establish the individual liable for that evil. The offender's mental condition was simply irrelevant to sentencing (Eigen, 2004). In 1230, Bartholomaeus Anglicus, a professor of theology in France, published *De Proprietatibus Rerum*. This contained descriptions of a wide variety of conditions such as *melancholie*. In England and Wales, legal categories classifying the mentally disordered first appeared in the *Statutes at Large* in 1324. These distinguished between lunatics and idiots. In both cases the property belonging to the individual could be transferred to the Crown or some entrusted person. The difference was that the idiot lost his or her property forever but the lunatic might have their property returned when they recovered from their lunacy. Thus the law enshrined the possibility that some mental disorders were temporary or curable. Legal changes allowing the detention of dangerous lunatics emerged at about the middle of the eighteenth century. Such persons could be held in workhouses, prisons or madhouses. By the end of the nineteenth century, legal categories such as idiot, insane, lunatic and person of unsound mind were well entrenched (Forrester, Ozdural, Muthukumaraswamy and Carroll, 2008). Other notable points are:

- The first English trial in which the accused was acquitted on the basis of insanity occurred as early as 1505. However, not until the eighteenth century did courts begin to develop criteria to assess insanity. The criterion developed at this time essentially held that insane persons are equivalent to wild beasts – which, of course, are not capable of committing crime. Such a definition was a difficult one to meet but nevertheless required no degree of psychiatric knowledge to apply – ordinary members of the jury could identify such an extreme case as this. So expert advice from the medical profession, such as it would have been at this time, was not needed. Insanity became an important issue in the nineteenth century when deluded reasoning became part of the legal test of insanity. Such a definition required the advice of experts much more than the wild beast criterion had. In the nineteenth century the *M'Naughten* case (see Chapter 22) and numerous books about the nature of insanity stressed the belief that a person suffering from a disease of the mind and reasoning should not be held responsible for their crime. Expert witnesses were required with increasing frequency and, as a consequence, lawyers became ever more concerned that evidence of experts might replace the jury in deciding the verdict.
- The notion that some individuals were unfit because of their limited intellectual ability had entered into legal considerations emerged quite early historically during the fourteenth century in England. The issue of competence to stand trial (see Chapter 22) was a development originating in eighteenth-century English common law (i.e. law not laid down by statutes but essentially by tradition). The basic idea was that the defendant must be competent at certain minimal levels in order to have a fair trial (Roesch, Ogloff and Golding, 1993). Although competence is a legal matter and one to be defined by the courts and not psychologists or psychiatrists, the emergence of the expert witness encouraged the eventual use of medical and other practitioners to comment on the mental state of the defendant.

All of this boils down to the question of the extent to which mentally impaired people (and also children) can be held responsible for their criminal acts and punished. Umanath, Sarezky and Finger (2011) review this especially from the viewpoint of somnambulism and crimes committed in such a state of night walking or sleepwalking. Umanath *et al.* see formal law dealing with somnambulism beginning at the latest in 1313. At this time, the Council of Vienne resolved that a sleepwalker, an insane person, or a child ought not to be found guilty of a crime if he or she attacked or murdered someone while in that state. Other examples of such thinking can be found in the declaration of the Spanish canonist Diego de Covarrubias, Bishop of Segovia, who claimed in the sixteenth century that sleepwalkers who killed committed no sin so long as they did not know of the risk that they might kill when they were asleep. Others developed similar principles in the seventeenth century: Sir George Mackenzie, a Scottish legal scholar, compared a sleepwalker to an infant and reserved punishment for sleepwalkers who had previously shown enmity for their victim. Sleepwalkers, somnambulists or nightwalkers, then, were not seen generally as sinning if they killed or injured in their sleep without sign of malice.

The first known trial of a somnambulistic killer was that of Colonel Cheyney Culpepper in 1686 at the Old Bailey in London. Fifty witnesses were lined up to testify about the strange deeds that the colonel had previously done in his sleep! Although the jury found him guilty, he was pardoned by the crown almost straight away. The Albert Tirrell case in 1846 was the first successful defence of a sleepwalking killer in the USA. It used what is known as the automatism defence – the idea that the sleepwalker is unaware of what they are doing.

Quinsey (2009) makes the observation that there has been little progress in concepts of how to deal with crimes committed by the mentally ill over the centuries. This could be broadened to make a more general point. Progress in forensic and criminal psychology cannot be described as being equal on all fronts. Some areas of research have progressed enormously and have been studied in depth for many years. Yet there are other topics which have scarcely been contemplated, let alone tackled systematically in any detail. Throughout this book you will find examples of impressive research traditions alongside much briefer discussions of topics which are only just emerging.

Links with the parent discipline

It is not possible to separate developments in forensic and criminal psychology from developments in psychology in general. To fully study the history of forensic and criminal psychology, it is necessary to understand the changes that have occurred in psychology in general as no branch of psychology has been unaffected. The following examples illustrate this:

- The new emphasis in social psychology on group dynamics in the 1960s was associated with a rise in interest in research on the dynamics of decision making in juries.
- Many of the psychological assessment techniques, tests and measurements used especially in the assessment of offenders for forensic purposes have their origins in other fields of psychology. In particular, their availability to forensic and criminal psychologists is contingent on developments in academic, educational and clinical psychology.
- The study of memory has been common in psychology since the pioneering work of Ebbinghaus. Obviously, the psychology of memory is very relevant to eye-witness testimony. Not until the 1960s and later did psychologists properly begin to address the important issue of memory for real events. This set the scene for expansion of research into eyewitness testimony beginning in the 1970s.

Social change

Both the law and psychology are responsive to changes in society in general, as can be seen in the following examples:

- Child sexual abuse: although nowadays concern about child sexual abuse (and rape and domestic violence for that matter) is extensive and ingrained, this has not always been the case. The history of the radical change in the way in which professionals regard child sexual abuse victims makes fascinating reading (e.g. Myers *et al.*, 1999). Dominant themes in early writings on sexual abuse contrast markedly with modern thinking. For example, a century or so ago, children were regarded as being the instigators of their own victimisation, mothers were held to blame for the fate of their children and sexual abuse was perceived as rare. The massive social impact of feminism during the 1960s and 1970s brought concern about a number of issues. Among them was child sexual abuse, which was found to be more common than had been previously thought. This interest brought to forensic and criminal psychology a need to understand and deal better with matters such as the effects of child sexual abuse, the treatment of abusers and the ability of children to give evidence in court. This does not mean that prosecutions for sexual offences against children were unknown prior to this. In the United States at least, they increased steadily during the twentieth century, although Myers *et al.* describe the rates as modest by modern standards. It is worth noting that countries may experience apparently different patterns. For example, Sjogren (2000) claimed that the rates of child sexual abuse in Sweden were as high in the 1950s and 1960s, before concern about sexual abuse rose due to American influences, as they were in the 1990s.
- Government policy: the work of forensic and criminal psychologists is materially shaped by government policy on any number of matters. For instance, government policy on the treatment of offenders (say, to increase the numbers going to prison and the length of their sentences) is critical. Similarly, the issue of the provision of psychiatric/psychological care (say, increasing the numbers managed within the community) profoundly changes the nature of the work of practitioners. Furthermore, changes in research priorities may well be contingent on such developments as researchers often tend to look for funding where there is political interest and governments fund research into changes they are planning.

We can now turn from the broad societal and legal framework in which forensic and criminal psychology developed to consider some of the key events in the history of research and theory in forensic and criminal psychology.

Early work in the disciplines of criminology, sociology and psychiatry

The intellectual origins of forensic and criminal psychology are to be found in related disciplines, especially criminology, sociology and psychology. Indeed, some of the earliest criminological contributions seem unquestionably psychological in nature. There are a number of aspects to consider:

- One of the first examples of forensic and criminal psychology is in the work of Italian Cesare Beccaria in the late 1700s. Beccaria regarded humans as possessing free will, which is subject to the principles of pleasure and pain. This is an 'economic' model in which we are seen to evaluate the costs and benefits (pleasures and pains) of our actions prior to engaging in them, such as when we decide to commit a crime. He believed that punishment for criminal behaviour is not desirable in itself, but is important in order to deter people from crime. Thus punishment needs to be proportionate or commensurate with the crime – and inflicted as a means of deterrence. It is argued by some that Beccaria's ideas led directly to the abandonment of barbaric torture of prisoners in a number of European countries (McGuire, 2000).
- The publication of the first official crime statistics in France in 1827 was a crucial development. Statistical data allowed the development of investigations into the geographical distribution or organisation of crime. This continues in criminology today, and geographical profiling of crime is important in areas of forensic and criminal psychology. The Frenchman André-Michel Guerry and the Belgian Adolphe Quetelet began the tradition of crime statistics. Modern computer applications have refined this approach enormously. It is now possible to study databases specifying the geographical locations of crime down to the household level.
- The idea of the biological roots of crime was an important late-nineteenth-century idea in the work of the Italian doctor Cesare Lombroso. He took groups of hardened criminals and carried out what might be called an anthropological study of their features. He compared the criminals' features with those of soldiers on whom he practised his medicine. Lombroso believed that certain structural anomalies of the skull were more common among criminals. These abnormalities, he said, were indications that criminals represented an earlier stage of evolution of humanity than the rest of society had achieved. According to Lombroso, criminal characteristics include a lack of skull-space for brain tissue, pronounced structural differences between the two sides of the skull, ears that stick out, a bent or flat nose, colour blindness, left-handedness and a lack of muscular strength! The differences could be even more specific since different characteristics distinguished murderers from sex offenders. Murderers' eyes are bloodshot, cold and glassy, whereas the eyes of sex offenders glint. Lombroso is largely remembered for being wrong and few give his ideas any credence. For example, Lombroso's findings could not be replicated just a few years later in Britain by Charles Goring. Harrower (1998) argues that the observation that some criminals are mentally deficient is indirect support for Lombroso's point of view. Her idea is that in Lombroso's time biological defects, including mental deficiency, were seen as linked, though Goring's evidence was that criminals had low intelligence, not that they showed the cranial characteristics Lombroso claimed. Just to confirm how wrong the theory was, Lombroso claimed that it could be used even to explain the lack of criminality in women. It was not that women are socially more evolved than men. Quite the reverse. They were so backward in terms of human development that they had not evolved to the stage at which it was possible to be criminal!

European psychology's early contribution to forensic and criminal psychology

One of the earliest concepts related to forensic and criminal psychology was that of *kleptomania*. The term appears in modern dictionaries and has some popular currency today among the general public. Mathey, in 1816, coined the term *klopemania*, which means 'stealing insanity', whereas Marc, in 1840, used the term *kleptomania*, to mean exactly the same thing (Fullerton and Punj, 2004). The main characteristics of kleptomania for these early physicians were as follows:

- impulses to steal things of negligible value;
- economic necessity was not a reason;
- the theft was accompanied by an elated state of exhilaration together with relief from feelings of tension;
- kleptomaniacs tend to be women.

Perhaps not surprisingly, given its emergence at a time of great economic growth in terms of industrialisation and commerce, the concept was popular throughout the nineteenth and twentieth centuries. Its explanation, though, was difficult since kleptomania was not fuelled by economic necessity – the things stolen were of little economic worth – and frequently the thief would not even unwrap the stolen item or use it. The motive was sexual, according to some, and the psychoanalytical psychiatrist Wilhelm Stekel held it to be suppressed sexual desire (Stekel, 1911). Women, it was argued, suffered from penis envy (envy at not possessing a penis) so might seek to replace their missing penis through symbolic objects that they stole (Fenichel, 1933). Kleptomania is not an outmoded concept in the sense that it is a diagnostic category in the American Psychiatric Association's current *Diagnostic and Statistical Manual of Mental Disorders* (DSM-IV). It remains in DSM-V (see Box 21.1).

Early interest in lie detection through hidden emotions (an idea which relates directly to the modern work discussed in Chapter 19) can be found in the writings of Charles Darwin (1872) who suggested that an angry person can control their body movements but not the muscles of the face which are not under wilful control. These ideas reflect very much the approach to the detection of lies through facial expression offered by Paul Eckman in his theory (see Chapter 18). Anyone wishing to find further evidence of the British roots of forensic and criminal psychology could draw on the fact that Sir Francis Galton, Darwin's cousin, tried to find a word association test that would serve as a procedure for lie detection. In this, the truth assessor would say a word such as 'thief' and study the response from the 'suspect' (Matte, 2002).

More important was the development of modern psychology at the University of Leipzig in the late nineteenth century, which quickly led to an interest in forensic issues. Generally speaking, it is accepted that the origins of modern psychology lie in the establishment of the psychological laboratory at this university in 1875. This was part of the legacy of Wilhelm Wundt to psychology. Some refer to this as a convenient 'creation myth' for psychology, but it was a number of his students, colleagues and co-workers who took the initial steps in developing forensic and criminal psychology. Other influences include:

- Albert Von Schrenk-Nortzing (*c.* 1897): in 1896, Von Schrenk-Nortzing appeared at a Leipzig court in a role that some might describe as the first true forensic psychologist. His was early testimony into the effects of the media on matters relevant to the courtroom. He argued that witnesses at a murder trial confused their actual memories of events with the pre-trial publicity given to the event in the media. They were not able to distinguish between what they had witnessed and what they had read in the newspapers. Von Schrenk-Nortzing described this memory effect as 'retroactive memory falsification'. Related issues continue to be studied although the researchers do not necessarily concur with Von Schrenk-Nortzing – for example, Roberts and Blades (1995) asked whether children confuse television and real-life events. Their answer was that children as young as four years are good at identifying the source of their memories correctly. Significantly, at the lower age studied, children can be confused into making errors by the way they are questioned.
- J.M. Cattell (*c.* 1895) investigated using the techniques of laboratory experiments into human memory on the quality of eyewitness testimony. He was an American who returned to the United States to research forensic issues after studying in Wundt's laboratory. His research included situational influences on eyewitness accuracy as well as the issue of whether some individuals tend to be resistant to error and outside influences. Binet, the originator of intelligence testing, in France, replicated Cattell's work. He focused particularly on the question of the amenability of testimony to outside suggestion in interrogations. In Germany, at about the same time, William Stern conducted research on similar themes to those of Cattell in relation to both adults and children.
- Sigmund Freud did not write about legal matters although his ideas about human nature so profoundly affected the legal system that he was given an honorary doctorate in law from an American university. Nevertheless, a number of the psychoanalytically influenced followers of the psychodynamic psychology of Sigmund Freud made contributions to the field. For example, in 1929, Theodor Reik wrote about the compulsion to confess; Erich Fromm, in 1931, discussed the psychological diagnosis of fact (Jakob, 1992). Also in Germany, around 1905, C.G. Jung experimented with using word association to test a criminal suspect – that is, the characteristics of the delay of responding to different words with another word. Emotional stimulus words tend to produce greater delay.
- Udo Undeutsch in 1953 presented arguments to a German Psychological Association meeting that moved the issue of testimony to the question of the veracity of a statement rather than the credibility of the witness.

'American' roots of forensic and criminal psychology

The timescale is short between what we may call the German origins of forensic and criminal psychology and its appearance in the United States. This is because a significant number of early American psychologists actually trained at Wundt's laboratory and either returned home or emigrated to the United States as academic positions became available. Thus early work in the United States involved both American researchers and European émigrés. It is interesting that it is not uncommon to find these migrants identified as the major figures in the history of forensic and criminal psychology. Hall *et al.* (2010) trace the interdisciplinary study of psychology and law to Hugo Münsterberg – especially his book *On the Witness Stand* (1908). On the other hand, Shaw, Öhman and van Koppen (2013) identify Wilhelm Stern (1871–1938) as the recognised originator of the tradition of witness psychology. He had founded the first journal *Beiträge zur Psychologie der Aussage* (*Contributions to the Psychology of Testimony*) in 1904. Whichever or whoever can best be described as the founder of eyewitness research, we should not overlook the convenience of naming American-based researchers for an America-centric view. Here are snapshot biographies of Stern, Münsterberg and other such pioneers:

- L.W. Stern (*c.* 1910) continued the tradition of testimony research in the United States. Among his achievements was the introduction of realism to the study of testimony in that he introduced staged events into lectures – such as a student brandishing a revolver, which was witnessed by the class of students! In 1903/4, Stern was the first to distinguish between two kinds of interview called *Bericht* and *Verhö* (Myklebust and Bjørklund, 2006). *Bericht* allowed the interviewee to give their account as a free narrative by the use of open questions. In the *Verhö* approach, the interviewees answered a set of preset questions which are known as closed questions. Generally, modern research suggests that open questions lead to longer responses and greater accuracy.
- Hugo Münsterberg was the first major applied psychologist – and one of the most resolute. He was another of Wundt's students and he developed a lifelong interest in forensic issues. While still in Europe, he worked in support of Flemish weavers who were being sued by a customer. They were accused of supplying material of a different shade of colour from that ordered. They disputed this. Münsterberg, with the help of the great physiologist of the visual system, Helmholtz, showed that the apparent difference in colour was a function of the different lighting conditions involved. The shades were *not* different. After migrating to the United States, he found that the adversarial Anglo-American system of law was not so sympathetic to hearing psychological opinion as the European system had been. Münsterberg's interests were wide in the field of applied psychology (Howitt, 1992) and included jury decision making as well as eyewitness testimony in the domain of forensic psychology. He developed what he believed to be a test of lying by the use of what was basically a timed word-association test. Generally speaking lawyers at the time were interested in Munsterberg's ideas about psychology and the law (Dalby, 2014). According to Dalby, the lack of psychologists with the appropriate skills was responsible for the extremely slow development of forensic psychology until the 1970s when there was an explosion in the number of psychologists graduating. However, others, including Weiss and Xuan (2015) are much more critical of Münsterberg suggesting, among other things, that he held back the development of forensic psychology by alienating the legal establishment.
- William Marston was one of Münsterberg's students. Under another name, he was the creator and cartoonist for the comic strip character Wonder Woman. He developed the lie detector test (polygraphy) in 1915. The prototype for this was known as the 'systolic blood pressure deception test' and employed repeated blood pressure measurements during questioning. Marston claimed that changes in systolic blood pressure are indicative of lying (Grubin and Madsen, 2005). Furthermore, Marston was the first psychologist to be appointed in an American university as a professor of legal psychology (Bartol and Bartol, 1999). Importantly, Marston was an expert witness in the *Frye* v. *The United States* case in 1923. In this, the Federal Court of Appeals laid down the principle that procedures, assessments and technique used in evidence should normally be well regarded in their field. Bunn (2012) points out that the development of the polygraph could not have occurred without the rejection of the dominant European ideas of criminology. The criminal in nineteenth-century criminology influenced by Cesare Lombroso could be described as *homo criminalis* since they were almost regarded as a separate criminal species. The polygraph would be superfluous as the signs of criminality were readily seen. The criminologist Frances Kellor not only refuted the idea of *homo criminalis* but suggested that psychological and physiological tests might be the means of identifying deceit. That is, the idea that psychologically normal people could be criminal meant that new ways of finding criminality in them became important and the potential of instruments like the polygraph was evident.
- Karle Marbe (*c.* 1911) testified in court that human reaction time latencies were such that an engine driver had no chance of stopping his train in time to prevent a crash. This was possibly the first psychological testimony at a civil rather than criminal trial. Less praiseworthy, Marbe also argued in court that the alleged victims of child sexual abuse made unreliable witnesses against their teacher. Society has changed a great deal since that time in terms of its attitudes to children.
- Henry H. Goddard was an American pioneer of intelligence testing. However, he is best known for his failed work which linked feeble-mindedness (sic) with criminality. His most famous book (Goddard, 1912) *The Kallikak Family*, was the study of the offspring of a soldier, Martin Kallikak, who fathered a son by a feeble-minded barmaid which led to generations of criminals, degenerates and deviants. Kallikak also married another woman and this led to a lineage of upstanding people such as doctors, lawyers, and educationalists. Goddard believed that it was low intelligence which led to the

criminality of the other line. He claimed that in excess of a quarter of the people in prison were feebleminded. He was much criticised and later changed his mind about his ideas.

- Louis Thurstone (1922) published the findings of a study of the intelligence of police officers in the United States. It was found that, in general, junior officers tended to be more intelligent than older ones. Thurstone suggested that the brighter officers tend to leave the force for more rewarding and stimulating work, leaving the less intelligent to be promoted within the police force. This, effectively, was the start of the study of police psychology.

The modern development of forensic and criminal psychology

The development of psychologists' involvement as expert witnesses in American courts was an important determinant of the growth of forensic psychology. Although psychologists could serve as expert witnesses, the general principle was that they should do so in circumstances where they were not stepping into the area of expertise of members of the medical profession. However, eventually it was established that an individual's knowledge of the topic in question was the determining standard for an expert witness (*The People* v. *Hawthorne*, 1940). This meant that the mere possession of a medical qualification was not a sufficient criterion for an expert witness. As empirically based psychology developed, the judicial system gradually became more prepared to employ the services of psychologists in courts of law, especially following the end of the Second World War in 1945 when the professional of clinical psychology began to expand substantially in the USA with an obvious interest in what happens in courts of law. However, psychologists' lack of medical qualifications was sometimes a stumbling block as the courts were reluctant to accept their evidence equally with that of the medical profession (Bartol and Bartol, 1999). However, gradually influential legal decisions contributed a great deal to the development of psychology and law in research and clinical practice. For example, the important case of *Brown* v. *Board of Education of Topeka* (1954) relied very much on the admission of psychological findings concerning the effects of segregation of children into the court proceedings. Crucially, in *Jenkins* v. *United States* (1962), the ruling of the Court of Appeals for the District of Columbia was that psychologists could act as expert witnesses on the matter of mental illness at the time when the crime was committed. The ruling said that expertise on mental disease was not the sole province of medics. The consequence was the increased acceptance of psychologists as expert witnesses on a wide range of legal matters by American courts. So, despite the slow headway that psychology made into courtroom, the 1962 judgement changed things forever.

Another factor was that key disciplines in the development of forensic and criminal psychology did not grow significantly until the second half of the twentieth century. This is especially true of social psychology and clinical psychology. Hall (2007) refers to the situation in the United Kingdom for psychology as being 'bleak' in these early years, owing to the small numbers of psychologists that were working in academic contexts. In this sort of setting, it was probably inevitable that the development of clinical psychology was slow in the United Kingdom. Things were different in the United States where the returning veterans from the Second World War led to the more rapid development of clinical psychology. Nevertheless, from about the 1970s onwards, psychologists were increasingly, though still in small numbers, turning their attention to matters of relevance to criminal psychology. In the United Kingdom, for example, Lionel Haward of the University of Surrey was beginning to speak of forensic psychologists and the work that they were doing to help, especially, defence lawyers. As an illustration of this, Haward carried out a study into the adequacy of a police officer's claim in court that the officer had recorded the licence plate of a motor cycle travelling at speed. A hundred trained observers tried to replicate this but none of them could identify licence numbers in such circumstances (Smith, 1977). Although, for example, Hans Eysenck was proposing his general theory of crime in the 1960s (see Chapter 5), by the 1970s others were making important contributions. For example, Ray Bull was beginning to apply social psychological principles to the work of police officers (e.g. Bull and Reid, 1975) and Philip Sealy was applying social psychology to the jury (e.g. Sealy and Cornish, 1973).

Forensic and criminal psychology has different historical antecedents in different countries. This is particularly the case in terms of the institutional basis of forensic and criminal psychology internationally. The institutional basis of the discipline is not the same in all countries. For example, although universities may provide the training in the legal area of psychology in Western Europe, the training is more likely to be in non-university settings in other countries. To illustrate how the origins of forensic and criminal psychology may differ in different countries, we can consider the example of Spain. The first textbook on legal psychology was written by a Spanish psychiatrist in 1932 (Royo, 1996). The author left Spain along with many other intellectuals because of the Spanish Civil War. It was not until 1971, when the Barcelona College of

Barristers created a Department of Sociology and Legal Psychology, that the field was reopened. The first international meeting on legal psychology in Spain was held in 1976. While the specific details differ from country to country (see accounts of the development of the discipline in Hungary in Szegedi, 1998; in Portugal in Goncalves, 1998), generally speaking, it would be a common experience in different countries that forensic and criminal psychology, despite early interest, was in the doldrums until the 1970s (cf. Wrightsman, 2001), certainly in the United States and Western Europe. Important things were happening, as we have seen, but these cannot mask the relative inattention to forensic issues until the 1970s and 1980s. It should also be noted that the pattern of the steady expansion of forensic and criminal psychology since that time is not characteristic of all nations, especially those in Eastern Europe (Kury, 1998).

In the period since the 1970s and 1980s forensic and criminal psychology has developed extensively as a discipline as well as in its institutional base. One might say it has burgeoned, flourished and prospered. (Heilbrun and Brooks (2010) date the rapid expansion of forensic psychology as from about 1980.) Royo (1996) suggests that there are four basic ways in which a discipline may be consolidated. These are the formation of associations, the creation of specialised books and journals, the legal institutionalisation of the discipline as part of the process of criminal justice and the creation of university courses devoted to the subject. All of these things can be recognised in forensic and criminal psychology to varying extents. Some of the key institutional happenings include:

- *Formation of Associations:* Particularly important in the development of any sub-discipline are meetings and associations of like-minded researchers which help them to form research relationships between universities and other organisations both nationally and internationally.
  1. The American Psychology-Law Association was established in 1969 (Grisso, 1991) and was influential in the creation of the Psychology and Law division (division 41) of the American Psychological Association (APA), with which it merged in 1981. The association began publishing the highly influential journal *Behavioral Sciences and the Law* in 1977. Often overlooked, however, Division 18 of the American Psychological Association – Psychologists in Public Service – formed a criminal justice section in 1975.
  2. The Division of Criminological and Legal Psychology was established by the British Psychological Society in 1977 but renamed the Division of Forensic Psychology in 1999. The division began publishing the journal *Legal and Criminological Psychology* in 1996.
  3. The Australia and New Zealand Association of Psychiatry, Psychology and Law was founded in 1972 and began publishing the journal *Psychiatry, Psychology and Law* in 1993.
  4. The European Association of Psychology and the Law grew slowly from initially small meetings, such as those held at the University of Oxford in the 1980s. Dominated initially by small fledgling research communities in countries such as Germany, the Netherlands, Sweden and the UK, the first European conference on psychology and the law was held in Maastricht, Netherlands in 1988. This led to a second European meeting in Nuremberg, Germany, which led to the founding of the European Association of Psychology and the Law.
  5. The Nordic Network for research on Psychology and Law began in Sweden in 2004.
- *Professional education:* According to Shaw *et al.* (2013), postgraduate psychology and law programmes are to be found in many countries. There are over 30 in the US, 20 in the UK, nine in Australia, four in Germany, four in Spain, three in Russia, three in Canada and one in Sweden, for example. Such a supply of qualified postgraduates contributes greatly to the future of any discipline.
- *Publications:* The number of journals which publish articles in the field of psychology and the law is large and includes important mainstream journals such as *Psychological Bulletin*. Black (2012) carried out a study of the most frequently cited articles listed in six forensic psychology journals, including *Behavioral Sciences and the Law* and *Law and Human Behavior*. He found nearly 22,000 citations to publications in a wide variety of journals. The top 68 most frequently cited journals contained only 15 specific to legal psychology. The top 68 journals only contained 47 per cent of the total number of citations. In other words, not only are there a substantial number of specialist journals in the field of forensic/legal psychology but there are numerous other publication opportunities available to researchers in mainstream and general psychology journals.

The field of forensic and criminal psychology is not now fixed with its foci, boundaries and future clearly defined. It is an evolving field that will inevitably change:

- Developments in both the law and psychology will ensure that new issues become incorporated into the field. For example, the development of the concept of stalking and its first incorporation into law in California in 1990 (Emerson, Ferris and Gardner, 1998) led to considerable psychological and psychiatric effort to understand stalking behaviour. Now it is a substantial research area in its own right. Right now there are probably new developments which will generate intense research interest from forensic and criminal psychology, but it would take a brave soul to predict precisely what they may be.

- Increased employment of psychologists as personnel within different components of the criminal justice system will bring its own developments. So too will increases in private practice in the field. For example, a broadening of the role of psychology in police organisations – such as the recruitment of officers – will bring a shift of interest in that direction.
- Increasing numbers of students training as forensic and criminal psychologists will ensure a fuller professionalisation of work and practice.

Main points

- The sub-discipline of forensic and criminal psychology deals with aspects of psychology relevant to the criminal justice system though, taken literally, the term 'forensic psychology' refers to psychology in the context of law courts. The wider definition of the field underlies the selection of material in this book. As a consequence of the broad definition, the field unites psychologists from a wide variety of academic and practitioner backgrounds.
- Forensic and criminal psychology began to become important in the 1980s and increasingly so afterwards. Its history can be taken back many centuries to the times when issues such as diminished responsibility and fitness to stand trial were first developed in the legal system and so the demand arose for expert help from outside of the court itself. There was a period of interest in forensic and criminal psychology during the early years of academic psychology around 1900. However, for most of the twentieth century there was very little interest in the field.
- Forensic and criminal psychology has developed an appropriate infrastructure to ensure its continued development. This includes specialist international organisations and journals in which the latest research is published.

Further reading

Bartol, C.R. and Bartol, A.M. (2014) 'History of forensic psychology' in I.B. Weiner and A.K. Hess (eds), *Handbook of Forensic Psychology* (4th edn). Chichester: Wiley (pp. 1–27).

Crichton, D.A. and Towel, G. (2015) *Forensic Psychology* (2nd edn). Chichester: Wiley.

Kapardis, A. (2014) *Psychology and Law: A critical introduction* (4th edn). Melbourne: Cambridge University Press.

Chapter 2

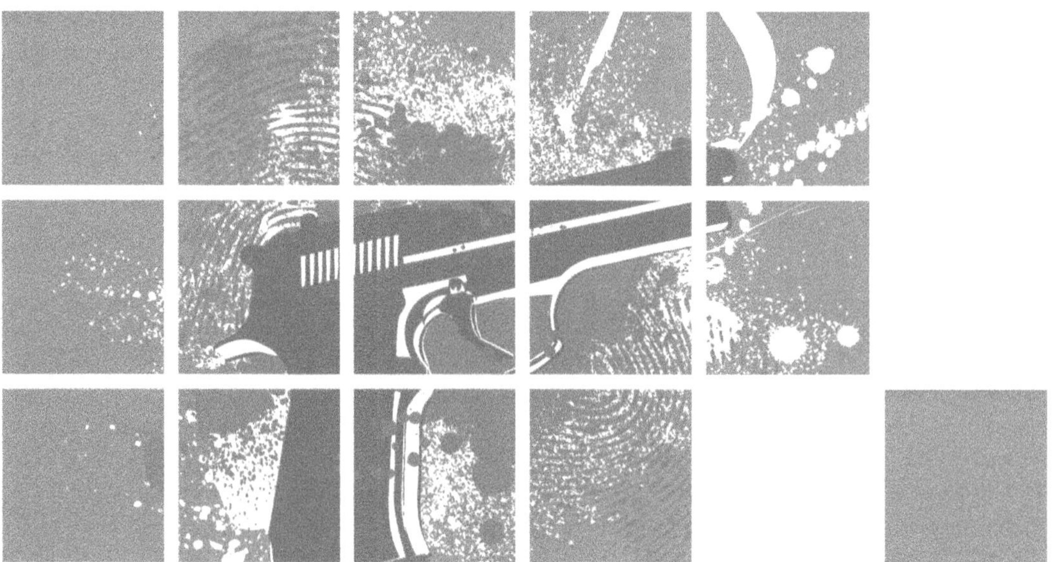

The social context of crime

Overview

- There are many sources of information about crime in society including the media, social media, the government, family, friends and acquaintances. Personal experience as a victim of crime or even a perpetrator can also contribute to our knowledge and beliefs. Nevertheless, misconceptions about crime and criminals are common.
- Crime statistics have their shortcomings yet can provide some useful information. The Internet is a ready and reliable resource for information on the most recent crime trends for many countries such as the United States and the United Kingdom.
- There are many sources of information which make up crime statistics. Sample surveys with members of the public and information recorded by the police are especially useful. Different types of statistical information may superficially appear incompatible because of the different types of data involved.
- Each method of data collection has its own advantages and disadvantages which need to be taken into account when assessing findings based on them. The various approaches should be regarded as complementary and incompatibilities seen as part of the challenge of understanding crime data.
- Crime statistics have to be interpreted and different researchers will interpret them differently. Consequently, there are alternative interpretations possible for crime statistics, depending on one's viewpoint.
- Extensive research has demonstrated that criminal behaviour is quite common – sufficiently so that it might be described as normal. Of course, relatively trivial incidents of stealing form the bulk of this criminal activity. Nevertheless, there is evidence that half of men and nearly a third of women admit to committing at least one crime such as burglary, theft, criminal damage, robbery, assault or selling drugs at some stage in their lives.
- International comparisons tend to suggest considerable variation in levels of crime in different nations. However, international trends in crime statistics do not indicate that levels of crime invariably increase over time. For some crimes (homicide is a good example), the trends are downwards or flattening out in some countries traditionally believed to be violent.
- Justice is administered differently and is based on different principles in different parts of the world. Even where the systems are closely related (e.g. the United Kingdom and the United States) there may be crucial differences in certain respects. It is important to avoid the assumption that the principles of forensic and criminal psychology are universally applicable.

Introduction

Our ideas about the world of crime come from a variety of sources. Personal experience clearly must play some part, but imagery of crime and the criminal justice system is everywhere. For example, Howitt (1998c) found that the largest proportions of UK media news stories concerned crime and the criminal justice system. Characteristically, almost by definition, the news is about relatively unusual, new or sensational events. As such, it is not intended to be indicative of the mundane reality of most crime. There is no precise correspondence between media coverage of crime and the more objective reality assessed from police reports and victimisation studies, for example. Studies demonstrating a lack of correspondence between the reality of crime and the contents of newspapers go back many years (Croll, 1974; Davies, 1952; Roshier, 1971, 1973). Compared to the reality, property crimes such as theft are grossly under-represented in newspapers, yet these are the very crimes that the general public is most likely to experience. Similarly, violent crime, including homicide, is disproportionately over-reported in the news media (Chermak, 1995). The situation is more extreme for movies and television which are replete with stories of cops and crime. In other words, to the extent that the media determine people's perceptions of crime, the risk is that they receive a rather distorted view.

It is difficult to overstate the extent to which most crime is relatively petty and mundane. It is intriguing that forensic and criminal psychology research dwells on the sensational and unusual much more than the typical. So much more is known about serial killers than shoplifters. So just what is the reality of crime? There is no research method or source of information that will give us anything other than an approximation to reality. Victim surveys are one way of quantifying the types of crime experienced by the public. In these, people are interviewed about their experiences of crime, perhaps in the previous six months or year. Although it is believed that such victimisation studies avoid some of the biases inherent in, say, police statistics they nevertheless have biases of their own. It is easy to see that statistics on crimes known to the police may be biased since the police may be unaware of crimes not reported to them. Victimisation surveys, on the other hand, have their own problems. For example, they are dependent on drawing a representative sample of the population and they cannot include crimes for which there is no victim. So victimisation studies omit vandalism and they cannot assess homicide since the victim is dead. Furthermore, victimisation studies may include as crimes events that are not strictly illegal. For these reasons and others, victimisation studies may not deal with so-called victimless crimes such as drug offences, as well as crimes against businesses. For reasons of sensitivity, victimisation studies may not include sexual offences routinely.

There are numerous victimisation studies carried out in a good many countries. One example is The Crime Survey of England and Wales (previously known, rather inaccurately, as the British Crime Survey). The following figures are taken from the Crime Survey of England and Wales for 2015. The study was based on almost 35,000 adults (Office for National Statistics, 2016). The commonest crime reported by respondents in the survey was theft, which accounted for 72 per cent of all crimes recorded in the survey. Theft is a broad category and includes robbery, domestic burglary, vehicle related theft and bicycle theft. Violent victimisation was much less common and accounted for 14 per cent of crimes. The remaining crimes were instances of criminal damage which would include malicious damage to a vehicle or stones thrown through house windows, for example. Criminal damage (vandalism) amounted to 13 per cent of crimes. In other words, a person is far more likely to be victimised through theft than through violence. Overwhelmingly, non-violent crime dominates. The figures for 2015 suggest that there are 6.4 million crimes against households and resident adults aged 16 years and above. The breakdown for the different types of crime can be seen in Figure 2.1. As already explained, as this was a victim study it does not include crimes such as drug offences, shoplifting and homicide. The survey involved adults of 16 years and above. Related research suggested that there was an estimated 829,000 additional crimes against children 10 to 15 years of age.

We can contrast this victim survey with statistics on crime recorded by the police. The police have a statutory requirement to report to the government the numbers of certain crimes known to them. One notable thing is that such reports include a substantially wider variety of crimes than included in the typical victimisation survey. We shall consider statistics on crimes reported by the police in England and Wales in 2015 (Office for National Statistics, 2016b), which can be compared with the victimisation study reported above. These crimes known to the police are classified under three separate headings: 1) victim-based crimes such as violence and theft (76 per cent); 2) crimes against society such as drug offences and public order offences (10 per cent); and 3) fraud (14 per cent). Victim-based crime is the largest group (76 per cent) followed by fraud (14 per cent) followed by crimes against society (10 per cent). The victim-based crimes category is obviously the one most directly comparable with the crimes in the victim survey. Theft is the biggest victim-based crime group (40 per cent of all crimes). It includes burglary and all other forms of theft. Violent offences accounted for 21 per cent of all offences. Criminal damage and arson accounted for another 12 per cent. Very broadly speaking,

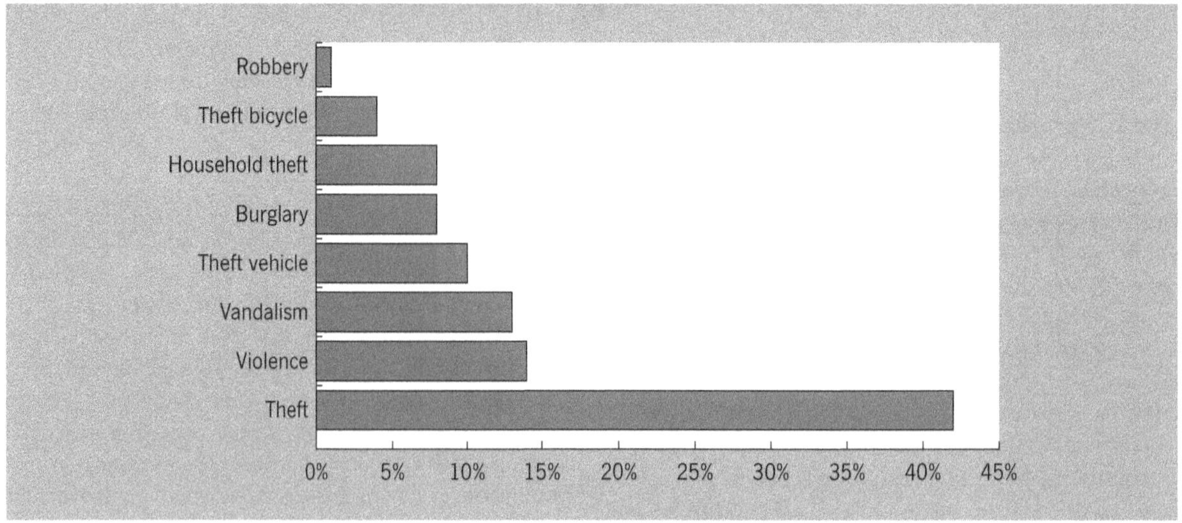

Figure 2.1 Percentages of different types of crime in the *Crime Survey of England and Wales* (2015)

these statistics support the broad trends found in the victim survey – that theft is far more common than violent offences – though the trends are far less strong. Sexual offences of all types were 2 per cent of all of the offences recorded by the police. Figure 2.2 provides more details.

Despite victim surveys and police-reported crimes being dominated by non-violent offences especially involving theft, it is the more sensational and lurid violent crimes which get media attention. Suffice to say that both the news and crime statistics are not objective accounts of crime. The news media manufacture what they regard as being newsworthy. It is also true to say that the criminal statistics are, to varying degrees, created through complex social processes. There is no ground-truth about the nature and extent of crime, but victimisation surveys and police statistics can be seen as ways of approximating it. So it is important to understand just where statistical data comes from and what factors influence the data in order not to over interpret the statistical trends.

There are many sources of information about crime and the criminal justice system. We have dealt with victimisation surveys and police statistics above. Victimisation surveys tend to produce the highest estimates of the rates

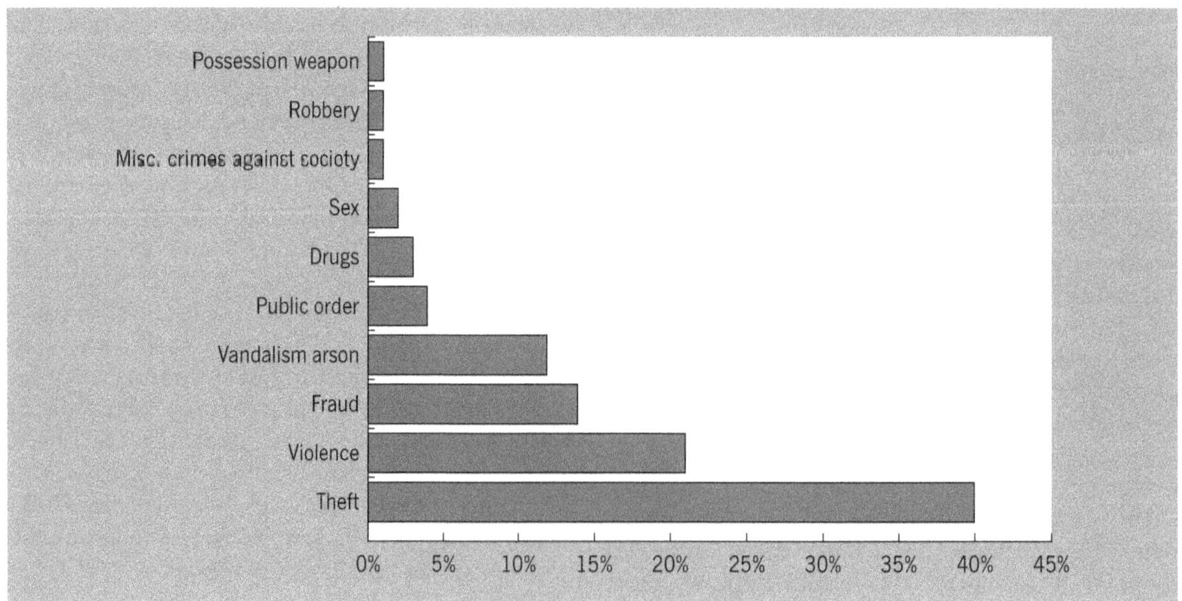

Figure 2.2 Percentages of different types of crime in *Police Reported Crime Statistics for England* (2015)

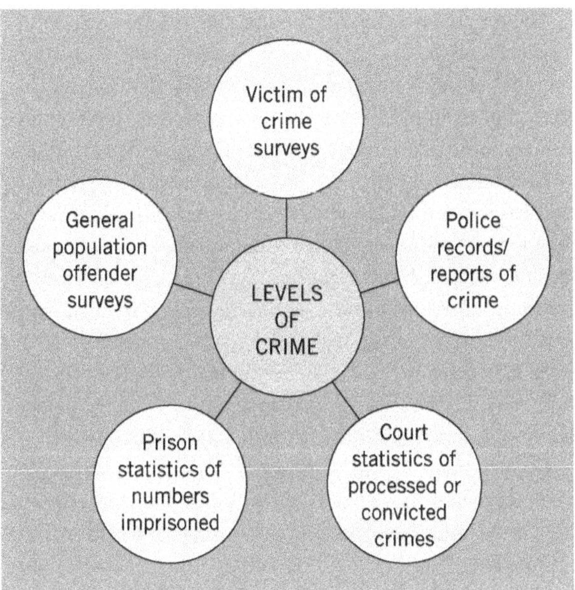

Figure 2.3 Different ways of estimating levels of crime

of crime for obvious reasons – that is, victims report to the researcher crimes which they have not reported to the police. Unfortunately, victim surveys cannot give information about every type of crime – such as where the crime is against a company rather than an individual, or crimes for which there is no obvious victim (such as vandalism in a public park). Police-recorded crime has its own biases in addition to reporting bias. For example, the police may decide that a 'crime' that a member of the public has reported is not actually a crime.

Other sources of information about crime and offenders include the following:

- *Court statistics:* these codify the numbers and types of offences being processed in a given year and the outcomes of these different cases in terms of sentencing. The obvious biases here are in terms of the factors that lead to prosecution as opposed to no charge.
- *Prison statistics:* these provide breakdowns of the numbers in prison at any one time (in terms of offence categories, sentences, and so forth). Biases here may be due to sentencing policies at the time. For example, a concerted clampdown on burglary may lead to an increase in the numbers of burglars in prison.
- *General population offender surveys:* these have recently been developed in which members of a random sample of households are interviewed about the crimes they have committed at any point in their lives and/or recently (for example, in the previous year). This is likely to include at least some crimes that would be ignored by the police and other components of the criminal justice system as being too trivial to warrant prosecution. Furthermore, there is probably a bias against the more serious crimes since those who have committed them may well have been arrested, prosecuted and sent to prison, with the result that they are excluded from such surveys.

For obvious reasons, the rates of crime that are estimated from these different statistics vary. One would rightly expect that surveys of victims produce substantially higher levels of crime in general than any of the other statistical indices. A number of points are worth mentioning before we move on to discussing what we know about crime from such sources:

- Crime statistics are rarely simply wrong. The fact that they are not always in agreement may indicate that each provides a different perspective on criminal activity.
- Each type of statistics has its own value and may be more useful for a particular purpose than others. Even though, say, crimes recorded by the police may be just a small fraction of crimes committed, they may still be very useful for examining changes in crime rates over time. This is especially true if the biases in reporting crimes to the police remain relatively constant over time. Unfortunately, this is difficult to ascertain. So, for example, if we find more cases of child sexual abuse in the 2010s than in the 1960s, is this due to higher levels of sexual abuse? The data are equally consistent with there being an increased awareness of the danger of abuse which makes people more vigilant and more prepared to report crimes. The change may also reflect an increase in retrospective (historical) prosecutions of previously unreported abuse that happened many years earlier.
- Care is always needed in the interpretation of any statistics. For example, legal and other changes may result in crimes being classified differently at different points in time. A change in the definition of rape to include, say, male rape may produce an increase in the number of rapes. While it is common practice for statisticians to signal changes in the basis on which the statistics are compiled, it is much more difficult to adjust previous years on the basis of such information unless the compilers do so. It may sometimes appear statistics have been manipulated to gain political advantage, but it may also reflect legal changes or genuine improvements to how the statistics are collected.

In short, while some will point to the inadequacies of crime statistics as being flaws in those statistics, it is better to regard crime statistics as being of limited usefulness in limited circumstances. This makes them very similar to much of the data that psychologists collect. That they are the result of a complex social process makes it all the more important to understand them; it is not an excuse for dismissing them as worthless. Often the problem is not the nature of the data but how they should be interpreted. The more familiar one is with a variety of different sorts of crime statistics and just how particular crime statistics are compiled, then the more adequate one's interpretations are likely to be.

The extent of crime

We have already seen that it is not easy to specify the reality of crime. Crime statistics do not present a single reality unproblematically. There are very basic questions that need to be asked, such as the point at which an event becomes construed as a crime. What is it about a set of circumstances that results in an eyewitness labelling events as a crime? There is undoubtedly a point at which an eyewitness will decide whether or not to report events to the police as a crime. The US Bureau of Justice Statistics (2003) indicated that 27 per cent of known violent crimes are reported by eyewitnesses. So how an eyewitness construes events is extremely important in determining whether what has been witnessed is reported to the police. In their research into bystanders' reactions to crimes, Langsdale and Greenberg (2006) showed participants a video of a conversation between a man and a woman which lasted just ten seconds before the man either walked or ran away. In other versions of the video there was a 30-second delay before the man walked or ran away. Simple differences like these affected whether the events were perceived as a crime. If the man *ran* away after ten seconds then the witness was more likely to see the events as a robbery than if it took 30 seconds before he ran away. If he *walked* away then the amount of time involved made no difference to the perception of the events as a robbery. In real-life situations, this may be the difference between a crime being reported to the police or not.

Trends in criminal statistics may change with the passage of time, and what may be the case in one country may not be the case in different country. There is plenty of information available on the Internet about crime statistics. Much of it is published by governments, but other organisations do so too: a good search engine and well-chosen search terms should readily find suitable sites. ('Crime statistics' and 'criminal statistics' are obvious examples of productive search terms.) Some governments publish extensive material, which is probably as up to date as any publicly available information since it is far quicker to update web material than books or pamphlets. As with any material on the Internet, it is important to always carefully assess the adequacy of the source and try to anticipate the sort of spin that may have been put on what the statistics mean or just what statistics are presented. This applies to all sources of information; it is not simply a consideration when using the Internet as a source.

The term 'crime index' is commonly used in relation to criminal statistics. This is merely a composite measure of the number of crimes, based, usually, on the more serious types. For example, in the US a violent crime index might be a composite of murder and non-negligent manslaughter, forcible rape, robbery and aggravated assault. A property offences index might include burglary, larceny theft, motor-vehicle theft and arson. Other countries may have their own variants on this, more appropriate to the major crime categories in those countries. These indices provide a very broad picture of crime trends. The sub-components of the index may actually show rather different trends. For example, rape may be increasing but since motor-vehicle theft is decreasing much faster, the overall trend is downward.

Governments spend substantial amounts of money on collecting various statistics about crime and the criminal justice system. They do not do so simply to inform the public. These statistics are obviously relevant to planning for the criminal justice system. Furthermore, the crime statistics may be used as evidence about the success or otherwise of policy initiatives. There are many reasons why crime is important to governments but an important one is the huge economic costs of crime and the criminal justice system. The economic cost of crime in the US is given in headline statistics by Ostermann and Matejkowki (2014). These estimates include:

- The US Criminal Justice System costs more than $200,000 million every year
- Crime victims suffer $876,000,000 in lost workdays.
- The average cost of a criminal career is $1,500,000.
- Preventing a high-risk juvenile from starting a criminal career is worth about $2,000,000 in savings.
- The national cost of crime exceeds $1.7 trillion when all costs are incorporated. This includes things like the cost of burglar alarms and other crime reduction commodities, the lost productive activity when individuals are involved in crime, and the transfer of assets from the victim to the offender.

These are extraordinary amounts of money and in themselves justify the search for solutions to crime and expenditure on crime reduction measures.

The extent of criminality

One of the classic ideas of criminology and sociology is that of white-collar or middle-class crime (Payne, 2013). The concept of white-collar crime was introduced by Edwin Sutherland (1949) to indicate the nature and extent of crime among the middle classes rather than it being primarily a working-class phenomenon. Sutherland defined white-collar crime as a crime perpetrated by 'a person of respectability and high social status in the course of his occupation' (Sutherland, 1949, p. 9). Although white-collar crime can be serious crimes such as fraud or embezzlement from a company, it can also include activities such as 'borrowing' stationery from the office or using the office telephone for private calls. This sort of petty crime is often regarded as acceptable or normal by perpetrators, but it is nonetheless crime. Similarly, tax evasion is seen as almost morally justified and hence not truly a crime by some people.

It is probable that everyone has committed what may be described as a trivial crime at some point in their lives: the extent of criminality in the general population is remarkably high. Taking the stringent criterion of imprisonment, in the United States the chance of a person going to prison during their lifetime is nearly 7 per cent according to estimates (Bureau of Justice, 2004). The odds are much worse for some groups, which may reflect biases in the criminal justice system:

- The figure is 11 per cent for men but only 2 per cent for women.
- A black person has a 19 per cent chance compared with 3 per cent for white people.
- The figure for black men is 32 per cent as opposed to 6 per cent for white men. That is, nearly one in three black men will spend time in prison.
- Over 64 per cent of jailed persons were of racial or ethnic minority origin in 2001.

More recently, Western and Pettit (2010) have pointed out that the risk of being imprisoned in the US is affected by generational factors, racial factors and school dropout. They compared men born in the 1940s (1945–9) with men born in the 1970s (1975–9). The key variable was whether the men had received a prison sentence by the time they were about 30 years of age. Table 2.1 clearly demonstrates that the younger generation had a much greater risk of imprisonment than the older one by substantial margins. It is also obvious from the table that black men were substantially more likely to serve a prison term than white men. Furthermore, dropping out from high school led to a greater likelihood of imprisonment. Putting all of these factors together, two-thirds of black high school dropouts in the younger generation received prison sentences compared to less than a third of white high school dropouts.

The extent of potential criminality can also be seen from other studies of youngsters. For example, Wilson (1980) took samples of 10–17-year-olds living in deprived housing estates in inner city or suburban settings. Evidence concerning their criminality was obtained directly from police records of convictions and cautions:

- 20 per cent of the boys had a record of crime. Theft and burglary were the commonest offences.
- This should be contrasted with self-reported misbehaviour. Crime is much more common in terms of self-reported offences rather than criminal convictions – over 40 per cent had shoplifted, 67 per cent had drawn graffiti in the street and so forth.

The British Crime and Justice Survey (Budd, Sharp and Mayhew, 2005) extended our knowledge of self-reported rates of crime. A national sample of the general household population in the age range of 10–65 years was asked in detail about the offences of burglary, vehicle-related thefts, other thefts, criminal damage, robbery, assaults and selling drugs. Over 50 per cent of men and 30 per cent of women said they had committed at least one of these core crimes in their lives. Given that other types of offences, such as sexual ones, were omitted from the survey, it is likely that the figure for people who had ever committed a serious offence could be higher. Of course, some of these crimes would have been less serious since they involved property of low value or involved assaults that did not lead to injury. About 20 per cent of the population had committed a serious offence at some stage and this usually involved assault with injury. The survey also assessed the numbers who had committed an offence in the last year. These figures are naturally smaller than the equivalent lifetime percentages. Six per cent of people had committed a property crime in the last year and 5 per cent had committed a violent offence. For juvenile offenders, the majority of offences were violent in nature though generally these did not involve injury. For people above the age of 25 years, the majority of offences were to do with

Table 2.1 Generational and racial trends in the likelihood of imprisonment in the USA by the age of 30–34 years

	All white	All black	White high school dropouts	Black high school dropouts
1945–9 Cohort	1%	10%	4%	15%
1975–9 Cohort	5%	27%	28%	68%

Source: Pettit, Sykes and Western (2009)

property. Drug offences were commoner than property offences and much more common than violent offences in the 18–25-year-old age group.

There is a long history of self-reported offending studies in criminology dating back to a hundred years ago. Farrington (2001) reviews a number of American and British studies and provides evidence of their validity and Zauberman (2009) concentrates on European work. They make an interesting contrast with victimisation studies and, especially, police crime statistics.

There is a further approach that warrants attention in this context: the field of experiments into honesty/dishonesty carried out by psychologists. Carefully staged situations, of a variety of sorts, have been contrived in order to investigate dishonesty. The origins of this were in the classic studies of Hartshorne and May (1928) who investigated aspects of dishonesty such as lying, cheating and stealing in pubescent children. Among their measures was the failure or not of children to return a coin they had been given. This and later research is reviewed in Farrington (1979). A range of other ways of assessing stealing has been developed. For example, some researchers have deliberately 'lost' money in the street to see whether the finder attempts to return the cash or merely just keeps it. Farrington and Kidd (1977) lost envelopes in the street containing varying amounts of money:

- With no money enclosed, 95 per cent of the envelopes were returned to the address in the enclosed letter.
- With £1 in cash enclosed, 75 per cent were returned.
- With £5 in cash enclosed, then 55 per cent were returned.

This is a notably high rate of dishonesty given that, in the United Kingdom, to keep money knowing that one is depriving its rightful owner of it constitutes theft. Many of these studies were carried out to investigate the effects of different environmental circumstances on the rates of honesty. They also indicate the baseline rates of dishonest behaviour in fairly general samples of the population. None of this should be too surprising given what we know about the illegal downloading of music from the Internet (music piracy). Wingrove, Korpas and Weisz (2011) showed that young people's attitudes to illegally downloading were very different from their attitudes to stealing a CD from a music shop – despite the fact that the illegal download and the CD might contain exactly the same music tracks. This goes some way to understanding why so many disregard the law on piracy.

Of course, there is an important implication for forensic and criminal psychology in all of this. That is, in many ways, the study of criminal behaviour is the study of the behaviour of normal people – a high proportion admit to having committed some sort of crime in their lives, no matter how trivial. That does not imply that there are no abnormal psychological features in any criminal, merely that much crime has to be explained in terms of normal behaviour.

Crime rates compared internationally

The rates of crime in different parts of the world are important sources of information. The International Crime Victimisation Survey (2001) compared countries in different parts of the world including Australia, Austria, Belgium, Canada, England and Wales, Finland, France, Germany (the West prior to reunification), Italy, Malta, the Netherlands, New Zealand, Northern Ireland, Norway, Scotland, Spain, Sweden, Switzerland and the United States. The crimes surveyed ranged from property offences against cars, such as theft of the car, damage to the car and theft from the car, on the less serious side, to sexual offences and assault and threat. To survey national populations in such diverse locations is, manifestly, logistically complex. Indeed, sampling in economically developing countries was very much confined to cities as a consequence. The surveys were not all conducted at exactly the same time in the different nations, so it is really only possible to describe the data as being collected in the 1990s. Since forensic and criminal psychologists are most likely to work in developed nations, the data for industrialised countries are the most pertinent. It should be stressed that this was a victimisation survey, not a collation of, for example, crimes known to the police. The information was obtained directly from the public, thus avoiding the sorts of reporting bias that can affect the numbers of crimes known to the police, but not avoiding the biases inherent in surveys (refusals to take part, for instance). The survey reported prevalence rates as opposed to incidence rates. The meanings of prevalence and incidence rates are as follows:

- Prevalence rates are simply the rates of people who report having been a victim of crime or a particular sort of crime in a particular time period. If they have been robbed twice, for example, this is not recorded in prevalence figures. So prevalence rates give the number of victims of a particular type of crime rather than the numbers of a particular type of crime.
- Incidence rates reflect the frequency of being victimised and, as such, would provide better estimates of the numbers of crimes committed annually.

In brief, the difference is between the number of a particular type of crime per person in the population (incidence) and average number of victims in the population (prevalence). These can be expressed as percentages but they can be given as the rate per 1000 people, for example.

Internationally there are noticeable variations between countries and over time in terms of crime statistics. Overall, the chances of victimisation were the highest in England and Wales of the countries surveyed. The prevalence rate was almost 31 per cent for victimisation for any sort of crime. Other countries had rates of 25 per cent or so. For example, the figure for the United States in the 1990s was 24 per cent. In general, Belgium and Northern Ireland had the lowest victimisation rates.

This international survey has been updated in recent years. Table 2.2 gives a few comparisons between England and Wales, the United States, Australia and Canada, based on the most recent available figures (van Dijk, van Kestern and Smit, 2007). Despite there being substantial differences between the US and England and Wales in terms of perceptions of the relative levels of crime, the victim data suggest relatively little difference in general. It should also be noted that, according to crime report figures, there were major reductions in levels of violent crime in the United States in the 1990s (Bureau of Justice, 2001a). The trend continues to be downwards (Bureau of Justice Statistics, 2011).

There have been other attempts to compare crime rates internationally. One study involved a cross-national comparison of eight countries – England and Wales, Scotland, Canada, the United States, Australia, the Netherlands, Sweden and Switzerland (Farrington, Langan and Tonry, 2004). The period studied was the two decades between 1980 and 2000. As with other studies, there are difficulties involved in making statistical comparisons among different countries. For example, in some European countries, burglary and vehicle theft are not distinguished in the legal code from other types of theft. This meant that the rates of burglary and vehicle theft in these countries had to be estimated from general theft data. One of the startling features of the findings was that different countries may show exactly the opposite trend rates of particular crimes. For example, in some countries, the rates of recorded burglary per 1000 population increased over time (e.g. Australia and the Netherlands); in other countries the rates of recorded burglary decreased over time (e.g. United States). Some countries have several times the rate of recorded burglaries found in other countries. Australia had the highest rate overall and Switzerland the lowest rate. Rates can change dramatically within a country over time. So the United States had far higher rates of robbery than England and Wales in the 1980s but at the end of the study period, rates in the two countries were virtually identical. Rates in the United States had declined markedly and rates in the United Kingdom had increased markedly.

Statistics rapidly go out of date, as does a psychologist's knowledge of them. Furthermore, what may be true of one type of crime (e.g. homicide) may not be true of other types of violent crime. It has been argued that homicide is the most valid statistic on which to base international crime comparisons (Eisner, 2008; Pratt and Godsey, 2003). Blackburn (1995b) is almost certainly correct when he points out national differences in terms of violent crimes, especially. He suggests that the United States is a nation particularly prone to such crime. The variation is remarkable, as Blackburn suggests, but crime statistics are not necessarily stable, even over a relatively short period of time. He argues that differential homicide rates may be due to socio-cultural factors: but just what socio-cultural factors could be responsible for rapidly changing homicide rates? Changes in crime policy may produce changes in policing, sentencing and punishment that result in a quick reduction in crime statistics. Of course, governments make claims about the efficacy of their criminal justice policy based on declining rates of certain crimes.

To be precise, for the United States the statistical evidence is that homicide, adjusted for the size of the population, has decreased in frequency in recent years. By 1999, it was at a low level equivalent to the figures for the latter part of the 1960s – in 1999, the rate was six homicides for every 100,000 people in the population (Fox and Zawitz, 2004). This is substantially less than the rate of ten homicides per 100,000 in 1980 – the United States' peak homicide year for the latter part of the twentieth century. Homicide rates in the United States have been more or less constant since 1999. The US homicide rates remained stable at about six per 100,000 inhabitants between 1998

Table 2.2 Prevalence rates of crime for England and Wales, the United States, Australia and Canada in 2003/4

	England and Wales	United States	Australia	Canada
Sexual crime against women	0.9%	1.4%	–	0.8%
Assault and threat	5.8%	5.3%	3.8%	3.0%
Burglary	3.5%	2.5%	2.5%	2.0%

and 2007. The figure for 2014 was 4.5 per 100,00 (Criminal Justice Information Services Division, 2015). These figures are lower than for the 1980s and 1990s in general. The figure for 1980 was ten, for example (US Census Bureau, 2011).

According to important international comparative data (Farrington *et al.*, 2004), homicide has also tended to decline since 1980 in some other countries included in the survey. In Australia, the homicide rate is about two homicides for every 100,000 people in the population, but has declined slightly; in Canada, the rate has dropped from three to two per 100,000. The Netherlands' homicide rate stayed remarkably constant over the period at one per 100,000. The UK figures have increased slightly over time but still are currently approximately 1.5 per 100,000 in the population. Other data (Barclay, Tavares and Siddique, 2001) show that the United States' homicide rates, although two or three times the rate for Western European countries, are comparatively low. For example, Finland has a homicide rate of 12, Russia a rate of 21 and South Africa a rate of 56 – nearly ten times the rate in the United States. National rates tend to disguise the fact that some areas within a country may have disproportionately high homicide rates. For example, the rate for Washington, DC, in the United States was virtually the same as the massive South African one at 51 per 100,000.

One interesting question is the extent to which countries worldwide have shown similar patterns in homicide – that is, are increases and declines over time similar across different nations. LaFree, Curtis, and McDowall (2015) undertook a study of 55 different nations with this question in mind. There is a broad agreement among researchers that violent crime rates began to increase in the United States and Western Europe around and about 1960 and continued to rise until around 1990 when violent crime rates began to decline as explained above. LaFree *et al.* found further evidence of this pattern. However, the pattern was not entirely reproduced in other parts of the world. For example, countries in Eastern Europe, despite showing a sharp decline in homicide in the 1990s just like the USA and Western Europe, do not show the same overall pattern. Eastern Europe had much higher levels of homicide than the West at the start of the 1950s but then showed a big decline in the 1950s to 1960s period. Overall this shows quite a different pattern from the US and Western Europe.

Anyone reading these comparative crime statistics will have concerns about the comparability of the definition of different crimes in different countries. This is a real worry. Recently the United Nations Office on Drugs and Crime has developed a system of definitions which may overcome concerns about comparability. This is known as the International Classification of Crime for Statistical Purposes (ICCS). The early research is promising (Bisogno, Dawson-Faber and Jandl (2015)). Such a scheme might be a boon to forensic and criminal psychology as well as criminology more generally.

Estimating the amount of crime

For certain types of offence, many crimes are not reported to the police. Assault has reporting rates of 38 per cent in England and Wales and 45 per cent in the United States. Sexual offences are less likely to be reported. The figures are 20 per cent for England and Wales and 28 per cent for the United States but the range is wide with a rate of 5 per cent in Spain and 43 per cent in Northern Ireland. Reporting rates found from victim surveys allow the 'true' rate of crime to be assessed from known numbers of crimes reported to the police. Thus, for example, the true rate of rape in England and Wales should be multiplied by approximately five (i.e. victim surveys suggest that just over 20 per cent of rapes are reported) in order to correct for the low reporting rate. Rates of reporting are highest for burglary in virtually all countries. The reason is probably the insurer's requirement that the crime is reported to the police if an insurance payment is to be made. Chapter 4 discusses, in part, the psychology of reporting crime.

Life-time likelihood of being a crime victim

Figures suggest that, in a lifetime, the vast majority of North Americans become victims of an index crime recorded by the police – 83 per cent will be victimised by violence in this way and 99 per cent by theft. Criminality may be common; victimisation is a virtual certainty (Bureau of Justice, 2001a). For every 1000 Americans from 12 years of age and above there are eleven simple assaults, three aggravated assaults, two robberies and one rape or other form of sexual assault (Bureau of Justice, 2011) each year. Based on the British Crime Survey of 2009/10, 22 per cent of the population had been the victim of violence that year (Flatley *et al.*, 2010). The British Crime Survey of 2000 (Home Office, 2001) found that 59 per cent had at some time in their life been the victim of a crime reported to the police. In contrast, only 10 per cent had been in court as a person accused of a crime. In other words, in terms of experiences of crime, the victim role is the commonest, despite the centrality of the offender in forensic and criminal psychology.

Conservative and radical interpretations

No matter how carefully obtained, criminal statistics are subject to interpretation. For any set of figures there are several equally viable interpretations. Crime statistics are aggregates of many distinct happenings and, by and large, we have little knowledge of the detail. For example, the US data on felony convictions in state and federal courts for 1994 (Bureau of Justice, 2001c) reveal that drug trafficking accounted for 20 per cent of convictions and drug possession for 12 per cent of convictions. That is, combined, the drugs offences are responsible for nearly a third of convictions. What should we conclude from these figures? One interpretation is that drugs offences are such a major crime problem that more should be done to arrest and punish offenders. This would imply a need for greater police activity, which ought to result in even more convictions. An alternative, more radical, view would be to point out that such high figures reflect the failure of policy on drugs to make significant inroads in reducing drug use. The country might be better off decriminalising drugs or some such strategy. The savings to the criminal justice system would be enormous simply in terms of time and money. Naturally, each of these positions can be criticised with further arguments. Nevertheless, the basic point should be clear – crime statistics do not carry with them implicit meanings: interpretation has to be imposed.

Take another example: black people are over-represented in both the homicide perpetrator and victim figures in the United States. In terms of rates standardised by population size, a black person has six times the risk of being a victim compared to a white person, and is eight times more likely to be a perpetrator (Fox and Zawitz, 2004). While some authors (Rushton, 1990) might interpret this as indicative of racial differences in the inheritance of criminal tendencies, for others they reflect the huge social inequalities experienced by black communities and biases in policing (e.g. Howitt and Owusu-Bempah, 1994; Stark, 1993). Of course, some explanations become more or less viable when other statistical information is incorporated. For example, the United States has achieved substantial reductions in violence between intimates (partners, spouses, etc.), which cannot possibly be accounted for by changes in the gene pool (e.g. Bureau of Justice, 2001d).

International variations in justice systems

Whatever the means by which crime rates are assessed, the socio-legal contexts in which forensic and criminal psychologists operate differ in many other respects. The variability in criminal justice systems, broadly defined, is immense. This is not generally problematic as most people will work solely within one criminal justice system. Nevertheless, it is important to understand that a given system is just one of many possibilities. Furthermore, each criminal justice system has many components of which practitioners need to be aware. By way of illustration, Table 2.3 gives some information from three criminal justice systems – Japan, France, and England and Wales (other parts of Britain have different systems). The data are taken from an international compendium of information about criminal justice systems around the world (International Crime Victimisation Survey, 2001). Despite the data being supplied by specialist researchers, certain information is unavailable from particular countries. A few areas of comparison have been taken to illustrate the similarities and diversities in countries both close together and far apart. The following points are fairly self-evident and are mostly illustrated in Table 2.3:

- *The legal system:* France, like most continental European countries as well as many African and Asian in addition, has an inquisitorial legal system in which judges or magistrates seek to obtain the truth about a particular case from various sources. In other words, they have a leading role in determining what evidence and expert advice is needed. In England and Wales (and other countries such as Canada, the United States and Australia, which derive their legal systems from Britain), the adversarial system is adopted: that is, the prosecution and defence are adversaries who battle to convince the judge or jury that theirs is the winning argument. Their success is then judged, often by a jury. The different systems vary in terms of the sorts of evidence that may be admitted as valid and the need to consider the fitness of the accused to stand trial. Japan basically moved from one system to another.
- *Jury system:* some legal systems do not use juries but rely on judges and magistrates to decide issues of guilt. Other systems use juries but there can be substantial differences in the sizes of the jury used or the rules used for determining the verdict of the jury. In some systems, it is possible for the judge to take part with the jury in determining guilt (see Chapter 23).
- *The age of criminal responsibility:* this is twice as old in Japan (20 years) as in England and Wales (10 years). Of course, there may be provision for treating young people separately, such as juvenile courts and other institutions, which reduce the apparent huge differences between the various countries. It may be helpful to note that Heilbrun *et al.* (1997) suggest that in most parts of the United States the trend is to allow younger people to be tried in adult courts. They report that, in the

Table 2.3 Some international comparisons of criminal justice systems

ASPECT	JAPAN	FRANCE	ENGLAND AND WALES
LEGAL SYSTEM	Influenced historically by French and German systems but more adversarial in recent times	Inquisitorial system – essentially the judge seeks the facts of the case from a variety of sources	Adversarial system based on cases put forward by prosecution and defence
JURY SYSTEM	Not in use in fact despite being available	Not used	Jury system for more serious crimes
AGE OF CRIMINAL RESPONSIBILITY	20 years of age	18 years of age	10 years of age but special provision up to 18 years
CRIMINAL STATISTICS: ASSAULTS AND THREATS IN ONE YEAR – VICTIM SURVEY**	0.6%	2.1%	5.6%
CRIMINAL STATISTICS: SEXUAL OFFENCES IN ONE YEAR – VICTIM SURVEY**	0.8%	0.3%	0.9%
CRIMINAL STATISTICS: ROBBERY IN YEAR – VICTIM SURVEY	0.2%	0.8%	1.4%
POLICE SYSTEM	Two-layered structure: (1) the national police and (2) the prefecture police	Three or more police divisions***	No national police force – separate forces at local level. Some smaller forces such as railway police
PRISON*	59/100,000	96/100,000	152/100,000
CIVIL CASES	–	A court can hear both civil and criminal cases	Separate systems for civil and criminal cases

Source: *Kings College London, Department of Law (2010)
**van Dijk, van Kesteren and Smit (2007)
***These include the police nationale, the gendarmerie nationale, and the compagnie republicaine de la securité

majority of jurisdictions, 14-year-olds can now be tried in criminal courts. This touches on fundamental beliefs about the nature of crime and how it is dealt with. This is discussed more fully in Chapter 3.

- *Crime statistics:* while, as we have seen, the figures vary among nations, it is equally important to note that crime classifications in different countries may not be the same. In other words, direct comparisons may be impossible. It is also notable that actual numbers of certain crimes such as murder and rape are probably rather lower than most people believe them to be. More recent data from international victim surveys have been added in the table.

- *Police system:* there are a number of differences among police organisations across nations. One particularly obvious dimension is the extent to which police organisations are national or local. Often there is a mixture of the two, but sometimes, as in the case of England and Wales, there are numerous small forces covering areas of just a few million people. The more small units there are then the greater the communication problems and, consequently, the greater the need for provision to ensure good inter-force communications.
- *Prison:* different nations differ substantially in their prison populations. This may be indicative of different base levels of crime, but it may also reflect profound differences in penal policies.
- *Civil cases:* civil law deals with legal cases that are about private rights rather than the public concern of crime. Criminal penalties (such as prison) do not apply in civil cases, where financial payments to the aggrieved party are the means of righting wrongs. In some jurisdictions, they are dealt with by the same courts, whereas in other jurisdictions there is a totally separate civil law court system. Civil courts may sometimes deal with criminal matters (e.g. civil actions have been brought against alleged criminals, but these do not result in criminal penalties).

Main points

- It is important for forensic and criminal psychologists to be familiar with trends in crime as reported in crime statistics and from surveys of the general population. A degree of sophistication is necessary in their interpretation since each source has its own particular characteristics. Crime rates obtained from victim surveys are different from those obtained by collating the number of crimes recorded by the police. Court statistics and prison statistics give us different sorts of information. It is unwise to regard the characteristics of different statistics as flaws.
- Quite high proportions of the general population are known to have been involved as victims and perpetrators of crime at some stage in their lives. Experimental studies have shown that various forms of dishonesty are very common. Of course, the precise figures will depend on quite how crime is defined. Clearly, the number of persistent offenders is a much lower figure.
- International comparisons reveal many differences between the criminal justice systems in different parts of the world. So research that is important in one country may have no bearing on what happens in another country. Similarly, crime statistics vary internationally in important ways. England and Wales seem to have disproportionately high rates of victimisation.

It is a substantial task to become sufficiently familiar with the legal system of any country to practise as a forensic and criminal psychologist. The international nature of research in the field should encourage researchers to develop a knowledge of these different systems of justice. If nothing else, such knowledge will help one to understand why certain sorts of research will be of interest in only some countries. Jury research may be relevant in the United States, Australia, Canada and the United Kingdom, but of much less interest to forensic and criminal psychologists from much of mainland Europe, for example. Some issues, such as inquisitorial versus adversarial systems, have been fairly extensively researched (e.g. Stephenson, 1992).

Further reading

Green, S., Johnson, H. and Young, P. (2009) *Understanding Crime and Criminal Justice Data* Buckingham: Open University Press.

Crime statistics are to be found in many locations on the Internet. These provide much more up-to-date information than is possible in most books.

UK Crime Statistics Collection may be found at: https://www.gov.uk/government/collections/crime-statistics

US Bureau of Justice, Bureau of Justice Statistics: http://www.ojp.gov/bjs/

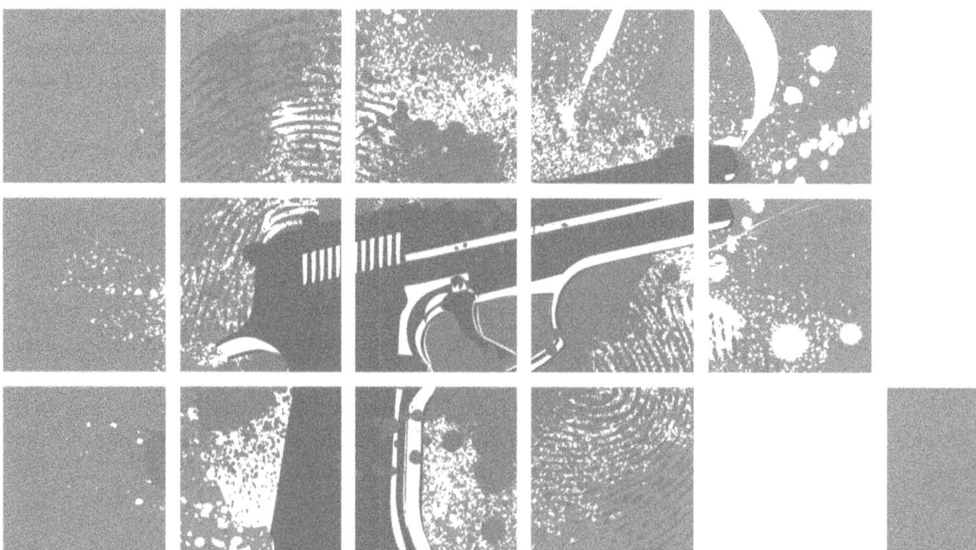

Chapter 3

Crime and the public

Overview

- What is a crime is defined by a complex social process. Identical events may be classified as crime or otherwise, depending on the circumstances. The decision to report events to the police as crimes is just one important aspect of this. Government policy may lead to certain crimes being targeted for police attention.
- There is evidence that the public appear to have a tough-minded attitude towards crime. This may affect the administration of criminal justice, perhaps by influencing politicians to be more tough-minded on crime.
- The public's knowledge about aggregate rates of crime and trends in criminal statistics tends to be generally inaccurate. This is partly because it is difficult to think statistically in terms of percentages and probabilities.
- Moral panics are essentially an overreaction to an event (such as a crime) that has been perceived as a threat or a risk to society's dominant values. The alarm generated may lead to demands for action to be taken against the source of the threat. The strength of feeling tends to be self-nurturing such that the panic escalates.
- The media and personal experience form the basis of the public's knowledge about crime. The links between the two are far from simple and not apparent in all research. There is often little or no relationship between an individual's risk of victimisation and their level of fear of crime. This is the fear–victimisation paradox. Understanding the psychological processes involved in the fear of crime seems to improve predictions about media influences on the individual and the consequences of victimisation.
- Theories about the origins of the fear of crime suggest that: (1) the distorted image of crime portrayed by the media affects heavy television viewers disproportionately (cultivation theory); (2) any source of information may provide the individual with a particularly vivid but negative impression of a particular crime or a particular sort of crime such that the individual responds to similar situations to the vivid imagery with fear (availability heuristic theory); and (3) fear of crime is the consequence of the independent influences of beliefs about the negative consequences of being victimised and the subjective risk of being victimised (cognitive theory).

Introduction

Crime does not just involve criminals. It is the result of a complex social process, which operates at virtually every conceivable level of social and psychological analysis. Crime is not merely (or even) the product of the mind of the criminal; it is a social product. According to Ainsworth (2000a), the path from the commission of a crime to the punishment of an offender is a long, complex and tortuous one. The factors involved include the following:

- what laws apply;
- what the set of circumstances surrounding the events is;
- what the public thinks about crime;
- what the victim thinks about crime;
- what the ethos of the policing system is;
- what the system for dealing with psychiatric cases is;
- who decides whom to prosecute;
- the rules governing court procedure;
- the skills of the lawyer;
- the characteristics of the judge;
- what the jurors have read in the newspapers about the case;
- any one of a number of other aspects of the crime, the criminal and the criminal justice system. Each is essential and, in some circumstances, any may become crucial.

The same event can be seen quite differently according to the prevailing circumstances. Defining when a crime has occurred is not merely complex but can involve a multiplicity of perspectives. It may seem that from one perspective a crime has been committed, but from another perspective a crime may not have been committed. All of these things are dependent on the jurisdiction involved since the practice of the law varies not only in different parts of the world but, in some cases, in different parts of a country. The thief who is so mentally impaired that he/she does not know that he/she is committing a crime may be not guilty of theft in the eyes of the court. The driver who inadvertently drives over the speed limit because his/her speedometer is faulty, in law may well be committing a crime even though he/she had not intended to, simply because this is a strict (i.e. absolute liability) offence. And some things which are illegal today, may once have not been subject to the law. For example, it is only in recent years that an offence of grooming a child for sexual purposes has been created in the United Kingdom and other parts of the world, despite it being a matter of concern for many years. Hate crimes are also a relatively new category of crime. Conversely, sometimes things that were illegal cease to be so, as in the case of suicide.

Legal processes are social in nature and cannot be understood simply in terms of knowledge of the relevant law. Figure 3.1 shows a little of the complexity of the processes involved. A number of issues should be considered:

- The figure suggests a relatively closed criminal justice system but this is an incomplete picture. It is a more open system than this implies and involves the wider social system (e.g. the media may put pressure on the police to find the culprit).
- Legislation is the result of a political process that may involve interest groups pressuring the government, for example. An illustration of this would be the pressure of feminist groups to change the laws and practices concerning domestic violence.
- Furthermore, some actions by the police – such as attempts to control private sexual practices that may be illegal in a technical sense – may bring media and public condemnation.
- The figure would seem to indicate that the criminal law is the recourse for the victim. However, there are other remedies available, such as using the civil law to achieve compensation. Private prosecutions of homicide suspects who have been acquitted by the criminal courts are an example of this. Standards of evidence are slightly less exacting in the civil law and the penalties are also less serious – financial costs rather than imprisonment being involved.
- Single arrows operating in just one direction join the elements of the system in Figure 3.1. In reality, each of the elements of the system may interact with other elements. For example, if it appears to the public that there is failure to lead to the conviction of the offender in sufficient numbers of rape cases, victims may be unwilling to report the crime to the police.

Attitudes towards crime

The views of the public about crime are of political importance. Governments are keen to demonstrate that they have the right policies on crime, prison and the police, for instance. For that reason, public attitudes may impinge on many aspects of the criminal justice system. Public opinion is widely surveyed on matters such as satisfaction with the police, judges and the prison system. For example, it became increasingly common for juveniles to be processed through the same courts as adult prisoners in Canada and the US. Research in the 1990s showed that the Canadian public supported processing youngsters in the same courts as adults (Sprott, 1998). Those who believed this tended also to have a harsher attitude to the punishment of juveniles. Although the public did not create the

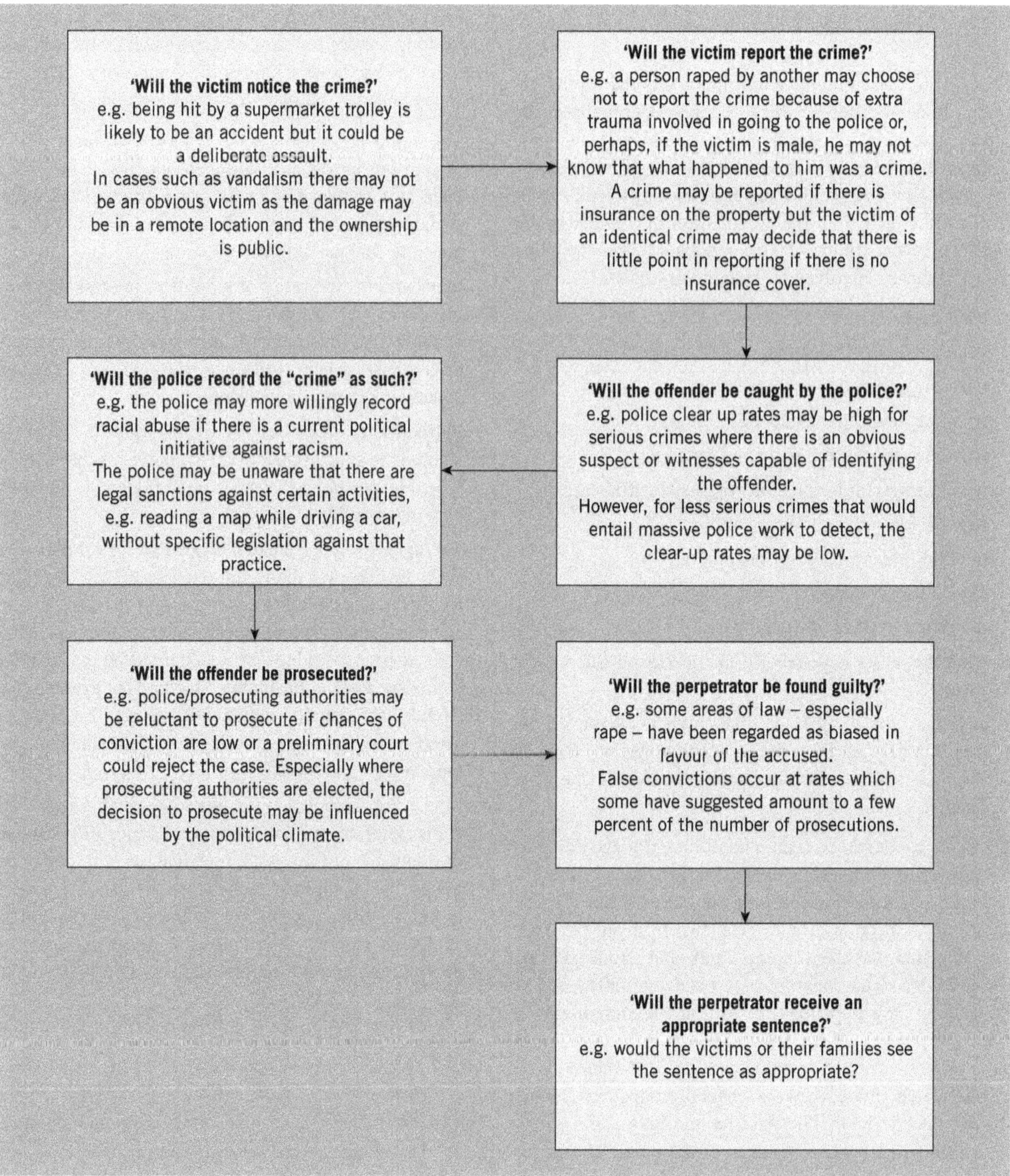

Figure 3.1 Stages in the process of crime described by Ainsworth

Source: After *Psychology and Crime: Myths and Reality*, Harlow: Longman (Ainsworth, P.B. 2000) Copyright © Pearson Education Ltd. 2000

situation in which the separate youth system of justice increasingly became eroded in Canada, the public supported it.

Another good example is the public's beliefs about recidivism after leaving prison. If recidivism was infrequent, the case for, say, keeping prison terms short would be stronger and, perhaps, attitudes towards the rehabilitation of offenders might be more positive. However, the public seems to believe that recidivism is rife and almost the norm for many types of offence. Evidence for this comes from a study of a range of individuals in Spain and Canada who have good educational backgrounds and, mostly, a close interest in criminology (Redondo, Luque and Funes, 1996). The Spanish sample believed that, for a first offender, the average likelihood of their reoffending for drug trafficking offences was high:

- On average, they thought that the likelihood of reoffending was 61 per cent within five years. The figure reached 100 per cent average prediction of reoffending for multi-recidivists (i.e. individuals having offended and been convicted many times). This contrasts with actual rates of 11 per cent and 44 per cent for the two types of offender in Spain. These figures are clearly much lower than the public's expectations.
- Similar findings were obtained for sexual offences. Recidivism estimates ranged from 31 per cent to 54 per cent in both the Canadian and Spanish samples for first offenders, recidivists and multi-recidivists. In reality, recidivism for sex offences tended to be rather low in sex offenders in both countries.

In other words, it would seem that the public strongly tends towards the view that once a criminal, always a criminal. Perhaps that is why custodial sentences are regarded favourably by many members of the public. Apart from being of interest in their own right, the public's knowledge, beliefs and concerns about crime need to be understood since they may impinge on how criminal justice is administered.

Knowledge of crime

People know all sorts of things about crimes they have witnessed, as well as those they have been told about or have read about or seen in the media. Nevertheless, the public's knowledge about criminal statistics suggests that the public's perception of rates of crime is rather inaccurate, no matter how it is measured. Feilzer (2015) reports that since the 1950s, numerous studies in different parts of the world have shown public knowledge of crime to be poor. For example, the public tends to assume that crime rates are broadly increasing despite the evidence being to the contrary in recent years. Lord Ashcroft (2011) conducted an online survey of over 2000 people about various things, including the crime rate in the UK. About three-quarters of the public thought that the crime rate had either risen or remained unchanged over the period 1997 to 2010. But the figures from the British Crime Survey (Crime Survey of England and Wales) suggested that the crime rate had actually fallen by 43 per cent during that period. Just 2 per cent of the public had said that this was the case (Kershaw, Nicolas and Walker, 2008; Chaplin, Flatley and Smith, 2011).

Another example comes from a survey of students at a British university (Ainsworth and Moss, 2000). These

Box 3.1 Key concept

Moral panics

The concept of moral panic has its origin in Stanley Cohen's study of the phenomenon of youth crime in Britain in the 1960s (Cohen, 1972, 1980). At the time, the two opposing teen gangs – Mods versus Rockers – came to the attention of the media and the public. Clashes between the two, often at seaside towns at weekends and holiday times, was reported in terms that, to Cohen at least, seemed out of proportion to the scale of the actual phenomenon. There was a sense of outrage and distress, fuelled by the media, which led for calls for action against such youth crime. Furthermore, there was a process of escalation in which the media overstated the situation and attributed to Mods and Rockers a far greater threat than existed in real life but, at the same time, the Mods and Rockers were attracted by the publicity and excitement that it brought. So there was a sort of spiral which fed public opinion.

A little later, Hall *et al.* (1978) applied the concept to an analysis of those street crimes commonly called mugging. Once again, the perceived threat was greater than the evidence of the real-life phenomenon. Nevertheless, the public feeling was that something had to be done about mugging. This encouraged police activity in the community which, again, could not be justified by the more objective evidence.

The term 'moral panic' has commonly been used to describe the circumstances in which demands for new legislation or other forms of legal action are intense. So, for example, the term has been used to describe situations in which there is a high level of demand that action is taken against a particular form of crime or criminal: for example, calls for legislation to deal with child sexual abuse, protests against paedophiles living in the community and so forth. While it may be true that emotions are intense in such cases, the term 'moral panic' is merely descriptive of the events rather than an explanation of why interest is at such levels. Hall *et al.* (1978) suggested that moral panics tend to occur when two ideologies are in conflict. For example, the emergence of the Mods and Rockers may have been the result of traditional moral values held by adults and emerging youth cultures with different ideas about the freedom and appropriate lifestyle of young people. It is the conflict between these two ideological positions that results in the moral panic.

students were enrolled on an undergraduate module on crime and deviance so they might have been expected to show more sophistication about the topic than the general public. This proved not to be the case. The students were asked a number of questions and were provided with a range of answers from which to choose. These included:

1. How many crimes were recorded by the (England and Wales) police per year in the 1990s?

   3 million
   5 million
   8 million
   12 million

   Only about a quarter correctly chose 5 million. There was a tendency to overestimate.

2. What proportion of officially recorded crimes do crimes of violence make up?

   5% 10% 20% 30% 40% 50%

   Again, about a quarter chose the correct answer, 10%. About a half said more than the true figure.

3. What percentage of crimes result in someone being convicted and sentenced in court?

   2% 5% 10% 20% 30% 40%

   Only one in ten chose the first option of 2%. In other words, the vast majority failed to appreciate what a low figure it is.

It can be questioned whether one would expect the public to know in any detail the sort of aggregate findings which are found in criminal statistics. The general public do not have a great interest in statistics and statistical data in general and is likely to dismiss statistics as misleading (Howitt, 1992, 1998b). It is likely that only specialists would be familiar with the detail of crime statistics. Of course, annual crime statistics sometimes feature in the news but this is infrequent by its very nature and, given the public's distrust of statistical data, even those reading about such statistics may take them with a grain of salt. Perhaps the most important thing is the public's general perception of the extent to which society is becoming increasingly criminal and risky (Docherty, 1990) irrespective of the trends to be found in criminal statistics.

The nature of the fear of crime

The disciplines of criminology, sociology, psychology and politics all share an interest in the topic of the public's fear of crime. It is of interest to political scientists since government's have an interest in measuring fear of crime. From the state's point of view, the less fear of crime, in a sense, the better job the government is doing. Different areas may have different levels of fear of crime which may be a pointer to where crime is a particularly difficult problem. It is probably easier to influence the public's fear of crime than the amount of crime in society. The general public demonstrates its fear of criminal victimisation in any number of different ways. Table 3.1 illustrates some of these indicators based on international data. The fear that one's home is likely to be burgled is particularly rife in England and Wales, Ireland and Australia, for example. The belief that one is unsafe in the street after dark is common among the public everywhere, but especially so in England and Wales and Scotland. Practical steps against crime, such as installing a burglar alarm at home, are especially common in England and Wales but more so in Ireland.

Surveys of the public's fear of crime are very common. Despite the abundance of statistics collected over more than fifty years, not too much is known about the psychological meaning of the concept of fear of crime. One might suggest that it is a political rather than a psychological concept. Long-term data is available from various sources, but one of the most useful is the British Crime Survey (now known as the Crime Survey of England and Wales). This regularly asks a random sample of the public about a

Table 3.1 Some international comparisons for indicators of fear of crime

Indicator of fear	England and Wales	Scotland	Ireland	Australia	Canada	USA
Burglary of house likely or very likely in coming year	35%*	21%	33%	36%	25%	16%
Feel unsafe or very unsafe in street after dark	32%	30%	27%	19%	17%	19%
% homes with a burglar alarm system	42%	33%	49%	27%	28%	28%

*Figures taken from van Dijk, van Kesteren and Smit (2007)

range of crime-related matters, including their fear of crime (Allen, 2004). Jansson (2007) reports data from the British Crime Survey over a period of 25 years ending in 2006. Broadly speaking, worry about a variety of crimes reached its peak in 1994 but, since then, the level of worry has declined. For the British Crime Survey of 2005/6, 17 per cent of respondents were very worried about violent crime, 14 per cent were very worried about vehicle crime, and 13 per cent were very worried about burglary. The highest rate of worry was found among women for the crime of rape. According to Allen (2004), some sectors of society are more fearful of crime than others. Women are disproportionately more worried about burglary and violent crime than men. Those over 75 years of age tend to be the least worried about these crimes in this particular study, though the literature on the fear of crime in general is somewhat ambivalent as to whether younger or older people have the greater fear of crime. People who reported that their general health was poorer tended to be more likely to be worried about crime – those with poor health were nearly twice as likely to report being very worried about burglary than those in good health. This is indicative that the fear of crime tends to be greater in those who might be seen as more vulnerable. Professionals were the least likely to be worried about crime and people living in the most deprived areas tended to be the most worried about crime. People who believed that crime rates had increased in the previous two years were more likely to have high levels of worry about crime.

Just what does the fear of crime imply? That the individual's life is dominated by the fear? Farrall and Gadd (2004) queried the extent to which fear of crime is a significant feature of most people's lives. It is not the same thing to suggest that many people have some fear of crime as to suggest that they constantly or frequently are in fear of crime. Do people generally feel anxious about the possibility of victimisation? Typically in surveys something like a quarter of people say that they are very afraid of certain crimes such as burglary and rape. However, just how often do individuals feel very afraid? Farrall and Gadd asked participants, 'In the past year, have you ever felt fearful about the possibility of becoming a victim of crime?' (p. 128). One-third of participants said that they had felt fearful in the previous year of which nearly a half said that they had felt fearful between one and four times. Fifteen per cent of the entire sample claimed to have experienced quite high or very high levels of fear, but only half of these said that they had felt afraid five or more times in the year. In other words, less than 10 per cent of people had experienced high levels of fear once every three months or so. In general, then, experience of a high level of fear of crime is uncommon and fear of crime is not a constant feature of people's lives.

It is usually beneficial to consider topics in forensic and criminal psychology from an international perspective in order to see how this extends, challenges and improves our understanding. In doing so, it is possible to see how the fear of crime is manipulable by the state. For example, the fear of crime in Poland under the Communist regime in the 1970s and 1980s found expression in ways which were very different from the West. It was important under Communism that the country was free from the high levels of crime which Western society suffered from. According to Szumski (1993), a survey conducted in 1977 showed that two-thirds of Polish citizens were not afraid of crime at all and another quarter said that they were rarely afraid of crime. In contrast with the West where fear of crime is common, very few Poles showed any fear of crime. The sorts of crimes which Polish people saw as a threat to society were very different from the violent crimes which dominate fear of crime in Western countries. Poles mentioned crimes like profiteering, bribery and corruption, appropriation of public property and theft of private property, and abuse of power by persons holding executive office as the most worrying. One reason for the very different situation in Poland compared to the West was the way in which crime statistics could be influenced by the activities of the police. At that time, the police in Poland could include in crime statistics only offences confirmed by them as crimes. In other words, they did not include crimes simply because they had been reported to them. Such a system left a lot of discretion for the police to influence what sort of crimes should be included in the recorded levels of crime. The police, for example, would know that violent crime rates should be kept low and so they may have decided that some acts of violence did not amount to a crime. This low level of recorded crime was held to indicate progress in building a Communist society. If crime rates increased then the state amended legislation, resulting in even more repressive social policies. Szumski argues that the figures were essentially manipulated. Fear of crime, it would seem, can be as much a social creation as an objective response to the reality of crime.

What influences fear of crime?

There are three main ways in which our levels of fear of crime might be influenced:

- Our direct knowledge about crime in our immediate community and beyond. In other words, all of those sources of information available to us including personal experiences of crime, knowing people who have been victimised, and gossip about crime at the local and international level.

- The coverage of crime news in the mass media and the coverage of fictional crime in popular entertainment.
- Personality and social characteristics which make us more or less afraid of crime. By way of illustration, Bazargan (1994) found that fear of victimisation at home related to factors such as feeling lonely, having poorer educational standards and believing that neighbours are not trustworthy and lack vigilance when it comes to crime.

But the relationship between sources of information about the risk of crime and the fear of crime is far from being a simple one to understand. Clark (2004) writes about what she describes as the fear–victimisation paradox following Lindquist and Duke (1982). This refers to the often unpredictable relationship between reported fear of crime and the actual risk of personal victimisation. Basically, it is found that those objectively the most at risk of being victimised are among the least likely to be afraid of crime. So we can say that the fear of crime has no clear and invariant relationship to the statistical risk of being a victim of crime. Asked about the risk of violence and their personal fear of it, the elderly tend to report the highest levels (Bazargan, 1994; Vanderveen, 2006). Yet, when we look to see who is statistically the most likely to be the victim of violence, the victims turn out to be much the same group as their victimisers for the most part: that is, males in their late adolescent and early adult years – the very group who in some surveys claim to be the least bothered by the risk of being victimised. The ability to deal effectively with an attack or assault is an element leading to differences in levels of fear of crime. Women, for example, who believe that they are unable to defend themselves from a sexual attack tended to have a higher level of fear of sexual violence (Custers and Van den Bulck, 2013). Such women also believed that they were more likely to suffer a sexual attack and that sexual violence has severe consequences.

Gender and the fear of crime

Women in general seem to have higher levels of fear of crime than men. Feminists have claimed that women are discouraged from being independent through being inculcated with a fear of an unpredictable attack by a stranger (Walter, 1996). Put another way, this is a means of keeping women 'in their place'. Women tend to fear the sorts of crime that could be perpetrated against them by strangers in public places (Stanko, 1995; Voumvakis and Ericson, 1982). However, crime statistics show consistently that it is men who are most at risk of an attack in public places and by a person who they do not know. In contrast, women are most at risk from physical violence by people they know. If they are sexually attacked, it is likely that the perpetrator will be familiar to them. Date and marital rape are neither rare nor trivial matters (Ainsworth, 2000a; US Department of Commerce, Economics and Statistics Information, 1996).

Sutton, Robinson and Farrall (2011) carried out an intriguing experiment on women's fear of crime which sheds light on the idea that women's independence is limited by the fear of crime. They took a sample of men and women in the UK and asked them to complete a fear of crime survey. The fear of crime questions were well-established ones from the research literature. Participants were asked to rate their level of fear of burglary, assault, vandalism, sexual assault and being mugged as well as a number of other questions. Responses to these fear of crime questions were combined to form an overall measure of fear of crime. As one might expect, based on other research, it was found that women did indeed have higher levels of fear of crime than men. But the researchers did something rather interesting. Participants in the study were split into two groups which were given quite different instructions about how to answer the questions. The first group were given the instruction to be 'totally honest and accurate' when giving their answers. The second group were told to answer the questions in a way which put the participant 'in the best possible light'. What emerged is intriguing. The men who were instructed to present themselves in the best possible light answered in a way which portrayed them as less afraid of crime compared to the men who were asked to be totally honest and accurate. It is perhaps easy to see why this was the case. It is normative to expect men to be brave and strong, so men faking their answers to appear in the best possible light gave low ratings of their fear of crime. That is, they behaved as if it is normative that men are not afraid of crime. The women who were asked to present themselves in the best possible light responded very differently. They presented themselves as being more afraid of crime than women who were instructed to be totally honest and accurate. In other words, the women behaved as if it were normative that they should be afraid of crime. Men underplay their fears and women overplay their fears. Sutton *et al.*'s research fits well with the idea that the inculcation of a fear of crime in women is a mechanism by which women's freedom is restricted as suggested by Brownmiller (1975).

Of course, other explanations of gender differences in the fear of crime have been put forward. The idea that some groups of people – women, for example – have higher levels of fear of crime because they are more vulnerable warrants more rigorous examination and cannot be taken for granted. It needs to be demonstrated that vulnerability is the explanation of the gender difference. Jackson (2009) attempted to find support for this. His basic research procedure was a postal survey in London. In the questionnaire sent to participants, he listed seven crimes including personal crimes and property crimes. Women had no greater worries about property crime than men so we can concentrate on the personal crimes which take place in the street. These included being attacked by a stranger, robbed or mugged, and being harassed, threatened or verbally abused. Participants had to make a range of ratings for each of the crimes. These ratings included their level of worry about the crime, their perception of their personal risk of being a victim of the crime, their perception of their ability to prevent the crime happening, and their perception of the seriousness of the consequences of being victimised. Women were more worried, felt more at risk, felt the consequences of being a victim would be more serious, and felt less in control of being able to prevent the crime. A statistical model of the relationship showed that women's worries about crime could be explained by the risk of being a victim, their perceptions of being able to control the crime from happening, and the more serious consequences of being a victim for them. In other words, vulnerability as measured by these three things explains the gender difference in worry about crime.

It is important to get any gender differences in the fear of crime into proportion. Gilchrist, Bannister, Ditton and Farrall (1998) argue that gender differences in fear of crime are overstated. They make the argument that fear of crime itself is at fairly low levels and that differences between men and women, where they exist, are not startling. For example, the British Crime Survey (Home Office, 2001) indicated that 18 per cent of men claimed to be very worried about burglary compared with 26 per cent of women. For mugging, 12 per cent of males claimed to be very worried compared with 26 per cent of females. And we have seen examples of crimes where there is no gender difference in terms of fear of crime.

Is fear of crime a fear?

There has tended to be a greater focus on the influence of perceptions of the risk of being a victim on fear of crime than on any psychological factors which contribute to fear of crime. Perceptions of the risk of being a crime victim are cognitive mechanisms which link causally crime to the fear of crime (e.g. Farrall, Jackson and Gray, 2007). However, the relationship between crime and the fear of crime is a complex matter. Decades of research on the relationship between perceptions of the risk of crime and the fear of crime have yielded somewhat mixed findings. According to Chadee, Austen and Ditton (2007), the size of the correlation between the two in the research literature has ranged from very small to very large. This leads to the question of whether more purely psychological mechanisms might play a part. One way of looking at this is to ask just what is meant by 'fear' in the term 'the fear of crime'? Is it fear in any psychologically meaningful sense? Clark (2004) asked whether the fear of crime is actually a crime phobia which, like other phobias, would be a debilitating condition that can severely constrain a person's day-to-day activities. Clark analysed Australian survey data which contained both fear of crime items and items related to various types of phobia. Fear of crime was measured for personal crime (violence), property crime and sexually based crime. She found that the three phobias that she studied – social phobia, blood-injury phobia and agoraphobia – tended to coexist. In other words, those who had a social phobia were more likely to have the other two phobias and so forth. If fear of crime is a phobia like these other phobias then one would expect that those with higher levels of phobias in general would tend to have higher levels of fear of crime. This simply was not the case. If anything, there is a slight tendency for fear of crime to be *lower* in those with greater levels of other phobias. The findings for each type of crime followed the general trend. So Clark's conclusion was that fear of crime is not like typical phobias. Reflecting on this, Clark pointed out that there is nothing in the vast fear of crime literature to suggest that fear of crime is dysfunctional or irrational in the way that other phobias are. This would imply a basic reason why fear of crime is different from phobias in general. She suggests that fear serves protective functions and so to reduce the fear may be to encourage the abandonment of protective strategies.

It is difficult, despite this failure, not to believe that fear of crime must relate to the affective/emotional system in some way. Chadee and Ng Ying (2013) considered it possible that fear of crime may also be shaped by other forms of fear, in particular, general fear which, of course, is not phobia. They describe general fear as being the typical level of (fearful) emotional response that an individual shows to real and imaginary events and things in the physical and mental world. Fear of death, illness, injury and animals typify the sorts of fear which are included in General Fear. Although perceived risk of victimisation is likely to be affected by an individual's knowledge about crime, general fear is far less likely to be influenced by an individual's knowledge about crime. Chadee and Ng Ying draw on the literature on self-interest to argue that people favour circumstances in support of their and their family's material well-being (Sears and Funk, 1990). In this regard, crime may result in financial loss but, more importantly, there are more abstract consequences such as feeling unsafe, feeling vulnerable, and feeling threatened. Chadee and Ng Ying set about testing their hypothesis that general fear was a more important antecedent of the fear of crime than perceived risk of crime victimisation. The latter has dominated previous research. They measured the three important variables in the ways:

- The Fear of Crime Scale (Ferraro, 1995) assessed fear of both personal crimes (such as violent assault) and property crimes (such as burglary).
- General fear was measured using Scherer's (1988) categories which involved scenarios such as death of an important person, a house fire, personal illness and loss of income.
- Perceived Risk of Crime Scale (Ferraro, 1995) which involved the participant giving estimates of the likelihood that they would be a victim of different types of crime in the next year.

The findings of the research supported strongly both General Fear and Perceived Risk of Crime as predictors of Fear of Crime. However, General Fear was the better predictor of the two. The important outcome, it should be stressed, was that a psychologically meaningful measure of fear was related to differences in Fear of Crime, suggesting in part that Fear of Crime involves genuine fear.

Theories of fear of crime

Whatever measures of the fear of crime actually indicate, concerns about fear of crime need explanation. The concept of fear of crime has spawned a great deal of research over the last fifty or more years. Despite this, the field lacks a degree of coherence which ought to be rectified – hence the importance of theory. In this section we will describe three rather different theories which deal with the fear of crime. These are cultivation theory, availability heuristic theory and cognitive theory. Each tackles a somewhat different area of concern. Cultivation theory is a theory of media influence on the fear of crime whereas availability heuristic theory and cognitive theory explain the psychological processes which contribute to the fear of crime.

Cultivation theory

Cultivation theory is an archetypal approach to the influence of the mass media on the public's perceptions of crime and media effects more generally. The basic assumption of cultivation theory is that the mass media and television in particular are means of cultural transmission (Gerbner, 1972). George Gerbner was a media researcher and theorist who carried out numerous extensive content analyses of American television to get a precise picture of the world as represented by the media. Many hours were spent by researchers coding television output to identify the way it portrays the world in both fictional and news output. The culture as represented in the world of television content was very different from the real world. There is a difference (the cultural differential) between the culture as represented by television and the culture of real life (see Figure 3.2). In terms of television, Gerbner was able to analyse the characteristics of portrayals of crime – what sort of person perpetrates criminal acts, what sort of person is a victim of criminal acts, what sorts of criminal acts are perpetrated, and so forth. Television distorts the nature of crime compared to what is regarded as reality as measured through crime statistics. A particularly good example of this is the overrepresentation of violent crime and the way that this is biased towards acts perpetrated by strangers. As we saw in Chapter 2, real-life crime is dominated by

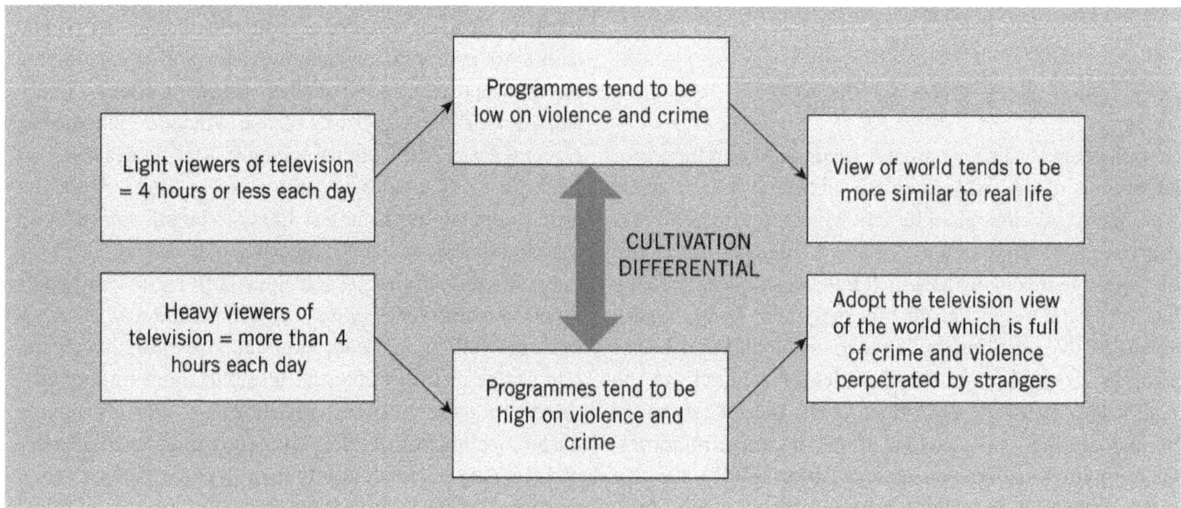

Figure 3.2 Media effects on viewer's worldview according to the cultivation analysis model

mundane crimes such as theft and fraud. In real life, violence is more common between people who know each other than between strangers. A great deal of information derived from Gerbner's analyses of the content of television showed that the message about crime it transmitted was a highly distorted world of crime (Gerbner, 1972; Gerbner *et al.*, 1977; Signorielli and Gerbner, 1988).

Heavy and light viewers of television differ not simply in terms of the amount they watch, but also in terms of what they watch. Heavy viewers typically watch a high proportion of fictitious programmes compared to, say, news programmes. In other words, heavy viewers experience a more distorted view of crime than light viewers. However, light viewers do not necessarily experience an entirely realistic view of crime from television. There is plenty of evidence to suggest that media crime news is selective in favour of the more serious and sensational crimes (Marsh, 1991; Schlesinger, Tumber and Murdock, 1991). Gerbner's argument was that the world that the heavy viewer witnesses on television is much more distorted than that experienced by the lighter viewer. The basic prediction of cultivation theory is that the culture of crime cultivated in the heavy viewer will be more like the television view than that inculcated in the lighter viewer. So, for example, since the world of television involves attacks by strangers, then the heavy viewer should be more likely to believe that he or she is at risk from strangers.

The main things to remember concerning the value of cultivation theory are as follows:

- In Gerbner's analyses, there does seem to be a very weak relationship between heavy viewing and having a distorted perception of crime and violence. This relationship is not due to 'third' variables such as social class which may be related to viewing and perceptions of crime and violence. Nevertheless, even shortly after Gerbner's studies were first published, other researchers were reanalysing the original data. They found evidence of the effects of third variables. When the influence of variables such as type of neighbourhood and other demographic characteristics of the sample were removed statistically, the relationship between media and fear of crime became negligible or even reversed (Ditton *et al.*, 2004).
- Gerbner's research relied on very large samples to achieve statistical significance. The relationships found were small or modest at best.
- There is evidence that Gerbner's findings, although modest, are not found in all countries or communities. For example, the evidence is that the relationship has not been found in the United Kingdom, despite a number of studies (e.g. Gunter, 1987). This may reflect a cultural difference, perhaps even a difference in media environments.

This style of research has not produced compelling evidence of the role of the media in creating fear of crime. This is not to suggest that the media are unimportant in people's response to crime but merely that a simple and direct relationship between media use and the fear of crime of the sort envisaged by Gerbner may be inadequate. More subtle processes may be involved. For example, it is assumed that people attend to all of the news which the media put before them whereas, in reality, people are very selective in terms of the crime news that they pay attention to (Graber, 1980) so it is somewhat unpredictable what information about crime they become aware of. Research that predicts rather subtler relationships between media use and fear of crime may be a little more successful. For example, Liska and Baccaglini (1990) examined responses to the questions 'How safe do you feel in your local neighbourhood in the day? At night?' It was possible to predict feeling unsafe in the neighbourhood by reference to the local media coverage. In the communities where people tended to feel unsafe, the local newspapers covered more local crime. The more news about, say, non-local homicides, the less the fear in the neighbourhood.

Gerbner's approach suggests that people act as statisticians adding up instances of crime in the media to get an overall picture of the world of crime according to television. This seems very unlikely. Is it not the case that people give prominence to particular crimes which may be notorious or geographically local for example? We can turn now to a theory that basically makes the assumption that certain events are more likely to be recalled from memory to influence fear of crime.

Availability heuristic theory

Information of certain sorts is more retrievable from memory than other sorts of information. Quite what this information is may vary substantially from person to person. Just what happens when an individual is approached by a researcher asking about their fear of crime in the local neighbourhood? It is likely that people do not spend their days routinely computing the risks of being victimised in different locations based on statistical knowledge of crime risks. Obviously they may feel unsafe in some situations, but this is different. A woman who steps into a car with a man she has only just met at a nightclub may become afraid when she suddenly remembers that a young woman was found murdered a few miles away recently, having left a nightclub in the same circumstances. Basically such vivid and recent images are more readily available from memory and may affect the individual's fear of crime. Shrum's (1996) *availability heuristic* approach is based on this simple idea. To the extent to which the media (or any other factor) creates vivid and readily accessible images of crimes in the mind of the individual, this sort of imagery will be more readily accessed from memory than less graphic imagery would be. This imagery will, in turn, partly determine the fear of crime.

In a study seeking to demonstrate the availability heuristic, Shrum (1996) studied the contents of television soap operas over a two-week period. The story lines of the soap operas were reviewed during this time for 'critical portrayals' (meaning those events that were dominant in the soap episodes). Crime was a major theme – and especially rape. Consequently, reasoned Shrum, the viewers of the programmes should have rape imagery more readily available from memory than those who did not watch the soap operas. The availability heuristic hypothesis was supported. Viewers were quicker in answering questions such as 'What percentage of women are raped in their lifetime?' This appeared to be a specific effect and not related to the general amount of television the individual watched.

These findings are supported by other research. For example, Vitelli and Endler (1993) used a more general measure of the availability heuristic. They based their index on the number of crimes participants knew of through the media, but with other information in addition:

- the number of times they had personally been victimised;
- the information they had obtained from other people.

For men, one study showed that the availability of media imagery went together with a lack of a belief that they could cope with victimisation situations. For women, the media were also important. Additionally, higher levels of fear of crime were also associated with their general levels of anxiety.

Riddle (2010) carried out an experimental study in which participants were shown different amounts and different extremities of violent fictional TV programmes. Those who watched a greater amount of vivid violent TV tended to see crime as being more prevalent than those watching less amounts of TV with low vivid content.

The availability heuristic has also been applied to how people form judgements as to the appropriate punishment for crimes, such as when a researcher asks how long a sentence should be given to someone who commits a robbery. Stalans (1993) suggests that recommendations for punishment are, in part, dependent on the image of robbery that the mind conjures up. If they conjure up a memory of a local crime which a friend has told them about, this may have involved little or no violence. So when they decide on their preferred punishment for the abstract, general case, they will be thinking of a robbery involving little or no violence. As a consequence, they may recommend a shorter sentence. If they recollect from memory a particularly sensational and violent robbery then they may recommend a long sentence when asked about their preferred punishment. Stalans found that participants whose source of information about robberies was the mass media alone tended to have imagery about robbery involving higher levels of violence. In comparison, they tended to have imagery about robbery as involving little or no violence if their source of memories was a mixture of both the mass media and interpersonal sources. This would amount to a more realistic view of robbery since crime statistics show that that most robberies have no or low levels of violence, the consequence being that either personal experience or the media could help determine preferred sentences depending on what was available in the memory of the participant. Two interesting trends were found concerning punishment. She found that participants who could readily recall a real-life robbery which took place locally were more likely to recommend harsher punishment in an abstract case. But, similarly, participants who knew of many instances of robbery from the mass media also tended to recommend harsher sentencing for the abstract case. In other words, the availability heuristic and stereotypes partly derived from the mass media are alternative sources on which to base crime judgements.

Cognitive theory

Winkel (1998) points out that much of the research indicates that there are two distinct components of emotional vulnerability:

- The subjective belief about the likelihood or risk of the event.
- The belief about the seriousness of the consequences of experiencing those events.

He suggests that these are much the same dimensions as those that emerge in the study of the fear of crime. The first element he calls the *subjective victimisation risk* and the second element is the *perceived negative impact* that would result from victimisation. Thus fear of crime might be seen as reflecting the product of risk and seriousness. The implication of this is that increased fear of crime will follow from events such as being a victim or seeing a news programme about a particular crime – that is, if the following apply:

- The event makes the individual aware of there being a risk of victimisation and of the consequences of victimisation (i.e. the priming effect).
- There is an increase in either or both the subjective victimisation risk or the negative impact as a consequence of being victimized (i.e. the change effect).

An example may be helpful. An American in, say, Dallas sees on the television news a serious bank robbery in Germany. This probably will not prime that person's awareness of his or her own risk of victimisation. The distant events in Germany will not impact on the viewer's fear of crime. On the other hand, take the case of a woman who sees a television programme about rape. She may discover for the first time the extent of the violence and humiliation that may be associated with rape. This may well increase her fear of victimisation.

An important aspect of Winkel's theory is the relative independence of risk and seriousness in the creation of fear. It is possible to imagine events in which the risk perception increases but the seriousness perception decreases. For example, a household has just been burgled. Members of the household rightly discern that the risk of their being a victim is higher than they previously thought. However, in their case, the burglar simply took some money and did not foul or ransack the place. The householders also find that they were less bothered and disturbed by the burglary than they had previously imagined. In these circumstances, the seriousness perception may move to regarding the crime as less serious. More generally, downward comparison processes may achieve adaptation or coping: that is, the development of the view that one got off lightly compared with what could happen or what has happened to other people. In this theory, fear is hypothesised to be a product of risk × seriousness. So, in some circumstances, although the perception of risk has increased, this may be compensated by the reduction in the perception of seriousness. In other words, there is no change in fear of crime. Figure 3.3 presents this schematically as a model. Of course, downward comparison processes may not be possible in all crimes. For example, does the rape victim whose rapist is acquitted in court following a court hearing in which her character is besmirched show such processes?

Winkel (1998) reports empirical evidence in support of the model based on research on a variety of crime victims compared with a control group:

- Over a data collection period of about two years, there was evidence that the subjective victimisation risk perceived by victims converged with that of the non-victim control group.
- If anything, in terms of the negative impact of being victimised, the gap between the victims and the controls increased. Victims saw less of a negative impact from further victimisation than did the control group. This is just what the theory suggests would happen.

Nevertheless, we need to understand better the victims for whom these compensatory processes do not appear to work. The evidence that some victims are profoundly affected by their victimisation in terms of stress and distress (Miethe, 1995) suggests that we have much to learn about the public's perceptions of and fears about crime. Predicting who is most at risk of the consequences of victimisation is one important task to be faced (Winkel and Vrij, 1998).

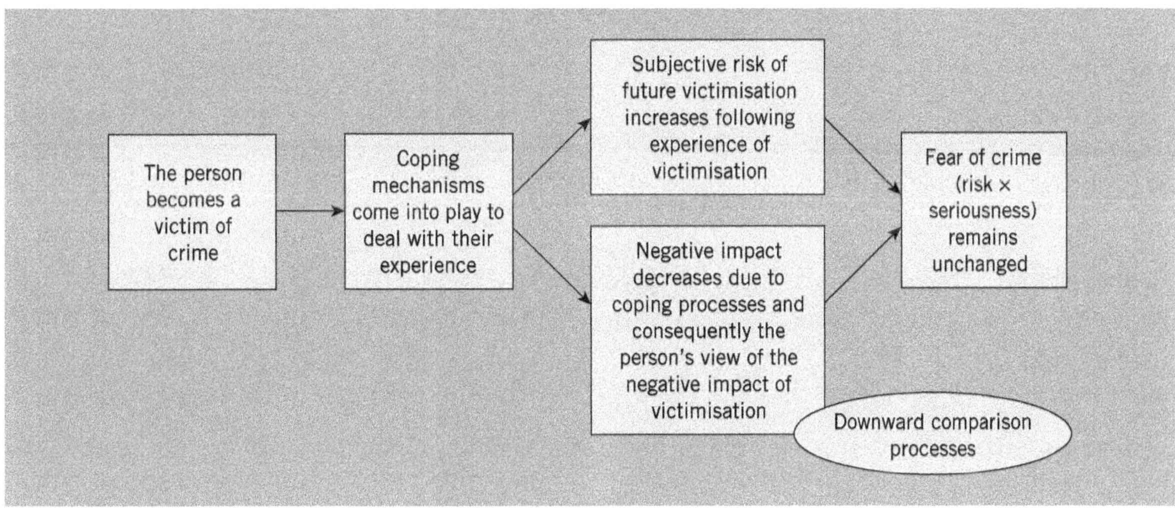

Figure 3.3 Winkel's model of the fear of crime

Source: Winkel, F.W. (1998) 'Fear of crime and criminal victimisation' *British Journal of Criminology* 38, 473–84. Reproduced by permission of Oxford University Press

Main points

- Although crime has an impact on the public, the public also has an impact on crime, either directly or indirectly. For example, victims of crime may or may not decide to report events as a crime and public opinion may influence government and police policy on crime. All aspects of the process of criminal justice may be influenced by the public, although perhaps in rather indirect ways.
- Surveys have demonstrated many aspects of the public's attitudes towards crime and there is at least some evidence that relatively tough attitudes are expressed about the ways in which criminals should be dealt with. However, it would appear that the public have a rather poor understanding of such matters as the extent of crime and trends or patterns in criminal activity.
- The fear of crime is both a researcher's and a policy maker's concept. Surveys of the general public's levels of fear of crime are now regularly conducted on behalf of some governments. The fear of crime is not at similar levels throughout all sectors of society. It has proven notoriously difficult to understand the fear of crime as it does not seem to follow commonsensical patterns. There is little relationship between fear of crime and the objective risk of being a victim. Researchers have questioned whether the fear of crime is as central to most people's lives as some surveys suggest.

Further reading

Wood, J. and Gannon, T. (2008) *Public Opinion and Criminal Justice* Cullompton: Willan Publishing.

Lee, M. and Farrall, S. (2008) *Fear of Crime: Critical Voices in an Age of Anxiety* London: Routledge Cavendish.

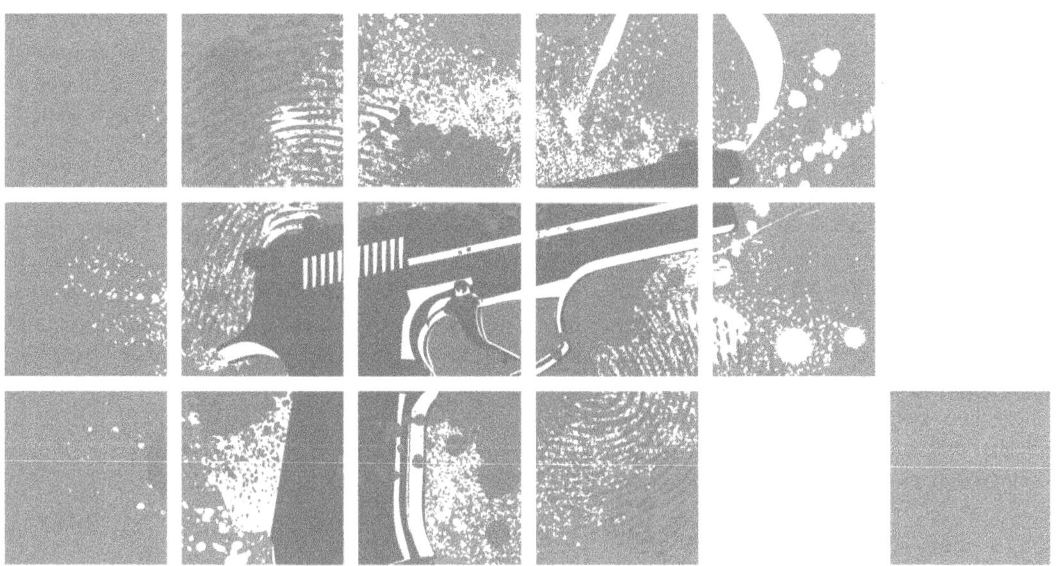

Chapter 4

Victims of crime

Overview

- In recent years, victims have become more of a priority in the criminal justice system; for example, the police have started to show greater sensitivity in the treatment of rape victims.
- Care has to be taken not to blame victims, either directly or indirectly, or in part, for their victimisation.
- Post-traumatic stress disorder (PTSD) is a consequence of serious trauma of which some crimes, such as rape and extreme violence, are examples. Flashbacks to the traumatising events and nightmares are among its characteristics. It is a psychiatric condition listed in the APA *Diagnostic and Statistical Manual* since 1980.
- A substantial minority of homicide offenders show PTSD symptoms caused by their offending. Suppression of the traumatic memories which re-emerge in flashbacks is counterproductive to the treatment of PTSD. The victim needs to work through the memories repeatedly, using methods such as structured trauma writing.
- Restorative justice concentrates on the harm done to victims by the offence. This may involve mediated interaction between the offender and the victim. There is evidence that this may be both helpful to victims and reduce recidivism in offenders.
- Victims, whether or not severely affected by the experience, have to make decisions about whether to report the crime to the police. Usually, it is the nature of the crime which determines this. It is common for victims to talk with other people before deciding to report the crime or not.
- Crime reporting decisions are also dependent on the rewards and costs of doing so, the emotion aroused by the crime, and the social push from those around the victim to report the crime. However, counterfactual thinking, which leads to victims holding themselves responsible for the crime, may inhibit reporting.
- Based on rational choice theory, there is evidence that self-protective behaviours may have an impact on the way in which a crime unfolds.

Introduction

Victims of crime should have access to justice and fair treatment in terms of compensation, social assistance and restitution according to The United Nations Declaration of Basic Principles of Justice for Victims of Crime and Abuse of Power of 1985. The needs of victims are not catered for by the massive resources that the criminal justice system put into the prosecution and punishment of, as well as treatment and support for, offenders. However, provision for victims is better developed now than, say, twenty or thirty years ago. Government financing for organisations providing victim support is one example, and victims will find that information is readily available about what resources they can access. In the UK, the website 'Get support as a victim of crime' (https://www.gov.uk/get-support-as-a-victim-of-crime) and, in the USA, 'Help for crime victims' (http://victimsofcrime.org/help-for-crime-victims) offer advice on sources of emotional support, counselling and safe accommodation, for example. Edwards (2004) argues that governments attempt to shift responsibility for dealing with crime more on to the community and less on to government. 'Good customer relations' (such as when the victim feels fairly treated by the criminal justice system) becomes the criterion for crime policy success rather than tangible reductions in crime figures. This chapter focuses on aspects of victimisation upon which psychology has shed light.

As a branch of the general field of criminology, *victimology* studies the victim–offender interface. Victimology's original focus was on victim characteristics that increased the likelihood of someone being victimised. This was sometimes criticised as holding the victim responsible for being victimised. Describing a rape victim as dressing provocatively is a good example of this. The proper study of victims avoids such an implication by, for example, regarding victimisation as being the consequence, in part, of the offender choosing an optimum victim for their offending. Consequently, in modern usage, the original term 'victim' is often replaced by 'target'. This has the advantage of emphasising the role of the criminal's decision-making rather than the characteristics of the targeted victim. It is worth bearing a number of facts about victimisation in mind:

- Victimisation does not occur equally or randomly. For instance, in the UK, just 2 per cent of the population are involved in over 40 per cent of property crimes as victims (Farrell and Bouloukos, 2001).
- In industrialised countries, approximately 40 per cent of crimes against individuals and households are repeat victimisations during the same year. The International Crime Victims Survey (van Dijk, van Kesteren and Smit, 2007) suggests, for example, that something like half the incidents of sexual crimes against women are repeat victimisations of women previously victimised in this way. Furthermore, there is a greater incidence of repeat victimisation for personal crimes against an individual than for property crimes.

Findings such as these point to the inescapable conclusion that crime victimisation follows patterns. These patterns cannot be understood solely on the basis of psychological characteristics of the victim. Indeed, much of this research uses by way of explanation geographic proximity and knowledge of the everyday activities of offenders in the territory that they inhabit and visit.

Victim–offender overlap

People who are perpetrators of crime are more likely to be victims of crime. The research on victim–offender overlap is reviewed by Jennings, Piquero and Reingle (2012). Their synthesis shows that being a victim (or being a perpetrator) is predictive of being in the combined victim–perpetrator category. The relationship is not perfect, of course, and the victim–offender overlap varies greatly by the type of crime in question. Part of the explanation of the overlap may be that the risk factors for being a victim are often much the same as those for being a perpetrator. For example, as shown in Chapter 8, the main perpetrators of violence are young men, who also tend to be the main victims of violence. Are there any other theoretical reasons for this overlap? Two main contenders can be identified:

- *Routine activity theory* (Felson, 1996). This regards offending as involving three things: 1) a target (which can be the actual victim); 2) a motivated offender; and 3) the absence of a guardian figure who could effectively intervene in the situation. The overlap between offender and victim lies in the opportunities for criminal activity and the generally risky lifestyles of some individuals. Osgood, Wilson, O'Malley, Bachman and Johnston's (1996) theory of 'unstructured socialising' possibly explains why this could happen. The theory argues that it is the time youngsters spend with delinquent peers without adult supervision which leads to the victim–victimiser overlap. This would help predict offending behaviour but how does it deal with being victimised? According to Schreck, Fisher and Miller (2004), the reason may be that delinquent peers frequently provide inadequate protection from victimisation
- *The general theory of crime* (Gottfredson and Hirschi, 1990). This emphasises the concept of self-control and the lack of it. Poor socialisation results in criminal

activity because the child's parents do not properly monitor the child's behaviour and do not punish criminal activity when it emerges. Inadequate socialisation leads to low self-control and consequent criminal involvement. Low self-control individuals show general riskiness in many aspects of their lives. So they are more likely to put themselves into situations which lead to offending but also those which put them in a higher risk of victimisation.

More recently, Averduk, van Galder, Eisner, and Ribeaud (2016) have developed what they describe as a decision-making perspective in order to understand how violent victimisation and violent offending relate. Although some theorists have claimed it to be a spurious relationship due to some common third factor such as the general theory of crime explanation given above, there is the possibility of it being causal due to altered decision-making processes. Averduk *et al.*'s basic idea is that suffering victimisation alters the way in which victims appraise future conflict situations. Victims of violence begin to see the benefits of violence as predominating over its costs. Criminological choice models, of which this is an example, generally assume that offenders are economic actors who evaluate potential criminal acts according to a cost–benefit analysis (Clarke and Cornish, 1985). More recently, researchers have included emotion in their models since emotions are strongly motivational (Lerner and Tiedens, 2006). Violent victimisation is associated with emotion, particularly negative emotions such as anger and injustice.

Violent victimisation can lead to a variety of responses, including the fear of retaliation which would reduce the likelihood of aggression in a conflict situation. Alternatively, it might lead to a greater likelihood of violence if victimisation leads to a loss of self-esteem and status which, in turn, results in a more positive evaluation of the costs and benefits of using violence. Experiencing anger, injustice and a desire for retribution may leave the individual seeing greater rewards in acting violently. They may also foresee less anger and shame in acting violently as they have moral justifications for doing so. Averduk *et al.* (2016) tested these ideas using data from a longitudinal study of Swiss youth. Their violence perpetration was measured using questions about simple assault, serious assault with injury, sexual assault, simple assault, sexual harassment and robbery. The number of these different types committed formed the measure of aggression. Violence victimisation was measured in a similar way for the same types of violence. Decision making was measured by presenting three different descriptions of violent situations. These vignettes included punching someone who was rude to you in public, threatening to beat someone up if they did not give you their mobile phone, and telling someone that you do not like to 'get lost'. For each vignette, the youngster was asked a number of questions about their thinking such as how bad they would feel doing these things, how ashamed, and whether their friends would admire them for what they did. The researchers found that victimisation was related to the youngsters' anticipated feeling about acting in the way described in the vignettes. Feeling good about acting aggressively predicted involvement in violence.

Psychology and the victims of crime

Victims of crime exhibit a wide range of responses to their personal crime victimisation. In DeValve's (2005) study, victims of crime mentioned the following consequences for themselves:

- angry at offender – 81 per cent;
- anxiety or panic attacks or some other psychological consequence – 67 per cent;
- fear of retaliation by the offender – 39 per cent;
- fear of the repetition of a similar event – 53 per cent;
- felt isolated and alone – 53 per cent;
- felt unsafe at home – 53 per cent;
- relationship with partner affected – 44 per cent;
- self-blame for the crime – 47 per cent;
- time off from work – 69 per cent;
- wanted revenge – 44 per cent;
- work affected – 61 per cent.

They had various feelings about the offender, including:

- wanting the offender committed to prison – 56 per cent;
- wanting an apology from the offender – 33 per cent;
- wanting the offender to receive help – 31 per cent.

Furthermore, 56 per cent wanted to tell the offender about how the crime had adversely affected them and 47 per cent wanted to understand why the offence happened. Some of these needs are met by the concept and practice of restorative justice which is discussed later in this chapter.

Many victims will be little affected, if at all, as a consequence of being a victim of crime. Even where the crime causes immediate distress, the victim may quickly return to normal with little or no evidence of lasting harm. Nevertheless, responses to crime can be varied and not everyone responds to victimisation in the same way. There can be serious, long-term consequences to victimisation which may profoundly affect the individual's day-to-day functioning. The psychological damage that victims suffer may have long term implications, such as making them more vulnerable to being re-victimised in the future.

PTSD and the victims of crime

The consequences of serious crimes such as rape, child abuse, and violence may be traumatic to the victim as well as witnesses, family members and friends. There are numerous negative psychological outcomes which can result from being victimised by crime, such as anxiety, depressive symptoms, eating disorders, hostility, poorer general well-being and somatisation. However, the most extensively researched outcome of victimisation is *post-traumatic stress disorder* or PTSD. Trauma due to accidents or combat in the military can also cause PTSD. Post-traumatic stress disorder is not the immediate consequence of trauma but can follow at some stage after the trauma. Winkel (2007) suggests that the prevalence of chronic PTSD following crime victimisation is of the order of 10–15 per cent when estimated from studies that include a later follow-up assessment, which indicates the chronic nature of the condition. This can be regarded as a conservative estimate and some studies report higher rates. In support of this, Norwood and Murphy (2012) cite rates of PTSD following intimate partner violence as having prevalence estimates ranging from 33 per cent to 84 per cent, according to the nature of the sample involved. Of course, from a psychological point of view, the precise rates are less important than the fact that significant numbers of victims of crime urgently need help to deal with the emotional and other psychological consequences of their victimisation. So the clinician should be alert to the possibility of PTSD following from traumatic victimisation even if it does not immediately manifest itself.

The following is a brief sketch of some of the common features of PTSD:

- Profound depression and possible thoughts of suicide.
- Sleep disturbances of all sorts. Some may have difficulty sleeping; some may sleep for abnormally long periods.
- Oversensitivity to noise. Noise can cause a startle response since the fight/flight reflex is heightened.
- Paranoia or fear of others: the victim may feel afraid of the reoccurrence of the traumatic event, which causes them to be uncomfortable with people who may be their future victimisers (Broken Spirits Network, 2004).
- Repeatedly reliving the trauma in the form of intrusive flashbacks of the traumatic events during waking hours. Because of the intensity of some flashbacks, victims can believe that they are experiencing the events once again. At night, the events may be incorporated into nightmares. Victims often go out of their way to avoid anything which remind them of the traumatic events. The anniversary of the occurrence of the traumatic events may lead to renewed upset.

The psychiatric diagnostic category of post-traumatic stress disorder was first introduced into the *Diagnostic and Statistical Manual of Mental Disorders* with the release of *DSM-III* in 1980. This manual, published by the American Psychiatric Association, details one of the most important schemes of psychiatric diagnosis. The fifth version of the *Diagnostic and Statistical Manual of Mental Disorders* (*DSM-V*) was released by the American Psychiatric Association in 2013. This makes a number of changes to how PTSD is regarded and diagnosed compared to earlier versions. Although PTSD was previously categorised as an anxiety disorder in *DSM-IV*, it is categorised as a trauma- and stress-related disorder in *DSM-V*. The following are the main criteria which need to be met in order for there to be a diagnosis of PTSD according to *DSM-V* (see Figure 4.1):

- *PTSD involves a traumatic event involving actual or threat of death, serious injury or sexual violation. The individual may have directly experienced the traumatic event or witnessed it happening to another person.* *DSM-V* has extended this to include close family members or close friends who learn about traumatic events which happened to a close family member or to a friend. A study by Zinzow, Rheingold, Byczkiewicz, Saunder and Kilpatrick (2011) in the US demonstrates how being a friend or relative of a victim of a traumatic crime can have an effect on PTSD symptoms. In this study the researchers defined homicide survivors as the

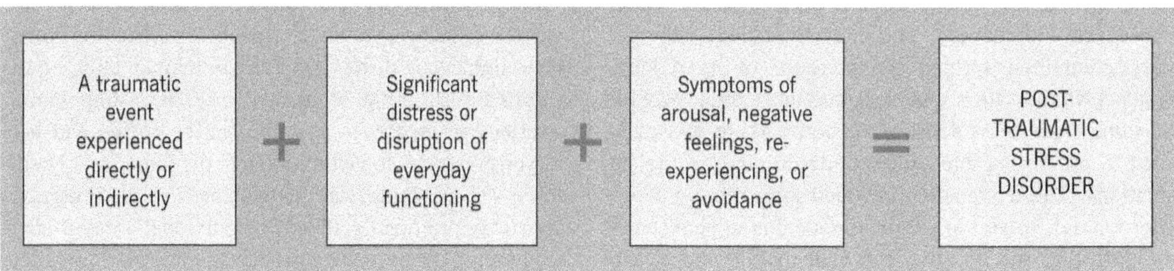

Figure 4.1 Some diagnostic features of PTSD

friends and family members of homicide victims. These were compared with victims of other forms of interpersonal violence. Those participating were interviewed using a structured telephone survey and asked, among other things, 'Has a close friend or family member ever been deliberately killed or murdered by another person or killed by a drunk driver?' Nearly 15 per cent of the homicide survivors (those who had had a close family member or friend killed in this way) met the criteria for all of the symptom clusters of PTSD (see below) compared to 8 per cent of victims of other forms of violence (rape, other forms of sexual assault, serious violent assault, and witnessing serious violence).

- *If a person experiences at first hand repeated or extreme examples of the disturbing details of traumatic events experienced by others, then PTSD may result.* Note that, in this instance, the individual does not witness the traumatic events directly at all. *DSM-V* specifically excludes the media as the source of the disturbing detail unless if the individual was exposed to this as part of their job. This suggests that professionals such as therapists or social workers dealing with distressing child abuse or rape cases might suffer PTSD as a consequence of repeatedly hearing disturbing details. Tabor (2011) reviews the concept of vicarious traumatization which may affect a therapist or other professionals dealing with the traumas of other people. This condition can affect the professional's relationships, perspectives on life, beliefs and values negatively. Vicarious traumatisation shares many of the features of PTSD.
- *There is clinically significant distress or significant impairment in important areas of the individual's functioning – socially, at work or other aspects of life.* *DSM-V* gives four symptom clusters (re-experiencing, avoidance, arousal and negative cognitions and mood) of PTSD. This is one more than was given in *DSM-IV*. A varying number of symptoms are required from each group in order to make a diagnosis. The symptom groups are:
  - *Re-experiencing:* This includes persistent images, thoughts, illusions, hallucinations, and so forth as well as flashback episodes or psychological distress to things which remind the individual of the traumatic event.
  - *Avoidance:* The individual will avoid and show a numbed response to things which are in some way associated with the trauma. So the individual will avoid talking and thinking about the traumatic event or they may avoid places and people that could remind them of the traumatic event.
  - *Arousal* (known as hyperarousal in *DSM-IV*): This may involve irritability, self-destructive behavior, concentration problems, sleep disturbance, and the like.
  - *Negative cognitions and mood:* This may involve an ongoing lack of ability to experience positive emotions or a persistent negative emotional state.
- The symptoms should be present for at least a month.
- The condition cannot be explained as a consequence of drugs or a medical condition.

The diagnosis of PTSD is not without its difficulties. According to Sparr (2015), the diagnostic criteria for PTSD are not particularly objective and they are not specific to PTSD. Symptoms like irritability and insomnia are common to a large number of other psychiatric conditions, for instance.

Very little, if any, research employs psychiatrists or psychologists to evaluate participants for PTSD. Instead, it seems universal to use one or other psychometric scales to measure it. These scales use questions to measure symptoms from the various symptom clusters which make up PTSD. One common one is the PTSD symptom scale (self-report version) (PSS-SR) (Foa, Riggs, Dancu, and Rothbaum, 1993).

There has been a shift over time in terms of the role specific trauma plays in the aetiology of PTSD, This begs the question as to what extent PTSD is associated with feelings of fear, helplessness or horror at the time of the trauma. These things are not essential to the development of PTSD but they do seem to be quite frequently involved. According to Brewin, Andrews and Rose (2000), 89 per cent of people who went on to have PTSD following a traumatic happening reported such intense responses. However, 44 per cent of those reporting intense levels of these emotions failed to manifest PTSD later. Thus it would appear that about 11 per cent of individuals who experienced traumatic events but did not experience intense emotions nevertheless developed PTSD. However, it is worth noting that the 11 per cent who did not manifest these emotions actually reported high levels of anger or shame.

What happens psychologically at the time of the trauma partly determines whether PTSD follows. If the victim experiences what is described as peritraumatic dissociation following a highly traumatic rape or violent crime then there may be an increased risk of PTSD. In peritraumatic dissociation the victim becomes detached from themselves psychologically and may experience the assault as being perpetrated on another person and not themselves – perhaps as if they were watching the assault at the cinema or on television. So dissociation is when the sense of possessing a single identity that links our life stages together is temporarily disrupted. It is a way of coping with the traumatic experience in that extreme emotions such as feelings of helplessness and horror are bypassed.

This is only of short-term benefit as the peritraumatic dissociation is believed to lead to PTSD (e.g. Marshall and Schell, 2002) and the adverse consequences involved in that. Peritraumatic dissociation is not necessary, however, for PTSD to develop. Although the onset of PTSD is more likely in those who demonstrate 'dissociation' during the traumatic event it is not more likely in those who show dissociation at a later stage (Brewin and Holmes, 2003). Actually, the cognitive factors involved can be somewhat wider than peritraumatic dissociation (Halligan, Michael, Clark, and Ehlers, 2003). For example, data-driven processing and lack of self-referent processing are also part of the process leading to PTSD. Data-driven processing is exemplified by statements such as 'the assault . . . was just like a stream of unconnected impressions following each other'. Lack of self-referent processing is exemplified by statements that describe the experience during the assault, such as 'I felt cut off from my past'.

Psychiatrists describe another condition known as *acute stress disorder* (ASD) which can last for up to a month following the traumatic event. It describes the intense and acute response that victims may show following the trauma. It can last from two days to four weeks following the traumatic event. After a month, these symptoms are likely to be diagnosed as PTSD which requires the symptoms to be present for at least one month. Acute stress disorder (ASD) involves substantial levels of impairment or distress. Victims of ASD show intense emotional reactions to the traumatic stressor together with many symptoms from various groupings of symptoms namely dissociation, arousal, avoidance and re-experiencing according to the *Diagnostic and Statistical Manual of Mental Disorder* (*DSM-V*) (American Psychiatric Association, 2013). These symptom clusters overlap with those for PTSD as we shall see. There is plenty of research demonstrating the relationship between ASD and PTSD. For example, Shevlin, Hyland, and Elklit (2014) showed a strong relationship between having high levels of ASD symptoms and the later development of PTSD.

There are other factors concerning the time of the traumatic episode which can materially affect the course of subsequent events. Kaysen, Lindgren, Lee, Lewis, Fossos and Atkins (2010) found relationships between the use of alcohol at the time of a sexual or physical assault and the process of recovery over the next three to six months in female crime victims. Participants who had consumed alcohol at the time of the crime had lower initial levels of PTSD symptoms from the re-experiencing cluster (i.e. intrusive symptoms) such as persistent images, hallucinations, thoughts and so forth. Alcohol can reduce stress responses and lower fearful memories. Recovery from the re-experiencing symptoms was slower in the alcohol group than in the non-alcohol group. In other words, alcohol was associated with lower levels of intrusive re-experiencing of cluster symptoms in those who had consumed alcohol but recovery from the symptoms was slower.

However, the same traumatic event may have both positive and negative consequences. For example, these days it is not an unfamiliar sight to see on television positive, community-centred responses to terrorist attacks. Kunst (2011) investigated *post-traumatic growth* and post-traumatic stress disorder in a Dutch sample of violent crime victims including sexual violence, severe or moderate physical assault, theft with violence and other types of violence. The concept of post-traumatic growth can involve various changes including one's philosophy of life, perception of self and interpersonal relationships. Kunst's research and that of others finds little or no relationship between PTSD and post-traumatic growth. That is, one can show both as a result of trauma. Given previous research findings, Kunst formed four different groups based on scores on positive affectivity and negative affectivity experienced by victims. These were measured using the PANAS-SF scale (Thompson, 2007). The participant simply had to indicate which, on a list of positive emotions and negative emotions, they experienced. A positive emotion word might be 'determined' and a negative emotion word might be 'nervous'. A person's pattern of high or low scores on positive and negative emotions was used to classify them as high affective, self-destructive, self-actualising and low affective as shown in Figure 4.2. PTSD was measured using a scale. Post-traumatic growth was measured employing a number of areas of growth such as appreciation of life, personal strength, new possibilities and spiritual change. The self-destructive pattern of affect was associated with developing PTSD symptoms and the high affective pattern influenced both PTSD and post-traumatic growth. It would seem to be the case that post-traumatic growth needs some negative emotion to develop.

So, in the case of terrorist attacks, the effect of the attack may not always be negative. In 2011, Anders Behring Breivik went on a killing rampage which led to the deaths of 77 young people at a summer camp on the Norwegian island Utoya. The young people were hunted for up to nearly two hours before they were killed. Nordanger *et al.* (2013) studied a large sample of over 10,000 young Norwegians to assess their reactions. About 20 per cent knew someone involved in the events. Questions related to PTSD included re-experiencing symptoms such as 'Frightening thoughts, images or sounds from the terror events pop up in my mind even if I don't want to.' PTSD symptoms were not high but nevertheless 5 per cent reported substantial avoidance symptoms, 1 per cent arousal symptoms and nearly 1 per cent re-experiencing symptoms. By substantial, the researchers meant that the symptoms were experienced between three or four times each week to everyday. There was evidence that that a high percentage changed their world view as a consequence of

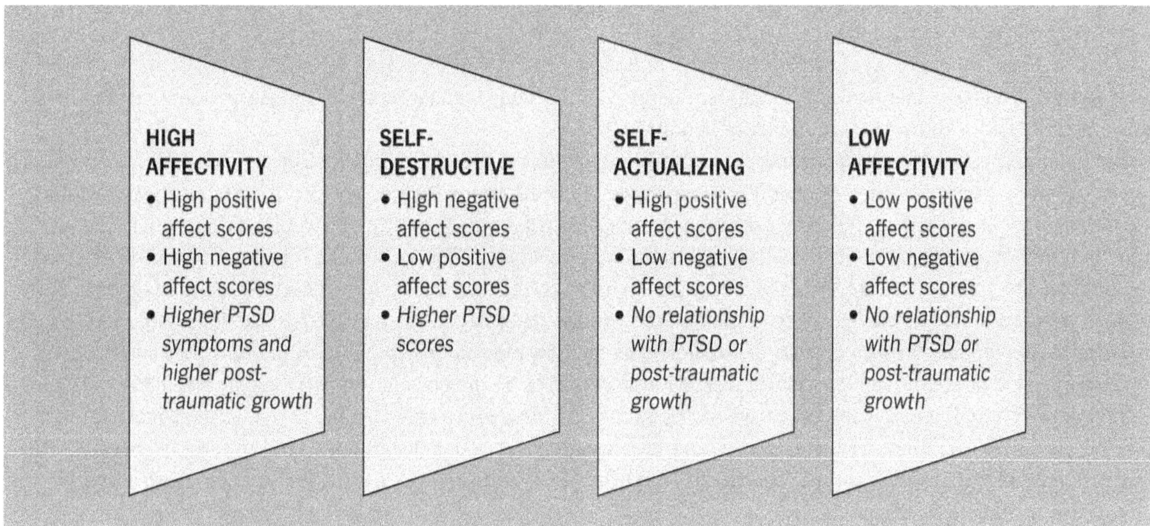

Figure 4.2 Affectivity types and effects of trauma

the attack. Eighty per cent reported that their worldview had changed to some extent as a consequence of the events. For 37 per cent, this change was in a positive direction.

Theories of PTSD

It is worthwhile pausing to examine the features of memory in PTSD. There is substantial research and theory to suggest that PTSD is associated with memory deficits. Normal autobiographical memory for life events is largely coded and stored verbally and is recalled in words primarily rather than pictures. In contrast, the flashbacks which typify PTSD overwhelm the victim with vivid sensory detail, such as loud sounds or other images, though these tend to be fragmentary in nature (Brewin and Holmes, 2003). Brewin, Andrews and Valentine (2000) suggested that good working memory capacity (an individual's ability to 'hold and manipulate' material which is the focus of attention) is necessary to help stop unwanted ideas from intruding into daily activities. Since flashbacks are also intrusions into thought, it might be expected that those with good working memory capacity should be less affected by flashbacks. Consequently, Brewin *et al.* point out that poor working memory may be associated with low intelligence which is a risk factor for PTSD. Morea recently, Ono, Devilly and Shum (2016) carried out a meta-analytic study of overgeneral memory (Williams and Broadbent, 1986) in relation to PTSD and other conditions. Overgeneral memory is a defect in the autobiographical memory which involves difficulty in remembering the details of personal events. Instead there is a tendency to remember a very general impression of events. This is the difference between a statement like 'I was assaulted that weekend by three members of my army unit' and 'I was miserable all the time that I was in the army'. Research has shown overgeneral memory to be a risk factor in PTSD (Anderson, Goddard and Powell, 2010). A meta-analysis (see Box 4.1) of 25 studies similar to this confirmed that there was a strong association between PTSD and overgeneral memory (Ono *et al.*, 2016).

Box 4.1 Key concept

Meta-analysis

Meta-analysis is based on statistical techniques. The purpose is to combine and summarise the findings of studies on a particular topic. The quality of the studies on which the meta-analysis is based is obviously important. In terms of the effectiveness of, say, cognitive behavioural programmes for the treatment of offenders, a researcher would search every possible database for empirical studies of the effectiveness of the treatment in the penal setting. Unpublished research, which may show different trends, is as important as the published research. The researcher needs to define the domain of interest for the analysis. For example, they may confine themselves to studies that

BOX 4.1 (continued)

use a control group and that measure recidivism in terms of its incidence (whether or not there is any reoffending) versus its prevalence (how often reoffending is done).

The meta-analyst then computes a measure of effect size – this is merely an index of how much effect the cognitive behavioural treatment has on recidivism compared with the untreated control group. Although the original researchers may have expressed this as a difference in means, percentages or any of a range of appropriate indexes, these are converted, using simple formulae, to a standard effect size index. Although there are a number of effect size indices, the commonest are Cohen's d and the Pearson correlation coefficient. There is a simple relationship between these two and one can easily be converted to the other. Howitt and Cramer (2008) provide a table for doing this. They also recommend the correlation coefficient as the best measure since it is familiar to most psychologists. So the effect size of cognitive behavioural therapy would simply be the correlation between the treatment variable (treated or not treated) and the outcome variable (reoffends within a given time of release versus does not reoffend). If treated is coded 1 and not treated coded 2, and then reoffends is coded 1 and does not reoffend is coded 2, the Pearson correlation between the two variables is the effect size expressed as a correlation coefficient. Some will refer to this as the phi-coefficient.

It is relatively easy to compute a (weighted) average of these effect sizes in order to assess the effects over a range of studies.

Another useful feature of meta-analysis is that it allows the researcher to refine the analysis by examining trends in selected aspects of the data. For example, it would be possible to compare the effect size of cognitive behavioural programmes carried out in the community with those carried out in prison. Any type of difference between studies – the type of sample, the size of sample and so forth – may also correlate with the effect sizes obtained by the researcher.

In recent meta-analytic studies you will find reference to the Collaborative Outcome Data Committee (CODC) study quality guidelines. These were developed by a group of 12 experts in the field to encourage researchers to include studies of a satisfactory quality in their meta-analyses. The guidelines contain 20 items which are structured into seven different categories: (a) administrative control was the independent variable manipulated by the researcher; (b) experimenter expectancies, involving the extent to which the researcher has some sort of interest in finding a particular outcome to the study and is aware of the group to which the individual has been assigned and so may inadvertently affect the outcome of the study; (c) adequate sample size; (d) information about attrition – that is, dropout rates from the study; (e) the equivalence of the groups; (f) the outcome variables; and (g) that the correct comparisons are conducted. The studies are categorised on the basis of these into various study quality categories from 'strong' through 'good' through 'weak' to 'rejected'. A strong study might have the following features:

- proper random assignment to experimental and control conditions without any compromise to the randomisation process;
- a minimum of five years for the follow-up period in the case of a recidivism study;
- less than 20 per cent loss (attrition) of participants;
- no pre-existing differences found between the experimental and control conditions.

Theoretical accounts of PTSD clearly have a variety of aspects of memory to explain as disturbing memory phenomena characterise the condition in many sufferers. Among the main theories explaining the condition, according to the important review by Brewin and Holmes (2003), are the following:

- *Stress response theory (Horowitz, 1986):* the traumatic event fundamentally disturbs the victim's beliefs about the world, the future and themselves. The new view of the world and the old view are very different. Prior to victimisation, the individual may feel competent and in control of their lives and the situations they face. Following the trauma, the victim may see themselves as vulnerable and driven by external events rather than being personally driven. Traumatic events produce a complex psychological situation in which the victim needs to avoid memories of the traumatic event since those intrusions are distressing; but, in order to deal with the traumatic events, the victim also needs to relive the traumatic events through memory. Flashbacks, intrusions and nightmares provide an opportunity to process the old cognitions of the world alongside those brought about by the trauma. So there is a defensive mechanism (avoiding memories of the trauma) and the healing mechanism (working with the memories) which are fundamentally in opposition to each other.

- *Conditioning theory:* Keane, Zimering and Caddell (1985) suggested that PTSD involves a two-state process along the lines of Mowrer's (1960) two-factor learning theory. The traumatic events naturally produce a fear response, such as when an individual's life is at risk in a hostage situation. At the same time, aspects of the traumatic situation which, in themselves, do not have fear-evoking properties actually are conditioned to be fear-arousing by association with the fear response. For example, if the hostage is threatened with death by a man wearing a red hat then a red hat may become capable of evoking fear. Avoiding memories of the event by blocking or suppression merely ensures that the normal processes of deconditioning cannot operate – that is, normally, thinking of red hats would gradually cease to evoke fear. However, avoidance of red hats is rewarding in that it is associated with reductions in fear levels. So avoidance is conditioned. The consequence of this is that the PTSD is maintained and healing cannot take place. Brewin and Holmes (2003) suggest that one of the weaknesses of the theory is that it deals ineffectively with the types of cognitions that are associated with PTSD since it concentrates merely on a simple conditioning process.
- *Dual representation theory (e.g. Brewin, Dalgleish and Joseph, 1996):* this suggests that ordinary memories and traumatic memories are fundamentally different processes. Trauma memories are problematic when they are dissociated from ordinary memories. Recovery from PTSD is partly dependent on transforming the trauma memories into ordinary memories (so-called narrative memory). This alternative memory system is known as 'perceptual memory' and it consists of information that has had little or no conscious processing. Perceptual memories are not verbally coded whereas narrative memories are. There is research which suggests that people fail to actively perceive things in their field of vision that are not expected. This is known as inattentional bias. Despite being unaware of these things, the individual may nevertheless be affected by them. Brewin *et al.* point out that some trauma victims claim that they have not noticed, say, shots fired at the scene of the trauma. Perceptual memories for highly emotional and important things may be long-lasting. Therapeutic improvement will occur when the elements of the traumatic situation are substantially encoded into the narrative memory. Until this stage, stimuli like the red hat will trigger the intense perceptual memory. Once the red hat is more likely to trigger the more reasoned and processed cognitive narrative memory, then the power of the intrusive memories of the trauma is disabled.

What leads to a greater likelihood of PTSD?

One obvious factor in PTSD is that of gender. It is clear from reviews of the research literature on this (Tolin and Foa, 2006) that females are more likely than males to meet the diagnostic criteria for PTSD. This is the case despite the fact that women are generally less likely to have experienced potentially traumatic events. Men were less likely to have experienced sexual trauma in childhood or adulthood, but they are more likely to suffer accidents, violent assaults, combat, and witness death or injury. Could the gender difference in PTSD simply be due to differential exposure to potentially traumatic stressors? The answer is no, because if one compares men and women on a like-for-like basis by comparing them in terms of particular types of stressors, women were still more likely to exhibit PTSD. That is to say, women were more likely to suffer PTSD than men for individual stressors such as accidents. However, for sexual trauma, women did not differ from men in terms of showing PTSD.

The nature of the trauma can make a difference to whether PTSD follows although subjective beliefs about the level of threat to life due to the traumatic event may have more influence on the development of PTSD than the objective size of the actual threat (Brewin and Holmes, 2003). Norwood and Murphy (2012) showed that different forms of intimate partner abuse are differentially associated with PTSD symptoms. They used measures of different sorts of intimate partner abuse which they related to PTSD:

- Sexual violence (e.g. 'My partner used force . . . to make me have sex').
- Sexual coercion (e.g. 'Had sexual intercourse with your partner even though you didn't really want to because he threatened to end your relationship').
- Physical abuse which was measured using the physical-assault subscale of the Conflict Tactics Scale. This includes slapping, shoving, and using a gun or knife.
- Psychological abuse was measured using the Multidimensional Measure of Emotional Abuse (Murphy and Hoover, 1999). This measures four different forms of psychological abuse – dominance/intimidation (such as putting his face into the woman's face to make a point), restrictive engulfment (such as checking with friends where the woman was), denigration and hostile withdrawal (such as refusal to discuss problems).

In a multivariate analysis of the data, it was found that sexual coercion predicted PTSD symptoms better than sexual violence. This fits with the more general finding that psychological abuse was independently associated with PTSD symptoms. Sexual coercion can be seen as a form of psychological abuse and sexual violence can be seen as a form of physical violence. If the specific symptom clusters that make up PTSD are considered separately then it emerges that psychological abuse alone was a significant unique predictor compared to sexual and physical abuse.

Research that looks for relationships between PTSD and aspects of the assault such as its severity or psychological aspects of the victim fail to take into account the social context surrounding a sexual assault. Brewin, Andrews and Valentine's (2000) meta-analysis (see Box 4.1) of a large number of factors which are implicated in PTSD found that social support had the biggest influence. Appreciation of the nature of the cognitive processes involved is important to understanding PTSD (Brewin and Holmes, 2003). One important explanation is that the trauma actually destroys core attitudes, beliefs and assumptions about the nature of their world and the victim's ability to cope with it. For example, the belief that other people are benevolent and well-intentioned may be shattered by the traumatic event. Someone who is subject to a malicious attack may find this difficult to reconcile with a sense of community conducive to positive social relationships. Of course, people will naturally try to cope with PTSD themselves. However, research suggests that simply attempting to avoid the disturbing thoughts is counterproductive since it may delay recovery. Social support is important in recovery, though the presence of negativity in the support network is worse than having little or no social support (Brewin and Holmes, 2003). Partners, friends and family are part of the social environment and the degree to which they are supportive or negative towards the victim also have a role to play. PTSD is affected by the social reactions experienced by sexual assault victims disclosing their assault to other people. Negative reactions include victim blaming, telling the victim that she could have done more to prevent the assault from happening, and forcing the victim to go to the police, for example. Positive reactions include listening support, holding, telling the victim that she or he is loved and helping to find resources that might be helpful to the victim.

Ullman, Townsend, Fililpas and Starzumslo (2007) studied a sample of over 600 women living in the community in order to examine the interrelationships between global support (the quantity and quality of the individual's social network to help deal with problems), negative reactions of friends and family, using avoidance coping techniques such as avoiding thinking about the traumatic event, self-blame for being victimised, the number of past traumatic life experiences and the severity of the assault on PTSD symptoms. There is evidence from other studies that, in isolation, suggests that all of these factors may affect the level of PTSD symptomology as was the case in the Ullman *et al.* study. Negative social reactions and avoidance coping mechanisms most strongly correlate with PTSD symptoms. The question raised by Ullman *et al.* was just how these factors interrelated. Multivariate analysis suggested that the commonly observed correlation between victim self-blame and PTSD symptoms may, in part be due to the influence of negative social reactions from other people on the victim. The mechanism through which this seems to work is that a victim who experiences negative social reactions to the sexual crime will probably self-blame and adopt an avoidance coping mechanism. It was found that assault severity also resulted in higher levels of PTSD symptoms. This is thought to be in part due the more serious assault producing more negative social reactions but also higher levels of self-blame.

There are various ways in which social reactions can facilitate or obstruct recovery from sexual assault. For example, negative reactions to the victim may affect the victim's ability to take responsibility for the recovery process or may discourage the victim from seeking further support from other people. The research of Ullman and Peter-Hagene (2014) investigated factors such as perceived control, maladaptive coping, and social versus individual adaptive coping strategies in the relationship between social reactions to disclosure and possible PTSD symptoms. They used a large sample of women who had suffered an unwanted sexual episode. Positive social reactions to disclosure led to increased perceived control over recovery which led to fewer PTSD symptoms. Perceived control is the individual's perception about their ability to cope with the assault. Such positive social reactions led to more adaptive coping (such as thinking hard about what to do) and individual coping (such as seeking the advice of other people about what to do) but PTSD was only predictable from adaptive social coping. If the social response to disclosure was a negative reaction then this led to PTSD directly but also mediated by maladaptive coping. Typical maladaptive coping strategies include denial, substance use, and isolating oneself socially.

Some victims have coping mechanisms which reduce the risk of PTSD. Others adopt a forgiving attitude towards the perpetrators of the crime against them. One example of research which combines these two elements is the study by Weinberg, Gil and Gilbar (2014). They investigated the relationship between the tendency to forgive, coping strategies and the level of PTSD experienced by Israeli victims of terror attacks who had received a physical disability but not brain damage as a consequence. Forgiveness involves mental, emotional and behavioural actions which can change negative responses into neutral or even positive ones. The tendency to forgive is regarded as a personality trait which can be divided into self (e.g. agreeing that learning from bad things one has personally done helps get over them); others (e.g agreeing that one can get past being disappointed by someone); and situations (e.g. agreeing with the view that with time the individual can come to be understanding of negative life situations). Coping strategies are mental and behavioural attempts to deal with the stress of the terrorist incident. Coping strategies may be *problem-focused* (concentrating on practical solutions, active coping, and planning); *emotion-focused* (concentrating on things like finding emotional social support and venting emotions); and *avoidance* (concentrating on ignoring problems, mental disengagement from problems, and behavioural disengagement from problems). There was very clear evidence that the tendency to forgive was related strongly to experiencing lower levels of PTSD symptoms. However, to some extent there was a pathway suggesting those who have a higher tendency to forgive also tend to adopt problem-focused coping strategy and that this also led to with lower levels of PTSD symptoms. Emotion-focused coping, on the other hand, was associated with higher levels of PTSD.

PTSD and re-victimisation

Evidence suggests that PTSD can lead to re-victimisation for a number of reasons. There are a number of features of PTSD which are obvious contenders to explain re-victimisation. For example, the arousal (hyperarousal) cluster of PTSD symptoms encourage the victim to be over-vigilant about possible attack. As a consequence, sufferers may have difficulty in differentiating between true danger and false alarms – simply because the victim has so many false alarms. Numbing and dissociative symptoms may make it hard for the victim to take the initiative of using resistance behaviours which otherwise may have dealt with using criminal approaches. Perhaps the most obvious of all, the association between PTSD and alcohol consumption may mean that alcohol consumption leads to the greater risk of being re-victimised. Being drunk may make a woman seem a better target to offenders, or women who drink may be more likely to go to bars and nightclubs where they may be seen as a target. Littleton and Ullman's (2013) research involved nearly 500 American women, both black and white, recruited through advertisements. Participants took part in two postal surveys about undesired sexual episodes. The researchers argued that PTSD would predict both forcible and incapacitated rape (when the victim, say, was too drunk or otherwise incapacitated by substance to resist rape) and hazardous drinking would predict incapacitated rape. The data supported all of this except that PTSD only predicted incapacitated rape in Black American women.

When revictimised, PTSD may have a role to play in whether the victim reports the crime to the police. Walsh and Bruce (2014) examined reporting behaviour in a large sample of mainly women who had experience an unwanted, forced sexual episode. The relationship between PTSD and reporting varied according to which of the symptoms of PTSD the victim manifested. Those who had higher avoidance symptoms of PTSD were less likely to report the crime to the police. Of course, to report the crime is to confront it rather than avoid it. So by not reporting the crime the victim need not think about it in the intense way they would have to had they reported to the police. Those who had higher re-experiencing and hyperarousal symptoms were more likely to report the crime to the police. These victims do not avoid thinking about their trauma so reporting the crime to the police would not change the status quo.

PTSD among offenders

Of course, there is nothing in the nature of PTSD which, in itself, implies that only victims can be affected by it. Pollock (1999) raised the superficially paradoxical question of whether perpetrators of crime also suffer PTSD. There are two main possibilities why there might be a link between offending and PTSD:

- A person suffering PTSD has a heightened propensity to act violently. Hence the assumption is that PTSD leads to violence. For example, battlefield trauma leading to PTSD has been implicated in later antisocial behaviour (Pollock, 1999).
- The person who commits a horrific violent act cannot cope with the act and develops PTSD. In this case, we have the reverse association that violent experiences lead to PTSD.

Both may be true, of course. However, Pollock notes research which identified 2 per cent of criminals as having PTSD before committing their crime but 15 per cent showing the symptoms after committing the crime (Collins and Bailey, 1990). This would be consistent with both of the above sequences. Pollock argued that homicide may lead to offender PTSD in circumstances where the offender's beliefs about themselves are undermined by the events of the crime. If the violence was unplanned, for example, then the risk of trauma is heightened because that violence is not seen by the offender as part of their personality or character. Pollock studied a sample of homicide offenders, of whom 42 per cent exhibited the criteria for a PTSD diagnosis. It was found that reactive violence tended to be associated with PTSD – that is, non-goal-directed, unplanned, angry aroused violence typically directed at a known victim considered by the participant to have contributed to the offence by provocation (p. 193). Typically, it is controlled and inhibited offenders who show PTSD – not psychopaths.

The experience of earlier traumatic events is far from uncommon among those who perpetrate violent crime, with Bojahr and van Emmerik (2016) claiming that over 80 per cent of offenders have previously experienced in excess of five past trauma events in comparison to about 60 per cent of victims. Chung, Xiaohu, and Wan (2016) investigated prevalence rates for different levels of PTSD and psychological symptom severity following committing a violent crime. Previous studies had found rates of PTSD as varied as 6 per cent and 52 per cent. Chung *et al.* also considered the condition of alexithymia to be possibly relevant. Alexithymia is a condition in which the person may have great difficulty in identifying their feelings and differentiating their feelings and body sensations. It may arise from the numbness which is a symptom of PTSD. Sufferers are not effective in describing their feelings to another person. Furthermore, individuals with high levels of PTSD tend to have high levels of alexithymia. Their fantasy and imaginative capacity is poor. Three hundred and thirty nine males who had perpetrated a violent crime (about half had committed homicide and the other half grievous bodily harm) completed the Post-Traumatic Stress Diagnostic Scale, the General Health Questionnaire, and the Toronto Alexithymia Scale. PTSD exists on a continuum and some sufferers show only partial symptoms compared to others despite both perhaps needing the same level of care. Partial symptoms can involve, however, similar psychological distress that full PTSD involves. About half showed no PTSD (49 per cent) but 14 per cent showed partial PTSD and 37 per cent showed full PTSD. Full PTSD cases had high levels of anxiety, depression and social dysfunction compared to the non-PTSD group. Levels of alexithymia were highest in the PTSD group and lowest in the non-PTSD group. PTSD experienced from a past trauma was the best predictor of PTSD following the commissioning of a violent crime. The most important previous trauma was the sudden death of someone close followed in importance by suffering a serious accident. PTSD from past trauma accounted for the path between difficulty identifying feelings and PTSD following committing violent crime.

Post-traumatic anger

It is possible to regard PTSD not simply as an anxiety disorder (as *DSM-IV* holds it to be) or a trauma-stress disorder (as *DSM-V* indicates), but also as an anger disorder. About 100 years ago, Walter Cannon's classic formulation of people's responses to emergencies (threat) proposed that, following the arousal of the sympathetic nervous system to the emergency, the individual may exhibit the characteristics of flight (fear) or those of fight (anger). It is readily seen that PTSD has characteristics associated with flight and fear but there is also evidence of a relationship between PTSD and anger. There is a conceptual problem since anger is among the defining symptoms of PTSD according to the *DSM*. So researchers tackling this question have compared the relationship where anger is included in the possible defining characteristics of PTSD and where anger-related items have been removed (Orth Cahill, Fos and Maerker, 2008). The correlations tended to be medium in size (of the order 0.4 to 0.5) between PTSD and anger – and it made little difference whether the anger-related items were removed from the measure of PTSD. Meta-analyses (see Box 4.1) have established that the relationship (correlation coefficient) is about 0.5 over numerous studies (Riggs *et al.*, 1992). There was not complete certainty as to whom the anger in post-traumatic anger is directed against because the measures of anger used in studies did not allow victims to specify the target of their anger. Orth and Maercker (2009) created an anger questionnaire which included a target by asking questions such as 'I was angry with the perpetrator because he caused so much harm in my life' and 'I was angry with myself because I did not prevent the assault'. The targets used were the perpetrator, the criminal justice system, third parties and the self. This questionnaire, together with the PTSD questionnaire, was administered to a sample of German victims of sexual and non-sexual assault. PTSD symptoms were predicted by anger at the perpetrator and anger at the self; they were not predicted by anger with the criminal justice system and anger with third parties. There were relatively low levels of these two forms of anger.

Trivial crime and PTSD

So far, we have discussed PTSD in terms of the traumatic consequences of very serious criminal acts. However, despite this, is the assumption of seriousness crucial to the development of PTSD necessary? We can readily apply the concept of PTSD to serious criminal acts such as rape or some other serious sexually violent incidents. What of the plight of people who suffer repeated but trivial criminal victimisation? Shaw and Pease (2002) argue that the police, for example, are not able to deal with multiple trivial incidents that profoundly impact a victim in the same way as they can deal with a clearly traumatic incident such as rape. (Some provisions for the support of rape victims are sophisticated multi-agency initiatives employing carefully trained personnel.) There is another reason why the neglect of seemingly trivial incidents is unsatisfactory. It fails to acknowledge that early trivial incidents may well lead to something much more serious. Shaw and Pease give details of an interview with a woman victim who had noted that children and drunkards were often to be seen hanging out around a hostel for the homeless which was close to her home:

> [they] use the wall outside as a toilet . . . the drunks sit at the bottom of the stairs and I'm scared of them throwing bottles through – this is what happened before. I wish someone would move them on. The police know but the CCTV doesn't cover that bit – the station and the alleyway on the back of the shops behind the building. About eight drunks loiter there most nights to drink because there's an old carpet they can sit on. I'd come down the next day and the windows would end up being put through again.
>
> (p. 43)

Her complaint was largely about what might happen to her and the sources of her concern were trivial taken individually. Despite this, events eventually culminated in a situation in which the victim and her property were attacked. According to Shaw and Pease, successive minor incidents may make it increasingly difficult for the victim to cope. Furthermore, if other stress is occurring in the individual's life – perhaps, say, as the result of a bereavement – then the effects of the repeated trivial victimisations may be worse.

Psychological help for victims

It is inevitable at the moment that the frontline psychological support for victims comes largely from friends, family, police officers and others largely untrained in psychology. Even in the medium term, psychological support is often provided by people less than fully trained in psychology, such as volunteers and police officers (Winkel and Blaauw, 2001). It is difficult to assess the value of such support. Winkel and Blaauw argue that one common error made by such personnel is to assume that victims compare themselves with someone better off than themselves by deciding that 'I am worse off than . . .'. This is termed an upward comparison process. However, victims are much more likely to employ a downward comparison process in which they compare themselves with someone who is worse off than themselves.

One approach to dealing with memories of trauma is through the use of structured trauma writing. This may employ homework exercises as well as one-to-one interactions with support workers. Structured trauma writing provides the victim with the possibility of self-confrontation, self-disclosure and emotional disinhibition, and something called narrativation. By employing self-confrontation, the traumatic events are effectively relived and so the intensive traumatic response to those events may become extinguished. Describing the traumatic events in words in a form of self-disclosure is therapeutic. Pennebaker (1995) provides a number of exercises based on the fundamental assumption that, when stressful/traumatic experiences are articulated into words, physical and mental health are improved. Thus he claims that talk about traumatic events may lead to fewer medical problems, better work performance and even better immune functions. In this context, narrativation is the construction of a story or narrative about the distressing and traumatic events.

Winkel and Blaauw (2001) asked a group of people to ventilate their deepest fears and emotions about a traumatic event; another group (downward comparison) was encouraged to write about the ways in which they were doing well in comparison to other groups; and a third group engaged in a rather trivial writing process (about, for example, their plans for the next day). The downward comparison condition was much more effective than the emotional expression condition in terms of clinically significant improvements in terms of intrusion symptoms. Examples of intrusions would include having difficulty sleeping because ideas and thoughts about the traumatic events keep occurring, and thinking about the events when one did not mean to. On the other hand, avoidance symptoms were better improved by emotional expression writing. Avoidance symptoms include avoiding letting oneself get upset by thoughts of the events and trying not to talk or think about the events. Stone, Smyth, Kaell and Hurewitz (2000) explored possible therapeutic processes which are involved in the use of structured trauma writing. There was no evidence that improvement was the result of lowered levels of perceived stress, improvement in the quality of sleep, changes in affect or changes in the use of medications.

Victim decision making

There are many reasons for not reporting a crime (Burcar, 2013):

- It may seem trivial.
- Reporting the crime may be seen as over-dramatisation of something unimportant.
- The victim may not see the events as a crime. For example, a fight may be seen as a normal part of interaction with other young men.
- Being a victim may be seen as suggesting weakness or loss of control and so the crime is best forgotten.
- Negative attitudes towards the police.

Equally, there may be special reasons for reporting a crime:

- In order to obtain a police report so that insurance compensation for a theft may be claimed.
- Crime reporting may be a symbolic act to draw attention to a wider social issue such as the vulnerability of staff to violence from members of the public.
- Reporting a crime can be seen as a preventative measure against future potential crimes.

Victims are the major gatekeepers in the process that brings a crime into the ambit of the criminal justice system. Three-fifths of crimes in the United States are reported to the police by the victims (Greenberg and Beach, 2001). Other important groups of people responsible for reporting crimes include the police themselves and bystanders who have witnessed a crime.

Whether or not a crime gets reported is largely determined by the nature of the offence. The characteristics of the victim are usually rather less important. Although the seriousness of the crime has an influence on reporting, the perception that there is a benefit to be gained from reporting the crime to the police is more important. Thus the theft of a motor vehicle is highly likely to be reported because it is necessary to do so in order to make an insurance claim. Although there is plenty of evidence from social psychological research, for example, that bystanders may be influenced by the social situation not to intervene (Darley and Latané, 1968), there is limited evidence to suggest that bystanders may influence the process by which a victim decides to report a crime. Experimental research has been carried out in which a bogus crime occurred and a bystander attempts to influence the victim to report the crime. The bystander was influential on the actions of the victim, especially when the victim was the sole victim – that is, there was no co-victim (Greenberg and Beach, 2001). Field research indicates further the extent to which victims of crime talk with other people about their victimisation. The precise figures vary somewhat according to the type of crime involved:

- The majority (78 per cent) of victims of sexual assault at a rape crisis centre talked to others about the crime. Of these, 76 per cent received advice and 84 per cent of these followed the advice.
- A similar pattern occurred for a sample of burglary, theft and robbery victims who had reported the crime to the police. Sixty-two per cent talked to others before reporting the crime, 58 per cent of these received advice and 95 per cent of these followed the advice.

Of course, these are victims who made the decision eventually to report the crime. It is difficult to generalise from this to victims in general, many of whom decide not to report the crime.

To understand both reporting and non-reporting of crime better, Greenberg and Beach (2001) contacted a sample from the community at random by telephone. Anyone agreeing to take part was asked whether they had been a victim of a crime in the previous 12 months. Those over 18 years of age who had been victims of burglary or theft and were personally responsible for the decision as to whether or not to report the crime to the police were interviewed in greater depth. About half had reported the crime to the police. Again, a majority (three-fifths) discussed the crime with others before making the decision whether or not to report the crime to the police. Family members (60 per cent) and friends (24 per cent) were the major categories of people with whom the events were discussed. Mostly (i.e. in 61 per cent of cases) this social contact was actually present when the crime was discovered. Forty-seven per cent of those who talked about the crime before making the reporting decision had also received advice from that other person. The researchers then studied the relative influence of a number of predictors of reporting or not, using logistic regression (see, for example, Howitt and Cramer, 2017, for a readable account of this complex statistical procedure). The most powerful factor in the decision to report the crime to the police (once demographic variables such as age, sex and race had been taken into account) was the type of advice given by those around the victim. So, if the advice was to call the police then this was extremely influential in the sense that the victim would call the police in a high proportion of instances. The type of crime was important since burglaries were much more likely to be reported than theft, for example. The financial loss had a significant but small influence on the willingness to report, as did generalised arousal, which is a sort of measure of the emotional response the victim had to the crime.

However, it would be wrong to think that reporting crime is simply the consequence of social influence. This would be to assume that the victim has no independent view of whether or not to report the crime since the other person may simply agree with what the victim decides in the first place.

Greenberg and Beach (2004) studied how victims of property crime decide to report the crime to the police. They tested the idea that the decision-making process includes three broad mechanisms:

- *Reward/costs-driven:* basically whether the gains of going through the reporting process and possibly court appearances as a witness are sufficiently warranted by the monetary value of their loss. If the value of the loss is small then victims will be less likely to report the crime to the police. In the study, this was measured on the basis of the amount stolen in dollars.

- *Affect-driven:* the arousal of emotion on being victimised may influence reporting in a number of ways. The more emotionally arousing it is, the more the victim's attention will continue to be focused on the crime and the more likely they are to report. Alternatively, a crime that raises fear or anger may arouse patterns of behaviour that involve seeking the protection of the legal system by reporting the matter. Emotional arousal was assessed by asking how the victim felt immediately after becoming aware of the crime – such as how angry, afraid and upset.
- *Socially driven:* the decision to report the crime is taken under the influence of significant social others who advise or inform the victim about what to do. If the victim had been advised to call the police immediately after the crime had been discovered then the report was classified as socially driven.

A sample of victims of burglary and theft was obtained, using random telephone contact methods. Eligible participants had to be 18 years of age, to have been a victim of either a burglary or theft but no other crime, and to have been the person who took the decision to report the crime to the police or not to do so. It was found that *all* of the above three explanations for reporting the crime to the police were influential in the reporting process. However, they worked independently in that the effect of each type of variable had an influence distinct from other types. There was no interaction between the predictors in the sense that, say, those who were very angry and who had received advice to call the police were not disproportionately more likely to report the crime to the police. The victims of burglary were above three times more likely to report the crime, irrespective of the dollar value involved, than the victims of theft were. Maybe burglary was seen as a more personally invasive crime than theft.

The decision to report being criminally victimised can be a difficult one involving all sorts of factors, as we have seen. But some crimes hit at the individual's self-identity, which may make reporting especially difficult. A case in point is to be found in Burcar's (2013) study of young Swedish men's narratives about contacting the police after being mugged or assaulted. These included their reasons for not making the complaint. The young men constructed in their narratives their own personal identities. Their understanding of why they were victims was congruent with dominant male norms.

Another aspect of the thought processes of victims is that of counterfactual thinking. We are all prone to this – such as when we imagine different outcomes to an event from what actually happened. For example, 'If only I had not gone to the bank then I would not have been carrying all the money that was stolen.' Counterfactual thinking may affect our decision whether or not to report a crime because it tends to increase the negative emotion experienced by the victim (Miller, Adya, Chamberlain and Jehle, 2010). The easier it is to complete the 'If only . . .' sentence, the greater the annoyance or anger that we feel about what had happened. But this is turned on ourselves and not the offender. One consequence of not reporting a crime to anyone is that we lose the protection of others, such as friends, family, police and mental health workers. Furthermore, because the offender cannot be punished for a crime which is not reported, the victim may be left with continuing feelings of vulnerability and injustice.

If the victim was engaging in their typical routine behaviours when the crime occurred then it is less likely that they will report the crime (see Figure 4.3). In the study by Miller *et al.* (2010), the participants were given one of several different stories in which their handbag or wallet was stolen as they walked home. So (a) in the typical behaviour version, the participants were told that they had taken their normal route home and (b) in the atypical behaviour version, it was explained to them that they took a rather unusual route home. The size of the financial loss is a factor which can increase the likelihood that the crime is reported. This was varied by indicating that a small, medium or substantial amount of money had been taken in the different versions. Both greater financial loss and taking an atypical route home increased the participant's subjective likelihood of reporting the crime. Furthermore, those who lost the most money and took a typical route home were disproportionately more likely to feel angry.

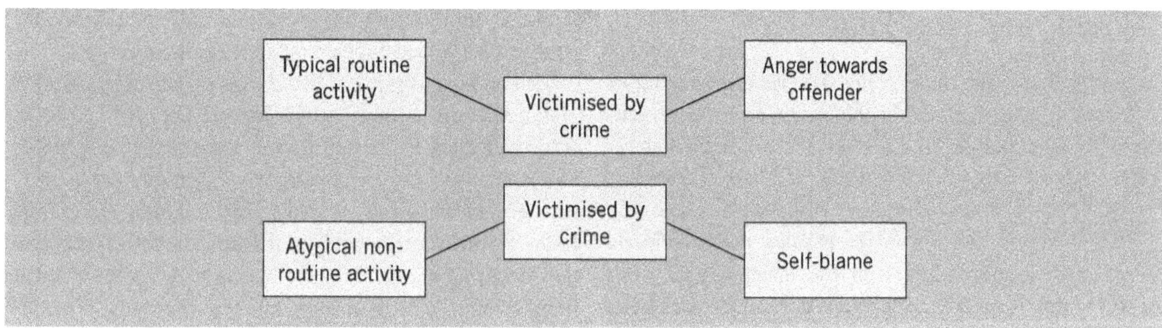

Figure 4.3 Counterfactual thinking and victim self-blame

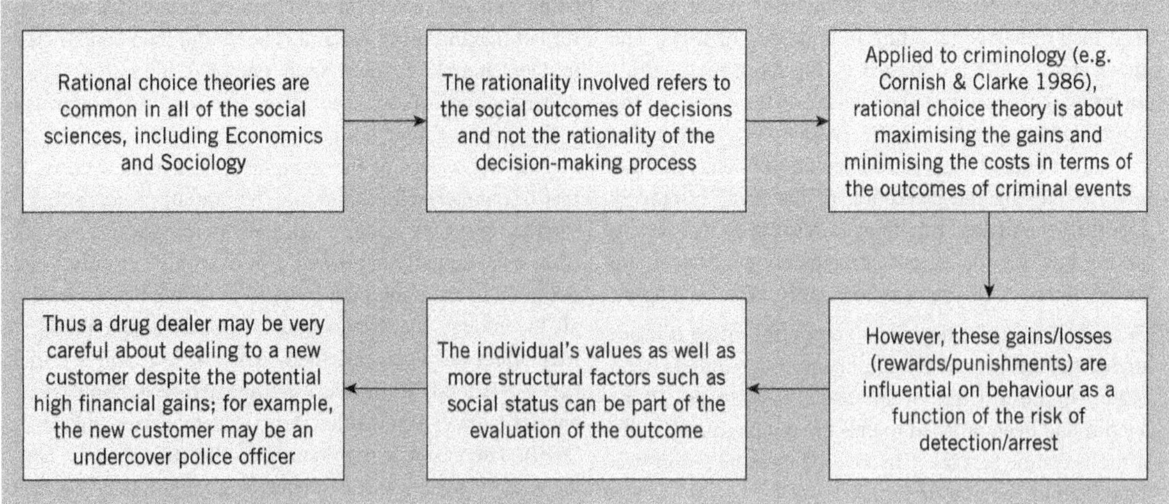

Figure 4.4 Elements of rational choice theory

However, it was not accurate to suggest that crime reporting was due to the feelings of anger since typicality did not predict anger levels – though typicality was related to reporting. The researchers argue that there was evidence that these findings were the result of counterfactual thinking because those who took an unusual route home tended to have a stronger belief that the incident was the consequence of luck and that it was preventable.

An important decision to make when being victimised is the question of whether to resist in any way or to be passive. There are a minimum of four different strategies that could be adopted in order to resist a rape or robbery, for example:

- *Forceful physical resistance:* things such as kicking, punching, scratching, and the use of judo or some other martial art.
- *Non-forceful physical resistance:* escaping from the offender's grasp, running away or trying to escape, and avoiding contact with the offender.
- *Forceful verbal resistance:* screaming, shouting, threatening.
- *Non-forceful verbal resistance:* begging, pleading, crying or reasoning with the attacker.

Clearly, the victim undergoing the crime is seeking to force the offender to abandon the crime, so a good measure of the success of the self-protective behaviour is whether the offender abandons the crime before completing it. Of course, what the victim would wish to avoid is personal injury to themselves. Generally, these methods are reasonably successful, with the exception of non-forceful verbal resistance, which did not reduce the likelihood of rape completion. Using forceful methods against a robber seems to increase the risk of violence to oneself.

Why should a victim's self-protective acts be effective at all? According to Guerette and Santana (2010), rational choice theory (Clark and Cornish, 1985) provides part of the explanation (see Figure 4.4). Criminals engage in decision making in preparation for and during a crime. Different crimes involve different decision-making models and are committed for a particular purpose. Offending is not a random occurrence but is dependent on both the offender and the immediate situation. According to ratio nal choice theory, offenders assess the effort, risk and reward involved in a potential crime so that they can decide whether or not to go ahead and commit it. It is a rational process but limited as such by the quality of information available to the offender concerning when, where and by what methods to commit the crime. The self-protective responses of the victim and other actions may alter their suitability as a target or, of course, risk alerting other people close by who may intervene. The latter are known as guardians in rational choice theory. Where the victim resists the offence, the chance that it will be successfully completed is reduced. Quite simply, the relationship between effort and reward is changed by victim resistance. Additionally, where the attack takes place (in a public setting or not) might have an influence, since the self-protective behaviour may alert guardians.

Guerette and Santana (2010) used data from the US National Crime Victim Survey for the years 1992 to 2004. Information collected in this was used to assess whether a rape attempt was completed, whether a robbery attempt was completed, and whether the victim was injured. Injuries were further categorised in terms of (a) whether they occurred before resistance to the crime or (b) whether they occurred during or after resisting the crime. For this study, only crimes involving a single offender were used. The level of resistance was coded on a scale ranging from verbal resistance to physical resistance to physical resistance with a gun or another weapon or an object. Robberies and rapes were completed on just over 60 per cent of occasions each. Only 20 per cent of injuries were received during or after resisting the crime. Robbers used less physical force than rapists, but this was because the use of guns was commoner during robberies. This might also explain the finding that more force was used by rape victims than robbery victims. All forms of resistance increased the likelihood that the offender would abandon the crime attempt. The higher the level of resistance used against the offender, the lower the chance that the crime would be completed. The situational variables had less effect on the likelihood of the crime being completed, though a public location or taking place at night did have some influence.

In personal crimes, the behaviours of the victim and the offender each affect the other. So the violence of the offender may help determine the extent and nature of the victim's response. A study of such crimes then needs to involve what both the offender and the victim were thinking in order to be complete. In the research by Beauregard and Mieczkowski (2012) the emphasis was the offender's viewpoint. Did, for example, the offender see the response of the victim as resistance and was this resistance seen as appropriate? The response of the offender to the resistance was assessed. Not all victims of sexual assaults put up resistance. Their motives for not doing so can vary from fear of being killed to the negative social consequence such as embarrassment. In their study, Beauregard and Mieczkowski found that aspects of the offender's strategy for committing the crime (use of weapons, violence, persuasion, etc.) were the most important factor in victim resistance. Where the offender began the offence with the use of violence, the likelihood was that he would continue with the violence when faced with the resistance of the victim. When the offender starts the assault using physical aggression, the victim is most likely to respond with physical resistance. The presence of a weapon during the crime also had important consequences and led to heightened patterns of violence during the offence. Possibly this reflects the fact that the victim would be in a better position to resist if her attacker did not have a weapon.

It has been argued that low resistance self-efficacy may be involved in the trend for those who have experienced sexual assault or PTSD as a consequence of sexual assault being at increased risk of re-victimisation (Littleton and Decker, 2016). Self-efficacy has a similar meaning to the concept of self-protective behaviours. Littleton and Decker (2016) took an online sample of American women who had a history of being raped. They were questioned about this history, rape-related PTSD symptoms, and a number of other things. Resistance self-efficacy included asking the man to leave, telling him nicely that you did not want sex, pushing him away, and using strong language. Having a history of childhood sexual abuse predicted lower levels of resistance self-efficacy. Having higher PTSD symptoms was also associated with lower levels of resistance self-efficacy. Lower resistance self-efficacy was related to a greater risk of a sexual assault. However, perhaps because it was a rare occurrence, using more violent resistance strategies (such as slapping, scratching or screaming for help) was not associated with lowered risk of sexual assault.

Restorative justice

Victims sometimes feel that they have undergone secondary victimisation by the insensitive response of the criminal justice system to them. Giving a voice to the victim alters this. The Victim Impact Statement (or the Victim Personal Statement) is one of the few ways in which victims can give communicate the effects of the crime on them in court. A victim statement allows the victim to describe to the court the consequences of the crime on them either orally or in writing. Do victim statements help with the emotional recovery of the victim? What little research that has been done on victim statements has concentrated on the victim's satisfaction with the criminal justice process they experienced (e.g. Roberts and Erez, 2004) but satisfaction cannot be equated with emotion reduction. Lens, Pemberton, Brans, Braeken, Bogaerts and Lahlah (2015) conducted a longitudinal study in Holland comparing the emotional recovery of those who gave victim statements with those who did not. The problem for the researchers was that victims who were experiencing high levels of anger and anxiety as a result of the crime self-selected to give victim statements. Those who experienced less emotion tended not to give victim statements. Did anger/anxiety decline markedly following giving a victim statement? There was little evidence that it did. There were changes in anxiety and anger levels in the victim statement group from before the trial to after the trial. However, these were small compared to the differences between the victim statement group and the non-victim statement group. Levels of anger and anxiety basically tended to remain stable. Lens *et al.* suggest that it is unlikely, based on previous research (Van Emmerik, Kapmphuis, Hulsbosch and Emmelkamp, 2002), that a single expression of emotion (as in making a victim statement) will have a therapeutic effect. It was found that a victim who felt in personal control of their recovery process tended to show bigger reductions in anger and anxiety feeling. However, this was not a consequence of making a victim statement since there was no evidence that giving a victim statement increased feelings of being in control. Also feelings that the justice process was procedurally fair (Box 4.2) were associated with reductions in anger and

Box 4.2 Key concept

Procedural justice

The psychological Theory of Procedural Justice (Thibaut and Walker, 1975) was a significant early step towards understanding why victim–offender mediation and similar strategies can be so important and what makes them effective. Although the procedural justice theory accepts that the outcomes of judicial processes are important in achieving a feeling of justice, the procedures involved in the judicial process are more important – especially knowing in advance that the procedures are fair. There are two factors which determine the sense of procedural fairness:

- *Process control:* This is the extent to which those involved are able to have an input throughout the decision-making process. That is, the degree to which it is possible for them to present information at all stages.
- *Decision control:* The extent to which the parties can control the outcome. To what extent is it possible for the parties involved to be able to accept or reject the decisions and recommendations made by a third party?

However, in Tyler and Lind's (1992) Relational Model of Procedural Justice, three factors are identified which lead to the sense of fairness about the procedures:

- *Trust:* The belief that the authority (the criminal justice system) is trying to do the right thing.
- *Standing:* The feeling that one is being treated with dignity and respect in a way which demonstrates the individual's rights. Respect is sometimes referred to as interactional fairness (Van den Bos and Lind, 2002).
- *Neutrality:* The term describing honesty and lack of prejudice with decisions being factually based.

All of this would imply that the ways in which professionals interact with victims is a crucial aspect of victim–offender mediation.

Many of these principles can be seen to be working in Wemmers and Cyr's (2006b) study of crime victims participating in a victim–offender mediation programme for young offenders. In terms of judgements of procedural justice fairness, 71 per cent of victims felt that the procedures were fair while 26 per cent of victims felt them to be unfair – only a few victims claimed to be neutral about the programme. There were significant relationships between feeling the process was fair and (a) feeling that they were heard, (b) perceiving that they had the ability to express themselves in the procedures, (c) having a good initial impression of the project workers, (d) feeling that they were given the information they desired, (e) faith in the mediator, (f) feeling respectfully treated, and (g) seeing the project worker as neutral. These relationships provide support for procedural justice theory and, more specifically, the concepts of trust, standing and neutrality found in Tyler and Lynd's (1992) theory. In a closely related report, Wemmers and Cyr (2006a) further investigated the experience of the victims who had been invited to join a victim–offender mediation programme. Once again, there was a tendency for victims to polarise towards the extremes and relatively few of them picked neutral points or milder versions of fair and unfair.

There is a substantial literature which shows that authorities which treat the public justly according to procedural justice principles encourage the public's cooperation and compliance by doing so. One recent study demonstrating this, Barkworth and Murphy (2015), surveyed the Australian public in two waves. Participants were asked to answer a number of questions concerning their most recent involvement with a police officer. Short scales were used to measure procedural justice and their emotions about that experience as well as their beliefs about compliance with the law:

- Procedural justice involved how approachable/friendly, polite/respectful/courteous and fair the officer was and whether they were able to give their views before a decision was made and whether what they said was considered in reaching the decision.
- The respondents' negative emotions in response to their experiences with measured in terms of being tense, anxious, angry, resentful and frustrated.

The above were measured in both the first- and second-wave questionnaires. Compliant behaviour was measured only at the second wave:

- Items making up the non-compliance questionnaire included disobeying the law is justified sometimes, sometimes it is ok to break the law and disobeying the police is sometimes justified.

The findings were very clear. Failure to apply the principles of procedural justice resulted in higher levels of self-reported non-compliance with the law and the police. However, this relationship is mediated by the negative emotions which were aroused by the police not applying procedural justice principles.

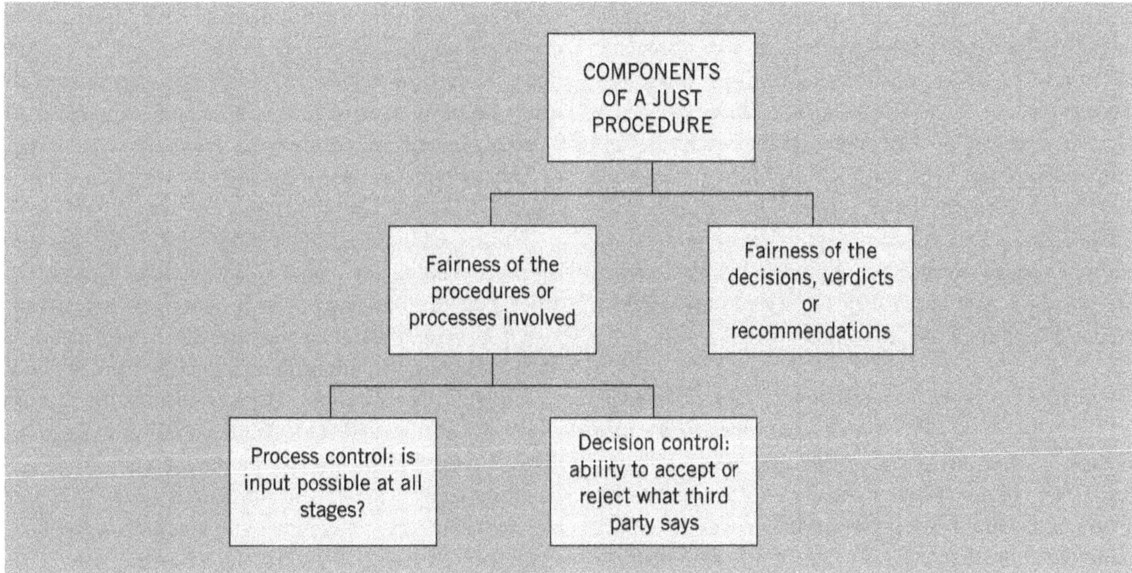

Figure 4.5 Elements of procedural justice theory

anxiety. Lens *et al.* suggest that there is no simple effect of giving a victim statement on the victim's emotional state. The question is more one of what sort of person will benefit from the victim statement.

A more thoroughly researched area is that of restorative justice which is a victim-oriented approach to dealing with the consequences of crime. The central issue in restorative justice is not the law-breaking but the injury it causes the victim. Some crimes, such as domestic violence, also damage the relationship between the victim and the perpetrator. Restorative justice initiatives provide victims with the opportunity to tell or confront those who offended against them (or offenders more generally) about the impact the crime has had on them. In this way, the offender may begin to appreciate the true impact of their crimes and its consequences for the victim. Not only should this help the victim come to terms with the crime better, but the offender, by taking responsibility for their own actions, may desist from further offending. One way in which restorative justice may work is by increasing the offender's empathy for the victim and other people in general. Although restorative justice programmes began in 1970s, the term itself was first used in the 1980s. Restorative justice is primarily a practice-led activity – though theoretical contributions are not insubstantial, as we shall see. Restorative justice generally involves some sort of formal mediation between the offender and the victim. Restorative justice works in parallel to the court-based trial process though in some cases it is an alternative to courts of law. Of course, such restorative justice procedures are not the only way in which the victim can take control and redress the balance. Victims may also have access to civil-legal procedures such as suing for compensation or even bringing a private prosecution against the perpetrator of the crime in order to obtain redress and the sense that justice has been done.

When laws are broken, there are two notions of justice which help determine responses. These are termed retributive and restorative justice. *Retributive justice* is about the repair of justice through a one-sidedly imposed punishment by the criminal justice system. *Restorative justice*, on the other hand, means the repair of justice by the reaffirmation of consensual shared values by all parties. A consensus is sought in terms of the nature of the harm done, the attribution of responsibility, and the values involved (Wenzel, Okimoto, Feather and Platow, 2008). So, according to Wright (2002), there are a number of characteristics of restorative justice:

- Restorative justice concentrates on the harm caused by the crime, not the criminal activity in itself.
- Healing and reintegration are its main objectives.
- The ideal outcome from restorative justice includes a satisfied victim and an offender who feels that they have been dealt with fairly. Thus the process of restoration is the focus, not merely financial compensation for the victim, for example.
- The community is involved in the outcome.
- Integration of parts of the system so that victims and offenders, in dialogue with one another, identify the factors that led to the crime (e.g. social and economic pressures). In this way, the process can inform community crime reduction strategies.
- All of those who are harmed are the focus, including the offender and the offender's family. Children may be

construed as victims of the crime because, say, their father has been sent to prison. Visits may be infrequent because of transport difficulties to a prison which may be very distant. They are then, in a sense, secondary victims, deprived of the benefits of their father's day-to-day parenting. Furthermore, the children of offenders may experience social stigma (Philbrick, 2002). The consequences of crime spread very widely. In addition, police officers, for example, may also be victims of the crime because of the trauma that dealing with a distressing crime may cause them.

The process of restorative justice may take quite some time. For example, some victims are not open to the idea immediately after being victimised but may be more receptive to talking about restorative justice processes after time has elapsed. Some victims may never be willing to be involved. Restorative justice is largely administered and organised by mediation services which work with both victims and offenders to facilitate the process. Attempts to pressurise the victim into participating may be counterproductive. The community benefits from restorative justice as well as the victim. Coates, Umbreit and Vos (2001) studied a substantial number of victim–offender mediation programmes in a number of different Western countries. Victims chose to participate for reasons such as understanding why the crime happened and to communicate to the offender just what effect the crime had had on the victim. Other benefits include the opportunity to express their emotions in the presence of the offender, the opportunity to be forgiving and the possibility of peaceful coexistence of the offender and victim in the community.

Wright (2002) suggests that, although a criminal act has taken place, the criminal courts may not deal with it effectively, especially in those cases which occur in the context of a relationship or involve a dispute between two or more parties. In these circumstances, victim–offender mediation may have more to offer the victim while avoiding the risk of further damage (secondary victimisation) by the criminal justice system. Some countries, such as Australia and England and Wales, have incorporated reparative procedures into legislation. Initially, reparative work was confined to young offenders (under the age of 18 years) though increasingly adult offenders may be involved. Restorative justice is seen as especially appropriate to young offenders.

Typically, following an instruction from a court, the mediation service elicits from the victim proposals for reparation or compensation. Direct offender mediation involves direct contact between the victim and the young offender in the form of face-to-face meetings which are supervised (mediated) by project staff. The aim is to reach some sort of agreement – possibly including financial reparation. Both the victim and the victimiser may ask questions, express their sentiments and proffer explanations. Failure to achieve a satisfactory agreement may result in an alternative punishment being applied to the offender. In contrast, indirect mediation involves no face-to-face meeting between the victim and offender – the mediator does the communicating between the two.

Wenzel, Okimoto, Feather and Platow (2008) provide a social psychological model of restorative justice. They argue that the consensus which is sought in restorative justice programmes attempts to reaffirm the shared and identity-defining values of the community from which the victim and offender come. The key issue is the extent to which the victim and the offender share at least part of their identities. Wenzel *et al.* define the concept of community broadly – it can be a community of the values and identity shared by the criminal and victim in question, for example. The result of the restorative justice process will not always be harmonious. For instance, where the victim and offender do not share identities in some way, the rebalancing process may result in the victim desiring to shame and humiliate the offender. To be successful, restorative justice needs the victim and offender to see themselves jointly in terms of an overriding or superordinate category. The victim and offender may share a subgroup identity which itself may contribute to defining the offender as deviant. This can result in punitive responses despite identity sharing. For example, if it transpired during the meetings that both victim and offender had suffered sexual abuse as a child, the victim's strong feelings about not using this as a reason for victimising others might lead to difficulties in reconciliation between victim and offender.

Perhaps the most influential theory influencing restorative justice work is Braithwaite's (1989) reintegrative shaming theory. His theory primarily sought to explain juvenile crime and, like other approaches to restorative justice, he regarded crime as causing damage to relationships between the offender, victim and the community. Reintegrative shaming theory draws from and essentially integrates several other theories. Among these, labelling theory (Lemert, 1951, 1967) is perhaps one of the best known. Labelling theory is based on the idea that labelling a person as deviant will lead them to being deviant. In keeping with this, Braithwaite proposes that, when society has as a primary goal of encouraging deviant individuals back into society, crime is more effectively controlled. In Braithwate's theory, two different types of shaming are identified: 1) disintegrative shaming which excludes individuals from the community and 2) reintegrative shaming which helps to reintegrate the offender back into society. Of course, reintegration back into the community lessens the risk of the offender reoffending at a later stage. Reintegrative shaming is characteristic of societies that retain positive regard for offenders despite disapproving of their crime. With time, disapproval turns to forgiveness (Braithwaite, 1989). Braithwaite indicates that Japan is a culture which favours reintegrative shaming. There the apology has an important role. A Japanese person who commits a crime affects their social environment, including family, school and workplace. In a collectivistic society such as Japan, the group adopts responsibility for the deviant behaviour. Shaming which labels offenders as deviant merely marginalises them from society and so has the reverse of the desired effect. Cultural shaming can explain variations in crime rates but can be seen also as a means of crime control.

Braithwaite's reintegrative shaming theory underpins the planning of what are known as diversionary restorative justice 'conferences' (Kim and Gerber, 2012) which originated from a police initiative in Bethlehem, Pennsylvania. These conferences are meetings employing restorative justice procedures between offenders and victims (especially young offenders, McGarrell, 2001). Offenders are brought face-to-face with the consequences of their criminal activities and, following this, efforts are made to encourage them to take personal responsibility for acting lawfully in the future. Negotiation, mediation, victim empowerment and reparation are the broad processes by which the damage of crime is repaired. The main features of the conferences should be familiar by now:

- The bringing together collectively of those with a particular interest in the consequences of the crime in question. These stakeholders are the offender, the victim, and the community. The conference focuses on the consequences of the crime and what needs to happen in the future.
- Offenders are given the opportunity to acknowledge the various impacts of what they did and to make reparation.
- The victim needs to have the harm done to them acknowledged and to have amends made in appropriate ways.

Victims were highly satisfied with such conferences when the crime involved was an offence against the person. However, this was not the case for property crimes. Importantly, recidivism among the juvenile offenders involved declined consequent to the conferences.

In the UK, the SORI (Supporting Offenders through Restoration Inside) programme has been implemented in adult prisons. It consists of a five-day prison-based programme. Day 1 is a taster allowing participants the opportunity to decide whether to undertake the full programme. The remaining four days are the main victim awareness component, including an introduction to the principles of restorative justice. Pilot courses have been carried out in a number of UK prisons (Beech and Chauhan, 2013). Three overriding aims are involved: 1) to encourage the offender's acceptance of personal responsibility for the harm they have done; 2) to increase the offender's feelings of victim empathy; and 3) to motivate the offender to desist from offending behaviour. Not all prisoners were eligible for the programme. All sex offenders and domestic violence offenders had a blanket exclusion since a restorative justice programme involving victims of these crimes might be counterproductive. Participants were required to be volunteers who had indicated acceptance of their guilt up to a point and accepted responsibility. It was also required that they had shown remorse. Offenders who could not cope in this sort of situation were excluded. In other words, participants needed to show signs that they could benefit from the SORI programme. At the end of the programme, the offender had to speak publicly in front of the victim group and others in order to accept their responsibility for their offending behaviour and to make statements about how they will make reparation for what they had done. Rather than meet with the actual victims of their crimes, the prisoners met with other victims who had been the victims of similar crimes to the ones the offender had committed.

The prisoners completed the following psychometric questionnaires both before and after the SORI programme:

- The Victim Concerns Scale (Clements, Brennen, Kirkley, Gordon and Church, 2006): this assesses how offenders view the impact of various sorts of offending on the victims of these crimes.
- The Locus of Control Scale (Craig, Franklin and Andrews, 1984): this measures the degree to which the individual sees themselves as controlling their own actions rather than their offending being the consequence of factors such as luck and accidental factors. It is not uncommon for prisoners to see what happens to them as being out of their control.
- The Stages of Change Scale (McConnaughy, Prochaska and Velicer, 1983): this assesses how much an individual is prepared to engage in life changes.

The results showed that the programme had improved empathy for the victim and motivation to avoid future offending. These are predicted outcomes from the research and indicate something of the SORI programme's effectiveness. Particularly important was that SORI moved offenders into the action level for change and away from merely contemplating change. However, there was no change in the degree to which the prisoners accepted responsibility for the damage they did to their victims. This may simply be a consequence of the relative shortness of the SORI programme in terms of shifting the locus of control from outside of the offender to within the offender. For victims, there was a reduction in post-traumatic stress symptoms resulting from the crime. They became less inclined to desire violent revenge. Both offenders and victims viewed the criminal justice system in a better light following restorative justice interventions.

Not everyone is convinced that victim–offender mediation is a boon to victims. Pease (2007) complains that 'there is more in the practice of restorative justice for the perpetrator than the victim, and the dangers of railroading well-intentioned and kindly victims into a process that is primarily for the benefit of the offender may, particularly in unskilled hands, become a form of secondary victimization' (p. 607). We have seen some evidence above of the influence of restorative justice procedures on victims and there is more. For example, Sherman *et al.* (2005), in a meta-analysis (see Box 4.1), found that, compared with conventional justice, those going through restorative justice procedures agreed with significantly fewer items dealing with revenge/anger.

The question of the effect of restorative justice on recidivism is bound to be a priority to sceptics. Research which concentrates more on the quality of the procedures than the outcome of procedural justice leaves this important question unaddressed. However, research has begun to emerge in the United Kingdom and elsewhere suggesting that there are reductions in offending associated with restorative justice (Shapland *et al.*, 2008). Over three different research sites, there were reductions in the frequency of reoffending and reconviction. Offenders involved in restorative justice committed a quarter fewer crimes during the follow-up period. This finding involved randomised allocation to restorative justice procedures. A statistical review of studies of restorative justice by Sherman and Strang (2007) indicated that restorative justice reduced the risk of future offending by the offender but also had positive consequences for the victim.

One compendium of research which draws on some of the above studies and others is Sherman *et al.* (2015). This summarises the findings from 12 randomised trials (randomised experiments) into one method of implementing restorative justice based on Braithwaite's ideas discussed earlier. These were randomised trials since arrestees were randomly allocated to either the restorative justice conference or to the normal criminal justice court procedure for the age group. Such randomisation is rare in field studies but it is particularly welcomed by psychologists. The studies took place in various locations in the UK and Australia. Sherman *et al.* explain in great detail the problems of trying to organise such research which depended a great deal on police and official cooperation generally. In every case the restorative justice conference was based on identical methods and procedures. This was achieved because members of the research team trained police officers and others who then ran the restorative justice conferences. Over 2000 victims and over 1000 offenders took part. There were lengthy follow-up periods of up to ten years for victims and nearly twice as long for offenders. Different categories of offences were concentrated on in the different studies such as violence, shoplifting, theft, drink-driving and burglary.

For the offenders, there was a reduction in the amount of repeat offending two years after the restorative justice conferences. However, this happened for violent crimes and not for property crimes. Generally speaking, the conferences were extremely cost effective in that the cost of running the conferences was offset by reductions in the numbers of crimes committed. The value in reduced repeat crime levels was eight times the cost of the conferences. The restorative justice conferences had their biggest effect on high-frequency offenders. There was some evidence that medium frequency offenders either showed no change or that they offended more following the conferences. Nevertheless, repeat offending was overall reduced in almost all of the studies except those involving drink driving which had no personal victims whereas increases in recidivism were found. Victims who had attended the restorative justice conferences showed a number of differences from the victim controls. They became less fearful of a repeat attack by the same offender and they wanted less a violent revenge against the offender. Satisfaction with the way in which the offence was handled was higher in the restorative justice conference condition. Victims of robbery and burglary showed significantly fewer symptoms of PTSD having gone through the restorative justice conference route compared with victims who went through the normal court route.

Along with many others, Van Ness and Strong (2013) have suggested that restorative justice may be used to avoid sending non-dangerous offenders to prison. Wood (2015) reviewed the evidence in this respect and concludes that restorative justice will not reduce incarceration in countries like the United States, the United Kingdom, Australia and New Zealand. Each of these has relatively widespread use of restorative justice while at the same time having the biggest increases in incarceration. There are a number of reasons why incarceration is unlikely to be reduced by restorative justice programmes, according to Wood. One reason is that restorative justice has by and large been applied to crimes such as vandalism, theft and relatively trivial assaults which would not normally lead to imprisonment for involving juveniles. Drug offences tend not to be involved in restorative justice possibly because there is no tangible victim. So even assuming that restorative justice programmes do deter the young offender from recidivism as research suggests, this can do little to affect incarceration rates simply because the offender is unlikely to have received a custodial sentence.

Main points

- The victims of crime have increasingly been regarded sympathetically as a consequence of a number of changes. The feminist movement, for example, pushed for public awareness of the plight of the victims of crimes such as domestic violence and sexual abuse. It was argued that often the victim was revictimised by the police investigation and the subsequent trial. While elements of this remain, the concept of restorative justice changes the focus of the criminal justice system onto the needs of the victims of crime rather than simply the disposal of the offender through the criminal justice system. It also allows for victims to express their emotions towards their victimiser. A court may seek a victim's proposals for reparation.
- There are many consequences of crime, such as cycles of abuse. Post-traumatic stress disorder is a psychological state in which the victim is unable to deal effectively with their memory of the traumatic events which the criminal subjected them to. Trying to suppress the distressing memories prevents the psychological processes of healing from taking place. Nevertheless, the memories are still there and burst through into consciousness in the form of nightmares and flashbacks, for example. Treatment involves working through the memories safely. These memories tend to be sensory motor ones rather than narrative ones. Trauma memories are converted to ordinary narrative memories and so can be dealt with by the victim through a normal healing process which was previously unavailable.
- Victims of crime are also the major source of information to the police. The process by which they choose to report the crime or not is therefore of great importance in the criminal justice system. It is clear that this is a social activity since a large proportion of victims of crime talk the crime over with friends, relatives and others, and solicit their advice. The decision to report a crime is influenced by a range of factors, including the emotional significance of the crime and the benefits/costs ratio involved in the decision to report the crime.

Further reading

Doerner, W.G. and Lab, S.P. (2015) *Victimology* (7th ed) London: Routledge.

Goulston, M. (2008) *Post-traumatic Stress Disorder for Dummies* Hoboken, NJ: Wiley Publishing.

Walklate, S. (ed.) (2017) *Handbook of Victims and Victimology* (2nd ed) Cullompton: Willan Publishing.

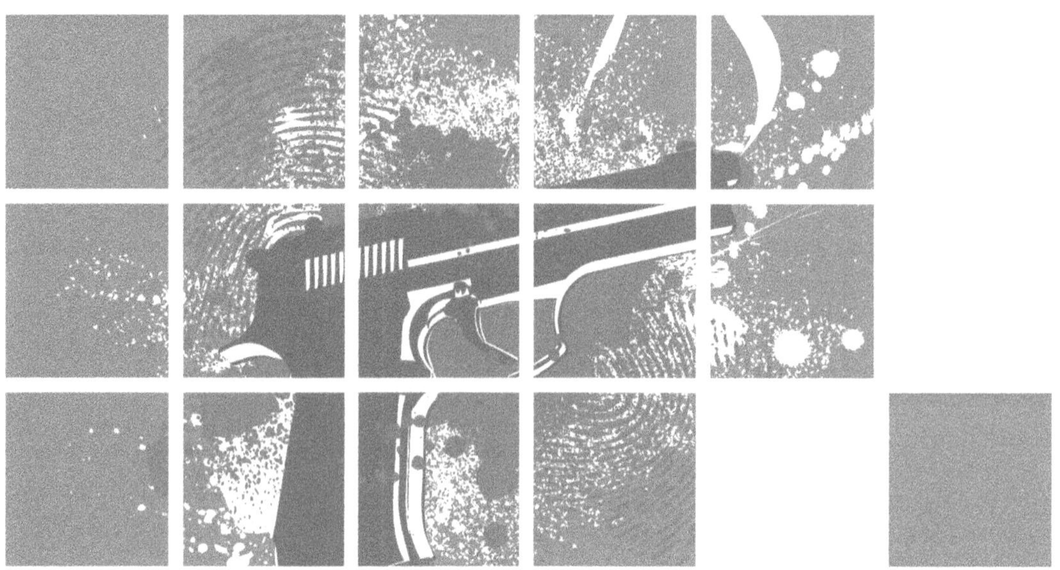

Chapter 5

Theories of crime

Overview

- There are many general theories relevant to the study of crime, only a portion of which can be classified as psychology. However, it is important to appreciate that crime can be understood from a variety of perspectives, and forensic and criminal psychologists can benefit from insights from other disciplines. Theories dealing with more specific aspects of crime are dealt with as appropriate in other chapters.
- Levels of explanation of crime range from the biological and genetic through to the social and economic. Psychological theories tend to be more limited but nevertheless cover much of that range between the biological and the social. The theories described in this chapter are fairly general theories trying to address the broad range of crime. Any reasonably complete understanding of crime should consider every different level of explanation. Few theories operate at more than one level of analysis.
- Theories of crime may be divided into: 1) societal or macro-level theories; 2) community or locality level theories; 3) group and socialisation influence theories; and 4) individual level theories. Most psychological theories of crime would be classified in the last two categories.
- Few, if any, of the theories compete in the sense that they make different predictions about crime and criminal activity. In other words, it is unlikely that one can reject a theory simply because another theory makes better predictions. Few of the theories have been falsified. Rather, they should be seen as complementing or supplementing each other.
- Among the theories described and evaluated here are: 1) physiological; 2) genetic; 3) intellectual deficits; 4) psychoanalytic; 5) addiction; 6) biosocial; 7) social learning; and 8) social constructionist approaches.

Introduction

This chapter takes a broad look at the role of theory in forensic and criminal psychology. Along with research, theory is the lifeblood of psychology. While the other chapters in this book are replete with theory, some theory does not fit into these because it is more all-embracing, or it may represent a perspective which can be applied to crime in general, or it is not a currently active aspect of forensic and criminal psychology. Theories of crime come in a variety of styles, types and shapes. Crime is of concern to a number of disciplines and it is possible to find economic, geographical, sociological, psychiatric, psychological and biological theories – and theories from other disciplines, such as social work, may have their own distinctive features. Of course, criminological theory itself is of great relevance and should be considered as an important resource for forensic and criminal psychologists. Figure 5.1 illustrates some of the main levels of analysis that may be applied to crime. While there is little space here to explore theories from all of these disciplines, they are very relevant to understanding crime from a wide perspective. Indeed, they are almost essential to anyone working in the field of forensic and criminal psychology wanting a broad perspective on crime. Figure 5.1 explains in some detail the operation of these different levels of explanation. (McGuire (2000) adopted a similar sort of scheme and some of the ideas are borrowed from him.) These are not theories in the sense that research can establish which one is the best empirically. They are alternative perspectives, sometimes on the same matters to do with crime and criminality but, more often, reflecting different aspects.

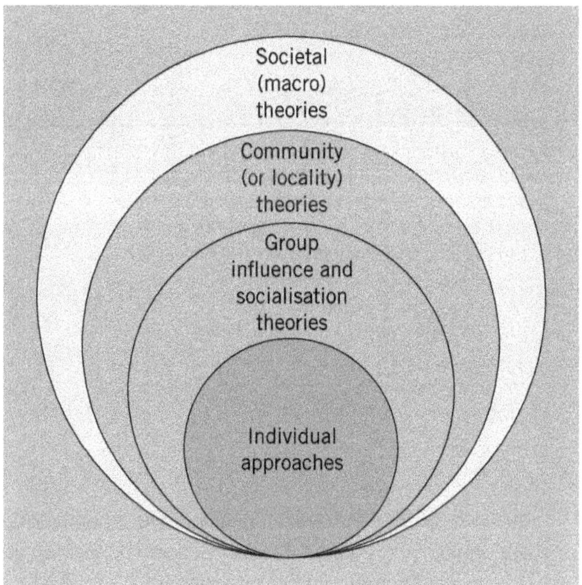

Figure 5.1 How crime can be explained at different levels of analysis

- *Societal or macro-level theories:* the broadest level of analysis, according to Figure 5.1, comprises the societal or macro-level theories, which basically suggest that crime is a consequence of social structure rather than, say, genetic tendencies or psychiatric problems. Marxist conflict theory regards the criminal justice system as a means by which the dominant or privileged classes retain their dominance and privilege. Possibly this is most clearly seen in the way land has become owned whereas once it belonged to nature. More immediately linked to psychology is the feminist analysis that fundamentally assumes that power is gendered in society and that male power is reflected in laws that, for example, have regarded females as the possessions of their fathers and husbands. Another example of a theory that links psychological process to macro-societal changes is the idea that there is a connection between hate crime (e.g. lynchings of black people in the United States) and prevailing economic conditions (Bailey, Tolnay, Beck and Laird, 2011; Bailey, Tolnay, Beck, Roberts, and Wong, 2008). Although early evidence claimed a link, the connection is questionable (Green, Glaser and Rich, 1998; Green, Strolovitch and Wong, 1998).
- *Community or locality theories:* crime is not randomly distributed geographically and neither is criminality. Some parts of cities tend to suffer more crime and others (perhaps the same areas) tend to be home to more than their fair share of criminals. If crime is geographically organised, why is this so? The answers vary somewhat, but basically the theories suggest that there is either something different about those areas or that different areas provide different opportunities for criminality. In general, crime tends to be committed fairly close to the offender's home base but, often, with a sort of buffer zone just around home where they do not offend because the risk of recognition is high. The people who migrate into these crime-prone areas may experience more extreme social problems. For example, they may be economically deprived thus heightening the risk that they offend.
- *Group and socialisation influence theories:* these are more about direct social influences on criminal behaviour. In a sense they are about the influence of the group (including the family) on criminality. They vary widely, but basically they assume that associates may determine whether or not the youngster gets involved in delinquent activities. These approaches are particularly important if they are regarded as a contrast with the purely individual theories that assume that the roots of criminality lie in the individual.

Societal or macro-level theories

Marxist conflict theory holds that society has evolved in a state of conflict between competing groups in society over material resources and institutionalised power. The dominant class uses laws to control other groups and maintain its command or hegemony.
Robert Merton's strain theory recognises that society's goals (prosperity, achievement, etc.) are only available to a limited few. The rest can achieve the goals only through deviant means. Some of these deviant forms of adaptation are innovative, as in some gang property crime. Others adapt to the strain by retreating into alcoholism, drug addiction, suicide and vagrancy.
Feminist theory holds that criminality is associated with males. Males seek to maintain power in the gendered social system through the deployment of violence against women and, by extension, children. Male control is through their access to power over social institutions such as the law, though relatively powerless men are inclined to the cruder expressions of power which lead to their imprisonment.

Community or locality theories

The *Chicago School* of the 1920s held that there are transitional zones of cities that harbour the greatest levels of crime. These were essentially twilight zones that had been deserted by the middle classes which gravitated to the suburbs. Migrants of all sorts would settle in the transitional zones and experience numerous social pathologies. As their affluence grew, these migrant groups would move to the suburbs and cease to be a crime problem.
Differential opportunity theory explains the patterns of crime likely to be exhibited by individuals in terms of the range of crime opportunities close to home. Different individuals display different modes of adjustment or adaptation to their particular social strains.

Group and socialisation influence theories

Subcultural delinquency theories: youngsters with problems especially to do with the home and school tend to associate with gangs and other groupings in which they can achieve some status. Through criminal activity, delinquent groups may provide an opportunity to achieve a sense of self-esteem.
Differential association theory: Edwin Sutherland viewed criminal behaviour as learned. The circumstances of an individual's upbringing determine their exposure to crime and pressure to commit crime. This theory claims to apply at different strata of society. The process of learning to be a criminal in middle-class communities may encourage exposure to fraud, tax evasion and similar, more middle-class, crimes.
Lifestyle and routine activities: most crime is trivial and impulsive with an element of opportunism. A mix of motivated offenders inadequately supervised by the community plus the availability of suitable targets for crime are the basic requirements of this theory, formulated by Cohen and Felson (1979).

Individual

Personality theories of crimes: Hans Eysenck's biosocial theory is a prime example of this. It emphasises the link between biological factors, personality and crime. Nevertheless, many others have attempted to find the particular patterns of personality associated with either specific crime or crime in general.
Biological theory: Many attempts have been made to identify the particular biological characteristics of offenders – their genetic make-up, brain activity irregularities and hormonal imbalances being typical examples. Evolutionary theories are related to genetic theories but concentrate on just how evolutionary factors lead to the selection of certain genes, including those associated with gender, to be passed on to the next generation (Quinsey, 2002).

Figure 5.2 Levels of explanation of crime

- *Individual approaches:* while no psychologists seriously believe that criminality can be divorced entirely from the social and societal context, some stress the importance of biological and psychological differences as a root cause of criminality. However, distinguishing between the influences of the individual characteristics and more social influences is not at all easy. Generally speaking, it is not possible to identify very precisely personality characteristics that are associated with criminality. Investigations using traditional psychometric measures

Table 5.1 Some theories of crime and the types of psychology they involve

Theory	Biological	Psychoanalytic	Cognitive	Individual differences	Learning	Social
Neuropsychology	✓	✗	✗	✗	✗	✗
XYY	✓	✗	✗	✗	✗	✗
Intelligence	✓	✗	✓	✓	✗	✗
Bowlby's attachment	✓	✓	✗	✗	✗	✓
Addiction model	✗	✗	✓	✓	✗	✗
Eysenck's biosocial	✓	✗	✗	✓	✓	✓
Learning theory	✗	✗	✗	✗	✓	✓
Social constructionism	✗	✗	✗	✗	✗	✓
Strain theory	✗	✗	✗	✓	✗	✓

of personality to try to understand the characteristics of particular offender groups (for example, paedophiles) have not, in general, produced very convincing findings and may be critiqued – for example, because they use incarcerated or arrested offender groups who may be different because of this. There are some aspects of personality types that are associated with criminality. Psychopathy and the somewhat similar antisocial personality disorder are among the exceptions.

Concentrating on psychological theories still leaves us with a considerable range of different approaches to deal with. The theories to be outlined are illustrative of psychological approaches. They also constitute a useful body of theory for any forensic and criminal psychologist since they reflect the range of levels of theory from the biological to the social. Since the theories may be associated with more than one level of psychological theorising, Table 5.1 lists the theories and the types of psychology they reflect. The classifications, on occasion, may be disputed, but it can be seen that, as we move down the table, the analysis tends to be more social. At the start of the table, the theories are much more biological in nature. Also, it should be clear that some theories are practically confined to a particular type of psychology (e.g. the biological only for the first two) but others, such as Eysenck's theory in particular, involve several different types of psychology.

One should appreciate that many of the colleagues that a psychologist works with will have been trained in fields which differ quite significantly from that of psychology. The better able a psychologist is to understand the theoretical orientations of these other disciplines, the better he or she will be able to relate effectively to colleagues such as medics, psychiatrists, social workers and the like. The perspective of psychiatrists is much more medicine-based than the typical psychologist's. Social workers probably will have been trained to eschew genetic explanations of criminal behaviour in favour of societal explanations which depend on social structures such as social class.

Neuropsychology of offending

Neuropsychology concerns the brain's structure and activity in relation to psychological processes. Can it do anything to explain criminal behaviour? Biological explanations of crime have not achieved great popularity among forensic psychologists (Miller, 1999a) and are overshadowed by the vast amount of evidence indicating the social and psychological causes of crime. Nevertheless, there has been a steady stream of research into physiological, anatomical, genetic and similar abnormalities in criminal subgroups such as rapists, child molesters, etc. From time to time, such differences are detected – or so it is claimed – but technical problems make their interpretation difficult. Neuropsychology was revolutionised by the use of CT (computerised tomography), magnetic resonance imaging (MRI) and positron emission tomography (PET). Prior to this, researchers studied lesions (areas of damage) to the brain (Beaumont, 2000) which were linked to cognitive and behavioural difficulties. Nevertheless, this does not mean that modern research into brain structures and behaviour is substantially less fraught with problems. Wolf *et al.* (2015) carried out a study which illustrates some of the limitations of neuropsychological research for the study of crime. They studied the brains of a sample of incarcerated criminal offenders looking for a difference in the brains of psychopaths compared to non-psychopaths. Psychopathy manifests itself in a callous, impulsive and antisocial personality. It is associated with criminality (see Chapter 21). Wolf *et al.* used diffusion tensor imaging which is a form of MRI scan. Based on previous research findings, they were interested in the left and right uncinated fasiculae. These consist of a band of fibres running from the frontal to the temporal lobes of the brain. Psychopaths showed reduced fractional anisotropy of the right uncinated fasciculus. By this is meant that the right uncinated fasciculus was distorted in shape from the norm. There was no such relationship for the left uncinated fasciculus and psychopathy. Other areas of the brain examined in this study showed no such trend. However, further examination causes us to question whether the anomaly led to criminality since it was the superficial charm, grandiosity, pathological lying, and manipulative aspects of psychopathy which showed the relationship. The antisocial dimension of psychopathy did not show the relationship. Another example is Stalenheim's (1997) study of the extent of psychopathy in a Swedish forensic psychiatric population. He found that the enzyme platelet *monoamine oxidase* was to be found at lower levels in psychopaths but the levels of the enzyme were not correlated with the amount of criminal behaviour exhibited. A further point should be considered. Even if an anomaly is found that is related to crime, there remains the question of why this anomaly should cause crime. Schiffer *et al.* (2007) provide an example of an attempt to locate the origins of paedophilia in abnormalities of the brain structures of such offenders. In comparison with control groups consisting of homosexual and heterosexual men, the paedophiles tended to have less grey matter volume in parts of the brain.

One particularly interesting area of neuropsychological research and theory involves traumatic brain injuries. Such injuries can occur in a number of circumstances: most commonly they are caused by falls, then road accidents, then being struck by or against an object, and finally assault being the most uncommon (Faul, Xu, Wald and Coronado, 2010). Traumatic brain injuries may involve unconsciousness lasting from just a few seconds to a much longer term. There are two main types of traumatic brain injury (Miller, 1999a,b):

- *Penetrative head injuries* in which an object penetrates the skull and enters the brain.
- *Closed head injuries*, which may involve fractures of the skull. The damage is actually caused by the force of momentum, say, on the head as an accident occurs and its sudden deceleration. Closed head injuries may cause generalised damage to important parts of the brain. The frontal, temporal and occipital lobes seem especially vulnerable.

Depending on the area(s) of damage and the intensity, different types of long-term impairment may follow from traumatic brain injuries. The effects of brain injury very broadly are predictable from knowledge of the site in the brain where injury has occurred. This is the consequence of the specialisation of different parts of the brain to serve different functions. Memory and attention are commonly affected cognitive functions. However, there may be long-term personality changes such as the loss of ability to plan and to see the likely consequences of one's actions. Lack of tact is another consequence. An apathetic personality may result from damage to the frontal lobe of the brain. Such injuries also cause a tendency to persist with inappropriate courses of action, a degree of irritability and unrealistic/grandiose thoughts. The individual may show *disinhibition* – a lack of response to the social niceties that makes behaviour acceptable in most people. We will see later how some of these impairments might be involved in crime.

Recent research into criminality in young people illustrates the neuropsychological approach to crime very well. There is compelling evidence that traumatic brain injury is more common in young offenders than in non-offending controls. Hughes, Williams, Chitsabesan, Walesby, Mounce and Clasby (2015) reviewed studies comparing the rates of traumatic brain injury in young people in custody compared with young people in the general population. There are various ways of measuring traumatic brain injuries and their seriousness. Loss of consciousness is an important measure used and it can be assessed from self-reports. Of course, varying definitions of traumatic brain injury result in different prevalence rates as with any measure. Only four studies involving a control group were found which produced prevalence rates for traumatic brain injury of 50 per cent for young people in custody compared to 42 per cent in young people in general, 55 per cent for those in custody versus 24 per cent of controls, 17 per cent for those in custody versus 11 per cent of controls, and 4 per cent for those in custody versus 2 per cent of controls. In other words, characteristics of the study had a big effect on the prevalence rates found. Nevertheless, the clear conclusion is that traumatic brain injury is more common in young people in custody than young people in the general population. Williams, McAuliffe, Cohen, Parsonage and Ramsbottham (2015) review some of the wider research literature on traumatic brain damage and point out that traumatic brain damage is three times more common in those who commit a violent crime compared with controls, the rate of traumatic brain injury is between three to eight times higher in populations of offenders compared with controls, and persistent reoffending into adulthood is more common among young offenders who have a history of loss of consciousness (in indicator of traumatic brain injury).

Adolescence is a period at which youngsters engage in risky behaviour which may lead them to criminal behaviour. But risky behaviour also leads to traumatic brain injury which means that, for some, their traumatic brain injury may not be the cause of crime. Williams *et al.* (2015) argue that traumatic brain injury affects important brain regions which are involved in acceptable social behaviour. This social brain network includes the amygdala, inferior parietal cortex, temporal pole and the medial prefrontal cortex amongst other brain structures (Ryan *et al.*, 2014). Traumatic brain injury characteristically causes pathology to the frontal areas of the brain and more general or diffuse injury to the white matter of the brain. The social brain network seems to be the most vulnerable to traumatic brain injury. This is a system involving self-regulation, planning, inhibition, and identifying emotion from another person's face and tone of voice, according to Tonks *et al.* (2008). Nevertheless, Williams *et al.* (2015) point out that one needs to be cautious about the link between these brain pathologies and crime. For example, pre-traumatic brain differences already present in the brain may be responsible for the brain being on a divergent criminal track. For instance, attention deficit hyperactivity disorder is related to neurological dysfunction and is also a risk factor for traumatic brain disorder.

Methodological difficulties abound in this sort of research:

- Violent people are likely to get into fights and consequently suffer brain damage. So their violence causes the brain damage rather than vice versa. Perinatal studies, for example, somewhat negate this possibility.
- Some of the samples used may be non-representative. Thus murderers on death row might be disproportionately black, poor and of low intelligence and may well suffer from other disadvantages. In essence, they may be on death row because of these handicaps rather than simply because of their crime.
- Pre-injury/post-injury comparison studies tend to use participants who have been on intensive rehabilitation programmes – that is, the most seriously injured – so a misleading picture may emerge.
- The appropriate comparison figures are difficult. Offender groups tend to be working-class – the group most likely to suffer head injury. So without careful matching on social class, the findings may be misleading.

The biological approach is fascinating in its potential but less practical than at first appears. For example, Evans and Claycomb (1998) found an abnormal EEG pattern in violent criminals with a history of violence who denied that they had been involved in a particular act of violence or claimed to have been guided by external forces such as Satan. They demonstrated extremely strong alpha-type brain wave patterns in the frontal part of their brains. While this is clearly of great interest, whether or not such patterns could be used to distinguish genuine cases of 'hearing voices' from those in which the offender feigns psychiatric problems requires much work.

Evaluation of the theory

Pros:

- Knowledge of a neuropsychological cause of criminality would contribute to better-targeted treatments. Medical treatments rather than psychological therapy might be considered for appropriate cases. Unfortunately, it is very difficult to establish such a relationship for individual cases except where changes have followed accidents, etc.
- The evidence to date suggests that biological factors have some influence on criminality although they are probably restricted to a small proportion of cases. This possibly applies to the notion of the genetic transmission of criminality too – though evidence on this is also almost always interpretable in terms of environmental influences.

Cons:

- We seem to be a long way from fully understanding any biological basis to criminality including neuropsychological explanations, let alone the mechanism by which this possible influence might operate.
- For most forensic and criminal psychologists, whatever the biological basis of crime, biological approaches at the moment do not deal with the immediate task of helping treat criminals through therapy or with the problems of making assessments about individuals and their future behaviours.

Intelligence and crime

It has been a traditional theme that offenders tend to be lacking in intelligence and, consequently, are somewhat under-equipped to cope with their social and work environments. Countless early criminological discussions of offenders would describe them as typically being feebleminded. Superficially, the idea that low intelligence leads to criminality is compelling. Low intelligence being indicative of poor learning skills might mean that the individual takes senseless risks, lacks the resources to avoid detection, is unlikely to have good earning power in the workplace and so forth. Some of the factors that are known to be associated with criminality are potentially associated with low intelligence. These factors would include school failure, unemployment and similar characteristics. Nevertheless, few criminal and forensic psychologists seem to regard intelligence as a particularly important factor in crime. There are, of course, some offenders of low intelligence but, in general, these appear to be seen as a special case, not the norm. We should also remember that there are many crimes for which a good intelligence would seem necessary – identity theft and other crimes based on fraud are examples.

One reason for the relative disinterest in intelligence in relation to crime is that the concept of intelligence has been seen in a bad light by researchers. This is most familiar in terms of the race and IQ debate but it is wider than that. Not too long ago, the argument that poor intelligence is associated in a causal way with any number of social ills reappeared – poverty, for example, being seen as a result of low intelligence, genetically determined, rather than resulting from social and environmental factors. More important to the work of forensic and criminal psychologists is the claim that low intelligence is associated with crime. Herrnstein and Murray (1994) essentially argued that cognitively limited individuals are almost invariably likely to experience and to be involved in social ills. Many psychologists reject this point of view on the grounds that intelligence, as measured by IQ (intelligence quotient) tests, is little determined by hereditary factors relative to environmental ones and that it is virtually impossible to separate the inherited from the environmental influence (Kamin, 1977). Is IQ a fixed characteristic largely determined by genetic potential? Is it, on the other hand, more or less affected by the quality of life experienced by the individual perhaps from before birth, but certainly in interaction with parents and others in the fastest stages of development in early childhood? This is an argument that became increasingly common in psychology from the 1970s onwards, especially in connection with the view that a person's race is associated with intelligence, so social disadvantage is an almost inevitable consequence of race rather than of racism and discrimination. A wide range of authorities has dismissed such a view (Howitt and Owusu-Bempah, 1994). Some would regard positions such as Herrnstein and Murray's as being part of a right-wing political agenda critical of liberal welfare and other service provisions. If social position is fixed biologically through intelligence, then it is a waste of money to try to change things. Of course, forensic and criminal psychology is subject to political influence in many respects (crime is a political issue) so the political implications of the theory in themselves are not a reason for its rejection.

Cullen, Genreau, Jarjoura and Wright (1997), going beyond general criticisms of the theory, have systematically integrated the research on intelligence and criminality. They reach the conclusion that IQ is only weakly or modestly related to criminality. More importantly, they regard criminality as being largely influenced by identifiable factors other than intelligence. These influential factors are largely amenable to change. If Herrnstein and Murray were right, social welfare policy is misdirected and tougher crime control policies would be a better strategy, Cullen *et al.* suggest. On the other hand, if crime can be affected by welfare provision, then tougher crime control policies are unnecessary and probably counterproductive.

- Cullen *et al.* (1997) reanalysed data crucial to Herrnstein and Murray's point of view. This concerns the relationship between the AFQT (Armed Forces Qualification Test) which was used as the measure of IQ and various measures of criminality including (a) being in the top 10 per cent on a self-reported crime scale and (b) having been interviewed in a correctional facility. The relationships are only modest at their highest. The correlation would be approximately 0.3 between low IQ and ever having been interviewed in a correctional facility. However, this correlation is the one obtained if no attempts are made to adjust for the influence of social class, which tends to be associated with both of these variables. If socio-economic status is removed in the analysis, then the correlations become much smaller – at best about 0.15. In contrast, in further analyses, it turns out that criminality is more strongly but inversely related to measures such as being religious, expectations of future work and academic aspirations. These relationships are not supportive of the theory as they suggest environmental influences are stronger. Furthermore, living in urban environments and low social class are implicated in criminality in precisely the ways that those who believe in environmental causes of crime would predict.
- A number of meta-analyses of studies of the relationship between IQ and criminality exist and are reviewed by Cullen *et al.* (1997). A meta-analysis is a sort of secondary analysis of several similar studies into a particular topic. So it provides us with understanding of the general trends in the research on related themes (see Box 4.1). At best, adult criminality correlates only 0.1 with low IQ although it is closer to 0.2 for juveniles. In comparison, other risk factors correlate with criminality at up to approximately 0.5. In other words, overall, research reveals the importance of environmental influences more than hereditary ones. This is simply because the other risk factors for crime have a much stronger influence than IQ: for example, criminogenic needs such as attitudes, values, beliefs and behaviours like associating with other delinquents.

Quite clearly, intelligence is a relatively minor aspect of criminality compared with many more social factors. The failure of the Herrnstein and Murray thesis to be sustained by the research evidence should be taken by psychologists as indicating the potential for social and psychological interventions to affect criminality.

Nevertheless, researchers continue to address the topic. One recent study (Bartels, Ryan, Urban and Glass, 2010) examined the relationship between estimates of intelligence in different states of the United States of America and crime levels in those states. With appropriate statistical adjustments having been included, it was found that there was a (negative) relationship between the average IQ in a state and murder statistics for aggravated assault and robbery and murder but also property offences such as theft, motor vehicle crimes, and burglary. So, states with lower IQ averages tended to have more crime. Beaver and Wright (2011) carried out a similar study but analysed at the county rather than state level. The average IQ in each of over 200 counties was assessed using the Picture Vocabulary Test and crime rates were obtained from the FBI Uniform Crime Reports for each county. There were substantial correlations of about –0.4 to –0.5 between IQ and crime rates for property crime, burglary, larceny, motor vehicle theft, violent crime and robbery. Finally, Rushton and Templar (2009) compared the comparative murder, rape and serious assault rates for over 100 countries in relation to the average IQ of the country. Countries with lower IQ averages tended to have higher rates of violent crime. As ever, the problem is knowing just what these relationships mean. One thing is important: these data tell us nothing about the relationship between IQ and crime rates within a country. This is because we do not have the data to compare the number of crimes that an individual commits with their IQ. The IQ and the crime data may well have been collected from very different people.

There is an argument that the reason why IQ tends to be negatively related to criminality is that cleverer offenders simply get away with their crimes more readily. Yun and Lee (2013), following a range of previous research, examined the possibility that arrests by the police are influenced by the offender's verbal intelligence. They used data from the large National Longitudinal Study of Adolescent Health in the USA to see whether self-reported arrests correlate negatively with their verbal intelligence as measured by the Peabody Picture Vocabulary test. In addition, there was self-reported data on offending in a number of categories and whether they had ever been stopped by the police. Verbal intelligence did have a substantial negative correlation with whether the young person had been arrested as a consequence. Furthermore, controlling for extent of delinquency made little difference to this relationship implying that any influence that verbal intelligence had on delinquency was not responsible for the findings.

All of this raises a question which has seldom been addressed. What is the nature of the criminality of high IQ individuals? Oleson and Chappell (2013) used a self-report survey of various types of violent criminal offending completed by nearly 500 adults with IQs at the level of genius. These were compared with another large sample of individuals whose IQs could be described as more average. Intriguingly, the genius level IQ sample reported rates of violent offending which were higher than for the control group. Convictions rates were slightly higher for the control group. The genius-level IQ sample self-reported more homicide, bomb making and aggregate violence in terms of prevalence rates but less threat and assault. In terms of incidence rates, the genius-level IQ sample reported more of all types of crime other than robbery. Of course, these findings may be biased by problems with self-report measures of violent crimes but, bearing this in mind, the findings are food for thought in the argument about the relationship between low IQ and criminal behaviour.

Evaluation of the theory

Pros:

- If we tease out the biological issue from the ability issue, knowledge that crime is associated to some extent with low ability, low educational achievement and low measured intelligence is useful to psychologists. It suggests that action to alleviate such factors may have a positive contribution to make. This is generally recognised as penal systems frequently offer educational and vocational courses to help remedy such deficits (see Chapter 25). Any assessment of offenders needs to include ability and intelligence testing as this suggests appropriate courses of action.
- We know that crime and criminality are not equally distributed through different levels of social structure. As such, it is attractive to seek simple explanations that justify the status quo. Unfortunately, this quickly turns to a con when it is realised that the case against the theory is strong.

Cons:

- The biological (genetic) approach to social policy generally receives little support from psychologists wherever it appears, though such notions have been disseminated through books and other media to the general public. The idea that social problems are basically intractable offers little for professionals dedicated to reducing criminality. Indeed, it is a good reason for not developing psychological services aimed at offenders as such.
- Even if the theory is regarded as true, it is of little practical value when working with offenders.

Psychoanalysis and crime

Psychoanalysis, especially that closest to Sigmund Freud's original writings, has little to say directly about crime (Valier, 1998). Freud carried out no analyses of criminals and lacked apparent interest in them. He regarded them as manifesting disturbances of the ego that resulted in their incapacity to be honest. Nevertheless, Freud had some impact on legal thinking. In 1909 Freud was given an honorary doctorate in law from Clark University, Worcester, Massachusetts. This recognised his impact on legal thinking through ideas of unconscious motivation and the like. Of course, Freudian theory deals with two extreme crimes – parricide and incest both the result and consequence of the Oedipal conflict. However, Freud wrote more directly about crime in a brief analysis known as 'criminality from a sense of guilt' (Freud, 1916). This is based on his observation that people commit what he calls 'forbidden actions' including theft, fraud and arson. This included extremely respectable people. Freud argues that these people suffer oppressive feelings of guilt which they did not understand the origins of. They committed these crimes because they were forbidden and committing them produced mental relief from the feelings of guilt. In other words, guilt plays a paradoxical role in crime by preceding the crime not following it. Although he did not see all criminality caused in this way, Freud saw it as the dominant motive for crime. Some followed this Freudian idea directly. For example, Melanie Kline argued that crime was not due to the weakness of the superego but the consequence of its overpowering strength in works such as 'Criminal tendencies in normal children' (Kline, 1927) and 'On criminality' (Kline, 1934).

Another Freudian influence was the way that psychology until the last third of the twentieth century regarded homosexuality as a clinical deviation rather than a chosen sexuality. Where homosexuality resulted in individuals being in trouble with the law, their homosexuality could be treated – that is, they could be diverted back to heterosexuality. This is an idea that now appears to be singularly old-fashioned. Valier (1998) quotes East and Huber (1939, p. 93) as saying of a gay man, 'In treatment every effort was made to release as far as possible his heterosexual drives . . . with treatment, stands an excellent chance of developing his heterosexual possibilities.'

John Bowlby is probably the most famous of the 'neo-psychoanalysts' to modern psychologists. This is largely because of his ideas about early separation of a child from its mother. These were enormously influential in terms of justifying social policy about the employment of mothers in the workforce, which was relatively uncommon at the time. Mothers, he indicated, should not work. The reason was that the severing of the ties between mother and baby destroyed the emotional bond between the two that was essential for the effective social development of the child. It was Bowlby's belief that there is a human predisposition to form attachment to others. The primary care-givers – usually the parents – are a sort of bedrock for future relationships (Bowlby, 1944, 1951, 1973, 1980). Positive, intimate attachments are required for attachment to be satisfactory, otherwise long-term problems of many sorts are likely. Once the bonds are broken, the child develops in ways indicative of an inability to form functional social relationships.

One of Bowlby's cases (he was a psychiatrist) was the child he called Derek, who had been hospitalised for nearly a year, starting before he was one. When he returned to the family, he addressed his mother as 'nurse' and lacked affection for any members of the family. The period of separation, in Bowlby's terms, resulted in Derek's inability to form social relationships. In his study 'Forty-four juvenile thieves', Bowlby (1944) showed the role of maternal separation in the aetiology of delinquency. He studied 44 delinquents, 16 of whom he classified as affectionless characters or affectionless thieves. These children were above average intelligence and seemed, in general, not to be socio-economically deprived. What characterised the affectionless thieves was that they had suffered broken mother–child relationships, major disruptions, by the age of three years. Maternal separation was rather rarer in the other youngsters he studied as his control group. Valier (1998) writes of the notion of the latchkey kid being a popularisation of Bowlby's ideas – for 'latchkey kid' simply read 'potential delinquent'. Attachment theory developed to be a major influence in a number of areas of psychology and way beyong (Holmes, 2014).

Evaluation of the theory

Pros:

- Some of the ideas, especially those of Bowlby, have been highly influential in directing the attention of researchers from many disciplines towards the impact of early life experiences, especially parenting, on later delinquency and criminality (see Chapter 6).

Cons:

- Few modern psychologists make direct use of Freudian concepts. This is because it is generally considered that, when subjected to research, the concepts fail to gain the support of researchers.
- Similarly, the evidence is that, in terms of efficiency and effectiveness, psychoanalytic therapies are not simply extremely-time consuming but apparently ineffective.

Addiction to crime

One of the mysteries of criminal behaviour is its persistence in some individuals despite its serious negative consequences. This basic observation has led some

(Hodge, McMurran and Hollin, 1997) to propose that crime can have many similarities to behaviours that are classified as addiction. At first, it would seem unlikely that a simple biological explanation of addiction could account for crime – after all, there is no substance that is being introduced to the body, no changes in metabolism or brain activity that have been identified. However, few psychologists specialising in the field of addiction hold resolutely to a purely biological model of addiction. There are a number of socio-psychological explanations to explain at least some aspects of addiction. From this wider viewpoint, addiction is a product of the interaction of personal and environmental factors of which stereotypical biological addiction is merely a part. One consequence of this is that concepts such as addiction to sex or addiction to gambling began to be seen in a different light. Reasons for considering some crime as an addiction include the following:

- Addiction, substance abuse and alcohol abuse all co-occur frequently in criminal populations. The co-occurrence of addictions may imply that addiction-prone personalities exist or a predisposition explanation of a similar sort. Co-occurrence does not happen with all types of offence. Take, for instance, sex offending. For such crimes, the evidence for co-occurrence is mixed, at best, and fairly weak overall (McGregor and Howells, 1997). However, there is evidence that the risk factors or antecedents or predictors of addictive behaviour are much the same as those for criminality (e.g. school problems, conduct difficulties in childhood, association with delinquent peers).
- Persistence and escalation: despite the well-known tendency for criminal activity to decline with age – to be a product of youth – this is not so for all offenders. For a minority, antisocial behaviour appears more like a lifelong career (see Chapter 6).
- The process of change: successful treatments are much the same for a variety of crimes and a variety of addictions. They tend to adopt a cognitive behavioural model (see Chapter 25). Furthermore, the processes of change in therapy are not dissimilar for substance abuse and crime (McMurran, Hodge and Hollin, 1997).

The disease model of addiction is a familiar concept in terms of alcohol and drugs. It assumes a genetic or biological predisposition for addiction. Problem drinkers, as in the Alcoholics Anonymous formulation, cannot be 'cured' but must always abstain. Use is followed by increased tolerance and more use. Withdrawal leads, in this account, to profound distress and craving. This is a disease that is out of control (e.g. McGregor and Howells, 1997). The model usually includes a component of 'predisposition' as well as increased consumption as a consequence of consumption. The consequences of withdrawal in the disease model are seen as severe but eventually the wanting and craving will decline as the disease disappears.

In contrast, the cognitive behavioural model of addiction concentrates on social-psychological influences that are distinct from biological vulnerability of individuals to drugs (McGregor and Howells, 1997). Learning processes are involved and the expectation of rewards from drug taking is powerful. Indeed, the learnt expectations may be more powerful than the biological properties of the substance. Drug taking is seen as adaptive since it is the individual's way of coping with stresses. It is not assumed in the cognitive behavioural model that sooner or later the 'disease' (the addiction) will become out of control. The notion of craving is replaced by the idea that withdrawal effects must be understood in terms of the user's expectations of the consequences of withdrawal.

Kilpatrick (1997) argued that the characteristics of addiction could be found in persistent joyriders in Ireland. She studied a sample of juvenile offenders incarcerated in a special centre for a variety of car-related offences, including taking and driving away, allowing oneself to be carried in a stolen car, careless driving, reckless driving, theft of goods from a car and so forth. Six common characteristics of addiction can be evaluated using the data collected from the joyriders:

- *Tolerance:* the need for more to produce the same effect. Multiple thefts were the norm, ranging from 50 to indeterminate numbers in the hundreds. Faster and more secure cars were particular targets. Universally, the offenders talked of stealing on demand or when they needed the money.
- *Salience:* the increasing importance of the addiction in the lifestyle. The joyriders frequently seemed to have abandoned their previous interests in activities such as boxing, snooker and video games. Car thefts tended to be episodic – that is, following a drinking session or glue-sniffing episode, the youngsters would steal cars over two or three days, exhaust themselves and take a break to get a decent sleep.
- *Conflict:* increasing awareness of negative consequences. While all of the youngsters were aware of the negative consequences, whether or not this is increasing was difficult to assess. Certainly, over half of them were trying to stop.
- *Withdrawal:* distress after a period of non-engagement. Some had absconded from the school to joyride, and absconding is a very common feature of joyriders at other institutions.
- *Craving:* distress associated with desire to re-engage. Some, but by no means all, had daydreams around the theme of joyriding.

- *Relapse:* reinstatement after decision to stop or reduce. There was some evidence of difficulty in those who were trying to stop but again this was not universal.

Similarly, Kellett and Gross (2006) also found evidence that the talk of young joyriders reflected ideas related to addiction. For example, the researchers regard the following quotation as indicative of the tolerance that can build up which effectively reduces the stimulating effect of a given level of activity: 'if it's getting a wee bit boring you know, just driving about or something, and you see them then you's, come on we'll get a chase, you know.'

Shoplifting and addiction are related. As many as a third of heroin addicts may finance their use through shoplifting. (See Chapter 7 which includes a more detailed discussion of the relationship between drugs and crime.) Among other evidence, McGuire (1997) describes three case studies that he examined for the components of 'addiction'. He found evidence for the following characteristics of addiction in shoplifting:

- *Salience:* the dominance of the addictive behaviour in thoughts, feelings and behaviour.
- *Arousal:* a depressed state may precede shoplifting and there is excitement at the prospect or actuality of shoplifting.
- *Tolerance:* the need for increasing amounts to achieve desired effect.
- *Withdrawal:* there are aversive states of feeling on discontinuation.
- *Relief:* this occurs for aversive feelings when activity is recommenced.
- *Cessation:* leads to a repetition of the activity with complete reinstallation even after a long period of cessation.

The fit of the data to the above cognitive behavioural model to shoplifting of this sort was generally good.

Taylor (2010) used an addiction model to explain the activities of young people who engage in graffiti as a form of vandalism. She interviewed a sample of young Australians who engage in this. She writes about the addictive adrenalin rush they experience from doing the graffiti. The risk of detection and arrest, she suggests, stimulates a rush of adrenalin into their bodies which the youngsters maintain eventually becomes addictive with repetition. The rush is unlike anything that they have previously experienced since it is so exhilarating. Furthermore, some of the graffiti offenders described the activity of drawing lines through someone else's graffiti work. This act like a declaration of a fight as it is so provocative. The anticipation of a fight creates its own adrenaline rush.

The evidence supporting the idea that crime is an addiction lies largely in studies drawing parallels between crime and addiction. Unfortunately, these have proven not to be numerous and there is, at best, a trickle of studies since Hodge, McMurran and Hollin's (1997) book *Addicted to Crime*? Although it has proven to be relatively easy to discuss crime using an addiction model, critical tests of the theory have not been forthcoming.

Evaluation of the theory

Pros:

- The main appeal of the concept of addiction to crime is that it could explain the continued involvement in criminality of those who are otherwise regularly punished for it.
- Criminals tend to be involved in a wide variety of crimes and relatively few are total specialists. Addiction to crime can be applied widely to the offending patterns of criminals.

Cons:

- Without a good deal of research, it is difficult to know whether the concept of addiction to crime explains anything that cannot be explained using other theories. There is a possibility that the theory merely describes features of some deviant behaviour without explaining why the individual is deviant in the first place.

Eysenck's biosocial theory of crime

Hans Eysenck was a highly influential personality theorist in the second half of the twentieth century. His contribution to understanding crime was largely an extension of his general psychological ideas. Eysenck (1996) suggested that it is wrong to ask why people break the law since it is perfectly rational to take whatever one wants since that is in the individual's personal self-interest. He suggested that the more cogent question is 'Why do we behave in a socially desirable fashion?' (p. 148). Put this way, we are asking about how we develop a conscience. Eysenck's basic answer is that we learn not to be criminal. His theory might best be described as biosocial since he believed that genetic factors contributed enormously to human behaviour but that they have their effects under the influence of environmental or social factors. Genetic variations substantially influence the psychological differences between people that lead to different propensities to crime (and other sorts of behaviour). During his lifetime, Eysenck was a controversial figure who, seemingly, pushed his theory to the limits. His views on crime tended to antagonise academic and practitioner colleagues who believed that his theorising did not follow from research findings quite so closely as he suggested. Further, his tendency to relate complex social phenomena to fairly gross differences between people did not appeal to many.

Figure 5.3 gives an overview of Eysenck's theory as it developed during the course of his writings. There are a number of shifts in his stance over the years which are highlighted in this figure.

Genetics

Perhaps the most familiar cautionary tale in this connection is to be found in the difficulties of the *XYY chromosome hypothesis*. The basic genetics of sex is that women have two X chromosomes and men have an X and a Y chromosome in the pair that determines sex. Occasionally, men are born with two Y chromosomes – that is, XYY rather than XY. Some of them tend to be big and have a low IQ. Since the Y chromosome is what makes males male rather than female, then, speculatively, one might suggest that the XYY male is extra-masculine. Masculinity

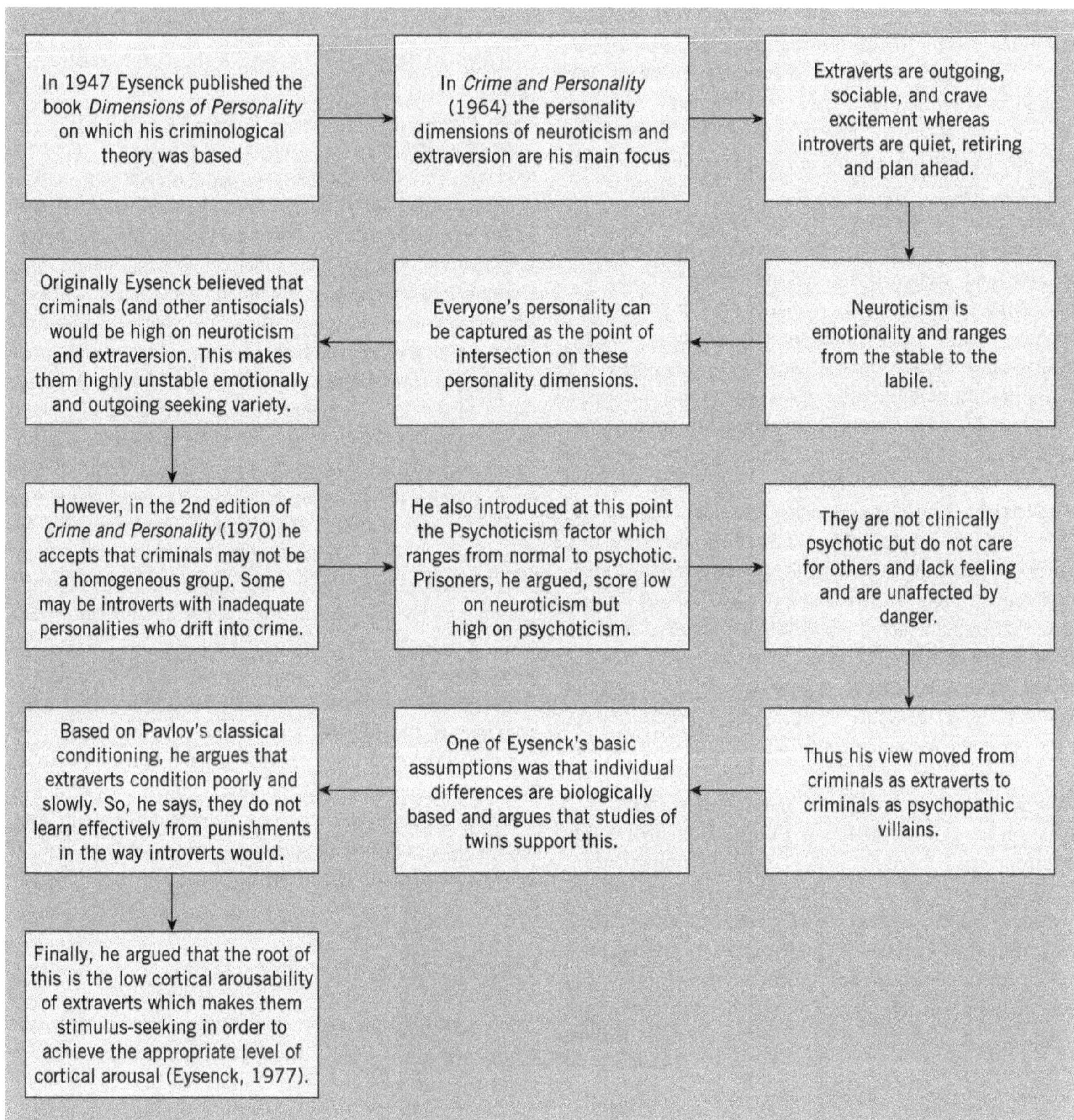

Figure 5.3 Changes and developments in Eysenck's theory of crime as outlined by Rafter (2006)

is associated with aggression, so the XYY male might be more aggressive – they are hyper-masculine after all. So the idea developed that offenders in places such as prison or hospital may well include a big proportion of XYY men (Price, Strong, Whatmore and McClemont, 1966). It is known as the Jacobs' syndrome after Patricia Jacobs, the British geneticist who described it in some detail. You will also see it described as '47, XYY'. Later research found that they were rare in the general population of men but more common in men involved in crime. The difficulty for the XYY theory was that these men were not particularly involved in violent crime, but only in non-violent crime (Epps, 1995; Witkin, Mednick and Schulsinger, 1976). It is reputed that an American serial killer of at least 13 women, Arthur Shawcross, had this chromosomal pattern. Nevertheless, we can be reasonably confident that, since this pattern has not been shown in other cases, irrespective of what caused Shawcross to kill, the XYY theory does not help us to understand other similar offenders (Coleman and Norris, 2000).

After more than fifty years of research on XYY men, clear evidence of a genetic link between the extra chromosome and violent crime has not been forthcoming. One of the problems is the evidence that there are men that have the XYY pattern but their abnormality does not show itself. In other words, it may be that it is only XYY men who show abnormalities who are detected. Abramsky and Chapple (1997) found that about three-quarters of XYY cases are not detected in infancy which may be because they show satisfactory mental and physical development. This does not mean that one does not find XYY men in samples selected because they are tall, aggressive, and with a low IQ. There are plenty of studies demonstrating this (Re and Birkoff, 2015) as well as those that find no such thing. The prevalence of XYY in all men is estimated to be 0.1 per cent. Witkin *et al.* (1976) found that the crimes committed by XYY prisoners were much the same types as those committed by XYY prisoners including robberies without violence and various minor crimes. However, they showed lower intelligence which may have made them vulnerable to detection thus giving them worse criminal records. Götz, Johnstone and Ratcliffe (1999) studied a population-based sample of men with sex chromosome abnormalities. They found that there were higher levels of antisocial and criminal behaviour in XYY men but this was related to their lower intelligence as a consequence of their chromosomal abnormality. At the end of their review of half a century of research on XYY men, Re and Birkoff (2015) concluded:

> . . . it is our opinion that the presence of an extra Y is only a genetic substrate, a probable risk factor, which cannot be the only cause of deviant behaviors. However, being normally associated with high stature and frequently with learning disabilities and increased aggression, it may contribute, along with other socio-cultural factors, to the development of antisocial and violent behaviors. (p.15)

XYY is not the only chromosomal abnormality that has been associated with crime. Epps (1995) describes a case of an adolescent boy with a very rare XXYY pattern. He was sexually abusive of children.

Some forensic and criminal psychologists accept a possible minor influence of genetics on crime though this currently is of little relevance to their day-to-day activities. For example, just how does genetics help psychologists, say, in therapy with sex offenders? In contrast, genetics is an essential feature of Eysenck's theory. In relation to crime, he was convinced that evidence from the study of twins brought up together and separately supported the hypothesis that there is a substantial inherited component to crime. Twins identical in their genetic make-up (monozygotic twins) tend to be similar in terms of being criminal or not compared with non-identical twins (dizygotic twins) who share only half of their genetic make-up. Thus he cites Cloninger, Christiansen, Reich and Gottesman's (1978) finding that there is a correlation of 0.7 between monozygotic twins in terms of their criminality versus non-criminality. This correlation reduces to the much lower figure of 0.4 for dizygotic twins. If everything else were equal, then this implies that genetics makes a substantial contribution to the criminality of individuals. Unfortunately for Eysenck's argument, all other things are not equal (e.g. Guthrie, 1998; Kamin, 1977). Monozygotic twins may be treated much more similarly because they are identical, which might enhance their similarity in terms of eventual criminality. He also placed importance on 'adoption' studies. For example, one study involved over 14,000 adopted individuals (Mednick, Gabrielli and Hutchings, 1994). There was no relationship between the number of criminal convictions the adopted child had and the number of criminal convictions of the adopting parents. However, there was a correlation between the criminal convictions of the adopted child and those of their natural parent. This finding was only true for property crimes such as theft; it was not true for violent crime.

Constitutional factors

Moving beyond genetic factors, Eysenck, again provocatively, argued that there are physical differences between criminals and non-criminals. Lombroso (1911) famously argued that criminals tended to show similar morphological features. While Eysenck accepted that Lombroso was wrong, he nevertheless was interested in the three somatypes or body types proposed by Sheldon (1940, 1942). Each body type was associated with a particular personality type. Sheldon's (1949) research suggested that compared with college students, criminals tended to have the mesomorphic body type:

- *Mesomorphs:* people with a preponderance of bones, muscles, connective tissue and heart/blood vessels. In terms of personality, they are assertive, adventurous, like power and dominance, enjoy risk and taking chances, and are ruthless (this was termed somatonia).

The remaining two body types were:

- *Endomorphs:* people who most characteristically lay on fat, especially around the abdomen. In terms of personality they are relaxed, love of physical comfort, love of eating, sociable, amiable, tolerant and communicate feelings easily (viscerotonia).
- *Ectomorphs:* people who have an overabundance of sense organs and the nervous system and brain compared to their body mass. In terms of personality they like privacy and need solitude, are not sociable, are very sensitive to pain and are physiologically overreactive (cerebrotonia).

In other words, body type is related to personality, which itself is related to criminality.

Personality

Eysenck believed that there are three major, largely unrelated, components of personality – *extraversion*, *neuroticism* and *psychoticism*. These dimensions were obtained by the analysis of numerous measures of personality that he developed based on the work of others and his own ideas. The following indicates the characteristics of each of these personality dimensions:

- *Extraversion:* active, assertive, creative, carefree, dominant, lively, sensation-seeking and venturesome.
- *Psychoticism:* aggressive, antisocial, cold, creative, egocentric, impersonal, impulsive, tough-minded and lacking empathy.
- *Neuroticism:* anxious, depressed, emotional, guilt feelings, irrational, low self-esteem, moody, shy and tense.

Which are characteristic of criminals? According to Eysenck, all of them. Criminals should show higher levels of extraversion, psychoticism and neuroticism. Extraverts condition poorly and so do not readily learn to behave in a socially acceptable way. Neurotics condition poorly because their anxiety interferes with learning. Psychoticism is very like what we refer to as psychopathy which is associated with antisocial behaviour.

Environmental influences

Nothing described, so far, explains why genetics may be associated with criminality. Eysenck's argument is that criminal behaviour (and other forms of antisocial behaviour) results from a failure of socialisation to stop immature tendencies in some individuals. These immature tendencies include being concerned solely for oneself and wanting immediate gratification for one's own needs. The process of socialisation is responsible for making individuals more social and thus less criminal:

- Antisocial behaviour of all sorts is punished by significant others in the life of the child, such as parents, siblings, teachers and peers. The process, according to Eysenck, is through classical Pavlovian conditioning – punishment of all sorts acts as an unconditioned stimulus, whereas the planning or execution of the behaviour is the conditioned stimulus.
- So socialisation leads to a situation in which even the thought of acting antisocially leads to the unpleasant pain or anxiety of the unconditioned stimulus. To avoid this pain or anxiety, the individual avoids thinking of or engaging in antisocial behaviour.

This argument requires one further step in order to explain criminality. Those low on extraversion (i.e. introverts) tend to learn quickly through conditioning, whereas those high on extraversion (extraverts) condition much more slowly. (Conditioning is the process by which associations are learnt between our actions and the consequences of our actions.) There is evidence to support the idea of the slower conditioning of extraverts according to Eysenck. Slow conditioning leads to poorer socialisation and hence to greater criminality. Such an argument also explains why crime is characteristically the activity of younger people – they have not had time to become completely socialised.

So why the association of crime with psychoticism? Eysenck explains this by pointing to the wider evidence that psychosis (i.e. severe mental derangement which may involve a poor grasp of reality or delusions) is associated with crime. Furthermore, the characteristics of psychoticism are patently associated with non-conforming and antisocial activities (making Eysenck's idea of psychoticism rather like that of psychopathy (see Chapter 21). And why neuroticism? One thing that may explain the criminality of neurotics is that their emotionality may make them rather difficult to socialise and condition. Hence, the conditioning process fails for a different reason from that employed for extraversion. The other possibility is that being emotional, volatile or hyper-reactive implies that one may well overreact to aversive situations (such as those that are stressful or emotional). If an individual's basic repertoire of responses to situations is antisocial or criminal, then these responses are much more likely in the neurotic individual than in the more stable individual.

From the point of view of forensic and criminal psychology, the question of the scientific adequacy of Eysenck's theory is perhaps not the key issue. Its practicality is much more important, although Eysenck believed that appropriate therapy for offenders is dependent on understanding their personality in relation to the socialisation or conditioning process. For example, younger offenders seem more amenable to treatment than older ones. Things to bear in mind include the following:

- Even if Eysenck is right about the socialisation process, a great deal of research has indicated that problematic childhoods are associated with long-term criminality. Understanding the failures of parenting and so forth may be a more practical way of dealing with criminality.
- Very few of the concerns of forensic psychology are addressed by Eysenck's theory of crime. Why, for example, do some men rape and others abuse children? Knowing that rapists and child molesters are extravert, neurotic and psychotic does not help us to understand their crimes in useful ways.

In the final analysis, Eysenck's theory was conceived to be part of a grand conception of human behaviour which became reduced to just a few key concepts. However, it bred research and hostility in roughly equal proportions. Most of us probably gain very little which is of benefit to our understanding of forensic and criminal psychology through exploring Eysenck's theory in depth. It does warrant some appreciation in so far as it tries to integrate the social, the psychological and the biological. Whether that is a futile exercise compared with the more pressing and immediate tasks of forensic work is another matter. Some issues are still current, such as the relationship between accidents and criminality, which were part of Eysenck's theory since they were both seen as having a similar genesis (Brace, Scully, Clark and Oxley, 2010). Furthermore, the impulsivity of delinquents continues to be actively researched (e.g. Sharma, Markon and Clark, 2014). Impulsivity, along with sociability, was regarded as Eysenck as a component of extraversion.

Rafter (2006) presents a thorough review of Eysenck and his theory, warts and all, and concludes sometimes in his favour, sometimes against. His contribution to sociobiological approaches to crime is highlighted as being influential in developing that field.

Evaluation of the theory

Pros:

- Eysenck's theory was remarkable in its scope. Like some other theories, it was an account of general criminality, although he believed that some patterns of personality might be more common in different sorts of offender. His evidence on this, though, was fairly limited.
- The theory brings together several different levels of theorising.

Cons:

- While other theories described in this chapter lack complete support from research findings, Eysenck's theory has tended to be seen by many psychologists as based on flawed data.
- Although the theory is impressive in that it operates at both the biological and the social levels, in fact the social input is little more than a matter of rewards and punishments. Sociological approaches, for example, have little place in the scheme of things.

Social learning theory

It is widely accepted that children and adults may learn effectively from the actions of another person through a process of imitation. 'Modelling' effects have been a central aspect of social psychological theorising since the early work of Miller and Dollard (1941). They regarded imitation as a form of *vicarious* learning. They extended the notion of learning through conditioning acting directly on the individual to include observing the experiences of other people being rewarded or punished. In other words, Miller and Dollard saw the process of learning as being mediated, in part, by the consequences of actions for other people. Much more crucial nowadays is the work of Albert Bandura (Bandura, 1973, 1983). This began in the 1950s and eventually led to his social learning theory. This became a relatively complex theory in its eventual form. His early studies demonstrated that young children imitate the actions of adults, modelling behaviours such as hitting an inflatable clown-doll with a hammer (Bandura and Huston, 1961; Bandura, Ross and Ross, 1963). This is taken as evidence that learning can occur in just a single experience of that behaviour (that is, it is not slowly built up through a process of conditioning).

That learning through modelling can take place is not controversial. What is more of a problem is the usefulness of the theory in explaining the acquisition of antisocial behaviours, such as crime, and the circumstances in which this behaviour will be reproduced. To suggest that people learn their violent and criminal actions from others is a weak argument. Unless violence and crime are entirely genetically transmitted then inevitably they must be learnt socially in some way. Quite clearly, any explanation of violence and crime in terms of learning is not particularly helpful unless the conditions under which it is learnt can be specified. Violence and crime are not the exclusive means by which goals are achieved. A variety of tactics are involved in achieving goals – working rather than stealing to get a television set being a simple example. As work is a major form of modelled behaviour, how can we explain why there is any crime at all if it is simply the result of social learning?

Bandura (1977), along with others, including, most importantly, Miller and Dollard (1941), recognised that rewards and punishments are involved in the reproduction of modelled behaviour. If a model were rewarded for theft then we would expect that the observer would be more likely to reproduce that behaviour, whereas if the model is punished, for example sent to prison, then we might expect the observer to be less likely to exhibit that behaviour. Bandura developed this aspect of his theory poorly in his later writings according to Bjorkqvist (1997). While this suggests that factors other than observing crime are needed to explain the involvement of individuals in crime, from the point of view of the forensic and criminal psychologist, even this does not take us very far. For example, it suggests that criminal behaviour is essentially goal-directed. This clearly contrasts with some sociological theories of crime, which emphasise the circumstantial/opportunity features of crime.

Evaluation of the theory

Pros:

- The importance of social learning theory lies in its dealing with the learning of complex forms of behaviour holistically rather than as a process of slow conditioning.
- Social learning theory stresses the importance of normal processes in the acquisition of behaviour. Hence there is no need to assume some sort of pathology in those who become criminal.

Cons:

- The theory's weak ability to explain under what circumstances criminal behaviour will or will not be learnt means that it has limited explanatory power.

Strain theories of crime

There have been a number of strain theories to explain criminality. The sociologist Robert K. Merton introduced the concept in the 1960s (e.g. Merton, 1968). His was an account of crime which was (social) structural in nature. The idea was that if normal opportunities to attain goals successfully are in some way blocked, this generates strain or frustration which acts something like a pressure towards criminality. The individual was said to be exhibiting a state of anomie or normlessness. So the desire for monetary success is an American value and (lower economic class) individuals thwarted in this wish because of, say, lack of opportunities in their immediate environment, may turn to crime to achieve that end, albeit illicitly. For example, a lower-class parent may be unable or unprepared to provide the economic resources required for schooling to a higher level. The strain that this imposes on the child is then dealt with by illegal means, such as drug selling or other forms of crime. There is a singular lack of support for this type of strain theory in the research literature and it is of almost exclusively historical interest now. Other theorists have suggested that strain is unlikely to operate in this way unless the individual is part of a deviant subculture (Cloward and Ohlin, 1960).

Social-psychological strain theories emerged with relative deprivation theory (Blau and Blau, 1982; Box, 1981). This basically suggests that structural factors which lead to inequality generate feelings of deprivation. The consequence may be aggression or some form of crime. Unlike Merton's earlier sociological theory, the strain (feeling of deprivation) was not measured against some absolute criterion but by reference to a group of individuals. This implies that poor people will not feel deprived if their reference group is other poor people, but they will feel deprived if their reference group is better-off friends, for example.

Agnew's General Strain Theory assumes that if people are treated badly (i.e. not as they would wish to be treated) then their consequent upset and distress leads them to respond with deviant behaviours such as aggression or crime. These negative relationships and the attendant emotions are known in the theory as 'strain' (Agnew, 1992). The theory is primarily concerned with young people and strain pressurises young people into delinquency through negative affect such as anger especially. Figure 5.4 illustrates this. Based on psychological theory dealing with stress, Agnew argues that there are two types of strain – objective and subjective strain. This is illustrated in Figure 5.5. Objective strain is strain which people in general would experience given a particular set of circumstances. Examples of this include a lack of food or inadequate shelter. Subjective strain is more particular to the individual. Thus being turned down for a job may be a major strain for some but inconsequential for others. Personality traits, life circumstances, self-esteem and a range of other factors contribute to subjective strain.

There are three major categories of strain in Agnew's General Strain Theory, as can be seen from Figure 5.5. The first category of strain is somewhat like Merton's theory in that it occurs when other people stop or threaten to stop a person from obtaining their positively valued goals. Within this category there are three types of

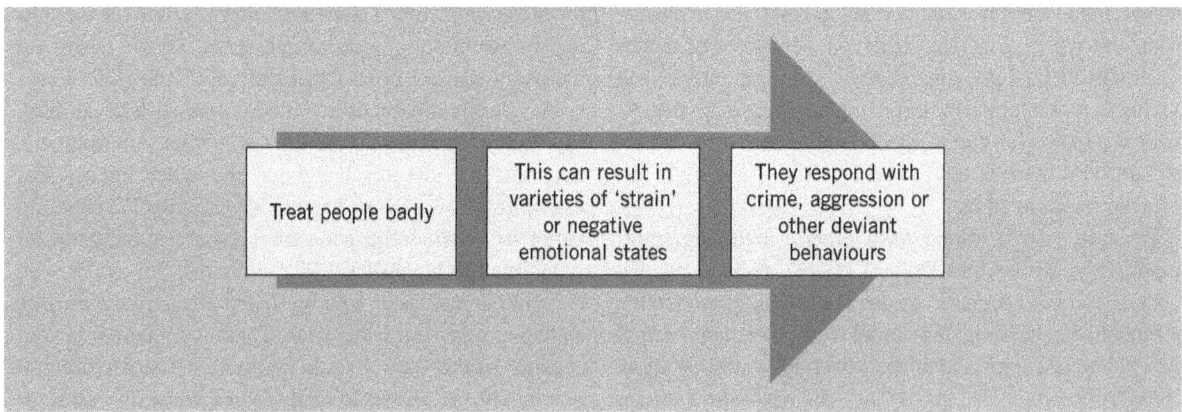

Figure 5.4 Basics of Agnew's Strain Theory

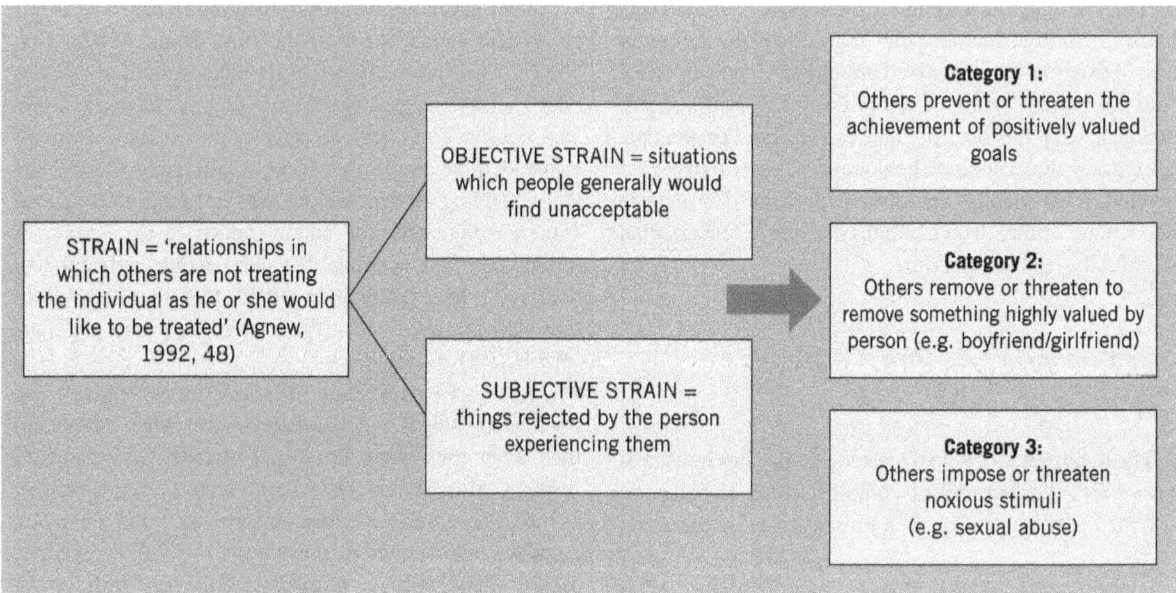

Figure 5.5 Agnew's main categories of strain

strain: (a) strain as a mismatch between an individual's expectations and their aspirations; (b) strain as a mismatch between their achievements and their expectations; and (c) strain as a mismatch between what would be a fair outcome and the actual outcome. This implies that an individual may have many and varied goals. According to Agnew (2001), the important goals for young people are the status and respect that they have in the eyes of others and autonomy. The second category of strain is the removal, or its threat, of positive things in the individual's life, such as the breakup of a romance. The third category of strain is to subject, or threaten to subject, an individual to negatively valued stimuli such as physical abuse.

The negative emotional or evaluative states created by strain include anger, depression, disappointment and fear. Anger is the most important since it promotes a desire to correct the situation or protect oneself, perhaps through revenge. So, in a sense, delinquency may be seen as a coping strategy. There are four aspects of strain which are likely to increase the likelihood of deviancy as a response in circumstances where:

- the events (strain) are perceived as unjust;
- the strain is extreme in magnitude or duration or is very recent;
- the young person lacks social controls;
- there are models for deviant coping strategies.

Not every coping strategy is available equally to every person. Individuals differ in terms of their coping resources. And traits such as self-esteem and intelligence will have their own impact. Similarly, the level of social support available to individuals differs widely. According to Agnew (1997), certain strains are more related to delinquency than others including:

- child abuse and neglect;
- failure to obtain goals easily through legitimate means which may be easily achieved through crime;
- harsh, erratic parental discipline;
- homelessness;
- rejection by parents;
- unemployment or very poor quality employment.

Evaluation of the theory

Pros:

- According to a major review by Froggio (2007), the last decade or so has produced a substantial number of empirical studies testing key aspects of General Strain Theory. These are detailed in depth in Froggio's report. Generally speaking, the research finds some but not complete support for the theory.
- There is research linking negative life experiences, anger and – less strongly – other negative emotions and delinquency.
- The theory is a fairly encompassing theory to explain deviant behaviour and criminality in particular.
- It is of relevance to forensic and criminal psychology especially as it is a clearly psychological approach to theory. Its level of analysis is largely socio-psychological.

Cons:

- This would appear to be a theory in development and so the strength of all of its principles is not known.

The social construction of crime

It is too easy to regard crime as an immutable thing and to regard the task of forensic and criminal psychologists as being merely to understand what leads some individuals to crime. Crime simply is not a static, universal thing that needs no explanation in itself. There is a very real sense in which crime is made, not done. As McGuire (2000) points out, there are no acts that can be called crime – crime is not a distinct type of behaviour. It is not always a crime to take something that does not belong to one against the owner's wishes (bailiffs, for example, may quite legally take away the goods of debtors in many countries). To kill another person is not always a crime. It may be an accident or that person may have seriously threatened one's life. To take a particular drug may be a crime in one country but not so in another. Even history changes what crimes are. In the United Kingdom and some other countries, for example, until recently men could not be raped. That is not to say that previously men had not been penetrated anally by other men but that the act had not been defined as a crime. Stalkers could not be readily prosecuted until stalking was made an offence in some jurisdictions. Furthermore, since in many jurisdictions a crime has not been committed unless there is criminal intent, the situation is even more complex.

Social constructionism can be banal as an explanation and, as such, is weak in terms of explanatory power. It is not helpful to speak of knowledge being socially constructed without knowing by whom it was constructed and what ends it served. Such a weak version of social constructionism largely serves to reaffirm that we live in a social world and this profoundly affects all we think and do. Social constructionism is sometimes offered as an 'antidote' to the positivist view that there are natural and largely immutable laws or principles of human behaviour that psychological research should strive to discover. Anyone entering forensic and criminal psychology with such a view will rapidly be frustrated to find how situationally specific and, sometimes, unreplicable findings in the field can be. Examples of the difficulties caused by this, for example, for expert psychological witnesses, are given in a number of later chapters.

A more powerful version of social constructionism is elite social constructionism (Howitt, 1992). This assumes that knowledge does not just happen in society but effective knowledge is that which is produced, disseminated and advocated by social groups of some status, standing or power. Much of this knowledge can be seen as partisan or in the interests of the group promoting that knowledge. This has profoundly affected the law, of course, and has implications for the study of forensic and criminal psychology. For example, the medical profession, especially during the nineteenth and early twentieth centuries, had an immense influence on the way in which many social issues were construed and dealt with (Haller and Haller, 1974). Characteristically, the medical model for studying social problems such as crime is based on the idea that a disease (or pathological condition) is the cause – hence the search for biological characteristics peculiar to criminals. Thinking about drugs is a good example since users are assumed to be seen as 'flawed' psychologically and physically susceptible to the substances in question (Howitt, 1991a,b).

Even more directly relevant to forensic and criminal psychology is the case of serial killers. This concept has its origins in the work of the FBI training establishment at Quantico in Virginia. According to Jenkins (1994), promoting the idea of serial killers was in the interest of the Behavioral Science Unit since they benefited as an organisation from public interest and fear. Indeed, there is some suggestion that rates of serial killing were defined in ways that made it seem more prevalent than it probably was. For example, statistics on serial killing have been manufactured that include all cases in which someone was murdered but apparently by someone unknown to them. This inevitably results in spuriously high estimates of the amount of serial killing. Other examples of the effective social construction of issues to do with crime include child abuse, domestic violence, sexual abuse, date-rape, marital rape and other issues which have been particular projects of feminist groups. That the way in which we regard crime and criminals is socially constructed does not mean that there are not serious problems such as child abuse to be tackled. In relation to child abuse, the development of public awareness of the problem does not mean that the problem has got worse, merely that the public nowadays regards violence against children in a different light. The involvement of feminists in these issues was essential to create a shift in the ideological foundations of the way they are regarded nowadays. However, one should be aware that the domination of such issues by ideas of male power might create a particular focus of interest and cause the neglect of others. For example, physical and sexual abuse by female perpetrators would be minimised by such a feminist viewpoint (e.g. Straus, 1992).

Evaluation of the theory

Pros:

- The theory encourages awareness of the societal processes that change our ideas of crime and criminals.
- Agencies in the criminal justice system may have their own viewpoints and priorities about the ways in which issues are understood.
- The theory should encourage one to explore the origins of new ways of thinking about crime. For example, the idea of a 'war' on drugs powerfully structures the way in which the policing of drugs may operate.

Cons:

- Social constructionism does not explain crime but it does help us to understand why conceptualisations of crime are what they are.
- Its relevance to the day-to-day activities of forensic and criminal psychologists may be a little remote.

Main points

- Crime can be understood at a number of different levels of analysis ranging from biological factors such as genes through to broad sociological and economic theories. Often they can be conceived as alternative conceptualisations of aspects of crime. Theories at all levels should be part of our understanding of forensic and criminal psychology since they all contribute to a full and rounded conceptual base for the advancement of the discipline.
- Many of the theories probably have very little day-to-day utility in the work of forensic and criminal psychologists. For this reason, the later chapters of this book rarely refer back to these theories but tend to employ much more specific and focused theories instead. Understanding something of the various levels of theory will help facilitate the forensic and criminal psychologist's interactions with other professional colleagues such as social workers and psychiatrists who were trained differently from most forensic and criminal psychologists.
- Most forensic and criminal psychologists will move between theoretical perspectives, depending on the matter under consideration. This flexibility can only contribute to the value of the discipline of forensic and criminal psychology.

Further reading

Marsh, I. (2006) *Theories of Crime* London: Taylor & Francis.

McLaughlin, E. and Muncie, J. (2013) *The Sage Dictionary of Criminology* (3rd edn) Sage: London.

Miller, J.M., Schreck, J., Tewsbury, R., and Barnes, J.C. (2014) *Criminological Theory: A Brief Introduction* (4th edn) New Jersey: Prentice Hall.

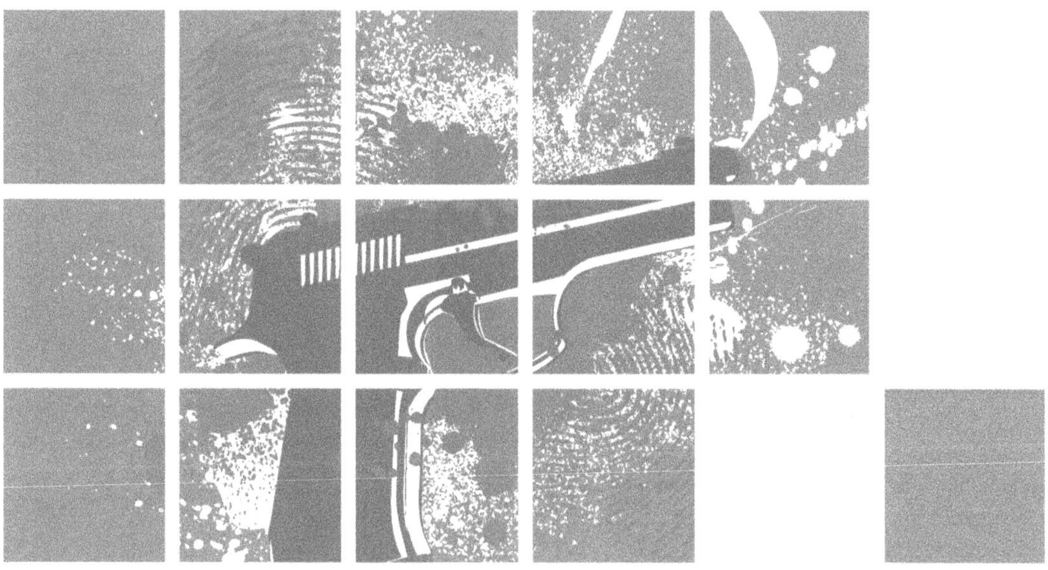

Chapter 6

Juvenile offenders and beyond

Overview

- Children commit a high proportion of criminal offences, and a small proportion of children commit a high proportion of these. Antisocial behaviour is common in the teenage years. Adolescents commit the highest proportion of criminal acts and males commit far more offences than females. Over two-thirds of adolescent males admit to committing one crime in their teen years.
- International comparisons show that self-reported delinquency varies somewhat from country to country. Nevertheless, there is considerable consistency in the factors that predict features of delinquency.
- A small proportion of individuals demonstrate a continuity between their antisocial behaviour in childhood, delinquency during adolescence, and offending in adulthood.
- Crime does run in families but the reasons for this are varied. One explanation is the impact of experiencing the arrest and imprisonment of a parent on the child.
- Genetic research has identified genetic conditions which lead to criminality when certain environmental factors are present.
- Although social disadvantage is associated with delinquency, the vast majority of youngsters from a disadvantaged background do not become seriously delinquent. Neighbourhood characteristics play an important role in determining whether crime will be committed.
- Moffitt's theory stresses the importance of neuropsychological problems which interact with family problems in the group showing a consistent antisocial tendency throughout life.
- Delinquents show less mature levels of moral reasoning than non-delinquents but moral reasoning is not helpful in predicting what type of crime they will commit.
- Strong evidence is available that early social interventions can have a substantial effect on children who are at risk. Educational programmes provided to very young children at kindergarten (or other forms of preschool education) are good examples of interventions that have demonstrated positive benefits.
- Diversion of young offenders away from the criminal justice system is to their future benefit.

Introduction

For some offenders, there is a trajectory towards antisocial behaviour and criminality which may begin even before birth. Research has demonstrated the association between a seeming myriad of precursors and later involvement in crime. These factors include poor parenting, erratic and inconsistent discipline, modelling by parents and others, the type of community the child is reared in, the opportunities for crime available locally, and many more. Delinquency is widespread among young people, though a small core of individuals are responsible for a large proportion of crime and criminal convictions. Morgado and Vale Dias (2013) describe what they term the *antisocial phenomenon in adolescence* which covers the teenage years mainly but applies to the majority of this age group. The antisocial behaviours of adolescents range from normative things like telling lies, to criminal acts such as theft, assault and animal cruelty. Antisocial behaviours are ones which violate the social rules of a particular society which generally promote respect for people and their property. They are particularly common during adolescence.

There is plenty of evidence which demonstrates that a high proportion of criminal offences are committed by young people. Budd, Sharp and Mayhew (2005) in a national UK offending survey found that 35 per cent of offences were committed by young people, though this included a lot of trivial offences. A similar picture emerges when statistics on offences proven in courts of law are considered (Cooper and Row, 2012). They studied the rates of youth crime on record on the Police National Computer in the United Kingdom. By extracting records on the basis of the offender's age, they found that young people aged 10 to 17 years were responsible for committing 1.01 million known crimes in the year 2009/10. Despite this age group amounting to only about 10 per cent of the population, they were nevertheless committing about 23 per cent of the total police recorded crime. Of all crime, 20 per cent was committed by young males. Shoplifting is the only category of offence in which adolescent females were more involved than males. In short, adolescents commit disproportionately more crime than any other age group. They are involved in the majority of robberies (which involve the use of force or threat of force in order to steal) though this is an infrequent crime. In contrast, they are proportionately unlikely to be involved in fraud compared with other age groups.

The fact that adolescents commit disproportionately more crime tells us nothing, in itself, about the proportion of youngsters who commit crimes. Do, for example, just a small percentage of adolescents commit a very large number of crimes? Among the sources of information about this is the study by Hales, Nevill, Pudney and Tipping (2009). This consisted of an analysis of self-reports of crimes by youngsters collected as part of the UK's *The Offending Crime and Justice Survey (OCJS) 2003–06*. The survey looked at criminal offending, antisocial behaviour and drug use in 10–25-year-olds, though here we will concentrate on the younger, adolescent, age group. A panel-study design was used whereby the respondents were interviewed each year over a period of four years. The method employed by the survey was innovative. The youngsters were interviewed in their home but the questions about offending behaviour were played to them through headphones. The survey asked question about crimes that included assault, burglary, criminal damage, other theft, selling drugs and robbery. Respondents typed their answers into a computer. In this way, privacy was maximised and the survey did not depend on the respondent's literacy level. One remarkable thing to emerge was the proportion of the youngsters who admitted to at least one criminal offence in the course of the four years of the study. It was found that approximately 60–70 per cent of males in their teenage years admitted a minimum of one crime. The corresponding figure for female adolescents was surprisingly large given their comparatively low level of involvement with the police. Approximately 50 per cent of female adolescents admitted at least one criminal offence in the four year period. As is typically the case with such surveys, much of this offending was relatively trivial but, of course, it does include more serious crimes.

So what of the young offenders who eventually find themselves in custody? Most young offenders in custody (in the United Kingdom) are convicted for a number of offences. Rarely are young offenders imprisoned for a single offence (Skett and Dalkin, 1999). Young offenders tend to have a varied repertoire of offence types and recidivism rates are high. Custody is not entirely effective as a deterrent since 75 per cent reoffend within two years of leaving prison. Research suggests that for 8–25-year-old males, most offending occurs at about 16–17 years (Farrington, 1990). After this, offending rates tail off to a plateau. Those convicted earliest tend to become the most persistent offenders. Those convicted six or more times are likely to have future adult convictions. Farrington (1987) reported that, in London, children rated most troublesome at 8–10 years of age by their peers and teachers amounted to about a fifth of the age cohort yet they made up over two-thirds of future chronic/repeat offenders. This is extended by Tracy, Wolfgang and Figlio's (1990) finding that, while boys with five and more contacts with the criminal justice system made up only 7.5 per cent of the age group, they were responsible for three-fifths of all recorded offences, including homicides, rapes and aggravated assaults.

The idea that there is a group of long-term or chronic offenders who commit high-frequency crimes goes back to the work of Marvin Wolfgang in the USA (Wolfgang, Figlio, and Sellin, 1994). This was the *Philadelphia Birth Cohort Study* which began in 1945. In terms of what is commonly accepted nowadays, the evidence seems to show that offenders may be broadly classified into two groups which show rather different developmental patterns:

- those with a 'career' of delinquency and antisocial acts by the time they become adolescent, which is likely to continue into long-term adult crime; and
- those whose delinquency is temporary and largely confined to their adolescence.

This distinction is important and crops up later in this chapter.

International comparisons

While juvenile crime is an international phenomenon experienced in many countries, rates of delinquency vary somewhat between different countries. Although by no means comprehensive, the *Second International Self-Report Delinquency Study* (Enzmann *et al.*, 2010) involved young people between 12 and 15 years in a total of 31 different countries. For analysis purposes, the countries were subdivided into clusters namely: 1) Anglo-Saxon which included Ireland, Canada and the USA; 2) Northern European; 3) Mediterranean; 4) Western European; 5) Latin American; and 6) post-socialist countries (e.g. Russia, Poland, and Estonia). The delinquency covered any of the following committed in the previous year:

- breaking into a building with the intention of stealing;
- carrying a knife, chain, or stick (not knife);
- deliberately hurting someone with a stick or knife or beating them up so badly that they had to see a doctor;
- purposely damaging something such as a window, a car, a bus or train seat, etc.;
- selling a soft or hard drug or acting as an intermediary in such a transaction;
- stealing a bicycle, moped or scooter;
- stealing a motorcycle or car;
- stealing from a shop or department store;
- stealing something from a car;
- snatching a purse, bag, or something else from somebody;
- taking part in a group fight in a public place;
- threatening someone with a weapon or violence in order to steal from them.

Consistent with other research, serious crime rates were low overall compared to delinquency in general. The highest levels of self-reported delinquency were found in the Western/European and Anglo-Saxon followed by the Northern European, Latin American and Mediterranean countries in that order. The youngsters in post-socialist countries reported the fewest crimes. There was a substantial variation in the numbers admitting at least one delinquent act in the previous year – 40 per cent for Irish youngsters but only 14 per cent of Venezuelan youngsters. The study's conclusions, although based on self-report measures which have their own characteristic distortions, were broadly supported by separate data on victimisation.

Relative numbers admitting delinquency are just one aspect of crime that international comparisons should report on. In particular, Rocque, Posick, Marshall and Piquero (2015) wanted to know if the correlates of high-frequency, serious crime are the same from country to country. Criminal careers are considered to have a number of important dimensions including their onset, duration, persistence, chronicity and desistance. Rocque *et al.* used the same data from the *International Self-Report Delinquency Study-2* to address cross-national variation in high-frequency offending and some correlates of offence specialisation. They took variables which are known to correlate with versatility/specialisation (i.e. whether the offender carries out a variety of types of crime or whether they tend to carry out just a single type) taken from the criminological literature. These included the variables sex, whether native born, attitudes towards violence, having delinquent peers, family bonding (how well the individual gets on with family members especially father and mother) and low self-control. In terms of the numbers of high frequency offenders, the Anglo-Saxon and Western European clusters has the most. Nevertheless, the differences between clusters of countries were, in general, not great so they were notable for their similarity rather than dissimilarity. In terms of diversity/specialisation, the evidence was that throughout the international data most offenders are not overwhelmingly versatile and are better described as specialists. Variables correlating with versatility/specialisation were all significant predictors when the entire sample is considered. However, at the level of country clusters, nativity status did not predict versatility in any of the separate country clusters. Being male and associating with delinquent peers were consistently correlated with versatile offending across the country clusters. Family bonding was not significant in the Latin America, Anglo-Saxon and Northern Europe country clusters. Low self-control significantly predicted diversity of crimes in each cluster except the Anglo-Saxon. Attitudes to violence predicted diversity for all clusters except the Latin America cluster.

So it would appear that there is some diversity in the amounts of self-reported delinquency in different countries, but the predictors of things like versatility/specialism show substantial similarity.

Adolescents, crime and the family

Crime runs in families (to a degree) and it is concentrated in a small number of families. Over a third of UK prisoners claimed that they had a family member also in prison (Walmsley, Howard and White, 1992). The trend for crime to run in families seems to be even stronger for juvenile offenders. Farrington, Barnes and Lambert (1996) assessed the prevalence of convictions among males with family members who had been convicted of an offence compared with those with family members who had not been convicted. Fifty-three per cent of those with a convicted family member had a conviction themselves whereas only 24 per cent of those without a convicted family member had a conviction. Most family relationships showed this trend – father, mother, older brother, younger brother and older sister. Only the criminality of the younger sister was not predictive. Genetic factors in the inheritance of criminality or adverse family circumstances are possible reasons for these intra-family trends. In truth, it is impossible to disentangle genetic from environmental factors in these data. Indeed, the strongest relationship between the family and one's own criminality is not explicable on either of these bases. Eighty-three per cent of males had a conviction *if* their wife had a conviction. Only 35 per cent of men whose wife did not have a conviction herself had a conviction. Wives share neither genetics nor parents with their husband. Thus factors such as early environment and heredity cannot explain this finding. The concentration of convictions in certain families is such that 1 per cent of the families were responsible for nearly 20 per cent of the convictions. Half of all convictions were the responsibility of just 6 per cent of families.

Family linkages in criminality are further demonstrated in a Finnish study by Putkonen, Ryynänen, Eronen and Tiihonen (2007). They were interested in intergenerational factors in repeat homicide offenders. They focused on a small group 35 repeat offenders. Criminal and prison records were obtained for their parents and for those of a matched control group. In addition, there were data available concerning the offspring generation (see Figure 6.1). The likelihood of committing any sort of crime was five

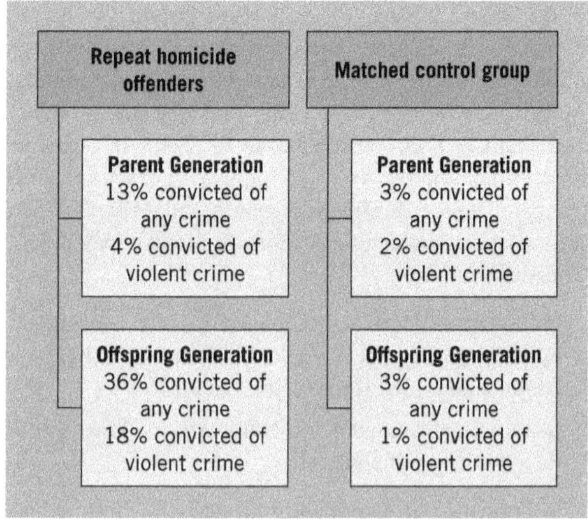

Figure 6.1 Criminal behaviour in the parent and offspring generations of groups of repeat homicide offenders and matched controls

times greater for the parents of the homicide recidivists than for the control group. The corresponding figure for the likelihood of violent offending was three times but this was not statistically significant. The prevalence of persons convicted for any crime was 13 per cent in the parent generation compared to 3 per cent in the controls. Turning to the offspring generation, the prevalence of being convicted of a crime was 36 per cent compared to 3 per cent for the control groups. Furthermore, the likelihood of violent offending was significant for the offspring generation whereas it had not been for the parent generation. In terms of statistical probabilities, this is evidence of intergenerational relationships for both crime in general and violent crime in particular. Nevertheless, the proportions involved strongly suggest that a minority of the parents and children of repeat homicide offenders show criminal patterns.

What possible explanations are there for the intergenerational transmission of criminal behaviour? Farrington (2011) provides a systematic list of the possibilities although not all of them imply that direct genetic or social learning processes are involved:

- There could be a genetic mechanism which results in the genetic transmission of a potential for criminality.
- The parents could teach criminal behaviours directly or indirectly to their child.
- Parents share the same environmental risk factors as their children, who will become criminal because of these just as their parents did. That is, they live in a criminogenic community.
- Parents share the same multiple risk factors for criminality with their children.

- Assortative mating may mean that crime-prone individuals get together and produce crime-prone offspring.
- The police and the rest of the criminal justice system may be biased against the parents for some reason and also biased against their offspring.

In recent years, there has been interest in the idea that parental involvement in the criminal justice system (e.g. arrest and imprisonment) leads to offending in the offspring. Of course, very young children may be unaware of their parent's contacts with criminal justice. Involvement in the criminal justice system has various consequences for the child and the rest of its family. Extra burdens are placed on the remaining parent and other family members. Other problems may arise as a consequence of parental imprisonment such as financial difficulties. The child will almost certainly experience emotional distress caused by the events. Negative emotions follow because the child has no legitimate ways of escaping the situation. Financial and other pressures on the family may lead to criminality and other problem behaviours according to General Strain Theory (Agnew, 1992). Prison visits, if they are allowed for children and are feasible, can be distressing and fear-provoking. A child may be searched for drugs and may not be able to hug and cuddle their parents. The child may even be old enough to understand that the parent's imprisonment is unjust, making problem behaviours worse. In terms of social learning theory, the loss of positive parental modelling and guardianship may leave the child vulnerable to peer and other negative influences. Stigma and labelling theory (Lemert, 1951, 1967) would suggest that the family may be stigmatised for the wrongdoings of the imprisoned parent. Bullying and teasing may contribute to the problem behaviour. Murray, Loeber and Pardini (2012) used longitudinal data from the *Pittsburgh Youth Study* in order to examine some of the issues associated with this scenario. Their study involved more than 1000 inner-city boys. The evidence for the adverse influence of parental imprisonment was zero for problem behaviours such as marijuana use, depression, and school performance. On the other hand, boys who had a parent imprisoned were more likely to steal than a control group. This was *after* the child's behaviour prior to the parent's arrest and other factors were controlled for statistically. The evidence suggested that changes in parenting and peer relationships were responsible for about half the effect of incarceration on the child's behaviour.

Since very young children are likely to be unaware of the involvement of their parents with the criminal justice system, there may be critical periods in the child's life when its impact is greatest. One possible critical period, according to Besemer (2012), might be between the ages of 7 and 13 years. At this stage, the child is still dependent on its parents while having an intellectual grasp of what the criminal justice system is doing to its parent. Bessemer used data from the *Cambridge Study of Delinquent Development* (see later) but also included the siblings of the boys (now men) in the study. This increased the sample substantially and also meant that females were included. She first established that parental arrest and imprisonment was associated with higher levels of criminality in the offspring. Children of parents with criminal convictions had a conviction rate three times that of controls – gender made little difference. Of course, other risk factors needed to be controlled before reaching a conclusion. Nevertheless, there was little support for Bessemer's ideas about critical periods when the child is particularly vulnerable to parental involvement with the criminal justice system. Although parents who only had criminal convictions before the child's birth tended to have children with criminal convictions, this is not very relevant to the idea that there may be a critical period between the ages of 7 and 13 years. Children whose parents were arrested while the child was in this 'critical period' did have higher levels of criminal behaviour but this was not statistically significant when risk factors for criminality were controlled for. These risk factors for crime included things like poor housing, large families, teenage mother at birth, parental conflict, and low socio-economic status. The evidence, then, for critical periods does not seem convincing. Consequently, Bessemer argued that the analysis seems compatible with Farrington's (2011) notion that a cycle of deprivation and antisocial behaviour is responsible for intergenerational transmission.

One well-documented research finding is that of birth order effects in the development of delinquency. Many, but not all, studies of delinquency have found that first-born children are less likely to be delinquent than later-born children. The first study reaching this conclusion was by Glueck and Glueck as long ago as 1950. Although the research findings in this field may be a consequence of poorly controlled research designs or analytic artifacts (Cundiff, 2013), it seems worthwhile to try to understand why birth order effects may occur. One possibility, of course, is that parents do not and cannot treat all of their offspring in exactly the same way. For instance, it would hardly be surprising to find that parents give less time to their younger offspring than the first-born. This might simply be a matter of time resources but other explanations are possible. It is known from a number of studies that parental control of their offspring has an influence in preventing delinquency. Parental supervision may encourage self-control, for example. So if first-born children are more likely to receive parental supervision, it is easy to see that they are less likely to become delinquent and, if they do, are more likely to offend trivially. Furthermore, the more time that a child is being supervised by its parents, the less opportunity that peers can influence the child adversely.

Bègue and Roché (2005) tested these ideas on French families. They took large samples of first-born and middle-born male and female adolescents. They measured parental control, using a standard measure which concerns things like children going out in the evening without their parents, adherence to return-home times fixed by their parents, and failing to tell parents where they were going when they went out. First-born children were more supervised than later-born children, according to this measure. Delinquency was measured using a self-report delinquency questionnaire including minor offences such as shoplifting and minor vandalism and serious offences such as arson, violent theft and serious violence. First-born children reported less minor and less serious delinquency than middle-born children. There was evidence that parental supervision had a moderate impact on delinquency.

Criminogenic factors in childhood

The continuity of criminal behaviour from the parent generation to the offspring is just one issue in the role of the family in delinquency and criminal behaviour. Many factors are associated with both delinquency and adult crime which many researchers believe have similar origins (Yoshikawa, 1995). Delinquency, Yoshikawa argues, is the product of the interaction of a multiplicity of factors occurring in a number of settings. These settings include school, home and the community. A great deal of research concentrates on the adequacy of parenting skills and methods within the family and the question of whether this affects the child's likelihood of delinquency and crime. While there is much evidence of such a relationship, it is harder to establish the causal linkage between the two.

Johnson, Smailes, Cohen, Kasen and Brook (2004) argued that problematic parenting is a mediating variable in the intergeneration transmission of aggressive/antisocial behaviour. That is to say, parents who show aggressive/antisocial behaviour employ problematic parenting methods which results in their children being aggressive/antisocial. Johnson *et al.* studied data from mothers in New York State who were interviewed when their children were between the ages of 1 and 10 years. Problematic parenting was assessed at various stages during the interviews. By problematic parenting the researchers were referring to things like inconsistent enforcement of rules by the mother, use of guilt to control the child's behaviour, arguments between the parents in front of the child, problems in controlling anger with the child and so forth. Official investigation records of arrests and charges during an individual's lifetime provided the key information on the dependent variable of criminal activity. The researchers found that there was a correlation between higher levels of aggressive/antisocial behaviour in the parents and higher levels of aggressive/antisocial behaviour in their offspring. Did problematic parenting mediate this relationship? Parents with a history of aggressive/antisocial behaviour did show poorer parenting behaviours even after taking into account variables like their level of education, income, age of the offspring and the gender of the offspring. Problematic parenting was shown to be the mediating variable because the relationship between parental aggressive/antisocial behaviour and that of their children disappeared when the researchers controlled for problematic parenting statistically. There is evidence from other countries of the relationship between inadequate patterns of interacting in families and delinquent behaviour. In Spain, Arce, Seijo, Farina and Novo (2004) found that a measure which assessed inconsistent, harsh or abusive parenting, parental rejection and coldness, inadequate supervision of the child by its parents, little parental involvement with the child, and lack of affection in the family was associated with more deviant and antisocial behaviour as well as delinquency.

Major childhood factors *associated* with future criminality have been well-known for many years. Some researchers might dispute whether these are causal factors rather than risk factors predicting future criminality. The research literature on factors associated with delinquency and criminality is extensive but it is not all high quality. In particular, cross-sectional studies taking place at a single point in time are difficult to interpret. For this reason, in their review of the research, Haapasalo and Pokela (1999) concentrated on the longitudinal research (that is, studies involving the assessment of children at different stages of childhood). These studies go back to the earliest and seminal studies of Glueck and Glueck (1962, 1968) whose work began in the 1950s. The evidence Haapasalo and Pokela reviewed strongly indicated that the following are antecedents of antisocial and criminal behaviour:

- deviant parental characteristics (criminality, substance abuse, mental problems);
- family disruption (separations, divorce, instability, marital conflict);
- lack of love or rejection;
- laxness (poor monitoring, lack of supervision);
- punitive child-rearing practices and attitudes (including corporal punishment, strict discipline, authoritarian attitudes).

However, the list probably should include more factors than this. Other studies overlap with and extend these findings. Hoeve, Dubas, Eichelsheim, van der Laan, Smeenk and Gerris (2009) conducted a meta-analysis (see Box 4.2) of a large number of studies (including unpublished work) into the association between parenting and delinquency. They found that the variables which had the strongest effects on delinquent behaviour were lack of parental monitoring and lack of disclosure by the child; neglect, rejection and hostility, and the use of psychological control (which includes the use of the withdrawal of love, using guilt as a means of controlling the child, and keeping the child dependent upon the parent). Permissiveness and the use of physical punishment were only weakly related to delinquency.

Of course, some might argue that the predictive factors are so intertwined that it is impossible to say exactly which factors cause later criminality. For example, conflict between parents and the self-confidence of the mother may be interrelated. If they both tend to occur together, it is difficult to know which is the most important. Furthermore, there are criticisms of some studies as they are dependent on how offenders remember their early family environment. Such recollections may be inaccurate or self-justificatory. However, there would seem to be enough evidence from studies that do not use such *retrospective* procedures to negate this view. For example, McCord (1979) used information from a study of parenting behaviours obtained from counsellors who had visited families. Thirty years later, she collected data on their children's criminal behaviour in the ensuing years. She found that characteristics (as measured between 5 and about 13 years of age) such as the following predicted the child's criminality:

- conflict between the parents;
- little or casual supervision of the child;
- mother's lack of affection for the child.

Statistically, such parenting variables in combination identified as serious adult criminals about two-thirds of men who had no record of offending as juveniles. Furthermore, if one considers those with juvenile criminal records, the parenting variables indicate reasonably well which ones go on to have an adult criminal record.

Mothers feature much more strongly in the literature on parenting and delinquency than fathers. Of course, the absence of the father from the family unit is regarded by some as potentially a risk signalling future delinquency. Where the father is present he is able to be involved with the child in the form of play, reading bedtime stories, outings and so forth. Unfortunately, few studies, if any, measure such involvement with the child and researchers have tended to concentrate on father present or father absent as a substitute. Sakadi, Kristiansson, Oerklaid and Bremberg (2007) reviewed a total of 24 studies which concerned the impact of fathers (including father substitutes such as stepfathers and live-in partners of the mother). They were interested in longitudinal studies in which key variables were measured at different points in time. This, of course, is beneficial to assessing causal influences of variables on each other. The researchers were not interested in single-stage cross-sectional or snapshot studies which lacked this temporal dimension. Some of the available studies controlled for socio-economic status but others did not. Children who engage interactively with their father or a father substitute have fewer behavioural problems if they are boys and fewer psychological problems as young women if they are girls. Among children from low socio-economic status families, the evidence showed that key variables such as criminality and economic disadvantage later in life were also affected by father absence. Although these effects happened irrespective of biological links between father and child, biological fathers seem to contribute other, more specific things. Having a biological father who does not live with the child but is nevertheless involved with the child has important influences on children from low-income families. The behavioural trajectory into adolescent delinquency for children with otherwise inadequate or criminogenic backgrounds is significantly reduced by the involvement of the biological father with the child. This remains the case irrespective of whether the father lived at home or not.

A study in northern Russia supports the importance of the father in delinquent behaviour. Ruchkin, Eisemann and Hagglof (1998a) studied a group of delinquents of 15 to 18 years of age. These were compared with a similar group of non-offenders. Their delinquency was fairly serious but consisted of repeated thefts in the main. A few were more serious cases such as rape and murder. Some types of aggression by the delinquents were best predicted by the father's rejection of the boy but, for the non-delinquent control group, it was rejection by the mother which was most strongly associated with aggression. According to the self-report data, delinquents scored higher than controls on rejection by both mother and father (Ruchkin, Eisemann and Hagglof, 1998b).

There is one issue that needs to be addressed before we move on. That is, to what extent do the same factors lead to delinquency in girls as they do in boys? There is substantial evidence to suggest that girls are increasingly to be found participating in delinquent activity. Of course, currently the proportion of girls engaging in delinquent acts is rather lower than that for boys. Zahn (2007) evaluated the many research studies into the correlates of delinquency in girls. In general it was found that the factors involved in the delinquency of boys are also involved in the delinquent activities of girls. One factor – sexual abuse – stands out as being commoner for girls than for boys and there is good evidence that abuse is predictive of delinquency. Intriguingly, the more girls associated with boys the greater their risk of delinquency – this may imply the adverse influence on males.

Continuity of childhood and adult antisocial behaviour

Among the factors associated with childhood and adult criminality according to Farrington (1995), Skett and Dalkin (1999) and West (1982) are having criminal parents or siblings, low family income, substandard accommodation, large family size and poor parenting such as a lack of interest in the child and inconsistent discipline. This list is very similar to the factors associated with the aetiology of psychiatric disorders. Not surprisingly, then, researchers have examined more directly the relationship between psychiatric disorder and criminality in childhood. Two psychiatric conditions (childhood) conduct disorder and antisocial personality disorder (ASPD) are of particular interest here since their diagnosis is partly dependent on criminal and antisocial characteristics. *Conduct disorder* is defined in the *Diagnostic and Statistical Manual of the American Psychiatric Association* (American Psychiatric Association, 2013) as a diagnosis which can be applied to young people under the age of 18 years (and much younger) who show a habitual pattern of violating social norms, the law and the rights of other people. Table 6.1 lists some of the diagnostic criteria for conduct disorder. In order for the diagnosis of conduct disorder to be applied, a child must exhibit four or more of the types of behaviour listed in the table. In other words, if not showing a range of criminal activities, they are demonstrating strong antisocial tendencies. Table 6.1 also lists the diagnostic criteria for *antisocial personality disorder* (ASPD), which is discussed further in Chapter 22. Basically, it is evidenced by an adult showing a range of criminal and other antisocial characteristics which are grossly at variance with social norms. The adult condition of antisocial personality disorder is not completely identical with the childhood condition of conduct disorder, nevertheless there are considerable similarities. Indeed, the individual must have exhibited signs of conduct disorder as a child, whether diagnosed or not, to be classifiable as having ASPD as an adult. Farrington (1996) argued on the basis of extensive research that conduct disorder and ASPD have much the same aetiological precursors. These include, according to Farrington: 1) having a convicted parent; 2) leaving school at a young

Table 6.1 Diagnostic criteria for childhood conduct disorder and antisocial personality disorder

Childhood conduct disorder: four or more of the following	Antisocial personality disorder
Aggressive behaviour towards other people/animals eg bullying	Non-conformity to social norms concerning lawful behaviour as shown by repeatedly doing things which actually or potentially result in arrest
Used a dangerous weapon to hurt other people	Deceitfulness as demonstrated by repeatedly lying or manipulating/conning other people for profit or pleasure
Deliberate physical cruelty to other people	Impulsive behaviour including failure to plan for the future
Deliberate physical cruelty to animals	Irritability and aggressiveness as shown by repeated physical assaults on other people or fighting
Frequent initiation of physical fights with other people	Reckless disregard for their own or other people's safety
Committed confrontational economic crime like robbery	Irresponsible lifestyle such as repeated failure to meet financial obligations or a lack of consistency in employment behaviour
Perpetrated a forced sex act on another person	Lack of remorse for harm done to others
Destroyed property through arson	
Destroyed property in other ways	
Committed non-confrontational economic crime like burglary	
Committed non-confrontational retail theft like shoplifting	
Ignored parents curfews under 13 years of age	
Ran away from home at least twice	
Truanted from school under 13 years of age	
Aggression to People and Animals	
Destruction of property	
Deceitfulness or Theft	
Serious Violations of Rules	

age; 3) harsh or erratic parental discipline; 4) large family size; 5) low family income; 6) low intelligence; and 7) poor housing. This is, of course, more or less the same list of things which predicted delinquency and adult criminality. Perhaps this is hardly surprising given the contents of Table 6.1.

Data from several stages of the *Cambridge Study of Delinquent Development* support the sequential progression of antisocial behaviour (Farrington, 1996). This study was begun in the 1960s by the famous criminologist Donald West, though the psychologist David Farrington became associated with the long-term project a few years later. This is a major longitudinal study of the same group of boys from childhood into adulthood. Data were collected on a large number and variety of factors and characteristics potentially associated with criminal offending. The study did not involve psychiatric diagnoses of the sort to be found in the *Diagnostic and Statistical Manual of the American Psychiatric Association*, nevertheless composite measures were available from the study which are very much like conduct disorder and ASPD. Antisocial personality as assessed from data collected at ages 10, 14, 18 and 32 years was explored in terms of possible predictors from the rest of the data. Table 6.2 gives the best predictors out of the vast range of different precursor variables for the variable antisocial personality.

Although it contains merely part of the findings, Table 6.2 reveals important things. Crucially, there is a very strong relationship between having characteristics of antisocial personality at one stage and demonstrating antisocial behaviour at later stages. These later stages include adulthood.

Table 6.2 Major predictors of antisocial personality at different ages

Age group	Best predictors of antisocial personality
10-year-olds	Poor parental supervision Low school attainment at age 10 Poor child-rearing by parents at age 8 High neuroticism
14-year-olds	Antisocial personality score at age 10 Separated from parent at age 10 Low non-verbal IQ at age 8–10 years Many friends at age 8
18-year-olds	Antisocial personality score at age 14 years Convicted parent at age 10 Father not involved at age 12 Father unemployed when child was 14 years
32-year-olds	Antisocial personality score at age 18 years Convicted parent at age 10 years Did not stay at school Hospitalised for illness at age 18 years

A word of caution may be appropriate at this point. Until we have a fuller picture, it is essential to avoid simplistic assumptions concerning how delinquency impacts adult criminality. This is a particularly difficult area for research and the numerous confounding ('third') variables which confuse the interpretation always need to be considered. A study by Sourander *et al.* (2007) illustrates something of this difficulty. They studied a large, representative birth cohort sample of 2600 males born in 1981 in Finland. The youngsters were researched until they were 25 years of age. The investigation employed a variety of sources of information:

- Stealing was assessed on the basis of information provided by the boy's parents and teacher.
- Parents and teachers also completed the Rutters Parent Questionnaire and the Teachers' Questionnaire, thus providing information about the child's mental and emotional problems.
- The boys themselves completed the Children's Depression Inventory.
- Other information was obtained from four different national registries. For example, Finnish men are required to do military service for up to a year and so Army medical records contained information about any psychiatric diagnosis they may have received. Criminal offences committed between 16 and 20 years were obtained from the Finnish National Police Registry. Another source was consulted for information about suicide and serious suicide attempts.

It was found that approximately 10 per cent of the sample reportedly had stolen in the year before they were eight years of age. There was a correlation between stealing at age eight and subsequent levels of crime, conduct problems, substance use and antisocial personality disorders. This was the case even when various background variables such as parental education level and conduct problems of the child were controlled for. However, things are not that simple because the comorbidity of stealing and aggression needs to be taken into account. Comorbidity simply means that stealing and aggression (or any other characteristics) are occurring together. Taking this into account, boys who both stole and were aggressive at the age of eight years were more likely to be involved in crime in later life and to have committed or attempted suicide. They were also more likely to have been given a psychiatric diagnosis at some stage. Boys who stole at the age of eight *without* showing high levels of aggression were no more likely than any other child to manifest any of these outcomes. Put another way, had the researchers not examined the question of comorbidity, they would have been left with a highly misleading research finding which essentially labelled children who steal as being deviant and problematic adults.

Biological factors in antisocial behaviour

Although there is a long tradition of twin studies seeking to demonstrate that criminality is inherited, it was not until quite recently that studies of specific genes in relation to criminal behaviour have become possible. Neuropsychological deficits may have a direct effect on antisocial behaviour. Some of this evidence is discussed in Chapter 5. Good self-control depends in part on good neuropsychological functioning and neuropsychological problems can lead to inadequate levels of self-control (Wikström and Treiber, 2007). Genetic imaging research has begun to show how particular genetic characteristics are closely related to differences between individuals in terms of the brain structure and its functioning. Of note is research on monoamine oxidase A (MAOA). This enzyme is involved in breaking down neurotransmitters such as dopamine, norepinephrine and serotonin in the brain. MAOA is configured by the MAOA gene which is to be found on the X-chromosome which means that MAOA-related genetic information is to be found in two places in females since they have two X-chromosomes. Males, having just one X-chromosome, may be more vulnerable to problems with the MAOA gene. The genotype for MAOA may be of one of two broad types: 1) high activity and b) low activity. Having the low-activity variant is associated with various brain characteristics such as having a smaller limbic system volume and lower than usual activity of the hippocampus and parts of the prefrontal cortex (Meyer-Lindenberg and Weinberger, 2006).

In ground breaking research, Caspi, McClay, Moffitt, Mill, Martin, Craig, *et al.* (2002) examined the interactive effects between an environmental characteristic and a gene characteristic on the delinquent behaviour of the individual. In particular, they believed that childhood maltreatment interacts with the monoamine oxidase A (MAOA) genetype to predict criminal and violent behaviour. So having the low-activity genotype was expected to interact with having had experienced maltreatment as a child to result in antisocial behaviour. Conversely, they thought that the high-activity version of MAOA would confer a resistance to the criminogenic consequences of childhood maltreatment. In their study, in line with their predictions, Caspi *et al.* showed that individuals who were maltreated as children were more likely to be convicted of violence, to have high antisocial symptoms, to have a high disposition to violence, to have high antisocial behaviour on a composite measure and to have conduct disorder. So, on its own, the environmental factor of being maltreated as a child was predictive of delinquency. In contrast, having the low-activity version of MAOA had no relationship with any of these measures of antisocial behaviour on its own. Crucially, however, those with the low-activity MAOA version who had suffered childhood maltreatment showed high levels of antisocial behaviour. Those with the low-activity type of MAOA who had suffered child maltreatment amounted to only 12 per cent of the sample yet they accounted disproportionately for 44 per cent of convictions for violence. The process is believed to involve the effects of low-activity MAOA on self-control.

Beaver, DeLisi, Vaughn and Wright (2010) confirmed and extended these ideas to involve this issue of self-control more directly. They expected that neuropsychological deficits are involved in the degree of self-control manifested by an individual as well as their degree of delinquency. MAOA was expected to have no direct influences on self-control or delinquency but MAOA in interaction with neuropsychological deficits would be associated with low self-control and higher delinquency. They used data from a USA national longitudinal study of adolescent health known as *Add Health*. Neuropsychological deficits were assessed using the Peabody Picture Vocabulary Test which assesses receptive vocabulary or the understanding of words when you hear other people use them. It is a measure of verbal and educational ability. It is known to correlate with specific tests of neuropsychological functioning. Self-control was measured using items from the study tapping self-control including asking the adolescents whether they had problems getting along with their teachers, keeping their minds focused on things, paying attention, and finishing homework together with a question which asked if the adolescent did things just right. Delinquency was measured by asking questions about how frequently they had sold drugs, shoplifted, damaged property and lied to other people, for example, in the previous year. An additional measure assessed more serious delinquency using items which asked about using weapons, physical fighting, and gang involvement. MAOA was assessed on the basis of cells collected by the respondent from their mouth. Just as in other studies, there was no relationship between low-activity MAOA and the measures of delinquency and self-control. On the other hand, there was a relationship between the measure of neuropsychological deficits (the Peabody test) and the measure of violent delinquency. However, the more important issue was whether or not there was an interaction between neuropsychological deficits and low activity MAOA. This proved to be the case. Furthermore, self-control was also predicted by the interaction and seemed to be a mediating factor in the relationship of the interaction of neuropsychological deficits and low activity MAOA with delinquency.

Similar interactions between genetic and environment factors in producing delinquency have been demonstrated or partially demonstrated in other research on the MAOA gene and various genotypes of this. For example, Roettger, Boardman, Harris and Guo (2016) looked at the interactive role of parental closeness and incarceration with the gene on delinquency. Zhang, Ming, Wang and Yao (2016) investigated the interaction of a MAOA genotype with childhood abuse on aggressive behaviours. Just what the complete picture will be about the role of MAOA in criminality depends on future research, nevertheless, the evidence of the involvement of genes in interaction with environmental factors in delinquent behaviour is important for our understanding of delinquency. Despite this, there are important questions such as the proportion of delinquency which can be assigned to such factors which need to be addressed.

Why don't all disadvantaged children offend?

The idea that youngsters from socially and economically disadvantaged backgrounds are most at risk of involvement in delinquency and crime is ingrained in our thinking. How is it then that the overwhelming majority of youngsters from disadvantaged backgrounds do not become delinquent and criminal? Wikström and Treiber's (2016) answer to this paradox is basically simple – delinquent acts are the consequence of the individual having a high propensity for crime being exposed to environments which are criminogenic. This is the basic idea of their Situational Action Theory (SAT) of crime. A high propensity for crime is the result of the individual having a weak personal morality and an inability to exercise self-control. A criminogenic environment is a geographical area (neighbourhood) where the community does not enforce rules of good conduct. Personal choice and social selection processes encourage socially disadvantaged individuals to spend more of their time in these criminogenic contexts. The implication of this is that people with the same propensity for crime and who are exposed to the same criminogenic contexts are more likely to commit crime irrespective of whether they are socially disadvantaged.

Wikström and Treiber tested out their theory as part of *The Peterborough Adolescent and Young Adult Development Study* in the United Kingdom. In overview, a sample of over 500 young people living in the city of Peterborough were studied more-or-less annually between the ages of 12 and 19 years. Their delinquent behaviour was measured through self-reports of the prevalence and frequency of their involvement in arson, assault, burglary from residential or nonresidential settings, car crime, robbery, shoplifting, theft from a person, and vandalism. Although 70 per cent of the youngsters claimed to have committed one criminal act during the duration of the study, very few reported many more crimes. The most prevalent crime was assault. More than half of the youngsters said that they had hit or beaten up somebody. Nearly one half of the reported crimes were committed by 4 per cent of the participants. Their propensity for crime was based on questions about personal morality (e.g. 'breaking into a building to steal something is wrong') and questions about self-control (e.g. 'I lose my temper pretty easily').

The participants also completed a detailed diary which described the activities each youngster was involved in and the location in the city where it took place. So the youngster would say what activity they carried out (e.g. roller skating), when they did it, the neighbourhood area where it was done, who it was done with (e.g. friends), and the functional place where it was done (e.g. the street corner). This was a massive undertaking as each youngster supplied data for 480 hours of their time. This diary information could be used to assess how much time each youngster spent in unstructured peer oriented activities in criminogenic environments. An unstructured peer-oriented activity is one which lacks a direction or goal – for example, media consumption and socialising. This sort of unfocused, unsupervised activity is regarded as encouraging delinquent behaviour. For example, using a large sample of Dutch adolescents, Weerman, Bernaso, Bruinsma and Pauwels (2015) collected detailed data on many aspects of how youngsters spent time with their peers. This included online time, time spent with peers in public places, time spent with peers not in public, and time spent with peers unsupervised by an adult. The researchers concluded that the amount of time spent with peers is related to delinquency when two of the following conditions were fulfilled: being in a public place, being unsupervised by adults, and just socialising.

Wikström and Treiber's theory also involves assessments of the physical environments frequented by the youngsters. Their study used very small areas of the city each covering a single postcode. So typically each neighbourhood would contain just over a hundred or so households. Each neighbourhood was assessed in terms of its collective efficacy. Basically, collective efficacy reflects the ability of residents in a neighbourhood to behave communally. It is maintained by informal social controls and social cohesion. Two different components of collective efficacy were measured: 1) social cohesion, which concerns how well people living in the neighbourhood get along and share much the same values; and 2) informal social control, which was measured by questions asking the probability that neighbours would intervene if young people were transgressing the shared values. Areas of poor collective efficacy show inconsistent social norms, neighbours not getting along so well, and poor ability to informally monitor and shape the behaviour of those using the area. Such neighbourhoods are ineffective at controlling the behaviour of young people when in that neighbourhood. Commercial and entertainment centres by their very nature lack collective efficacy since they are visited by many non-residents. So they lack shared norms and it is difficult for residents to monitor and control the behaviour of youngsters there.

Social disadvantage for each participant was assessed on the social disadvantage of the neighbourhood and the social disadvantage of the family. So their measure of neighbourhood social disadvantage was based on the proportion of households in the postcode area which was working class, unemployed, not living in a detached house, and having minimal or no educational qualifications. They measured also the youngster's family social disadvantage based on the family's household income, the highest educational level of the parents, and their highest occupational class. Only very few of the most advantaged families lived in highly disadvantaged neighbourhoods and a disadvantaged family could live in an advantaged neighbourhood.

The Peterborough Study revealed something very important. That is, youngsters actually spend a great deal of their time outside of their home neighbourhood. If the youngster has a high propensity for crime, they are susceptible to delinquency when they go to areas of poor collective efficacy. They are not resistant to the possibility of crime so when in places in which social controls on their behaviour are weak they are likely to carry out an act of delinquency. There was a relationship between the amount of delinquent acts committed by the participants and their level of family and neighbourhood deprivation. This agrees with the idea that deprivation leads to offending. Nevertheless, only a small number (7 per cent) of those from disadvantaged backgrounds had persistent offending patterns despite 70 per cent of youngsters with persistent offending patterns having disadvantaged backgrounds. If crime propensity and exposure to criminogenic settings are controlled for statistically, the relationship between family and neighbourhood disadvantage and crime involvement disappears. In other words, deprivation is not the cause of the delinquency. The vast majority of youngsters from disadvantaged backgrounds do not offend and they show levels of criminal propensity similar to those of youngsters from more advantaged backgrounds. They do not spend as much time as offenders with peers unsupervised by adults and they spend less time at locations where collective efficacy is low. So crime propensity and criminogenic exposure are related to involvement in crime irrespective of the youngster's level of family and neighbourhood disadvantage. The theory assumes that more children who are born into and live in disadvantaged circumstances develop a higher level of crime propensity and are more likely to be exposed to criminogenic settings. To understand the relationship of delinquency with disadvantage depends on understanding why some youngsters from a disadvantaged background develop higher levels of propensity to crime and spend more time in criminogenic environments. There are many reasons but lack of self-control could be the result of psychoneurological deficits and a lack of money may lead to them spending time in unstructured socialisation in public places. Box 6.1 discusses other explanations of why some youngsters avoid becoming delinquent.

Box 6.1 Key concept

Factors protective from delinquency

There are four major methods of crime prevention (Farrington, 1998):

- Situational prevention, which involves targeting the physical environment in ways which make it difficult to commit a crime, while maximising the risk of getting caught.
- The traditional criminal justice approach which involves deterrents, incapacitation and rehabilitation. For example, rehabilitation programmes for young offenders target factors such as criminal thinking, pro-social interpersonal skills, socio-moral reasoning, impulsivity reduction, challenging pro-offending cognitions and helping tackle substance abuse. Anger management courses appear effective at reducing angry events, as measured from staff checklists, by about a third or more (Ireland, 1999).
- The community prevention interventions which are designed to change social conditions and institutions (e.g. families and parenting).
- The final category of crime reduction strategy Farrington calls *developmental prevention*. This involves tackling the risk factors involved in youthful criminality.

In addition, he mentions protective factors. Just what is a protective factor? If, say, poor parenting is a factor putting the child at risk of criminality then good parenting may be seen as a protective factor. This would be to equate protective factors with unrisk factors – that is, merely the opposite of the risk factor. We need to go one stage further. Many children who experience poor parenting will not become delinquent and criminal. Not everyone who smokes gets cancer, but smoking is a strong risk factor for cancer. There may be other factors which protect the health of the individual and make it less likely that they will become ill. There may be factors which, if they co-occur with risk factors, will reduce the impact of those risk factors. For example, poor parenting may be a risk factor for antisocial behaviour but some at-risk children may have grandparents close by who take a great interest in the child. Grandparents in these circumstances can be described as a protective factor.

One way of looking at the risk factor approach is to conceive of it as a deficit model – that is, something is missing in childhood which pushes the young person towards crime. They are, for example, deficient in social skills because of the poor parenting they received. There is a more positive approach that tries to see what it is about some youngsters who are faced with the most unpromising start in life that leaves them capable of resisting the impact of a raft of grave life stressors that turn some youngsters criminal.

One approach is to be found in Bender, Bliesener and Lösel's (1996) study of adolescents in a residential institution. As one might expect, the family and social backgrounds of many of these left much to be desired. Bender *et al.* asked the residential staff to nominate examples of youngsters who, despite the risk factors in the background, nevertheless turned out to be pretty decent young people who were not problems. They were also asked to nominate risk-succumbing youngsters who similarly manifested high levels of risk factors but exhibited serious behavioural disorders.

These two groups were loaded with similar risk factors (deaths, divorces and separations, parental unemployment and financial problems, marital conflict and drug and alcohol abuse within the family). What was it about the resilient youngsters that helped prevent them from succumbing to the effects of the risk factors? The researchers found that the protective factors which distinguished the resilient youngsters from the rest included the following:

- *Personal resources*: resilient youngsters had better technical/spatial intelligence, had flexible temperaments, were approach-oriented, had more positive self-esteem and had active coping styles.
- *Social resources*: the resilient youngsters were more satisfied with their social support and experienced the climate of their residential institution as socio-emotionally oriented (openness, autonomy and low conflict).

In an earlier, similar study, Bliesener and Lösel (1992) found an association between intelligence (especially that involving problem solving) and resilience. The resilients seemed to actively face up to problems rather than simply responding passively – they did not see themselves as in some way fatalistically helpless.

Given the involvement of forensic psychology in the aftermath of parental separation and the ensuing divorce, the work of Czerederecka and Jaskiewicz-Obydzinska (1996) is important. While not specifically concerned with criminal behaviour, the research investigated Polish children involved in divorces for signs of emotional or social problems. Children classified as having no disorder were found to have stayed with their mother as the custodial parent but they also had a 'clearly defined' relationship with their father. By this is meant either having regular contact with their father or *no* contact. They also found that the amount of conflict between the parents did not necessarily lead to problems for the child. It was when the child was put into a position in which they were expected to take sides that the problems arose. A child passively observing parental conflict did not appear to be so affected. In other words, despite our expectations about divorce, these effects can be essentially neutralised in some cases by other factors. A good psychological relationship with both parents seems to be the neutralising agent.

The research literature on protective factors has tended to dwell on listing variables which lead individuals not to involve themselves in crime or antisocial behaviour. This produces very long lists of variables which are not particularly stimulating in terms of the development of systematic theories that could focus research in this field. One exception is Agnew's (2016) *Theory of Crime Resistance and Susceptibility*. It attempts to explain resistance and susceptibility (which are seen as opposite ends of a dimension) especially in relation to Agnew's General Strain Theory of crime (Agnew, 1992, 1997 and 2001). Strain is the result of a failure or inability to achieve one's own goals, being victimised by negative events including both verbal and physical assaults, and the loss of something positive in one's life such as through bereavement. Strain pushes the individual towards antisocial ways of dealing with circumstances, such as stealing money to achieve an economic goal or taking drugs to deal with the pain of a loss. Some situations may be conducive to crime which means that they are criminogenic. However, whether the individual acts criminally or resists it depends on various contingencies such as how the individual perceives and interprets the situation, their emotional reaction to the events and their behavioural inclinations. People differ in

BOX 6.1 (continued)

their response to strain and this process leads to either resistance or susceptibility by the individual. Agnew stresses that resistance and susceptibility are not the same thing as restraint which involves controls internal to and external to individual. A person who is resistant to the criminal pathway, though, faces the same situations that would lead other people towards crime. The resistant individual fails to perceive these experiences as either pressure or attractions towards crime. Strains in the individual's life such as economic problems, discrimination, and victimisation by crime push some individuals towards crime yet they are not perceived in this way by everyone. Other factors which can be involved include spending time with criminal or delinquent peers, the consequences of crime such as cash and thrills, and awareness of criminal models. Agnew suggests four factors which he assumes influence both resistance and susceptibility to criminogenic circumstances: 1) Negativity is the general tendency of a person to see circumstances as unjust or bad in some other way. Once seen negatively, such an individual is likely to respond antisocially in an aggressive/aggressive manner because the circumstances upset them. 2) Pleasure and sensation seeking is the degree to which a person emphasises money, material goods, physical pleasure and thrills and excitement in their motives but does not see hard work and personal sacrifice as important. Such an orientation will make the individual more prone to the crime pathway. 3) Conventional efficacy and perceived social support is how much a person believes that they can deal with the strains and stresses in their lives in legal ways and that they will be able to seize any opportunities which come to them in the lives. Crucially they assume that other people will help them in their endeavours. If the individual thinks this way then they will follow legal routes rather than criminal ones. 4) General sensitivity to the environment reflects the tendency for some individuals to be responsive to the environment whether that is good or bad. Variables such as beliefs, values, identity, biological characteristics, social experiences including situational factors, Agnew states, are contained within these four factors or overlap with them. According to Agnew: 'Susceptible individuals are more likely than resistant individuals to perceive or imagine strains; view them as very bad, unjust, and uncontrollable through legal channels; experience negative emotional reactions to them; and be inclined to respond to them in an aggressive or rebellious manner.' (p.189) For Agnew, the essential point is that people vary in their response to exactly the same strain in their lives.

Two types of delinquents

By this stage we have touched on quite a few of the risk factors for delinquency as well as indicating that among delinquents there seems to be a hard core of lifetime antisocial individuals. These seem to have disadvantaged family, social and educational backgrounds. Yet are there not many youngsters who, maybe, shoplift just once in adolescence but, apart from that, show little sign of lifelong antisocial behaviour? One theory of delinquency which assumes that there are two types of delinquency – the life-long antisocial trajectory and the temporary delinquent blip – is the work of the clinical psychologist Terrie Moffitt. Moffitt (1993) points to a statistical pattern in delinquency and antisocial behaviour which warrants explanation. Criminal statistics show that adolescence is the peak time for crime and that crime is most common at about the age of 17 years. There is a rapid drop in the amount of crime following this. Of course, the years before adolescence do not appear in these statistics simply because children under the age of ten are rarely charged with crimes. Moffitt believes, however, that these early years of life may show antisocial behaviour though this is not necessarily regarded as criminal. She points to the research on (childhood) conduct disorder as evidence for this. Moffitt argues that the steep decline in criminal behaviour occurring between 17 and 30 years of age is matched by a steep increase in antisocial behaviour between the ages of 7 and 17 years. Antisocial behaviour begins early in childhood and remains a feature into and through adulthood though it is increasingly labelled criminal behaviour as the child gets older. Adolescence, then, is a period in which antisocial behaviour increases markedly. To explain this, Moffitt proposes that there are two types of offender. The first type she labels as *life-course-persistent* for whom antisocial behaviour is persistent, regular feature of childhood, adolescence and adulthood. These are just a few per cent of individuals – substantially less than 10 per cent in all probability. The other group is described as *adolescence-limited* which reflects the temporary nature of their antisocial behaviour. This is restricted largely to the teenage years and adolescence. These two types, in combination, explain the statistical data on crime and, especially, its peak in adolescence according to Moffitt. Of course, in her paper, Moffitt supports all of her points with a wide range of research studies which cannot be mentioned here.

Antisocial behaviour in life-course-persistent antisocial individuals is continuous throughout life, of course, but its manifestation varies by age. Moffitt suggests that in a four-year-old it might consist of biting and hitting, in a ten-year-old it might be school truancy or shoplifting, in a 16-year-old it might be drug dealing or vehicle theft, and at the age of 22 years it might be robbery or rape. The expression of antisocial behaviour changes though the core antisocial disposition remains unaltered. The life-course-persistent type is consistent in that they demonstrate antisocial behaviour across many different sorts of situation. So the life-course-persistent individual might lie at home, shoplift, and cheat in exams at school as a youngster, but fight in pubs and steal from their employers as an adult. This can be described as *heterotypic continuity* which means merely that there is a continuity of antisocial behaviour but that this may take various forms in different settings and at different life-stages. Behaviours such as theft, alcohol abuse, promiscuous sex, irresponsible driving and violence, substance abuse, debt problems, homelessness, employment issues, spousal battery, abuse and neglect of children, multiple unstable relationships and so forth are listed by Moffitt as being characteristic of individuals whose antisocial behaviour/criminality extends past their mid-twenties.

The antisocial behaviour of life-course-persistent individuals often manifests itself in infancy. This implies that the origins of their antisocial behaviour must lie in things which happen before birth or shortly afterwards. Moffatt believes that factors which cause neuropsychological functioning problems are involved. Neuropsychological is a concept which describes the ways in which anatomical and physical processes of the nervous system affect psychological aspects of the individual such as their level of activity, speech, attention, learning, language, coordination, self-regulation and memory. Among the things which can affect neural development are maternal drug abuse and inadequate nutrition before the child's birth, brain injury at birth, exposure to toxic substances, and genetic inheritance. Moffitt states that research overwhelmingly finds a link between neuropsychological impairment and antisocial behaviour and some of the evidence for this was discussed earlier in this chapter. Neuropsychological deficits may not be recognised because they occur at subclinical levels even though they affect the child developmentally. These impairments may be in the form of temper tantrums, poor school performance, or overactivity, for example. Neuropsychological deficits associated with antisocial behaviour involve 1) verbal and 2) executive functions. The verbal problems include poor problem solving, memory, and expressive speech/writing. The executive function deficits include inattention and impulsivity. Moffitt states that persistently and extremely impaired levels of verbal and executive function are related to antisocial behaviour. This does not mean that such children show particularly low IQs as the effects of neuropsychological deficit may be quite subtle. Environmental factors play their part in the expression of neuropsychological deficits. Given the causes of these deficits such as parental drug abuse, it is not surprising that Moffitt suggests that many of these children will be born into families which do not supply the kinds of support which might reduce the effects of the neuropsychological problem. Moffitt argues that a child's vulnerabilities may be compounded with their family's imperfections. Thus a family where prenatal care is poor, the infant's nutritional needs ignored, and substances abused in pregnancy may be circumstances where a neuropsychological problem may be present alongside a criminogenic environment. The problematic behaviour of the child may, in its turn, affect the behaviour of its parents such as the manner and nature of discipline. A child who is persistently difficult to rear may, eventually, cause its parents to abandon attempts to discipline. There may be a process of antisocial continuity where the antisocial child attracts peers who are also antisocial or, as adults, partners who are similarly antisocial. Generally speaking, life-course-persistent individuals are not popular with their peers.

Life-course-persistent individuals are just a small percentage of offenders. The adolescence-limited antisocial behaviour group is far more common and includes the vast majority of adolescents. This is the group which creates the bulge in criminal statistics at about the age of adolescence. They may have gaps when they do not offend and they are not antisocial in all situations. Such a youngster may, for example, diligently follow school rules yet shoplift. They may involve themselves in antisocial behaviour when they see it as profitable but adopt prosocial styles of behaviour when that appears to be profitable. Moffitt sees the beginnings of their antisocial life style in social mimicry of the antisocial lifestyle of the life-course persistent offender. Mimicry is the way in which the individual can learn from the successful individual. Why would the adolescent choose to imitate such individuals? Adolescence-limited antisocial behaviour is a consequence of the gap between biological maturity (as signalled by adolescence) and social maturity, according to Moffitt. Historically speaking, a youngster's biological maturity came later than nowadays and adult status arrived at an earlier age. Modern youngsters enter the labour market, for example, at a much later age than their forebears. Social changes leave modern teenagers with a five or ten year gap between becoming biologically mature and being treated as an adult. This is seen in age restrictions on being allowed to drive, marry, vote, buy alcohol, leave school and so forth. Modern young people are able only infrequently to make important decisions and they remain generally dependent on their parents to substantially older age than in the past. Yet they want to do the things that adults do such as to form intimate relationships, make their own choices about things, and accumulate material possessions. They also wish to be regarded as consequential by adults, Moffitt argues, and not as just kids. Awareness of this maturity gap comes about the same time as youngsters move to a secondary or high school dominated by older youngsters who have developed ways of dealing with this self-same maturity gap.

According to Moffitt, healthy adolescents can see that some of their peers seem to be able to avoid the problem of the maturity. These peers are not so controlled by their parents and very much go their own way doing what they want and deciding what rules they wish to live by. These peers are largely members of Moffitt's life-course-persistent category. They can take risks and do dangerous things which most parents would disapprove and they are skilled at deviant behaviour which means that they can get material goods through stealing or being involved in vice. So they can have pseudo-adult things such as cars, fashion, and drugs which the typical teenager without an income cannot afford. Furthermore, they are sexually experienced and may have children despite their youthfulness. They impact on the adult world and may have their own social worker, probation officer, or lawyer. Moffitt suggests that from the perspective of the adolescent culture, the 'antisocial precocity' of the life-course-persistent group is seen as a 'coveted social asset'. So during adolescence, the life-course-persistent delinquent moves from the periphery of the adolescent social structure to a position of some influence. That is, their style is admired and emulated by youngsters at the stage. Prior to adolescence they are either simply ignored or even rejected by their peers because of the erratic and aggressive behaviour which they display. After adolescence they often seem to lack the capacity for loyalty or friendship. This does not mean that they are befriended by other youngsters during adolescence in order to be emulated. Social mimicry, Moffitt suggests, does not require affectionate bonds to occur. It is the style of the life-course-persistent offender that is influential – this is not mediated by friendship bonds. The life-course-persistent offenders are at the core of a somewhat unstable delinquent network. In this context they exploit their peers by using them as fences, sexual partners, lookouts or drug customers. It is not necessary, though, for the life-course-persistent offender to be even aware of their peers who are influenced by them. Adolescence-limited delinquents can use antisocial behaviour as a way of showing that they are independent and independent of their parents. According to Moffitt, the negative consequences of delinquency act as reinforcers by provoking a response from people in authority and by providing ways of looking more adult such as by smoking or being tattooed. 'I suggest that every curfew violated, car stolen, drug taken, and baby conceived is a statement of personal independence and thus a reinforcer for delinquent involvement' claims Moffitt (1993, p. 688–689)

Although Moffitt's theory concentrates primarily on two groups of adolescents, there is obviously a third group which we have not mentioned yet – the small number of adolescents who abstain from all delinquency including drugs. The percentage of such youngsters may be as low as 10 per cent (Boutwell and Beaver, 2008). Moffitt in her theory suggests that they are isolates who do not get involved with their peer group or, for some reason, do not want to or have the opportunity to engage in adult-like behaviours such as smoking cigarettes or drinking. Possible reasons for their abstinence are described by Moffitt as: 1) structural barriers such as close parental supervision which restricts opportunities to interact with delinquent peers; 2) they may not experience the maturity gap because they are given responsibilities which makes them feel like adults; and 3) they may have negative personal characteristics such as being socially inept, overly self-controlled, timid, morose or fearful. Characteristics like these may ensure that the individual is excluded from adolescent culture. Owens and Slocum (2015) studied American teenagers who abstained from a range of delinquent acts up to the age of eighteen and then abstained from criminal acts into adulthood. Very few abstainers in childhood became offenders in adulthood. Abstainers were much more likely to have received high school honours and to be a virgin at the age of 18 years. Abstainers tended to have prosocial peers and tended not to have antisocial peers. Those who abstained from delinquency in their teenage years were more likely to have high levels of undesirable personal characteristics such as being very compliant, very fearful, very apprehensive, very shy and withdrawn, very flat emotionally with unchanging facial expressions, and poor verbal communication. However, it was rare for the abstainers to claim to have no or few friends when they reached adulthood and they generally seemed more successful as adults than those who were not abstainers.

Moffitt's theory has been highly influential (Beaver, DeLisi, Vaughn and Wright, 2010), nevertheless there have been studies critical of aspects of it. For example, Rulison, Kreager and Osgood (2014) tested the idea that life-course-persistent offenders become more accepted by their peers during adolescence when they provide models for antisocial behaviour as well as whether delinquency abstainers become less accepted as friends. They studied friendship networks in a very large sample of adolescents approximately 12 to 15 years of age. Participants provided nominations of friendships among their peers. This information was turned into the number of nominations each participant received as a friend, attractiveness as a friend, and centrality in the peer network. The evidence suggested that life-course-persistent offenders did not achieve greater acceptance between early and middle adolescence. The persistently delinquent individuals showed the cognitive deficits such as lower academic grades, hyperactivity in the form of sensation seeking, and family risk factors predicted by Moffitt's theory. They were the most likely to live in a lone parent household. Friendship choices and centrality in the peer network data did not support Moffitt's theory well. There was better support for the theory from the measure of attractiveness as a friend which suggested that life-course-persistent offenders became more attractive as a friend during adolescence. Delinquency abstainers, however, were less accepted in early adolescence but became more accepted with time which is not in line with Moffitt's theory. Abstainers lived more often in two-parent families, had the strongest family relationships with low harsh or inconsistent discipline, and were low on sensation seeking. Other research on abstainers has tended to suggest that they do have friends who they spend considerable amounts of time with (Brezina and Piquero, 2007, Chen and Adams, 2010) so they are not the isolates that the theory suggests. There is a problem with Beaver *et al.*'s study, since Moffitt did not assume that friendship was the process by which the life-course-persistent adolescent achieved influence on the adolescence-limited group.

Specific explanations of antisocial behaviour in childhood

A number of research areas relevant to the development of criminality in childhood which are substantial have developed in their own right. These warrant some discussion in this chapter.

Moral reasoning development and moral disengagement

It is easy to assume that young offenders have deficits in terms of their moral reasoning. Kerby and Rae (1998), to the contrary, show that moral reasoning is subtly articulated by young offenders especially when the issue of their own personal moral identity as a good or bad person is under consideration. It is well-known that the nature of moral reasoning changes and develops during childhood as exemplified in Kohlberg's theory of moral reasoning (Kohlberg, 1963, 1984) which extends Piaget's theory of cognitive stages in thinking (Piaget, 1970). The basics of Kohlberg's theory are to be found in Figure 6.2. According to Kohlberg, moral reasoning develops in six relatively discrete stages grouped into three levels – the pre-conventional, the conventional and the post-conventional – which the child goes through in order. The difference between the stages lies in the reasons for a particular moral decision not in the nature of that decision. Delinquents tend to reason at an earlier level than non-delinquents do at a given age (Blasi, 1980; Gibbs, 2003; Palmer, 2003). Nelson, Smith and Dodd (1990) carried out a meta-analysis (see Box 4.2) involving as many as 50 separate studies have shown a delay in moral reasoning development in delinquents compared to non-delinquent youngsters (Nelson, Smith and Dodd, 1990; Stams, Brugman, Dekowic, van Rosmalen, van der Laan and Gibbs, 2006).. Youngsters with less developed moral reasoning were more likely to commit crimes. This relationship was particularly strong for male offender groups, late adolescents, incarcerated, and lower-intelligence delinquents. The relationships held even where socio-economic status, gender, age etc. were controlled. Stams *et al.* suggest

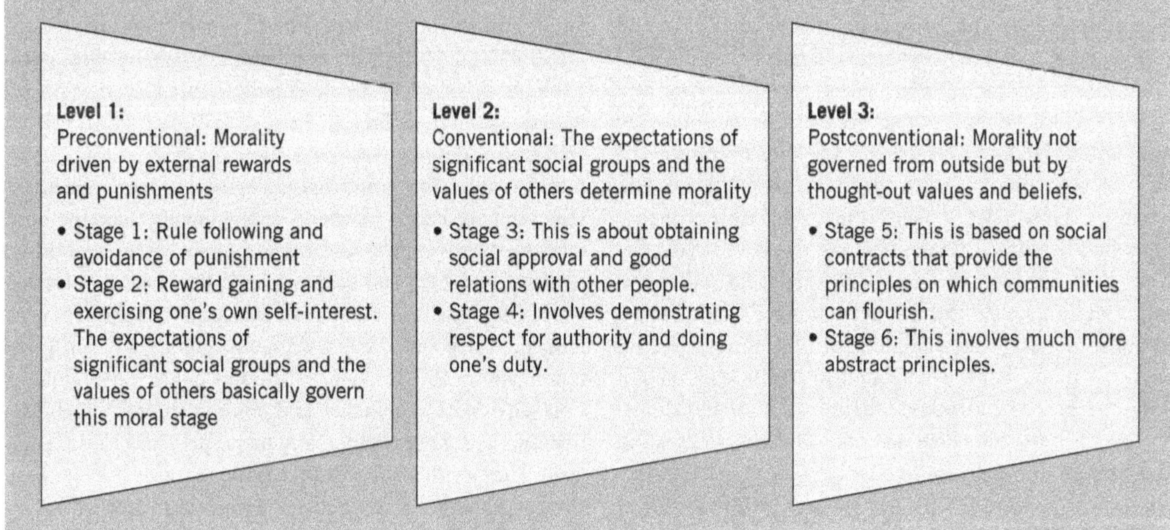

Level 1:
Preconventional: Morality driven by external rewards and punishments
• Stage 1: Rule following and avoidance of punishment
• Stage 2: Reward gaining and exercising one's own self-interest. The expectations of significant social groups and the values of others basically govern this moral stage
Level 2:
Conventional: The expectations of significant social groups and the values of others determine morality
• Stage 3: This is about obtaining social approval and good relations with other people.
• Stage 4: Involves demonstrating respect for authority and doing one's duty.
Level 3:
Postconventional: Morality not governed from outside but by thought-out values and beliefs.
• Stage 5: This is based on social contracts that provide the principles on which communities can flourish.
• Stage 6: This involves much more abstract principles.

Figure 6.2 Kohlberg's Model of Moral Development

that the superficiality and self-centredness associated with lower levels of moral development may become criminogenic in late adolescence.

There are a number of difficulties with Kohlberg's theory applied to delinquency. Famously, Gilligan (1982) argued that the theory is gender biased in that female characteristics in moral reasoning are attributed to a lower stage of moral development. Level 3 reasoning seems to be more female in nature. Nevertheless, there is evidence to suggest showed that when age and verbal IQ were controlled for or equated, girls, whether or not delinquent, tend to be at a morally more advanced stage than boys (Gregg, Gibbs and Basinger, 1994). There is an argument in the child development research literature that children actually have far more developed moral thinking than the theory seems to allow (Tisak, 1995). That is to say, even three-year-old children can distinguish between moral behaviour and mere conventions which we follow. Furthermore, the development of moral judgement is not the same irrespective of the domain or matter in question (Turiel, 1983; Turiel and Nucci, 1978). All this suggests that the developmental stages approach may have fundamental problems.

Moral reasoning development differences between delinquents and non-delinquents are greatest for issues that are especially relevant to criminal behaviour. Palmer and Hollin (1998) surveyed convicted offenders between 13 and 21 years of age and a comparison group of non-offenders in the UK. The offenders were typically at Kohlberg's pre-conventional level of moral development whereas the non-offenders were at the conventional reasoning level. The scale to measure moral reasoning development included questions tapping five distinct norms: contract and truth; affiliation; life; property and law; and legal-justice. For each of these areas, male delinquents were at a lower stage of moral development than other males. Interestingly, non-offending boys tended to be at a lower stage of moral reasoning development than the non-offender females. Delinquent males tended to score at a lower level of development than controls for the following moral issues: helping your parents; keeping a promise to a child; keeping a promise to a friend; keeping a promise to a stranger; lying even if you do not want to; not taking things that belong to others; obeying the law; saving the life of a friend; sending criminals to jail; and telling the truth. Only on saving the life of a stranger was there no difference between the offenders and the non-offenders. When the moral issue was related to crime, such as not taking the property of others, there was a greater difference between the offenders and non-offenders suggesting poorer moral development in offenders.

Is it possible to link different types of crime to differences in moral reasoning development? According to Chen and Howitt (2007), moral reasoning development has a fairly limited power to differentiate between offenders committing very different types of crime. Moral reasoning development is commonly assessed using the Socio-moral Reflection Measure (Gibbs, Basinger and Fuller, 1992). However, this measure is actually a composite based on several different moral values, including contract, affiliation, life, property and law, and legal-justice, which derive from Kohlberg's ideas. Researchers have questioned whether these different aspects of moral reasoning development mature at the same rate. For example, Brugman and Aleva (2004) found that young offenders tended to show relatively slower moral reasoning development for the value 'obeying the law'. Assuming that moral reasoning development is partly the consequence of the internalisation of actions (as Piaget accepted in his theory) rather than being the externalisation of cognitions, then such differential development in different areas of moral values is possible. In other words, the different experiences of different types of delinquent may produce differential moral value development.

Chen and Howitt (2007) studied Taiwanese young offenders divided into drug, violent and theft types to see whether the offence type was related to different levels of the development of the different moral values. The research findings provided only limited support for this. Only the moral value 'life' helped differentiated members of the different offence-type groups. This moral value was relatively poorly developed in violent offenders compared with the theft and drug offenders. Using this moral value 'life' together with age was capable of differentiating among drug, violent and theft offenders with an overall accuracy of about 60 per cent. So what is the moral value 'life'? Well, it is measured by the question 'How important is it for a person to live even if that person doesn't want to?' That people who act violently have less well-developed moral reasoning in relation to this seems understandable, although why drug offenders do not share this is less clear.

Studies of this sort compare delinquent and non-delinquents using arrest or conviction as the criterion of delinquency. In contrast, Tarry and Emler (2007) used self-report delinquency measures in their study. They found that self-reported delinquency was not related to structural measures of moral reasoning level of the sort discussed above after controls for demographic and other relevant variables had been applied. This leaves open the possibility that the means of measuring delinquency is crucial. Tarry and Emler argue strongly for their self-report approach. Brusten, Stams and Gibbs (2007) question self-report approaches and point to studies which say that they are more problematic than Tarry and Emler suggest. They criticise Tarry and Emler's study for using a sample which was too young to demonstrate moral reasoning development influences which they say only emerge later in adolescence, according to research.

The moral development stage of an offender is related to offending but another strand of research, moral disengagement, may tell us more about moral thinking and offending. Moral disengagement involves a number of psychological processes which lead to the nullification of one's internal self-sanctions against doing wrong. This allows antisocial and criminal behaviours harmful to other people to be employed in order to achieve a desired outcome without negative emotion such as guilt. In other words, it makes a wrong seem right. Moral disengagement may be applied to: 1) the act in question; 2) the consequences of the act; and 3) the victim of the act as well as responsibility for the harm caused by the act. Niebieszczanski, Harkins, Judson, Smith and Dixon (2015) studied an incarcerated sample of offenders and found that those who had been involved in street gangs were more likely to use moral disengagement to 'turn off' their moral standards when offending. The theory underlying moral disengagement starts from research demonstrating that offenders proffer a wide range of justifications or excuses for their criminal actions. Some of these are referred to as cognitive distortions or neutralisations. They allow the offender to commit the crime while letting them retain self-esteem and a positive self-regard without feeling ashamed or socially stigmatised. A more general account of this sort of strategies is the theory of moral disengagement (Bandura, 1991; Bandura, Barbaranelli, Caprara and Pastorelli, 2001). People have internal moral standards which are the result of socialisation processes involving the observation of other people and more direct teaching by parents, family and so forth. These internal moral standards form part of our self-regulatory behaviour in that they guide us in our actions and deter us from doing unacceptable things. If we transgress, these internal moral standards cause us to self-sanction resulting in, for example, feelings of guilt or shame. Of course, we might also be criticised or worse by other people or there might be some other negative outcome such as arrest.

According to Bandura, there are eight mechanism which can be invoked in moral disengagement. These are listed next together with an item from Bandura *et al.*'s (1996) self-report scale of proneness to moral disengagement in a variety of contexts (Fontaine, Fida, Paciello, Tisak and Caprara, 2014; Niebieszczanski, Harkins, Judson, Smith and Dixon, 2015): 1) Moral justification: an action is presented as having a moral or socially worthy purpose ('It is alright to fly off the handle to protect your friends.'); 2) Advantageous comparisons: an act is compared to worse transgressions ('Damaging some property is no big deal when you consider that others are beating people up.'); 3) Euphemistic language: an act is sanitised so that it appears not to transgress moral standards ('Slapping and shoving someone is just a way of joking.'); 4) Diffusion of responsibility: an act is carried out by several people making the individual appear unaccountable for their actions ('If youth are living under bad conditions in their neighborhood they cannot be blamed for behaving aggressively.'); 5) Displacement of responsibility: attributing responsibility to a perceived authority figure ('A member of a group should not be blamed for trouble the group causes.'); 6) Distorting consequences: changing or ignoring the consequences of an act so that the harm is overlooked or minimalized ('Teasing someone does not really hurt him/her.'); 7) Dehumanising the victim: this makes the act against the victim seem acceptable since no sympathy or empathy is necessary ('Some people deserve to be treated like animals.'); and 8) Blaming the victim: again the act is made more acceptable by holding the victim responsible ('People who get mistreated usually do things that deserve it.'). The deactivation of internal moral standards takes place over a period of time but leaves the individual's internal moral standards to remain intact while, nevertheless, taking part in an act which otherwise would result in self-sanctions.

Moral disengagement strategies have been shown to be associated with a variety of antisocial behaviour such as bullying (e.g. Pornari and Wood, 2010), serious offending (e.g. Schulman, Cauffman, Piquero and Fagan, 2011), drug use (e.g. Passini, 2012) and violence and aggression (e.g. Barnes, Welte, Hoffman, and Dintcheff, 2005).

Cycles of abuse

Cycles of abuse and cycles of violence, in particular, have been part of the thinking of researchers and practitioners in child care for half a century. The violence-breeds-violence hypothesis originated in the work of Curtis (1963) who believed that violent social environments create violent youngsters and adults. The range of factors which appear to be involved in the development of aggressiveness is also well-known (Haapasalo and Tremblay, 1994) and can be seen in Figure 6.3. This shows that the task of trying to develop integrated approaches to the development of aggressiveness is complex. It is abundantly clear that there is a relationship between being a victim of violence and being a perpetrator at a later stage. There are several meanings of the term 'cycle of violence' or 'cycle of abuse':

- The effects of early experience on later behaviour. Put simply, does the child who is subjected to physical abuse grow up to be a violent teenager and adult?
- The child who is physically abused by its parents grows up to be a parent who abuses their own children.
- Sometimes the phrase is used to refer to the process by which women physically abused domestically by their partners are persuaded back by the man with promises of

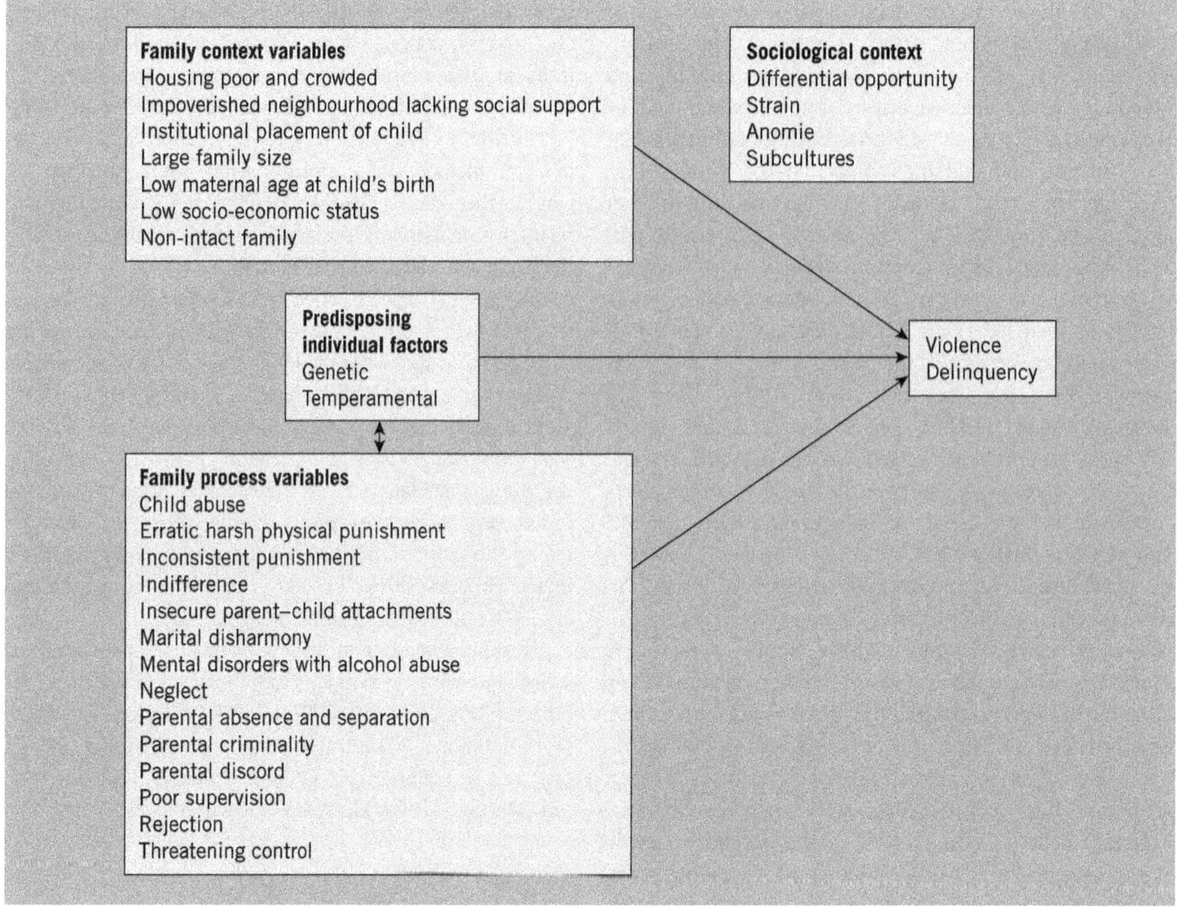

Figure 6.3 Widely established psychological model of aggression according to Haapasalo and Tremblay (1994)

love and that the episode will not be repeated. Events then build up to another episode of violence and another 'reconciliation'. While these violent acts are frequently severe and warrant criminal prosecution, this is a meaning of cycle of abuse which is not intended in the context of this chapter on the childhood development of crime.

There are a number of methodological issues involved in assessing cycles of violence:

- Abuse is usually not directly observed in research. This means that there may be difficulties in interpreting the data obtained retrospectively in interview. For example, abusive parents may be asked they themselves were physically abused as children which may encourage self-justificatory replies: that is, 'My excuse for abusing my child is that my parents did it to me.'
- The retrospective character of much research means that memory issues may affect recollections.
- Definitions of physical abuse vary from study to study. This means that knowing what sorts of and what degrees of violence lead to the abusive cycle.
- Child abuse is associated with a wide range of other family characteristics that are also harmful to children. Consequently, teasing out what factors are responsible for the cycle of abuse may be very difficult.

Cycles of abuse involve processes that, generally, are somewhat unclear or speculative. Figure 6.4 brings to our attention the contrast between generalised effects of abuse and specific isomorphic ones. While violence may lead to violence, some researchers believe that the effects of violence are more generally pathogenic than that. Figure 6.5 describes something of the range of possible models of cycles of abuse.

Bullying and bullying victimisation

Research has established that school bullying is associated with many antisocial outcomes in the long term (Bender and Lösel, 2011). It is a good predictor of later delinquency, violence and aggression. This is particularly the

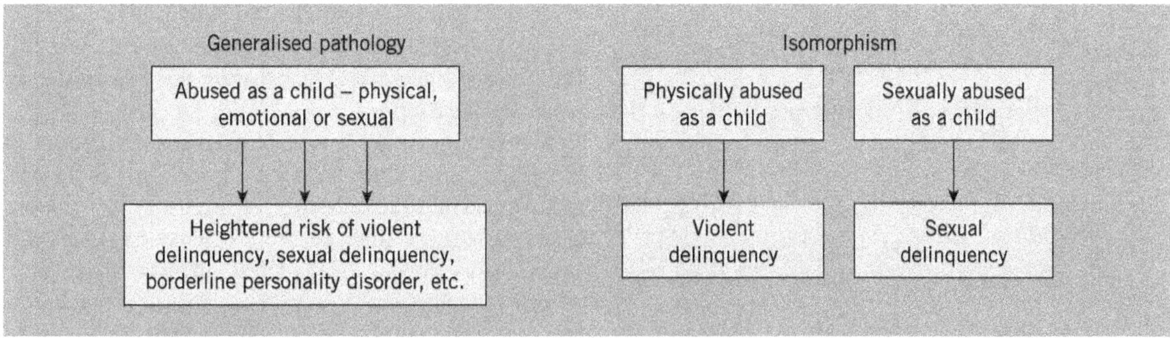

Figure 6.4 Isomorphism versus generalised pathology as a consequence of abuse

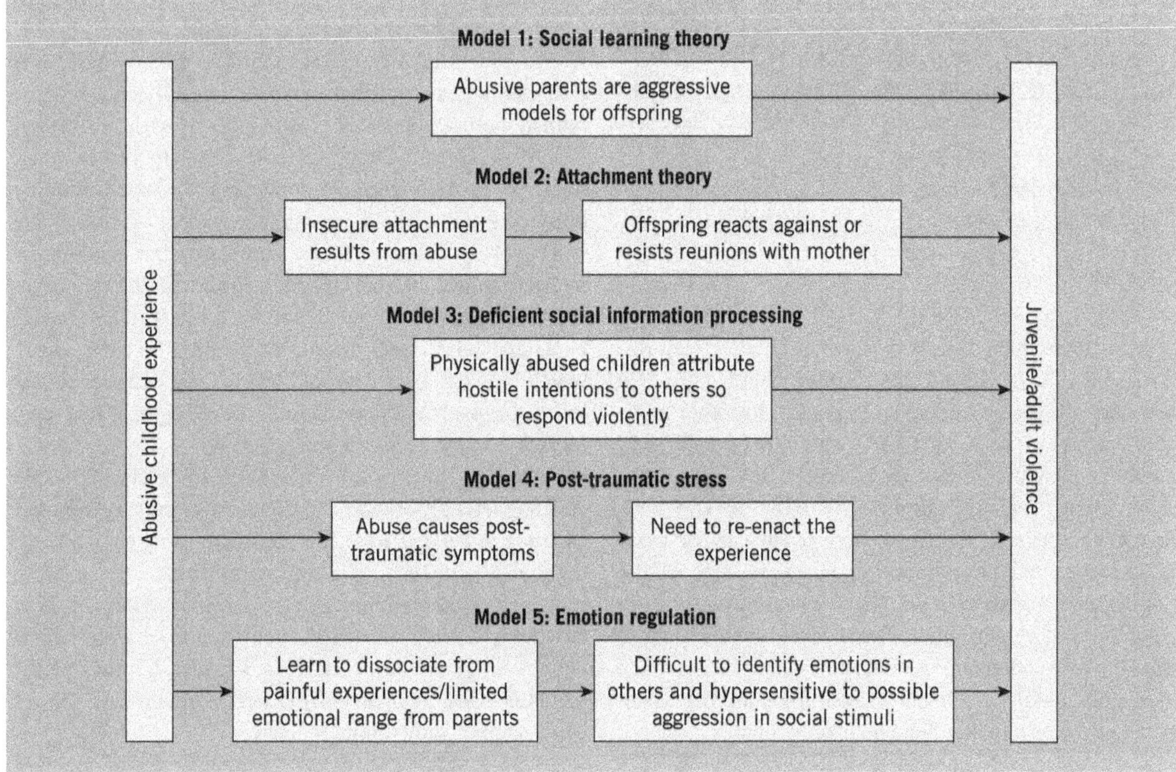

Figure 6.5 Psychological models of the cycle of violence

case for physical bullying but also for verbal/indirect bullying. Serious bullies are at a high risk of developing long-term antisocial problems. It is easy to understand the relationship between bullying and violent delinquency, but just why do bullies often engage in non-violent delinquency too? One suggestion is that anger mediates between bullying and non-violent delinquency. Sigfusdottir, Gudjonsson and Sigurdsson (2010) carried out a study of over 7000 adolescents in Iceland of between 15 and 16 years of age. Various measures were employed:

- Bullying was measured by questions such as whether, in the last year, they had been involved in a group starting a fight with another group or hurting an individual.
- In order to measure the experience of being a bullying victim, the participants were asked whether, in the last year, they had been attacked and hurt or teased by a group of people when they were alone.
- Delinquency was measured in terms of the individual reporting that they had stolen things, etc.
- Anger was measured by the question whether they wanted to break or damage things.

The relationships between the first three variables above (excluding anger) were analysed, using the complex statistical technique known as structural equation modelling (see Howitt and Cramer, 2017 for a discussion). Structural

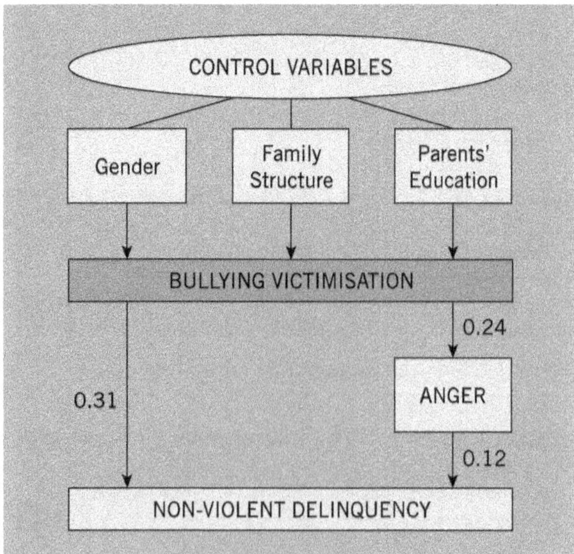

Figure 6.6 How anger partially mediates between being a victim of bullying and non-violent delinquency (based on the work of Sigfusdottir, Gudjonsson and Sigurdsson (2010))

equation modelling attempts to develop 'models' describing the best-fitting account of the interrelationships. The procedure allows the researcher to control for other influential variables, such as family structure, gender and parental education in this case. Figure 6.6 shows the model linking being victimised by bullying and non-violent delinquency. The arrows indicate the paths between the variables and the numbers indicate the size of the relationship. As can be seen, the pathway through anger shows modest relationships but it is clear that a more direct pathway between victimisation and delinquency which does not involve anger is also important. The model for the effect of bullying behaviour on delinquency is not given here, but is very similar. So bullying is a factor in non-violent delinquency for both bullies and their victims. But it is also clear that at least part of this relationship is mediated by anger.

Sigfusdottir, Gudjonsson and Sigurdsson (2010) discuss their findings in terms of Agnew's social-psychological revised general strain theory (see Chapter 5). This theory acknowledges the important role of emotions. Agnew's strain theory argues that adolescents who experience adverse circumstances are pushed towards delinquency because of the negative emotional reactions these experiences produce. The list of negative emotions includes anger, which was the focus of Sigfusdottir *et al.*'s study. According to Agnew (1992), strain arises in relationships where an individual is not treated in the way they would like to be treated (see Figure 6.7). The underlying idea is that people treated badly behave badly. Bullying and being bullied are both part of the delinquent lifestyle, so youngsters experiencing these are more likely to express their negative emotions through delinquency. Victimisation by bullying is an example of Agnew's concept of *strain*. That is, it is likely to cause distress and frustration plus it has a negative impact on mental health. Although the same cannot be said of the bullies themselves, it has to be remembered that bullies tend to come from a stressful background, which amounts to a form of strain. They experience low levels of parental warmth and the discipline that they receive tends to be harsh and physical.

Given this, it is worth mentioning the work of Karnik and Steiner (2007) who argued that psychology's understanding of the developmental originals of juvenile offending behaviour has advanced significantly. However, it remains the case that much more needs to be known about how interventions may be best targeted in order to reduce delinquent behaviour. They, too, suggest that therapeutic methods need to take much more seriously the role of aggression of in juvenile offending.

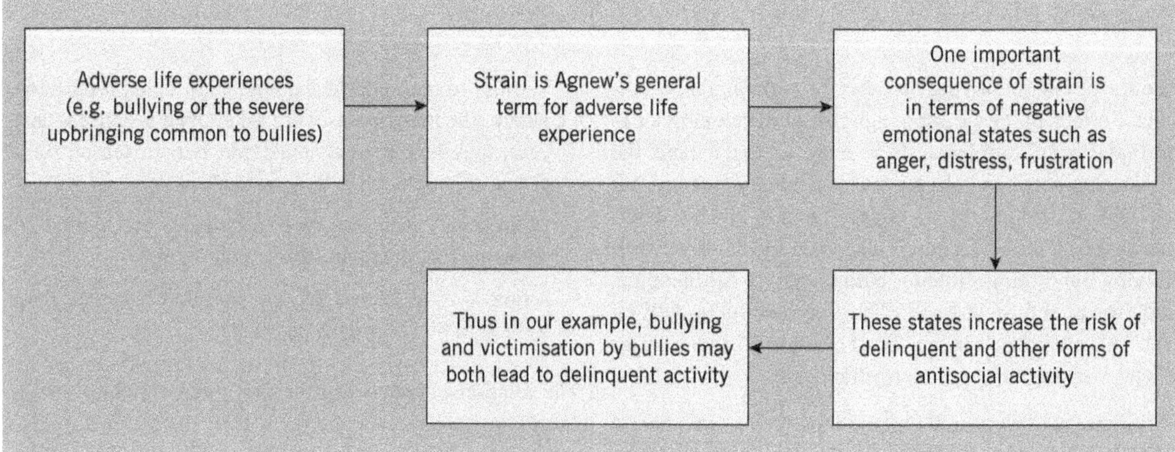

Figure 6.7 Theory summary: Agnew's Strain Theory applied to bullying and its victims

How childhood risk factors such as school bullying lead to adolescent and adult problems is not yet clear. For example, there is an attractive simplicity in the idea that bullying in childhood leads to violent crime in adulthood, which makes sense in terms of an individual's disposition to aggression. This implies that there should be a closer relationship between childhood bullying and adult aggression than between, say, childhood theft and adult aggression. Perhaps a more sophisticated view is the alternative idea that antisocial behaviours in childhood and adulthood are the result of the common risk factors influencing antisocial behaviour. In other words, the individual brought up in a deprived environment is exposed to a multitude of risk factors which result in childhood antisocial characteristics. Often they will continue to be exposed to the same risk factors in adulthood and so exhibit adult antisocial behaviour patterns too. If this version is true, we should not simply expect, say, the child who bullies to grow up to become a violent offender – they are likely to commit non-violent crimes, attempt suicide, and so forth.

In the light of this, research by Ttofi, Farrington and Lösel (2012) is important. They carried out a systematic review and meta-analysis of the relationship between school bullying (both perpetration and victimisation by bullies) on later aggression and violence. Furthermore, they wished to know whether or not the relationship obtained remained after controlling for major childhood risk factors. They studied bullying and victimisation because they argue that, generally, perpetrators of violence tend also to be victims of it. Fifteen studies were found in the research literature investigating the relationship between bullying in childhood and violence in later life. Initially in the analysis it was found that there was indeed a substantial relationship between bullying perpetration and aggression/violence in later life. However, when the influence of the risk factors for violence was controlled, the relationship was reduced, though it still remained fairly strong. In the example they give, the risk of being a violent adult increased by two-thirds if the child was a bully. Similarly, being a victim of violence also increased the likelihood of adult violence but the level of risk increased by about a third if the child was a victim of violence. Ttofi, Farrington and Lösel were inclined to conclude that these findings were not the result of a specific violent tendency but more likely the product of a more general antisocial tendency, much as we discussed earlier. This is because the relationships found in this study were on a par with the size of relationships found, for example, between bullying and adult crime in general in other studies. This is difficult to explain without reference to a common cause relationship. Specific violence, theft, suicide and other separate antisocial behaviour propensities cannot account for this. In other words, school bullying and other externalising behaviours are merely age- and context-related manifestations of a more general antisocial tendency.

BOX 6.2 Controversy

Do predictors predict participation in crime or frequency of participation?

Sometimes researchers overlook what, in retrospect, seem important questions about crime. For example, Ramoutar and Farrington (2006) became interested in whether factors associated with participating in criminal behaviour are the same factors as those associated with the frequency with which the offender participates in crime. Most theories of crime seek to explain why some people become delinquent or criminal, and scant attention is paid to the frequency with which they carry out criminal acts. Gottfredson and Hirschi (1986) promoted the view that different features of a person's criminal career, such as frequency, participation, onset and desisting from crime, are part and parcel of a single propensity to be criminal and that they need not be differentiated. Clearly this is an assumption which has to be tested.

Ramoutar and Farrington systematically looked at factors associated with (a) participating in crime and (b) frequency of participation in serious violence and property crimes. They took several broad categories of explanation which might be associated with crime. These were (a) Bandura's social learning theory and (b) personality theory dimensions such as those proposed by Eysenck (both of these are discussed in Chapter 5) together with (c) labelling theory. This suggests that the adverse reaction of the criminal justice system and other people to an individual's crimes leads to them becoming defined as deviant. This can lock the individual into further involvement in crime. Ramoutar and Farrington developed a total of 24 explanatory variables based on these three different categories of explanation. Data were collected from male and female

BOX 6.2 (continued)

prisoners in Trinidad. As far as participating in violent crimes was concerned, there were 19 significant relationships for the male sample and 16 significant relationships for the female sample. In terms of participating in property crimes, there was a total of 12 significant relationships for the male sample, for example. However, what was the case for participating in these crimes was not the case for the frequency of participation measures. For violent crime, only seven significant relationships were found for male offenders and only three significant relationships for female offenders. For property crime, there was only one significant relationship between frequency and any of the 24 explanatory variables. In other words, variables that are associated with participation in a type of crime may not be associated with frequency of carrying out that criminal activity.

The conclusion, for the time being at least, is inescapable that important theories of crime may only explain participation in crime rather than the frequency of participation in crime. So there is a case for suggesting that important theories of crime such as social learning and personality explanations need to be re-examined in order to improve their ability to explain frequency of involvement in crime.

Social interventions to reduce delinquency

Given what we have learned about the origins of teenage delinquency and adult criminality in early childhood disadvantage, is it possible to intervene to stop this happening? Initiatives to prevent future delinquency should begin in the first few years of childhood and it is a mistake to wait until the child has become delinquent before intervening (Yoshikawa, 1995). The question is what works? Yoshikawa reviewed forty evaluation studies of early childhood intervention programmes which met his criteria:

- The children should be from groups most at risk of future delinquency/antisocial behaviour. Low birth weight and living in low-income families would be among the criteria for this.
- The intervention took place somewhere between the prenatal stage (i.e. prior to birth) and going to primary school.
- The evaluation study of the intervention programme included juvenile delinquency or, failing that, risk factors for future long-term delinquency among its outcome measures.

The interventions studied were either educational programmes, parent-focused family support programmes, or a mixture of the two. The educational programmes provided children with part-time kindergarten or a pre-school of some sort. There was consistent evidence that children receiving the educational intervention were cognitively (intellectually) more advanced than those who did not. However, the evaluation studies did not consistently demonstrate improvements in terms of antisocial/delinquent behaviour. *Parent-focused family support programmes* involved things such as regular home visits from a professional in childcare. The results of these studies seem a little more varied and show mixed success. Some found improvements in the intellectual functioning of children whose parent receives the intervention but others show little difference. Parenting skills also showed mixed outcomes. There were few if any improvements in terms of antisocial/delinquent behaviour. *Combined family support and early education programmes* showed the most promising outcomes of all. Cognitive abilities of the children and parenting abilities were improved. Most significantly in this context, antisocial behaviour (aggressive and delinquent behaviour in the long term) was reduced by this mixed intervention.

This sort of intervention is costly but less so than the delinquency they prevent. The cost of the programmes was less than the cost of dealing with delinquent children in the criminal justice system. Welsh *et al.* (2008) estimated the economic costs of the self-reported crimes of a cohort of young males in the 7–17 year range in the metropolitan areas of Pittsburgh, USA. The self-reported crimes of these boys were dominated by assaults (69 per cent) followed by larcenies (25 per cent). Virtually no sexual crimes were reported. The estimated cost of this delinquency ranged from about $90 to $110 million. This was for 500 boys!

Turning to youngsters who are currently at high risk of offending in the near future or who have already begun their delinquency, evaluation studies of intervention programmes for them are not uncommon (Nee and Ellis, 2005). One difficulty, of course, is the long time-scale involved if the outcome measure is delinquent offending itself. So, instead, in their evaluation study Nee and Ellis used scores on a powerful risk and needs assessment tool as the outcome measure. They used Andrews and Bonta's (1995) Level of Service Inventory – Revised or the LSI-R.

This measures many of the risk factors known to be associated with offending and also indicates the level of help/intervention required for a particular offender to reduce their risk of reoffending. The support services which they require are known as their criminogenic needs. In short, the Level of Service Inventory forms a convenient indicator of the success of an intervention programme and it is assumed to be predictive of delinquent behaviour. Information about the number of police charges each youngster had was also available though it may be biased as a measure of delinquency because the police may choose not to criminalise the youngsters if at all possible. The programme (The Persistent Young Offender Project) included a range of practices:

- one-to-one mentoring in order to help the youngster reintegrate into the school;
- group work addressing life problem-solving, anger management, victim awareness, interpersonal skills, substance misuse, appropriate sexual behaviour and health;
- self-esteem and social skills building activities such as music, art and drama.

The youngsters on the project were overwhelmingly male and they had largely committed offences against property although a small number had committed sex offences. In some cases, they had referred themselves for help but more usually they had been referred by social workers, their parents and so forth. Compared with a control group, the number of police charges for members of the treatment group declined during their time on the programme. Furthermore, risk of offending as assessed by the LSI-R also declined in the treated group. This is evidence that interventions may be effective even on active delinquents.

There are many types of interventions seeking to reduce delinquency. For example, cognitive behavioural therapy, drug court, family therapy, victim–offender mediation and prison visitations among many others. An important question then is just what is it about a programme that makes it effective? To answer this question, Lipsey (2009) carried out a meta-analysis (see Box 4.2) of intervention programmes for young or juvenile offenders. As might be expected, a very large number of research reports of evaluation studies were included, giving a total of over 500 samples of young people with the age range of 12 to 21 years. Recidivism was an important outcome variable and was standardised across the different studies. The following were important factors associated with reducing recidivism:

- a therapeutic intervention philosophy – initiatives strongly based on the concept of discipline were generally much less effective at reducing recidivism;
- higher treatment effectiveness was found for high-risk offenders with two or more previous convictions, though violent or aggressive youngsters were not likely to benefit in this way;
- the quality of the intervention.

Different types of therapeutic intervention did not differ much in terms of their effectiveness and the size of the effect across all of the studies was small. This remained so when variables such as study design and the method of measuring recidivism were taken into account. While it was true that generally the different types of intervention differed little in their effectiveness, there were exceptions. Counselling-based treatments were relatively ineffective whereas behavioural and cognitive-behavioural interventions were somewhat more effective than the other forms of intervention. The effect sizes for some studies were negative, implying that treatment made recidivism worse, not better in those cases!

Matjasko, Vivolo-Kantor, Massetti, Holland, Holt and Cruze (2012) argue that violence among young people is a 'pervasive public health problem' leading to numerous injuries and deaths. Not surprisingly, many interventions to reduce violence have been implemented and a great deal of research has been carried out into their effectiveness. These vary in important ways – they can be community-based, school-based, family-based, or specific to a particular form of treatment. This research has resulted in several meta-analyses (see Box 4.2) attempting to collate the research findings. It is possible to carry out meta-analysis of meta-analyses! Matjasko *et al.* synthesised 25 years of meta-analytic and systematic reviews into the effectiveness of youth violence prevention programmes. Out of the ones found, 57 meta-analyses and systematic reviews met the researchers' criteria for inclusion. As the quality of research studies is known to be associated with apparent treatment outcomes, the researchers rated the quality of each of the studies using a standard instrument (AMSTAR – Assessment of Multiple Systematic Reviews). A rigorous study would use randomised controlled trials, experimental designs, or correlational/non-experimental evidence.

The reviews concentrated largely on family- and school-based programmes with the trend being towards school-based approaches which, typically, involved parenting training. A clear majority of the previous reviews had found a moderate programme effect. That is, broadly speaking, school-based programmes which dealt with family factors were slightly more effective than those which did not. Some of the previous meta-analyses, however, had found strong effects. These seemed to suggest that programmes which targeted particular selected populations tended to be the most effective. Similarly, the inclusion of cognitive-behavioural approaches was associated with more effective outcomes compared to just the behavioural component or neither. Experimental designs (randomised control trials), seen as being the more rigorous type of study, actually showed the largest effects among these violence reduction programmes. This makes the conclusions from Matjasko's study more convincing.

There is a fundamental risk with any intervention programme – that is, they inevitably bring together groups of individuals with problems. The risks are fairly evident if the programme involves youngsters showing criminal tendencies and other forms of antisocial behaviour. In other words, there may be a peer contagion effect. The technical medical term for a treatment which has negative consequences is an *iatrogenic effect*. So bringing together adolescents with the same sorts of problems may, quite simply, reinforce those problems. According to Cécile and Born (2009), there is considerable evidence in favour of the idea of an iatrogenic effect of treatment in such studies. Granting that this is the case, there are some fairly obvious ways of avoiding such iatrogenic effects in treatment programmes. For example, treating a delinquent youngster before their trial may be less damaging than treatment following conviction, which may risk greater iatrogenic effects simply because of the mix of offenders under-going treatment post-sentencing. To reduce problems due to delinquent peers, adults could be used as group leaders or contact with non-deviant peers/family arranged. Social interaction during the programme should be structured in order to minimise the opportunities for deviant behaviour among the youngsters involved.

Diversion from the criminal justice system

Worldwide, it is not unusual for young offenders to be imprisoned. Examples can be found of jurisdictions which process young offenders through the adult criminal justice system. However, the *United Nations Convention on the Rights of the Child* of 1989 provided for the special protection for children in the legal system. That is, persons under the age of 18 years should be separated from adult offenders. Most jurisdictions in Western countries employ what is termed a *modified justice model*. Typically, young offenders are processed through the formal judicial system, at the end of which they receive sanctions such as punitive prison terms or rehabilitation measures. The balance between punishment and rehabilitation varies between jurisdictions and even within a country. The findings of research on the imprisonment of young offenders clearly indicate that imprisoning young offenders has negative effects, especially when they are processed through adult facilities (Lambie and Randell, 2013). The incarceration of children fails to meet their developmental and criminogenic needs. Imprisoning young offenders is counterproductive because they risk mixing with 'expert' criminals, thus escalating their criminality, for example. Prison imposes limitations on the effective rehabilitation of young people. The most obvious negative outcomes include increased likelihood of future criminality and criminal justice system involvement. In terms of financial costs and social benefits, the imprisonment of young offenders is simply not effective. Punitive and disciplinarian regimes (as in the case of boot camps) are no different in this respect.

Young offenders, like any other youngsters, are undergoing important maturation processes, which prison distorts. Being in prison makes it much more difficult for the young offenders to 'age out'. Normally, young offenders become less likely to reoffend as they age through their adolescence (Mulvey, 2011). Prison takes away the prosocial aspect of their adolescent environment and replaces it with the negative consequences of immersion in the criminal justice system. Prison does not encourage prosocial behaviour but can make young offenders feel that they have lost their childhood. They may feel that they have to abandon any positive aspirations they had for their futures. Lambie and Randall (2013) stress the importance of keeping juveniles out of prison while providing effective rehabilitation appropriate to their age and criminogenic needs.

Youth diversion programmes have been available since the 1970s in the USA. They divert youngsters from the formal justice system into other resources for help and support. The underlying assumption is that the criminal justice system is in itself criminogenic for young people. Among the theories which might account for the success of diversion programmes are labelling theory (Becker, 1963) and differential association theory (Cressey, 1952). Thus diversion programmes avoid labelling by preventing the stigma of a conviction. Furthermore, they ensure that the youngster does not associate with more serious criminals. They provide a way of speedily taking youngsters out of the criminal justice system and its possible adverse effects. Diversion can be either pre-or post-charge:

- Pre-charge means that the police divert the youngster onto a youth diversion scheme quickly following arrest. This minimises contact with the police and avoids court processes, etc.
- Post-charge means more involvement with the police but then no further contact with the criminal justice system.

The programmes vary widely in content. Some are merely caution/warning programmes, after which there is no further contact. Other, more intensive, programmes impose conditions for participation, such as admission of guilt. So long as the youngster attends satisfactorily and fulfils any other requirements, they will face no further sanctions. Community service may be part of the programme but sometimes therapy may be involved. Do such programmes actually reduce recidivism? Wilson and Hoge (2013) used meta-analytic techniques (see Box 4.2) to review the relevant research evidence on this. They also explored the aspects of diversion programmes which make them more or less effective. Forty-five studies were identified as relevant to Wilson and Hoge's research questions. Being on a diversion programme resulted in decreased levels of reoffending. This broad conclusion applies to programmes involving therapeutic strategies as well as the diversion programmes involving only warning/cautions. The programmes accepting young offenders pre-charge were demonstrably more effective than those dealing with them post-charge. In other words, the further the youngster was processed into the criminal justice system, the more likely they were to reoffend.

Main points

- The study of juvenile offending is one of the most thoroughly researched areas of crime. A great deal is known about delinquency, its antecedents and consequences. Not surprisingly, various sorts of deficiencies in the functioning of families have been found to be associated with later delinquency. So deficiencies in parenting (e.g. abusive behaviour leading to cycles of abuse) are closely associated with delinquent and other forms of problematic behaviour in children. Nevertheless, it would be wrong to suggest that all delinquent children are the result of such family inadequacies. Delinquency is the result of many different influences, not all of which are directly to do with the family. Peer pressure to engage in delinquent activity is an obvious example.
- There is very good reason to believe that social interventions in early childhood intended to counteract some of the deficiencies of families known to be associated with delinquency can be very effective. Certain interventions with older children, maybe after they have become delinquent, can also be effective. Especially effective are those programmes which combine early childhood education with direct support for the parents of high-risk children.
- Despite knowing a great deal about the development of delinquent behaviour, there is a gulf between what we know about the risk factors for delinquency and the causes of delinquency. There is strong evidence that violence is transmitted generationally through cycles of abuse but we are less clear about how, say, moral development affects delinquent behaviour

Further reading

Loeber, R. and Farrington, D.P. (eds.) (2012) *From Juvenile Delinquency to Adult Crime: Criminal Careers, Justice Policy, and Prevention* Oxford: Oxford University Press.

Miller, M.K., Chamberlain, J. and Wingrove, T. (eds) (2014) *Psychology, Law and the Wellbeing of Children.* New York: Oxford University Press.

MacLeod, J.F., Grove, P. and Farrington, D. (2012) *Explaining Criminal Careers* (2012) is available free from Oxford University Press on open access and the link to the pdf is: http://fdslive.oup.com/www.oup.com/academic/pdf/openaccess/9780199697243.pdf

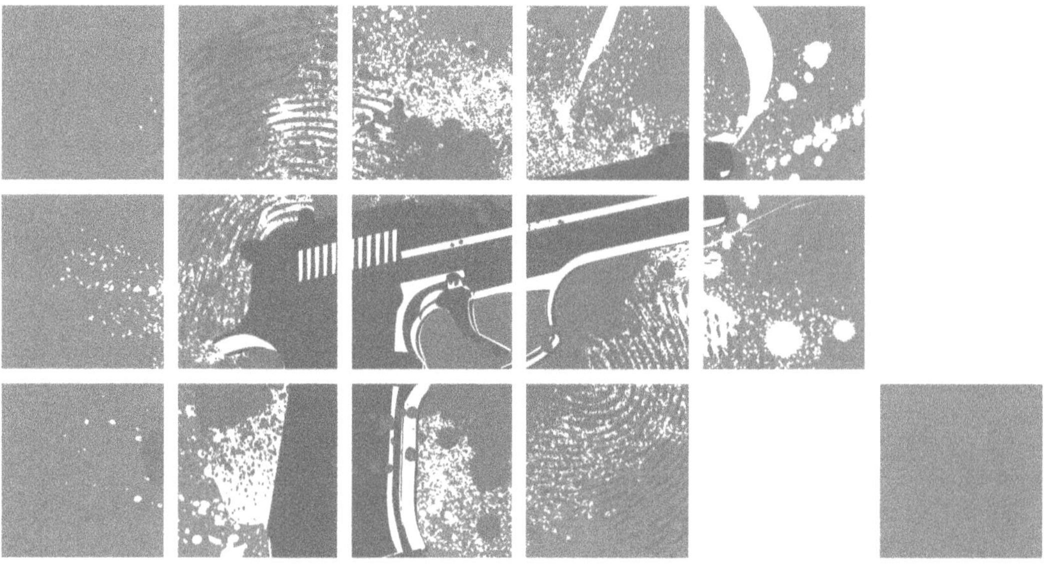

Chapter 7

Theft and other crimes against property

Overview

- Property crime is the most common sort of crime. Two in every five males admit committing a property crime such as theft, burglary and criminal damage at some time in their lives.
- There is a problem with research into shoplifting because of biases towards targeting those who fit the 'offender profile' or stereotypes about that crime.
- Kleptomania is rare among shoplifters. This is the impulse to steal without there being a need for the property or money and is said to be associated with some form of positive emotion when committing the offence.
- Burglary has a strong connection with drug use. This may be because drug users associate with criminals or because of financial needs. Property offences are more common when supplies of drugs are scarce and consequently expensive. Methadone support therapy, which helps heroin addicts come off of the drug, is associated with a reduction in property crime.
- Decision making by burglars often appears to be expert. For example, burglars may be deterred by the presence of security measures from burgling a house even though it is an ideal target otherwise.
- Arson is largely committed by youngsters – perhaps for reasons of boredom or thrill seeking. The psychiatric disorder pyromania is a deep-seated urge to set fires. Few arsons are committed by pyromaniacs – indeed, the figure may be as low as 1 per cent. Fewer than one in five arsonists suffer from a mental disorder.

Introduction

Historically, forensic and criminal psychology has tended to ignore property crime since psychological factors seem only marginally relevant to such commonplace offences (McGuire, 2004). By property crime we mean theft, shoplifting, motor vehicle theft, fraud, arson and vandalism. In other words, property crime is the stealing of property or, as with arson and vandalism, the destruction of property. What these crimes have in common is the absence of violence in commissioning the offence. Robbery, which involves violence or its threat, would not be classified as a property crime. Most of us have probably taken something that did not belong to us at some time in our lives – including trivial things such as keeping change, not going back to the shop when undercharged, taking paper or paper clips from the office to use at home, illegal downloading and so forth. The normality of property crime is underlined by a survey of households in England and Wales in 2003 (Budd, Sharp and Mayhew, 2005) which revealed that a high proportion of the general population reported committing some sort of property offence (theft, vehicle-related theft, burglary and criminal damage, and robbery) at some time in their lives:

- 40 per cent of men and 22 per cent of women reported committing a property crime.
- 35 per cent of men and 21 per cent of women reported committing theft although these were minor (e.g. theft from a person, work, school or a shop).
- 11 per cent of men reported vehicle-related thefts (e.g. theft of a motor vehicle or theft from a motor vehicle) though the corresponding figure for women was only 2 per cent.
- 4 per cent of men reported committing burglary in their lifetime but only 1 per cent of women (though this was primarily commercial burglary and not domestic burglary).
- Only 1 per cent of men reported domestic burglary and a fifth of this number of women did so.
- Thefts from an individual (as opposed to thefts from work, school or shops) were actually very uncommon. Less than 1 per cent of men and half that percentage of women reported ever committing the crime of theft from a person.

Participants were also asked about crimes that they had committed in the previous year. These figures are naturally lower than the life-time figures. So, in the year before the survey, 8 per cent of men and 4 per cent of women had committed some sort of property offence. Most property crime was committed by just a few offenders – only 2 per cent of the sample committed 82 per cent of the total number of offences (Budd *et al.*, 2005)!

Illegal downloading of music files from the Internet illustrates some of the issues associated with property crime – especially its normality. Legally, such downloading amounts to a form of theft yet it is endemic among otherwise law-abiding citizens. Steinmetz and Tunnell (2013) analysed the 'conversations' on an online discussion board concerning illegal downloading. Motivations for doing so included: 1) the desire to share content/culture among people; 2) to listen to content before purchase thereby not buying disliked items; 3) to get content that could not be afforded; and 4) a subversive wish to undermine the laws of copyright and the music industry which is seen as making unjustifiable profits. Various techniques of *neutralisation* were used (Sykes and Matza, 1957) by the illegal downloaders to justify their illegal acts. Questioning who the victim of illegal downloading is is an obvious example. But other participants question the morality of royalties being paid for so long. One illegal downloader claimed the housebuilder doesn't get a cut every time a house is sold – they are paid once and only once, no matter how many people take advantage of their skills.

Just what is it about illegal downloaders that stops them heeding warnings about the illegality/criminality of downloading? Robertson, McNeill, Green and Roberts (2012) wondered if illegal downloaders were characterised by a greater willingness to engage in other illegal acts and ethically dubious behaviours. Did they have a greater propensity towards stealing a CD from a music shop if the risk of being apprehended was minimal? Three-quarters of their sample engaged in illegal downloading. They showed less concern for the law (they were more likely to use marijuana, shoplift, not wear a seatbelt, and drive substantially over the speed limit), were not so concerned with ethical behaviour, and were more likely to say that they would steal a CD from a music shop in circumstances in which there was no risk they would be detected. Those who subscribed to the view that 'no harm, no foul' showed the greatest antisocial tendencies.

Shoplifting

There is a distinction to be made between shoplifting and other unethical customer behaviours (Egan and Taylor, 2010). The latter includes returning an item to a shop which you have damaged for a refund because the item is faulty, and trying to buy items that you are too young to purchase legally. Proportionately, crime against business is more common than crime against individuals. For example, 80 per cent of retailers and 63 per cent of manufacturers in the United Kingdom had experienced crime in 1999, whereas the corresponding figure for the general population was about 30 per cent (Hopkins, 2002). Theft by customers was the most common (47 per cent of retailers reported this) followed by burglary (24 per cent), theft from vehicles (23 per cent) and vandalism (22 per cent). Certain sorts of businesses are more likely to be victims of crime – alcoholic drinks shops and DIY stores were the most likely to be burgled. Perhaps the view that it is worse to steal from a person than a wealthy business is responsible for this. It is wrong to assume that shoplifting is always a casual form of criminal activity. In their review, Krasnovsky and Lane (1998) discussed several typologies of shoplifters which involve distinctions between 'professional' shoplifters and other types such as the opportunistic shoplifter.

Situational Action Theory (SAT) combines environmental explanations with internal psychological explanations in a novel way. It has been applied to adolescent shoplifting by Hirtenlehnera and Hardie (2016). The theory brings together the individual's morality, environmental factors, self-control and social controls (deterrents) to predict whether an individual will shoplift in any given circumstances (see Figure 7.1). Deterrents include the perceived adverse consequences of being caught for committing a crime and the likelihood of being detected. We are likely to commit crime either if we have a propensity to crime due to a moral acceptance of crime or because we are in a situation which is conducive to crime. A situation may be conducive to crime (criminogenic) because of the presence of delinquent others or because social controls exercised by the community are weak, for example. When both these things – the characteristics of the individual and the situation – are congruent, in that they favour criminal acts, then we do not deliberate about what we are about to do. We are highly likely to carry out the criminal act. When neither our individual morality nor the setting are conducive to crime, then we are unlikely to offend.

When the situation is not conducive to crime but our personal morality is, then we will deliberate about offending. The decision to offend will be determined by our perceptions of deterrents such as the risk of being caught for the crime. If our personal morality is against offending but we are in a setting conducive to offending, then whether or not we offend will be determined by internal control (the exercise of self-control) mechanisms. SAT theory does not entirely regard criminal activity as a rational choice and it can be routine or habitual for some individuals.

Hirtenlehnera and Hardie (2016) tested SAT theory in relation to shoplifting using data from the Austrian Adolescent Shoplifting Survey of nearly 3000 students. Shoplifting was a self-report measure of how often the youngster had taken something from a shop without paying for it in the past year. About 5 per cent reported some shoplifting. Shoplifting-relevant morality was based on the youngster's perceptions of the wrongfulness of stealing from shops and their feelings of guilt and shame about shoplifting. Self-control was measured by a questionnaire which tapped into impulsivity and risk-taking in particular. The moral context or setting was measured in terms was based on the youngster's perceptions of their friends' moral beliefs about shoplifting and the extent to which their friends were perceived to engage in shoplifting. Finally, deterrence was measured in terms of the perceived likelihood of being caught if they shoplifted. The findings of the research indicated that not shoplifting is related to deterrents when the adolescent has weak morality in relation to shoplifting. However, youngsters with a strong sense of morality against shoplifting probably will not shoplift irrespective of how likely they think it is that they would get caught if they shoplifted. Exposure to a criminogenic environment (as measured by the adolescent's perceptions of their peers' moral position on shoplifting and whether their peers shoplifted) was related to shoplifting if the adolescent had poor self-control but not if the adolescent had good self-control. Internal (self-control) and external (deterrence) controls were shown to be less important in determining whether the youngster shoplifted than were internal morality and external morality. All of this supports SAT theory.

	Individual's morality conducive to crime	Individual's morality NOT conducive to crime
Situation is conducive to crime	Both the situational and the individual's morality are favourable to crime CRIME (shoplifting) HIGHLY PROBABLE	Only the situation is favourable to crime CRIME DEPENDS ON LOW SELF CONTROL
Situation is NOT conducive to crime	Only the individual's morality is favourable to crime CRIME DEPENDS ON PRESENCE OF DETERRENTS	The situation and the individual's morality are NOT favourable to crime CRIME (shoplifting) HIGHLY IMPROBABLE

Figure 7.1 The relationship between personal morality and situational morality and shoplifting

Shoplifters, obviously, do not want to be apprehended and adopt various tactics to avoid being spotted. Lasky, Jacques, and Fisher (2015) describe some of the tactics used by shoplifters to appear like normal shoppers by blending in with them. There is a tendency for shoppers and shop staff to be reluctant to perceive the actions of shoplifters as shoplifting in the absence of unambiguous evidence or without the support of other shop workers or shoppers (Bickman, 1979). Shoplifters avoid suspicion by the use of gestures or actions which communicate the normalcy of their activities. Shoplifters employ a mental schema of how a normal shopper speaks, looks and acts based on their actual experience of normal shopping. The researchers used a sample of shoplifters who took part in a simulated shoplifting episode which was videoed. The shoplifters were then interviewed about the strategies they employed in the video. At the first stage of shoplifting, the shoplifter enters the shop and searches for the item(s) to thieve. Among the signs of normalcy they employ is taking a shopping trolley and examining items which they have no intention of stealing. The second stage of shoplifting is taking possession of and concealment of the item to be stolen. Tactics of normalcy that might be employed at this stage include examining the target item as a normal shopper would and putting a mobile phone close to the object so that they can remove the phone and the object at the same time. The third stage of shoplifting is exiting the shop which may involve purchasing another item before leaving the shop or taking a circuitous route around the shop before exiting.

Such tactics make shoplifting difficult for security workers to deal with. Shoplifters merge with a large number of shoppers who serve as cover for or to hide the shoplifter. With so many shoppers, how does one choose possible shoplifters for surveillance as they move around the shop? If arrests for shoplifting are systematically biased, such as when a profile of the typical shoplifter is used, targeting a particular type of customer may simply reproduce that bias and may be considered oppressive by the targeted group. Dabney, Dugan, Topali and Hollinger (2006) were not satisfied by previous research, which is almost entirely based on official statistics and self-reports of shoplifting. Instead, they believed that the use of strict observational methodologies with strict sampling criteria would be more productive of useful data. So they planned a study based on unobtrusive observations in a retail pharmacy/drugstore. The data were collected from high-resolution, closed-circuit (CCTV) cameras used for shopper surveillance. The observers were rigorously trained about all aspects of their work.

During the first six months of the research, the observers were required to select every third shopper for observation. In this way, purposeful selection on the basis of characteristics such as race or youthfulness could be avoided. Unfortunately, these exacting standards were expensive, both in terms of time and money. Very few shoplifters were identified in this way. So the sampling protocol was relaxed a little. Instead of every third shopper, the new protocol required that every third shopper should be selected if their manner of dress gave them opportunity to conceal shoplifted items. So a person who was wearing tight clothes would be excluded from the sample since such a style of dress would make shoplifting difficult. So before the change in sampling there was no flexibility and discretion as to who was observed – every third person coming through the door was observed without any deviation. After the sampling method change, the observer had to decide whether a person's clothing was amenable to shoplifting and then select every third such individual. This gave the opportunity for preconceptions about likely shoplifters to have an influence. What appears to be a small change in the sampling method made a big difference to the sort of person who was selected into the sample – the numbers of African American and Hispanic people surveyed increased markedly.

BOX 7.1 Controversy

Are shoplifters kleptomaniacs?

Psychology's neglect of property crime is surprising since one of the earliest 'psychological' (psychiatric) explanations of crime concerned theft. This concept, *kleptomania*, has a 200-year history (see Chapter 1). It is currently included as a diagnostic category of the *Diagnostic and Statistical Manual* (V) (APA, 2013) under the heading of 'impulse control disorders'. To be diagnosed with kleptomania, the individual should show the following symptoms:

- A recurrent inability to resist stealing things but not for their monetary value or to be used personally.
- Immediately prior to the thing being stolen, the individual experiences increasing feelings of tension.
- The act of stealing is accompanied by feelings of gratification, pleasure or relief.
- There is no conduct disorder, antisocial personality disorder or manic episode due to bipolar disorder involved.

BOX 7.1 (continued)

- The stealing is not to exact revenge or because of anger and is not carried out while the individual is in a delusional or hallucinatory state.

These criteria are very similar to those in earlier editions of the *Diagnostic and Statistical Manual.*

Since kleptomaniacs are aware that the thefts they commit are both wrong and 'senseless' then the condition is not a psychotic one. Addiction Hope (2013) suggests that the 'typical' person with kleptomania is a woman of 35, who started stealing at the age of 20. They give the prevalence rate for kleptomania in the USA as 0.6 per cent and claim that kleptomania is responsible for 5 per cent of shoplifting. A study of students in the US suggests a similar prevalence rate of 0.4 per cent of the population, even though 30 per cent of the students admitted acts of stealing and theft (Odlaugh and Grant, 2010). They simply failed to have the required symptoms for the diagnosis. Kleptomania is very frequently comorbid with substance use and mood disorders (Addiction Hope, 2013). Suicide attempts seem common in kleptomania (Odlaug, Grant and Kim, 2012). Nearly a quarter of their sample had attempted suicide and this was related to their kleptomania in the vast majority of cases. Sufferers who also had bipolar disorder were particularly prone to suicide attempts.

On the face of things, kleptomania then seems not to be characteristic of shoplifting given the above prevalence estimates. Sarasalo, Bergman and Toth (1997) studied shoplifters to assess the extent to which any of the APA diagnostic criteria for kleptomania could be found in them. The shoplifters had, literally, just been apprehended by store security staff. Those who agreed to take part in the study were interviewed in the short period prior to the arrival of the police. The researchers assessed each shoplifter for the presence of four of the main criteria used in the APA *Diagnostic and Statistical Manual IV* for identifying kleptomania (see Figure 7.2) at the time of this research (which are much the same as in the current edition V):

- Criterion A is the 'recurrent failure to resist impulses to steal items even though the items are not needed for personal use or for their monetary value' (American Psychiatric Association, 2000). A lot of shoplifters (78 per cent) mentioned needing the stolen object; 90 per cent said that the stealing was a sudden impulse; and 56 per cent mentioned that they had had similar impulses in the past.
- Criterion B is 'a subjective sense of tension before the theft'. Over 84 per cent mentioned a sense of thrill before their offence.
- Criterion C is the 'pleasure, gratification, or relief' experienced on carrying out the theft. Only 40 per cent of shoplifters mentioned that they had experienced a feeling of relief or gratification during their offence.
- Criterion D is that the offence is not due to anger or vengeance and is not the consequence of a delusion/ hallucination. On average, only 14 per cent of shoplifters agreed that their offence was the consequence of anger or a need for revenge.

According to Sarasalo *et al.*, in order for an individual to be classified as a kleptomaniac, they should meet all of the above criteria and more. Few met all of these as we have already seen. For example, they argue that 34 per cent of the sample were stealing with the assistance of other people so it is difficult to classify them as suffering from kleptomania since kleptomania is a psychological condition of individuals. Of course, it is possible that the co-offenders were also kleptomaniacs, but this is not a realistic possibility since very few of the offenders met all of the Criteria A–D above anyway. Of those who acted alone, only a very few (8 per cent) mentioned an inability to resist impulses to steal unneeded items (Criterion A). However, half of this 8 per cent did not experience the rising sense of thrill before committing the crime and the others did not meet Criterion C since they did not feel pleasure, gratification or relief when they committed the theft. In

Figure 7.2 DSM criteria for a diagnosis of kleptomania (American Psychiatric Association, 2013)

other words, although a number of shoplifters met certain of the criteria, when more than one criterion is used then there is no evidence of kleptomania in the sample. The commonest reason for taking the thing in question was to use it personally (64 per cent) while 12 per cent intended to sell it and 6 per cent intended to give it away or discard it.

Virtually none of the criminals in this sample was in full-time employment. Some were students and others were unemployed. Another remarkable finding was that about a third reported a history of chronic bodily illness (the mean age of the sample was actually quite low). Furthermore, two-thirds of the offenders reported a history of psychiatric disorder.

Not surprisingly, kleptomaniacs can have considerable levels of involvement with the criminal justice system. Grant, Odlaug, Davis and Kim (2009) studied a group of kleptomaniacs attending a clinic seeking treatment. It was found that 27 per cent had never been stopped by a shop security staff member or arrested. Most had been arrested for their offences (68 per cent) but, despite this, 37 per cent were not convicted. Twenty-one per cent had been convicted and incarcerated. Of those with a history of being arrested, 10 per cent had been arrested more than four times. Thus those suffering from kleptomania are at significant risk of being disposed of as criminals in the criminal justice system.

So it is incorrect to equate kleptomania with shoplifting. Shoplifters may be kleptomaniacs in a small minority of cases but kleptomaniacs do not have to shoplift. They can steal in other contexts. Grant, Odlaug, and Kim (2010) argue that kleptomania has a lot in common with substance abuse disorders. So they may be responsive to the same sorts of treatment. Cognitive behavioural therapy incorporating relapse prevention seems beneficial. Therapy seeks to develop insight into behavioural and other patterns associated with thieving, dealing with high risk situations, and making lifestyle changes. Pharmacological treatments which seem to be effective at treating substance abuse disorders also seem to be efficacious for kleptomania. Naltrexone is an example of such a pharmacological treatment.

Shop workers and shop theft

Not all theft from retail shops is the work of shoplifters. It is widely accepted that some shop stock losses can be attributed to shop assistants and other shop workers. Something in excess of half of employees steal from their workplace (Wimbush and Dalton, 1997) and largely this goes undetected. What they steal is not just goods but fiddling time records and taking information for personal gain also. Crime by shop workers in the United States may involve losses ten times those due to street crime. Estimates as high as $40 million a year in the US can be found. About a third of employees admit to some form of stealing when questioned (Kulas, McInnerney, Demuth, and Jadwinski, 2007). Some factors are conducive to workplace theft, whereas others reduce it. Older employees are helpful in keeping stock loss etc. at lower levels. Avery, McKay and Hunter (2012) looked at age variability within shops, whistle blowing climate, and stock 'shrinkage' in a retail chain. Shrinkage is essentially stock loss including theft by employees in a shop. There was an inverse relationship between mean age and shrinkage. That is, shops employing older workers have less shrinkage. Older workers seem to act as guardians to prevent theft by other employees. This is related to the openness of the store to whistle-blowing. If the shop climate was conducive to whistle-blowing then the influence of older workers on theft reduction was greater.

It is tempting to believe that dissatisfied employees are primarily responsible for these losses at the hands of shop workers. Although employee dissatisfaction is an antecedent of some theft, there are many dissatisfied employees who do not steal. Kulas *et al.* (2007) argued that theft is more likely in organisations where there is a climate or ethos conducive to theft. Characteristically such organisations are ones in which it is easy to steal, staff perceive that their co-workers and management perpetrate a great deal of crime, the likelihood that thieves will not get caught is high, perceptions that those caught stealing will suffer sanctions are high, and co-workers are permissive about theft.

The researchers studied a number of supermarket companies, using the Employee Perceptions Study which has 74 questions covering demographic information, desirable and undesirable employee workplace behaviours, including theft, sick leave abuse and so forth. Job satisfaction, as measured in the Kulas *et al.* study, included pay, supervision, co-workers and global satisfaction (such as 'All in all, I am satisfied with my present job and I would recommend this job to a friend'). It was found that employee dissatisfaction proceeds to employee theft through the employee's perceptions of the workplace's climate for theft. Dissatisfied workers carry out more thefts than other employees. There was an association between dissatisfaction and theft-permissive work environments which produced higher levels of theft. The implication is that organisations should avoid a permissive attitude towards theft since the organisational climate in this regard forms an explanatory mechanism linking job dissatisfaction with employee theft.

Restaurants also suffer theft by the workforce of various sorts. This is a multi-million dollar loss which is a common cause of business failure. Shigihara (2013) studied the neutralisation techniques used by restaurant workers when accounting for their thefts from their employers. Data were collected in the form of semi-structured interviews. Time, merchandise and cash thefts were all reported. Everyone who was interviewed in the study knew other workers who practised such thefts. But substantial proportions also admitted doing these things themselves in the interview. For example, some would use discount vouchers intended for customers in order to get extra cash for themselves. In their accounts, workers used numerous examples of neutralisation. Neutralisation is characterized by verbal devices which justify theft, avoid self-blame, and maintain a favourable self-image despite the worker actually being a thief. Mostly these were well-known neutralisation techniques documented in many previous studies. They included minimising the extent of theft, economic need, and deserving the cash. In addition, two new ones unfamiliar in the previous research were identified. Denial of excess was where the worker suggested that if the workplace thefts were moderate then the other workers would not be concerned. 'No one cares' was when the restaurant employee believed that co-workers and managers have few qualms about small-scale theft.

Burglary

Although there have been a number of attempts to identify the major different types of burglar, mostly these have been based on qualitative methods. Vaughn, DeLisi, Beaver and Howard (2008) chose instead a more quantitative approach. A sample of over 450 career criminals provided a wide variety of information. The offenders were interviewed by a researcher working for a bail bond agency so the data, unusually in research, were collected under oath. A range of topics was covered, including the offender's employment, residency and criminal history supplemented by other officially recorded data. Using insights from some of the previous typologies of burglars, 15 different variables were extracted from the data set, including aliases, drug use, length of criminal career, sex offences, tattoos and so forth. The interrelationships between these variables led to four different types of burglar being identified statistically:

- *Versatile burglars:* These were characteristically young and had a variety of different types of offences in their criminal history.
- *Vagrant burglars:* They had been charged with numerous offences which were primarily a consequence of their adopted vagrant lifestyle. Their offending was primarily for material gain and to ensure survival during the winter months.
- *Drug-oriented burglars:* Their background offence history involved drug possession and trafficking. They often had numerous theft and weapons charges, which probably reflects the risks of their drug-user lifestyle. Criminality was to meet their need to pay for drugs. Not surprisingly, then, they had a history of charges to do with drug possession and trafficking as well as numerous theft and weapon charges. Typically they used aliases and were tattooed.
- *Sexual predator burglars:* These showed the indications of involvement in deviant sexual acts. For instance, their criminal histories tended to include rape- and prostitution-related offences. This group was the most violent and they had the longest-lasting criminal histories, which also tended to have an early onset in childhood.

Such a typology is useful, especially in suggesting a number of motives for burglary. The identification of a group of drugs-oriented burglary offenders is salient, given that there would appear to be a strong connection between drugs use and acquisitive crime,

Burglary–drugs connection

Not all burglars use illicit drugs and not all illicit drug users are burglars. Nevertheless, there seems to be a connection between burglary and illicit-drug use. Of course, there are at least three possible bases to this relationship:

- Drug users tend to associate more with criminals which may lead to a greater involvement in crime.
- Drugs are expensive and some users cannot finance their drug use through legitimate means. So theft, robbery and sex work may be used to finance their drugs habit. Many users, though, use legally obtained funds to pay for illicit drugs.
- A third factor may influence both drug use and criminality. For example, it is possible that inadequate parenting in childhood leads separately to criminality and drug use.
- Drugs may have pharmacological effects which in themselves may lead to offending such as violent or reckless behaviour (Bureau of Justice Statistics, 2013).

These are not mutually exclusive pathways to crime in drug users. A more systematic categorisation of theories linking drugs and crime can be found in Figure 7.3 in

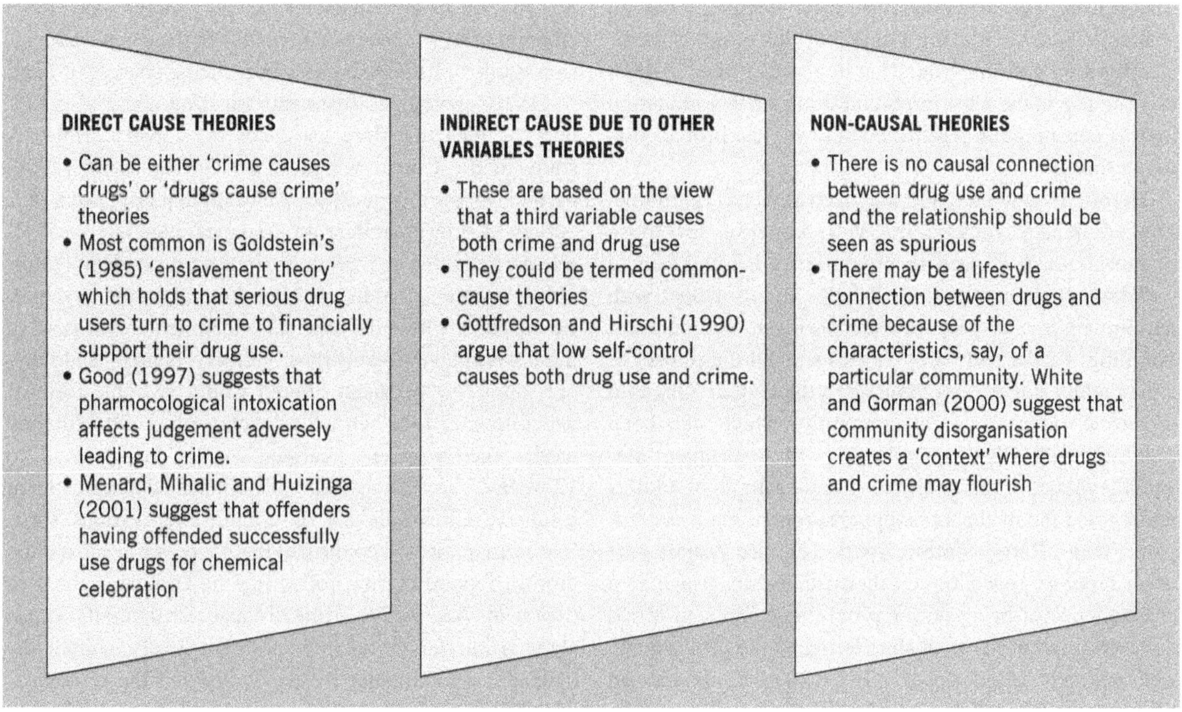

DIRECT CAUSE THEORIES	INDIRECT CAUSE DUE TO OTHER VARIABLES THEORIES	NON-CAUSAL THEORIES
• Can be either 'crime causes drugs' or 'drugs cause crime' theories • Most common is Goldstein's (1985) 'enslavement theory' which holds that serious drug users turn to crime to financially support their drug use. • Good (1997) suggests that pharmocological intoxication affects judgement adversely leading to crime. • Menard, Mihalic and Huizinga (2001) suggest that offenders having offended successfully use drugs for chemical celebration	• These are based on the view that a third variable causes both crime and drug use • They could be termed common-cause theories • Gottfredson and Hirschi (1990) argue that low self-control causes both drug use and crime.	• There is no causal connection between drug use and crime and the relationship should be seen as spurious • There may be a lifestyle connection between drugs and crime because of the characteristics, say, of a particular community. White and Gorman (2000) suggest that community disorganisation creates a 'context' where drugs and crime may flourish

Figure 7.3 Some of the main theories concerning the drugs–crime relationship according to Bennett, Holloway and Farrington (2008)

which examples of relevant theories are mentioned. This is based on the conceptualisation by Bennett, Holloway and Farrington (2008).

There is plenty of evidence showing a relationship between illicit drug use and property crime – evidence that this is a causal relationship is harder to come by, of course. An Australian study showed that 70 per cent of heroin users admit committing acquisitive crimes (Degenhardt, Conroy, Gilmour and Collins, 2005). In the UK, over half of crimes are committed by drug users and the figure is much higher for shoplifting (85 per cent) and domestic burglary (80 per cent) (Home Office, 2002). Heroin and crack cocaine are the main drugs involved in the economic cost of drug-related acquisitive crime. Following a familiar pattern, just 10 per cent of drug users are responsible for half of the cost of drug-related crime. If there is a causal link between illicit drug use and crime then one might expect that property crime fluctuates with the economic cost of drugs in the open market. There is evidence in support of this from a study by Degenhardt *et al.* (2005). There was a sudden change in the availability of heroin in Australia. In a market economy, the cost of products (including illegal drugs) is partly determined by the scarcity of the product. Thus, if heroin use causes acquisitive crime because of their cost, users would be expected to engage more in acquisitive crime when supplies were short. Using a variety of data sources to confirm trends in availability and cost, the researchers were able to show that, during the period of scarcity of heroin, property crime rose including robbery without a weapon, robbery with a weapon other than a firearm, and breaking and entering homes. When supplies began to return to normal, property crime also dropped to its previous levels.

Similarly, when drug users cease to take drugs, we would expect to find that their criminal activity declines. McIntosh, Bloor and Robertson (2007) used data from the Drug Outcome Research in Scotland (DORIS) study – a longitudinal study of over 650 people, mainly males, some of whom were in prison, seeking treatment for problematic drug use. Each person was interviewed four times over a period of 33 months. The researchers were concerned with whether the offender had been involved and/or arrested for an acquisitive crime in the previous three months or since the previous interview:

- About 35 per cent of the participants claimed to have committed an acquisitive crime.
- 25 per cent said that they had been arrested for such a crime.
- Drug users were seven times more likely to have committed an acquisitive crime than those who had been abstinent for three months (excluding marijuana). This was true of both prisoner and non-prisoner participants.

The researchers concluded that drug treatment has an indirect effect of reducing crime, but this effect is mediated by drug consumption. That is, the treatment's effect on drug use is the most important thing since a reduction in drug consumption is reflected in lower levels of acquisitive crime.

Heroin is a semi-synthetic derivative of morphine. Methadone is a synthetic drug with properties like those of morphine. It is used in programmes helping people withdraw from heroin since it helps the user deal with heroin withdrawal symptoms such as fever, insomnia and vomiting. Parker and Kirby (1996) studied the impact of a methadone support programme in the United Kingdom on crime. They chose a community which had been going through a heroin epidemic, with consequent elevated levels of property crime. A large sample of addicts undergoing the methadone-support programme was compared with a large control group. The vast majority of users reported reductions in their illicit drug usage as a consequence of being on the programme and a fifth had not used illicit drugs at all since being on the programme. The treatment sample spent only a fifth of the amount on illicit drugs than the non-treated community control group sample. During the period of the methadone-support programme, there were dramatic declines in the crimes of burglary from a dwelling and theft from a motor vehicle. In keeping with this, those on the methadone-support programme claimed to have been involved in less crime.

More evidence of the effectiveness of methadone maintenance treatment in reducing property crime comes from Lind. Chen, Weatherburn and Mattick's (2005) Australian study. A reoffending database was used to track the offending patterns of drug users when they were undergoing methadone treatment compared with when they were not. Another database was used to obtain information of any periods that the users were in custody to adjust the data for the amount of time that the offender would not have been able to offend. In terms of theft offences (mainly robbery, theft and related, burglary and breaking and entering, and fraud and forgery), there were reductions in the rates of criminal charges when the offender was undergoing treatment. The extent of the impact depended on gender and age group. Expressing the reductions as numbers of charges per hundred drug users:

- men under 30 years of age: a reduction of 8 theft charges;
- women under 30 years of age: a reduction of 20 theft charges;
- men 30 years and over: a reduction of 11 theft charges;
- women 30 years and over: a reduction of 20 theft charges.

So this methadone-maintenance programme was more effective with women than men, though the general conclusion is one of its effectiveness in reducing charges of theft.

Do psychological treatments for drug abuse also support the idea that drug use leads to property crime? A study in the United Kingdom by Gossop *et al.* (2003) partly answers this question. They studied drug users on a variety of drug treatment programmes including methodone programmes and treatment in drug dependency units. Drug dependency units are often housed within psychiatric hospitals where the available treatment would involve multi-disciplinary teams mostly of psychiatrists and nursing staff. The treatment offered would be some form of detoxification together with psycho-social rehabilitation work. The in-patient treatment would last from 2 to 12 weeks. The findings generally confirmed that treatment resulted in lower levels of drug use of various sorts. Furthermore, it was confirmed that there was a substantial drop in reported crime following the commencement of treatment. Acquisitive crime dropped substantially to just about a quarter of the pre-treatment levels in both the methadone community treated group and the residential drug dependency units. Unfortunately, it is not possible to fully separate the effects of detoxification from the effects of the psycho-social work.

Surprisingly, few attempts have been made to synthesise the sizeable body of research into the relationship between drug misuse and crime. Bennett, Holloway and Farrington (2008) carried out a meta-analysis (see Box 4.1) of 30 studies into this. They fine-tuned their analysis by breaking it down by different drug types and different crime types. Compared to non-drug users, drug users were three or four times more likely to be involved in crime. The basic relationship was true for the offences of burglary, prostitution, robbery and shoplifting. The increase in offending due to drug use was the greatest for users of crack cocaine (about six times greater) and least for recreational drug users such as marijuana:

- Amphetamines 2×
- Cocaine 2.5×
- Crack cocaine 6×
- Heroin 3×
- Marijuana 1.5×

More expensive drugs such as crack cocaine and heroin seem to be more strongly related to criminality which may reflect the greater financial burden they place on users. Löbmann and Verthein (2009) dismiss the challenging theory that criminality preceded illicit drug usage on the basis of a similar study showing that heroin replacement therapy led to a reduction in crime. If the theory were true then stopping taking the illegal drug should have no effect on criminality.

As a coda to this, do we get similar trends in terms of the impact of alcohol on acquisitive crime? There is plenty of data to suggest that offenders often commit their crimes while under the influence of drink. Not unexpectedly, much of this research concentrates on alcohol as a cause of violent crime. To what extent is acquisitive crime used to support problem drinking? Of course, relatively speaking, alcohol is much cheaper than illegal drugs in general so the financial pressures on the drinker are probably much less than on the drug user. McMurran and Cusens (2005) studied self-reported data from 126 offenders in British prisons. Some financially motivated crime includes violent offences (e.g. robbery) and so these were studied alongside other forms of acquisitive crime. The researchers found that self-reports of crime were about 80 per cent accurate against what was recorded on official records. The offenders were screened using the Alcohol Use Disorders Identification Test (AUDIT) for hazardous drinking (i.e. high frequency, poorly controlled, and resulting in adverse consequences). Those who had been violent when drinking were higher on this measure than those who were not drunk when they committed a violent crime. Among the important findings concerning the role of alcohol on acquisitive crime were:

- Half of those in prison for acquisitive offences said that they were drunk at the time of the offence and the scores on the hazardous drinking measure were higher when the offender had been drunk when committing their acquisitive offence.
- About one in five indicated that their acquisitive offending was carried out in order to get alcohol.
- Crime in order to finance alcohol consumption characterised only a small number of violent and acquisitive criminals. Such crime was more common where the offender scored highly on the measure of hazardous drinking.

A more general view of the relationship between alcohol and acquisitive offending can be found in the work of Felson, Savolainen, Aaltonen and Moustgaard (2008). They acknowledge that there is a strong relationship between alcohol use and criminal behaviour but ask just how much the relationship is causal and just how much is spurious. Their study involved data on over 5000 participants in the Finnish Self-Reported Delinquency Study of 2004. This study compared the size of the correlations between:

- delinquent behaviour when the offender was sober at the time of the offence with their alcohol consumption in general;
- delinquent behaviour, irrespective of whether the offender was drunk or sober, with their alcohol consumption in general.

If these correlations are the same then quite clearly alcohol consumption cannot be responsible for the criminal behaviour when drunk; if there is a weaker correlation when the offender is sober then this is evidence that alcohol consumption led to criminal behaviour. For every crime-type studied by the researchers, a strong relationship was found between drinking and the amount of crime committed when sober. This clearly indicates that much of the relationship between alcohol use and crime may be spurious (i.e. alcohol use does not cause crime). However, a more detailed analysis was quite revealing. For some crimes of petty theft, such as shoplifting and theft from one's home, there was virtually no difference between the total crime relationship, whether drunk or sober. For these offences, the alcohol–crime relationship is totally spurious as the relationship was the same when offenders had been drinking at the time of the offence. On the other hand, for some crimes including violence, vandalism and car theft, there was a difference between the sizes of the two relationships. In these cases, alcohol is having a direct causal effect. These seem to be the sort of crimes which we might expect to be affected most directly by drunkenness.

Burglar decision making

The naïve burglar might find the challenge of looking for valuables in a modern house in broad daylight rather daunting.w (Robson, 2015). What should they grab? The antique silver? Where would they find it? How about the flat-screen TV? Picking the TV up quickly reveals that it is heavy and awkward to carry – a fast escape with one of these would not be easy. What about upstairs? There are lots of drawers there, but which ones contain valuables? Back downstairs. What about the kitchen? Surely nothing there is of any value – but what if car keys are kept there? There is so much that is unfamiliar which needs attention and thought that the naïve burglar is likely to be almost transfixed. In contrast, most experienced burglars would know what to do and where to find the sorts of small, portable, high-value items which bring good financial rewards. Cash in a wallet, car keys, and credit cards are obvious possibilities.

There are several theories which seek to explain how burglars go about their crimes. One of these is routine activity theory. In routine activity theory the emphasis is on the day-to-day activities of individuals and the structure of their daily lives which provide them with opportunities to commit crime. So, to illustrate this, it is useful to note that studies show that low-income households as well as inner-city ones have the greatest risk of burglary. This is simply because they are the locations most likely to be in close proximity to where the burglar lives – that is, are encompassed within the routine ambit of the burglar.

Felson (1996) identified three different factors which contributed to property crime:

- There are motivated offenders around in the locality.
- There is a suitable property which makes an attractive target for burglary.
- There is an absence of guardians capable of protecting the property.

Guardians may simply be members of the household or neighbours whose presence is obvious to the potential burglar. Social guardianship involves such things as household composition, house occupancy and the presence of neighbours willing to watch over the dwelling when it is unoccupied (Johnson and Bowers, 2004). A high proportion of burglars avoid occupied premises in their offending for this reason. Physical guardianship includes things such as burglar alarms, CCTV, and high quality locks. Much of this sort of information is available to the potential burglar going about their usual daily business.

Suitable properties for burglary characteristically show: 1) greater value as judged by the burglar; and 2) a lack of physical characteristics which increase the risks of offending. Accessibility of the property to the offender and a lack of visibility of the offender's actions to the public will be part of the decision about whether to burgle the property. A prospective burglar will assess a property in order to decide whether it is occupied or unoccupied. There is a general preference among burglars to try to avoid the risk of being disturbed by householders – which increases the likelihood of the offender being arrested. In a study pertinent to this, Nee and Meenagham (2006) found that over three-quarters of burglars preferred unoccupied homes and check that the property appears empty before breaking in. Of course, their assessment is not always successful and the presence of members of the household may result in the offender perpetrating acts of violence or opportunistic sexual crimes such as rape as well as increasing the risk that the offender will be arrested.

Tseloni, Witterbrood, Farrell and Pease (2004) attempted to test routine activity theory applied burglary victimisation across three countries (the Netherlands, United States, and England and Wales). They took the major assumptions of routine activity theory and tested whether the predictions of the theory worked in such a wide variety of settings. Many variables related to routine activity theory were coded using crime survey data. The following are among the general findings:

- The social guardianship variable lone parent (there are fewer adult social guardians) increased the risk of burglary to a similar extent in all three countries.
- Households that had preventative measures against burglary were actually more likely to be burgled than those that did not. This is contrary to expectations. The researchers suggest that the use of precautions against burglary may be the result of previously having been burgled. In some of the cases, the preventative measures were token efforts which would not deter burglars. The authors warn against assuming that burglars target houses which have taken preventative measures.
- Living in inner-city or urbanised areas increased the risk of burglary, perhaps due to living closer to where offenders live.

With the above exceptions, it should be stressed, though, that there was a degree of inconsistency as to the factors which related to burglary rates in the different countries. It is important to note that the researchers found that their variables measuring aspects of routine activity theory left a great deal unexplained in burglary rates. That is, a great deal is yet to be found out about why certain households are more likely to be burgled than others. So, taken overall, there is evidence in support of routine activity theory, but it is also true to say that the fit of the theory to the data on burglary was far from complete.

Rational choice theory is possibly the most important alternative to ideas which suggest that offenders are driven to crime by a personal propensity to crime. Gary Becker (1968) introduced the theory into criminology though it is often (somewhat erroneously) credited to Cornish and Clarke (1986). Rational choice theory regards offenders as decision makers who seek to gain advantage for themselves using means which are rational within the constraints of the information available, the offender's ability to reason, and the amount of time available to make the decision. Quick decisions may not be the most rational decisions. Although the theory deals with the initial decision to become criminal, its most significant contribution concerns the rationality of decisions when the offender is faced with a particular opportunity for crime. Rational choice theory accepts that background factors such as low intelligence or poor upbringing as well as situational factors such as being drunk, having had a row with one's partner, and pressure from friends may play a part in offending. Pease (2001) suggested that rational choice theory freed researchers from seeking explanations of crime in the pathological character of the offender. Instead, it led researchers to investigate offenders' criminal methods and the precautions they employ in the course of their offending.

Sometimes it is suggested that rational choice theory works better for property crime than for expressive crime. Certainly, some of the more profitable research has explored the activities of burglars. Detailed interviews with burglars have led to the view that they are far less opportunistic than was once believed. They plan and search out targets rather than make impulsive choices. Nee (2004) studied the motivation and decision making of burglars in Ireland. She employed a control group of householders who were not burglars in order to assess the extent to which burglar decision making was truly distinctive. The method involved simulating vulnerable residential areas by the use of numerous photographs of five houses. Decisions that a particular house would be good to burgle depended on patterns of factors and not individual ones in isolation. The same combination of cues to decision making did not apply in every circumstance. For example, the least popular target house for burglars would have been somewhat easy to enter because it had timber doors and sash windows. However, it had a scruffy and 'downmarket' appearance and was exposed to the gaze of passersby. Had it been next to cheaper housing, the house might well have been seen as a better target by the burglars. The burglars' preferred target house had a mature appearance and appeared to be easy to get inside. The house next to it looked as if it might yield more profits, provided a lot of cover for the burglar and was easy to break in at the rear of the property. Despite this, the burglars were deterred by the number of security measures installed – such as double glazing, a visible burglar alarm box and mortice locks on the doors. In contrast, when householders assessed the same houses in terms of how desirable they would be as burglary targets, they lacked an appropriate strategy or plan for making their decision. They did not choose the same target houses as the burglars did. Furthermore, the householders took rather more time over reaching a decision than the burglars did. They explored a greater number of photographs of the properties before selecting what for them appeared to be the best target. Burglars had more experience and expertise than the householders.

Some researchers have questioned whether all criminal thinking follows the cool, cognitive decision-making processes assumed by the rational choice model. For example, Based on a good deal of evidence, Shover and Hochstetler (2002) took the view that burglars are not the calculating beings which rational choice theory suggests they are.. That is, they often carry out offences without a plan or forethought. Van Gelder (2013) argues for a two-process (hot-cool) model which suggests that 'cool' cognitive process and 'hot' affective feelings both influence offender choices but in rather different ways. Individuals are often unaware of the influence of emotion on their decision making so may not be able to identify its influence on their crime-related decisions. Affect-based thinking encourages the criminal to make choices that have an immediate rather than long-term benefit. Closely allied to the hot/cold approach to criminal decision making is the difference between an impulsive crime and a planned crime. An impulsive crime is one which is committed in hot-blood and is considered to demand lesser punishment than the cold, calculated offence.

Rational choice theory (Clark and Cornish, 1985) assumes that a number of different sorts of cues are considered when deciding whether to commit a particular crime (see also Chapter 4). According to Snook, Dhami and Kavanagh (2011), the rational choice model regards criminals as entirely rational decision makers using what is essentially a compensatory process – they attach weights or values to the potential rewards and costs of a particular course of action. For example, the possibility of a large financial gain is considered against the risk of arrest. In other words, the positive and negative aspects of a possible crime are weighted in terms of their likelihoods of occurrence and these evaluated jointly when deciding whether to offend. That is, the burglar maximises gains and minimises costs. So if the probability of a large financial gain is big and the probability of being punished by the law is low, then the burglary is more likely to go ahead.

There are alternatives to this including the possibility that burglars use a non-compensatory strategy or matching heuristic (Dhami and Ayton, 2001). In this, the burglar examines a number of homes one by one until a home that meets certain requirements sufficiently is found and targeted. Heuristics are step-by-step information processing procedures. So, for example, the process employed by the offender is to use different sorts of information sequentially. Once a cue supporting a particular decision by the offender is found, the search stops. It is a quick process which relies on a minimal amount of information. Snook, Dhami and Kavanagh (2010) used Dhami and Ayton's matching-heuristic approach. This is used for binary classification tasks such as deciding whether a house is unoccupied or occupied. Imagine that a particular burglar's matching heuristic model is based on using three cues – vehicle absent, windows above ground level closed, and landscaping to hide behind. Each of these cues is used in turn when making the decision to burgle or abandon the attempt. This is illustrated in Figure 7.4. As can be seen, the burglary attempt will be abandoned at each stage if the cue that the house is unoccupied is missing. For example, if a vehicle is seen on the house drive then the burglar will abandon this particular burglary attempt – this explains why this model requires a minimal amount of information. There is no point in looking for the other cues as an important one is present.

In order to study the processes involved, Snook *et al.* asked convicted burglars to make judgements about whether homes were occupied or not from photographs of each of the properties. The actual occupancy at the time of the photograph was checked and the permission of the householders to use these photographs in the research obtained. The researchers had deliberately included properties which had different sorts of cues to possible occupancy. These clues seem to be ones that burglars

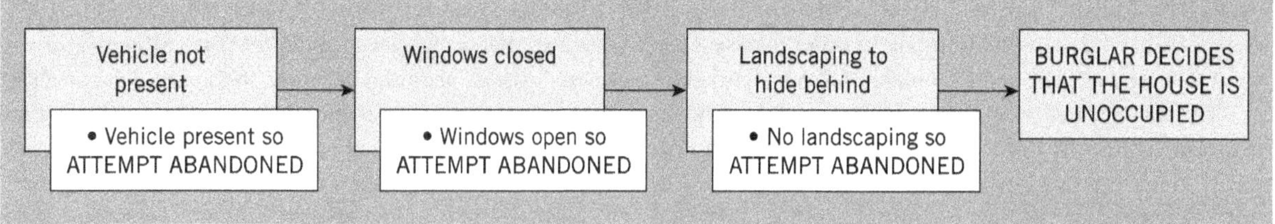

Figure 7.4 The Matching Heuristic Model applied to a burglar's decision-making process

themselves identify as being involved in their decision-making about occupancy:

- attached garage (or none);
- curtains above ground level open (or closed);
- deadbolt present (or not);
- landscaping to hide behind (or none);
- security system visible (or not visible);
- vehicle present on the property (or absent);
- windows above ground level open (or closed).

As they examined the photos, the burglars assessed whether each property was occupied. Then they explained to the researchers just how they had made their decision. Additionally, they rated the importance of a range of cues when making their decisions. The burglars were relatively good at the task since their predictions of whether the house was occupied or not were better than chance levels, though not spectacularly so. However, the most important cue to occupancy by far was the presence of a vehicle at the house. With this cue excepted, in general, the cues in the above list had poor ecological validity. That is to say, most of the cues were actually not strong indicators of whether or not the property was truly unoccupied. This, perhaps, emphasises the difficulty of the decision facing the burglar (though, of course, in real life they would be able to use surveillance and other methods which are not possible from photographs alone). The researchers attempted to fit both the more complex rational decision model and the simple heuristic model to their data on how the burglars actually made decisions. Their analysis strongly suggested that the matching heuristic model – the simple model – characterised burglars' thinking better than did a more complex, compensatory model. Basically, this means that burglars employ an unsubtle model when making their decisions.

There is a geographic dimension to burglary decision making since certain areas tend to have a high concentration of the crime – hot spots. It should be remembered that this may result in the police paying much more attention to an area. Johnson and Bowers (2004) suggested that a perspective from behavioural ecology, optimal foraging theory, may be of help in understanding burglars' thought processes which lead to such hot spots. The theory suggests that animals, when seeking food (and so burglars when seeking money), adopt strategies that keep the rate of rewards to a maximum. At the same time, an animal will keep to a minimum the amount of time spent foraging since this increases the risk of being caught by another animal – or the police in the case of burglary. Thus one would expect that the burglar will try to keep rewards at a maximum and the time spent commit the offence at a minimum. This implied to Johnson and Bowers (2004) that a burglar would tend to burgle one property then continue to target ones close by if: 1) they are unlikely to be observed/overlooked; 2) ready escape routes are available; and 3) there is a likelihood of stealing valuable goods. Since this strategy is likely to eventually be recognised by the police or public, the wise burglar will limit the duration of offending in a particular area. That is, there will be a hot spot for burglary which lasts for just a short time. This is what Johnson and Bowers' (2004) research showed – hot spots for burglary move dynamically. Hot spots involve potentially lucrative households in an area, but the burglars' strategy is to move on to another location when the yields are poor and/or the risk of arrest is high. This may have important practical policing implications. It may be an ineffective for the police to target those areas which have been shown to have high burglary rates in a particular month, since the hot spot is likely to have moved – most probably to a nearby area. The most affluent areas are not necessarily where burglary is most frequent though they are likely to be hot spots. None of this is the consequence of certain households being repeatedly targeted as such properties were excluded from the study.

Expertise among criminals

Researchers have begun to realise that burglars have at their disposal a whole array of complex cognitive skills which, for the most part, are automatic and require relatively little thought to implement. We have already seen that often the crime begins well in advance when the burglar becomes aware of possible targets when walking to the shop or taking the kids to school. The preferred target may be dropped in favour of another on the actual day if it is obvious, say, that the owner's car is on the drive. Once inside the house, the burglar may be largely on automatic pilot. Skilled, experienced burglars by and large will follow much the same plan which generally will be a search of the bedrooms and then the downstairs living rooms. The search is not the focus of their attention, it happens almost subconsciously, with their attention being on things like the householder returning or suddenly becoming confronted by someone unexpectedly being in the house. The burglar will rely on schemas to help them through the varied scenarios which may befall them. They may have extensive knowledge of the internal layouts of different types of house as well as plans for their escape.

Burglars vary greatly in their offence-related skills – some being very skilled burglars and others little other than amateurs. This was investigated in an Australian study (Clare, 2011) but there is much more research. Most previous research had compared burglars with controls without considering the domain-specific skills that some of them possess and others do not. Clare defined expertise in terms of a formula which included offending frequency, offending-related income, burglary charges and estimated length of burgling career. Two burglar groups – experts and novices – could be defined in this way. The expert group had better domain-specific (burglary) skills: 1) they show generally homogeneous patterns when selecting and searching property – i.e. a relatively standard set of procedures; 2) they operate in a largely automatic manner; and 3) they can deal with big quantities of information both speedily and effectively. This fits well with findings from other research. For example, often burglaries are virtually repeats of previous ones. That is, burglars target similar properties to ones they have successfully targeted before (Pease, 1998). Expert burglars and novice burglars seem to be different in terms of their first burglary offence:

- The experts started younger.
- The experts were less afraid of being arrested.
- The experts' first burglary was more likely to involve co-offenders.

There were other differences:

- Compared with novices, expert burglars more often claimed that their most recent offence typified their offending style, perhaps implying a greater stability in their burglary methods.
- Novices were more likely to burgle an acquaintance.
- Novices were more likely to be deterred by difficult targets (e.g. places where there was an alarm system).
- Experts were more likely to travel further to burgle.
- Experts were more likely to seek out small, high-value, easily disposed of items. They were also different in terms of how they disposed of items they stole. They found out the prices of items before selling them on and they were less likely to involve family and friends when selling the items, preferring more discrete avenues. It was common for stolen property to be traded for drugs, for example.

Burglary is far from the only crime to demonstrate elements of expertise. Carjacking or taking a vehicle by force also shows features of expertise (Topalli, Jacques, and Wright, 2015). Two important aspects of carjacking which involve expertise are 1) the perceptual (targeting or choosing a vehicle) and 2) the procedural (commandeering the vehicle). Skills and knowledge are essential when the offender selects a target vehicle, such as its value and the ease of disposing of the vehicle for profit. The driver's characteristics can have a bearing on what target vehicle is selected because the driver may resist, for example by screaming, driving off or attacking the offender with a weapon. Different carjackers have different preferences for different reasons. Female victims may be preferred by some because they may offer less resistance in a physical confrontation but other carjackers may avoid female victims because they are more likely to scream. Generally the car and driver were considered as part of the decision. Topalli *et al.* interviewed one carjacker who said:

> 'When I'm looking for a car, I look at the car then the driver. See if he's intoxicated, see if he might be a police or something. How he's dressed. To see if he might have a pistol or something. That's why I look for old people. They are easier. They don't fuss with you.'
>
> (Topalli, Jacques and Wright, 2015, p. 22)

The process of commandeering the targeted vehicle is a critical and highly dangerous business. The carjacker, if skilled, will have a sophisticated script which is accessed without pausing to consider in detail what they are about to do. Commandeering has to be done quickly since, for example, the target car may move off when the lights turn to green. Another carjacker recounts what can happen with an inexpert carjacker:

> 'So we was walking along the street, me and my little cousin, and he always wanna do the shit I do. He was talkin' a lot about doing a carjacking and I was like, no man, you need to practice or watch me do it if you wanna do it right. Anyhow, he seen this car go by and was like, is that a good car to get? I looked at it and I was like, well it's a Honda and there's a lady driving it and yeah its cool I guess, blah blah blah. And before I know it, he ran up on her on put the gun to the window. I was like, God damn it! Stupid ass. Because, you know, he put the gun up on the passenger window, not the driver window. And there was two cars behind her and we was at this intersection in the middle of all this

traffic. And he was like give me the keys!! And she just took the keys out the car but the window wouldn't open and the car was just sitting there with her screaming and shit. I was like, Oh Lord this is some bullshit. So, I ran up on the driver side, reached in and open the door and took her keys. I did it right you know? And I yelled at his stupid ass to get in. I had to back the car up and drive over a sidewalk to the parking lot to get outta there because the intersection had cameras. So stupid. I hit him in his face with the pistol I was so mad. He don't know shit.'

(Topalli, Jacques and Wright, 2015, p. 22)

The idea of expertise in criminal activity has begun to emerge as a coherent account of the process of committing a crime. Nee and Ward (2015) argue that the activities of the offender around the crime scene can be construed as expert behaviour just as exhibited by skilled gymnasts, ball players, guitarists, conductors, and medical staff, for example. Expertise is regarded by them as a continuum from the unskilled to the expert rather than simply a skilled-unskilled dichotomy. Cognitive psychology has conducted a wide range of basic research studies on expertise. Nee and Ward and like-minded researchers argue that this provides an important knowledge-base when describing the functioning of experts and, importantly, the activities of burglars, sex offenders, and identity thieves for instance. Expertise is a continuum and not everyone will reach the heights of expertise in their chosen area of activity. The question is why and how expertise confers advantage to experienced offenders.

Nee and Ward (2015) extract the following from the basic research on expertise from which they developed what they call their dysfunctional expertise model:

- *Chunking:* Novices begin to learn to recognise, as a consequence of repeated experiences and trial-and-error, what factors lead to a successful decision or outcome while, at the same time, learning to ignore the factors which lead to bad outcomes. As our expertise develops, we come to recognise the cues which lead to successful patterns and the cues leading to disastrous outcomes. These cues and patterns are drawn together into 'chunks' or groupings which are readily and speedily capable of being retrieved from memory so they allow us to quickly and effectively deal with challenges and problems. These chunks which result in success eventually become organised into cognitive schemas. These schemas are abstractions and amount to shortcuts to employ when dealing with situations. So instead of having to consider many different aspects of a situation in reaching a decision about what to do, the schema simplify decision-making processes and the consequent actions we adopt. One advantage of the schema is that the need only for low levels of cognitive processing capacity thus leaving capacity for the working memory to do other more resource-intensive tasks at the same time. Learning to drive or cycle are good examples of the way in which a complex, demanding task becomes increasingly or totally automatic with practice. Once we have some expertise, we no longer have to pay full attention to steering, gear changing, and the like and we begin to be able to have conversations, for example, while carrying out these tasks.
- *Automaticity:* An activity can be described as automatic when it does not need intention, awareness, control and high demands on cognitive resources. Some would argue that many thousands of highly similar repetitions of the experience must be involved. However, research in cognition suggests that automaticity can occur after far less practice than this. Furthermore, an activity may be more-or-less automatic even if the individual intends to do the activity or is aware that they were carrying out the activity.
- *Situational awareness and selective preconscious attention:* Experts are skilled at attending to, processing and storing information with the potential to be relevant to decisions that they may make in future relevant to their area of expertise. The consequence of this is that they are better able to evaluate what is happening around them than the non-expert. This can generalise to new situations so long as they have some familiar elements. New elements may rapidly accommodated into a schema though there are limits to this and there may be too much information to incorporate.
- *Multi-tasking:* The automatic, highly learned, unconscious decision-making processes of the expert take up little cognitive capacity which means that there is room for other thinking and problem-solving tasks which are much more resource intensive to be carried out. So the expert burglar has more capacity to listen out for signs of danger than the novice who has a multitude of new decisions to take at every step.

Nee (2015) uses Nee and Ward's (2015) dysfunctional expertise model based on mainstream cognitive psychology to integrate what is known about burglary from research. This seeks to understand how offender's minds work prior to, during and after their crime. Many of the processes, as is common in skilled performances, become automatic without involving conscious awareness as a consequence of frequently carrying out a type of crime. This frees the offender's mind to carry out more thoughtful, conscious activities. For example, burglars engage in automatic, continual appraisal of their environment during their everyday activities when preparing for burglaries and seem to have fast offending scripts based on what is known to work when engaging in the crime. Such ideas help to relate current thinking with some of the classic studies of burglars. Bennett and Wright (1984), for example, showed that about half of the convicted burglars they studied used their knowledge of environmental cues to decide what property would be the most satisfactory target based on ease of entry, likely monetary gains, and so forth. Once a decision had been made to commit a crime, the offender would travel to a location which he regarded as conducive to committing a crime. Researchers who followed Bennett and Wright tended to conceptualise burglary in terms of the planned versus spontaneous dichotomy. It takes little thought to see that the planned burglary might be equated with the expert burglar who employs automatic decision making whereas the spontaneous burglary is equivalent to the inexpert burglary who uses deliberative decision making. Nee (2015) describes the route through the dwelling commonly employed by burglars being the master bedroom first, other adult bedrooms next, and followed by a short search of downstairs bedrooms. Expert burglars go for smaller items such as cash, drugs, handbags, jewellery and wallets. They avoid items which are more identifiable such as antiques, artworks, china, and silver. These are, generally speaking, more difficult to sell and increase the risk of detection.

One difficulty with regarding criminal activity as expert behaviour is that the theory of expertise employed is not based on criminal behaviour but on basic research on the acquisition of expert performance. This is applied to crime but largely in ways which are just illustrative. That is to say, it remains to be shown that criminal expertise is learnt in the way that other expertise is. For example, would it really take a slow learning process involving multiple repetitions to decide to focus on small items like cash and jewellery rather than massive television's when burgling a house? Or to avoid easily identifiable items for that matter? Yet to consider the expertise of criminals as an important part of understanding their activities seems to have many advantages in relation to certain crimes. Identity theft is one such area (Vieraitis, Copes, Powell and Pike, 2015). Identity theft is the criminal use of another person's means of formal identification such as passwords, credit and debit cards, personal information such as birthdates, and driving licenses. Stealing a person's identifying information and then using that information for personal gain can involve a wide range of skills. There are many ways of stealing personal identifying information ranging from low to high tech. At the low-tech end the offender may obtain identifying information from wallets, dustbins, handbags, cars, or filing cabinets containing records, for example. Some identity information is stolen through working in an office or some other organisation dealing with financial matters. The Internet is another source of information which might include addresses, hobbies, dates of birth, and the like which are sometimes revealed on social media. But more sophisticated methods can be used such as setting up scam, online businesses which require information to be entered when making a purchase or signing up. Skills may be developed through engaging in illegitimate activities such as handbag or wallet theft or by engaging in legitimate work in banks, department stores, and other organisations who supply credit or loans. Identity thieves develop skills and expertise which help them pass themselves off as someone they are not. These include practical skills, social skills and cognitive skills:

- *Practical skills:* The identity thief, in order to be successful, must have or know someone who has, practical skills such as knowing how to steal information and knowledge of financial systems like mortgage processing and credit card checking systems employed by shops. They may need the skills to forge documents or watermarks or to obtain specialist inks. Having legitimate experience in the relevant organization may be of value. For example, what is the maximum value of a cheque before it would have to be verified by a manager? This sort of information can be chunked into group memories which provide patterns of how to deal with different companies or situations.
- *Social skills:* Social skills are required to pass oneself off as an account holder at a bank. They need to regulate their emotions such that nothing appears to be unusual about them. Are they convincing and seemingly honest and trustworthy? They also need to be able to deal appropriately with any problems which arise. Can they appear to be of a high social status? Can they appear friendly, naïve, respectful or assertive as the situation requires?
- *Cognitive skills:* The offender needs to develop a highly tuned sense of situational awareness which may be only semiconscious. They need to analyse this crime-relevant information. Expert identity thieves often claim to have super-sensitivity to circumstances and possibilities for illicit activity. This includes a knowledge of when to desist, or knowing when it is likely that you are being checked, which is a cue to leaving quickly. Being expert means that the offender has the cognitive capacity to monitor for problems and difficulties and the like which may signal that things are getting too risky.

Arson and pyromania

Many arsonists come from impoverished home and social environments and may have extensive criminal and antisocial histories from childhood onwards (Horley and Bowlby, 2011). Despite this, majority of firesetters are motivated by retribution, revenge and financial gain. The UK government's statistics show a very clear downward trend in the numbers of deliberately caused fires (Home

Office, 2016c). According to the Arson Prevention Forum (2014), nearly half (45 per cent) of the 70,000 fires attended by the fire service were deliberate. Although accidental fire rates are dropping due to innovations such as fire-resistant furniture and smoke alarms, the rate for deliberately set fires is falling rather more slowly. Care needs to be taken since not all deliberately caused fires can be classified as criminal (i.e. arson) since some are set by children and others who cannot be held to be criminally responsible. Over a five-year period ending in 2014, there were 348 fatalities in fires deemed to be deliberate of which 45 per cent were down to suicide. The evidence is that arson without endangering life has one of the poorest detection rates of all crimes although arson endangering life has a considerably better clear-up rate (Smith, Taylor, and Elkin, 2013). One might assume, then, that many arsonists escape punishment for their crime. Figures from the US suggest that there were 300,000 intentionally started fires each year from 2003 to 2006 which resulted in nearly 500 deaths and cost over $1 billion (Stockburger and Omar, 2014). There, one arson in six is prosecuted for being a danger to life (Hickle and Roe-Sepowitz, 2010).

The UK government's Crime Reduction Toolkit (Home Office, 2005a) for arson identified the major categories of motivation for arson and indicated the percentage of arsons that are in each category:

- *Malicious:* revenge and racism are among the motivations for this – 5 per cent of total.
- *Psychological:* triggered by a mental illness or suicide attempts – 5 per cent of total.
- *Criminal:* concealment of another crime is one example of this or where the perpetrator may profit financially from the fire such as insurance frauds – 4 per cent of total.
- *Youth disorder and nuisance:* boredom and thrill-seeking may be associated with this – 80 per cent of arsons.

Given the last point, it is not surprising that male youths under the age of 18 years comprise about half of the total of individuals either found guilty in court or cautioned by the police for an arson offence. Similarly figures are found elsewhere. Approximately one-third of US juveniles arrested for arson are under 15 years of age (Hickle and Roe-Sepowitz, 2010). The proportion of females involved is less than 15 per cent. About 10 per cent suffer from mental illness. So many firesetters begin at an early age. This tends to suggest that an explanation for arson lies more in delinquent behaviour than in deep psychological problems underlying the arson. Nevertheless, we should not overlook that half of the firesetters were adult.

Almond, Duggan, Shine and Canter (2005) investigated Shye's (1985) action system model in relation to arson. Four different 'modes' of arson emerge in the analysis and there is empirical evidence in support stemming from a study of arsonists in a British psychiatric prison:

- *Adaptive mode:* an external event is exploited for some sort of gain. Setting fire to a crime scene to hide evidence of a crime is an example of this. Because of the links of this mode with criminal activity, it includes variables such as more than one offender involved, business, vehicle, force and theft.
- *Expressive mode:* internal psychological factors are expressed against external targets. The choice of the target for the arson would have a symbolic or emotional significance for the arsonist. Variables associated with this include school and civic buildings.
- *Integrative mode:* internal psychological factors are dealt with by using arson as a means of seeking attention. Variables associated with this include self, own home and hospital.
- *Conservative mode:* an external source of frustration has an effect on the individual, who responds by setting a fire which restores their sense of well-being. Using fire to exact revenge on another person is an aspect of this. Variables associated with this include victim known, prior threats of violence or arson, arguments and planning.

Of course, it is a common criticism that most research is carried out on convicted offenders. There is only a little evidence from non-convicted samples. Borrowcliffe and Gannon (2015) reported the findings of an online questionnaire partially related to firesetting. Nearly 12 per cent of those responding admitted firesetting. A number of differences were found between firesetters and non-firesetters. Psychological difficulties were found in the firesetter group as exemplified by a history of self-harm but having a family member who had deliberately started a fire was also predictive. Curiously, the non-firesetters began experimenting with fire at a younger age than the firesetters. Firesetting was only rarely carried out alone and generally with a number of other people. In terms of motive, 82 per cent claimed curiosity or experimenting with fire and 55 per cent claimed that they did it to create fun or excitement or to alleviate boredom.

Females are under-represented among arsonists as they are for most crime. Nevertheless researchers have paid them some attention. Gannon (2010) in her review of what is distinctive about female arsonists suggests the following features:

- Female arsonists are relatively less to watch the consequences of fire-setting, such as firefighting.
- Female arsonists show a higher prevalence of depression and psychosis.
- Females do not demonstrate sexual fetishism involving fire.

- Females do not typically carry out arson for reasons of profit and the concealment of crimes.
- Sexual abuse is much more prevalent in the childhoods of female arsonists.
- Various forms of attention seeking and cries for help predominate in the motives of female arsonists.

Evidence is beginning to accumulate about the background factors associated with female arsonists and these do not seem very different from those of male offenders. Some features of the backgrounds of male firesetters are given in Figure 7.5 Hickle and Roe-Sepowitz (2009) carried out a study of juvenile females charged with arson in a southern state of the USA. Generally, the findings replicate those of fire-setting boys. Young female arson offenders frequently (70 per cent) came from extremely unstable home environments – often with little or no contact with one or more of their parents (55 per cent). Behaviour at school and attendance was problematic. Usually, their arson offending happened at a time of substantial crisis such as a loved-one's death or parental separation or divorce. Physical, sexual and emotional abuse may also be involved. The commonest location for their offences was at school, which accounted for nearly 40 per cent of the arson crimes.

When the girls tried to explain their offending, they suggested that their offences were essentially impulsive or accidental rather than planned in origin. Sixty per cent of offences were committed with peers. If girls offended alone then they tended to demonstrate high levels of home instability and they had poorer school attendance records. Contact was likely to be highly unsatisfactory with one parent. The girls tend to have anger, upset and suicidal thoughts if they were solo offenders. These factors tended to encourage Hickle and Roe-Sepowitz to regard arson as a signal or warning sign of the high levels of distress being experienced by these girls. Serial arsonists were not common.

One popular view about such fires is that they are caused by individuals who get pleasure out of setting fire to property (Doley, 2003). They might be regarded as pyromaniacs who are driven by deep-seated urges to light fires. So it is believed that flames have an irresistible attraction for them and that they even get sexual satisfaction from their activities. As a consequence, they begin to carry out more and more arson attacks of increasing seriousness purely for reasons of self-gratification. The concept of pyromania was put forward by Charles Chrétian Henry Marc in 1833 to refer to the strange behaviour of repetitive fire-setters whose behaviour could not be put down to understandable motives such as revenge. Clearly not all fire-setters are pyromaniacs. In 1842, James Cowles Pritchard stipulated two conditions for a diagnosis of pyromania. Not only had the perpetrator to display a morbid propensity for fire-setting but that propensity had to be beyond their conscious control. This was not necessarily an excuse for their crimes as arson was seen as an extreme crime. So in 1835 Franz Josef Gall suggested that murderers and arsonists had much the same mental faculties and, hence, deserved the same fate (i.e. execution). Clearly not all firesetters are pyromaniacs.

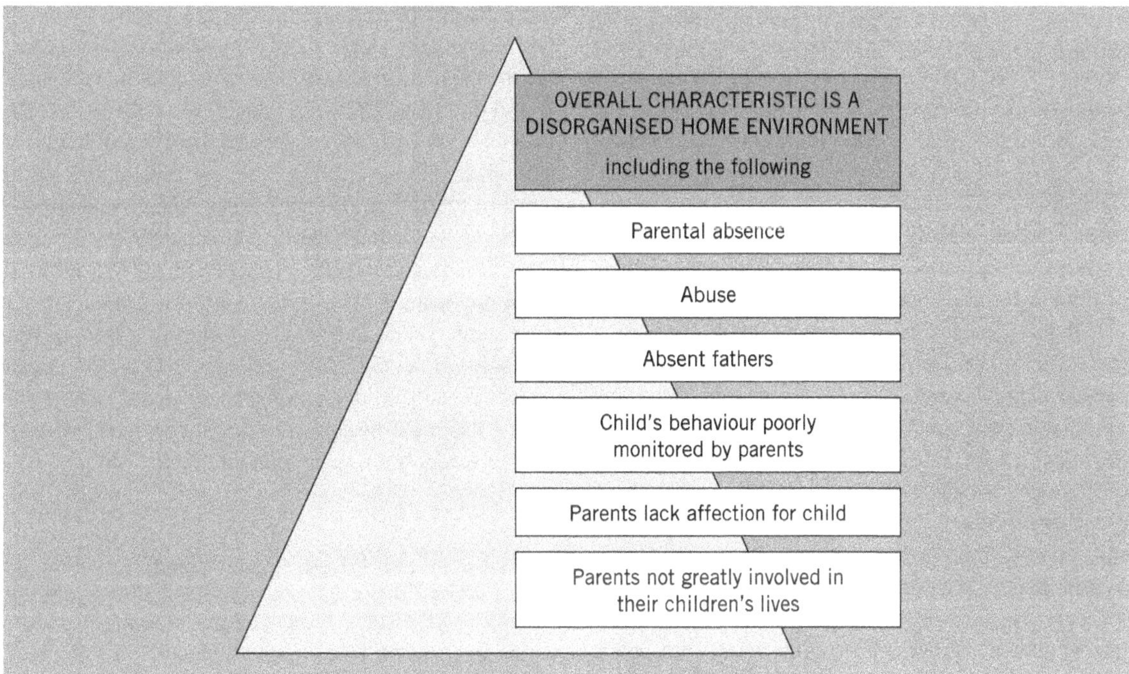

Figure 7.5 Background factors in male arsonists

Pyromania is a psychiatric disorder which has the same diagnostic criteria in both the IV and V editions of the *Diagnostic and Statistical Manual* of the American Psychiatric Association (see Box 21.1). These criteria include:

- deliberately and purposefully starting a fire on two or more separate occasions;
- experiencing a state of emotional arousal or tension before starting the fire;
- a fascination with or curiosity about fire and the context of fires (such as being fascinated with lighters, fire engines or the aftermath of fires;
- a feeling of gratification, pleasure or relief when starting a fire or about a fire's aftermath;
- contra-indications of pyromania include monetary gain, political ideology, concealment of a crime and acts of vengeance. Furthermore, impairments of judgement such as when intoxicated, having limited intellectual ability and suffering dementia are also contra-indicative of pyromania;
- there should not be a better way of accounting for the fire starting, such as indications of conduct disorder, antisocial personality disorder or a manic episode.

Pyromania seems rare among arsonists (Doley, 2003). It is difficult to say precisely what proportion of them are pyromaniacs as the reported figures vary somewhat in the studies which Doley reviewed. Only between 0 and 1 per cent of arsonists met Doley's criteria for pyromania though other studies give higher percentages. Mental disorders in general are uncommon among arsonists as only 17 per cent of arrested arsonists manifest mental disorder (Almond *et al*., 2005). Furthermore, the old idea that arson or even pyromania is motivated by sexual urges has little force. Lewis and Yarnell (1951) found that out of more than 1100 arsonists only 3 per cent reported sexual arousal in association with their crime.

There is some evidence that firesetters relate differently to fire from non-firesetters. Ó Ciardha, Barnoux, Alleyne, Tyler, Mozova and Gannon (2015) studied a variety of published questionnaires related to fire setting. They had a sample of British prisoners known to be firesetters which they compared to a sample of prisoners with no fire setting record answer questions taken from the questionnaires. A statistical analysis revealed that there were five underlying dimensions to these questions. Four out of the five dimensions distinguished firesetters from the controls. These were 'identification with fire' ('Fire is a part of me' and 'I have to have fire in my life'), 'fire safety' ('Playing with matches can be very dangerous') for which firesetters showed the riskiest attitudes, 'firesetting as normal ('Most people's friends have lit a fire or two'), and 'serious fire interest' (thinking that it is exciting, fun, or lovely to watch a house burn down). 'Everyday fire interest' (watching an ordinary coal fire burn in a grate or watching a bonfire) did not discriminate the two groups. However, only 'identification with fire' distinguished between firesetters who had offending a few times from those who had offended many times.

Other evidence suggests that firesetting is just part of a general propensity to offend. If firesetting is somehow based on a deep-seated propensity to setting fires then it might be expected that firesetters are a specialist form of offender whose reoffending is confined to setting fires. A number of studies over the years put this idea into considerable doubt. Reoffending figures for firesetters, like any reoffending data, is dependent on the population in question (psychiatric versus prison, for example), how recidivism is measured, and how offending is measured. These differences affect the exact findings of studies. However, the research literature (e.g. Gannon and Pina, 2010; Ducat, McEwan and Ogloff, 2015) is generally very consistent in finding that firesetters are in fact generalists when it comes to their reoffending. That is, they are unlikely to reoffend with arson but likely to reoffend with a generality of criminal acts. Indeed, the best predictor of whether an arsonist reoffends is their general criminality.

As a topic, firesetting has for two centuries attracted a mass of opinion theory and research which demands a comprehensive synthesis of disparate elements into a meaningful overview. The Multi-Trajectory Theory of Adult Fire-Setting (M-TTAF) (Gannon, Ó Ciardha, Doley and Alleyne, 2012) seeks to do just that. A variety of theoretical developments by a number of researchers were subject to what Gannon *et al.* refer to as 'theory knitting'. In this, the best elements of existing theories are constructively synthesized with the aim of rectifying weaknesses in the separate theories. Gannon *et al.*'s theory suggests that there are several different trajectories which lead to firesetting. Each trajectory has its own antecedents, involves different vulnerabilities in the arsonist, and the critical risk factors which result from the vulnerabilities such as when they are moderated by mental illness or proximal factors of various sorts. The final stage for each of the trajectories is the actual fire-setting. The five trajectories leading to firesetting are: 1) the antisocial trajectory; 2) the grievance trajectory; 3) the fire interest trajectory; 4) the emotionally expressive and need for personal recognition trajectory; and 5) the multi-faceted trajectory. The trajectories and their antecedents are to be found in Figure 7.6.

Developmental context

Gannon *et al.* discuss the developmental context of firesetting in terms of the distal factors involved – that is, the origins of firesetting in childhood. (Proximal factors would be the immediate, short-term influences which lead

TRAJECTORY 1 ANTISOCIAL	IMPORTANT RISK FACTOR: General criminality-supporting attitudes and values.
	ADDITIONAL RISK FACTORS: Problems in self-regulation.
	CLINICAL FEATUREES: Impulsivity. Antisocial attitudes and values. Conduct disorder. APD.
	MOTIVATORS: Crime hiding. Vandalism and boredom. Revenge. Financial gain.
TRAJECTORY 2 GRIEVANCE	IMPORTANT RISK FACTOR: Self-regulation problems.
	ADDITIONAL RISK FACTORS: Communication difficulties.
	CLINICAL FEATURES: Low assertiveness. Poor communication.
	MOTIVATORS: Retribution and revenge.
TRAJECTORY 3 FIRE INTEREST	IMPORTANT RISK FACTOR: Inappropriate fire interest/scripts.
	ADDITIONAL RISK FACTORS: Firesetting-supportive attitudes.
	CLINICAL FEATURES: Fire fascination. Impulsivity.
	MOTIVATORS: Thrill. Stress. Boredom.
TRAJECTORY 4 EMOTIONALLY EXPRESSIVE	IMPORTANT RISK FACTOR: Communication problems.
	ADDITIONAL RISK FACTORS: Self-regulation problems.
	CLINICAL FEATURES: Poor communication. Impulsivity. Depression.
	MOTIVATORS: Cry for help. Suicide. Need for recognition.
TRAJECTORY 5 MULTI-FACETED	IMPORTANT RISK FACTOR: Offence-supportive attitudes. Inappropriate fire interest.
	ADDITIONAL RISK FACTOR: Self-regulation issues. Communication problems.
	CLINICAL FEATURES: Pervasive firesetting. General criminality.
	MOTIVATORS: Wide range.

Figure 7.6 The different trajectories leading to firesetting

to firesetting.) Multi-trajectory theory does not seek to identify one or two decisive childhood determinants of firesetting but assumes multi-causality, as indicated by the wide range of the available research. The strategy behind the theory was to identify the childhood influences behind each of the trajectories. These are summarised in Figure 7.7. Furthermore, it is not assumed that the childhood antecedents of fire-setting are necessarily different from those for other forms of antisocial and deviant behaviour. They see the main aspects of the developmental context of fire-setting as being:

- The role of the caregiver environment in childhood (e.g. abusive experiences);
- Social learning (including experiences with fire and coping scripts developed in childhood);
- Cultural forces which provide beliefs and attitudes about fire;

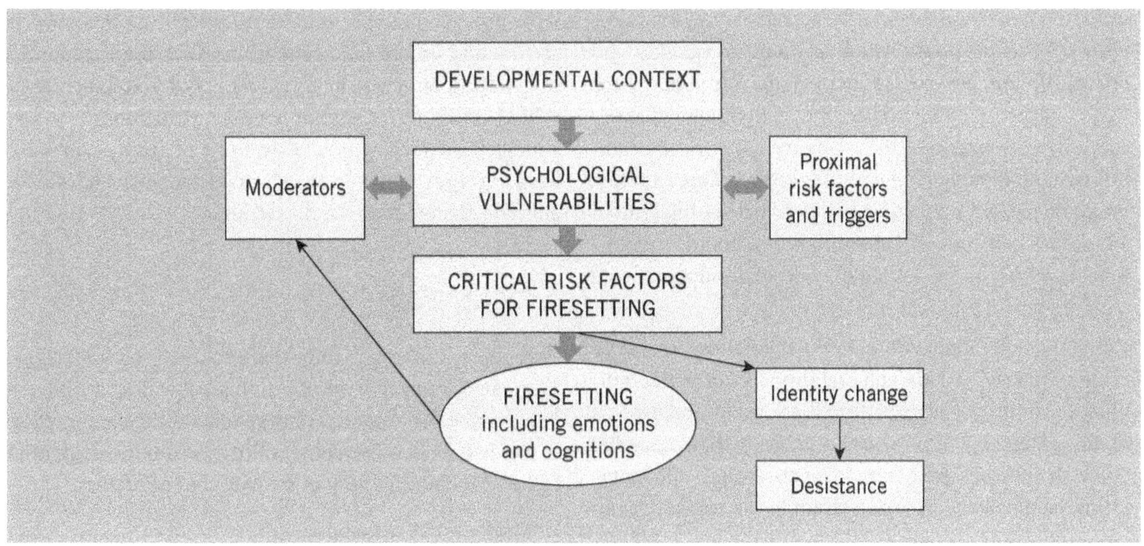

Figure 7.7 Gannon *et al.*'s model of firesetting

- Biological and/or temperamental factors such as impoverished brain structure which may intertwine with other aspects of the individual's development.

An example may be helpful. Culturally, there may be a reverence for fire, which is held in awe or esteem. This reverence is learned socially and may influence the selection of fire-setting as a means of revenge against another person. The developmental context basically serves to create various vulnerabilities, which continue to manifest themselves in adolescence and adulthood. Certain patterns of experiences in childhood may lead to certain characteristic vulnerabilities.

Psychological vulnerabilities

The major vulnerabilities leading to firesetting are identified by Gannon *et al.* as follows:

- *Psychological vulnerability 1: Inappropriate fire interest/scripts:* A fascination with fire may be reinforced by the intense sensory stimulation which surrounds fire, such as flames, excitement and the noise of sirens. The negative aspects of fire can be reinforcing for some individuals too. In Western cultures, children are restricted by parents, etc. in terms of learning about fire and using it naturally. So playing with fire with other children without adults knowing may be reinforcing. Feelings of power and self-efficacy may result from such experiences with fire and handling fire may become a way of gaining self-control and self-efficacy. Inappropriate fire-scripts may develop, such as learning to regard fire as a means of physically hurting others rather than simply a means, say, of keeping warm and cosy.
- *Psychological vulnerability 2: Offence-supportive cognitions:* These are the cognitive accounts (e.g. attitudes) built upon experiences which are used to quickly and effectively interpret social interactions. For some, these ways of accounting for and dealing with life are offence-supportive. Sometimes, these offence-supportive cognitions would directly deal with fire-setting. One example might be the individual who believes that setting light to a building is harmless. Other offence-supportive cognitions involved in fire-setting may be those supportive of a more general criminal lifestyle.
- *Psychological vulnerability 3: Self-regulation/emotional regulation issues:* This vulnerability concerns the individual's ability to monitor emotional states and aspects of the external world so as to achieve their personal goals. It involves problems in goal-setting, self-monitoring, and evaluation which result in the fire-setter not being in proper control of what happens to them. Gannon *et al.* cite impulsivity, low frustration tolerance, inappropriate goals and poor coping skills as instances of this sort of vulnerability; a deficit in the ability to control anger is a further example. The use of drugs can lead to this sort of vulnerability.
- *Psychological vulnerability 4: Communication issues:* Firesetter research provides evidence that some firesetters have impoverished communication ability due to poor social skills, the inability to be assertive, and a tendency to be passive in interaction. Some firesetters are social isolates with few if any sources of social support. For them, firesetting may be used to achieve positive outcomes such as status and power. Gannon *et al.* suggest that firesetters who then act heroically at the scene of the fire they themselves caused are examples of this.

Proximal factors and triggers

Psychological vulnerabilities are to be found in a dynamic relationship with a range of proximal factors and triggers. These include:

- Proximal factor/Trigger 1: Internal affect/cognition
- Proximal factor/Trigger 2: Contextual factors
- Proximal factor/Trigger 3: Life events
- Proximal factor/Trigger 4: Biology
- Proximal factor/Trigger 5: Culture

These factors/triggers are both internal and external to the individual but they interact with vulnerabilities in ways which lead to firesetting. They worsen and amplify the psychological vulnerability to such an extent that firesetting becomes likely. In other words, the factors/triggers work on a psychological vulnerability by priming or exacerbating it. In this way, the psychological vulnerability is turned into a *critical risk factor*. For example, the person with a psychological vulnerability such as inappropriate scripts and emotional regulation issues may respond to, say, failing an exam in a critical way by setting fire to a school building. Communication vulnerabilities could similarly interact with adverse life experiences, making it hard for fire-setters to seek social support and so their anger is channelled into firesetting.

Moderators

These are different from the proximal factors/triggers. They also interact with psychological vulnerabilities and may reduce the potential of the vulnerability or increase it. In the latter case, the vulnerability becomes a critical risk factor. Moderating factors include the following:

- Moderator 1: Mental health
- Moderator 2: Self-esteem

Gannon *et al.* see mental health as a moderator which determines how and how strongly a proximal trigger interacts with psychological vulnerabilities leading to a critical risk factor which makes firesetting likely. A person with poor mental health may have the psychological vulnerabilities of poor coping skills and impulsivity. Such a person is at increased risk of being severely affected by triggers since poor mental health reduces their ability to cope. Similarly, self-esteem can play an important role in criminal behaviour. High self-esteem may, for example, may reduce the impact of the other psychological vulnerabilities.

Critical risk factors

We have already seen how psychological vulnerabilities may become critical risk factors under the influence of proximal factors and triggers and moderators. So we need to add little here. The critical risk factors have same names as the vulnerabilities, though they are, of course, different things:

- Critical risk factor 1: Inappropriate fire interest/scripts
- Critical risk factor 2: Offence supportive attitudes
- Critical risk factor 3: Self-regulation/emotional regulation issues
- Critical risk factor 4: Communication issues

Reinforcement is crucial to the maintenance of firesetting behaviour, according to Gannon *et al.* Fire-setting can be reinforcing due to consequent financial gain and feelings of power and emotion. A criminally inclined individual may find rewards in escaping being arrested for a fire-setting incident. Self-esteem may be affected too by firesetting. So built into the M-TTAF theory is a feedback loop which is primarily from the firesetting episode back to moderators of mental health and self-esteem. But, of course, there are many other feedback and reward loops to be found for different aspects of the theory. Negative feedback loops similarly may make fire-setting worse – the individual who suffers rejection for a fire-setting incident may well have some of their psychological vulnerabilities adversely affected.

Desistance from firesetting is also tackled by the theory. Changes in the individual are possible from a variety of sources, including therapy. But, for example, the social skills of an individual may well develop and improve under some peer group influences. Factors such as these will work to reduce the potential for critical risk factors to develop.

Main points

- Property crime is commonplace and it is probably impossible to find anyone who has not committed some sort of trivial theft at some time in their lives. Perhaps as a consequence, psychologists have not devoted so much activity to researching property crime as a specific topic. Relatively large proportions of the general population admit to committing some sort of property crime at some time in their lives. Mainly these are thefts and the proportions reporting having crimes such as burglary or robbery are much smaller. There is clearly a need to develop psychological approaches to the understanding of property crime much further.
- Psychiatric classifications such as kleptomania and pyromania seem to have little to do with the vast majority of property crimes or fire-setting offences against property. Their lack of importance to the majority of crimes contrasts somewhat with the familiarity of these terms among the general public. Some forms of theft such as shoplifting, just like fire-setting, are offences overwhelmingly carried out by youngsters. As such they are probably best considered as crimes of delinquency (Chapter 6).
- It is not surprising that financial motives underlie a great proportion of thefts of all sorts. One of the most disturbing property crimes is burglary. There seems to be clear evidence that this sort of crime is partly carried out in relation to the need to finance drug usage. Research has shown that times when heroin becomes expensive because of supply shortages are associated with increases in property crimes such as burglary. Furthermore, methadone treatment (a replacement for heroin to help users come off heroin) is associated with a decrease in the amount of crime carried out by heroin users.

Further reading

Canter, D. and Alison, L. (2000) *Profiling Property Crimes* Aldershot: Ashgate.

Mawby, R.I. (ed.) (2007) *Burglary* Aldershot: Ashgate.

Nee, C. (2015) 'Understanding expertise in burglars: from pre-conscious scanning to action and beyond' *Aggression and Violent Behavior* **20**, 53–61.

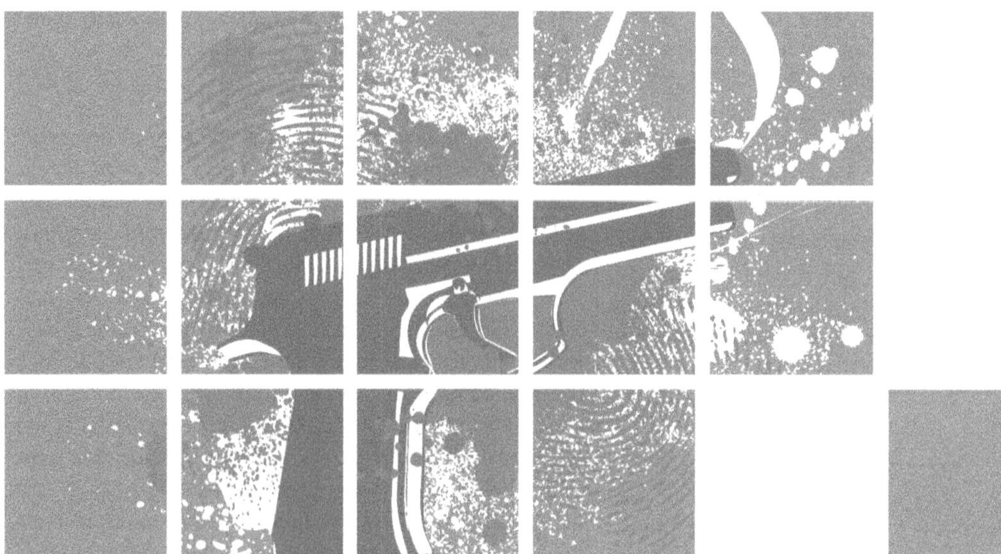

Chapter 8

Violent offenders

Overview

- Despite the public's belief that violent crime continues to rise, trends in violent crime indicate that the rate of increase for some types of violent crime may be relatively modest, even assessed over the period since records began a hundred years ago. Homicide, the most serious violent crime, has only doubled in that time although all violence against the person has multiplied greatly.
- Explanations of violent crime can be at a number of levels of analysis – the sociological, the psychological and the biological, for example. Of course, societal trends in violent crime (e.g. gender differences) need explanation and cannot be effectively dealt with at the level of individual psychology. Most forensic and criminal psychologists would accept that extreme acts of violence are multiply determined by a variety of predisposing, maintenance and situational/triggering factors.
- The effects of media violence on violent crime have rarely been seriously considered by forensic and criminal psychologists. Nevertheless, it is a major area of psychological research relevant to criminology. Mostly, the studies of media influences are contrived. Ignoring laboratory studies, field research does not strongly indicate an influence of media on violent crime.
- A lot of violent crime is perpetrated by offenders who only perpetrate violently once in their lives.
- Alcohol is associated with violent crime but whether this is a causal relationship may be hotly debated.
- Violence between intimates in the form of domestic violence and stalking is a significant part of violent crime, especially as far as gender relationships are concerned. There are many complex forensic issues surrounding both of these types of violence and they make an important case study in the understanding of how crime is gendered.

Introduction

The sheer variety of crimes of violence makes it difficult to understand them comprehensively. For example, how does one compare the violent riots in England in 2011, which resulted in five deaths and numerous injuries to the police and public alike (Newburn, 2015) with, say, a domestic violence incident? As a consequence, we can only illustrate some of the issues concerning violent crime which have drawn the attention of forensic and criminal psychologists. Violent crime tends to loom larger in the public's mind than it does in crime figures. Increasingly, research is beginning to grasp important questions with regard to violent crime, its nature, and how to deal with it. However, without such understanding, it is too easy to regard the criminal world as being populated with violent individuals who spend a lifetime notching up one violent crime after another. So in this chapter we shall try to clarify the nature of perpetrators of violent crime in order to better understand not only the origins of such crime but also how it manifests itself through offenders' lives and the process of stopping offending. Violence can be regarded as being a public health problem which has consequences of enormous importance for government crime policy. In the USA and elsewhere, considerable public funds have been allocated to violence research and interventions to deal with it. Partly, the research effort has sought to identify 'the violent offender' and the steps which can be taken to help reduce their risk of reoffending.

Statistically speaking, the vast majority of crime consists of relatively trivial property offences (Chapters 2 and 7). Nevertheless, violent offences occur frequently, according to crime statistics. Violent crime appears to be among the most salient determinants of the public's perceptions of crime in general. The level of violent crime is used as an indicator of society's malaise. Official crime statistics for the last century or so have generally shown increases in all sorts of crime. Violent crime is no exception to this long-term trend, although it has reversed in some countries in recent years, as has that of other crimes (Table 8.1). In the United Kingdom, for example, crime in general increased 46-fold during the period 1900 to 2014/15. The figures for violent crime reflect a high growth rate of 408 times in the same period. These are recorded crime rates.

It is generally held that homicide is one of the most accurately recorded crimes. So changes in homicide rates may be a better indicator of the true underlying trend in crime statistics. With other forms of violent crime, reporting rates may be the consequence of changes in the acceptability of violence in society. Domestic violence is an example of a violent crime that is likely to have gone unreported to the police or been ignored by them in the past but not nowadays. Table 8.1 shows us that crime statistics escalated markedly in the second half of the twentieth century. Care is always needed when interpreting changes in crime statistics especially since the definitions of crime and the way in which crimes are grouped for classification purposes can change over time. Nevertheless, according to the Home Office (2005b, 2007, 2010, 2016a) figures, in England and Wales the trend for homicide is actually quite modest in comparison as can be seen in Table 8.1. For example, in 1900 there were 312 homicides in total, in 1950 there were 346, in 1975 there were 515 and in 2014/15 there were 534. Overall, these statistics reflect a slow growth rate for homicide followed by a decline in recent years. The figures for crime in general and violence against the person

Table 8.1 The growth of violent and other crime in the twentieth century

Year	Notifiable crimes recorded by police	Total violence against the person	Homicide recorded crimes
1900	78,000	1,908	312
1925	114,000	1,495	318
1950	479,000	6,249	346
1975	2,106,000	71,002	515
1980	2,688,000	97,246	620
1985	3,612,000	121,731	616
1990	4,544,000	184,665	669
1995	5,100,000	212,588	745
2000/1	5,171,000	600,922	850
2002/3	5,791,000	709,101	1,047
2003/4	5,844,000	799,000	904
2004/5	5,477,000	846,000	868
2005/6	5,426,000	839,000	764
2006/7	5,332,000	815,000	758
2007/8	4,881,000	748,000	775
2008/9	4,630,000	709,000	664
2009/10	4,265,000	699,000	620
2010/11	4,078,000	665,000	639
2011/12	3,903,000	627,000	553
2012/13	3,553,000	601,000	558
2013/14	3,507,000	634,000	533
2014/15	3,581,000	779,000	534

show much more dramatic increases and declines. Remember that adjustment is also needed for population growth to obtain a reasonable comparison. So the growth in homicide is even less than it appears to be from these figures, owing to the increase in population size – the UK population in 2015 was 1.7 times the size that it was in 1900. Improved medical services saving more lives might have also affected the trend somewhat, but this would decrease the levels of apparent violence. Taking all of these things into account, as an indicator of violence, homicide seems not to show the pattern that is generally expected.

Crime costs the community dearly. For example, the average cost of a case of violence against the person was put at £19,000 in 1999 (Brand and Price, 2001). A murder cost £1,100,000 and a burglary (£2,300). A similar study (Dubourg, Hamed and Thoms, 2005) suggested that in 2003/4 the cost of the typical sexual offence was £31,438, a typical homicide was £1,459,000, and the typical common assault £1,440. In 2010 in the UK, the cost of a theft of a motor vehicle was £7,507, a sexual offence £36,952, an assault £9,790 and burglary £4,267 (Home Office, 2011). These prices need inflating by a quarter or a half to bring them up to current values.

Forensic and criminal psychology has concentrated on the more serious offences and has neglected the commonplace crimes in comparison. Violent crime has been a major focus as have been sexual crimes. The heading of violent offences includes an array of rather different crimes which need disaggregation. Can a bar brawl be explained in the same terms as a serial killing? Intuitively, we would say that they are very different. Yet there are a number of matters to consider. One very obvious thing uniting violent crimes (and all forms of crime) is the profound gender difference in terms of involvement with the criminal justice system. Males make up the majority of violent criminals in categories ranging from simple assault to serial killing. Age is another important factor in violent crime. Violent offenders tend to be young. These things need to be taken into account when studying violent crime. Several other chapters in this book also deal with aspects of violent crime:

- The development of violent crime through childhood was discussed in Chapter 6.
- The role of mental illness in the aetiology of violent crime is discussed in Chapter 21.
- Serial killers are a special focus of Chapter 14 on offender profiling.
- Anger management and other therapies for violence are covered in Chapter 26.
- Risk assessment for violent offenders is dealt with in Chapter 27.

Are violent criminals specialists?

Is there a type of criminal who specialises in violent crimes such as assault, homicide, rape and robbery? Piquero, Jennings and Barnes (2012) reviewed the extensive literature on violent criminals and reached a number of well-founded conclusions which may require us to rethink some of our assumptions. Their conclusions included:

- The majority of offenders who have violent crime in their records have only committed one violent offence. Recidivistic repeat violent offenders constitute a very small percentage of the total. One possible explanation for this is that the criminal justice system is very good at taking serious violent offenders out of contact with the public.
- Non-violence is the rule in criminal careers. Violent crime is relatively rare in most offenders' patterns of offending. This conclusion is especially true for official crime record data. Self-reported crime data tends to suggest a higher level of violence amongst criminals.
- Higher frequencies of violent crime are associated with higher rates of criminal activity in general. The more criminal acts, the more violent ones occur. Some researchers, including Piquero *et al.*, describe this as being a case of offenders 'rolling the dice of crime' more often and thereby increasing the risk of violence.
- The pattern of onset of violent offending is older than for theft and other sorts of crimes. Adolescent offending which is largely non-violent usually runs its course by the late teens and early twenties. Those who remain criminal are more likely to start violent offending in their late teens and early twenties. This is another area where self-reported offending suggests that violence is more common and actually starts earlier in life than the official crime statistics indicate.
- Reoffending rates for violent crime are lower than for many other crimes. Generally, however, recidivism rates for other crimes are high. The low recidivism tendency for violent offenders may simply reflect the general infrequency of violence in criminal careers. As a consequence, some researchers doubt that attempts to predict future violence amongst offenders is likely to be successful. The proportion of false positives (those predicted to violently offend but who do not) compared to 'hits' would be unacceptably large. Rather than concentrate on risk factors for violence, reducing crime in general may be a more effective way of reducing violent crime specifically.

- There is a small core of persistent and long-term violent offenders but violent offenders do not generally fall into this category.

Different factors affect criminality at different life-stages and in different contexts (Thornberry, 1997). Though there are changes in criminal activity over the life-span, these are not random but orderly progressions affected by developmental changes in the offender's lifetime. This developmental life-course approach also stresses the underlying view that the vast majority of offenders are not specialists in any particular sort of offending. They are criminal jacks-of-all-trades. Violence may be a limited part of this, but rarely the dominant feature.

Moffitt's (1993) developmental taxonomy of criminality was discussed in Chapter 6. It is helpful to our understanding of some basic features of violent criminality. To recapitulate, Moffitt's idea is that there are two distinct groups of offenders: 1) the adolescence-limited group and 2) the life-course persistent groups. The adolescence-limited group is of little concern to this chapter. One could describe them as well adjusted, well-socialised, and generally followers of social norms. They generally offend to achieve power and status in their adolescent social world through the process of social mimicry. They mimic others, including life-course persistent offenders. But their criminal activity is best described as non-violent. Their offending comes to an end with the end of adolescence and it consists largely of things like petty theft, illegal drinking and vandalism.

Life-time persistent offenders show a very different pattern as illustrated in Figure 8.1. As can be seen, taxing/difficult behaviours begin in the first few years of life and move to problem behaviours in late childhood prior to adolescence. In adolescence serious crimes are engaged in, but they are usually not violent in nature. Violent crimes such as robbery and rape typify early adulthood from about 20 years of age. In later adulthood there are further changes such that fraud or domestic violence are more typical. The point is that the criminality and other problematic behaviours are not static but in a state of change during the criminal lifespan. Different environmental and other contingencies (risk factors) apply at different stages. Basically, due to various impairments in development, this group lacks self-control, which hampers normal socialisation processes. The manifestations of all of this at different points in the individual's life vary. Lifetime persistent offenders may make up something like 5 or 10 per cent of the criminal population.

As a consequence, we should begin to see why the notion of the specialist violent offender is inadequate in the light of the weight of the research evidence. This may be difficult to accept for psychologists familiar with ideas like aggressive personality traits. But that is to miss the point that life-course criminality is characteristically a process of change and development. This, it should be stressed, does not mean that there is no relationship between youthful offending and that in adults in a proportion of offenders. In his developmental study, Farrington (1991) did find a relationship between childhood aggressiveness and adult violent crime. That is, about 20 per cent of the most aggressive boys at 8–10 years of age had committed a violent offence by their early 30s but only 10 per cent of the less aggressive in childhood did so. However, this does not mean that Moffitt's ideas are not generally valid.

Alcohol and violent crime

The idea that alcohol is involved in violence is deeply ingrained in our culture – the drunken brawl is a familiar notion. Research support for this is readily available. Substantial amounts of crime are alcohol-related. However, this may merely mean that the offender had been consuming alcohol at the time of the crime rather than that they were drunk. So it is interesting to note that figures from a study of London police stations seem to suggest fairly low levels of drunkenness in arrestees (Robertson, Gibb and Pearson, 1995). Furthermore, even serious violent offences tended to involve drunkenness relatively infrequently. Nevertheless, only 69 per cent of grievous bodily harm cases were free from signs of drunkenness when they arrived at the police station. It is known

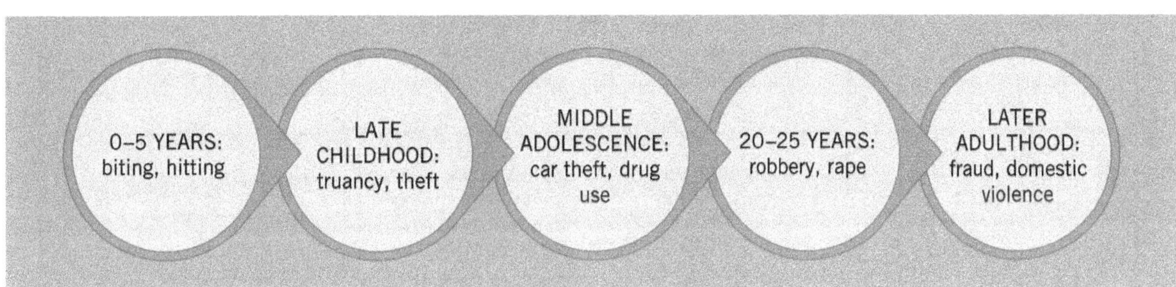

Figure 8.1 The life-course persistent offenders

from the British Crime Survey that 44 per cent of victims of violence believed that their assailant was under the influence of alcohol (Smith and Allen, 2004).

According to McMurran, Jinks, Howells and Howard (2011), three distinct types of violence may be identified:

- violence when pursuing material goals;
- violence related to social dominance goals;
- defensive violence to deal with threat.

This typology was used to classify the violent crimes committed by a sample of males between 18 and 21 years of age whose offences were alcohol-related. Many had drunk to excessive levels prior to committing their crimes. The study used semi-structured interviewing together with psychological measures of anxiety and anger. The three different types of violence were not differentiated in terms of the extent of alcohol consumption prior to the offence or in terms of the level of violence shown. Nevertheless, there were some differences between the groups on the psychological measures:

- *Gain or material goals:* 24 per cent of the alcohol-related violent offences involved violence in the course of achieving their material goals. High aggression and anxiety characterised this group. There was some evidence that they made efforts to inhibit their anger since they were higher than average on a measure of the inward expression of anger. Their violence was typically quick but severe.
- *Social dominance:* 62 per cent were classified in this category which was the most common. They were similar to the gain or material goals group in term of their aggression and anger traits. However, their violence tended to be accompanied by strong anger feelings. They rarely expressed remorse for their crimes.
- *Self-defence:* 14 per cent were in this category. Unlike the other two groups, they were lower on aggressive traits. They were the most likely to offend alone.

Why should being drunk lead some to behave violently? McMurran, Hoyte and Jinks (2012) believed that the thoughts of young male offenders on this might be helpful when planning treatment programmes. They obtained accounts of incidents of alcohol-related violence from nearly 150 young offenders. The amount of alcohol consumed between getting up and before the criminal incident took place was considerable – the average was 46 units. The researchers identified 16 types of triggers to violence, which are summarised in Figure 8.2 in order of frequency. McMurran *et al.* identified six distinct groups of triggers using thematic analysis (see Howitt, 2016). These groupings together with the triggers which made them up were:

- being offended by someone (triggers = insult, inappropriate comment, grudge) – 25 per cent;
- opportunities for material gain (friend initiates robbery, opportunity for material gain, refusing to pay, a joke gone wrong, asked to do a friend a favour) – 23 per cent;
- seeing someone in need of help (male friend in fight and harm to female acquaintance) – 19 per cent;

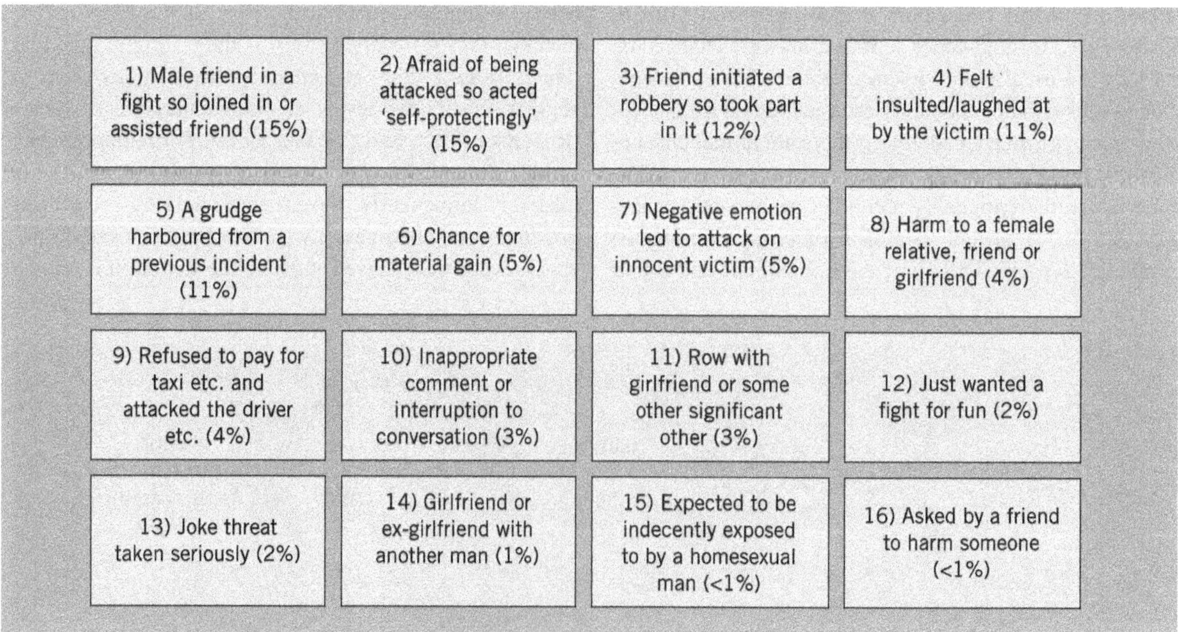

Figure 8.2 Triggers to violence in coding scheme

- perception of threat (fear of attack, indecent exposure) – 16 per cent;
- distress (negative emotion from previous event, row with significant other, girlfriend with another man) – 4 per cent;
- wanting a fight for fun (only this one trigger) 2 per cent.

The percentages indicate the frequency with which each grouping occurred.

Quite clearly being offended by someone, opportunities for material gain, seeing someone in need of help, and perception of threat are the dominant types of triggers. These findings encourage us to consider the triggers to alcohol related violence as being rather wider than merely being reactions to perceived insults or injury.

That there is a relationship between alcohol abuse/dependence and violent crime is reasonably well established. Answering the question of whether this is a causal relationship is rather more difficult. Many variables possibly account for this relationship other than the direct causal influence. Boden, Ferguson and Horwood (2012) describe the results of a longitudinal study into the effects of alcohol abuse/dependency on violent offending and victimisation, including intimate partner violence. They used sophisticated statistical techniques which allowed them to remove the effects of a wide range of confounding variables from the relationship. A birth cohort of babies in New Zealand was followed until the age of 30 years. Alcohol abuse/dependence was assessed annually using the Composite Diagnostic Interview (World Health Organization, 1993) between the ages of 17 to 30 years of age. This is based on the criteria for alcohol abuse/dependence which are described in the APA *Diagnostic and Statistical Manual* (*DSM-IV*). Violent offending was measured using annual self-report data about assault, fighting, use of a weapon, and threat of violence against a person. The possible confounding variables included anxiety, depression, and major depressive disorder, each measured annually.

Initially, the researchers found a strong relationship between alcohol abuse/dependency symptoms and violence perpetration and victimisation. Those with five or more symptoms showed rates of violence perpetration and violence victimisation between four and 12 times those for people with no symptoms. Gender made no appreciable difference to the size of the relationship. However, the relationship was much smaller when the confounding variables were included in the analysis. The adjusted figures controlling for the confounding variables indicated that those with five or more alcohol abuse/dependence symptoms were between two and four times more likely to show the violence outcomes than those with no symptoms. The authors suggest that this implies that 5 to 9 per cent violent crime perpetration, violent crime victimisation, and intimate partner violence is down to alcohol abuse.

Anger and its management in violent crime

There is a tendency to regard violence as an impulsive response to a perceived threat. However, the legal concept of pre-meditation itself questions the simplicity of this by regarding some violence as pre-meditated and warranting the most serious charges and the severest punishments. Crimes of passion are excused somewhat because of their impulsive and emotional nature. The impulsive offence is often contrasted with the planned offence. Planning is taken to imply a colder, more calculating approach. In psychology the distinction is made between reactive and instrumental aggression (Berkowitz, 1989). Reactive aggression involves the desire to hurt or harm the other person. Instrumental aggression has other motivations and involves the use of violence as a means to achieving other goals. Whether or not this boils down to a simple conclusion that homicides and assaults are reactive aggression and most robberies and sexual assaults involve instrumental aggression (as Berkowitz would have it) is far from certain. That is, there are instrumental and reactive versions of violent crimes like homicides, robberies, and so forth. Tedeschi and Felson (1994) also suggested that reactive aggression can involve instrumental behavioural patterns, such as when the motivation is retribution or thrill seeking. They saw the impulsivity in crimes not as 'automated' responses to frustration or threat but due to the poor decision making of offenders. Their lack of self-control, their drunkenness and high levels of arousal lead to a failure to consider their actions more carefully. Whether or not the reactive/instrumental dichotomy in aggression is the most useful approach has been questioned by some. Felson (1993) distinguished between dispute-related and predatory behaviour as opposed to reactive/instrumental aggression. Crimes like murder and assault generally are the result of interpersonal disputes of one sort or another. Homicide and assault usually stem from disputes and they are more likely to spontaneously emerge due to contextual factors. Predatory crimes include robbery and sexual assaults. The planned–spontaneous distinction is also of a wider theoretical interest. For example, the general theory of crime boils down to the idea that criminals lack self-control or that they are impulsive (Gottfredson and Hirschi, 1990; see also Chapter 9). The more that crime is planned, with costs and benefits carefully weighed up, the less sustainable becomes the general theory of crime.

Research has had relatively little to say about the planning of offending. One exception is a study by Felson and Massoglia (2012). They obtained self-reports from offenders about the planned/unplanned nature of their offences. This involved 7000 prisoners in state and federal facilities in the US. Participants were interviewed individually about demographic, social and behavioural indicators and the index of violent crime. The offences included homicide, physical assault, sexual offences and robbery, amongst others. The measure of planning simply required a yes/no answer and was: 'Did you plan the (name of offence) ahead of time?'. Some of the main findings were:

- Planning is much more characteristic of robberies than homicides and assaults.
- Dispute-related offences are more likely to be unplanned than predatory offences.
- Robberies are about eight times more likely to be planned than physical assaults.
- Sexual assault offenders are more likely to plan than physical assaulters.
- Planning is no more common for sexual assault than homicide.
- Female perpetrators of violence against their intimate partner were more likely to plan their offending than male perpetrators. Generally, however, domestic violence tends not to be planned.
- Offenders who had been drinking were less likely to plan. Forty per cent said that they had been drinking at the time of the offence.
- Better-educated and better-off offenders were more likely to plan.
- Older homicide and assault offenders were less likely to plan than younger ones.
- Only a quarter of robbery offenders said they planned their offence.

Perhaps, though, overall figures for offence planning are the most informative. Only 12 per cent of the offenders said that they planned their offence. Clearly, these data raise big questions about the nature of violence in offending. For some crimes, their instrumentality seems clear but there are other crimes for which impulsivity seems to be the most important feature. This is an area where there is insufficient basic data and a deeper analysis of the issue of planning than the above study provides is desirable. For example, more detailed accounts by offenders of their crimes might allow researchers to judge the presence or absence of planning more objectively. The above data predominantly portray the reactive nature of much violent crime.

So where does anger come into the equation? How important is it in understanding criminal violence? Novaco (2011) is one researcher who argues that forensic and criminal psychology fails to prioritise the role of anger appropriately. His basic assumption is that anger is closely involved with and the consequence of perceived threats such as insults, unfair treatment, and so forth. Anger drives violent offending in circumstances of threat *if* the individual has poor control over their anger. Developmentally, poor anger control may be the result of prolonged negative life experiences such as histories replete with themes of abandonment and rejection, psychoses, acute traumas, and biochemical imbalances among other things. Those with better anger control may well respond to a threat-provoking situation in a more constructive and socially positive way. In contrast, those without appropriately developed resources for dealing with anger may respond with aggression and violence. The model is pictured in Figure 8.3. Problems with the handling of anger may result in an offender being referred to anger management programmes by the criminal justice system. Rage, hate and revenge can be seen as closely linked to – or even as varieties of – anger. Referring back to Figure 8.2, we can see how several of the triggers to alcohol-related violence can be construed as perceived threats in various ways (even the possibility of an act of indecent exposure by another male). It is the perception which is important here, not the intention of the other person. To the angry person, their anger is experienced as justified by the wrong that the other person

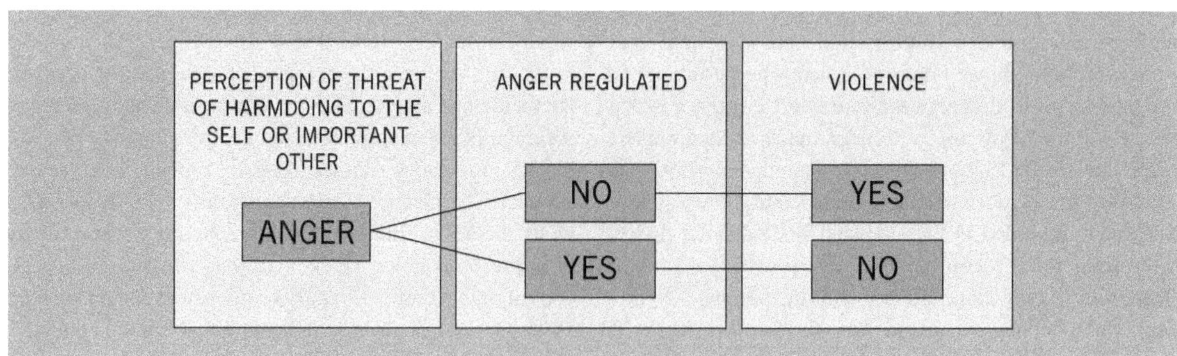

Figure 8.3 The relation between threat and violence

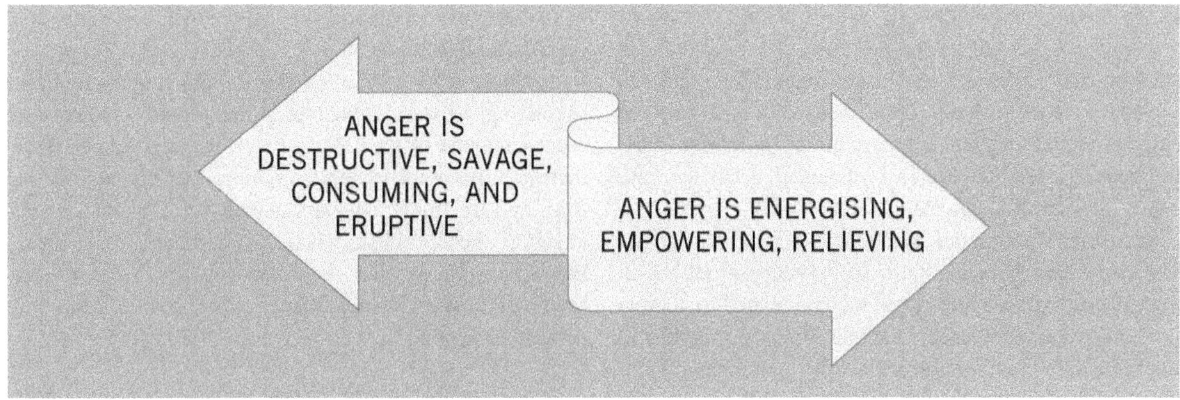

Figure 8.4 Contrasting conceptualisations of anger

has done. Once angry, we may have thoughts justifying why the anger is appropriate. In the future, these thoughts may readily be recalled as justifying anger. They encourage antagonistic responses to others, which may reinforce the likelihood that anger is aroused.

Novoco's definition is: 'Anger is a negatively toned emotion, subjectively experienced as an aroused state of antagonism toward someone or something perceived to be the source of an aversive event' (p. 651). This does not mean that anger is simply a bad thing. It needs to be understood that anger is a functional human emotion and not one which simply releases destructive forces. There are two different conceptualisations of anger – one implies that it needs controlling and the other that it should find expression and utilisation in one's life (see Figure 8.4). The latter is not frequently part of psychological thinking, which is dominated by the first conceptualisation, in which anger needs to be controlled. Things are worsened by the tendency of offenders to blame others and to see hostile intention in their actions. This can be described as a hostile attribution bias. There is also a tendency to blame things close to the situation for one's anger, rather than the actual cause of that anger. In order to function effectively, we need to employ self-monitoring capacities to good effect. But when angry, we cannot self-monitor well and we lose objectivity. So anger that has its roots in past events and experiences is treated by the individual as if it were caused by proximal events in the immediate environment. Anger makes us think imprudently, perform poorly at work, promotes poor health, and damages close relationships. When anger is not properly regulated, this can be seen in the frequency, intensity, duration, and ease of arousal, according to Novaco. Anger is not simply reactive. There are individuals who manifest recurrent anger. Such individuals are, in a sense, the agents of their own anger – as when they choose to live in highly conflictful settings or live with highly hostile people. These are the very circumstances which maintain anger.

Not surprisingly, anger is generally regarded as a dynamic risk factor indicative of potential violence. Its regulation, then, is a vital skill. Emotional regulation, in general, is important in life – not just the regulation of anger. Someone who manifests adaptive emotional regulation can function more successfully in their day-to-day environment. They can contain an emotional experience in ways which allow the emotional experience to run its course whilst avoiding anger-based goal-directed actions. Maladaptive emotional regulation means that the individual 1) cannot contain their emotional experience or 2) fails to let the emotional experience run its course. These are 1) underregulation and 2) overregulation respectively. Often the word *dysregulation* is used to refer to these.

Little research work is available on the regulation of emotion in aggressive behaviour beyond the issue of under-controlled anger and aggression. Roberton, Daffern and Bucks (2012) believe that focusing on this issue alone is a fragmentary way of looking at dysregulation. They argue that concentration on underregulated anger leads to a neglect of the sorts of problems that overregulated anger can lead to. Furthermore, it leaves aside the possibility that other emotions than anger may also be associated with aggression. For example, emotional dysregulation in which the emotions are poorly differentiated, or where there is poor awareness of emotion, can be correlated with 'aggression' (Cohn, Jakupcak, Seibert, Hildebrandt and Zeichner 2010). One form of overregulation is when the individual repeatedly uses strategies to block the emotion from running its full course. The individual may avoid thoughts, situations and people which arouse the emotion, or manipulate situations in such a way that emotion is not aroused. Overregulation employs much mental effort and consequently depletes the cognitive resources needed to deal with events. Depleted of these resources, the individual may more and more readily respond aggressively in anger-provoking situations. In support of this idea, it has been shown that emotional suppression is associated with poorer memory capability. A study by Tull, Jakupcak, Paulson and Gratz (2007) demonstrated that the avoidance and suppression of anger may be associated with increased aggression. The lowered cognitive resources associated with emotional overregulation might compromise decision making, lead to the loss of social networks, and reduce inhibitions against aggression.

Roberton, Daffern and Bucks (2014) set about testing their belief that poor regulation of aversive emotions in general, rather than anger alone, may be related to aggressive behaviour. They used a sample of adult offenders in Australia. These authors regard adaptive emotion regulation as being a balance involving allowing the emotional experience to run its course but controlling the emotion sufficiently to avoid impulsive responses such as aggression while at the same time allowing the individual to engage properly in their normal, goal-directed behaviours. Each of the offenders in their study was individually assessed in terms of how proficient they were on three different emotional skills. These were:

- Emotional awareness in which the individual recognises and can describe the emotional experience they have. For example, such an individual will agree that they pay attention to the way they feel.
- Emotional acceptance which involves a non-judgemental response to emotions and a lack of adverse response to those emotions. For example, such an individual will disagree that they become angry with themselves when they are upset.
- Having a variety of emotion regulation strategies. For example, such an individual would agree that when they are upset they believe that they will eventually get to feel better.

The participants were subdivided into those showing adaptive emotion regulation and those showing maladaptive emotion regulation. Given that this was an offender sample, it perhaps is not surprising that there were more maladaptive emotion regulators that adaptive ones. Aggression was commoner in the maladaptive emotion group. They had more substantial histories of aggressive behaviour. This was not accounted for by them having normative beliefs supportive of violence since the influence of maladaptive emotion regulation on aggression was additional to the influence of normative beliefs.

Howells (2004) had a straightforward answer to the question of whether anger is an essential component of human aggression and violence. He points out that a psychopath's violence may be entirely instrumental and dispassionate. Furthermore, anger is a common occurrence in human interaction but the vast majority of times when we become angry we do not become violent at the same time. Anger can lead to constructive as well as destructive behaviours. As a consequence, Howells labels anger as a contributing factor to violence especially if it co-occurs with certain other conditions. It is important that a forensic psychologist assesses whether an individual's violence is a consequence of their poor management of anger since there is little point in applying anger management in the form of a treatment programme (see pages Chapter 26) if anger is not problematic for a particular individual. Howells suggests that the following are some of the important aspects which the clinician should assess in relation to anger:

- Just what sorts of events trigger anger in the individual?
- How is anger experienced subjectively?
- How does the individual about and appraise anger triggering events? For example, does the individual regard them as threats to their social status?
- Does the individual manifest a particular action strategy in relation to anger? Perhaps, for example, they tend to strike out or they may 'bottle up' their feelings.
- Does the individual show good self-regulation strategies for anger? For example, do they make opportunities to cool off?
- What behavioural reactions does the individual have in response to anger? For example, do they become more confrontational?
- What functions do the angry behaviour have in terms of their social environment? For example, if they live in a macho culture then violent responses may be seen as reflecting their manliness.

Chapter 26 discusses therapeutic approaches to dealing with maladaptive anger responses.

Media influences on violent crime

Forensic and criminal psychologists have traditionally ignored the role of the media in the genesis of crime. One exception is Blackburn (1993). He reviewed the research evidence on media violence and concluded that the violent content of the media was influential on the violence exhibited by the audience. Harrower (1998), again unusually for the field, devoted considerable space to the topic, though her conclusions are largely rhetorical rather than research-based. If one relied solely on general psychology textbooks rather than on forensic texts, there would be no other conclusion but to accept that media violence has a significant effect on societal violence (e.g. Passer and Smith, 2001). However, there have been a number of reviewers who dispute the media violence causes societal violence notion (e.g. Cumberbatch and Howitt, 1989; Fowles, 1999), though this is far from a universal view (Browne, 1999; Pennell and Browne, 1998a). This is not to argue that the media have had no impact on society – that would patently be an absurd suggestion. Nevertheless, apart from laboratory experiments, research employing a variety of methods seems to indicate little or no influence of the media on real-life violence (e.g. Howitt, 1998b).

Criminologists have generally neglected media influences on violent crime (Cumberbatch and Howitt, 1989; Howitt and Cumberbatch, 1975). There are a number of reasons for this:

- Much of the research on media violence effects is based on laboratory experiments that are of little interest to many researchers.
- Explanations of media violence effects have largely been in terms of social influences rather than the clinical perspectives favoured by some forensic and criminal psychologists.
- Research findings in the field appear somewhat chaotic at first, with some studies suggesting effects and others suggesting no effects. Consequently, the complexity of the research is difficult for non-specialists in media research to comprehend.
- Few media researchers have much knowledge of crime. Indeed, the media violence research very rarely involves acts that are likely to be illegal since the 'victim' has agreed to the aggression or it is directed against an inanimate object or it may be verbal aggression.

What is the case for believing that media violence causes violence in society? This can be broken down into several broad research strategies including laboratory experiments, developmental studies, studies of crime statistics and studies of delinquent individuals:

Laboratory experiments

There have been numerous laboratory studies of the effects of media violence. This style of research is still current, for example, in relation to video games (e.g. Rothmund, Bender, Nauroth and Gollwitzer, 2015). Essentially one group of participants are shown a violent film/video snippet and another a non-violent snippet. Then their aggression levels, as measured by an electric shock machine in the fashion of the classic Milgram experiment on obedience (Milgram, 1974) are compared. Alternatively, as in the case of the Bandura studies of social learning through modelling (Bandura, Ross and Ross, 1961; 1963), children watch a model of knocking over and otherwise maltreating a blow-up plastic clown, which is regarded as analogous to other forms of violence (Howitt, 1998b):

- It is clear from meta-analysis (Box 4.2) that the findings of laboratory experiments overwhelmingly suggest the strongest effects of media violence compared with other types of study (Hearold, 1986; Paik and Comstock, 1994; Wood, Wong and Chachere, 1991).
- However, a number of studies have failed to reproduce findings using different methods and, in some cases, the effects are so specific that they are likely to apply only in the laboratory setting. For example, in Berkowitz's famous studies (Berkowitz and Rawlings, 1963; Berkowitz, Corwin and Heironimus, 1963) the aggression effects claimed were very short-lived and applied only to the person who had deliberately insulted participants.
- Howitt (1998b) called for the criminological relevance of research to be the basis for deciding whether research on media violence should be taken seriously by forensic and criminal psychologists. Research on four-year-olds imitating the modelled, seemingly play aggression against a squeaky blow-up plastic clown that cannot be knocked over without it bouncing back up, is hardly the sort of activity that warrants the description 'criminal' (Howitt, 1998b). Ultimately, the concern with media violence is its influence on the development of serious violence in the audience.

Studies of the development of aggression during childhood

We saw in Chapter 6 that there is a strong tradition of developmental studies of delinquency. Rarely do these studies research the effects of media violence. One exception is the work of Leonard Eron. In the early 1960s he published a study into factors associated with aggression in a large sample of youngsters of about eight years of age (Eron, 1963). Peer and teacher ratings of aggression were obtained, as well as a range of other measures such as the number of hours of television watched each week. In addition, the violence level of the child's favourite television programmes was assessed. This was based on the nominations *each child's mother* made about their child's favourite television programmes. The amount of television watched did not correlate positively with the aggression exhibited by the youngsters. Indeed, for boys, the less television watched, the more aggressive they were – the reverse of the 'media causes violence' hypothesis. Although, maybe, this ought to have been the end of the story, it was not. The reason was that the *mothers' nominations of the aggressive boys' favourite television programmes* were more often violent programmes than were those of the non-aggressive boys. No such relationship was found for girls. This seems, overall, rather weak evidence that television is responsible for violence.

A few years later, with a number of collaborators, finance was obtained to study the same youngsters when they had reached their late teens (Eron, Lefkowitz, Huesmann and walder, 1972). This additional stage is probably the most famous and influential. It showed that the violent television variable at age eight years predicted aggression at age 18 years ... apparently. One major problem was that this measure at age 18 years was actually retrospective. Peers were rating each other as they were quite a few years earlier. In other words, these were ratings of aggression going back close to the time of the original phase of the study. It is hardly surprising that media use at age eight predicted aggression at age 18 years since aggression at age 18 years was simply not what it appeared to be. There were more follow-ups. The final stage studied the same group when they had reached adulthood. It was possible to check the actual crimes and motor traffic offences they had committed. Remarkably, it looked as though adult criminality could be predicted from those ratings of favourite television programmes decades earlier. One interpretation of this is that it is an effect of liking violent television that persists into adult behaviour and results in criminal and other antisocial behaviour (e.g. Newson, 1994a,b). There are other possibilities. For example, we saw in Chapter 6 the continuities between childhood antisocial behaviour and adult antisocial behaviour. Perhaps the mothers, when they nominated their son's television viewing favourites, were conscious that sometimes their son was a little wayward in his behaviour. Thus when they answered about television programmes they nominated a violent programme because this fitted with their son's personality; the boy was not asked. Consequently, this adult behaviour was merely a continuation of the difficulties that some mothers recognised in their sons' behaviour and nothing to do with television at all. If it were television that caused their behaviour, would we not expect the problems to be associated with watching more television, not with watching less?

- Milavsky, Kessler, Stipp and Rubins (1982), in a major replication in the style of the above study, found little to support the Eron *et al.* data (Eron *et al.*, 1972; Huesmann and Malamuth, 1986; Lefkowitz, Eron, Walder and Huesmann, 1977).
- A later American study by Huesmann and Eron (1986) failed to detect similar effects for boys. This time, quite unlike the original study, some evidence was found that girls' viewing was associated with aggression.
- International studies of the development of aggression supervised by Eron and his co-workers (Wiegman, Kuttschreuter and Barda, 1992) found, at best, extremely varied results with very little support other than in North American research. There were many zero relationships between television viewing indexes and violence in viewers. Indeed, the relationships were very inconsistent even within countries.

Studies of the criminal statistics

While crime statistics can be difficult to interpret (see Chapter 2), they have been used in two ways to study media effects on societal violence:

- Messner (1986) took the crime statistics of different states of the United States and related them to the public's viewing of media violence obtained from surveys of media use. The areas with the greatest amount of public consumption of media violence then should have the greatest levels of societal violence – according to the 'media violence causes violence' hypothesis. Of course, it is essential in such a study to control/adjust for demographic characteristics when making the comparisons. After that was done thoroughly, Messner (1986) found that the *more* television violence watched, the *less* the violence in the community. This is the reverse of expectations if the media violence causes violence hypothesis were true.
- Centerwall (1989, 1993) took a different approach. He studied changes in violent crime rates in the United States for the period from before the introduction of television to many years after its introduction. Previous research had found no immediate impact of the introduction of television on US violent crime rates (Hennigan *et al.*, 1982). Nevertheless, Centerwall argues that one would not expect effects until several years later, when children have grown into adolescents – the time when they are most likely to demonstrate violence. This is a reasonable idea, although many other researchers had studied the immediate effects of witnessing media violence and found effects in the laboratory. At first sight, the crime data appear to support this thesis – a rapid rise in societal violence occurred several years after the introduction of television in the United States. In comparison, in South Africa, where television was not introduced until many years later, there was no such rapid rise at that time. Howitt (1998b) applied Centerwall's idea to Great Britain, where television was introduced as a mass medium during the 1950s. He found that there was a steady growth in violent crime during the period researched by Centerwall but no rapid rise at the time predicted by Centerwall's argument. In other words, there is no general effect of television violence on violent crime statistics, which casts considerable doubt on Centerwall's interpretation of the US data.

Studies of delinquent offenders

There have been some studies of the media use of delinquent offenders (Hagell and Newburn, 1994; Halloran, Brown and Chaney, 1970; Kruttschnitt, Heath and Ward, 1986). These generally fail to produce evidence of the influence of media violence on offenders. For example, one study found initially that there was an association between serious delinquency and television use (Browne and Pennell, 1998; Pennell and Browne, 1998b). A sample of violent teenage boys in a young offenders' institute for violent offending was studied. The young offenders were compared with appropriate control groups – including a similar group of incarcerated young offenders *not* convicted of violence, community controls of the same age range, gender and so forth:

- Differences were found in the media use of the incarcerated groups and the community groups – for instance, the offenders tended to prefer violent videos, though they also liked soap operas even more.
- There were psychological differences, such as the lower level of moral reasoning in offender groups, which might have contributed to their offending (see Chapter 6).
- Physical abuse by parents was far commoner in the childhoods of the offenders.

Despite the initial finding that media violence and offending were correlated, when experience of childhood abuse was controlled differences between the groups in terms of liking violent videos disappeared. Their violence then results from their abusive childhoods as does their greater interest in violent videos.

Does media violence cause violent crime?

In the context of forensic psychology, the answer to the question of whether media violence leads to societal violence needs to concentrate on criminologically relevant research. This means that much of the voluminous literature on media violence effects is irrelevant, as it does not deal with criminal acts. A lot is now known about the development of criminality and violent criminality in particular from longitudinal studies of child development (see Chapter 6). It is clear that early experience, especially inadequate parenting, leads to problem children, problem teenagers and problem adults. Taking this into consideration, the following summarises the main issues concerning media violence and criminal violence:

- Virtually no developmental evidence exists concerning the influence of the media on criminality. The studies that deal with the media tend to be associated almost exclusively with the work of Leonard Eron and his co-workers. Despite being frequently cited in the debate on media violence effects, the original findings are inconsistent and apply to boys and only in terms of their mothers' assessments of their favourite television programmes. When the amount of television viewed is considered, the evidence suggests that the more television watched, the less impact it has on aggressive behaviour! Later studies fail to reproduce these findings, or find similar outcomes but for girls and not boys, which is the reverse of the original findings, or produce inconsistent outcomes for different parts of the world. In short, there is less than convincing evidence of the effects of media violence.
- Crime statistics do not show a relationship with the levels of violence viewed in communities – the reverse trend exists in fact. Crime statistics in the United States have been interpreted as demonstrating a delayed effect of the introduction of violent media but this claim has not been substantiated for the United Kingdom.
- Violent delinquents do seem to have a preference for certain sorts of programme, including violent video. Despite this, the biggest factor in their violence is their abuse by their parents in childhood. Once this is taken into account, then their media consumption can be regarded as no different from non-violent controls.

In summary, a forensic and criminal psychologist should exercise great caution before assuming a role of the media in generating violent criminality. Although there have been claims that offenders have been influenced by movies, no court in the United States has accepted such arguments (Lande, 1993). Nevertheless, there have been accusations that movies such as *Child's Play 3* (directed by Jack Bender in 1991) and *Natural Born Killers* (directed by Oliver Stone in 1994) influenced youngsters to kill, the latter in very substantial numbers. However, the evidence in support is weak. For example, whether the culprits actually saw the movie in question is doubtful in some cases and that an accused person attempts to excuse their acts by blaming a movie might be expected. It is not the sort of rigorous evidence that forensic and criminal psychologists normally seek. The inhibition of aggression is socialised from early in childhood, long before the child is capable of giving much attention to television programmes. Failures of parenting at an early age have clearly been shown to be associated with later criminality and violence.

An independent, review of the evidence (Felson, 1996) makes a number of related points. They are worth mentioning as they reinforce some of the comments made above:

- Violent offenders tend to be versatile offenders as we saw earlier in this chapter – they do not confine their activities to violent crime but commit a variety of types of crime. This is somewhat incompatible with the idea that violent offenders have a problem caused by their violence socialisation, either via the media or any other source.

- The contents of the media concerning violence do not appear to give a radically different message about violence than any other source of socialisation. The media give much the same message about when it is appropriate to use violence and when it is not appropriate. The one area where Felson makes an exception is illegitimate violence that is, by definition, unacceptable. The media show this sort of violence being punished more so than does any other source of socialisation.

Savage and Yancey (2008) also expressed surprise that, out of the thousands of studies relating media exposure to aggressive behaviour, very few have studied criminal violence. There are probably rather fewer than 40 such studies, even if one stretches the definition of criminal violence a little. Savage and Yancey included studies which used measures of exposure to media violence about whose validity they had doubts. For example, they used studies, among others, which employed violence ratings of the individual's favourite programmes, even though they say that studies using violence ratings of general viewing would be preferable. When they estimated the effect size of studies they found no significant effects of media violence on real criminal violence for studies using female participants or studies combining female and male participants. Even for male participants alone, the size of the effect of television violence on real-life criminal violence was tiny at 0.07, which is virtually no effect. Even this, they claim, was a highly biased estimate because some important control variables were missing from some studies.

If that were not enough, Ferguson (2009) launched a technically sophisticated critique of the same body of research which Savage and Yancey had meta-analysed. But he went further in terms of the forensic implications of the media/violence research debate. He points out that forensic psychologists can (and have been) asked to provide sound information concerning media violence research. He mentions two main contexts for this: as an expert witness, and when speaking to the media or more directly to the public. Ferguson says that the psychological community has failed to properly inform the legal system and the public about the many significant difficulties with media violence effects research. He writes, 'I submit here that psychologists have an ethical responsibility to provide full disclosure of research limitations to the courts and public so that an informed conclusion can be reached' (p. 117). The failure of psychologists to do this has a long history.

Similar arguments have been made about the impact of violent video games on the user's violent behaviour as were made about the effects of media violence. Ferguson, Rueda, Cruz, Ferguson, Fritz and Smith (2008) discuss the issue and mention that meta-analyses (see Box 4.2) of research studies into the effects of violent games on interpersonal violence have found very small effects with between 1–4 per cent of the variance in interpersonal violence being accounted for by playing violent video games. But they say that these are overestimates because unpublished studies tend to have insignificant findings and were excluded from these meta-analyses. When unpublished studies are incorporated then the relationship effectively becomes zero.

An interesting coda to all of this can be found in Ferguson and Dyck's (2012) discussion of media violence. In part this can be seen as a response the events of *Brown* v *EMA* in which the US Supreme Court 'struck down' a Californian law banning selling violent video games to minors. A number of prominent psychologists had signed an *amicus curiae* statement in support of the view that such games increase aggression in children – that is, harmed them. (There was, it may come as no surprise, an opposing *amicus curiae* denying this.) *Amicus curiae* means literally 'friend of the court' and is information offered to the court by someone who is not directly involved in the case. The psychologists in question generally advocate the general aggression model, a psychological theory. Quite clearly, their comments did not sway the Supreme Court to their view. Ferguson and Dyck (2013) see the origins of the general aggression model in Bandura's (1961) Bobo doll experiments mentioned earlier. In these he demonstrated that children could learn and reproduce modelled behaviour. This behaviour was construed as aggressive as it involved knocking down an inflated self-righting plastic doll. Various social cognitive models elaborated on this and various related ideas such as 'priming', desensitisation, excitation-transfer, etc. have been put forward and extensively researched. Despite such considerations, the basic premise of the general aggression model is that young humans have an innate proclivity to reproduce (imitate) what they observe. Ferguson and Dyck argue that little prevents the assumption that reproduction of observed behaviour is inevitable in this modelling. Modelling has its longer-term effects, according to the model in terms of social schemata. Nevertheless, this cognitive component does not stop the researchers acting as if children cannot tell/do not know the difference between reality and fiction. There is no benefit in rehearsing the case that Ferguson and Dyck make against the general aggression model here. The point that should be apparent here is that research evidence which some psychologists might be inclined to accept as pertinent to legal matters may not have the same impact on judges, juries, and lawyers who have a different perspective. Psychologists often sloppily generalise from their laboratory studies to real-life issues. In some circumstances this may go unchallenged. So the test is not whether your fellow-researchers see things your way but whether the data withstand the scrutiny of other perspectives. This would apply to other academic disciplines too. Particularly important for forensic and criminal psychologists is the question of just what would a criminologist, for example, make of their ideas? Understanding something of the criminological foundations of the subject matter of forensic and criminal psychology has to be a useful starting point – something that is obvious but easily overlooked.

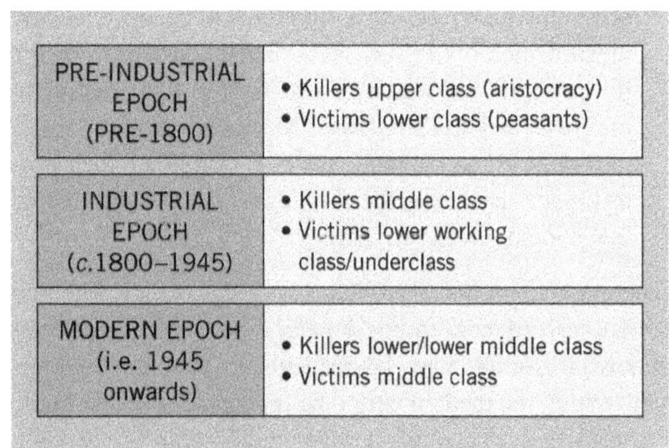

PRE-INDUSTRIAL EPOCH (PRE-1800)	• Killers upper class (aristocracy) • Victims lower class (peasants)
INDUSTRIAL EPOCH (*c*.1800–1945)	• Killers middle class • Victims lower working class/underclass
MODERN EPOCH (i.e. 1945 onwards)	• Killers lower/lower middle class • Victims middle class

Figure 8.5 Leyton's epochs of murder

Theories of homicide

Societal level theory

There is a tendency to assume that violence is the result of an individual's psychological make-up. Since most of us do not murder then there must be something 'odd' about murderers. For most homicides, there is little to implicate psychiatric factors, which suggests that other factors are involved. The evidence that homicide rates tend to increase in times of war, for example, suggests that that broad societal events may significantly affect the criminal acts of individuals (Pozgain, Mandic and Barkic, 1998). Nevertheless, psychiatric factors simply cannot be discounted entirely. For example, Steck (1998) found that spouse murderers in a German sample characteristically had a history of psychologically deviant development, especially involving psychiatric disorder, and were the individual is disengaged socially.

One of the more interesting societal level explanations of homicide is Leyton's (1986) view that multiple murder can be understood of social structure. A problem in understanding multiple killing (including serial killing) is that the targets of such crimes tend not to be a random sample of potential victims – i.e. victims tend to have particular characteristics. Leyton's key insight was recognising that multiple killers are not merely a recent phenomenon but one with roots in history. He identified three major historical periods in which multiple killing was common and realised that they differed markedly in terms of who became killers and who the victims. The historical epochs in question are the *pre-industrial period*, the *industrial period* and the *modern period*. The typical killer during these times and the typical victim are given in Figure 8.5.

What appears to be happening, very broadly, is that killers have been from ever lower social classes since the pre-industrial period. In contrast, their victims have become of higher social class. In the pre-industrial epoch, the typical multiple murderer was Gilles de Rais, a French nobleman who killed peasant children by the hundred. The typical multiple killer of the industrial epoch was a middle-class man who killed housemaids or prostitutes. Finally, in the modern epoch, the multiple killer is largely of a lower social status than the victim. If this is true, then the question is why do these changes occur? Basically, Leyton argued that multiple killings are indicative of *homicidal protest*. This means, essentially, that at different times in history one social class comes under threat from another social class. The general dissatisfaction, concern and anxiety felt by the threatened class become expressed by a few of the discontented class through multiple murders of the threatening class. In other words, the murders are symbolic of structural discontent. The epochs differ in the focus of this discontent:

- In the *pre-industrial period* there was challenge to the social order by the peasant classes as well as merchant classes. Revolts and the like illustrate the challenge.
- In the *industrial period*, the middle classes held their position through a 'moral' superiority over the working class. Consequently, the threat to their social position came largely from those in society who most threatened that moral order. Prostitution was by its nature a threat to the family and the patriarchal social organisation of the family. Women who engaged in sexual activity willingly outside marriage would threaten the moral basis of family life. Housemaids, of course, were the lowest level of employment; the sexuality of single women was also a threat. They were also in the sector of employment that somewhat morally disgraced young women could be encouraged to enter if their chances of marriage had been sullied. Killing such women symbolically reinforced the moral superiority of the middle class. Jack the Ripper would appear to represent this type of killer – if he were a member of the middle class rather than royalty, of course, in the light of some claims about the Ripper's identity.
- In the *modern period*, according to Leyton, the challenge to the social order comes from the changed social

order in which rigid class structures have loosened and upward mobility is seen as a realistic ambition of the lower social classes. It is when those who expect to progress feel thwarted that *homicidal protest* comes into play. Hence students may be victims of such protest since they have the privileges that the disaffected feel should have been theirs.

There are a number of problems with this theory. The historical record concerning crime, especially in the pre-industrial period, may be inadequate. Can the findings concerning the modern period be replicated away from the North American context? Grover and Soothill (1999) took Leyton's ideas and attempted to apply them to serial killing in recent British criminal history. A total of 17 serial killers (three or more victims) were found for the period beginning 1960. According to Grover and Soothill, it was clear that the victims were simply not middle-class people, as the theory predicts that they should be. They were in fact typical of the weak and powerless groups in society – gay men, women, children, young adults and pensioners. The serial killers included Ian Brady, Myra Hindley and Beverly Allitt who killed children, and Dennis Nilsen, Colin Ireland and Peter Moore who killed gay men. While at least a substantial number of the killers could be described as working class, the data do not support the idea of a class-based homicidal protest. Grover and Soothill suggest that the idea of homicidal protest may be useful if the idea of its basis in social class conflicts is abandoned. It should be replaced by consideration of broader social relations which make certain groups vulnerable.

Psychological disposition theories

There is no easy way of explaining homicide. While it is tempting to regard murderers as exceptionally violent personalities suffering from extremes of psychopathology, this is to ignore the large number of killers who are non-aggressive and not suffering from an identifiable psychopathology. Murderers have been divided using various typologies. After studying murderers in a psychiatric prison hospital, Blackburn (1971) suggested that there are four types of murderer:

- depressive;
- over-controlled repressors (of aggression);
- paranoid-aggressive;
- psychopathic.

This pattern has been found in a non-psychiatric group of offenders so it is not merely the result of the extreme psychiatric difficulties of a selected group of offenders.

Biro, Vuckovic and Duric (1992) carried out a standardised interview with Yugoslavian men convicted of homicide offences. As in Blackburn's research, the MMPI (Minnesota Multiphasic Personality Inventory) scores of the men were an important aspect of the categorisation. Four categories were identified:

- Normal profiles (28 per cent).
- Hypersensitive-aggressive (49 per cent): this group consists of people with the characteristics of being easily offended, prone to impulsive aggressive outbursts and intolerant of frustration. They are very rigid, uncooperative and permanently dissatisfied with things.
- Psychopathic (17 per cent): these tend to score highly on emotional instability, impulsivity and immaturity. They tend to have poor control of their aggression.
- Psychotic (5 per cent): these seem to be 'mistakes of the system' since they are individuals who show extreme psychiatric signs and would normally have been confined to a special psychiatric unit. Their crimes appear to be bizarre, such as the man who cooked his own child in a pot. These offenders had not been psychiatrically evaluated before being sentenced.

The percentages in each category seem to indicate that only in a large minority of the cases is the issue primarily to do with aggression. A quarter plus show normal profiles overall. The normal personality category seems to act aggressively out of a situational pressure, not because its basic personality structure leads to aggression.

Sociobiological theory

At the opposite pole, there are biologically based ideas about murder, which on the surface would appear to be as different as possible from the societal approaches such as that just described. While it is tempting to believe that there may be some biological factor (e.g. brain dysfunction) in extreme violence such as serial killing, the research evidence in its favour is best described as minimal (Coleman and Norris, 2000). There are two important issues here:

- Research on the biological basis of criminality, and criminal violence in particular, is somewhat patchy. There is a lack of a coherent body of knowledge as a consequence. This situation is no help to forensic and criminal psychologists.
- Biological factors are generally beyond the scope of psychologists to change materially.

The typical biological approach seeks to find the biological 'defects' which result in criminal behaviours.

When one considers the topic of violence including homicide, it is tempting to point to the statistics that show that violent crime is an overwhelmingly male activity. This, surely, must be irrefutable evidence of a firm biological basis to violent crime. A little care is needed. Bjorqkvist (1994) argued that men and women do not differ in their aggressiveness. What is different is the way in which it is expressed. Bjorqkvist goes so far as to indicate that the claim that men are the more aggressive is nonsensical. Aggression is largely seen from a male perspective that equates aggression with physical aggression. It is this male perspective that has dominated research on human aggression. If men are the most aggressive, then the fact that same-sex aggression (female vs. female, male vs. male) seems to be more common than cross-sex (male vs. female) is difficult to explain. Bjorqkvist argues that the physically weaker sex, women, is likely to learn different aggressive strategies from those used by the physically stronger sex, men (Bjorkqvist and Niemela, 1992; Bjorkqvist, Osterman and Kaukiainen, 1992). It is inappropriate then to extrapolate from animal studies to human aggression since animal aggression is mostly physical. For adults, the reasonable assumption is that physical aggression is the least common form of aggression.

The putative link between testosterone and aggression is commonly believed yet is a very much a dubious proposition for humans. According to Bjorkqvist, the closer an animal species is to humankind, the less is the link between testosterone level and aggressiveness. If the theory is correct, injecting testosterone experimentally should lead to higher aggression levels. Unfortunately, the research evidence on this does not have clear-cut results. Sometimes such experiments seem to suggest no link between the testosterone and aggression. Edwards (1969) and Edwards and Herndon (1970) found that female mice given the male hormone androgen at birth grew up to be more aggressive as adults than non-treated mice. While this appears to support the view that maleness = aggression, perhaps this is not the case. Similar female mice given the female hormone oestrogen at birth also tended to fight rather more than non-treated mice as adults. Bjorkqvist proposed an effect/danger ratio theory for human aggression. This is based on the notion that there is a subjective estimation of the ratio between the effect of the intended strategy (such as physical aggression) divided by the danger involved of such a strategy. This operates in such a way that risk is minimised while the effect of the strategy is maximised. Hence, women have a greater risk if they engage in physical aggression than men, so they may prefer other strategies. There is some evidence that aggression in human males is expressed directly (perhaps in the form of fighting) whereas aggression in females is expressed indirectly (perhaps in the form of maliciously telling a teacher something).

Bjorkqvist and Niemela (1992) had peers rate Finnish seven-year-olds, indicating what each child did when angry. Direct responses were kicks/strikes, swearing, chasing the other child and pushes/shoves. Indirect responses included gossiping, becoming friendly with another child in revenge, and suggestions that the other child should be shunned in some way. The study was essentially repeated with a similar sample of 11-year-old and 15-year-old adolescents. At the younger age, it was clear that boys used direct forms of aggression more than did girls. There was no difference in terms of indirect aggression. But during adolescence girls were still using direct aggression less than did boys, whereas they used more indirect forms of aggression. The girls seem to manipulate their friendship networks as a means of effecting some of this indirect aggression. Similar findings were found concerning indirect aggression in females cross-culturally (Osterman, Bjorkqvist and Lagerspetz, 1998).

Others have found that relational victimisation of this sort (telling lies about another person so they will be disliked or leaving another person out of social activities when one is angry with them) is more characteristic of girls (Crick and Bigbee, 1998) even at the pre-school age level (Crick, Casas and Mosher, 1997). There is evidence that girls see social aggression as little or no different from physical aggression in terms of its hurtfulness (Galen and Underwood, 1997). Thus if aggression is seen as the intention to hurt or harm another then the use of indirect aggression by females relates more closely to physical aggression. It might be argued that it is physical aggression that is punished in law, not the indirect forms of aggression. This is to ignore, for example, libel and slander laws, which are clearly about controlling what might be described as 'verbal social attacks' on individuals. Lindeman, Harakka and Keltikangas-Jarvinen (1997) had Finnish adolescents rate themselves in terms of their strategies in conflict situations. In this context, in late adolescence, the preferred mode for male adolescents was to join in with any verbal aggression. In contrast, girls said that they would adopt a strategy of withdrawal from the situation or used a more social model of response such as 'I would clearly tell the backbiters that their behaviour is mean and I would ask them to stop' (p. 343). Of course, some have argued that direct forms of physical aggression are becoming more characteristic of females. Much of the physical aggression between girls concerns their relationships with males and threats to those relationships (Artz, 1998). As such, the aggression is regarded as the right thing to do.

It is worthwhile noting Crick's (1997) findings concerning social-psychological adjustment as assessed through self-ratings and teacher ratings. Gender normative aggression was associated with good adjustment ratings. Boys who engaged in aggression through relationships and girls who were overtly aggressive tended to be perceived as less well adjusted. In other words, there is evidence of the deeply seated nature of these gender differences in aggression.

There is a substantially different perspective concerning gender differences in aggression. Daly and Wilson (1988) put forward a socio-biological explanation of homicide. They worked primarily on the basis of the following established socio-biological principles:

- The process of natural selection shaped human nature: that is, random genetic variation produces diversity of offspring and those best fitted to survive tend to pass on their genetic material. While the ideas are essentially those of Charles Darwin, Herbert Spencer's phrase 'survival of the fittest' is the most familiar way to describe it. In this context, survival is survival of the genes or species rather than a particular individual. Fitness really refers to those who are able to transmit their genes – individuals who do not win out in mating may live to an old age, but they have not passed on their genes so they were not fit in terms of the species.
- Daly and Wilson use the term 'adaptively constructed' to describe the way we are – that is, we are what we are because that is what allowed the species to survive. There is a competition in mating whereby the fittest (best genes) tend to be transmitted to the next generation.
- People (as well as other creatures) have evolved such that they spend much of their efforts on the posterity of their genes: that is, sex is not some sort of secondary motivation that comes into play when hunger and thirst, for example, have been satiated. It is much more to the forefront than that.
- Homicide, like any other field of human activity, should show characteristics that reflect in some way the characteristics of how we have been adaptively constructed.
- Daly and Wilson accept that there is cultural variation over and above socio-biological influences on homicide. Some cultures seem to exhibit higher levels of killings than others. Nevertheless, part of the pattern of homicides is socio-biologically determined.

These basic ideas, in themselves, did not take Daly and Wilson far. Something else needs to be considered. They recognised that much of the available statistical evidence was incapable of answering crucial questions about homicide. Furthermore, the available database needed reanalysis to provide helpful answers. To illustrate, in the context of the family, socio-biological thinking would suggest that both parents should have an interest in ensuring that their offspring (their genes) survive. At the same time, Daly and Wilson argue that we are often encouraged to believe that the family is a dangerously violent place in which the offspring are at considerable risk. In other words, rather than preserve their genes, parents may kill their offspring, thus destroying the future potential of their genes. This is certainly the impression created by the research literature on family violence. There is a problem with this. When homicide of children is subdivided into killing by natural biological parents and by step-parents, interesting findings emerge. Natural parents kill their offspring rather rarely in comparison with step-parents, who kill the children of the family relatively frequently. Step-parents are not destroying their own distinctive genes by killing, say, a child fathered by the woman's previous partner.

Another example is their argument concerning intrasexual homicide – that is, men killing men, women killing women. The genes of men, they argue, are best helped to survive by fertilising as many women as possible. Hence other men are a handicap to genetic survival since they monopolise women. Women help their genes survive best by protecting and nurturing their offspring. Thus Daly and Wilson argue that men should kill men much more frequently than women kill women. The data on homicide suggest that this is the case. Indeed, young men are much more in competition for mating than older men – and crime statistics suggest that young men kill each other much more frequently. There are a number of matters to bear in mind:

- The socio-biological approach, since it attempts to explain society from the point of view of biology, competes with social explanations of the same phenomena. For example, step-parents may murder children of the family more often simply because the stresses in step-parent families are likely to be greater. Furthermore, bonds between step-parents and step-children may have had less opportunity to develop. It is difficult to decide which is the better explanation. Socio-biological approaches tend not to have any verifiable genetic evidence: both they and societal explanations rely on observations of the same social processes.
- Socio-biological approaches to a variety of social phenomena tend to be a little unhelpful because of the assumption that what is genetically fixed becomes incorporated into social structure. Forensic and criminal psychologists are more interested in changing individuals than in regarding their criminality, for example, as a built-in feature.
- Whatever the long-term value of Daly and Wilson's approach in helping us to understand homicide, it teaches a valuable lesson about crime statistics: that is, statistical compilations of data may sometimes hide important relationships simply because very different things are classified together in published tables.

The multi-factorial approach to homicide

Generally speaking, most forensic and criminal psychologists would take the view that extreme acts of violence, including homicide, have multiple causation. Rarely is a

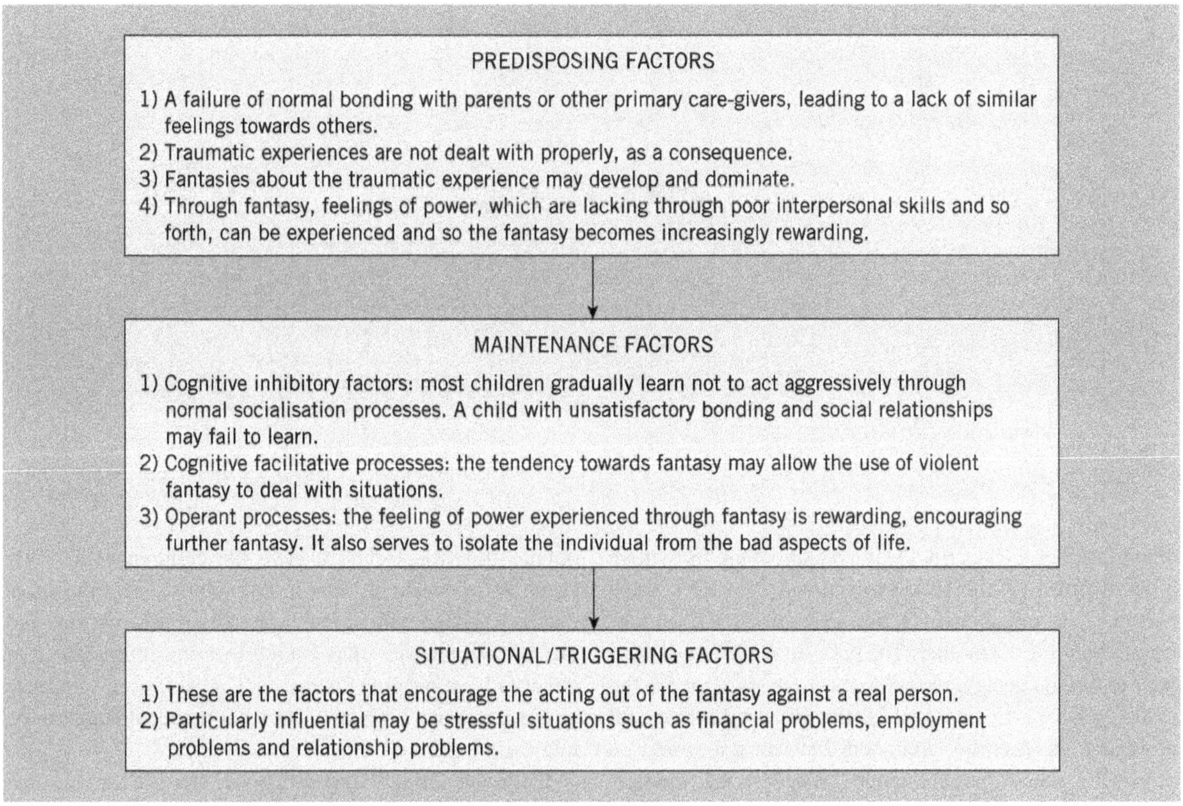

PREDISPOSING FACTORS

1) A failure of normal bonding with parents or other primary care-givers, leading to a lack of similar feelings towards others.
2) Traumatic experiences are not dealt with properly, as a consequence.
3) Fantasies about the traumatic experience may develop and dominate.
4) Through fantasy, feelings of power, which are lacking through poor interpersonal skills and so forth, can be experienced and so the fantasy becomes increasingly rewarding.

↓

MAINTENANCE FACTORS

1) Cognitive inhibitory factors: most children gradually learn not to act aggressively through normal socialisation processes. A child with unsatisfactory bonding and social relationships may fail to learn.
2) Cognitive facilitative processes: the tendency towards fantasy may allow the use of violent fantasy to deal with situations.
3) Operant processes: the feeling of power experienced through fantasy is rewarding, encouraging further fantasy. It also serves to isolate the individual from the bad aspects of life.

↓

SITUATIONAL/TRIGGERING FACTORS

1) These are the factors that encourage the acting out of the fantasy against a real person.
2) Particularly influential may be stressful situations such as financial problems, employment problems and relationship problems.

Figure 8.6 Multi-factorial model of serial killing

Source: Gresswell, D.M. and Hollin, C.R. (1994) 'Multiple Murder: A Review' *British Journal of Criminology* 34, 1–14. Reproduced by permission of Oxford University Press

single factor seen as sufficient to explain violent crime. Since extreme violence, such as serial killing, is such a rare phenomenon, it is unlikely that a single factor could be identified which is only associated with serial killing. Extremely violent behaviour may, then, best be understood by the application of the sort of multi-factorial framework suggested by Gresswell and Hollin (1994, 1997). This is illustrated in Figure 8.6. Basically, it involves three levels of factor – *predisposing factors*, *maintenance factors* and *situational/triggering factors*. These three types should be considered as part of the explanation of a homicide. No particular specific factor is assumed to be essential to homicide. Nevertheless, the accumulating pattern of factors when applied to a particular case may help understand that case. It is clear from Figure 8.6 that serial killing is rare because the contributing factors in themselves may not be common and the presence of several of them together may be a rare situation.

Equally, when considering the many frequent minor assaults that pervade the criminal statistics concerning violence, we might look for commonly occurring factors. However, the likely influence of factors acting separately may not be the same as factors acting in combination. For example, Haapasalo (1999) examined intergenerational cycles of physical abuse by taking a Finnish offender sample. He collected a variety of information about physical abuse as well as other matters such as marital conflict and involvement with the child protection services. In a sense, studies such as this are particularly important for forensic and criminal psychologists since they are about their main clientele. Studies involving the general population are less relevant to their work and may show less strong or even dissimilar trends. Following a complex statistical analysis (Lisrel), it became clear that the paths leading to the sons being physically abused in childhood can have unexpected twists. As shown in Figure 8.7, there was clear evidence that the variable *mother physically abused in childhood* leads fairly directly to her son being *physically abused in childhood*. This is probably very much what one might expect on the basis of the assumption that aggression is, in part, socially learnt.

What of the influence of another variable *economic stress* (financial and related difficulties)? We would expect, surely, that the more stress on the mother, the more likely she would be to physically abuse her children since stress makes her irritable and moody, among other things. Take a look again at Figure 8.7. Starting with the factor *economic stress*, we can see that it leads to a higher level

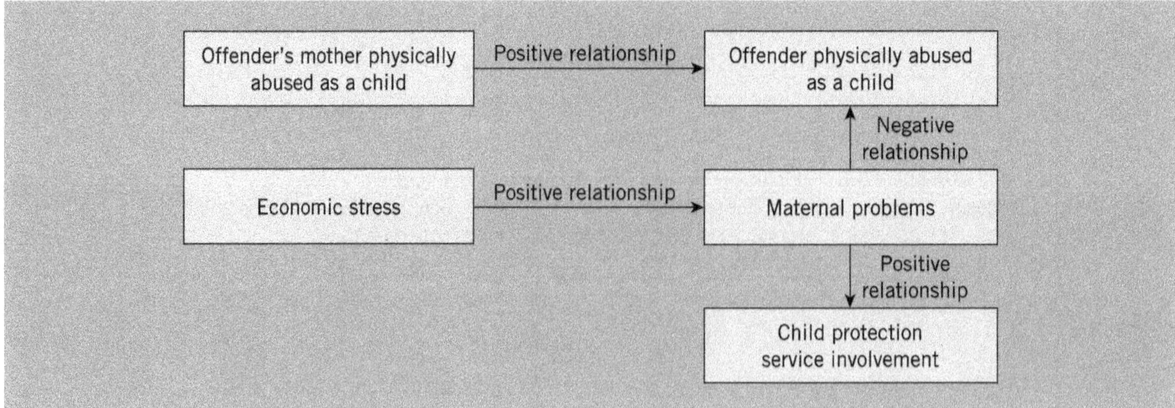

Figure 8.7 The relationship between cycles of abuse and economic stress

of *maternal problems*. But the most likely route from there is involvement of the child protection services for some reason. This might include, for example, some sort of respite help for the mother. The path from *maternal problems* to the son being *physically abused in childhood* is the reverse of expectations: that is, the greater the maternal problems, the *less* the likelihood that her son would be physically abused in childhood. Whether the mothers regard economic stress as a warning sign that they are not coping cannot be addressed simply from these data. Nevertheless, this is feasible, which may make them more inclined to seek the help of social services. This completely unexpected finding tells us to avoid making simplistic assumptions about how social and psychological factors influence violent behaviour.

Domestic violence: forensic issues

Much of this chapter has dealt with explanations of extreme acts of violence. It is important for a forensic and criminal psychologist to understand the range of theoretical approaches that can be brought to the discipline. At the same time, forensic and criminal psychology is not merely a branch of psychological research and theory; it is also a practical discipline that seeks to help deal with otherwise tricky questions for the criminal justice system. Let us take a particularly difficult issue – that of domestic violence within a family. There are a number of aspects to this. One is that this is the sort of situation with which social workers, the police and sometimes psychologists may have to deal. So what can we say if we know that a man at 25 Beeches Road has split up with his partner? There are children in the household and social workers insist that he lives at another address. He attempts to obtain visitation rights to have the children at his new home at the weekend. The mother objects. Her reason is that he has been violent to her on numerous occasions and that every time there has been a meeting in the past, the children have become distressed. Called in to give advice or even evidence to court, just what practical suggestions might a psychologist make?

Common notions suggest that violence is a trait in some people, and that such people act aggressively in a wide variety of situations. The suggestion is sometimes heard that a particular person has a short fuse, for example – that is, the person is readily provoked to be aggressive. Unfortunately, one cannot rely on folklore as a definitive treatise on human behaviour. Put more formally, the issue is one of the co-occurrence of spousal abuse and physical child abuse – if the one is present, how likely is it that the other is also present? This has been sporadically an issue for research since the 1970s, when it was first suggested that, if there was spousal abuse in the family, the risk of that child being abused was increased. It was not until the 1990s that it became recognised that child abuse and spousal abuse were simply different aspects of family violence (Appel and Holden, 1998). This has clear implications for forensic issues such as whether spouses who batter their partners are fit to be the custodial parent on divorce or separation. According to Appel and Holden, what at first appears to be a relatively simple question becomes a complex one when the research literature is addressed. Issues include the following:

- The criteria employed to decide whether spouse abuse and child abuse had occurred. The mother's report, the father's report, the child's report and professional assessment may all be expected to produce somewhat different findings.
- The sorts of act classified as abuse may profoundly influence rates of co-occurrence. For example, if a

gentle slap of a child were to be regarded as physical child abuse, then, since a gentle slap is a very frequent form of discipline in families, it is extremely likely that a man who has abused his partner will also have abused the child.

- What period of time was covered by the retrospective reports? The greater the time period, the greater co-occurrence.

Appel and Holden reviewed studies of different types of sample: community (or non-clinical) samples, samples of battered women and samples of maltreated children. Self-reports, agency records, hospital records and clinical impressions were included. The detail of the outcomes of the studies differed quite widely, although it is fair to suggest that, generally, co-occurrence does take place but the magnitude of this varies:

- Most of the work on community samples (i.e. general population samples) has been carried out by Gelles (e.g. Gelles, 1979; Gelles and Cornell, 1985), using the *Conflict Tactics Scale*, which consists of a list of ways in which conflict between family members has been resolved during the year. Figures on violent means of conflict resolution give a 6 per cent occurrence figure for spousal and child abuse. This increases substantially when the period under consideration is extended. If violent methods of conflict resolution are considered for any time during the relationship (i.e. if violence ever occurred), then the figures increase: 11–21 per cent overlap, depending on the study in question (Silvern, Karyl and Landis, 1995).
- Studies using data from battered women showed bigger variation. Overlap between spousal and child abuse varied from 10–100 per cent. The studies using the Conflict Tactics Scale tended to suggest 51–72 per cent overlap between spousal and child abuse. Of course, battered women as a group might be expected to produce more extreme tendencies than those in the general public. For example, the battered women may go to the shelters not for their own safety but for the safety of their child.
- Child abuse reported to the authorities gave figures of co-occurrence varying between 26 per cent and 59 per cent.

In other words, just basing one's assessment of risk to the child on the fact that the spouse claims to have been beaten seems unsatisfactory. The increase of risk is very difficult to know with any precision. Furthermore, we have already seen that the risk of violence by step-parents is greater than the risk from natural parents: that is, there is more to put into the equation than the act of spousal abuse alone.

There are still further considerations. Appel and Holden argue that the structure of violence within families falls into a variety of types which are, at least, theoretically feasible:

- *Single perpetrator model:* the man beats the woman and the child.
- *Sequential perpetrator model:* the man beats the woman who then beats the child.
- *Dual perpetrator model:* the man beats the woman and the woman also beats the child.
- *Marital violence model:* the woman and man beat each other and both beat the child.
- *Family dysfunction model:* all three family members beat each other – including the child who beats the adult perpetrators.

There is at least some evidence in favour of each model. Each of them may apply at least in a proportion of cases. So, if we do not understand the family dynamics in more detail, we may make unfounded assumptions. The child may be at risk from the mother as well in some types of family.

Quite clearly, simplistic commonsense assumptions about violence may prove woefully inadequate in the setting of professional forensic and criminal psychology work. Confirmation of this comes from US data on homicide of partners (Walker and Meloy, 1998). Estimates suggest that, annually, a minimum of 2.5 million women are battered by their partner/spouse. Twelve hundred are killed annually by their partners/spouses. Thus domestic violence is quite a poor predictor of murderous outcomes, given the ratio of abuse to deaths, statistically stated: there is a 2100 to 1 chance of a death compared with the numbers of battering households. What makes this an even more problematic interpretation is that about half of such homicides were not preceded by violence/battering at any stage. While it is clear that domestic violence is predictive of homicide, at least weakly, just about half of the spousal murders are not associated with prior abuse. See Chapter 27 on risk assessment for more details.

Domestic violence by women against men

Radical changes have occurred in the ways police forces around the world deal with domestic violence. Once the police regarded violence within an household as a domestic matter not normally warranting police involvement but now they are proactive about the issues. It would seem obvious that most domestic violence is the actions of men against women. In a study in the United States, Stalans (1996) found that the public estimated that two-thirds of the victims of domestic violence where the police are called out were women; 17 per cent thought that the victim was the man and another 17 per cent saw the injuries as being to both. The message from the public seems to be that women are overwhelmingly regarded as the injured victims of domestic violence. However, one researcher in particular, Murray Straus, seems to take a different view. Straus was one of the first researchers to carry out major studies into the extent of domestic violence. His work with Gelles (e.g. Gelles and Straus, 1979) was profoundly influential by exposing the extent of the problem. These authors used the Conflict Tactics Scale which, as we have seen above, has been extensively used by family violence researchers (Straus *et al.*, 1996). The scale does not ask directly about family violence but, instead, how conflicts are resolved within the family. Various means of dealing with conflict are considered, ranging from verbal conflict resolution techniques (e.g. 'discussed issues calmly' or 'got someone to help settle things') to minor physical aggression (e.g. threw something, pushed or slapped), to severe physical aggression (e.g. burned, used a knife, or fired a gun).

Straus (1992) argued that a neglected aspect of his work was the extent and seriousness of violence by women against men. Numerous US family violence surveys, he commented, have demonstrated that violence by women against men is almost as common as men's violence against women. 'Husband battering' (Steinmetz, 1977), he suggested, has been ridiculed and not taken seriously. Critics have taken issue with Straus because of problems in knowing just what the Conflict Tactics Scale measures. For example, the general nature of the measure may mean that it fails to differentiate effectively between a woman slapping a man once and a man beating a woman on several occasions. In addition, on the basis of the 'act' alone it is not possible to know the motivation for the violence. For example, if a person slaps another, one does not know whether this was unprovoked or in retaliation. In contrast, some claim that the legal system treats violence by women as more serious. For example, it has been suggested that homicides of the female partners of men are relatively leniently treated compared with where a woman kills her male partner (Roberts, 1995).

Can we regard female domestic violence against men as symmetrical or asymmetrical with that of men against women (Dobash and Dobash, 2004)? That is, does women's violence against men have the same damaging consequences as that by men against women. Straus's view is an example of the symmetrical argument. Even if women are as likely to resort to violence as men in domestic situations, does it, for example, lead to the same level of serious injuries? Dobash and Dobash studied the reports of men and women involved in court cases involving domestic violence. A number of things were clear in terms of violence against partners:

- Women were less likely to have acted violently against their partner in the previous year.
- Men were more likely to have carried out a series of violent acts than were the women.
- Men were much more likely to punch, scratch, slap, kick the body, use objects as a weapon and so forth. To take an extreme example, men were about 50 times more likely to choke their partner. There was no category of violent act in which the rates by women exceeded those by men.
- The injuries sustained by women were much more common – bruises, black eyes, cuts, scratches, split lips, fractured teeth or bones, and unconsciousness.
- Ratings of seriousness of the violence were on average higher for men's violence than for women's violence. Somewhere between a quarter and a half of the ratings for men's violence were in the serious or very serious category whereas only about 1 in 20 of the acts perpetrated by women were placed in these extreme categories.

Care is needed not to assume that women's violence is relatively benign as there is evidence of the serious injuries that women perpetrators of domestic violence can inflict (Nowinski and Bowen, 2012).

Although this is rather convincing evidence of the dangerousness of men's domestic violence, it does not mean that we can totally disregard those cases where women are initiating extremely serious acts of violence against their partner. However, there is considerable evidence that women's violence against male partners is judged differently. Morgan and Wells (2016) used qualitative data analysis in an interview study of male victims of domestic violence. In their interviews, the men failed to mention their personal emotional reactions to their physical abuse and thought that their abuse was different because they were men. Their gender limited their means of coping with the abuse. They adopted a strategy of merely describing the events. They were rather more emotional when they discussed the impact of the abuse on their children. Indeed, they felt that their children were used as methods of controlling them by their abuser. For example, once children had come along the victim felt a sense of self-imposed lifetime involvement in the relationship. It reduced the likelihood of leaving the relationship while at the same time providing new means by which the woman could control the man. Gendered sterotypes of abuse were also seen as means of manipulating them.

And the issue does not stop there. We can turn to stalking, which frequently follows the break-up of a relationship.

Stalking: what sort of crime?

There are various types of stalking and it is motivated by a number of different factors. It frequently arises out of intimate relationships and often involves individuals previously close to the victim. The origins of anti-stalking legislation were a consequence, initially, of cases of stalking famous people though this belies the way in which it commonly occurs. Among the famous victims of stalking are actress Brooke Shields, who was stalked for 15 years; the actress Jodie Foster – stalked by John Hinckley, who shot President Ronald Reagan in the belief that this would gain her attention; David Letterman; Madonna; Rihanna; Jennifer Aniston and Rebecca Schaeffer, who was killed by her stalker in 1989. Some of these could be described as cases of *erotomania*, which is obsessive, excessive, unwanted or delusional love, according to Fitzgerald and Seeman (2002). Perhaps this appropriately describes cases such as Madonna, David Letterman and Rebecca Schaeffer since their stalkers held delusional beliefs that the celebrity was in love with them. Erotomania is defined as a delusional disorder in the *Diagnostic and Statistical Manual* V (American Psychiatric Association, 2013). Delusions need to have lasted for at least a month and there should be no evidence of a psychotic disorder. While these high-profile examples have been important in developing anti-stalking legislation, they do not define the typical stalking offence or offender. Stalking had not really been established as criminal behaviour until after the Rebecca Schaeffer killing.

Many of the people who become fixated on public figures are severely mentally ill and often this fixation is associated with mental illness (Mullen *et al.*, 2009). For example, Ronald Dixon went to Buckingham Palace and claimed to be King Ronald, the son of Edward VIII and the rightful king of England. He said that he would kill Queen Elizabeth II because she had had him tortured by an electronic crown put into his head which prevented him sleeping. After being legally sectioned to the local mental health services, he was eventually discharged. Weeks later, he stabbed a mental health worker to death. His response to all questions in court was: 'King!' Relatively little is known about the risk factors for violence perpetrated against high-profile people. James *et al.* (2010) employed what they term 'proxies' for violence against the British royal family. By this is meant examples of inappropriate approaches to the royal family, such as unauthorised entry to royal events by deception. The list of 'proxies' was obtained from the files of the Metropolitan Police Service Royal Protection Unit. Most of the instances were simple approaches in which someone behaved inappropriately at a royal residence or a royal event (58 per cent) and a further 10 per cent included cases where the person had previously communicated, say, by letter to a member of the royal family but then approached that royal in person. The more serious approaches tended to be attempts to breach security barriers or cordons. Seven per cent of the total approaches were failed attempts to breach security barriers or cordons and 25 per cent were successful crossings of a barrier or security perimeter (including those involving the use of deception).

Different legal jurisdictions do not take identical approaches to stalking (Sheridan and Davies, 2002) and no legal or research definition effectively distinguishes dangerous, predatory stalkers from what they term 'the over-attentive suitor'. US legislation requires the fear of physical injury or death whereas the United Kingdom merely requires a minimum of two acts of harassment. Australian legislation includes the word 'intends' in aspects of the definition, such as intending to cause serious physical harm or intending to cause fear (ibid., 2002). Quite clearly, these various definitions are very different and allow the police to intervene at different stages of stalking. Furthermore, it needs to be understood that the public may recognise some acts of stalking as examples of unreasonable behaviour without necessarily regarding them as criminal (Scott, Rajakaruna, and Sheridan, 2014). Similarly, McKeon, McEwan and Luebbers (2015) have identified community attitudes which minimise, justify, and normalise stalking thus, possibly, leading to inaction by victims and the police. These were: 1) 'stalking is not serious' (e.g. 'If there is no actual violence, it shouldn't be a crime.'); 2) stalking is romantic (e.g. 'Women find it flattering to be persistently pursued.'); and 3) victims are to blame (e.g. 'Victims of stalking are often women wanting revenge on their ex-boyfriends.'). These attitudes were associated with acquitals in a mock jury stalking trial.

Sheridan and Davies (2001) had participants in their research rate a number of vignettes concerning stalking. Different groups were given different instructions about the criteria to employ. One group had a US legal definition, another group a British legal definition, and a third group an Australian legal definition to work group. A fourth group simply based their assessment on their own opinions. Different vignettes exemplified the different penal codes more effectively than others. For example, the following was more likely to be judged stalking according to the US principles than those of any of the other countries:

> After our divorce, whenever I saw my ex-husband he would use obscene and threatening language towards me when such was entirely inappropriate (i.e. not during an argument situation). He also threatened to kill me. I also received an obscene threatening telephone call from his girlfriend.
>
> (p. 11)

The following is perhaps even more illustrative since it was seen to illustrate stalking using the UK legal definition but unlikely to illustrate stalking from the point of view of the US legal definition:

> A chap in the recent past kept turning up at my house uninvited and just walking in. He was sometimes difficult to get rid of. The relationship was flirtatious at first but his behaviour I considered inappropriate and I therefore cooled off a bit in friendliness towards him. He failed to acknowledge or accept this and chose to write weird poetry and one particularly worrying letter to me which was menacing and full of 'magical thinking' abstract type stuff. This behaviour stopped after a few weeks.
>
> (p. 11)

This is another reminder that jurisdictions differ and what is true in one may not apply elsewhere.

Stalking is a form of predatory behaviour that is characterised by repeated patterns of harassment of a particular individual to a degree which may frighten the victim or worse (Sheridan and Davies, 2001). Examples of stalking/harassment behaviours described in a number of studies are annoying telephoning, letters, visiting the victim at home, following the victim; verbally threatening violence, physical assaults, gift-giving, visiting the place where the victim works, face-to-face contacts, aggressive letters and property damage. Stalking behaviour is common according to a number of surveys. The precise figures obtained depend somewhat on the style of the survey and the sources of information. A good example was Tjaden and Thoennes' (1998) national violence against women survey in the USA. This telephone survey of a sample of the general population in the United States was not restricted to female victims. The survey used the following three key characteristics to define stalking behaviour:

- The victim is spied on, sent unsolicited letters or receives unwanted telephone calls, finds that someone is standing outside their home and other behaviours of this sort.
- The behaviour had to be carried out by the same person on at least two occasions.
- These incidents had made the victim either 'very frightened' or fear violence.

Of the people in the survey reporting that they had been stalked, 78 per cent were women and 22 per cent were men. For the women, 94 per cent of stalkers were men and, most importantly, 48 per cent of these stalkers were intimates such as a past husband or partner or having had a brief sexual relationship. The average stalking continued for 1.8 years. Approximately 1.3 million American women would be stalked annually extrapolating from these base rate figures (Tjaden and Thoennes, 2000). Being afraid that the stalker could be violent is not unrealistic. Meloy (2002) summarised a number of studies of inter-personal violence among obsessional followers, stalkers and criminal harassers. Typically rates of violence between 30 per cent and 50 per cent were found. Furthermore, studies where the stalker was a former 'intimate' of the victim yielded figures of around the 60–90 per cent level for violence.

Roberts (2005) examined stalking by former romantic partners after the relationship broke-up. British undergraduate female students completed a self-report questionnaire which showed that a third had been a victim of stalking, a third had suffered harassment and a third experienced neither from their previous partner. The stalking behaviours included unwanted letters, telephone calls and gifts, and violence such as physical violence or destruction of property. Stalking was differentiated from harassment in terms of its involving unwanted attentions on two or more occasions. Those who experienced harassment or stalking were more likely to have been subject to controlling behaviours and denigration during their relationship with the offender. So they were more likely to report that during the relationship they were discouraged from having contact with friends and relatives, sex was demanded when the woman did not want it, and the partner would humiliate her in front of others. These are behaviours which are commonly reported in surveys of domestic violence. Roberts argues that these findings are in line with the idea that stalking is a variant of domestic violence.

Long-term or persistent stalkers are not generally deterred from their activities by the involvement of the police or other authorities. On the other hand, they may desist from stalking in these circumstances for some time only to return to stalking in the future – perhaps with a different victim. McEwan, Mullen and MacKenzie (2009) studied 200 stalkers who had been referred to a community mental health clinic, for example, by a court. About a quarter of the stalkers persisted with their stalking for more than a year. The nature of the prior relationship involved was a major predictor of persistence. Those who stalked prior acquaintances rather than strangers were significantly more persistent. Characteristics of persistent stalkers included:

- They tended to be over the age of 30 years.
- They were seeking intimacy or be motivated by resentment.
- They tended to have symptoms of a psychosis.
- They tended to send victims unsolicited things through the postal services.

It is a misunderstanding, however, to equate persistence with high risk of violence. Persistent stalkers were not more violent.

Inevitably there is concern about the characteristics of stalkers which make it more likely that they will carry out the more extreme acts, including violence. Psychopaths are relatively uncommon among stalkers, though their stalking patterns are not typical. A Canadian study by Storey, Hart, Meloy and Reavin (2009) used Hare's Psychopathy Checklist Revised, which is a common assessment tool for psychopathy (see Chapters 21, 22 and 27). Actually, only one diagnosable psychopath was found in this study, indicating a very low prevalence of psychopathy amongst stalkers. The sample was obtained from attendees at a forensic psychiatry clinic. The victims of this sample of stalkers were mostly female, with an average age of about 50 years. There was evidence of the secondary victimisation of members of the primary victim's family in about 20 per cent of cases. Evidences of any psychopathic symptoms were uncommon among stalkers but, where they occurred, the stalker tended to target casual rather than close acquaintances. They also tended to have higher levels of some standard risk factors for reoffending. Figure 8.8 summarises some of the characteristics of stalkers with psychopathic characteristics.

However, the research evidence using victimisation surveys in various parts of the World including the UK, US and Australia is that ex-partners stalkers are typically more violent and persistent than stranger stalkers (Scott, Gavin, Sleath, and Sheridan, 2014). Furthermore, the majority of stalking is done by partners, ex-partners, and friends of the victim. Thus the most violent of stalkers are the most common type of stalker. Those who were violent as part of their stalking were also the most violent during the relationships. There is a paradox, however, in that stranger stalkers are the most likely to be arrested – intimates are less likely to be arrested. This can be partially understood when we consider that the Crown Prosecution Service in the UK is more likely to abandon cases where the offender is an ex-partner of the victim (Harris, 2000). Scott *et al.* (2014) showed that victims of ex-partner stalking were perceived as more responsible for the stalking especially where the offender was persistent and threatening! Furthermore, a study of English and Scottish police officers found that they rated stalking behaviour as harassment and believed that police intervention was necessary when the perpetrator was described as a stranger (Sheridan, Scott, and Nixon, 2016).

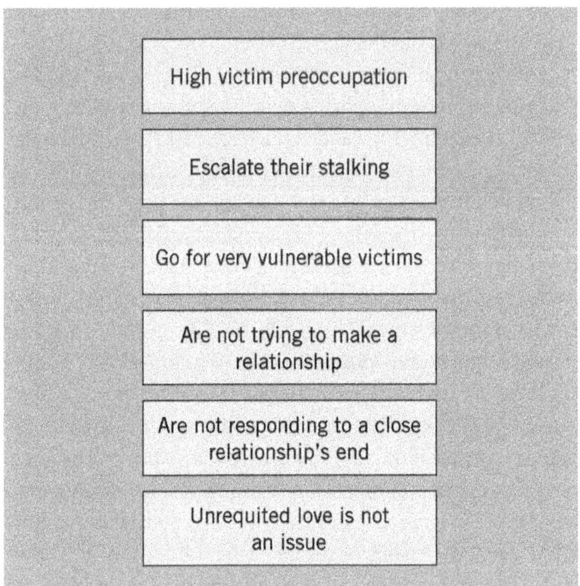

Figure 8.8 Psychopathic stalkers are uncommon but they show some of the characteristics above

Finally, we should not forget the potential of the Internet in relation to many sorts of crimes. The concept of 'cyberstalking' has been mooted, though without a clear distinction being made between cyberspace being used as an extra way of stalking victims and cyberstalking being an entirely new and different form of stalking behaviour. Some of the ways in which the Internet can be used to frighten and harass victims include deluges of unwanted e-mail, ordering goods and services in the name of the victim without the victim's immediate knowledge, posting unpleasant material about the victim, and threatening the victim in some way on the Internet. Some regard cyberstalking as a form of cyber-bullying along with such activities as harassment and denigration in which repeated messages are sent in order to harm the victim (Langos, 2015). Cyberstalking includes these components of harassment and denigration to an extent to which the victim becomes worried about their personal safety and fear their self to be in imminent danger (Willard, 2007). Cyberstalking can involve behaviours such as using e-mail to contact the victim, employing social networking sites such as Facebook to address the victim or to post comments about the victim of a derogatory nature, and to obtain information about the victim to be used in the stalking behaviour. Alexy, Burgess, Baker and Smoyak (2005) found that cyberstalking was more likely to involve behaviour such as threats to the victim and threats of suicide by the victimiser – and the victims were less likely to contact the police.

Sheridan and Grant (2007) studied victims of four different types of stalking: (1) pure online-only cyberstalking; (2) crossover from cyberstalking to real-life stalking; (3) real-life stalking with crossover to cyberstalking; and (4) pure real-life stalkers. The researchers developed a series of characteristics which distinguish cyberstalking. These included the fact that the stalking began online first of all and the stalking was solely online for a minimum of four weeks. Most (74 per cent) of those victims who met these criteria of being cyberstalked had originally come into contact with the offender over the Internet. It was found that there were no differences in terms of the psychological and medical effects of stalking and cyberstalking on the victim. In terms of social and economic effects of victimisation, the only significant effect was that the victim, not surprisingly, was more likely to change her e-mail address. Compared with real-life stalking, cyberstalkers were likely to have been former romantic partners and more likely to have been people who had been met on the Internet. Given that the study involved several hundred different variables to assess the differences between stalking and cyberstalking, the main finding was of great similarity between the two.

There is relatively little evidence about cyberstalking which is based on studies of cyberstalking offenders rather than information provided by victims. An exception is an Australian study by Cavezza and McEwan (2014). Generally speaking it was difficult to differentiate the stalker from the cyberstalker on the basis of various demographic, behavioural and clinical statistics. Indeed, most of the cyberstalkers also employed off-line stalking tactics. Cyberstalkers tended to be ex-intimate partners and they approached their victims less often than did stalkers.

Desistance from violent crime

As with other offenders, the criminal careers of violent offenders eventually end. Desistance is used to both describe the process by which crime is given up and the state of having given up crime. The general perspective on desistance is that it is the result of a complex interplay of internal and external factors. Many questions need to be addressed about desistance. Just what triggers it and how it is maintained is unclear. In part the difficulty is the lack of a clear definition of desistance. Just how should desistance be defined?

- Is it meaningful to speak of desistance for offenders who only ever commit one crime?
- Does desistance have to be absolute or can a reduction in criminal activity be termed desistance?
- Is a crime-free period (crime-free lull) the same as desistance – that is, is this a failed desistance?
- Crime-free is not the same as arrest-free, though they are often not differentiated.
- Researchers seem to regard desistance as being more-or-less akin to permanent retirement from crime. This begs the question of how long it is before desistance can be regarded as permanent.

Very little is known about the protective factors which are involved in desistance from crime. Statistical trends based on aggregated data from samples of offenders need to be treated with great caution. Such figures may show statistical trends, but these trends need not represent any one offender's experience of desistance accurately. These statistical trends differ somewhat, according to the nature of the crime under consideration. The trends for violent crime are relatively clear. The violence–age curve is one which climbs steeply during adolescence, peaking in early adulthood and then declines smoothly and steadily up to when the offender is 30 or beyond. Even though there is a correlation between beginning violence early and ending violence in adulthood later, nevertheless many adolescents stop acting violently before they reach their adulthood.

Just how the age-decline part of the age–crime curve can be explained is uncertain. The bad consequences of arrest, decline in physical powers, being contentedly married, and being in an employed career are among the possibilities. There are also potential biological factors to consider (Walker, Bowen and Brown, 2012). For example, they point out that levels of neurotransmitters are related to ageing and violence. So men who are interpersonally violent tend to manifest lower levels of serotonin. Interestingly, given the age decline in violent crime, levels of serotonin tend to increase with age (Rogers and Bloom, 1985). Also nor-epinephrine and dopamine are both associated with aggression and its decline with age. Marriage is a recognised factor in desistance from crime, though the quality of the relationship involved seems to be important. Anticipating marriage may be responsible for kick-starting desistance, but other consequences of marriage could be involved. This is redolent of Sampson and Laub's (1990) idea that involvement in adult institutions affects how criminal behaviour progresses in the individual's life. These adult institutions include the community, family, military and work. These institutions are considered to be effective because of the informal social controls that they exert. Haggård, Gumpert and Grann (2001) found evidence that desistance followed from a triggering or turning point such as being arrested; that offending declined gradually with relapses prior to cessation; and that offenders saw informal social controls like having children as being important. Desistance involves a complex interplay between the individual's characteristics, their cognitive processes relevant to desistance, and social influences of various sorts. It may be that different combinations of these things are involved in desistance at different stages in life.

Desistance theory has to have at its core the concept of agency. In other words, the offender's sense that they are capable of doing what is necessary in order to abandon crime. If we discuss this in terms of the analogy of giving up smoking it may be clearer. A smoker may believe 1) that giving up smoking will have financial and health benefits and 2) that carrying on smoking will result in cancer and other diseases. However, unless the smoker believes that they have the personal resources to be able to quit smoking then they will simply carry on smoking, no matter their beliefs about its dangers. Figure 8.9 provides us with a formula for giving up crime based on this sort of rationale. It is basically the model of desistance put forward by Caleb, Lloyd and Serin (2012). Quite clearly, there are many influences which affect beliefs about what will happen if crime is continued, beliefs about what will happen if crime is stopped, and the belief that one has 'what it takes' to give up crime – that is, the feeling of self-efficacy or agency. Caleb *et al.* refer to *outcome expectancies* to describe beliefs about what will happen if a particular course of action is followed (more crime or desistance). Basically, they propose that expectancy beliefs and agency beliefs need to be in line with each other for effective desistance from crime to occur. The offender needs to believe that:

- continuing with crime will lead to bad outcomes;
- giving up crime will lead to good outcomes;
- they have the personal wherewithal to be able to desist from crime.

No research has comprehensively examined the entirety of this approach to desistance. However, Caleb *et al.* took a step in the right direction when they developed measures of each of the above three things. Did their measures correlate in the way they might be expected to? That is, did negative crime expectations, positive desistance expectations, and a personal sense of agency relate to each other? Among the battery of questionnaires which the offenders completed were the following measures of each of these things:

- *Personal Outcome Expectancies for Crime Scale:* This measured the benefits and costs of criminal activity from the offender's point of view. An example of these is 'You will feel a good thrill or excitement'.
- *Personal Outcome Expectancies for Desistance Scale:* Examples of items measuring positive desistance outcomes are 'You won't worry about arrest or prison again' and 'You will have a healthier life-style'.
- *Personal Agency for Desistance Question:* This essentially measured the offender's sense of personal agency for desisting from offending. This is indicated by the following item from the scale 'I feel helpless when I try to stop myself from committing crimes; the world always somehow forces me to keep going back to crime' which is, of course, reverse scored.

Participants in the research were approximately 140 male inmates of a Canadian minimum-security institution. They ranged in age from 20 to 71 years, with an average of 41 years. Half were non-sexual violent offenders whose offences included murder and assault, and about a fifth were sex offenders, with the remainder being made up of non-violent offenders. The researchers found that these different aspects of desistance tended to be associated together – that is, they all had a tendency to be present if any of them were. Caleb *et al.* therefore argue that offenders' expectations about crime and desistance are consistent and coherent. The evidence seems to suggest that agency beliefs are at the core of this cluster – that is, the belief that one can change is at the core of the process. Other data from the study indicate that offenders understood the difficult requirements that the process of desistance would involve and were aware of the demands – they could divide their overriding goal of desistance into smaller, more immediate objectives. Put another way, offenders with the will to desist knew better how to desist. A final point is that measures of static risk factors did not correlate with desistance expectancies, although they did correlate with crime expectancies. That is, the development of desistance beliefs may not be dependent on changes in risk factors.

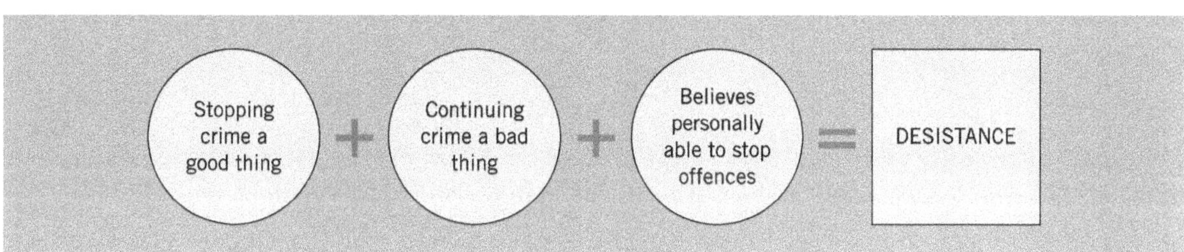

Figure 8.9 The main factors leading to desistance

Main points

- As violent crimes range from the most trivial of assaults to the most disgusting of serial killings, a range of theoretical perspectives is needed in order to begin to explain such crimes. Similarly, given that violent crime has traditionally been found to be commonest among young men, we should not expect to find a single psychological explanation to be sufficient. The explanations of violent crime are varied and stretch from the influence of alcohol to psychological predispositions. There is a great deal to suggest that violence is socially learnt. It has often been claimed that media violence is part of the cause of violence in the young, though this has not been a major theme in forensic and criminal psychology – or criminology, for that matter. Evidence in support of the media causing violence is strongest from laboratory studies and much less a feature of field studies asking the same question. There is only a small amount of evidence concerning the media and actual acts of criminal violence.
- Homicide might seem to be largely determined by psychological factors, but evidence of psychiatric abnormalities in such crimes is generally fairly exceptional. Furthermore, it has been shown that broad societal factors (e.g. periods of wartime) may affect levels of homicide. Leyton (1986) claimed that homicide is related to social structure (social class). Others have provided socio-biological explanations of such phenomena as the different rates of killing of step-children and biological children by their parents.
- There are a number of issues concerning violent crime which are particuularly psychological in nature. Desistance from crime has yet to be fully understood. Violence risk assessment and violence treatment programmes will be discussed in Chapters 26 and 27. Stalking is not necessarily a violent crime but often it can be and it can be threatening and intimidating to the extreme. The different patterns of violent criminal careers are important in that they help us to be more sophisticated in our understanding of such crimes.

Further reading

Delisi, M., and Collis, P.J. (eds) (2012) *Violent Offenders: Theory, Research, Policy and Practice* (2nd edn) London: Jones and Bartlett Learning.

Kocsis, R. (ed.) (2008) *Serial Murder and the Psychology of Violent Crimes: An International Perspective* New Jersey: Humana Press.

McMurran, M. (2012) *Alcohol-Related Violence: Prevention and Treatment* Chichester: Wiley-Blackwell.

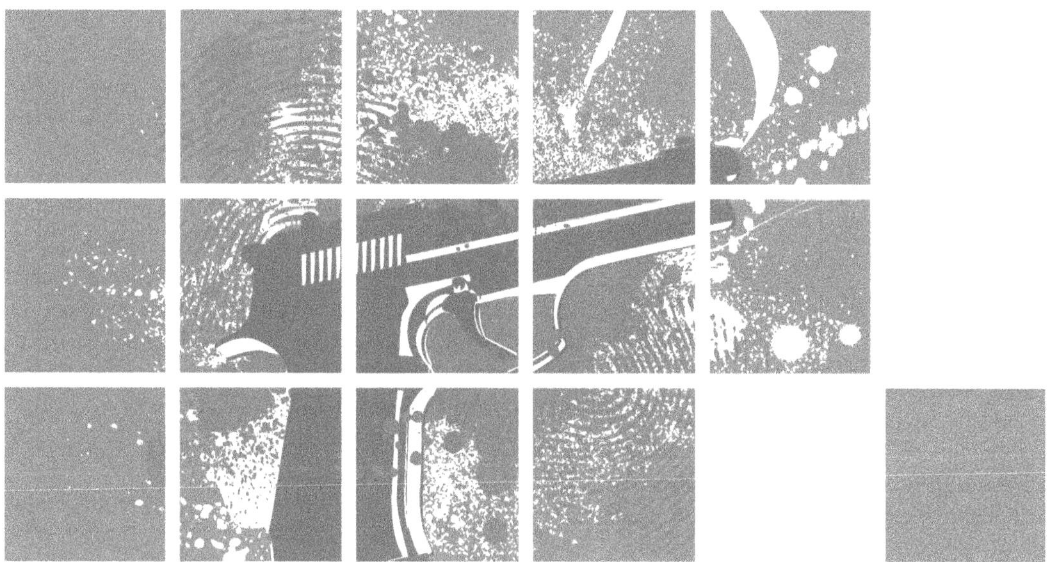

Chapter 9

Sexual offenders 1: rapists

Overview

- Legal definitions vary, but recent definitions of rape hold it to be the unwanted penetration of the vagina, anus or mouth of another person. Statutory rape is penile penetration of any child below the age of consent to sexual intercourse.
- Many sex offences are committed by young people, including those against children. Their sex offending can be restricted to adolescence but not always so.
- Feminist thinking has been enormously influential in establishing rape and other sexual offences as significant social problems. Feminism changed views of rape such that now it is generally regarded as an act of power and control rather than of sexual gratification.
- It is seen as a substantially underreported crime to an unknown extent. In a British survey, approximately 5 per cent of women claimed to have been raped at some point in their lives.
- Despite radical improvements in how rape victims are treated by the criminal justice system, rape remains a crime with relatively low conviction rates.
- In terms of theory development, one important issue is whether sex offenders are crime generalists or specialists. There is evidence supporting both views. Rapists may be crime generalists and offenders against children more specialist.
- An early example of classifying rape was Groth, Burgess and Holmstrom (1977), who classified rape as power-assurance rape, power-assertive rape, anger-retaliatory rape and anger-excitement rape.
- Rape myths are beliefs about women and their sexuality which place the blame on the woman rather than the rapist. However, there is no convincing balance of evidence which demonstrates that sex offenders are more extreme in their acceptance of rape myths than other men.
- Offenders use pornography, but developmental studies tend not to hold pornography responsible for creating their deviance. Furthermore, research on sexual fantasy tends to indicate that fantasy has a potentially complex relationship with offending.
- Phallometry or plethysmography is a technique for measuring the volume or circumference of a penis as an index of sexual 'arousal' in a man. There are doubts that it is sufficiently precise to identify men likely to offend and there is reason to believe that it is somewhat outmoded as alternative, simpler ways of achieving the same end are available.

Introduction

Legal definitions of rape, historically, referred almost exclusively to vaginal penetration by a penis. Commonly, nowadays, the forcible anal penetration of either sex by the penis is included in the legal definition of rape, as is oral penetration and penetration with the use of a foreign object such as a bottle in some jurisdictions. A conviction for rape requires that the victim has not given consent to the sexual act. In some jurisdictions, intercourse with youngsters regarded as too young to give their consent is classified as rape – this is known as statutory rape. However, in the research literature on rape, there is a tendency to employ definitions which do not correspond to the legal definition of the crime. Feminists, in particular, tend to extend the definition far beyond its typical legal meaning to include all forms of sexual act that women may find unacceptable (e.g. Kelly, 1988, 1989). For example, some researchers may well include salacious comments to a woman about her breasts in the definition.

Frequency of rape

The 2004/5 figure for recorded rapes of females age 16 and above in the UK was 8192 and that for 2014/5 was 18, 292 (Home Office, 2016b). The corresponding figures for rapes of males were 444 and 1024. Surveys based on data collected between 2009 to 2012 in England and Wales (Ministry of Justice, Home Office and the Office for National Statistics, 2013) revealed that, on average, 2.5 per cent of females and 0.4 per cent of males claimed to have been the victim of a sexual offence or an attempted sexual offence in the previous year. Offences such as indecent assault and unwanted touching formed the great majority of sex offences. However, 0.5 per cent of females but less than 0.1 per cent of males claimed to have been raped or suffered sexual assault by penetration in the previous 12 months. This amounts to about 97,000 victims in total each year. Furthermore, about 5 per cent of adult females reported that they had been a victim of the most serious offences (rape, attempted rape and sexual assault) at some time in their lives above the age of 16 years. About 20 per cent of adult females reported victimisation from any sort of sexual offence in their adult lives. One notable statistic is that about 90 per cent of the victims of these most serious sexual offences knew the perpetrator, but this figure falls to less than 50 per cent for what the report describes as less serious sexual offences such as indecent exposure and voyeurism. Remarkably, only 15 per cent of victims of the serious sexual offences said that they had reported the crime to the police. Reasons like embarrassment and thinking that the police could not do anything were given for avoiding reporting the rape to the police. In contrast to what we know from victim surveys, only about 54,000 sexual offences were recorded by the police. The vast majority of these were serious sexual offences. In other words, a lot of minor sexual offences do not get reported to the police.

The use of victimisation surveys probably has fewer biases than using police reports as the measure of crime. The Crime Survey for England and Wales (formerly but inaccurately referred to as the British Crime Survey) allowed participants to use a computer-assisted self-interviewing procedure using a lap-top computer which may have reduced interviewer biases considerably (Myhill and Allen, 2002). However, there was some disparity between episodes which the victims described as rape and the way in which the researchers classified the same events. The researchers defined rape as the woman being forced to have sexual intercourse (vaginal or anal penetration) though they did not require penile penetration in their definition. A sexual assault was anything identified as sexual which did not meet the requirements of rape. The women in the survey and the researchers agreed that the events were rape in about 60 per cent of the cases.

There is considerable uncertainty about whether a rape will result in a conviction as there is considerable attrition in the process (Ministry of Justice, 2013). This is illustrated in Figure 9.1. Based on national victim surveys, it can be estimated that the number of rapes in England and Wales is somewhere between 60,000 and 95,000 cases on average per year. However, the police only record about 15,670 rapes, partly because of non-reporting by the victim but sometimes because the police do not think that a crime has been committed. The police investigation may not identify a suspect, or the Crown Prosecution Services will decide that there is insufficient evidence, or the victim may decide not to proceed with a prosecution. This leaves an average of 3850 potential prosecutions. There may be no trial for various reasons, such as the magistrate decides that there is no case to answer. So only 2910 on average go to trial. The number of offenders finally committed for rape is 1070 although some may have been convicted of another sexual offence. A minority of men accused of rape in court plead guilty. The majority of these are found guilty of rape or another sexual offence. The majority of suspects plead not guilty and the majority of these are found not guilty of rape or another sexual offence.

Research by Hohl and Stanko (2015) helps us understand how conviction rates for rape in the UK are amongst the lowest in Europe. They studied a large and representative sample of allegations of rape made by female victims to the London Metropolitan Police. The available data included considerable detail about the attack, the victim, any suspects and the police investigation process. The *attrition problem* or *justice gap* refers to the fact that the

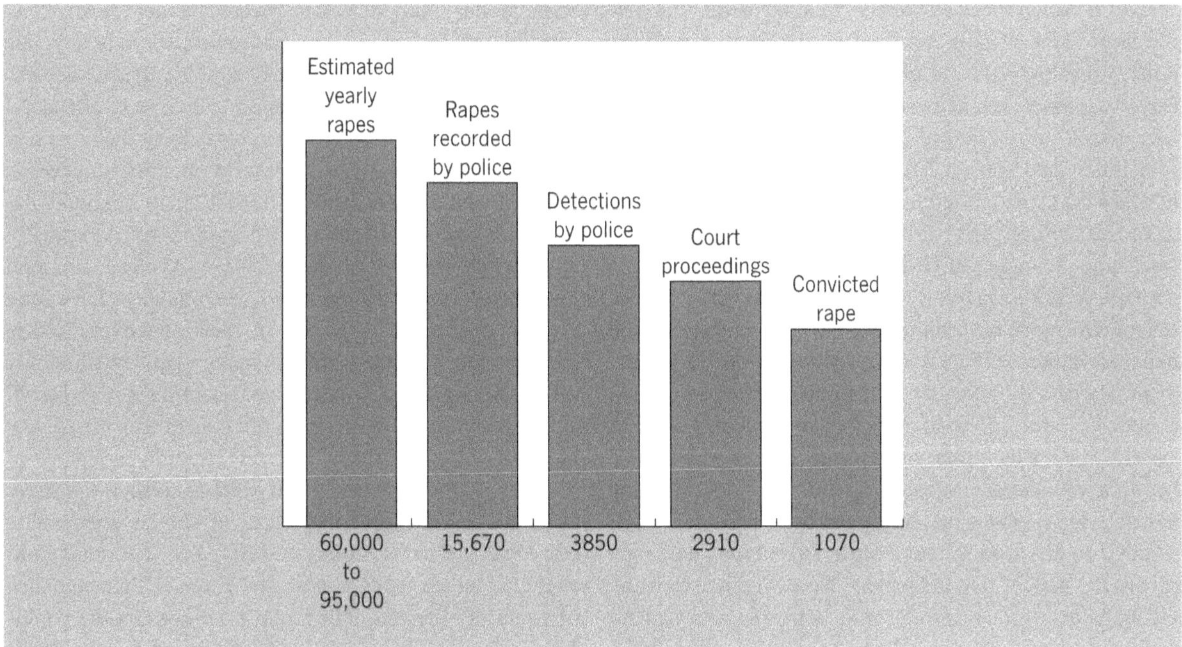

Figure 9.1 The process of attrition in the processing of rape allegations

majority of rapes are not reported to the police and, of the ones which are, only a minority lead to a conviction. Women do not report rape to the police for any of a number of reasons. These include the victim not trusting the criminal justice system, the victim fearing that she will not be believed, and police interview tactics which may make the woman feel that she is being raped over again. How are rapes that go to court different from those which do not? What factors make a rape allegation credible to the police and public prosecution service and what discredits an allegation in their eyes. A major factor leading to attrition are things which the police and prosecutors regard as being evidence against the rape allegation. In Hohl and Stanko's study, no cases were prosecuted where the victim had a previous false allegation, evidence or opinion from police officers casting doubt on the allegation, and inconsistencies in the victim's evidence.

The police and prosecutors were more likely to persist with a case in which the suspect has a previous police record and where the suspect is not a white man. The attrition of cases is at its greatest in the early stages following the allegation and is most likely to be the consequence of the victim withdrawing. As many as two-thirds of victims withdraw. A second route leading to attrition is a decision to drop the case by the police or prosecutors. This may take the form of no-criming the allegation. No-criming is supposed to happen if the investigation yields credible evidence that the crime did not, in fact, happen. However, sometimes the police will no-crime the allegation if they merely suspect a false allegation or think the crime would be difficult to prosecute. In other cases, the investigation may fail to find the culprit or fail to find sufficient evidence against him. In these instances, the case is closed with a decision for no further action. The Crown Prosecution Service may also close a case for no further action if they believe that the evidence is insufficient or because a prosecution is not in the public interest. Of the cases in which the victim does not withdraw her allegation, police no-criming accounted for nearly 20 per cent of attrition, a police decision to take no further action accounted for 67 per cent of attrition, and a prosecution service decision to take no further action was responsible for 14 per cent of attrition.

Hohl and Stanko argue that decision makers in the criminal justice system (police officers, prosecutors, judges and jurors) use 'schematic processing' which are cognitive heuristics which allow beliefs, attitudes and stereotypes to enter decision making. Estrich's (1987) conceptualisation of 'real rape' is a rape by a weapon-wielding stranger in a dark outside location, using force, which is met with resistance by the victim, and results in tangible injury. In a demonstration relevant to this, Sleath and Woodhams (2014) had a large sample of students rate the frequency of a wide range of perpetrator and victim behaviours during rape (such as bind or tie up the victim, scream, and freeze). The students grossly overestimated the likelihood of such behaviours in nearly every case. In other words, there was an expectation of violent and extreme behaviours in rape which did not reflect the reality of rape. Another study, demonstrated that rape scenarios which included stereotypical elements (the victim resisted the attacker and was fully cooperative with the police) resulted in same culture perpetrators being perceived as less to blame, deserving of less punishment and less likely to be guilty of the offence (Bongiorno, McKimmie and Masser, 2016). A complaint of rape which matches these pre-conceptions of 'real rape' is more likely to progress through the criminal justice system. But the 'real rape' is quite unlike the typical rape in which the perpetrator is known to the victim. A victim who does not reflect an ideal of femininity has less chance to be believed. Police officers and prosecutors work to performance targets in a context of resource limitations which results in them prioritising for progression through the system cases which they assess will have a good likelihood of conviction in court. In order to do this they develop expectations of how members of a jury will respond to the case – and gender stereotypes and rape myths are part of this judgement. So cases in which the victim knows the perpetrator, did not resist and had no apparent injuries, has mental health problems, had drunk alcohol, and gives an inconsistent account are more likely to suffer attrition.

Youthful sex offenders

Despite the public image of sex offenders as being dirty old men, there is considerable evidence that young offenders are responsible for significant proportions of sex offences. According to the Home Office (2003), in the UK 20 per cent of those convicted for a sexual crime are under the age of 18 years. About a third of rapes of adult women and 30–50 per cent of child sexual abuse is carried out by adolescents. Following a major review of the research literature on young sex offenders, Grimshaw (2008) wrote:

> 'The needs of young people who sexually abuse are complex and often ongoing. Young people have typically suffered abuse, which can have important mental health consequences and may affect the impact of future intervention for their sexually abusive behaviour. They show poor social skills and a tendency to impulsiveness, and are coping with disrupted and neglecting family backgrounds.'
>
> (p.51)

Nevertheless, Vitacco, Viljoen and Petrila (2009) argue that the burgeoning of interest in adolescent sexual offending was fuelled by legislation to *protect* the public from adolescent sex offenders. In particular, the USA's Sexual Offender and Notification Act of 2006 (also known as the Adam Walsh Act) made provision for including adolescent sex offenders on public registers. According to Vitacco *et al.*, public policy was made before relevant research was carried out which might have had an impact on policy. For example, researchers may doubt the idea that adolescent sex offenders go on to become adult sex offenders. Adolescent sex offenders seem to have much the same risk of reoffending sexually as adolescent offenders in general. Many juvenile sex offenders do not show continuity in their future offending and do not go on to offend sexually after adolescence (Caldwell, 2007). Another common assumption is that treatments for sex offenders have little impact, despite the evidence of their effectiveness (see Chapter 26). In other words, thinking about youthful sex offending is politically determined and not research based.

Graves *et al.* (1996) carried out a meta-analytic review of studies of youthful sex offenders by studying empirical research studies from 1973–93. Meta-analysis is the study of trends across different studies of similar phenomena (Howitt and Cramer, 2008) (see Box 4.1). The study concentrated on the demographic and parental characteristics of youthful offenders. The authors believe that the youthful offenders could be classified into three different, exclusive categories:

- *Paedophilic:* generally their first offence was committed between 6 and 12 years of age. They consistently molest younger children and prefer female victims.
- *Sexual assault:* these are youthful offenders whose first reported offence is between 13 and 15 years but their victims may vary substantially and include both older victims than themselves and younger victims.
- *Mixed offence:* these are youngsters who commit a variety of offences such as sexual assault, molesting younger children, exhibitionism, voyeurism, frotteurism, etc.

Overall, youthful sex offenders in general tended to have the following characteristics:

- lower socio-economic class origins;
- pathological family structures and interaction style;
- their fathers were physically neglected as a child;
- their mothers were physically abused as a child;
- substance abuse was common among the fathers.

There were considerable differences between the three different types of youngster, as shown in Table 9.1. Care has to be exercised since, despite the rather pathological picture painted of the families of youthful sexual offenders, these are only trends in the data. A substantial proportion of youthful sex offenders came from homes identified as healthy.

An important question is whether the childhood experiences that predict general delinquency are the same as those that predict sexual delinquency. If they are the same, then this has obvious implications for how young sexual

Table 9.1 The family and social characteristics of different types of youthful male sexual offenders obtained from meta-analysis

Characteristic	Paedophilic	Sexual assault	Mixed offence
Low to middle social class	✓	✓	✗
Low social class	✗	✗	✓
Lives in foster care	✓	✗	✗
Lives in lone-parent family	✗	✓	✗
Mother physically abused as child	✓	✗	✗
Mother neglected as child	✗	✗	✓
Mother abuses drugs	✗	✗	✓
Father abuses alcohol	✗	✓	✓
Father abuses drugs	✓	✗	✗
Maladaptive, dysfunctional family	✓	✗	✓
Rigid family	✗	✓	✗
Maternal neglect	✗	✗	✓
Protestant religion	✗	✗	✓

A ✓ indicates that this characteristic is especially common in that group of youthful offenders.

offenders are managed in the criminal justice system as well as for theory. Langstrom (1999) studied 15- to 20-year-olds who had been subject to the *Forensic Psychiatric Examination* over the period 1988–95. These young sexual offenders had extensive previous histories of sexually abusing others. Young sexual offenders brought to the attention of the authorities for the first time already had an average of seven victims. The predictors of sexual offending included:

- early onset of sexually abusive behaviour;
- male victims;
- multiple victims;
- poor social skills.

These are not the same sort of factors that predict non-sexual delinquency. If sexual recidivism is excluded, then the predictors of general reoffending are much more familiar:

- early onset (childhood) conduct disorder;
- previous criminality;
- psychopathy (Psychopathy Checklist–Revised, PCL-R – see Chapters 21 and 27);
- use of death threats/weapons at the time of the index offence (the offence which led to the offender being included in the researcher's sample).

This raises the possibility that the origins of child sex offending are specific ones to that type of offence. However, sexually abusive children are not specialists in sexual delinquency. It is not uncommon to find that juveniles who commit sexually harmful acts against others also offend more generally. Indeed it has been suggested that sexually harmful behaviours may be a marker for (i.e. predictor of) a future more general crime pattern (McCrory, Hickey, Farmer and Vizard, 2008). According to Moffitt (1993) and Moffitt, Caspi, Harrington and Milne (2002), a group of children can be identified who persistently engage in antisocial behaviours at the different stages of their life history – from their pre-school period into adulthood. Children as young as ten years of age carry out a sizeable minority of sexually inappropriate acts. Deficits in their self-regulatory abilities, cognitive functions and temperament are manifested in various aspects of their life. McCrory *et al.* found that:

- early sexually harmful behaviours which have begun before the age of ten years predict a general crime offence trajectory into adolescence and adulthood;
- sexually harmful behaviours first begun after the age of ten years did *not* predict a child's long-term future of general crime.

Early onset sexual abusers need to be distinguished from those who begin offending in their adolescence. McCrory *et al.* found that the childhoods of early onset sexual abusers were generally characterised by a lack of parental supervision and inadequate sexual boundaries in the family. Generally, there was evidence that that the early onset of sexually harmful behaviour serves as a clinical marker of the increased likelihood of future risk of general delinquency. Consequently, any treatments and interventions they receive should not be limited to their sexually abusive behaviours but extend more generally to factors related to delinquency. However, there was evidence that the early onset of sexually harmful behaviours was linked to a number of factors such as a history of educational difficulties, a continuous pattern of non-sexual anti-social behaviour throughout childhood and adolescence, and serious background issues such as maltreatment, temperament problems, aggression and mental health problems. Inconsistent and harsh discipline, disruption of the primary care-giver, and parental mental health problems were more influential on the early onset sexually abusive children because of their heightened levels of vulnerability in early childhood. Furthermore, educational and personality difficulties restrict these children's opportunities for change. Thus, early onset sexual abusers may become adults manifesting characteristics such as violence, mental health issues, and psychopathic traits.

Seto and Lalumiěre (2010) reviewed explanations of adolescent sex offending in boys and tested them using meta-analysis (see Box 4.1). Figure 6.2 summarises some of the possible explanations. The data came from 59 separate studies which compared male adolescent sex offenders with male adolescent non-sex offenders. A big problem is that adolescent sex offending is treated as part of a single group as if youngsters who rape adult women and children who molest other children sexually are the same. This failure to distinguish sub-types of offenders makes interpreting research findings more difficult or even impossible. Various theoretically derived variables were coded which dealt with general delinquency risk factors (antisocial tendencies), childhood abuse, cognitive abilities, exposure to violence, family problems, interpersonal problems, psychopathology and sexuality. Adolescent sex offending could not be explained in terms of general antisocial tendencies alone. They had more restricted criminal histories, fewer antisocial peers, and fewer substance abuse issues. However, more specific explanations such as sexual abuse history, exposure to sexual violence, other abuse or neglect, social isolation, early exposure to sex or pornography, atypical sexual interests, anxiety, and low self-esteem were shown empirically to be possible factors in adolescent sexual abuse. The largest effect sizes were for atypical sexual interests, sexual abuse history, criminal history, antisocial associations and substance abuse in that order.

A study by Lussier, Van den Berg, Bijleveld and Hendriks (2012) concerning the offending trajectories of juvenile sex offenders produced particularly interesting findings. A sample of almost 500 young sex offenders in Holland was studied from adolescence into adulthood. All of them had either been convicted of or confessed to a hands-on sex offence. Their initial assessment in a special unit was at approximately 14 years of age on average and their final assessment at about 29 years on average. Most had sexually offended against pre-pubertal victims at least five years their junior (52 per cent of sample). Thirty-two per cent had abused peers and 16 per cent had abused in groups. The researchers tracked the patterns for both 1) non-sexual and 2) sexual offending separately into adulthood, using a complex statistical method (semi-parametric group-based modelling). To stress, this was done separately for both type of offenders. Beginning with the non-sex offending, five different offending statistically-based trajectories were identified:

- Non-sex trajectory 1: very low rate offenders (53 per cent of total). This group's non-sexual offending stayed around zero for the entire study period. On average, they committed just one non-sexual offence. Recidivism was unlikely, obviously.
- Non-sex trajectory 2: late starters (21 per cent). This group was not very criminally active during their childhood and adolescence. However, their offending increased during the period when they were 20–25 years of age. They were very often recidivists in adulthood but less than half had been recidivists as adolescents.
- Non-sex trajectory 3: adolescence-limited offenders (11 per cent). This group showed rapid growth in offending during adolescence which peaked when they were 17 years of age. Then their offending declined gradually, resulting in very low rates by the age of about 25 years.
- Non-sex trajectory 4: high-rate offenders (4 per cent). These were early starters and had the highest rate of adolescence non-sexual offending. They were chronic offenders with many convictions. They were commonly recidivists in adulthood.
- Non-sex trajectory 5: late bloomers (10 per cent). This group had a trajectory which looked much the same as for the high-rate offenders (Trajectory 4) but they started and peaked their offending somewhat later.

Thus for non-sexual offending, the most common pattern was a low frequency of offending from adolescence into adulthood. The second most common trajectory was not to become active offenders in their adulthoods. The long-term, high rate trajectory involved only a very small percentage of offenders.

Turning to the patterns of sex offending, only two distinct trajectories were found:

- Sex offending trajectory 1 (90 per cent of the sample): Adolescence limited: This group peaked in terms of their sexual offending at the age of 14 years. There was then a rapid decline and sex offending terminated by approximately 20 years of age. About one third showed recidivism in childhood but only 2 per cent reoffended sexually in adulthood.

- Sex offending trajectory 2 (10 per cent of the sample): High rate slow desisters: This group started sex offending younger and peaked in terms of sex offending younger at the age of 12, but then their sex offending declined rather slowly from that age onwards and reached similar low levels to the adolescence limited group at about the age of 30 years or so.

In other words, for the vast majority of these juvenile sex offenders, sex offending was confined to adolescence. Only one in ten continued to offend significantly into adulthood. There was generally very little, if any, relationship between the non-sexual and the sexual trajectories. There was a lack of synchronicity or correspondence between the non-sexual trajectories and the sexual trajectories. Most (95 per cent) of those in the adolescence limited non-sexual trajectory group were also in the adolescence limited sexual offence trajectory group. This was the only indication of synchronicity between sex and non-sex offending trajectories.

So there are questions to be raised about the role of sex offences in the criminal history of juvenile offenders. One possibility is that having a sex offence conviction is predictive of a different pattern of offending in general. The evidence seems to be against this view. This may be made clearer if we consider McCuish, Lussier and Corrado's (2016) study of a large group of juvenile sexual offenders and non-sexual offenders in the USA. They identified four distinct offending trajectories: 1) low-rate offending which ended roughly by mid-adolescence; 2) a bell-shaped offending trajectory which seems similar to Moffit's (see pp. 96–98) adolescent limited type of juvenile offender; 3) slow-rising and chronic offending from adolescence to adulthood with no sign of ending; and 4) high rate chronic offending which slowed down with the coming of adulthood. The offending in general by juvenile sex offenders did not correspond to any one of these patterns. Indeed, the juvenile offenders appeared relatively equally frequently in every trajectory. That is, juvenile sex offending does not allow us to predict a youngster's general offending behaviour.

In some jurisdictions such as the US, precisely the same policies are applied to juvenile sex offenders and adult sex offenders. Especially important is that sex offender laws concerning sex offender registration and notification affect juvenile sex offenders. Calleja (2015) points out that this may be inappropriate since these sanctions assume that sex offenders are frequent recidivists. However, the research evidence suggests that juvenile sex offenders have low risk of sexual recidivism. For example, Colleja reported a study of juvenile offenders who had been treated in a residential facility. Only 3 per cent of juvenile sex offenders reoffended in (up to) two years post release. In contrast, 19 per cent of substance-using young offenders and 33 per cent of juvenile general offenders reoffended. Unarmed robbery and vehicle theft were the commonest recidivistic offences. Absolutely none of the juveniles in any of the three offence groups reoffended with a sexual crime. This does not mean that juvenile sex offenders never reoffend sexually. Vandiver (2006) studied a sample of 300 male juvenile sex offenders into their adulthood. Recicivism was assessed for a period of three to six years when they reached adulthood. Adult sexual reoffending was relatively uncommon in about 4 per cent of the sample. Nevertheless, in excess of a half of the sample reoffended at least on one occasion for a non-sexual offence. Rather similar figures were found in a ten-year follow up of two groups of treated juvenile sex offenders (Waite, Keller, McGarvey *et al.*, 2005).

Sex offenders as specialists and generalists

There are at least three conceptually distinct models of sex offenders which deal with sex offending in relation to offending in general:

- The first is based on the general deviancy model, which says that sex offenders offend sexually as part of their general tendency to engage in all sorts of deviant behaviour. In other words, sex offenders are generalist offenders.
- The specialist model of sex offenders assumes that they are not likely to commit other types of crime. Broadly speaking, the idea is that sex offenders are exclusively/predominantly/persistently to be found committing sex offences of one sort or another. Harris, Mazerolle and Knight (2009) put this slightly differently by suggesting that there is an 'implicit' assumption that those who commit sex offences are not the same as non-sexual offenders.
- There is a variant on the specialism model which involves specialisms within the sex offending specialism. Sex offending itself is a broad category and involves a variety of seemingly different forms of offending. So it is possible that some sex offenders are limited in their range. For example, it may be that some sex offenders confine themselves to offending against children and never offend against adults.

The idea of the sex offender as a criminal generalist fits well with modern criminology theory – especially Gottfredson and Hirschi's (1990) General Theory of

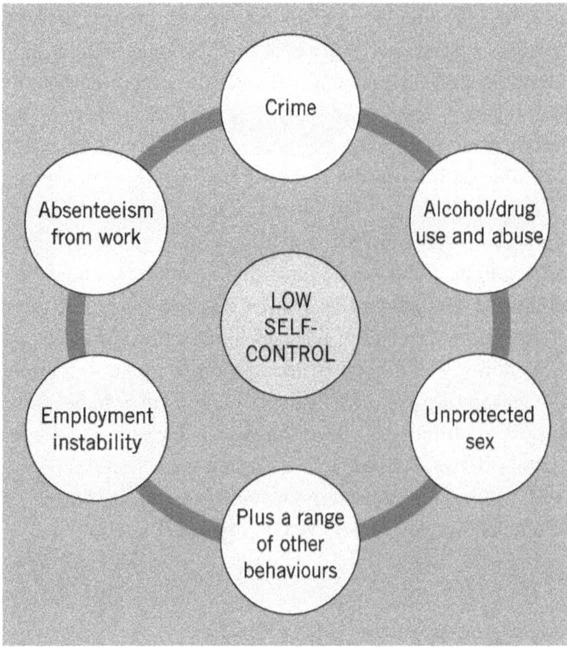

Figure 9.2 The General Theory of Crime
Source: based on Gottfredson and Hirschi, 1990

Crime. This argues that offending is a manifestation of a broader and more pervasive antisocial character which involves not just crime but other deviant behaviours (see Figure 9.2). Offenders lack self-control. As a consequence they engage in crime-analogous behaviours which result in other, broadly antisocial, behavioural patterns as well as crime itself. According to the General Theory of Crime, these other behaviours include absenteeism from work; alcohol and drug use and abuse; cigarettes; employment instability; irresponsible driving; marital instability; truancy; and unprotected sex (Simon, 2000). It should be added that Gottfredson and Hirschi (1990) accept that there is some crime specialisation but they believed that, overwhelmingly, criminals are generalists. No serious criminological analysis would deny that Gottfredson and Hirschi's General Theory of Crime is well supported by research evidence, though it is debatable just how general a general theory of crime should be. How well the General Theory of Crime accounts for sex offending is not so clear.

According to Lussier, Leclerc, Cale and Proulx (2007), sex offenders include both generalists and specialists. The case for them being generalists is quite extensive and compelling. Previous histories of non-sexual offending are common among sex offenders. Furthermore, when they reoffend following a conviction for a sex offence it is most likely that it will be for a non-sexual offence. Equally important is that the risk factors for sexual reoffending are much the same as the ones predictive of generalist patterns of a broadly antisocial lifestyle. Typical of these risk factors are any sort of prior offences; a background of involvement in violent and property crimes; an antisocial personality; and psychopathy. Of course, all that this might imply is that researchers have not identified the appropriate risk factors which are conducive to a particular sort of criminal activity. The specialist view of sex offenders would lead us to expect specifically sexual risk factors to be involved – such as having been charged with a sex offence; having committed sexual offences early in life; a preference for male victims and stranger/extrafamilial victims; and sexual deviance. Evidence that sex offenders can be characterised as having poor self-control can be found in Cleary's (2004) findings. Her in-depth interviews with sex offenders found that offenders were frequently injured in motor accidents, had fathered illegitimate children and were involved with alcohol and drugs.

One study followed a large sample of juvenile sex offenders for a follow-up period of 35 years since their adolescent offence (Hargreaves and Francis, 2014). The reconviction rates for sexual offences were low at 7 per cent after five-years – the figure reached only 13 per cent at the end of the 35-year follow-up period.

One problem is that global categorisations such as 'sex offender' subsume a variety of different types of offences which may mask the degree to which they are specialists. The failure to differentiate, say, rapists from child molesters in a great deal of research may mean that important differences between the two are simply not recognised. Indeed, Knight and Prentky (1990) suggested that rapists show the signs of criminal versatility of the generalist, whereas child molesters tend to be crime specialists. It may be of some importance that well-regarded theories of sex offending tend to treat them as sexual crime specialists and not as generalists, as implied by the General Theory of Crime. For example, several theories of sex offending claim that it is the result of conditioning or, alternatively, based on social learning (e.g. Laws and Marshall, 1990). Similarly, explanations of sex offending which suggest that it is the consequence of sexually deviant experiences (Ward *et al.*, 2006) help promote the idea that sex offenders are specialists in a particular type of crime.

Harris, Mazerolle and Knight (2009) studied these issues in order to clarify the extent to which:

- There is a group of generalist (versatile) sex offenders who tend to show the mix of antisocial behaviours predicted by the General Theory of Crime. For example, they are more likely to show signs of psychopathy. In addition, there is a group of specialist sex offenders who are likely to manifest characteristics associated with specialism, such as emotional congruence with children, preferences such as for male victims or victims known to themselves, and sexual preoccupation.

- Rapists are generalist (versatile) offenders showing the characteristics of generalist criminals.
- Child molesters tend to be specialist offenders, showing different criminal characteristics from the generalist offender.

Harris *et al.*'s (2009) study was based on a sample of over 570 sex offenders convicted in Massachusetts between 1959 and 1984. Specialisation in sex crime was determined using 'the specialisation threshold'. This essentially assumes that if an offender has a majority of offences for a particular type of crime then they are a specialist in that type of crime. Charges rather than convictions were used in this study. It was found that:

- Sex offenders who were classified as generalists (versatile) tended to exhibit the characteristics identified in the General Theory of Crime. For example, school maladjustment and delinquency were much more common in the versatile offenders group and they were typically rearrested shortly after release much more frequently.
- The victims of specialist sex offenders tend to be known to the offender.

However, the researchers subdivided sex offenders further into four groups: specialist rapists, versatile rapists, specialist child molesters and versatile child molesters. Only about 12 per cent of the rapists could be described as specialists in this sample using the criteria employed for specialism. Figure 9.3 shows this breakdown and some of the characteristics associated with each subdivision. Once again, these characteristics are associated with the General Theory of Crime for versatile offenders and indicative of specialism for the specialist subgroups of offenders:

- Versatile child molesters were more likely to abuse alcohol and other substances; to have had difficulties in their early years at school; and to show behavioural problems during adolescence.
- Specialist child molesters were more likely to be sexually preoccupied, to have emotional congruence with children and to offend against male victims.

Others have specifically dealt with stranger sexual killers and failed to find substantial evidence of specialism. Greenall and Wright (2015) studied a group of sexual killers in the UK. Thirty-six per cent of them had no previous convictions. The evidence broadly indicated that this group of killers were generalist offenders. They had criminal histories which were diverse in nature and few had past convictions for interpersonal violence. What criminal specialism that occurred mostly involved acquisitive crime. What about their previous convictions for sexual violence? Only 16 per cent had previous sexual convictions and 28 per cent previous violent convictions. When their sexual homicides were examined in detail,

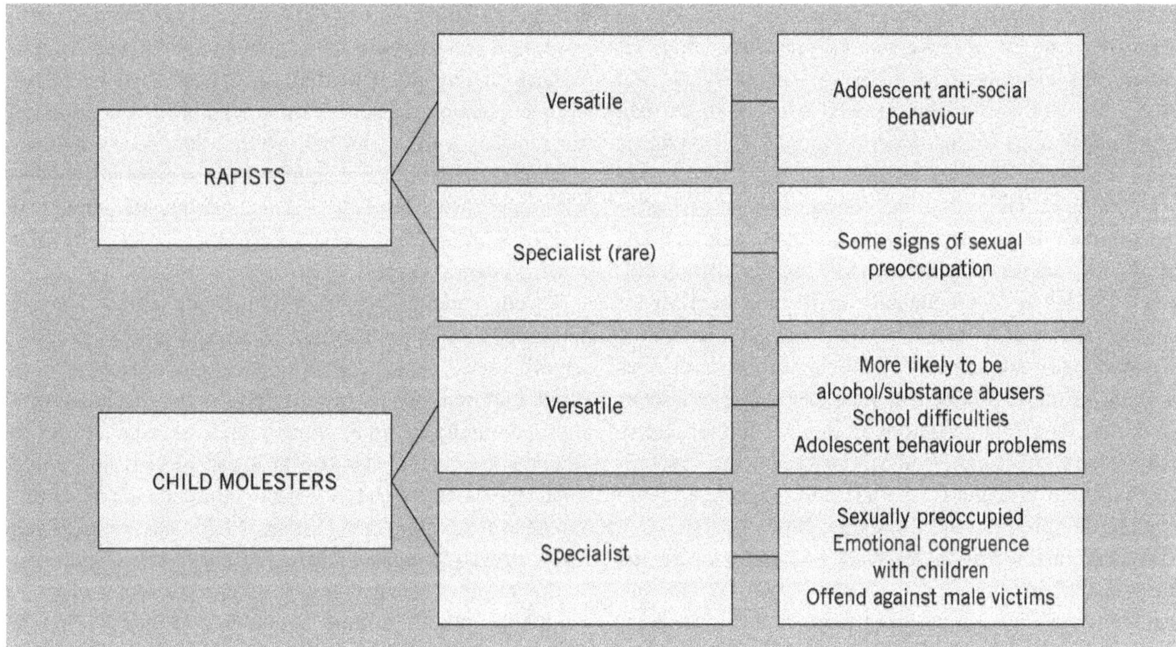

Figure 9.3 Rapists and child molesters as versatile and specialist offenders

mostly they showed very different behaviours from those they exhibited in any sexual convictions they may have had. In other words, overwhelmingly the evidence was that stranger sexual killers were generalists in terms of their previous offending.

Another aspect of sex offender generalism–specialism is related to the issue of victim category crossover. Crossover is the extent to which a sex offender offends against victims in a variety of categories. For example, one offender might offend against adult women only, whereas another might offend against adult women and boy children. The more crossover there is, the more difficult it is to explain sexual offending in terms of different patterns of conditioning or social learning, for example. Similarly, the more crossover there is, the harder it is to predict the sort of sexual reoffending that a sex offender may engage in. Of course, it is not easy to define exactly what constitutes the same type of offence and what constitutes a different type of offence. A study by Cann, Friendship and Gozna (2007) looked at crossover among sexual offenders in terms of their choice of victims defined in terms of victim age, gender and relationship to the offender – intrafamilial versus extrafamilial. Their sample consisted of nearly 1350 adult male sex offenders. Each had offended against multiple victims and each had been sentenced to a minimum of four years for a sexual offence. The data were collected from UK police records at New Scotland Yard's National Identification System. These records include written offence summaries describing the offender's convictions and, usually, details of the victim. These were supplemented with data collected from the Offenders Index (OI). Twenty-five per cent of the offenders showed evidence of crossover in their offending on a minimum of one dimension. Of course, this also shows that the vast majority did not cross over. Some offenders crossed over on more than one dimension, as is illustrated in Figure 9.4. This figure gives the percentages of all types of crossover in the entire sample. The crossover offenders were at higher risk of reoffending according to Static-99 calculations. (Static-99 is an assessment method which predicts recidivism, though it is not actually in itself a measure of recidivism (see Chapter 27).) Furthermore, crossover offenders had more convictions for any sort of offences as well as more sexual offences than non-crossover offenders. One interpretation of this is that offenders cross over from a preferred victim type when circumstances make it difficult to find their preferred victim type (Heil, Ahlmeyer and Simmons, 2003).

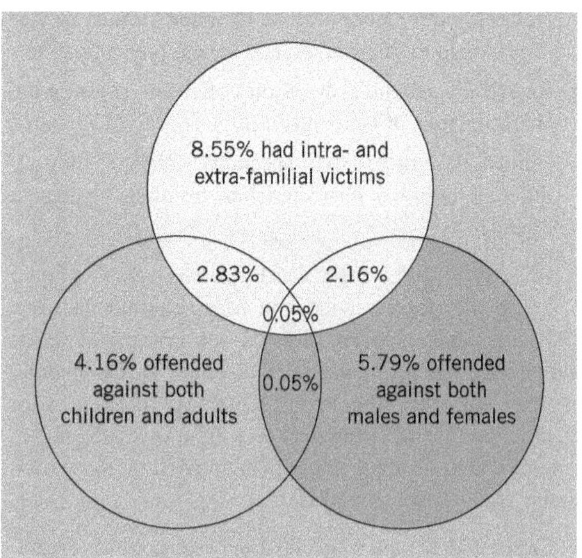

Figure 9.4 Crossover behaviours in offenders showing the percentage of crossovers of various types in the total sample of offenders

We can turn briefly to the work of Lussier on sexual criminal careers (Lussier and Cale, 2013) for another perspective on generalism–specificity in sex offending. The criminal career approach involves a wide range of different aspects of criminal careers, some of which are illustrated in Figure 9.5. Lussier and Cale have a much longer list. Criminal careers actually involve dynamic processes which are difficult to capture. But the problems go beyond being able to capture these dynamic processes. The most simple of questions from Figure 9.5 can be remarkably difficult to address. Sometimes the research has focused on things like sexual recidivism yet has largely neglected issues like the onset of sexual criminality. Sometimes the answer to the question varies, depending on the sort of data which is regarded as relevant. So, for example, what percentage of men rape a woman at any point in their life? Just what does that simple question mean? Is it men who have been arrested for rape? Is it men who believe that they coerced someone into sex? Is it men who have been accused of rape by a woman? Just what is it? If we take almost any other of the questions about sexual criminal careers similar uncertainties abound.

Briefly summarising, there is no simple answer to the question of whether sex offenders are specialist or generalist offenders. Those committing certain crimes such as child molestation are more likely to be specialists but those committing other crimes such as rape are more likely to be generalists. Too little can be said for certain about the essential features of the criminal careers of different sorts of offenders. Almond, McManus, Worsley and Gregory (2015) suggest that there remains no clear answer to the question of whether sex offenders are specialists or generalists. The failure of a great deal of research to differentiate different types of sex offender they give as one reason why uncertainty remains.

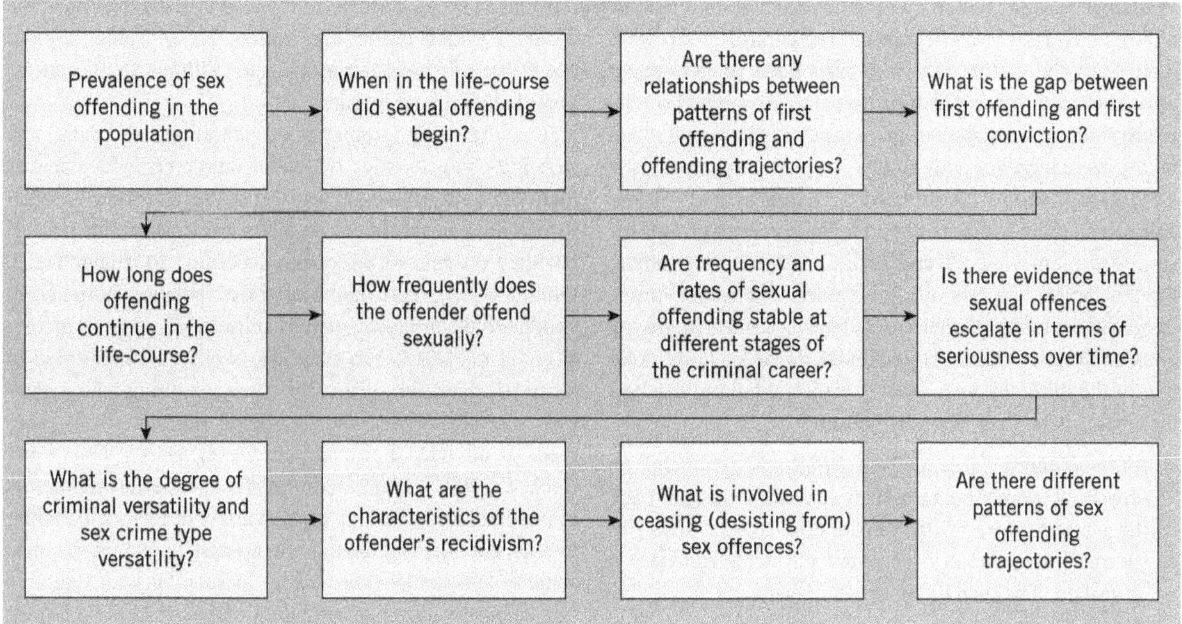

Figure 9.5 Some aspects of criminal careers

Is rape a sexual orientation?

The idea that sex offenders are generalist offenders who just happen to include rape in their toolkit of offending does not sit easily with a search for distinctive features of rapists which make them different from other men. So to ask the question of whether rape is a distinct sexual orientation perhaps appears to go against the flow of the statistical analyses of offending patterns in criminals. The feminist idea that all men have the capacity to rape, for example, fits with the statistics on crime patterns and would suggest that rape is part of the sexuality of the male gender. So it is quite a radical step to consider the possibility that rape is a distinct sexual orientation, as Harris, Lalumiěre, Seto, Rice and Chaplin (2012) chose to do. It is well established that rapists respond to coercion and violence in a distinctive way according to the research on using plethysmography (see Box 9.1 for a detailed discussion of the use of the plethysmography (also known as phallometry) in sex offender research and practice). The plethymograph is simply a physiological instrument which measures the degree of tumescence of a man's penis. As such, it is used as a way of assessing sexual arousal to various sexual depictions, for example. The first thing to say is that if a rapist is shown a picture of a nude mature adult woman he will typically respond with quite a substantial erection, but no more so than non-sex offenders. Where the big difference comes is in terms of how aroused rapists are by representations of forced sexual assault. When played audio tapes of stories about a sexual assault, rapists show higher levels of sexual response than to stories about mutually consenting sex. The reverse pattern applies to non-rapists. According to Lalumiěre *et al.* (2005), the degree of erection to rape stories is the only characteristic which can differentiate reliably between rapists and other violent offenders.

However, past research is not clear enough about just what it is about rape depictions which produces the increased sexual response in rape offenders. Studies have so far failed to differentiate effectively between the non-consenting aspect of rape and its violent aspect. Depictions of violence and injury, however, tend not to produce much erectile response in either rapists or non-rapists. So increasing the amount of violence in rape stories does not reliably produce an increasing erectile response in rapists. What seems to happen is that non-rapists respond sexually less to the stories when they contain violence and injury. This leaves the possibility that non-consent is the key feature of rape stories which produces the most erectile response by rapists to rape stories.

In order to disentangle the different elements of the rape stories, Harris, Lalumiere, Seto, Rice and Chaplin (2012) created stories which varied in terms of the presence of:

- violence and injury;
- non-consent;
- sexual activity.

Participants were men charged with sexual assault against a female over 16 years of age and the control group were men from the community who responded to newspaper advertisements for research participants. Responses on the plethysmograph to stories involving sexual activity and nudity were large for both groups – rapists and non-rapists. Both groups then were aroused by sexual activity in the stories and there was a strong preference in both groups for stories without violence and severe injury to the woman, though rapists had less of a preference. The major difference was in terms of their responses to stories involving consent or non-consent. Here is how Harris *et al.* describe two of the different types of story which should give a better idea of what they mean by consent:

> Rape Without Violence and Injury. A man and an unwilling woman engage in sexual activities. In vain, the woman pleads with him to stop. She is forced to submit but no injury or overt physical violence is described. The man experiences orgasm.
>
> p.224)
>
> Mutually Consenting Sexual Violence. A man and woman engage in mutually consenting sexual activities. The man also beats, stabs, or whips the woman who is an eager participant, verbally encouraging the man throughout even though she also describes extreme pain and serious injuries, including broken bones or considerable blood loss. Both experience orgasm.
>
> (p. 224)

The study concluded that the main difference between rapists and other men is in terms of their erectile response to active non-consent on the part of the woman. This is clearly important as it implies something about the sexual make-up of rapists which contributes to their rape offences.

Evidence that other types of sex offenders had a distinctive sexuality would be helpful to this question. Sexual homicide can be considered as pertinent here. The definition of sexual homicide is not universally agreed (Kerr, Beech and Murphy, 2013) which makes basic questions about its frequency hard to address. Francis and Soothill (2000) pointed out that, for the period 1985–94, in England and Wales just under 5000 people were found guilty of homicide. Only 4 per cent of these were identifiably sexual or sex-related in character. Even in those cases where a sex offender later kills someone it may be difficult to identify a sexual motive for the killing. Most attempts to decide whether a homicide is sexual in nature utilise evidence available at the crime scene. For example, there may be evidence of 'symbolic' sexual acts such as genital mutilation of the victim. Revitch (1965) argued that a sexual murder may not necessarily show evidence of a sexual nature since the violence may be a substitute for sexual activity. There is little likelihood that such crimes would be regarded as sexual homicide, however. Some killers may deliberately introduce sexual elements to mislead investigators as to the motive for their crime (e.g. Folino, 2000). Since they did not happen for sexual reasons, such killings should not be regarded as sexual murders.

Leaving aside problems of definition, are there any defining characteristics of sexual murderers which makes them different from other sorts of sexual offenders? Mental illness does not differentiate them from people in general but they do tend to be loners, according to research (e.g. Grubin, 1994). This theme of social isolation is linked to childhood disturbances such as abuse of one sort or another (Kerr *et al.*, 2013) and they also seem over-controlled in terms of anger. But, generally, there is nothing which identifies the sexual murderer as being different from other types of offender. For example, Oliver, Beech, Fisher and Beckett (2007) compared rapists and serial murderers imprisoned in the UK on a wide variety of factors including intelligence, developmental characteristics, pathology, personality and sexual functioning. In keeping with Grubin's (1994) observation that sexual murderers tend to be loners, it was found that sexual murderers were less likely to have been in an intimate relationship prior to the offence than were rapists. By and large, sexual murderers and rapists wee much the same on the measures used in this study.

All of this makes Seto, Lalumiěre, Harris and Chivers' (2012) study of sexual sadists important. Are sexual sadists different in terms of their sexual responses to stimuli using the plethysmograph? The study actually compared the very sample of rapists used in the Harris *et al.* (2012) study discussed above with a group of sexual sadists. The two studies used virtually identical methodologies. Rapists, as we have seen, tend to respond differently to community controls to the lack of consent by the woman in the story. It emerged that sexual sadists were more aroused by violence and injury in the story than by the lack of consent. In other words, evidence that the sexual stimulus for sexual sadists is violence and injury has to be pertinent to the idea that sexual sadism is a distinct sexuality.

It is not easy to draw conclusions about the specificity of sexual offending. At the clinical level, it does seem that rapists and sexual sadists are aroused by different things. But at the statistical level of analysis, the evidence that many sex offenders are likely to also offend in non-sexual ways is also compelling.

Anger and hostility and sex offending

We saw in Chapter 6 that it is a general trend for sex offending to begin in the early life of an offender. This sort of crime tends to follow the same sort of pattern as that associated with violent crime thus begging the question of whether anger and hostility are features of sexual crime. Violent crime is also most commonly a youthful offence that declines sharply in middle age and beyond. Putting these things together, one may ask whether rape is best conceived as a crime of violence rather than one of sexual lust. Certainly, there is good reason to believe that rape is associated with anger in many offenders. There is also good evidence that sex offenders are more likely to experience abuse in childhood:

- Worling (1995) carried out a study of adolescent sex offenders – one group had offended in a 'hands-on' fashion against peers and older women. The other group had offended against younger children. Various measurements were taken, including acceptance of rape myths (see pp. 195–197) and experience of physical punishment and sexual abuse. Those offending against a woman rather than a peer had experienced greater levels of physical punishment. Interestingly, sexual abuse by male perpetrators tended to lead to abuse against younger children by the victims. In contrast, victims of sexual abuse by females tended to become the offenders against peers and older women.
- Haapasalo and Kankkonen (1997) studied the self-reported experiences of childhood abuse in men whose victims were women above 18 years. These were compared with violent offenders with no record of sexual offences. The two groups were matched according to a number of family problems – including matters such as being in care in childhood; having experienced parental divorce in childhood; having parents who were substance abusers; and a number of other factors. Sex offenders claimed to have experienced more psychological (verbal) abuse (such as yelling, threatening, ridiculing) than the violent offenders. Furthermore, psychological rejection and isolation were commoner in sex offenders' childhoods. For example, their parents were more openly hostile and negative towards them as children; they tended to be ignored; other siblings were favoured; and they were locked up in closed environments more frequently and isolated from other people. There were further differences, sex offenders reporting:
  - father threatened to hurt me;
  - father belittled me;
  - father did not want me near him;
  - mother threatened to hurt me;
  - mother belittled me;
  - mother did not want me near her;
  - father made me do shameful things.

What is true of the childhoods of rapists may not be true of the childhoods of other types of sex offender such as paedophiles and child molesters. Often in research it is important to differentiate these various types. Jespersen, Lalumière and Seto (2009) published a meta-analysis (see Box 4.1) of publicly available research articles, theses and dissertations which examined childhood experiences of sexual abuse in offenders. The studies included in the analysis were those which compared sex offenders with other types of offender. Studies which compared sex offenders with non-offender groups were not included. The analysis compared sex offenders with offenders for other types of crime and also men who had sexually offended against an adult and those who had sexually offended against a child. The meta-analysis included physical abuse if it had been part of the original study. Sex offenders overall were much more likely to have been sexually abused, but the trend for physical abuse to be commoner in sex offenders was not statistically significant. Subdividing sex offenders into those offending against children and those sex offending against adults revealed some interesting trends. Sex offenders against adults were less likely to have been sexually abused in childhood than those who offended against children. On the other hand, those who offended sexually against adults were more likely to have been physically abused in childhood than offenders against young people.

It is easy to understand the origins of the hostility that some rapists feel. A number of researchers have commented on the role of this. For example, Hall and Hirschman (1991) suggest that there are a numbers of precursors to rape which may motivate the crime:

- sexual arousal: deviant sexual arousal;
- cognitive motivation: rape myths (see later);
- developmental problems;
- emotional factors (e.g. anger towards women).

While anger as a component of rape appears to be common, very little is known about precisely how it contributes to offending. It is generally accepted that some rapes are driven by sadistic fantasies which eventually are acted out in behaviour (e.g. MacCulloch, Snowden, Wood and Mills, 1983). Moreover, anger has been more directly associated with sex offending than this indirect route implies. For example, 94 per cent of rapists report that anger is associated with the offence, a figure that is not much lower in other types of sex offender (Pithers, Kashima, Cumming and Beal, 1988).

There is a general assumption that rape is a crime committed by younger offenders and a number of surveys have demonstrated this. However, the type of rape can make a significant impact on these age trends. Muir and Macleod (2003) showed that rapes in an unspecified UK metropolitan area were generally committed by offenders under the age of 40 years; however, this figure was lower for the rape of intimate partners such as spouses. In the case of rape by strangers, 61 per cent of offenders were under

30 years of age; for the rape of acquaintances, again 61 per cent were under 30 years of age; for the rape of intimates, only 24 per cent of offenders were under 30 years of age. Furthermore, rape is an offence where the victims tend to be younger women – only 8 per cent of rapes were committed against victims of 40 years or older. Seventy-five per cent were committed against women of under 25 years of age and 30 per cent were against 14-year-olds and under. Probably a high proportion of the latter were statutory rapes in which consent cannot legally be given because of the victim's young age. The 15- to 24-years-old age group was the most at risk, but this was largely the case for stranger and acquaintance rape.

Patterns in rape

McCabe and Wauchope (2005) studied Australian rapes based on a sample of 130 police reports involving the penetration (or attempted penetration) of a woman. Just what acts take place during rapes and just how frequent are they? Surprisingly, until recently, such seemingly basic information rarely gathered together systematically in order to obtain a picture of typical rape behaviours. The researchers identified different behavioural themes in these reports at the following rates:

- The *vaginal theme,* which included digital penetration, foreign object insertion, hand/fist insertion and so forth (92 per cent of rapes);
- The *kissing/hugging theme* (32 per cent);
- The *oral theme*, which included cunnilingus, fellatio, analingus (25 per cent);
- The *anal theme*, which included foreign-object insertion and anal penetration (22 per cent);
- The *brutal-physical theme* (9 per cent) (including biting, beating, kicking, choking and strangulation).

Certain themes are more likely to co-occur in combination than others. The most common combination was kissing/fondling with the vaginal theme. These occurred together in 29 per cent of rapes. The oral and vaginal themes co-occurred in 22 per cent of rapes.

The language used in the assaults could be largely accounted for by four themes:

- A caring, persuasion or reassurance theme – 'I won't hurt you, I just want sex' (characteristic of 24 per cent of rapists);
- A sexually abusive or explicit language theme – 'I want you on top, play with yourself' (19 per cent);
- An angry, demeaning or threatening theme – 'Keep your voice down or I will kill you' (18 per cent);
- A revenge or payback theme – 'I will kill your new boyfriend' (just 2 per cent).

The search for the characteristic patterns linking some rapes is an important step. This is a form of analysis of rapes related to profiling (Chapter 15). Häkkänen, Lindlof and Santtila (2004) studied the police database for rapes by strangers in Finland. Case files included various records: witness statements, medical statements, forensic evidence, the interview with the victim and the interview with the suspect. A long list of possible characteristics of the rape was compiled and each case record coded in terms of the presence or absence of this context. A complex statistical technique, multidimensional scaling, was used to identify what sorts of rape behaviours tended to be associated with each other. For example, in some of the rapes the offender had apologised to the victim whereas, in others, the offender had bitten the victim. Do these characteristics tend to coexist together or does the presence of one characteristic tend not to be associated with the other?

Some behaviours were virtually universal in the rapes. Vaginal penetration from the front was achieved or attempted in 89 per cent of the rapes. In contrast, vaginal penetration from the rear, or an attempt at this, was relatively uncommon (7 per cent of rapes). The rapist revealed information, true or false, about themselves in 40 per cent of cases. In 23 per cent of rapes, the offender carried out multiple acts of violence against the victim – more than those required to simply control the victim. Among the rare characteristics were that the offender had taken a weapon to the scene of the crime (6 per cent); penetration was achieved more than once (6 per cent); and the offender implied knowing the victim before the attack (5 per cent). Three separate rape patterns were identified:

- *Theft:* the offender had stolen identifiable items such as credit cards from the victim; the offender rummaged or searched through the victim's property; a condom was used; the offender stole things such as money which cannot be identified.
- *Involvement:* the offender tried to reassure the victim, though this might include reassurance that he did not intend to carry out the act; the offender complimented the victim; the victim was drugged by the offender; the rapist implied that he knew the victim; the offender attempted an intrusion into the victim's home.
- *Hostility:* the offender carried out vaginal penetration from the rear; the offender bit the victim; the offender carried out a single act of violence but not to control the victim; the offender penetrated the victim's vagina digitally; the weapon had been taken from the scene of the crime.

An earlier study using British data by Canter, Bennell, Alison and Reddy (2003) had generated a similar classification of rape, based on the transcripts of statements made verbatim by rape victims. This provided information about a number of characteristics of rapes which could be analysed statistically for patterns in stranger rape. The terminology is much the same, though the rape characteristics used to define each pattern were not the same in every case:

- *Control:* the victim was bound or gagged; use of mask or blindfold and using a weapon were characteristic of this. About a tenth of rapes were in this category. This pattern did not emerge in the Finnish study discussed above, whilst the following patterns are similar in both studies though slightly differently defined.
- *Theft:* goods were demanded from the victim; the personal property of the victim was stolen; identifiable goods were stolen; unidentifiable goods were stolen. About a twentieth of rapes were in this category.
- *Involvement:* the victim might be complimented about her appearance – for example, the offender might make sexual comments in the course of the offence; the victim was kissed; and the offender implies that he knew the victim. About a third of rapes were in this category.
- *Hostility:* the offender removed the victim's clothing in a violent manner; there was an attempt to penetrate the victim anally; the victim was threatened at some time in the offence; the victim was demeaned or insulted, for instance by the use of verbal insult. This amounted to about a quarter of rapes.

Some rapes showed mixed patterns.

Canter *et al.* (2003) argue from these crime activity typologies that rapists are best distinguished in terms of the sorts of interpersonal behaviours that occur as part of the rape. It is less important and profitable to study the types of sexual behaviours involved.

The nature of rapists

So, it is clearly too simplistic to regard rape as the result of an uncontrolled, intense sexual lust. There are many reasons to be dubious about this formulation. For example, there is some evidence that sexual deprivation is not an essential component of rape (Howitt, 1991a). Rape commonly involves physical violence, of course. This, in some cases, goes substantially beyond the levels required to force the victim to participate in sex. Lloyd and Walmsley (1989) found that rapes in the United Kingdom typically were accompanied by violence. Around 25 per cent contained no violence. About one in eight resulted in the victim being hospitalised owing to the level of the violence. Thus the explanation of rape must go beyond libidinous needs alone or in part.

Rape may manifest itself in a variety of forms. Hazelwood (1987), an offender profiler, suggested that the following types of rapist should be considered (following Groth *et al.*, 1977):

The power-assurance rapist:

- This describes the commonest type of rapist.
- The rape is concerned with dealing with the rapist's insecurities about his masculinity.
- As the offence may not help with the insecurities and because the insecurities are deep, there may be only a short interval before he needs to offend again.
- Force is not great and threats may be involved. Weapons are not common in this form of rape.
- Usually, the rape is planned – there may be prior surveillance of the victim.
- If the victim is sufficiently passive to allow this, sexual fantasies may be expressed during the course of the rape.
- 'Trophies' such as clothing or some other article may be taken. These may be used, for example, in future masturbation.

The power-assertive rapist:

- This type of offender is sexually confident.
- Rape expresses his virility and sexuality, and power over women.
- Victims may be found in social locations such as discos, pubs or parties.
- Initially, his manner may be friendly but may quickly change.
- Violence is extreme, especially in the later stages. He does not appear to be the stereotypical rapist as he is socially skilled.
- Offences may be scattered and irregular in terms of frequency of occurrence.
- This pattern may be common in date-rape.

The anger-retaliatory rapist:

- The offender has extremely high levels of anger towards women such that, for example, degrading activities may be involved in the rape.
- The rape involves short, intense attacks (blitz).
- Characteristically, there is a similarity between the victim and the woman he has a grudge against.
- Attacks may be fairly regular as a consequence of the build-up of anger.

The anger-excitement rapist:

- This is the least common type of rapist.

- The rapist gains pleasure and sexual excitement from viewing the distress of his victim.
- Thus the infliction of pain is common and violence is at such high levels that the victim may be killed. Torture is common.
- There is careful, methodical planning.
- The rapist will bring such items as blindfolds, gags and ropes to the rape.
- Victims are usually total strangers to the offender.
- Photographs and video-recordings may be taken.
- Usually attacks are irregular, in part determined by the time at which his careful planning is complete.

Clearly, then, rape takes a variety of forms in terms of the motives and behaviours of the rapist. Understanding the different types of rapist may be helpful in deciphering the different crime scenes. This is an issue which we shall return to in Chapters 14 and 15 when discussing offender profiling.

BOX 9.1 Forensic psychology in action

Phallometry (also known as plethysmography)

The phallometer is a device that measures the amount of penis enlargement as an indicator of sexual arousal. There are two types:

- *Volume phallometry* measures the volume of the penis. Essentially, a man's penis is put inside an air-tight glass tube. Changes in the size of his penis will cause changes in the pressure inside the tube. These changes may be measured through a meter or recorded on an electrical, moving pen device (much like a lie-detector machine – see Chapter 19).
- *Circumference phallometry* measures the circumference of the penis with a flexible 'tube'. Changes in circumference lead to changes in the electrical signals that are fed to the recording device.

The underlying theory is obvious – the size of a man's penis is an indicator of his level of sexual arousal. Thus, if a man is shown a pornographic video of a rape, then the potential rapists should show greater increase in penis size than so-called 'normal' men. There are a number of practical difficulties that need consideration:

- Penises vary in size both between men and over time. One consequence of this is that the measures used tend to be expressed in relative terms: that is, rather than the change in penis volume or circumference being used, the *percentage increase* in volume or circumference would be the measure of arousal. Alternatively, the man may be encouraged to masturbate to full erection and his response to the sexual stimuli assessed as a percentage of this maximum.
- Phallometry is undertaken in circumstances that are not conducive to sexual arousal for all men. These investigations are relatively public, cold, clinical and intrusive: for example, being connected up to the apparatus by a clinician, being sat in a chair in a small room or cubicle in a corner of a hospital or clinic, and being shown pornography which might be alien to one's sexuality. These factors mean that for some men, at least, the assessment process is ineffective as little or no sexual response is produced.
- It is possible to fake responses in a number of ways. Secret masturbation may allow the offender to show apparent arousal to 'normal stimuli'. Fantasising to alternative arousing imagery and tensing muscles in the area of the anus/scrotum may allow the same control on arousal. Disinterest in certain stimuli may be faked by fantasising about non-arousing themes while the clinician is showing otherwise arousing material to the man. For example, the man may be carrying out mental arithmetic while the arousing material is being shown. Alternatively, by pressing heavily on a nail or splinter in the chair he may cause an unpleasant and distracting sensation.
- Attempts may be made to detect or prevent faking. One way of doing this is to ensure that the participants are concentrating on the video material by setting them a task such as answering questions about what they have seen or, for example, signalling when a light flashes in the video.

There are a number of techniques using phallometry which assess sexual arousal to different types of 'sexual' stimulus and possibly, then, the different types of victim. For example, Abel, Barlow, Blanchard and Guild (1977) developed the *rape index*. This compares a man's responses to various types of erotic material, including that with force and coercion. Men highest on response to the latter type of material are regarded as those with the greatest rape potential. Similarly, Avery-Clark and Laws (1984) put forward a *dangerous child molester index* which identifies the men with the greatest response to coerced sex with children.

As ever, a crucial question is that of the extent to which the different types of offender can be differentiated using phallometry: that is, if one is trying to identify paedophiles, just how many of them would be correctly identified as such and just how many of them would not be identified? Furthermore, how many normal men would be classified as paedophiles and how many would be identified as normal by the test in question? The evidence seems to be that circumference measures are fairly poor at correct identifications (Baxter, Barbaree and Marshall, 1986; Baxter, Marshall, Barbaree, Davidson and Malcolm, 1984; Murphy, Haynes, Stagaitis and Flanagan, 1986). Volume phallometry is better (McConaghy, 1991). Unfortunately, all that can be said currently is that if you have two groups of men, one group normals and the other group paedophiles, phallometry will help you correctly choose the group of normals and the group of paedophiles. It is rather less good at deciding for any group of men who is a paedophile and who is not.

The important question, to the clinician, is whether phallometry can identify rapists and paedophiles from the rest of the population. If high proportions of normal men are wrongly classified as paedophiles or rapists, and offenders are often misclassified as normal, then it is an ineffective test. For example, Quinsey, Steinman, Bergersen and Holmes (1975) found that normal men showed erections to pictures of pubescent and young girls that were 70 per cent and 50 per cent of their responses to erotic pictures of adult females. In a study by Wormith (1986), the classification accuracy based on circumference phallometry was 64 per cent for groups of paedophiles, rapists and non-sex offenders. Only 50 per cent of paedophiles were correctly classified as such, and 42 per cent were classified as normal.

Perhaps more importantly, Hall, Shondrick and Hirschman (1993) carried out a meta-analysis (see Box 4.1) of a number of published studies. These studies compared penile responses when shown sexually aggressive materials in men known to be sexually violent with appropriate control participants. These studies only used audiotaped materials, which included both consenting sexual activity and sexual violence (rape). Using tables in Howitt and Cramer (2008), the correlation (effect size) obtained over the varied studies was about 0.14. This is a rather small correlation despite showing a relationship between responses to rape stimuli and being a rapist: that is, many men would be misclassified.

Using the rape index (Abel *et al.*, 1977), the correlation was much higher at the equivalent of 0.33. This proved to be a rather inconsistent finding since some studies obtained large relationships and others small relationships. According to Hall *et al.*, the studies finding large effects were those comparing rapists with non-sexually violent men. Smaller differences were found for the studies in which rapists were compared with paedophiles, for example.

Other worries include the simplistic equation that links erections to sexual offending. This assumes that sexual motives underlie rape and other forms of sexual offending, whereas there is considerable evidence that offenders may suffer sexual dysfunction in that they cannot achieve penetration and that there are non-sexual motives involved in some of the crimes.

Some recommend confronting suspected sex offenders with phallometric evidence in order to elicit a confession (Travin, Bluestone, Coleman, Cullen and Melella, 1985). This has its own risks, such as false confession. While phallometry may be effective enough for research purposes, it appears to be rather risky for clinical assessment purposes. Indeed, there is some evidence that self-reports may be at least as effective as phallometry in detecting offenders (e.g. Howitt, 1995a). Furthermore, the results appear to be better for co-operative (admitting) offenders than unco-operative (non-admitting) offenders. This again lessens their attractiveness as an objective assessment technique.

Penile plethysmography is problematic in a number of obvious ways. It involves relatively expensive instrumentation which needs time and appropriate space to administer. Furthermore, there is no universal standard way of administering the phallometry which is applied consistently from one clinical setting to another. Laws and Gress (2004), among a number of researchers, have increasingly regarded viewing time of 'erotic' imagery as an alternative to phallometry since it involves no equipment attached to a man's genitals and is equally suitable for assessing women. (For a review of plethysmography for females see Staunton and Harold (2016)). Viewing time measures are simply the amount of time that, say, a sex offender spends looking at particular types of erotic stimuli. It is now possible to administer viewing time procedures using computers, which can also be used to generate standard imagery without having to recourse to pictures of real people.

Rape myths

Cognitive factors conducive to rape increasingly became a focus for researchers following Burt's (1980) work on the cultural myths concerning rape. She developed the *Rape-myth Acceptance Scale* based on the observation that Western culture had essentially blamed the victims of rape for the attacks on them. Such victim-blaming strategies have in the past been identified as characteristic of the criminal justice system. In a male-dominated culture, ideas develop that, by essentially blaming the victim, either encourage men to rape or provide them with an excuse for their sexually aggressive acts against women. Women, it is held, deserve to be or want to be raped. Men, according to the myths, are almost justified in raping. This is best illustrated by considering a number of items taken from the Rape-myth Acceptance Scale:

> If a girl engages in necking or petting and she lets things get out of hand, it is her own fault if her partner forces sex on her.
>
> If a woman gets drunk at a party and has intercourse with a man she's just met there, she should be considered 'fair game' for other males at the party who want to have sex with her too, whether she wants to or not.
>
> A woman who is stuck-up and thinks she is too good to talk to guys on the street deserves to be taught a lesson.

The final item above also illustrates the idea that rape is part of male domination/control of women. There are other measures, which reflect similar ideas such as the *Mosher Scale Sexually Callous Attitudes Towards Women* (Mosher and Anderson, 1986). This appears to measure somewhat tough, unsympathetic and heartless attitudes on the part of men towards sex with females and female sexuality:

> You don't ask girls to screw, you tell them to screw.
>
> You never know when you are going to meet a strange woman who will want to get laid.

There is evidence that this sort of measure of the cognitive aspects of rape is associated with views about a man's willingness to offend. The most controversial of these measures is Malamuth's *Self-reported Likelihood to Rape* measure (Malamuth and Ceniti, 1986). This is also known as the proclivity to rape. It is basically a single-item measure: 'How likely do you think you would be to commit rape if you can be assured of not being caught?' This is a controversial measure because of the inherent difficulty in knowing quite what men mean if they agree with this statement. Does it mean that they are likely to rape even if they might get caught? Does it mean that they are unsure of why they do not rape so feel that they might rape in some circumstances? Or what do the answers mean? A number of researchers have shown that there is a small or modest relationship between acceptance of the rape myths and proclivity to rape. For example, Tieger (1981) found that the men who score higher on the *Likelihood to Rape* measure also tend to see rape as an enjoyable seduction for the victim and hold the victim to blame for her victimisation. Men who report regarding rape as a serious crime and who are not overtly stereotyped in their thinking about sex roles tend to score lower on the *Likelihood to Rape* measure. Some researchers stress these cognitive components and, for an extreme version of this viewpoint, Russell's (1988, 1992) model warrants attention in so far as she draws together much of the work in this area to make the case for the cognitive basis of rape.

The acid test of this cognitive model has to be whether these cognitive factors help us differentiate between rapists and non-rapists. Here the theory seems to fail. There is some evidence suggesting that such cognitive factors do not differentiate rape offenders from others. For example, Overholser and Beck (1988) found no evidence that rapists differed from non-rape offenders and non-offenders on a number of attitude scales including acceptance of rape myths as well as attitudes to sex and attitudes to the use of violence. Stermac and Quinsey (1986) found no evidence that rapists were different from other groups in terms of their attitudes to women. The finding that adolescent sexual assaulters against women did not differ from the less overtly aggressive offenders against younger children supports this. Perhaps this is no surprise, given what we know about the offending and reoffending patterns of rapists. They tend to have been previously imprisoned for non-sexual offences and their reoffending is likely not to be sexual (Lloyd and Walmsley, 1989).

It is not easy to make the case that rape myths are a crucial factor in rape because of such evidence. Nevertheless, work on the cognitive aspects of sex offending, including the factors discussed in this section, is extremely common in the psychological treatment of sex offenders (see Chapter 26). There is no distinct evidence of the effectiveness of therapy on rape myths on recidivism separate from the total effects of the treatment programme. Any improvement in the social functioning that might enable an offender to establish a non-offending lifestyle is welcome, irrespective of what aspect of the therapy is responsible.

Leaving to one side the question of whether rape myth acceptance distinguishes rapists from other men, there still remain numerous questions about its role in the criminal justice system. Grubb and Turner (2012) reviewed the research literature on the factors which can influence attitudes towards victims of rape. This included rape myths. Their review concluded that men demonstrate the highest levels of rape myth acceptance overall when compared to women. They also tend to attribute more blame to rape victims than women do. The more that the victim violates traditional gender roles (such as by drinking), the more she is blamed. Grubb and Turner, however, point out that the major thrust of research in this area came in the 1980s and 1990s and so question whether renewed research interest in the field today would show previous findings to be valid. Rape myths are about how victims of rape are seen in society and so its ramifications in the criminal justice system may be more widespread than their role in offender thinking suggests. Egan and Wilson (2012) studied the role of victims' attitudes to rape and rape-reporting in a sample of nearly 40 rape victims. For this sample, reporting the rape was uncommon and only about one-third of victims had reported the offence to the police. The researchers had a comparison group of women who had been victims of non-sexual crimes. Reporting non-sex victimisation was slightly higher at about 40 per cent.

The research design considered victim type (rape versus non-sexual) and whether the crime was reported (yes or no). All participants completed a number of questionnaires dealing with rape myth acceptance (The Illinois Rape Myths Acceptance Scales: Payne, Lonsway, and Fitzgerald, 1999). There are six separate subscales of this: 1) She asked for it; 2) It wasn't really rape; 3) He didn't mean to; 4) She wanted it; 5) She lied; and 6) Rape is a trivial event. Other measures included locus of control, attitudes towards the police, the pro-victim and the anti-victim scales. The women who did not report their rape disturbingly had higher levels of rape myth acceptance than the women who did report. This finding is the same as a number of other studies. They also had higher levels of internal locus of control – that is, they saw themselves as responsible for things that happen to them. One possible explanation of the higher levels of internal locus of control may have been that these women felt relatively more in control of the rape.

Egan and Wilson argue that it is not uncommon for rape victims to blame themselves as a means of getting to feel more in control of the events. Feeling that nothing could be done to stop the rape becomes unacceptable to the victim, who then, according to Egan and Wilson, blames herself. However, another explanation could be that the non-reporting rape victims saw no resolution through the criminal justice system and regarded the resolution of their issues as lying in their own personal resources. For the non-sexual crime victims there was a correlation between rape myth acceptance and just world beliefs. 'Just world' theory (Lerner, 1980) is based on the idea that people tend to operate on the basis of the belief that the world is a fair and just place. The consequence of this is that any misfortune which befalls a person is seen as the victim's fault in some way. In this case, believing that the world is a fair place was associated with blaming rape victims for their victimisation. However, there was no such relationship for the rape victim group. So one might suggest that at the root of rape myths is the 'just world' idea the world is a fair place and you reap what you sow in life. Some individuals strongly believe that we inhabit a just world and that calamities which befall us are partly our fault. In theory, then, the stronger the belief in the just world, the more likely the victim is to be blamed for her rape.

Stromwell, Alfredsson and Landstrom (2013) studied the effect of the 'just world' belief on blaming victims and perpetrators in rape scenarios. A Swedish community sample of nearly 170 participants read one of a number of different scenarios dealing with different levels of relationship (e.g. strangers, acquaintances, dating and married). Generally, high levels of blame were attributed to perpetrators and low levels to victims. The victim of stranger rape, however, was blamed more than the victim of an acquaintance rape, which is the reverse of previous research findings, which suggested that the closer the relationship between the victim and the attacker, the more the victim is blamed. In line with the just world theory, the researchers found that those who held strongly to just world beliefs tended to blame the victim more and the perpetrator less than those without a strong belief in the just world. Interestingly, female participants attributed the most blame to the victim for the stranger rape scenario. Within these findings there would seem to be hints that victim blaming may be coming to an end – at least in Sweden. Furthermore, perpetrators were blamed and not victims. There were no differences between male and female participants either in this study. All of this may reinforce Grubb and Turner's call for more modern research.

One may wonder whether modern police officers trained in anti-stereotyping ideas continue to operate on the basis of societal rape myths. Goodman-Delahunty and Graham (2011) were interested in how contextual factors such as intoxication of the victim and the victim's clothing influence the way in which police officers process sexual assault victims. The study involved a simulated sexual assault and 125 detectives from the New South Wales Police Department read witness statements and looked at photographs related to a case of date rape. Unlike expectations and previous research, complainant intoxication, provocative dress, and the officer's gender had no influence on whether or not the officer would charge the suspect with the offence. Important factors predicting charging were the perceived credibility of the complainant and culpability of the offender. The rape myth acceptance level of the officers influenced credibility and guilt judgements. This is clearly a mixed message in terms of progress.

Socio-cultural factors and sexual violence

Hall and Barongan (1997) argue that socio-cultural factors may be involved in rape. By this they mean that certain sorts of cultural organisation may encourage males to rape and others may reduce the risk of rape. One dimension on which cultures differ is the *individualist–collectivist* orientation. Western culture, and that of the United States especially, holds that individuals should strive to achieve the best they can for themselves. Collectivist cultures, on the other hand, value those who work for the collective good. Within a nation – especially nations built on migrant communities such as the United States – there may, of course, be different subcultures. The argument is that collectivist cultures are less conducive to rape than individualist cultures. Unfortunately for Hall and Barongan, superficially their idea does not fit the available statistical evidence well. For example, despite the fact that African-American communities may be regarded as relatively more collectivist in orientation, African-American men tend to be over-represented in the rape statistics. Hall and Barongan suggest that this may be illusory – a function of socio-economic status differentials between black and white Americans. Low socio-economic status is a risk factor in committing rape and also more characteristic of black rather than white Americans.

International crime statistic comparisons are problematic since one is unsure whether like is being compared with like. For example, rape might be defined differently; women less likely to report rape; police less likely to seek prosecutions for rape and so forth. There is some evidence when American and collectivist Hong Kong Chinese college students are compared that the American men were rather more likely to report using coercion sexually such as when touching a woman's genitals against her will. Among the reasons why collectivist cultures will show lower levels of sexual violence are:

- interpersonal conflict (including violence) tends to be minimal in collectivist cultures partly because of the sharing of group goals;
- individual needs are subordinated to the well-being of the group in collectivist cultures;
- a personal sense of shame at letting down the community is a major deterrent against crime.

Similarly, socio-cultural values are intimately related to rates of rape in different parts of the United States (Baron and Straus, 1989). Their research design was statistically complex but essentially simple. They took the 50 American states and compared them in terms of rates of rape based on publicly available statistics. Of course, such statistics are gathered from official sources and are subject to a degree of error since they are dependent upon reporting by the victim, recording by the police and other factors that may lead to a degree of inaccuracy. While accepting that there is inaccuracy, Baron and Straus argue that, in relative terms, such indexes are satisfactory for their purposes. Some states, such as Alaska and Florida, tended to have high rates of rape, given the size of their population, and other states, such as Maine and North Dakota, tended to have substantially lower rates of rape compared to their population size. The crime figures were rape reports in the Uniform Crime Report statistics from the early 1980s.

The researchers also collected a number of other indexes of significant differences among the 50 states, based on sociological theory. These included the following, which essentially constitute three different theories about why rape rates vary across different communities:

- *Cultural spillover:* this was measured in terms of the *Legitimate Violence Index* which involved state-approved violence such as the acceptance of corporal punishment in schools and capital punishment rates for murder.
- *Gender inequality:* this was an index of the economic, legal and political status of women compared with men. The measures included the proportion of the state's senate that was female and the average income of employed women compared with that of employed men.
- *Social disorganisation:* this was based on indicators of social instability due to weakening forces of social regulation. Factors such as geographical mobility, divorce, the proportion of lone-parent families and a lack of religious affiliation were included here.

There was support for the *gender inequality* and *social disorganisation* explanations of rape. *Cultural spillover theory* was rejected on the basis of the data. In other words, the findings suggest that the greater gender inequality in favour of males and the greater social disorganisation then the greater the amount of rape.

BOX 9.2 Controversy

Sexual fantasy and sex offending

It is commonly accepted that sexual fantasy, especially violent sexual fantasy, has some role to play in the most serious sexual crimes, including sexual murders. The work of MacCulloch *et al.* (1983) was particularly influential in this regard. Clinicians believe that there is a process by which somewhat obsessive sexual fantasies escalate in frequency and extremity. Eventually, these may lead to violent and sexual criminal acts. Following this, there may be satiation. This sort of escalating cycle of fantasy is described in the writings of clinicians dealing with paedophiles (e.g. Wyre, 1990, 1992). Fantasy-reduction and fantasy control are important themes in the therapy employed with sex offenders. Some therapists employ the term *directed masturbation* in which the offender is encouraged to masturbate to sexual imagery which is appropriate (e.g. consensual sex with two adult women) in an attempt to recondition appropriate sexual preference (Cooper, 2005). It is also useful to note that research seems to have established that child molesters tend to have more fantasies about children when they are in a negative mood state (feeling depressed or miserable, for example) than at other times (Looman, 1999).

Others, dealing with non-offender populations, have taken a rather different view about the role of fantasy in sexual relationships (e.g. Cramer and Howitt, 1998). It would seem clear that, in sexual relationships, there may be a big difference between the contents of fantasy and expectations about sexual relations. Sexual thoughts that lead to sexual arousal are commonplace for both men and women (Jones and Barlow, 1990). Sexual fantasy within the relationships of ordinary couples may be at variance with principles such as monogamy, tenderness and sharing. This is as true of women as it is of men. Sexual fantasy in sexual intercourse and masturbation occurs at very high rates (Knafo and Jaffe, 1984). In other words, sexual fantasy may be construed as normal and somewhat unacceptable themes are commonly found in fantasy. For example, Kirkendall and McBride (1990) established that more than a third of men and a quarter of women fantasised about being forced into sexual relations.

A number of possible links between sexual fantasy and offending may be hypothesised (Howitt, 2000, 2004). One crucial piece of information would be to assess whether the reduction of sexual fantasy through therapeutic intervention actually reduces offending. There is little direct evidence on this. Hall, Hirschman and Oliver (1995) describe a meta-analysis (see Box 4.1) of studies of the effects of sex offender treatment programmes on recidivism. There was a negative effect of behavioural therapies directed mainly towards fantasy reduction: that is, more recidivism where sexual fantasy had been reduced. Also of significance is Daleiden, Kaufman, Hilliker and O'Neill's (1998) finding that the difference between offenders and non-offenders is not in terms of having 'deviant' sexual fantasies but that offenders have fewer normal fantasies! The lack of normal fantasy is what is dangerous. Interestingly, a small study involving largely homosexual paedophiles found that those engaging in deviant fantasy were less likely to use coercion and more likely to engage in 'friendship formation' in the process of offending (Looman, 1999).

Where do fantasies come from? They seem to emerge developmentally at a quite early stage. More than 80 per cent of offenders reported having deviant sexual fantasies by the age of 15 years (Bates, 1996). Such fantasy might have its origins in childhood sexual abuse since some claim that there is a close link between early fantasy and features of their abuse (Howitt, 1995a, 1998a). Others find no such link (Waterhouse, Dobash and Carnie, 1994). Fantasy, in this formulation, is regarded as rising out of experience. If this is the case, then it becomes feasible that offenders engage in offending not because they are driven by their fantasies but in order to provide fantasy imagery. Sex offences are quite frequently non-consummatory since penetration and orgasm do not take place (Howitt, 1995a). An offender, for example, might limit his sexual contact to touching a child through its clothes. One explanation of such behaviour may be that it is to provide material for fantasy rather than to act out the fantasy.

In an attempt to see whether preventing masturbation could reduce sexual fantasy, Brown, Traverso and Fedoroff (1996) had outpatient paedophiles randomly assigned to a masturbation-allowed or masturbation-not-allowed condition. Self-report measures were used to assess the effectiveness of masturbation prevention. Only about a fifth of the paedophiles were able to abstain from masturbation for the required four-week period. There seemed to be no differences between the two groups in terms of intensity of sexual urges, urges to masturbate, urges for sex with adults and urges for sex with children. The low compliance of the offenders with the therapist's request not to masturbate should be evaluated with the finding that paedophiles masturbated about four times each week in mind. The authors regard what they see as a low sexual interest in this group as reason not to employ masturbation prohibition.

Sheldon and Howitt (2008) studied Internet child pornography offenders compared with regular contact paedophiles in terms of their use of sexual fantasy and the contents of their sexual fantasies. The most common sexual fantasies among these offenders with a sexual interest in children were the same as the typical heterosexual fantasies of men in general. So fantasies such as 'having vaginal intercourse with a willing female

BOX 9.2 (continued)

adult'; 'giving oral sex to a willing female adult'; and 'masturbating a willing female adult' were among the most common fantasies (Sheldon and Howitt, 2007, p. 195). Fantasies involving force were among the least common (e.g. 'overpowering a woman and forcing her to give me oral sex', Sheldon and Howitt, 2007, p. 197). Interestingly, the contact offenders reported fewer girl-oriented sexual fantasies than did the Internet child pornography offenders. There was also some evidence that contact offenders had a greater tendency to use confrontational fantasies which involved things like 'exposing my genitals to an unsuspecting adult or adults' and 'making obscene phone calls', which implies that for them fantasy has to stray into the realms of experience (Sheldon and Howitt, 2007, p. 199). If anything, there seems to be a deficit in the amounts of sexual fantasy in contact offenders compared with Internet child pornography offences. This, of course, leaves open the possibility that contact offenders need to contact offend in order to stimulate their fantasy rather than offend to fulfil their fantasies.

Given that it is commonly assumed that deviant sexual fantasies are played out behaviourally by sex offenders (Williams, Cooper, Howell, Yuille and Paulhus, 2009), why does not every deviant sexual fantasy lead to deviant sexual behaviour? Sexual deviance may be defined by the criterion of an unusual source of sexual arousal. However, according to Williams *et al.*, the rates of deviant sexual fantasies are very similar for offender and non-offender samples. Given this, just what determines whether a fantasy will be acted out in the form of a crime or not? The researchers used nine different deviant behaviours for their study, including bondage, exhibitionism, fetishism involving objects, frotteurism, paedophilia, sadism, sexual assault, transvestism and voyeurism. The study involved non-offender male university students at a large Western US university who completed a self-completion questionnaire pack anonymously. An 80 per cent return rate was obtained. The core of the research questionnaires was the Multidimensional Assessment of Sex and Aggression by Knight, Prentky and Cerce (1994). The items from this were rearranged into the nine areas of deviant sexual behaviour listed above in order to provide a measure for each of them. The researchers also obtained self-reports of the nine different deviant fantasies and behaviours.

Ninety-five per cent of the participants reported having had at least one deviant sexual fantasy, though only 74 per cent had actively engaged in one or more of these activities. The mean rate for experiencing each fantasy was 52 per cent. This was higher than the mean rate for engaging in the corresponding sexually deviant behaviour, which was much lower at 21 per cent. Despite there being a moderately high correlation between having a deviant fantasy and carrying it out, this relationship was not statistically significant for paedophile fantasies. To put it another way, fantasisers were behavers in only 38 per cent of cases but behavers were fantasisers in 96 per cent of cases. Sixty-three per cent of the sample claimed to use pornography currently and the mean fantasy score was significantly greater for those who did than for those who did not. Users also reported significantly more carrying out of fantasy. The use of pornography had a partial but statistically significant mediating effect on the relationship between fantasy and fantasy-related behaviours. Pornography's influence on deviancy was mediated in part by an increase in deviant fantasy.

Are there any factors which determine whether a fantasy will be acted out in behaviour? A second study by Williams *et al.* (2009) examined the possible mediating influence of different variables including eight personality characteristics – these were agreeableness, conscientiousness, extraversion, Machiavellianism, narcissism, openness to experience, psychopathy and stability. It emerged that the link between fantasy and deviant behaviour applied only to those individuals who reported high levels of deviant sexual fantasy. Furthermore, the association between pornography use and sexually deviant behaviours only applied to those participants who were also high on psychopathy. It has to be stressed that this research involved seemingly normal university students rather than offenders. The equivalent research has yet to be carried out on offenders. Nevertheless, it is important to know that the prevalence rate for deviant sexual fantasies in offender samples has been found to be approximately 80–90 per cent.

In a systematic review of sexual murderers which involved seven different studies and a total of 171 sexual murderers, Maniglio (2010) concluded that sexual fantasies might lead to sexual murder when the offender had early traumatic life experiences or more extreme social and/or sexual dysfunctions. There are problems for researchers since legal definitions of sexual homicide in the US exclude many crimes which appear to have a sexual element and, in addition, sexual killing is relatively rare among homicides.

More on the theory of rape

There has been one systematic attempt to compare the different theoretical explanations of rape that should be considered. Ellis (1989) identified three major theories of rape:

- feminist theory;
- social learning theory;
- evolutionary theory.

In many ways influenced by the socio-biological approach to crime (see Chapter 5), Ellis suggests that it is possible to generate testable hypotheses from each of these theories.

Feminist theory

This essentially argues that rape is built into the gender structure of society. A dense network of different ways of controlling women buttresses male power. As such, one would expect this control to be manifest in many aspects of society. It has been manifest in the law (e.g. the denial of women's property rights, considering it reasonable that a man should be allowed to beat his wife and so forth) as well as domestic relations between men and women. Basic tenets of feminist theory, according to Ellis, are the following:

- Rape should be associated with sex disparities in social status and power. (p. 20)
- Rape is primarily motivated by a desire for power and dominance rather than a desire for sex. (p. 21)

From these basic ideas of feminist theory, Ellis derives what he considers to be formal hypotheses that can be tested against empirical data concerning rape:

- Societal trends toward sexual egalitarianism should be associated with a lessening of rape victimisation. (p. 28)

The evidence does support the idea that gender equality in society is associated with fewer rapes, as we have already seen.

- Rapists should hold less egalitarian and more pro-rape attitudes toward women than non-rapists. (p. 29)

This hypothesis is not clearly supported by the studies which find that rapists are no different from other offenders in terms of their cognitions about rape and women, as we saw above.

Social learning theory

This basically suggests that rapists learn to be rapists by learning pro-rape beliefs and attitudes from their social milieu. For various reasons, rapists tend to learn the pro-rape cognitions more effectively than non-rapists do. Ellis mentions the following hypotheses based on social learning theory, among others. Notice that the hypotheses derived from social learning theory are not necessarily very different from those proposed by feminist theory:

- Rapists should hold attitudes that are more favourable towards rape, and towards violence in general, than other men. (p. 33)

We have seen that this hypothesis is not clearly supported.

- Exposure to violent pornography should increase male propensities to commit rape, and otherwise to behave violently toward women. (p. 35)

This is one of the pornography-related hypotheses listed by Ellis, who regards pornography as an almost essential learning course for rape. This is a somewhat controversial area and Ellis's views reflect just one side of the controversy (see Box 10.1).

Evolutionary theory

Socio-biological theory is largely about one's adaptiveness for the transmission of one's genetic material to the next generation. Rape, according to a socio-biological perspective, should reflect this basic principle of behaviour. In other words, the hypotheses for evolutionary theory should emphasise the functionality of rape for the transmission of genetic material to the next generation. The following hypotheses are feasible:

- Tendencies to rape must be under some degree of genetic influence. (p. 43)
- Forced copulations should impregnate victims, at least enough to offset whatever risks rapists have of being punished for their offences. (p. 47)
- Rape victims should be primarily of reproductive age. (p. 50)
- Rape should be vigorously resisted by victims, especially when the offender is someone to whom the females are not sexually attracted. (p. 50)
- Rapists (especially those who assault strangers) should be less likely than other males to attract voluntary sex partners. (p. 52)

To the extent that these hypotheses are clear, there is generally some evidence to support them. Ellis's (1989) position is that basically each of the different theories has some commendable features and that a synthesis of various elements is essential to understanding rape. Unlike some recent writers, Ellis is an advocate of the view that rape is partially a sexual rather than a violent crime.

More recently, another theory about rape, claiming to be based on evolutionary psychology, has received a great deal of publicity, especially in the United States. Thornhill and Palmer (2000) are not psychologists, despite this. Their argument is that, subject to conditions, all men are capable of rape. Rape, they argue, has to be considered to be motivated by sex. Men who are essentially disenfranchised from society, lacking status in the sexual order, are still driven to procreate. Cognitions may play a part in that men are calculating beings capable of evaluating the benefits and costs of rape. In the theory, women are regarded as contributing to their victimisation by rapists by failing to avoid dangerous situations conducive to rape attack. The trauma that follows rape is regarded as a beneficial matter since the women would be less inclined to put themselves in any of the situations which are conducive to rape in future. Many of their ideas have placed Thornhill and Palmer at the centre of significant criticism from academics and others.

Others have recently outlined their own theoretical relationships between evolutionary concepts and crime. A good example of this is Quinsey (2002) who relates evolutionary theory to sexual crimes as well as other types of crime. Evolutionary theory, he suggests, is environmental and selectionist in nature because the environments of our ancestors have helped select particular characteristics of individuals which are genetically transmitted over generations. Those characteristics that tend to be emphasised as a consequence of natural selection are termed *adaptations*. They are related to successful reproduction strategies since if they were not then the adaptations would die out. Quinsey gives a simple example. He suggests that a man in the 'ancestral environment' who had a genetically produced sexual proclivity for trees would have little reproductive success with females and so would not sire future offspring. So males would demonstrate features that lead to reproductive success with females, which may not be the same as those that lead to reproductive success in females themselves. Males and females, in the evolutionary view, do not share reproductive interests entirely. Quinsey argues that sexual coercion illustrates this divergence between males and females. While, according to the environmental psychologists, it is in the interest of women to seek a male who provides the greatest advantage in terms of protection and care and genetic potential, sexual coercion essentially prevents women exercising choice in this respect. So one argument from the evolutionary perspective is that, in circumstances where the costs of disregarding the mating preferences of females are insignificant, coercive sexual behaviour is more common. Circumstances in which this would happen include the situation of soldiers in an occupying country or when the man expresses sexually callous attitudes towards women anyway. The problem is, of course, that without the crucial evidence that links sexual coercion to genetic make-up in some way, many other explanations of sexual coercion are equally viable. For example, Quinsey points out that psychopathy and sexual deviation as measured by plethysmography together predict new sex offences. Unfortunately for this explanation, psychopaths commit many types of crime more frequently than others and not just sexually coercive crime.

Finally, based firmly in the evolutionary psychology perspective, McKibbin, Shackelford, Goetz and Starratt (2008) propose a tentative typology of rapists which are based individual differences and the likely circumstances in which they are likely to perpetrate rape. They assume that rape is a possible act of all man though only or largely in specific conditions. The five types of rapist are: 1) disadvantaged men; 2) specialised rapists who are sexually aroused by violent sex; 3) opportunistic rapists; 4) high-mating-effort men who have a need to be dominant and may show psychopathic traits; and 5) partner rapists motivated by heightened risk of sperm competition. These will become clearer:

- *Disadvantaged men:* Research evidence suggests that there is a tendency for some rapes to be committed by men who lack the means of obtaining sex by any other means. They include men of very low socioeconomic status and those with very assymetric faces which is an indicator that their genetic quality is poor as they tend to suffer poorer physical and psychological health, for example. They are seen as less desirable as mates. According to some, rapists show this facial asymmetry (Krill, Lake and Platek, 2006).
- *Specialised rapists:* McKibbin *et al.* see the special feature of this group as lying in their potential to be sexually aroused by violent sexual imagery. The evidence supporting this has already been discussed in this chapter.
- *Opportunistic rapists:* This group includes men who usually seek out willing sexual partners. However, in the absence of this or where the costs of rape are low (perhaps there is little chance of getting caught) then these men may resort to rape. A good example of this sort of rapists is the soldier in wartime who rapes when the chances of detection and punishment are low.
- *High-mating-effort rapists:* These are typically sexually experienced men with high self-esteem who characteristically are dominant and aggressive. They put a lot of effort into mating and so seek many partners though without emotional investment. When this tactic fails, they may turn to coercive sexual behaviours.
- *Partner rapists:* McKibbin *et al.* suggest that this group involves men who rape their partners when faced with increased risk of sperm competition. This simply means when there are other males around to fertilize the female. So they suggest that when faced with the actuality or

possibility that his long-term partner is unfaithful. There is evidence that partner rape is most likely during a breakup due to the man's concerns about his partner's sexual faithfulness (Thornhill and Thornhill, 1992).

The evidence in support of this typology is heavily dependent on ideas developed from evolutionary psychology. The extent to which the typology helps forensic and criminal psychology can only wait to be seen as McKibbin *et al.* stress its tentative nature.

Synthesising explanations of sex offending

Certain concepts commonly reoccur in the research literature on sex offending. Lussier, Leclerc, Cale and Proulx (2007) point to three major concepts which tend to dominate in explanations of sex offending. They concentrated on empirically testing the role of the concepts of internalisation, externalisation and sexualisation, using data from interviews with members of a large sample of sex offenders. According to Lussier *et al.*, each of these concepts consists of several, interrelated components:

- *Externalisation* is undercontrolled behaviour and involves authority conflict, recklessness, covert externalised behaviours and overt externalised behaviours.
- *Internalisation* is overcontrolled behaviour and is made up of social isolation, depression and anxiety/somatic complaints.
- *Sexualisation* is a pattern of precociously oversexualised behaviours and can involve things like impersonal sex, sexually compulsive behaviour, and a preoccupation with sex. The view is that offenders are essentially driven to engage in deviant sexual behaviours. Lussier *et al.* use the term *sexualisation* to describe the lack of control offenders have over their sexual behaviour and feelings and the high strength and frequency of their sexual libido.

Examples of each of these components are given in Figure 9.6. For each of the individual concepts, the individual components are likely to co-occur. Thus depression, social withdrawal and anxiety are described as commonly occurring prior to the commission of sexual offences by offenders. Of course, not every researcher uses the same terminology in order to describe these different constructs.

The research team interviewed more than 500 convicted sex offenders in Quebec concerning their developmental history. They collected a wide variety of information but concentrated on internalisation, externalisation and sexualisation. Their analysis employed advanced statistical techniques (structural equation modelling and confirmatory factor analysis) to test various models (patterns of relationships) which might account for the data. For example, the first model they tried was based on the general deviancy model, which would suggest that internalisation, externalisation and sexualisation were highly interrelated. If an offender was high on one, then he would be high on the others. This model fitted the data badly – that is, the assumptions of the general deviancy model found poor support from the data. The best-fitting model was one in which internalisation, externalisation and sexualisation are largely independent of each other. Slight modifications had to be made to the model as it was found that impersonal sex was related to both sexualisation and externalisation (not just to sexualisation, as was originally thought) and compulsivity was related to both sexualisation and internalisation. These are empirical linkages, of course, and not conceptual ones.

You will also see in Figure 9.6 that sexualisation and externalisation were the more powerful constructs in explaining the extent of sexual offending. Internalisation was only weakly related to it. However, the construct of internalisation was important since where the victim was a child there tended to be higher internalisation. The evidence of a clear sexualisation pathway probably reinforces the importance of this in explaining why some offenders may specialise in sexual offences.

Offence Seriousness Escalation

The detection of sexual assaults by strangers is difficult. A substantial amount of research has been carried out on sexual offender's offending patterns over the last few decades (e.g. Lussier, Leclerc, Healey and Proulx, 2008) aimed at helping investigations. Sex offenders tend to be stable or versatile according to the aspect of their crimes is being considered. Offenders are likely to be stable in terms of the age of their chosen victim and the relationship they have with the victim. They may be less stable when, say, the type of sexual acts inflicted on the victim is concerned. However, situational factors such as victim resistance in a particular crime may have an influence on the stability of the crime pattern. If possible, situational variables ought to be taken into account during an investigation. It is frequently conjectured that there is a likelihood of offenders becoming more extreme with successive offences. The sexual acts and the level of force employed are thought to escalate in their seriousness. This idea of escalating offence severity may be contrasted to circumstances in

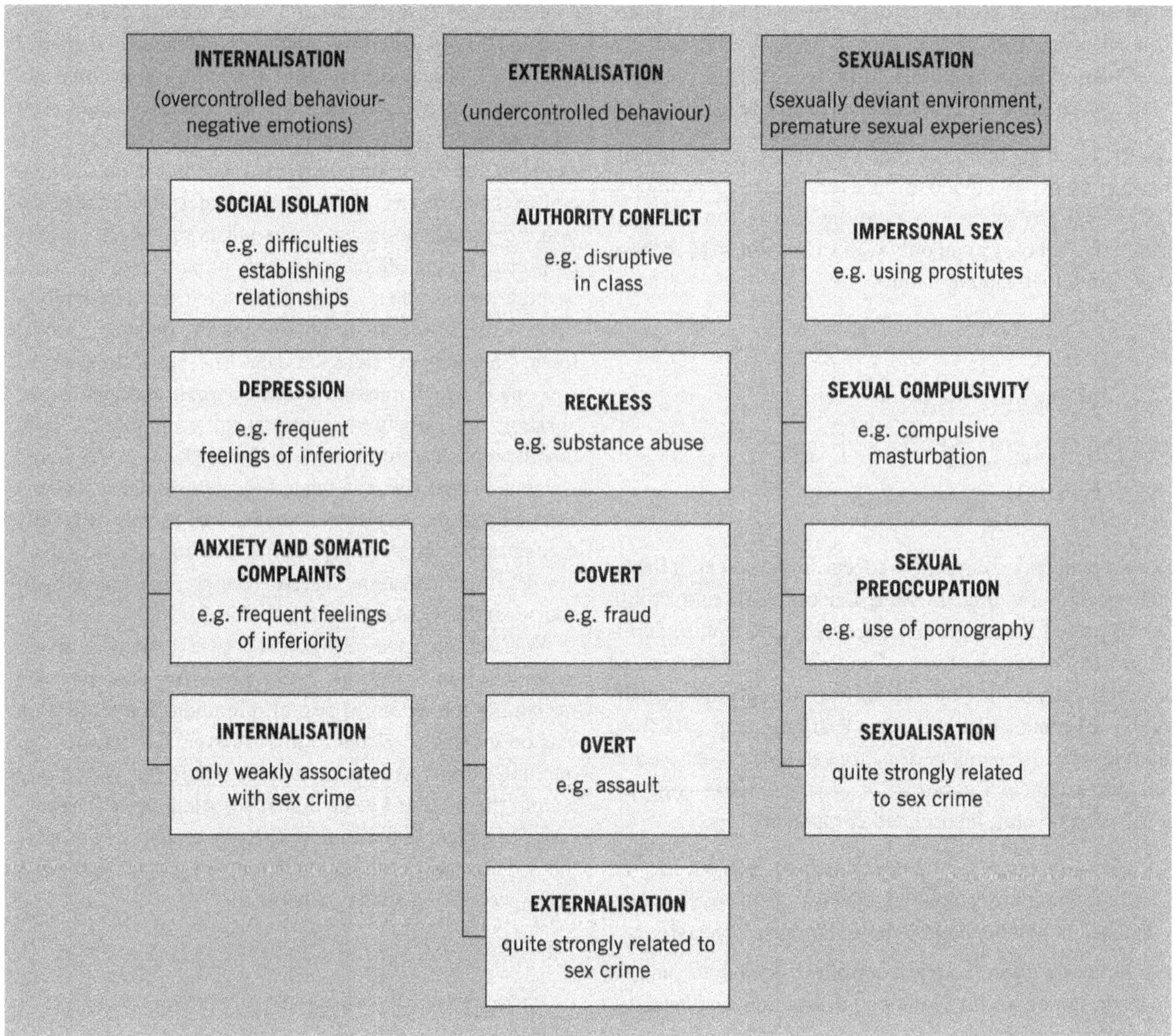

Figure 9.6 Internalisation, externalisation and sexualisation as concepts in the explanation of sex offending

which the offender becomes less extreme in their treatment of future victims. Hewitt and Beauregard (2014) used data on 72 serial stranger offenders in Canada. This sort of offender tends to show the most consistency in research. The researchers were interested in patterns of escalation, stability, and de-escalation over a series of crimes for measures of the intrusiveness of the sexual acts committed by the offender and the level of violence involved. The data were collected from the incarcerated offender using lengthy semi-structured interviews and police reports on their crimes.

Amongst the data collected was information concerning pre- and post-crime variables, the selection of victims, modi operandi, and geographic information. Other information collected included victim resistance, the offender's use of drugs, and whether the victim was alone prior to the crime. Whether stability or variability dominated depended somewhat on the aspect of the crime under consideration. Stability and variability. There was a lack of stability in the sexual acts performed especially in relation to contact versus non-contact sexual acts. This may be due to time being limited by situational factors or differences in the offender's sexual arousal at the time of the different offences. On the other hand, more serious sexually intrusive acts showed more consistency. Such activities included oral sex, penetration, and manually stimulating the victim's genitals. It would appear that actions which reflect the offender's sexual preference tend to be stable. The use and level of physical force by the offender showed consistency too. The majority of offenders did not use physical force in their offending. However, there was some versatility which may, partly, be the consequence of victim resistance. Higher levels of physical force were associated with more intrusive sexual acts. De-escalation depended on the resistance of the first victim compared with the second victim. If the first victim resisted then de-escalation of violence was more likely; if the second victim resisted then de-escalation was less likely. Overall, the issue of escalation is a complex matter and the result of quite a complex interplay of factors.

Main points

- The legal definition of rape often now includes non-consensual anal and oral penetration with a penis, as well as that of a vagina. In the last two decades or so, conceptions of the nature of rape have changed, especially under the influence of feminist thinking, which construes rape not simply as a sexual crime but as another aspect of male control of women. Rape, defined legally, has happened to 1 in 20 women at some time in their lives, although the annual rate is much lower. This is according to victim studies. Rape is a relatively under-reported crime and is much more often carried out by men whom the woman knows than by strangers. It is a crime more commonly carried out by younger offenders and shows much the same characteristics in terms of offender characteristics as other crimes of violence.
- Anger is a component of some rapes but not all. The commonest type of rape is described as the power-assurance rape. The offender is insecure in his masculinity, which he tries to assert through his use of power. As a consequence, he does not actually get the reassurance that he needs from his actions and is likely to reoffend after a short period of time. Other researchers find that other patterns can be identified in the characteristics of the rape itself without reference to psychological motives. One pattern is involvement, in which the offender tries to reassure the victim throughout the act in some way – so he may compliment her, or he may indicate that he knows her, or try to intrude into her home. It is commonly accepted that rape myths are conducive to rape offenders. Rape myths are exemplified by ideas such as 'If a woman wears sexy clothes, she is to blame if she is raped'. However, there is no evidence that such ideas distinguish rapists from other men. Evolutionary explanations of rape also tend to emphasise traditional gender-stereotypical ideas and seem, in many ways, the antithesis of feminist ideas about rape.
- In the forensic setting, there are a number of issues that are especially pertinent. One is the use of phallometry/plethysmography, which is basically a technique for assessing a man's sexual responsiveness to different types of sexual imagery. It involves using a tube or cuff around the penis. Changes in the volume or circumference of the man's penis can be recorded from this apparatus and are held to be indicative of sexual arousal. In this way, a man's responsiveness to rape imagery can be assessed, for example. Sexual fantasy, although commonly accepted as a driving force in sexual offences, is poorly understood and inadequately dealt with in forensic and criminal psychology. The common view is that sexual fantasies will be acted upon and, sometimes, this will be in criminal ways in the form of sex offences. This contrasts with what we know about sexual fantasy in non-offender groups, which indicates that fantasy does not always need to be acted out in order to have erotic effects.

Further reading

Proulx, J., Beauregard, E., Lussier, P. and Leclerk, B. (eds) (2014) *Pathways to Sexual Aggression* London: Routledge.

Ward, T., Polaschek, D.L.L. and Beech, A.R. (2006) *Theories of Sexual Offending* Chichester: John Wiley.

Ward, E. (2017) *The Wiley Handbook on the Theories, Assessment and Treatment of Sexual Offending.* Wiley-Blackwell: Chichester, West Sussex.

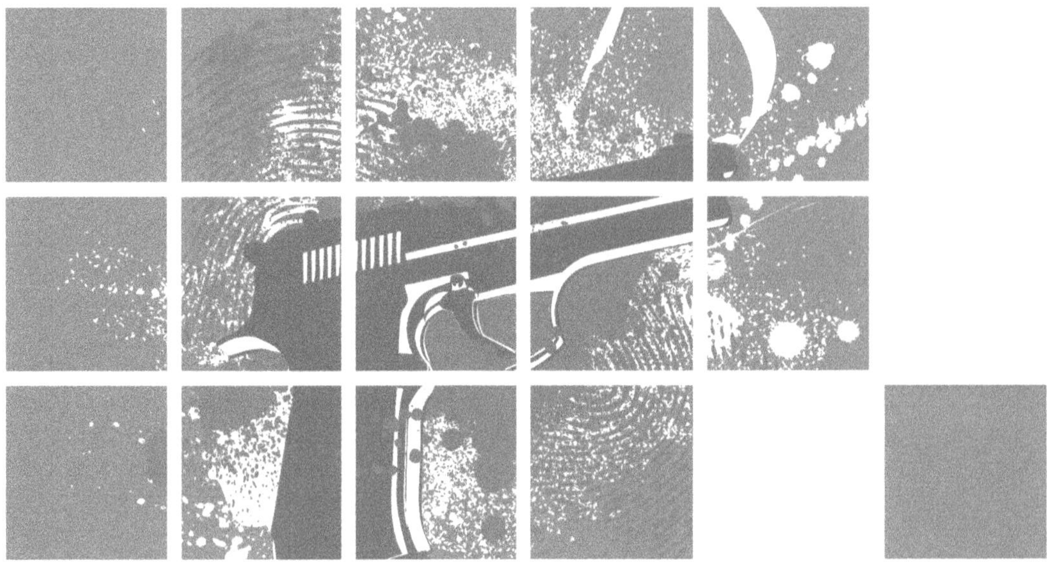

Chapter 10

Sexual offenders 2: paedophiles and child molestation

Overview

- Public opinion is more negative about sex offenders than any other sort of crime. One problem with this is that it may contribute counterproductively to attitudes towards treatment.
- Child molesters are often classified as fixated or regressed. Fixated offenders are halted in their psychosexual development so that they retain a sexual interest in children. Regressed offenders have matured sexually but have returned to an earlier stage of psychosexual development. Regressed offenders are most likely to be intrafamilial (incestuous) offenders.
- Estimating the incidence of paedophile orientation is difficult. A quarter of men show a greater deviant sexual response to stimuli involving children than to those involving adult women. About 4 per cent claimed to have engaged in paedophile activity.
- Only a minority of child molestation acts involve penile penetration and many involve non-contact offences such as flashing and peeping. Bribery rather than other more violent forms of coercion is typical.
- There are a number of important theoretical models which attempt to explain sexual offences against children. The *preconditions model* suggests that the paedophile needs: emotional congruence with children; sexual arousal by children; blockages against social contact with other adults; and the removal of inhibitions against sex with children. The *pathways model* suggests that there are several routes to paedophile offending, which include intimacy and social skills deficits, sexual scripts learnt in childhood being distorted due to early sexual experiences in some individuals, and emotional dysregulation when offenders avoid guilt when offending against children or when they fail to learn the coping skills to help them deal with stress development.
- The link between pornography and sex offending has been subject to controversy. On balance, studies of actual sex crime rates and the availability of pornography suggest that there is no causal relationship.
- Internet paedophile offenders can commit a number of offences but ones associated with child pornography are the commonest. They appear to be desisters from acting out their sexual interest in children by contact offending, thus making the link between paedophile orientation and paedophile offending less clear-cut than is often suggested.

Introduction

According to Bolton (2012), we are at one and the same time both fearful of and fascinated by sex offenders. But our view of them tends to be that of violent bogymen/monsters and not one of troubled sexual nuisances. Sexual offenders against children are regarded with a special hostility by the general public. Sex crimes are sensationalised by the mass media especially by highlighting atypical instances (Ducat, Thomas and Blood, 2009). Levenson, Brannon, Fortney and Baker (2007) surveyed public attitudes in Florida to the therapeutic treatment of sex offenders. The majority were in favour of castration as a treatment and most of these were still in favour of castration even if there was no scientific evidence that it worked. Some researchers (e.g Carabian and Hogan, 2015; Kleban and Jeglic, 2012) argue that negative attitudes towards sex offenders and their treatment might have an adverse impact on initiatives to rehabilitate and reintegrate offenders. Paradoxically, as a consequence these negative attitudes might result in increased rates of sexual violence. A meta-analysis (see Box 4.1) of relevant studies (Rade, Desmarais and Mitchell, 2016) suggested that not only do the public have a more negative attitude to sex offenders but that there is less variability about this than for attitudes to other crimes.

Attitudes towards sex offenders held by the public may be shared by some professionals. This is a serious matter as it is possible that their professional judgement may be affected by this antagonism. Not only are the attitudes of the general public important; the views of staff working in the criminal justice system have an even more direct impact on how offenders are treated in the system. Radley (2001) used the Attitude Toward Sex Offenders Questionnaire with samples of police officers, prison officers, and probation workers and psychologists. The sorts of items involved include (p. 6):

- sex offenders are different from most people;
- sex offenders never change;
- I think I would like a lot of sex offenders.

Although attitudes varied, it was clear that police officers were more hostile than probation workers and psychologists. There was also evidence of similar differences between prison officers and probation workers/psychologists. Female staff members were more favourably disposed to sex offenders. There was also, possibly, evidence that attitudes towards sex offenders have become less hostile in recent years.

Similar processes can be seen in research in the US into the registration of sex offenders. Levenson *et al.* (2007) found that nearly three-quarters of participants in their survey said that they would support sex offender registration even though there is no evidence that it reduces sexual abuse. Extending this to deal with beliefs about the registration of juvenile sex offenders in the US, Salerno *et al.* (2010) found that family law lawyers were less supportive of registry laws for juveniles than for adult sex offenders. However, the general public (in this case represented by a sample of university students) and prosecution lawyers supported registration laws for juveniles as strongly as they did for adults. The public tend to envisage an extreme prototype of the juvenile sex offender when making their judgement, but if they envisage or are encouraged to envisage a less extreme prototype, their support for registration tends to be less extreme. These effects are mediated by the perceptions of threat posed by the juvenile sex offender (utilitarian concerns) but also by moral outrage (retributive concerns).

Research in the UK has provided a mixed picture of the public's ideas about sex offenders (Browne, 1999). This postal survey investigated stereotypes about sex offenders and attitudes towards their treatment. Generally, a mixture of custodial sentence together with treatment was seen as acceptable. The vast majority (88 per cent) believed that treatment without a prison sentence was unacceptable. Mostly, the public felt that the treatment of sex offenders was desirable:

- 51 per cent of the public felt treatment of sex offenders was a good idea;
- 35 per cent were undecided;
- 13 per cent said that sex offenders should never be given therapy.

Of those who were favourable towards the idea of treatment, a small majority (51 per cent) believed that treatment facilities should be available in both prison and the community. Nearly as many (45 per cent) thought that treatment should *only* occur as part of the term of imprisonment. Virtually no one thought that treatment should be confined to community settings. Nevertheless, the need for punishment dominated over the need for treatment.

However, faced with the concrete situation of a sex offender treatment centre being located in their community, participants were not so positive:

- Only 36 per cent were in favour of a treatment centre to be located in their community.
- As many as 44 per cent said that they would not be prepared to move house into an area in which there was a treatment centre for sex offenders.
- Those who were against a treatment centre in their community expressed willingness to take action in support of their views. Twenty-six per cent would start a campaign against it and 33 per cent said that they would join an existing campaign against it; 80 per cent would sign a petition against it.

- Those in favour of a treatment centre in their community were much less willing to take action in support of their belief. Only 9 per cent of them were prepared to start a campaign in favour and just 7 per cent said that they would join a pre-existing campaign; 50 per cent said that they would sign a petition in support of the treatment centre.

There is some evidence that being against therapeutic treatment for sex offenders was associated with acceptance of certain 'myths' about sex offenders. Mancini and Budd (2016) found that those in the US public who believed that sex offences against children were 1) mostly perpetrated by strangers or 2) that sex offenders usually escalate the seriousness of their offending over time were less likely to endorse sex offender treatment. However, this was not the case for all of the myths that Mancini and Budd studied.

Female sex offenders tend not to be viewed with quite so much hostility as male sex offenders, according to research by Gakhal and Brown (2011) in the United Kingdom. They point out that most studies of public and professional attitudes to sex offenders fail to specific the gender of the offender, though it is inconceivable that male offenders were not in participants' minds. Gakhal and Brown edited the Attitude to Sex Offenders Questionnaire so that it specifically dealt with female sex offenders. They surveyed various groups, including members of staff at a chain store; probation officers and staff at a regional sex offender unit (the forensic professional sample); and undergraduate students. Attitudes to female sex offenders were less hostile than previous research with the 'same' questionnaire had shown for male sex offenders. The non-professional groups were best seen as having 'undecided' attitudes rather than favourable ones. Forensic professions tended to be the least hostile, reflecting, according to Gakhal and Brown, a more generally favourable attitude to female offenders on the part of professionals. They find it relatively easy to display empathy and warmth to female offenders compared to male offenders (Marshall, Marshall, Sachdev and Kruger, 2003).

The Community Attitudes Towards Sex Offenders (CATSO) scale was developed by Church, Wakeman, Miller, Clements and Sun (2008) and has attracted some interest from researchers. For example, Shackley, Weiner, Day and Willis (2013) assessed the Australian public's attitudes towards sex offenders. One of the researchers' intentions was to understand better the underlying dimensions of public attitudes to sex offenders. They recruited more than 500 participants, using online social media sites such as Facebook and Twitter. The volunteers completed the Community Attitudes Towards Sex Offenders (CATSO) scale and a number of other measures. The results of the analysis are presented in Figure 10.1. As can be seen, four distinct categories of belief about sex

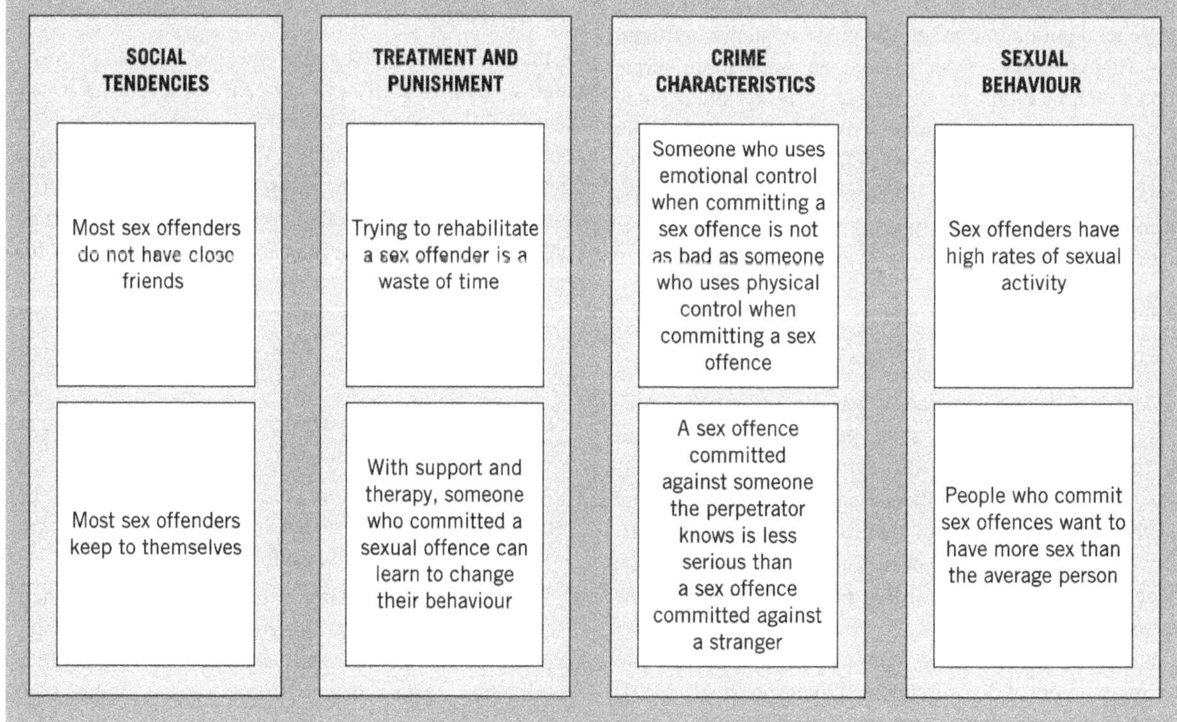

Figure 10.1 The main groups of attitude to sex offender items with examples

offenders were identified: sex offender social tendencies; the treatment and punishment of sex offenders; the characteristics of sex offender crimes; and the sexual behaviour of sex offenders. The general public tends to believe that highly recidivistic sex offending is associated with stranger perpetrators; that recidivism rates are very high for sex offending; and that sex offenders often have been previously victims of sexual abuse themselves. Those with the most negative attitudes towards sex offenders also tended to be in favour of community notification of sex offenders. The better-educated participants rated sex offenders less negatively. A Canadian study using the CATSO scale found four similar dimensions underlay the answers of a mixed sample of sex offenders, undergraduate students, and professionals working with sex offenders (Corabian and Hogan, 2015). High scorers on each of the factors are associated with different views about sex offenders. That is, their social tendency is to be loners, in terms of treatment and punishment they are likely not to change, their crimes characteristically are serious and dangerous, and in terms of their sexual behaviour they are sexually preoccupied. However, not all researchers have found the identical four factors in the CATSO scale described above. Wevodau, Cramer, Gemberling and Clark (2016) found evidence for just two factors in a study of jury-eligible US participants. These were more or less like the first two factors found by other researchers – that sex offenders have a tendency to be loners and that they are unlikely to change.

BOX 10.1 Controversy

Pornography and sex offending

Ted Bundy, the notorious US serial killer, claimed to have been influenced to commit his violent sexual crimes by pornography. The role of pornography in creating sexual attitudes has been part of the feminist debate for three decades at least. Here, we are concerned only with the evidence that pornography might lead to sex offending. Analyses of the content of pornography indicate that at least some of it contains anti-women themes such as rape, violence and degradation. The extent differs according to the study. For example, Thompson (1994) found little to support the view that pornography was full of such imagery, whereas others (e.g. Itzin, 1992) find the reverse. This is partly a matter of how a particular image is interpreted and codified.

The range of studies is wide and stretches from laboratory experiments to case studies. Here are some of the more important studies:

- *The Danish experiment:* Kutchinsky (1970, 1973) carried out research into the social consequences of liberalising the law in Denmark in the 1960s. Pornography became increasingly available. The crime statistics over this period tended to decline. The crimes affected were those such as indecent exposure, peeping, indecent language and so forth. These are the relatively trivial crimes which might be most affected by changes of public attitude towards sex such that they are less inclined to report trivial crimes to the police. There was no such change in the reporting of rape. In later studies, Kutchinsky claimed to find that the liberalisation of pornography laws has not brought about increases in the rates of sex crimes: things have either held more or less steady or rape rates have declined. These researches were carried out in Denmark, Germany and the United States (Kutchinsky, 1991).
- *Court's propositions:* Court (1977, 1984) put forward several hypotheses about the effects of pornography on sex crimes. For example, he has suggested that in parallel to the availability of increasingly violent pornography, the amount of violence in rapes will have increased over time. Although Court has evidence for this proposition, it should be pointed out that he is a little selective in that he does not examine every country where crime statistics are available. For example, Howitt (1998b) showed that there is evidence that, over a fairly lengthy period, rape in the United Kingdom shows trends upwards, which cannot be explained by changes in legislation (which became more controlling). Since the contents of pornography have tended to remain relatively free of violence, the steady rise in rape cannot be explained by that either (Thompson, 1994).
- *Developmental studies:* a number of researchers have studied the aetiology of interest and use of pornography in the life cycle of sex offenders. There is some evidence that masturbation comes early in the adolescent lives of sex offenders and earlier than use of pornography (Condron and Nutter, 1988; Howitt and Cumberbatch, 1990). Their deviancy seems to precede their use of pornography in general. This sequence of events suggests that pornography is

BOX 10.1 (continued)

not a cause of this deviancy, although their interest in it may be a consequence of their deviancy.

- *Area studies:* Baron and Straus (1984, 1989) and others (Gentry, 1991; Scott and Schwalm, 1988) looked at the relationship between the amount of pornography circulating in different states of the United States and rape rates in those states. Although they found a relationship between the two, since this was strongest for the circulation of pornography aimed at women, it seems unlikely, according to Baron and Straus, that this sort of pornography actually caused the rapes.
- *Paedophile preferences:* in terms of paedophiles, the few available studies have concentrated on the use made of pornography by paedophiles. Marshall (1988) found, for example, that sex offenders show little preference for and arousal to pornography redolent of their offending. They tend to use a variety of pornographic stimuli. Similarly, Howitt (1995b) describes how paedophiles will use a variety of imagery in their fantasies, including Walt Disney films featuring children; television advertisements for baby products; and adult heterosexual pornography. This material is used to generate personal paedophile fantasy.

It would appear that, like many non-offenders, sex offenders use pornography and other imagery. It is difficult to argue that this material causes their offending. However, see Box 9.2 on sexual fantasy and sex offending. In recent years, the focus has been on child pornography rather than adult pornography of the sort that we have discussed in this box. See later in this chapter for a discussion of child pornography offending.

Classifications of child molesters

Classifying sex offenders against children, if successful, should enable both research and treatment to be better focused. The question is, of course, just what taxonomy will help us achieve this. Research on child molesters is replete with examples of taxonomies but some of these confuse issues rather than clarify them. One does not have to dig too deeply in the literature on paedophiles to find discussions of taxonomies such as incestuous versus non-familial offenders (Williams and Finkelhor, 1990) and fixated versus regressed offenders (Cohen, Seghorn and Calmus, 1969). The dichotomy between the fixated and regressed offender is a good example of a taxonomy and the sort of potential difficulties which can arise. Based on Groth and Birnbaum (1978), the following are the main features of this taxonomy:

- *Fixated offenders:* these are said to be developmentally fixated on a permanent or a temporary basis such that their sexual interest is in children rather than adults. Although they may have had sexual contact with adults, this contact is more coincidental than intentional since peer relationships are not psychologically an integral part of their sexuality.
- *Regressed offenders:* these are men who matured in their sexuality but demonstrated a return to an earlier level of psychosexual development. Their psychosexual history would show primary interest in peer age or adult individuals rather than younger ones. Interest in the latter seems to reflect almost a reversal to a more childlike sexuality.

Important differences are found between the two types, especially in terms of their relationship history. This is perhaps not surprising, given the above descriptions, but fixated offenders rarely marry (something like one in eight have been married) whereas about three-quarters of regressed offenders have been married. Perhaps even more significantly, the fixated offenders offend most commonly against strangers or acquaintances, whereas the regressed type offend commonly within the network of friends or relatives. This is the very sort of victim whom feminist writers on child sexual abuse have regarded as incestuous in its broadest terms (Howitt, 1992). While it may seem commonsensical to suggest that adult men who have sexual relationships with women have 'regressed' when they offend sexually against children, this is actually somewhat naive. Some offenders target women with children for the primary purpose of gaining access to the children. While they may engage in sex with the mother, in some cases they describe this as being accompanied by paedophile sexual fantasy (Howitt, 1995a).

Another taxonomy differentiating among child molesters is that separating them into incest offenders versus non-familial offenders (Williams and Finkelhor, 1990). It is related to the fixated-regressed dichotomy in that often the incestuous offender is regarded as being regressed whereas the non-incestuous offender is regarded as fixated. According to Marshall, Smallbone and Marshall (2015), the research literature is somewhat confused about what is incestuous. In some cases, researchers mean by this biological fathers only whereas in other cases researchers include all men acting as fathers whether or not they are biological fathers or even uncles, grandfathers and cousins. In other words, there is no standardisation in terms of whether an offender against children within the family will be defined as an incestuous offender of not. Incestuous offenders seem to show patterns of sexual arousal to 'erotic' depictions of children (Howitt, 1995a), despite the argument that they are 'forced' by circumstances to regress to sex with children. That is to say, explanations of family factors such as stress leading to offending against children by offenders possibly serve merely as excuses. An example of the lack of clarity in the definition of incestuous can be found in a study by Studer, Alwyn, Clelland, Reddon and Frenzel (2002). They used phallometry (see Box 9.1) in order to assess child molesters' responses to slides of different ages, sexes and body shapes. The molesters were grouped into incestuous and non-incestuous offenders against children. In this particular study, biological fathers, adoptive fathers, step fathers and foster fathers comprised the incestuous category. Grandfathers, uncles and brothers were considered to be among the non-incestuous offenders. It was not possible to differentiate the two groups effectively on the basis of their responses to the slides. Just over 40 per cent of each group showed their strongest erotic response to the slides that featured pubescent children. More of the incestuous offenders showed their major response to slides of adults (37 per cent) compared with 19 per cent of the non-incestuous group. More of the non-incestuous group (30 per cent) showed their primary erotic response to pre-pubescent children, compared with 13 per cent of the incestuous group. So, clearly, there are some differences, but, equally clearly, there are sizeable numbers of incestuous offenders who show exactly the same sort of sexual interest in under-age persons that non-incestuous offenders do.

This boils down to whether biological fathers who offend are different from non-biological fathers who offend and whether family members who offend are different from non-family members who offend in terms of their arousal to paedophilic stimuli. In the literature, only a study by Greenberg, Firestone, Nunes, Bradford and Curry (2005) demonstrated that stepfathers showed greater deviant arousal using phallometry than did biological fathers – but there were no significant differences between the two on a wide range of demographic and psychological measures such as cognitive distortions and psychopathy. However, this is against the general run of the evidence. For example, a wider study by Blanchard, Kuban, Blak, Cantor, Klassen and Dickey (2006) found that three groups of offenders against underage girls all differed from each other. The groups were: 1) biological fathers and stepfathers who offended against their daughter or stepdaughter; 2) offenders against other related girls such as sisters and nieces and offenders against unrelated girls; and 3) offenders against an adult female and men with no known victim. It was the second group, those offending against girls other than daughters or stepdaughters, which showed the highest paedophilic arousal. The biological father and stepfather group was midway between the other two groups. Importantly, there were no differences between biological fathers and stepfathers in terms of paedophilic arousal. That is the highest phallometric paedophilic deviancy was found for a mixed group of offenders against related girls. One implication of this study is that the definition of incestuous molestation used might have a profound influence on the results of a study. If incestuous abuse is defined in terms of offences perpetrated by the biological father then, as Marshall *et al.* (2015) suggested, one is likely to come up with different findings than if incestuous abuse is defined in terms of, say, any relationship within the biological family.

Another problem is that even when incestuous fathers are distinguished from other types of offender, only limited comparison groups may be provided. For example, Rice and Harris (2002) studied men who had molested their biological daughters and stepdaughters and compared with extrafamilial offenders against children. The evidence from plethysmography indicated that the incestuous fathers and stepfathers showed less sexually deviant response to imagery involving children. Nevertheless, this should not be taken to mean that they had no deviant sexual arousal to child images. The incestuous fathers had an absolute response to paedophilic imagery greater than to imagery involving adults. We know nothing, of course, about intrafamily offenders who were not fathers. In their meta-analysis of a large number of studies comparing intrafamilial with non-familial sexual abusers, Seto, Babchishin, Pullman and McPhail (2015) merely used these two categories thus merging several subgroups of intrafamilial offenders. Compared to non-familial offenders, familial offenders were lower in terms of various measures of anti-social tendency and atypical sexual interests such as paedophilia and excessive preoccupation with sex. As is found in other research, extrafamilial offenders also had related victims in the majority of cases.

What seems to be clear is that incestuous offenders often show deviant arousal to images of underage children as do non-familial offenders though to a greater extent it would appear. There are other reasons to be cautious about the taxonomy:

- Despite claims to the contrary, incestuous fathers have frequently also offended against children outside the family or raped women (Abel *et al.*, 1983). In other words, offending against children is a sexual preference, not the product of family circumstances such as stress or sexual privation. In Studer, Aylwin, Clelland, Reddon and Frenzel's (2002) study, over 40 per cent of incestuous offenders self-reported that they had committed sexual offences against children outside the family. This does not mean that the groups are not, to some extent, different. For example, Miner and Dwyer (1997) found that incestuous offenders were more able to develop trusting interpersonal relationships than exhibitionists and child molesters.
- Groth and Birnbaum (1978) argue that homosexual men are never regressed offenders. By homosexual we mean men whose adult sexual orientation is towards men. (This is in order to differentiate them from heterosexual paedophiles and homosexual paedophiles, who are defined in terms of the sex of their child victim, not their sexual history with adults.) This is a remarkable claim in some ways and difficult to accept. The implication is that sexual privation and stress do not affect gay men in the same way as they do heterosexual men. This clearly needs support, if it is true, which has never been provided.

Reading the literature on child molestation and paedophile, it is easy to reach the conclusion that many of the research findings are confusing and incoherent. According to Marshall, Smallbone and Marshall (2015) this is partly the result of a lack of standard ways of allocating offenders to the different categories of the various taxonomies. For example, by what criteria should we differentiate a fixated offender from a regressed offender? Does having sex ever as an adult with another adult mean that if that individual molests a child that they should be classified as a regressed offender? What criteria should be used to decide whether a man is a familial/incestuous or a stranger abuser? Marshall *et al.* suggest a simple taxonomy of child molesters which they believe has important implications for research and treatment. The taxonomy consists of two categories: 1) the non-affiliative child molester and 2) the affiliative child molester. Non-affiliative child molesters are true strangers to their victims up until the crime; affiliative child molesters characteristically are involved in some sort of caregiving relationship with their eventual victim for a while before they commit the offence. For Marshall *et al.*, the difference is essentially between men who groom their victim and men who do not.

Among affiliative child molesters, apart from fathers and other familial abusers, would be caregivers (e.g. teachers, clergy and childcare professionals) and volunteers working with children (e.g. sports coaches). Crucially, for Marshall *et al.*'s argument, all of these different groupings of offenders have been shown not to differ on important psychological and demographic variables. So these groups are not different in terms of factors like sexual functioning, sexual interest and personality. Grooming is seen as a major characteristic of professionals and volunteers who molest children in their care as well as familial abusers. Offenders who find their victims within their work or voluntary organisation environments groom the child by giving them extra attention, telling the child that they are special, telling the child personal things about themselves, giving the child gifts, ignoring misbehaviours and treating them generally favourably (Leclerc, Proulx and McKibben, 2005). Thus the strategy is to create a special, affectionate relationship. One objective of this is to discourage the child from subsequently reporting the abuse. The point is that grooming is a feature of every sort of offender–child relationship (father, stepfather, more general familial relationships, professionals involving childcare, and voluntary workers with children) except where the offender has no relationship with the child. Members of these groups of offender who know the children that they offend against have quite high rates of marriage. Grooming does not happen in true stranger offences and these offences are more likely to involve violence. Context and grooming align in that true stranger offenders do not use grooming whereas molesters who know their victims display caring behaviours which turn to sexually intrusive acts. One study found that nearly three-quarters of child molesters had known the victim for more than six months prior to the abuse. Over 60 per cent of non-familial offenders had known the victim for more than this time (Smallbone and Wortley (2000). Only 5 per cent were truly stranger offenders.

Non-affiliative or true stranger molesters are more likely to use force than the affiliative offender (Smallbone *et al.*, 2008). Furthermore, non-affiliative offenders often seem to be loners who show arousal to paedophilic imagery during phallometry. They are also more likely to be recidivist offenders against children.

Marshall *et al.* see as part of the explanation of child molestation ideas taken from Routine Activities Theory (Felson, 2002) (see p. 120). This suggests that if a potential and motivated offender and a suitable victim are present together without the presence of a guardian, the likelihood of a crime ensuing is high. They also draw on research evidence which suggests that unsatisfactory adult attachment styles may lead to offending against available children by the affiliative molester. Marshall *et al.* put it as follows: '. . . we suggest that men who have continued supervisory access to children may be at heightened risk. Under these circumstances, when the offender has lost a source of sexual and intimacy satisfaction, he will be primed to offend and will be likely to employ 'adult-like' grooming strategies as a prelude to offending.' (p. 209).

As interesting as Marshall *et al.*'s suggested typology is, it has its problems. In particular, it splits child molesters into a large group of affiliative offenders (90 per cent) and a much small group of non-affiliative offenders (10 per cent). The larger group are described by Marshall *et al.* as if they share psychological and demographic characteristics. This means that on the basis of the typology, researchers are left seeking an explanation of offending which applies to all of the affiliative group as well as one applying to all of the non-affiliative group. This seems to be quite a tall order. On the other hand, the lack of consistency that researchers have shown when applying some of the older typologies does warrant attention if a coherent body of knowledge is to be developed.

How common is paedophilia?

The word 'paedophile' refers to sexual offenders against pre-pubescent children according to the research literature. This, of course, excludes offenders against pubescent children and other offenders against young people. The development of adult sexual characteristics does not occur at precisely the same age in all children and paedophiles are often defined in terms of offending against children under 10 or 11 years of age. Members of the general public may not use the term paedophilia in this technical sense. There is a distinction between paedophiles and hebephiles which is inconsistently applied in the literature. DSM-V does not recognise hebephilia (APA, 2013). A paedophile offends against (or has strong sexual feelings for) pre-pubescent children while a hebephile offends against a sexually mature pubescent youngsters. However, research suggests that it is possible to distinguish between the paedophile and the hebephile fairly accurately using penis volume phallometry (Cantor and McPhail, 2015). That is to say, some men respond to paedophilic imagery and others to hebephilic imagery. Some men are sexually responsive to both pre-pubescent and pubescent children. But things may not be that simple. One theoretically important question concerns the extent to which paedophilic sexual arousal can occur in 'normal' men. Is sexual arousal to imagery of children confined to offenders? Research on this is sparse. Hall *et al.* (1995) recruited a sample of American men through a newspaper advertisement. Each man was assessed in several different ways, including plethysmography (see Box 9.1) in which changes in the size of a man's penis is regarded as an indicator of sexual arousal. A number of slides of nude pre-pubescent girls, nude women and clothed pre-pubescent girls were shown in random order to each participant. Generally, there were fairly close correspondences in terms of a picture's effects on participants – that is, there was a tendency for the men who were aroused by one type of stimulus to be aroused by others.

Most importantly, about a quarter of the ordinary men showed more arousal to child stimuli than to those of women. About a fifth of the total sample reported that they had 'paedophile' interests. Only about 4 per cent of the sample reported that they had actually engaged in paedophile behaviour. This is a low figure compared with the figures for physiological arousal to paedophile stimuli and interest in children sexually. Nevertheless, one should be cautious when generalising from the findings of any single study:

- It is important to note that the men who were aroused by the paedophile stimuli were also aroused by other sexual imagery. This might indicate that they were not paedophile in their sexual orientation, because they found all imagery, including that of adults, arousing. The men most easily aroused by the explicit pictures of adult women often could be aroused by the paedophilic stimuli too.
- The men in the study were encouraged to allow themselves to be aroused. While this is not uncommon in studies using plethysmography, it may be a limitation in that it may result in more men showing signs of sexual arousal. The researchers have no way of knowing what was actually causing the arousal – what was in the experimental stimuli or personal fantasies created by the participant in order to become aroused? (See Boxes 9.1 and 9.2.)

Despite these criticisms, this is of theoretical importance since it may mean that paedophile orientation does not necessarily have to be acted out in the form of sexual abuse – that is, it is possible to desist from sexual crime against children.

There has been a small stream of evidence to suggest that some men in non-clinical and non-forensic samples show a sexual interest in children. For example, about 10 per cent of men said that it was possible that they would engage in sex with a child or view child pornography – if they could get away with it (Wurtele, Simons and Moreno, 2014). The figure for women was 4 per cent. Furthermore, 20 per cent of men said that they had used child pornography on the Internet (Ray, Kimonis and Seto, 2014). An anonymous online survey of a community sample of German men measured the extent of this for pre-pubescent children of under 12 years of age. Over 3 per cent (3.2 per cent) reported that they had sexually offended against a prebubescent child and 4.1 per cent reported sexual fantasy involving this age group (Dombert, Schmidt, Banse,

Briken, Hoyer and Osterheider, 2016). A very small percentage (0.1 per cent) had a clearly paedophilic sexual preference – that is, their sexual behaviours and fantasies involved prepubescent children more than adults. Overall, 5.5 per cent of the participants indicated some form of paedophilic interest. Those with a sexual interest in prepubescent children generally thought that they needed help.

There is plenty of evidence that sexual abuse of youngsters below the age of consent is not a rarity. Surveys on child sexual abuse provide a range of different answers to the question of how common such abuse is. Depending on the definition of abuse used – e.g. self-definition by the victim or legal definition – various estimates will be obtained. Furthermore, relatively unintrusive sexual acts, such as passing suggestive remarks, may be very common but nevertheless experienced as abuse (Kelly, 1988, 1989), whereas penetrative sex is relatively rare in this abuse (Nash and West, 1985). Non-reporting confuses the issue still further since they make police reports poor measures of the extent of child sexual abuse. Conviction data are poor indicators of the extent of victimisation. Victim surveys are possibly the most accurate indicators but there are reasons why victims may fail to answer questions accurately. In a major UK survey, Radford, Corral, Bradley *et al.* (2011) found that 0.6 per cent of male and 1.5 per cent of female young adults claimed to have been sexually abused by their parents or guardians as children and adolescents. For contact sexual abuse by adults not living in the home the corresponding figures were 1.1 per cent for males and 4.7 per cent for females. This amounts to very small numbers even in a sample of, say, two or three thousands. Furthermore, it is known that sexual abuse by peers or older children is a substantial proportion of sexual abuse.

Just how does the *Diagnostic and Statistical Manual of Mental Disorders* (*DSM-V*) (APA, 2013) deal with paedophilia? It does not refer to paedophilia as such but to paedophilic disorder. The manual makes it clear that paedophilic disorder involves repeated sexual urges, fantasies or behaviours towards prepubescent children (13 years of age or younger) for a minimum of six months or longer. There is an age differential in that young people under the age of 16 years cannot be given the diagnosis and the subject of their sexual interest should be five years younger than themselves. Pedophilic disorder is described as a paraphilia which is a strong sexual arousal to atypical stimuli – such as sadism and masochism. The American Psychological Association describes paedophilia as a mental disorder (APA, 2013).

There is an assumption in the professional literature that to be a paedophile a person should have their primary sexual interest in prepubescent children. A person with a sexual interest in adult women, for example, cannot be a paedophile as a consequence and should be described as a child molester if they offend against children. Whether this is intended to imply that the explanation of child molestation is different from that of paedophilia is not clear. Their denial of a sexual interest in children makes it difficult to establish its frequency as does the requirement that sexual interest in children dominates their sexuality. As a consequence, one should think carefully as to whether to ever use the term paedophilia rather than that of child molester which can be more readily defined especially in terms of committing a sexual crime against children.

The normal sex lives of paedophiles

The research literature on paedophiles and other sex offenders against children tends to portray them as either fairly regular, if placid criminals, who just happen to engage in sex offending against children or as specialist abusers of children. But what of the non-forensic aspects of such offenders' lives and their sex lives in particular? This can be posed in a slightly dramatic form by asking the question of whether paedophilia is a sexual orientation. This was raised by Howitt (1995a) but was revived by Seto (2012). In other words, is paedophilia much the same as other sexual orientations such as bisexuality, heterosexuality or homosexuality? To answer this question, the obvious starting point is a definition of sexual orientation. This brings all sorts of problems and difficulties but core features of gender orientation involve long-term preference for a particular sort of sexual partner; it appears quite early in life, and it is not changeable by therapy, for example. One problem in answering the question of whether paedophilia is a sexual orientation is the evidence that, in some circumstances, a substitute for the preferred type of sexual object can be adopted. Homosexual behaviour of seemingly life-long heterosexual men in prison is an example of this. But when one tries to compare paedophilia with other sexual orientations, it is remarkable how difficult it is to avoid the conclusion that paedophilia has all or most of the features of a sexual orientation. The main difference is that paedophilia is characterised more in terms of an age dimension than a gender dimension. However, this is only relative as heterosexuality and homosexuality are age-specific in that they involve attraction to sexually mature individuals.

Paedophilia is characterised by attraction to sexually immature individuals and it is not so clearly gender-specific. Seto's definition seems to boil down to the following: 'male sexual orientation can be defined as the direction(s) of a male person's sexual thoughts, fantasies, urges, arousal and behaviour' (p. 232). That is, sexual orientation is a directing force in terms of all aspects of the individual's sexual behaviour and gives a sense of coherence to the individual's sexuality. Understanding Seto's argument does involve setting aside considerations of legality which have beset discussions of sexual orientation in the past. Paedophilia is a sexual attraction to prepubescent children and, like heterosexuality, etc., it is associated with urges, fantasies, reoccurring sexual thoughts, arousal and sexual behaviour. Seto points out that the age of onset of paedophilia is similar to that for other sexual orientations. That is, some paedophiles, at least, report having a sexual interest in other children before their adulthood. Some report this from the age of 15 years or earlier. Paedophiles often report high levels of emotional congruence with children and that sex with children fulfilled their emotional needs. There are paedophiles who seek a romantic relationship with children and describe their relationships as loving. The implications for the treatment of paedophiles are among the many ramifications of construing paedophilia as a sexual orientation. It should be noted, though, that *DSM-V* (APA, 2013) abandoned the use of the term sexual orientation in favour of sexual interest in relation to paedophilia although accidentally misused it (Brauser, 2013).

Cale, Leclerc and Smallbone (2012) asked just what is the nature of the non-offending sexual behaviour of sex offenders. That is, what is the bigger picture about the sexual lives of sex offenders beyond their offending behaviour? Rather than look at the development of deviant sexuality, what leads to their deviancy, and the relationship of these to sexual abuse, the researchers studied offenders' non-criminal sexuality. The researchers obtained a sample of over 500 incarcerated Australian sex offenders. These included offenders against prepubescent children and those against adult women, as well as some that offended across age boundaries. The main findings were:

- Some sex offenders have a successful non-criminal sexual lifestyle. For many, it is difficult to identify any remarkable features of the sexual development and their non-criminal sexual lifestyles.
- Taken as a group as a whole, sex offenders had diverse non-criminal sexual lifestyles compared with their deviant sexual behaviours.
- Although many sex offenders have generally normal non-offending sex lives, there are some sex offenders whose non-offending sexual lifestyles show characteristically unusual patterns.
- Sexual victimisation in childhood was reported by nearly one half of the offenders in the study. Using the duration of the abuse as an indicator of its severity, it was found that severe sexual abuse led to early activation of various sexual behaviours such as sexual contacts and self-directed sexual behaviours such as masturbation, fantasy, and the use of pornography. These sexual behaviours generally began about a year after the sexual abuse terminated.
- Sexual abuse in childhood led to adult feelings of being less competent sexually than others. As adults they were less likely to be satisfied with their sex lives. Despite this, the feelings were not reflected in the amount of sexual activity engaged in. The mechanism involved in this is not clear. Possibly it is the consequence of sexual abuse lowering self-esteem and so adversely affecting psychological adjustment in general.

  To highlight some ways in which sex offenders against children seem to be different: sexual abuse was almost twice as common in the early lives of sex offenders against children compared to sex offenders against adult women. Furthermore, they tend to have experienced a longer duration of sexual victimisation.
- Offenders who victimised children had an earlier onset of masturbation but sexual intercourse began later in life. This pattern was reversed for sex offenders against women.

The contrast between sex offenders against women and those against children was strong. Offenders against women had positive beliefs about their sexual competence, had a higher frequency of adult sexual partners and more consenting sexual partners, and they were more satisfied with their sex lives. In contrast, those who victimised under-aged children tended to have poor self-esteem and were less satisfied with their sex lives overall. There were also differences between those who victimised adolescents (and mixed-age-group offenders) and those who chose pre-pubescent children. This group were more likely to feel sexually somewhat incompetent, were dissatisfied with their sexual lives and had fewer sexual successes than sex offenders in general. The researchers argue on the basis of their data that this group offends because they are not successful in seeking appropriate sexual partners but they do not have a sexual preference of pre-pubescent children. So they seek out adolescent children and may use coercion and aggression in their offending. In general, then, they are rather like the men who offend against adult women, but they lack the element of self-confidence.

The nature of paedophile offences

The general public learn about sex offending through the media. The media, of course, have their own agenda (Los and Chamard, 1997) in which sensational and extreme acts are presented as the image of sex offenders and what they do. Paedophiles are mainly seen as murderous child abductors. Some are. However, in the United Kingdom, for example, convictions for child abduction averaged 44 annually in the 1990s. Of these abductions, 60 per cent were motivated by sexual factors (Erikson and Friendship, 2002). Research suggests that, as a group, molesters carry out a wide range of different types of activity. Some, such as frotteurism and peeping behaviour, may not be recognised by the victim as such.

Like most crime issues, the picture of paedophile offending varies according to one's source of information. The context in which data are collected is also important. Studies of victims of child sexual abuse illustrate this. In a Los Angeles study, Wyatt (1985) found non-contact incidents such as flashing, improper comments and the like formed 40 per cent of the abusive experiences. Intercourse/attempted intercourse made up about a quarter of the incidents. A study of the perpetrators of child sexual abuse coming before the court in an area of south-east London over a period of two years also reveals something of the varied nature of such offending (Craissati and McClurg, 1997). The offences with which they were charged were overwhelmingly indecent assault (68 per cent). Gross indecency (11 per cent), buggery, i.e. anal intercourse (9 per cent) and rape (7 per cent) were much less common. Under a third (29 per cent) of the men were convicted of penetrative offences. Nearly three-quarters (71 per cent) were convicted of offences against just one child (at that hearing) and 14 per cent were involved with offences involving a total of three or more victims. Male victims tended to be abused outside the home, whereas female victims were relatively more likely to be victimised by relatives at home. The methods of grooming were: 40 per cent used bribery to gain the participation of the victim; 24 per cent used verbal threats; and 16 per cent used physical threats. One of the subgroups, and the one most at risk of recidivism, tended to show the following characteristic pattern:

- to have been sexually abused as a child;
- to offend against boys;
- to have more victims;
- to have victims outside their family;
- to exhibit cognitive distortions;
- to have previous convictions for sexual offences.

Whatever the overall pattern, individual offenders may have very distinctive patterns of offending. For example, Robert Black, a lorry driver who killed girls and left their bodies in locations in various parts of the United Kingdom, had a pattern of penetrating the child's vagina with his finger and then killing her (Wyre and Tate, 1995): in other words, extreme violence but less extreme sexual acts.

Theories of paedophilia

There have been a number of attempts to explain paedophilia. None of them is completely satisfactory in itself, although most have at least some virtues. The ones that we will consider in some detail are:

- the preconditions model;
- the psychotherapeutic/cognitive model;
- the sexualisation model;
- the pathways model.

The preconditions model

Araji and Finkelhor (1985) proposed the preconditions model of abusive behaviour. It is illustrated in Figure 10.2. As can be seen, several different types of factor are listed,

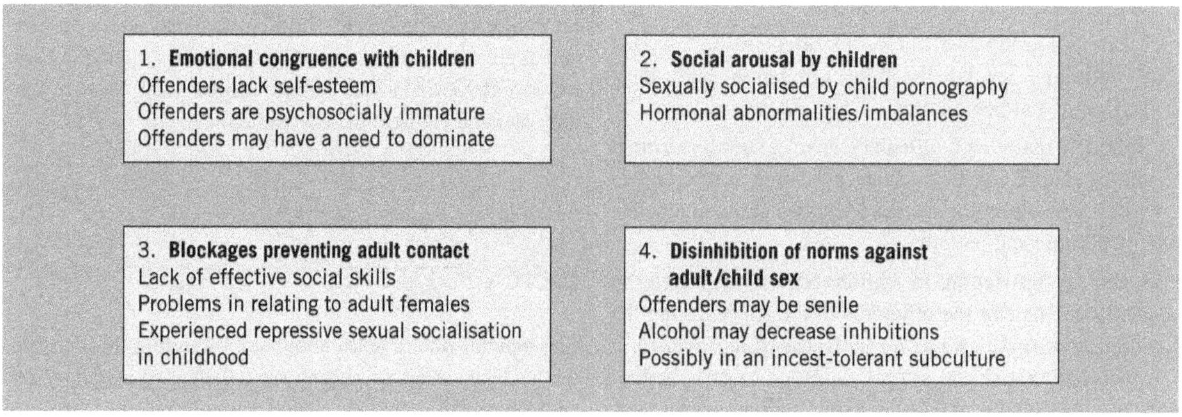

1. **Emotional congruence with children**
Offenders lack self-esteem
Offenders are psychosocially immature
Offenders may have a need to dominate

2. **Social arousal by children**
Sexually socialised by child pornography
Hormonal abnormalities/imbalances

3. **Blockages preventing adult contact**
Lack of effective social skills
Problems in relating to adult females
Experienced repressive sexual socialisation in childhood

4. **Disinhibition of norms against adult/child sex**
Offenders may be senile
Alcohol may decrease inhibitions
Possibly in an incest-tolerant subculture

Figure 10.2 The preconditions model of molestation

which are seen as partial preconditions for sexual abuse to occur. These broad types of factor include emotional congruence, sexual arousal, blockage and disinhibition. The following points should be made:

- This model is relatively old and was developed at a time when empirical research on sex offenders was very limited in its scope.
- It is based on a number of almost common-sense assumptions, not all of which have or had been supported and some of which have not even been adequately tested.
- It assumes that child molestation is multiply caused and does not assume that any of the preconditions are necessarily involved in any given case.
- It has the advantage of linking the theory with therapy that has tended to assume the multi-causality of abusive behaviour and, consequently, the need for complex therapeutic methods.
- Unfortunately, as was acknowledged by Arajii and Finkelhor, very few of the preconditions have been shown in empirical research to be associated with abusive behaviour.

Furthermore, it is descriptive in the sense of merely describing the characteristics of abusers rather than trying to identify the root cause of the abusive behaviour, say, in their own childhood.

The preconditions model was among the earliest attempts at a comprehensive theory of sexual offending against children and among its achievements was its help in clarifying the goals of treating such offenders. In particular, according to Ward and Hudson (2001), the model encouraged the following: concentration on deviant sexual arousal; working with problems of intimacy; showing offenders how to effectively identify and manage situations in which they are at high risk of offending; and the incorporation of socio-cultural factors such as the possible role of pornography. However, it could be argued that the theory has merely encouraged a highly unspecific multi-faceted approach to the treatment of offenders which, consequently, has not helped develop our understanding of the process of becoming an offender.

The psychotherapeutic/cognitive model

This model is rarely systematically described in total, although elements of it are very common in the literature (e.g. Salter, 1988; Wyre, 1987, 1992). The main emphasis of this model is on the cognitive and behavioural steps involved in offending behaviour. Broadly speaking, the model suggests that there are four steps in the process:

- Cognitive distortions or distorted thinking of the sort effectively captured by the Abel Rape Index Scale (Abel *et al.*, 1977). Such distorted beliefs include 'Having sex with a child is a good way for an adult to teach a child about sex', and include other beliefs about the sexual nature of children, how children's behaviour signals sexual interest and so forth.
- Grooming – these are the methods by which offenders contact children and gain their trust and confidence. Violence or threats of violence may be part of this, but probably more typical are bribes of sweets, money, trips out and the like.
- Planning through fantasy – this is the idea that the offender plans in fantasy the likely scenarios of events in, for example, finally trying to seduce the child. What will they do, say, if a child says they are going home?
- Denial is the mental process by which offenders appear to be denying the consequences of their actions and perhaps blaming someone else. For example, they would tend to agree with the following statements from the Abel scale (Abel *et al.*, 1977): 'Sex between an adult and a 13-year-old (or younger) child causes the child no emotional problems' and 'A man (or woman) is justified in having sex with his (her) children or step-children, if his wife (husband) doesn't like sex'. Denial can take a wide range of forms according to Salter (1988) and others:
  - denial that abuse actually took place;
  - minimisation of the abuse by claiming few victims, for example;
  - denying seriousness – by admitting fondling but not anal sex, for example;
  - denying that there is anything wrong with them – they have found God so do not need therapy;
  - denial of responsibility – blaming the child for seducing the offender.

While it is fairly well established that there is cognitive distortion or distorted thinking in paedophiles and other sex offenders, this idea is often mixed together with that of paedophiles being adroitly manipulative people. They are keen to manipulate others, including psychologists and others working with them. Hence, they will try to convince the other person of whatever they think will be to their advantage. Thus it becomes a little unclear whether or not they really do think in particular ways or whether they are simply trying to manipulate their therapists, researchers and any other individuals who become involved. The writing on this is not particularly coherent in the sense that concepts are somewhat inconsistently used. Sometimes similar words are used to describe very different processes, so one finds the terms 'minimisation' and 'denial' used somewhat interchangeably. Figure 10.3 presents aspects of this model as a diagram.

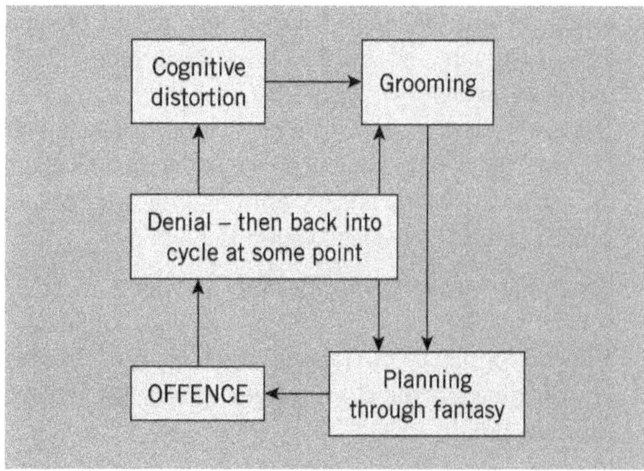

Figure 10.3 The clinical/cognitive model

Studies of cognitive distortions in paedophiles and other sex offenders are rather rare compared with the numerous mentions of them in the professional literature. Nevertheless, research does seem to suggest the importance of cognitive distortions. Barbaree (1998) found that substantial numbers of paedophiles and rapists denied carrying out the offences they were charged with. This Barbaree refers to as denial. Some adopted strategies that essentially minimised the offence in some way. Approximately 30–40 per cent of the offenders sought to minimise the seriousness of the offence or the extent of their culpability by strategies such as:

- blaming the victim;
- suggesting that the amount of force used was smaller than it actually was;
- holding personal factors such as stress or unemployment responsible.

Interestingly, the effects of psychological therapy on the men who initially denied the offence were quite impressive. About two-thirds changed from denying to admitting their offence. Denial of the offence was replaced by minimisation of the seriousness or their culpability for the offence. The excuses were largely about their use of force and just how sexually intrusive the sexual acts involved were. Of those in the study who initially admitted involvement in the offence but minimised other activities, the tendency was overwhelmingly for them to continue to minimise but at reduced levels. Hence, Barbaree argues that these cognitive strategies are amenable to change through therapy and recommends that they are tackled early in therapy. At the same time, it should be noted how strongly offenders persist with minimisation, despite admitting the offence itself in general terms.

Of course, there is nothing unusual about the denial of an offence since it occurs among all sorts of offenders. Any court of law will demonstrate this on a daily basis.

The sexualisation model

Howitt (1995a) regards paedophilic orientation as developing out of the characteristics of early sexual experiences. In particular, he suggests that experience of sexual abuse in childhood is the start of a process that ends in paedophile activity. Not all abuse is equally likely to lead to sex offending of this sort but penetrative sex, abuse by females and similar uncharacteristic abusive acts are more likely to have this effect. Furthermore, it is possible that sexual experiences in childhood with other, probably older, children may also be influential. In this approach, paedophilia is seen more as a developmental process beginning from early sexual experiences but often continuing through adolescence into adulthood. One possible consequence of this early experience is the way in which the paedophile regards sexual activity between adult and child. He will see adult–child sexual contact as normal since it is the normal thing in his experience. The following should also be considered:

- This account also partly explains the apparent relationship between the characteristic abuse experienced by the paedophile-to-be and the characteristics of his offending against children in the future. Others have noted similar tendencies in abused children. Haapasalo, Puupponen and Crittenden (1999) describe the concept of isomorphic behaviour. They point out 'Physically abused children tend to commit physically violent crimes whereas sexually abused children are prone, in adulthood, to sexual violence, including pedophilia, child molestation, and rape' (p. 98). Groth and Burgess (1978) mention that there are age and type of act similarities between offender and victim and Howitt (1995a) gives other examples. One reason for the isomorphism of sexual offending may be that it involves repetition of strategies for achieving basic feelings of safety and security. It could equally be simply a further instance of the importance of childhood experiences in determining adult behaviour.
- One potential difficulty with the explanation lies in the mixed support for cycles of sexual abuse in the literature. Box 10.3 suggests that the evidence is stronger than some researchers have indicated. Furthermore, not all acts of sexual abuse are as damaging as others.
- Another potentially crucial problem is that not all children who are abused become abusers themselves. The sexualisation model, since it assumes that the more extreme/repetitive forms of abuse have greatest effect, actually has an explanation of why some abused youngsters become abusers. Howitt (1998a), for example, points out that sexual abuse of boys by women seems to be particularly associated with later sexual offending by the victim.

Box 10.2 Key concept

Cycles of abuse

The childhoods of young sex offenders often involve experiences which make them vulnerable to developing patterns of sexually harmful behaviours. Vizard, Hickey, French and McCrory (2007) studied a substantial sample of nearly 300 children referred to a UK national assessment and treatment service for young people who perpetrate sexually harmful behaviours. For 54 per cent of these youngsters their abusive behaviour began before the age of ten years. Fifty-seven per cent offended against one or more victims who was at least five years younger than them. Overwhelmingly they knew their victims. Most (88 per cent) had abused female victims and 57 per cent had abused male victims. Half of them had abused both male and female victims. Their childhoods were far from normal. Vizard *et al.* argue that during the development of children there is a matrix of risk factors which may contribute to the emergence of sexually abusive behaviours (see Figure 10.4). The childhoods of the children involve extremes of emotional deprivation including abuse, family instability and family dysfunction. Ninety-two per cent had suffered at least one of neglect, witnessing domestic violence, or had been victims of one form of abuse from sexual, physical and emotional. For three-quarters, this began under the age of six years;

- 76 per cent had been removed from home into the care of the local authority;
- 61 per cent had been sexually abused by members of their family;
- 50 per cent approximately had been sexually abused at the age of seven years, usually suffering serious abuse such as anal penetration (38 per cent);
- 50 per cent or more had experienced inconsistent or overly punitive parenting;

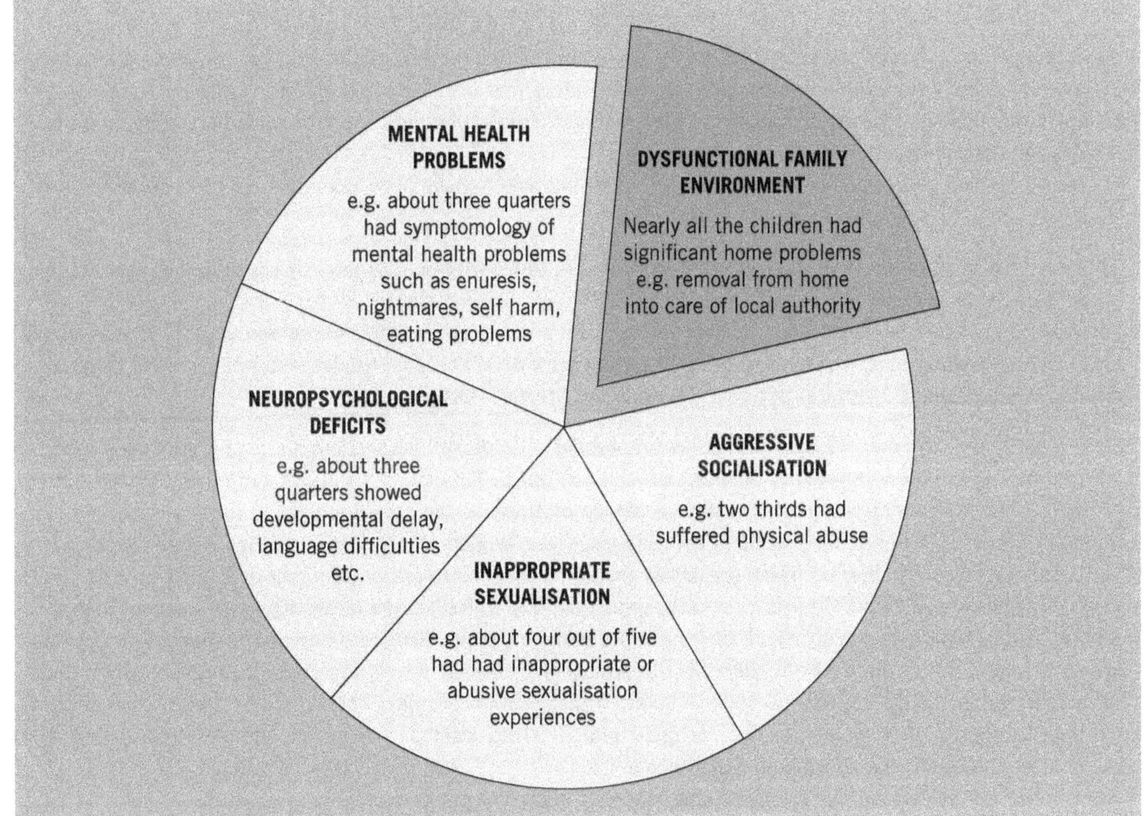

Figure 10.4 Vulnerability factors in the childhoods of young sex offenders

BOX 10.2 (continued)

- 44 per cent were exposed to lax sexual boundaries within the family, such as access to sexually explicit materials and exposure to adult sexual behaviour;
- 35 per cent of the biological mothers had mental health problems and 29 per cent of fathers had criminal records;
- 22 per cent had been admitted into a therapeutic community or other psychiatric unit;
- 21 per cent had been abused by a female abuser;
- only 13 per cent had stayed in the same family home throughout childhood and only 5 per cent of the children were living with both of their biological parents when assessed.

This level of dysfunctionality and problems extended into the young offender's educational environment:

- 71 per cent exhibited disruptive behaviour in school;
- 63 per cent had been required to move school at least once and up to five times;
- 45 per cent had special educational needs;
- 42 per cent had been excluded from school because of their behaviour.

All of this adds to a distressing picture of the difficult childhoods experienced by young sex offenders.

From this and other research, it is fairly uncontroversial to suggest that a sizeable proportion of sex offenders had been victims of sexual abuse as a child. What is controversial is the issue of whether this abuse is a causal influence on sex offenders. Imagine, for example, that there is evidence that 100 per cent of sex offenders had been sexually abused as children. These are some of the comments that might be made:

- Many youngsters who are sexually abused as children do not grow up to be abusers themselves.
- Girls are the commonest victims of sexual abuse but women are much less likely to be abusers than men are.
- This merely provides offenders with excuses and inappropriate justification for their offending.

The first two points, although correct in themselves, do not mean that the sexual abuse had no effect on later offending. They may merely imply that one needs to explore factors that insulate some children from growing up to be offenders or that there may be further characteristics of their victimisation which lead to some becoming victimisers themselves and others not.

On the other hand, what if 10 per cent of sex offenders claimed to have been sexually abused as children? What might be argued in these circumstances?

- This does not seem to be a very high percentage and is in line with low estimates of abuse in the general population. Hence abuse cannot be causal.
- Offenders might be reluctant to admit their abuse or may not even see their childhood experiences as sexual abusive. Hence the data are inadequate. Men known to have been abused sexually tend not to regard their experiences as sexual abuse in a ratio of 6 to 1 (Widom and Morris, 1997).

These are really the extremes. Certainly, there are a number of authorities who deny the strength of the cycles of abuse argument (Finkelhor, 1984; Hanson and Slater, 1988) for the reasons given above and others. Equally, there are a number of studies which suggest that the incidence of abuse in the childhoods of sex offenders is low. For example, Waterhouse, Dobash and Carnie (1994) suggest that offenders are little different from non-offenders.

Unfortunately, these studies are based on survey methods that tend to ask quite direct questions such as 'Were you sexually abused as a child?' This is a sensitive issue that may well elicit denial from any person abused in their childhood. It may be a matter with which they have not come to terms. Hence it is not surprising that studies that examine the question in groups of offenders post-treatment find that the admission rates of sexual abuse in childhood increase dramatically from 22 per cent to about 50 per cent (Worling, 1995). Howitt (1998b) provided evidence that, using a more sympathetic style of questioning, 80 per cent of young sex offenders (compared with 25 per cent of non-offenders) admitted having been abused.

Salter *et al.* (2003) carried out a longitudinal study of male victims of childhood sexual abuse who had been referred to a sexual abuse clinic in the UK. A wide variety of information was obtained from sources such as social service and clinical records including later criminal acts. Of the 224 victims studied, 26 committed sexual abuse offences. That is about 12 per cent. Only a quarter had been cautioned or convicted of the sexual abuse and, for most, the evidence of them abusing came from various records reviewed. Mostly they offended outside of their family. Half offended against girls, a quarter against boys, and a quarter offended against both sexes. The average age of them starting to abuse was 14 years. More victim-abusers had committed crimes of violence than non-abusers but other types of offence were committed equally by both groups. The two groups did not differ on a range of demographic variables. The researchers wished to identify factors which resulted in some becoming victim-abusers whereas most were victims only. About two-thirds of both groups had suffered some amount of physical abuse though the victim-abusers had suffered more severe physical abuse. Eighty-one percent of victim-abusers had witnessed family violence compared to 58 per cent of the non-abusers but the victim-abusers had witnessed significantly more serious violence. About twice as many (37 per cent) of the victim-abusers had been sexually abused by a woman which is more than twice the rate for non-abusers. However, the seriousness of the abuse did not correlate with becoming a victim-abuser. A study, of people referred to a forensic clinical in the UK, involved individuals who had experienced sexual abuse as a child and those which hadn't (Glasser, Kolvin, Campbell, Glasser, Leitch and Farrelly 2001). 'Their sample included sexual abusers and non-abusers. About a quarter of those who had not been sexually abused in childhood. Of those who had suffered intra-familial abuse, 51 per cent became sex abusers as adults. Of those who had suffered extra-familial abuse, 61 per cent became sex abusers as adults; and of those who had suffered both types of abuse, 75 per cent became sex abusers as adults. Although women were hardly ever perpetrators of abuse they were commonly victims of abuse. As in the previous study, one of the factors which led to a higher likelihood of being a perpetrator was being abused as a child by a female adult such as mother or sister.

Quite clearly, there is less than perfect evidence that being abused as a child sexually leads to sexual offending as an adult. Quite why this is the case has not been satisfactorily explained although there is evidence that there is considerable neglect in the childhoods of those who go on to be offenders.

There has been a growing recognition that sex offending in childhood is a matter that should not be neglected and that it is actually rather extensive in scope. Coleman (1997), for example, has mentioned the following 'explanations' of adolescent offending – that the offender is experimenting or curious, that sexual aggression is common in adolescence, or boys will be boys. She sees the denial of juvenile sex offending as a problem as part of the means by which such offending is cultivated. If it is not a problem then nothing needs to be done about it and adolescent offenders proceed to adult offending. Of course, increasingly juvenile sex offending is being recognised as a significant problem. Although it is generally assumed that 'consensual' sexual activity between children is harmless exploration, this is an assumption rather than an established fact.

This sexualisation model is illustrated in Figure 10.5.

The pathways model

Ward and Siegert (2002) integrated the best features of several important multifactorial theories of child sexual abuse into a single, comprehensive model. This they call the *pathways model*. The term *multifactorial* means that, for a particular form of behaviour, there are many determinants of that behaviour which the theoretical model needs to take into account. These determinants should be considered individually or in combination in order to understand sex offending against children. Virtually all of the theories of paedophilia discussed in this chapter accept that child sexual abuse is multi-determined in this way. They differ in important ways. Finkelhor's (Finkelhor, 1984) approach tends to imply that offenders are diverted from the path of a normal sexual interest in adults by a variety of factors which push the offender towards children or remove inhibitions against sex with children. The psychotherapeutic/cognitive model makes very similar assumptions in that it claims that the way to stop the sexual abuse of children is to change a wide range of cognitions and behaviours which are conducive to child sexual abuse. Howitt's sexualisation model (Howitt, 1995a) is different in a key respect. Sex

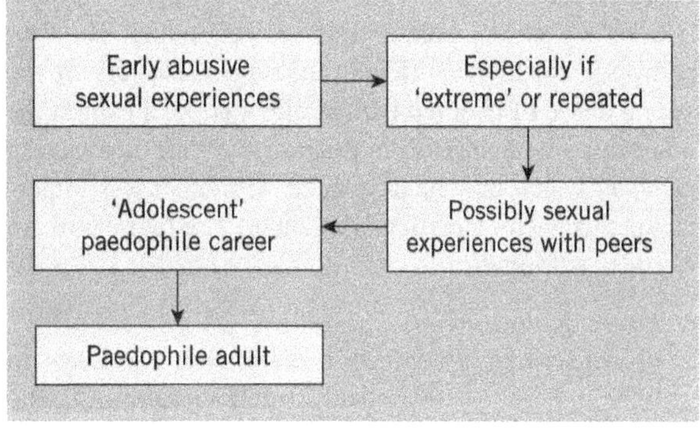

Figure 10.5 The sexualisation model

offending in this model is regarded as a part of a lifestyle starting in childhood in which sexual orientation to children begins early and remains into adulthood. This does not mean that sexual abusers of children never involve themselves in sexual relationships with adults: they do. However, the model does imply that the task of the researcher is to understand the origins of the offender's sexual interest in childhood rather than regard it as a substitute for sexual activity with adults. In other words, sexual interest in children should be regarded as more akin to a sexual orientation.

Theories operate at three different levels according to Ward and Siegert. Level I is the multifactorial level; level II is a theory which postulates a single factor – though in many respects these amount to little more than a hypothesis about the relationship of a variable to the sex offending against children; and level III is the micro-level or offence process level, which is little more than descriptions of the behavioural sequence leading to offending or possibly relapsing into offending behaviour.

A distinction is made by Ward and Siegert between *distal* and *proximal* factors in relation to the offending behaviour:

- *Distal factors:* these are causal factors which lie in the predispositions of the offender. They may have a number of origins. They may be in the genetic make-up of the offender or in his childhood development and beyond. They are long-term psychological mechanisms which may lead to offending when the environmental situation encourages offending.
- *Proximal factors:* these are the factors in the environment that change the distal factors into actual offending. They, in other words, trigger the predispositions into action. Possible proximal factors could include negative mood states or stress.

Ward and Siegert (2002) propose four psychological mechanisms which may be involved in an offender's offending behaviour: 1) intimacy and social skill deficits; 2) deviant sexual scripts; 3) emotional dysregulation; and 4) cognitive distortions. These are distal factors which make the offender vulnerable to offending against children but are not the immediate trigger for offending. The four pathways constitute different aetiological factors in the sexual abuse of children though offenders will exhibit the other three with varying intensities. So there is a central pathway which may be associated with other less important pathways for a particular offender. The four pathways are then as follows:

- *Intimacy and social skill deficits:* as a consequence of abuse and/or neglect in childhood, the ways in which a child understands relationships and 'the emotional availability' (p. 331) of important others are adversely affected. They may have difficulties in emotional disclosure to others. Furthermore, other people may not be valued as people as a consequence of these adverse early experiences. The attachment style corresponding to this is best described as insecure since the offender may fail to develop the appropriate trust of others and see the social world as a dangerous place. So they lack socially and emotionally intimate contacts and avoid such contact. According to Ward and Siegert, insecure attachment can result in lasting difficulties in managing mood and problem solving.

  This sort of offender is hypothesised by Ward and Siegert to offend only at specific times such as when their normal adult sexual partner is unavailable. The child in the abuse is effectively an 'adult substitute'. The intimacy deficits are the result of insecure attachment and abuse is directly consequent on the offender failing to achieve satisfactory relationships with adults. Other pathways, such as cognitive distortions, will be involved. In particular, the offender may believe that he has a right to sex with whosoever he pleases. According to Ward and Siegert, this sort of offending is likely to have its origins in adulthood. When faced with rejection or emotional loneliness, the offender diverts his attentions towards children.
- *Sexual scripts:* 'A sexual script spells out when sex is to take place, with whom, what to do, and how to interpret the cues or signals associated with different phases in a sexual encounter. These cues can be internal to the individual, interpersonal, or broadly cultural in nature' (p. 332). Sexual scripts are learnt during psychological development and represent the broad framework of understanding how complex social behaviours play out. As a consequence, the scripts, in part, guide social behaviour. It is argued that sexual experiences before the child is capable of cognitively and emotionally handling them lead to distortions in the script in comparison with those developed by others. The distorted script might involve inappropriate sexual partners (e.g. age discrepancy), inappropriate behaviours (deviant practices) or inappropriate contexts (e.g. sex devoid of interpersonal feelings).

  Sexual abuse in childhood may be the basis of their offending. These offenders seek emotional reassurance through sexual activity and sexual behaviour is equated with intimacy. Sexual cues are not differentiated from or are confused with the cues to affection and closeness. Offenders also fear rejection in intimate relationships. They choose children sometimes because of opportunity or because of intensified sexualised emotional needs. Sexual abuse of children is likely to emerge in adulthood in this group.

- *Emotional dysregulation:* we need to regulate our own behaviour in order to function effectively. This self-regulation allows an individual to achieve their goals. For example, we might be afraid of flying but wish to travel abroad for holidays. To achieve that goal we will have to adopt behaviours that allow us to succeed in that goal. That is, we have to control our anxieties about flying. Part of self-regulation is the regulation of emotions. Sometimes we may seek to elevate our emotional state (perhaps by listening to particularly evocative music or watching an emotional film) but equally we may need to reduce emotions in some way. The offender may exhibit emotional dysregulation when, for example, avoiding guilt and other emotional feelings while offending against children or when they fail, for whatever reason, to use coping skills to deal with stress, leaving them at greater risk of offending against children.

  This group develops essentially normal sexual scripts. However, their emotional regulation system has substantial problems. For example, they may have difficulty in using social support effectively in times of distress or some may have difficulty in accurately identifying particular emotional states in themselves. They may have problems in dealing with anger and resort to the sexual abuse of children as part of an attempt to punish a partner who has angered them. Sexual fantasies help ameliorate negative feeling states and, consequently, increase the risk of offending. Such offenders are unlikely to attempt to develop emotional intimacy with their victim but have profound sexual arousal when they are strongly emotionally aroused.
- *Cognitive distortions:* these have already been discussed but Ward has suggested that cognitive distortions are generated by a much smaller number of schemata or implicit theories held by the offender. Ward's view is that many varied expressions of distorted thoughts which are manifested by offenders actually reflect a small number of implicit theories which the offender holds. We all have such theories or schema about the world but the offender's are maladaptive because they can lead to offending behaviour. Five important implicit theories are listed by Ward:
  - *Children as sexual objects:* just as the offender regards adults as sexual, children are equally regarded as able to enjoy and desire sexual relationships with adults.
  - *Entitlement:* offenders regard themselves as being entitled to have their sexual needs met because they are more important than other people.
  - *Dangerous world:* children are not seen as being the threat that other adults are and their reliability and trusting nature give the offender comfort against the danger.
  - *Uncontrollable:* the offender is not in control of his actions but is driven by external factors such as those resulting in stress or the effects of drugs or alcohol.
  - *Nature of harm:* not all sexual activity with a child is harmful and children can benefit in a variety of ways from sexual activity with adults.

These offenders tend to be antisocial generally and demonstrate strongly criminal attitudes. They are patriarchal in their attitudes towards children and believe in their own superiority. Their sexual offences against children do not reflect a sexual preference but more their general antisocial behaviour pattern.

Although the idea of implicit theories has gained popularity in the field, there are many questions to be asked of offenders. Gannon, Hoare, Rose and Parrett (2012) wanted to know whether the implicit theories suggested by Ward and Keenan (1999) apply to the offence-supportive beliefs of female sex offenders. The women in their research had all offended against children. In half the cases the women had offended against their own children but invariably with their male partner. The researchers claim that they could code the female offenders' implicit theories using Ward and Keenan's implicit theories scheme. But the fit was rather uncomfortable when Gannon *et al.* studied the contents of the women's implicit theories in detail. Gannon *et al.* suggest that, instead of complete support for Ward and Keenan's implicit theories, they found evidence of gender-specific interpretations. Missing from the female offenders' was evidence that they regard all children as if they were sexualised beings (children as sexual objects) and they did not appear to see themselves as entitled to use children sexually – this despite the researchers attempting to tap this belief. Furthermore, the implicit theory of 'dangerous world' also did not apply in the same way to female offenders. They did not see the world as a hostile and dangerous place but they did see men in particular as hostile, dangerous and violent. On the other hand, some of them did see men as being entitled to do what they wanted with both women and children. Like men, they tended to see themselves as uncontrollable but their uncontrollability was due to the influence of male perpetrators.

Finally, there is a fifth group of offenders which Ward and Siegert suggest may represent the 'pure paedophile' in the sense that they have critical deficits in all four of the above pathways, not just a preponderance of just one sort of deficit. They idealise the relationship between an adult and a child in their sexual scripts.

BOX 10.3 Controversy

Cognitive distortions

Cognitive distortions are a virtually indispensable concept in most explanations of sex offending and, especially, that against children. They serve as a cornerstone of several different theories of sex offending, including that of Finkelhor (see main text of this chapter). For many clinicians, cognitive distortions are common in their conversations with sex offenders and can be regarded as routine in their day-to-day work. So it would be a surprise to these clinicians to know that some researchers express doubt over the centrality of cognitive distortions in the explanation of sex offending. This controversy about the value of the concept may reflect problems with the relevant research just as much as inadequacies of the concept.

Historically, there seems to have been a shift in how cognitive distortions have been construed. According to Sheldon and Howitt (2007), there are at least three distinct views of what cognitive distortions are:

- *Cognitive distortions* are beliefs held by offenders which help them overcome inhibitions about offending and serve as a defence in so far as they serve to reduce the guilt that sexual offending creates. A presumption of this view is that sexual offenders are predisposed to being sexually interested in children and that their cognitions are modified such that, for example, children and childhood sexuality are seen in ways which justify their sexual assaults on children. Such a conception of conceiving cognitive distortions reflects the original formulation put forward by Abel, Becker and Cunningham-Rathner (1984). As such, cognitive distortions can simply be regarded as a special instance of drift or neutralisation theory (Sykes and Matza, 1957). Drift/neutralisation theory argues that offenders effectively neutralise the psychological impact of their offending. Many techniques of neutralisation are similar to cognitive distortions and the denial processes which psychologists have seen as characterising sex offenders. Although the original formulation of cognitive distortions is absolutely clear, confusion has developed as to whether neutralisation through cognitive distortions comes prior to or follows after offending. However, Maruna and Copes (2005) insist that conceptually cognitive distortions can only apply post-offence and that they cannot explain the aetiology of offending.
- Cognitive distortions are *rationalisations* which emerge when offenders need to account for their crimes. Thus they are little other than justifications or excuses for unacceptable behaviour. In other words, the accounting process required in many forensic interviews yields characteristic cognitive distortions. Gannon and Polaschek (2005) describe these as 'transient post-offence justifications and excuses' (p. 184). Thus cognitive distortions do not have a significant role in offending in this conceptualisation. Instead, cognitive distortions are essentially face-saving devices which come into play when the offender is held to account for their crimes by psychologists, police officers and others in the criminal justice system.
- Cognitive distortions should not be construed as altered cognitions at all but, instead, they reflect the distorted life-experiences of offenders. In this sense, cognitive distortions can be regarded as essentially narrative accounts of the sex offender's childhood experiences of sexual abuse by adults and sexual play with other children (Howitt, 1995a). In this formulation, cognitive distortions may pre-date offending but they have close links to offending behaviour. Accounts of childhood experiences are difficult to obtain from offenders and they are often and characteristically fragmentary. Nevertheless, many offenders describe their early experiences of very sexualised behaviours including histories of sexual abuse, sexual play or both. Thus cognitive distortions involving 'Children are sexual beings' simply reflect the sexualised childhood of the offender and the child's sexual involvement with others. Cognitive distortions, then, are consequent on particular childhood experiences which themselves are grossly different from the childhood experiences of most of us. The term 'cognitive distortion' is, therefore, a misnomer since the cognitions reflect a child's subjective reality.

Maruna and Mann (2006) have questioned the value of the concept of cognitive distortions to sex offender research. The term 'cognitive distortion', they argue, lacks a singular and clear meaning. It is used as an umbrella concept for (a) a variety of attitudes which seem supportive of sex offending; (b) cognitions common during the offence sequence; and (c) *post hoc* neutralisations of or excuses for offending. Cognitive behavioural treatment programmes for sex offenders focus on cognitive distortions, of course. Therapists want offenders to take responsibility for their actions and eschew rationalisations. The identification and confrontation of cognitive distortions is a major part of this. Maruna and Mann argue that the *post hoc* excuse aspect of cognitive distortions is problematic since, after all, such after-the-fact excuses for one's behaviour are regarded as part of the psychology of normal, healthy individuals. The therapeutic process should shift attention from *post hoc* excuses to concentrate, instead, on those offence-supportive attitudes and cognitive schemas which have been clearly linked empirically to offending.

Evidence abounds that in Western societies individuals formulate excuses and justification for their unacceptable actions. Furthermore, there is a wide variety of criminological research which has shown that, for offences ranging from poaching to attacks on prostitutes, offenders seek to justify their offences. Generally, these studies show that offenders tend to blame external and unstable causes as being responsible for their offending. The explanations avoid blaming the offender in terms of their personal responsibility. In other words, there is a human tendency to claim that it is not our fault when we behave badly. Bandura's (1990) theory of moral disengagement suggests that individuals avoid sanctioning themselves for their immoral behaviour through processes such as displacement of responsibility; diffusion of responsibility; distortions of the consequences of our actions; dehumanisation of the victim of our crimes; and by presenting themselves in the role of a victim.

What is strange is that what is considered as normal for most people becomes pathological when we consider prisoners and other offenders. These explanations employed by offenders have been called aligning techniques because they align the offender with the rest of society. Maruna and Mann (2006, p. 158) argue:

> Pathologizing such aligning techniques when used by criminal justice clients places them in a no-win situation: If they make excuses for what they did, they are deemed to be criminal types who engage in criminal thinking. If, however, they were to take full responsibility for their offences – claiming they committed some awful offence purely because 'they wanted to' and because that is the 'type of person' they are – then they are, by definition, criminal types as well.

Besides conceptual problems with the idea of cognitive distortions, it has not always fared well in terms of empirical research. There has not been a consistent research finding that child molesters differ from controls in terms of their use and acceptance of cognitive distortions. There are some studies which demonstrate such differences in terms of mean scores on cognitive distortions questionnaires (e.g. Bumby, 1996). On the other hand, there are those researchers who suggest that child molesters are reluctant to overtly agree with cognitive distortions. These researchers tend to suggest the difference between sex offenders and control groups is that child molesters tend to reject the cognitive distortion less extremely than appropriate controls (e.g. Arkowitz and Vess, 2003; Marshall *et al.*, 2003). Thus, for instance, where the non-sex offender ticks the questionnaire it is to *very strongly* disagree with the cognitive distortion, whereas the sex offender is likely to just *disagree*. Among the explanations of this is the possibility that offenders fake a socially acceptable response by rejecting the distortion (Blumenthal, Gudjonsson and Burns, 1999; Horley, 2000; Kolton, Boer and Boer, 2001). Such faking 'good' is consonant with the image of sex offenders as being liars and manipulators (Wyre, 1987, 1990). Nevertheless, experimental studies with sex offenders have indicated that social desirability response sets are not responsible for the answers which sex offenders give to such questionnaires (Gannon and Polaschek, 2005). Offenders' answers are also unaffected by convincing the offender that if they lie are likely to be found out (Gannon, 2006).

An alternative possibility is that some cognitive distortions questionnaires include very extreme questions which perhaps most offenders actually disagree with. Hence low scores on such extreme cognitive distortions are to be expected if offenders are responding honestly to them.

It has been held for a long time that child molesters and other sex offenders have a variety of criminogenic and distorted cognitions. These cognitive distortions are seen as a problem to be addressed in treatment. In other words, cognitive distortions are causally linked to offending behaviour. Others see them as post-offending rationalisations which distance the offender from accepting responsibility for their offending. In contrast to these points of view, Marshall, Marshall and Kingston

BOX 10.3 (continued)

(2011) claim that there is no convincing evidence that cognitive distortions are criminogenic or require treatment. They reject forcefully the idea that cognitive distortions explain the crimes of sex offenders. Marshall *et al.* use some of the research that we have already discussed and more to suggest that excuse making is characteristic of normal day-to-day life. Excuse making is actually a positive feature of everyone's thinking and not making excuses can have negative consequences. So if excuses are part of normal life then why use them to explain offending behaviour? For example, there is evidence that excuse making is healthy and not to engage in it is unhealthy. Depression can be the result of accepting full responsibility for one's own actions (Abramson, Seligman and Teasdale, 1978). On the other hand, excuse making can prevent loss of self-esteem (Blaine and Crocker, 1993). In terms of a more forensic example, there is some research suggesting that offenders who excuse their own offending have a lower risk of being re-convicted compared to those who accept full responsibility (Hanson and Wallace-Capretta, 2000). Marshall *et al.* point out that by making an excuse for his crimes, the sex offender tacitly accepts that he did something wrong. So perhaps the process of desistance from crime begins sooner in these individuals. Bearing these things in mind, they question whether cognitive distortions expressed by child molesters are truly important in their offending behaviour. Marshall *et al.* directly equate cognitive distortions with excuses. The case for doing so is not completely spelt out and they thus ignore the possibility that cognitive distortions have deeper implications than that in sex offending. Sex offender thinking becomes 'normal' thinking in Marshal *et al.*'s formulation.

Related to the idea of cognitive distortions is the emphasis that some therapists place on full disclosure by the offender. Some sex offender treatment programmes require that the offender accepts the truthfulness of the victim's account. The basic idea behind this is that if the two do not match then the sex offender is engaging in distorted thinking and distorted thinking undermines the goals of treatment. But is this an adequate way of conceptualising such a disparity? Marshall *et al.* (2011) argue that such a viewpoint basically ignores the fallible and constructive nature of human memory. That is, should we expect perfect correspondence between what the offender says and what his victim says? Why should the reports of child molesters match the accounts of their victims? We would not expect that any two people will give identical accounts of any events that they have been involved in, after all. The police interviewing method, the constructive nature of memory, and modifications to the victim's memory over time are all possible factors leading to a mismatch between the offender's and the victim's stories. Memories are characteristically error-prone.

They also make a point which has been made before. That is, sex offenders actually tend to disagree with the cognitive distortions. They merely disagree less strongly with cognitive distortions than do control group members. That is, sex offenders actually reject cognitive distortions, but not so strongly as other people do. Taken at its face value this is difficult to reconcile with the idea the cognitive distortions are criminogenic. The research evidence favouring the view that cognitive distortions are criminogenic is relatively scant. Hanson and Bussiere (1998) and Hanson and Morton-Bourgon (2004) included 'attitudes tolerant of sexual crime' in their meta-analysis (see Box 4.1) and related these to recidivism data. They found a relationship only for the rapist sample and not for child molesters. Most other studies in Marshall *et al.*'s review involve risk-assessment measures as the dependent variable and tend to paint a very unclear picture overall. Marshall *et al.* also point out that their treatment programme no longer excludes those manifesting denial, with no apparent detriment to the success of treatment.

The extent to which one accepts Marshall *et al.*'s argument that treating and challenging offenders' cognitive distortions during treatment may be more to do with one's definition of cognitive distortions than anything else. This is the point that O Ciardha and Gannon (2011) make in reply to Marshall *et al.* (2011). They are insistent that the cognitive distortions of child molesters warrant treatment. Cognitive distortions have been understood in a variety of different ways, which causes some confusion among researchers. The definition of cognitive distortions adopted by Marshall *et al.* is 'thoughts, perceptions, beliefs and ideas that are understood to present obstacles to the offender taking responsibility for his crimes' (p. 118). This seems to be a broad definition on the face of things. However, O Ciardha and Gannon point out that in their writings Marshall *et al.* actually focus on a much narrower variety of cognitions – in brief, 'excuses for offending'. In contrast, Ó Ciardha and Gannon take the view that the important and theoretically significant conceptualisation of cognitive distortions is to regard them as 'stemming from cognitive structures, cognitive processes and cognitive products. . . . Cognitive structures refer to the beliefs, schemas, scripts and implicit theories that people resort to when interpreting their social worlds' (p. 131). That is, cognitive distortions are central and integral to offending –Ó Ciardha and Gannon are adopting Ward's cognitive schema discussed earlier. Actually, they suggest that the term cognitive distortions would be best replaced. However, its ubiquitous use in the sex offender research literature would make this difficult. Furthermore, they suggest that the confrontational style of psychotherapy often used with sex offenders (Salter 1988) may be outmoded. In this early style of treatment the offender is required to fully confess to their crimes precisely as their victims describe the abuse. Gannon *et al.* point out that there is a big difference between cognitive processes which are involved after offending/arrest to neutralise and excuse their offending and the cognitive processes, whatever they may be, which may be more criminogenic and involved in the committing of the offence. This difference is important and may go some way to help sort out the conceptual muddle which has become associated with the idea of cognitive distortions.

Denial and sex offending

It has been argued that the use of denial is exceptionally common among sex offenders (e.g. Abel *et al.*, 1987). According to Nugent and Kroner (1996), clinical experience suggests that child molesters are more likely to admit to their offences than rapists, though this appears not to be supported by Barbaree's (1998) study. There are claims that, for example, sex offenders who admit the offence may differ from those who do not in terms of the self-justification strategies they employ. Men who are offence deniers tend to attribute responsibility to the victim (Scully and Marolla, 1984) whereas the admitters attribute the cause to their emotional problems or substance abuse, in particular. The idea that denial of the offence is a risk factor for future recidivism has a great deal of intuitive appeal among some professionals working in sex offender treatment (Howitt, 1992). By denying their offending, offenders may fail to deal with the factors which contribute to their offending.

One special sort of denial is what may be termed 'categorical denial' – this is where the offender claims not to have committed the offence. According to Ware, Marshall and Marshall (2015), estimates for the rates of categorical denial vary. In studies of sex offender outpatients and convicted offenders it is 25–30 per cent approximately but much higher for men who had been accused but not yet convicted. The figures for offenders who had been through a treatment program were very much lower at just a few percent. Categorical deniers tend to minimise sexual interest and show little deviant sexual response to appropriate stimuli in plethysmography. They also self-report less interest in girls, boys and men than offence admitters. Categorical deniers also have a lower risk of reoffending.

Admission of one's misdemeanours is encouraged by many criminal justice systems. Sentence discounts may be available for suspects who admit their offending early. Not only does this save the criminal justice system money and facilitate closure for victims, it also signals that the offender is a promising case for treatment. But, of course, there are rewards for those who successfully deny their guilt. Many of those working with sex offenders argue that denial of the offence is commonplace. The term *denial* seems to be used very inconsistently by different authors. At one extreme would be denial in which the offender truly believes that they did not commit the crime (Jenkins-Hall and Martlatt, 1989); at the other extreme are offenders who are fully aware of their offending but choose to deny it to friends, family or those in authority. Of course, it is extremely difficult to know where a particular offender lies on this continuum.

There are many reasons for denial of the offence other than trying to escape the punishment of the criminal justice system. Ware and Mann (2012) suggest that among the reasons for categorical denial are: (1) in order for offenders to maintain their status and reputation and support of family and friends; (2) in order to maintain a sense of self-esteem; and (3) in order to continue with their offending in the future. The first motive appears to be the most common. There also may be a wish not to be labelled as a sex offender. Of course, some categorical deniers may be telling the truth.

But there is very little about the process of coming out of denial available in the research literature. Blagden, Winder, Thorne and Gregson (2011) carried out an Interpretative Phenomenological Analysis (IPA) (Howitt, 2010; Smith, 2008) of the experiences of sex offenders emerging from denial. IPA basically seeks to describe the 'lived experiences' of individuals and has been applied now in a wide variety of medical, social and other settings. It involves an interview, usually, in which the individual is encouraged to describe as fully as possible their experience of, in this case, denial. The interview or interviews are then carefully reviewed with the aim of identifying the important themes that they contain, as well as wider-embracing superordinate themes. The men Blagden *et al.* interviewed were all prisoners at a UK prison. This also is the largest sex offender treatment location in Europe. Participants volunteered for the study and, by and large, they had 'emerged' from the denial stage while in prison although they had not always arrived at complete acceptance.

The interview was semi-structured and broadly based, including questions about offenders' life experience at the time of the offence but also specific questions about details of their story, such as why they denied at a particular stage. The data analysis is illustrated in Figure 10.6. As can be seen, the overriding themes were viable identity maintenance, being in denial and wanting to change.

Denial is part of a meaning-making process which is intrinsically driven. It provides offenders with an understanding of their offending experiences. Although the literature tends to portray denial as counterproductive and maladaptive, in the context of the life of the individual as experienced by that individual, denial may be adaptive for their circumstances. Denial, suggest Jenkins-Hall and Martlatt (1989), is the end product of a process. It involves the individual seeking to make sense of and deal with what is a highly problematic, confusing and threatening situation. Denial is affected by a wide range of factors, such as the context of the denial; the situation as faced by the offender; the offender's motivations; and their personal narratives concerning their experiences. Consequently, denial ought not to be regarded as being maladaptive. Coming out of denial is based on wanting to change:

- *Superordinate theme 1: maintaining a viable identity.* Being arrested for a sexual crime threatens the self-identity of the offender. One reason is that the offender's activities are made public and his persona as a good father, decent neighbour, or whatever else is difficult to maintain. Arrest brings with it embarrassment and shame; concerns of being stigmatised as a sex offender well into future life; fears about the reactions of friends and family; and the need to create a new identity for himself. All of these things are themes subsumed under this superordinate theme. Of course, by denying the offending, the offender may create for himself the persona of victim.
- *Superordinate theme 2: 'being in denial'.* One important finding was that denial was construed by the offenders as a conscious decision. The researchers suggest that denial should be seen as a social act which serves a purpose, often in terms of relationships. In their situation following arrest, denial has a sort of survival value, especially where it helps the offender avoid the consequences of the stigma of being seen as a sex offender. In many respects, being in denial did not stabilise the offender's life. Denial was experienced as a very unstable and chaotic phenomenon. Some offenders might engage in impulsive acts – one in the study decided to get baptised, for example. Although fear of the response of family and friends was part of the reason for denial – for example, the offender might not want to hurt them – it was also true that the support of family and friends could contribute to the process of coming out of denial. This makes understandable why

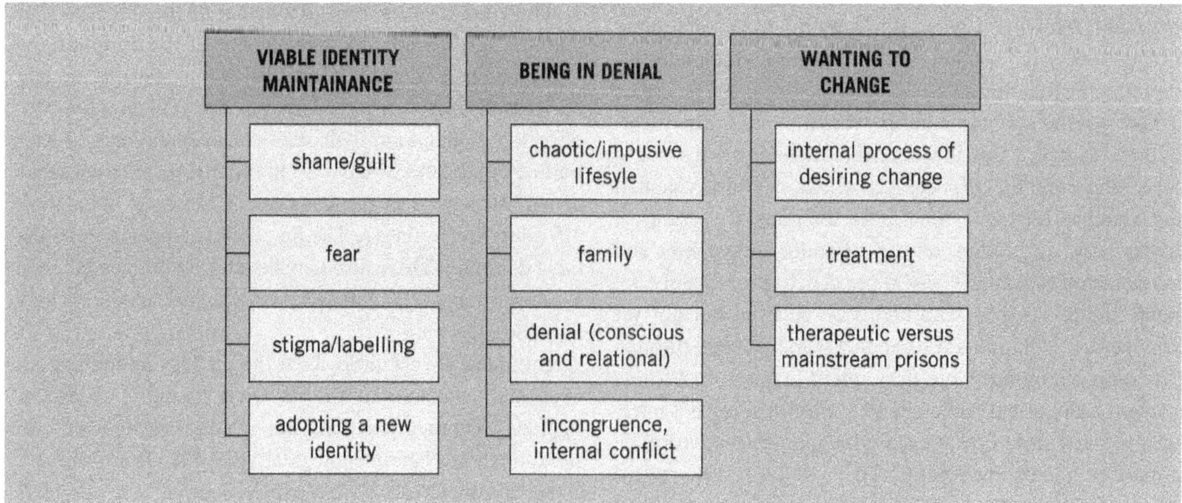

Figure 10.6 Major themes and sub-themes in sex offender denial

denial is not absolute. That is, offenders may admit their offences to prison staff but continue to deny culpability to their family and friends.

- *Superordinate theme 3: wanting to change.* Internal processes are largely responsible for overcoming denial. It builds from a desire to change. Gradually, the offender begins to feel that denial has ceased to be a viable choice. The reasons for this realisation are numerous, including the recognition that denial is actually becoming counterproductive in their life. For instance, the offender may want to move to a sex offender-only prison where they would be less at risk of attack by other prisoners. This would be unlikely if they continued denying. Furthermore, denying means exclusion from many sex offender treatment programmes. The more therapeutic environment of the specialist prison creates an ambiance which facilitates coming out of denial. They might feel safer and more trusting in such an environment.

One of the more confusing aspects of the literature on denial in sex offenders is the question of its relationship to other minimising and offence-excusing cognitions. Probably this is an area where there has been too much reliance on scales and measurement and too little in-depth research on offender cognitions. Not too much is known about denial, cognitive distortions and minimisation techniques from detailed studies of all of these in terms of the cognitions of individual offenders. If they all share the underlying strategy of offsetting responsibility or blame for offending then it is difficult to see why they should not intercorrelate highly. To be sure, cognitive distortions are more general statements about child abuse, compared to denial and minimisation, which concern a particular offender's culpability for a particular crime. But why should an offender who denies responsibility for the events not blame the child?

Nunes and Jung (2013), in Canada, carried out a number of secondary analyses on existing data sets, employing well-established measurement scales which contained relevant variables to this research question. Two samples of child molesters and one sample of rapists were available and primarily analysed separately. Generally, endorsements of cognitive distortions about child sex offending were associated with variables which involved denial/minimisation tactics. Superficially, this would seem to support the idea that the evasive cognitive strategies which help the offender to reject responsibility are associated. But we should look a little more carefully at the size of these associations. Endorsement of cognitive distortions correlated .2 with high levels of denial/minimisation of guilt and deviance. It correlated .3 with denial of harm to the offender's own victims, .2 with denial of the need for treatment, and .2 with denying responsibility for one's own sex offences. These are very small correlations, which either means that, as yet, we have only very poor measures of each of these variables, or that they are distinct constructs, which was the researchers' interpretation. Quite how the different variables might play a causal role in sex offending is not at all clear – if, indeed, they do. Cognitive distortions are seen as functioning to condone, excuse, rationalise, justify, minimise and generally support sex offending. They can be seen as being concerned with sex offending in general. Denial involves claims of innocence which the offender may only be making strategically and which may not actually be believed by the offender, as we saw above. So cognitive distortions may just be what the offender thinks of sex crimes in general without having a clear bearing on their own offending.

The general upshot of studies of the recidivism of deniers has generally been to find little if any consistent relationship (e.g. Hanson and Morton-Bourgon, 2004; Thornton and Knight, 2007). Yates (2009) reviewed the literature on deniers and also concluded that there was little to support the assertion that denial is a signal of a greater risk of recidivism. Some studies even point to the possibility that categorical deniers are less likely to reoffend. Possible explanations of some of this include the likelihood that categorical deniers tend to be first-time offenders who tend to have lower levels of recidivism anyway. There have been meta-analyses of the relationship between denial and recidivism (Hanson and Bussière, 1998; Hanson and Morton-Bourgon, 2004). Again, what emerges is that there is very little or no relationship between denial and reoffending in the future. Perhaps this implies that, despite their claims, denying offenders tend to be well aware of what they have done. One of the negative consequences of denial is that the sex offender may be refused a place on a sex offender treatment programme. They may also find parole difficult to obtain and they may remain in a higher-risk prisoner establishment than if they had not remained 'in denial'. Nunes *et al.* (2007b) studied Canadian sex offenders (predominantly those offending against children) in an attempt to discover whether other variables might, in some way, be masking the relationship between denial and recidivism. In this study, deniers were those who denied committing all index offences for which they had been convicted, whereas admitters admitted at least one of their index offences. As part of a detailed analysis, the researchers found the offender's relationship to the victim – that is, whether the case involved an incest offender or an extrafamilial abuser – was a key factor. For incest offenders, denial correlated with increased risk of recidivism, but this was not the case for extrafamilial offenders. Sexual recidivism was 17 per cent for incest offenders who denied but only 6 per cent for those who admitted their offending. The reverse pattern applied to the extrafamilial offenders. Extrafamilial deniers reoffended at a rate of 15 per cent, but extrafamilial admitters recidivated at a rate of 24 per cent. Among the various explanations of this is that incest offenders need to gain the trust of their family before they can reoffend. Admitting the offence is not a way of gaining this trust and so recidivism in this group is lower. For extrafamilial offenders, regaining their family's trust is not relevant to reoffending outside of the family.

Despite the thrust of the research in this area, many in the criminal justice system believe that an offender who denies their offence is at greater risk of reoffending in the future, partly because they cannot benefit fully from any available treatment. Deniers are regarded as poor candidates for sex offender treatment who will progress poorly in treatment or drop-out prematurely. However, there is considerable variability in terms of how forensic psychologists think about deniers and how they should go about risk assessments and recommendations about eligibility for parole (Freeman, Palk and Davey (2010)).

Internet paedophile offenders

The Internet has provided the legal impetus for a range of new offences in countries everywhere. According to Robbins and Darlington (2003), 27,000 people throughout the world go onto Internet child pornography sites each day and over 1 million images of child sexual abuse are in circulation. Ray, Kimonis and Seto (2014) obtained a sample of Internet pornography users by using the Internet to recruit volunteers. Twenty-one percent of the men who had used pornography on the Internet had also viewed child pornography. Although 8 per cent of the pornography users said that they would be interested in having sex with a child if they could get away with it, 32 per cent of the child pornography users said they would be interested. However, this meant that over two-thirds of the men who viewed child pornography would not be interested in sex with a child if they could get away with it. While child pornography involves the sexual abuse of children, Internet offences may be committed by those who have not made physical sexual contact with children themselves. Internet offences are important in that they raise the possibility that some adults may be sexually interested in children but never have contact children sexually. There are, of course, differences between child pornography only offenders and men with both child pornography and contact abuse offences. Long, Alison, Tejeiro, Hendricks and Giles (2016) found evidence that the latter group were more likely to: 1) have a criminal record; 2) have unsupervised close access to children; and 3) to demonstrate precursors to contact offending such as grooming and taking indecent images of children. A meta-analysis (see Box 4.2) of studies attempting to differentiate child pornography offenders, contact only offenders, and mixed contact-child pornography found fairly consistent a number of differences (Babchishin, Hanson and Van Zuylen, 2015). The meta-analysis supported the idea that contact offenders have greater access to children. Child pornography offenders had greater psychological obstacles to contact sexually offending because they had greater empathy for children. What is important is that child pornography only offenders desist from sexual activity with children despite their sexual interest in children (cf. Howitt, 1995a). Understanding more about how paedophiles may avoid contact sexual offending against children might help us to understand better how to help paedophiles cease offending despite their sexual leanings (Howitt, 2005). There is evidence that 97 per cent of UK Internet paedophiles have no previous convictions and have not previously come to the police's attention (Brookes, 2003).

Internet pornography offences have come to court in increasing numbers in recent years, mirroring the rapid growth in the spread of the Internet. In jurisdictions such as Britain and the United States, Internet pornography offenders risk lengthy prison sentences. Child pornography is a graphic representation of the sexual abuse of children and, it is argued, downloading the material contributes tangibly to the sexual abuse of children by encouraging further production of such material. However, the suggestion that Internet child pornography users will then go on to offend against children is based more on speculation than evidence. Sullivan and Beech (2003) are among the psychologists who believe that fantasising to imagery of child abuse encourages men to act out their fantasies through the direct sexual abuse of children. This, of course, does not mean that there are no contact offenders who also offend on the Internet. In this context, it is worth noting Seto and Eke's (2005) study which found that, although 17 per cent of child pornography offenders reoffended in some way in the following 30 months, it was just 4 per cent who were reconvicted for a contact sexual offence against a child. Sheldon and Howitt (2007) studied the explanations given for desisting from contact offending by Internet child pornography offenders. The following is a typical explanation:

> I have been in the position shall I say if I'd wanted to I could have done . . . on many, many occasions, but I always drew the line of actually touching [a child]. I got to the point where if I was looking at something that to me was my, like a drug addict, that was my fix for the day . . . my end release was looking at the pictures. I never got to the point where I would want to touch . . . looking at the images is enough, though a lot of people will disagree . . . I mean I've met people in prisons . . . who are in for the same thing and . . . their talk was never of actual sexual contact. Definitely. No. No. I would never.
>
> (Sheldon and Howitt, 2007, p. 227)

It is not easy to answer the superficially simple question of whether child pornography offenders can be regarded as paedophiles. One way of conceiving paedophiles is that they have a sexual interest in young children under the legal age of consent to sexual intercourse. Just as there are people with heterosexual interests who remain virgins all their life, there is no reason why a paedophile has to act out their sexual interest. What evidence there is suggests that many Internet pornography offenders collect substantial quantities of the material and that a good proportion of these will masturbate to such imagery while at their computers (Sheldon and Howitt, 2007). So in this sense, Internet child pornography offenders can be seen as paedophiles. However, if one insists that a paedophile is someone who commits a sexual offence directly against a child then, of course, Internet-only offenders are not paedophiles.

Researchers are only just beginning to identify the ways in which contact offenders and Internet offenders differ and are similar. Sheldon and Howitt (2007) compared groups of Internet child pornography offenders and contact sex offenders against children in terms of a great many characteristics. For example, Internet child pornography offenders tend to have had a longer education than contact sex offenders. On the other hand, both types of offender, quite contrary to the usual stereotypes, tend to be in relationships with adults at the time of their offending, though there is some evidence that these relationships are often fundamentally inadequate or troubled in some way. Nevertheless, Internet child pornography offenders tend to be more psychologically secure in their adult relationships than contact sex offenders against children. Both types of offender commonly experience rather adverse and neglectful childhoods. The lack of adequate relationships with their parents seems often to push the offender as a child to seek emotional warmth from other children or adults, which can result in early sexual experiences or exploitation. Sheldon and Howitt (2007) indicate that sexual experiences with peers in childhood are common in both groups, though abusive sexual activities were less common in Internet offenders and sexual activities with adults were more common in the contact offenders.

One promising line of research involves the cognitive distortions of these offenders – the ideas and beliefs which facilitate the offence. There is evidence that Internet offenders are cognitively similar to contact offenders in terms of the broad pattern of their cognitive distortions. For example, it has been claimed that Internet offenders who view pictures of children involved in sexual intercourse tend to interpret a child's smiles just as contact offenders do (Drake, Ward, Nathan and Lee, 2001). That is, the children's smiles are seen as indicating that children are sexual beings and are enjoying their abuse (Taylor and Quayle, 2003).

Using a conceptualisation developed by Ward (Ward, 2000; Ward and Keenan, 1999), the patterns of cognitive distortions in contact and Internet offenders have been explored by Sheldon (2004). Sheldon interviewed both Internet-only and contact offenders about many different aspects of their lives and analysed the interview transcriptions for evidence of the above, Ward's five 'implicit theories'. She found similarities throughout in terms of the use of these theories by both types of offender. For example, take the first implicit theory – children as sexual objects. One of her interviewees, who had Internet as well as contact offences, said of his victim:

> She was a bit of a tart dressed in a provocative manner *the way she put herself to you verbally and physically* . . . the way she walked, the clothes she wore you pick it up straight away . . . probably even blokes think she's a puller.
>
> (p. 27)

This clearly demonstrates how that offender regarded a child as a sexual being – much of the language is more commonly used to describe adult women and would not be used of a child by many people. Sheldon found evidence of similar beliefs in Internet-only offenders. For example:

> My favourite [fantasy] would be consensual sex with a child . . . the most arousing thing would be to give the child pleasure.
>
> (GA: Internet)

Notice that this ideal sex is described as consensual and that the child in the fantasy has an orgasm. If it were applied to an adult woman, such a fantasy would not be regarded as deviant in any way. Because of their similarities in the use of cognitive distortions, we should hesitate in assuming that the two groups are essentially distinct. However, Merdian, Curtis, Thakker, Wilson and Boer (2014) found that child-pornography only offenders were less likely to use cognitive distortions especially in terms of seeing children as sexually active or blaming the child for the offence.

One of the tasks facing the criminal justice system is that of how to deal with an offender caught with a large amount of child pornography on their computer. Is this person a threat to children and should they be treated as if they were? Is there any way of knowing the likelihood of them contact offending against children? Lee, Li, Lamade, Schuler and Pfentky (2012) suggest that there are two possibilities. The first is that an Internet child pornography offender has contact offences against children lurking in their offending background. They refer to such an offender as a dual offender. The second is that, once child pornography attracts the offender's interest, they are likely to go onto contact offending in their future offending career. In their study, Lee *et al.* had three groups of offenders:

- Internet child pornography only offenders;
- child molesters with no Internet child pornography offences;
- dual offenders, who had both child molestation and Internet child pornography convictions.

The research used self-report information from sex offenders in the community and those in prison. All three groups had a similar average age of 41 years. There were differences, such as the higher educational and employment achievements of the Internet-only group. The researchers developed two different scales. The first measured antisocial behaviour and the other was a measure of Internet preoccupation. The antisocial behaviour items were things like childhood conduct disorder, juvenile delinquency and non-sexual criminal activity as an adult. Internet preoccupation involved agreeing with items like: 'Did you prefer the excitement of the Internet to intimacy with a partner?' and 'How often did you lose sleep because of late-night log-ins?' Using both of these scales, it was possible to predict membership of one or other of the two groups involved in child molestation with 75 per cent accuracy. The research also found that the offenders could be fairly accurately classified into the three different groups on the basis of these two measures. The basic differences are illustrated in Figure 10.7. If an offender is known to have Internet child pornography offences, then the probability of him being a hands-on offender was 27 per cent when he scored zero on the antisocial behaviour scale but the probability was 84 per cent when he was at the top of the antisocial behaviour scale

It is always an underlying concern in the design of research studies that offenders who have been processed through the criminal justice system are in some way different from those who have not been caught for their offending. In the case of sex offenders, this is particularly problematic in the light of mandatory reporting of sex offences in some countries. However, this is not required everywhere. Neutze, Grundmann, Scherner and Beier (2012) studied over 300 self-referred paedophiles and hebephiles recruited from the community. All of them met *DSM-IV* diagnostic criteria for these classifications. Included in the sample were child sexual abuse offenders, dual offenders, and child pornography offenders only. A wide range of self-reported risk factors were measured in the research, including sexual preference; problems in sexual-self-regulation; cognitions supportive of offending; and low educational attainment and unemployment. Undetected sexual abuse offenders were younger, more educated and more likely to be employed than detected offenders. The undetected child sexual abuse offenders reported higher levels of sexual self-regulation problems, such as higher masturbation frequency, compared to detected offenders. The dual offence group reported more paraphilic interest than the detected offenders in this group. This fits with previous studies of undetected offenders as compared with detected offenders. On the other hand, the authors point out that this pattern may simply be a matter of the undetected offenders over-egging things since they are likely to be keen to get therapeutic help for their problems. In general, despite some differences, similarity between the detected and undetected groups dominated the findings. The researchers claim that the offence-supporting cognitions of the two groups did not differ. Detected offenders, however, employed an emotion-oriented coping style, which means that they tend to regulate their emotions by ruminating about things, wishful thinking, or blaming. This may be a consequence of being arrested, with the ensuing fear of bad consequences, feelings of helplessness, and losing control. These factors may discourage a task-oriented style of coping.

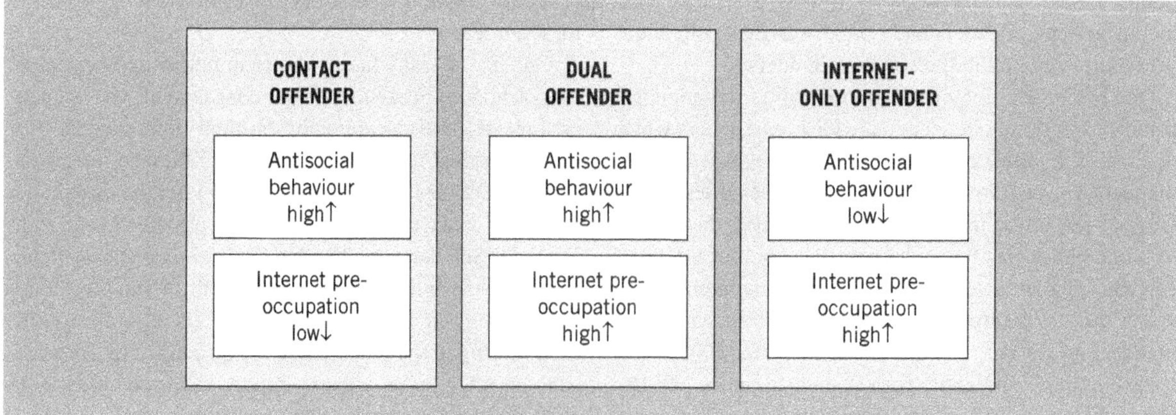

Figure 10.7 Characteristic patterns of offender types

Very little of the research on Internet child pornography makes explicit its role in stimulating its users to offend against children directly. One exception is Wood (2013) who argues that paedophilia in some people is not a stable characteristic but can be episodic over time. She suggests that child pornography can tip such an individual into active paedophilia.

Main points

- Sex offenders against children are in many ways much the same as anyone else, except for their offending. Various attempts have been made to categorise different types and one of the most common is that of fixated versus regressed offenders. There are problems with this, especially because regressed offenders typically offend against children in the family. Some data suggest that paedophile response to erotic images of children is quite common, though self-reported paedophile acts are relatively uncommon. A fuller understanding of sex offending against children must recognise that adolescents perpetrate a high percentage of all sexual offending.
- The evidence is that sexual reoffending is relatively uncommon after conviction, even several years after release (see also Chapter 27). Recidivism for other types of crime is more frequent. Similarly, the previous criminal histories of sex offenders against children are more likely to involve non-sexual crimes. There are claims that paedophiles have numerous victims, though this seems untypical of the majority. Recidivism in sex offenders has to be considered in the light of the monitoring of sex offenders after release back into the community.
- There are a number of theories to account for sexual offending against children. The preconditions model is of historical importance for the most part and very few of its principles have been established empirically. The psycho-therapeutic/clinical model stresses cognitive aspects of the offending cycle such as fantasy and cognitive distortions. There is more support for this model and it has a degree of validity in terms of describing the abuse process, though it does not address the issue of the aetiology (development) of offending behaviour. There is reasonable evidence to suggest that offenders' early abusive and other sexual experiences are associated with sexually offending against children. However, it is clearly untrue to suggest that all sexually abused children will grow up to abuse others. Nevertheless, there are some indications that certain types of sexual abuse and repeated abuse in childhood are more conducive to the development of sexually abusive behaviour towards children. This supports the basic idea of sexualisation theory. One question is whether a single-factor cause of offending is adequate. The pathways model suggests that there may be a number of different developmental routes to offending, though it accepts much of what is central to the other models of sexually abusive offending.

The treatment of sex offenders is dealt with in Chapter 26.

Further reading

Seto, M.C. (2008) *Pedophilia and Sexual Offending Against Children: Theory, Assessment, and Intervention* Washington: American Psychological Association.

Sheldon, K. and Howitt, D. (2007) *Sex Offenders and the Internet* Chichester: John Wiley.

Ward, T., Polaschek, D.L.L. and Beech, A.R. (2006) *Theories of Sexual Offending* Chichester: John Wiley.

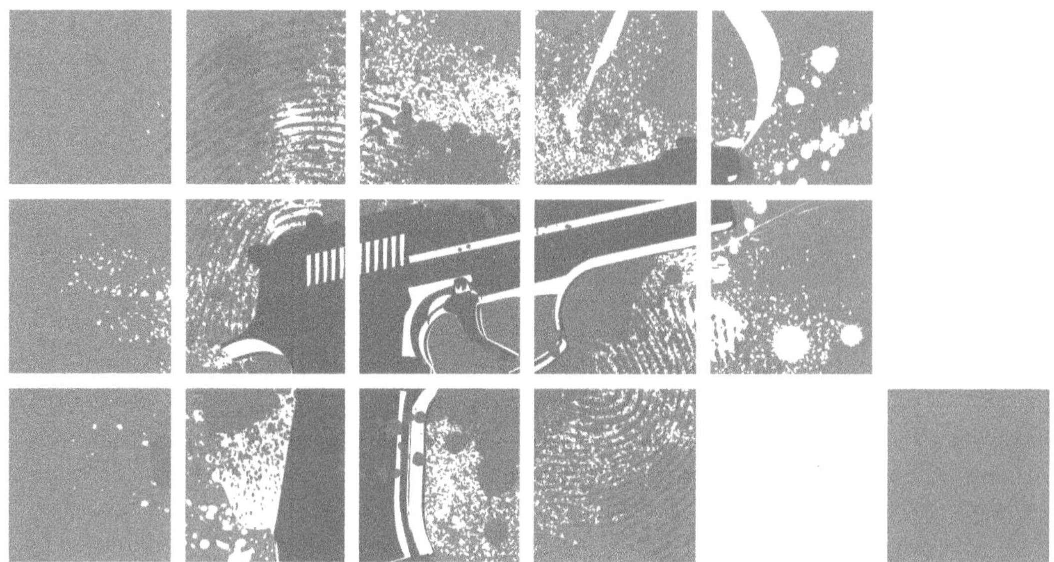

Chapter 11

Police psychology

Overview

- Within the criminal justice system in the UK, the police force tends to be the most highly regarded by the general public.
- Police psychology, as with all work organisations, falls within the remit of organisational psychology. Working group dynamics, occupational stress and many other factors such as these are aspects of the psychology of policing. Other chapters in this book pertinent to policing include Chapters 12 to 21.
- In the past it has been claimed that the police force manifests a distinctive organisational culture that emphasises heterosexual, white male attitudes. It also stresses the importance of confessions obtained through interview.
- Researchers have studied police interviewing techniques in some depth. Many bad practices have been identified over the years, though good practice is also to be found. *Intimidation* by maximising the seriousness of the event, *robust challenges* such as accusing the interviewee of lying, and *manipulation* in which the officer suggests that the interviewee was not totally responsible for the offence or that the offence was not so serious, are among the most common bad practices identified in police interviews.
- Language inconsistencies in statements taken by the police can reveal fabricated evidence.
- The *cognitive interview* consists of techniques designed to improve the quantity and quality of eye-witness evidence based on principles developed from the psychological study of memory. The *enhanced cognitive interview* adds elements from good interview techniques in general, such as establishing rapport and asking questions effectively. There is evidence from a range of studies that cognitive interviewing is effective at eliciting greater quantities of good-quality information, although there is an attendant risk of more inaccurate information.
- The broad consensus, until recently, was that police officers, in general, are no better as eyewitnesses than other people. However, there is emerging evidence that, where the events witnessed were stressful, the police tended to be at an advantage and produced better eyewitness testimony – possibly as a result of their experience and training.
- Being witness to the consequences of offending has a stressful and traumatic effect on a proportion of the officers involved. Dealing with the aftermath of a suicide is a particularly traumatic experience. The stress of working in a bureaucratic organisation also takes a toll on officers.
- Among other issues that psychologists have raised in relation to the work of the police is the clarity of the police caution. There is evidence that police cautions are poorly understood by many of those who receive one. Furthermore, there should be concern when arrestees waive their rights in law since they may be unaware of the impact of this decision.

Introduction

Of all the component parts of the criminal justice system, the police are consistently the most highly regarded by the public (Howitt, 1998b). For example, Londoners in a survey (Metropolitan Police Service, 2013) were asked the question: 'Taking everything into account, how good a job do you think the police in this area are doing?' Sixty-seven percent of the public indicated that they thought that the police were doing a good job. This despite seemingly not knowing a great deal about police activity. For example, only 47 per cent claimed to feel informed about what the police are doing in their local area and only 12 per cent knew local policing priorities. It has long been known that objective evidence about police performance was irrelevant to such judgements about confidence in the police (Christensen, Schmidt and Henderson, 1982). The Crime Survey of England and Wales showed that although 69 per cent of the public regarded the police as being effective at catching criminals, only 55 per cent thought that the Crown Prosecution Service was effective at prosecuting those accused of committing a crime (Ministry of Justice, 2015). The figures were far worse for the probation service which was seen as effective at stopping criminals from recidivating by 26 per cent of the public and only 22 per cent thought that the prison service was effective at rehabilitating offenders. Generally speaking, confidence in the police tends to have improved over the time since previous surveys (Chapman, Flatley and Smith (2011); Mirrlees-Black, 2001). Of course, criticisms of the police are common too as exemplified by police shootings and deaths in custody.

The nature of policing has changed in recent years from being a police force to being a service industry to the public. Issues like security, safety and harm reduction have taken over from law enforcement and crime control as the focus of policing. In the light of this, it is an interesting question just why the police tend to be appreciated more than other sectors of the criminal justice system. An Australian study by Elliott, Thomas and Ogloff (2012) provides some understanding of the positive evaluation of the work of the police. In-depth interviews were conducted with over 100 victims of personal and property crime. Over 70 per cent of them had been repeatedly victimised. Violent crime, sexual assault, thefts, burglaries and stalking were the categories of offences. The interviews were transcribed and subjected to qualitative analysis using grounded theory (see Howitt, 2016). Grounded theory requires researchers to exactingly code and recode the data, seeking to identify the main themes which summarise effectively the range and scope of their data. A major finding was that satisfaction with the police is far from determined by their crime-solving effectiveness. What made the difference was 1) that the police showed willingness to do their best to solve the crime, and 2) that the police related to the victim humanly and respectfully as a person, independent of the crime itself. In other words, the researchers suggest that victims value highly the procedural justice of their dealings with the police. The public wants, above all, to be fairly and respectfully treated by the police. The police officer demonstrably finding the crime unacceptable played a part in the victim's response to the police. Non-blaming attitudes towards the victim and prompt action on the case led to higher satisfaction. The public also valued courtesy actions such as keeping the victim informed of their progress on the case. Much of this equates to the police negating some of the harmful consequences of victimisation.

Police culture

The idea that there is a particular set of personal characteristics (or 'police personality') which good officers possess is somewhat dubious. Such a personality, if it exists at all, is probably at least as much to do with the requirements of police work as it is to do with any pre-existing personality predispositions or any selection and recruitment practices (Bull, 1984). Stress seems endemic in police forces and indicators such as suicide have been claimed to be high in police officers (but see Box 11.1 for evidence of the mythical status of this claim). Furthermore, often it has been required that all officers progress through the ranks to achieve promotion. This not only brings about problems of reorientation towards one's previous peer group but may well be the prime way in which the police occupational culture is transmitted.

Ainsworth (1995) suggests that no two days of police work are ever the same. He lists among the diverse situations with which police officers have to deal the following: attending road traffic accidents; going in pursuit of a teenage vandal; taking drunks to the police station; attending domestic disputes; helping to police a riot and working through backlogs of paperwork. At the same time, the police officer is required to have a good working knowledge of the law and to act lawfully. Finally, the officer is expected to promote a positive image of the police force. This is a range of tasks with which, say, the average supermarket checkout assistant or psychologist does not need to cope. The training of police officers is, consequently, a compromise between what is practical to include in training and what would be ideal. While earlier generations of police officers received little training except that provided by on-the-job experience, there is now a growing emphasis on fairly extensive training.

Ainsworth (1995) indicates that police training in the past encouraged rote learning of legislation and the powers available to police. Nowadays, it increasingly concerns how to deal with the wide variety of incidents that come under the rubric of police work.

It seems clear that the process of becoming a police officer leads to changes of which even the trainees themselves are unaware. Garner (2005) carried out a longitudinal study involving police trainees. They were assessed in terms of their attitudes to policing and their 'distinctive impact or effectiveness in law enforcement' during training and a year later. There was a marked shift to an increasing pro-police position in terms of a range of attitudes, despite the officers in the research overwhelmingly believing that they had not changed.

Part of the training of new recruits is through contact or on-the-job training with more seasoned or experienced officers. While this can be regarded as teaching the recruits the job at a practical level, seasoned officers may employ practices that are less than ideal, or even unacceptable to their managers. Consequently, the novice police officer may merely learn bad practice from his or her colleagues. This is particularly important when we consider the transmission of the occupational subculture or *police culture*. Skolnick (1966) was the first to suggest that the culture of the police influences the work of the police force. It is fairly easy to recognise the different cultures typical of different organisations. The organisational culture of a hospital is obviously different from that of a school. Similarly, there are typical characteristics of the organisational cultures of police forces that are not found in the same measure or the same combination in the cultures of other organisations. Police culture refers to the characteristic patterns of belief, behaviour, thinking and interaction that police officers tend to share. They are essentially *normative* as they are the accepted and prescribed standards of police personnel. This does not mean that they are fixed and unchanging. Although personnel may be recruited because they seem to reflect the characteristics of a 'good' police officer, they learn police culture by interacting with other police officers. The occupational culture may be in some ways at odds with what new officers have learnt at police college. There may be a painful reality shock when they try to put their college knowledge into practice. They may find that their new ways of doing things clash with what is acceptable to the transmitters of police culture – the old school of officers. Another way of putting this is that organisations have two parallel aspects. There is the structural aspect of the organisation which is formal and deals with what is supposed to happen in the organisation. The cultural aspect of the organisation is informal and deals with what actually happens in the organisation. These two aspects may be at odds with each other.

Canteen/cop culture

While police culture is a generic description of the cultural characteristics of the police, there is also evidence of the prevalence of certain sorts of attitude that characterise the general thinking of ordinary police officers. We may call this *canteen* or *cop culture* in order to differentiate it from the more general police culture. There may actually be a clash between the management subcultures and the subculture of the rank-and-file officers. Wootton and Brown (2000) summarise canteen culture as involving and valuing action, cynicism, conservatism, mission, pessimism, pragmatism, solidarity, suspicion, and racial prejudice. One review suggests that police culture has a number of important elements. These include: the police have a strong orientation towards the deployment of direct action; a concurrent cynicism about members of the community which is accompanied by pessimism about whether police work can improve society; they emphasise how important solidarity among the ranks is; they tend to be socially isolated from the more general community and socialise within the police community; they stereotype or categorise some groups within society in an evaluative manner; they are suspicious of members of the community and about the dangers of situations they face; they manifest moral and political conservatism; and they are practical and down-to-earth in their orientation to getting things done (Reiner, 2010). This combination of traits is best interpreted as an 'ideal-type'; a synthesis of police values and perspectives into a unified analytical construct.

The list might be extended further since apart from racism, sexism, homophobia and heterosexism have all been claimed by some to be characteristic of the culture. Research evidence seems to suggest that many of the features of police culture have remained resistant to change (Loftus, 2009). For example, police officers verbally expressed to Loftus things which can be interpreted as indicating that police work is a moral mission or that crime fighting is central to police work. Essentially, cop culture determines the rules followed by police officers that allow them to be seen as being effective in their work. This means that the standards of the dominant group within the police and their styles of interaction determine what is regarded as effective policing and the effective police officer. Gay and lesbian officers, for example, can then be seen as subordinate to the dominant group, their values disregarded. The nature of the canteen culture is such that homosexual officers do not 'come out'. This choice can do nothing to challenge the homophobia and, in a sense, reinforces it. Cop culture has been held to be responsible for a number of the problems in police work including resistance to new innovations, how members of ethnic minorities are treated, the lack of accountability, and failures to stick to conventional rules. Marenin (2016) argues that many of the cases of the police using deadly force in the course of their work are influenced by police culture. In this case, the tendency of the police to believe that the dangers of their work are greater than objectively is the case.

After joining the police, the processes of occupational socialisation may create a situation in which the individual's police identity is not psychologically compatible with other aspects of the individual's identity (e.g. their sexuality). In-group identification refers to the sense of a common identity shared by members of the force. This sexist, heterosexist and homophobic culture would readily identify gays and lesbians as out-groups. This may encourage hostility and discrimination by the majority group towards the out-group. Women, ethnic minorities, lesbians and gays are not readily tolerated because they are 'other' or different from the accepted norm. The problem for officers with these characteristics (e.g. they are women or homosexual) is that the dual identities of police officer and being homosexual, for example, can be extremely difficult to reconcile and handle.

Wootton and Brown (2000) studied police officers. One group consisted of officers who belonged to one minority (e.g. the officer was female). The other group had two minority positions (e.g. they were black women or they were homosexual black men). The officers were interviewed and what they had to say was coded in terms of the presence or absence of a number of themes. A grid was then created in which the different officers were listed against the different themes emerging in the interviews. This was then analysed, using a complex statistical technique (multi-dimensional scalogram analysis). This essentially plots people into a chart indicating their similarity/ dissimilarity across the themes. There seemed to be a cluster of heterosexual officers who shared similar experiences. Lesbians and gays were not among them. Furthermore, officers with just one minority characteristic (e.g. being black or being homosexual) tended to group together as similar in terms of their experiences. Individuals with two minority characteristics (e.g. black homosexuals) tended to be at the periphery – separate from the dominant heterosexual group and the minority group. Wootton and Brown recommend that it is members of the heterosexual core, those demonstrating the discriminatory attitudes, who should be seen as having the problem – not their victims.

One reason why the social attitudes and beliefs of police officers are important is the considerable discretion that officers have in the way they carry out their duties. For example, there is discretion in terms of whether they make an arrest. While the police as individuals and as institutions may try hard not to let such factors influence their decisions, good intentions may not be totally effective in preventing this happening. Thus, potentially, police officers' social attitudes and beliefs relevant to a particular suspect may be influential on their decisions. Further indications about how homophobic attitudes might influence policing decisions can be found in the work of Lyons *et al.* (2005), who studied anti-gay attitudes in a sample of largely male US police officers. The officers completed an *Attitudes Towards Gay Men* subscale which includes items such as 'Male homosexuality is a perversion'. Generally speaking, homophobic attitudes tended to be typical of the officers.

In another part of the study, these police officers were given a crime scenario in which the offender's sexual orientation was described as either heterosexual or homosexual. The officers judged culpability of the offender in a scenario which incorporated a moral dilemma adapted from the work of Kohlberg on moral development. In this, a person steals from a pharmacist drugs which might help save his dying partner. The pharmacist is grossly overcharging for the drug, which the offender cannot afford to buy. When the suspect was gay, the officers were more likely to think that he should be convicted than if the suspect was heterosexual. Those with most extreme homophobic attitudes were more likely to endorse the conviction of the offender. Most officers believed that the offender ought to be arrested (82 per cent) and the sexual orientation of the man made no difference to this. Eighty-six per cent believed that the man should be indicted (charged) but only 72 per cent thought that he should be convicted. However, this figure was only 64 per cent where the offender was described as heterosexual, but 79 per cent for the homosexual offender. In the homosexual condition, there was a relationship between the level of the officer's homophobia and believing that the defendant should be convicted. This was not the case for the heterosexual condition.

There are other aspects of police culture that warrant attention. In particular, there is some evidence that the police have systematically different beliefs about the criminality of men and women. Horn and Hollin (1997) took a sample of police officers and a broadly similar comparison group who were *not* police. A lengthy questionnaire was used to extract, in particular, ideas about female and male offenders. Factor analysis, a complex statistical technique, revealed three dimensions underlying ideas about criminals:

- *Deviance*, which includes beliefs such as 'Trying to rehabilitate offenders is a waste of time and money' and 'In general, offenders are just plain immoral'.
- *Normality*, as reflected by agreeing with statements like 'There are some offenders I would trust with my life' and 'I would like associating with some offenders'.
- *Trust*, which is measured by such matters as 'I would never want one of my children dating an offender' and 'You have to be constantly on your guard with offenders'.

There were two versions of the questionnaire – one with female offenders as the subject, the other with male offenders as the subject. Women offenders were seen as less fundamentally bad (deviant) than men who offend. This was true irrespective of the sex of the police officer. Compared with the non-police group, police officers saw offenders as fundamentally deviant or bad. The police viewed offenders as less normal than the general public (factor 2), though they tended to see offending women as more normal and like the general public than they saw male offenders. They also regarded offenders as less trustworthy than did the general public and male offenders were seen as less trustworthy than female offenders.

There are problems with the idea of cop culture. It is obviously questionable whether all police officers share the same core of policing-related attitudes. That is to say, cop culture is monolithic within police organisations. Researchers have shown that there may be a number of different types of officers which are to some extent differentiated in terms of cop-culture attitudes. For example, Cochran and Bromley (2003) identified three subtypes of officers – the traditionalist, the cynic, and those who accepted and were receptive to change. A study by Ingram, Paoline and Terrill (2013) explored cop-culture among US patrol officer working groups. They found that there tended to be a degree of similarity among officers within the same work group in terms of their attitudes. However, there was considerable variation between different work groups such that the idea of a monolithic cop-culture was undermined. These different variants of cop-culture were different ways of adapting to the strains of the work of the patrol officers. It should be remembered that rapid changes occur within police organisations as a consequence of the pressures on police management coming from political sources as well as legal judgements and reviews of particular policing episodes. These will differ from country to country and force to force but nevertheless they put established practices continually under review.

BOX 11.1 Controversy

False facts and forensic psychology

False facts, according to Aamodt (2008) are to be found in a number of areas of forensic and criminal psychology. By false facts we mean notions which are commonly promulgated for which there is simply no research foundation. Among these is the idea that police officers are more prone to suicide and divorce (Kappeler, Blumberg and Potter, 2000). Apparently, the FBI held a conference seeking remedies for this only to find that the suicide rate among police officers may even be lower than would be expected and that much the same motives apply for suicide in police officers as in the general public. Or is this a myth too? Some beliefs – such as that the police are good at detecting deception – may have a bad influence simply because they encourage misplaced faith in the ability of the police. There is plenty of evidence concerning this in Chapter 18. According to Aamodt, perhaps the most alarming feature of these myths is that they are perpetuated despite sound evidence that they are untrue. He lists other false facts, such as that crime increases during a full moon and that the typical profile of a serial killer is a white male in his twenties. These are feasible but which of us knows whether they are true or not? Aamodt argues that a number of principles might help reduce the amount of misinformation circulating. For example:

- Check the primary source for the facts – relying on secondary sources is not good.
- Be sure that like is compared with like – there is no point applying what might be the case for apples to pears.

So what of the claim that police officers are more likely than people in general to get divorced? Aamodt reports several Internet claims of this sort, e.g. 'Police officers, for example, face divorce rates averaging average between 66 and 75 per cent' (Aamodt, 2010, p. 1). What is the source of this 'fact'? No sources are given for this or numerous other examples on the Internet. McCoy and Aamodt (2010), however, used census data and found that the rates of divorce and separation for police officers are somewhat lower than the national average. Aamodt stresses primary sources because he is aware of secondary sources which are substantially inaccurate compared to the relevant primary source. For example, the Kitty Genovese murder has often been used to illustrate the principles of bystander intervention and how bystanders fail to intervene when there are several of them. The truth is that two bystanders called the police in the Kitty Genovese murder case, despite the impression created by textbooks.

What of the claim that police officers are particularly prone to suicide? This apparently, according to Aamodt, was based on a study of insurance claims which found that the police officer suicide rate was 22 per 100,000 as opposed to 12 per 100,000 in the general population. This led to many claims, including the idea that police suicide had reached epidemic proportions. The problem is that this statement simply compares apples with pears. Police officers in the US are predominantly white males between the ages of 25 and 54 years. The suicide rate for these 'apples' in the general populations is 22 per 100,000. That is, the police suicide rate is exactly what it should be if the police are merely regarded as a random sample from the general population with those particular demographic characteristics.

Into this mix of dubious facts, Lilienfeld and Landfeld (2008) throw claims about the role of pseudoscience in relation to law enforcement. Pseudoscience has many of the superficial appearances of science; however, it does not work by the rules of science. The responsiveness of pseudoscience to negative evidence about its precepts is not the same as that which science ideally shows (no matter how reluctantly initially). Thus falsifiability does not feature as a criterion. Lilienfeld and Landfeld (2008) provide a whole list of pseudoscientific endeavours related to law enforcement, such as the belief in truth serums, profiling and the polygraph. They also mention graphology – the idea that handwriting can be used to assess personality or psychopathology. There is no evidence of its validity.

Explaining police bias

Officers are at risk of developing negative stereotypes of groups of people with whom they interact during police work. Smith and Alpert (2007) proposed that this can result in a form of unconscious racial profiling which leads to disproportionate actions against minority group members during police work. Black (and Hispanic) people have repeatedly been shown to be over-represented in the activities of the US police such as stops, searches and arrests. Smith and Alpert (2007) argue that social-psychological research concerning stereotypes can go a long way towards explaining this. These authors claim that racism is not the root of this bias but nevertheless the bias acts against black people. There are instances of differential treatment of racial minorities motivated by what Smith and Alpert call *racial animus* as part of an intentional strategy to deal with crime. Instead, social conditioning and the phenomenon of the illusory correlation may lead to police officers believing that black people are disproportionately criminal. Because of this, at each stage black people are disproportionately involved in police activity and they are likely to receive tougher treatment and charges. The exercise of discretion is a feature of much police activity which leads to the over-representation of certain minority groups.

Unconscious racial stereotyping may be part of the explanation of these biases, according to Smith and Alpert. Attitudes, beliefs and stereotypes emerge when the police have repeated contact with people from a particular social grouping. Stereotypes are the outcome of both social and individual cognitive processes. As members of communities, police officers share with other members of the community stereotypes which appear to them as collective knowledge and beliefs about minority group members. Officers are also in regular contact with criminals and develop cognitive schema concerning black people and crime. These schema are activated to help the officer understand new situations based on familiar features of the situation. The consequence of this is that beliefs about black people as a group and crime are generalised to individuals from that group, irrespective of the personal characteristics of the individual minority group member.

Why might illusory correlation play a part? This is the idea that there appears to be a correlation between two things (e.g. race and crime) whereas in reality there is no – or a smaller than believed – correlation between the two. Smith and Alpert mention one study (Hamilton and Gifford, 1976) in which 1) an arbitrary majority group of 26 persons and 2) an arbitrary minority group of 13 persons was created. Each group was presented as engaging in different and unique behaviours proportionate to the size of the group, such that the ratio of desirable to undesirable behaviours in the two groups was identical. In other words, the researchers created a situation in which the behaviours of the majority group and the minority group were exactly equal. Despite this, the two groups were perceived differently such that the majority group was seen as the more desirable and, also, the proportion of undesirable behaviours in the minority group was perceived as being greater than it actually was.

Of course, the consequences of such stereotyping can be serious. For example, African Americans are approximately four times more likely than white people to be killed in encounters with the police in the United States. Furthermore, simulation research suggests that the police are more likely to make the right decision to shoot if the target is an armed black man and not to shoot if the target is an unarmed white man (Correll, Park, Judd and wittenbrink, 2002).

In a rather different sphere of police activity, it has been frequently shown that the personal characteristics of a driver can affect police officer's decisions to stop motorists and sanction them. In particular, there seems to be a gender bias in the decision to given a sanction (citation or ticket) in that female drivers seem to be less likely to be punished (e.g. Makowsky and Stratmann, 2009). The only problem is that there seems to be some variation between different police areas in terms of the extent of this differential. A police officer will make the decision about whether to punish a traffic violator speedily and on the basis of only a small amount of information. To achieve this, the police use stereotypes in order to classify the offending motorist. Race, gender and age are obvious contenders given this. A form of 'chivalry' may encourage the male officer to be more protective of female offenders. The less an organisation is dominated by males, the weaker should be the influence of this paternalism. Farrel (2015) studied nearly 150,000 traffic stops in various Rhode Island communities. Among her hypotheses were that gender disparities in sanctioning would be greatest for police agencies with low proportions of female officers and where organisational pressure to punish motoring offending was highest the greater the gender disparity. The primary factors in decisions to issue tickets were individual factors such as the nature or severity of the offence. However, there were differences in issuing citations which were down to differences between the communities involved. Women, overall, were less likely to be given a citation for speeding offences than men. It was also true that black drivers and older drivers were also less likely to receive a citation. In communities where the police force had higher percentages of women officers, there was less likelihood of a ticket being issued and the less disparity between the genders. The evidence was that where the police organisation was under more pressure to give out citations (perhaps for revenue reasons) there is an increase in the gender disparity in the number of citations issued. In short, both hypotheses were supported.

Confession culture and police interviewing

Not all people detained by the police are formally interviewed. Robertson, Pearson and Gibb (1996) found that only about 30 per cent were interviewed in London (many minor offences do not require one) and interviews are largely conducted by junior officers. Nevertheless, the interview was common for some offences and, in particular, serious offences. Despite the belief among psychologists that coercive interviewing by police runs the risk of false confession (Chapter 17), police officers regard the interview as a crucial stage during criminal investigations which may encourage them to adopt a range of tactics, some of them dubious. The interview situation is different from a normal conversation because one person, the police officer, is the prime controller of the content, structure and direction of the exchanges. Suspects are discouraged from interrupting, initiating conversation or challenging the officer's authority at any level. In the United Kingdom, concerns about miscarriages of justice led to legal changes. The *Police and Criminal Evidence Act* of 1984 changed the underlying ideology of interviewing to discourage practices which courts of law in the United Kingdom have found unacceptable (Sear and Williamson, 1999). This has resulted in substantial differences between the United Kingdom and the United States. In the *United Kingdom*: a number of principles underlie modern UK training in investigative interviewing. These are:

- the function of interviewing is the search for the truth rather than justification for a prosecution;
- the interview should be approached with an open mind;
- the interviewing officers should behave fairly and recognise, for example, the special difficulties of the groups who may be most at risk of making false confessions – such as those with very low intelligence.

Unreliable confession evidence may have drastic consequences for the prosecution of a case. A number of things may render a confession unreliable. These include questioning which is hostile and aggressive, confessions following the offering of inducements such as bail or freedom from prosecution, not providing an appropriate adult to sit in at the interview where the law requires it, and so forth (Crown Prosecution Service, 2017).

There has been research demonstrating the importance that the police place on obtaining a confession. Police officers listened to various real-life, audiotaped interviews (Cherryman, Bull and Vrij, 2000). These varied in competence levels (as judged by researchers) and in terms of whether or not a confession was obtained. The police participants rated the interviews on a large range of factors that experts regard differentiate good from bad interviews. The following are among the characteristics of a good interview:

- all information is released at the beginning of the interview;
- appropriate use of pauses or silences;

- appropriate use of pressure;
- communication skills;
- conversation management;
- development of and continued rapport;
- empathy/compassion;
- information is released appropriately;
- interview has structure;
- interview is kept to relevant matters;
- knowledge of the law;
- open-mindedness;
- planning and preparation;
- purpose of interview is explained;
- officer responds to what interviewee says;
- officer summarises appropriately;

whereas the following are characteristics of a bad interview:

- apparent use of tactics;
- closed questions;
- closure;
- creation of apprehension;
- inappropriate interruptions;
- leading questions;
- over-talking;
- questions are too complex or long;
- undue use of pressure.

Overall, the police officers tended to rate the interviews as better when they resulted in a confession or admission than when no confession or admission was obtained.

Not all police interviewing is skilled. At a minimum, what would constitute a skilled interview performance on the part of a police officer? Griffiths and Milne (2006) make some suggestions and indicate that the following elements and structure are important:

1. The skilled interview would begin with an open question intended to obtain a preliminary account of what had occurred. Closed questions are only used to clarify details at this stage. These would be described as appropriately closed questions.
2. There would be probing questioning to gather finer details.
3. The interview might involve challenges to the suspect about inconsistencies that remain unclarified after the probing questioning. Closed questions such as 'Did you do the crime?' Might be asked at this stage though the suspect might be asked open questions instead such as 'Why doesn't your story match with what witnesses have told us?'
4. The suspect may be asked to confirm that any police summaries of what has been said are correct. A closed question may be sufficient for this.
5. The skilled officer will keep to a minimum unproductive categories of question such as the following: a) inappropriately closed questions such as 'Did your father visit you that day?' or only encourage 'yes/no' answers (a productive open question such as 'Who visited you that day?' may solicit rather more information); b) forced choice questions, which also encourage limited answers such as 'Was it your father or your mother that visited you that day?'; c) leading questions which imply the preferred answer such as 'It was your father who visited, wasn't it'; d) compound questions consisting of more than one question and complex overlong questions are avoided as they are difficult for the interviewee to know quite what to respond to; e) expressions of opinions or making statements are also avoided as these can lead to responses from the suspect and provide the suspect with indications of the interviewer's biases.

The situation may be very different in other parts of the world such as the United States where obtaining a confession is still regarded as important. What the British police might regard as unacceptable trickery and deception are seen as appropriate techniques in other parts of the World. The training of officers involves instruction in these techniques as well as others. Training is frequently by outside agencies. Part of the US approach is to present the suspect with an acceptable justification for their offending. These are appealing psychologically whether or not they have any basis in law. The self-respect of the offender is ostensibly redeemed by these 'excuses'. Examples include justifying theft by suggesting that the company is rich or that the offender was stealing to help support their family. Another example is feigning support for the offender with comments such as 'Her mother dresses her in those little tiny pants, deliberately turning you on . . .' (Sear and Williamson, 1999, p. 76). A further strategy is to minimise the crime such as suggesting that this was the first crime or that there are far worse crimes.

There is a distinction to be drawn between a police interview and a police interrogation. The latter is more applicable to the American situation. The literature on interrogation is extensive and so it is difficult to get an overall impression of what it involves in its various manifestations including the military. There is an argument that much of the research literature on methods of interrogation concentrates on individual techniques without presenting a full picture of the underlying nature of interrogation methods. Kelly, Miller, Kleinman and Redlich (2013) reviewed the vast literature on interrogation methods and generated a long list of the many interrogation methods available. This list was greatly shortened by looking for duplicates etc. leaving a final list of 71 methods. Examining this list led to the development of six taxonomic categories to describe interrogation methods. An interrogation may involve techniques from a variety of the categories:

1. Rapport (and relationship building) is achieved when there is an interactional, working relationship between interrogator and interviewee is established. Each understands the others goals and needs in the interview. It is based on mutual trust and respect, empathy and reciprocity according to Kelly *et al.* Among the interrogation methods related to this are:
   - attempts to find common ground or similar experiences;
   - appearing kind and respectful;
   - expressing concern for the interviewee and their situation in some way
2. Context manipulation involves interrogation techniques in which the physical and temporal environment of the interrogation are manipulated. These methods include:
   - carrying out the interview in a small or informal room;
   - the interviewee is isolated before the interrogation begins;
   - choosing the time of day for the interrogation – perhaps night.
3. Emotion provocation includes tactics at the interviewee's raw emotions in the hope that the interviewee will respond by providing more information. These methods include:
   - appeals to conscience;
   - carrying out the interrogation while the interviewee is very distressed;
   - encouragement of a feeling of helplessness in the interviewee.
4. Confrontation and competition involves the use of threats and perceptions of punishments in order to achieve compliance on the part of the interviewee. These methods include:
   - the interrogator emphasises their authority and expertise over the interviewee;
   - the interrogator repeatedly asks the same question;
   - the interviewee is asked a rapid sequence of questions without being given an opportunity to reply.
5. Collaboration is essentially the antithesis of confrontation and competition. It may involve:
   - the interrogator makes bargains with the interviewee;
   - the interrogator offers inducements in return for the required information;
   - the interviewee is provided with scenarios of how they can regain or achieve control.
6. Presentation of evidence involves various ways in which the interrogator can show to the interviewee that they already know or pretend to know important information. The hope is that this leads to the disclosure of additional information. These techniques include:
   - providing for the interviewee photos or statements from witnesses etc.;
   - confronting the interviewee with fabricated or partially fabricated evidence of their involvement in events;
   - employing polygraphic or other physiological indicators of the interviewee's involvement.

Some of these tactics have been noted by British researchers studying police interviews in the UK. According to the research of Pearse and Gudjonsson (1999), police tactics in interviews with suspects of serious crimes may be classified empirically into six main categories:

- *Appeals:* this might be appeals to tell the truth, appealing to the suspect's good character and suggesting that it is in the suspect's interest to confess.
- *Intimidation:* in this the seriousness of the event and the anxiety felt by the suspect are maximised. Long silences, attempts to manipulate the self-esteem of the suspect and the use of more than one officer to ask questions while not giving the suspect time to answer are additional features of this.
- *Manipulation:* minimising the seriousness of the offence; minimising the suspect's responsibility; suggesting themes to explain events; and so forth.
- *Questioning style:* leading questions are used; echoing the answer; asking more than one question in a single sentence.
- *Robust challenge:* this involves direct challenges such as suggesting the suspect is lying. This is often repeated at different stages.
- *Soft challenge:* soft, friendlier tone; challenges with questions such as the possibility that the witness is lying; attempts to reduce shame of the acts, especially in child sexual abuse cases.

It was found that the greater use that was made of the first three tactics above (the authors call these the overbearing tactics), the greater the likelihood that the court in the UK would dismiss the evidence as inadmissible.

The cognitive interview

Much of the psychological literature on traditional police interviewing skills paints a picture of officers using less than optimum techniques to elicit information from witnesses. In contrast, the psychological research literature is replete with findings about what makes a good interview and there is plentiful advice and assistance about the best techniques to use. Often police investigative interviews fail to meet the standards recommended in these publications. Wright and Alison (2004) analysed a number of interviews with adult witnesses in Canada. The interviews were characterised by a number of features: 1) there was frequent interruption of the witnesses by the officers; 2) more closed questions of the sort which produce short (e.g. yes/no) answers were asked than open questions designed to elicit more information; and 3) psychological techniques of the sort discussed later in this section designed to facilitate the witness's memory were not fully used. The police spoke about one-third of the time, interviewees two-thirds of the time, and lawyers scarcely spoke at all in comparison – just about a third of 1 per cent of the total time! Questions were asked at a high rate of frequency – there was on average one question posed every 16 seconds. Multiple (complex) questions were asked once in just over four minutes on average. The officers paraphrased what the witness had said once every seven minutes. In every minute of interview time, on average, 0.4 questions were asked by way of clarification; 0.3 leading questions were asked; and 1.2 closed questions were asked per minute about clarification.

There was a common structure to the interviews whereby firstly the interviewing officers helped the witness to construct an account of the events and then, secondly, they used a sequence of 'yes/no' (closed) questions to confirm that account. It appeared possible that the interviewing officers had a version of the events which they were pursuing through the interview.

Given evidence like this, it is not surprising that police interviewing techniques have come under intense and potentially damaging public scrutiny. In Norway, a notorious child sexual abuse case led directly to new efforts to improve the police's skills in interviewing children. This is known as the *Bjugn case*. Seven adults were arrested for the suspected sexual abuse and rape of children in the town. The police conducted a substantial number of interviews with children and there was a judicial hearing involving 40 children. However, charges against six out of seven of the suspects were dropped, though the remaining suspect underwent a ten-week trial before being acquitted. Criticisms of the affair included doubts about the competence of the interviewers; the style of questioning adopted; and the large delay between the allegations being made and the interviews finally taking place.

Norwegian police officers' use of open and closed questions was studied during investigative interviews with children. The officers were divided into two levels based on their competence assessed through the amount of training and experience. The questions that they asked of the children were classified as open or closed. Closed questions predominated and were ten times more frequent than open ones. However, there was not a significant difference due to competence. Open questions became less frequent as the interview progressed, whereas the frequency of closed questions showed an inverted U distribution, with most occurring in the middle of the interview. The use of closed questions is not a recommended interviewing technique.

The cognitive interview attempts to enhance recall by witnesses, using techniques deriving from psychological research into memory retrieval. Recall does not just happen; it is dependent on the types of probe used to retrieve the memory. If one type of probe does not work, then another may (Tulving, 1974). Cognitive interviewing is a practical reality, at least up to a point, since it has been adopted in police work. For example, since 1992 it has been part of the standard interview package used to train officers in England and Wales. It takes just a few hours for a police officer, for example, to obtain improvements in the information obtained from witnesses (Memon, Holley, Milne, Koehnken and Bull, 1994). The cognitive interview is not recommended for use with suspects or witnesses who are uncooperative or resistant to the interview. In this case, the recommended best practice is to use the conversation management approach (Shepherd and Milne, 1999). This involves the building of trust and confidence in the interviewer. It is known as GEMAC (greeting, explanation, mutual activity, close). Thus the initial greeting signals equality. The interviewer discusses the reason for the interview; the agenda of activities; routines employed, such as the taking of notes or the recording of the events; and the expectations of the interviewer, e.g. that the interviewer regards silence as positive and interruptions to these will be avoided. Mutual activities include monitoring activities such as active listening. Finally, the close of the interview can be an opportunity to summarise what has been said in order to check on the detail. Shepherd (2007) has presented in great detail a manual giving details of how to conduct an investigative interview, using the conversation management approach.

The original cognitive interview adopted two basic principles (Geiselman, Fisher, Firstenbeg, Hutton, Sullivan, Avetissian and Prosk, 1984):

- Recall in an environment that successfully reproduces features of the original encoding context is likely to be superior (Tulving, 1974).
- Memory is a complex thing and there is no whole representation of events stored in the brain. Instead there is a complex array of events and happenings which may not be stored in a coherent manner but will require a variety of strategies to tap in their entirety.

The cognitive interview then consists of four 'strategies' for improving the process of retrieving memory. Incorporating these simple instructions can improve eyewitness memory reports compared with standard police interview (Geiselman and Fisher, 1997). Witnesses should be encouraged to do the following:

- Report everything that they can think of about the witnessed events, even including trivial or incomplete fragments that they might feel irrelevant. Such an instruction might be: 'Tell me everything you remember, no matter how big or how small a detail' (Goodman and Melinder, 2007, p. 11).
- Mentally reinstate the circumstances of the witnessing. This includes their feelings at the time (e.g. they felt scared) or external factors that they recall (e.g. the noise of the building work in the background). So it should be explained at the start of the interview that they should mentally recreate the external physical environment and their internal state including affective (emotional), physiological and cognitive states at the time of witnessing the events (Fisher, Brennan and McCauley, 2002). This instruction may be phrased, perhaps, as follows: 'Think back to where you were at the time' (Goodman and Melinder, 2007, p. 11).
- Vary retrieval methods. For example, the interviewer should encourage the witness to report events in a number of different sequences and not just in chronological order. So recall could be obtained from the point when the police arrived or perhaps by recalling in reverse order. The underlying idea is based on research evidence that different components of a complex event may be recalled when different cues are present to aid retrieval from memory. Fisher *et al.* (2002) stress that these methods need care, otherwise the interviewer may be dissatisfied with the evidence presented. This might be phrased, for example: 'Now that you have told me what happened, try to remember it again but this time starting at the end and recounting it in reverse chronological order' (Goodman and Melinder, 2007, p. 11).
- Report events from alternative perspectives, such as that of another witness, the offender or from another physical location. This instruction might be phrased: 'What would the perpetrator have seen and heard?' (Goodman and Melinder, 2007, p. 11).

Additional considerations have been added as interest in the cognitive interview has grown. For example, witnesses should be encouraged to concentrate on their senses. Although we memorise in terms of concepts, we also memorise in terms of events' sensory features. So one simple technique for improving retrieval is to have the witness close their eyes and visualise the events.

Eventually, a number of problems with the cognitive interview became apparent that are not to do with memory directly. For example, the witness may be nervous and anxious, inarticulate and very unsure of what is expected of them in the context of the interview. For that reason, Fisher and Geiselman (1992) introduced what is known as the *enhanced cognitive interview*. This can be seen as the cognitive interview combined with techniques from communications psychology to help alleviate communication problems. For example, an interview can be ineffective because it fails to take into account the fact that people have limited mental resources to cope with the information flow. The interviewer may have a too complex task if they have to frame the questions, pay attention to the interviewee and make notes at the same time. As a consequence, they may fail to hear all of the information being provided, perhaps because they are distracted by the need to frame their next question. Similarly, if the interviewee is faced with a barrage of questions, they may be so overloaded cognitively that they can only search their memory superficially (Fisher *et al.*, 2002).

The enhanced cognitive interview hands control of the interview to the witness by making it clear that they have as much time as they require to respond to questions. Instead of the police officer determining, say, when as much has been recalled as could be recalled, this, among other things, becomes the prerogative of the witness. Other changes included training in the following:

- The process of building rapport or easy dialogue between the officer and the witness.
- How to use appropriate body language in the interview to reduce the feeling of intimidation experienced by some witnesses being interviewed, for example.
- How to ask effective questions – that is, for example, questions asked in a way that facilitates both understanding and a clear reply.
- How to use pauses effectively – for example, allowing the witness time to think and reply rather than rushing from one question to the next.

So the main principles of the cognitive interview seem to be effectively based on detailed and well-founded research on effective memory retrieval. Nevertheless, simply knowing the basics of the cognitive interview is insufficient to effectively conduct one. Fisher, Brennan and McCauley (2002) explain that the cognitive interview should be structured into five different sequential components (these are expanded on in Figure 11.1):

- *Introduction:* this is a crucial stage in that it provides the witness with an appropriate psychological and social setting for the cognitive interview to work. So it is at this stage that the interviewer must develop rapport with the interviewee, explain the need for as much

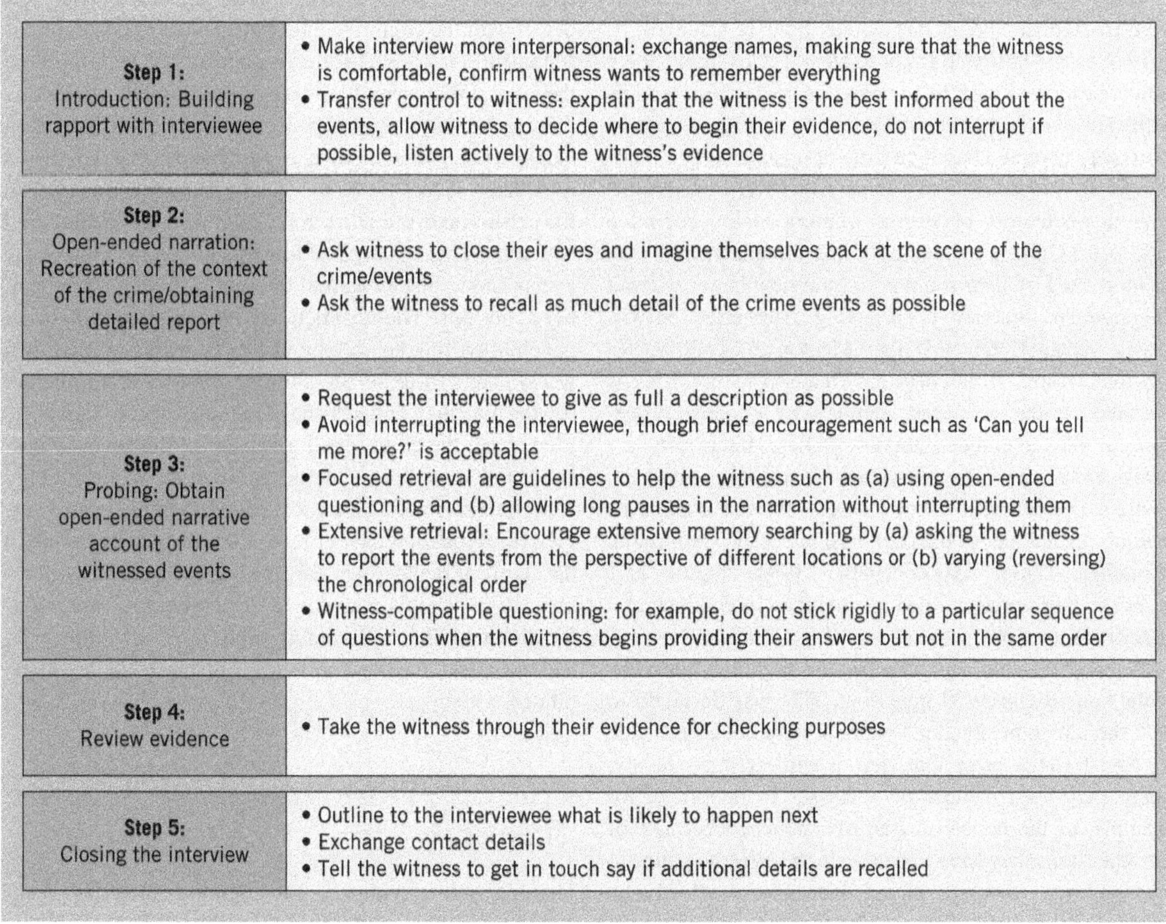

Step 1: Introduction: Building rapport with interviewee	• Make interview more interpersonal: exchange names, making sure that the witness is comfortable, confirm witness wants to remember everything • Transfer control to witness: explain that the witness is the best informed about the events, allow witness to decide where to begin their evidence, do not interrupt if possible, listen actively to the witness's evidence
Step 2: Open-ended narration: Recreation of the context of the crime/obtaining detailed report	• Ask witness to close their eyes and imagine themselves back at the scene of the crime/events • Ask the witness to recall as much detail of the crime events as possible
Step 3: Probing: Obtain open-ended narrative account of the witnessed events	• Request the interviewee to give as full a description as possible • Avoid interrupting the interviewee, though brief encouragement such as 'Can you tell me more?' is acceptable • Focused retrieval are guidelines to help the witness such as (a) using open-ended questioning and (b) allowing long pauses in the narration without interrupting them • Extensive retrieval: Encourage extensive memory searching by (a) asking the witness to report the events from the perspective of different locations or (b) varying (reversing) the chronological order • Witness-compatible questioning: for example, do not stick rigidly to a particular sequence of questions when the witness begins providing their answers but not in the same order
Step 4: Review evidence	• Take the witness through their evidence for checking purposes
Step 5: Closing the interview	• Outline to the interviewee what is likely to happen next • Exchange contact details • Tell the witness to get in touch say if additional details are recalled

Figure 11.1 The basic procedural steps for the revised cognitive interview according to Wells, Memon and Penrod (2007) and Fisher and Geiselman (1992)

information in as great a detail as possible, and encourage the interviewee to engage actively in the interview and freely offer information without waiting for a direct question pertinent to that information.

- *Open-ended narration:* by allowing the interviewee an opportunity to freely indicate what they remember of the witnessed events, the interviewer is provided with the basic material needed to plan what aspects should be probed using the techniques of the cognitive interview. During the course of the witness's narration, the interviewer notes what appear to be the mental images of important aspects of the events: for example, the images the witness has of the perpetrator and significant objects such as weapons.
- *Probing:* because the interviewer has established the general features of the interviewee's recollections, the aspects of memory which might be the best sources of information are focused on. So the interviewer 'guides' the interviewee to these aspects and provides the cognitive interview techniques which help maximise the information gathered. The interviewer might suggest that the witness closes their eyes and thinks about the best view that they had of the offender (Fisher *et al.*, 2002). This best view is then described in as much detail as possible. Of course, the interviewer may ask additional questions (probes) in order to get more information.
- *Review:* the interviewer takes the interviewee through the evidence that the interviewee has provided in order to find any inaccuracies in what has been recorded. Naturally, in the course of this the witness may recall more things.
- *Close:* this may include fulfilling the official requirements in respect to interview, such as signing any required forms and the like. The witness may be encouraged to get back in touch with the officer when new things occur to the witness that were not recalled in the interview.

Unquestionably, the cognitive interview works better than traditional approaches. Quite how it achieves its objectives and how well is not so clear. For example, there is the question of what to compare the cognitive interview with. The standard police interviewing techniques can be extremely poor and based on little or no appropriate training. So is it reasonable to compare this sort of interview with the outcomes of special training in the cognitive interview? Officers trained in the cognitive interview may be motivated by their training to interview better without the cognitive interview itself having much effect on witnesses' recall (Kohnken, Milne, Memon and Bull, 1999). For that reason, researchers have chosen to use what is described as the structured interview as a control procedure to the cognitive interview. These interviews are similar to the cognitive interview in terms of the good and positive characteristics they possess but the mnemonic memory techniques of the cognitive interview are missing (Kohnken, Thurer and Zoberbeier, 1994). Figure 11.1 gives the basic procedural steps involved in conducting a cognitive interview.

A recent development based on the cognitive interview is the self-administered interview. This was designed to help the police in situations where it may not be possible for logistic reasons to interview a witness immediately. There may be a number of witnesses to interview, for example, or the police may be overstretched because of the other tasks they have to complete. It helps the police to manage their resources at the scene more effectively. Gabbert, Hope and Fisher (2009) developed the self-administered interview (SAI) as a tool to be used when interviews cannot be carried out promptly. It employs some of the procedures used in the cognitive interview to improve interviews. The self-administered interview consists of a booklet, the cognitive interview-based instructions, and questions designed to facilitate recall of the events the witness had just observed. Of course, the self-administered interview does not replace the police interview with the witness but it is designed to help ensure that this is not affected by any delay. In a study, Gabbert *et al.* (2009) found that adult witnesses who used the self-administered interview immediately after witnessing the events were better at recall a week later than those who did not complete the booklet.

Hjelmsater, Strömwall and Granhag (2012) investigated the usefulness of the cognitive interview with children and whether its use made children more resistant to social influences which might affect their testimony. The experiment involved the child helping a man choose which present to take to a young child's party. Following this, the child completed one or other of two versions of the self-administered interview or nothing. One version of the self-administered interview was structured, while the other version had an open-ended response style. The structured version of the self-administered interview began with the cognitive interview device of context reinstatement. That is to say, the respondent had to think about the events, think about how they had felt while witnessing the events, think what they seen or had heard. They then had to write as much down as possible of what they could remember, including minor details. They then focused on the person involved and wrote down what he/she had said and done. They finally had to focus on the location of the events and write down all of the details they could remember about this. The unstructured version simply involved the child writing an account of the witnessed events. Two weeks later, some of the children underwent an attempt (by the man they had helped) to influence them. That is, he tried to get the child to tell a version of the events which contained some untrue elements. Then all of the children were interviewed. The use of the self-administered interview in the structured form resulted in improvements in the recall of details over the open-ended version or nothing. However, this was not at the expense of more confabulations. The self-administered interview, however, had no effect on the children's resistance to the social influence attempt.

The cognitive interview in police practice

There is some evidence that cognitive interview techniques are well received by police officers. Kebbell, Milne and Wagstaff (1998) surveyed police officers about the cognitive interview. Officers trained in the method showed evidence of using some of the techniques more often, in particular the mental reinstatement of context, changing the order of events and describing the events from another perspective. Features of cognitive interviewing such as reporting everything, establishing rapport and transferring control did not seem to differ between trained and untrained officers. In terms of the usefulness of different components of cognitive interviewing, establishing rapport was rated as the most valuable. Some of the cognitive interview techniques, such as changing perspective, trying different orders and transferring control, were seen as much less useful, even though these are key aspects of cognitive interviewing.

Memon *et al.* (1994) trained police officers in cognitive interviewing and examined their performance with witnesses to a simulated robbery. The police had some difficulties. For example, they tended to continue with the faults of conventional police interviewing such as rapid-fire questions with little opportunity for the witness to respond and questions about specific matters. They incorporated, most commonly, the cognitive interview strategies of context reinstatement, perspective changing,

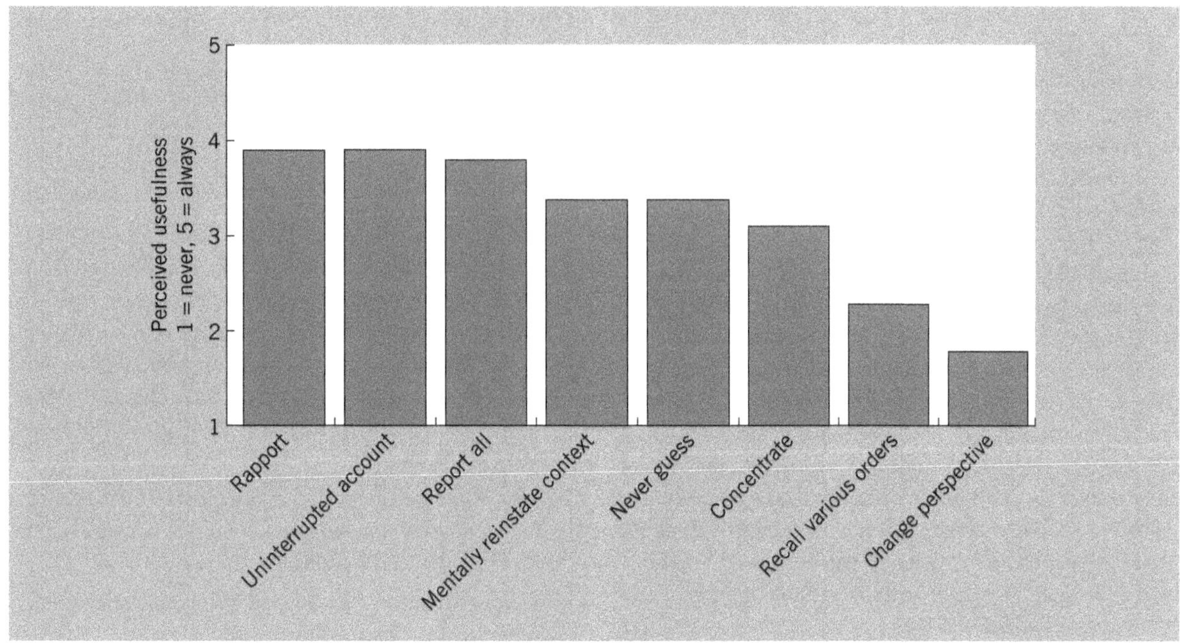

Figure 11.2 Police officers' perceptions of the effectiveness of different aspects of the cognitive interview

reporting everything and focused retrieval. On the other hand, officers trained in structured interviewing techniques (see above) also commonly used context reinstatement and reporting everything. After cognitive interview training, context reinstatement, perspective changing and focused retrieval were used more. Overall, it would appear that despite its successes, there are problems in implementing the cognitive interview entirely.

Nevertheless, in Wright and Alison's (2004) study mentioned above, cognitive interview techniques were rarely used. For example, none of the interviews encouraged the witness to recount events from someone else's perspective and it was virtually unknown for the witness to be encouraged to mentally reconstruct the physical and emotional context of the events they had witnessed. Other cognitive interview techniques were used more frequently. One in five interviews encouraged the interviewees to report any detail or to recall events in any order. Much more common were verbal demonstrations that the interviewing officer was listening to what was being said, giving the interviewee an opportunity to contribute information which had not specifically been asked for, and questioning sequences compatible with the witness's recollections. These were found in over three out of five interviews.

These findings are broadly reflected in more recent research by Dando, Wilcock and Milne (2008). In this, over 200 young non-specialist police officers completed an anonymous self-completion questionnaire concerning the role of the cognitive interview in their day-to-day work. This is, of course, not a cross-section of police officers in general. Many of the components of the cognitive interview were regarded as being effective in their interviewing work. The perceived effectiveness of some of the components of the cognitive interview is shown in Figure 11.2. It is notable, though, that the procedures of recalling in various orders and changing perspective during recall were regarded as the least effective. This pattern was reflected in the officer's frequency of use of these same techniques. Most cognitive interview elements were quite frequently used though, once again, recalling events in various orders and changing the perspective during recall were the least frequently used. They are perhaps the most psychological and least obvious aspects of the cognitive interview which perhaps do not equate with common sense as much as the others. The officers generally lacked confidence in their interviewing training and expressed a desire for more.

There is greater resistance to the use of cognitive interview methods elsewhere. Compo, Gregory and Fisher (2012) describe how in 1999 the US National Institute of Justice introduced guidelines for the conduct of interviews with witnesses based in part on the principles of the cognitive interview (Technical Working Group: Eyewitness Evidence, 1999). These were the first attempt to improve the amount and quality of information obtained from witness interviews in the USA (although cognitive interview principles are long established in the training of police in the UK and elsewhere in the world). These guidelines were well publicised and were issued to every police department along with copies of a training manual. Compo *et al.* obtained a sample of 26 audio-taped real-life interviews involving experienced police detectives in southern Florida. The transcribed interviews were coded for aspects like question type, the use of positive interviewing techniques along the lines of the cognitive interview, and the presence of undesirable techniques in the interview. The findings were rather damning in terms of the influence of the working group's recommendations. The average number of words said by the witnesses in the interviews was over 1200 per interview. About a quarter of these words came in response to open-ended questions. During the interviews, on average, over 60 questions were asked. About 60 per cent were yes/no questions, a quarter closed questions, and just over 10 per cent were open-ended questions calling for narrative-type answers. Only 4 per cent were multiple choice questions in which several possible answers were provided from which the witness would choose. Positive recommendations such as rapport building and context reinstatement rarely appeared in the interviews. In contrast, negative practices, such as using complex questions or interrupting the witness, were common.

Infrequently used positive interviewing techniques included making the interviewer's expectations explicit; context reinstatement; focused concentration; mental imagery and visualisation; encouraging detailed responses; encouraging the witness to take their time and allowing them to say they did not know were extremely rare in the interviews. The only positive techniques that were at all common were positive rapport building and, by far the most common, long pauses. Whether the inclusion of these positive techniques was due to knowledge of the cognitive interview is in some doubt. The use of negative techniques was much more common. In decreasing order of frequency these included suggestive leading questions; interruptions; multiple questions asked in one; and negative rapport building. The lesson from this study remains much as elsewhere. It is difficult to get interviewers to employ with any consistency anything like the full range of cognitive interview procedures. This is not simply a problem in the USA, as we have seen.

The evidence from studies of the impact of the cognitive interview on memory quality is broadly positive. There are numerous studies and too many to consider here individually. The technique of meta-analysis (see Box 4.2) allows trends over a range of studies to be assessed. Kohnken *et al.* (1999) put into such an analysis studies that involved recall (rather than recognition) as the measure of memory. Their main selection requirements for including a study were that a full cognitive interview strategy was employed and that the outcome was compared with some form of standard interview (non-cognitive interview). Over 40 studies were found meeting these criteria:

- Compared with the standard interview, the cognitive interview produced more correct details. Translated into a correlation coefficient, the type of interview correlated 0.4 with the amount of correct details recalled.
- Factors that led to poorer outcomes in the cognitive interview included the length of delay between the witnessing of the event and the interview; how little the interviewees were involved in the events they witnessed; and the research laboratory where the study took place. It was the research carried out in the laboratory of the originators of the technique that had the best effects on recall.
- There were no identifiable differences between the effectiveness of the original cognitive interview and that of the enhanced cognitive interview.
- The cognitive interview tended to increase the number of errors (incorrect recollections) made.
- The type of cognitive interview made a difference. The enhanced cognitive interview was especially error-prone. Again, the research conducted in the laboratory of the originators of the technique tended to get the highest error rates. To clarify matters a little, while increases in errors may be undesirable, an increase in the correct detail is more important as this aids detection. If one calculates the proportion of correct details remembered to the total number of details, the cognitive interview produces a 40 per cent increase in the relative numbers of correct details. It has been recommended for work with children (Milne and Bull, 1994). Milne, Bull, Koehnken and Memom. (1995) showed children to be resistant to leading/suggestive questioning after the cognitive interview (also Hayes and Delamothe, 1997, and Milne and Bull, 1996, for children with mild learning difficulty).

Do psychologists always know best about how to conduct effective interviews? The literature on the cognitive interview tends to offer a one-size-fits-all approach to best practice. The cognitive interview does provide a useful summary of strategies for obtaining good information, especially when interviewing witnesses. But not all police interviews can afford the luxury of the cognitive interview strategies – primarily because of time constraints. The tendency of officers to 'cherry pick' the most convenient aspects of the cognitive interview may be seen in this light. Some cognitive interview strategies are awkward to use in real-life settings. We also lack clear research-based knowledge of exactly what aspects of the cognitive interview work best and in what circumstances. Furthermore, it is beginning to emerge from research that some of the interviewing techniques which psychologists regard as effective may have their limitations. Sex offenders actually seem especially sensitive to negative aspects of police interviews compared to other offenders (in this case murderers) (Holmberg and Christianson, 2002). That is, sex offenders may respond aggressively to the dispassionate but increasingly confrontational approach employed by some police officers. So some researchers, such as Gudjonsson (2006), argue that sex offenders should be interviewed in an understanding or empathic fashion. Oxburgh and Ost (2011) surveyed the literature on the use and efficacy of empathy in interviews with suspected sex offenders. Although there are many reasons for expecting empathy to work well with sex offenders, empirical research on the effectiveness of empathy is actually quite sparse.

Oxburgh, Ost and Cherryman (2012) set about the task of researching the effectiveness of empathy. They chose not to use confession as the outcome measure of effectiveness. Confession alone without further evidence can be weak evidence in court. Instead 'investigation-relevant information' (IRI) was used as the yardstick of a successful interview. The assumption is that the main purpose of the police investigation is to find out what happened; how it happened; who did what; when they did it; and where they did it. Oxburgh *et al.* managed to obtain sample transcripts of real-life police interviews with suspects in child molestation cases in England. They looked at the use of empathy and the influence of question type on the amount of investigation-relevant information generated in the interview. The officers who had carried out the interviews had been trained in methods including the cognitive interview and were experienced in interviewing sex offenders. The analysis of empathy involved the use of the empathy cycle (Barrett-Leonard, 1981). In this approach, the researcher examines the interview for 'empathic opportunities' provided by the offender. This is something that is said which may indicate that the suspect is feeling emotional in some way. The interviewing police officer may then respond with what is termed 'a continuer'. This is a phrase or sentence which acknowledges this emotion and, possibly, provides an opportunity for the suspect to talk further about their feelings. The alternative is that the police interviewer responds to the indications of emotion by using what is termed 'a terminator'. So if the officer replies to the empathic opportunity with a sentence like 'Let's get back to my question' then the empathic opportunity has been lost. This raises the question of whether there were any other expressions of empathy by the police in the interviews other than the ones encouraged by the suspect. There were none. Empathic opportunities were present in only about half of the interviews and, of these, two-thirds were conducted by female officers. The research findings were very clear. The use of good question types (along the lines of the cognitive interview) was related to the amount of investigation-relevant information produced. However, empathy itself did not encourage the provision of more investigation-relevant information by the suspected offender.

Finally, as far as can be ascertained, the use of interviews based on the cognitive interview has rarely been contentious in courts of law, even in the US. For example, Fisher *et al.* (2002), experts in the field, indicate that they are aware of only two court cases in which the use of the cognitive interview was raised as a point of contention. One of these is American and the other British. It is significant that these instances both occurred around the 1990s, when the cognitive interview was new.

Other types of police interview

Leeney and Mueller-Johnson (2012) suggest that police investigations can be conceived as a series of interviews (see Figure 11.3). Often the first contact that a victim or witness has with the police is the phone call they make to report a crime. Their call will be received by a police call centre and the call handler essentially interviews the victim/witness. This 'interview' usually begins with an open question about the reason for the call. Most likely, this will be followed by a sequence of closed questions aimed at getting further information from the victim/witness. The call handler creates a computer-based record of the main aspects of the conversation. A decision will be made on the basis of this about what sort of police action should follow – that is, a police staff controller will allocate an appropriate officer to deal with the incident. Generally, a patrol officer will be sent out to the scene of the incident. Once again, the witness/victim will be interviewed. At the police station, the investigating officer may well interview the victim/witness further. On the basis of the information gathered, a suspect may be interviewed further by the investigating officer. Finally, a decision is made whether or not to process the case through the courts. The centrality of interviewing in all of this makes it clear that interviewing skills are an important part of the quality of police work.

In their research, Leeney and Mueller-Johnson analysed 40 typical phone calls to an English police call centre. Calls are sound recorded in real time and this call centre handles 70,000 emergency and other calls each month. The main research findings were:

- Characteristically, the call handler talked much of the time (44 per cent). This is a higher percentage of the time than would be expected in interviews at the later stages of the investigative process.

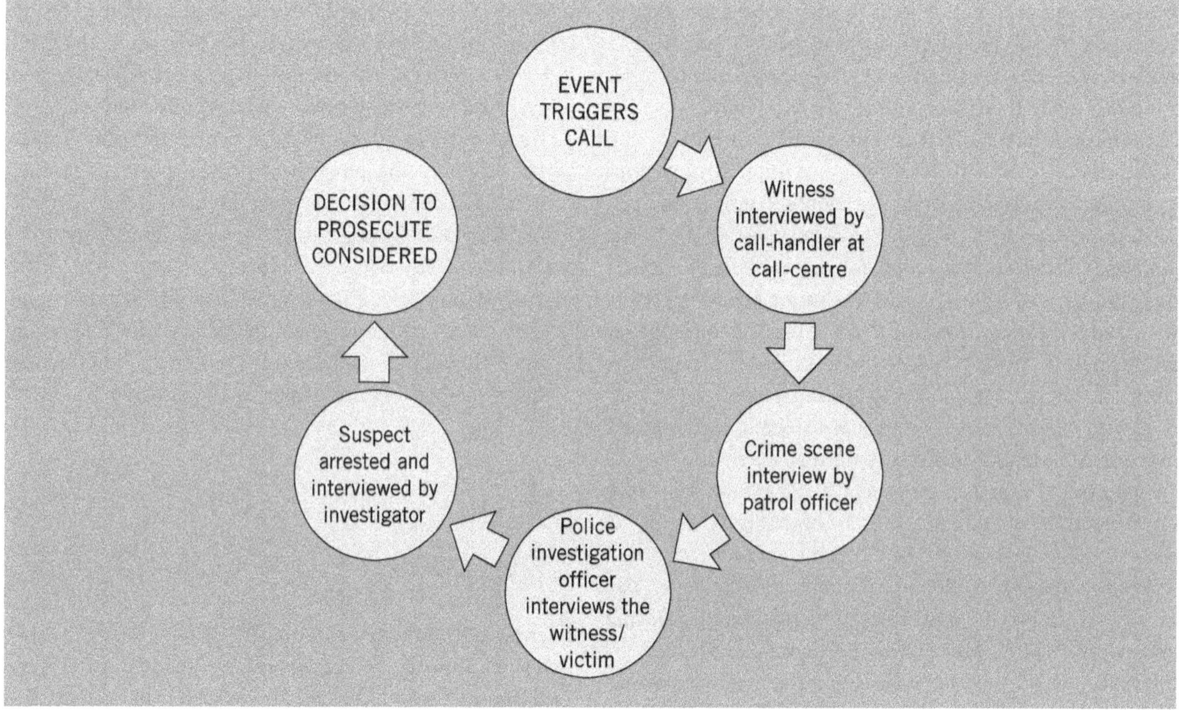

Figure 11.3 The sequence of interviews in a police investigation

- Very few questions asked by the call handler were open questions (about 2 per cent).
- Overwhelmingly, however, 89 per cent of the questions by the call handlers asked were productive in the sense that they gathered information relevant to the complaint to the police. The majority of these were specific 'yes/no' and 'wh. . .' questions (who, what, where, when).
- About 11 per cent of the questions were categorised as unproductive. They consisted of leading, suggestive and forced choice questions.
- The call handler failed to note on the computer record about 22 per cent of the details mentioned by the victim/witness.
- A call script was used in 43 per cent of the interviews. Their use resulted in no loss in the amount of detail collected. Fewer questions in total were asked with a call script and unproductive questions were reduced.
- Errors did creep in: 5 per cent of details were changed by the call handler and 3 per cent of details were added in error. A typical example was when a caller said:

> 'No, he's just punched the light off the ceiling and I've just grabbed the door off him cos he was about to slam the door into me . . .'.

But the call log reads:

> 'HE HAS PUNCHED THE LIGHT OFF THE CEILING AND SLAMMED DOOR ON INF[ORMAN]TS HAND . . .'
>
> (p. 683)

How should we regard these call centre interviews? Quite clearly, they reveal little evidence of cognitive interview techniques being used but nevertheless they seem reasonably effective for their purpose. That is, the fast closed-questioning method employed generated the information necessary to make appropriate decisions about the deployment of staff to the case. But the summarised information entered on the computer can contain substantial errors of both omission and commission. These errors may be partly counterproductive for immediate purposes and at later stages as they provide misinformation. Quite unlike the cognitive interview, the call centre interview strategy is best seen as a form of box ticking. That is, the flurry of 'yes/no' questions asked speedily obtains by-and-large useful information. This information is not always accurate but speed may be more important than complete accuracy. It is not obvious that the cognitive interview would have anything to contribute to call centre interviews. The time-consuming nature of the cognitive interview might make it inappropriate.

Forensic hypnosis

Hypnotic suggestion as a defence against criminal charges has occurred from time to time. There is evidence that the public regard 'automatism' due to hypnosis as the basis for seeing the defendant as less responsible for the offence than a similar crime carried out under duress (Roberts and Wagstaff, 1996). Potential jurors with experience of hypnotism tend to be less inclined to believe that hypnotism had affected individuals' behaviour (Wagstaff, Green and Somers, 1997). Another aspect of hypnosis in forensic contexts is the investigation of crime. This seems to be regarded favourably by the media (McConkey, Roche and Sheehan, 1989). Many psychologists who are experts in the field are less than enthusiastic about forensic hypnosis compared with, say, the cognitive interview (e.g. Wagstaff, 1996). It also needs to be said that hypnosis has had a somewhat chequered history in courts of law. This is documented for the United States by Lynn, Neuschatz and Fite (2002). The use of forensic hypnosis only became popular in the 1960s. Even then it attracted controversy and legal ambivalence about where and when hypnosis is appropriate in testimony. The Hurd rules (or Orne rules after the famous psychologist Martin Orne) may be used as procedural guidelines and safeguards. Briefly they include, according to Lynn *et al.* (2002):

- Qualified expert: the psychiatrist/psychologist conducting the hypnotic session needs to be experienced in the use of hypnosis.
- Independence: the hypnotist should be independent of the major parties in the case (prosecution, investigation and defence) and should not be in the regular employment of any of these parties.
- Recording of information: the information received from any of the major parties should be recorded in writing (or another acceptable form).
- Pre-hypnosis gathering of facts: a full account of the events should be obtained from the witness prior to any hypnotic session. The hypnotist should not influence the description by their interview technique or add details in error to the description.
- All contact between the hypnotist and the 'witness' must be recorded.
- No other persons should be present during the hypnotic suggestion phase – including any pre-hypnotic testing and any interview after hypnosis.

Despite all of this, the American judiciary have tended to accept hypnotically obtained evidence rather than reject it.

While it would appear reasonable to ask 'What is hypnosis?', a clear and consensual answer is not forthcoming (Wagstaff, 1997). To suggest that it is a different or altered mental state compared with normal conscious behaviour is to ignore a lot of evidence. This would imply that people who have not been hypnotised will carry out much the same behaviours and at similar rates as those who have characteristically been seen as showing hypnotic behaviour. The latter viewpoint is the non-state view of hypnotism, which argues that it is not a distinct psychological state but basically normal psychological processes. Its proponents see hypnotic behaviours as the result of less than extraordinary psychological mechanisms such as conformity, compliance and expectations. According to Wagstaff, one of the reasons why hypnosis remains a point of contention is that simply because a non-hypnotised person will do the same things as a hypnotised person (e.g. handle snakes), this does not mean that hypnosis is not a distinct state of consciousness. Any given behaviour may have a number of different determinants, of course.

Not surprisingly, there is an extensive academic research base evaluating hypnotically induced testimony. While hypnotic practitioners may have a different view, the academic consensus tends to doubt the value of hypnosis compared with other methods of improving witness recall (Kebbell and Wagstaff, 1998):

- Inaccurate recall sometimes results from hypnosis, thus decreasing the overall accuracy rate. According to Lynn *et al.* (2002), meta-analyses (see Box 4.2) of a large number of studies have pointed to the conclusion that, although hypnosis increases the amount of material remembered, this is at the cost of also increasing the amount of false recollections. This is much the same criticism as for the enhanced cognitive interview. The reason for this appears to be that hypnotised witnesses simply report more recollections – both inaccurate and accurate. When witnesses are required to recall a fixed number of memories, there is no difference between hypnotised and non-hypnotised individuals in terms of their accuracy.
- Confidence in hypnotised witnesses may increase without commensurate improvements in accuracy. Indeed, they may well have more confidence in what they inaccurately remember under hypnosis than in the accurate information (Lynn *et al.*, 2002). This is of particular concern in the legal context, given the importance of witness confidence in persuading courts of the value of a witness's testimony. Some witnesses appear to be more suggestible to the effects of leading questions and misleading information. Nevertheless, Lynn *et al.* state that 'vulnerability to suggestive information' may be commoner among those who are high or medium on hypnotisability, who tend to report false memories (pseudomemories) much more commonly than those low on hypnotisability. As high and medium hypnotisability is characteristic of most of the population, then

Lynn *et al.* puts the figure of those susceptible to suggestive memory recovery techniques as high as 60 per cent. Even those low on hypnotisability sometimes report false memories.

- It should be considered that the hypnotic interview may be technically better executed than the typical police interview. So memory performance may actually be better, but not because of hypnosis.

It should be stressed that most of the findings are based on generalisations from laboratory situations. Consequently, there may be some reason for caution before hypnotism is rejected entirely by forensic psychologists.

While there are advantages in using hypnotism, it has been suggested that the cognitive interview outperforms it. It is a particular concern to some that hypnotism may have a distorting effect on memory. That does not mean that it invariably does so. Wagstaff (1996) argues that, without detailed knowledge of the process of hypnosis involved in a particular case and other details, it is not possible to draw firm conclusions about the degree of adverse influence of hypnosis on the witness. Others (Berry, Robinson and Bailey, 1999) suggest that hypnosis, irrespective of its effectiveness, may have a variety of drawbacks for practitioners. These include the number of lengthy hypnotic sessions necessary and the possible need for aftercare in cases where the memories emerging in hypnosis are particularly distressing.

Although the value of hypnosis in interviewing has generally not been held to be great, as we have seen, there remains some interest in aspects of it. Hammond, Wagstaff and Cole (2006) studied two techniques which may facilitate the quality of eyewitness memory during interviews. One has its origins in the cognitive interview and the other is essentially the hypnotic method with-out hypnotic states being achieved. Although there is considerable evidence that other techniques may work better, it is true that hypnosis may be better than using no technique at all. Furthermore, in some studies the cognitive interview produces high levels of false recollections which may reach unacceptable levels when poorly trained interviewers are used. However, it is fairly generally accepted that the cognitive interview does not seriously increase the amount of incorrect information recalled nor does it increase susceptibility to leading questions. But there are problems with the cognitive interview – especially since it leads to lengthier interviews and officers need considerable training to become effective at using the techniques. There is evidence that officers may fail to comply with the procedures of the cognitive interview despite being trained in the method. Children seem to have difficulty with cognitive interview techniques and may be error-prone as a consequence. In Hammond *et al.*'s study, both adults and children viewed a video of a crime which involved an armed robbery of a shop selling alcohol. They were then either put through a focused mediation procedure which derives from hypnotic interviewing techniques or the context reinstatement procedure from the cognitive interview. A control group received no memory procedure.

The context reinstatement procedure used asked participants to close their eyes and try to clear their head of other thoughts apart from the crime that the participant had witnessed. They were to picture the events as if they were happening at this very moment in front of their eyes. They were asked to replay the events in their minds as if they were watching a film. They then had to ask themselves questions such as the location of the crime and what the environment surrounding the crime looked like. The instructions continued in this vein and encouraged witnesses to remember as much detail as possible. The focused mediation procedure is similar to hypnotic induction but does not have the context of hypnosis, which itself might be responsible for the false alarms and mistaken confidence that hypnotic methods may create. The focused mediation group were taken through a short focused breathing mediation procedure and were asked to continue these exercises while they completed the memory questionnaire.

The sort of open-ended questions used were: 'Describe the scene where the crime occurred' and 'What did the first robber look like?' whereas the closed questions were, for example: 'What weapon did the second armed robber use?' and 'What was on the shop counter?' Both methods improved memory compared with the controls. This was for both open-ended and closed interview questions. Context reinstatement produced more correct responses though than the focused mediation methods and the context reinstatement group showed higher confidence levels when they gave wrong information in reply to the closed questions.

The conduct of a forensic hypnotic interview itself is problematic. Indeed, in the US, guidelines are available for the conduct of such interviews for legal purposes. The hypnotic interview contains many opportunities for suggestions to be implanted into the interviewee's mind. Scheflin (2012) describes his involvement as an expert witness at the time of the appeal in a case that had involved hypnosis. There were numerous violations of the guidelines. The consequences of these errors may have included the guilty verdict and the long time spent in prison by the suspect in this case.

The historian Alison Winter has painted the story of forensic hypnosis as one ascending in the 1950s and 1960s when hypnotically obtained evidence was first admitted by the US courts, through the 1970s and 1980s when it remained in its ascendency, to its descent from that point on (Winter, 2013). She suggests that its fortune was partly due to the public's understanding of memory as 'something' hidden deep in the mind just waiting to be retrieved just as a motion picture film retrieves images from the past when played through a cine projector. In contrast, psychologists studying memory were overwhelmingly regarding it as a reconstructive process which is characteristically malleable. If a traumatised witness could have their 'fuzzy or unreliable' memories restored to their original state through hypnosis then the problems of collecting evidence would be lessened. This was a point of view which juries would find acceptable. The alternative view that memories lacked permanency and reliability also fed into the idea that forensic hypnotists inadvertently and unknowingly made suggestions to the witness which became enmeshed into the newly exposed memories. The evidence emerging in psychology from experts such as Elizabeth Loftus and Martin Orne of the malleability of not only memory but perception and testimony for that matter led to the demise of forensic hypnosis. These experts, and others, were readily recruited as expert witnesses in court to question the extent to which lay-persons' understanding of memory could be used to evaluate issues to do with the recollection of events. That is, questioning the ability of juries to do this. All of this based on extensive research evidence.

Police as eyewitnesses: how accurate are they?

Common sense suggests that the police, because of their training and experience, should be accurate witnesses. They are, after all, experienced professionals. Whether or not police officers make especially accurate witnesses is probably not the most important issue. Crucial is whether those responsible for making legal decisions believe in the superiority of police eyewitness evidence. A majority of the general public believe that officers are more accurate than people in general (Clifford, 1976). Not only that, but there is evidence that the majority of legal professionals, such as judges, lawyers and police officers, also believe in the superiority of police evidence. To the extent that this leads to greater acceptance of the evidence of the police, then this is a significant social fact.

Forensic and criminal psychologists have argued differently. Police officers and others were asked to identify crimes that had occurred at a street corner depicted in a video. They seemed to be no more skilful than civilians (Ainsworth, 1981). Actually, there were differences in the sense that the police officers were more suspicious that a crime was taking place when, in fact, it was not. Clifford and Richards (1977) found that police officers could give better descriptions than could civilians of a person who stopped them to ask for directions. Briefer encounters than this produced no differences.

In Sweden, Christianson, Karlsson and Persson (1998) studied students, teachers, trainee police and police officers. These groups were shown a series of somewhat gory photographic slides of a violent incident – a man's gloved hand holding a bloody knife; a woman with slashed throat and copious bleeding; and a distant shot of a woman lying bleeding. They were then shown photos of the perpetrator making his escape. The next stage was a filler stage in which participants were shown photographs of faces. The findings were somewhat different from those of earlier studies. In terms of the proportions able to recall information related to the crime slides correctly, serving police officers were clearly superior to the other groups – especially schoolteachers. Specifically, the police tended especially to recall more about the perpetrator. In a line-up/identity parade situation, 'hits' (correct identifications) were highest for police officers. False alarms (the wrong person selected) were little different between any of the groups. Incorrect rejects were the least for the police officers. That is to say, the police officers failed less often to identify the culprit when he was actually in the line-up. Length of service more than age or any other factor tended to be associated with better recall. While memory in general was not superior in police officers, it may be that the emotive nature of the task here worked to the advantage of police participants.

Lindholm, Christianson and Karlsson (1997) wondered whether experience in policing brings with it a knowledge of crime events which facilitates the way in which officers remember events. This would follow from early research indicating that familiarity with a particular domain of memory tends to facilitate recollection of events relevant to that domain. This is possibly because previous experience provides a structure for the organisation of memories. Swedish police recruits, police officers in service and students were shown to be similar on all measures. The memory material consisted of one or other version of a video of a robbery of a grocery store. It takes the viewpoint of an eyewitness who picks up items such as lettuce and spaghetti before arriving at the checkout. At this point, a man runs through the store, threatening the people queuing. He then robs the cashier, slashing his face with a knife. There were two versions of the robbery which differed in terms of the robber's ethnicity – in one case he had a Scandinavian blonde appearance, whereas in the other he had a dark, more southern European appearance. After a short filler task, participants were asked to write down as much detail as they could remember. They were also given a multiple-choice questionnaire concerning: 1) people in the video (such as their clothing) and 2) the sequence of events in the film. A photo line-up and a line-up of the knife from the video and others were also employed. The findings were:

- Police officers were better at identifying the actual knife.
- Police officers were better at identifying relevant crime information.

One possible reason for the superior performance of the serving police officers may be that the stress of the events in the video was less for them because they were used to dealing with violent events in their work. Their lower emotional responses to the video may have provided them with more freedom to form an accurate opinion rather than rely on stereotypes. In the light of the earlier comments, it is worth noting that the police officers seemed less affected by the ethnicity of the offender than the others.

Whether or not features of the training of police officers in Scandinavia contribute to their superior performance over the public is not known. Comparative data collected in similar circumstances from police officers in other parts of the world are simply not yet available.

One might describe police officers, military personnel and emergency service personnel when they are called up to act as witnesses as operational witnesses. What they have in common is the possibility that the challenge and stresses of their jobs together with the mental demands of their active roles may serve to impair recall of the events at a later date. Hope *et al.* (2016) carried out a study in which they compared the memory recall of operational active witnesses with that of non-operational observer witnesses for a scenario which involved an armed perpetrator. Each active witness was twinned with a nonoperational observer. The active witness had a gun and was told to behave in the scenario as if it were an operational setting. The other non-operational observer simply had to observe the events as they progressed. Afterwards, the witnesses completed a free report questionnaire and closed questions. There were no differences between the two types of observer in terms of the accuracy of their recall of things that might have happened while they were being briefed. Things were different when it came to the operational phase. The heart rates of the witnesses were recorded and the active witnesses exhibited a stress-like pattern. The active observers were significantly less accurate about the details of the scenario and this was related to the 'stress' they exhibited. The more stress then the less accurate they were. Although in the scenario a gun remained in the belt of the perpetrator throughout, approximately 20 per cent of the active observers mistakenly claimed that the perpetrator had pointed the gun at them. Nevertheless, it needs to be stressed that overall both groups demonstrated high recall accuracy for both phases of the study. Things were not the same in terms of the closed questions when both groups only answered the questions correctly just over half of the time.

Finally, irrespective of typical memory ability of the average police officer, it has to be remembered that some individuals may be far better at a memory task than other. The London Metropolitan Police appreciates that there is a small number of specialist police officers who are extremely good at recognising suspects from CCTV images and used this to improve performance. Only 0.29 per cent of police and civilian staff working for the Metropolitan police were part of this group of superior recognizers. Sixty-nine percent of identifications made from CCTV were identified by this group of super-recognisers. These are known as super-recognisers and it is a phenomenon well-known to memory researchers. For the most part they are front-line officers and rely on their local knowledge to make the identifications. Davis, Lander, Evansand Jansari (2016) compared a group of police officer super-recognisers with a group of non-police super-recognisers and a group of members of the public who were not super-recognisers. Memory ability was measured using the Famous Face Recognition Test, the Glasgow Face Matching test, the Object (Flowers) Memory Test, the Old/New Unfamiliar Memory Test, and the Unfamiliar Face Memory Array Test. Both recogniser groups were similar in their measured memory ability which in both cases was better than that of members of the general public. So the London Metropolitan police super-recognisers were generally better than the general public on familiar and unfamiliar face memory and unfamiliar face matching. However, they did not differ from the non-police super-recognisers. It was not the case that the super-recognisers did uniformly well in all of the memory tasks – they varied according to the task in question. This may simply reflect the unreliability of the measures though it may be that, for example, some officers have a greater interest in popular culture than others so do especially well on tests involving famous faces. Of course, even the super-recognisers made errors in recognising suspects and this is made worse when the images are poor though recognition remains quite good even in these circumstances.

The police caution

The police caution is the 'warning' that police officers are required to give when arresting a suspect. The current police caution in much of the United Kingdom is: 'You do not have to say anything, but it may harm your defence if you do not mention when questioned something which you later rely on in court. Anything you do say may be given in evidence.' In other words, it informs the suspect about their right to silence, that whatever they say may be treated as evidence, and that relevant information should be supplied at an early stage. Police cautions to suspects vary from legal system to legal system. In the United States, the police caution reminds the suspect of their right to remain silent so as not to incriminate themselves. This, along with the right to a lawyer, forms the basis of informing the suspect of what are known as his or her Miranda rights. Thus British and US systems are rather different. Previously, in the United Kingdom, citizens had the right to remain silent and exercise of this right could not be considered by the court. One key issue, despite the variation among nations and over time, is the extent to which statements of rights are actually understood by the public.

Research going back several decades suggests that the public, in general, has a poor grasp of the meaning of police cautions. For example, a survey of the modern police caution in Britain (Shepherd, Mortimer and Mobaseri, 1995) found that relatively few members of the public could explain the components of the caution (Police and Criminal Evidence Act 1984):

- 'You do not have to say anything.' This was understood by 27 per cent.
- 'But it may harm your defence if you do not mention when questioned something which you later rely on in court.' This was understood by 14 per cent.
- 'Anything you do say may be given in evidence.' This was understood by 34 per cent.

Scotland has a different tradition of caution that does not depend on quite such a precisely prescribed position, although the officer should explain it. Under Scottish law, in order for a statement to be admissible in court it must be made under caution and the information obtained fairly. The meaning of fairness fundamentally depends on the totality of the circumstances surrounding the statement. The basic common law caution is that a suspect is not obliged to say anything but anything she or he does say will be noted and may be used in evidence. (Common law is that established by custom and the decisions of judges. It is law that is not contained as such in statutes or legislation.) There is no standard wording for the police caution in Scotland. Cooke and Philip (1998), however, provide an example of the typical wording that might be used: 'You are going to be asked questions about the assault. You are not bound to answer, but, if you do, your answer will be noted and may be used in evidence. Do you understand?' (Cooke and Philip, 1998, p. 18). Young offenders are known from previous international research to have particular difficulties with the standard cautions. In other words, they do not understand their basic rights. Cook and Philip (1998) studied the comprehensibility of the Scottish caution in a number of ways. One of the things they did was to ask the young offenders to decide whether phrases actually meant the same as the phrase in the caution:

- 'You are not bound to answer' was seen by 59 per cent as equivalent to 'You do not have to say anything until the police ask you questions' though its legal implications are quite different from this.
- The phrase in the caution 'Your answer may be used in evidence' was interpreted by 90 per cent as meaning the same as 'As long as you are polite to the police, whatever you say will not be used against you in court.'

While on the topic of the police caution in Scotland, we should perhaps mention the research by Hughes, Bain, Gilchrist and Boyle (2013) into ways of improving the administration of the caution. They investigated whether providing suspects with a written version of the police caution improved its comprehensibility. A relatively highly educated group and a relatively poorly educated group were used for comparison purposes. These were then allocated at random to one of three conditions – verbal presentation, written presentation, or both written and verbal presentations. The researchers measured comprehension using the same procedure as Cooke and Philips – that is the Scottish Comprehension of Caution Instrument (Cooke and Philips, 1998). Overwhelmingly, 95 per cent of participants claimed to understand the caution used. However, objectively only 5 per cent fully understood the caution delivered verbally. Full understanding was better in the written-only (40 per cent) and the combined verbal/written conditions (35 per cent). For pragmatic reasons, the researchers recommend the dual format of both verbal and written cautions, though the written-only format actually produced the best results. Having the caution in writing may reduce the load on the individual's working memory. It is possible to pace oneself through the text and scan backwards if necessary. No matter how promising the idea of dual presentation is, the bottom line of the study was that less than half of the participants in the research fully understood the caution even when presented in this optimum written/verbal format. That is, a lot of the participants may not have exercised their right to silence simply because they do not understand that this choice is available to them under the terms of the police caution.

The Canadian police caution includes a statement about the right to silence and one about the right to have a lawyer present. The right to silence is as follows: 'You need not say anything. You have nothing to hope from any promise or favour, and nothing to fear from any threat, whether or not you say anything. Anything you do say may be used against you as evidence.' The right to a lawyer is: 'You have the right to retain and instruct counsel without delay. You have the right to immediate access to advice from duty counsel (lawyer) free of charge. You also have the right to subsequently be represented by a lawyer free of charge if you meet the criteria set up by the Newfoundland Legal Aid Commission.' It was found in a study by Eastwood and Snook (2010) that participants in the research (and they included a very substantial minority of individuals on a programme for police recruits as well as students on a range of other degree programmes) poorly understood these two elements of the caution. Only 3 per cent fully understood the right to silence and only 7 per cent fully understood the right to a legal counsel. This is when the caution was read aloud to the participants; they were much better when the statements were in a written form, when 48 per cent and 32 per cent understood the two elements of the caution fully. It did not matter significantly whether police recruits or the others were considered. When the caution was broken down sentence by sentence, it was clear that there were problems with the second sentences in both cases. They were poorly understood and appear to be somewhat complex but nevertheless contain important information in the context of the research. While it would seem that the caution could be presented sentence by sentence in written form in order to optimise its comprehension, this is problematic. Many of those arrested by the police may have literacy limitations so they lack the ability to deal with material in this format. In contrast, the participants in the study were well educated and well versed in reading skills. Clearly what should be done is far from obvious or straightforward.

Whether or not psychologists could develop phraseology that would improve matters in any of these jurisdictions is a moot point if the precise legal implications of the caution are to remain unchanged. Nevertheless, the bottom line is that offenders in the normal intelligence range often have difficulty understanding their legal rights.

Other studies show similar findings. For example, the UK Police and Criminal Evidence codes of practice are available at police stations. They supplement the statutory verbal and written material. Various matters are covered. These include the rules governing detention. Very few arrestees actually ask to see the code of practice. When they do, based on the observations of Joyce (1993), they read a passage or two and then discard the booklet. Readability of text can be analysed. For example, the average sentence length is a useful index. One example of this approach is the Flesch Index. This is the average sentence length adjusted by the average number of syllables in a word. Joyce took 40 passages from the code. Overwhelmingly, they fell in the 'fairly difficult' to 'very difficult' range. An IQ in the range above average to above 126 is needed in order to comprehend material of this level of difficulty. What is the readability of the paragraph you are reading? It is in the 'fairly difficult' range. This means that this paragraph is easier to read than nearly all of the samples of text in Joyce's study!

In some countries, such as England and Wales, there is no longer a right to remain silent with no possibility of legal consequences. In the United States, the constitution gives suspects 1) the right of silence, 2) the assurance that this silence may not be used against them, 3) the right to have a lawyer, 4) the assurance that the state will pay for the lawyer if they cannot afford one, and 5) that they have a right to become silent at any stage. These are known as the Miranda rights in the US. In these circumstances, the issue of understanding the police caution becomes even more salient. Kassin and Norwick (2004) report an intriguing laboratory study in which groups of 'suspects' were subjected to different styles of interviewing by a 'detective', including sympathetic and hostile styles. The 'detective' was trying to get the 'suspect' to forego their Miranda rights so that more evidence could be obtained which would be legitimate in court. The style of interview actually made no difference of note to the decision to waive one's Miranda rights. However, the researchers had included a guilty–innocent dimension into the study. Some participants 'stole' money from a nearby teaching laboratory, others did not. Actually, they had received instructions about what to do from the experimenters. Nevertheless, some were 'guilty' because they had taken the money on instruction and others were 'innocent' because they had not taken the money. When put under some pressure by the 'detective', it was found that the 'innocent' group were more likely to waive their Miranda rights than the 'guilty' group. Kassin and Norwick (2004) argue that Miranda warnings may not protect the most vulnerable from the actions of the police. False confession is not uncommon and we need to understand the process that includes waiving Miranda rights. One important case involved an 18-year-old who confessed to the murder of his mother and was imprisoned until independent evidence showed that he could not have possibly committed the crime. When asked why he did not remain silent during the interview, he said: 'I hadn't done anything wrong and I felt that only a criminal really needed an attorney, and this was all going to come out in the wash' (reported in Kassin and Norwick, 2004, p. 218). Thus the innocent may be put at risk.

Rogers, Fiduccia, Drogin, Steadham, Clark and Cramer (2013) wondered whether Miranda warnings had outlived their usefulness since if the public are well versed in their rights then the warning just becomes a routine ritual rather than serving a useful purpose. Rogers *et al.* used samples taken from a pool of potential jurors. They were asked to report the Miranda warning and then given questions which tapped their actual knowledge and misknowledge of their Miranda rights and police activities having a bearing on Miranda rights. The final Miranda right (the right to return to silence at any stage of the interrogation) was rarely recalled. One-third of the participants claimed to be truly uninformed about their Miranda rights. They tended to perform poorly on a measure of misconceptions about one's Miranda rights (such as agreeing with the statement 'Your family pays if the court appoints you a lawyer'. Even those who claimed to be informed about their Miranda rights did badly on the right to free lawyer support and the continuing nature of their right to remain silent at any stage. Rogers *et al.* concluded that there was still a need for Miranda warnings. Of course, we have all heard police cautions in the mass media so one function of giving the caution might be that it helps rectify misconceptions that the individual might have. Rogers, Fiduccia, Robinson, Steadham and Drogin (2013) repeatedly presented Miranda warnings to a group of participants. Over two-thirds did not show any tangible improvement in that their previous misconceptions were not corrected.

One final point. It is worthwhile noting that the issue of the police caution (Miranda warning) in the USA has led to some difficult courtroom decisions. While the police may have a vested interest in encouraging suspects to abandon their rights, it remains important that those arrested by the police need to be treated fairly by the system in terms of their rights. The Grisso Tests for Assessing Understanding and Appreciation of Miranda Warnings are psychologically based methods which may help to assess an individual's likely ability to understand and appreciate the significance of the Miranda warning (Frumkin, Lally and Sexton 2012).

Use of lethal force

In the United States in 2016, 135 police officers died in the line of duty, of which about half were killed by guns (Chan, 2016). Nevertheless, the police are more likely to kill than to be killed (Blau, 1994). US police killed more than 1000 civilians in 2015 (*The Guardian*, 2015). The officers were not killed by deranged individuals. Killers of police according to Blau, are not 'mad psychopaths' but, generally, criminals attempting to escape a crime scene. So a strong cue to danger for a police officer is when the suspect attempts to escape arrest. The following may be particularly dangerous:

- suspects who have a history of dangerousness;
- suspects who associate with people with a history of dangerousness;
- suspects who live or work in situations or settings where violent and dangerous events are likely to occur.

There is a buffer zone which, when breached, greatly increases the likelihood that the suspect will react violently (Blau, 1994). A dangerous stimulus moving from 4 ft (1.2 m) to closer is especially likely to produce a dangerous response in the officer.

The costs of being involved in armed violence as a victim are not merely personal. In the United States, four-fifths of police officers involved in shooting incidents left their police department consequently. Police officers who get involved in shooting incidents are not a random sample of officers. Research has shown that they tend to show certain characteristics. McElvain and Kposowa (2008) studied nearly 200 shooting incidents over a 15-year period which involved more than 300 officers in a particular Californian sheriff's department. The researchers obtained data concerning the shootings and the officers involved from the department. Almost all of the shooting incidents happened while the officer was on duty. The researchers selected a comparison group of officers who had *not* been involved in a shooting incident during that period. Among their findings were:

- College-educated officers were about 40 per cent less likely to be involved in a shooting.
- Female officers were only one-third as likely as male officers to be involved in a shooting.
- Lower-ranking officers were more at risk of being involved than higher-ranking ones.
- Older officers were substantially less likely to be involved in a shooting.
- Those officers that had previously been involved in shootings were about 50 per cent more likely to be involved in another shooting incident.

Of course, very different patterns may exist in other countries. This is especially so for countries with lower levels of violence in the community in general, or those where the police are not normally armed. Surprisingly, figures on the use of force in police work, such as when making an arrest, are not always available. For example, Rappert (2002) explains that such figures were unavailable for the United Kingdom. Instead, he had to rely on the data collection initiative of a particular UK police force to provide any systematic data. (The United Kingdom has no national police force.) In one area, force was used in 6 per cent of arrests. This contrasts with a figure of almost 20 per cent for arrests in the United States. In the British data, evidence was found that the arresting officers sustained injuries in about 16 per cent of these instances. In other words, in roughly 1 per cent of arrests police officers sustain an injury. Rappert puts the situation this way: 'As the police patrol the boundaries of respectability in society, the resort to the use of force is always a possibility' (p. 690). In the United Kingdom, *armed response unit* personnel are likely to be called in when there is a critical incident that appears to be sufficiently dangerous. Such officers are likely to drive or be driven at high speeds to the incident. Barton, Vrij and Bull (2000a,b) argued that this sort of situation might have potential for encouraging violent responses based on the *excitation transfer theory* of aggression (Zillmann, 1979, 1982). Basically, this proposes that:

- emotional events are physiologically arousing;
- we become aware of physiological arousal from cues such as heart rate, breathing getting heavier and sweatiness;
- this internal state is generally labelled by us according to the environmental stimuli available at the time;
- failure to recognise the true cause of the emotional arousal will result in other factors being identified as the cause of the emotion.

This is relevant to the work of the armed response unit since their rapid travel to the scene of the incident is physiologically arousing. If the officer attributes his or her physiological arousal to the suspect at the incident, this may well result in their acts being labelled differently.

Previous research has shown the efficiency of 'incident' simulators to research in this area. Generally, officers are very accurate in their marksmanship when they appropriately evaluate the situation as being a risk to themselves or others. When they *inappropriately* decide to shoot then their accuracy is relatively poor (Doerner and Ho, 1994). In their study, Barton *et al.* (2000a,b) had officers drive either at normal patrol speeds or at a high 'emergency' speed. Normal driving should produce less physiological arousal than high-speed driving. Based on the theory, it might be predicted that high-speed driving may produce physiological responses that may or may not be identified correctly as being the consequence of the high speed of driving. The officers were then exposed to one of two simulated incidents. In one case they would be justified to shoot under British law. In the other case shooting would not be justified:

- Shooting justified: they enter a shopping centre and see the suspect kneeling by cash machines picking up money. Following a warning of 'armed police' the suspect fires a handgun at the officer.
- The unjustified situation: the suspect pulls a small child to his body as protection, then releases the child, lifts a firearm and places it on the table and surrenders.

The findings were:

- The speed of travel affected the officers' self-rated willingness to shoot.
- Another variable known as *field dependence* (Witkin and Goodenough, 1981) (this is, essentially, the perceptual dependency of the individual on the environment around them) affected outcomes where the shooting was justified. Field-dependent officers rated themselves as more likely to shoot the suspect.

The issue of the racial bias in the use of deadly force has been a dominant theme especially in relation to the American police. Police killings of black suspects has produced considerable response from the public and has led to protests and organisations such as 'Black Lives Matter'. Quite clearly this is a difficult area for researchers to investigate although the basic finding that disproportionately more black people are shot by the police is generally accepted. The question of whether this is the result of black people being a greater threat or because of police racial bias demands difficult methodologies. James, Klinger and Vila (2014) argue that previous research in this area is problematic since it lacked a realistic setting.

The impact of their work on the police

Practices will vary in different police organisations, but one British police force has experimented with a system of requiring members of its staff and officers to attend a 'counselling' session with an independent counsellor on a twice-yearly basis. This is recognition that stress is an important adverse factor on police performance. Karlsson and Christianson (1999) asked Swedish police officers to describe the most stressful and traumatic event that had happened to them. Commonest among the stressful/traumatic policing episodes were:

- being threatened with a weapon;
- complex investigations requiring them to deal with relatives of the victim and handle the press, and being under pressure to find the perpetrator;
- homicides and suicides;
- notifying next of kin about deaths;
- taking children into custody;
- traffic accidents, especially being the first to arrive at deaths and bad injuries.

Armed threats and traffic accidents accounted equally for a total of about half the events reported. Their memory for the events was highest for suicide but each of the other categories of events was not much different. The commonest consequences of the event were 22 per cent of officers felt depressed; 19 per cent felt fear when reminded of the event; and 15 per cent mentioned feelings of guilt. Tension, sleeping problems, nightmares and overreacting were also included.

Just what is the impact of stress in police work? Police officers in Baltimore, USA were studied by Gershon, Barocas, Canton, Li and Vlahov (2009). The main components of their analysis can be seen in Figure 11.4. In

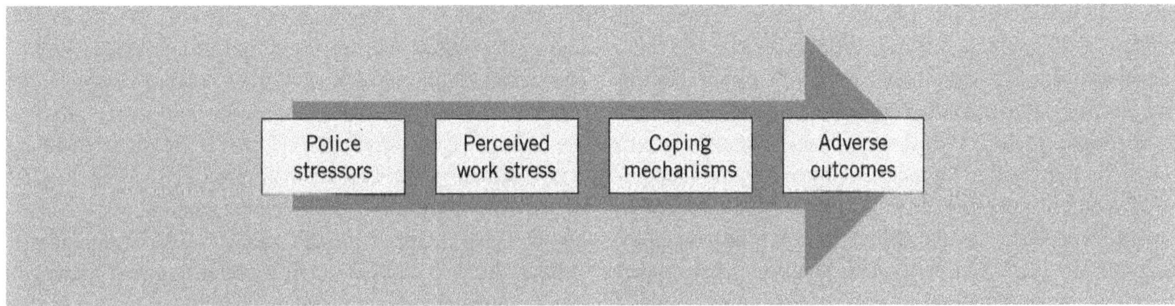

Figure 11.4 A model for the effects of police stress

this, stressful things which are perceived by the individual as stressful may have their influence modified by coping mechanisms, though they may nevertheless lead to negative consequences. The main components of this model are:

- *Perceived stress:* The range of self-perceived stressors included the categories (a) critical incidents (e.g. violent arrests and shooting suspects); (b) workplace unfairness; (c) lack of cooperation from colleagues; and (d) job dissatisfaction. The sorts of individual questions used to measure perceived stress included 'I want to withdraw from constant demands on my time and energy at work' and 'I think that I am not as effective at work as I should be.' Exposure to critical incidents had the highest rating as a stressor, followed by job dissatisfaction – 93 per cent of officers in the survey reported exposure to critical incidents. The greatest emotional impact was attending police funerals (64 per cent mentioned this); being subjected to an internal affairs investigation at work (52 per cent); and shooting someone in the line of duty (32 per cent).
- *Coping strategies:* Four different coping strategies were measured: (a) cognitive coping strategies, such as making a plan of action and carrying it out; (b) faith-based coping strategies, such as relying on religious faith to get through a difficult time; (c) avoidance coping strategies, such as acting as if nothing is bothering you; and (d) negative behaviour coping strategies, such as drinking, smoking and acting aggressively. Common coping strategies among the police officers were making a plan of action and following through (45 per cent); talking to family members or professionals when they felt stressed (39 per cent); and faith-based include relying on their faith in God (39 per cent); and praying (32 per cent). Less common were avoidance coping methods including acting as if nothing was bothering them when they were actually feeling stressed (27 per cent) and negative strategies such as smoking more than usual (12 per cent).
- *Adverse outcomes:* Measured in terms of a checklist including aggressive behaviour, anxiety, burnout, depression, interpersonal family conflict, post-traumatic stress symptoms and somatisation. Among the adverse items, the highest levels were for the post-traumatic stress symptoms, burnout, depression, somatisation and anxiety in that order. Work stress was particularly associated with feeling tired at work despite adequate sleep (84 per cent); feeling moody or irritable or impatient about small things (70 per cent); and feeling that their efficiency at work was not what it could be (63 per cent). The most commonly reported individual psychological symptoms were low energy (81 per cent); feeling blue (64 per cent); headaches and pressure in the head (58 per cent); self-blame (47 per cent); stomach pains (47 per cent); no interest in things (46 per cent); and pains or pounding in the chest (46 per cent). Post-traumatic symptoms included having intrusive/recurrent thoughts, memories or dreams about distressing work events (33 per cent) and feeling detached from people and activities that were believed to be related to the stressful events (24 per cent).

What is notable about the findings from this study is that, of the five major categories of stressors, the strongest relationships with stress were for common workplace issues such as the lack of fairness of the organisation and job satisfaction. That is, critical incidents and the like were less important than the general workplace environment. Of the psychological adverse outcomes, depression, somatisation and post-traumatic stress symptoms were stably related to stress when demographic and similar variables were controlled. Physiological and behavioural outcomes were all associated with perceived work stress. Positive coping behaviours such as problem solving and faith were predictive of lower levels of perceived stress, whereas negative and avoidant coping strategies were associated with more stress.

The finding that relatively routine workplace issues are particularly stressful led Garner (2008) into an attempt to help officers deal with such problems. Survey research had indicated to Garner that criticism from others in the workplace was difficult to deal with. Not only that, but those in a supervisory role indicated that they experienced extra stress when they had to evaluate or hand out criticism to others. To counter this, Garner developed a stress-inoculation training programme for police officers which tried to help officers deal with the criticism issue, among other things. It involved: 1) a conceptual phase which included examining coping skills and cognitive restructuring; 2) skills acquisition, including relaxation training; and 3) application and follow-through, including role-playing scenarios etc. Officers following this programme reported that (a) they were better at dealing with criticism in relevant situations; (b) they felt less general job stress; and (c) they had fewer health complaints compared to a control group which did not go through the programme. Interestingly, the ratings of supervisors about interpersonal performance and conflict handling were higher for the officers who went through this programme.

Police work is built around working teams that are, to a degree, mutually interdependent. Consequently, it is wrong to regard police officers solely as individuals acting in isolation. The problems of a stressed-out or underperforming colleague are actually shared by the team in that the team has to cover for the inadequacies of their colleague, which will extend stress far beyond the individual officer.

Generally, the officers felt a lack of support from superiors and a lack of preparation for what they were going to experience. It was brushed aside with a joke – one should be able to deal with that sort of thing. Significantly, half mentioned fellow workers; half mentioned close family members; a quarter mentioned neighbours, friends and relatives; and about a sixth mentioned other persons at the event as those who helped with the effects of the stressful events. Doctors, psychologists and priests were mentioned by about 1 in 20. A tenth reported that nobody had helped them.

A further study compared ratings of the impact of a particular event ten months and four-and-a-half years after the event. The event was a mass shooting incident. Things remained fairly stable in terms of emotional impact – if anything getting worse or more negative with time (Karlsson and Christianson, 1999).

This brings us to the question of the impact of traumatic incidents on the officers involved. It is obvious that some of the situations faced by the police during their work are horrific. Equally, a great deal of police work involves following largely bureaucratic procedures. According to Rallings (2002), there is little direct information about the impact on the police of the offences they come across. The way in which the media tend to cover police work encourages the impression that their work is dangerous, morbid and gruesome. As a consequence, the idea is encouraged that police officers are resilient and immune to any psychological consequences that their work may have on them. Some describe this as the impervious perspective or the John Wayne syndrome. However, there is another, more realistic, view which construes police officers as hidden victims suffering from much the same adverse consequences that members of the public would experience in similar circumstances but their problems go unrecognised. Post-traumatic stress disorder (PTSD), an extreme and debilitating response to severe trauma, is to be found within the police at a prevalence rate of about 7 per cent. (See Chapter 4 for a detailed discussion of PTSD.) This is probably a fraction of the figure that would be achieved if exposure to traumatic events invariably led to PTSD. There are far higher rates of exposure than cases in which particular events lead to PTSD, which implies that other, mediating factors may be at work. Among these factors would be good social support at home and at work.

Shooting incidents produce quite profound emotional reactions in the majority of officers. The typical reports are of crying, depression, anger, elation, nightmares, flashbacks of the incidents, bodily and emotional disturbances, loss of interest in work. Some officers had problems with readjusting to work on the streets after a shooting incident. The sorts of incident that seem to be most associated with psychological symptoms are those in which the officer is subjected to violence; a colleague dies; children are dead; sudden deaths and mutilated bodies or decomposed ones. In this sort of study, the officers nominate the most traumatic work-related event that they have experienced. These can then be compared with the symptoms of trauma experienced by the officers.

Two recommendations made by Rallings are particularly important:

- It may be possible to focus resources on affected officers rather than all officers, following a traumatic policing episode. By examining the immediate effects on physiology, emotion and mental dissociative responses then the at-risk personnel may be identified.
- Workplace characteristics have an impact on whether or not a traumatic event will lead to psychological trauma. So workplaces should be perceived by officers as supportive; morale should be good; and communications in the workplace should be improved.

There have been suggestions that vicarious traumatisation may affect an officer's ability to behave in a seemingly neutral manner when interviewing child victims. Oxburgh, Williamson and Ost (2006) researched the use of emotional language by police officers who interview both a child victim and the suspect during a child sexual abuse investigation. The prior expectation of the researchers was that officers who had interviewed the victim before they interviewed the offender typically would use more emotional language during their interview with the offender. It was also predicted that the amount of emotional language used would depend on the gender of the interviewer as well as the type of offence. For example, there might be differences between intrafamilial offenders compared with extrafamilial offenders. Transcripts were obtained from police forces but an analysis of the numbers of negative emotional utterances expressing contempt, disgust and anger indicated that those who had *not* interviewed the child before tended to use this emotional language more. Gender and type of offence made no significant difference. However, one limitation of the study was that very few officers had received specialised training to deal with child sexual abuse cases. One explanation of the findings is that the experience with the child is less emotional in fact than the general view of the effects of abuse on children. Thus those who did not interview the children would have the highest levels of emotion.

Emotional labour (Hochschild, 1983) refers to the process by which all of us manage our emotions as part of our working lives. Display rules are the expectations, implicit or explicit, governing emotional display at work. In most jobs, the display rules confine emotional expression to positive emotions. However, naturally, sometimes how an employee feels emotionally will not be positive at all. Thus there is a state of emotional dissonance between the two. Problems at home may lead to negative emotions but, at work, the requirement generally is for a display of positive emotions. There are many situations in which individuals may, as part of their role, need to express negative emotions. This is not normally in relation to the general public but to subordinates who may, for example, need to be reprimanded in some way. The police force seems to require more negative emotion display in daily interactions between its members than is common in other workplaces. Positive emotional expression is expected in police work with the community, for example. So it can be said that the police force demands a variety of positive and negative emotional expression which changes continually. This requires officers to know when a particular strategy is needed.

Usually two factors are held to describe the emotional labour of people whose work involves significant amounts of interpersonal contact with the public:

- *Surface acting:* This refers to the masking/hiding of the emotions one feels so as to meet the rules of emotional display that govern conduct in the work environment. This does nothing to reduce emotional dissonance, of course, and, according to research, the outcome is that surface acting leads to emotional exhaustion.
- *Deep acting:* This involves modifying one's emotions to meet the expectations of emotional display in that particular work environment. This requires that an effort is made to experience workplace-appropriate emotions. This might be achieved by focusing on the work situation to the exclusion of other difficulties or by reappraising the situation entirely. In effect, emotions are brought in line with what is expected in the workplace. As a consequence, deep acting protects against emotional exhaustion.

As might be expected, researchers have studied the negative psychological consequences of such emotion regulation strategies. These include burnout (i.e. the experience of chronic exhaustion and loss of interest especially in relation to one's job). It has also been suggested, however, that deep acting leads to a better identification with one's work. So for example, the need of a job change may be felt less soon. But more is involved than merely presenting a positive face in organisations. The research by Larissa, Grawitch and Trares (2009) involved nearly 300 officers from a US police department. The researchers distributed a survey to all employees although just over a fifth replied. An established questionnaire assessing surface and deep acting was adapted for the study. This included items such as officers pretending to have negative feelings that they don't really have, pretending to have positive feelings that they don't really have, and so forth. Emotional exhaustion was measured by three items asking how drained their work makes them feel, how burned out their work makes them feel, and how used up they felt at the end of the day. The researchers' analysis of the data suggested that there were three different components, not two, to the work of police officers. These are illustrated in Figure 11.5. As is commonly found, surface acting predicts emotional exhaustion. However, it was force-oriented deep acting (not service-oriented deep acting oriented towards the general public) which was associated with greater job involvement. Force-oriented deep acting involves negative emotions that have to be expressed within the police force.

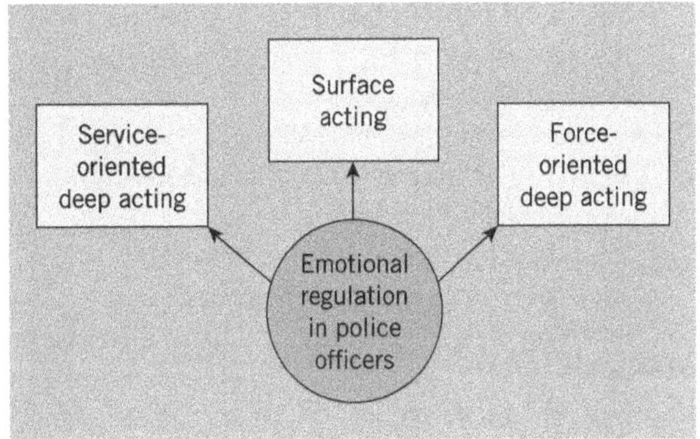

Figure 11.5 The components of emotional regulation in police officers

BOX 11.2 Forensic psychology in action

Why investigations go wrong

A Swedish man, Joy Rahman, was convicted of the murder of an elderly Swedish woman but the verdict was reversed by the Court of Appeal (Ask and Granhag, 2005). Rahman was identified as the prime suspect because he had bought coffee at the same time and place as two bottles of a particular brand of cigarette-lighter fuel were sold. The fuel was used in an attempt to burn the victim's body. The victim had been killed using the decorative edging from a Christmas decoration which was believed to have come from the home of a woman that Rahman had visited on the day of the murder. The appeal was granted on the basis that: 1) it had not been established that he had bought the lighter fuel or that it was the same as that found at the crime scene and (2) it had not been established that the murder weapon had been taken from the other woman's home that day or that no one else but Rahman could possibly have taken it.

This case offers some support for the idea that 1) the police, when conducting an investigation, are driven by theories which guide the process and evaluations of the evidence etc., and 2) the working hypotheses used by the police are not always firmly based on the facts of the case.

Causal hypotheses and theories are common in human thinking (Pennington and Hastie, 1986, 1988, 1992). Jurors, for example, tend to incorporate evidence into coherent memory structures which equate to causal explanations. The well-known processes which may affect police thinking include the following:

- Confirmation bias is a well-known and well-established phenomenon which occurs throughout human thinking. The term refers to the tendency for people to seek information which supports their existing beliefs and opinions.
- People also interpret information in a way which supports their existing beliefs and tend to avoid anything which contradicts their beliefs – things which might support alternative explanations.
- When given the opportunity to search for new information, people tend to go for information which is more likely to confirm their beliefs and also tend to interpret new information in ways which support their existing beliefs.

Evidence supporting this can be seen in the role of confirmation bias in the interviewing of suspects (Hill, Memon and McGeorge, 2008). Scottish university students acted as 'interviewers' whose task was to formulate questions to ask in order to assess the guilt of a suspect. One group of 'interviewers' were led to assume that there was a high likelihood that their interviewee was guilty, whereas the other group were led to assume that their interviewee was more likely to be innocent. The 'interviewers' read a resumé of the events in which two people were completing intelligence tests in the same room. They were being supervised by the researcher's assistant, who eventually left the room for a few minutes. The assistant had left the answer sheet for the IQ test on the desk. When the researcher's assistant returned, the answer sheet had been moved. In the guilty expectation version the 'interviewers' were told that most (80 per cent) of people cheat in these circumstances (i.e. there was a high presumption of guilt), whereas in the innocent expectation version the 'interviewers' were told that most people (80 per cent) do *not* cheat (i.e. there is a low presumption of guilt). The 'interviewers' were asked individually to formulate ten questions to help them to determine whether or not cheating had occurred. A team of evaluators rated the questions on a scale from 'extremely presumptive of innocence' to 'extremely presumptive of guilt'. Much as the researchers expected, where there was a presumption of guilt then the questions formulated were presumptive of guilt; where there was a presumption of innocence then the questions formulated reflected this presumption.

Powell, Hughes-Scholes and Sharman (2012) extended this argument somewhat by showing how confirmation bias may be built into police interviews because of poor interviewing techniques. Their basic premise is that leading questions in interviews, because they point towards the sort of answer the interviewer expects, provide a mechanism by which confirmation bias can work in practice. In their study, they established the ability of Australian police interviewers to keep with an open question format when requested to do so. Nearly two-thirds were female officers. All of the participating officers had completed some special training in child interviewing and were authorised to do so within the police service. The interviewers were provided with a certain amount of background information about a hypothetical child abuse investigation just prior to conducting the interview with the child. No leading information was provided at any of the interview's stages. The interviewee was an adult playing the part of a child, but this procedure is known to work well as a training exercise. The interviewers were instructed by the researchers to start the interview stage with the substantive question 'Can you tell me what you're here to talk about today?' They then were required to obtain accurate, detailed information using open-ended questions. As might be expected, even experience police officers varied in their ability to do this. This assessment phase was simply there to measure each officer's ability to stick to best practice interview guidelines when asked to do so. Some, of course, would use a lot of closed-format questions against the instructions and best policy.

The main stage of the research involved each police officer interviewing a child of about five to eight years. Each officer interviewed a different child. The set-up of this stage of the research was that a special event had happened at the child's school. This was known as the Deakin Activities. There were a number of activities including some key ones: 1) a story about an elephant; 2) interaction with a koala bear puppet; and 3) finding a sticker by surprise. However, each child only experienced two out of the three events. Which event was the non-experienced one was varied from child to child. These were the events that the police officers interviewed the children about just one week later. The police officers were split into two different groups. One group received biasing information and the other group did not. The non-biased instruction involved the officers being told that a lady had gone to the school and carried out the Deakin Activities – they were told that there were specific activities but not what they were. For the biased condition, the interviewers were provided with biasing information about the activities which may or may not have occurred. So these officers actually had a mixture of correct and incorrect information since some of the information was incorrect, of course, because the children did not do one of the activities. Each officer then interviewed one child. The researchers analysed their data by counting the numbers of open questions and the number of specific questions separately. Open questions were defined as ones which encouraged the child to give elaborate responses and did nothing to indicate the sort of information. The numbers of open versus specific questions were counted separately. The specific questions were largely of the why, what, where, and when sort plus some 'yes/no' answer questions. Leading questions were also assessed and these were defined as those which included detail which the child had not given the interviewer.

The findings overall were that the best interviewers at the initial assessment, who were capable of sticking to the open question format, showed less confirmation bias in the interviews. That is, compared to poorer interviewers, they asked more open questions and fewer leading questions if they had received the biasing information. A poor interviewer, then, essentially biased their questioning in a way which meant that they got what they wanted to hear. The better interviewers asked the same proportion of open and leading questions, irrespective of the biasing information. That indicates that even the best interviewers had difficulty avoiding using leading questions.

Of course, in the context of a police investigation, the risk is that these normal, everyday cognitive processes work against the interests of the innocent suspect and affect the quality of the investigation in other ways. The concept of 'the need for cognitive closure' may also play a role, since police officers can be under considerable time pressure to complete an investigation. It can be measured by statements such as 'I don't like situations that are uncertain' and 'I usually make important decisions quickly and confidently.'

In an experiment, police officers were given a vignette by Ask and Granhag (2005) about a crime in which *either* an alternative suspect was indicated as a possibility *or* a plausible motive for the murder was presented. Half of the participants were given each version. Thus, one mindset was the guilt of the potential culprit whereas the other was of the possibility of another potential culprit. This manipulation was followed by a 20-item list of things noted in the preliminary investigation of the murder. Some of these things were compatible with one or other of the different viewpoints on the crime and others were incompatible with them. There was only mixed support for the hypotheses. Police officers' guilty ratings were in line with the hypothesis. Participants with a high need for closure tended to be less likely to notice that observations were inconsistent with the condition of the study.

Main points

- Psychologists from a wide variety of backgrounds have contributed to our understanding of the police and their work. It is particularly important to note that the police as organisational cultures tend to have particular attitudes and values, some of which may make the problems of a psychologist working in this context more difficult. It is commonly held that the police have a somewhat macho culture, which may make helping them deal with stress or certain groups difficult.
- A major area where psychological research and theory has contributed to our understanding of the work of the police is in terms of interviewing techniques. Of particular note in this context is the enhanced cognitive interview, which is part of the training of some police officers. The enhanced cognitive interview takes concepts and techniques from laboratory studies of memory and communications psychology in an attempt to improve interviewing of eyewitnesses. The research evidence tends to point to the superiority of the enhanced cognitive interview in extracting good-quality, accurate memories of the eyewitnessed events, despite an increased risk of generating inaccurate memories. There is generally little support for the use of forensic hypnosis as it is felt that there are no respects in which it is superior to the enhanced cognitive interview.
- Stress affects police work in a number of ways. As in any other work organisation, aspects of the bureaucratic structure may add to felt stress levels. Stress is relevant to police work in ways that are not characteristic of other organisations. In particular, police work involves being involved in highly stressful situations such as the aftermath of crimes or suicides, for example. The requirement sometimes to use lethal force and the risk of being victims of lethal force are also characteristics of police organisations not shared by other organisations. Features of the organisation may make dealing with the stress more difficult, such as the macho-ness of police culture and attitudes towards the working team. However, the police may be better able to perform under stress than others since there is some evidence that they make better eyewitnesses of stressful events than the general public.

Further reading

The following cover important topics in relation to policing, including those covered in later chapters in this book:

Bull, R. (ed.) (2014) *Investigative Interviewing* New York: Springer.

Kebbell, M.R. and Davies, G.M. (eds) (2006) *Practical Psychology for Forensic Investigations and Prosecutions* Chichester: John Wiley.

Kitaeff, J. (ed.) (2011) *Handbook of Police Psychology* Abingdon: Routledge Academic.

Chapter 12

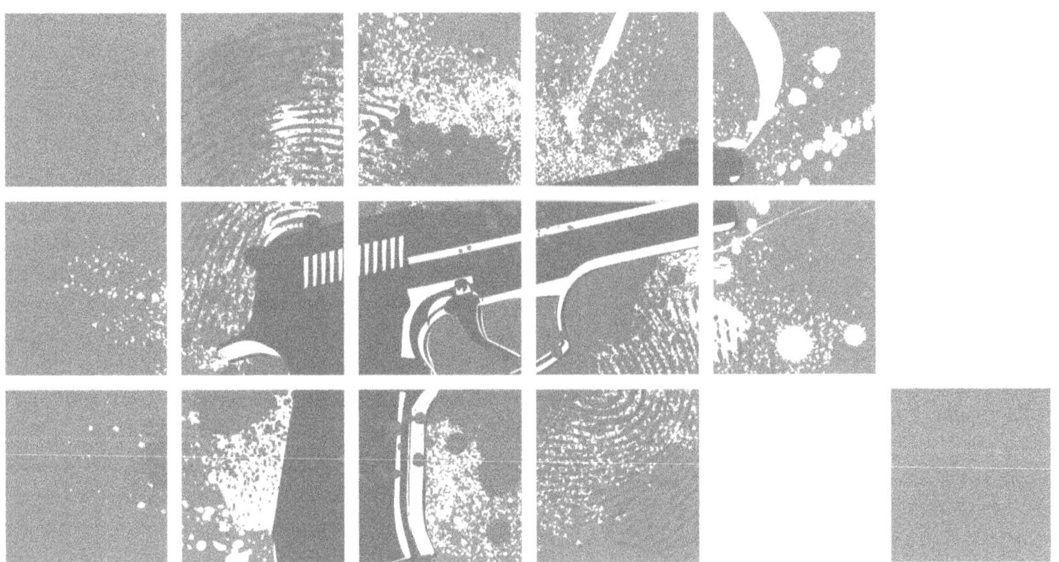

Terrorism and hostage-taking incidents

Overview

- Experts in the psychology of terrorism take the view that the field lacks scientific rigour and has failed to provide an adequate psychological perspective on terrorism.
- The definition of terrorism involves force or the threat of force being used in a political way in order to bring about social or political change. However, universal agreement on which groups are terrorist or not is missing.
- There is clear evidence that major acts of terrorist violence can have substantial psychological effects on the victims and the community from which they come. The effects are greatest on those closest to the attack, with direct victims being particularly affected.
- While it is conventional to use terms such as 'mad' to describe those who commit extreme violence, the typical terrorist is a normal person. Furthermore, suicide bombers do not conform to the usual psychological profile of the suicidal person.
- Growing evidence suggests that terrorists are produced by certain cognitive and social processes.
- Hostage barricade incidents are difficult situations to which psychological research has made an important contribution. However, it is not clear that the police are always well trained to accurately identify the risk factors involved in real-life incidents
- Hostage negotiation involves the psychological principles of negotiation developed in organisational psychology.
- Hostage negotiation involves the use of 'active listening skills'. These are generally very simple techniques such as mirroring what has been said. Nevertheless, research using real hostage-taking incidents suggests that active listening skills are employed in only a minority of the exchanges and then mainly using the simplest techniques.

Introduction

While terrorism has a long history, its impact on governments has escalated disproportionately in the last few years. This escalation seems to have been one consequence of the Twin Towers attacks in New York, often referred to as 9/11. The heightened security environment raised annual UK spending on counter-terrorism (homeland security) from £1 billion to £2 billion between 2004 and 2009 (Mythen and Walklate, 2005) and it was estimated to be £3.5 billion in 2010/11 (Security Service, 2007). Before 9/11 the UK spend was only about £950,000 per annum. The US has suffered approximately 3000 deaths in the last decade or so as a result of terrorism. Compared to other causes of death, this is a low figure. Nevertheless, the US spends in excess of approximately $500 million dollars on anti-terrorism for EACH of these 3000 deaths. In comparison, deaths from strokes are the third most common cause of death in the USA but only $2000 is spent on measures to combat strokes for each stroke death (Sinn, 2017). Terrorism itself is cheap and needs relatively few personnel. For example, the material cost of a suicide bomb which, on average kills 12 people is only $150 (Lomborg, 2008).

If we take a moment to look at the history of modern terrorism, authors such as Rapoport (2004) and Post, McGinnis and Moody (2014) suggest that there have been four distinct waves of terrorism starting at the end of the Victorian period and continuing to the present day. Modern terrorism can be said to have begun with the anarchist wave which began in Russia in the 1880s. This was modern in the sense that it spread globally and used modern methods of communication effectively. The second wave of terrorism was the nationalist-separatist anti-colonialist movement which was dominant between the First and Second World Wars and beyond. Often these terrorists sought to fulfil the mission of their parent generation for national freedom from their imperialist masters in countries such as Algeria, Cyprus and Ireland. The third wave of terrorism involved the social-revolutionary new left which generally opposed their parent generation. This began in the 1960s and was frequently organised around opposition to the Vietnam War. Groups such as the Weather Underground in the USA, Shining Path in Peru, and the Red Army Faction in Germany exemplified this sort of terrorism. The fourth wave of terrorism began in the 1980s and centred, in various ways, around religion. This does not only include Islamic fundamentalism such as Islamic State but other religions such as Jewish and Christian fundamentalism, according to Post *et al.* The use of the social media by religious terrorists continues the emphasis on communications which Rapoport suggests characterises modern terrorism. Religious fundamentalists (e.g. Hezbollah and al-Qaeda) employed the terrorism of mass destruction (Hudson, 1999). These new terrorist groups had a very different attitude from earlier ones. Previously, terrorist groups frequently showed concern not to alienate the public through the use of indiscriminate, excessive, mass violence. The IRA (Irish Republican Army), for example, usually gave specific warning of the terrorist acts that they were about to perpetrate. Another big change in recent years is the growth of suicide terrorism. The first modern example of suicide bombing occurred in 1981 and involved the car-bombing of the Israeli embassy in Beirut. Evidence of the escalation in the rates of suicide bombing can be seen in the fact that three-quarters of the suicide bombings between 1981 and 2004 took place between the years 2000 and 2004 (Merari, 2007). Lone-wolf terrorism is suggested by Post *et al.* (2014) as a fifth wave of modern terrorism and, once again, the use of novel technologies of communication is an obvious characteristic. Perhaps the most famous US case of a lone-wolf terrorist was Theodore Kaczynski or the 'Unabomber'. For 17 years he sent letter bombs to academics and airline executives as part of his protest against modern technology and its consequences for the environment and society in general (Weissman, Busch and Schouten (2014). One thing seems clear, it is likely to be very difficult to develop explanations of terrorism which apply in all of these cases.

There has been a great deal of terrorism research over the past 40 years or so. However, in purely academic terms, much of this research lacks scientific rigour (Borum, 2004) and is often less than convincing. Empirical research is far from easy in this field, for obvious reasons, and many of the publications of terrorism researchers are highly conjectural and speculative. Data constitutes a challenge and many of the basic methods of psychological research cannot be employed or are meaningless in this context. Research on terrorism was largely ignored by mainstream psychology and dwelt in the 'cracks and crevices' between academic disciplines such as politics and sociology and psychology (Silke, 2004).

The nature of terrorism

Differentiating terrorist violence from other forms of criminal violence is problematic because it depends on both the objective of the violence and its motivation. So, for example, it seems difficult to distinguish between violence at a political rally from terrorism if we use what appears to be a perfectly sensible definition of terrorism such as the following:

> terrorism is generally understood to be the use of violence and intimidation to disrupt or coerce a government and/or an identifiable community. Terrorism has

> traditionally been distinguished from routine criminal violence because it is driven by a particular political and/or religious motivation.
>
> (Mythen and Walklate, 2005, p. 381)

Similarly, if a letter bomb is sent through the post to a politician what further information would we need to decide that it was an act of terrorism?

If we assume that terrorist crimes involve action against a national government or specific communities, does this depend on assuming the government or community to be legitimate or is legitimacy not a relevant criterion? There may be no international agreement about the legitimacy of, say, a particular government which may make the definition of certain groups as terrorists difficult. Some may see exactly the same group as freedom fighters rather than terrorists, for example. A terrorist from one perspective is a martyr or freedom fighter from another – that is, a value judgement is involved.

Are there underlying patterns in terrorism which suggest different types? Fortunately there are databases which have collected together substantial sets of data concerning terrorist incidents. One such data base is ITERATE (International Terrorism: Attributes of Terrorist Events). This, together with sophisticated statistical methods (non-metric multi-dimensional scaling), was used by Yokota, Fujita, Watanabe, Yoshimoto and Wachi (2007) in order to identify patterns in terrorist attacks. Each incident in this large data set of terrorist incidents was coded in terms of a number of dimensions. The associations between these ratings for the different incidents led to the identification of the main clusters or groupings of terrorist attack types. Three attack strategy types emerged, as can be seen in Figure 12.1. In more detail, they were:

- *Terrorist attacks as threat:* In this the terrorist organisation seeks to intimidate people and society. The intention is not primarily to cause casualties.

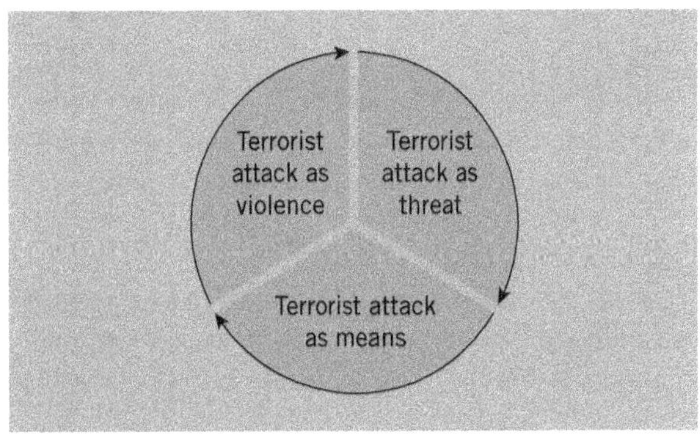

Figure 12.1 Types of terrorist attack according to Yokota *et al.* (2007)

- *Terrorist attacks as means:* The victim is used as a way of negotiating about the goal of the terrorist group.
- *Terrorist attacks as violence:* In this individuals or groups of people are targeted to be injured or killed.

Terrorist organisations generally used one of these three forms of terrorist incident but not the other types. That is to say, one terrorist organisation would primarily use terrorist attacks as threat, another would use terrorist attacks as means, and so forth. Eighty-seven per cent of terrorist organisations had over 50 per cent of their incidents in one category. This, nevertheless, leaves some variation in strategy which Yokota *et al.* suggest may be the result of instability within the terrorist organisation. Deaths were quite common where the strategy was terrorist attack as means or terrorist attack as violence, despite the fact that the motivation for terrorist attack as means was not the killing or otherwise harming of the victim. Modern policing policies in many countries now aim to resolve potential stand-offs (or barricade incidents) peacefully without harm to terrorist, hostage or police officers.

BOX 12.1 Controversy

Is fingerprint evidence unreliable? Confirmation bias in legal settings

In March 2004, terrorist bombs exploded on commuter trains in the region of Madrid, Spain. A bag of detonators was discovered, on which was found a crucial fingerprint. This was identified by the FBI's Integrated Automated Fingerprint Identification System as that of Brandon Mayfield, an American Muslim lawyer, married to an Egyptian professor's daughter. In fact, Mayfield was one of several matches identified for the crucial fingerprint and was only the fourth closest match found. Nevertheless, among the 'incriminating' facts was that he had associates who themselves were suspected of being terrorists and that once he had acted as lawyer for a known terrorist in a child custody case! Four fingerprint experts expressed complete confidence that

BOX 12.1 (continued)

the print from Madrid was a match for Mayfield, who was subsequently arrested – putatively because his prints were an absolute match for those on the detonator bag (Busey and Loftus, 2007).

Fortunately for Mayfield, the Spanish police had other suspects – one of whom was identified using a better fingerprint. This man was an Algerian terrorist who was believed to have al-Qaeda links. Mayfield was released and subsequently successfully sued the FBI. According to the FBI, the error was due to the poor digital image of the original fingerprint and the exceptional similarity of Mayfield's fingerprint to that on the bag of detonators. However, independent reviewers blamed the first fingerprint examiner for not completely analysing the crucial fingerprint and so failing to see the decisive differences between the two. Possibly, the judgement of the first expert influenced those of the other three. This was a public, high-profile case which pressured the fingerprint experts who probably had too much confidence in the fingerprint analysis system in use.

This is, of course, a salutary lesson for those who believe that fingerprint evidence is without problems. Recent research has looked at the influence of extraneous (psychological) factors which may affect the decisions of experts, as in this case (Dror and Charlton, 2006). The researchers had the cooperation of a laboratory which employed fingerprint experts of considerable experience and capability. Consequently, they had access to fingerprints which had been involved in real criminal cases. The Tenprints System is essentially a database of 'rolled' fingerprints which can be compared with latent prints collected from the crime scene. The research design was very imaginative. The researchers had access to archival information about previous decisions made about fingerprints by the experts at this laboratory. The researchers wanted to know if the experts' previous decisions about fingerprints could be influenced by additional contextualising psychological and cognitive information. So the researchers might introduce biasing information – for instance that the suspect had confessed to the crime or that the suspect was in police custody at the time of the crime. The researchers selected (for each fingerprint examiner) (a) some fingerprints that they (the fingerprint examiner) had previously judged to be individualisations (that is, the fingerprint matched a known person's fingerprint) and (b) some fingerprints that had been judged to be exclusions (that is, the fingerprint did not match that of a known person). Independent experts confirmed that there was enough information in the fingerprints to make a definite individualisation or exclusion decision. Half of the prints were selected because they were hard to evaluate, whereas the others were easy to evaluate. There was also a control sample of prints for which no contextual information was provided.

Two-thirds of the experts made inconsistent decisions compared with what they had decided previously about the same fingerprints. However, some experts (a third) were perfectly consistent with their previous decisions throughout. About 17 per cent of inconsistent decisions were made due to the biasing context.

Dror, Charlton and Peron (2006) carried out a similar study which was even more directly relevant to the Madrid bombing case. The fingerprint experts looked at what they believed to be a pair of fingerprints, one from the Madrid train terrorism case and the other being the rolled fingerprint of someone else. They were told that the prints were those which the FBI had erroneously matched with the Madrid bomber. In other words, contextual information suggested that the prints were a non-match. Only one of the fingerprint experts decided (counter to the contextual information) that the prints were a match, although this expert had five years previously concluded that these prints were not a match! Of the other experts studied, three of the experts judged the 'new' pair as a non-match. Only one decided that there was insufficient information to form a judgement and only one did not change their mind at all! Dror *et al.* (2011) suggest that the degree of inconsistency is not consistent across experts or across fingerprints.

What makes the studies of Dror and his co-workers especially important is their use of forensic experts as the participants in their studies. Less convincing but nevertheless relevant are studies which use alternatives to experts as participants. One otherwise important study is that of Smalarz, Buck, Madon, Yang and Guyll (2016) which looked at the influence of criminal stereotypes on fingerprint matching. This is a different form of contextual information compared to that in the Dror studies described above, but nevertheless a process by which bias might develop. The study used students as participants. Actually there were two parts to their study. The first part was intended to assess the extent to which a wide range of offences had a stereotype shared by most people. Participants rated vignettes describing the different crimes which formed the basis of the assessment of the stereotypes. Some crimes such as identity theft had poor consensus in terms of the assumed characteristics of the offender whereas others such as child molestation had high consensus. In the second part of the study, participants read a brief incident report concerning either an identity theft or a child molestation and had to rate how similar pairs of fingerprints potentially from the suspect were to each other. They were also given information about the suspect's address, date of birth, address, weight, height and hair and eye colour plus, in addition, a photograph. Half of the participants were told that the suspect was a middle-aged white man, and the other half were told that the suspect was a middle aged Asian woman. In other words, some received a stereotypical description of a child molester (a middle-aged white man) and the others received a description of a suspect which did not meet the stereotype of any type of offender. They then had to judge whether a pair of fingerprints, one from the suspect and the other obtained from the crime scene, were a match or a mismatch. Briefly, for the identity theft condition, the same proportion of participants rated the fingerprints as matching irrespective of the description of the offender given. This is as the researchers expected as there is no consensual stereotype of identity theft offenders. However, in terms of the child molestation offence, significantly more participants claimed the fingerprints matched when the suspect corresponded to the stereotype of a child molester – that is when the suspect was described as a middle-age white male. In fact, none of the pairs of fingerprints were a match. In other words, judgements concerning fingerprint matches were affected by the sort of information which would usually be available to fingerprint examiners.

All of this suggests that forensic science is far from perfect despite it giving the appearance of scientific rigour to the general public. Kassin, Dror and Kukucka (2013) argue strongly that contextual cues in forensic judgements lead to confirmation bias. Confirmation bias is a well-established idea in psychology and Kassin *et al.* review the wide variety of evidence supporting the idea that expectations can seriously affect decision making. This evidence comes from basic psychological research into cognitive processes. Some forensic science methods are highly dependent on the judgement of the expert in question. So, for example, there are no satisfactory objective methods of saying how similar two different fingerprints are. Kassin *et al.* suggest a number of ways to avoid confirmation bias due to contextual information. For example:

- The use of blind analysis procedures in which the examiner is not presented with any contextual information or as little as possible is a starting point. This would include not having contact by the investigating police officers, for example. Unfortunately this does not deal with the base-line assumption problem which is that it is likely that an individual suspected by the police is likely to be guilty.
- Verification procedures should avoid the possibility of contextual information. That is, for example, the expert chosen to check a previous expert evaluation should be unknown to the first expert and most certainly not selected by the first expert.

More generally speaking, it is argued by Haber and Haber (2013) that the broad strategy for improving the quality of forensic work and, hence, fewer mistakes should be encouraging a scientific culture in forensic testing organizations. The well-known research on the biases that can occur in psychological experiments is, perhaps, some indication of what needs to happen in the forensic context. Without the development of a scientific culture, it is not known the extent to which forensic conclusions are inaccurate and unreliable or the degree to which bias has a role.

The consequences of terrorism

Despite ideas which abound concerning the resilience of the general population to the effects of terrorist violence, there is considerable evidence that terrorist incidents can have quite profound effects on members of the public. DiMaggio and Galea (2006) describe the results of a meta-analysis (see Box 4.2) of the aftermaths of terrorist incidents such as 9/11 and the 2005 London tube and bus bombings. They found that the rate of post-traumatic stress disorder (PTSD) in directly affected populations was between 12 per cent and 16 per cent.

An exceptionally deadly major terrorist incident took place on 11 March 2004 with the commuter train bombings in Spain. Bombs exploded on four different early morning trains destined for Madrid's Atocha station. More than 400 people were taken to hospital and nearly 200 died from the blasts. A loosely structured Moroccan Islamic combatant group (GICM) was responsible and some of those associated with it had been trained at al-Qaeda camps. Gabriel *et al.* (2007) studied the aftermath of these terrorist attacks on three different groups of people. These were: 1) those injured in the bomb blasts; 2) the residents of the local area in which many of the victims lived and in which few did not know a victim; and 3) the police officers involved in the rescue operation. Members of each of these three groups were interviewed on a one-to-one basis within three months of the attacks. The researchers used standard psychiatric diagnosis instruments such as the mini international neuropsychiatric interview (which is used to assess major depression, panic disorder, social phobia, generalised anxiety disorder and agoraphobia) and the Davidson trauma scale to assess the mental health of the participants. The group of injured commuters showed the greatest evidence of current mental disorders when interviewed after the attack (58 per cent). For the local area group, 26 per cent showed signs of a current mental disorder. However, only 4 per cent of the police officer group showed mental health problems. Post-traumatic stress disorder (PTSD) (see Chapter 4) was the commonest category of mental disorder manifested by the injured group (44 per cent). The equivalent figures for the local group were 12 per cent and for the police 1 per cent. One striking feature of the data was the extent of the comorbidity (co-occurrence) of two or more mental disorders. Fifty-three per cent of the injured group showed this, compared with only 22 per cent of the local group. This is, perhaps, a clearer demonstration of the impact of direct victimisation on the mental health of victims.

As one might expect, there have been numerous studies of the impact of 9/11 on mental health. One study (DiMaggio, Galea and Richardson, 2007) concentrated on mental health-related admissions to hospital emergency departments for psychological reasons before 9/11 and the changes which occurred after that date. The researchers put forward the simple hypothesis that the impact of the terrorist attacks would vary according to the distance that people lived from the terrorist incident – the closer they were, the more likely they were to attend an emergency department for psychological health reasons. Four different geographical areas were selected which represented increasing distances from the World Trade Centre target of the 9/11 incident, in the New York and New York State areas. Also four time periods were stipulated representing periods before 9/11 and the period after 9/11. The findings were in line with other mental health studies: compared with periods prior to the terrorist attacks, after 9/11 there were 10 per cent more behavioural and mental health diagnoses at hospital emergency departments. Furthermore, in support of the hypothesis, there was evidence that these increases were stronger in the areas closest to the 9/11 attacks.

Perhaps by way of a summary and coda to this, Jhangiani (2010) brought together and reviewed 118 research studies into the psychological consequences of the 9/11 attacks. There is evidence of poorer mental health in New York and Washington DC consequent upon the attacks. However, these levels returned to pre-attack baseline levels after about six months or, it would seem from some studies, mental health was better than before. The precise details of this varied from study to study. The effects of the terrorist attack were worse if the individual:

- had a history of mental illness;
- was physically very close to the attacks;
- knew someone involved in the attacks.

Outside of the target areas, research showed a much more minimal effect of the impact of the attacks on mental health. For countries outside the US the impact of the bombings was virtually indiscernible over the various studies. There was a positive response to the attacks, too, which included long-term increases in helping behaviours, religion, and even an increased level of life satisfaction.

Of course, the victims of terrorism are all of us and not just those directly and immediately effected. Just how do we respond to terrorist attacks and what determines the nature of this response? Ferguson and Kamble (2012) report a study of the responses of Indian and British students to the Mumbai terrorist attack of 2008. Briefly, the events involved a coordinated series of bombings and shootings at various notable locations in central Mumbai over a period of three days. A minimum of 173 people died and many more were injured. They chose to examine the impact of just world beliefs on responses to the attack. People are motivated in their judgements by the belief in the justice and fairness of the world according to the just world theory (Lerner, 1980). Consequently, an individual's good fortune and fate in general are seen as the result of their intrinsically good character. Dreadful happenings are not easily reconciled with this belief. Initially, people want to help the victims but they can also blame the victim for the events because of their bad character or irresponsibility. According to Ferguson and Kamble, the theory amounts to us getting what we deserve and deserving what we get. Despite this, it was not thought that victims of terrorism would be responded to in that way. Indeed, modern research on the just world theory has tended to move away from the victim-blaming aspect to the more positive effects of holding strong beliefs in the just world.

The methodology first of all involved the participants completing the *Global Belief in a Just World Scale* (Lipkus, 1991). Examples of items from this are:

- 'I feel that people get what they are entitled to have.'
- 'I feel that a person's efforts are noticed and rewarded.'

In addition the participants completed a number of questionnaires assessing distress, revenge, and denial:

- The terrorism-related distress scale: e.g. 'I feel threatened by terrorism targeted against India.'
- The desire for revenge scale: e.g. 'I would support any retaliatory military action taken by the Indian government after this attack.'
- Denial of terrorism: e.g. 'I often avoid the news about terrorism because it worries me.'

Following this, they read an account of the Mumbai terrorist attack based on contemporary newspaper accounts. The Indian participants demonstrated significantly higher belief in a just world than did the UK students. This could be a cultural difference. They also had higher levels of terrorism-related distress; more desire for revenge action against the terrorists; and higher levels of terrorism denial. However, irrespective of nationality, those with greater belief in a just world also tended to have a higher desire for revenge and more terrorism denial. The researchers suggest that their findings indicate that multiple strategies are employed in order to attempt to maintain the belief in a just world. Firm action against terrorists and denying terrorism they see as part of this.

The public's response to terrorist incidents is complex, judging from the available research. Systematic research on the public's response to terrorist incidents is difficult to plan and often the available research has to be planned and executed at great speed. As such, it becomes hard to be systematic and theoretical in orientation, as opposed to being pragmatic about the possible objectives of a study. It seems generally accepted that terrorists seek to instill fear into the community and population in the hope that this will put pressure on governments to agree to the terrorists agenda. At the same time, it is noteworthy that governments do not seek to reduce fear of terrorism in the public but to maintain it at a high level (Braithwaite, 2013). Braithwaite suggests although this may be motivated by the wish of governments to avoid blame for previous assurances that the public is safe when a terrorist attack occurs. But a higher level of fear may encourage the public to report anything they see which may suggest that a terrorist incident is being planned.

Is there a terrorist personality or psychopathology?

Just how to conceptualise people who do extreme things has long been a difficulty for psychologists. For example, are the terrorists mad who hijack aircraft, force them to another country and then hold passengers as hostages? Are suicide bombers already suicide-prone? There is a temptation to label out-of-the-ordinary actions as insane, since such a label seems to justify the behaviour. There is a danger of assuming that terrorists necessarily conform to a particular type given the characteristics of a particular terrorist episode. For example, the media feed us with the idea that suicide bombers are religious zealots, which leads us to the assumption that religion is strongly associated with terrorist acts. The Tamil Tigers of Sri Lanka were not based on religion but politics. Nevertheless this group has committed a good proportion of all suicide bombings worldwide.

Given our assumptions about the relationship between the male sex and violence, there can be surprisingly large proportions of women who become suicide bombers. There is evidence that the Kurdistan Workers Party (PKK) and the Tamil Tigers of Sri Lanka used women as frequently as men as suicide bombers (Ergil, 2001).

There is a remarkable consensus in the research literature: 1) there is no such thing as a terrorist personality and 2) that mental abnormality is simply not an important consideration when trying to understand terrorist attackers (Silke, 2004). Borum (2004, 2014) summarises the research literature by stating that the consensus among commentators is that terrorism is at best poorly accounted for on the basis of psychopathology (widely defined to include conditions referred to as mental disease and mental disorder). There will be terrorists with such conditions, of course, but there is no tendency for terrorists to be more likely to have these conditions. Equally, there appears to be no useful or consistent profile of the typical terrorist. Maghan (1998) suggested that terrorists range through all character types from the self-doubting wretch to those haunted by indescribable demons. But madness, as an explanatory concept, has no role to play. Other reviewers followed suit:

- Silke (1998) summarised the findings of researchers by suggesting that terrorists are normal people but who commit acts of terrorism.
- Ruby (2002) commented that terrorists are rational, lucid people.

An article in a popular psychology magazine by Perina (2002) had the subtitle 'Suicide bombers have distinctive personality traits'. Despite this, Perina also points out that psychologists tend to agree that suicide bombers cannot be explained in terms of some personal psychopathology but it is also difficult to understand how other factors such as those of a religious, social or cultural nature in themselves can just turn some normal young people into suicide bombers. He reports that Ariel Merari, director for the programme for political violence at the University of Tel Aviv, studied 32 suicide bombers and found no evidence of social dysfunction or suicidal characteristics which could account for their actions. Terrorist groups such as Hamas in Palestine may take advantage of their recruits' religious fanaticism and nationalism, but these fail to account for why these particular people and not others with similar characteristics become suicide bombers. Merari has made a number of observations based on his studies of terrorists (*The Michigan Daily*, 2002). Like others, he argues that terrorists are just normal people who can be seen as a cross-section of their societies. There was no significant evidence of any psychopathology among them. Neither is it correct to suggest that suicide bombers can be seen in simple terms as extreme religious fanatics.

Many of the acts of terrorists are atrocious and difficult for most people to understand. The humiliation of hostages and, for example, their slow decapitation which is videoed and broadcast on the Internet are instances of this. This naturally has led some to ask whether psychopathy is characteristic of terrorists. After all, we know that psychopaths commit some of the most extreme murders and rapes. Borum (2004) reviewed the evidence on psychopathology and antisocial personality disorders in terrorists in the light of this general assumption that terrorists are callous, cold-blooded killers. According to Borum, however, the characteristics of psychopaths do not make them good members of any sort of organisation (although this seems to contradict the evidence that psychopaths can do extremely well in organisations, see p. 391). While dedication and selflessness may be required of terrorists, Borum argues, these are very different from the defining characteristics of psychopaths.

We need to consider why it is even expected that terrorists will have some sort of personality extremity or defect, despite this being common in discourse about terrorists (e.g. 'these madmen', 'these fanatics'). This accords with the general tendency to associate deviant activity with madness and badness. But this is to assume that terrorism is driven by characteristics of the individual and that it needs some particular personality to commit extreme acts. However, the lesson taught by social psychology is quite different. Social psychological research has pointed to the rationality rather than irrationality of participants in extreme behaviours. The classic studies of Milgram (1974) on obedience demonstrate how ordinary citizens can obey dangerous commands that might harm others. So, the atrocities of Nazi Germany may be the consequence, in part, of normal social processes. Taylor and Quayle (1994) made a telling analogy between terrorism and careers in terms of personality. One would not expect that university lecturers all had a similar personality profile or that all students shared a similar personality, so why should one expect that terrorists would be any different as a group?

Borum (2014) argues that the understanding of terrorism might progress faster if we adopt a more complex model of how the psychology of the individual involving ordinary mental states and processes might explain why a person may become involved in terrorist activity. He acknowledges that there is a contextual and situational aspect to this (terrorism is more common in some settings than others). However, four different worldviews that the individual may have need consideration. These are authoritarianism, fundamentalism, dogmatism and apocalypticism. These are different but overlapping worldviews.

Authoritarianism is in the modern formulation an enduring learned attitude which involves hostility and anger towards out-groups, submissiveness to authority figures, and conventionality. Dogmatism is in many ways similar to authoritarianism. A dogmatic person manifests a closed system of thought including beliefs and disbeliefs which are strongly held and resistant to change. They see authority as absolute and are generally intolerant of most other people.

Fundamentalist thinking involves absolutist religious thinking about right and wrong and how people are categorised morally. Paranoia is a characteristic of them in the context of their group and they rage against those they believe have humiliated them. The group is constituted around a charismatic leader who has intense conviction.

Apocalypticism is an aspect of fundamentalism and involves a belief in a future cataclysmic event such as a confrontation or massive change. Only a few have been selected to be warned of this event and make preparation. The past and future develop as if from a blueprint.

But there is more to Borum's idea than contextual factors, situational factors, and a person's worldview or mindset which are the psychological climate to their thoughts and actions. These further considerations include a number of psychological vulnerabilities and a number of propensities. They have the role of 'shaping' the individuals thoughts and actions and can lead to an increased probability of involvement in terrorism. The psychological vulnerabilities, which can be considered as need states, include the need for meaning/identity, the need to belong, and the person's perceptions of injustice and/or humiliation. These may make the individual receptive to influences conducive to terrorism. One can perhaps see how a terrorist ideology may provide the individual with meaning and a sense of identity and a sense of belonging. Equally it is not hard to see that a feeling of injustice or humiliation, perhaps living under an occupying army, may push the individual towards terrorism. Motivational, attributional, attitudinal and volitional propensities of various types may also play a role. For example, the hostile attributional bias is the tendency to see hostility in what others say or do. Again, it is not difficult to see this as facilitating the push towards terrorism. In other words, a psychology of terrorism does not need to focus on mental disorder as an explanation but can be directed towards more ordinary psychological processes.

Suicidal characteristics and suicide terrorism

It is important to note that suicide bombing is rare in terrorism, although it is responsible for a high proportion of deaths. So is it possible to regard suicide bombers as being like anyone else who commits suicide? The answer is no, according to Silke (2003). Suicide bombers do not share characteristics and motivations with the typical person who commits suicide. Suicide bombers are psychologically stable and very much ordinary personalities when judged from their own cultural context. Furthermore, suicide bombers' families regard their actions positively as being heroic, in contrast to the families of people who commit suicide for other reasons.

All of this and more is reinforced in Townsend's (2007) views on the question of whether suicide bombers are indeed suicidal. Quite evidently this is a technically difficult issue to address. Her strategy was to assess the extent of similarity and dissimilarity between:

- what we know from research on suicide in general;
- known psychological characteristics obtained from research on (potential) suicide bombers.

There was little correspondence between the two. One possibility considered was that suicide terrorists are similar to 'altruistic suicides'. There is an obvious difficulty since suicide terrorists takes the lives of many others and not just their own. Researchers have found from suicide notes and interviewing suicide attempt survivors that a variety of motivations underlie suicide. Amongst these are financial problems, mental health issues and relationship problems. Based on this, one could take the view that there is no such thing as a typical suicide, but terrorism research suggests that there is no such thing as the typical suicide terrorist either.

There is plenty of evidence of a higher incidence of diagnosable mental illness in both attempted and completed suicides. Depression, not surprisingly, is particularly associated with these. In contrast, what is known about suicide terrorism strongly links it with feelings of martyrdom which are accompanied by positive feelings. These do not appear to be at all like the sense of being abandoned by everyone around and the feeling of being a burden to loved ones and others characteristic of suicide in general. The suicide bomber regards their violent acts as being in the service of Allah. This martyrdom is known as *istishhad* (Abdel-Khalek, 2004). Suicide, itself, is not acceptable in the Islamic faith in any circumstances. Given that we know that suicide bombers (a) are religious, often to an extreme and (b) believe that their acts are supported by Islamic principles then these facts fit better with the view that so-called suicide bombers lack suicidal intent.

So is religion a factor in suicide, since it is strongly implicated in suicide bombing (though not all terrorism)? Once again there seems to be a mismatch since, according to Townsend, good modern research indicates that religion may be a protective factor against suicide. Frequency of praying and the importance of religion to the individual predict having lower levels of suicidal thoughts on average and not having attempted suicide in the past (Nonnemaker, McNeely and Blum, 2003). One clear characteristic of suicide bombers is that vengeance is frequently a motivation. For example, research suggests that terrorists have often been victims of state violence or even torture in their earlier lives. Again this does not match with the motivations of suicidal individuals in general, who rarely mention revenge as a motive – with the exception of some abused women. But, even these, unlike the suicide bombers, do not act violently to others prior to their suicide.

Remarkably, among all of this consensus, Merari, Diamant, Bibi, Broshi and Zakin (2010) report data from interviews with failed suicide bombers to suggest that marked depressive and suicidal symptoms were found in 53 per cent of them. This compared with a figure of 21 per cent of organisers of suicide attacks and 8 per cent of non-suicide-attack insurgents. One finding was exclusive to the suicide bombers in that 40 per cent of them showed suicidal tendencies which were not associated with their desire for political/religious martyrdom. These findings were strongly criticised by Brym and Araj (2012) who suggested that the differences were not statistically significant and the judgements of depression and suicide symptoms may well involve a degree of wishful thinking on the part of the original researchers. Furthermore, Brym and Araj provide evidence from their study of members of the family and close personal friends of suicide bombers in Palestine. Their data tell a different story from Merari *et al.*'s. Seventy-six per cent of their sample of suicide bombers showed no indications of depression or of personal crisis potentially leading to depression as far as the immediate family or close friend knew. Of the others, the immediate social and political situation surrounding them possibly may have led to their depression. In any case, the rate of depression in the sample and that for Palestinians living on the West Bank or in Gaza was much the same. Merari (2012) defended his research suggesting that it used stringent reliability checks for the assessments of depression etc.

The problem created for risk assessment

The question of how to rehabilitate terrorists has become a practical concern for modern governments. For example, Horgan and Braddock (2010) describe different de-radicalisation programmes employed by a variety of nations. The idea that terrorists are by-and-large psychologically normal, lacking indications of mental illness, leads to difficulties for any psychologist. At some stage, decisions have to be made about the release of convicted terrorists from prison. Just how should psychologists and psychiatrists go about a risk assessment of such an individual? Although risk assessment is a feature of the work of forensic psychologists (see Chapter 27) little of what is known applies well to terrorists since it is based on psychiatric patients and prisoners. Terrorists do not represent either of these groups well. Dernevik, Beck, Grann, Hogue and McGuire (2009a) argue that, as a consequence, psychologists and psychiatrists do not have an appropriate knowledge base upon which to formulate risk assessment for terrorists. The sort of approaches taken to the prediction of violent recidivism described in Chapter 27 are simply inapplicable because the causes of terrorists' violence are not the same as the causes of interpersonal violence in general. They are particularly dubious about the value of psychometric methods of risk assessment which were developed on very different groups of offenders from terrorists.

Among the problems involved in applying established risk assessment methods to terrorist prisoners are the following:

- Different groups of terrorists come to terrorism through very different pathways, according to Dernevik *et al.* (2009a). As we saw earlier, in the 1970s, research suggested that the typical terrorist was middle-class, young, unmarried and lived in an urban location – and they were university-educated (Russell and Miller, 1977). This is not the profile of the typical violent offender and is also not representative of modern terrorists.
- What about mental illness and psychopathy in modern terrorists and the possibility that terrorists are typically recidivist criminals? Dernivika *et al.* place a great deal of emphasis on the research of Sageman (2004) in addressing this. He obtained biographical data on a reasonably large sample of people who were members of the worldwide Salafijihad fundamentalist Islam network, of which al-Qaeda is part. There was virtually no evidence of criminality – other than very minor petty offences – in the histories of those who committed major terrorist incidents. Furthermore, the outrages that they committed could not be conceived as for personal gain. Using *DSM-IV* criteria of mental illness (see Box 21.1), Sageman sought evidence of major mental illnesses such as psychosis or delusions as well as antisocial personality disorder among terrorists. These searches led nowhere other than to the common conclusion that terrorists do not generally have identifiable mental illnesses. Hence psychological and psychiatric measures which predict violent recidivism discussed Chapter 27 simply do not apply to terrorists.
- The lack of significant personal criminal histories among terrorists means that criminal history cannot be used to predict recidivism. Or to be more accurate, the lack of a personal criminal history would imply that terrorists in general pose little or no risk of future violence on release.

Gudjonsson (2009) regards the views of Dernevik *et al.* (2009a) as somewhat negative. He suggests a number of things which potentially may be of relevance to the prediction of future risk among terrorists. For example, political changes may have removed some of the major grievances which motivated the terrorism. Alternatively, in making the risk assessment, the present situation with regard to the terrorist's support network needs to be taken into account. These and similar factors may well be relevant to terrorist assessment, despite the fact that they have little or nothing to do with conventional ways of assessing risk as discussed in Chapter 27. Dernevik, Beck, Grann, Hogue and McGuire (2009b) point out that both historical and psychological research indicate that some of the most appalling acts of violence during the twentieth century were committed by individuals who functioned normally in general and appeared to be mentally within the healthy range.

What makes a terrorist?

There is another consensus view in the psychology of terrorism literature (Luckabaugh *et al.*, 1997). That is, that it takes time to turn even a vulnerable individual into a terrorist. The psychological motivations of terrorist recruits tend to be the very human needs of 1) wanting to feel that one belongs and 2) the development of a satisfactory personal identification. Social alienation followed by boredom leads to dissidence or protest on a minor scale, then eventually terrorism. Although histories of childhood abuse, trauma, perceived injustice and humiliation are common in terrorists' backgrounds, Borum (2004) feels that these do not help explain terrorism (though this view is not universally shared, as we shall see). Perception of injustice combined with the need for a sense of belonging and a need for identity can frequently be seen as vulnerabilities among potential terrorists.

Merari (2007) may be referring to such general vulnerability factors when he suggests that susceptibility to indoctrination may be the key to understanding suicide bombers. Most suicide bombers that he studied were young and unattached – the very sort of person at the greatest risk of becoming involved in violent organisations of all sorts. Merari believes that suicide terrorism should be understood in terms of the consequences of terrorist organisation systems. Terrorist groups recruit members largely through interpersonal connections and then support the recruit through to becoming a suicide bomber. Highly committed members of the terrorist group will spend hours speaking with the recruit, promoting the idea that martyrdom is the will of God and focusing on the illustrious past of Islam. The suicide bomber becomes enmeshed in a group contract which is designed to increase their allegiance to the other group members. Finally there is a 'formal contract' which constitutes a final personal commitment before the suicide bombing.

Merari (2007) makes the analogy that terrorist groups act like a suicide production line. There is empirical support for this from data on Palestinian suicide bombers. Merari refers to the stages of indoctrination, group commitment and personal commitment:

- *Indoctrination:* throughout the process leading to the suicide mission, high-authority members of the group continue to indoctrinate the potential bomber in order to maintain the motivation to engage in the terrorist act and to prevent changes of mind. For the Palestinian terrorists, the major indoctrination themes were nationalistic (such as Israel's humiliation of the Palestinian state) and religious (such as the guarantee that the suicide bomber will go to paradise).
- *Group commitment:* by mutually committing to carry out suicide attacks some of the consequences of doubts are dealt with and motivation for the suicide attacks is maximised.
- *Personal commitment:* this may take the form of a video-recording in which the terrorist describes his or her intention to engage in such a suicide mission. This is partly for the bomber's family. It is a way of getting the individual's irrevocable commitment to the suicide mission. The bomber also prepares farewell letters to friends and family at this stage for later distribution. Mirari points out that the bomber is often referred to as the 'living-martyr' at this stage.

This is sympathetic with Horgan and Taylor's (2001) view that terrorists usually do not make a conscious decision that they wish to become a terrorist. Instead, they gradually become involved in a process which socialises them towards their ultimate terrorist activities. The process leading towards becoming a terrorist is not absolute, since there is a high rate of turnover in membership of terrorist groups (Crenshaw, 1986). Taylor and Louis (2004) suggest that:

> young people find themselves at a time in their life when they are looking to the future with the hope of engaging in meaningful behavior that will be satisfying and get them ahead. Their objective circumstances including opportunities for advancement are virtually nonexistent; they find some direction for their religious collective identity but the desperately disadvantaged state of their community leaves them feeling marginalized and lost without a clearly defined collective identity.
>
> (p. 178)

It is easy to get into a way of thinking about terrorism which holds that terrorist acts are the consequence of group processes. However, Taylor (2010) asks whether terrorism incidents can truly be understood as group phenomena. Just what does it tell us when we say that terrorism is a group process? He makes a distinction between involvement with terrorist groups and the like and taking part in terrorist events. Group processes may be important as a backdrop to terrorism where social, political and cultural factors can be seen to play their part. But do they explain the episode of terrorist violence itself? Taylor suggests that there are two broad issues:

- Do we have an adequate definition of what terrorism is (apart from being what terrorists do)?
- Do we have a clear idea of what is meant by group processes in relation to terrorism?

To illustrate his point, he gives a number of examples of terrorist incidents in which group processes seem to be minimally or not involved. For example, Theodore John Kaczynski was the notorious Unabomber who conducted a successful terrorist campaign beginning in 1978 and lasting for about 17 years in the USA. He appears to have been a recluse living in a log cabin in Montana. During that period of time he sent 12 bombs which resulted in the deaths of three people. He had an environmentalist agenda largely of his own making. This is an extreme example, but Taylor provides others where it is difficult to understand the relevance of the idea of group processes.

Life story studies

Borum (2004) argues that the life experiences of terrorists tend to include the themes of injustice, abuse and humiliation. However, Borum suggests that these are not sufficient causes of terrorism but may help identify individuals who are susceptible to the influence of terrorist groups. In some ways, this viewpoint fits in with narrative studies of terrorists in that other factors need to be brought into account to understand just what turns one potentially vulnerable young person into a terrorist while another equally vulnerable young person will fail to go down the route to terrorism.

Since 1992, suicide terrorism has been a feature of Israel's relationship with Palestine. Soibelman (2004) also subscribes to the view that terrorism should be regarded primarily as the consequence of group processes rather than individual psychological factors (such as personality). Group solidarity and shared ideologies combine to create the terrorist. Obvious ideas such as that suicide bombers are young religious fanatics are rejected by Soibelman, who believes that less extreme personality characteristics are often responsible for the creation of a suicide bomber. He bases his ideas on published research as well as his interviews with five suicide bombers who had either been arrested before they could detonate a bomb or whose bomb failed to detonate (this occurs in about 40 per cent of suicide bomb attempts) in order to understand the process by which they had become bombers. He argues that there is no single explanation of why someone becomes a bomber and that there is a mixture of circumstances that are responsible, which may be different in different cases.

Group solidarity and shared ideologies combine to create the terrorist. Mostly the interviewed suicide bombers shared at least some of the following characteristics:

- Bad direct or secondary experiences of involvements with the Israeli military forces. These included a friend being shot dead and having been beaten by them.
- Political factors were commonly mentioned as the reason for becoming a suicide bomber.
- Most had previously been involved in demonstrations or other forms of assembly.
- As the situation escalated, participants' beliefs became more extreme.

Not surprisingly, given the nature of the sample used by Soibelman, all of the suicide bombers and their families followed the secular Fatah movement. Furthermore, for this group of terrorists, there was no tendency for them to have criminal backgrounds, although a few may have had.

A much more detailed analysis of the structure of life history narrative accounts of becoming a terrorist is to be found in Sarangi and Alison's (2005) study of left-wing Maoist terrorist groups in Nepal and India. These Maoist terrorists regard the state as the instrument serving the needs of the rich and so the state needs to be violently overthrown. The use of the individual terrorist as a storyteller, Sarangi and Alison suggest, may help us to understand how different life trajectories are shaped in terms of how the terrorist creates his or her own personal relevance.

The 12 terrorists studied included three women and three men who were no longer actively involved in terrorism. The terrorists' average age was about 26 years and they generally lacked a formal education. Police and court records validated the fact that they had been actively involved in violent incidents. An example of a member of the study is as follows:

> RM is 25 years old. He was involved in the assassination of a prominent political leader, explosions in two industrial units, and an attack on a police station that led to the killing of a police officer. His father died when he was a small child and so his mother brought him up. He was influenced by the personality and ideas of a prominent terrorist leader and joined the terrorist movement at the age of 15 against the wishes of his mother. His mother died in his absence. He surrendered to the police because of differences with a commander and is now in prison.
>
> (Sarangi and Alison, 2005, p. 73)

The participants were interviewed by a researcher with social scientific knowledge for whom rapport-building was a priority. This was achieved by having each terrorist talk about their childhood together with other matters not directly involved with their terrorist activities. The researchers suggest that there are common rhetorical structures in the interviews:

- *Images of self (us):* these include Me, parents, siblings and friends, my people, such as villagers in the community. The descriptions of the self(us) are simple and naive, poor, short of food and water, exploited and cheated. These images of the self are referred to as imagoes, using McAdams' (1990) concept. An imago can be seen as the personification of the self in an idealised form. The imago serves as the central character in the individual's life story. For these terrorists, the imago would be characterised as good, simple, brave, loyal and so forth. Imagoes may change according to whether it is the self in the past, present, or future which is being referred to (Figure 12.2).
- *Significant others (interpersonal figures):* this includes the major categories of Other: (a) the descriptions of They for

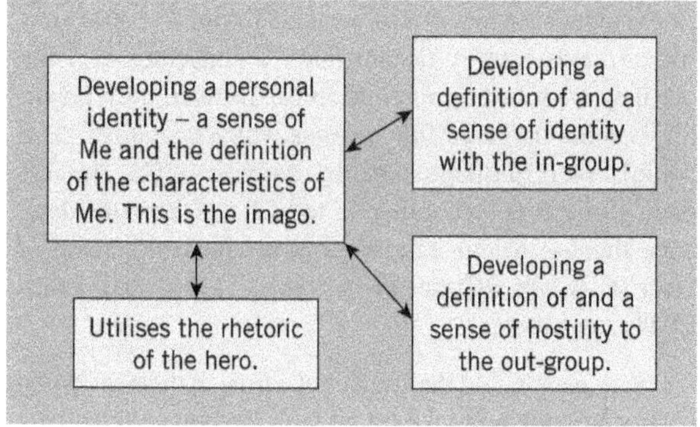

Figure 12.2 The process of terrorist identity formation

the Government, etc. which include characteristics such as villains, rich, powerful, exploiters, uncaring and inhuman and (b) the descriptions of They for the liked (e.g. global terrorist leaders) which would include characteristics such as heroes, saviours, brave-courageous, admired by people, knowledgeable and committed.

- *Visions of the future (the generativity script):* the life trajectory is from the past (which included ideas such as nobody, hungry, insignificant, marginalised, suppressed, exploited and ruled by the evil They) to the present (which includes sacrificing, courageous, disciplined, fighter, cadre, and influence and significance) to the 'future' in the trajectory, which includes creator of an exploitation-free society, leaving behind a legacy, plenty of land and food, goodies of life, victory over the evil They, and powerful and respected. The terrorist accounts show a commitment to achieving an exploitation-free society in the future. They were ideologically committed to a rhetoric which justified violence of the worst sort.

Terrorist ideologies and cognitions

A common approach to explaining the development of ordinary people into terrorists is to concentrate on their ideologies and the way in which their cognitions change over time as they become more involved in terrorist groups. In his important review of the psychology of terrorism, Borum (2004) includes the following as important to the understanding of terrorists:

- Terrorist ideologies are often favourable towards and justify particular behaviours.
- There is an erosion of the normal human inhibitions against killing as a result of the influence of social and environmental variables or changes in the perception of the situation.

There is reason to believe that the violent environments which are sometimes associated with the rise of terrorism may have as their consequence effects which were unintended. These unexpected consequences can be illustrated by Atran's (2003) observation based on a large study of Muslims in Gaza who were adolescent at the time of the first Palestianian Intifada, which occurred between 1987 and 1993. Exposure to violence at this time was more predictive of pride and social cohesion than it was with depression or antisocial behaviour. These Gaza teens had more hope for the future than did a control sample of Bosnian Muslims. According to Borum (2004) three conditions result in an ideology being supportive of terrorism:

- the ideology must involve beliefs which both guide and justify the terrorist acts;
- it must be characterised by rigid orthodoxies which do not allow these beliefs to be challenged or questioned in any way;
- the terrorist acts must have clear goals which can be seen as part of a meaningful cause, such as the struggle between 'good and evil'.

Part of the cognitive changes which are needed in order for normal people to engage in terrorist acts include what Bandura (1990) refers to as the *techniques of moral disengagement* which would allow terrorists to insulate themselves from the psychological consequences of their violent actions. These include:

- moral justifications, such as the belief that the terrorist is fighting some evil;
- the displacement of responsibility to their leaders or others in the group, which may allow the individual to psychologically disown their agency in terrorist acts;
- the minimisation of the suffering of victims;
- the dehumanisation of the victims.

In a cognitive model applicable to terrorist ideologies, Beck (2002) proposed that the thinking of terrorists exhibits the sort of cognitive distortions that are often found in people who commit other sorts of acts of violence. These cognitive distortions include the tendency to overgeneralise the enemy's perceived failings to encompass the entirety of the population. Perceptions of people are also dichotomised so that they are either good or they are bad, with no shades of grey in between. There is a form of tunnel vision in that the terrorist focuses entirely on the destruction of their target.

Planning terrorist attacks

One would not expect terrorists to be the most enthusiastic of research participants. Researchers into terrorism have difficulties in obtaining viable data on topics of importance and they have to settle for data which probably would be regarded as minimal or unsatisfactory in many other areas of study. Not surprisingly, then, a large proportion of the scholarly publications contain no empirical data and are theoretical/conjectural/speculative in nature. These may be helpful up to a point but after that we are in desperate need of sound empirical research. The question of just how terrorists go about planning their attacks is the sort of research issue which is expectedly difficult to address directly. So the approach taken by Romyn and Kebbell (2013) fills a need to some extent while remaining a little removed from terrorist reality. The researchers essentially simulated the planning process using non-terrorists. They had 'red-teams' who were involved in planning a terrorist attack on an important city. These teams consisted of Australian people without anti-terrorism training and others who did have anti-terrorism training. There was also a 'blue team', which had the task of anticipating how the terrorists would plan their attack. This was made up of people who had anti-terrorism training, including a group of police officers. The participants in the research ranked the tasks involved in the attack in terms of their sequencing. There was good consistency in terms of how the elements of the attack were ordered. This overall order is presented in Figure 12.3. The order of the sequence was the same for those with and those without previous military training. Not all of the steps were regarded as being as important as each other. Acquiring weapons and identifying targets were seen as the most important. In terms of the blue team members, those with previous experience did not differ from the red team in terms of the sequence expected to be planned, though those with police experience were not so good at identifying what the untrained members of the red team would choose as their sequence. The choice of targets also manifested a lot of consistency. The order was: 1) underground railway station; 2) football cup final; 3) military march; 4) airport; 5) religious gathering; 6) electrical substation; and 7) military base. Again there was a lot of similarity between the red and blue teams in terms of ordering. The expectation of casualties and the ease by which they could be attacked were the reasons for the primary targets. The least preferred targets were generally seen as not easy or not occupied and hence casualties would be low.

Such research is clearly of interest and it is questionable whether it is any less pertinent to terrorism research because of its artificiality than the research on mock juries is to jury research, for example. No doubt the methodology could be improved in numerous ways. By providing choices, the role of this sort of planning exercise for identifying less predictable targets is weak. But one could image the methodology being adapted to identify the nature and process of terrorist attacks on particularly important targets. The availability of this sort of study hopefully is encouraging of further research using different methodologies such as interviews with captured to 'retired' terrorists.

The end of terrorist organisations

Terrorist organisations eventually cease their activities, just as criminals abandon their criminal careers. The processes involved in this are poorly understood and have not been the subject of study until recently. Reinares (2011) discusses the disengagement of members of the Basque terrorist organisation Euskadi Ta Askatasuna (ETA) over the three decades beginning in 1970. His study was based on 35 long interviews with ex-members of ETA who decided to abandon their active militancy over this period. Key to understanding his findings is the death of the Spanish dictator Franco in 1975. Reinares writes that the mid-1980s marked a change in the nature of the decisions to leave ETA. Spain moved to democracy and there was political decentralisation. For some terrorists, abandonment of terrorist activity came when they saw that political and social changes had become sufficient. Some of the terrorists were aware of the effect that such changes were beginning to have on the Basque people's attitudes to separatism and they abandoned violence because of this. After this time, the dominant reasons changed. Issues like the internal functioning of the organisation and the leadership's tactics became more important. Some left for reasons that can be best described as personal. Those who left did not abandon their militancy and they had not become deradicalised in general. Among those who left there were some who still accepted the doctrine of violence that they agreed to when they joined. A few left because they were expelled by the ETA leadership. The circumstances of their abandoning their membership also shed some light. Sometimes they left ETA while still active gunmen but this was relatively uncommon. Terrorists were more likely

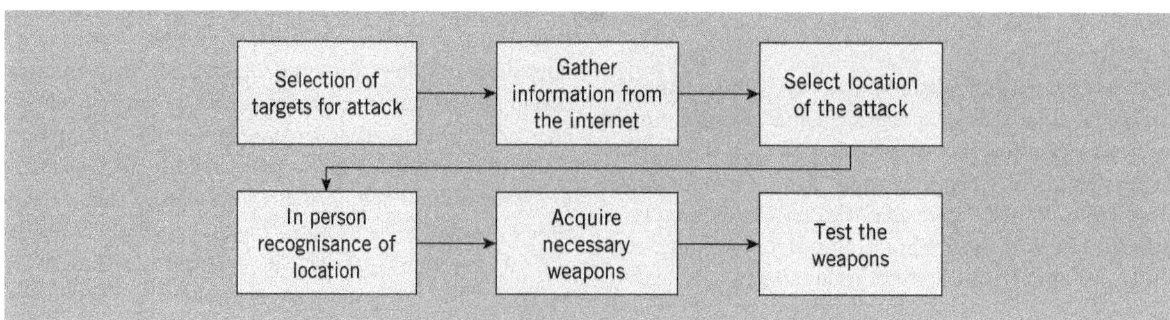

Figure 12.3 The sequence of activities planned by the 'attackers'

to abandon the organisation when hidden away for long periods in France and Latin American countries to avoid arrest. The vast majority, however, made the decision to quit during (often very lengthy) prison sentences. Among those who had spent a lot of time in prison, new relationships such as fatherhood influenced their decision to quit. In the terrorists' accounts there may be patterns but overall there is no single reason for abandoning terrorism. Factors internal and external to the organisation all had their impact. What seems clear is that the abandonment of ideology and radicalism was not a key feature in abandoning terrorist involvement.

Miller (2012) approached the decline of terrorist organisations in a radically different way by seeking statistical patterns in their onset and decline. To speak of terrorist organisations is to brush over the fact that this can refer to anything from highly structured hierarchies to a few loosely interconnected cells. She points out that the usual unit of analysis in terrorism research is the terrorist attack. The terrorist organisation, as such, is seldom the research focus, except for some case studies of individual organisations. Just what are the conditions which lead organisations to desist from terrorism? The answer to this was sought in the data contained in the Global Terrorism Database. This contained relevant data on over 500 terrorist organisations which had been active between 1970 and 2008. The included terrorist organisation had to have been active for a minimum of a year. There are two main patterns to be found: 1) those which show rapid desistance after their peak year of attacks and 2) those which show minimal decline after their peak year of attacks. The former involves something like 80 per cent of the terrorist organisations studied and the latter group about 20 per cent. It was found that terrorist organisations that had a fast-climbing onset curve for terrorist attacks were the most likely to reach moderate to high levels of attack annually. They also tended to be the organisations which soon after their peak attack year showed persistent and steady decline. Remember, though, that the end of one group may merely signal the start of other, maybe splinter, terrorist groups.

Hostage barricade incidents

The phrase 'hostage barricade incident' describes the police or security forces besieging a house, business or aeroplane, for example, where people are being held against their will. A simple siege does not involve a hostage but an individual who the police are trying to get out from a particular physical location. In hostage barricade incidents, whatever intermittent communications occur are likely to be determined by the hostage takers rather than the police. Potentially, of course, the forcible release of the hostages may be extremely risky, as we have seen, so some form of assessment is necessary into the inherent risks of an immediate forceful intervention compared with the risks of continuing the barricade into the future. Just how do police officers go about assessing risk in these situations? Is there a correspondence between the risk factors identified by police officers and known risk factors obtained from real-life barricade incidents?

Research by Yokota, Iwami, Watanabe, Fujita and Watanabe (2004) studied risk factors established from real-life hostage incidents and compared them with the beliefs that police officers have about different aspects of incidents which may make them especially risky. In two out of four of these real-life incidents firearms were present, but this is a poor indicator of risk because the possession of firearms occurs very frequently in barricade situations. Hostages were most likely to be injured in domestic situations where domestic violence had led to the hostage taking or the hostage taker's purpose was to get his ex-partner to come back to him. Expressive situations such as suicides, suicide attempts or domestic situations were the most likely to lead to injuries among the hostages. The risk of injury was quite low where the perpetrator was mentally ill.

The majority (73 per cent) of the Japanese police officers studied believed that a highly excited state among the hostage takers was dangerous. In contrast, if one examines real-life hostage incidents then other factors including 'a long siege' tended to increase the risk of death. Nevertheless, the risk of death is small since fewer than 4 per cent of the real-life hostage incidents studied ended in a hostage's death. The second most common perceived risk factor was 'an incident is caused due to interpersonal problems', which was mentioned by 24 per cent of the police officers, while 16 per cent mentioned the stage at which the hostage taker was told that their demands were not to be met as being risky. About a third of the police officers mentioned offence characteristics as risk factors. Another third mentioned police activities more frequently, such as where there was no effective communication between hostage taker and the police (16 per cent). Offender characteristics such as mental illness (13 per cent), attempted suicide (11 per cent) or drug use (9 per cent) were mentioned by 27 per cent of officers.

In a second aspect of the study, the researchers presented the police officers with 22 hypothetical situations which they evaluated in terms of the level of risk inherent in each. Situations described to the officers included such things as: hostages have been injured/killed; the siege duration is very long; hostage taker demands an escape route; a plane is hijacked by the hostage taker; and the hostage taker is a member of a political group such as a right-wing one. Generally, the officers rated all of the situations as high-risk. Where hostages had been injured/killed was the highest risk situation according to the ratings of the police officers, followed by 'hostage taker takes illegal drugs' and 'hostage taker is mentally ill'. Low-risk characteristics included the perpetrators making tangible demands to the police, including demands for money, coverage by the media or a means of escape. Thus the officers seem to rate emotional and impulsive situations as more risky than instrumental ones.

There was only a very weak relationship between the risk assessment of situations by police officers and actual risk of deaths and injuries to hostages obtained from a sample of real-life incidents. One obvious conclusion is that the officers were unaware of the true nature of risks in these situations. This is possibly the result of inexperience but, of course, these officers may well be those responsible for at least the early stages of hostage barricade incidents.

The majority of officers managing major enquiries (80 per cent) have less than five years of policing experience. A model dealing with the experiences of senior police officers who managed significant incidents in the United Kingdom is described by Crego and Alison (2004). The lack of control the officers believed they had, together with the blame that they felt they would receive as managers, resulted in these incidents being seen as complex and difficult by them. The researchers used electronic conferencing to bring together a focus group of officers who had managed critical incidents. The method systematically explores the experiences of officers who had managed critical setting. There were several aspects to the research:

- unstructured accounts where participants considered their experiences and outlined the significant issues as they saw them;
- theme building: the officers taking part in the electronic conferencing were split into teams which were given the task of reviewing the data that had been collected in the first stage;
- plenary session where the themes developed are discussed and agreed;
- first sort: the focus group organises the items generated in the first stage into the agreed themes;
- summation in which the themes are synthesised into key statements;
- prioritisation: in which participants rate the issues according to different criteria such as, in this case, impact and ease of implementation.

Officers use two co-occurring issues as the defining features of the criticality of incidents:

- The impact of features of the situation directly on the enquiry – for example, creating a good teamwork atmosphere and keeping local and national authorities aware of what is going on.
- Whether the issue will affect how the police will be judged by others, such as the community, the media or the victims. Thus the officers recognised that engaging with the community early on in the enquiry and anticipating possible leaks to the media were important. But they also appreciated that the media is a resource.

Box 12.2 Key concept

The Stockholm syndrome

The *hostage identification syndrome* (or the Stockholm syndrome) refers to the tendency in hostage-type situations for hostages to develop a psychological affinity with their captors. Negative feelings may develop against the authorities trying to rescue them. This is a two-way thing in some cases, which may work to the hostages' advantage in that their safety is improved by such positive interpersonal feelings. The term was coined by a Swedish psychiatrist, Nils Bejerot, who was used by Swedish police to help in a hostage incident at the Kreditbanken in Normalmstorg, Stockholm in 1973. During the aftermath of a botched robbery attempt, four members of the bank's staff were used as hostages and forced into the bank's vault, where they had dynamite strapped to them and nooses prepared to place around their own necks. This situation lasted for five days. Victims and robbers became somewhat close during this time and, afterwards, the hostages would defend the robbers almost as if they were the victims. Indeed, one of the hostages organised a defence fund and it is reputed that one of the women hostages later married one of the robbers Adorjan, Christensen, Kelly and Pawluch (2012). In the terrifying situation that hostages face, they begin to see good in any slight act of kindness on the part of their captors. Even not being beaten or otherwise badly treated can be seen positively by hostages. De Fabrique, Romano, Vecchi and van Hasselt (2007) indicate that the characteristics of the Stockholm syndrome are as follows:

- The hostages have positive feelings about their captors.
- The hostages manifest negative feelings to the authorities, including the police, such as anger, fear and distrust.
- The perpetrators begin to display positive feelings about the hostages as the hostages begin to be seen on a more personal level as human beings.

The hostages may show hostility towards the police. According to Adorjan *et al.* (2012), the emotional bonds may be reciprocated by the captors, which has been described as the Lima syndrome.

So what are the conditions which lead to the development of the Stockholm syndrome? According to de Fabrique *et al.*, there are several conditions which experts generally agree are required (de Fabrique *et al.*, 2007):

- The hostage is unable to escape and it is in the hands of the hostage taker whether the hostage lives or dies. The hostage taker is in control of the hostage's basic survival needs and their life.
- The hostage is kept isolated from other people and so only has the hostage taker's perspective. The hostage taker usually discloses little or nothing about the outside world to the hostage, which further ensures the dependency of the hostage on the hostage taker.
- The hostage taker threatens the life of the hostage convincingly. The hostage then aligns themselves with the hostage taker as the safest option. The hostage realises that they simply have to accept the discomforts of being held captive and to go along with what the hostage taker wants. The alternative is to resist and risk being killed.
- The hostage taker shows the hostage kindness in some way. Without this, the Stockholm syndrome will not develop.

Given that the Stockholm syndrome may help protect the hostage, crisis negotiators encourage its formation in hostage barricade incidents.

Hostage negotiation

Hostage taking is a terrorist technique but it is more likely to occur in domestic situations and robberies, among others. The practicalities of how to deal with such hostage situations have been addressed by psychologists, especially in hostage crisis negotiations. This is partly because of the realisation that extreme situations may have a core of normality – especially so far as relations between the hostage takers and police are considered. Wilson and Smith (2000) argue that behaviour during hostage-taking situations is bound by two sets of rules: 1) rules about the 'normal' behaviour that should be followed in hostage-taking situations and 2) rules about everyday behaviour which act as a fallback if the specific rules cannot be applied. They propose the importance of the following:

- *Motivation:* although it may be a complex task to understand the motives of the hostage takers, there may be clues to motive in their behaviour in the situation. They may give information to newspapers and television about the reasons for their action. If the demand is solely for money, according to Wilson and Smith, then this suggests a personally motivated crime rather than a politically motivated one. If the hostage takers demand the release of fellow terrorists then the hijacking may be a strategic attempt to fill a gap in the organisation. On the other hand, if the demand is to release prisoners in general, then this may be a simple expression of ideological beliefs about injustice as it applies widely.
- *Planning and resources:* the amount of planning that goes into a terrorist situation may indicate various things. For example, it may indicate the determination of the terrorists to fulfil the mission. Their behaviour should be more predictable than in circumstances in which the incident occurred spontaneously. Resources – or the lack of them – may give other insights into the planning of the operation.

In negotiations with hostage takers, the underlying 'rules' include the following:

- Both parties should demonstrate a willingness to negotiate.
- The parties should show willingness to demonstrate 'negotiability' by, for example, being willing to extend deadlines.

The hostages are the 'currency' of exchange with which the terrorists may bargain and negotiate. The release of all hostages is a bad strategy because only things such as the aircraft remain with which to bargain. At the same time, not releasing some prisoners may also be regarded as a bad strategy. The reasons include the good publicity accruing to the terrorists if some prisoners are released, especially women, children and the sick. Wilson and Smith suggest that breaking the rules of hostage taking may lead to a direct response by the authorities. They give the example of 'bluffing' about the situation, such as the terrorists claiming to have hostages when they do not. Negotiations may break down in these circumstances.

According to Flood (2003) 82 per cent of incidents were dealt with without injury or death to the hostages or the hostage takers. This is probably in part the result of modern crisis negotiation techniques introduced by Frank Bolz and Harvey Schlossberg of the New York Police Department in the early 1970s. Schlossberg had a doctoral degree in clinical psychology (Strentz, 2006). They worked together following the Munich Olympics massacre (where the policing tactics of a hostage incident had been disastrous) to produce soundly based guidelines for negotiators in such situations. Instead of the hard-nosed, confrontational techniques which had previously been employed, revolutionary techniques based on ideas from conflict and dispute resolution were introduced. The overriding strategy is that of buying time in order to facilitate a rational ending to the episode. The fundamental approach of crisis negotiation is to:

- negotiate with the hostage taker while at the same time containing them within their immediate environment;
- use whatever methods are available to establish the motivation of the hostage taker and the personality factors which may underlie the incident;
- proceed at a deliberately slow pace, thus stretching the timescale of the negotiations. This is partly a way of dealing with the stretched emotions of the hostage takers by giving them the opportunity to express their feelings. As a consequence, the hostage taker may respond in a more rational way.

The phrase 'active listening skills' describes the strategies, such as emotion labelling and mirroring, used in crisis negotiation to achieve its goals. These skills are involved in establishing social relationships between the negotiators and the hostage takers and lead to the defusing of the situation. Noesner and Webster (1997) describe the different active listening skills used in crisis intervention negotiations, which include the following:

- *Minimal encouragements:* these are verbal demonstrations that negotiators are listening carefully to the hostage taker's words and that the hostage taker is understood. These are very ordinary, everyday responses such as 'OK' or 'I see'. These keep the conversation going and eventually may help shift control of events to the crisis negotiator.
- *Paraphrasing:* in this, the hostage taker's talk is repeated back to them by the negotiator in the negotiator's own words.
- *Emotion labelling:* the negotiator must deal with the hostage taker's emotions in relation to the hostage-taking situation. The negotiator gives a 'tentative' label to the emotions that the hostage taker is communicating. So the negotiator may say something like 'It seems that you are angry with the way the Americans have treated Muslims all over the world.' The response of the hostage taker to this emotion labelling further helps the negotiator understand his or her emotional state.
- *Mirroring:* in this the negotiator repeats a few words of what has just been said by the hostage taker or the idea that has been expressed. For example, if the hostage taker says something like 'There's no way that I am going to be pushed around by Americans' the mirrored response might be 'You won't be pushed around by Americans.' Mirroring provides one way of avoiding confrontational exchanges between the hostage taker and the police. It may also lead to the disclosure of valuable information as well as allowing the hostage taker to vent his or her emotions.
- *Open-ended questions:* the negotiator cannot learn effectively from the hostage taker unless the hostage taker does most of the talking. So open-ended questions inviting the hostage taker to tell the negotiator more about something would be appropriate as these are known to promote lengthier replies.
- *'I' messages:* these are non confrontational personal comments by the negotiator expressing the way he or she feels in response to the hostage taker's words or actions. Phrases suggesting that the negotiator feels frustrated at the lack of progress in the negotiations would be an example of this.

Hostage negotiation is a skill which can be taught and so is included in police training programmes. Perera *et al.* (2006) describe their evaluation study of one particular training programme in crisis negotiation. This programme involved many important topics in crisis negotiation, including basic principles of effective negotiations, suicide interventions, abnormal psychology and the use of third-party intermediaries in negotiations. Apart from these psychological aspects of hostage negotiation, training in the use of equipment and technical aspects involved in the use of, for example, communication systems and command posts was included. Initial crisis negotiation training cannot be done 'on the job' for obvious reasons. So the necessary psychological skills involved in active listening are developed through role-play and enactments of risky negotiation situations. They list direct instruction, performance feedback, modelling, behavioural rehearsal and positive reinforcement as the basis of learning crisis negotiation skills.

A group of FBI special agents took part in a role-play assessment of their crisis negotiation skills prior to intensive training and afterwards in order to assess the practical consequences of the programme. The role-play test for crisis negotiation skill was based on audio-taped narrative versions of real hostage incidents. Active listening skills in general improved significantly after the training. But equally important was the fact that attempts at problem solving declined with training. It is generally considered that making statements directed towards providing a solution to the hostage taker's problems (problem solving) is actually dangerous in crisis negotiation as it may lead to premature interventions. This is especially the case early in the negotiation before sufficient rapport between the negotiator and hostage taker has developed.

While it is clear that hostage negotiation skills can be taught, there is some evidence that active listening skills may not be commonly employed in practice. Webster (2004) obtained tapes of a number of crisis negotiations and was somewhat surprised to find that the use of active listening skills only occurred in about 13 per cent of turn-takings in the negotiations. In fact, two-thirds of these active listening skills were very basic indications of attention to what the hostage taker was saying (attending skills) or the use of minor encouragers. The sort of thing that characterises these active listening skills is the use of such expressions as 'I see', 'sure' and 'right'. The use of complex active listening skills is a rather smaller proportion of the total turns. Paraphrasing what the hostage taker has said amounted to about 12 per cent of the total, emotion labelling amounted to 8 per cent of the total, summarising what had been said so far was 7 per cent of the total, and mirroring was 6 per cent of the officer's speaking turns. If the minor encouragers are left out, the actual use of active listening skills reduces to about 6 per cent of all of the turns.

Models of hostage negotiation

One of the unexpected features of the terrorism and crisis negotiation literature is the number of models related to negotiation processes. These are predominantly theoretically rather than empirically based. Mostly psychologists tend to adopt empirically driven models rather than more hypothetical ones; however, empirical work on terrorist processes is patently very difficult or impossible. Nevertheless, crisis negotiation is a deadly serious issue which demands to be better understood for the safety of all concerned. The purpose of the models is to provide a degree of conceptual clarity to otherwise intrinsically complex and confusing situations. As such, a shared framework of understanding is available to officers as well as a basis for proceeding through the negotiation. The authors of these models almost invariably stipulate that they are to be used flexibly and that it may be appropriate to move back to an earlier stage in the negotiation process in appropriate circumstances. One such model is the FBI's Behavioural Influence Stairway Model of crisis negotiation (Vecchi, van hasselt and Romano 2005). This, according to Ireland and Vecchi (2009), is the prototypical version of this sort of model. It is also a model which has influenced strategies in the United Kingdom, for example. The Behavioural Influence Stairway Model (Van Hasselt, Romano and Vecchi, 2008) is an update of the FBI's crisis negotiation process. This is illustrated in Figure 12.4. The metaphor of a stairway or steps is common in models of crisis negotiation.

The stairway starts at the bottom step where there is no relationship between the negotiator and the hostage holder/terrorist and ends at the top step where there is a good relationship between the negotiator and the hostage holder/terrorist. Progress up the steps is through the use of active listening skills over a period of time which is, of course, flexible according to circumstances. There is no reason why the negotiator should not step back down should there be difficulties advancing up the steps. There is no fixed timescale for carrying out this sort of negotiation. There is no need to have information about any mental disorders involved and it is not essential to know just what the motives of the terrorist are. The process is about bringing the situation to a peaceful halt with no harm done to any of those involved. The staircase is a relationship-building process in which the development of a trusting, positive relationship between the terrorist and the negotiator is the underlying aim of the enterprise. The aim is not for the negotiator to understand the reasons behind the incident. Concentration on motives can divert attention onto emotionally driven aspects which can make matters worse. Neither is it about solving the terrorist's problems in some way as that also is about understanding the motive of the offender and may lead to a counterproductive urgency to find a solution.

The stairway model is intended to be dynamic since the terrorist may alternate between steps. Active listening is fundamental throughout and can be thought of as a way of moving from the emotional to the rational. One possibility is that the negotiator may find that the terrorist wishes to go to a bargaining stage straightaway. In the process of active listening, the negotiator may appear to be making trade-offs but nothing is really given away. But doing so may help reassure the terrorist and also buy time. Terrorists in such incidents may be less concerned about themselves and their personal interests and more concerned with how they will look in the eyes of their peers. Some terrorists may be keen to die in an act of martyrdom but probably many more would prefer to live to fight for their cause another day. Judgements about such matters may have a bearing on the negotiation. The flexibility of the Behavioural Influence

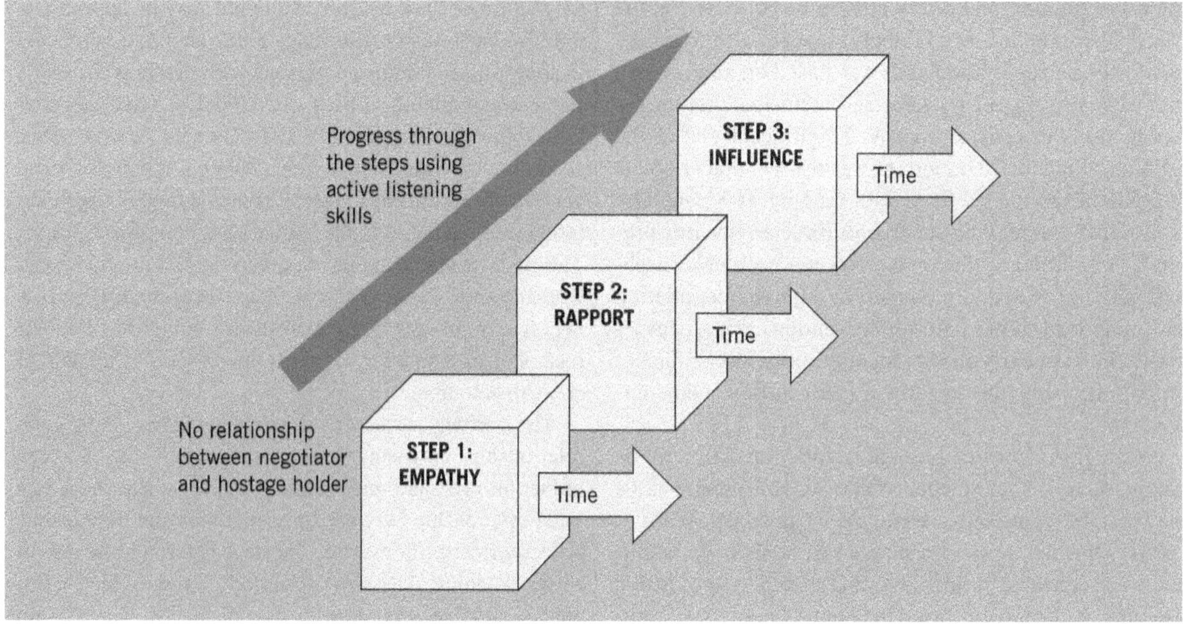

Figure 12.4 The Behavioural Influence Stairway Model

Stairway Model is important but the model nevertheless brings a sense of structure to a situation which may otherwise be chaotic to the negotiators involved.

Others have proposed not too dissimilar models. Madrigal, Bowman and McClain (2009) suggest a four-phase model of hostage negotiation which concentrates on the actions of the negotiator and indicates what style of language and talk should be used at each stage (see Figure 12.5). That is to say, the sorts of verbal statements which are utilised by the negotiator change during the negotiation process – each phase of the model is communicatively different. Generally, the sequence given will be followed, but this is not always the case and backtracking is a distinct possibility in this model too. The negotiator should not move too quickly through the phases since this may result in anger or some other reaction from the hostage taker. If this happens, then the situation may be corrected by backtracking to the earlier phases.

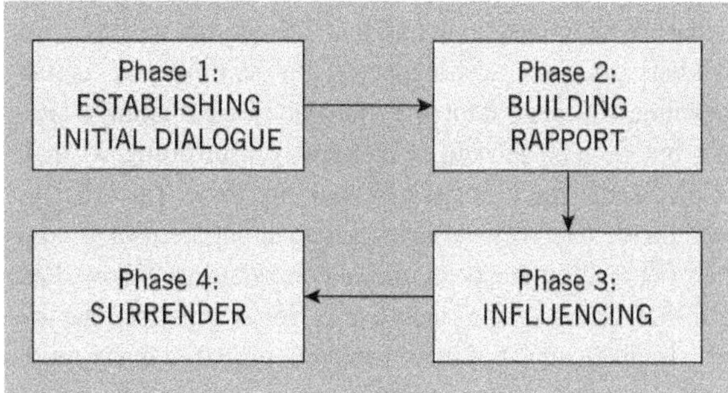

Figure 12.5 The four phases proposed by Madrigal *et al.* (2009)

- *Phase 1: Establishing initial dialogue.* In this approach, it is assumed that the hostage taker may be reluctant to engage in negotiation and may demonstrate hostility. So the process is one of initiating dialogue through whatever means seem to be appropriate. The initial statements of the negotiator will tend to be situational or more general. The weather may be such a general topic but asking about the condition of the hostages may also be appropriate. Even sport on big match days might be a good way into the dialogue. This phase can be difficult because the hostage taker may be decidedly resistant to speaking with the negotiator.
- *Phase 2: Building rapport.* Some degree of rapport has been achieved when this phase of the negotiation is instigated. The task of this phase is to create a personal relationship and trust between the hostage taker and the negotiator. In this way, a free exchange of personal information becomes possible. If Phase 1 requirements have not been achieved then problems may occur in Phase 2 and the hostage taker's response may become very negative. If this is the case, backtracking to Phase 1 may be necessary. This phase will involve many of the active listening techniques which have already been discussed. Mirroring, paraphrasing, minimal encouragers are all part of this. If Phase 2 is executed successfully then it will result in personal information including emotional information being revealed by the hostage taker, who holds the negotiator in some sort of positive

regard if not friendship. These may appear to be reciprocated by the negotiator. This signals the possibility of moving on to the third phase.

- *Phase 3: Influencing.* Building on the achievements of the previous phase, the negotiator's task is to persuade the hostage holder to free the hostages and bring the stand-off to a peaceful end. The risk is that the hostage taker will perceive the negotiator as engaging in trickery. This stage involves little active listening since the necessary personal relationship will have been developed. The negotiator may make suggestions and promises, and reframe the situation to present a positive outcome from surrender. The primary task of this stage is to reassure the hostage taker of their safety should they decide to end the stand-off by surrendering. It is not really about bargaining or providing solutions to problems, though sometimes these may be part of this phase.
- *Phase 4: Surrender.* In this phase the hostage taker will have decided to surrender. The task of the negotiator is to give the hostage taker the important instructions about how to do this in a way in which they will stay safe and also ensure that the hostage taker fully understands what is required. This is a relatively pragmatic stage since the major negotiation skills will have been used in order to get to this final phase. But this is regarded as a very risky phase for both the hostage taker and the police officers involved, so everything needs to be done with great care.

Models like this are not built on vast bodies of research work but they are extremely useful in helping to clarify and conceptualise the negotiation process such that those involved can structure their experiences around a meaningful framework.

Terrorism and hostage negotiation

Most hostage crisis incidents tackled by the police do not involve terrorism. However, there are examples of hostage taking by terrorists which can strain the available research and theory in this area. Terrorist attacks on the Moscow theatre, the Beslan school, and the Kenyan shopping mall suggest new and disturbing trends in barricade/hostage incidents. The Beslan school attack led to the deaths of over 300 adults and children in 2004. More than 1200 hostages, mainly children, were held at the school by more than 50 hostage takers strategically located around the school. There were 21 hostages killed the first day and their bodies thrown outside through a window. Any one of four terrorists located in different parts of the school could detonate the 130 explosive devices left in different locations. The terrorists could monitor each entrance to the school through security cameras. The terrorists had gasmasks to protect themselves against incapacitating gas should it be used at the school. Heat exhaustion was a major problem inside the school. The terrorists made demands which seemed impossible to meet. Angry parents were also outside the school, threatening to kill the rescue team if they attempted a rescue. In the light of such incidents, Dolnik and Fitzgerald (2011) paint a picture of the 'new terrorists':

- They are difficult to trick because they have carefully studied past hostage incidents and have read hostage crisis training manuals.
- They use religious rhetoric which is extreme and far beyond anything experienced by hostage crisis negotiators in general.
- The new breed of terrorists seem more willing to harm hostages to achieve their ends than was the case in the past.
- They have good communications with terrorist colleagues in distant locations.
- Because they are tactically knowledgeable it is difficult to use threats coercively or to bargain hard. They have good weapons and are prepared to die.

So what resources are available to help the negotiator deal with such situations? Dolnick and Fitzgerald suggest that the following are important.

- Hostage negotiation is about influencing the thinking, behaviour and decision making of the other person. Just being in conversation may provide important information.
- Hostage negotiators need to constantly question their own assumptions, biases and characteristics in relation to the terrorists. Jumping to conclusions which cannot be challenged may lead to missed opportunities or information.
- The negotiator needs to remember that they are negotiating with a rational human being, albeit one who has involved in an extreme action. Regarding them as a 'terrorist' can engender stereotypes of terrorism, which may be counterproductive.
- Active listening should be employed along with good questions which enable the negotiator to understand as fully as possible the terrorists' grievances and motives. Asking in detail about the terrorists' justifications for their actions may provide useful information for later use.
- Looking for ways of empathically responding to legitimate grievances underlying the terrorists' actions can make it more difficult for the terrorist to label the authorities negatively as unreasonable.

As a research area, terrorism research is extremely important, though its advances are slowly made and rather insecurely based.

Main points

- Psychological research on terrorism may lack discernible achievements. One difficulty has been that terrorism research has often adopted a traditional personality/mental disorder model to explain why individuals become terrorists. It is becoming increasingly clear that terrorism cannot be explained in terms of pathology. Terrorists are best regarded as normal people who commit extreme violence. Recent work into the cognitive processes of terrorists, their identity development, and the influence of group socialisation practices may form the basis of future research in this field.
- Adopting psychological principles from organisational psychology and the psychology of negotiations has provided police with skills to deal with a range of situations, not all terrorism-based, where hostages are being held. Although these methods are essentially simple ways of maximising talk between the authorities and the terrorists, it is notable that very few hostage-taking situations end in the death of or injury to the captives.
- The psychological literature on terrorism and hostage incidents is somewhat demanding because, as yet, no dominant or commonly accepted theoretical perspective has emerged. The problems are compounded by the difficulty of carrying out research in these areas which are probably not conducive to any traditional psychological research methods. Much of the available research is based on fortuitous opportunities which bring the researcher and terrorist together. What research there is is spread thinly across numerous terrorist groups. This is a good example of researchers having to do make the best of whatever opportunities arise.

Further reading

Broad issues related to psychology and terrorism are to be found in the following:

Bongar, B., Brown, L.M., Beutler, L.E., Breckenridge, J.N. and Zimbardo, P.G. (eds) (2007) *Psychology of Terrorism* Oxford: Oxford University Press.

Silke, A. (ed.) (2010) *The Psychology of Counter-Terrorism* Abingdon, Oxon: Routledge.

The following have extensive reviews of the literature on the psychology of terrorism:

Borum, R. (2004) *Psychology of Terrorism* Tampa: University of South Florida: http://www.ncjrs.gov/pdffiles1/nij/grants/208552.PDF

Hudson, R.A. (1999) *The Sociology and Psychology of Terrorism: Who becomes a Terrorist and Why?* Library of Congress: http://www.loc.gov/rr/frd/pdf-files/Soc_Psych_of_Terrorism.pdf

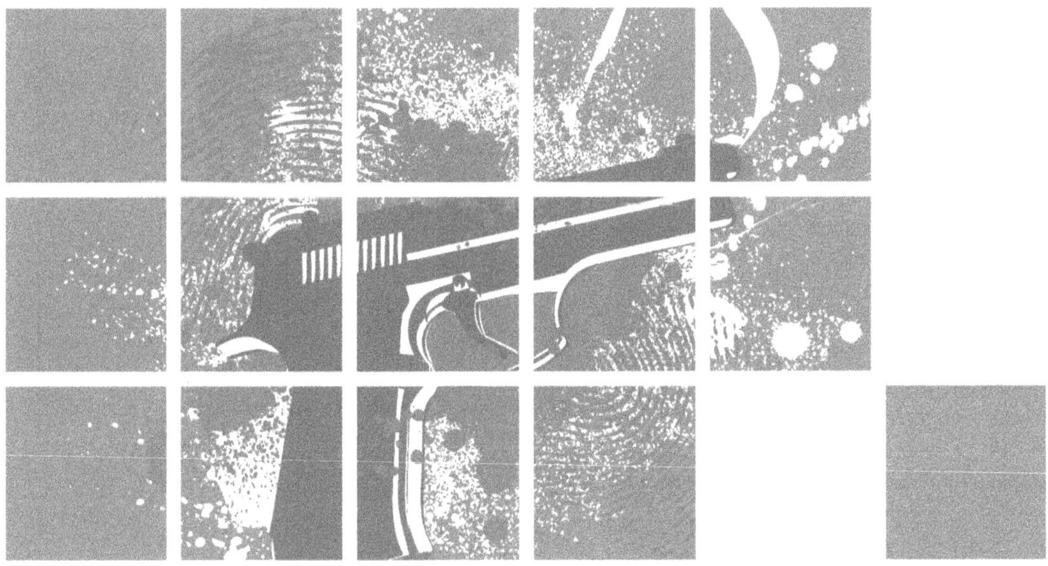

Chapter 13

Eyewitness testimony

Overview

- DNA evidence has proven beyond doubt the innocence of some people wrongfully convicted of crimes. Despite this, surveys of police officers show that they value eyewitness evidence and believe that eyewitnesses are usually correct. Jurisdictions differ according to whether convictions based solely on eyewitness evidence are not acceptable.
- There is a sizeable literature on the characteristics of eyewitness memory. Of importance is the evidence that events following the incident (e.g. interviews) may affect what is remembered, as does the type of questioning.
- The confidence of eyewitnesses in their testimony and their accuracy are quite distinct things. Traditionally in forensic psychology, it was claimed that there is, at best, only a weak correlation between the two. However, more recently it has been argued that this is a misinterpretation and too dependent on witnesses' confidence in court rather than at the time of the initial identification.
- The line-up or identity parade needs to be planned and executed following a number of rules to minimise errors. Features that researchers build into designing psychology experiments may be appropriate. For example, the person conducting the line-up should be unaware of the identity of the suspect in order to avoid the risk of biasing the situation.
- Relative judgement theory suggests that an eyewitness tends to choose someone similar to the culprit if the culprit is not in the identification parade. Procedures which indicate that the culprit may not be present in the line-up may reduce the relative judgement effect.
- CCTV footage does not readily lead to the identification of individuals unknown to the person viewing the tape. Facial composites are not particularly recognisable even for well-known individuals.

Introduction

Few would doubt that human memory is fallible. Ost, Granhag, Udell and Roos afHjelmsäter. (2008) asked samples of British and Swedish people about the events in Tavistock Square, London, when, on 7 July 2005, a Number 30 bus was blown up by a terrorist at roughly the same time as tube trains were bombed. Within three months of the events, the researchers asked whether the participants remembered seeing the video of the bus being blown up. No such video exists, but some participants claimed to have seen it. For the combined samples, 28 per cent claimed to have seen the material which did not exist, though this was more common in the British sample than the Swedish sample. When adjustments were made for the percentages of the two samples who had seen any coverage of the events (the Swedes were less likely to have seen such material), the trends remained much the same. Crombag, Wagenaar and Van Kopen (1995) in a study of an air crash found that people claimed to have seen film of the events despite the fact that no such film exists. A key finding of the research is the failure of participants to recognise the falsity of their claims. That is to say, they did not realise that they were manufacturing memories.

The implications of these studies for forensic and criminal psychology are obvious. Imagine the following circumstances. Police officers show a photograph to a woman who has witnessed a crime. They ask her whether the man in the photograph is the offender. She decides that it is the man who committed the crime. Just what degree of confidence should one have in a conviction based solely on this identification? There are many reasons why the witness identified the photograph as being that of the offender:

- She may feel that the police must have strong reasons to suspect this particular man.
- The man in the photograph may have a passing resemblance to the offender.
- She may believe she has seen the man in the photograph somewhere before.
- She may be concerned that she would appear foolish if she says that she cannot remember whether or not this is the man.

Clearly, this is a very unsatisfactory procedure for identifying an offender with accuracy. Nevertheless, this was common practice in the United States until the Supreme Court of the United States recognised the risk of a miscarriage of justice brought about by such procedures (*Simmons* v. *United States*, 1968).

Nevertheless, there is evidence that police officers have great faith in eyewitness evidence. A survey of British police officers found that, generally speaking, they valued witness evidence positively. The majority believed that witnesses are usually correct and three-quarters thought that they were never or rarely incorrect. On the other hand, about half felt that witnesses remember less than the officer needed (Kebbell and Milne, 1998). In other words, witness evidence may have an important role in police investigations, irrespective of its validity.

Of course, risky identification evidence is an issue in only a minority of crimes. Criminal statistics, as we have seen, show quite clearly that many victims already know their victimisers socially. Thus the risk of innocent misidentification in these circumstances is minimal. In other words, identification evidence is unproblematic in the vast majority of cases. It is in circumstances in which the witness and the offender are strangers that difficulties arise.

Eyewitness testimony as a central issue in forensic and criminal psychology

As we saw in Chapter 1, as long ago as 1896 the German psychologist Albert Von Schrenk-Nortzing testified at the Munich trial of a triple murder. Basing his argument on the then emerging academic research into the nature of suggestibility and memory, Von Schrenk-Nortzing unsuccessfully argued that witnesses confuse real-life events with events they read about in the press. He used the phrase 'retroactive memory falsification'. Just a few years later, Munsterberg, who may be seen as the founder of the field of applied psychology, returned to this field. He argued that there was probably no relationship between the accuracy of an eyewitness and the eyewitness's confidence in the accuracy of his or her testimony. This conclusion still more or less accurately reflects available research findings.

Eyewitness misidentification is the greatest contributing factor to wrongful convictions proven by DNA testing, playing a role in more than 70 per cent of convictions overturned through DNA testing nationwide.

The topic remains important in terms of justice. According to the Innocence Project (2017), eyewitness misidentification played a role in over 70 per cent of proven (DNA exonerated) cases now known (see also Weber, Brewer and Wells, 2004). Work in this area goes back more than twenty years now (e.g. Wells *et al.*, 1998, which extended an earlier review by Connors, Lundregan, Miller and McEwen, 1996). DNA exoneration refers to false convictions established in US courts using genetic fingerprint (DNA) testing. At the time of Wells' paper, forty trials that led to wrongful conviction were available for review. In each of these, the testing of genetic material with new techniques established the unjust conviction beyond any doubt.

These were serious miscarriages of justice. All of the men who were convicted served prison sentences. Five of them spent time on death row awaiting execution. The testimony of at least one eyewitness was involved in 90 per cent of these forty proven miscarriages of justice. In one instance, as many as five eyewitnesses were involved. The case of Ronald Cotton is typical. Cotton spent ten years in prison for a rape actually committed by another man, Bobby Poole. There was remarkably little evidence against Ronald Cotton. One victim had identified him from a photographic line-up (a selection of photographs possibly including the offender). In a line-up/identity parade, just one witness identified him as the rapist. Eventually, the DNA evidence from semen left by the actual rapist resulted in Cotton's release. Remarkably, the real rapist, Bobby Poole, had already confessed to the crimes and this confession had been rejected by a court as reason to release Cotton.

DNA evidence is minimally relevant to a great many crimes. So naturally, for crime in general, it would seem impossible to know the extent to which eyewitnesses make errors which incriminate innocent people in a line-up/identification parade. Nevertheless, Wells, Memon and Penrod (2007) suggested a novel way of obtaining minimum estimates of this. Their approach is based on the frequency with which a filler (stooge) is picked out erroneously as the target from line-ups/identity parades. They refer to a number of studies of real police line-ups in which the rates of identifying a filler as the suspect incorrectly ranged from about 20 per cent to about 24 per cent (i.e. in about 20 per cent of line-ups a filler is erroneously selected). In these studies, a filler was picked out in about a third of the line-ups in which someone was selected by the eyewitness (some line-ups would result in no one being identified). These filler identification rates provide a conservative estimate of the likelihood of an innocent party being picked out. This is on the assumption that the innocent party was at the same level of risk of being selected as any of the filler persons. So if the line-up consisted of six people (the suspect plus five filler people) then the five fillers would have a 20 per cent chance of being picked out *in total*. Since there are five fillers in this example then, overall, a particular filler has a one fifth of 20 per cent chance of being picked out – that is a 4 per cent chance of being identified as the criminal erroneously. The quite reasonable assumption is that the innocent person has the same risk of being picked out.

The accuracy of witness evidence

Eyewitnesses, of course, can be very accurate in their descriptions, despite failing to identify offenders precisely. Very little research is available that compares the characteristics of offenders with those descriptions given to the police. What evidence there is suggests that witnesses can be accurate in terms of describing individual characteristics, but are not always so. One intriguing study which warrants attention concerned witnesses to the murder of Anna Lindh, the Swedish Foreign Minister (Granhag, Ask, Rebelius, Öhman and Giolla, 2013). She was stabbed several times by a lone attacker when visiting a department store. The attack lasted less than 15 seconds before the killer escaped the crime scene. There were 29 witnesses to the stabbing, mainly women. Each one was interviewed up to five times by the police. Descriptions of the offender provided by the witnesses were the main data for the study. One notable event in the course of the study was that the police released pictures of the suspect three days after the killing – some witnesses were interviewed both before and after the release of pictures. The availability of CCTV video of the offender a few minutes before the attack provided the baseline information of the offender characteristics for the researchers. This was sufficiently informative most of the time, though we have already seen some of the limitations of CCTV in Box 13.1. So the researchers used additional photographs in order to obtain finely detailed characteristics such as eye colour or the logo on his cap. Overall, the eyewitness descriptions of the killer as recorded by the police included a total of 43 different unique attributes. These could be grouped into 20 categories and then into four broad categories – clothes, face, hair and general. The accuracy of the details provided was coded into the categories of correct, partly correct, incorrect, and not verifiable, using a formal schedule for each category. The main findings were that, in this case, the accuracy of the witnesses was not good. Only 35 per cent of the details provided were correct, with a further 24 per cent only partly correct. This left a high percentage of details which were actually misleading or potentially misleading in the investigation. The researchers suggest that these accuracy figures are relatively low compared to previous studies. And it made little difference whether physical features such as height were being considered, for example, or whether the descriptions concerned clothing. The release of pictures to the media did result in more details being provided to the police afterwards than before. But the increase was confined to details about clothing and not anything else. Accuracy of the details of clothing also improved. The researchers suggest that the poor quality of the released photographs may have meant that new fine detail could not be picked up from the media.

One of the best large-scale studies in this field was carried out in the Netherlands (Van Koppen and Lochun, 1997). Data were obtained from official court records in store at the offices of prosecutors. The researchers targeted offences involving robberies of commercial buildings and dwellings. Street robberies (muggings) were not included.

In the Netherlands, witnesses are rarely questioned in court. Instead, the prosecution depends on statements obtained by the police from witnesses. In the cases studied, there was very little delay between the offence and the collection of witness statements:

- 80 per cent had been collected within two days – about two-thirds in one day;
- over 400 different robberies were studied;
- 1300 witnesses were involved;
- 2300 offender descriptions were obtained;
- only 1650 descriptions could be used since not all could be verified against the robber's true appearance;
- mostly, the witness had seen the robbery (over four-fifths);
- the remaining witnesses had seen the escape or preparations being made for the robbery.

Other information was available from various sources on the characteristics of the witness and the circumstances of their evidence:

- witness characteristics such as their sex and age;
- the amount of delay before they gave their statements;
- the quality of the lighting conditions at the robbery;
- whether the witness's view was obstructed;
- the estimated distance between the witness and the robbery.

The actual offender characteristics were assessed using the police's own descriptions of the arrestee, which were available from official forms designed for that purpose. The correspondence between the witness description and the police description of the suspect varied according to the physical feature under consideration. The greatest correspondence was found for:

- sex (100 per cent agreement);
- eye shape (100 per cent);
- hair colour (73 per cent);
- face shape (69 per cent);
- race (60 per cent);
- height (52 per cent);
- ears protruding (50 per cent).

While the correspondence for some of the above is generally impressive, some features were rarely mentioned in the witness descriptions. Sex and height were the most commonly mentioned features. Overall, the witness descriptions were relatively sparse. So, out of the maximum of 43 different characteristics that could be mentioned, on average each witness mentioned only eight features.

Of course, offenders have an interest in altering their physical appearance either specifically for the offence or after the offence. So it is of some interest to note that the characteristics that are the most easily altered tend to be those with the lowest agreement:

- beards (1 per cent);
- moustaches (3 per cent);
- accents and dialects (32 per cent).

Some variables predicted the accuracy of the eyewitness description. For example, the longer the statement, the greater the eyewitness accuracy. Given the large sample size involved, the relationships between predictors and accuracy were not strong, despite being statistically significant. Generally speaking, the relationships were much as would be expected. Factors such as the distance between the offender and the witness; the duration of the crime; the physical position of the witness in relation to the offender; and the feelings of threat experienced by the witness all had predictable relationships with witness accuracy. Counterintuitively, the longer the delay between the crime and the statement by the witness, the better was the accuracy of the witness's description.

The overall impression, nevertheless, is of rather vague descriptions that are dominated by very general characteristics such as the offender's sex, race, height and age. The witnesses were accurate in their description of these characteristics. However, these are the very characteristics that are poor at distinguishing offenders from others who are suspects. For example, knowing that the offender is male is not very much use in identifying the particular person in question.

This is about accuracy in describing characteristics of offenders; who gets picked out in line-ups is a different issue.

Later intrusions into eyewitness memory

The early studies of human memory in the first part of the twentieth century largely consisted of the memorising of nonsense syllables following the work of Ebbinghaus (1913): hardly a situation conducive to the study of eyewitness testimony. Things gradually changed from the late 1960s onwards in ways that encouraged psychologists to investigate eyewitness psychology. Increasingly, the importance of studying real-life memory was recognised. For example, Neisser (1982) and Neisser and Winograd (1988) published seminal work on human memory in real-life contexts. Consequently, from the 1970s onwards, academic memory researchers carried out numerous studies of eyewitness memory. Nevertheless, coming, as they did, largely from the laboratory tradition of psychology, their emphasis was on theoretical rather than practical matters.

Some of the most important theory in this area emerged from the work of Elizabeth Loftus. Her interests eventually extended into practical matters such as recovered memories (see Chapter 16). Perhaps the most famous of her studies were demonstrations that subsequent events influenced testimony about incidents. Witnesses to a robbery or accident may be exposed later to new information – perhaps during a police interview, for example. In some circumstances, that new information can influence how they recollect the incident. Furthermore, information in one modality may affect memory for events held in a different modality. Thus verbal information may affect visual recall. The most familiar study is that of Loftus and Palmer (1974). Participants witnessed images of a car accident and were later asked a series of questions in which key information was embedded. There were alternative versions of the key question:

- 'About how fast were the cars going when they *hit* each other?'
- 'About how fast were the cars going when they *smashed* into each other?'

Other variants on this theme had the cars colliding, contacting each other, bumping and so forth. Estimates of speed were affected by the word used in the questioning. The estimates gave speeds about a third faster when the word 'smashed' was used compared to the word 'contacted'. It might be objected – and it was – that, in itself, this does not mean that what was stored in the brain changed. Subtly leading questions may have simply encouraged faster estimates without affecting the 'memory trace'. It is not possible to get into the mind of the witness to measure the speed the cars are travelling in the brain trace. Perhaps this is a theoretical issue rather than being of practical importance. Nevertheless, researchers, including Loftus herself, pursued this issue with some vigour.

In this series of studies, a visual recognition procedure replaced the problematic verbal statement (Loftus, Miller and Burns, 1978). Participants in the research were shown a series of colour slides of the stages of a car–pedestrian accident. The car in question was a red Datsun that was seen driving towards a road intersection where there was either a stop sign or a yield sign (give way sign), depending on the experimental condition. Later a series of questions was asked in which were embedded one of two variants of the key question:

- Did another car pass the red Datsun while it was stopped at the stop sign?
- Did another car pass the red Datsun while it was stopped at the yield sign?

After a short diversionary activity, a 'yes/no' recognition test was administered immediately or a week later. The crucial recognition slides were the stop and the yield slides. Essentially, then, the experimental design was as follows:

- Some participants saw a stop sign and were asked about a stop sign.
- Some participants saw a stop sign but were asked about a yield sign.
- Some participants saw a yield sign and were asked about a yield sign.
- Some participants saw a yield sign but were asked about a stop sign.

In other words, some participants were asked questions *consistent* with what they had seen and others were asked questions *inconsistent* with what they had seen. Some of the findings were:

- Questioning consistent with the contents of the original experience enhanced correct visual identification for the crucial slide immediately after exposure.
- Questioning inconsistent with the original experience depressed correct identification initially.
- Generally speaking, these effects tended to reduce after a week, such that the initial differences disappeared.

Given the great numbers of laboratory studies of eyewitness testimony, it is not possible to review all of the findings. We can, nevertheless, turn to some major forensic issues that illustrate the implications of research findings for court decisions.

BOX 13.1 Forensic psychology in action

CCTV video evidence

There has been a vast increase in the use of closed-circuit television (CCTV) video cameras in public areas such as town and city centres. One of their prime purposes is to act as deterrents to crime. They can also be considered as evidence collection systems. We are all familiar with footage of crimes observed in this way from

BOX 13.1 (continued)

TV programmes. Figure 13.1 presents a model of the influence of CCTV cameras based on Williams (2007), which involves consequences for the policing of an area but also the influence of such cameras on the general public. CCTV cameras do not provide irrefutable evidence of a crime and offenders in practice. This is partly the consequence of the rather poor images produced sometimes because of over-enlargement. One thing is very clear, CCTV does not necessarily lead to crime reduction but it can. Take, for instance, the effect of introducing CCTV into car parks on vehicle crime. In a Canadian study, Reid and Andresen (2014) found little in police and insurance claim records to indicate that CCTV was effective. On the other hand, in the UK, Gill, Little, Spriggs *et al.* (2005) found it to be beneficial. Research suggests substantial issues to do with current CCTV technology and claims of its effectiveness:

- There is evidence that CCTV systems do reduce crime in the *short term* in locations where they are installed, although there is a return to previous levels in the longer term (Brown, 1995). The growing awareness that the system is not altogether effective in ensuring arrest leaves some people willing to take the risk. Overall, there are rather mixed findings from research on CCTV as a crime deterrence and reduction method. Welsh and Farrington (2002) found that the majority of studies did not demonstrate that the cameras led to a decrease in crime. Actually, three studies out of 13 showed an increase in crime rates following CCTV's introduction and four others showed no effect one way or the other.
- The issue of displacement cannot be overlooked. This is the idea that the criminal merely shifts their activities to spots where there is no CCTV surveillance. That is, reductions in crime with the introduction of CCTV is possibly illusory. Scott, Higgs, Caulkins, Aitken, Cogger and Dietzel (2016) looked at the effect of the introduction of CCTV on the self-reported drug taking of a large sample of addicts. There was evidence that injecting moved from the public toilets to the street, for example. Waples, Gill and Fisher (2009) suggest that CCTV does displace crime but this is found rather infrequently.

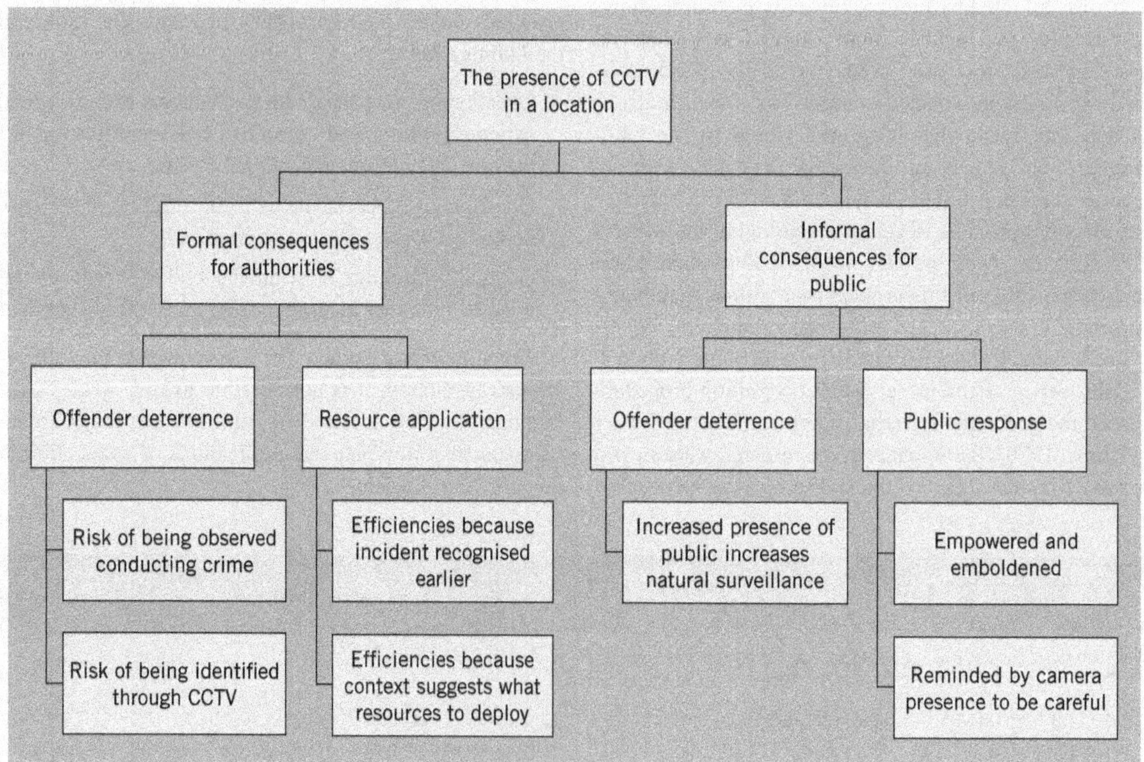

Figure 13.1 A model of the effects of CCTV loosely based on Williams (2007)

- Familiarity with the person in a low-quality video makes it far easier to recognise them compared with strangers. Nevertheless, there is not a proportionate increase in the recognition of strangers as the video quality increases (Burton, Wilson, Cowan and Bruce, 1999). Henderson, Bruce and Burton (2000a) investigated the effects of allowing participants to become modestly familiar with individuals by showing them a short video clip of a face they would later be asked to identify. The consequence was no improvement in recognition of faces in a photo line-up of similar faces compared with a no-familiarisation condition.
- With strangers, it is very difficult with even high-quality videos to determine whether two different images are of the same person (Kemp, Towell and Pike, 1997). For example, Davies and Thasen (2000) found that 65 per cent of viewers of a CCTV video of a woman in an 'incident' in a car park in which she was seen in close-up actually picked out another 'innocent' person from a line-up. Only 29 per cent correctly identified the woman, the remainder made no choice.
- When they compared various measures of the recognition of CCTV-simulated video and stills taken from the video, Kemp, Pike, Brace and Badal (2000) found evidence of the superiority of the video clip. Participants made more correct identifications and were less likely to make false recognitions from the (moving) video. This involved recognition of familiar faces, *not* strangers.

Henderson, Bruce and Burton (2000b) recommend that great caution is needed in assessing evidence from CCTV from people who are not very familiar with the person(s) in the video. Part of the solution lies in the improvement of CCTV images which are poor in comparison with those from broadcast television or domestic camcorders, with which many of us are more familiar. They see CCTV as more important in assessing what happened at a crime scene.

Cerezo (2013) reports the findings of a study of the introduction of CCTV to the historic centre of Malaga, Spain. The study used a pre-test/post-test, quasi-experimental design. In this, measures of crime were taken for the year before and the year after CCTV began. The streets having the cameras were compared with similar streets close by. A control area of Malaga was also used. Streets similar to those which had CCTV were studied as well as streets similar to these. The data collected varied greatly and included interviews with police and other officials as well as survey data of the public using these areas. Crimes including homicide, injury, theft, robbery, theft from vehicles, damage and drug trafficking were involved. The findings of this study were very much in line with the consensus from previous studies. Generally speaking, CCTV cameras made little difference to the levels of crime on streets which had them. The reduction based on police data was about 2 per cent or nearly 4 per cent based on surveys of the public. There was also evidence of increases in the control streets implying a small displacement effect of the CCTV. However, it was crimes against property rather than crimes against people which showed this displacement. Although one might argue that any benefits are worthwhile, the 17 CCTV cameras installed on the streets of Malaga had a capital cost alone of about £400,000. Mucchielli (2011) points out that the cost of personnel to use of CCTV cameras is far in excess of the capital cost.

Of course, the CCTV cameras themselves do not identify which activities are worth monitoring and possible subsequent action. This is the task of human monitors using them. There has only been a little research on this. Just how do the operators of CCTV systems decide what is potentially criminal? The information available from the screen is relatively degraded by many things. A person who is aware of the cameras may decide to modify their behaviour according to whether or not they have any criminal intent. Playful behaviours within the context of a light-hearted conversation may appear to be aggressive or potentially violent on screen. The lack of sound to further inform the human monitors can make interpretation difficult. There is evidence from Lassiter, Geers, Munhall, Handley and Beers (2001) that persons depicted in relative close-up with the wider situation excluded tend to be perceived as problematic. The persons selected for closer observation are those who fit a criminal stereotype – such as younger males or younger black men (Norris and Armstrong, 1997). Williams (2007) studied such decision making in a control room and made comparisons with demographic and similar information collected directly from the locations where the cameras were in use. As in other studies, it became obvious that it was young men of a scruffy appearance who were disproportionately selected by the operators. The operators' justifications for selecting them as targets tended to be that they were loitering. Males were

BOX 13.1 (continued)

selected and followed by the cameras for rather longer, on average, than females.

Grant and Williams (2011) investigated the extent to which the visual cues in CCTV images could accurately be used to predict whether a criminal act was taking place. They used a group of CCTV operators and a group of novices who were shown some video scenes leading to antisocial acts and others not leading to antisocial acts. As far as was possible, the scenes were matched on things such as location and the number of people to be seen. That is, scenes leading to crime were broadly similar to those which did not. The videos were obtained from YouTube. The research utilised actual control rooms. An eye-gaze direction tracker was used to help understand what visual cues were attended to by the observers. That is, measures were taken of the point of gaze during viewing the video. The observer's task was to predict which scenes led to criminal behaviour. A specially constructed measure of Criminal Intent Prediction was used. The participants reported suspicious aspects of the scenes that they observed. Good predictions about criminal actions to follow were associated with visual concentration on the face or head of a lone individual and the bodies of individuals interacting socially. Not unexpectedly, an awareness of the more general social context of the scene led to better predictions of criminal behaviour. Experienced and inexperienced operators were similar in terms of their accuracy of predicting which incidents would lead to crime.

Eyewitness evidence in court

Witness confidence

The issue of eyewitness confidence markedly divides the legal and the psychological views. The United States Supreme Court decided in 1972 that witness confidence was an indicator of witness accuracy. Thus witness confidence can be regarded as a 'marker' (Weber, Brewer, Wells, Semmler and Keast, 2004) or assessment variable (Sporer, 1993) which might help when assessing the value of any witness's testimony. Equally, confidence should also be taken into account when assessing the risk of misidentification. Furthermore, research has shown that lawyers, by-and-large, accept the validity of the confidence–accuracy link and jurors tend to subscribe to this view too. In contrast, researchers have generally argued that confidence is a rather poor predictor of accuracy. Recently, this sort of conclusion has been challenged and it has been suggested that confidence if measured at the time of the initial identification is actually a rather good indicator of accuracy.

It is probably best to survey some of the arguments that have been made over the last few decades about the confidence–accuracy link. For example, Cutler and Penrod (1989) studied a wide range of investigations of confidence expressed before an identity parade/line-up and correct identification of the offender. The overall correlation between pre-line-up confidence and accuracy was 0.20 or less for these studies though it was substantially higher for post-line-up confidence with accuracy. While this is evidence of a relationship, it is nevertheless a rather weak relationship, statistically speaking. Consequently, Cutler and Penrod felt it important to stress that this poor relationship was good reason to consider positively the evidence of witnesses lacking in confidence and not just that of the confident ones. Confident witnesses are not much better, in general, than non-confident ones in their identifications.

An observant reader will spot various values of the size of the confidence–accuracy relationship reported in this chapter. Superficially this may seem a little confusing, but the problem boils down to whether we are comparing like with like or apples with pears – that is, the figures vary according to precisely what is being studied. For example, the correlation between confidence and accuracy may be different if all witnesses are included, whether or not an identification is made, compared to when only witnesses who make an identification are included. Hence the different correlations for the relationship. If the calculation is confined to witnesses who actually made a choice (but not those who do not make a choice) then the correlation between confidence and accuracy could be as much as 0.4, according to studies. This is quite a respectable effect size, given what is typical in psychological research – though, of course, it could be regarded as the best-case scenario. Naturally, including witnesses who do not make an identification would lead to a much lower correlation.

Just what does this correlation of 0.4 mean? In order to make things more intuitively meaningful, Wells and Quinlivan (2009) compare the witness confidence–accuracy correlation with another, more familiar, relationship.

Predicting someone's eyewitnessing accuracy from their confidence is about the same as predicting their gender from their height, they say! Nevertheless, this does not mean that a correlation of 0.4 between accuracy and confidence is useless. Wells *et al.* point out that, in a sample of 100 eyewitnesses, half of whom had accurately made an identification and the other half inaccurately, approximately 70 per cent of the witnesses who were above average on confidence would be accurate in their selection and only 30 per cent who were below average on confidence would make a correct identification. Of course, it is a judgement-call to decide whether such figures warrant the use of accuracy assessments in court.

As might be expected, after the line-up (identity parade) witnesses demonstrate a slightly better association between confidence as measured after the line-up and accuracy. Nevertheless, this remains a modest correlation (Bothwell, Deffenbacher and Brigham, 1987). In eyewitness testimony, the size of the confidence–accuracy relationship may be affected by a range of factors. There is a slightly bigger relationship between confidence and accuracy in the target present line-up than for the situation where the target is absent from the line-up. A comparison of target present and target absent line-ups reveals differences but this is starting from a low base and does not get very strong. According to Krug's review (2007), the correlation between confidence and accuracy is only about 0.3. Of course, in reality, target present and target absent line-ups are a research notion and not a practical one since the police simply do not know which applies to line-ups in their day-to-day work as opposed to the psychology laboratory. The relationship between confidence and accuracy tends to be lower for recognition memory tasks – the line-up is, of course, a recognition memory task for the witness. The relationship is higher for recall tasks, which is the sort of activity a witness does when he or she describes the offender to a police officer.

Kebbell, Wagstaff and Covey (1996) were among those to question such a counterintuitive finding as the suggestion that there is only a poor correlation between confidence and accuracy. They pointed out that researchers have avoided memory tasks that are either very easy or very hard. So, for example, witnesses may be asked the culprit's gender or their eye colour. Gender is a relatively easy thing to identify but seeing the offender's eye colour requires a close view. The optimality encoding hypothesis (Deffenbacher, 1980) suggested that the confidence–accuracy relationship will be at its highest level in circumstances where encoding, storage and retrieval conditions are optimal. Eyewitnesses may well be less confident in circumstances which are suboptimal for any of these aspects. The witness to a crime which took place at night, in the dark, might understandably be reluctant to claim great confidence in their ability to pick out the offender. In Kebbell *et al.*'s (1996) study, student eyewitnesses watched a short video showing the implied murder of a man by a woman. Following a filler or distracting task, they were asked to complete a 33-item questionnaire about the video. The questions were open-ended and varied in terms of difficulty. Confidence was fairly closely related to item difficulty – that is, easy questions produced a high correlation between accuracy and confidence. Difficult questions produced a low correlation between accuracy and confidence. Interestingly, virtually every time that a participant rated themselves as being absolutely certain about the accuracy of their answer to a question they were correct – that is, their accuracy was 97 per cent in these circumstances.

Memory confidence is an instance of the general phenomenon of meta-memory which refers to the way in which we monitor, predict and control our own memory. There are many instances of this, such as our assessment of how much we have learnt, the feeling that we know something well, or even that our memory for names has declined as we have got older. It is difficult to be precise about the relationship between how good our memories are and our meta-perspective on our memories (Krug, 2007). In some areas of memory, there is quite a strong relationship between our confidence in our memory and the accuracy of our memory. So, for example, confidence and ability are fairly well related in the domain of general knowledge. On the other hand, school students when assessing their own knowledge show a poor relationship between confidence and their true level of knowledge.

Some researchers (Juslin, Olsson, and Winman, 1996) have suggested that eyewitness confidence–accuracy correlations are not the ideal way of indicating exactly what the relationship is. Calibration is recommended in preference. Essentially, calibration is about how well the eyewitnesses' assessment of the likely accuracy of their recollections corresponds with the probability that the identification choices made are correct. So a perfectly calibrated relationship between confidence and accuracy would be one where the confidence rating is the same as the actual accuracy. So individuals who say that they are 80 per cent confident will be correct 80 per cent of the time. Individuals who say that they are 60 per cent confident should be correct 60 per cent of the time. Perfect calibration occurs then when there is a perfect relationship between the objective and subjective probabilities concerning the correctness of an answer (see Figure 13.2). Metacognition – our cognitions about our cognitive processes – come into play in this (Nelson, Gerler and Narens, 1984). For example, we may feel that a lower confidence estimate is appropriate where the questions are about a topic we know little about, or we may not feel confident because what we saw was over so quickly, or we may feel very confident because it was a

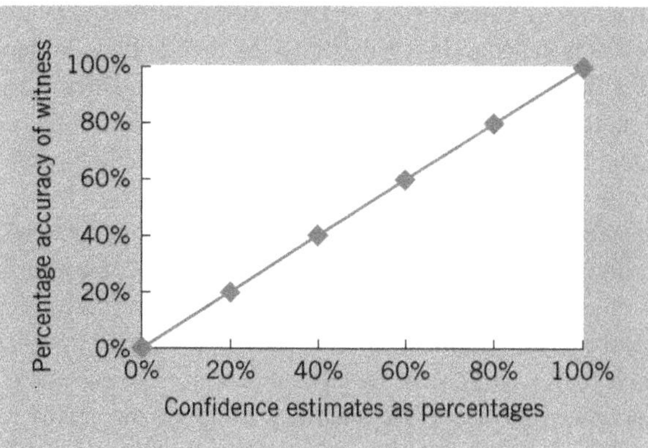

Figure 13.2 The perfect calibration between confidence and accuracy

bright summer day and everything was very clear. Luna and Martin-Luengo (2010) carried out a number of studies into recognition and recall of a criminal event. For example, in one study they asked 'witnesses' direct questions concerning events which happened in a video of a bank robbery. A typical question might concern what the robber had in his hand while he was in the car. Participants had to rate their confidence on a percentage scale, with 0 per cent being the rating for a guess. Overall the findings suggested a good calibration between confidence and accuracy at the higher and lower levels – though it was not so good at the middle levels of accuracy. Witnesses appeared to be over-confident in general. Calibration has one important advantage over correlation – if calibration is good then one can say things such as 'If the witness is 60 per cent confident then it is 60 per cent likely that the witness is correct'. On the other hand, if we know that the correlation between confidence and accuracy is 0.2 how many of us know whether this tells us that the witness is likely to be accurate or inaccurate.

This leads us to the important conclusion by Wixted, Mickes, Clark, Gronlund and Roediger (2015) that eyewitness confidence reliably predicts eyewitness identification? (That is, almost the opposite conclusion from that drawn by early researchers in this field.) They reach this conclusion partly on the basis of findings from this sort of calibration graph. This conclusion is only for the relationship between the earliest assessment of confidence and the identification made after this. That is, if the witness is asked about their confidence that they will be able to identify the offender prior to, say, the line-up, then there is a strong relationship between this confidence assessment and accuracy at the original line-up. This assertion is based on the analysis of substantial numbers of studies. However, this does not mean that confidence assessments carried out later, perhaps in court, will show such a strong relationship. For one thing, a witness may be affected by intervening events which bolster their feelings of confidence and thereby contaminating the confidence–accuracy relationship adversely. So how could researchers in the past have been so wrong when they concluded that the confidence–accuracy relationship was poor. The answer, according to Wixted *et al.* is that earlier researchers were misled because they used correlation coefficients rather than calibration graphs in their analyses. Actually the correlation coefficient used is that known as the point-biserial correlation coefficient, which is a version of the common Pearson correlation coefficient. The big difference is that the point-biserial correlation coefficient is used when one of the variables, in this case accuracy, takes just one of two values – i.e. correct versus incorrect identification. An almost perfect calibration plot, if turned into a point-biserial correlation coefficient, may yield what appears to be a relatively small value of the correlation coefficient such as .4. This is a technical matter and depends to some extent on the distribution of the scores on the two variables. So what one can see with one's own eyes is hidden when correlational statistics are used in place of a calibration graph. Wixted *et al.* indicate that studies using calibration methods show that identifications made with low confidence have about a 40 per cent accuracy rates, those made with high confidence have an accuracy rate of about 80 per cent. Such figures might suggest the value of initial accuracy assessments.

Earlier we mentioned the case of Ronald Cotton who was eventually exonerated from rape by the use of DNA evidence. His case is relevant here since the witness, Jennifer Thompson, confidently asserted in court that Ronald Cotton was the man who raped her. However, at the early stage of the investigation, she had demonstrated hesitation and indecision during a photo-lineup before she eventually chose Cotton and said 'I think that this is the guy'. She received supportive feed-back from a police officer which may have been part of the reason why she eventually became confident in court. That is, her memory had been contaminated by subsequent events. The point is that had emphasis been placed on her initial lack of confidence, as Wixted *et al.* recommend in general, then it is possible that Cotton would not have been falsely convicted. In a review of cases of DNA exoneration, Garrett (2011) found evidence in nearly 60 per cent of cases that the all-important eyewitness had initially expressed some doubt about their ability to identify the culprit. In support of the idea of confidence inflation in witnesses, Steblay, Wells and Douglas (2014) reviewed, using meta-analysis (see Box 4.1), the experimental research literature on the effects of feedback about their identification choice by another person. Confirmatory feedback affected eyewitness positively in terms of the confidence they had in their identification choice. This was true whether or not the witness had made a correct identification or, indeed, any identification at all.

Improving the validity of the line-up

Identification evidence is not totally synonymous with identification parades or line-ups. The police may seek identification evidence shortly after a crime has been committed especially when the crime took place in a public place. So the police may present a suspect to an eyewitness for identification (i.e. a street identification) or the eyewitness may be driven around the streets in the hope of spotting the offender (i.e. a drive by). In the UK, these procedures are only legitimate if 1) the witness has provided a description of the offender and 2) there is insufficient evidence to arrest the offender otherwise (Davis, Valentine, Memon and Roberts (2015). Street robberies are an obvious example of where street identifications and drive-bys would be appropriate. If there is sufficient evidence to arrest the suspect without using a street identification procedure, then the identification by witnesses should take the form of a formal identification parade or line-up. Practices concerning line-ups or identification parades vary from country to country. Basically these procedures include the suspect and a number of similar foils or fillers. Photospreads are collections of photographs including one of the suspect. The United Kingdom is particularly advanced in its thinking on identification evidence, largely because of a record of wrongful convictions on the basis of identification evidence. In the 1970s, critical reviews of identification evidence were published, most importantly the influential *Devlin Report*. Nowadays, many 'identity parades' in the UK are digitally produced video lineups employing 'libraries' of video clips of lineup members – that is, virtual identity parades. Other countries do not have quite the same procedural protection for suspects as the United Kingdom.

Researchers have been aware for a long time of various problems with line-ups, some of which are more intractable than others. According to Busey and Loftus (2007) these include the following:

- *Inadequately matched fillers:* in this, the foils or fillers do not match the descriptions of the offender provided by eyewitnesses. Busey and Loftus suggest that having poorly matching fillers effectively reduces the functional size of the line-up. That is, one should calculate the number of effective foils by subtracting the number of foils who do not match satisfactorily with the witnesses' descriptions from the total of foils.
- *Physical bias (oddball):* the suspect's picture in a photo line-up may be noticeably physically different from the others (e.g. it may be larger or the background may be different). The witness infers that the odd picture must be the suspect. It has been suggested that facial expression may have a similar sort of influence. In an identity parade, the suspect may be dressed differently from the foils.
- *No double blind procedure:* this is the idea that the officer conducting the identity parade should not know which member is the suspect. Busey and Loftus describe a situation where one of them was present at a two-witness line-up in which the first witness was concentrating attention on one of the fillers in a photo lineup when the officer in charge, who was aware of who the suspect was, asked the witness if the offender could be someone in one of the other photographs. That is, the officer essentially indicated that the witness had chosen the wrong person. The second witness was concentrating on the actual suspect whereupon the officer told that witness to sign across this photo (which is the way of indicating that this is the person that has been identified).
- *Unconscious transference:* this occurs when the witness has seen the suspect before but not at the crime scene, though the witness does not realise this. For example, they might both live in the same neighbourhood.

Consequently, attempts have been made to formulate procedures that would help prevent the wrong person being identified in a lineup. Wells, Small, Penrod, Malpass, Fulero and Brimacombe (1998) proposed four general principles given below, to protect the suspect. They apply both to line-ups/identification parades as well as photospreads. All of these seek to identify the offender. An analogy is drawn between a good line-up and a good psychological experiment:

- A properly designed experiment should be a fair test of the research hypothesis.
- A good experiment should be, as far as possible, free from biases.

Wells *et al.* suggest that two broad issues need to be taken into account:

- structural properties, e.g. the appearance of the line-up in terms of how similar to and different from each other its members are;
- procedural properties, e.g. the instructions given to the witnesses, the numbers in the line-up and so forth.

Consider some of the ideal characteristics of a study of human memory. The participants in the research listen to a list of words. They are then shown a sequence of words that may or may not have been in the original list. If the researcher testing their memory knows which words are in the original list then he or she may subtly and non-consciously give clues as to what these words were. For example, the researcher might pause fractionally longer over the critical words. There are indications that researchers are able inadvertently to bias an experimental outcome such that it favours the researcher's favoured hypothesis (Jung, 1971; Rosenthal, 1966). One way of reducing this influence is to keep the actual researcher in the dark about the hypothesis or leave them blind as to other aspects of the procedure (such as the list of words to be remembered). The rule for line-ups and photospreads is:

> Rule 1: The person who conducts the line-up or photospread should not be aware of which member of the line-up or photospread is the suspect.
>
> (p. 17)

Even where the experimenter does not have knowledge about the list of words to be remembered, the participants may think that they do. Thus participants might inadvertently and wrongly read into the experimenter's behaviour what they believe to be cues about the correct words. For example, the experimenter might find certain words amusing and respond differently to these. Explaining to participants that the experimenter is unaware of what words are correct may reduce the effect.

> Rule 2: The eyewitness should be told explicitly that the person administering the line-up does not know which person is the suspect in the case.
>
> (p. 19)

The participant in the memory research might be inclined to pick out certain words simply because they are more interesting, more dramatic or in some way different. They may be inclined to pick these words as the correct ones as a consequence. Applied to eyewitness evidence, the following needs consideration:

> Rule 3: The suspect should not stand out in the line-up or photospread as being different from the distracters based on the eyewitness's previous description of the culprit or based on other factors that would draw extra attention to the suspect.
>
> (p. 19)

In the light of what we know about eyewitness confidence (see above), the recommendations also include the following:

> Rule 4: A clear statement should be taken from the eyewitness at the time of the identification and prior to any feedback as to his or her confidence that the identified person is the actual culprit.
>
> (p. 23)

Kassin (1998) felt that there is an omission from these recommendations. He recommended that the identification parade/line-up and witness identification should be videotaped. This is because records of the line-up are often not carefully kept such that the police and eye-witnesses differ markedly in terms of their recollections of events at the line-up. He points out that police procedures in relation to evidence of various sorts have been subject to a variety of criticisms. For example, in the United Kingdom, the Police and Criminal Evidence Act of 1984 requires that all custodial interviews with crime suspects are taped. This, of course, is primarily to protect individuals against police malpractice.

Relative judgement theory answers the question of how eyewitnesses choose the culprit from a line-up/identity parade. In the absence of the culprit, the theory suggests that the line-up members most similar to the culprit will be picked out. In other words, the eyewitness acts as if the culprit is present and forms a judgement on the best of what they recall of the culprit. No mechanism exists for deciding that the offender is not in the line-up (Wells, 1984). If participants were responding using absolute judgements, then each line-up member would be compared with the memory of the culprit. Then unless the line-up member meets the criteria they will be rejected. Evidence demonstrating the validity of relative judgement theory comes from studies such as that of Wells (1993). In this, some witnesses were shown the line-up including the culprit and others were shown exactly the same line-up with the culprit absent. Despite being told that the culprit may not be present, 54 per cent of those who identified the culprit when the culprit was present would have identified someone else in the culprit's absence! When the offender was present, 21 per cent failed to make a choice but this increased to only 32 per cent when the culprit was actually absent. In other words, mostly when the offender is absent other, innocent, line-up members are chosen.

Obviously a major factor in this is that explicit warnings that the culprit may not necessarily be present substantially reduce incorrect identifications (Malpass and Devine, 1981). They do not affect correct identifications when the culprit is present.

A number of studies have shown some of the factors that affect relative judgements in real cases. For example, Doob and Kirkenbaum (1973) reported on a Canadian robbery at a department store. The accused was said to be one of two men who had committed the crime. The cashier who witnessed the events recalled that the offenders were neatly dressed, good looking and could be brothers. Despite this somewhat sketchy recollection, she picked out the accused from a line-up. One of Doob and Kirkenbaum's studies had 20 women pick 'a rather good looking man' out of 12 parade participants from the original line-up. The women chose the accused extremely frequently, despite not having witnessed the crime. This would appear to be evidence of the unfairness of the system employed.

Similarly, in Poland, Wojcikiewicz, Bialek, Desynski and Dawidowicz. (2000) were involved in a pertinent court case. The suspect was actually a man of 29 years of age. They were asked by the defence to assess how likely it was that a particular man, from the viewpoint of a 12-year-old rape victim, could be described as being a 40–50-year-old man with a rat-like face. Adult participants in the research did see him as the 29-year-old that he was. About a fifth of the children saw the accused as being in the 40–45-year-old age group. Adults described him as having a rat-like face although children did not have a significant tendency to do so. In view of this evidence, it remained possible that the accused was indeed the perpetrator. Nevertheless, the research evidence is indicative of a possible problem and was used in court by the defence.

One way of assessing the likelihood that a person will be susceptible to relative similarity effects when choosing is their performance in the *dual line-up or blank line-up* method. This involves an initial (or blank) line-up, containing only people known to be innocent, followed by a second line-up, containing the suspect. The blank line-up was first suggested by Wells (1984). Basically it is a way of identifying inaccurate, profligate choosers in line-up situations. It is a two-stage process. The blank line-up is the first stage and consists of known-to-be-innocent foils. Should the witness make a choice on the blank line-up then they are clearly more likely to be a witness who will make a mistaken choice in a later, normal, line-up. Those who do not make a choice at the blank line-up are likely not to make a wrong choice in the later regular line-up. The use of computerised line-up methods would perhaps makes it more feasible to use blank line-ups. Wells (1984) showed that:

- if a witness resists choosing from the blank line-up, it is more likely that they choose accurately in a proper line-up later;
- witnesses who did not go through the blank line-up first were more likely to make mistakes in the second line-up.

Sequential procedures (though this is a somewhat controversial matter) are claimed to work better than conventional line-ups. In these, the group of people selected to be in the line-up is shown in sequential fashion – one individual at a time, usually through the use of photographic images. This makes it much more difficult simply to use a process of elimination in choosing the guilty party (it cannot be a, b or d so it must be c). It is less likely that relative similarity will operate in the sequential line-up (Dunning and Stern, 1994). Another identification method, very common in parts of the United States, is the show-up. This is a single individual who the eyewitness has to identify as the culprit or not. In one sense, this should be more effective than a line-up since relative judgement cannot apply when there is just person to decide about. On the other hand, the fact that the police have picked out this individual for the show-up may be strongly suggestive that he or she is the prime suspect.

Steblay, Dysart, Fulero and Lindsay (2003) carried out a meta-analysis (see Box 4.1) of studies which compared the single-person line-up (the show-up) with six-person line-ups (these included both sequential and simultaneous versions). Furthermore, both single-person show-ups and six-person line-ups included conditions in which the target suspect was present in the majority of the studies. Interestingly, the line-up was much more likely to result in a choice by the eyewitness than the show-up. If the target were present, on average 71 per cent out of 10 line-ups resulted in a choice, whereas the figure was only 46 per cent for the show-up. Where the target was absent, 43 per cent of line-ups resulted in a choice, as opposed to 15 per cent of show-ups. Correct identification where the target was actually present did not differ between line-ups and show-ups. Around 46 per cent correctly identified the suspect when the suspect was present in either type of identification procedure. Furthermore, when the target is absent, the false identification rate is approximately the same at about 16 per cent for both show-ups and line-ups. What is happening when the eyewitness makes a wrong identification in a target absent line-up? Simply the errors are spread across all of the foils. This results in a situation in which, if one classified all of these latter errors into a non-identification category with other non-identification outcomes, then line-ups show no difference from show-ups in terms of outcomes. It is important to note that those studies in which the foil is more similar to the target resulted in a worse performance in show-ups than in line-ups. False identification of an innocent foil is more common in show-ups than in line-ups.

Steblay, Dysart and Wells (2011) brought Steblay's earlier meta-analysis discussed above up-to-date for sequential line-up research. They included research carried out since that time comparing simultaneous with sequential line-ups. They found more than 70 relevant studies. A wider variety of laboratories were involved in the research (23 in number) and in total over 3,000 witnesses were involved in the included studies. The overall finding of the research was that sequential line-ups are better at discriminating between a guilty suspect and an innocent foil than simultaneous line-ups. Nevertheless, the sequential is less likely to lead to the identification of the suspect – i.e. sequential line-ups involve over 20 per cent fewer errors of this sort. The researchers chose to measure the accuracy of witnesses using what is termed the diagnosticity ratio. This is the ratio of percentage identifications of the offender when they are present in the line-up over the percentage likelihood that a particular innocent suspect will be chosen when the offender is not present in the line-up. The diagnosticity ratio for sequential line-ups was 8 but it was rather lower for simultaneous line-ups, which had a diagnosticity ratio of 6. When similar foils to the suspect are included in the line-up then the diagnosticity ratios decline. It should be pointed out that this is known to cause problems in the sequential line-up since, when a similar foil appears just before the suspect, there is an increased likelihood that the innocent foil will be selected. Thus far, we have ignored the issue of just how a sequential line-up is conducted. There is more than one way of doing this. One possibility is that the witness can make their choice at any stage in the sequence but then the line-up ends. But there may be a different rule about stopping such as one not allowing the witness to make their choice until they have seen all of the photographs. Or there may not be any stopping rule defined in a study. Accuracy at identifying the suspect is better when the session stops after an identification is made.

Recent research may help to provide a theoretical explanation of some of the findings concerning sequential line-ups. Palmer, Brewer and Weber (2012) carried out two studies relevant to blank line-ups. In their first study they found that participants who made a choice at the blank line-up stage were *less* likely to make a choice at the regular line-up. The researchers suggest that this can be explained in terms of a cognitive bias to confirm their original decision, or alternatively that they simply remain committed to it. The implication is that following the use of a blank line-up, the guilty suspect may not be picked out in the subsequent regular line-up. Their second study indicated that choosers at the blank line-up stage tend to have poorer memory of the offender, which may explain why they were less likely to identify anyone at the second line-up. Compared to other witnesses, initial choosers were more inclined to reject a second line-up than to positively identify someone in that line-up. This is in line with confirmation biases and commitment effects.

The procedures actually employed by police officers when they plan identification line-ups have been investigated by Wogalter, Malpass and McQuiston (2004). Over 200 police jurisdictions in the United States were surveyed about their practices. There were examples of good and bad practice as verified by laboratory studies. Some of the common good practices included:

- Officers tended to choose line-up foils on the basis of upper facial features such as race/ethnic group, facial hair characteristics, colour of hair and overall shape of face. Whatever the reason why the officers chose to do this, it is important to note that there is a substantial amount of research evidence which suggests that people recall such upper facial features more readily than lower facial features (e.g. shape of the chin).
- Substantial numbers of officers report that they gave witnesses the option of not choosing anyone from the identification line-up, which is known to reduce errors, as we saw above. Very few warned eyewitnesses that facial features may change or that photographs may be of poor or insufficient quality. These factors may affect eyewitness accuracy according to research.

Examples of bad practice included the following:

- Most respondents (83 per cent) claimed to base their choice of foils in the line-up on their similarity to the suspect. In contrast, only a small number (9 per cent) based their choices of foil on the verbal descriptions provided by eyewitnesses. Research evidence has suggested that there may be problems with the use of similarity to the suspect as a criterion for choosing foils. This may seem to be a strange assertion given that it would seem common sense to use identification line-ups of similar-looking people. The problem is not in the theory but the practice. What actually happens is that the foils are chosen because of their similarity to the suspect rather than to each other. As a consequence, the suspect stands out because they have characteristics in common with many of the foils but the foils do not look too much like each other. In other words, there is a powerful clue in the situation which encourages the selection of the suspect.
- Generally, assessments about the fairness of the procedures being used by an officer are made by that officer (94 per cent). They also might ask the advice of another officer (77 per cent) or a prosecution lawyer (51 per cent). These are not completely independent judgements as they are all on the side of prosecuting the suspect. Asking the advice of the defence lawyer was fairly uncommon (only 15 per cent) although this sort of advice might be regarded as a much more acid test of fairness.
- The use of video line-ups that do not require the direct recruitment of foils was relatively uncommon. But this is the sort of line-up that enables things like the editing out of any biasing behaviours on the part of members of the line-up.

One view of the field based on the research literature is to be found in Brewer and Palmer's (2010) guidelines for line-ups/identity parades. This is summarised in Figure 13.3. They do not offer their guidelines as a cure-all for the mistakes that witnesses make when providing identification evidence. Nothing can entirely prevent such errors. Nevertheless, it is possible to do something about arrangements which are more likely to lead to errors and the way in which courts respond to eyewitnesses claims about the accuracy of their evidence. Unfortunately, the link between research-based recommendations and good practice by police officers is less than certain. For example, Greene and Evelo (2015) who surveyed Canadian and American robbery detetectives about the use of procedures which have

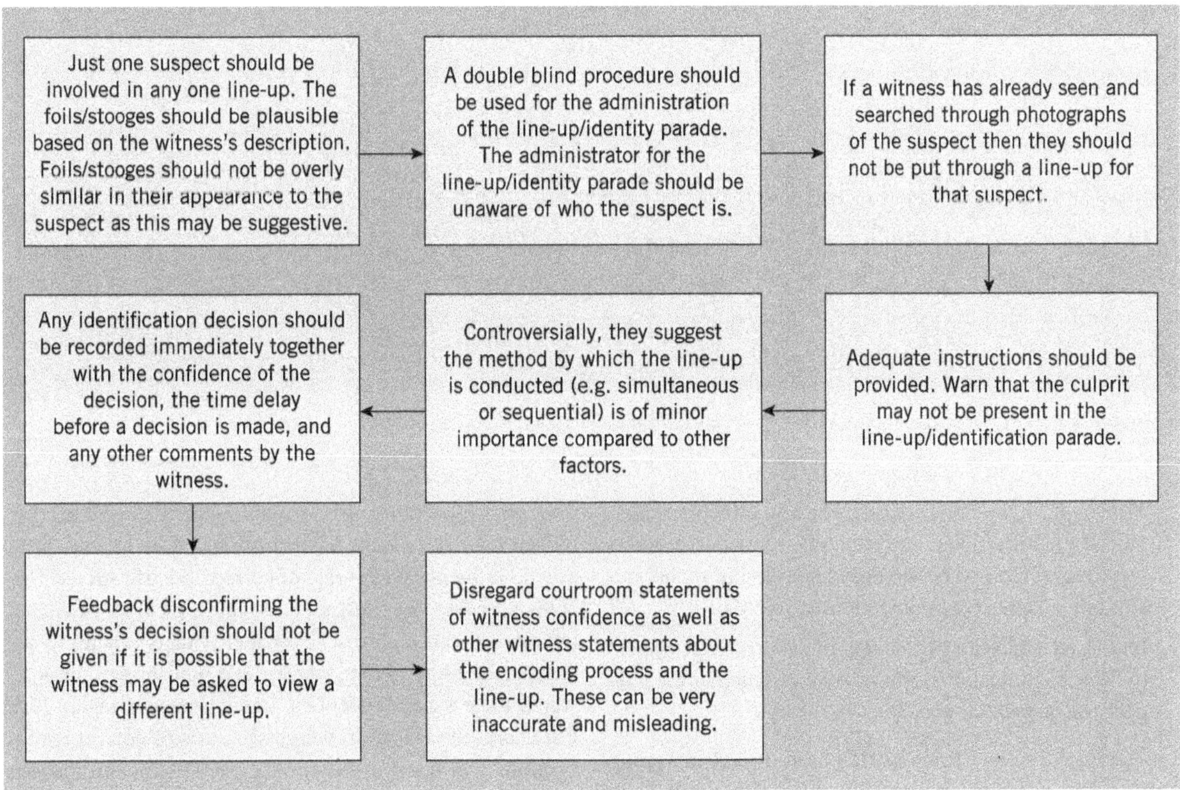

Figure 13.3 How to plan a satisfactory line-up according to the suggestions of Brewer and Palmer (2010)

been recommended on the basis of research or are regarded as bad practice. A high proportion of the American officers did not use double blind procedures though this figure was much lower for the Canadian officers. However, high proportions of both groups would tell the witness that the suspect may or may not appear in the lineup and that the suspect may not look the same as when first seen by the witness. There was evidence that at critical times in the lineup detectives from both countries used subtle questioning tactics with the witness which may boost the witnesses' confidence or encourage them to make a choice.

Suspect–filler similarity

The issue of suspect–filler similarity is more complex than at first appears. There is no simple formula for deciding the degree of similarity. Luus and Wells (1991) argued that there may be an inverted U curve between similarity and line-up diagnosticity (i.e. picking out the suspect). When the similarity is close then correct identification is impeded, but when similarity is not close then false identifications may be more likely. In other words, having the suspect–filler similarity too close may not protect innocent suspects – unlike what previously had been thought. Matching is not easily achieved either as it is unclear what, in general, the best characteristics are to match on. These may actually be substantially dependent on the circumstances of the line-up. Matching, though, can be of two broad types. It may be 1) matching the line-up members to the descriptions provided by the witnesses or 2) it may be matching the line-up to the characteristics of the suspect. These are not the same thing. Description identified suspects may be picked out in the line-up simply because they are the most similar to the description provided by witnesses.

Price, Oriet and Charman's (2013) meta-analysis of studies (see Box 4.1) of suspect–filler similarity involved the researchers coding the original studies as low, moderate or high in terms of similarity. They made these decisions on the basis of the information contained in the methodology section of each of the articles used. Among the main findings were:

- Low-similarity line-ups were more likely to produce an identification (ignoring accuracy).
- Filler misidentifications were more common in medium- and high-similarity line-ups.
- Filler similarity did not increase refusals to identify a culprit, whether or not the suspect was present.

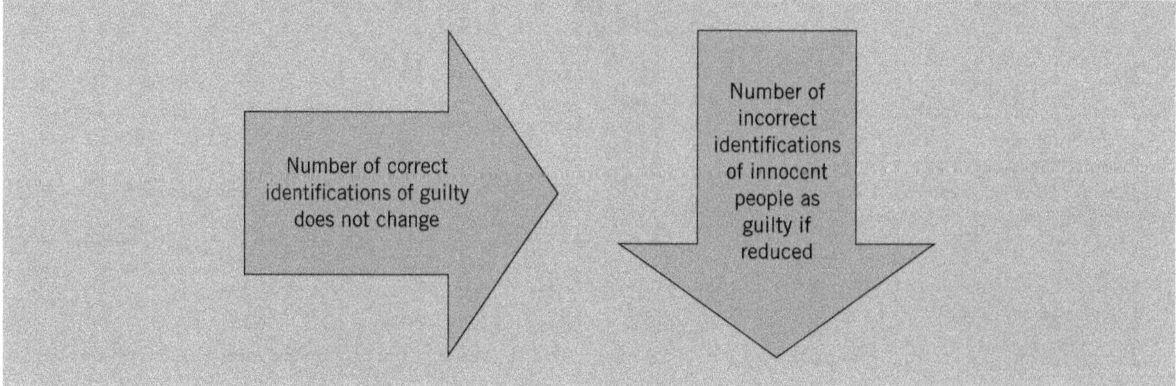

Figure 13.4 The no-cost view of eyewitness procedure reform

- Moderate-/high-similarity fillers had no effect on actual culprit identifications. Nevertheless, innocent suspects were more likely to be wrongly identified in moderate-similarity line-ups compared to high-similarity.
- Increased similarity shifted identifications from suspect to filler identifications, irrespective of whether the suspect was present or absent.

Fitzgerald, Oriet and Price (2015) used digital morphing software in order to generate line-ups with moderately high and very high similarity to the suspect. Line-ups in the very high similarity category made correct identifications more difficult.

Broadly speaking, these findings support Clark's (2012) argument that policies designed to prevent innocent suspect misidentifications actually come at the cost of reducing correct identifications as well – that is, the guilty will also tend to go free. Increasing suspect–filler similarity reduced culprit identifications but at a lower rate than the reduction of innocent suspect misidentifications. Clark's ideas are interesting and difficult to dismiss. He points out that psychology has helped in the drive to reform eyewitness identification procedures. Underlying this is the firm view that procedures are available which can be used to reduce the risk of false identifications while having virtually no influence on the rate of correct identifications. This is the no-cost view illustrated in Figure 13.4. However, all but one of the changes advocated actually increase the number of guilty people who escape punishment. In other words, there is a trade-off of the sort illustrated in Figure 13.5. For Clark, the task is to weigh the costs of correct identifications lost against the benefits of false identifications avoided. This is not really a matter for psychological research but it is a public policy issue. Where to strike the balance in the trade off is not the sort of question that psychology can normally address.

From laboratory to field

The deeper one gets into the research of eyewitness line-up evidence, the more intractable seem the problems of translating intriguing laboratory study findings into recommendations for running real-life line-ups. The findings of O'Connell and Synnott (2009) illuminate some very basic problems. One of the difficulties of the simultaneous

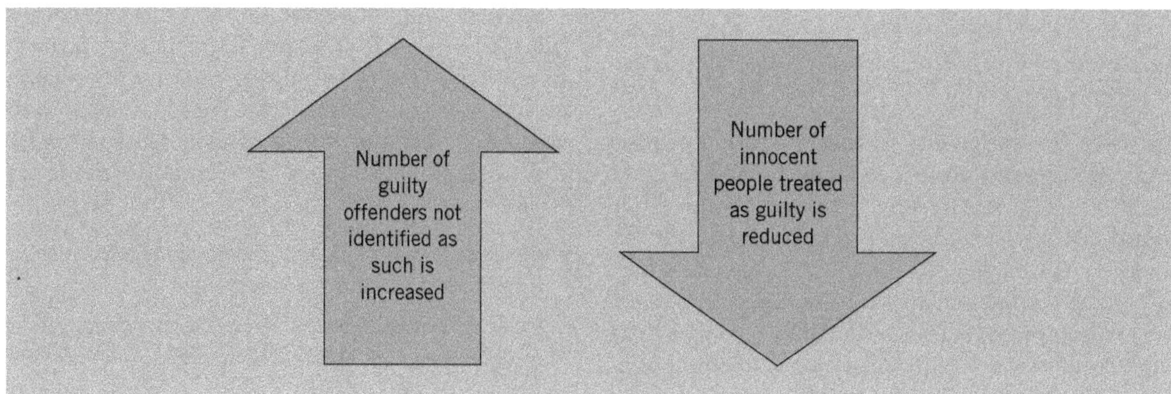

Figure 13.5 The trade-off view of eyewitness reform

line-up is that the eyewitness may process the array of faces in front of them using a variety of different strategies. The strategy employed by witnesses is not in the control of the researcher – or the police, for that matter. In O'Connell and Synnott's study, participants watched a simulated crime – a handbag snatch – and then they were later shown a live line-up which included the offender and four fillers or foils. Imagine that there then are several possible positions in which the suspect could be placed. The researchers did not use position 2 for offenders in this particular study, but the suspect was placed in the other positions for different runs of the study. What they found was a profound position effect:

- Position 1: 7 per cent correct offender identifications, 3 per cent misidentifications
- Position 3: 50 per cent correct offender identifications, 31 per cent misidentifications
- Position 4: 64 per cent correct offender identifications, 34 per cent misidentifications
- Position 5: 21 per cent correct offender identifications, 15 per cent misidentifications.

In other words, the offender would stand a far better chance of escaping recognition if they stood in Position 1 than if they stood in Position 4. The police would have a much better chance of identifying the offender as the guilty person if they stand them in Position 4. Although these are actual data, whether or not they are reliable need not concern us here. But what would be the appropriate policy recommendation stemming from these data? 'More research is needed' would obviously be a contender. But what are the alternatives? Maybe randomising the position of the suspect in a line-up is a possibility. But the consequence of this would simply be that guilty offenders would, on average, not be identified so often. Should the suspect be made to stand somewhere in the middle of the line-up? This would maximise the number of correct identifications – but what if the strategy got out and the public became aware of it? This might suggest to witnesses that the offender is in one of the middle positions and so might encourage them to pick someone from there. Or should we allow the suspect to choose where they stand? 'Whoopee!' we can hear offenders exclaim. 'Position 1 for me please.'

Not surprisingly, then, researchers have begun to look for simpler solutions to improving line-up evidence. Weber and Perfect (2012) went back to basic research and noticed that forensic researchers have tended to overlook the simple alternative of encouraging eyewitnesses to say that they don't know in the line-up if this is appropriate. The research design involved a show-up of either the offender or an innocent person. The participants viewed a mock crime video before either being tested immediately or after about a three-week delay. The video shows the thief approaching a car and trying to force a door open. A witness shouts, thereby alerting the thief, who runs off. The offender's face is in full view for six seconds of the video. The participants in the research either 1) reported their decision spontaneously in their own words without restriction by the researcher; 2) they chose between identifying or rejecting the person in the show-up; or 3) they made a choice between identification, rejection, or *don't know* in the show-up. That is, they were given the opportunity of not identifying the offender if they so wished. The spontaneous use of *don't know* in these circumstances was very rare. In the spontaneous free-report condition only 2 per cent responded in this way. When they were offered *don't know* as an option, use of this response was much higher at 19 per cent. What was the net effect of this relative to the forced choice between guilt and innocence? Free reports allowing *don't know* were more accurate and effective at distinguishing the guilty from the innocent. Participants in the spontaneous free-report condition largely made a clear decision. Most important, in terms of wider concerns, is the effectiveness of offering witnesses the use of the *don't know* category.

Or perhaps Levi's (2012) suggestion might be considered. He noted that previous research on sequential line-ups had shown that using a large number of photographs led to a reduction in the number of identifications made. A witness faced with 40 or more sequentially presented photos may regard this as overload. Levi's idea was to present the sequential line-up but group the pictures into pages. With grouping, identification and mistaken choice rates were by and large the same, irrespective of the number of pictures in the line-up. In the research, the researcher and a helper solicited the help of Israeli office workers and others to take part in a memory study. The second person was in fact the memory target and was not present when the researcher returned to complete the memory test. The task of the participants was to identify the foil from sets of photographs. It was explained to participants that the pictures might not include the 'foil'. In addition, once a decision about the photographs had been made that decision would be final. Generally speaking, only in the case of a very large line-up of 160 photographs did size affect the number of mistaken choices adversely. Although increasing line-up size reduced the probability of a mistaken identification, a point is reached when the trade-off between the number of correct identifications and the number of identifications becomes too large. Having too many photos on a page can result in problems. In other words, if the object is to reduce the number of mistaken identifications, then the use of large line-ups in which the photographs are presented in groups has a great deal to commend it. Given that some researchers stress the importance of reducing mistaken identifications by using sequential line-ups, the use of large grouped sequential line-ups would seem to be helpful in that regard.

Research on video line-ups

Increasingly, video-based systems are being used by police forces. Setting up a line-up or identity parade is a time-consuming matter. Pike, Brace and Kynan (2002) carried out a major survey of identification parades in the United Kingdom, using several different police forces. They found that the typical delay (median) between a parade being requested and its being run was about ten weeks. Over half of the parades were cancelled before they had even begun. There are many reasons for this. The commonest reason was the absence or late arrival of the suspect (51 per cent), followed by the witness not showing up or refusing to take part (21 per cent) and the problems associated with getting suitable foils or sufficient numbers for the parade (7 per cent). Video-based alternatives such as the VIPER (Video Identification Parade Electronic Recording) and PROMAT (Profile Matching) systems are used increasingly in the United Kingdom. They have enormous practical advantages – they are ten times *less* likely to be cancelled than a normal (live) line-up. In the VIPER system, a short video film of the suspect is shot. The 14-second sequence begins with a frontal head and shoulders view, then the right followed by the left profile, and finally back to the front. This can be transmitted by computer to the national centre where an electronic identification parade is created using in addition about ten additional videos of suitable 'foils' from the VIPER database. This contains thousands of video clips of volunteers. The electronic database is sent back to the original police station where officers to run the identity parade with the witness. Not only is it a very speedy process but costs a fifth or less of the regular live line-up.

A further advantage of the VIPER system is that it may result in less stress for participants compared with the traditional line-up/identification parade. Brace, Pike, Kemp and Turner (2009) carried out a study using student participants in which a live incident was staged involving two men fighting over a bag. There was some degree of pushing and shouting involved but no further violence. The identification stage was a month later. A regular line-up/identification parade was completed and then a video identification parade, based on the VIPER system. In half of each of the two identification procedures the target suspect was included and in the other half the target suspect was not included. Police officers of inspector rank conducted all of the identification procedures using standard police procedures. The VIPER-style procedures involve more of the witnesses' time than the line-up/identification parade, which only involves a witness walking up and down the line. The findings were that the participants believed that the line-up/identification parade was rather more stressful a procedure than the VIPER video method.

Finally, evidence from a large-scale study of VIPER reinforces the positive findings of earlier studies in general but raises other important issues too (Memon, Havard, Clifford, Gabbert and Watt, 2011). Data from over 1700 witnesses/victims using the VIPER system in Scotland were made available to the researchers. A wide range of different types of victim was involved, including a large number who could be described as vulnerable because of their age, their abilities, or simply because of the nature of the offence involved. The police suspect was identified 44 per cent of the time but the identification rate of the foils/fillers was almost as large at 42 per cent. These figures are for suspects not known to the witness. Of course, it is not feasible to assess what proportion of the police suspects was the actual offender. Consequently, it is impossible to estimate what proportion of the identifications were of innocent suspects. Why the false identification rate was so high could be due to a number of considerations. For example, the VIPER data base is replete with foils so it may be that the suspect-foil similarity is very close so encouraging false identifications because of this similarity. Another possibility is the consequence of the VIPER procedure. Witnesses are required to view the video identification parade twice before making their decision about the offender. Such a procedure is known to increase foil/filler choices. Recent legislation has made the use of identification parades for young people and children more common. It is notable then that the best witnesses using the VIPER system were the children and young adults in the sample. They had a higher rate of suspect identification and made fewer erroneous choices of a foil.

The importance of eyewitness evidence research

It is an interesting question whether substantial aspects of eyewitness identification research are becoming outmoded, given modern trends towards using electronic systems. The available electronic line-up systems are sequential in nature and it is to that part of the research literature that one has to look to understand the characteristics of electronic line-ups better. Just how best to conduct the video line-up would have to be a focus of future research as it is not sufficient to argue merely that sequential line-ups are better than simultaneous ones. Just what is the best way to organise a video line-up? For example, what is the optimum stopping rule for the sequential video line-up? In this context, the low identification rates in Memon *et al.*'s (2011) study and the stopping rule employed by the police using VIPER need to be noted. Other issues also become increasingly important. In particular, the suspect–foil similarity issue. What is the ideal similarity of the foils to the suspect and how should this similarity be determined, given the ease of obtaining foils for electronic line-ups? Choices increase generally with increased foil similarity. Systems like VIPER have many foils available in their electronic databases. So it is no longer a time-consuming and frustrating struggle to recruit members for an identity parade. In other words, modern systems have the potential for using optimum strategies if only we know what they are from top-quality research.

It is also possible to get a misleading impression of the importance of eyewitness evidence in the criminal justice system from the emphasis of research in this area. The issue of mistaken identifications which lead to injustices tends to be the main context of research on line-ups. But, if we take a wider point of view, it is notable that eyewitness identifications are rarely sufficient in themselves in many jurisdictions. If, like the UK, eyewitness evidence cannot form the only evidence against the accused, then the simple formulae applied by some eyewitness researchers are unrealistic no matter how they might apply elsewhere. Furthermore, we also need to study statistics on the extent to which eyewitness evidence leads to prosecution. Flowe, Mehta and Ebbeson (2011) studied archival data concerning over 700 felony cases (assault, rape, and robbery) from the archives of a very large District Attorney's Office in the USA. Prosecutors there have the power to decide whether a suspect should be charged with an offence and what that offence should be. But they are also there to protect innocent felony suspects in fact and in law. Thus charging decisions must be guided by the question of whether the police evidence is legally sufficient and admissible in court. The researchers were interested in the role of the availability of eyewitness identification evidence in the decision to prosecute a case. Relatively few cases went to prosecution solely on the basis of the evidence of eyewitnesses. It would seem that where eyewitness evidence was the only available evidence then the police tended to avoid forwarding the case for possible prosecution. Mostly, other types of evidence were available (such as physical evidence or previous records) in addition to any eyewitness identification evidence where cases were sent for possible prosecution. However, positive identification evidence was commoner in cases accepted for prosecution than in rejected cases. But this was only true for cases involving acquaintances and not for cases involving strangers. The strength of the eyewitness evidence was appreciably greater in prosecuted cases when the eyewitness testimony was the only evidence against the accused. In other words, it would seem that precipitous reliance on dubious eyewitness evidence was filtered out of the system.

BOX 13.2 Controversy

Critiques of expert evidence in court

Any psychologist, especially laboratory researchers, offering his or her professional expertise in court may be faced with struggle. Take, for example, the events in a Toronto coffee shop. A man entered the café and said that he would choke his hostage to death there and then unless one of the witnesses gave him a few dollars. Someone complied and the man made his getaway, having released his hostage. The hostage was a Canada goose. Just what insights could be brought from the lab to bear on this situation? Could one rely on the eyewitness testimony in circumstances like these? Ebbesen and Konecni (1997, also Konecni, Ebbesen and Nehrer, 2000) offered a seminal, fierce critique of how expert witnesses in court deal with eyewitness research. The critique made the cogent charge that psychologists acting as expert witnesses have systematically misled courts of law about the validity, consistency and generalisability of research findings on eyewitness testimony. They argued that there is no generally accepted theory of eyewitness testimony. This is despite a number of sophisticated models of memory available to psychologists. As a consequence, valid assessments of the accuracy of eyewitness testimony in particular cases are not possible.

Part of the difficulty is the gulf between the context of real eyewitnessing and that of the psychology laboratory which limit the usefulness of research findings in court. According to Ebbesen and Konecni (1997):

- Studies of eyewitness testimony show many inconsistencies in their outcomes.
- The vast majority of eyewitness testimony research involves the use of college students only (Yuille and Cutshall, 1986).

BOX 13.2 (continued)

- The length of exposure to the criminal events vary substantially between real life and the laboratory. The median exposure duration in real life lies somewhere between five and ten minutes but in the laboratory exposure is six seconds give or take a little. That is, laboratory studies involve a fiftieth to a hundredth of the exposure time that real life crimes do (Moore, Ebbesen and Konecni, 1994).
- Researchers are not in a position to translate such key variables as length of exposure to the crime into the likelihood that the witness is wrong. Although it is correct to suggest in broad terms that greater exposure leads to greater accuracy, the precise risks of error cannot be calculated. So it is not possible to say things like after two minutes of exposure correct identification rates are 60 per cent or any other figure.
- Research generally shows that increasing exposure time is associated with increased accuracy in offender identification (Shapiro and Penrod, 1986). A precise mathematical function describing the relationship between these two factors is not known. Even if it were, things are not simple. Increasing exposure time for the witness to the crime is also associated with an increased risk of identifying the wrong person as the criminal (Ebbesen and Konecni, 1997).
- An analysis of transcripts of trials involving expert testimony on eyewitness accuracy shows overwhelmingly that these problems in interpreting the implications of longer exposure to the crime are not mentioned.

Ebbesen and Konecni (1997) argued:

> Because the evidence is either inconsistent or insufficient in almost every area in which eyewitness experts testify and because there is no research that provides the experts, much less the jurors, with rules to use when translating the evidence to particular decisions in particular cases, we believe that eyewitness expert testimony is more prejudicial than probative and should not be allowed in courts.
>
> (p. 24)

Faigman (2008) argues that:

> The task of applying general research findings to specific cases is, to be sure, a monumental intellectual challenge. Hard tasks are easy to ignore, but ignoring them does not make them go away. In a sense, then, this comment is a cry for attention, imploring psychological scientists to begin considering more carefully the inferential leap they make when they bring population-level research to individual-based trial processes.
>
> (p. 313)

Of course, this is a problem which applies to most, if not all, psychological research findings. Trends are found in conglomerates of data and what may be true in general may not apply to specific instances. So although many psychologists may have the skill to comment effectively on the general case, where do their skills to comment on individual cases come from? Are psychologists taught this skill? So the issue is in two parts: 1) general application – does the scientific evidence support a particular perspective on an issue? and 2) specific application – does the psychological scientist have any basis for taking an established general finding and applying it in a particular case? Passive smoking is a useful analogy here – while the evidence may be that passive smoking increases the risk of lung cancer, the question remains whether it was passive smoking or some other factor which caused the lung cancer in a particular individual. So, in court, can a psychologist legitimately say that a woman's post-traumatic stress disorder was the result of a violent sexual assault or is it merely possible to say that her post-traumatic stress disorder was simply the consequence of some other severe stressor that has occurred in the woman's life? Faigman proposes two ways in which the psychologist may operate:

- *The limits model:* in this approach it is inappropriate for the researcher to testify on matters about which there is no empirical support. Furthermore, where there is support for a particular proposition, the researcher would need to provide evidence that it is appropriate to generalise to a particular individual case.
- *The no-limits model:* this approach would allow the researcher to comment on the individual case even where there is a lack of data to establish that opinions about individual cases can be validly made.

The question is who should apply the general research findings to the specific case? Of course, in a court of law a psychologist may make an assessment based, say, on the research on eyewitness testimony that a particular eyewitness may not be reliable but the alternative is to leave this to the judge and jury – the triers of fact.

This is clearly an issue that all psychologists working as expert witnesses in courts of law should address. But according to Yuille, Ternes and Cooper (2010) psychologists still fail to distinguish between laboratory witnesses and crime witnesses and ignore the problems of generalising from research on the former to research on the latter. They acknowledge the feeling among some psychologists that certain laboratory-based findings are robust enough to use in court, but point out some very relevant areas of memory research where the opposite appears to be true. At this point we can return to the case of the Canada goose hostage. These would have been circumstances in which the weapon focus effect might be relevant. There may not have been a weapon present in the crime scene but nevertheless it is an example of a more general phenomenon in which an incongruous object (a weapon – or a goose in this case) pulls the attention of the eyewitnesses towards it. Numerous laboratory studies have shown that the weapon focus effect is a robust phenomenon and that laboratory witnesses are affected adversely by the presence of a weapon or other incongruous stimuli. They report fewer details of the events and are less able to identify the culprit (e.g., Davies, Smith and Blincoe, 2008; Pickel, Narter, Jameson and Lenhardt, 2008). In comparison, the presence of weapons seems to have very different effects on witnesses to real crime (e.g., Behrman and Davey, 2001; Wagstaff *et al*., 2003). In some cases the detrimental effects found in laboratory studies are not found – sometimes more detail is recalled where weapons are present. Fawcett, Russell, Peace and Christie (2013) carried out a meta-analysis (see Box 4.1) of studies in this area and found comprehensive support for the effect. However, they point out that these robust effects do not appear to manifest themselves in real life. The study by Cooper, Kennedy, Herve and Yuille (2002) is a graphic example of how the weapons effect can fail to emerge in real-life settings. The study asked sex workers to recall sexual assaults against them and provide as much detail as possible. In some cases, they had been assaulted with a weapon present and in other cases there was no weapon present. No weapons effect emerged as there were no differences in terms of the amount of detail provided whether or not a weapon was present. It could be that the trauma of the assault may have overwhelmed any possible weapons effect. But the key thing is that the effects of weapons found in laboratory studies seem different from those found in real crime incidents. Also, in the typical laboratory experiment, the presence of the weapon is actually drawn to the attention of laboratory witnesses – which may be the reason why they notice other things less. Yet, according to Yuille *et al*., the findings obtained in laboratory studies have been discussed in American courts without reference to these problems.

Generally speaking, research shows that stress in laboratory memory experiments worsens the accuracy of witnesses in the laboratory (e.g., Bornstein, Liebel and Scarberry, 1998; Payne *et al*., 2006). By way of contrast, crime witnesses demonstrate very mixed findings in terms of memory improvements and detriments (Yuille and Daylen, 1998). Nevertheless, despite the disparity, one expert witness said in court:

> it's my opinion, and I think it's shared by most, that when we are looking at the very high levels of stress, fear and arousal, witnesses are scared to death, in fear of their lives, that eyewitness memory for faces, facial identification accuracy is decreased.
>
> (*People* v. *Bacenet*, 2002 cited in Yuille *et al*., 2010, p. 244)

Finally, a study of Norwegian psychologists and psychiatrists by Melinder and Magnussen (2015) provides food for thought. They surveyed psychologists and psychiatrists who served regularly as expert witnesses and another group who had not served in that capacity. They were asked to complete a questionnaire concerning basic 'facts' about human memory. Among the questions were:

> 'At trial, an eyewitness's confidence is a good predictor of his or her accuracy in identifying the defendant as the perpetrator of the crime.'
>
> 'A witness's ability to recall minor details about a crime is a good indicator of the accuracy of the witness's identification of the perpetrator of the crime.'
>
> 'Sometimes people become witnesses to dramatic events. Do you think the memory for such events are worse, as good as, or better compared to the memory for everyday events?'

Remarkably, there was no difference between those who had served as expert witnesses and those who had not in terms of the accuracy of their knowledge about memory as established in the current research literature. Worryingly, a substantial number of the experts held unproven ideas about human memory thus making them liable to offer bad advice in court. By the way, the correct answers to the above questions were disagree, disagree and better in that order.

The strange case of alibi research

One somewhat neglected aspect by eyewitness evidence researchers is something greatly relied on in court – the alibi. Of course, only some of the time do alibis involve a witness. Although it is assumed that innocent suspects should be able to produce alibis indicating their innocence, research has failed to place this centre-stage. The Innocence Project (2010) showed that many of the DNA-exonerated cases actually involved an alibi provided by the defendant. However this alibi was not believed in 25 per cent of cases. Yet the DNA evidence means that they all must have been somewhere else at the time. Ronald Cotton, the DNA exonerated rapist, provided an alibi for himself which was not correct. There are a number of theoretical reasons which might result in an innocent suspect failing to produce convincing alibis:

- They may lack memories of the potential alibi. That is, they do not remember where they were on the night of 3 April. This is more likely if they were engaged in a routine task. The key stage for memory is the encoding of the memory at the time of the events. If the individual is not motivated to remember at this stage they would have no reason to do so. (Why, for example, would one want to remember that one was watching television on the night of 3 April?) Of course, being accused of a murder on the night of 3 April might motivate the search for an alibi but this motivation does nothing to improve recollection. But if the investigator believes that motivation at the time of recall should improve recall then this undermines the suspect. Even if the events are encoded initially, long periods of delay can degrade memory for events naturally.
- They may produce mistaken alibis. That is, they may believe that they were in Aberdeen on that night whereas in reality they were in Penzance. Or they may think that they have till receipts from a shopping trip in Penzance when in fact they threw them away almost immediately. They may produce 'script consistent details' such as being at university on 3 April because they routinely go to college on Wednesdays but have forgotten that on that particular Wednesday they had had a surprise visitor and did not go.
- They may generate weak alibis which cannot be corroborated. For example, the person who could validate the alibi cannot remember where they were on 3 April and whom, if anyone, they were with.
- Most of the available research concentrates on evaluating how police investigators and jurors estimate how strong alibis are. Police do not take alibis at their face value but seek proof of their accuracy. In other words, they seek to validate the alibi. This can take the form of either physical evidence or the corroboration of the alibi by another person. Little research has been done on the generation of alibis, especially by innocent people. One question is the strength of alibi production – it may be rather difficult in some circumstances and can be erroneous, thus putting the innocent suspect at risk of prosecution. A lab-based study by Olson and Charman (2012) simply asked undergraduates to report alibis concerning where they were for each of four different dates/times, together with the supporting physical evidence and supporting witnesses. They were given 48 hours to produce this evidence. At the end of this period, they returned to the research site and reported what they had found. It emerged that 36 per cent of the alibis given were simply erroneous, which meant that the individual had to modify their story or change the corroborating evidence. Most of the alibis the researchers regarded as weak evidence and the problem is worse for distant events. Of course, changing an alibi is regarded with suspicion, though this study indicates that it is a common occurrence in innocent people.

Asking people their memory of what happened at a particular point in time in the past is a notoriously fallible way of accessing memory. So, in many circumstance, asking a question like 'Where were you at 10.30 am last Wednesday?' may produce wrong answers. This is because people do not generally encode events well in terms of time. Consequently cuing a person's memory using a time cue such as the question about last Wednesday, risks memory failure because they resort to general schema about their life in order to address the question. If normally an individual would be at a lecture at 10.30 am on Wednesdays then they may claim to have been at the lecture. But the lecture may have been cancelled or the individual may have overslept and missed the lecture. As a consequence, relying on the schema would lead to a mistaken alibi ('I was at a lecture') which is not true of that specific occasion. If, at a later point after providing the alibi, the individual remembers that the lecture had been cancelled they may change their alibi which may be regarded with suspicion by the police. In other words, when searching our memory we will activate schema before we find specific memory events. If the memories according to the schema seems accurate then the individual may search their memory no further and provide a mistaken memory.

Leins and Charman (2016) compared several methods of asking a suspect for alibis – time cuing, location cuing, and paired time + location cuing. Asking a time cue such as 'What were you doing in the evening of last Thursday?' is less likely to be successful than 'What were you doing at the Curzon cinema?'. Location is encoded normally in the memory whereas time is not. Mixed cues such as 'What were you doing at the Curzon cinema last Thursday evening?' might be the most effective. In the experiment, students took part in two apparently independent studies. The first study involved the students completing a questionnaire about what they normally did between 2.00 and 3.00 pm on various days of the week along with a number of filler tasks such as rating a cartoon in terms of how humorous they found it. That is, the participants' schema was being assessed by the first questionnaire. Using a ruse about a mistake occurring in the study, the students were offered participation in another study a week or so later in order to obtain their course credits for serving as a participant in research. In the second stage of the study, the participants attended a very different location with a different researcher from the week before. It was indicated to them that they were participants in a study of interrogation methods. Some other participants had taken part in some staged crimes the week before (the guilty participants) but they were the innocent participants since they had not been involved in the crimes. They were asked about their whereabouts for two time periods. These were supposedly the times when the mock crimes had occurred. One of the time periods was actually the time that they had taken part in the first study session. Some of the participants were asked about damage that had occurred to equipment at the time corresponding to the first part of the study. Other participants were asked about damage to equipment which had happened at a particular location. The remaining third of participants, the mixed cue group, were asked about damage to equipment at that particular time in that particular location. Memory accuracy was substantially better for the location cued participants (44 per cent accuracy rate). The time-cued and the mixed-cued groups did not differ from each other and were only 13 per cent and 6 per cent accurate respectively. Accurate participants in the time-cued and the mixed time-cue and location cue groups were inconsistent with their schema as assessed in the first part of the study. Had they been consistent with the schema then their 'alibi' would have been in error. Those who were mistaken about their 'alibi' tended to be were consistent with the schema they had reported in the first part of the study. The poor performance in the mixed cue session was not expected by the researcher and would seem to be the consequence of the ease of retrieval of the time schema. Schemas are more readily retrieved by the memory than discrete specific events. In other words, honestly given but mistaken alibis may be quite common.

Just how do the police and prosecutors make decisions about whether to believe alibis when making decisions to charge or prosecute suspects? Dysart and Strange (2012) questioned approximately 60 senior law enforcement personnel about alibi investigations and stories. Time emerged as a critical element in whether or not an alibi was believed. Part of the reason for this is that memory fades with time. Furthermore, relevant physical evidence is increasingly likely to be tampered with or even disappear with time. Nor should it be forgotten that interference with witnesses is more likely as time passes. It was found that suspects actually provided information about physical evidence supporting alibis in only about 20 per cent of instances. Unmotivated strangers are regarded as lying to the police in 12 per cent of cases. Law enforcement officers are sceptical about alibi statements and are very distrustful of suspects. However, just 28 per cent thought that the suspect might be mistaken if asked for an alibi one week after the events in question. Crucially, the law enforcement personnel would regard a suspect who changed their alibi as lying. Over 80 per cent regarded changing one's alibi as an indicator of lying.

An experimental study by Marion, Kukucka, Collins, Kassin and Burke (2016) further adds to the impression that alibi evidence is fraught with dangers. Basically the study had a participant paired with a 'stooge' to carry out a task. However, later, the stooge was accused of stealing money. The participant had the opportunity to provide an alibi for the stooge indicating that the stooge had never left the room and so could not be the thief. The participant was then told that the stooge had admitted the crime. In these circumstances only 45 per cent of the participants maintained the truth of their alibi against 95 per cent of another group of participants who were told that the stooge had continued to claim to be innocent. This has particular significance for cases in which an innocent person succumbs to police pressure and falsely confesses. Any alibi might be less forthcoming from witnesses because of the false confession.

Facial composites, age progression and identification

One investigative technique familiar to the general public is the police's use of facial composites – that is, images of the 'suspect' based on the reports of victims and other witnesses. These have changed with changes in technology. Originally, an artist would sketch a picture of the face based on the information supplied by the witness, then in the 1970s Identikit (based on 'sketched' material) and Photofit (based on photographs) approaches were used. These used 'kits' of facial features from which, say, a nose with the appropriate shape was selected from a range of noses in the kit. The different elements of the face were then built into the total image. More recently still, technological advances have enabled the use of computer techniques to produce the images. These allow the size, for example, of the feature to be adjusted quickly, so increasing the flexibility of the approach. Such computerised facial composite approaches include E-FIT and PRO-fit, which are used by some police forces. E-FIT is used by 90 per cent of British police forces and is used in 30 countries around the World (Visionmetric Forensic Imaging, 2017). Research into earlier methods of creating facial composites before computerisation generally found that the quality of the composites was not good. So are the newer methods more satisfactory?

Frowd *et al.* (2004) had the 'witness' work with a facial composite operator to produce an image of a target person (popular personalities but ones identified as not being known to the 'witness'). The image of the target was shown for about one minute and there was a delay of three to four hours before the next stage of the research. The operator did not know the identity of the 'target' and worked solely on the basis of the descriptions given by the 'witness' and the normal interactions between the witness and the operator. These facial composites could then be shown to people who were asked to identify who the celebrity was. Accuracy was not outstanding. E-FIT and PRO-fit produced 20 per cent of recognition from the composite, artist's sketches resulted in 10 per cent recognition, and Photofit yielded 5 per cent recognition. The results were essentially replicated when participants were asked to match the facial composite to an array of photographs including that of the target. In other words, the composites were not very good matches to the original photographs. One other feature of the design should be mentioned – the 'witnesses' underwent a cognitive interview (see pages ***) before engaging in the facial composite construction task. Of course, a delay of three or four hours between exposure to the target and reconstruction was relatively short compared to most forensic situations.

A study by Frowd *et al.* (2005) followed many of the above procedures but extended the delay between exposure and facial reconstruction. The witnesses were shown pictures of celebrities (in this case, actors and pop music performers) until they came across one which the witness did not recognise. They looked at this for one minute. Two days later the facial composite recognition task was carried out. This again involved a cognitive interview and witnesses were asked to think of the time that the target photo was seen and the context of this. This is the reinstatement of context procedure from the cognitive interview. Then, once a clear picture had been formed, the witness described the face, taking as much time as they needed. This was then followed by cued recall where the descriptions of each feature were read to the witness, who then added anything further that came to mind. The precise procedures used for creating the 'likeness' varied but were similar to the standard practice employed with each particular method.

A separate group took part in the 'identification' process based on the composites. Overall, only a small percentage of composites were correctly named (2.8 per cent). This is partly a function of the composite method employed. Actual sketches were the most frequently recognised. Of course, this could be a consequence of the target individual not being recognisable from the original photograph. However, this group of participants were asked a number of questions about the person in the photograph. The recognition figures for the composites were adjusted on the basis of the answers to these questions to allow for these differences in recognisability of the personalities. This resulted in a modest increase in naming to 3.3 per cent over all the composites. Once again, sketches were the best named (8.1 per cent) with E-FIT and PRO-fit only being recognised by less than 2 per cent.

Just why do facial composite methods produce such inadequate composites? The temptation is to regard the problem as being the consequence of weaknesses in the methods and the inadequacy of memory for faces. There is another possible explanation which suggests that the problem may *partly* lie in the communications between the witness and the facial-composite operator. Brace *et al.* (2006) also used recognisable famous faces which had been created by a computerised facial composite system (E-FIT). The facial composites were either produced by the E-FIT operator following the verbal instructions of the 'witness' (describer) or by the E-FIT operator working alone without a 'witness'. In some conditions the facial construction was done from memory and in others a photograph of the famous person was used. Thus the composite was produced by: 1) the E-FIT operator working alone from memory; 2) the E-FIT operator working alone using a photograph; 3) the E-FIT operator following the instructions of a 'witness' who worked from memory; and 4) the E-FIT operator following the instructions of a 'witness' who could see a photograph when the operator could not.

This was followed by an evaluation phase in which the E-FIT composites were shown to a large group of evaluators, who made judgements about the quality of the composites in one study or had to name the famous person from the composite in another study. The general pattern of results was similar for both studies. Where the operator worked alone, the composites were more accurate and it made no difference whether they worked from memory or photographs. On the other hand, where the operator followed the verbal description of the 'witness', the facial composite was more accurate when the 'witness' was working from a photograph than from memory. The implication of these findings is that part of the difficulty in constructing good facial composites lies in the communication between the operator and witness; it is not simply problems to do with the witness's memory or the facial composite system in use.

Clearly there is a need for ways of improving the recognition of facial composites given the inadequacy of many of the composites. One approach to this is based on our tendency to process images of faces holistically. McIntyre, Hancock, Frowd and Lanton (2016) suggest that this adversely influences the recognition of facial composites. Even where facial composites appear to be satisfactory likenesses to an individual, quite often they achieve unsatisfactory rates of identification. A range of celebrities was chosen including film stars, TV stars, musicians, sport stars, and politicians. Initial participants were shown a picture of one of these and then produced a likeness from memory using computer software with the aid of an experienced composite operative. In addition to these original composites, enhanced versions were produced using computer software which corrected the shape of the face. In order to interfere with holistic face recognition processing, the original and the enhanced composites were doctored such that the lower half of the face was offset from the upper part of the face. Participants were shown different ones of these four versions. The data clearly revealed that the enhanced images were better recognised than the original composites. However, it was the effects of the misalignments which produced the interesting findings. Misaligning the enhanced composite made recognition significantly worse. However, misaligning the original composite led to it being better recognised than if it were not misaligned. In short, it would seem that there is promise in preventing the holistic processing of ordinary facial composites.

Turning to age-progressed photographs, the research is not so encouraging. Missing children can be high-profile, newsworthy stories for the media and distressing even where the child is quickly found and returned to its parents. The availability of photos and videos of the missing child increases the story's news impact. It sometimes happens that a child is missing for several years. There are well-known high-profile instances of this, such as the case of Madeleine McCann, the four-year-old English girl who disappeared in 2007 on a family holiday in Portugal. In such cases, age-progressed pictures of the child may be made public through the media in various ways. Age progression takes a picture of the child at the age they went missing and shows what they are likely to look like currently. The procedure uses a combination of 1) statistical anthropomorphic data concerning how faces usually change in time (e.g. the ratio between head width to head length at different ages) and 2) photographs of close relatives of the child taken at the age that the missing child is currently. The statistical data gives trends but the relatives' photos provide more global information. Just how effective are they?

This was the question that Lampinen, Arnal, Adams, Courtney and Hicks (2012) set out to answer. They obtained photos of particular individuals at about the age of 7 years and about 12 years. The picture at about 12 years provided an 'objective' picture. The researchers had the picture of the 7-year old age-progressed to 12 years of age. So they had:

1. Real photos of each child at the age of 7;
2. Real photos of each child at the age of 12;
3. Age-progressed photos from the age of 7 progressed to the age of 12 years.

In the study proper, photos were presented via a computer programme and the participants had to imagine that the children were missing. In different conditions of the study, one of each of the three different types of image was presented. The memory test for recognition consisted of a large number of different pictures of children of approximately 12 years of age. Included in this large set of photos were target pictures of the 'missing' children at age 12 years. The key finding from the research was that the outdated pictures from age 7 years were just as good as the age-progressed pictures at age 12 years in terms of the participants being able to spot the 'missing children'. On the other hand, the good news was that, even given the lack of advantage of age-progressed pictures, recognition of the 'missing children' was rather better than chance. In other words, the photos were of some use, even though age progression did not improve things. This would, at first sight, seem to be something of a mystery. However, it has to be remembered that age-progressed pictures are statistical averages. Since it is well known that small changes to a face's dimensions can make recognition difficult then perhaps it is not surprising that statistically age-progressed pictures are not that effective. Furthermore, Keenan (2007) suggested that people know about facial growth patterns. For example, we recognise our friends in pictures from their childhoods. Using this implicit knowledge, it may be that seeing the outdated photograph allows us to imagine the child at an older age or at least recognise key features.

The use of age-progressed photographs may serve other purposes, of course. They may stimulate fresh media coverage of a case and, with it, public interest. The increased vigilance of the public may, then, be the important thing.

It is important to remember that age-progression is done by forensic artists based on some science. Different artists can produce rather different age-progressed images. Can anything be done to improve the age-progressed image? One idea is simply to use the work of several different artists and combine the results (Lampinen, Erickson, Frowd and Mahoney, 2015). Doing this for different degrees of age-progression resulted in somewhat disappointing results. It was clear that the work of individual artists varied in terms of how close to actual images of the individual at the older age, as one might expect. Using morphing techniques to combine the eight different artists' work into one image did, in general, lead to a more satisfactory image. However, the actual similarity was judged to be better than the midpoint of the scale but generally not reaching the next point up – somewhat similar. Also, the best of the work of the individual artists was better than for morphed pictures.

Main points

- Eyewitness testimony is a proven source of wrongful convictions in jurisdictions in which conviction is possible on the basis of such eyewitness evidence alone. Police officers place a great deal of reliance on it. It should not however be assumed that eyewitness evidence is without worth. Research has shown that for some types of physical features, eyewitness descriptions can be quite accurate. However, little credence has until recently been placed on the idea that confident eyewitnesses are also accurate eyewitnesses.
- Memory can be influenced by a range of factors and there is evidence to show that memory can be affected by later events and questioning style. Much of the pertinent research tends to come from laboratory studies, which can be problematic to apply to real-life situations with precision. For example, it is difficult to generalise the effects of time of exposure to the witnessed event from the laboratory to real-life settings for very mundane reasons such as that exposure times in laboratory studies are a fraction of the time that a real-life eyewitness observes the offender for.
- The planning of the line-up or identification parade should proceed with care as there are many pitfalls. There is evidence that police line-ups may sometimes reflect good practice but sometimes bad practices prevail – for example, it is much more common to choose the foils (stooges) in a line-up on the basis of their similarity to the suspect, whereas good practice holds that they should be like the eyewitness's description of the offender. In line-ups, eyewitnesses tend to identify someone who is like their memory of the offender even when the offender is not present in the line-up. This is in accordance with the theory of relative judgement. Factors that may improve eyewitness performance in line-ups include informing the eyewitness that the person administering the line-up does not know who the suspect is and making sure that that person indeed does not know who the suspect is.

Further reading

British Psychological Society Research Board (2010) *Guidelines on Memory and the Law: Recommendations from the Scientific Study of Human Memory* British Psychological Society.

Thompson, C.P., Herrmann, D.J., Read, J.D. and Bruce, D. (2014) *Eyewitness Memory: Theoretical and Applied Perspectives* New York: Psychology Press.

Toglia, M.P., Ross, D.F., Pozzulo, J. and Pica, E. (eds) (2014) *The Elderly Eyewitness in Court* New York: Psychology Press.

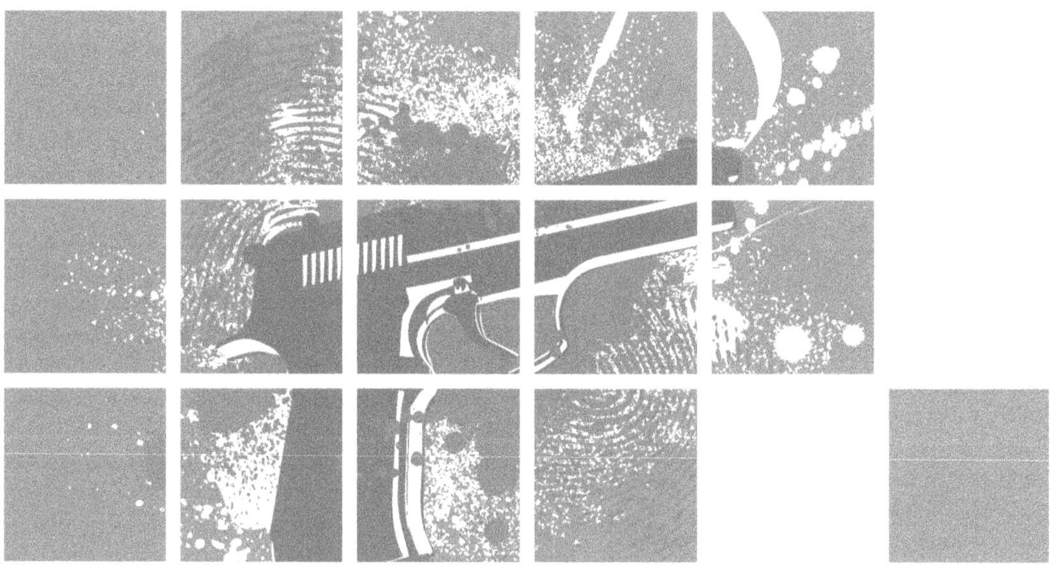

Chapter 14

Profile analysis 1: FBI-style offender profiling

Overview

- Two main branches of offender profiling are carried out – FBI-style profiling which is described in this chapter and the more actuarial or statistical style, associated with the British psychologist David Canter, which is described in Chapter 15.
- Offender profiling dates back to the nineteenth-century case of Jack the Ripper, although its modern origins are in the work of the Behavioral Science Unit of the FBI located in Virginia in the 1970s. This form of profiling is based on clinical intuition, whereas more recent approaches have been more research-based and statistical in nature.
- Offending profiling of all sorts is based on the work of the police in gathering information, especially from the scene of the crime. Obviously, offender profiling only helps where the police have problems identifying suspects and organising the information collected.
- Information from the crime scene is used to classify the crime scene into *organised* (where there is evidence that the crime has been carefully planned) or *disorganised* (where the crime scene looks chaotic and there is little sign of preparation for the crime. An organised crime scene suggests, for example, a sexually competent, charming person who lives with a partner. The disorganised crime scene is indicative of an offender with low intelligence, unskilled occupation and who lives alone.
- FBI-style profiling has been subject to intense media interest and coverage which has influenced its development. The lack of clarity about just what profiling applies to and the paucity of empirical evidence concerning it have left the topic somewhat moribund.

Introduction

Offender profiling emerged in the US at about the same time as forensic and criminal psychology began its rapid expansion. Indeed, offender profiling may have fueled the interest of many people in the broader discipline. Despite its high profile, profiling as practised by the Federal Bureau of Investigation (FBI) has generally failed to convince many psychologists of its effectiveness. For many, including law courts, the question is whether the work of profilers amounts to reliable scientific evidence or whether it is little other than *ipse dixit* – the unfounded opinion of the profiler. According to Kocsis (2015), the problem of a lack of convincing evidence of the validity or accuracy of the method is only part of the difficulty. A second issue is the lack of theoretical coherence which might ensure a substantial body of knowledge for application. That final issue is that the interest of the public in the topic has resulted in a misplaced emphasis on sensational cases rather than coherent scientific development.

Offender profiling is generally taken to mean the use of information gathered at the crime scene in order to predict the characteristics of the offender. Sometimes it is referred to as criminal investigative analysis. According to Jackson and Bekerian (1997, p.2) offender profiling is based on the following formula: 'Behaviour is exhibited at a crime, or a series of similar crimes, and studying this behaviour allows inferences to be made about the likely offender.' Jackson and Bekerian suggest that profile analysis includes offender profiling, psychological profiling, criminal profiling and criminal personality profiling. According to Homant and Kennedy (1998), the following three types of profiling should be carefully distinguished among others:

- *Crime scene profiling:* uses information from the scene of the crime (physical and other evidence) to generate a full picture of the unknown offender.
- *Offender profiling:* the collection of empirical data in order to collate a picture of the characteristics of those involved in a certain type of crime.
- *Psychological profiling:* the use of standard personality tests together with interviewing in order to assess the extent to which the individual fits the known personality template of a certain type of offender such as child sex abusers.

There is, then, self-evidently a degree of confusion or, at least, inconsistency in terms of what is often referred to simply as profiling.

In profiling work there is a marked difference of opinion between two points of view. There are those who argue that profiling is akin to clinical judgement – informed by research but ultimately a subjective matter, dependent on the insight and skill of the profiler. On the other hand, some argue that profiling must be led by research and aspire to objectivity. The former best reflects the FBI approach, which is featured in this chapter, and the latter is David Canter's approach, which is dealt with in Chapter 15. The contrast between the two is stark in many ways – as reading this and the next chapters will demonstrate. The bottom line, however, is that both approaches have contributed a great deal to the public and research interest in profiling.

Herndon (2007) provides extensive information about the impact of offender profilers on popular media including both fictional and factual. For example, he gives a remarkably long list of the motion pictures which have featured offender profilers. The most famous of these is probably *The Silence of the Lambs* (1990) but the list also includes *Manhunter* (1986), *Kiss the Girls* (1997), *Copycat* (1998), *The Bone Collector* (2000), *From Hell* (2000), *Along Came the Spider* (2001), *Citizen X* (2001), *Hannibal* (2001), *Blood Work* (2002), *Red Dragon* (2003), *Twisted* (2003), *Mindhunters* (2004), and *Taking Lives* (2004). This is not to ignore the myriad of newspaper and magazine articles, books, and TV programmes which involved profiling. Herndon sums up this material in the following way:

> 'Profilers are portrayed as flawed individuals, in some ways not unlike the criminals they seek to identify: obsessed, driven, and troubled. In the non-fictional/biographical books, profiling is touted as truly remarkable in its effectiveness; profilers sell themselves and their claimed skills. And, in documentaries, general readership articles, and news magazines, there is more likely to be found a balanced presentation of profiling and profilers—the good and the bad.'
>
> (p. 319)

Crime fiction is littered with numerous insightful, subjective profilers who make amazing interpretations based on small quantities of evidence. Remarkable deductions lead inexorably to the culprit. Fictional detectives have incredible insights into the psychological motives behind crime. The great fictional detective Sherlock Holmes was inclined to make statements redolent of the ideas of offender profilers. A good example is that a criminal returns to the scene of the crime – a theme which modern profilers echo (Canter, 2004). Much of this media coverage has produced somewhat hostile responses from psychologists concerned about what they see to be extremely weak psychology (e.g. Williams, 1994).

Bosco, Zappala and Pekka (2010) reviewed examples, in various parts of the world, in which profiling evidence was considered for admission in court. In the US, in recent years, the *Daubert* decision (1993), and the closely linked *General Elec. Co.* v. *Joiner* (1997) and *Kumho Tire Company, Ltd.* v. *Carmichael* (1999), decisions basically held that to be admissible in court, evidence had to be reliable and scientifically sound (see Box 1.1 for a discussion of *Daubert*). Furthermore, the American Federal Rules of Evidence (The National Federal Courts Rules Committee, 2017) require that expert testimony should be based on 'reliable principles and methods'. Quite obviously, these criteria bring into doubt the value of offender profiling to courts of law. Bosco *et al.* chose to divide profiling into three different aspects – motivation analysis in which an opinion is expressed about the motive for the crime based on the crime scene, profile analysis in which an opinion is expressed about whether a particular type of behaviour committed by an offender is associated with a particular type of person, and linkage analysis indicating whether two or more crimes are linked in the sense that they have been committed by the same person. Although they do not state this as such, Bosco *et al.*'s examples following *Daubert* in the US are generally refused by the court except for the case of linkage analysis. Other countries too seem to have been less than enthusiastic about the use of profiling in court.

The origins of offender profiling

According to Canter (2004), offender profiling probably began in 1888 when a medical doctor, Dr Thomas Bond, provided what might be regarded as a profile of Jack the Ripper. Bond was of the opinion that:

> [t]he murderer must have been a man of physical strength and great coolness and daring. There is no evidence he had an accomplice. He must in my opinion be a man subject to periodic attacks of homicidal and erotic mania … The murderer in external appearance is quite likely to be a quiet inoffensively looking man probably middle-aged and neatly and respectably dressed. Assuming the murderer be such a person as I have just described, he would be solitary and eccentric in his habits, also he is likely to be a man without regular occupation, but with some small income or pension.
>
> (cited in Canter, 2004, p. 2)

Dr Bond's profile of The Ripper was remarkably similar to profiles of sexual murderers in recent times according to Canter.

The origins of offender profiling in modern times are usually traced back to 1956 and the work of the psychiatrist James A. Brussel on the New York bomber crimes of that time. Brussel, basing his theorising on psychoanalysis, studied the crime scene. Based on his assessment of this, Brussel gave a description of the bomber containing the following features among others:

- heavy;
- middle-aged;
- male;
- single;
- living with a sibling.

This is held by some to be a convincingly accurate picture of George Metesky who was eventually convicted of the crime. He was actually living with two siblings but this is held to be of little consequence. Brussel, at first sight, had demonstrated the power of psychological approaches to detective work. Accounts vary but the general consensus is that Brussel's profile was not responsible for Metesky's arrest. Nevertheless, the case demonstrates another feature of offender profiling – the seemingly mysterious nature of the profile. Just how can this information be deduced simply on the basis of the characteristics of the crime scene?

One of the students of Brussel was Howard Teten who pioneered profiling when he became the first chief of the FBI's Division of Training and Development at Quantico, Virginia. This housed, in a nuclear bunker, the Behavioral Science Unit which produced research, consultation and training in the application of psychology and the other social sciences to crime and detective work. It was disbanded in 2014. Among the famous agents associated with the Unit were Robert Ressler and John Douglas. During the 1970s, the unit began to research the personality, behaviours, crimes and motivations of serial killers showing sexual aspects in their crimes. This formed much of the research base for their method of profiling (Douglas, Burgess, Burgess and Ressler, 1992). The term 'serial killer' is held to be an innovation of members of the Unit. It should be stressed that there may well be serial killers who do not show sexual elements in their crimes. For example, a bank robber may kill on several different raids, yet it would be difficult to identify this as being in any way sexually motivated. The FBI investigators defined serial homicide as 'three or more separate events in three or more separate locations with an emotional cooling off period in between homicides' (Douglas *et al.*, 1992, p. 21).

Ferguson, White, Stacey, Lorenz and Bhimani (2003) argue that there is a lack of an agreed definition of serial murder that makes progress in the field difficult. They reject the idea put forward by Douglas *et al.* (1992) that serial killers seek to express their need for power. Every crime, it could be argued, is an expression of power. Instead, Ferguson *et al.* (2003, p. 4) suggest the following three criteria are crucial to the definition of serial (sexual) murder:

- Three or more victims are killed during multiple and discrete events.
- Killing the victim is pleasurable to the offender at the time. It may be stress-relieving or otherwise consistent

with the perpetrator's internal set of values. The attacks themselves do not fulfil only functional purposes.

- The murders do not occur under the direction or blessing of any political or criminal organisation.

Notice that this definition does not necessarily define the crime as sexual. It is questionable whether the elements achieve much other than excluding serial killings for reasons of gain, for example.

The FBI profiling process

There are several stages in a Federal Bureau of Investigation profile.

Stage 1: Data assimilation

The earliest stage of FBI profiling involves the collection of a variety of information, as seen in Figure 14.1. A crime usually has a variety of associated documentary materials: for example, the pathologist's report about the medical circumstances that led to death, photographs taken at the crime scene, witness statements and police reports and so forth. This information may not appear at first sight to be of any value at all. Nevertheless, there is always the potential for unpromising materials to be crucial in terms of the ultimate profile. The time of death, for example, may have an important implication for the psychology of the offender. Basically, the process is one of seeking to identify the psychological signature of the offender. This psychological signature is different from the *modus operandi* (see Box 14.1) – the latter broadly refers to the style of committing the crime. It is the characteristic way in which that particular criminal works. The psychological signature concerns what can be gleaned from the crime scene about the personality of the offender. This is most likely to include the fantasies of the offender.

Stage 2: Crime scene classification

Remember that serial sexual murders are the most important crimes profiled by the FBI psychologists. Profilers developed a dichotomy to describe two characteristic crime scenes – the *organised,* the *disorganised,* and the *mixed* crime scenes.

- Organised = evidence of planning.
- Disorganised = chaotic.
- Mixed = elements of both

The organised/disorganised crime scene classification was based on offenders' reports of their crimes in the early study by profilers (Douglas *et al.*, 1992). Early research indicated that crime scenes could be reliably classified by profilers (Ressler and Burgess, 1985). There was, on average, nearly 75 per cent agreement between different profilers on whether a crime scene was organised or disorganised. However, there was considerable variation among profilers and some profilers made a very different assessment of the sort of crime scene involved than others did.

The two main types of crime scene reveal different aspects of the psychology of the offender. According to Geberth (1996), the organised offender is characterised by features such as: following the news media; has a decent car; alcohol is associated with the crime; his father had a stable pattern of employment; experienced inconsistent childhood discipline; the offender controlled their mood during the crime. The disorganised offender demonstrates virtually the reverse pattern: little or no interest in the

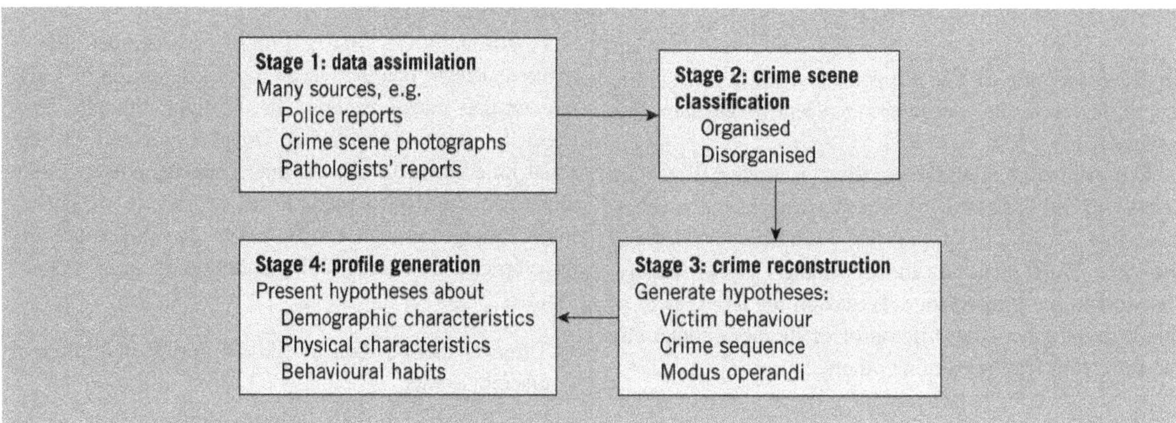

Figure 14.1 Major stages of FBI crime scene profiling

news media; lives or works close to the crime scene so a vehicle is not needed; alcohol was uninvolved in the crime; the offender's father had an unstable employment pattern; their childhood discipline was harsh; and the offender exhibited anxiety when committing the crime. Further, perhaps more important, differentiating characteristics of organised and disorganised offenders are to be found in Table 14.1. This is based on the work of Holmes and Holmes (1996) which, as can be seen, extends into matters such as which interview techniques are appropriate to which type of offender. The mixed crime scene may be the result of a planned crime going wrong because the victim does something unexpected. As a consequence, the body may not be carefully hidden as it might be in a typical organised crime.

Gierowski, Jaskiewicz-Obydzinska and Slawik (1998, 2000) studied 120 murderers classified by their crime scenes as planned or not planned, which appears to be very similar to the FBI profilers' organised versus disorganised dichotomy. The factors associated with a planned crime include the choice of weapon and the manner in which death was inflicted; the location and time at which the crime occurred; and other aspects intended to hide the identity of the culprit. Disordered socialisation factors (e.g. inconsistent upbringing methods and running away from home) were associated with the organised crime scene. Organised crime scene offenders had frequent changes of sexual partners, were low on alcoholism and showed evidence of psychopathy.

They also tended to have higher regard for their personal appearance.

Stage 3: Crime scene reconstruction

The crime scene is not a simple fixed event. Instead, it is the result of a complex set of circumstances. Consequently, there are aspects of the crime scene that cannot be understood unless attempts are made to understand the events as a dynamic process involving a minimum of two people – offender and victim. There may be witnesses, actual or potential, to consider. The information collected in *Stage 1* is essential to the reconstruction. Inference and deduction are involved. Reconstruction does not have to involve playing out the events as in a television reconstruction. The purpose of the reconstruction may be to clarify the offender's *modus operandi*. Knowing this may help tie the crime to other crimes. The sequence of events (for example, where there are signs that the victim was stalked) would be considered. Also, could the victim's response have affected the offender? For example, if she fought and struggled then this may have affected the offender's ability to act out his fantasies.

Stage 4: Profile generation

Hypotheses about the profile of the offender are drawn together. These hypotheses are not necessarily psychological in nature and may include, for example, demographic features (social class, type of work, employment/ unemployment); lifestyle (such as living alone, being in a relationship); behavioural habits (e.g. poor at mixing socially, solitary hobbies); and personality dynamics (e.g. offending linked to depression).

In FBI offender profiling, the profile may serve a number of possible functions Obviously, helping police improve the efficiency of information processing by suggesting features of the offender which would narrow the search is a major one. Another function of profiling is to help answer questions of links between a series of crimes and the possible number of different offenders involved. Linking crimes to offenders in this way means that information and resources can be pooled by different police teams investigating seemingly unconnected crimes.

Table 14.1 The relationship between crime scene type and aspects of investigation

	Organised offender	Disorganised offender
Personal characteristics	Sexually competent Lives with partner Has charm	Low intelligence Unskilled Lives alone Poor personal hygiene
Post-offence behaviour	May move body Police 'groupie'/follower	May turn religious May change job
Recommended interview technique	Use direct strategy Be accurate about details	Show empathy Interview at night

Source: Holmes and Holmes (1996)

The methodology of the FBI profilers

In strict scientific terms, the methodology employed by the FBI team in developing their ideas about serial killers was far from rigorous. Indeed, it is remarkable that so much developed from just one study (Ressler, Burgess and Douglas, 1988) of a mere 36 offenders. Little formal research methodology was employed which consisted of ad hoc interviews (Canter, Alison, Alison and Wentink, 2004). Furthermore, importantly the methodology drew on the collective experience of members of the unit as much as it did on research findings. Crime scene profiling, the basic form of FBI-style profiling, nevertheless has been widely publicized in a number of popular accounts by ex-FBI profilers of their work (e.g. Douglas and Olshaker, 1995, 1997; Ressler and Shachtman, 1997). The FBI style of profiling is presented by these authors more as a 'special art' (Canter, 2004) rather than a scientific endeavour. FBI profiling's main features are as follows:

- A willingness to encompass experience and intuition as a component of profiling.
- A relatively weak empirical database, which is small in comparison to the extent to which the method is used.
- A concentration on the more serious, bizarre and extreme crimes, such as serial sexual murder.
- A tendency to involve an extensive contact with the investigating team of police officers at all levels of the investigation rather than simply providing a profile. For example, the profiler may make recommendations on how to respond to letters and similar communications from someone who appears to be the offender.

Figure 14.2 is a schematic diagram of some similarities and differences between FBI-style clinical profiling and statistical profiling. What sorts of crime should be profiled? This may be decided on a number of bases:

- There is little point in profiling trivial crimes since, by their nature, they are unlikely to be actively investigated.
- A crime that shows few distinguishing characteristics at the crime scene is a poor candidate for profiling.
- Are the investigating officers unaware of a likely offender? Frequently, offenders are friends or family members of the victim. Offender profiling may not be helpful in these circumstances.
- Profile analysis is especially appropriate if the crime scene indicates pathological psychological features. For instance, objects may be found inserted in the victim's genitals or even body parts taken as 'trophies'.

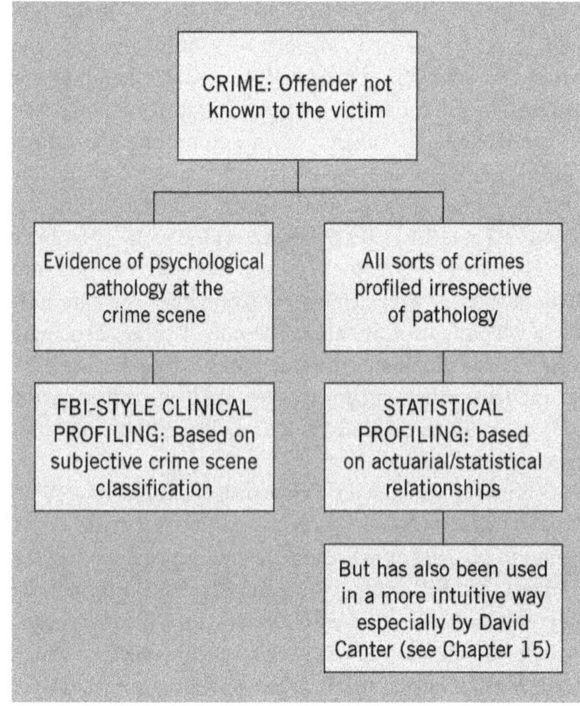

Figure 14.2 Features of FBI-style clinical profiling and statistical profiling

Despite this, as will be seen in Chapter 15, profiling has been extended to a much wider variety of types of crime than the FBI profilers ever considered (e.g. fraud).

Box 14.1 Key concept

Crime signature and *modus operandi*

Two concepts which have a bearing on offender profiling need to be distinguished: (a) *modus operandi* (MO) and (b) crime signature:

- *Modus operandi* simply refers to the characteristic way in which a person performs a particular task, although it is commonly specifically applied to the way in which an offender commits a particular crime. According to Keppel, Weis, Brown and Welch (2005, p. 14) a *modus operandi* refers to 'the offender's actions during the commission of a crime that are necessary to complete the crime'. (The plural of *modus operandi* is *modi operandi.*) *Modi operandi* are not necessarily fixed and offenders may well change their *modus operandi* in the light of their experiences while committing a crime or on the basis of what they learnt from previous crimes.

- A criminal signature, in offender profiling, actually uses an archaic meaning of the term signature which is 'a distinctive action, characteristic, etc.' (*The Concise English Dictionary*, 1990, Clarendon Press, Oxford p. 1129). A crime's signature characteristics reflect things which happen during the commission of a crime but which are more or less idiosyncratic to or characteristic of the offender. The criminal signature is believed to reflect aspects of a particular offender's nature. Unlike the *modus operandi*, a criminal signature is believed to be a relatively fixed and unchanging thing at its core. However, it may evolve in certain respects during a sequence of crimes.

Of course, this distinction is not absolute in practice but it is helpful in the sense that signature characteristics are more likely to be associated with a particular offender than is their modus operandi. According to Keppel *et al.* (p. 14), signature analysis is widely used in the United States and it is also the only crime scene assessment technique that courts in the United States accept as part of testimony and that may be used in appeals.

It is helpful to consider the 11 Jack the Ripper killings which occurred in Whitechapel, London, between 1888 and 1891, since they illustrate the difference between the concepts of *modus operandi* and crime signatures. There has been controversy as to just how many killers were involved in the Jack the Ripper murders. Nevertheless, there is some consensus that five of the murders were committed by the same killer. However, Keppel *et al.* suggest that six crimes were committed by the same offender on the basis of their signature analysis of various Scotland Yard case files.

The earliest of the cases attributed to this killer was that of Martha Tabram. She was found face-up with clothing disarranged in a way which exposed the lower part of her body and genitals as the killer left her with her legs wide open. The evidence clearly established that she had been killed at a spot on a landing at the Working Lads' Institute in Whitechapel. There was no indication at all that the body had been dragged from one location to another. Her body was found at around 4.45 a.m. – probably three hours after the time of death. Martha was a heavy-drinking, known prostitute of about 36 years of age. She had about 39 stab wounds, especially to the left-hand side of her body. There were 17 stabs to her breasts and 13 in her lower body. There were wounds to her neck, liver, spleen and stomach as well as her genitals. All of the wounds were inflicted before she died from a stab to her heart.

The last of the series of murders believed to have been committed by this one killer was that of Mary Jane Kelly. She was found in a room of a house in Spitalfields, London. Again she was a known prostitute and heavy consumer of alcohol. Her body was found on its back on a bed. There were considerable levels of mutilation: her nose and ears were severed and the flesh had been removed from the body to leave it in a skeletal state. Her heart and other organs were missing, though some body parts had been left on a table nearby. She had been disembowelled and her viscera placed around the body. Her uterus and one breast were placed under her head. Her neck was severed down to the bone and her right thigh was revealed down to the bone. Mary Jane's vulva and right buttock had been removed. It was concluded that some of the mutilation had occurred after the death of the victim.

Of course, to appreciate the murder series in full, each should be carefully considered in its entirety. The *modi operandi* of the six murders in question, while not identical, were highly similar in certain ways. Each victim was a poor woman prostitute almost invariably in the 24–45 year range. Once they lifted their clothing to have sex with the killer, they were strangled and lowered to the ground. Usually, their heads were facing to the left of the killer. The attacks took place during the night, after midnight and before 6 a.m. The geographical locations of the murders were within a one square mile (2.6 km^2) area and it was no more than a mile (1.6 km) from each successive murder to the next. The victims were found where they were killed, which was by a sharp, long-bladed knife after they had been strangled near to death. The first victim (Martha Tabram) was stabbed from the front, which meant that the killer was covered in a great deal of blood, putting him at risk of detection.

Consequently, his *modus operandi* changed to attacking his victims from behind, which meant that less blood was transferred to his body.

Interestingly, there was a change in the location of the killings. The early killings took place outdoors and the killer had been interrupted by the arrival of others at the location. The later killing of Mary Jane Kelly took place

BOX 14.1 (continued)

indoors as she lay on a bed. This change in the modus operandi meant that the killer was less likely to be disturbed but it also enabled him to extend the process of mutilation, as revealed by the extensive cutting up of her body.

According to Keppel *et al.*, the signature for the six linked Jack the Ripper killings includes the following:

- *Picquerism:* this describes the sexual pleasure that some obtain from cutting or stabbing others or observing such acts. It should be stressed that there was no evidence at all of physical sexual activity on the part of the killer in any of these crimes.
- *The killer needed submission of the victim:* all of the victims suffered multiple stab wounds, slashing of the throat, etc. which would incapacitate and subdue them.
- *Overkill to have complete domination of the victim:* the violent acts of this particular Ripper were far in excess of what was needed to kill or subdue the victim.
- *Degradation of the victim:* this was exemplified by the killer's leaving of the bodies in very public places which might suggest that he felt invincible and beyond the authority of the police.
- *Posing of victims' bodies:* except in circumstances in which he was disturbed in the course of his crime, the killer posed the bodies of his victims in a characteristic and sexually revealing manner.
- *Escalation of violence:* the violence became more extreme as the series of killings progressed.
- *Planning:* the killer left no evidence at the crime scene other than the remains of the victim and took his weapon to the crime and carefully removed it.

Finally, a signature is helpful only if it reveals very idiosyncratic behaviours. Keppel *et al.* compared this signature with a database of homicides. It is important to note that, for example, only 0.03 per cent of the murders on this database involved mutilated prostitutes, and there were no cases of prostitutes who had been mutilated and their bodies left in unusual poses. In other words, the Ripper signature for these cases is very unusual.

The process of police investigation

Profiling is seen as an adjunct to the police investigation process. Innes (2002) carried out a qualitative study of how the police in an English police force investigated homicides. The national clear-up rate for homicide is very high, with approximately 90 per cent of cases being 'solved'. This is less than surprising since most homicides are committed by associates of the victim. Nevertheless, there may be problems in solving some crimes that often lie in the complex set of events involving a number of people which culminates in the murder. This can make it difficult to know precisely who did what and the reasons why. The police make an informal distinction between cases which are 'self-solvers' and those that might be termed 'whodunnits'. Different processes of investigation would be involved in the case of the self-solvers from that of the 'whodunnit'. Something like 70 per cent of cases of homicide could be classified as self-solvers. A suspect emerges very early because there are witnesses, or the offender goes to the police, or the physical forensic evidence points to a particular individual. However, these are not always easy cases – they can be highly emotive – and deconstructing the events to provide a 'coherent, explanatory account' (Innes, 2002, p. 672) taxing. Often self-solving cases are investigated using a three-stage approach:

- The collection and analysis of information from the crime scene.
- Pursuing lines of enquiry relevant to the suspect, such as a formal interview with the suspect; tracing and interviewing witnesses who may have seen the suspect with the victim earlier; inquiries involving neighbours; and inquiries into family background.
- Case construction: selecting and organising the material into an account of the events which is appropriate to the needs of the legal system and presented in appropriate legal language. For example, it can be important to carefully define the events as murder or manslaughter in the UK.

The 'whodunnit' investigation is somewhat more complex and involves five stages:

- *The initial response:* the primary task is to deal with the evidence available at the crime scene. Witnesses are interviewed and the area of the crime scene subjected to a systematic search for forensic evidence.

- *Information burst:* the police quickly generate substantial amounts of information. There may be a variety of sources, including interviews with the immediate relatives of the victim and ex-partners, business associates and local house-to-house inquiries. Other sources include criminal intelligence resources to identify the victim's criminal connections. A number of suspects might be arrested and released without charge on the basis of having committed similar crimes in the past.
- *Suspect development:* the police proceed to elicit more detail about possible suspects. Some suspects may be dropped at this stage and others may come under suspicion as the evidence becomes clearer. A prime suspect is being sought even on the basis of hunches.
- *Suspect targeting:* once other suspects have been eliminated or a prime suspect has been identified, the police will change their approach and start targeting this particular individual in terms of their information gathering.
- *Case construction:* this is the stage at which the police attempt to formulate an account of the events of the homicide in a way that is in keeping with legal considerations.

It is the whodunit crime which might attract profiling.

An example of FBI profiling

It can be difficult to explain exactly how a profile emerges out of the different inputs available to the profiler. FBI profilers have rarely, if ever, made totally clear the inferential processes involved and there is plainly a degree of subjectivity inherent in the method. Some insight into profiling can be obtained by comparing the inputs with the actual profile. The following case is reported in detail in Ressler, Burgess and Douglas (1988):

- A nude female body was found at 3 p.m. on the roof of the apartment block where she lived.
- She had left home for work at 6.30 in the morning.
- She was 26 years of age, 90 pounds in weight, her spine was deformed and she was not dating men.
- Both of her nipples had been removed and placed upon her body.
- Her face was severely beaten.
- She had been throttled with the strap of her bag.
- A blunt instrument had caused many face fractures.
- Virtually all items used came from the victim's bag.
- The phrase 'You can't stop me' was written in ink on her inner thigh and 'Fuck you' on her torso.
- The pendant that she usually wore was missing.
- The victim's underwear had been taken down and pulled over her face.
- Her stockings were tied around her ankles and wrists but very loosely.
- A pen and an umbrella were inserted into her vagina.
- A comb was stuck in her pubic hair.
- There was no semen in the victim's vagina. The offender had ejaculated over her body from a standing position.
- There were bite marks on her thighs and various bruises/lacerations all over.
- Faeces from the murderer were very close by. They were covered with the victim's clothes.
- There was no evidence of similar crimes being carried out in the area.

This is a shortened list of the available information. Nevertheless, there is enough, perhaps, to form an impression of the murderer.

The psychological profile developed included the following major features:

- A white man.
- Age between 25 and 35 years – similar in age to the victim.
- Alcohol and drugs were not material factors in the crime.
- Any dates would be younger so that they could be more easily controlled and dominated.
- Average intelligence but dropped out of education.
- Difficulties in personal relationships with women.
- Disorganised offender – confused and perhaps mental difficulties in the past.
- He would fit into the context well – might reside in the apartment or could be employed there.
- Never married.
- No military background.
- Possibly unemployed.
- Sexual fantasies have been harboured by the offender for a long time and he possibly uses and collects sadistic pornography.
- Sexually inexperienced and inadequate.
- Unskilled or skilled occupation.

So what is it about the information about the crime scene that leads to this profile? The following is some of the threads in Ressler, Burgess and Douglas's thinking:

- Killers tend to be similar in terms of age and race to their victim.
- Fantasy tends to be embedded at the core of such extreme cases. The crime may be the result of the offender using the fantasy as a plan or blueprint for offending. Thus the contents of the fantasy may be seen in the characteristics of the offence. For example, the sadistic nature of this crime is indicative of the contents of the offender's sadistic fantasy. Keeping a pendant as a 'trophy' indicates that the offender has a need to fantasise in the future.
- There is little evidence that this crime was prepared for – except in fantasy. The crime scene was disorganised. The offender used whatever was to hand in the course of the crime: things were taken from the victim's bag.
- Although the crime was clearly sexual in nature, the offender used substitutes for sexual penetration. This suggests that he had sexual inadequacies. Consequently, the likelihood is that he lacked sexual experience and had never married.
- The offence has elements of control and domination, thus explaining his choice of victim.
- That the offender defecated near the crime scene indicates that the offence took place over a lengthy time period. Remember, though, that the murderer was in an exposed location and there was a great risk that he might be seen. One explanation linking these features together is that the killer was very familiar with that locality. Perhaps he was an employee or resident in that area.

Once this profile had been made available to the police, they studied their investigation records for possible suspects. They found a prime suspect – a man whose father lived in the apartments. Although they had been led to believe that the man was in mental hospital, it was discovered that security there was not perfect. He was eventually convicted on the evidence of the bite marks on the body, which matched his dental pattern.

What research says about profiles

Some researchers have studied numerous profiles and have identified problems. In a nutshell, the profiles generally lack justifications for the claims and assertions they make about the offender. In the United Kingdom, the Association of Chief Police Officers required that profilers must explain the thinking behind the contents of their profiles. Alison, Smith and Morgan (2003) and Alison, Smith, Eastman and Rainbow (2003) obtained a selection of real offender profiles – largely from the United Kingdom and the United States. Using a systematic coding scheme, they analysed the 3090 statements these profiles contained. The vast majority of the statements merely reiterated facts that were already known to the police, gave information about the profiler's professional competence, or gave warnings about the limitations of the use of the profile. This left only 28 per cent which were profile material about the offender. Mostly these were unsubstantiated claims (82 per cent of the 28 per cent). Only about 16 per cent provided some justification for the statement being made. A further 1 per cent were simply illogical.

It has been suggested that anecdotes concerning the success of profiling dominates assessments of profiling's validity (Wilson, Lincoln and Kocsis, 1997). Nevertheless, they provide a table of what they claim to be qualitative evaluations of selected case studies involving techniques related to profiling. The profiles produced were judged to be accurate in 22 of the 32 cases listed plus a few more that are described as partially accurate. Four of the cases were essentially not solved which means the accuracy of the profile against the offender could not be judged. At one level it is possible to argue that this is good evidence of the validity of profiling but, unfortunately, there is no explanation of how the accuracy of the profiles was actually judged. The authors, however, hint that this data augurs well in terms of the validity of profiling. However, one might expect a clear explanation of how the profiles were judged accurate. One of the cases, for example, was Brussel's mad bomber – there has been controversy over whether this profile was accurate yet Wilson *et al.* claim that it was.

BOX 14.2 Controversy

Is criminal profiling just common sense?

Just what is the status of offender profiling as presented in the professional literature? Snook, Eastwood, Gendreau, Goggin and Cullen (2007) systematically reviewed publications discussing criminal profiling literature by employing what they refer to as a narrative review. The concept of narrative review is based on the work of Gendreau, Goggin, Cullen and Paparozzi, (2002) who classified publications into whether the author used common sense or empirically based arguments to make their case or evaluate an idea. Common sense sources of knowledge are those which essentially regard criminal profiling as a skill or art based on experience or intuition. This would be exemplified by references to authorities, testimonials, intuition and anecdotal information to make the case for criminal profiling. Such common sense rationales are very different from an empirical rationale in which the following, for example, might be used: 1) empirical research drawn from scientific writings; 2) data based on surveys; 3) experiments or similar scientific methods; and 4) the issue of causality is regarded as problematic. Another aspect of this more scientific perspective is that theory needs to be revised in the light of new empirical findings. Snook *et al.* (2007) searched the electronic databases *PsycINFO* and *Criminal Justice Abstracts*, using the keywords 'criminal', 'psychological' and 'offender profiling'. A wide range of different sorts of publications were included, namely peer-reviewed journal articles; book chapters (including those from a previous edition of this book); research reports; published conference papers; and magazine articles.

Coders independently coded the materials using the following broad categories:

- Knowledge source (e.g. quantitative versus qualitative);
- Analytic processes (e.g. experimental or biased towards hindsight);
- Evidence integration (e.g. idiographic versus nomothetic focus).

In addition, *post hoc ergo propter hoc* (often shortened to *post hoc*) reasoning (i.e. reasoning after the event – the phrase literally means 'after this, because of this') was added into the codings. The coders were generally good at coding material into the same categories since overall inter-coder agreement was 76 per cent, though there was more disagreement on some of the codings than others.

In many ways, the findings were remarkable. Out of a total of 130 articles on criminal profiling, the *sources of knowledge used* tended to be common sense types of arguments rather than the use of scientific evidence. For example, 42 per cent of the articles used scientific evidence, but anecdotal arguments (60 per cent), testimonials (45 per cent) and authority (42 per cent) were all at least as frequent or more frequent. Common sense rather than science was also dominant in the analytic processes used. Hindsight biases, illusory correlates, availability heuristic, *post hoc ergo propter hoc* and self-serving biases were all more common than the scientific processes of surveys, correlational methods, case histories, quasi-experimental procedures and experiments. It was only for the category of integration of evidence that scientific categories were found to be generally more common than for common sense ones. So the most frequent categories in this broad category were 'recognition that causality is complex' and 'the expectation that theory will be revised'. A simple summary of all of this is that over all of the articles, common sense arguments were used in preference to empirical evidence on 58 per cent of occasions.

Snook *et al.* found, not surprisingly perhaps, that the use of common sense arguments was associated with publications which were generally more favourable to criminal profiling. Interestingly, articles from the United States were substantially more common sense-based than, for example, those from the United Kingdom. This may reflect the more objective forms of criminal profiling that are used by British profilers. Snook, Cullen, Bennell, Taylor and Gendreau (2008) describe FBI-style offender profiling as 'smoke and mirrors' with nothing behind them. They suggest that people are led to believe that profiling is effective because of dramatic anecdotes describing its success, the idea that there are profiling experts and the concentration on a few correct predictions when there may be many more incorrect predictions to counterbalance these.

Does profiling work?

The issue of the effectiveness of profiling for good policing outcomes is clearly most important. The theoretical adequacy of FBI-style profiling is, perhaps, more an academic interest but one which impinges on the issue of whether profiling works. Devery (2010), like others, argued strongly that FBI style profiling has never shown itself to be devoted to scientific rigour. He suggests that there are a few rather circumspect articles by the famous profilers which, at least superficially, are manifestations of scientific care but these contrast with the more upbeat nature of the popular books on profiling by these self-same authors. He goes on to describe profiling as a 'compendium of common sense intuitions' which boil down to mere 'educated guesses and wishful thinking'. He claims that examples of where FBI-style profiling has contributed positively to a police investigation are hard to find. On the other hand, examples of where FBI-profiling hampered a police operation by diverting attention in the wrong direction are more common. For example, there have been instances of where police officers have pursued the wrong person when they have sought to match a profiler's profile. This include DNA exonerated cases.

Amongst the exceptions to the lack of research evidence on profiling was Canter and Wentink's (2004) empirical assessment of Holmes and Holmes' serial murder classification scheme (Holmes and Holmes, 1998). In this, five types of serial murder were proposed, based on case material concerning serial killings. These are visionary, mission, lust, thrill, power/control. Canter and Wentink used archival data of public domain accounts of American serial killings. In order to give Holmes and Holmes' typology the maximum possible chance of success, the researchers coded each serial killing case in terms of the presence or absence of characteristics relevant to the typology. There were 37 such characteristics. The researchers then identified which of these are pertinent to each serial killing type. The following is indicative of the type and the sorts of variables that Canter and Wentink identified as being especially relevant to each category:

- *Visionary killers:* this type of killer is largely acting on voices or visions from God, angels, devils and the like which tell him that he should kill a particular person or type of person (e.g. prostitutes). Thus, for example, the visionary killer is claimed by Holmes and Holmes to leave behind a chaotic crime scene – the typical disorganised pattern. Variables such as scattering of belongings, clothing spread around, weapon left in victim, ransacking and bludgeoning ought to help identify this type.
- *Mission killers:* this type of killer has decided that a certain group or type of person is unacceptable or valueless and that the world should be free of them. The crime scene characteristics that should identify this type in Canter and Wentink's data include murder weapon missing, firearm use, bludgeoning, throat cutting.
- *Lust killers:* this type is a subcategory of hedonistic killers. Lust killers kill as part of the process of fulfilling their sexual lusts. Sex is the point of the process. As a consequence, typical crime scene characteristics would include multiple sexual acts, penetration with object, vaginal rape, abdominal mutilation, torture and violence to genitals.
- *Thrill killers:* this is another subcategory of hedonistic killers. The thrill killer basically enjoys the process of killing in the sense that they get pleasure and excitement from it. Death may deliberately be extended to take a long time and may involve torture. Characteristics of thrill killing can be similar to those of lust killing (e.g. torture, vaginal rape and penetration with objects) but others are different (e.g. bite marks, manual or ligature strangulation, body covered after death and concealed perhaps in an isolated spot, and burns on body of victim).
- *Power/control killers:* the gratification in the killing is that the killer has control over the victim. Dominance over another person is the motive. Enjoyment of the killing is maximised by extending the process over time. Typical crime scene characteristics include the use of restraints, torture and gagging, body parts missing, evidence tampered with, decapitation. Some characteristics are shared with thrill killing such as vaginal rape, ligature strangulation and the body concealed.

Canter and Wentink (2004) claim that their data offered some rather limited support for the typology. Nevertheless, simple, direct support for the typology categories did not emerge. The following summarises some of the more important findings:

- Power/control killing characteristics were actually very typical of the entire sample of cases and did not form a distinct group. Such acts as bludgeoning, attacks on the face, strangulation and violence to the genitals, then, are a feature of the other types of serial killing.
- There did appear to be a group of thrill killing variables which tend to go together, though these seem to be best considered largely in terms of the restraint pattern that the killer used. For example, gagging, ligature use and covering the dead body seem to form a cluster. However, other characteristics which seem to imply a thrill according to Canter and Wentink were not so clearly identified with this particular pattern. So details such as the weapon being missing and the victim being alive during the sexual attack were likely to be part of other patterns.
- There did appear to be some support for the idea of visionary killers. Characteristics such as bludgeoning the victim to death and leaving a trail of clothing around tended to co-occur frequently in crime scenes. On the other hand, some of the key characteristics of visionary killers according to Holmes and Holmes were not particularly close to this core of variables – e.g. leaving the weapon in the victim. The researchers add that facial disfigurement, which is characteristic of lust killing according to Holmes and Holmes, seems to be more associated with the core of visionary killer variables.

This is, of course, progress in academic terms. That it may make Holmes and Holmes' ideas more difficult to use by profilers is not the point. Canter and Wentink's findings indicate that the simple typology lacks sufficient clarity and empirical justification to be used without further modification.

Canter and his co-workers tackled another basic categorisation in offender profiling – the contrast between the organised and the disorganised crime scenes which predicts rather different offender characteristics according to the FBI profilers as discussed earlier (Canter, Alison, Alison and Wentink, 2004). What they did was to use a database of 100 serial sexual murders by 100 serial killers. They assessed each crime scene for 39 different characteristics which corresponded to those claimed to represent organised and disorganised crimes according to the *Crime Classification Manual* (Douglas, Burgess, Burgess and Ressler, 1992). The researchers were looking to see whether there was a distinct organised pattern and a distinct disorganised pattern, In other words, did disorganised crime scene characteristics tend to co-occur and did organised crime scene characteristics tend to co-occur together while the co-occurrence of organised and disorganised characteristics was uncommon. Statistical analysis (multidimensional scaling) failed to reveal two distinct subsets of these characteristics which could be described as organised and disorganised respectively. There was a subset of characteristics which corresponded to the organised type and this was typical of the majority of serial killings. The reason for this is that serial sexual killings overall tend to show organised features – not that there is a distinct group of organised characteristics. Disorganised characteristics not only failed to group together as a subset but they were also much less common.

Wilson, Lincoln and Kocsis (1997) suggested that anecdotes about the success of profiling had dominated assessments of the validity of the method. Nevertheless, they provide a table of what they claim to be qualitative evaluations of selected case studies involving techniques related to profiling. The profiles produced were judged to be accurate in 22 of the 32 cases listed plus a few more that are described as partially accurate. Four of the cases were essentially not solved which means the accuracy of the profile against the offender could not be judged. At one level it is possible to argue that this is good evidence of the validity of profiling but, unfortunately, there is no explanation of how the accuracy of the profiles was actually judged. The authors, however, hint that this data augurs well in terms of the validity of profiling. One of the cases, for example, was Brussel's mad bomber – there has been controversy over whether this profile was accurate, yet Wilson *et al.* claim that it was. Deciding whether a profile is accurate is probably a relatively easy task – the problem is establishing that the profile would discriminate between possible offenders effectively.

Nevertheless, perhaps the most important aspect of profiling – at least in the minds of the general public – is its contribution to the work of the police. There are a number of points to be made about the seemingly straightforward issue of the adequacy of profiling for police work: it is a deceptively simple question to ask whether profiling is effective. Try to imagine a research study to definitively answer the question of whether profiling is worthwhile. How would such a study be done? What crimes would be studied? Would a profiler be randomly assigned to some cases and not others? What is the criterion of success – arrests, reduction in time to arrests, the satisfaction of the senior investigating officers with the profiler, or what?

- Purely in terms of psychological research methods, the issue might be thought of as a simple technical exercise in evaluation research. As soon as we plan this research in detail, the practical and conceptual difficulties grow. A researcher might select, say, crimes and assign a profiler at random to half the crimes and no profiler to the other half. The outcome of this might be evaluated in terms of the proportion of crimes that were solved with and without a profiler. Even if the profiler condition seemed more successful, this in itself would not be definitive evidence that profiling worked. Profilers are usually very familiar with police methods and their apparent success might be the result of their good advice on how to conduct and prioritise the investigative operation. The profile itself may well be poor. Profiling has traditionally been applied to extreme crimes. Serial rapes and serial sexual murders may result in pressure on the police for an arrest. At the same time, the investigating police officers may have little experience of such rare crimes. Expert profilers may simply bring wider experience of such crimes. Their profiling skills, as such, may not be very helpful.
- The involvement of a profiler may be diverting resources away from other lines of enquiry. If other options are ignored simply because of the profile then this might reduce the success.
- Claims about the importance of profiling in a particular high-profile crime may appear impressive because an arrest is achieved. What does this tell us about crimes in which profiling was used but no arrest achieved or about the improvement in the chances of arrest due to profiling? It is a bit like a heart surgeon parading their living patients as evidence of the success of their techniques while ignoring those who ended in the graveyard.
- It is generally believed that only certain crimes are suitable for profiling or potentially helped by profiling. People with certain characteristics, for example, may commit car break-ins, but it is unlikely that resources will be found to mount an investigation of the vast majority of these crimes. So profiling could not make a contribution.

- Is detection of a particular crime the main objective of profiling? There are circumstances in which the role of the profiler is rather different: for example, when trying to assess whether crimes are linked to a particular offender or whether they are the work of several different offenders. Sometimes in high-profile cases there is the need to assess the likely validity of letters of confession which may be hoaxes. The hoax potentially could waste much police time. Just what strategy should the interviewing officers take when interviewing suspects? All of these seem worthwhile profiling endeavours but may impinge little on the question of whether the offender is arrested.
- The information provided by profiling research may be operationally useful in general without it having a discernible impact on individual cases. Potentially, ideas of what sorts of rapist are associated with particular crime scenes may generally inform police work without the direct input of a profiler, for example.
- Profiling can inform the sorts of data collected at the crime scene and lead to improvements in the collection and recording of information. The better the crime scene information, the better profiling research can be, and the better profiling research becomes, the more we will know about what crime scene information is useful.
- There have been studies of user satisfaction with profiling. By user satisfaction we mean in this case that of the senior officers managing a particular crime. It is notable in these that relatively few offenders are arrested as a result of the profile. Gudjonsson and Copson (1997) found that 3 per cent of detections were attributed to the profiler's work. Do not forget that these figures are based on what the senior officers say and it may be that they are not keen to give credit to the profiler. It is interesting to note, nevertheless, that most senior officers express positive attitudes to profilers for other reasons.
- Of course, a profile may be good but the offender arrested without its help. In these circumstances, comparing the fit of the profile to that offender might better assess the validity of the profile. The difficulty is the lack of a clear standard for doing this. For example, is a count or tally of the similarities between the profile and the offender sufficiently sound for evaluating profiling? For example, if the profile of a killer was young, male, of average education, lived near the crime scene and has at least one previous arrest, most of us would not be impressed with the profile even if all of the listed characteristics proved to be true. On the other hand, if the killer was predicted to be a hotel worker, supporting his arthritic mother, living within two minutes of a railway station, with a history of exhibitionism and transvestism and it all turned out to be correct, we would be more impressed.
- Despite allegations of its less than scientific status, FBI crime scene profiling has been subject to more validity assessment than the statistical or actuarial approach discussed in the next chapter. By validity assessment we mean its validity in relation to police work rather than its psychological methodological validity. Few, if any, studies have been conducted on the operational value of statistical profiling.

One of the perplexing findings on offender profiling is the claims made by the police that the profiles were useful but did not lead to the arrest. Alison, Smith and Morgan (2003) carried out a study in which they took a genuine FBI profile and asked police officers to evaluate the accuracy of the profile against the known facts about the criminal finally convicted. In this particular case, the offender was 19 years of age; a stranger to the victim; was unemployed in his work as an actor; had attempted suicide and suffered depression; had no previous convictions; had no relationships in his life; had no sibling; denied the offence; and had not suffered abuse within the family. Among the statements that the profile contained were the following:

- The offender will be a white male between 25 and 35, or the same general age as the victim and of average appearance.
- He will be of average intelligence and will be a secondary school (high school) or university (college) dropout.
- He will not have a military history and may be unemployed.
- He will have a pornography collection.
- The subject will have sadistic tendencies.
- The sexual acts show controlled aggression, but rage or hatred of women was obviously present.
- He did not want the woman screaming for help.
- He probably will be a very confused person, possibly with previous mental problems.

The police officers overwhelmingly claimed that the profile was useful for crime investigation. Another group of forensic professionals tended to be less enthusiastic.

However, the study went further than this and for another, similar group of officers the procedure was varied and a fabricated picture of the offender was provided. For example, in this condition he was 37; he knew the victim; he worked for the water board but had just been made redundant; he was an alcoholic; had several previous convictions for assault and burglary; had lived with a girlfriend and had had several relationships with women but each one was violent; he had two sisters; admitted the offence; and suffered an abusive family background. Despite the fact that the two descriptions of the offender were virtual opposites, the officers were just as likely to see the profile as being as useful for the bogus description as the real description. In other words, accuracy had no impact on how useful the officers regarded the profile!

Not surprisingly, FBI-style profiling is treated with a degree of scepticism by psychologists and others. For example, Torres, Boccaccini and Miller (2006) describe the findings of an Internet-based survey of American forensic psychologists and psychiatrists. These professionals were likely to believe that profiling was a useful tool in law enforcement. Ninety-five per cent of the psychiatrists and 85 per cent of the psychologists believed this. Nevertheless, there were doubts about its scientific basis. Over 97 per cent of the psychologists and psychiatrists thought that profiling needed empirical research to support it. It was only a minority who thought that profiling was a scientifically valid method for linking a defendant to a crime. Even fewer believed that profiling was scientifically reliable. Interestingly, the group of forensic psychologists and psychiatrists generally did not feel themselves to be knowledgeable about profiling – only about a quarter claimed to be knowledgeable. Similarly, only about one in eight of these forensic practitioners had testified in court concerning profiling or had been asked for their opinion about profiling in court.

Do professionals produce better profiles than lay persons? There is some evidence that profilers, psychologists and the police produce more informative and detailed reports containing more predictions than non-experts such as comparison groups of students (Kocsis, 2003b; Kocsis, Middledorp and Try, 2005). In a similar vein, Pinizzotto and Finkel (1990) found that profilers and other expert groups produced profiles which were better than chance in terms of their accuracy of their contents compared with the known facts. Profilers were the best, with 67 per cent accuracy compared to no more than 57 per cent for the other expert groups. The research design used was essentially quite simple. Groups of experts in profiling and non-expert comparison groups read the details of a criminal case. The usual research design compares expert profilers with non-profilers such as students and others. Then the participants rate the characteristics that they think the offender is likely to have, using a standard form. The offenders' known characteristics are then compared with these predictions. Basically, then, the research tests the hypothesis that the expert profiler is more accurate in their assessments than the non-expert. Generally speaking, these studies suggest that expert profilers are better profilers than non-profilers. This hardly sounds controversial. Nevertheless, there are some limitations to the method employed and, consequently, the findings are only partially convincing. For one thing, the situation in which the profiles are generated is somewhat artificial, with the participants completing a checklist rather than generating their profiles themselves.

Figure 14.3 summarises available data on the accuracy of criminal profiling using this sort of methodology, according to Kocsis, Middledorp and Karpin (2008). It is a composite of several different studies. It would seem to show that profilers, overall, are substantially more accurate in the profiles that they generate. The superiority of experts is, nevertheless, not consistent across all aspects of profiling. For example, there is very little difference between the expert and non-expert profilers in terms of the quality of

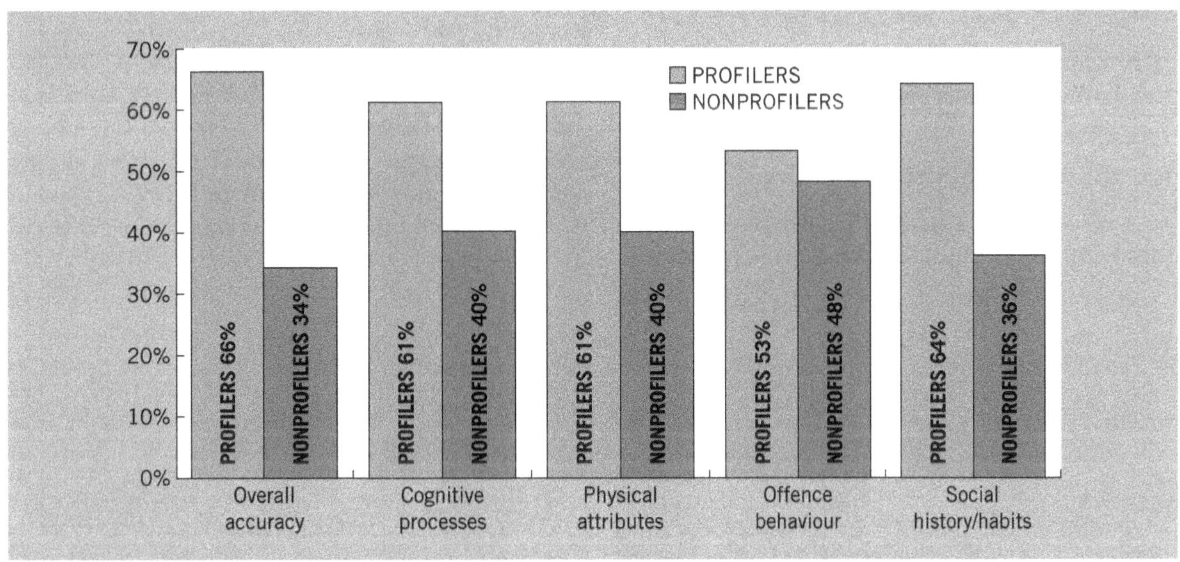

Figure 14.3 Comparing profilers with others in terms of accuracy

their predictions about offence behaviour. It has to be said that Kocsis, Middledorp and Karpin make relatively modest claims about the trends shown in the data. However, offender profiling is not the most neutral of topics for researchers to study. Perhaps, then, it is not surprising that others chose to dispute Kocis, Middledorp and Karpin's conclusions. In particular, Snook, Eastwood, Gendreau and Bennell (2010) evaluate the data differently and argue that the profiling groups 'did not decisively outperform' the comparison groups. This disagreement is difficult to explain briefly and it is even more perplexing because Kocsis (2003a) and Snook *et al.* (2010) largely use data from the same set of studies in their analyses but reach radically different conclusions. Partly the issue is of just what is strong evidence in favour of offender profiling. But there are other difficulties. For example, who should be classified as an expert profiler and who is not (Kocsis, 2010)? If expert profilers are defined as those who have training and expertise in FBI-style profiling then the evidence suggests strongly that profiling experts are better than non-profilers at producing accurate profiles is stronger. On the other hand, if we include serving police officers who provide profiles to courts in the US but who lack the formal training then the expert group of profilers is little different from non-profilers in their profiling ability. Just which of these alternatives is correct? Well neither is correct since the issue of definition is a complex one and involves judgements which are not consensual. One cannot simply claim the superiority of one approach over the other. Factors such as these account for some of the disagreements between researchers looking at essentially much the same data. (See Kocsis, 2013, for a summary of the argument.)

Finally, any evaluation of profiling needs to assess the theoretical underpinnings of profile generation. We will return to this in the next chapter. Among the theoretical assumptions of FBI-style profiling are the following:

- the characteristics of the offender are reflected in the characteristics of the crime scene;
- crime scenes can be effectively categorised;
- an offender's crimes tend to show characteristic patterns.

One approach to evaluating is to examine what has increasingly been termed the homology hypothesis (see Figure 14.4). Quite simply, this asserts that crime scene characteristics and offender characteristics converge. Snook, Cullen, Bennell, Taylor and Gendreau. (2008) argue that typologies commonly used in offender profiling actually have no substance in the relevant empirical literature. So they point to the example that the organised/disorganised crime scene typology has not been empirically validated by the little research that has so far been carried out into it. Snook *et al.* suggest that it is intrinsically a problem that FBI-style profiling is built on trait approaches to personality. Modern conceptualisations in psychology recognise that situational characteristics are probably more important determinants of a person's behaviour than whether they do or do not possess a particular personality trait. For the homology hypothesis to work, the offender should show consistency in terms of their style of offending over the course of a number of offences. This often is not the case because, for example, the offender learns by experience what does and does not work. This may lead to the abandonment of ineffective strategies while effective ones are repeated subsequently.

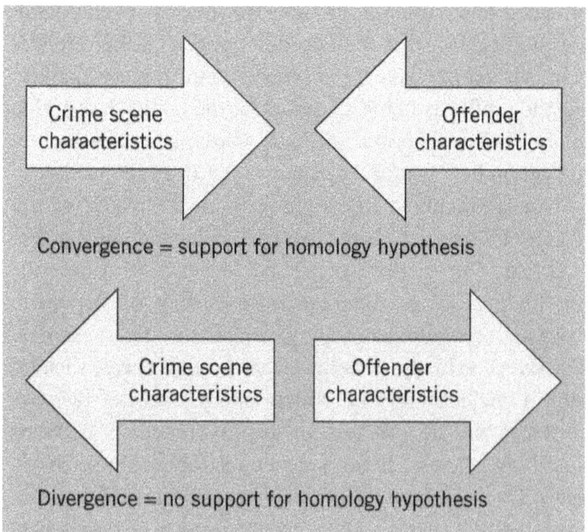

Figure 14.4 The homology hypothesis that there is a convergence between characteristics of the crime scene and the characteristics of the offender

Main points

- Offender profiling seeks to use information from the scene of a crime to assess characteristics of the sort of offender likely to have committed the crime. It ranges from somewhat intuitional approaches to those based on the careful analysis of aggregate statistical data. The latter is becoming increasingly characteristic of research in the field, as is discussed in Chapter 15. All forms of profiling assume that there is some sort of homologous relationship between the crime scene and the offender in question. It is unclear whether the simple distinction between organised and disorganised crime scenes stands up to empirical scrutiny, despite its impact on the work of FBI profilers.

- There is considerable evidence that the police regard offender profiling favourably. There is evidence that police officers find profiles equally useful even when they are given virtually opposite profiles for the same crime! There is evidence that FBI profiling is less accurate than statistical profiling in circumstances in which it is possible to assess the validity of elements of the profile. Research indicates that some profiles may contain a very high proportion of information which is little more than the facts already collected by the police themselves. Only a small proportion of statements in profiles include some justification for what was being claimed. There are clear signs that offender profiling is regarded as helpful though it is just one of many sources of support that supervising officers find very useful without it necessarily leading to an arrest.
- Profiling has had a high public profile in recent years thanks to the various media depictions of profilers. Furthermore, profiling is intimately associated with the concept of serial killing. Given this, one would expect that public interest in the topic will continue to be disproportionate to the tangible achievements of profilers. One of the achievements of profiling is that it has moved research into serious crime away from the search for psychological abnormalities to the manifestation of individual characteristics in the behaviours of criminals when committing crimes.

Further reading

Britton, P. (1997) *The Jigsaw Man: The Remarkable Career of Britain's Foremost Criminal Psychologist* London: Bantam Press.

Douglas, J., Burgess, A.W., Burgess, A.G. and Ressler, R.K. (2013) *Crime Classification Manual: A Standard System for Investigating and Classifying Violent Crimes* (3rd edn) Chichester: John Wiley.

Holmes, R.M. and Holmes, S.T. (2009) *Profiling Violent Crimes: An Investigative Tool* (4th edn) London: Sage Publications.

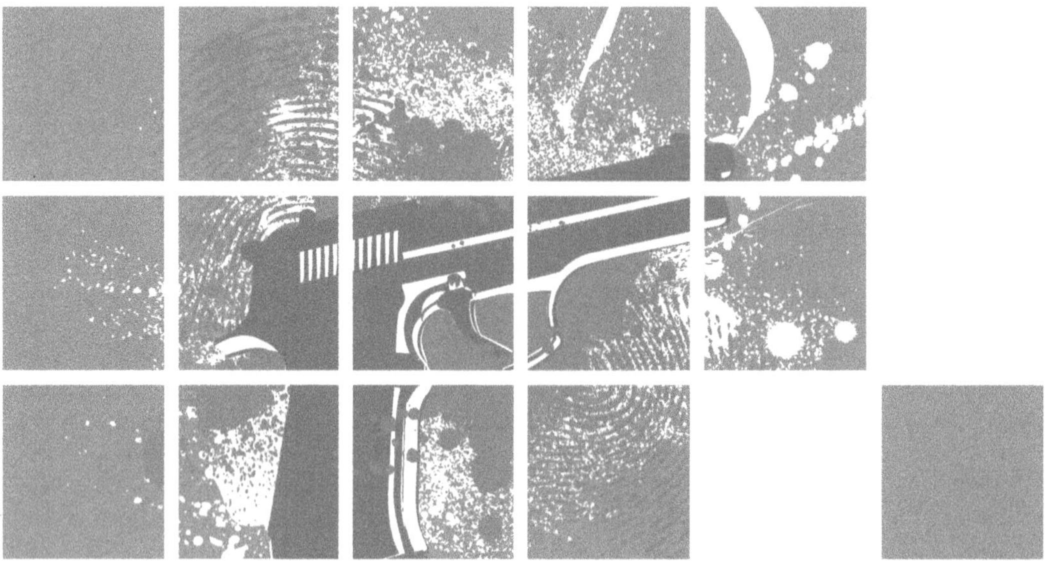

Chapter 15

Profile analysis 2: investigative psychology, statistical and geographical profiling

Overview

- The actuarial or statistical approach to offender profiling originated in the work of David Canter which led to investigative psychology. Statistical offender profiling has been applied to a wide variety of crimes beyond those of the initial FBI focus (serial sexual homicides and rape) to arson and property crimes, for example.
- A somewhat broader term to describe the activities of psychologists working with the police is, in the UK especially, *behavioural investigative advice* (BIA).
- The essence of Canter's approach emerged in his earliest work on offender profiling. This can be seen as statistically based attempts to identify patterns in different crime characteristics and the consideration of geographical factors in the commission of crimes.
- Geographical profiling primarily seeks to identify the likely 'home base' of the offender.
- Statistical profiling uses statistical techniques such as smallest space analysis in order to plot the relationships between various crime scene characteristics on a diagram or plot. The crime scene characteristics that tend to co-occur frequently are physically close to each other on the plot. At the centre of the plot are the common characteristics of crime scenes; at the periphery are the uncommon characteristics of crime scenes. The researcher then identifies the major segments of the plot and identifies their linking characteristics.
- Despite its origins, this form of profiling has lost some of its roots in police work in favour of statistically based academic research.
- The evidence of the effectiveness of this sort of profiling is varied. It would seem that the police like and value it, although it is seldom the basis for an arrest. The profiler acts as a processor of the mass of information available to the police and provides advice which facilitates the policing process.

Introduction

Before his work on investigative psychology, the social psychologist David Canter made important contributions to developing the research field known as *environmental psychology*. This seeks to understand the interaction between people and the environments within which they live. Some basic principles of environmental psychology were incorporated into Canter's distinctive approach to profiling. In the 1980s, he began to meet with senior police managers about using psychology to aid police work (Canter, 1994). According to Canter, shortly afterwards, he became intrigued by a number of unsolved rapes in the London area which were receiving media attention. In 1986, Canter began to assist the police in the investigation this series of rapes which we now know were committed by John Duffy, either alone or with David Mulcahy. The media labelled them as the railway rapes and, later, the railway murders. During the course of this investigation, Canter created the first offender profile in the United Kingdom.

Characteristically, Canter incorporated quantitative data into his analysis and had drawn up simple information such as: 1) maps showing the locations where the crimes had taken place; and 2) chronologies of when the offences occurred. Initially, Canter was faced with a list of rapes which might or might not have been committed by the same person(s). So in order to assess which rapes had been committed by the same person(s), he examined how similar each of the rapes was to the others in terms of their manifest characteristics. The essential features of each crime (such as precisely what sort of things took place during the sexual activity) were coded and then the data collated. Using computers, it was then possible to generate an index of how similar the various crimes were to each other. Some crimes were very similar (i.e. contained many of the same elements) and so they were likely to have been committed by the same person. Features of the highly similar rapes, for example, were acts like tying the victim's thumbs together behind her back and asking her questions about herself and her home's location. In this way, Canter isolated a group of rapes from the series which appeared to be very similar and likely to have been carried out by the same offender(s). These rapes became the focus of his attention and, eventually, resulted in his first, tentative offender profile.

The profile Canter sketched out for the police included 17 different elements, most of which are now known to be accurate. The profile included:

> Has lived in the area circumscribed by the first 3 cases since 1983.
>
> Possibly arrested some time after 24 October 1983.
>
> Probably semi-skilled or skilled job, involving weekend work or casual labour from about June 1984 onwards.
>
> (Canter, 1994, p. 39)

How did Canter reach such highly specific conclusions as these? By gradually superimposing maps of successive years of offences in this series on top of each other, it could be seen that there was no offending at certain times. Hence, because of the length of the gap in offending, the possibility that the offender had been arrested became apparent. Furthermore, the geographical locations of the crimes in relation to their chronology did not indicate that the offender was moving from area to area committing several crimes before moving on to another area. Instead it looked as though the offender was increasingly willing to travel further in whatever direction from his home to commit the offences. Therefore Canter concluded that the location of the first three offences mentioned in the profile essentially determined where the offender lived. Duffy, although he had been a bottom-of-the-list police suspect for quite a while, was arrested shortly after the profile was discussed with the police. His co-offender was not found until many years later when Duffy finally revealed his identity.

Characteristics of Canter's approach to offender profiling can be seen in this early investigation. In particular, his commitment to empirical evidence to back up the profile. The search for patterns associated with different types of offenders and the consideration of geographical factors are strong features of his work. Recently, some have preferred to replace the term *offender profiling* with that of the broader term *Behavioural Investigative Advice* (BIA). This refers to the evidence-based knowledge that psychologists, especially in the United Kingdom, provide to the police to help with particular investigations (Alison, Goodwill, Almond, van den Heuvel and Winter, 2010).

Geographical profiling

Canter's early work involved a form of geographical profiling. We will consider this first and then move on to offender profiling more generally. Criminologists have long recognised the importance of environmental factors in crime. It is known that crime is not spread out evenly throughout cities but tends to be concentrated in crime hot-spots which attract much police attention relative to the size of the area (Sherman, Gartin and Buerger, 1989). The Chicago School of Sociology (Shaw and McKay, 1942) established that offenders tend to be concentrated in particular zones of a city. Another example, Routine Activity Theory (see also Chapter 7), stresses the relationship between a criminal's general, daily activities and the crimes which are committed. In other words, crime is often the result of everyday opportunities combined with three key factors occurring together: 1) there being a suitable target for the crime; 2) the risks of being seen are minimal since, for example, a property has no neighbours who can act as guardians of the property, perhaps because it is secluded; and 3) there is a potential offender available. Routine Activity Theory originated in the work of Lawrence Cohen and Marcus Felson. Their main interest was in the theory of crime prevention rather than crime investigation. Geographical profiling primarily aims to suggest the offenders likely base (his home or some other frequently used place) in order to limit the area of police investigation. It is also often used to assess whether different offences could be linked to the same offender.

The earliest use of geographical profiling is a matter of debate. It has been suggested that it first occurred in the infamous UK Yorkshire Ripper case in 1980, when an investigator examined the locations of the Ripper's attacks and calculated a sort of central point in this distribution, which turned out to be the city of Bradford where the Ripper actually lived. Others attribute its invention to the work of Detective Kim Rossmo of the Vancouver Police Department in Canada. He uses a computerised algorithm technique called RIGEL to analyse the spatial locations of serial crimes. Rossmo (2000) summarised the early findings of geographical profiling as including: 1) criminals tend to offend close to their homes; 2) there is a decline in the number of offences the further away one gets from the offender's home; and 3) the precise patterns vary with the crime type in question. Sometimes a close-by target is less desirable than, say, an affluent city centre (see Figure 15.1).

Of course, a psychological approach to geographical profiling would seek to examine the association between crime geography and more psychological factors. For example, Snook, Cullen, Mokros and Harborts (2005) studied the way in which a group of 53 German serial killers' location decision making was mediated by their social, economic and cognitive characteristics. On average, each killer had killed 4.6 times. In 63 per cent of murders the killer lived within 10 kilometres (6 miles) of the place where the body was found. Younger killers tended not to travel so far from their home base and killers with a higher IQ travelled further. Not surprisingly, those with their own transport travelled further than those with access to public transport only. There is reason to question whether the initial killing is the best indicator of where the killer lives, since fewer than one in five of initial killings were the closest of the series of killings to the killer's home. Of course, it is important to realise that averages (means) can be a little misleading. The mean distance between the killers' homes and the body sites in Snook *et al.*'s study was 30 kilometres (19 miles), whereas the median distance was only 8 kilometres (5 miles). That is, half of murder sites were 8 kilometres away from the killer's home. This suggests that some killers murdered a long way from home, although very few homicides were in excess of 100 kilometres (62 miles) away.

Crime linkage using spatial factors has been a theme in the research literature. That is to say, are crimes by the same offender similar geographically? Bennell and Canter (2002) found that there is a degree of stability in an offender's choice of crime site locations, which may be useful in helping identify linkages between crimes. In particular, linked burglaries tend to occur closer together. Of course, depending on what cut-off point is selected, different numbers of serial crimes would be identified as linked. So if the cut-off point was 0.7 kilometres then 52 per cent of linked and 93 per cent of unlinked burglaries would be correctly identified. However, using a less

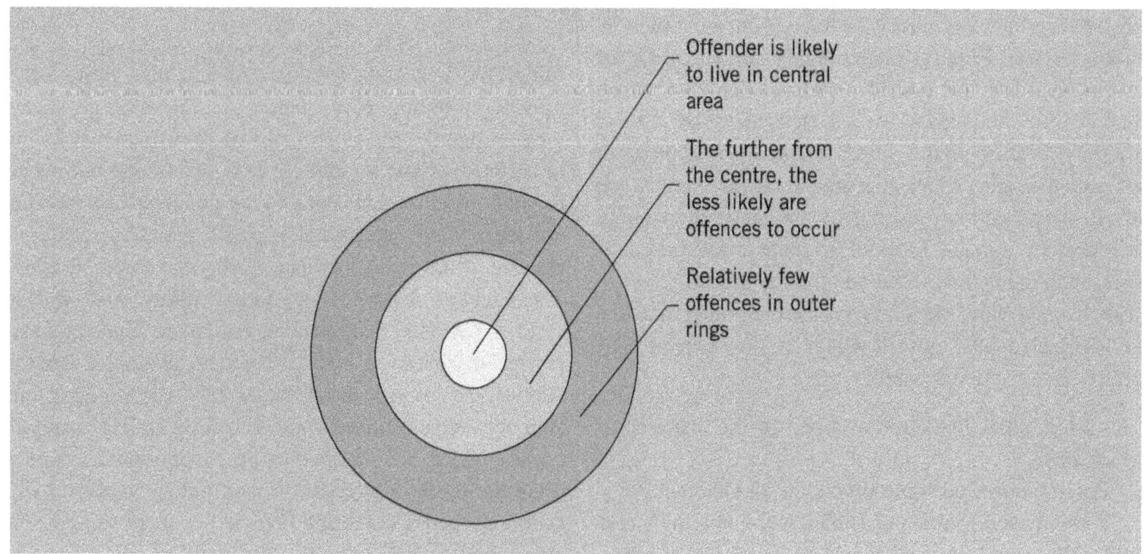

Figure 15.1 The basics of geographical offender profiling

stringent threshold of 2.5 kilometres then 62 per cent of linked burglaries but only 68 per cent of the unlinked ones would be correctly identified as such. In other words, great care needs to be exercised in the setting of the decision point which differentiates the likely linked crimes from the likely unlinked crimes. Bennell and Jones (2005) followed up this by studying commercial and residential serial burglaries using different elements from the *modus operandi* exhibited. They used a variety of types of crime characteristics, such as the way in which the property was entered; characteristics of the target location of the burglary; and the type of item stolen. In addition, the distance between the crime sites in kilometres was used. By using data from crimes where the offender was known, it was possible to distinguish between isolated crimes and those involving a serial offender. They claim that the shortness of the distances between crime sites were a better way of assessing whether crimes were linked than were other crime scene characteristics. Linked burglaries tended to have the smallest inter-crime distances.

According to Haginoya (2014) there are two main ways of predicting offender place of residence from spatial information about various, presumed linked, crime scenes. The first is Canter's circle hypothesis (Canter and Gregory, 1994). In this, the two crime locations which are the furthest apart are identified and a line drawn between them. Then a circle is drawn from the midway point so that it cuts both of these locations. Every offence location (and probably the home of the offender) will lie within this circle. 'Marauder' is the name given to offenders who live within the circle and 'commuter' is the name for those living outside of the circle. The alternative is the suspicious area model (Mimoto and Fukada, 1999). This assumes that the offender's home is at the point which gives the shortest sum of distances to all of the offence locations. The average of the distances to each offence location from this point is used as the radius of a circle drawn around this point. The offender is assumed to live within this circle. This method gives a smaller search area than Canter's method. Hammond (2014), however, warns that there may be rather different parameters needed when geographical profiling is used in locations in which it was not initially developed.

Optimising the decision criterion involves using a receiver operating characteristic, or ROC curve. This is used for binary decisions such as whether a crime is a linked or unlinked one. Basically, it is a graph of the true positive rates against the false positive rates for the different values of the decision criterion. The ideal decision rule is the one which maximises the true positive rate and minimises the false negative rate. The true positive rate is the number of linked offences detected, whereas the false negative rate is the number of linked crimes wrongly identified as being unlinked crimes. Of course, these are assessed against crimes which are already known to be linked and those known not to be linked.

What about other questions which may be important to crime investigators? For example, can geography be used to help differentiate between crimes committed by a single offender and those committed by multiple offenders? Bernasco (2006) looked at whether co-offending burglars were different in terms of their choice of target areas for crimes. The study was carried out on data from The Hague. The assumptions underlying the research were that areas are more likely to be targeted: if they are affluent; where the properties are physically accessible; where social disorganisation is rife (which tends to reduce the number of guardians to watch over neighbouring properties); depending on the proximity of the neighbourhood to the city centre; and depending on the proximity of the neighbourhood to the offender's home. Of course, some of these factors may be particularly salient to burglar groups rather than solo burglars. For example, a group of burglars is more visible than a single burglar, so it could be that burglar groups are more likely to offend in areas of social disorganisation where neighbours are less likely to watch over each other's properties. The findings were clear-cut. No matter how the distance from the burglars' homes to where the offence was committed was calculated (i.e. which member of the group of burglars was chosen), these distances failed to differentiate the solo from the group burglar. Burglars, however, tended to recruit their burglar partners from their own neighbourhood.

One rather unexpected use of geographical profiling has been that of obscene telephone calls made to children in southern Sweden. Dragnet, a geographical profiling program, was used to estimate the most likely area that the obscene telephone caller lived. Remarkably, given that the telephone calls potentially could have been made to any part of Sweden, the program identified very precisely the area in which the offender lived (Ebberline, 2008).

If a crime is committed somewhere, other crimes are likely to follow shortly afterwards close-by. Burglaries committed close together in terms of both distance and time are likely to be committed by the same offender. That is, geographical profiling works on the assumption that spatial decision-making (the offender's decision about where to commit the next crime) is not a random process. Unfortunately, knowing this does not tell us exactly how the next crime will be located spatially. Johnson (2014) drew attention to the possibility that the spatial locations of crimes obeys the principles of animal ecology – that is, it follows the same principles as animal foraging. What does not seem to work is that foraging occurs fairly randomly from a central place. Instead, offending according to Johnson's data follows both Brownian and Levy walks patterns. A Brownian walk in animal ecology involves movements in a random direction at every step (that is, the location at which the animal feeds – and, perhaps, the offender offends) but the length of each step is more or less constant. The animal may return to the same spot quite often. In the Levy walk the length of a foraging step varies with more short distances than long distances. This sort of walk means that the animal is rather less likely to return to the same locations so often than if the Brownian process was involved. For animals, the Brownian pattern is more likely when food is abundant but the Levy process more common when food is scarce. Johnson studied police crime records and found evidence that both Brownian and Levy processes are involved. The importance of this for geographical crime linkage is in the basic assumption that crimes which occur close together are likely to be committed by the same offender(s). So an offender who operates using Brownian processes may be more likely to be caught because he is operating according to the geographical profiling assumption. However, if the offender is offending in the Levy pattern, things are harder because he will, some of the time, offend at some distance. As one might expect, Johnson's use of the animal ecology analogy has attracted some critical attention (Eck, 2014; Pease, 2014). There may be rather more 'foraging' strategies employed by offenders than Johnson implies (Felson, 2014). For example, there may be some who do not forage from a particular central place, co-offenders may influence patterns, how the offender reaches the crime scene (bus, car, on foot, etc.) may vary, the offender may be well-known locally which may affect his offending locations, and some may employ different patterns at different stages of the week or even change from morning to afternoon.

Criminal Profiling – the research based approach

One of Canter's important insights was how little was known about the behaviours of criminals in their real-life environments. This contrasted with the great deal of information that was available about offenders after they had been arrested and processed through the criminal justice system. As we have seen, empirical, statistically based methods in conjunction with careful attention to theory had served Canter well in relation to the railway rapes. Subsequently, he turned his attention to systematically studying the behavioural characteristics of offences. The statistical model of offender profiling is illustrated in Figure 15.2, which is based on data collected by House (1997). As with FBI profiling, the assumption is that features of the crime scene contain evidence of salient behaviours carried out by the offender in the course of the crime. These then may help reveal the distinguishing features or characteristics of the offender. The essential difference between statistical profiling and FBI profiling is that the former concentrates on establishing the relationships empirically, using statistical techniques which identify patterns in large data sets. FBI-style profiling is weak in terms of this empirical core. Thus, statistical profiling is based on its own distinct research orientated ethos without reliance on intuition and clinical insight. Indeed, the application of research directly in the police setting would not seem to be a primary objective of much research on statistical profiling and it seems increasingly geared to addressing theoretical issues.

There are a number of matters that manifest themselves much more clearly in statistical profiling than the FBI approach:

- What degree of stability is there in the crime scenes of individual offenders? Will an offender leave similar patterns behind at a crime scene? To what extent do patterns remain stable and consistent over time?
- How best can the crime scene be classified? This really refers to two distinct things: (a) the information that is collected about the crime scene and (b) whether there are features of certain crime scenes which warrant them being classified as being of a particular type, grouping or cluster.
- Do these types, groupings or clusters of crime scenes reveal psychological and other features of the offender?

In Canter's statistical approach, the classification of crime scenes is empirically based, using specialised statistical methods such as smallest space analysis (see Box 15.1). This is a method of identifying just how likely a feature of a crime scene is to exist and coexist with another feature. Take the following features of rapes: offender apologises; binding the victim's limbs; victim's clothing removed; offender disguises; element of surprise; fellatio of the offender; gratuitous violence; humiliation; inquisitive; offender kisses victim; multiple violence;

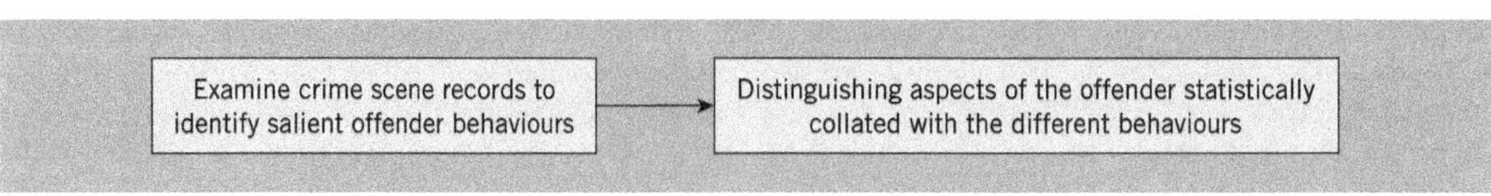

Figure 15.2 The statistical approach to profiling

offender confident; offender reassures victim; use of sex language by victim; sodomy by offender; takes time; theft of money; theft of personal belongings; torture; use of blindfold; vaginal penetration; and verbal aggression. Some of these features are very common in rape (e.g. vaginal penetration is practically universal in rapes of women), whereas others are quite rare (e.g. cunnilingus). Some of the behaviours frequently occur together if they occur in a rape; other behaviours are rarely found together. House (1997) analysed the co-occurrence and frequency of these behaviours in rapes. The statistical analysis produced a pattern shown stylistically in Figure 15.3. This gives a visual representation of a smallest space analysis of data on the above and other characteristics of rape crime scenes. Vaginal penetration, the element of surprise and clothing removed are central in the diagram – this indicates that they are very common features of rape. As such they are not very useful for differentiating different types of rape crime scene:

- Characteristics at the extremities of the diagram (such as the rapist apologises) are relatively rare in rapes.
- Characteristics that are close together occur together relatively often, such as theft of the victim's money and theft of the victim's personal property. Theft of the victim's money and sodomy rarely occur together. This is shown by the distance between them in Figure 15.3.

Also notice that labels have been given to the characteristics in the four different quarters of the diagram – sadism, aggression, intimacy and criminality – which seem to reflect the major integrative themes underlying the pattern of associations among characteristics. This is as if there are several major themes in rape – a variety of scripts for carrying out rape.

One practical implication of House's work is his finding that the type of rape is associated with the offender's past criminal history:

- The sadistic group were less likely to have an arrest and conviction history; the criminality group were the most likely to have been imprisoned (they are committing other types of crime alongside the rape, after all, as can be seen from Figure 15.3).
- The sadism and intimacy groups tended to be low on convictions for property crime; the sadistic group were the least likely to have convictions for violence.
- The sadism and intimacy groups were the most likely to have convictions for deception.

A potential application of this is in prioritising searches of offender databases in the hunt for possible suspects for a rape attack. If rapists commonly have a criminal record and these records contain good-quality relevant information, then there may be something to be gained from

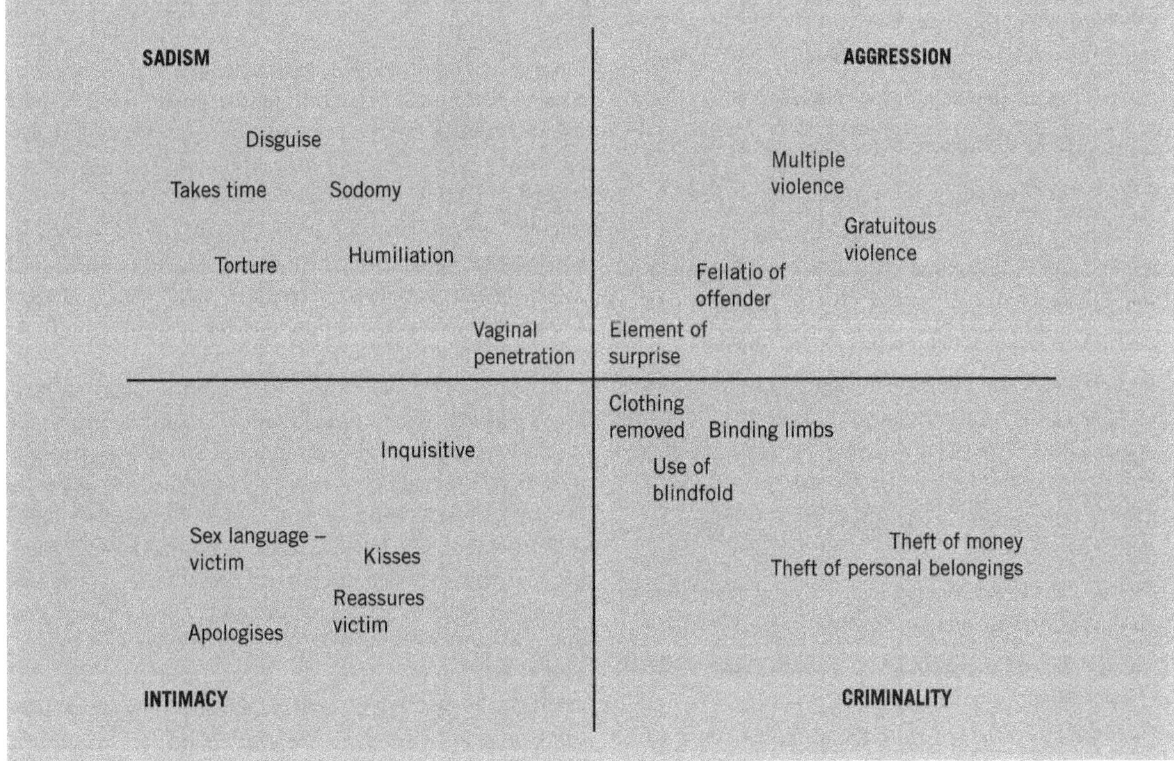

Figure 15.3 Schematic representation of crime scene characteristics

searching the criminal records. This would merely help manage routine investigative police work of interviewing, record keeping and so forth more effectively. It could never in itself prove that a particular individual is the rapist – unless, of course, there is a record of his DNA that matches the new crime scene sample, for example.

While this is interesting and does point to some characteristics of the offender, it is desirable to extend this sort of analysis to include indications of the relationship between the major crime scene 'scripts' and the psychological and other characteristics of the offender. Salfati and Canter (1998) examined the relationship between murder crime scenes and the murderer's characteristics. They used methods much like those used by House (1997) described earlier. A major hypothesis was that the murderers would show similar modes of interaction during the homicide as in much of the rest of their lives. A sample of 82 British homicides in which a single offender attacked a stranger was studied. These were murders in which the police did not know the assailant at the time of the discovery of the crime. Although these are described as stranger murders, this is something of a misnomer. Seventy-four per cent of the offenders knew the victim at least slightly. Information about the crimes was drawn from police records. Some 48 variables were extracted from these records. Broadly speaking, they fell into the following categories:

- characteristics of the victim;
- information which reflected characteristics of the offender;
- things or actions done by the offender to the victim;
- traces of behaviours left at the crime scene.

There were a number of informative features of the crimes:

- 12 per cent of offenders had served in the armed forces.
- A further 23 per cent had previously been married.
- About half of offenders were married or cohabiting (48 per cent).
- Few involved sexual elements (12 per cent).
- Imprisonment was common in the histories of offenders (40 per cent), with the commonest previous offences being theft (22 per cent), burglary (18 per cent) and violence against people (15 per cent).
- Mostly the homicides had taken place in the evening (66 per cent).
- Mostly the offenders were male (72 per cent) and the victims female (55 per cent).
- Mostly the victims were left at their place of death (76 per cent).
- Nearly half of victims were found in their own home (44 per cent).
- Offenders were much younger, with an average age of 27 years and a range of 15 to 49 years.
- The majority of offenders (79 per cent) were local or familiar with the area in which the crime occurred.
- The victims averaged 45 years of age with a range of 1 to 70 years.
- Unemployment was common in offenders (41 per cent).

Using smallest space analysis (Box 15.2), the researchers found three major groups of crime. These were classified as having instrumental opportunistic, instrumental cognitive and expressive impulsive themes. Two-thirds of the homicides could be classified fairly readily into one of the three categories. Very approximately, a third of the classifiable crimes fell into each of the three groupings. Each of the themes was associated with different typical offender characteristics. Table 15.1 gives the major crime scene characteristics and the associated offender characteristics. This is impressive but with a few caveats – just how well can offender characteristics be predicted from the crime scene? Just how useful is the analysis in police work? What does it tell the police about where to search for the offender? How effective will this search be?

Mostly these questions cannot be answered at the present time. Most statistical profiling remains research-based with no direct input into the conduct of police investigations. So, in that sense, it is not known whether such profiling could enhance police work. The potential is there but the success of the application of the methods may be a matter for future collaborations between researchers and the police. Importantly, Canter's statistical profiling recognises better than FBI profiling that relationships established between crime scene and offender characteristics are only probabilities and not certainties. Thus an instrumental cognitive crime scene merely indicates that the offender has an enhanced probability of having served in the armed forces.

In another important example of statistical profiling, Davies (1997) investigated a large sample of rapists from the British National Crime Identification Bureau records. Eighty-four per cent of them had criminal records which implies that such a database could potentially be important as a source of possible offenders. It should be stressed, though, that sexual offences were among the least common previous offences and that burglary and violence were the most common. Of course, there is a bias in Davies's sample as it only included offenders who had been arrested, it was not a random sample of offender. Davies found that different types of behaviour at the rape scene were associated with different sorts of prior convictions. So, for example, 15 per cent of rapists had taken fingerprint precautions such as wearing gloves or wiping off fingerprints. Such offenders were four times more likely to have a past

Table 15.1 The relationship between crime scene theme and offender characteristics

Crime theme	Crime scene characteristics	Corresponding offender characteristics
Instrumental opportunistic	Face hidden	Previous theft offences
	Female victims	Familiar with the area of the crime
	Manual attack	Having previously come to police notice
	Multiple wounds in one area	Knew victim
	Neck attacked	Unemployed
	Old victims	Knew victim
	Partially undressed	Previous vehicle theft offences
	Premises of the victim	Knew victim
	Sexual	Previous burglary offences
Instrumental cognitive	Body transported	Served in the armed services
	Body hidden	Served a prison sentence
	Body carefully placed	
	Blunt instrument	
	Face up	
Expressive impulsive	Limbs attacked	Previous traffic offences
	Multiple wounds all over body	Married at the time of the offence
	Single wound	Previous marriage
	Slash/cut	Female offender
	Torso attacked	Previous offences for public disorder
	Weapon taken to scene and also removed	Previous violent offences
		Previous drugs offences
		Previous marriage
		Previous offences for damage to property
		Previous sexual offences

burglary conviction. Failing to use such precautions indicated a threefold greater likelihood of being a one-off rapist. Twenty per cent of rapists stole from the victim. These had a fourfold greater likelihood of a previous robbery offence. Twenty-five per cent of rapes involved forced entry into the property where the rape took place. Such offenders were five times more likely to have a previous burglary offence. It was shown that combinations of characteristics of the rape could predict previous criminal history well. For example, a previous record for burglary could be predicted with almost complete certainty on the basis of a combination fingerprint precautions being taken, theft from the victim, a forced entry to the premises and the presence of alcohol at the scene or immediately before the crime. Previous convictions for violent offences are predicted by a combination of the use of extreme violence, comments about the police and deliberately lying to mislead about the offender's identity. In other words, crime scene characteristics could generate a list of possible offenders assuming that the offender was on the database.

Box 15.1 Key concept

Facet theory and smallest space analysis

Facet theory can be used to relate crime scenes with offender characteristics. Shye and Elizur (1994) and Borg and Shye (1995) provide accounts of facet theory and Canter (1983) describes its role in psychology. Canter explains how the use of facet theory requires the researcher to abandon many of the ideas which are held dear by psychologists. In particular, it involves the exploration of the area being researched thoroughly rather than quickly and developing a simple hypothesis which can be tested using simple tests of statistical significance. Those who can act on the findings of research (policy makers of all sorts) are usually only concerned about things under their control. Isolating factors in a situation (variables) one from another may be part of psychologists' training, but policy makers may be much more concerned with the total situation. Furthermore, Canter believes that facet theory allows the

BOX 15.1 (continued)

researcher to explore the definition of concepts at a theoretical level so eschewing the tendency of researchers to define concepts operationally by reference to the measurement procedure and other similar measures of similar concepts. He stresses that facet theory is a broad method for research – it should not be regarded as a narrow measurement technique or way of analysing data.

Consequently, there are a number of ideas that need to be understood in order to see its role in profiling:

- What is a facet? In facet theory, any domain of interest is a complex system. Research can only partially sample this system. Variables are seen as continuous throughout the system in facet theory. Each variable has other variables that differ only slightly from that and from other variables. This is just like the faces or facets of a diamond, which are just one view of that thing that is the diamond. The same diamond can be cut in many ways and each facet is merely one of many minutely different ones that might have been cut.
- In crime scene analysis, the presence of multiple stabbing of the victim, for example, in itself fails to capture the fullness of the crime scene. Bloodiness, depth of penetration, the multiplicity of weapons used and other variables would be needed to capture crime scene ferocity more completely.
- Shye and Elizur (1994) describe a facet as 'A set playing the role of a component set of a Cartesian set' (p. 179). 'Cartesian' means that facets can be represented in terms of a physical space. Usually, it implies the use of axes at right angles to each other. Put this way, a scattergram or scattergraph would represent the position of individuals in a two-dimensional physical space defined by the horizontal and vertical axes. In terms of crime scene analysis, the two axes might be:

1) Amount of effort by offender to hide own identity (rated on a scale from 'Very high' to 'High' to 'Fairly high' to 'Fairly low' to 'Low' to 'Very low').
2) Amount of effort by offender to hide the identity of victim (rated on a scale from 'Very high' to 'High' to 'Fairly high' to 'Fairly low' to 'Low' to 'Very low').

Crime scenes could be rated on these facets and each crime scene represented on a scattergram by a single point. This would roughly correspond to the Cartesian approach. The analogy is with a map and facet theorists speak of 'mapping'.

The matrix in Table 15.2 takes a simple case of three murders A, B and C and four different characteristics of the crimes, such as whether they took place at night. It is obvious that there are patterns in this matrix – Murders A and B are similar in terms of the presence of three of the four characteristics, whereas Murder C is rather different. One step forward is to produce a matrix of the correspondence of the four facets across the three murders in order to see what sorts of thing tend to occur together. So, if we consider 'Multiple weapons' and 'Sexual humiliation', the three different murders show complete agreement as to whether these things co-occurred or not. There is a match for these variables on the three murders, so a score of 3 is entered into Table 15.3. 'Night-time' and 'Multiple weapons' match twice over the three murders so 2 is entered as the amount of match or similarity between 'Night-time' and 'Multiple weapons' in Table 15.2.

Each of these numerical values (similarity scores if you like) can be represented in space. The Cartesian basis of the approach comes into play here. It is not quite like drawing a scattergram since we do not know where the axes should be. Nevertheless, the information in the above table can be represented in physical space. All that we know is how close or distant the points representing the table would be. Three of the four facets ('Multiple weapons',

Table 15.2 Crime scene characteristics at three different murders

	Murder A	Murder B	Murder C
Multiple weapons	1	1	2
Sexual humiliation	1	1	2
Night-time	2	1	2
Victim left naked	1	1	2

1=yes, 2=no

Table 15.3 A simple matrix of the co-occurrence of crime scene characteristics

	Multiple weapons	Sexual humiliation	Night-time	Victim left naked
Multiple weapons				
Sexual humiliation	3			
Night-time	2	2		
Victim left naked	3	3	2	

'Sexual humiliation' and 'Victim left naked') are at the identical point in space. The remaining facet ('Night-time') is 1 away from a complete match with the other three facets (according to the data in the table). We can arbitrarily place any of the facets and plot all of the other facets in relation to it. This plotting would look something like this:

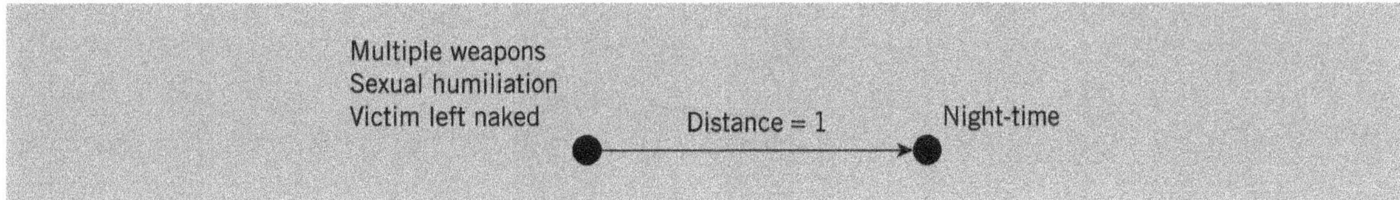

In this simple example, 'Multiple weapons', 'Sexual humiliation' and 'Victim left naked' all lie at the same point in space – there is no difference between them and they match perfectly. Only 'Night-time' fails to match completely with the other three. The maximum match for this and the other three variables is 2 so it is different by just 1.

It may take several dimensions in order to reproduce the case. Take for purposes of illustration this little puzzle: Greater Aston, Middle Aston and Little Aston are three different villages. Each of them is four miles by foot from each other as the crow flies. You can probably work out that the three villages would look like they were at the points of an equilateral triangle on a map. The sides of the triangle are four miles long each. There is another village – Great Spires – that is three miles exactly from each of the other three villages. How can that be? Well the answer has to be that either Great Spires is on the top of a hill in the middle of the other three villages, or that it is in a valley with the other three on the ridge above. In other words, the first three villages can be represented by a two-dimensional map (a triangle is two-dimensional) but the four villages require an extra dimension to represent their relative distances from each other.

Statistical techniques, in an analogous way, can plot a multitude of distances or differences into Cartesian space. We need not know precisely how it is done and it is best left to computer programs. There are numerous techniques available. They are all built on indexes of similarity or closeness or correlation between the variables. In the case of crime scene analysis, they are based on whether Variable A and Variable B tend to occur *together* at different crime scenes. This is then extended to include the relationships between *all* possible pairs of crime scene variables. This can be expressed as a matrix of similarity or a matrix of correlation. Smallest space analysis (often just referred to as SSA in research publications) is one of the statistical techniques available that will represent matrices of similarity or correlation matrices in multidimensional space. As mentioned earlier, this process is known as mapping. One important question is: how many dimensions? One, two, three, more? (Yes, it is possible to have more.) The computer programs doing smallest space analysis will produce the best outcome they can for the number of dimensions specified by the researcher. If the researcher wants a two-dimensional plot then that is what they should request from the computer. The computer gives something called the *coefficient of alienation*. This is simply an index of how well, say, the two-dimensional plot fits the data. If the coefficient is zero then this means that the data fit the two-dimensional plot perfectly. The poorer the fit, the greater the need for more dimensions. There is something of a trade-off between the adequacy of the plot and how useful it is for most analysts.

What emerges is a two-dimensional map. On this map are placed the attributes of a crime scene. The closer two attributes are to each other, the more likely they are to coexist at the crime scene. Attributes that are common to crime scenes tend to be at the centre of the map. The more central, the more crime scenes they are found at. The figure illustrates this using a few facets of a crime scene.

BOX 15.1 (continued)

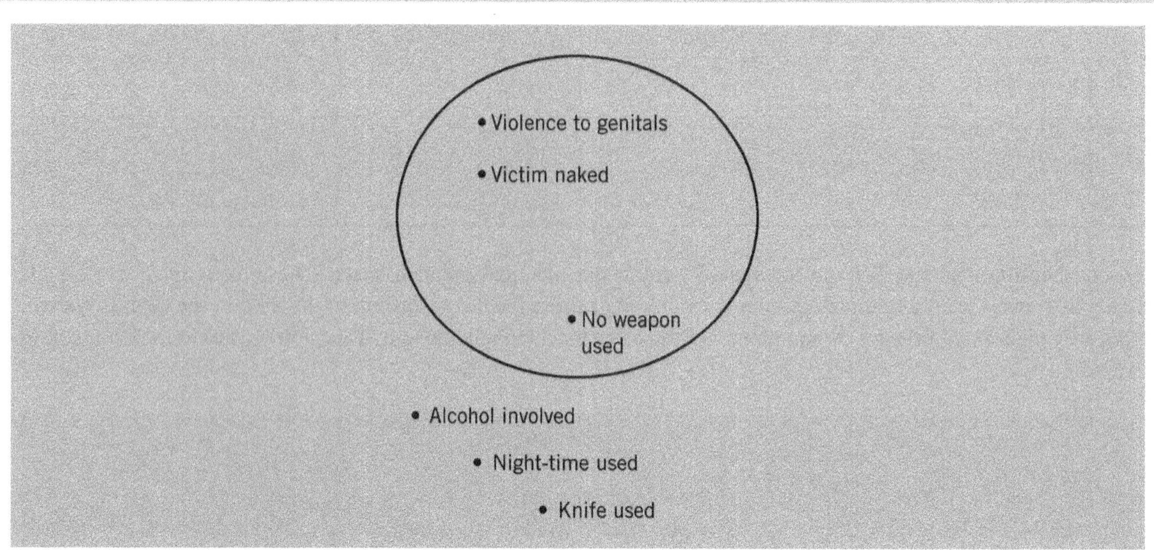

This (imaginary) plot tells us the following:

- Where a knife is used it is likely to be night-time and alcohol is involved, since these three things tend to be close together on the plot.
- Typically, no weapons are used in the murders (since 'No weapon used' is close to the centre of the plot).
- Where the victim is naked and there are signs of violence to the genitals, then it is unlikely to find a knife used.

The researcher is also likely to segregate or partition the plot into sectors, largely subjectively, in order to identify the broad types of crime scene. This is somewhat difficult with the simple example above, but one obvious sector consists of the murder crime scenes with a sexual component. That is, lines would be drawn (usually from the centre) to enclose the aspects of crime scenes that are sexual in nature (i.e. a naked victim, violence to the genitals). Examination of real analyses will demonstrate the value of this better.

Profile analysis is dependent on the measures of similarity used. The simple total of matches between two crime scenes is not the only possibility. Woodhams, Grant and Price (2007) consider two methods:

- *Jaccard coefficient:* this method is quite well established. The Jaccard coefficient is simply the number of crime scene characteristics shared by two crime scenes divided by the total number of different crime scene characteristics present in at least one of the two crime scenes. This means that crime scene characteristics which are present at neither crime scene are not used in the calculation of crime scene similarity.
- *Taxonomic similarity:* in this procedure, the similarity calculation is calculated in a way which considers that certain behaviours are similar, despite the fact that they are nominally different. So, for example, a crime scene behaviour such as 'bites victim's breasts' can be seen as very similar to 'bites victim's buttocks', even though they are not exactly the same. Both, for example, can be seen as very different from say 'cuts off some hair from the victim'. Taxonomic similarity thus takes into account the fact that some crime scene characteristics can be seen to belong to much the same category.

The researchers used offence information which was on file with a Social Services department in the United Kingdom. Seven young offenders under the age of 16 years were studied. A list of 55 offence behaviours were coded from this information. The researchers knew from police information which offenders had committed which crimes. So they explored the data to find out how similar offences committed by the same offender were compared with offences committed by different offenders. They found that the taxonomic similarity measure worked somewhat better than the Jaccard coefficients at distinguishing the linked from unlinked offences. Interestingly, the researchers also omitted a proportion of offence behaviours in order to see whether the indexes of similarity were affected by incomplete data. They found that the taxonomic similarity measure was more resistant to dropping information than the Jaccard coefficient.

The homology issue and basic theory

We briefly touched on the concept of homology in Chapter 14. So, to be clear, in profiling the basic form of homology is the assumption that the characteristics of the offence (crime scene) are predictive of the characteristics of the offender. Some evidence for such a relationship has already been given earlier in this chapter but there are conceptual issues which need to be raised. The evidence supporting the homology hypothesis cannot be said to be overwhelming but neither can it be dismissed. The idea that there are consistencies in offending can manifest itself in various forms (see Figure 15.4):

- *Consistency/Crime linkage:* The first type is crime matching which is built on the belief that there is a consistency in the characteristics of the offences of a particular offender. This is sometimes referred to as the consistency hypothesis (Canter, 1994). It refers to the expectation that the manner of carrying out a crime on one occasion will be reflected in the characteristics of the manner of offending on a later occasion. This form of consistency is primarily used to assess the likelihood that a particular offender was responsible for a series of crimes or whether different offenders were involved in the different offences.
- *Matching:* The second type of consistency is that there is a simple match between a characteristic of the offence and the typical characteristics of offenders who commit that sort of crime. This is illustrated by the suggestion that there is a relationship (negative) between the age of the victim of a sex attack and the age of the offender. Of course, the potential for such research is enormous as there are so many different measurable aspects of crime scenes and a multitude of characteristics that may be ascribed to the offender.
- *Homology:* The third type of consistency seeks relationships between particular patterns of crime scene characteristics and particular characteristic patterns in the individual offender.

Consistency in offending

No simple summary can describe the findings into the various studies of homology, matching and crime linkage. As we saw at the end of Chapter 14, Snook *et al.* (2008) argued strongly that the evidence for these relationships is very weak – so weak that they suggest that the fundamental theory underlying traditional FBI offender profiling is invalid – but this does not adequately reflect the range of findings and expert opinion on this matter. In terms of Cantor's approach to profiling, probably a more adequate conclusion would be that overall there is some tentative support for the idea that crime scene characteristics reflect offender characteristics, but largely at only modest levels. However, better methods and data may well improve our understanding.

It is worthwhile starting with what appears to be a successful demonstration of the potential effective use of profiling. The basic idea of this research was to calculate the mathematical similarities between one crime scene and other, possibly related, crime scenes. Thus Yokota *et al.* (2007) created a profiling system based on a general crime data base. Ninety-six variables concerning different aspects of offences were recorded, including things such as the type of victim, the place of victimisation, the time of victimisation, interaction with the victim, and the sexual behaviours involved. The computer database contained about 1250 incidents of rape and forced indecency involving 868 offenders. Most of the offenders (78 per cent) had just one record. The computer program allowed the researchers to compare a new crime scene with all of the other crime scenes in the database. It picked out those old offences which were most like the new offence. Since this particular database involved old offences where the offender was known then this essentially generated a list of likely suspects. Actually, the method was slightly more sophisticated than all of this implies. Because this was a research trial, the 'new' offences were really the most recent offence in the series of offences where the offender had committed three or more crimes. Thus, the offender for the 'new' offences was actually known to the researchers. The 'new' offences were not included in the database for the trial.

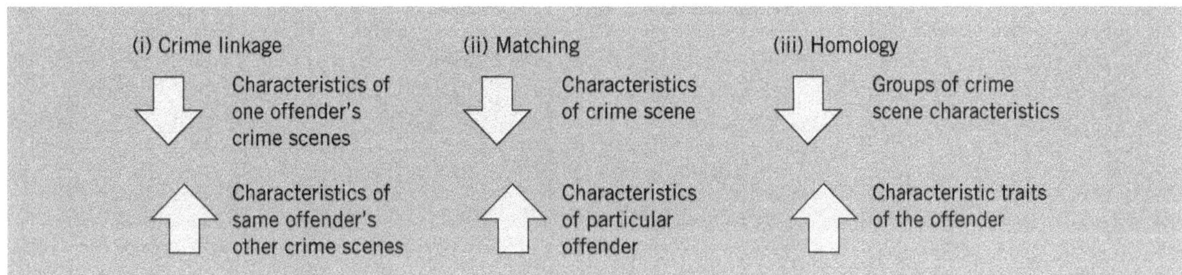

Figure 15.4 Some of the different types of consistency between the crime scene characteristics and the offender

The computer calculated similarity scores between the old offences (those in the database) and the new offences (the most recent offences of 81 offenders).

The system showed a lot of promise in terms of identifying 'potential offenders'. For 81 'new' offences, the system picked out the actual offender from the other records on 30 per cent of occasions and the actual offender was picked out as in the top four likely suspects for half of the 'new' crimes. The hit rate for the actual offender being the number one suspect increased to 56 per cent when the area of Japan involved was added into the calculations. The researchers could also use the most likely offenders to generate a profile of the sort of offender who was likely to be involved. Interestingly, this approach allows for the inclusion of low-frequency behaviours, which are dealt with by the similarity calculation (algorithm). Most studies tend to dispense with very infrequently and very frequently occurring behaviours as they are either too discriminating or not discriminating enough.

Sorochinski and Salfati (2010) provided an analysis of what they term the 'consistency of inconsistency' in serial homicide. They point out that some research has painted a rather muted picture of the consistency between crime site behaviours in serial homicide offenders – the very sort of offenders for whom offender profiling was originally developed. Earlier research by Bateman and Salfati (2007) found just four crime scene behaviours which showed consistently over all of the offences (bringing equipment to the crime scene to help them commit the crime, destroying evidence, oral sex by the victim, and using a ligature). This is only very modest evidence of crime scene consistency. Sorochinski and Salfati essentially replicated this research but using groupings of different types of crime scene behaviours rather than individual crime scene behaviours. Three groups of behaviours were used. Each of these was broken down into two different themes. These were:

- *Group 1: Planning:* A strategy to complete the crime and avoid arrest (e.g. body transported; evidence of forced entry; forensic evidence removed; and weapon brought to scene). It was found that this group could be fairly effectively differentiated into pre- and post-planning themes.
- *Group 2: Wounding:* The strategy for killing the victim (e.g. biting; blunt instrument; injury to face; injury to neck – stabbing; and ligature strangulation). It was found that this could be differentiated into (a) process-oriented and (b) goal-oriented themes which strongly separated wounding behaviours into one of the two dominant themes.
- *Group 3: Offender–victim interaction behaviours:* (e.g. body posed; face covered after death; masturbation at the scene; necrophilia; and prostitute victim). It was found that this group could be differentiated into the themes of (a) the victim as object – acts such as necrophilia basically treated the dead victim as an object and (b) the victim as vehicle – this included various types of sexual acts with the live victim and the victim being a prostitute.

The different crime scenes were coded using these three different groups and themes for 19 serial homicide cases with solo killers in the USA (Sorochinski and Salfati, 2010). On average, each offender had killed more than five people. However, for the purposes of the analysis, only the first three killings were studied. The question is just how consistent the offenders were in terms of their behaviours over these three groups. As shown in Figure 15.5, the consistency of the offender's placement in each of these groups and their themes was most evident for the

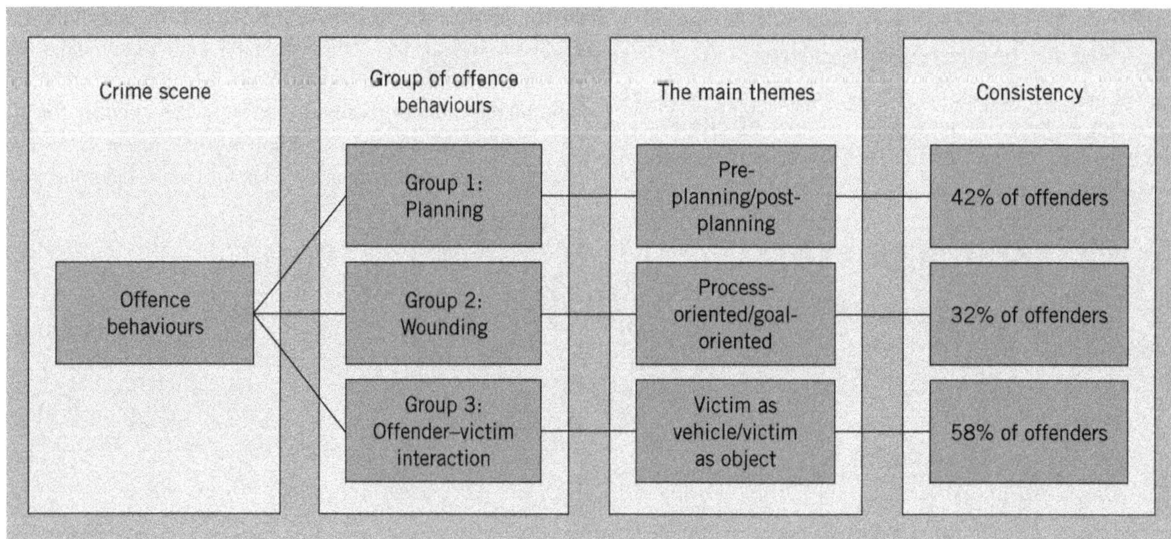

Figure 15.5 Consistency of crime scene themes over serial killings

victim–offender interaction behaviours group. It was found that there was 58 per cent consistency for this group for crime scene categorisation into the different themes. Consistency for planning was 42 per cent and for wounding 32 per cent. However, consistency was not a characteristic across all three crime behaviour groupings. That is to say, for example, if an offender was consistent in terms of victim–offender interaction, they were unlikely to be consistent for planning and wounding as well.

Of course, the classification of crime scene behaviours into groupings and themes has consequences. Most importantly, it inevitably loses some of the specific detail which, in some circumstances, might show consistency. Grouping variables together is only clearly advantageous if the research outcomes are more informative as a consequence. One study suggests that grouping crime scene behaviours may be a problem (Goodwill, Alison and Beech, 2009). They used data from a sample of stranger rapists acting alone in order to evaluate the extent to which three different profiling models predicted previous rape offences from crime scene information. The three models were:

- Hazelwood's (1987) Power and Anger model. The basis of these ideas is discussed in Chapter 9.
- Behavioural Thematic Evaluation (Canter, Bennell, Alison and Reddy, 2003). This suggested that there are four styles of rapist plus a mixed group.
- The Massachusetts Treatment Centre's Rape classification scheme, which involves five types of rapist.

Details of the different subcategories in each of these models may be found in Figure 15.6.

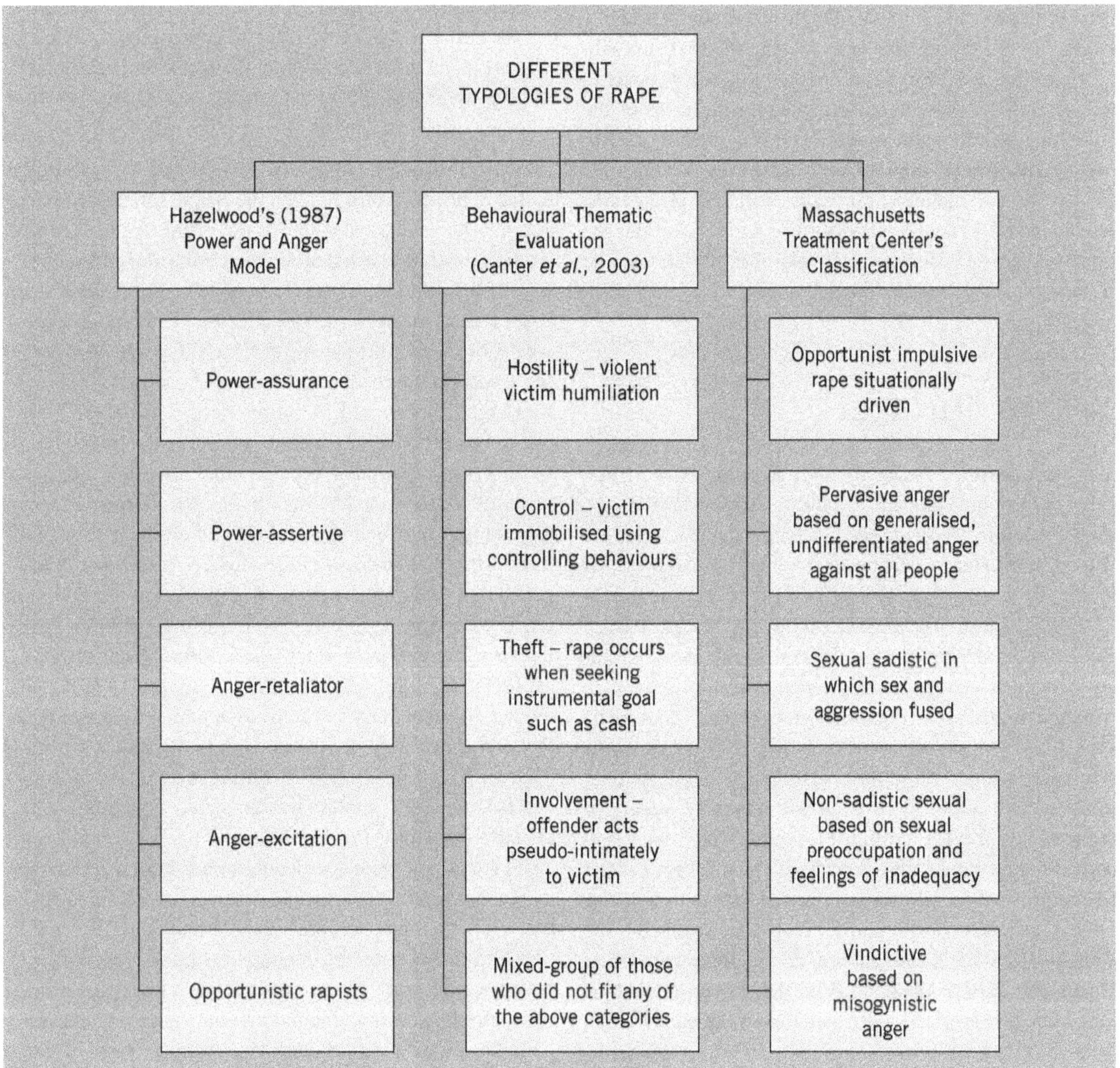

Figure 15.6 The different typologies of rape evaluated in Goodwill *et al.*'s (2009) study

Each of these three models is commonly used when profilers give advice about sex offences (Goodwill, Alison and Beech, 2009). The researchers used the coding schemes developed by each model's original author(s). In order to ensure high-quality coding, the coders underwent a period of training involving practice together with feedback on how they coded the data for each model. Then the coding stage proper began. Information about the rapists' previous convictions was obtained from the UK Police National Computer. The researchers were looking for previous convictions for the same type of offence – that is sexual, violent, drug and/or weapon, property, or other offences.

Hazelwood's Power and Anger model and the Massachusetts Treatment Centre's Rape classification scheme were just about equally as effective at predicting whether or not the offender had previous offences, though fairly modestly so. Canter's Behavioural Thematic Model was decidedly less effective. This is fairly typical of the findings in this broad area of research.Alison, Goodwill, Almond, van den Heuvel and Winter (2010) decided to analyse the data but without organising it in terms of the requirements of the three models. By using the raw data to make predictions (as opposed to using the raw data to code into theoretical models), far more accurate predictions were achieved. Thus the categorisation process in this case may be responsible for the relatively poor fit between the crime scene data and previous offences.

Crime linkage

The idea of crime linkage through an analysis of crime-scene behaviours may have validity irrespective of the value of profiling as such. An interesting application of the issue of consistency can be appreciated in the work of Tonkin, Bond and Woodhams (2009). This took a slightly unusual but intriguing approach to testing the basic principles of offender profiling – the consistency and homology principles – using forensic evidence of footwear worn by burglars rather than the more typical crime scene characteristics. Footprint analysis has been one of the stalwarts of forensic science work. Of course, only a small number of offences (8 per cent) provide the necessary quality of footprint to provide strong evidence. The make and model of shoe can be identified from about 40 per cent of the footprints. Special databases are available to help the forensic scientist identify the footwear worn by the offender from the tread pattern in the footprint. Other information may be obtained from the shoeprint, such as estimated shoe size and wear patterns on the shoe, which make identification of the actual shoe involved more certain. Tonkins *et al.* applied profiling methods to evidence from nearly 160 domestic burglaries where a suspect had been found in possession of footwear corresponding to the make and model of the shoe leaving the footprint. A total of 100 different offenders were involved. The information collected included:

- The estimated price of the footwear: This was the key crime scene variable studied. The researchers trawled shoe shops in the area in order to find the typical local cost of each model involved. Nearly all of the shoe-prints were from training shoes. The manufacturers were mainly well known 'designer labels' such as Adidas (9 different models), Nike (28) and Reebok (8). The Reebox Classic was very frequent but there was a great deal of variety in the shoe models involved.
- Background information on each crime from police records: This included whether they were employed or unemployed, their age, and a measure of the relative deprivation level of the place of the burglar's residence. The last was based on the UK government's Index of Multiple Deprivation (which includes education/skills, employment, health and disability, and income amongst other factors).

In some instances, more than one burglary was known to have been committed by the same offender. Where similar shoeprints were left at the crime scene then this would illustrate consistency. As a control, random pairings of the other burglaries were made. Where the crimes were linked to the same offender the difference in footwear cost was quite small, at £5 on average. However, the price difference for the random (unlinked) pairings was much larger, at £16 on average. Thus there was a closer correspondence in shoe prices for the linked pairs. In this way evidence for the matching or similarity principle was found. Was there also correspondence (homology) between shoe prices and offender variables? Similarity in shoe costs in the offence pairs was found to correlate with the amount of deprivation in the area where the offender lived. Shoe cost similarities were linked to employment status similarities. One intriguing aspect of this, though, was that the unemployed burglar tended to wear more expensive trainers. Interesting as these findings may be, it seems unlikely that a criterion such as living in an area of deprivation narrows things down sufficiently that it would materially improve the chances of identifying an offender.

There is a range of evidence supporting crime linkage to some extent. Nevertheless, there are problems in its use. For example, Burrell, Bull, Bond and Herrington (2015) studied whether behavioural crime linkage principles would work for group offences as well as crimes committed by an individual. Of course, any offender may commit all of their offences in groups, none of their offences in groups, or some of their offences in groups and some of their offences alone. One might expect, and there is research to support it, that the group has an influence on offending. So is there the same degree of consistency between pairs of offences committed in a group, pairs of offences committed alone, and pairs in which one offence was group and the other offence was individual? Using police records, it is possible to draw up samples of offenders with pairs of most recent offences in one or other of these three types of pairings. Because of conviction evidence, the link between the culprit for each pair of offences was known. That is, an offender could be classified into one of three categories on the basis of their two recent offences – group-group, individual-individual, or group-individual. The researches took personal robbery offences in two English locations as the basic sampling strategy. Behaviours at the crime scene were also available from police records which formed the basis for calculating the similarity between the two separate offences involving a particular offender. The crime scene behaviour characteristics used in the studies included: 1) the time between the offences; 2) the distance between the offences; 3) a target selection characteristics including things like the day of the week of the offence and whether the offender knew the victim; 4) a control behaviour measure which included the presence of a weapon at the offence and violent actions; and 5) a property measure including the different types of property stolen and whether the robbers gave any of the property back to the victim. This enabled the researchers to calculate indexes of similarity between the two crime scenes for each offender. For comparison purposes, random pairings of offences irrespective of offender were also obtained and the same statistical analyses applied. It was found that there were no differences between group-group levels of behavioural similarity and individual-individual levels. It was possible to distinguish between linked pairs of offences and unlinked (randomly paired) offences. That is, crime linkage worked for both the group-group and the individual-individual category. The group-individual crime pairs seemed to be different and showed lower levels of offence-pair similarity than for the other two types of crime pairing. The group-individual crime pairings were not so differentiated from the random pairings in terms of behavioural similarity so crime linkage would be rather less effective in this case. This suggests that linking crimes when comparing a group crime with an individual crime needs special care. However, this does not apply to all behavioural features of crime scenes. For example, it was possible to identify linked offences in terms of physical distance between the two crimes for all three conditions of the research.

A study by Bouhana, Johnson and Porter (2016) has potential for unpinning some of the mysteries in crime linkage research. Their study was carried out on prolific burglars in an English county who had committed at least five offences. We saw in Chapter 7 that burglars have strategies not only for carrying out their crimes but also for deciding locations. Bouhana *et al.* were, firstly, seeking to know the extent to which a burglar showed consistency across all of their offending. Unfortunately, even if they show consistency, it could be the case that burglars, in general, demonstrate much the same pattern. If this were the case, then crime scene characteristics would not be helpful in identifying possible specific offenders. So, in addition, Bouhana *et al.* wanted to know the extent to which it is possible to differentiate offenders in terms of their offending characteristics – this is technically known as specificity. One novel thing about this study was that the similarity between ALL of each burglar's offences was studied. Most studies of crime linkage use just two recent crimes per offender. The offences studied were from an English county. The burglaries were assumed to be linked to the same offender in the study when the same offender had been charged by the police or the offender had asked for the offence to be taken into account so that they could not be prosecuted for them in the future. The offence characteristics used included spatial coordinates for the offence (i.e. its location), the sort of home burgled, entry method, whether the inhabitants were at home at the time of the burglary, and the point of entry used. Sophisticated measures of similarity were calculated for these offence characteristics. Of course, for there to be consistency then all of the individual's crime scenes should have high measures of consistency. For there to be good specificity then there should be low similarity between the crime scenes of different offenders. The study showed that burglars manifest consistency in their offending behaviours. That is, one of the key principles of linkage analysis (and profiling in general) was met. Things were a little more complicated when it came to the question of the specificity of a burglar's modus operandi. Some burglars did indeed show specificity so that their crimes could be differentiated from those of other burglars but not all of them did. In other words, some burglars were more identifiable from their offending behaviour patterns than other burglars whereas others were not. This is only partial support for the specificity criterion. Some features of offender's *modus operandi* (such as choice of crime location and type of house targeted) were the most likely to help differentiate one burglar from another. There was poorer specificity for the point of entry and whether the house was empty. It should be noted that a good portion of the consistency in *modi operandi* is down to the majority of burglars adopting the same offending strategies. If it were possible to decide from the crime scene which offenders are the most likely to manifest specificity, then crime linkage could concentrate on these as they are the cases where crime linkage has the best chance of being effective.

There are a number of reasons why the crime scenes of an offender may change over a period of time thus reducing the consistency between an offender's crimes:

- Criminals change and develop new tactics and become more effective with time – their confidence in their ability to commit the crime increases.
- The offenders' goals may change over time – maybe their sexual fantasies have changed.
- The victim's resistance may change what the offender needs to do in order to complete the crime on a particular occasion.

Profiling and personality

One reason why profiling may not be too successful at predicting personality characteristics from the crime scene may simply be irrelevant or poor theories of personality are employed. Anyone examining the research on profiling will find relatively little that relates criminal activity to conventional personality theory. There is, of course, some research which tries to make the link between criminality and personality such as Eysenck's biosocial theory (see Chapter 5) but this is too general to be used in profiling. The profiling literature does make reference to personality characteristics but these are rarely based on theoretically advanced understanding of human personality, it has been argued. According to Youngs (2004), little research is available into the relationship between *styles of offending* and personality as opposed to studies of the personality of, say, violent offenders. Perhaps not surprisingly, most of the measures of personality used in these studies are ones created for clinical purposes. Their value, then, may be limited in the extent to which clinical (abnormal) factors are responsible for criminal style. The alternative is to use non-clinical measures of personality. The upshot of these studies is less than clear. Some studies claim a relationship, whereas others suggest that there is no relationship. Quoting Youngs (2004): 'it remains unclear, then, whether personality is differentially related to offending style and, if so, which aspects of personality will relate to which aspects of offending style' (p. 101). Youngs argues that the circumstances in which there will be a differentiating relationship between personality and style of offending are as follows:

- Conceptions of personality employed must be appropriate to criminal behaviour.
- Empirical research must be informed by an understanding of the way that behaviour is shaped by personality.
- Offending styles must be empirically defensible and defined.

In other words, the research in this field requires a rather more sophisticated understanding of both personality and criminal behaviour than has generally been the case.

Some modern ideas about personality have been introduced into profiling by a number of researchers. In an expert review of the evidence on crime linkage involving psychological methods, Woodhams, Hollin and Bull (2007) carefully evaluated the evidence and concluded that the assumption of some consistency in an offender's behaviours across crimes is supported. Not only this, they suggest that the variation between different offenders in their crime patterns is sufficiently great that the offences of a particular offender can be differentiated from the other offenders' crimes with a degree of confidence. Nevertheless, consistency in the successive crimes of criminals is not always the rule. That is, there is both usable consistency but problematic inconsistency. Researchers need to develop understanding of the latter. Woodhams *et al.* argue that profilers have tended to adopt an outmoded conception of personality which was abandoned by personality researchers several decades ago. They argue that if forensic researchers adopted a more modern approach to personality, then a better fit could be achieved between personality and the different crime scenes of the same offender. There are two fundamental aspects to all of this:

- Consistency across an offender's successive crime may not be the same irrespective of the behaviour in question.
- Situation-dependent behaviours show less consistency than the behaviours initiated by the offender.

Woodhams *et al.* argue that that research trying to link different crimes has ignored the 'if' in the 'if-then' relationship (Mischel, 1999). What this means is that people respond in distinctive but stable ways to situations but that this response is dependent on the type of situation under consideration. A person may be open and communicative when interacting with their friends but quiet and unresponsive when in a meeting with their boss at work. The situations are the 'if' and the stable behaviour patterns are the 'thens'. Crudely, this can be expressed as in Figure 15.7. Essentially, the argument is that, by taking into account the general situation of crimes, one can make better assessments of whether the same offender carried them all out. Generally, the situation is that as experienced by the offender rather than something more objectively defined by the researcher. Consequently, the situation to which the offender is responding is not totally reflected in the crime scene. Even where the offender chooses a crime scene to be similar to the others, events may happen to cause changes. For example, a victim may resist the attack, a passerby disturb the offender, and so forth.

Goodwill and Alison (2007) make a similar argument about the incorporation of the situation into profiling. They

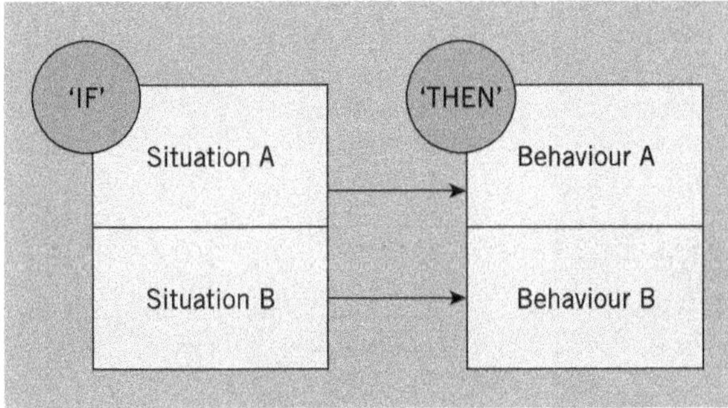

Figure 15.7 Behaviour involves personality characteristics plus situational characteristics

stress the well-known basics that profiling is only possible if 1) offenders are consistent in the manner in which they commit their crimes and 2) they are differentiable from other offenders in their offending behaviours. Some things are so unique to a particular offender that they can do nothing to help when comparisons are being made between a number of offenders. Nevertheless, a feature which is exclusive to an individual is a 'signature' of that individual and so reliably indicates that this particular individual was responsible for the series of crimes. Goodwill and Alison explored the simple idea of an inverse relationship (negative correlation) between the age of the offender and the age of the victim in sex offending (Figure 15.8). Thus if the victim of a sexual attack is young then the offender is more likely to be older and vice versa.

Other relevant features of a crime which can be assessed from the crime scene are:

- *Planning:* Has the crime been planned and organised in advance? Planning may be assessed by such factors as whether the offender brings to the scene equipment to help carry out the rape, such as handcuffs to control the victim, a gag for the victim, or a disguise or blindfold for himself. Research has shown that such planning enables the offender to target a victim of choice rather than someone at random. In these circumstances, the relationship between the age of the offender and victim may be apparent. Where the crime is unplanned, then the expected relationship between offender and victim age may not be apparent.
- *Gratuitous violence:* The level of aggression/violence involved in the sexual crime is predictive of the age of the offender. Younger sex offenders tend to be more violent than older ones (Grubin and Kennedy, 1991), for example. Gebhard *et al.* (1965) found that violent sexual aggressors were typically younger than non-violent sexual offenders. The fact that these findings tend not to be consistent across different studies suggested to Goodwill and Alison (2007) that the level of aggression/violence may be a moderating factor in the relationship between offender age and victim age.

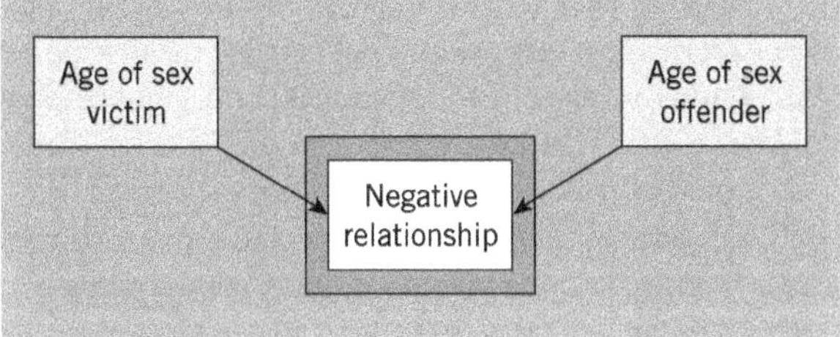

Figure 15.8 Illustrating the negative relationship between victim and sex offender age

Goodwill and Alison investigated data from 85 stranger rapes in order to examine the question of whether the situational factors strengthen the relationship between victim age and offender age. The researchers' expectations and the findings of the research were as shown in Figure 15.9. Their analysis showed that there was the expected, modest negative relationship between victim and offender age. If one simply takes either the gratuitously violent group or the planning group then the relationship gets stronger. This indicates that gratuitous violence and planning separately have a moderating effect. However, the relationship between age of offender and age of victim is strongest when the moderating effects of gratuitous violence and planning are considered. Where there is evidence of both planning and gratuitous violence then it is possible to predict the offender's age from that of the victim to within less than three years.

It can be argued that criminal behaviour is an interpersonal activity. The extent to which crimes differ in this regard is enormous and, in some cases, the relationship is extremely remote. For crimes such as rape and murder there has to be some sort of direct relationship, whereas for other crimes, such as burglary, the relationship is not direct but 'implicit'. So, for example, a burglar is affected by the behaviour of a victim even if this is merely in terms of when the victim is away from home. This is a very indirect level of interpersonal activity. It might be noted also that many of the concepts used to explain the characteristics of offenders really describe interpersonal relationships – 'controlling', 'dominant' and 'hostile' are examples.

Youngs (2004) suggested that, potentially, Fundamental Interpersonal Relations Orientation (FIRO) theory could be a means of assessing interpersonal interaction characteristics which might have a bearing on criminal style (Shutz, 1994). A person's interpersonal style will be reflected in the characteristic behaviours they receive from others. The theory's core personality characteristics

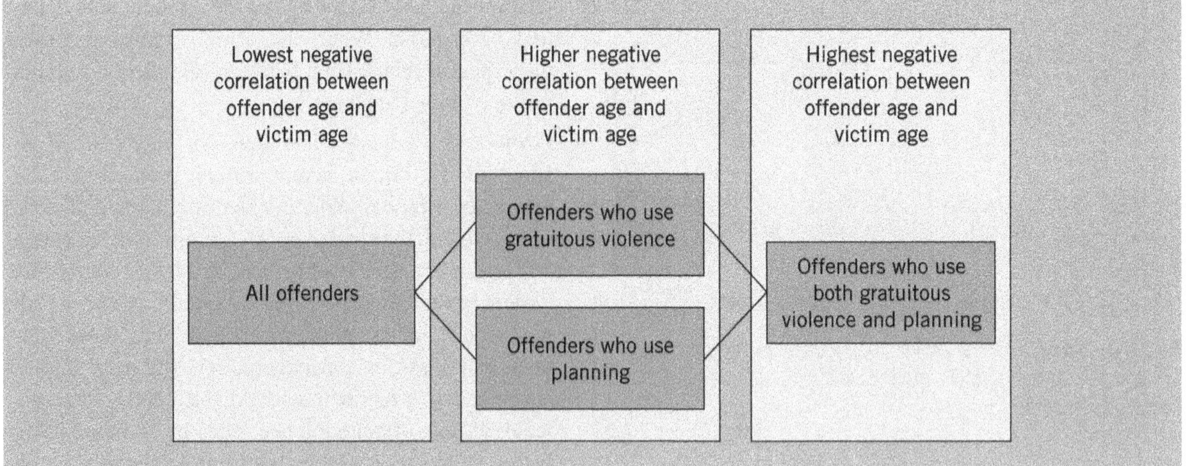

Figure 15.9 Age of victim and offender relationships taking into account the moderating effects of planning and gratuitous violence

of control, inclusion and openness may be defined as follows:

- *Control:* this consists of two components that are not strongly related to each other. Expressed control is essentially the exertion of control over others, whereas received control is the individual's willingness to submit to the control attempts of others. Someone who attempts to control others may be willing to be controlled or resistant to control.
- *Inclusion:* expressed inclusion is basically the manifestation of the desire to receive attention, interact and to belong to others. High received inclusion refers to those persons who tend to receive the attentions of others.
- *Openness:* expressed openness refers to those who relate to others with affection and closeness. So they are not private and withdrawn in their relationships.

Received openness refers to those who tend to receive the affection and closeness of others.

The offending behaviours of young men in the age range of 14–28 years (the median age was 19 years) were studied, using a lengthy questionnaire. This included behaviours such as cheating at school in tests, being drunk regularly under the age of 16, and trying to pass a cheque by signing someone else's name. A statistical analysis found two major modes or styles of offending behaviour. Expressive behaviours included breaking into empty buildings to cause damage, arson and sex in public. They are expressive since these acts are the aim of the behaviours. Instrumental behaviours included forging a cheque, shoplifting and burglary. Another dimension of the offence concerned the seriousness of the behaviours.

Among the findings was that the expressed control group tended to target their offending against others – commonly through the use of violence. Offences involving the use of a weapon and the carrying and use of a gun were especially common in this group. In terms of the received control dimension, higher scorers tended to be more involved in property offences, with the highest levels being for vandalism. These, taken with other findings, can become support for Youngs' assertions about the circumstances in which offence style might relate to personality.

Conclusion

One remarkable thing about all forms of offender profiling is that none of the various methods has attracted research which demonstrates its value in relation to specific crimes. To be sure, there is some statistical evidence that some crime scene characteristics may be associated with some offender characteristics. But this is different from being able to say that offender profiles lead to the identification of the offender or have been operationally useful. At the end of a long and detailed review of the evidence, Chifflet (2015) concluded that:

> 'Assessing evidence of the validity of offender profiling does not yield an entirely reassuring picture. There still appear to be fundamental gaps and shortcomings in the theories that serve as a foundation for the discipline as well as in the research undertaken to validate and advance this framework. Furthermore, there is little empirical evidence to conclude unequivocally that profiling works in practice or that profilers offer significantly more accurate predictions than non-profilers . . . This has undoubtedly led many to wonder how the discipline succeeded in permeating criminal investigations and legal proceedings.'
>
> (p. 251)

Main points

- Canter's approach to offender profiling, although originating in an interest in solving the railway murders, is probably best regarded in terms of its characteristic empirical basis involving the collation and analysis of substantial systematic data sets describing numerous crime scenes and of descriptions of crime scenes and characteristics of known offenders. As such, it can be seen as systematically testing some of the basic assumptions of FBI-style profiling rather than being aimed at directly supporting specific criminal investigations.
- Statistical profiling has abandoned many of the shibboleths of FBI-style profiling. This can be seen most easily in the much wider range of types of crimes which it covers compared to FBI profiling's emphasis on serial violent sexual crimes containing 'bizarre' elements. So statistical profiling is increasingly likely to look at crimes such as arson and fraud, which are very different from the focus of the original FBI profilers.
- It would be wrong to describe Canter's approach to offender profiling as a purely empirical endeavour, as researchers adopting his methods have emphasised new and different theoretical perspectives in their writings, as we have seen, for example, in the work of Youngs (2004) described above. Nevertheless, many of the writings in this field are dominated by statistical approaches to pattern finding which are characteristically a little inaccessible. Consequently, it is important to understand how these methods are used following explanations such as those in this chapter and not to be overwhelmed by the detail of the analysis. There is a great deal of work to be done if the statistical approach is to inform police investigations in ways as influential as those of the FBI profilers.

Further reading

Alison, L. and Rainbow, L. (2011) *Professionalizing Offender Profiling: Forensic and Investigative Psychology in Practice* Abingdon, Oxon: Routledge.

Canter, D. and Youngs, D. (2009) *Investigative Psychology: From Offender Profiling to the Analysis of Criminal Action* Chichester: John Wiley and Sons.

Youngs, D. (2013) *The Behavioural Analysis of Crime: Studies in David Canter's Investigative Psychology* Farnham, Surrey: Ashgate.

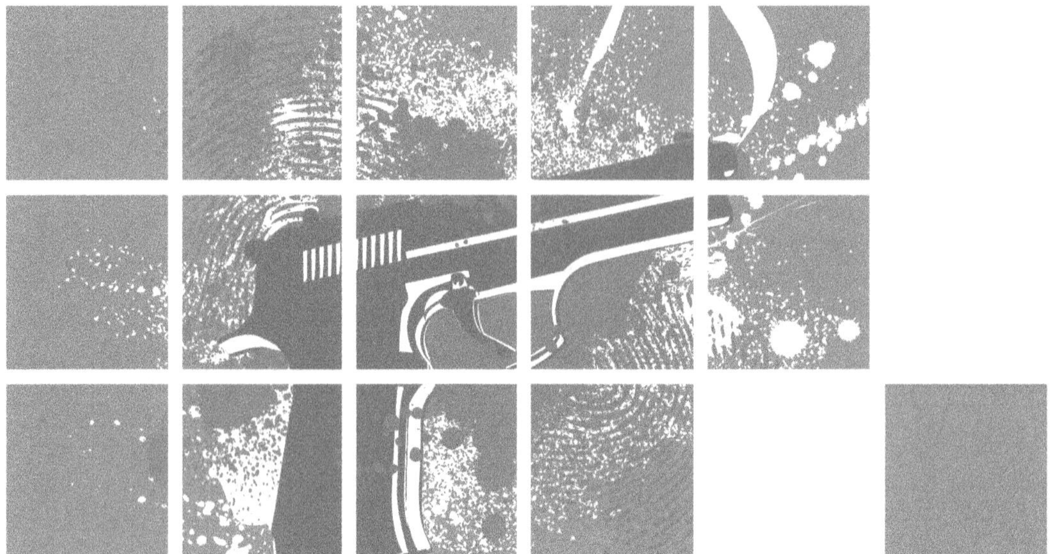

Chapter 16

False allegations

Overview

- Miscarriage of justice is a legal rather than psychological concept and may involve procedural rather than factual matters. Psychologists have focused on the more limited issues of false allegations and false confessions.
- False allegations may be made for a number of reasons – they are not simply motivated by malice in every case.
- Bad interviewing practices can lead to false information. In some circumstances, persistent leading questioning can result in individuals being falsely implicated in crime. Some children, especially, seem vulnerable to the implantation of false memories of events that are resistant to challenge in some cases.
- The recovered memory/false memory debate reflects opposite ways of understanding some allegations of sexual abuse dating back to childhood experiences. Recovered memory implies that the abuse happened and was lost to memory for a while, whereas false memory implies that the memories are of events which did not take place. The debate centres around radically different perspectives on memory.
- A rather sceptical view of recovered memory comes from those experimental psychologists primarily using laboratory-style experimentation in developing memory theories. A more favourable view of recovered memories comes from psychologists who regard memory as being affected by repression, especially following trauma. Some individuals retract claims of having had memories of childhood recovered in adult life.
- There are a number of graphic experimental demonstrations that children can be encouraged to make false claims about events which may been interpreted as sexually abusive. The *Mr Science* studies involved a classroom visit and later stories told to the children by their parents about that visit which contained inaccurate information. Some children claimed to remember events that happened in real life which were only to be found in the stories. 'Experts' in interviewing were not able to distinguish between the children's accounts of the real and fictional events.
- Professionals may make false allegations because they fail to understand the limited value of certain signs in diagnosing child sexual abuse. The risk of false positives and false negatives should be part of any such assessment.

Introduction

Miscarriage of justice involves a wrong decision by a court of law which results in an innocent person being punished. It is clearly a legal rather than psychological concept. Miscarriages of justice are identified when an appeal court overturns a conviction (Naughton, 2005). Overturning a previous decision does not necessarily mean that the appeal court believes that the convicted person was, in fact, innocent. In England and Wales, the requirement for a conviction is that the legal standard of proof has been met – that there is sufficient evidence that establishes beyond reasonable doubt the guilt of the accused. A previous decision may be overturned because legal procedures had not been followed correctly.

It is difficult to give a true rate of false allegations since this depends on the definition of false allegations being used. For example, it would be highly problematic to define false allegations in terms of the proportion of trials that end in 'not guilty' verdicts. A 'not guilty' verdict may or may not mean innocence and there is an obvious distinction to be made between false allegations and false convictions. Unfounded claims where the supporting evidence of, say, sexual harassment is not available are conceptually different from false allegations where no offence actually took place. Furthermore, recanted accusations are not in themselves evidence that no offence occurred, since there are numerous reasons for recanting – such as a reconciliation between partners.

One area where concern about false allegations has been extensive is that of child sexual abuse. Poole and Lindsay (1998) suggested that false allegation rates might vary from 5–8 per cent for child sexual abuse – if we take into account only *intentional* false allegations. Such malicious motives exclude a great number where the police and social workers among others raise suspicions of abuse against families. When false suspicions of this sort are included, the false allegation rate increases markedly to between 23–35 per cent, depending on the study in question (Howitt, 1992). Underlying these figures may be a reality of trauma, stress and distress for the child and its family. Risks consequent to false allegations include children being removed from their homes, fathers being forced to live away from home and imprisonment. Even if they do not lead to criminal convictions, well-intentioned false allegations may still take their toll on family life (Howitt, 1992). Of course, false denials of abuse by the victim may be equally damaging to the victim as false allegations are (Lyon, 1995).

The problem of false allegations

Although crime reports by the police seem an obvious source of information concerning false allegations, this is actually quite problematic. The International Association of Chiefs of Police (2005) stipulated that to count a case as a false allegation there must be proper evidence that no crime had actually occurred. This evidence might be the absence of physical evidence when such evidence should be available or evidence contradicting the accuser from one or more credible witnesses. The tendency of the police to classify a rape as a 'no crime' without obtaining positive evidence that the alleged crime did not take place is a fundamental problem. If allegations are judged to be 'no crime' as a consequence of sloppy investigative work, the figures for false allegations become inflated. The rules which should be employed by the American police can be found in the *Uniform Crime Reports (UCR) Handbook* (Federal Bureau of Investigation, 2004) and for the UK in the Home Office's (2014) 'counting rules'.

In the USA the term 'unfounded' is used to describe a report to the police by a victim which is found to be false or without foundation after a proper police investigation. In the United Kingdom, the phrase 'no crime' is used instead of 'unfounded'. These terms are not altogether synonymous with false allegations since they also include other circumstances. For example, a drunken woman at a party who claims to have been raped but does not know whether sexual penetration occurred might be in this category. This is because it is not known whether the basic legal requirement for a charge of rape (penetration) has been met.

Research has repeatedly shown that the police do not always obey the rules to the letter when classifying crimes. Specifically, they use 'unfounded' or 'no crime' rather more frequently than a strict interpretation of the rules allow. The following are some of the circumstances in which the police wrongly classify a crime as 'unfounded' or 'no crime' (Lisak, Gardinier, Nick and Cote, 2010):

- The police fail to obtain sufficient evidence to bring a prosecution.
- The victim, for whatever reason, acts uncooperatively with the police.
- Cases where the victim offers inconsistent accounts or directly lies.
- Cases in which the victim delays reporting the crime to the police.
- Cases in which the victim was intoxicated.

Lisak *et al.* (2010) carried out a slightly unusual study in order to assess rates of false allegations of sexual assault. They collected a sample of sexual assault cases reported to security police at an American university over a ten-year period. Rather than rely solely on the original investigation, the researchers coded the sex assault allegations into four categories, using victim descriptions of the assault and notes made by the investigators from the interviews with the victim, perpetrator, and any witnesses. The four categories used and their frequencies were as follows:

- *False reports* (6 per cent): This judgement was to be based on the preponderance of evidence that a crime had not been committed.
- *Case did not proceed* (45 per cent): These were cases not referred for prosecution or other action. The reasons for this included a lack of sufficient evidence; the victim withdrew their complaint; the perpetrator could not be identified; and the allegations did not constitute a crime in legal terms.
- *Case proceeded* (35 per cent): This category was used if, after investigation, the case was referred for prosecution or some other action by the university.
- *Insufficient information for assignment to above categories* (14 per cent): This included cases where neither victim nor perpetrator was named or where the record contained virtually no information.

These codings had 95 per cent inter-rater agreement; agreement for the false report category was perfect. Hence the researchers were confident in their false allegation rate of 6 per cent which is well within the false allegation rates claimed by other researchers. This figure is for substantiated false allegations and it is possible that other instances of false allegations were subsumed under other categories. For example, if the complaint was withdrawn it would be placed in the 'case did not proceed' category, though it may in truth a false allegation.

The largest study of false reports should be considered (Kelly, Lovett and Regan, 2005). This was commissioned by the British Home Office. A large number of rape cases covering a 15-year period were studied. Information drawn from a variety of sources was considered, including forensic reports; medical examinations; interviews with victims; content analyses of victim and witness statements; and so forth. The most important finding was that the police used the 'no crime' category as a 'dustbin' category for a variety of different things. Just over 8 per cent of the rapes studied were classified as false allegations. However, sometimes this classification was the result of police scepticism about the accuser. They might have mental illness or give inconsistent evidence based on factors such as mental illness or inconsistency in their evidence. The police, it should be stressed, did not have evidence that a crime had not happened. In these cases, the police did not have evidence that no crime had taken place. The researchers reanalysed the data using the relevant Home Office crime reporting rules. If the rules had been followed, according to Kelly *et al.* (2005), the rate of no crime or false allegations was only 3 per cent.

Such low rates contrast with what staff working in the criminal justice system believe. Saunders (2012) interviewed both police officers and Crown Court prosecutors in the UK. They appeared to think that false allegations are rather more common than research suggests. Academics generally argue that false allegation rates are low and that the inflated estimates of the police simply reflect biases by the criminal justice system against victims of rape. Academics need to be rather more forthcoming about what should be included in estimates which would yield very different outcomes from data based on police crime recording procedures. Researchers, however, need to clarify just how they know that the offence did or did not actually occur. Saunders argues that studies which require positive evidence that the crime did not occur tend to result in relatively low estimates of the rates of false allegations – typically in the range of 2 to 11 per cent of cases. This might be the end of it except that these studies do not systematically investigate false allegations of rape. Instead, they often merely subject police 'no criming' decisions to scrutiny.

A 'no crime' decision should be made, according to the Home Office rules, when the reported incident is subsequently found to involve further verifiable evidence to indicate that a notifiable crime had not actually been committed. Saunders argues that this cannot be equated with a definition of false allegation. She says that it merely indicates when the rules say that a reported crime may be struck off of the total tally of reports for this sort of crime. A good example of the sort of allegation not included in 'no crime' statistics are the cases in which the false allegation actually goes to trial. Perhaps that figure would be the most important of all to know. Saunders interviewed police and prosecutors about false allegations. Their understanding of a false allegation is one where no crime had been committed. However, the police and prosecutors did not stick to this. For example, they also talked of genuine rapes in which the victim's account was not entirely true as if it were a false allegation. In some cases, the accuser's account was entirely false – such as when it eventually transpires that the alleged perpetrator was on holiday. But it was common to find police and prosecutors referring to cases as false allegations where the victim's account was not completely true though parts of the events narrated actually happened. This leads Saunders to make a distinction between 1) the false complaint and 2) the false account. A false account does not mean that no rape occurred. One of Saunders' examples was of a woman who accused the wrong man of rape because she said she was afraid of naming the actual perpetrator! It became clear to Saunders that the police and prosecutors saw false allegations as being relatively rare. Nevertheless, they believed that partially or entirely false accounts of events were common and this influenced their perceptions of rape victims.

Pathways to false allegations

Beliefs about rape allegations have changed over past decades. Historically, the presumption was to blame the victim of sexual crimes and to treat the offence as trivial. The phrase *pseudologia phantastica* was once use to refer to the hypothetical condition in which a woman in a deluded state falsely believes that she has been raped (Bessmer, 1984). Historically, the general belief was that women 'cry rape' and make false allegations for reasons of revenge and so forth. Famously, Sir Matthew Hale, a chief justice in England, writing in the seventeenth century, remarked that true rape is a detestable crime warranting to be punished by death but it is an easy accusation to make and hard to prove. Furthermore, it is a crime that the accused will find hard to defend. These sentiments formed the basis of instructions to juries in rape cases until well into the twentieth century. The current preference is to assume that victims of sexual crimes are telling the truth. The presumption, then, generally favours truth telling.

Child sexual abuse has been replete with examples of wrong accusations being made against parents and others. The reasons why such false allegations occur in the context of child sexual abuse include the following:

- In many cases, no physical evidence of sexual abuse can be detected. While penetrative sexual intercourse might damage the sexual organs or anus of a physically immature child, sexual abuse takes many other and less invasive forms. Almost certainly, oral sex will leave no physical signs. As a consequence, allegations may not be supported by medical evidence.
- What evidence there is often comes from interviews with relatively young children. Unskilled interviewing may generate false information from the child.
- Professionals and the public in general are sensitive about the dangers of abuse and feel it is important to protect children wherever possible. As a consequence, they may over react to things a child says.

Some family circumstances seem especially conducive to children making false allegations of sexual abuse (Lipian, Mills and Brantman, 2004). These include the following:

- During the course of divorce proceedings, one parent influences an impressionable child in some way to make false claims related to abuse.
- In dysfunctional families, an adolescent makes allegations of sexual abuse for secondary gain – for example, as a way of getting back or deflecting family outrage in family conflicts about a teenage pregnancy or unacceptable boyfriends/girlfriends.
- A child has learned from past abuse about the power that the disclosure of abuse brings. So years later they make an allegation of abuse which acts as a bombshell to try to stop something from happening that they don't want to happen.
- The child in a dysfunctional but non-abusive family makes allegations of sexual abuse as a sort of cry for help.
- There can be contagion effects when other youngsters have come forward claiming abuse.

One cannot overestimate the extent of problems facing investigators in difficult child abuse cases, especially when young children are involved. Not only is independent evidence of sexual abuse often difficult to find but the offender is unlikely to confess. Lippert, Cross, Jones and Walsh (2010) are among the researchers who have studied the confession rates in those suspected of sexual abuse. Included among the cases studied were 38 per cent involving allegations of vaginal or anal intercourse. The children averaged nine years of age at the time of their abuse and 88 per cent were girls. During the stages of the criminal justice process only 30 per cent of the participants confessed either to the allegations in full or partially. This sort of figure is also typical of this sort of study although where polygraph testing is available in the community then confession is more likely. A number of factors seem to encourage confession: 1) when the suspect is young; 2) when there is a greater amount of evidence; 3) when the victim is older; 4) if it is a case of abuse outside of the family; 5) when the abuse is more severe; 6) if the child discloses the abuse fully; 7) if another child alleges abuse by the same person; and 8) where there is corroborating evidence. Quite clearly, then, in many cases the investigators can expect denial from the suspect since the optimum circumstances for a confession simply are not present.

Psychological research has yet to embrace the full range of motivations and processes involved in producing false accusations. A useful perspective on the complexity of false allegations is O'Donohue and Bowers' (2006) theoretical analysis of sexual harassment allegations. They propose a number of pathways which can be involved lying, psychosis, substance abuse, dementia, false memories, false interpretations, biased interviews and mistakes in the investigation. Most of these pathways can be complex in themselves. So, for example, what are the reasons why people knowingly lie by making false allegations of sexual harassment? They include the possibility of financial gain; that some people enjoy the status of being a victim; simply to hurt an individual or organisation; and to serve as an excuse for poor work performance.

This line of largely speculative theorising has been extended by Engle and O'Donohue (2012) by including psychological conditions conducive to false allegations of sexual assault. It has to be stressed that actual evidence supporting each of these pathways is, at best, limited. However, the list is important since its primes us to look at a number of possible routes to making a false allegation. Some of these are less obvious than a consideration of motivational factors alone would suggest. Their suggestions about factors leading to false allegations are:

- *Lying for conscious and unconscious secondary gain*: This is the usual pathway considered when false allegations are suspected. Examples of this would be to make difficulties for the accused or to make an excuse for a pregnancy.
- *Denial of consent for the sexual contact:* Sexual relationships are not formal contracts and consent may be expressed non-verbally. So there is room for mistakes and misunderstandings though some offenders may take advantage of this possibility by deliberately misunderstanding their victim's intention. Consent for one sort of sexual activity may be withdrawn for another. So the legal issue may well be not that of whether or not sexual activity took place but whether consent was given.
- *A false memory:* Research has now shown that false memories may be formed in certain circumstances. As a consequence, false memories of sexual assault may lead to false allegations.
- *Intoxication:* Alcohol and other drugs can lead to inadequate information processing. Perpetrators may use Rohypnol and amphetamines, for example, which can reduce a woman's resistance to sexual activity. Nevertheless, drugs may lead to confusion about what did and did not happen. According to Engle and O'Donohue (2012), in many states in the US a person cannot give consent to sexual intercourse in an intoxicated state. This is also the case in the United Kingdom (Sexual Offences Act, 2003) and elsewhere.
- *Antisocial personality disorder (or conduct disorder in adolescents):* This refers to a general pattern of violating and ignoring the rights of other people. Its diagnostic characteristics include deceitfulness, remorselessness, and nonconformity to social norms. These may encourage false reporting. People with this condition report being sexually victimised more often than other people and they are also more prone to being perpetrators (Burnam *et al.*, 1988).
- *Borderline personality disorder:* The features of this include impulsivity and interpersonal relationship difficulties, frequently involving feelings of abandonment. The individual may experience disturbances of cognition such as dissociation, extreme feelings of badness, and delusions/hallucinations. They can rapidly shift from idealising partners in relationships to devaluing them. This may result in them seeking revenge for past behaviours.
- *Histrionic personality disorder:* Widespread and excessive emotionality coupled with attention seeking are the main characteristics of this. Such individuals need to be the centre of attention and are uncomfortable otherwise. When interacting with other people, they may be inappropriately sexually provocative or seductive. A false allegation may be stimulating to them and they may misconstrue, say, a casual compliment as a sexual pass or accidental physical contact as deliberate.
- *Delirium:* This is a disturbance of consciousness involving cognitive changes which are not the product of dementia. Perceptual disturbances such as illusions and misinterpretation can be present. Causes include medical conditions and substance abuse. Sufferers need close supervision and care which might be construed by them, incorrectly, as sexual.
- *Psychotic disorders:* These are states characterised by delusions and hallucinations. A number of common delusions may be experienced – for example, erotomanic delusions that another person is in love with them. Not only are these beliefs irrational and unsubstantiated, they may involve a famous person. The condition can be associated with persecutory delusions. Hence the condition may lead to false allegations of a sexual kind.
- *Dissociation:* this refers to the absence of normal integration of cognitions into consciousness and memory. Memory, personality, identity etc. are split off from each other. It is related to fantasy-proneness, memory fragmentation and absent mindedness. Individuals may recall events that did not happen. So in sexual relationships they may fill in what is left out of their memory due to their dissociative state. Such manufactured material could be sexually abusive in nature and so lead to false allegations.
- *Intellectual disability:* Limited intellectual ability is associated with poor adaptive functioning. Consequently, the individual manifests social, work-related and self-care deficiencies. Disproportionately, they are victims of sexual assault. However, they are suggestible and otherwise vulnerable in interviewer influences. So they may readily agree with leading questions concerning possible sexual assaults against them.

The value of this list lies in possible indications that an investigator or court needs to be especially wary of possible false allegations. This is not a one-sided matter because such an extra-vigilant investigation may help be helpful in establishing the facts and so may lead to a decision to prosecute.

The recovered memory/ false memory debate

It is hard for the inexperienced to believe how, in some cases, bad interviewing technique can create false evidence. The psychiatrist Bernet (1997) described a case in which an allegation was made against a parent through repeated suggestive questions (i.e. leading questions). A babysitter developed suspicions about the family for whom she worked. As a precaution, she taped an interview she conducted with their child, known as Betsy, then five years of age. As a consequence, the parents were reported to child protection services and Betsy was removed from the family home for nearly two years. Generally speaking, repeated sessions of suggestive interviewing are not necessary to produce such effects. Notice how in the following extract the child very quickly begins saying untrue things. The babysitter had formed the opinion (or developed a theory) that Betsy was afraid of sweeping brushes or brooms because her parents played a game they called 'sweep the bootie' with her. There were several hundreds of questions on the tape. The following is representative of some of the things that could be heard on the tape:

Joyce: [the babysitter]: Okay. So Daddy plays sweeping the bootie with his hand. How does he use his hand? What does he do with his hand?
Betsy: Touches.
Joyce: He touches you. Did he touch your pee-pee where you go number one or did he touch where you go number two?
Betsy: Number two.
Joyce: Okay. You're saying he touched you where you go do-do at or where you go pee-pee at?
Betsy: Do-do.

(Bernet, 1997, p. 968)

Notice the way the babysitter gives forced-choice alternatives that gradually shape in the mind of the child the idea that the parents had molested the child's genitals and anus. The net effect of all of the questioning is that the parents appear to be being accused by the child of molesting her genitals and anus with a sweeping brush. Processes like this underlie the recovered memory/false memory debate.

The recovered memory/false memory issue has been one of the most controversial in modern psychology (Ost, Wright, Easton, Hope and French, 2013) It has involved arguments in courtrooms as well as the pages of academic journals. It is a long-standing matter which still attracts a degree of acrimony. A flavour of the debate can be seen in Kristiansen, Felton and Hovdestad's (1996) caution that beliefs about recovered/false memories are '[more] closely tied to autocratic misogynism and self-interest than they are to social values or science' (p. 56). It is an area where 'facts' seem to have been readily supplied for any position that one wishes to defend. The introduction of historic child abuse legislation is part of the backdrop to this. A very significant factor in the origins of the debate were the allegations made by an American professor of psychology, Jennifer Freyd (1996), against her parents, John and Pamela Freyd, concerning sexual abuse (Calof, 1993). These claims led to the False Memory Syndrome Foundation being set up. In adulthood, Freyd had undergone therapy and her recollections of the abusive events emerged following this. The basic issue is whether such memories are simply the product of suggestions made during psychotherapy by therapists (false memories) or reflect the uncovering of true childhood memories of repressed, stressful events (recovered memories). In other words, this is a two-step argument. The first step is that children subjected to sexual and other abuse deal with this trauma by a state of amnesia (blocking out memory) for the events; the second step is that therapists can reliably help an individual recover these memories. If these two steps are fulfilled, then recovered memory exists. However, if say therapists 'create' these memories in their client, then we have a situation where the memories are false. The so-called false memory syndrome is a severe psychopathology involving pseudo-memories relating to beliefs about early sexual abuse. It is identified in terms of a belief in such memories; patterns in their current interpersonal relationships; symptoms of trauma in their life history; and characteristics of their therapeutic experience (Hovdestad and Kristiansen, 1996a). Only a small proportion (less than about one in eight) of women with claims of recovered memories actually meet the diagnostic criteria for false memory syndrome. The central issue, then, in the recovered memory/false memory debate concerns therapists and their clients. One client has expressed this in the following terms:

> He [therapist] kept pressuring me by telling me that if I wanted to recover from my depression at that point and become a better mother, then I better look at these memories and do some work with them. He also thought if I left my children with their grandparents, they might be in danger. He kept insisting that I had all of the symptoms and I might as well admit it. He acted like he could see right through me and that he knew my story better than I did.
>
> (Ost, Costall and Bull, 2002, p. 4)

The recovered memory issue inevitably became important in legal settings. What has been a fairly acrimonious debate within psychology has been rehearsed in front of judges in many courtrooms. MacMartin and Yarmey (1998) regard the debate as being a dispute over who possesses the expertise on the matter. The battle involves confrontations between academic psychology (experimentalists for the most part) and clinician/practitioners (including clinical psychologists and psychiatrists):

- Support for the idea that recovered memories are reliable evidence of childhood sexual abuse comes largely from practitioners – the people who counsel the victims of abuse. They believe that, through repression and dissociation, early memories of real events become unavailable to memory. The writings and evidence of this category of expert suggest that repression and dissociation help the traumatised victim of sexual abuse defend themselves psychologically against the resulting psychological pain. Broadly speaking, repression is regarded as the burial of memories of abuse deep in the mind whereas dissociation is a sort of setting aside of memories normally available within our conscious experience. There are a variety of positions within the clinical perspective. The primary evidence for this idea is, of course, the case studies of recovered memories. There is also a long tradition in clinical theorising (starting with Freud and Janet) which adopts such a perspective. In addition, there are some examples from the research tradition of experimental laboratory studies that can be or have been used in support of this. While these do not directly study trauma – for obvious reasons – they include studies in which forgetting is directed under hypnosis and could be seen as evidence of similar processes. Sheehan (1997) suggests that the cases in which a woman has forgotten her abuse but the offender validates that she was abused are persuasive evidence of repression.
- Academic psychologists are more likely to be dismissive of the value of recovered memories as evidence of childhood abuse. Some of them, according to MacMartin and Yarmey (1998), claim that clinicians work with what could be described as 'robust repression'. Such clinicians are suggesting that repression in the clinical formulation screens off what is an accurate memory trace of the traumatic events of the sexual abuse. The difficulty with the notion of robust repression is that it relates poorly to the main theoretical assumptions of experimentalists researching memory. Experimentalists tend to view memory as a reconstruction that blends fact and fiction. Experimentalists may be rather more accepting of the notion of dissociation. Doubters of the veracity of recovered memories sometimes point out that a person in a dissociative state is usually aware that there is something missing from their memory. This does not seem to apply to the cases of recovered memories. These sceptics generally believe that there is no definitive evidence favouring repression and dissociation as applied to multiple repeated experiences of sexual abuse. One of the fiercest critics of the idea of recovered memories is Elizabeth Loftus (Loftus, Garry and Hayne, 2008), who views the evidence of the process of repression as crucial to the debate. She argues that 'there is no empirical evidence for repression and that claims of repression (in cases where the event really happened) are merely instances of plain old everyday forgetting' (p. 178). Nevertheless, she points out that the majority of people in forensic settings, such as judges (50 per cent), jurors (73 per cent) and police officers (65 per cent), believe that the phenomenon of repression exists (Benton, Ross, Bradshaw, Thomas and Bradshaw, 2006) whereas only 22 per cent of psychologists of a scientific orientation did.

While not feeling able to prefer one side of the debate over the other, Memon and Young (1997) stress the importance of exploring the possible mechanisms of recovered memories. Their conclusions echo those of others:

- They describe the 'grand' idea of repression to be of dubious validity if by repression we mean something other than the gradual forgetting of events.
- Repression (in the sense of cognitive/emotional processes which essentially 'keep the lid' on events and memories that we would otherwise remember) lacks supporting laboratory evidence convincingly mimicking the process.
- There is evidence in favour of the ideas that memories may be suppressed, the dissociation of memories (as in multiple personality disorder) and inhibition.

Flashbulb memories, it should be mentioned, can be the result of highly emotional events and they can be highly accurate forms of memory (Brown and Kulik, 1977). This is in contrast, of course, to the idea that emotional events are repressed.

Of course, sceptics have to explain how false memories are created and the mechanism by which these 'memories' are recovered. This may be through a retrieval process of the sort that has frequently been described in the research literature. An especially graphic example of this is a study by Loftus and Pickrell (1995). Their study involved stories apparently recalled by older relatives about the early childhood of each participant. Three of the stories were in fact true recollections by the relatives, but the fourth one was untrue. The participants remembered 68 per cent of the true stories. Many fewer claimed to remember the fictitious events but, nevertheless, a quarter of them indicated that they at least partially remembered the fictitious

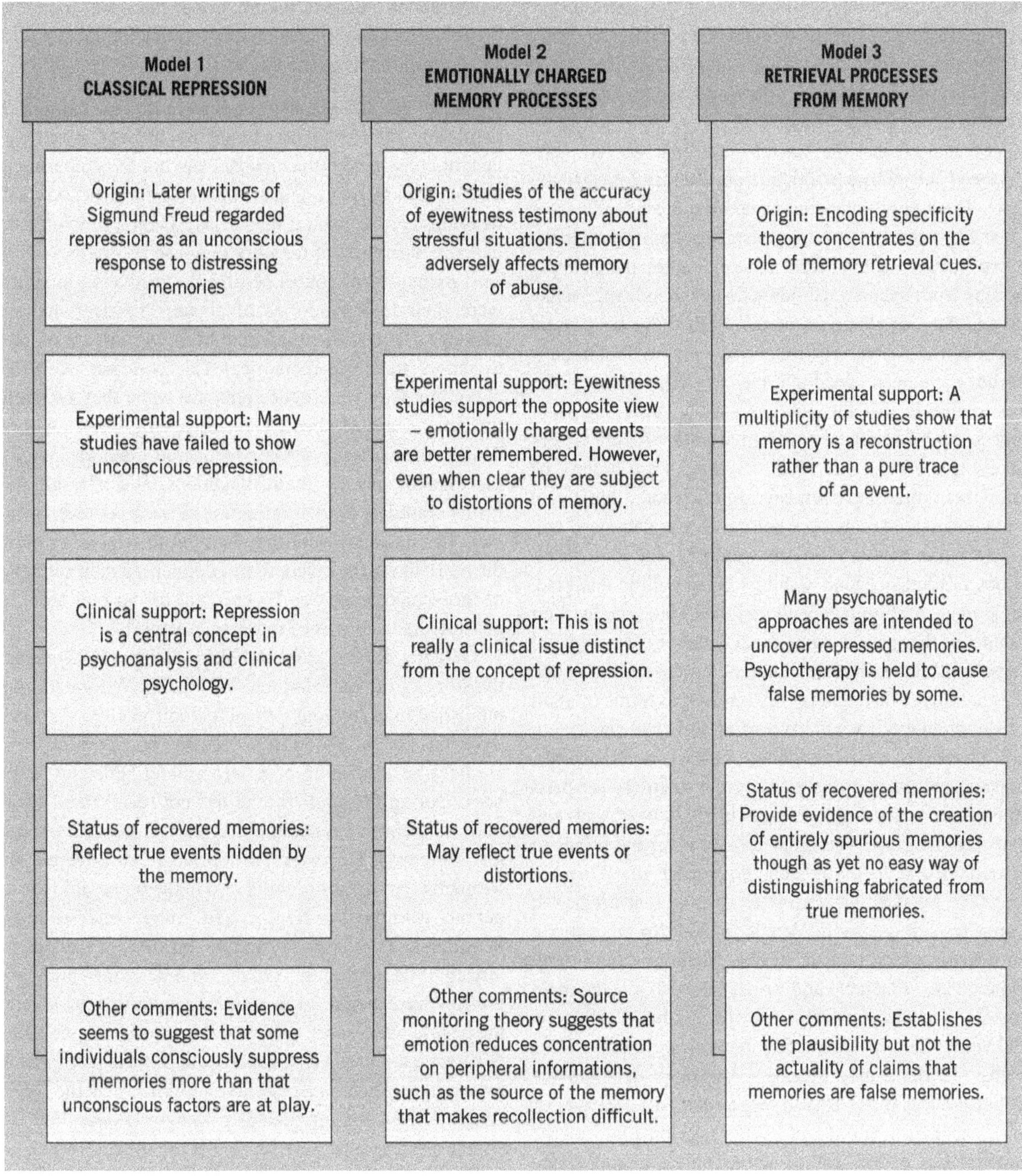

Model 1
CLASSICAL REPRESSION
Model 2
EMOTIONALLY CHARGED
MEMORY PROCESSES
Model 3
RETRIEVAL PROCESSES
FROM MEMORY
Origin: Later writings of Sigmund Freud regarded repression as an unconscious response to distressing memories
Origin: Studies of the accuracy of eyewitness testimony about stressful situations. Emotion adversely affects memory of abuse.
Origin: Encoding specificity theory concentrates on the role of memory retrieval cues.
Experimental support: Many studies have failed to show unconscious repression.
Experimental support: Eyewitness studies support the opposite view – emotionally charged events are better remembered. However, even when clear they are subject to distortions of memory.
Experimental support: A multiplicity of studies show that memory is a reconstruction rather than a pure trace of an event.
Clinical support: Repression is a central concept in psychoanalysis and clinical psychology.
Clinical support: This is not really a clinical issue distinct from the concept of repression.
Many psychoanalytic approaches are intended to uncover repressed memories. Psychotherapy is held to cause false memories by some.
Status of recovered memories: Reflect true events hidden by the memory.
Status of recovered memories: May reflect true events or distortions.
Status of recovered memories: Provide evidence of the creation of entirely spurious memories though as yet no easy way of distinguishing fabricated from true memories.
Other comments: Evidence seems to suggest that some individuals consciously suppress memories more than that unconscious factors are at play.
Other comments: Source monitoring theory suggests that emotion reduces concentration on peripheral informations, such as the source of the memory that makes recollection difficult.
Other comments: Establishes the plausibility but not the actuality of claims that memories are false memories.

Figure 16.1 Possible mechanisms of repressed memories

events. Figure 16.1 provides a summary of some of the possible mechanisms of repressed memory.

What is generally known about adult recall of things from childhood may help us set limits as to what we expect about memory from different stages of childhood. This knowledge may also be useful when trying to assess the veracity of adults' claims of abuse in their childhood. Historic sex abuse involve an adult's recollection of abuse that may have occurred many years earlier when that person was a child or adolescent – sometimes in the first few years of life. These cases may involve no other evidence. The adult supplies a witness statement to the police which involves first of all free recall of the events by the adult but then they answer detailed questions such as what they felt at the time, what the accused person was wearing, information about conversations, and the time at which the abuse occurred. The police officer asks for details over and over again and provides summarises the contents of the interview. According to Howe and Knott (2015) the product of this process is a detailed, elaborate and fluent description of what the adult believes to be the truth. Yet these details refer to things which may have happened fifty or more years earlier in life. The question for Howe and Knott is just what is possible knowing what we know now about the development of memory.

They suggest that the sort of detail that we have just described is beyond an adults' memory ability for early life events. The sort of rich detail sometimes provided in cases of historic sexual abuse suggests most strongly that the adult is reconstructing from memory rather than simply reporting from memory. Children do not encode things like time and date into their memories. So if these are present in recollections from early childhood then the likelihood is that they have been added into memory. The counterargument to this is that the adult is simply retrieving from memory things which they put into in adult terms. It is very unlikely that a child will recall anything from before the age of about three and even later. Furthermore, things that are not understood properly when they are experienced will be distorted in memory. So one would expect adult recollections of things beyond a child's grasp will be distorted. People may recall things from childhood but usually their accounts of these are lacking much detail about peripheral things. So if memories from childhood seem to be rich and fluent narratives then this is very unusual in terms of adult recall of childhood events. According to Howe and Knott, adult memories from childhood consist of fragments, things are presented in the wrong order, memory for parts of the events is missing, context is likely to be absent, and details are incorrect. The brain adds in plausible things to the memory but the adult does not realise that they are doing this. So it is not correct to assume that a detailed account providing specific details is likely to be accurate than a fragmentary, undetailed one. Memories from early childhood are vulnerable and we are left with just the main elements. The detail may simply be the brain doing its usual work when reconstructing memories. So the reverse of what we think may be true – the more detail in the account the less likely it is to be correct. After the age of about ten, then memories of events take on more of the characteristics of the mature autographical memory system. Comprehension of the more complex concepts of emotion, for example, may be beyond, say, a four-year-old. So it might not be expected that an adult recollects some aspects of emotion surrounding childhood events if the events occurred early in life.

Not only are claims of recovered memories made, they are also sometimes retracted. De Riviera (1997) suggested that retraction of claims of abuse may be the result of a set of circumstances in the creation of these memories:

- an authority figure used techniques of emotional, information, behavioural and thought control to control their thoughts;
- the client creates a narrative that helps put their lives into a meaningful systematic structure aided by a few suggestions from the therapist.

Ost *et al.* (2002) also studied retractors. Almost by definition, their evidence might be suspect, given their lack of consistency (the change from not remembering the events, then recovering memories of the events and finally denying their recovered memories). Only a few retractors had any indication of memory of abuse before they recovered memories of abuse. Mostly the recovered memories were their first memories of abuse. The overwhelming majority claimed that there had been *no* pressure on them to retract the false memories. This contrasts with their claim that they were under pressure when they recovered their memories of abuse. Generally, they were not confident in the veracity of their recovered memories even at the time of making their allegations. Virtually all were firmly confident in their retraction of the recovered memories. The more pressure they had felt to remember abuse, the more likely they were to be confident in their retraction of those memories. See Figure 16.2 for an outline of the possible mechanisms of repressed memories.

Geraerts, Raymaekers and Merckelbach (2008) recount the story of famous clarinettist Binjamin Wilomirski who published his autobiographical memoir in 1996. In this he describes his childhood in a German concentration camp. He became something of a hero among Holocaust survivors. During his adult life he did not recall these events until he went through something called dream interpretation therapy. However, a journalist discovered that Binjamin had spent his childhood in the home of his foster parents who lived in Switzerland! Some began to regard Wilomirski as a fabricator but he, himself, remained convinced of the truth of his childhood ordeal. Research laboratories have begun to examine the question of whether the people who report 'recovered' memories might also be those who are prone to the induction of false memories by researchers. There is a cognitive test known as the Deese-Roediger-McDermott (DRM) paradigm (Deese, 1959) in which participants look at a list of words which are strongly associated with another word not included on the list. This word is the *critical lure* and reflects the essential features of the whole list. Geraerts *et al.* (2008) give the example of the list 'awake', 'bed', 'rest', 'tired', etc. and its critical lure word 'sleep'. Tested later, some people claim to have seen the critical lure word 'sleep' among the words presented on the list. In fact, they tend to 'remember' the word 'sleep' as well as any of the presented words in the middle of the list.

People who had experienced recovering child sexual abuse memories tended to erroneously recall the critical lure as being on the list compared with a control group of people with no history of abuse or those who had been

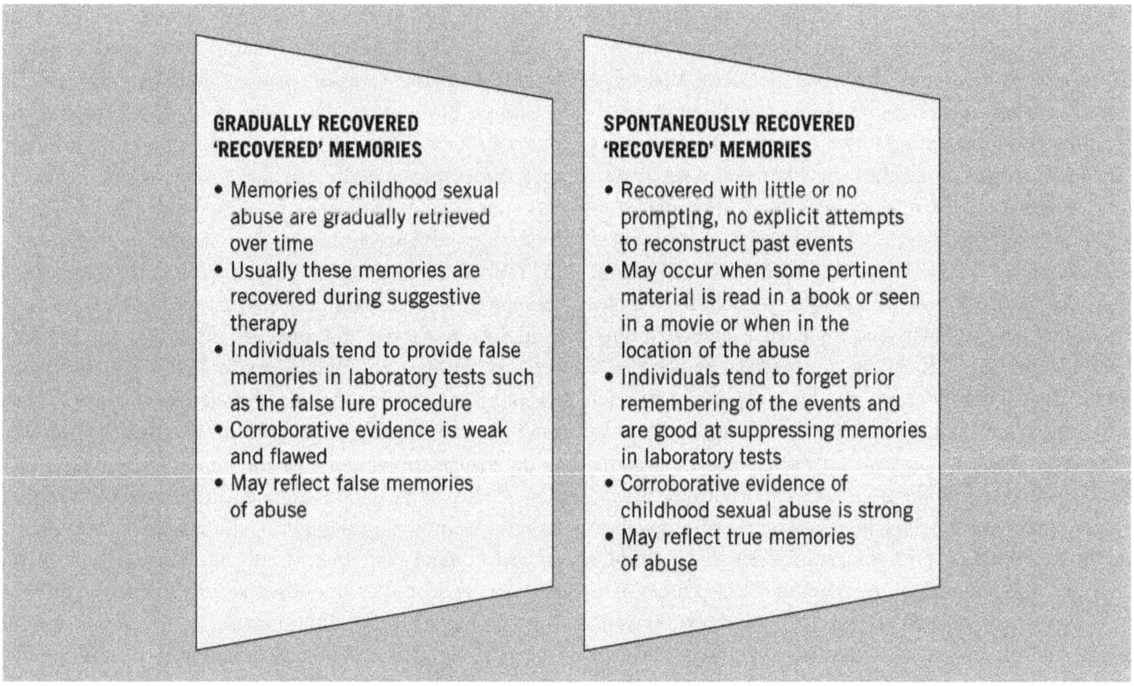

GRADUALLY RECOVERED 'RECOVERED' MEMORIES

- Memories of childhood sexual abuse are gradually retrieved over time
- Usually these memories are recovered during suggestive therapy
- Individuals tend to provide false memories in laboratory tests such as the false lure procedure
- Corroborative evidence is weak and flawed
- May reflect false memories of abuse

SPONTANEOUSLY RECOVERED 'RECOVERED' MEMORIES

- Recovered with little or no prompting, no explicit attempts to reconstruct past events
- May occur when some pertinent material is read in a book or seen in a movie or when in the location of the abuse
- Individuals tend to forget prior remembering of the events and are good at suppressing memories in laboratory tests
- Corroborative evidence of childhood sexual abuse is strong
- May reflect true memories of abuse

Figure 16.2 Two types of recovered memory claims (Geraerts *et al.*) 2008

abused but had never forgotten these events (also Clancy, Schacter, McNally and Pitman, 2000). Of course, such a research procedure may be criticised for its artificiality compared to the recovered memory phenomenon – a problem which Geraerts *et al.* partially address by using more emotional, sexually charged lures such as 'assault', 'rape' and 'violence'. Much the same findings emerged, with people claiming recovered memories of sexual abuse believing that they remembered the (emotional) lure as being on the list. Case examples suggest that some people who claim to have recovered memories of childhood sexual abuse had actually talked to others previously about this abuse. Although the other people clearly remember these discussions, the person themselves claims to have no recollection of these discussions and so believes that they had no recollection of the abuse since childhood until the memory was eventually recovered – apparently spontaneously.

According to Geraerts *et al.* (2008), interviews with those who had recovered memories suggested that there are two types of recovered memory, as illustrated in Figure 16.2:

- One type of recovered memory experience is fairly slow and is usually associated with involvement in suggestive therapies, including hypnosis. This is the gradual type of recovered memory.
- The second type of recovered memory is much quicker and almost takes the individual by surprise. This is the spontaneous type of recovered memory.

The two types may begin to explain why some adult recoveries of memories of childhood abuse seem to be accurate, whereas others seem to be false. In order to examine this further, the following four groups of participants were used:

- a control group who had never claimed as an adult or child memories of child sexual abuse;
- a spontaneous recovery group who reported forgetting memories of their sexual abuse as a child with no prompting from others;
- a group who recovered memories of child sexual abuse during therapy perhaps encouraged by suggestive therapeutic techniques – that is, sexual abuse memories were actively reconstructed;
- a continuous memory group who had never forgotten their childhood experiences of sexual abuse.

It was expected that the group recovering memories of child sexual abuse during suggestive therapy would be particularly prone to showing source monitoring deficiencies as assessed by the DRM or false lure test and that the spontaneous memory recovery group would show a tendency to underestimate their prior remembering of events as assessed by the false lure test. The spontaneous recovery group was expected to be more capable of suppressing memories when asked to do so under laboratory conditions. Both of these expectations proved to be correct. Of course, the implication is that the memories recovered under suggestive therapy are mistaken and fabricated whereas the spontaneously recovered memories are not really recovered memories at all but memories that have been accessed before and forgotten about (see Figure 16.2).

It is intriguing the extent to which psychologist practitioners such as clinical psychologists believe in recovered memories and have experience of clients who claim to have them. There are a number of relevant studies but a good example is that of Ost, Wright, Easton, Hope and French (2013). They surveyed online the beliefs of chartered clinical psychologists and a separate sample of hypnotherapists in the UK about recovered memory and possible false memory amongst other topics. Although they had quite substantial samples, the response rate was quite poor at about 12 per cent for both samples so some caution is needed about the findings. As part of the survey, the participants were asked how many clients they had seen who had reported past amnesia for abuse which they came to recall. A quarter of the combined sample claimed to have experience of such clients. Quite high proportions said that such memories were accurate. Only just over a quarter said that such reports with either 'never' or 'rarely' true. Over a fifth said that such memories were 'usually' or 'always' true. They were also asked whether it was possible for a person could come to the false belief that they had been abused. Over a third of those responding said that personally they had had such clients. Ost *et al.* interpret their data as suggesting that a proportion of practitioners hold beliefs which most memory researchers would view as dubious.

The flurry of experiments designed to show that in the laboratory what appear to be illusory memories could be created have received an evaluative review by Brewin and Andrews (2017). Three broad types of experimental procedure have been used to demonstrate illusory memory creation some of which have been illustrated already in this chapter. These are: 1) false feedback studies in which participants are told that they are likely to have experienced a particular event; 2) imagination inflation studies in which the participant imagines and re-imagines over again an event which was fictitious; and 3) memory implantation studies in which the truth of a suggested false event is supported either by parents and other family members or by the use of individually manipulated photographs appearing to confirm that the event happened. This resulted in claims that it is easy to induce false memories or that a relatively high proportion of people are susceptible to such false memories. Of course, these conclusions are understandable if merely thinking about falsehoods about one's past can create false memories. But, of course, this assumes a lot of things such as the participants were convinced that these false memories were real. It is hard to make this decision. Brewin and Andrews point out that it is possible to know that something occurred (e.g. from family photos) without one being able to recollect that experience. So belief that something happened in the past is different from recall of that incident. Brewin and Andrews argue that there are three different types of memory judgement. The first is an autobiographical belief that something actually occurred. The second is that the individual has recollections of that experience. Finally, there is confidence in that reality of their recollections. If the individual does not have confidence in the truth of their recollections this is termed 'partial memory'. Brewin and Andrews reviewed the research literature on the three types of study in the light of these three different types of memory judgement. Memory implantation studies largely relied on recollective belief with little by way of follow-up to determine the veracity of the belief. Imagination inflation studies largely concentrated on the autobiographical belief. Memory implantation studies have not demonstrated copious amounts of full autobiographical memories as opposed to recollective experiences. In brief, Brewin and Andrews do not find a lot to support the idea that it is easy to create false memories of childhood in experimental participants. This, however, is not the end of it since some, at least, experimental participants seem to meet all three of Brewin and Andrews's memory judgement criteria and may be susceptible to false memories in real life. At best, based on memory implantation studies, a little under 50 per cent of participants showed some recollection for the implanted events according to Brewin and Andrews. But these largely meet the description of partial memories. Full memories seem to be induced into only 15 per cent of experimental participants.

Of course, such a conclusion is controversial especially among memory researchers who favoured the idea that false memories are easily induced. Criticisms of Brewin and Andrews' work varied from moderately supportive, through the questioning to the downright hostile. Some support for Brewin and Andrews came from Pezdek and Bladon-Gitlin (2017) who argued that it is far harder to implant false memories than true ones. For McNally (2017) the problem with their estimate of 15 per cent was that it fails to take into account factors in the psychotherapy setting such as the level of dissociation manifested by the client and the belief that it is possible through therapy to recover otherwise repressed memories. These characteristics of the therapeutic situation would increase the percentage susceptible to false memories. On the other hand, Smeets, Merckelbach, Jelicic and Otgaar (2017) regard the 15 per cent figure as alarmingly high rather than being low as Brewin and Andrews so. Becker-Blease and Freyd (2017) argue that the idea of false memory lacks clarity since it fails to distinguish between memory accuracy and memory accessibility. These should be seen as separate dimensions. So memories which have ceased to be hidden, memories which are unavailable, and memories which have continuously been available should be regarded as different things. Others argue that it is surprising that the rather minimal procedures of the experimental studies so effectively induce false memories (Nash, Wade, Garry, Loftus and Ost (2017). This contrasts markedly with the hours and weeks of suggestion that the clinical therapist is able to deliver to their clients. Nash *et al.* further argue that the original paper by Brewin and Andrews should not have been published as it did not meet the requirements of peer review processes for journal publication. So fierce were some of the criticisms that Andrews and Brewin (2017) were left wondering whether scientific debate was being suppressed. What is very clear from this is that false memory/recovered memory research remains a fraught and conflictful as it has since the first research was published in the 1990s.

Research into recovered memories can be a minefield, as epitomised by the experiences of Elizabeth Loftus (Geis and Loftus, 2009). Briefly, Loftus is somewhat sceptical of the idea that there are repressed memories of sexual abuse which can be recovered or retrieved during therapy. She was interested by a published article by a psychiatrist concerning the pseudonymous 'Jane Doe' who was first interviewed at five years of age and again at the age of 17 years. Jane Doe had putatively recovered memories of sexual abuse by her mother. Loftus and Guyer (2002) reviewed this article and critically evaluated the evidence that it contained. A psychiatrist involved in this case had claimed that Jane Doe's experiences represented an example of recovered memories (Corwin and Olafson, 1997). One oddity was that Jane Doe had been known to the mental health authorities since she was a young child and had told them of the abuse by her mother – and of abuse by her father which she eventually retracted. There was documentary evidence that the allegations were repeated. However, the psychiatrist claimed that Jane Doe had suffered traumatic amnesia and the abuse was eventually revealed during interviews with him. Loftus and Guyer decided to track down Jane Doe, which they did from clues to her identity in video of the interviews and so forth. On the basis of their investigations, Loftus and Guyer (2002) not only doubted the evidence of recovered memories but also whether the alleged abuse had ever happened.

Jane Doe sued Loftus and Guyer and others for alleged harms that had been done to her in terms of emotional distress, defamation and invasion of privacy among other things. The basis of the claim of defamation was that Loftus had supposedly publicly questioned Jane Doe's mental health and fitness. The point of describing all of this is not only that it led to lengthy proceedings against Loftus and others in the courts but it also led to obstacles being placed before Loftus and Guyer's academic research by their then respective academic institutions. Recovered memory and false memory research has been a tricky, thorny road indeed for academic researchers.

Ultimately one might asked if it is necessary to be pro or con either false memories and recovered memories. The evidence for one does not invalidate the reality of the other. Gleaves and Smith (2004) following their review of the literature came to the conclusion that there was good, tangible evidence in support of both.

False claims of abuse and young children

A little different from the issue of false memories of abuse is the evidence that children, during the course of being interviewed, may be encouraged by the interviewer to claim that things happen which didn't. Interest in this grew in the 1980s with the McMartin School case in the US and others. In this preschool children seemed to be making accusations of satanic abuse and teachers were accused of kidnapping them and taking them by helicopter to a remote farmstead and forcing them to have group sex! Charges against the teachers were all eventually dropped. Using interviewing methods based on recordings of the original interviews with the McMartin School children, such as reinforcing children by suggesting, for example, that they had good memories, it was possible to extract false accusations from children (Garven, Wood and Malpass, 2000). It seems relatively easy to demonstrate how false claims of abuse can be obtained from preschool children (e.g. Bruck *et al.*, 1995; Ceci, Loftus, Leichman and Bruck, 1994). Essentially, researchers interview children about events that had happened to the child and also what were actually fictions (according to the child's parents). The studies involved, for example, a fictitious episode in which the child was supposed to have caught his or her finger in a mousetrap. As a consequence, a hospital visit was necessary to deal with the injury. For all (or the vast majority) of children in the studies these events had not happened. During the course of an interview, children were read a list of things that might have happened to them. They were required to think hard about each of them and to try to remember if the event really did occur.

How resistant are preschool children to the pressure of the interview? About a third of children accepted fictitious events as real. This percentage remained much the same when they were interviewed on several occasions. There was some inconsistency since a number of the children switched one way or the other at each stage, balancing the changes in each direction. If the children were told by the interviewer that the fictitious events really did happen to the child, there were increases in the percentage of the children accepting the fictitious experiences as real (Ceci *et al.*, 1994). The extent of 'false memory induction' depended somewhat on the age of the child. Children who accepted the fictitious event as real would sometimes provide additional detail about the events. The event would be elaborated and they would describe the emotional feelings associated with it.

Of course, such evidence as this is only suggestive of the extent to which, in interview conditions, young children confuse fiction with fact. Limitations include the following:

- This age group is not representative of those involved in sexual abuse allegations and false memory induction may not apply to these older children.
- The questioning by the interviewers in these studies went way beyond what would be expected in a police interview or social work interview of a child involved in possible sexual abuse.

That is to say, the findings of the studies might not generalise to real-life situations. In order to disregard the suggestion in the question, the child must be able to do the following, according to Poole and Lindsay (1998): 1) understand that the interviewer actually wants them to report only their individual, personal experiences and 2) know what the sources of their knowledge actually are (i.e. they require source monitoring ability). Given this, Poole and Lindsay's *Mr Science* study was an important experiment. In essence, this can be summarised as follows:

- At school, a group of three- and four-year-olds experienced vivid science lessons given by Mr Science.
- Very soon afterwards, they were interviewed and requested to tell the interviewer everything about the science lesson. Their reports were extremely accurate and very few of them made false claims.
- Three months later, the parents of the children were sent a storybook to read to their child. It contained descriptions of the *Mr Science* lessons that had actually happened, but also descriptions of lessons that had not happened. The fictitious material, for example, describes how the child was touched by Mr Science who then put a 'yucky' object in their mouth. The stories were told to the child three times.
- This was followed by another interview session in which open-ended and then leading questions were put to the child about whether or not the events were real or just from one of the stories.

The major findings from the study were as follows:

- Two out of every five children mentioned as if real events that originated only in the stories.
- Leading questions increased the rates of false reporting. Over half of all children answered yes to a question about whether Mr Science had put something 'yucky' into their mouths. When requested by the interviewer, the majority of these children went on to describe details of the fictional event.
- The interview also included quite severe challenges to the children about the truth of what they said. Nevertheless, the majority of the children when challenged in this way continued to maintain that Mr Science had truly put a yucky thing into their mouth.
- Increasing the age range from three to eight years of age did not result in a decline in false reports. These remained stable in free recall conditions.
- Challenges about the truth of their claims meant declines in false claims for the older children but not the younger ones.
- There was a fairly high degree of stability in the false claims. Follow-up of those who had made false claims a month later revealed that two-thirds were still making the same false claims.

There is another important study which reinforces the view that even young children are somewhat resistant to suggestive or leading questioning. It also shows that, as children get older, even the simplest of challenges to their false claims rapidly produces recantation. Leichtman and Ceci (1995) had children aged three to six years watch as a stranger named Sam Stone visited their pre-school, walked about and left. They were interviewed four times about Sam Stone's visit. There was no leading or suggestive questioning up to this point. Then the children were asked about two fictitious events: did Sam Stone do anything to a book or a teddy bear? A high level of accuracy was produced. Only 10 per cent said that he did do something and this figure reduced to 5 per cent when they were asked if they actually saw him do it. When they were gently challenged about their false claims – 'You didn't really see him do anything to the book/teddy bear, did you?' – this figure declined further to 2.5 per cent. For the older children, this sort of questioning challenge was especially effective.

Another group of preschoolers was exposed to repeated conversations about Sam's clumsiness and proneness to breaking things. They were subsequently interviewed with suggestive questions such as 'Remember the time Sam Stone visited our classroom and spilled chocolate on that white teddy bear? Did he do it on purpose or was it an accident?' In the final interview:

- 72 per cent of the youngest preschoolers reported that Sam did something to the book or teddy;
- 44 per cent said they actually saw him do these things;
- 21 per cent maintained their false stories when gently challenged;
- 5–6-year-olds were less malleable since only 11 per cent said they actually saw the misdeeds and less than 10 per cent maintained that the story was true when challenged.

Forensically, the issue is more complex than this. Children in sexual abuse cases are in the hands of professionals such as the police, social workers, psychologists and psychiatrists, all of whom must form judgements and make decisions. So one question must concern us: just how good are professionals at detecting false information? Poole and Lindsay (1998) argue that the ability of professionals is relatively poor. For instance:

- When clinical and research psychologists specialising in interviewing children were shown videos of children in the mousetrap experiments described above, they were unable to differentiate between fictional and real experiences at better than the chance level (Ceci *et al.*, 1994).
- Horner, Guuyer and Kalter (1993) showed workers in the mental health field a two-hour case study containing interviews with the parents, interviews with the child and child–parent interaction, and they could request additional information. In addition, groups of the workers discussed the case together for over an hour. The researchers found no relationship between whether or not the health worker believed that child abuse had taken place and recommendations about future contact of the child with its father – they all recommended that the child–father contact should be supervised, irrespective of their judgements about abuse!

Bruck and Ceci (1997) construe the above research and others as evidence of the creation of suggestive interviews based on interviewer bias. Such biases are seen as involving a failure to challenge what children say when it supports the interviewer's preconceptions, and events inconsistent with the interviewer's preconceptions are not touched upon.

The concept of suggestibility has a long history in psychology but, perhaps more importantly, it is a notion familiar to professionals working in the criminal justice system and child protection. Over 100 years ago, William Stern (1904) regarded the predisposition to succumb to suggestion as suggestibility. Nevertheless, it was important to distinguish two different types of suggestion:

- *Active suggestion:* the activity of suggesting something to another person.
- *Passive suggestion:* the state of a person who is currently under the influence of suggestion.

These can be totally unrelated processes since 1) a suggestion may be made but *not* responded to, but 2) a suggestion which has *not* been made may be responded to. In other words, one cannot simply find a suggestion's influence in circumstances in which a suggestion has been made. According to Ceci and Bruck (1993), suggestibility refers to the extent to which all aspects of a child's memory for events are influenced by a variety of social and psychological factors. Suggestibility may influence the ways in which events are encoded into memory, the processes of retrieving the memory, and just what is reported to others in interviews and elsewhere. Thus it is a mistake to assume that suggestibility is exclusively the consequence of a particular interview or interview style.

Motzkau (2004) argues that 'suggestibility is itself suggestive' (p. 7), meaning that the widespread knowledge of the concept of suggestibility itself has an effect within the criminal justice system over and above what could be warranted by our current research-based knowledge. Some psychological concepts spread into common knowledge among other professions and the general public. The public finds out about psychological ideas in part through the media. Of course, the concept as understood by the public may be quite a simplistic one and involve rather overstated accounts of the findings of research (Motzkau, 2004). So, for example, the general public may be led to believe that children are extremely suggestible and easily influenced by parents and misguided professionals into making allegations that are simply untrue. The danger in this is that because of high-profile cases in which children have made unfounded allegations of abuse, others will be reluctant to report the abuse simply because it is felt that no one will believe their story. As a consequence, there will be a decline in the number of reported child abuse cases. In Germany, argues Motzkau, people became concerned that the criminal justice system could be undergoing an 'epidemic' of false allegations of child sexual abuse, especially in relation to child custody disputes, since there had been a great deal of scientific, media and public interest in the issue of suggestibility. Objectively, this was totally unfounded as there were virtually no cases in which false allegations of sexual abuse were an issue. The issue focused on the disputed child custody cases in which allegations of abuse could result in unfair child custody decisions.

The important practical consequence of this can be illustrated by one of Motzkau's interviews with a police officer. The police had been called in by staff at a care home. A 12-year-old girl with a learning disability had apparently reported to one member of staff that another staff member had behaved inappropriately sexually towards her. The alleged perpetrator denied this. The police officer was concerned about his role as an interviewer, fearing that he might not have interviewed the girl correctly since she disclosed nothing about her apparent abuse. The officer was also apprehensive about interviewing the girl again since this repeated interviewing might devalue the evidence in the eyes of others. It finally emerged in a chance comment from a different child that the alleged perpetrator had actually accidentally hurt the putative victim of abuse with a food trolley. With this information, it was possible to clarify with the 'victim' that this was the incident that had resulted in the allegation. Furthermore, the staff member who had reported the matter to the police initially did not discuss it with the girl because she feared the suspicion that she had suggested the allegation to the girl in some way!

BOX 16.1 Forensic psychology in action

Testing for suggestibility

While it is extremely important to understand just how questioning styles, age and other factors influence responsiveness to suggestion, there is another fundamental issue – do certain individuals tend to be more suggestible than other people in more situations? That is, is it reasonable to regard suggestibility as a characteristic of the individual rather than the situation? Gudjonsson (2003) explored this route using the Gudjonsson Suggestibility Scale (Gudjonsson, 1984), which attempts to establish the general suggestibility level of an individual. Quite clearly, if suggestibility is a characteristic of individuals then a test that measures it would have potential in the context of the work of forensic psychologists. The Gudjonsson Suggestibility Scale is more than a questionnaire – it is a procedure in which the practitioner gives the individual material to learn and then examines the way in which that individual responds to leading questions and other pressures. The point is, however, that the procedures are reasonably standardised. The steps in the process are as follows:

- *Material presentation:* a tape-recording of a short piece of narrative is played to the person being assessed.
- *Immediate recall:* the person being assessed is requested to remember as much of the narrative as possible in as much detail as possible.
- *First asking of list of leading questions:* the assessor asks a standard list of 20 questions about the narrative. Fifteen of these questions are leading questions that imply an answer which is actually inaccurate. A score is computed, known as 'Yield 1', which is simply the number of the leading (inaccurate) questions that the person being assessed agrees with.
- *Negative feedback:* once the questions have all been answered, then the assessor says things like 'You have made a number of errors. It is therefore necessary to go through the questions once more, and this time try to be more accurate.' This is an attempt to influence the individual being assessed further.
- *Second asking of list of leading questions:* the assessor reads out the same list of leading questions again. After this stage, two additional different scores are calculated: 'Shift' is simply the number of questions that the person being assessed actually answers differently from the first time. It does not matter if the question is a leading question or one of the five other questions. 'Yield 2' is the number of leading questions which the person being assessed agrees with after the negative feedback. It indicates the direction of any change from the first leading question stage to the second.
- There is another measure – total suggestibility – which is simply the sum of 'Yield 1' + 'Shift'. Research suggests that 'Yield 1' and 'Shift' are two quite distinct aspects of suggestibility. They are independent dimensions. Of course, this is quite a complex assessment and it is perhaps not surprising to find that procedural differences may have some but not necessarily a crucial influence on the outcome. For example, the negative feedback can be expressed in a more or a less hostile fashion (Boon and Baxter, 2004). It is also valuable to know that it is difficult to fake suggestibility on Gudjonsson's test (Baxter and Bain, 2002) since of course it would be in some offenders' interests to be able to appear suggestible when they are not. Some participants in a study were requested to pretend to act like a suggestible person on the test. The researchers found that it was possible to fake suggestibility well on the 'Yield 1' measure but, having done this, the participants' 'Shift' scores did not correspond to the pattern of a suggestible person. So, quite clearly, the participants knew some of the things that they needed to do in order to appear suggestible but they could not anticipate all of what was needed to put on an entirely convincing display.

Does the scale work with children? Scullin, Kanaya and Ceci (2002) studied an adaptation of the Gudjonsson measure which is known as the Visual Suggestibility Scale for Children. This is very similar except that the material is presented visually as well as aurally and a number of other modifications were made to ensure that the measure was suitable for this younger age range. What they did was to set up an independent field study in which the children were repeatedly interviewed about an event that occurred at school and things that did not actually happen. The question was, then, whether being influenced in these interviews actually was predictable on the basis of scores on the Visual Suggestibility Scale for Children. The 'Yield' and 'Shift' measures both independently predicted aspects of suggestibility in the field interviews.

Great care needs to be exercised over the question of the extent to which you children are suggestible. As we saw above, there is evidence that they can be influenced to make accusations that turn out to be simply untrue However, just because they may be influenced, say, by leading questioning does not mean that they are always influenced or that they are more susceptible to suggestion than older children or even adults. Similarly, just because young children may be susceptible to influence on some matters does not mean that they are equally susceptible on all matters. A good example of this is Eisen *et al.*'s (1998) research. They studied a group of children who had been hospitalised for several days for assessment of abuse. This involved a medical examination which included an analysis of their genitals and anus as well as an interview concerning their possible abuse or neglect. Before they left hospital, they were subjected to an interview which included misleading questions about the genital and anal examination and about other much more mundane matters. There were clearly signs that younger children were more susceptible to suggestion than older children. When asked suggestive questions about mundane matters, preschool children were led to give untruthful responses nearly one-third of the time whereas the figures for older children were half this and for teenagers a fifth of this. But when faced with leading questions on the topic of abuse such as 'The doctor did not have any clothes on, did he/she?' then preschool children succumbed one-fifth of the time, older children rarely and teenagers never. That is to say, that the youngsters were not so suggestible about the crucial issue of abuse.

There is little consistency across studies in terms of the percentages of children who succumb to suggestive questions. Poole and Lindsay (2002) describe the proportions across different studies which are affected by suggestive questioning as showing 'vast variability' (p. 369). Consequently, it is difficult and perhaps impossible to assess the likelihood that suggestion plays a role in real-life cases involving children. One remarkable suggestion Poole and Lindsay make is that there is a case for the use of leading questions in some circumstances. They urge professionals such as social workers not to use leading questions when working in areas where the baseline rates of abuse are low. Children disclose about abuse without interviewers using leading questions, which risk increasing the risk of false claims by the child. On the other hand, professionals working in areas where sexual abuse is common may be justified in using leading questioning as their 'hit' rate is likely to be high. They can reduce the risk of false information by the use of instructions or procedures which clarify to the child what is expected. For example, they can be told that they can give answers such as 'I don't understand' or 'I don't know.'

The problem with this is that it is difficult to make a judgement about just what proportion of false allegations is tolerable. If one seeks to minimise the number of false allegations then what Poole and Lindsay have to say is unacceptable. On the other hand, if the objective is to maximise the number of correct identifications of child sexual abuse then what they have to say is appropriate. These are not matters for psychology but are issues such as fairness, justice and ethics.

It should not be assumed on the basis of the studies of false claims by children that high base rates of falsehood are likely. The extent of false claims is dependent on the quality of the interviews with children. If good quality interviewing methods are used then false claims may be kept to a minimum or possibly eliminated entirely. One way of improving interviewing is to use the interview protocols produced for professional use. Hershkowitz, Lamb and Katz (2014) carried out a study of Israeli children in the age range of 4 to 13 years of age. All of them had been referred for investigation because of suspected child physical or sexual abuse by family members. They used the NICHD Investigative Interview protocol. (NICHD stands for National Institute of Child Health and Human Development and is an American organisation.) This is a research-based instrument which deals with the linguistic, cognitive and social factors which place limits on how informative children's accounts of child abuse are. It is designed to increase rapport within the interview with the child. For example, the interviewer expresses interest in what the child had been doing. Actually two different versions of the protocol were used – the standard version versus a revised version. It was found that the revised version of the protocol resulted in more allegations by the child than did the standard version of the protocol as well as improving rapport of the interviewer with the child.

Importantly, there became available independent evidence about any abuse that had taken place. About 56 per cent of the children made allegations about physical or sexual abuse in a sample of over 400 children. All of these were supported by the independent evidence – meaning that there were no false allegations made by the children. The use of the protocol led to allegations being made at a rate which was higher than would otherwise be expected. That is to say, the protocol seemed to encourage allegations which were true without there being any false allegations.

The diagnosticity of signs of abuse

Forensic and criminal psychologists and other clinicians usually spend their time forming judgements about a limited range of individuals. For example, they may work almost exclusively with sexually abused individuals. It is not surprising, therefore, to find that their expertise is largely limited to this group. They may take characteristics of such clients as indicators that there is a problem in people in general. For example, many of their sexually abused clients may report bed-wetting or enuresis in childhood and assume that this indicates a relationship between sexual abuse and bed-wetting. In other words, the psychologist may come to believe that bed-wetting is symptomatic of child sexual abuse. The trouble is that this is an illusory correlation since no comparisons are being made with non-abused children. If the psychologist dealt with non-abused individuals then he or she might well find that bed-wetting is just as common in this group. Hence bed-wetting would have no power to differentiate between the abused and the non-abused.

So clinical experience may result in practitioners having false beliefs that certain indicators are signs of abuse. Denials by a child that they have been abused do not always seem to carry the evidentiary weight that might have been expected had the denial been made, say, by an adult. It is widely assumed that children are reluctant to disclose abuse for many reasons. A study, in Texas, took children in the age range of pre-school to 18 years on the files of the local child protection service (Bradley and Wood, 1996). Nearly three-quarters of them had already disclosed to someone that they had been abused. Only later did most of them come to the attention of the police or the child protection service. Denial of abuse by the children was rare, at 6 per cent of the cases. The recantation by the child of their claim to have been abused was also rather rare, at 4 per cent of the cases. One simple lesson to be drawn from these statistics is that children who deny abuse are probably not hiding the fact that they have been abused. It is more likely that abuse simply did not happen.

Berliner and Conte (1993) argue for caution when implementing the conclusions of studies that find a greater prevalence, say, of behavioural disorders in clinical samples of sexually abused individuals than in community controls. Most behavioural correlates of abuse are non-specific to abused children. That is to say, there are few, if any, factors that manifest themselves only in the behaviours of sexually abused children. Furthermore, the behavioural differences between abused and non-abused children are rather stronger when the behaviour is assessed through parents' ratings than when they are assessed through the children's ratings. It is possible, then, that the parents are aware of the possibility of abuse and consequently their ratings are affected by that knowledge. In this context, some of the indicators that have been claimed to be characteristic of sexually abused children do *not* emerge in the self-reports of those children. These are depression, anxiety and low self-esteem.

A key concept in understanding false allegations is that of diagnosticity. Broadly speaking, this is the extent to which certain features of a child's behaviour indicate that he or she has been sexually or physically abused (but see below). Howitt (1992) listed some of the many factors that have been suggested to be indicative of abuse. Textbooks for teachers about abuse, for example, sometimes suggest that regularly being late for school is a sign of abuse. Medics in Cleveland, location of the first major sexual abuse scandal (Butler-Sloss, 1988), similarly accepted that the response of a child's anus to being touched by a doctor was a sign that that child had actually been abused (Hanks, Hobbs and Wynne, 1988). These are examples of the indicators approach to the identification of sexual abuse.

Their use may be flawed in practice, but it is encouraged by research findings. For example, Slusser (1995) reviewing six studies concluded that overt sexual behaviour that is inappropriate for a child of that age is an indicator of sexual abuse. Nevertheless, any practitioner working with children should be aware that the baseline rates of childhood sexual activities are sometimes high. Gordon, Schroeder and Abrams (1990a,b) obtained parental reports on two- to seven-year-olds:

- 29 per cent of the families claimed that their child had been exposed to sexually explicit materials;
- half of the children were known to have masturbated;
- 30 per cent of the children had been involved in exploratory sex-play.

The value of any indicator of sexual abuse is dependent on the following factors:

- The frequency of this possible indicator of sexual abuse in the group in question;
- The frequency of the indicator in similar but non-abused children.

It is particularly important for an indicator to be common among abused children but rare or non-existent among non-abused children. Very often, the relative frequency of the indicator in the population is unknown. Diagnosticity of a sign of sexual abuse depends on how common the sign is in abused children compared with its frequency in non-abused children. If the sign is equally common in both groups of children then it is useless in the diagnosis of sexual abuse. Munchausen's syndrome by proxy is a condition in which the offender fabricates symptoms and may deliberately injure a child in order to obtain repeated medical attention (Plassman, 1994). Some of the suggested indicators of the syndrome are actually diametric opposites (Howitt, 1992). So, for example, it has variously been suggested that evidence of the syndrome is demonstrated by confession to the crime but also by denial of the crime, or by over-concern about the child's health on the part of the parent as well as unconcern about the child's health!

A study of paediatric psychologists (Finlayson and Koocher, 1991) suggested that their interpretation of the extent to which an indicator may be indicative of abuse varies enormously. The psychologists were, for example, given a short description of a child whose school performance declined fast, who wet its bed, who was saying things about a bad man and who became anxious at the prospect of separation from its parents. On the basis of this evidence, 9 per cent believed that the likelihood of abuse was above 75 per cent certain, and 35 per cent suggested that the probability of abuse was less than 25 per cent certain. According to Slusser (1995), certain indicators, such as bed-wetting, may be the result of a multiplicity of different aetiologies. Consequently, especially because they are common among children (i.e. high base rate of occurrence), these indicators are of little diagnostic value at all. Why is this?

The diagnosticity issue is illustrated in Table 16.1. This shows the possible outcomes of using an indicator to predict whether abuse has occurred. For an indicator to be useful, true positives and true negatives should be maximised but false positives and false negatives should be kept to the minimum. Otherwise, the guilty will escape detection and the innocent will be falsely accused.

The lack of knowledge of how common an indicator is in the non-abused population affects the confidence that one can have in its diagnosticity. So, for example, it is fairly widely held that precocious sexual behaviour is an indicator of sexual abuse. Just how common is it in the non-abused population of children? Research is the only sure way to answer the question. Friedrich *et al.* (1992) have carried out extensive investigations into parents' reports of sexual behaviours in abused and non-abused children. Certain sorts of behaviour seem to occur at similar rates in groups of abused and non abused children. So, for example, touching the breasts of a woman is equally common in both sexually abused girls and non-abused girls. Thus any psychologist who took such touching as an indicator of sexual abuse would be profoundly wrong. There are dangers in inadvertently choosing a variable as an indicator of abuse which, actually, does not discriminate between abused and non-abused children.

Even if we take an indicator such as masturbation that does differentiate between the two, there remain dangers, despite the fact that this is commoner in abused children. Data collected by Friedrich (undated) demonstrated that in the 2–5 years of age female group, 28 per cent of the sexually abused children masturbated whereas 16 per cent of non-abused children did. In conventional psychological research terms this suggests that there is clearly an association between masturbation and sexual abuse. In terms of diagnosticity of indicators, things are not this simple. Take, for example, a class of 30 children. It is difficult to state precisely just how many of this class will have been sexually abused on average. Given the age group and the results of a variety of surveys, it is not unreasonable to suppose that 10 per cent of the class will have been abused, whereas the remaining 90 per cent will not have been abused. Taking Friedrich's figures on rates of masturbation, we would expect the following outcome:

- *True positives* – one child correctly identified by the indicator as sexually abused.
- *False negatives* – two children who were abused are not correctly identified as such by the indicator (because they do not masturbate).
- *False positives* – four children wrongly identified as abused (because they are in the non-abused sample but masturbate).
- *True negatives* – 23 children correctly identified as not being abused.

Thus using this test, only a third of abused children are identified as being abused. For every abused child the test

Table 16.1 The outcomes of using an indicator (or sign) to predict abuse

	Child abused in reality	Child not abused in reality
Indicator of abuse present	True positive	False positive
Indicator of abuse absent	False negative	True negative

picks out, a further four are identified incorrectly as being abused. This is an unimpressive outcome, especially given the distress that follows from false accusations.

So it should be clear that the requirements of the indicator approach are much more demanding than would appear initially (Wood, 1996). It has been suggested that an indicator that is three times commoner among abused children than non-abused children nevertheless is only very weak evidence of abuse. An indicator that is 14 times more common in abused than non-abused children might be described as a moderate to strong indicator. It is far from being perfect proof (Poole and Lindsay, 1998). The interpretation of ratios such as this may be difficult for practitioners and other professionals to appreciate and apply. It may be helpful to point out that Friedrich *et al.* (1992) found that imitation of intercourse occurred in precisely this ratio. Imitation occurred in 14 per cent of abused children but only 1 per cent of non-abused children. Another reason for caution about such indicators is that sexual interest in sexually abused children may be heightened by the child sexual abuse investigation itself: that is, that part of the apparent effect of child sexual abuse is actually a consequence of the interest in sexual matters among the professionals and parents involved.

Of course, it might seem sensible to seek two indicators rather than a single indicator of abuse. But the consideration of two indicators may not be much of an advance, given the weak predictive strength of most predictors of abuse. Furthermore, one might expect that different indicators of abuse might quite commonly occur together, which would do very little to improve the diagnosticity of combining two or more indicators.

In what ways are genuine allegations different?

Obviously, if there were simple ways of differentiating a true allegation from a false allegation then false allegations would be easily dealt with. But, of course, there is no way of doing this with complete certainty in every case. Chapter 18, which deals with the assessment of truth, is clearly pertinent here and, for example, it discusses how statement validity analysis has been used to differentiate rape allegations which the police believe to be genuine from those which appear to be false. In a similar way, Marshall and Alison (2006) have used what they term *structural behavioural analysis* to differentiate the characteristics of genuine rape allegations from simulated ones. Marshall and Alison obtained actual rape allegation statements held by the police and compared them with the manufactured accounts of women instructed to imagine that they were trying to convince the police that they had been raped. None of this group had been the victim of any form of attack in their lives. The analytic task was straightforward – what characteristics differentiate the genuine rape allegations from the manufactured ones? The researchers examined each of the accounts, real or fabricated, for the presence of 37 different characteristics. These characteristics included things like: the offender made sexual comments; kissing was involved; fellatio occurred; cunnilingus occurred; the victim was bound; something personal was stolen from the victim; the offender was apologetic; and there was anal penetration. There were points of difference between the two. For example, there were more different behaviours reported in the real accounts, pseudo-intimate features (such as the offender giving the victim compliments and telling the victim details about himself) occurred more frequently in the genuine accounts, and there was a tendency for genuine accounts to provide behaviourally more coherent accounts than fictitious ones. Fictitious accounts tended to involve sexual acts which were 'normal' such as vaginal intercourse whereas other acts, such as anal intercourse, fellatio and cunnilingus, were relatively uncommon in fictitious accounts. Fictitious accounts were also more likely to include violent acts such as the victim's clothes being torn, the woman subjected to insulting or demeaning language, and more different acts of violence. There were indications from the analysis that the methods employed were much better at identifying truthful allegations than they were at identifying fictitious allegations.

This does not mean that it is easy to distinguish false allegations from truthful ones. Peace, Porter and Almon (2012) report a study into whether people (in this case students) can discriminate between genuine and false sexual abuse allegations. The researchers had undergraduate students evaluate four truthful and four deceptive written allegations of sexual assault. The traumatic and true narratives had been collected from participants in another study by the researchers. The sources of these traumatic narratives were women who had referred themselves to a sexual assault centre. The women also provided police reports to the researchers which confirmed the broad details of the narratives and in each case the narratives had resulted in the conviction of the perpetrator. Other women who had never been victims of sexual assault were asked to report a fake trauma as convincingly and using as much detail as possible, as if it had happened to them. The number of words used in the narratives was more or less the same for both types of report. In addition, the emotionality of each of the narratives was rated by independent people so that the narratives were categorised as high and low on emotionality. Despite the use of emotional narratives, accuracy at detecting false narratives was only at about chance level.

More precisely, participants performed worse than if they had simply flipped a coin to determine accuracy. They were accurate on only 45 per cent of decisions overall. Furthermore, there was a bias towards judging the sexual assaults narratives as truthful. They did tend to be more accurate at assessing truthful accounts but still only at chance level. The researchers concluded that emotionality leads to poor accuracy in truth judging tasks like this.

Chapter 20 discusses methods of assessing the value of a child's evidence and provides more information about how interviews can be better constructed to prevent the influence of suggestive and leading questions.

Main points

- The problem of false allegations is only one component of miscarriages of justice. It has proven particularly problematic in relation to allegations of child sexual abuse, given the young age of many victims and the difficulty in interviewing them adequately. There is considerable evidence that some false memories for events may be created in children. Persistent leading questions can have an effect. One can overstate the fallibility of children's memories since there is plenty of evidence that they can be very accurate at recalling events. Nevertheless, some children in some circumstances will be affected by suggestion and make incorrect reports. However, a proportion of these will be retracted by the child when the interviewer questions their answer.
- There are a number of mechanisms that lead to repressed memories according to the theoretical approach in question. Freudian/classical repression refers to an unconscious process by which the person is protected from distressing memories. An alternative are those studies that investigate the accuracy of eyewitness memory for emotionally charged events, although the evidence seems to suggest that these tend to be well remembered. The repressed memory/false memory debate in psychology has attracted a great deal of public attention. Fundamentally, it sets different theories of memory in opposition to each other. It seems likely some recovered memories are indeed false memories because they are retracted.
- The issue of the diagnosticity of signs ought to be understood better by professional groups working with children. There are frequent claims in the professional literature of various professional groups that certain things are predictive of, say, sexual abuse. These include, for example, precocious sexual behaviour. Thus, say, a teacher who sees such behaviour exhibited by one of their students should be alerted to the risk that the child is being sexually abused. While it may be true that sexually abused children do demonstrate this more often, precocious sexual behaviour may not be a good indicator that a child has been sexually abused. The balance between the correctly identified abused and those mistakenly identified as abused is important. A seemingly good indicator may result in many more false positive identifications of abuse than correct ones. The number of errors depends on the base rates of sexual abuse in the population and the frequency with which a sign occurs in the population in question.

Further reading

Innocent website: challenging miscarriages of justice since 1993. https://innocent.org.uk/about/

Loftus, E., Garry, M. and Hayne, H. (2008) 'Repressed and recovered memories' in E. Borgida and S.T. Fiske (eds) *Beyond Common Sense: Psychological Science in the Courtroom* Oxford: Blackwell, pp. 177–94.

Shaw, J. (2017). The memory illusion: remembering, forgetting, and the science of false memory. London: Random House.

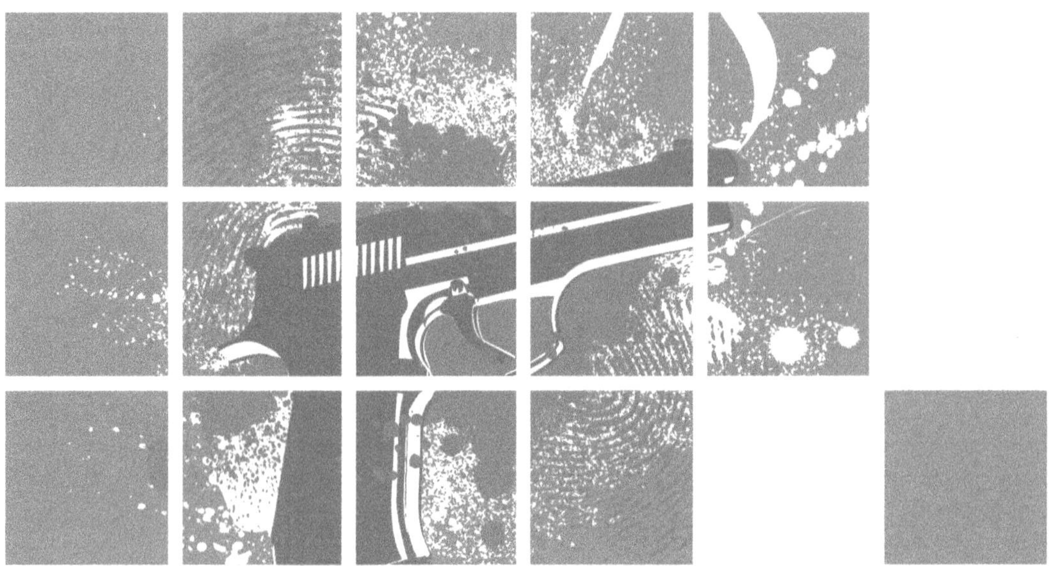

Chapter 17

False and true confessions

Overview

- There is plenty of advice available to the police on how to elicit a confession during interrogations of suspects. The environment for the interview should isolate the suspect and leave the officer in total command. The suspect may be intimidated by overstating the crime's seriousness or the strength of the evidence against them or by making claims which are simply not true. Alternatively, a more sympathetic approach can be used in which excuses for the crime are provided.
- It is argued that the decision to confess is a rational process and false confessions follow similar rational processes.
- There are a number of different processes leading to false confession. Stress-compliant false confession is where the suspect confesses falsely merely to escape the stress of the police interview. Coerced-compliant false confessions may be induced by threats or offers of leniency subject to a confession being made. Persuaded false confession involves the suspect becoming persuaded that they may have committed the crime – perhaps because they were drunk at the time and cannot remember it.
- False confession seems to be commoner among those with previous convictions in real life. Nevertheless, laboratory studies have shown how remarkably easy it is to induce someone to confess falsely and sometimes the confessor comes to believe their confession.
- The evidence in the United States shows that as many as half of the confessions which eventually were established to be false nevertheless led to criminal convictions. Furthermore, there is evidence that a jury, knowing that certain confession evidence has been obtained by illegal means, nevertheless may be affected by that evidence, even when warned by a judge of the inadmissibility of such evidence.

Introduction

Confession has traditionally been seen as the important outcome of police interviews with a suspect. Confession serves both as evidence and a means of speeding a case through the criminal justice system. Between 40 and 76 per cent of police interrogations end in a confession (Gudjonsson, 2003). While the factors which lead to confession and false confession can be very similar, the fallout from a false confession can be as serious as for a true confession. A false confession may be made for many reasons but, once made, it can be difficult to reverse. It has consequences in the courtroom and the jury room. Kassin (2008) presents a detailed argument about false confessions in relation to the criminal justice system. This is summarised in Figure 17.1. Kassin's view is that a confession, true or false, has a powerful effect on the criminal justice process. The long-term consequences of a confession made for short-term reasons may be immense. There are many factors which lead to confessions but police interrogation techniques are important ones. The inability of the police to effectively and accurately distinguish the truth from a lie means that innocent people may be at risk of being subjected to interrogation techniques which are based on the assumption of guilt.

Some false confessions are entirely voluntary in the sense that the confession does not come from police pressure such as that consequent on certain interviewing techniques. An early example of a voluntary false confession dates back to 1666 when Robert Hubert made the false claim that he had started the Great Fire of London. In actual fact, he had not arrived in London until two days after the fire had started. Kavanaugh (2016) suggests that there are a number of different reasons why a person should voluntarily falsely confess other than interrogation techniques. These include:

- Not understanding the implications for doing so in the adversarial system and the possible outcomes for making such a confession.
- A wish to achieve fame or notoriety.
- To help someone who was actually the offender.
- Mental illness

However, sometimes there may be a relationship between these and interrogation techniques. Redlich, Kulish and Steadman (2008) studied incarcerated prisoners with a serious mental illness (usually schizophrenia). About half claimed to have made a true confession and about half to have made a false confession. True confessors were much more likely to mention issues relating to guilt and honesty as their reason for confessing compared to the false confessors. They were also more likely to perceive that there was proof against them and that they were confused or ignorant about things. The false confessors sometimes mentioned threat from the interrogation as their reason for falsely confessing whereas the true confessors never did. False confessors also were protecting someone else more often than the true confessors.

Various reasons are given by people for falsely confessing. Gudjonsson and Sugurdsson (1999) analysed data from the Revised Gudjonsson Confession Questionnaire, which offers a wide variety of possibilities which respondents indicated applied to them or not. The researchers found that these clustered around the themes of external pressure, internal pressure and perceptions about the proof surrounding the case. Figure 17.2 gives examples of each of these. Taking the blame for what someone else has done seems to

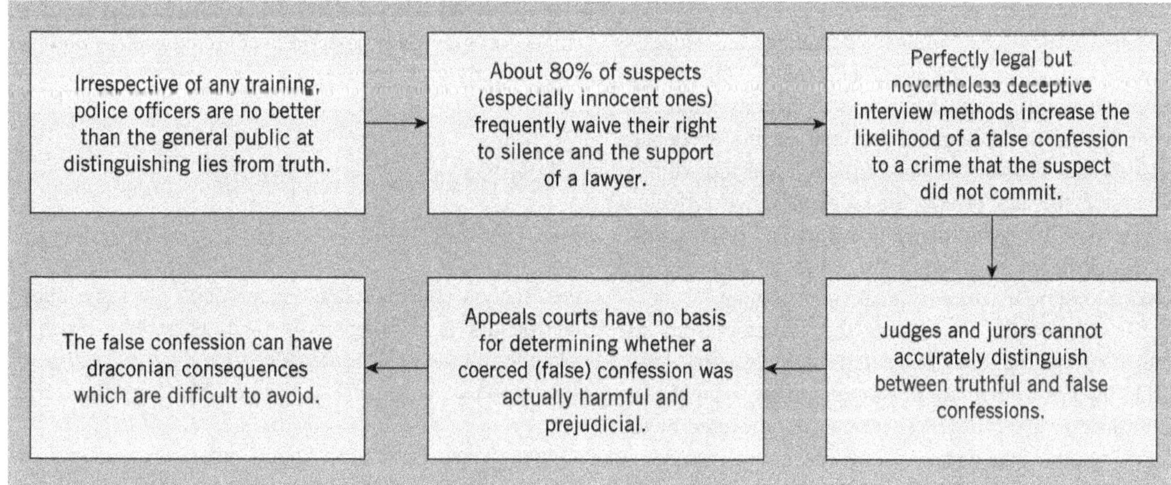

Figure 17.1 Kassin's argument concerning the power of confession evidence

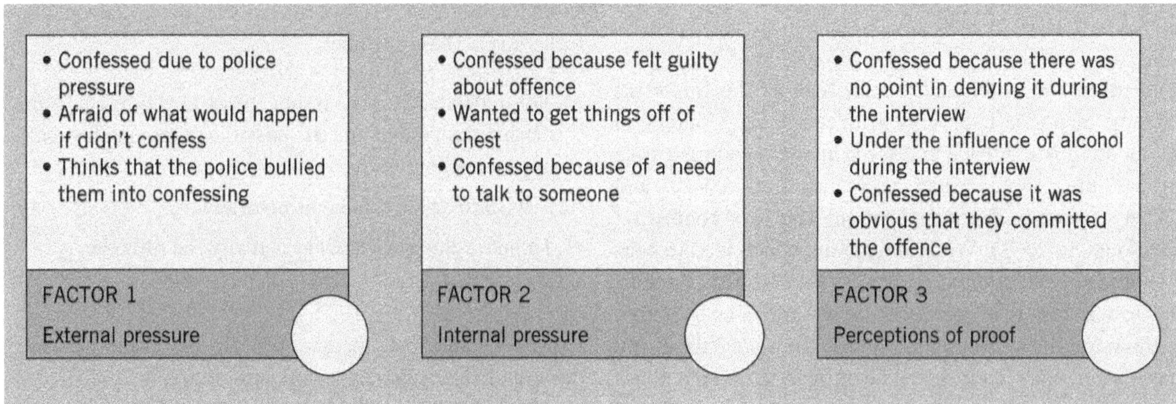

Figure 17.2 The major types of reasons given for confessing based on Gudjonsson and Sigurdsson's (1999) analysis

be fairly common. About 12 per cent of prisoners in Sigurdsson and Gudjonsson's (1996) research claimed to have taken the blame for an offence for someone else. In a purely experimental study, Pimental, Arndorfer and Mallow (2015) found that 59 per cent of adolescents and 39 per cent of adults confessed falsely to protect another. Malloy, Shulman and Cauffman (2013) found that in incarcerated adolescents who falsely confessed over 50 per cent did so to protect another person. Willard, Madon and Curran (2015) surveyed college students about situations in which they could have decided to take the blame for others – whether or not they actually did so. They were also asked about why they did take the blame or why they did not. Sixty-seven per cent of the students said they had been in a potentially blame-taking situation at some time in their life and 40 per cent had taken the blame for the misbehaviour of another person(s). Two-thirds of those who took the blame did so for friends or partners, with acquaintances (17 per cent) and family members (13 per cent) being much less frequently mentioned. Blame taking was primarily done for cheating, disorderly conduct and stealing. Conscientiousness was associated with not ever being in a potentially blame-taking situation. Delinquency was associated directly with being in such a situation. It was also related to actually taking the blame for another person. Situational factors were also involved such as the closeness of the relationship with the perpetrator, the lack of seriousness of the offence, feeling some responsibility for the events which led to the crime, and the difference between the consequences for the offender to those for the person taking the blame.

It is worthwhile mentioning that some reasons for falsely confessing are associated with gender. Jones (2011) interviewed 50 adult women serving sentences in an English prison. From these interviews informed by the extant literature, the women were subject to pressures to falsely confess which are gender-specific. Family responsibilities are one aspect of being female which encourages women to be compliant with suggestions made to them by police and prosecutors. The statistics suggest that two-thirds of women in prison have dependent children under 18 years of age (Prison Reform Trust, 2009) and that half of these women will not receive visits from their children. This sort of factor can encourage women to do whatever they feel may help them avoid imprisonment. But Jones also found evidence that some women falsely confessed to crimes committed by their male partners due to coercion from the man. There is also a 'stand by your man' pattern in which a woman pleads guilty to a crime they did not commit. They see this as an act of love to protect their male partner who had actually committed the crime.

For this chapter, we are concentrating on confessions, true or false, made to the police. There are other forms of confession. For example, sometimes individuals confess to a friend, an authority figure or some other third party such as a cellmate in prison. These confessions may then be reported to the police etc. as secondary confession evidence. There is little research on this but Wetmore, Neuschatz and Gronlund (2014) found that this form of confession may have as serious consequences as confessions directly to the police.

Methods of inducing confessions

Interrogation and interview are not quite the same thing. Interrogation is more aggressive and deliberately aimed at obtaining a confession. Interviews are about collecting as much accurate information as is possible. Interrogation is more characteristic of the system in the USA; interviewing is more characteristic of the UK. Confession evidence can be decisive and, in some cases, constitutes the most important evidence available to the police. In the American system, in particular, once the police have collected evidence leading to a particular suspect, a process of interrogation takes place with the primary objective of obtaining a confession. As a consequence, influential American police investigation manuals (Inbau, Reid and Buckley, 1986; Inbau, Reid, Buckley and Jayne, 2013) contain a great deal of advice on how to encourage a suspect to confess. In this approach known as the Reid model, a two-phase strategy is employed. The first phase is an information-gathering exercise during which the interviewer gathers information relevant to the investigation and behavioural information based on a behavioural analysis interview. The behavioural analysis interview is a list of questions investigators can ask in order to differentiate between a suspect telling the truth and telling lies. An example of these questions is 'What do you think should happen to the person who did this?' (Kassin, 2015, p. 28). Changes in the suspect's behaviour such as fidgeting, eye contact, and posture are then supposed to reveal to the investigator when the suspect is lying. Information gathered in this way is then used to assess the guilt of the suspect and whether an interrogation is necessary. If the suspect is believed to be guilty, then the second phase – the nine-step interrogation – begins. The interrogator avoids using legal terms to refer to the crime according to one recommendation, but there are many others. King and Snook (2009) describe in some detail the characteristics of Reid-style interrogations carried out by the Canadian police. The procedure is not rigidly adhered to but most of the elements of the Reid system seem to be utilised.

Inbau *et al.*'s advice based on the Reid interrogation approach includes suggestions about the arrangement and style of the room in which the interview is conducted. Recommendations include:

- It should take place in a small, bare room.
- Controls for things such as lighting should be inaccessible to the suspect.
- Invasion of the suspect's physical space by the officer is desirable.
- If possible, the room should be fitted with a one-way mirror so that another officer can secretly view the suspect for signs that he or she may be becoming distressed or tired. These times are when the suspect may be especially vulnerable to pressure to make a confession.

Generally speaking, such an environment will make the suspect feel socially isolated, and experience sensory deprivation. They will feel not in control of the situation. Figure 17.3 gives a résumé of the nine steps in obtaining a confession as put forward in the police manual. Advice is

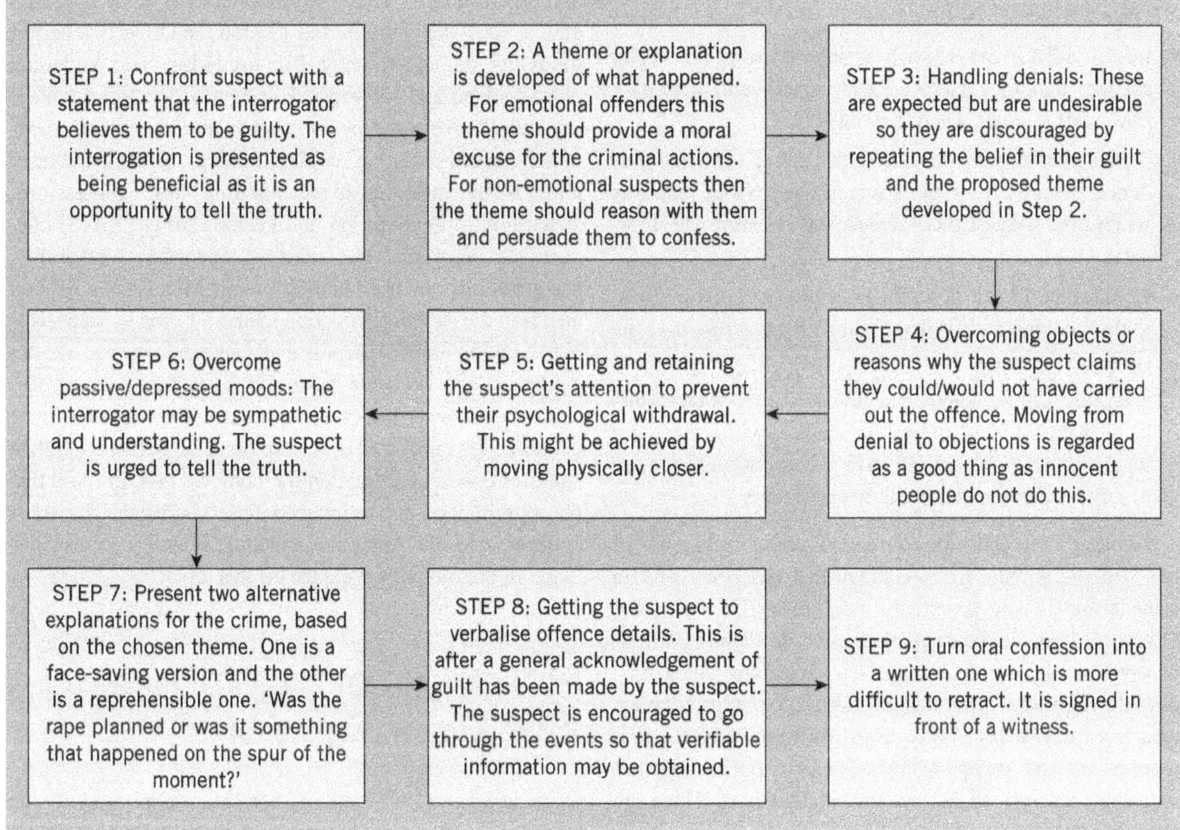

Figure 17.3 The Reid steps during the interrogation process

also given on how to distinguish guilty and innocent suspects. The manual suggests that there are verbal and non-verbal cues to lying. Innocent people give concise answers, sit upright but show little rigidity of posture and they make direct eye-to-eye contact (see Chapter 18 for a discussion of the characteristics of lying).

Two processes are involved in the interview:

- *Maximisation:* this consists of 'scare' tactics employed with the intention of intimidating the suspect. The officers overstate how serious the crime was and also the charges involved. Sometimes false or exaggerated claims are put forward about the evidence or its nature.
- *Minimisation:* this consists of the soft-sell techniques designed to encourage a sense of security. The techniques include offering sympathy, tolerance, giving face-saving excuses and moral justification by, for example, blaming the victim for the crime. The seriousness and extent of the charges may also be minimised.

Kassin and McNall (1991) found evidence that these strategies were effective in communicating high and low sentence expectations respectively, as might be expected. While these practitioner-oriented guidelines are of interest, there is more systematic information available about the process of confession. There are a number of different deception ploys used by American police according to Woody and Forrest (2009):

- false evidence ploys, such as where the police tell a suspect that they have a DNA match and that they never fail in court when they have;
- demeanour ploys occur where the police fabricate evidence gleaned from the suspect's behaviour, such as when they suggest that the suspect's posture etc. indicates guilt;
- testimonial ploys where, for example, the person is told that others have identified them as being present at the scene of the crime;
- scientific ploys, where it is claimed that fingerprints have been found at the crime scene – while these are legal in the USA, they do have a bearing on the value of any confessions which they encourage.

Another more elaborate example of police techniques of this sort is the 'Mr Big' technique that has been used in Canada and is also apparently used in the USA (Kassin, Drizin, Grisso, Gudjonsson, Leo and Redlich, 2010). It involves setting a complex and elaborate trap which may unfold over weeks or months. The aim is to obtain a confession from the suspect away from the custodial setting. It requires massive deceptive input from the police, together with the necessary social and financial support. There are (possibly) implied threats involving harm to the suspect or some form of punishment. Like other confession-inducing techniques, it is likely to be effective when used against a crime perpetrator but it has clear risks in relation to innocent suspects. The dangers are well illustrated by the case of Kyle Unger, a Canadian, who confessed and was convicted along with another man in 1992 for sexual assault and murder but was eventually exonerated on the basis of DNA evidence. He was convicted of beating and sexually assaulting a 16-year-old girl, Brigitte Grenier, at a rock music concert. He was young and naive and financially in poor circumstances. Two undercover Canadian police officers posed as tourists who gave him copious amounts of money for doing odd jobs. They also went drinking with him and provided him with luxurious accommodation. Eventually, they offered that he could join their criminal organisation. He falsely confessed to Brigitte's murder to impress a fictitious gang leader who was looking for someone with the capacity for violence. The confession contained numerous factual errors but Kyle Unger was nevertheless convicted. Other evidence was jailhouse evidence of a confession told to another prisoner and a wrongful claim by a forensic expert that one of Unger's hairs was found on the victim's body.

The Reid interrogation method is not the standard worldwide. Actually, it is likely that some aspects of the methods used for collecting evidence may be illegal in countries such as the United Kingdom. In the UK the PEACE model (Preparation and Planning, Engage and Explain, Account and Clarification, Closure, and Evaluation) is the approach employed. It was first used in 1993 in the UK and is part of the police training strategy. It is used elsewhere, including New Zealand and Norway. PEACE was developed collaboratively between the police, researchers, and other practitioners, based partly on research findings. Among its stated aims is the wish to avoid eliciting false confessions. According to Gudjonnson and Pearse (2011) PEACE concentrates on things like fairness, openness, workability, accountability and truth finding – confession is not a fixation as it is in the Reid interrogation method. Lying to suspects is not an option for the UK police and neither is the use of false evidence. This does not mean, however, that false confessions do not occur under this approach. They do since false confession is motivated by a wide range of factors other than stressful police interrogation methods. So bear in mind that the extremes of police-induced false confession are most applicable to the American situation, which also provides much of the research evidence on this topic.

Police interrogation and false-confessions

Ofshe and Leo (1997) regard false confessions as being the result of much the same type of factors that result in any other type of confession. Others have expressed similar views. Confession is largely the result of a *rational decision-making process* in which people optimise any situation for themselves in the context of the possible alternatives. Just as the police manual suggests, the police obtain confessions by leading the suspect to believe that the evidence against them is insurmountable. For example, it is certain that they will be convicted, irrespective of any additional confessional evidence. By confessing, the suspect may gain some advantage, such as a sentence reduction or a lesser charge. Following the confession, it remains possible that the suspect may be found to be innocent. For example, their confession may contain inaccurate information – they may describe using a weapon different from the one the police believe to have been used, for example. Leo (1996) likens the process to a confidence game in which the suspect exchanges trust and confidence in the police for the confession or other evidence. Only in this way, he argues, does the irrationality of not remaining silent (the suspect's right under the US Miranda rules that govern police interviews) become understandable.

Various types of false confessions have been identified by Ofshe and Leo (1997), based on the interrogation strategies of the police who obtain the confession:

- *Stress-compliant false confession:* being accused of a crime is a stressful situation that may be compounded by insistent and seemingly endless questioning by the police. The suspect may have no answer to what they say. In an attempt to escape such a punishing situation, the suspect may confess.
- *Coerced-compliant false confessions:* threats of harm or promises of leniency may coerce the suspect into confession. For example, the detectives may appear to agree that the offence is an accident rather than a crime. Nevertheless, they insist on a confession in order to confirm this.
- *Persuaded false confession:* the suspect becomes convinced that the chances are that they actually committed the crime although they have no recollection of doing so. For example, the suspect may be persuaded that drugs or alcohol have induced a blackout, thus explaining the lack of memory of the event.

One false confessor describes his interaction with the interviewing police officer as follows. It clearly shows some of these techniques in action:

> He goes, 'If you'd just say it was an accident,' he said 'you all were having rough sex,' you know, 'and just got carried away and you accidentally killed her, they won't charge you with first degree. They will charge you with second-degree murder and then,' you know, 'your future looks so much brighter,' you know, he goes, 'because you're a clean-cut, respectable man from what I see. Your bosses think highly of you, and so do all the people I've talked to.' He goes, 'Now why would you throw your life away for some drunken coke whore who is nothing but a piece of white trash,' you know. And he goes, 'Well, if you say it was an accident I think I can possibly talk these guys into letting you go home.'
>
> (Ofshe and Leo, 1997, pp. 1103–4)

More recently, Leo (Davis and Leo, 2012) has proposed a very psychological description of the process by which Reid-style stressful police interrogations sometimes result in false confessions on the part of some suspects while others manage to resist such pressures. To summarise, these interrogations involve certain stressors which mean that confession evidence cannot be adequately described as voluntary. Among the stressors are fatigue, disturbing amounts of sleep deprivation, and emotional stress. The interrogations may also be excessive in length and involve aversive tactics. Furthermore, the suspect may already be tired and fatigued before the interrogation begins. Various aversive procedures, such as DNA testing, blood testing, and polygraph assessment, can add to the stress, as will the endless accusations, dismissal of any attempt by the suspect to have their account of events considered, multiple and sequential interviewers and so forth. Put together, these factors can reduce the resistance of individuals to interrogation tactics.

What is the mechanism by which this happens? Davis and Leo (2012) put forward the concept of *interrogation-related regulatory decline* in order to describe and account for the failures of resistance. The idea of interrogation-related regulatory decline is quite powerful as it allows Davis and Leo to explain why a wide range of factors can contribute to the process. They are not solely concerned with false confessions, which may be relatively few as a percentage, but also with those suspects who confess against their own best interests. Nor are they concerned merely with those individuals who have particularly vulnerable personalities but with normal people with normal personal resources. Certain personal resources are needed to resist the power of the interrogation situation, but these are much more easily depleted than is commonly supposed. Many types of force within situations may adversely affect our ability to effectively marshal and employ our personal resources to best effect. According to theories of resistance to persuasion, two resources are required: 1) the ability to resist influence and 2) the motivation to resist influence. Resistance can involve the following:

- the ability to properly assess information in order to come to the optimum decisions and to act in way which will enable one to achieve one's goals;
- the ability to exert one's will and carry out what one believes is the optimum course of action – all of this requires that the individual can focus on the goal of achieving the best legal outcome for themselves.

In addition, the suspect needs to avoid adopting goals which are counterproductive, such as trying to please the interrogator (perhaps in order to get out of the interrogation as quickly as possible). The long-term goal of the best legal outcome must not be sidelined in favour of short-term goals. Several things need to happen. The focus of attention should be goal-relevant information. Irrelevant or distracting information needs to be ignored or else speedily dismissed from the individual's mind. Information stored in the individual's long-term memory relevant to the situation should be retrieved and integrated and evaluated in the light of the new information coming in during the interrogations. The individual's working memory should have sufficient capacity to handle all this relevant information. Emotion needs to be controlled to allow abilities to be used to their best effect. Sufficient willpower must be available to allow continuous resistance to persuasive influences and not to be defeated by early failures.

Interrogation tactics are there to reduce the motivation to resist by convincing the suspect that resistance is futile and not in their interests in the long term. Among the things that will have to be resisted in the interrogation are:

- The 'choice architecture' (Thaler and Sunstein, 2008) which seeks to limit the individual's beliefs about the choices they have. In particular, the possibility of establishing one's innocence is not contemplated in the police account.
- The police interrogator may seek to overcome resistance to them personally by presenting themselves as a sympathetic character and trustworthy 'ally'. Nevertheless, they must appear as an authority figure who can influence outcomes such as whether the suspect will be charged.
- Attempts to redefine the interrogation situation as one in which the suspect is given the opportunity to explain themselves. Through this they may be able to influence the nature and seriousness of the charge that will be made against them. Nevertheless, the real purpose of the interrogation is to establish guilt.
- Attempts to minimise the seriousness and legal outcomes of the crime.
- Tactics such as speaking quickly, the invasion of personal space, and interrupting the suspect are there to ensure that the suspect focuses on what the interrogator wishes to discuss.

The concept of *self-regulation* is important in this sort of situation. It is the process of controlling one's own thoughts, actions and emotions when pursuing a goal in many aspects of life. Clinical psychopathology, school performance and risk taking are just some areas in which it has been researched. Self-regulation is a limited resource which is depleted when we exercise self-control (Baumeister, Bratslavsky, Muraven and Tice, 1998). The technical term for this depletion of resources is *ego depletion*. This depletion makes the individual more likely to fail in subsequent self-regulation activities. This is the case when the self-regulation task is complex. Simple self-regulation tasks will not deplete resources. All of the stressors in the interrogation such as tiredness can effect adversely the availability of resources.

Another, but rather different, approach to understanding why people falsely confess involves the analysis of conversation between an interrogator and a suspect (as an interview may be regarded). It is based on the classic linguistic theory of speech acts – that is, the way that language does things. Shuy (1998) argues that:

- confessions are constructed through dialogue;
- the suspect and the interrogator each contribute to the dialogue;
- the dialogue will contain uncertainties and lead to questions about what was actually confessed and what is admitted, i.e. things may be admitted ('I did have sex with the woman') but these may not be seen as a confession to the crime ('She readily agreed to having sex').

The interrogator may make rather different inferences about what is admitted. This interpretation forms the central thrust of subsequent legal action.

Shuy (1998) provides an analysis of a number of transcripts of police interrogations. The transcripts of the interrogation were analysed linguistically by Shuy for inconsistency. In the example to follow, he points out that the police may have misunderstood the language of the suspect. The verb 'to know' has a series of dictionary meanings but, in addition, it has a number of non-dictionary meanings. The verb may be used in the following contexts to mean rather different things such as in the sentences 'I know that Jones is going to win the election' and 'I know it's going to rain tomorrow when we have our picnic.' A strict dictionary definition of these words actually makes these sentences taken literally unintelligible.

In the case that we will consider, Jerue is one of the suspects for a crime. The investigator asks him a question that uses this verb 'to know'. Jerue's reply is:

> No
> Yea, but I didn't know he was gonna shoot him though
> We didn't plan to kill him when we were goin' over there.

This can be interpreted as a statement by Jerue that there was no intent to murder. That is the implication of saying that he did not know that the other man was going to shoot the victim.

This theme of intent occurs at other stages in the dialogue. The police, in their attempts to obtain an admission of the intent to kill the man, employed other words. Read through the following exchanges – it may be useful to read the passage first of all as the police seeking an admission of intent would and then from the perspective of the accused who was essentially trying to deny intent:

> You guys intended to go over there and rob him and kill him, didn't you?
> No, we didn't plan to kill him at all.
> But it was an understanding and a plan between the two of you for him to do it, right?
> Yeah.
> You both planned to do it – before – up to two hours before you and Lavon actually shot him, you both planned on shootin' him, right?
> Right.
> OK, that's what we thought, and you just had to kill him to rip his stuff off.
> No, we were just gonna hold him at gunpoint, that's what I thought.
> But about two hours before he actually shot him is when he changed your mind and decided to shoot him, right?
> Right.
> Then, if I understand you right, you guys changed your mind from robbin' him to shootin' him about two hours before he actually shot him, right?
> Yeah, about that, yah.
> That's when both of you changed your mind, you both agreed on it at that point, right?
> Right.
>
> (Shuy, 1998, pp. 35–6)

Early on, the suspect seems to be admitting intent but the interpretation depends on how the word 'it' is to be understood in the officer's second question. Does 'it' refer to killing the man or to going to his house with the intent to steal? Similarly, how is one to understand the penultimate sentence just before the suspect's comment 'Right'? It might appear to indicate that the suspect had finally capitulated and admitted the intent to kill. This may be an erroneous interpretation. Notice the structure of the final questions from the police officer. They are somewhat complex and it is not definite exactly what the suspect is agreeing to. It could be planning to kill but it may be that he was a little confused by the structure of the question and thought he was agreeing that the decision to rob was made two hours before.

The suspect was convicted of aiding a planned homicide.

There seems to be some consensus on the view that some interrogation/interviewing methods are more conducive to false confessions than others. A good way of demonstrating this is the sort of meta-analysis (see Box 4.1) carried out by Meissner*et al.* (2014). They identify the 'Reid Model' of interrogation but refer to it more generically as 'accusatorial'. This they compare with what they refer to as the 'information-gathering' approach which is the sort of method used in the UK and several other countries. That is to say, interviews following the PEACE model in which coercion and deception are not allowed. Meissner *et al.* also made comparisons with direct interviews – routine interviews which are not informed either by the PEACE or the Reid-models. The study involved two meta-analyses. One was based on field studies and the second was based on experimental studies. Actually rather few studies met the criteria for inclusion which Meissner *et al.* had set. So only five field studies and 12 experimental studies were analysed. Field studies, of course, do not have access to the truth or otherwise of any confession. The meta-analysis of the field studies showed that both the Reid-model of interrogation and the information-gathering approach associated with PEACE yielded more confessions than did the direct interviewing approach. However, the findings from the experimental studies were more interesting. This is because these studies address both confession and false-confessions. The Reid-style interrogation increased the rates of both true and false-confessions. In contrast, the PEACE-based information gathering style of interview reduced the number of false confessions but either did not affect or reduced the number of true confessions. In both cases, the comparison is with the direct questioning approach.

None of this would be of any great significance if police officers, prosecuting lawyers, and others in the criminal justice system were good at distinguishing false-confessions from true confessions. The evidence seems to be that they are not. The police investigator may be, for various reasons, over-keen to accept the false confession as true. In particular, they may have workload pressures or be under pressure to close the case for other reasons. Kassin, Meissner and Norwick (2005) compare US police officers with college students in their ability to say whether a confession is true or false. Students were better at the task than police officers! But since only 54 per cent of decisions were correct then this is a dismal outcome overall anyway. A not dissimilar study by Honts, Kassin and Craig (2014) investigated ability to differentiate true from false confessions made by incarcerated juveniles. All of the participants in this study were American college students. The evidence suggests that false confessions are not likely to be weeded out. Kavanaugh (2016) stresses the importance of a post-confession review of the evidence consistent with the confession, the consideration of alternative hypotheses, and seeking mismatches between the evidence the police have and the contents of the confession.

BOX 17.1 Forensic psychology in action

Who confesses falsely?

False confessions are often the result of the interaction between the police and suspect. The factors which lead investigators to suspect a particular individual of a crime may be the starting point of a pathway which, in some cases, end with a false confession. This is known as investigator bias. Some aspects of a suspects demeanour may contribute to this. For example, Heath (2009) points out that there is a considerable amount of evidence that the emotionality of suspects and accused is often regarded as appropriate and indicative of their innocence or truthfulness. Lacking appropriate emotionality may be regarded as a sign of guilt. Evidence that investigator bias can lead to false confessions comes from several studies including Narchet, Meissner and Russano (2011). They set up a laboratory analogue of the police investigation by, firstly, inducing participants to cheat by sharing information with each other despite being told not to. So guilt was established. Some other participants were not put in this situation and these were the innocent participants. The researchers put into the minds of people who were to be the 'interrogators' the suggestion that the participant was likely to be guilty, or the suggestion that the participant was likely to be innocent, or no suggestion at all. The interrogators had been trained for several weeks in the sort of interrogation technique employed by American police. They chose what interrogation technique to use. For the guilty participants, confession was very common whether or not a non-coercive interview method was used or if maximisation or minimisation technique was employed. However, for the innocent participants, things were different. Few falsely confessed if non-coercive methods were used but maximisation and minimisation techniques resulted in a high proportion of false confessions. In other words, coercive techniques risked increasing the false confession rate considerably.

Heath (2009) reports the case of the American Marty Tankleff, who was just 17 when he reported to the police that his mother and father had been attacked. This was a homicide case as both were to die from their wounds. The officer leading the investigation grew suspicious because of the remarkable calmness of Marty and his lack of emotion. This suspicion was not altered by comments from relatives that Marty's demeanour was always like this. The officer then used the tactic of (falsely) claiming that Marty's father had come out of the coma and claimed that Marty had attacked him. The only way Marty could understand this was to assume that he had blacked out or something since he remembered nothing of the (false) attack. Following this, Marty made a confession (but never signed it) and recanted it soon afterwards. He was sentenced to 50 years in prison and only was released after 17 years.

What sort of person is most likely to falsely confess? The Birmingham Six were the group of men convicted of the Irish Republican Army's bombing of a Birmingham pub, killing several people. Flawed forensic evidence suggested that they had been involved with explosives. There was a serious degree of ill treatment of the men by the police. Four of the six had made confessions. Eventually, they were acquitted of the crime after many years in prison. Gudjonsson (1992) had collected psychological data from the men in 1987. His data on compliance and suggestibility indicated that the two men who were the most resistant to the pressure of the police to confess were the two men who scored lowest on these measures.

Another study examined 56 prison inmates in Iceland who had claimed to have made a false confession to the police and compared them with over 400 other prisoners (Sigurdsson and Gudjonsson, 1997). The researchers suggest that there are two types of explanation of false confession:

- Inexperience of police methods and procedures makes some suspects especially susceptible to police manipulation and attempts at coercion. It is known from previous research that those who score highly on interrogative suggestibility as measured by Gudjonsson's Susceptibility Scale had fewer previous convictions.
- False confession is part of the criminal lifestyle of some offenders. It is known from previous research that false confessors tended to be illicit drug users and to have a history of drug dependency.

The findings of the research included the following:

- The false confession concerned only their current sentence in 5 per cent of cases.
- False confessors had previously served prison sentences more often than the control group (65 per cent versus 38 per cent).

- False confessors were younger than people who did not falsely confess when first convicted or when they first went to prison.
- False confessors had more previous prison sentences and had spent more time in prison prior to their current offence.
- Nearly all had a criminal record before the false confession (88 per cent).
- The commonest offence associated with false confession was property crime (59 per cent). The second category was serious traffic violations. Violent offences amounted to 7 per cent.

Pearse, Gudjonsson, Clare and Rutters (1998) carried out forensic clinical interviews with suspects at a police station in order to assess their psychological vulnerability. Measures included anxiety, intelligence and reading as well as suggestibility. There was no evidence to indicate that such clinical assessments of vulnerability related to confession. Indeed, the best predictor of confession was whether the suspect had taken illegal drugs in the previous 24 hours. The reasons for this are not yet clear – it could be merely that they confessed so as to get out of the police station into an environment where they could obtain drugs. They tended to confess less if a solicitor was present.

Of course, it is not possible for researchers to validate claims of false confession among those subject to police interrogations. But such claims are useful data nonetheless when no better data exists. Gudjonsson, Sigurdsson, Asgeirsdottir and Sigfusdottir (2007) obtained questionnaire data from nearly 1900 Icelandic students aged between 15 and 24 years. These were youngsters who had reported having undergone police interrogation. Seven per cent said that they had made a false confession to police officers. The major predictive factors for false confessions were multiple experiences of victimisation (e.g. bullying, death of a significant other) and substance abuse (i.e. having had substance abuse therapy or used LSD). In other words, having experienced a lot of unpleasant or traumatic experiences was conducive to falsely confessing. Figure 17.4 gives more details about this. Some factors, such as alcohol use, cannabis use, parental separation/divorce, and having serious arguments with their parents, did not

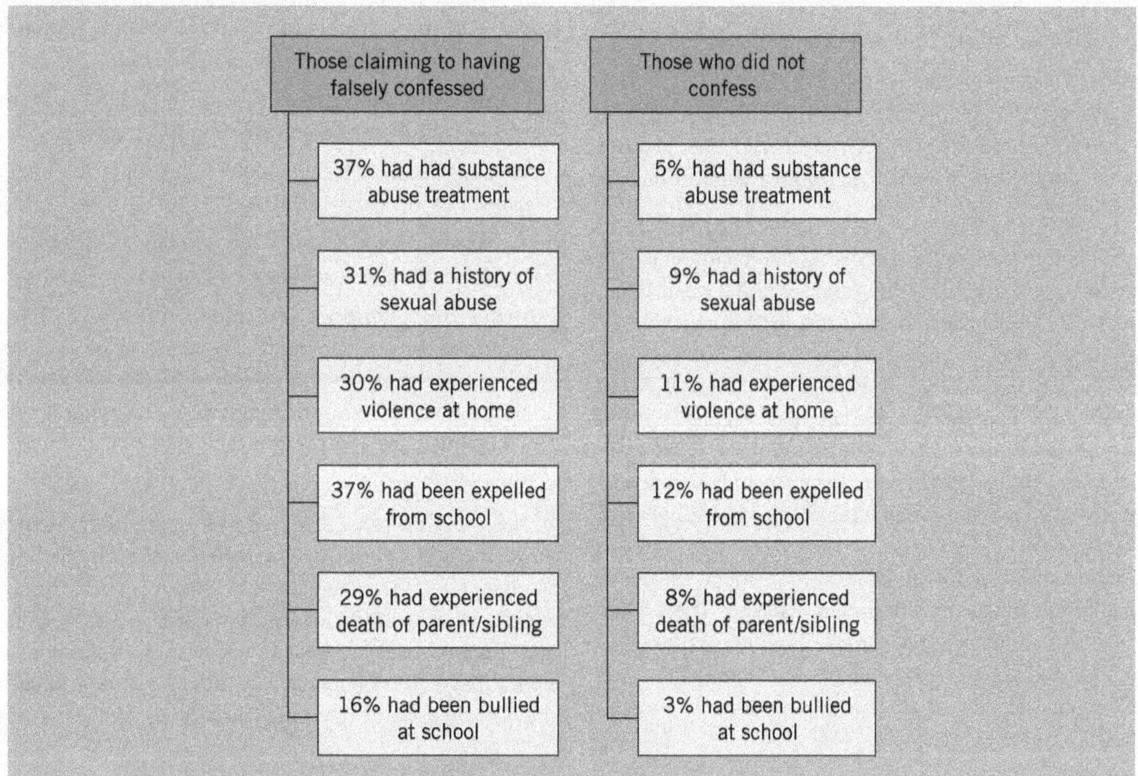

Figure 17.4 Some of the differences between false confessors and other youngsters according to Gudjonnson *et al.* (2007)

BOX 17.1 (continued)

differentiate false confessors from others, however. A similar study by Gudjonsson, Sigurdsson and Sigfusdottir (2009) involved a smaller age range – just Icelandic 15–16 year olds. Eleven per cent had been questioned at a police station as a suspect – this was commoner for boys than girls. Mostly, they had been questioned just once. However, some 7 per cent of those who falsely confessed had been questioned six or more times. In this study too, life adversity variables seemed to discriminate between the false confessors and the rest quite effectively. The most discriminating aversive factors were sexual abuse within the family; death of a parent or sibling; sexual abuse outside of family; and witnessing serious violence between adults at home.

Demonstrating different types of false confession

Kassin and Kiechel (1996) describe three different types of false confession which are not entirely dissimilar from those used by Ofshe and Leo (1997) and described earlier:

- *Voluntary false confession:* this is personally motivated and occurs in the absence of external pressure from others;
- *Coerced-compliant false confession:* the suspect confesses in order to escape an aversive interrogation, secure a promised benefit or avoid a threatened harm;
- *Coerced-internalised false confession:* the suspect comes to believe in their own guilt of committing the crime.

It is difficult to believe that individuals come to believe in their own guilt over something that they have not done. Perhaps it is more understandable that people may confess when they find themselves in a no-win situation and are offered a way of making things easier for themselves. In an intriguing experiment, Kassin and Kiechel (1996) simulated aspects of false confession in a laboratory experiment. Remarkably, participants could be encouraged to make up details of an offence that they simply had not committed.

American university students were assigned to one of four different groups by Kassin and Kiechel. These were defined by the independent variable high versus low vulnerability and by a second independent variable, which was the presence versus absence of a false incriminating witness:

- Participants worked on an individual basis with a female 'plant' or confederate of the experimenter.
- Both the participant and the plant worked together on a reaction time study.
- A list of letters of the alphabet was read aloud by one of them and typed on the computer keyboard by the other.
- Initially, the confederate did the typing but after three minutes the roles were reversed.
- They were warned not to press the ALT key because a software fault would crash the computer and so the data would be lost.
- Some of the participants had to type fast and others could type slowly because of the speed of reading out the letters. This is known as the vulnerability manipulation – the more quickly one works, the less opportunity one has to self-monitor what one is doing.
- Typing errors were greatest for the high rate, confirming the validity of the procedure in this regard.
- After 60 seconds the computer crashed, as had been planned by the experimenter.
- The experimenter accused the participant of pressing the forbidden key – all denied this.
- At this stage, false incriminating evidence was introduced for some participants. The confederate admitted that she had seen the participant hit the ALT key on the computer. In the control condition, the no witness condition, the same confederate said that she had not seen what had occurred.

So, the experimental situation had resulted in the participant being accused of doing something that they had not. In some cases, there was also a witness claiming to have seen the participant doing that thing. These are much the same circumstances as those in which false confessions in real life have been obtained. The different aspects of false confession could be identified according to the participant's behaviours:

- *Compliance:* the experimenter wrote a 'confession' for the participant ('I hit the ALT key and caused the program to crash') which counted as compliance if the participant then agreed to it.

- *Internalisation:* a second confederate asked the participant later what had happened. If the participant said they had hit the wrong key without qualification (i.e. without saying something like 'I think') then this counted as internalisation.
- *Confabulation:* the experimenter reappeared and asked whether the subject could recall specific details to fit the allegation.

The outcome of the research suggested that the fast or pressurised version of the study tended to increase all three forms of influence. Each of these was increased by the presence of the witness who claimed she had seen the participant hit the wrong key. Confabulation was common where there was a witness and a fast pace but not otherwise. These findings have been effectively replicated on a number of occasions. For example, Candel, Merckelbach, Loyen and Reyskens (2005) used young Dutch children in the age range of six to nine years. Over a third of the children falsely confessed when they were questioned and there was evidence that the vast majority of these internalised their confession. Interestingly, a measure of suggestibility used by the researchers did not predict false confession in this study.

One criticism of this research is that falsely confessing to something one had not done had no adverse consequences. Falsely confessing in a police interview may lead to punishment in the form, say, of a prison sentence. Horselenberg, Merckelbach and Josephs (2003) essentially replicated the Kassin and Kiechel (1996) study but added a punishment in that the false confessions led to a financial loss by the confessor. That is, they lost part of their fee for participating in the study by accepting that they caused the computer to crash. Despite this, the findings of the new study were much the same as those of Kassin and Keichel's. That is to say, the majority of participants falsely confessed. However, despite the evidence that there are personality factors that might lead to false confession (see Box 17.1 for details), falsely confessing in this study was not associated with Gudjonsson's Compliance Scale and a measure of compliance tendencies. In circumstances in which over 80 per cent of people will falsely confess, would one expect that personality traits would be a factor? The situation is enough to create the confession so this will be little affected by some people being more prone to confess falsely than others.

There are a number of fairly self-evident limitations apparent in the Kassin and Kiechel study (Russano Meissner, Narchet and Kassin, 2005):

- The participants may be uncertain or confused about whether they did press the 'ALT' key accidentally since it is very plausible that they did in these circumstances. This is rather different from what happens in real cases where the accused would be accused of deliberately committing a crime.
- All of the participants in the study were actually innocent of the misdemeanour they are accused of, so it is not possible to compare true confessions with false confessions.

Attempts have been made to address these issues. Horselenberg *et al.* (2006) replicated the essence of the Kassin and Kiechel study but cleverly designed procedures which meant that the participant actually may have done something wrong. Participants had the opportunity to cheat by taking a look at an exam paper which had been left accessible to them. The researchers found that it was possible to get participants to confess to cheating (i.e. looking at the examination paper) even though they had not actually done so. Only a small number confessed falsely but, even so, this limited evidence effectively neutralises this criticism of the Kassin and Kiechel study. In perhaps a more effective approach, Russano *et al.* (2005) also attempted to address the issue of the lack of culpability in the Kassin and Kiechel study. In this method, guilty and innocent participants were accused of cheating since they broke one of the rules of the experiment in which they were participating. In the study, participants were paired with a confederate and they were required to solve a number of logical problems. Some were asked to solve the problems on their own, whereas some were required to solve the problems together in a 'team'. The manipulation of guilt was achieved by having the confederate of the experimenters ask the real participant for help. Some participants gave the confederate the answer and so could justifiably be accused of cheating. In the innocent condition, the confederate did not ask for help. It could be argued that this cheating is a serious infringement knowingly committed by the participant – that is, a very different situation from accidentally pressing the 'ALT' key on a computer keyboard.

In one of Russano *et al.*'s studies, the researchers investigated the influence of the police interrogation tactics of (a) maximisation versus minimisation and (b) offering a lenient deal in return for a confession. Maximisation techniques are intimidating since the suspect is accused of guilt, the police officers will not accept denials of guilt of the crime, and the seriousness of the situation is inflated by the police officers. In contrast, minimisation is essentially the reverse of this, so the officers present the crime as being relatively trivial. When dealt with by the minimisation and lenient-deal tactics, guilty individuals were three-and-a-half times more likely to confess than innocent individuals. Compared with the condition in which there was no tactic used, offering a deal, minimisation tactics and deal plus minimisation tactics all resulted in more confessions. True confessions were nearly doubled from

46 to 87 per cent with the use of a deal and minimisation. The risk of a false confession increased from 6 per cent with no tactic to 43 per cent with minimisation and a deal! In other words, confession evidence is seriously degraded by the use of this sort of interrogation tactic since they disproportionately raise the likelihood of a false confession. On the basis of this research, Russano *et al.* argue that police officers should not be involved with any suggestion of leniency as this tends to reduce the diagnostic value of any confession resulting.

Distinguishing between true and false confessions

Researchers have begun to ask the question of whether there is anything quantitatively different about the actual text of confessions which might help distinguish true ones from false ones. For example, is there more evidence of remorse in a false-confession? Appleby, Hasel and Kassin (2013) took 20 instances of major crimes in which a false confession had been made. Forty per cent of the confessions either included some form of apology or an expression of remorse. Without a comparison group of true confessions this figure is of limited value. Participants in an Australian study by Villar, Arciuli and Paterson (2014) were female undergraduate students. They were asked indirectly to provide both a true and false story (i.e. confession) about a recent social transgression. It was presented as a study of lying compared to truth telling. The participants were given for the false confession a list of six topics on which they were to choose one to lie about (such as being unfaithful to their romantic partner). If the participant indicated that their story was based on truth then the participants were asked to tell a story about the next topic on the list. They were required to present the true and false 'confessions' twice – once in written form and again in spoken form. Orders were counterbalanced. The confessions were analysed for remorse, vocal pitch, and loudness. Remorse was assessed in terms of expressions of feeling guilty, regretful, apology, repentance, sorrow, feeling responsible, wishing to make reparation, and the intention not to repeat such a transgression in the future. The use of expressions of remorse was three times as high in the true confessions than for the false confessions irrespective of whether the confession was in a written or spoken form. However, rather more remorseful words were found for the spoken confession than for the written one. Although there were no differences in pitch between the spoken true and false confessions, there were differences in loudness. Expressions of remorsefulness were spoken more softly for the true confessions. This is preliminary evidence that features of a false confession might be indicative that it is a falsehood

Consequences of a false confession

Confession is common. It has been estimated that in the United Kingdom something like 60 per cent of all police detainees confess (Pearse *et al.*, 1998). Just how many of these are likely to be false confessions is anyone's guess. Not all false confessors are victims of police interviewing methods. Some false confessions are nuisances and in no way solicited by the police. There is such a phenomenon as voluntary false confession. For example, 200 people confessed to the kidnap of the US aviator Charles Lindbergh's baby in the 1920s. The Innocence Project in the United States has identified wrongful convictions, using DNA evidence. In about 20 per cent of these proven wrongful conviction cases there was a false confession (Russano *et al.*, 2005). Berger (2008) argues that false confessions are likely to come to the attention of authorities when: 1) the inconsistency of the confession causes charges to be dropped; 2) the false confessor tries to recant or retract the confession; 3) a claim of false confession is made in proceedings occurring after the conviction; or 4) when the real perpetrator is found – though this is exceptional.

At one extreme is the anonymous false confession which, if followed up by the police, may take up a lot of time. The classic example of this in Britain was the Yorkshire Ripper case of the 1970s. The police investigating this case were hampered severely by a number of highly publicised tape-recordings purporting to be from the Yorkshire Ripper himself. He appeared to be taunting the officers. Senior officers mistakenly regarded them as genuine. This diverted police resources along a false trail. It, possibly, may have delayed arrest of the Ripper and allowed further murders. McCann (1998) mentions another example of false confession that is not the result of police pressure. Young members of gangs may be pushed into confessing by other members of the same gang in the belief that the court will deal leniently with young people.

The availability of confession evidence has a corrupting effect on other sources of evidence (Kassin, Bogart and Kerner, 2012). Not only has this been shown in laboratory studies, evidence in favour of this idea can be found in real cases with potentially serious outcomes. Kassin *et al.* used the evidence from DNA-exonerated cases held by the Innocence project. They found that multiple evidence errors are more likely in false-confession cases than cases which depended, say, exclusively on eyewitness evidence.

These errors also tended to corroborate the confession. The most common additional errors following false confessions were found to be invalid/improper forensic scientific evidence, followed by information from informants. However, they were rather less likely to involve eyewitness errors. Furthermore, the sooner the suspect falsely confessed, the more likely it was that the other evidence irregularities would occur. It is well known that evidential standards can require more additional evidence in confession cases, though this is far from universal. The problem, as highlighted by Kassin *et al.*'s research, is that this additional evidence may well not be independent of the confession.

Leo and Ofshe (1998) studied some of the numerous documented cases of police-induced false confession. They systematically searched media, case files and secondary sources for examples of false confession. All cases selected for inclusion in the study satisfied the following criteria:

- no physical or other credible evidence indicated the suspect's guilt;
- the State's case consisted of little other than the suspect's confession;
- the suspect's factual innocence was supported by evidence.

In this way, they found 34 proven cases of false confession: for example, the murder victim turned up alive after the trial, or the true offender was eventually found guilty, or scientific evidence proved the innocence of the false confessor. In addition, there were another 18 cases that seemed highly likely to be false confessions. Eight cases were classified as probably false confessions, since the majority of the evidence indicated the innocence of the accused.

Whatever the reason for false confession, the consequences for suspects in the United States are often great, as these US data show:

- 8 per cent were fortunate and suffered only arrest and detention by the police;
- 43 per cent were prosecuted but the case was eventually dismissed;
- 48 per cent of the cases ended up with a criminal conviction.

This final figure included:

- 17 per cent who were sentenced to more than ten years;
- 5 per cent who were given death sentences;
- 2 per cent who were actually executed.

Nearly three-quarters of all of the false confessors were found guilty if they went to trial. Considering the certain false confessors alone showed that 55 per cent were released prior to going to trial. Of this group who were eventually established as not guilty by further evidence, 3 per cent were acquitted by the court; 29 per cent were convicted despite their 'not guilty' plea; and 15 per cent pleaded guilty in court despite their eventual proven innocence.

The consequences of wrongful convictions for crime can be serious in other respects. Grounds (2004) gives evidence from a British sample exonerated after they had wrongfully been convicted of a crime. Among the serious symptoms found which appeared after incarceration were lasting anger; panic disorder; permanent personality change; substance abuse; and post-traumatic stress disorder. Two-thirds showed the symptomology of post-traumatic stress disorder (PTSD). Others argue that the consequences of miscarriages of justice can spread beyond the individuals immediately affected. The high-profile nature of some wrongful allegations and miscarriages of justice can affect the public's beliefs about the nature of crime and facts about crime and its perpetrators (Cole, 2009). He gives the example of the false cases of organised sexual abuse of children which led to numerous reports and prosecutions in the 1980s and after. These included claims of human sacrifice and cannibalism as well as satanic ritual abuse. In terms of US cases alone, there were ten or more mass prosecutions for organised sexual abuse and a minimum of 72 people were found guilty. Most of these were released though generally without exoneration. The public's belief in organised ritual abuse waned as a consequence of this as well as confidence in the child protection system.

One intriguing possibility is that experience of coercive interrogation and falsely confessing may have a negative impact on young people's attitudes to the police and criminal justice system. Arndorfer, Malloy and Cauffman (2015) tested this possibility on a sample of nearly 200 incarcerated adolescent males in a California facility. These were among the juvenile offenders with the most serious criminal backgrounds. The youngsters were given the General Procedural Justice scale as a measure of the fairness of the justice system in general. This yielded a measure of attitudes towards courts (e.g. 'The courts generally give everyone a fair trial') and another of attitudes towards the police (e.g. 'Police officers often unfairly harass high school kids'). Their experiences of confession, both true and false, were assessed by a separate measure. This asked questions about them having ever confessed to a crime which they did not actually do but also about confessing to crimes that they had done. A third measure concerned the interrogation strategies that the police had employed such as befriending, deception about having more evidence, use of threats, and so forth. The findings showed a relationship between having experienced highly coercive interrogation methods and having negative perceptions of the police. However, there was no relationship with attitudes towards the courts. Similarly it was found that having falsely confessed to a crime was also associated with negative attitudes towards the police. Again there was no relationship with negative attitudes towards the courts. Also important was that having made true confessions to the police did not relate to attitudes towards the police or the courts. It is interesting that the relationships between false confessing and experiencing coercive interrogation strategies with negative attitudes only applied to the police. This gives some strength to the argument that falsely confessing and experiencing coercive interrogation tactics causally influence attitudes towards the police though we cannot be certain of this.

Can evidence of a confession be disregarded?

On the face of things, it is hard to understand why people confess to horrific crimes which they simply did not commit. Nearly two-thirds (64 per cent) of members of the public agreed or strongly agreed that a confession is a powerful indicator of guilt (Henkel, Coffman and Dailey, 2008). Just about half (51 per cent) believed that if a person confesses to a crime then they are probably guilty. People in general agreed with the statement 'Criminal suspects sometimes confess to crimes they did not commit' and only 14 per cent disagreed to any extent. Perhaps more troubling is that even more people strongly agreed that 'Once someone has confessed to a crime, there is no need to continue searching for other evidence, such as fingerprints.' The public tended to believe that they would be unlikely to confess to a crime they had not committed and believed that they would only do so under torture.

What is it about false confessions that makes them influential? It is important to understand that false confessions generally involve a lot more than a simple acknowledgement of guilt. They can be rich in detail and there are no established methods of readily distinguishing a confession from a false confession. However, the simple admission of guilt can be enough to lead to a conviction (Appleby, Hasel and Kassin, 2013). Remarkably, the power of confession evidence applies even when the false confession is by a third party and not the individual in question. Appleby *et al.* (2013) sought to analyse what the main features of false confessions are in the hope that these would reveal something about why false confessions seem to be so readily believed. The study concentrated on police interrogation-induced false confessions. The researchers obtained examples of false confessions from the records of the Innocence Project and elsewhere. Coding was carried out to identify the following features of the false confessions:

- the medium and format of the confessions;
- whether various types of crime details were present;
- any indications that the false confession was voluntary.

Universally, false confessions included details about the crime's location and when it occurred. All of the false confessions contained visual details concerning the crime scene (such as that there was blood everywhere). Ninety-five per cent referred to people such as co-perpetrators, witnesses and others. The victim was described in 80 per cent of cases and 45 per cent described the victim's mental or emotional state. Surprisingly, 45 per cent of the false confessions included illustrations, such as maps of the crime scene, which might suggest first-hand knowledge of the crime, thus enhancing the credibility of the confessions. About two-thirds of the confessions contained material that psychologically justified or excused the false confessor's blameworthiness for the crime. The authors suggest that this may reflect the minimisation tactics used by police in interrogations. About half of the false confessions included material indicative of their voluntariness in some way.

In an interesting comment, Appleby, Hasel and Kassin (2013) mention Inbau, Reid, Buckley and Jayne s (2001) error correction ploy. That is, the advice that police officers deliberately introduce into the written confession minor errors such as incorrect crime details which the suspect will correct and initial before finally signing the confession. The ploy is introduced to create the 'guilty knowledge' required to spot the error. At least one error was corrected in 44 per cent of the false confessions. But these are false confessions, so the 'guilty knowledge' must have been obtained from the police during the interrogation or in some other way. Although Appleby *et al.* tend to point to similarities between the contents of true and false confessions, this should not be seen as definitive evidence that there are no informative differences between the two. Villar, Arciuli and Patterson (2013) point out that a true perpetrator of a crime has to act ignorant of their 'guilty knowledge', whereas a false confessor may pick up these details from being shown photographs or from leading questions during interrogation. The result of this is the impression that the false confessor is telling the truth rather than lying. They carried out a study in which participants had to come up with accounts of a social transgression in which they had been involved and about which they felt guilty. Using quite a sophisticated and complex methodology, they also asked the participants to create a fabricated account of something embarrassing which had

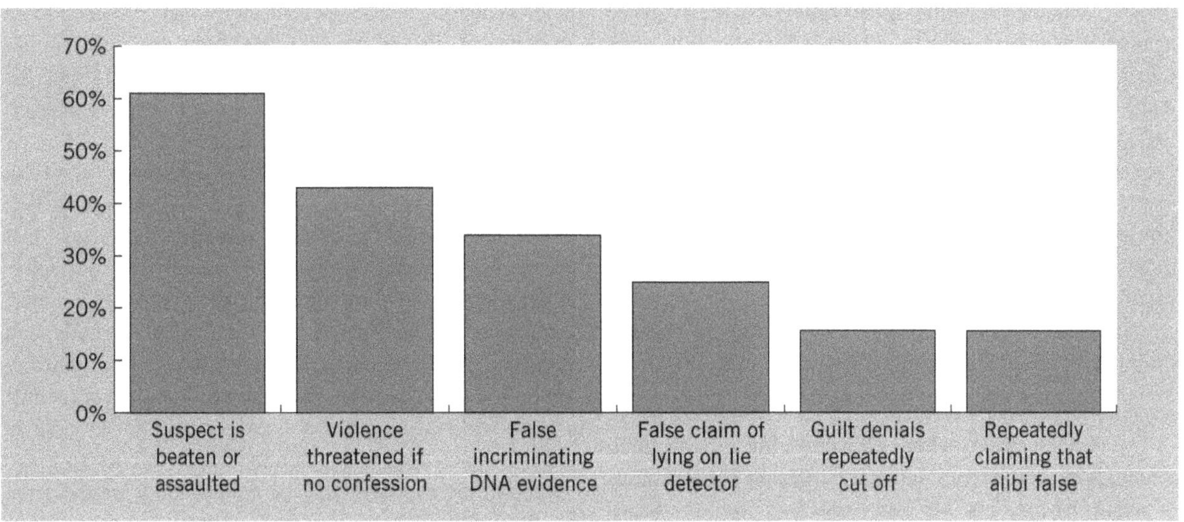

Figure 17.5 Interrogation tactics and the percentage believing that they would lead to false confessions

not actually happened to them. The analysis was simply the number of nouns, verbs and adjectives found in truthful versus false accounts. The number of nouns and verbs did not differentiate the two but the number of adjectives did. There were fewer adjectives in the false confessions.

Just what do the public understand about the factors which lead to false confessions? Their knowledge is vital when they come to serve on juries where this might be an issue. Leo and Liu (2009) surveyed a sample of 264 jury-eligible students about the likelihood that a range of interrogation tactics would lead to a false confession. Some details about the factors jurors thought might induce false confession can be found in Figure 17.5. Quite clearly, potential jurors believed that torture and the like were likely to encourage people to confess falsely. However, they were far less likely to believe that psychological tactics such as repeatedly interrupting any denials that the suspect tries to make would work. Leo and Liu argue that these findings demonstrate the public's failure to completely appreciate the power of coercive interrogation to encourage false confessions.

There is evidence from experimental studies that confession evidence is especially potent. Studies by Kassin and Neumann (1997) found it to produce higher conviction rates than character testimony and eyewitness identification. Confession evidence is subject to rules. In the United States, confession evidence is not normally admissible in court if it was elicited by any of the following (Kassin, 1997b; Kassin and Sukel, 1997):

- brute force;
- deprivation of food or sleep;
- prolonged isolation;
- promises of immunity or leniency;
- threats of harm or punishment;
- omitting to notify the suspect of his/her constitutional rights, except in exceptional circumstances.

Of course, this confession evidence may be given in court before its admissibility is challenged. This begs the question of whether, in these circumstances, the jury members can completely disregard the confession evidence, as is required in accordance with legal principles. The alternative, of course, is that the confession evidence, despite its inadmissibility, sways the jury.

Kassin and Sukel (1997) set out to test, experimentally, this hypothesis. In one study, introductory psychology students in the United States were randomly assigned to one of four confession groups. The groups were those produced by the following variables:

- high-pressure versus low-pressure interrogation;
- admissible versus inadmissible confessions, as ruled upon by the judge during the 'trial'.

Each 'mock' juror studied a trial transcript that took 20–25 minutes to read. They then completed questionnaires without jury deliberations.

The transcript was of the trial of a man charged with murdering his estranged wife and a male neighbour. The district attorney charged that the man, Wilson, killed the pair after coming across them together. The defendant, on the other hand, claimed that he merely found the bodies when he went back to his former abode to collect financial papers. With the exception of the confession, the evidence against Wilson was entirely circumstantial (the killer was 6 feet tall and left-handed), incomplete (there was no murder weapon) and ambiguous (before calling the police he fled the scene and phoned his attorney). The transcripts consisted of opening statements, closing arguments, the examinations of five witnesses and a brief judge's instruction on the charge of first-degree murder and the requirements of proof: presumption of innocence, burden of proof and reasonable doubt.

Other participants rated interrogation situations based on Inbau *et al.*'s (1986) manual for police officers:

- *The high-pressure condition:* 'They drove me back to the police station, where Officer Heffling handcuffed me, took out his gun and started asking me questions about the murders. My arm really hurt from the handcuffs, but he wouldn't remove them . . . I told him that my right arm had just come out of a cast and was very sore.' When asked 'Were they trying to pressure you to confess?', the defendant replied 'Yes he was angry and yelling'. The police officer also testified but rejected the suggestion that Wilson was under so much stress that he would confess to a crime he did not commit.
- *The low-pressure condition:* the defendant was said to have confessed immediately upon questioning. He was not handcuffed, verbally abused or threatened with a weapon.
- *The no-confession control group:* the defendant and police officer both testified that Wilson denied murdering his wife and neighbour during his interrogation.

The remaining condition to be manipulated was the admissibility or not of the confession:

- *Admissible condition:* the defence lawyer raised an objection to the police officer's mentioning the confession material. The judge overruled the objection. The prosecuting lawyer mentioned the confession in the closing argument.
- *Inadmissible condition:* the judge supported the defence's objection to the police evidence about the confession. The confession was deemed inadmissible and struck off the transcript of the trial though, of course, the jury was aware of it. The jury was then instructed by the judge to disregard the police officer's remarks about the confession.

The evidence showed that the inadmissible evidence affected the mock jurors' perceptions of the guilt of the accused. They gave more guilty verdicts when they knew of this evidence. This was the case even in circumstances where they believed that the confession was a coerced one and they knew that information about that confession was inadmissible in court. A second study that contained more evidence in support of the prosecution produced similar findings. The US Supreme Court's view was that the admission of coerced confession is a harmless error. Kassin's findings are clearly at variance with this.

Jurors seemed to discount confessions where the false evidence ploy was used. The false evidence ploy is a police tactic where the officers pretend to the suspect that they have evidence which they actually do not have. However, the extent to which this ploy is totally counterproductive in the jury room is not clear. Woody and Forrest (2009) gave mock jurors transcripts of an interrogation to read. The transcript either did or did not include a false evidence ploy and either did or did not involve an expert witness commenting on the false evidence strategy. Although the evidence and the confession were the same in all conditions, the presence of false evidence ploys resulted in a lowering of the likelihood of conviction and shorter prison sentences. The transcripts with ploys were rated as being more coercive and deceptive. The presence of an expert witness commenting about ploys cut down the convictions and increased perceptions that the interrogation involved deception and coercion.

What should be done?

Kassin and other experts on police drew up a list of recommendations which, if implemented, would help ensure that the problem of false confession is reduced. This was published by the AP-LS (American Psychology and Law Society) and is generally referred to as a white paper (Thompson, 2010). The main recommendations (reforms) were as follows (Kassin *et al.* 2010), though it cannot be stressed too much that they are specifically aimed at the American context and may already be employed elsewhere:

- *Electronic recording of all interrogations and interviews:* The requirement is for every custodial interview/interrogation to be videotaped in its entirety, using a camera position which places equal focus on the suspect and the interrogator.
- *Limit custody and interrogation time:* There should be movement towards restricting the maximum length of interrogations such that it can only be exceeded with the permission of an authority (e.g. a senior police officer). This is already a requirement in the United Kingdom.
- *Presentation of false evidence:* The white paper encourages the criminal justice system to be more sensitive to the effects that false evidence in the context of interrogations can have. For whatever reason,

perhaps political, the white paper falls short of recommending a complete ban on the use of false evidence in interrogation. It suggests that vulnerable groups such as young people and those with intellectual restrictions perhaps should not be subjected to the presentation of false evidence.

- *Protection of vulnerable suspects:* A trained professional advocate (ideally a lawyer) should sit in on interrogations involving juveniles. Similarly, those who conduct interviews with vulnerable group members should be required to have specific training with the objective of maximising their sensitivity and skills when dealing with the problems that vulnerable suspects bring.
- *Reform of interrogation practices:* In many countries, there should be a move from the Reid model of interviewing (as found in the police training manual) and its assumption of guilt to an investigatory style of interviewing (more characteristic of the United Kingdom's approach).

These seem wise suggestions. Nevertheless, there are potential problems with them especially the recommendation to electronically record interviews and interrogations. There is a growing use of video in some states of the USA (Snyder, Lassiter, Lindberg and Pinegar, 2009). It is felt that videoing 1) encourages the police not to employ the most extreme coercive methods of getting a confession and 2) the video may be evaluated later by the judge and jury. Besides these advantages, there can be a number of problems with video. If only part of the interrogation is recorded then the result may be misleading since it omits important information about what happened in the rest of the interview. Furthermore, the use of 'recap' videos is problematic – these are essentially videos in which the suspect is asked to repeat their confession for the camera. As such, they may lack the important evidence about the emotionality accompanying the original confession. Entire interview recording, then, is important.

In addition to all of this is the camera position chosen. Frequently, the video shows the suspect clearly but also part of the interrogator's body as the camera points from behind them. Researchers have identified a difficulty with this, known as the *camera perspective bias*. It was first identified by Lassiter (2002) and has been repeatedly demonstrated by researchers since. The conspicuousness of the suspect compared to the interrogator is perceived by people viewing the video in terms of the suspect having a causal role in what happens during the video. If this was reversed and the interviewer dominated the video then the interviewer would be perceived as having the causal role in determining what happens. This is all down to the higher salience of the action attributed to the most conspicuous person. This is known as *illusory causation* and goes back to the work of Taylor and Fiske (1975, 1978). Most of the evidence for the camera perspective bias is based on simulated confessions but recently Lassiter, Ware, Ratcliff and Irvin (2009) have demonstrated it, using real confession interviews.

So the solution would appear to be to have both the suspect and the interrogator portrayed with equal conspicuousness by using two cameras simultaneously and a split screen format for the video. Snyder, Lassiter, Lindberg and Pinegar (2009) carried out such a study and found that the dual camera yielded largely unbiased judgements of both the guilt of the suspect and the voluntariness of their confession. However, things are not quite straightforward since the researchers obtained actual videos of true and false confessions. The participants then watched these confessions and had to say whether or not each one was true. There were a variety of video formats. It transpired that the dual presentation was poor at obtaining accurate decisions about the truth or falsehood of the confession. This would seem to be because the participants concentrate on facial cues and ignore other information which might be more pertinent in making the decision. In other words, the white paper may require revision in this respect.

Main points

- Confessions and false confessions may be motivated by a range of factors. Particularly problematic are those false confessions that are the consequence of police interrogation methods. These are designed to encourage confession by the guilty but may encourage confession by the innocent. Although in some cases false confessions may be made simply to obtain relief from the interview situation with the police, sometimes the decision to confess falsely is the result of a rational choice when faced with apparently strong evidence.
- There are some remarkable demonstrations of false confessions in laboratory experiments. These are important since they suggest that virtually anyone, given appropriate circumstances, can be put into a

situation where they confess to doing something that they have not done. What is more remarkable is that some false confessors do not simply acquiesce under certain circumstances but they seem to believe that they did what they confess to.

- The consequences of falsely confessing may be as serious as those for a true confession. People who are eventually proven to have falsely confessed stand a high risk of retractions not being accepted. As a result, there is a high risk of being convicted by a court of a crime they did not commit. Perhaps even more disturbing is the evidence that juries can be influenced by inadmissible confession evidence that a judge has warned them to disregard.

Further reading

Gudjonsson, G.H. (2003) *The Psychology of Interrogations and Confessions: A Handbook* Chichester: John Wiley.

Inbau, F.E., Reid, J.E., Buckley, J.P. and Jayne, B.C. (2013) *Criminal Interrogation and Confessions* (5th edn) Burlington, MA: Jones and Bartlett.

Lassiter, G.D. and Meissner, C.A. (2012) *Police Interrogations and False Confessions* Washington, DC: American Psychological Association.

Chapter 18

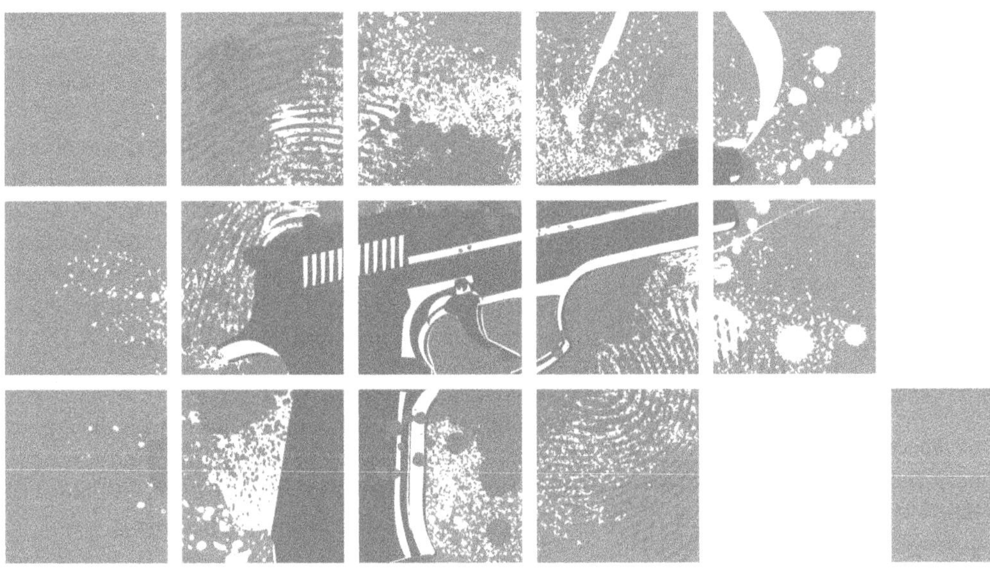

Lies, lie detecting and credibility 1: the psychology of deception

Overview

- Lying can be defined as the intention to deceive without making the other person aware of this intent.
- Assessing the accuracy of testimony is a complex process. No serious researcher nowadays would suggest that there are simple, infallible indicators of untruthful testimony such as characteristic body language.
- Good indicators of false emotion are asymmetrical facial expressions and the overly quick facial expression of emotion.
- It used to be claimed by researchers that most professional groups – police officers and psychologists, for example – are little better than chance at detecting lies without specialised training. This is not the case if police officers and others are given training in lie detection.
- Experience may lead to confidence in one's abilities to detect lies, irrespective of actual ability.
- The complexity of interview situations makes it difficult for the interviewer to concentrate on indicators of lying and truth telling.
- The lack of accurate feedback about whether they have successfully identified a liar or not is one reason why professionals cannot improve their lie-detection ability.
- Detecting lying may be difficult because the police officer uses incorrect cues to lying when making their decision.
- It is possible to increase lie detecting ability by creating cognitive overload in the suspect. ur cognitive capacities are essentially finite and the liar has a more complex set of tasks than the truth teller. By increasing cognitive load on the liar during the interview (e.g. by asking unexpected questions), the leakage of cues to deception is encouraged.

Introduction

If only we could identify liars accurately then a good number of the problems of the criminal justice system would be solved. Police, prosecutors, judges and jurors, for example, routinely assess who is telling the truth and who is lying, without their ability to do so being questioned. There is no perfect way of distinguishing the liar from the truth teller. Nevertheless, psychological research has provided at least some insights about how to train people to tell them apart. In the time since the first edition of this book was published, researchers have stood much of the established wisdom of lie detection on its head. So in this chapter we will try to reflect the changing nature of the field while respecting the contribution of earlier research. A good example of how ideas have changed in this field can be seen in the long-held view that professionals such as police officers and others are no better than the general public at detecting lies. There is some partial truth in this but, nevertheless, some police officers in certain circumstances have shown themselves to be good at sorting out the difference between truth and fiction.

When it comes to simplistic indicators of lying such as those to do with body language, language and physiological signs then there is no good news in this chapter. Such simple signs are often poor and misleading indicators of lying.

Ekman's theory of lie detection

The modern study of lie detection began with the work of Paul Ekman published in the book *Telling Lies: Clues to Deceit in the Marketplace, Politics and Marriage* (Ekman, 1992). Unfortunately, despite being the initial stimulus to research, Ekman's ideas are generally somewhat outmoded. To begin with the basics, according to Ekman (1992, 1996), a lie has to include two components:

- the intention to mislead the victim of the lie;
- the victim is not informed about this intention.

It follows from this that not all forms of deception are lies – magicians, for example, are open about their intention to deceive. Keeping secrets is not a lie if the secret is known to be a secret – such as consistently refusing to reveal one's age. Giving false information with no intention to deceive is not lying. Not revealing information may be a lie if the intention was to deceive. Ekman's definition disregards the accuracy of statements made if there was no intention to deceive. That means that false memories of child abuse would not be considered a lie, despite their extreme consequences for the accused. However, the accused is probably more concerned about the accuracy of the claims made against him or her in general than the motivation for the false allegation.

Much of the current research on lie detection concentrates on developing interview settings and procedures which make it difficult for a suspect to hide the cues to lying from police officers and the like. Nevertheless, Ekman's work laid down some of the basics which need to be appreciated. Among the reasons why lie detecting is difficult, according to Ekman, are the following:

- Assessing a person for lying is overly complex since everything from facial expressions through gestures to vocal utterances need our attention. So sometimes we concentrate on verbal and facial aspects which the liar finds the most easy to monitor and change.
- We may not have baseline measurements of things called *manipulators* (touching, stroking and otherwise manipulating one's own body), for example, though they can be a clue to deceit. Unfortunately, people vary markedly in the extent to which they use manipulators. Many signs of lying are actually signs of strong emotion. So a deceitful individual may be in fear of being caught lying. However, these same emotions may be raised by factors other than lying. Taken on their own, emotions are often misleading guides to deceit.
- The context of the lie may vary enormously. So, for example, it is easier to tell a lie if one can anticipate when it will be necessary to tell a lie. If one has to lie unexpectedly, then there is little time to formulate a convincing lie.

According to Ekman (1992), the emotions which lying arouses manifest themselves in *leakages* – that is, in the form of observable characteristics. These are possible clues to emotion that may reveal that someone is lying. Included among the clues that should be looked for are: 1) frequent swallowing, faster/shallower breathing, sweating, increased blinking, pupil dilation; 2) louder speech – most likely indicates anger; 3) pauses and speech errors – these suggest a lack of preparation of the 'story' or strong negative emotions, especially fear; and 4) the whitening of the face – which suggests anger or fear.

Ekman argues that there are clues in facial expressions of emotion which indicate that the emotion may not be real. Asymmetrical facial expression and abrupt onset of the emotion are characteristics which suggest that the emotion is false. Expressions of happiness should involve eye muscles otherwise they are false. False fear and sadness lack a characteristic forehead expression involving the eyebrows. Anger is very difficult to fake, according to Ekman's (1985) theory. The muscles involved in expressing anger are very hard to control. A falsely accused innocent person may find their anger difficult to control and the guilty accused person will find it difficult to feign anger realistically. Of course, anger should be more common in high-stake situations than for trivial matters.

In the first part of their study of this, Hatz and Bourgeois (2010) used both real transgressions and mock transgression scenarios in order to induce lying (and truth telling). In the real transgressions scenario, college students were asked to cheat or otherwise. The task involved working independently and then collectively with another 'student' on a series of mathematical problems. The other 'student' was a confederate of the researchers who asked the real student for help – which was against the rules. Because the cheating pairs submitted identical answers they were accused of cheating by the researcher. The cheating was 'reported to a professor' who said that it could be considered as a case of academic dishonesty and could involve the academic disciplinary committee. Although cheating was a matter of choice in the study, all of the participants did cheat, given the opportunity, and all of them chose to lie about cheating. The design also included a mock transgression situation in which participants largely went through the same procedures as before but instead they were told that the confederate was the researcher's assistant – and the researcher's assistant told some of them that they should cheat. The participants in all conditions were secretly videotaped as they replied to a number of questions such as 'Did you two cheat on these problems?'

The videos were shown to a panel of judges in order to have the behaviours of the participants assessed. The findings were clear. First of all, the judges perceived the truth tellers in the real transgression situation as being significantly more angry than the liars. For the mock transgression groups there was no difference between liars and truth tellers in this respect. The researchers also examined the numbers of anger-related words used by participants. In the mock transgression situation, the mean number of angry words used by truth tellers was much the same as the mean number of angry words used by the liars. On the other hand, in the real transgression situation, the truth tellers used more angry words than the liars.

Although people in general do little better than chance when attempting to distinguish a liar from a truth teller, some individuals are better than others at lie detecting (Ekman, O'Sullivan and Frank, 1999). Furthermore, Ekman believed that it was possible to train people to be better at lie detecting. But the basic bottom line position is that there is no simple way of detecting lies with a single indicator – such as body posture – which instantly reveals who is lying.

BOX 18.1 Forensic psychology in action

Are people good at telling lies to the police?

One of the common activities of the police is that of taking the names and addresses of people. This maybe because they have been a witness to a crime or maybe they have been stopped on suspicion. Much of the time most of us would have no reason to lie about our home addresses but this is not always the case. A person acting suspiciously may provide a false address in the hope that this will help them avoid further police action. A perfectly innocent young person might choose to give a false address simply because they do not want their parents to know where they were at a particular time.

Just what is the psychology of making up a false address? It sounds like an easy thing to do but there are problems. Roach (2010) researched the fabrication of addresses in situations like this. The act of giving a false address, suggests Roach, is likely to be spontaneous rather than planned as one cannot predict being asked for one's address by a police officer. Research on human memory suggests that it is cognitively quite difficult to fabricate an entirely false address – remember that while fabricating the address the individual needs to avoid arousing any suspicions. When they choose to give a false address, people are likely to resort to using something relatively familiar since they employ established schemas in their thinking. Another way of putting this is that there is likely to be more than just a mere element of truth in this sort of lie. So just how is the false address fabricated? To understand this further, Roach (2010) adopted a simple strategy – he asked a substantial sample of university students in the north of England to respond to a scenario in which they had been stopped by a police officer and asked for their personal details. They do not wish to give their correct address. They are to generate a false address very quickly within a space of ten seconds. It was required that the address included the number of the house, the name of the street or road, the town, and country plus the postcode (zip code).

It was often very clear that elements of the address actually gave clues about their real addresses. In other

▶

BOX 18.1 (continued)

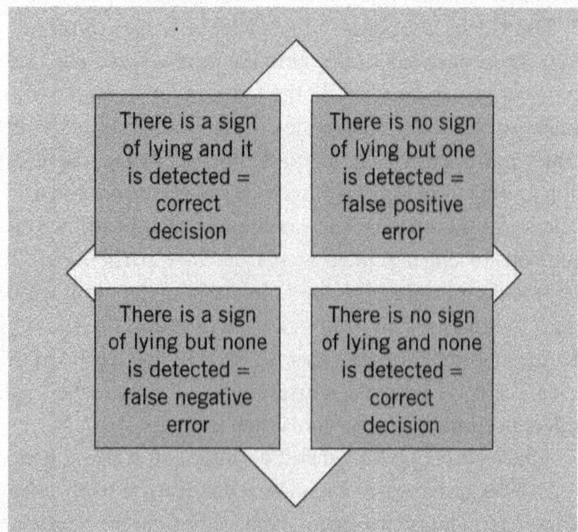

Figure 18.1 Showing the tendency to invent a 'false' postcode but which reveals the place lived in

words, many of the false addresses were only partial fabrications. Participants also indicated the nature of their thought processes which led to the false address. Eight per cent said that they gave an old address of theirs, 21 per cent gave the address of someone they knew, 16 per cent used an address made up of real and fabricated elements such as giving their own address but with a different house number, 20 per cent claimed that the address was created randomly although this is doubtful in some cases as they contained recognisable elements, and 36 per cent gave complex explanations sometimes of a rather fanciful nature. Quite a high proportion, then, of putatively false addresses contained information which might be useful in tracking down the person in question. Of particular interest were the data on postcodes (zip codes). These in general locate a house within quite a small geographical boundary in the UK. Roach found that the majority of the postcodes given were real in terms of the first two letters of the code at a minimum (see Figure 18.1) and a small number gave exactly their own postcode. In other words, the postcode given was a good predictor of the town in which the individual lives but sometimes located the individual even more precisely than that.

Another analysis checked whether or not the postcodes given were real ones despite being part of a false address. The 'false' postcodes were checked against an available list of postcodes. It was found that where the participant had given a postcode based on reality, they overwhelmingly checked out against the list of postcodes. However, where the participant had given a totally fictitious postcode then this only existed in about a third of cases. See Figure 18.2.

These findings do not simply fit with established theory about memory but they are of some practical value. First of all they imply that an individual may be found because the false address reflects aspects of their current address or it is an address of someone known to the individual or it is a previous address. Secondly it might be expected that if someone lies by giving a non-existent postcode then they may be more generally untrustworthy. This is a matter for further research, however.

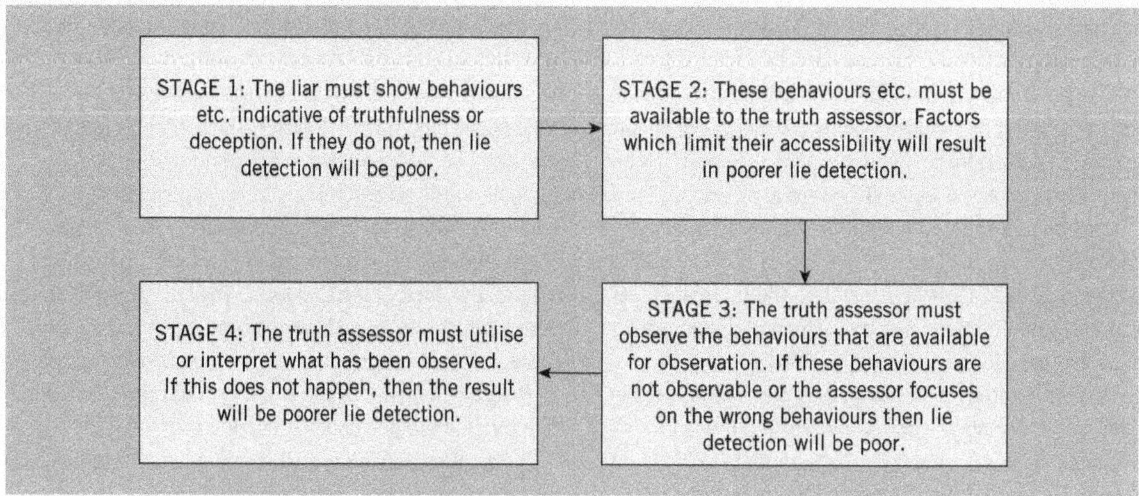

Figure 18.2 Illustrating how false postcodes do not correspond to real ones

Are professional lie detectors really no better?

It is hardly surprising that lies are hard to detect – their function is to mislead. Indeed, if, as research suggests (Vrij, Ennis, Farman and Mann, 2010), a quarter of everyday conversations involve lying, then we exist in an environment in which lying largely goes unnoticed. There is a general consensus that the detection of lies is a skill that can be learned but is nevertheless a rare talent. The traditional view based on research has been that that the police, psychologists, lawyers and the medical profession can detect lies only marginally better than the chance level (Ekman, 1992, 1996). Garrido and Masip's (1999) review of police lie detection skills based on studies from many parts of the world is typical of this point of view. In this review, they concluded as follows:

- An officer's confidence in their lie-detecting ability is unrelated to their actual ability to detect lies.
- Experienced officers are over-confident about their lie-detecting ability.
- Experienced police officers and newly recruited ones do not differ in their lie- and truth-detecting ability.
- Police officers are no better than the general public at detecting lies.
- Police officers use worthless indicators that a person is lying (e.g. social anxiety and assertiveness).
- Usually, police officers are no better than chance at identifying truth telling and lying.

This is a damning summary of the ability of police to distinguish between honesty and deceit. However, the standard methods used in research supportive of these conclusions can be criticised. One reason is that the studies fail to reflect the sorts of situations in which police officers make their professional judgements about lying. Increasingly, research is indicating that the pessimistic conclusions from such early research may have to be modified. Taken overall, there has been variable research findings concerning the accuracy of police professionals' lie detection ability. Some studies have suggested that the police are reasonably accurate lie detectors, while others suggest that their ability differs little from chance, just as Garrido and Masip had concluded.

Why such conflicting conclusions? O'Sullivan, Hurley and Tiwana (2009) argue that some conditions are suboptimal in terms of lie detection accuracy and others are nearer optimal. There are a number of issues following from this. In particular, we might question the relevance of studies in which police officers make judgements about lying in contexts very dissimilar to those of the typical police interview. Of course, the evidence that people in general are bad as distinguish truth from lies tends to support the contention that police officers are also bad at detecting lies. Sullivan *et al.* point out that meta-analyses (see Box 4.1) leading to the conclusion that people are poor at detecting lies generally used students as participants. Young people are poorer at lie detection than older people. Meta-analyses (e.g. Aamodt and Custer, 2006) may be 'swamped', Sullivan *et al.* suggest, by data from students such that overall they misleadingly indicate that all people are poor lie detectors. The studies also often involve relatively low-stake outcomes if the lie is detected – that is, in the studies the unsuccessful liar often does not get punished. There are some studies in which the consequences of lying are much more serious – such as where major crimes are involved. Sullivan *et al.* suggest that these variations in the characteristics of studies may be responsible for the rather confusing array of research findings in the early research.

Another problem is that researchers tend to write as if a simple signal detection theory applies to the detection of lies. Signal detection theory developed out of situations in which a radar operative had to decide whether a signal had been detected in circumstances where there may or may not have been a signal. So the basic task of lie detection is conceived as shown in Figure 18.3 from the signal detection perspective. O'Sullivan *et al.* (2009) argue that since there are no universal indicators of lying, the lie detection situation needs a more complex model than that implies. They adopted Funder's (1999) Realistic Accuracy Model (RAM), which was originally developed in order to study the accuracy of people's assessments of another person. One advantage of the RAM model is that it does not assume that there is a signal (indicating a lie) which has to be detected in order to decide whether or not the person has lied. The features of Funder's RAM model applied to lie detection are illustrated in Figure 18.4. Each of the four stages illustrated can potentially improve or worsen the truth assessor's accuracy:

- Stage 1 requires that the liar should manifest a range of behaviours indicative of lying, otherwise lie detection will be poor. Research suggests that, where the outcome or stake is trivial, the cues to deception are much less likely to manifest themselves. That is, the liar has to be motivated to deceive before deception cues will manifest themselves. Furthermore, any procedure which encourages their manifestation (e.g. cognitively overloading the suspect) will improve lie detection.
- Stage 2: The signs which are indicative of lying involve potentially many parts of the liar's body and what they have to say. If the truth assessor cannot see or hear these things, for example, then their lie detection ability

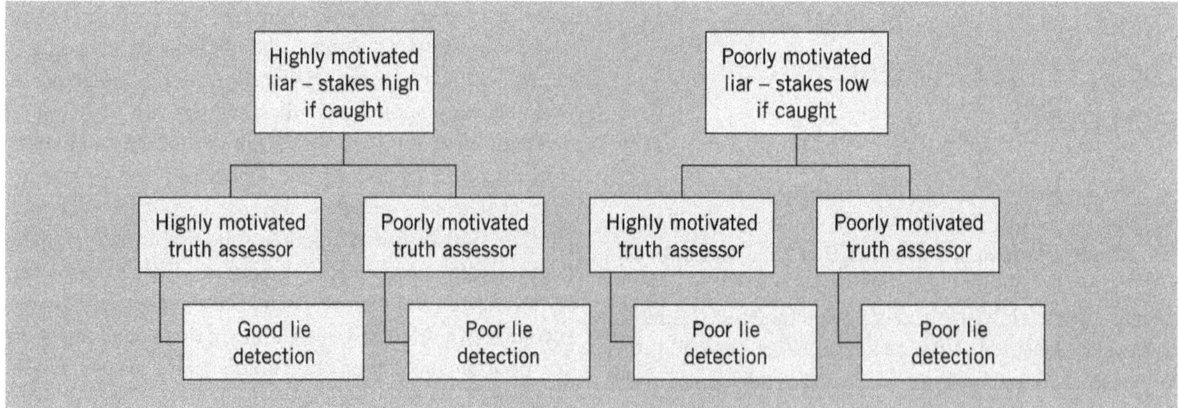

Figure 18.3 Signal detection theory applied to lie detection

will be reduced. So fuzzy, inaudible video or video solely concentrating on the face will adversely affect lie detection.

- Stage 3 is more about the activity of the truth assessor when observing the suspect. The truth assessor may simply fail to concentrate properly or they may concentrate on the suspect's face when the cues to deception are in what the suspect does with their hands.
- Stage 4 is about what the truth assessor does with what is observed in the previous stages. If the truth assessor does not know what behaviours are truly indicative of lying and so uses invalid signs then, of course, the detection of lies will be poor.

It is fairly easy to see from the theory how problems at any of these stages can hamper the detection of lies. Furthermore, the theory also gives strong hints about how the particular methodological features of a research study may mask the true level of lie-detecting ability among professions such as police officers.

Laboratory-induced lies, because of their lack of serious implications for the liar, are quite clearly problematic. It is probably inevitable that research relies on a fairly narrow range of procedures when a research field is new. Nevertheless, studies using significant lies with significant risks and police officers as lie detectors are what is needed – though they are at a premium. Such procedures are often known as *high stakes*, reflecting that there are serious consequences involved for not being believed. Vrij and Mann (2001) used videos of press conferences in which a relative of a missing or murdered person appealed for help in finding the missing person or their killers. These televised appeals in some cases are highly deceptive since the relative involved was actually the killer. These obviously

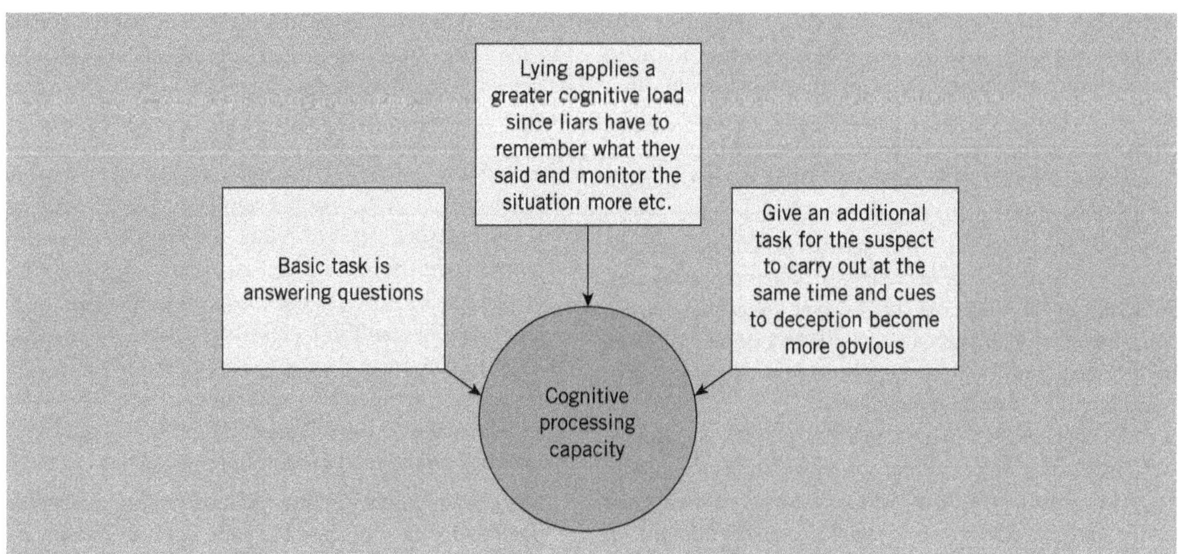

Figure 18.4 The lie detection process according to the RAM model

involved high-stake lies of the sort that might heighten the number of cues to deception available. So are such high-stake lies more readily detectable? Dutch police officers were shown videos of a number of such press conferences as well as similar ones that did not involve such lies as 'fillers'. The murders were all British ones, hence the decision to carry out the research with Dutch police officers who were much less likely to have prior knowledge of the events. These officers identified the liars at exactly chance level – 50 per cent accuracy. As with other studies, accuracy was unrelated to (a) the amount of time served as a police officer and (b) the amount of experience interviewing suspects. Confidence in these decisions was also unrelated to accuracy; although officers with more interviewing experience were more confident about their judgements. A variety of reasons were offered by the officers to explain their decisions about lying and truth telling. For example, they frequently mentioned fake emotions, real emotions and gaze aversion. Nevertheless, there was no correlation between these reasons and accuracy with one exception. That is, those who mentioned real emotions were actually less accurate in detecting lies than those who did not!

Curiously, a rather similar study to that of Vrij and Mann (2001) using similar high-stakes lying situations came out rather more positive about the ability of the police to judge lying and truth telling. Whelan, Wagstaff and Wheatcroft (2015) used police firearms officers, police detective and students at an English university. The high-stakes material was videos of public appeals for missing or killed relatives such as when the relative speaks to a press conference for help finding or finding the killer so much the same as the earlier study. Half of the appeals where honest and the rest lies made by the actual culprit. The findings of the study were more optimistic about detecting high-stakes lies. Over 50 per cent of the police officers were better than 74 per cent accurate at detecting the truth whereas the figure was rather lower at 27 per cent of the students. The police were a little more accurate at judging dishonest appeals correctly whereas the students did better with the honest appeals. There was also a positive relationship between judgement confidence and judgement accuracy unlike the findings of low-stakes studies. Whelan, Wagstaff and Wheatcroft (2015), however, do mention that past work of high-stakes accuracy involving the credibility of suspects in police interviews with suspects. Over this series of studies police credibility assessments varied in accuracy from between 64 per cent to 72 per cent. There is clearly some support for the view that the police are better than chance at detecting liars in this study.

In another high-stakes study of police lie detection ability, Carlucci, Compo and Zimmerman (2013) used just about as natural a source of truthful and deceptive material as possible. Traffic stops are routinely videoed by a dashboard camera in the US. In Carlucci *et al.*'s study, videos of the conversations of the police with those they had stopped were shown to participants in the research. In some of the stops, a search of the vehicle revealed something suspicious (e.g. illegal aliens or illegal drugs). These searches were edited out of the videos. But the fact that a search had taken place is strongly indicative evidence that the drivers involved had a motivation to lie to the traffic officers. Similarly, no suspicious evidence can be seen as suggesting strongly that those involved had no reason to lie. The drivers all denied any wrongdoing in the videos. So these are realistic and relevant lie detection situations for police officers. A sample of experienced police officers watched the videos and made truth or lie calls for each of them. There was an additional sample of novice students who watched the videos and also made judgements of lying or truth telling. Overall accuracy for students was 63 per cent correct assessments while that for the experienced police officers it was 60 per cent. The hit rates for lying and truth telling are slightly above chance levels. This hides the fact, though, that police officers manifested a bias to saying that the drivers were lying in the videos. They were actually quite good at detecting liars accurately (80 per cent correct lie calls) but they performed slightly below chance when detecting truth telling in the drivers (42 per cent correct truth calls).

So professional lie detectors sometimes may be poor at lying because of their inherent biases in making credibility judgements. Lay people may be poor at detecting lies because of their own biases, which are different but nevertheless produce inaccuracy. Nahari (2012) compared lay people and professionals who are involved in lie detection. The aim was to understand their different ways of going about credibility judgements. He took a sample of nearly 50 professionals in lie detection (police officers, interrogators, and intelligence and secret service agents) and compared them with a sample of 40 students in Israel. The participants simply read a story and had to say whether the narrator was being truthful in that the events had actually been experienced. The findings suggested that the professionals and lay lie detectors differed in a number of important respects:

- The professionals tended to be sceptical and believe that the story was a lie. The lay lie detectors tended to be biased towards believing the story true.
- The professionals tended to adopt a systematic approach to the judgement. That is, they checked the internal details against other internal details or against knowledge external to the story. So they were more likely to see, for example, that the colour of the narrator's coat changed during the telling of the story. Nahari suggests that is because they have a tendency to being suspicious which previous research has indicated tends to lead to systematic processing.
- The lay lie detectors, however, adopted a different strategy – the heuristic strategy. Basically this is built

on making judgements about the richness of the different sorts of detail in the story. So there may be contextual, emotional, perceptual and semantic details. This strategy is a relatively automatic judgement, with the level of detail being indicative of truthfulness.

- Professional lie detectors would use the same detail as lay lie detectors but conclude often that it was indicative of deception, as the narrator was seen as putting in the details to convince the reader of the truthfulness of his story. At the same time, some would argue that a lack of detail indicated deception.

In other words, the strategies for detecting lies might be different between ordinary people and professionals but they both are problematic in terms of accuracy. We can now turn to other explanations of what prevents professionals from being good lie detectors.

Reliance on invalid cues to deception

Recently the research literature has stressed two main problems that lead to people making poor shows when making deception decisions. The first is that most people (including professionals) mistakenly use invalid cues to deception when making decisions about when another person is lying. If people use cues which research has shown don't work effectively to sort out liars from truth tellers, it is not surprising that most people make poor lie detectors. If we look in the wardrobe for the milk then no wonder we don't find it! The second is that even the best cues to deception are at best mediocre predictors. Researchers can always look for better indicators of deception but whether they are there are to be found is quite another matter. Many would doubt that they exist. Nevertheless, many 'experts' in the criminal justice system remain convinced of their ability to detect lies. But because they think they are good does it follow that they are good? Stromwall and Granhag (2003) studied three separate groups of legal professionals in Sweden – judges, prosecutors and police officers. The researchers compared what the professionals believed about lie detection with what has been substantiated through research. For example, Stromwall and Granhag mention such cues as higher-pitched voices when lying and fewer body movements of the leg, foot, hand and arm. So to what extent are the beliefs of professionals working in the criminal justice system? The evidence from a survey of these professional groups demonstrates major discrepancies between what research evidence suggests overall and the beliefs of the professionals:

- *Body movements:* police officers tended to believe that liars made more body movements, whereas the prosecutors and judges believed that body movement could not be used as a sign of lying. The research evidence suggests that liars may actually make fewer body movements than truth tellers.
- *It is easier to detect a liar in face-to-face situations:* the professionals tended to believe that interrogators interacting with witnesses in face-to-face situations would be better at identifying lying. Observers would be worse at detecting lying. This view held by professional groups in the criminal justice system reverses what research evidence suggests. That is, objectively, observers are better at detecting liars than interrogators.
- *Lack of detail:* all three groups of professionals tended to believe that untruthful statements contain little detail. This is supported by the mass of relevant studies into the relationship between truthfulness and the amount of detail.
- *Liars avoid eye contact (are more gaze-aversive):* most police officers subscribed to this belief. However, the prosecutors and judges tended to believe that there was no difference between liars and truth tellers in gaze aversion. The research evidence is that there is no relationship between lying and gaze aversion – some studies even suggest that liars make more eye contact. (There is evidence of one exception which is worth mentioning as it illustrates something of the complexity involved. Lundi *et al.* (2013) had pairs of liars and pairs of truth tellers interviewed together by a single interviewer. The truth tellers had had lunch together in a nearby restaurant, whereas the liars had to claim that they had lunch together. Eye contact between the suspects and the interviewer was coded. The expectation of the researchers was that liars would make more eye contact with the interviewer in order to assess the effectiveness of their lies. But liars were expected to make less eye contact with each other – perhaps to avoid cognitive overload or perhaps to avoid revealing their deception. Liars did look less at each other and more at the interviewer as predicted, thus making a very particular exception to the research evidence.)
- *Pitch of voice:* this was not generally seen as an indicator of lying in any of the groups of professionals. The research evidence does, however, suggest that there is a relationship.
- *Untruthful statements are less consistent over time:* all professional groups tended to believe this. There is some research evidence to suggest that this idea is correct.

It is not surprising then that incorrect decisions are being made about deceit if those decisions are based on worthless indicators of lying.

The wide acceptance of the idea that bad lie detection rates are the consequence of the wrong use of cues has been challenged. Hartwig and Bond (2011) took the idea of invalid cues and tested it. One of the things which they point out is that simple claims by the decision maker (the person trying to detect lies) that a particular cue is used in lie detection (by a suspect) may not reflect what actually was involved. Hartwig and Bond make a distinction between:

- cues which are associated with *perceiving* that the individual is lying;
- cues which are actually associated with individuals lying.

Decision makers about lying may pick on a common but flawed idea and offer it in explanation of what they look for when they make decisions about truthfulness. But they are wrong in their claim and actually use other cues which they do not mention. That is, the decision maker's perceptions of their task and what actually happens in the decision-making task itself are not necessarily the same thing. The decision made about whether a person is lying or telling the truth is a function both of the cues that differentiate truth tellers from liars and the extent to which the decision maker uses those cues rather than other cues in making their truth/lie judgements. Hartwig and Bond carried out a number of meta-analyses (see Box 4.1) of studies which provided evidence about the relationship between deception cues and judgements that the individual is lying. Impressions of incompetence in interviews (a cue to deception) correlated substantially (r =.6) with judgements that the individual was lying. Similarly, evidence of ambivalence in the interview correlated .5 with judgements that the individual was lying. For comparison, eye contact was only weakly correlated with judgements that the individual was lying (.15). To test the wrong subjective cue hypothesis, a further meta-analysis was conducted. The researchers collected together those studies in which cues to judgements of deception were compared with cues for actual deception. Cues to perceived deception and cues to actual deception correlated substantially (.6). However, lying judgements and lying itself correlated much lower at .2. In other words, these findings do not support the wrong cues explanation of poor deception detection.

The quest for lie detection wizards

One of the problems with any form of professional decision making lies in the adequacy of the feedback that follows the decision. In the case of assessment of deceit and truth telling, there is no accurate feedback as to whether the decision was correct. This lack of feedback means that professionals cannot improve and, worse still, may come to believe that their strategy for detecting lies is a good one. Granhag, Andersson, Stromwall and Hartwig (2004) carried out a study in Sweden which was founded on this idea that adequate feedback is required in order that skills at detecting deception may be improved. They reasoned that among the groups of people who actually get feedback about the best cues to deceptions would be criminals who gain from telling lies successfully but are punished if, for example, the police do not believe them. So the researchers compared three groups – prisoners, prison personnel and students – in terms of their replies to a questionnaire concerning beliefs about the characteristics of lying. The questionnaire included a number of questions that had several responses from which to choose. For example:

> Liars include fewer details than truth tellers.
> Liars include more details than truth tellers.
> There is no difference in the amount of details given by liars.
> Don't know.
>
> (p. 108)

The answers to the various questions could be assessed against the findings of research. So, for the above question, the correct answer according to research was the first option – liars include fewer details than truth tellers. Other research-based correct answers would include that liars move less than truth tellers and that planning of deceptive things to say increases the impression of honesty. The findings of the study tended to indicate that the prisoners did have different beliefs about the cues to deception from prison staff and students. They tended to have fewer stereotypes about cues to deception than the other two groups. Relatively, prisoners had the greatest insight into deception psychology – evidence in favour of the feedback hypothesis. Suspects who cannot lie effectively will quickly get feedback on their lack of skills by being charged with the offence. Those who lie effectively will have positive feedback on this as they walk out of the police station without being charged.

If there are some criminals who are more expert in detecting lies, are there some police and related personnel who might be particularly good at this too? There is a tradition in the research literature which accepts that there are expert lie detectors, despite the general lack of lie detection ability among people. The idea of lie detection wizards has little to do with the general view that police officers are just about as poor as the average student at detecting lies. Ekman's research (O'Sullivan and Ekman, 2004), which is held to demonstrate such lie detection skills, contained very obvious weaknesses since it involved self-scoring by participants and a show of hands to indicate how accurate they were! Methodological objections to this procedure are obvious and need no explication here. Ideally, to search for lie-detection wizards involves assessment over a number of occasions. Those who are very good lie detectors in each of the sessions can be designated as being experts. Of course, given a big enough sample, there is a probability that some people will consistently do well simply on the basis of chance – that is, by guessing.

Bond (2008) set about addressing the question of whether there are deception detection experts, using more demanding methods and criteria. Four lie detection tests were given over two occasions. Participants who showed 80 per cent or better accuracy over each of the two assessments at the first session were invited back for more tests the next day. They were classified as deception detection experts if they did better than this criterion again. These experts were further studied in order to try to understand just why they were so good, using eye gaze tracking of them viewing suspects giving evidence and 'think aloud' data where they attempted to say what they were doing in their observations of the suspects. The liars and truth tellers were former prison inmates with histories of serious offending. They were required to lie and truth tell in four different contexts: 1) a mock crime interrogation; 2) their work history during a job interview; 3) talking about people who had had a positive or negative impact on their lives; and 4) when describing videos they had watched. An elaborate counter-balanced procedure was used to obtain video of the each of the offenders lying and truth telling. These offenders were videoed during the lying and truth telling episodes in such a way as to show their body in full, except where occasionally their feet went out of shot.

Potential lie detection wizards were recruited from various locations where police officers and other frontline personnel from the criminal justice system were to be found. A total of 112 participants were involved. A similar number of American university students were also recruited to go through the testing procedures. At their first testing session, the participants were shown 14 video excerpts which they had to assess for truthfulness or lying. There were equal numbers of truthful and deceitful video clips. Accuracy scores (based on accurately detecting lies and deceit) were calculated for the participants. The range was 34–63 per cent correct for students and 31–94 per cent correct for the police officers. There was a tendency for the police officers to suggest that the 'suspect' was lying. If they claimed the suspect was lying all of the time, this would ensure perfect accuracy for the detection of lies – but perfect inaccuracy for the detection of truth. This bias has been found in other studies which we discussed earlier. However, this sort of bias is more or less controlled for by using figures for overall accuracy (which includes both lie and truth) and not just lie detection accuracy.

After the first session (i.e. two lie detection trials) it was found that 10 per cent of the police officers achieved more than 80 per cent accuracy on both occasions. These were invited to take part in the second day of assessment. For the students, basically, a random sample of the better-performing individuals were invited back for their second day. None of the students actually reached anywhere near the 80 per cent accuracy of the best of the police officers. In the second session, the participants' accuracy was again assessed and some police officers who continued to perform very well were invited to take part in an eye-tracking study and other investigatory procedures on yet another occasion. Two corrections officers, both female, performed at better than 80 per cent accuracy on all of the testing sessions. The chances of this occurring on the basis of random guessing are incredibly small and so it is unlikely that chance is the explanation of their skill. The research found that the lie detection wizards were very quick to come to a decision about truth or lie. They also showed distinctly expert strategies in terms of their eye gaze pattern on the 'suspect'. That is to say, they focused rapidly on non-verbal cues that they had found helpful in lie detection in their careers, which led to them not only making fast decisions but also extremely accurate ones.

These findings are a little more promising than the traditional view in terms of the accuracy of police officers and related professionals when assessing for deceit or truthfulness. But it remains something of a difficulty that some reviews of the evidence seem to suggest that inaccuracy typifies truth assessors. O'Sullivan, Frank, Hurley and Tiwana (2009) also argue that the stake of the liar in the outcome is an influential factor in the detection of deceit. Of course, most police interviews involve higher-stake outcomes than the average laboratory experiment in this area. They argue that, where the stake was high because the lie was personally very involving or it would lead to substantial rewards or punishments, police lie detection ability would be high compared to circumstances in which the stake was low. The broad scheme of this is given in Figure 18.5. Furthermore, it is likely that

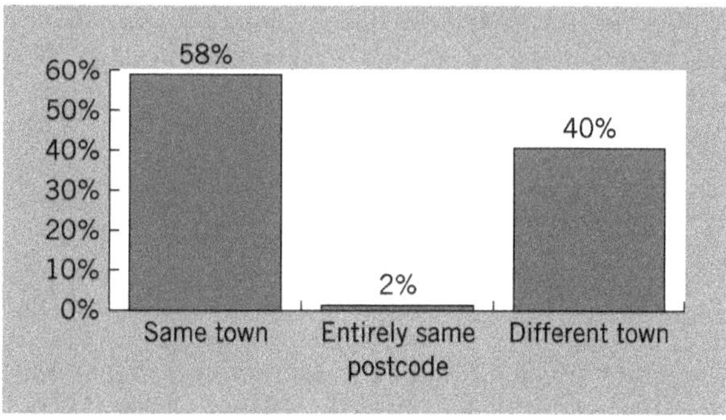

Figure 18.5 Possible circumstances where lie detection would be good

the high-stake situation would be one which is also relevant to the occupation of the truth assessor. From a total of eight different countries, 23 research studies were located which involved the police as participants.

Some of the characteristic high-stake scenarios would be:

- having to lie about something important personally to themselves;
- having to lie when they are in an intense emotional state;
- lies told by real suspects under police interrogation are high-stake, whereas the ex-prisoner who is encouraged to lie under laboratory conditions will be telling low-stake lies;
- where there is a (personally) big reward for a successful lie as opposed to a minor reward (such as a cinema ticket).

The scenarios used in the studies identified for inclusion in the new analysis were rewritten in a more standard form and assessed by a panel of raters in terms of how distressed or afraid or upset or feeling guilty the person telling the lie would be. This resulted in a group of studies involving high stakes and a group of studies involving low stakes. For the high-stake studies the average accuracy was 64 per cent, whereas for the low-stake studies the average accuracy was 55 per cent (i.e. little different from chance). Quite clearly, this is indicative that some police when assessing lies in appropriate conditions are far from being the random guessers that some researchers have suggested they are. This, though, only applies to some officers and not to police officers in general. Furthermore, there is evidence that some types of professionals are better at assessing some types of lies than others. For example, expert therapists are better able to detect lies about the emotions a person is feeling while the police are poor at detecting this type of lie (O'Sullivan, 2008).

It is doubtful whether the issue of the accuracy of police lie detection is yet settled, but the balance seems to be changing somewhat. This does not mean, however, that it is not possible to improve lie detection rates substantially. Changing the interview situation can make the cues to lying more apparent.

Improving lie detection hit rates – cognitive overload

Research has addressed ways in which professional lie detector can improve their 'hit' rate above the derisory levels noted in the past. Many of these newer developments

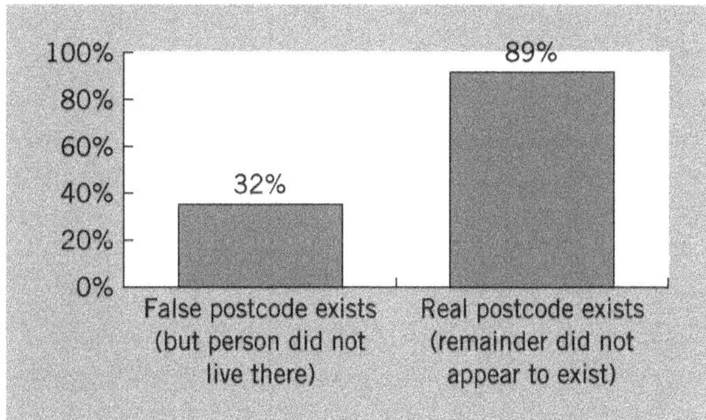

Figure 18.6 The cognitive load approach to making lie detection easier

work by impose an increased cognitive load on the interviewee. We are all familiar with the idea that multi-tasking can be very difficult. Since our brains have a finite processing capacity, increasing the cognitive load (such as by multi-tasking) may make it difficult for the interviewee to think about the things they need to do to lie convincingly. Such techniques interfere with the individual's ability to inhibit, mask, or disguise their deceptiveness. The procedure can be very simple such as asking the interviewee to elaborate on what they had just said but in much greater detail (Vrij, 2004). So by placing increased cognitive demand on the interviewee the likelihood that signs of deception are revealed is enhanced (see Figure 18.6). The cognitive overload ensures that suspects find it difficult to manage the situation without revealing evidence that they are lying. It would seem that lying is more demanding on our mental resources than telling the truth is – the liar has to do more mental work and carry out more different kinds of task than the truth teller in many circumstances. This increased task complexity simply gets too much for the brain to handle. The greater cognitive load on liars is the result of a number of factors including:

- It is cognitively more demanding to invent the lie than to merely report the truth.
- Truth tellers will assume that the other person sees what they say as truthful, whereas the liar may feel it necessary to put more effort into appearing credible.
- The liar may need to monitor the other person more actively and carefully for indications that the lie is being believed or not.
- The truth has to be suppressed by the liar, which itself may be cognitively demanding.

This does not mean that all lies are cognitively more demanding than the truth, but they will be in certain circumstances. For example, lying may not be more demanding where the liar has no strong motivation to be believed. On the other hand, the liar needs to be able to access the truth from their memories quickly and easily – otherwise it will be more difficult for them to suppress the truth. There are some circumstances in which the cognitive load on the truth teller will be bigger than that on the liar. For example, if the truth teller is trying to recall largely forgotten events then their cognitive load may be higher than that for the liar who is simply making up events.

To demonstrate this cognitive load effect, Vrij, Mann, Fisher, Leal, Milne and Bull (2008) set up a situation in which the participant was playing a game with another person during which a wallet belonging to a third person was recovered but the owner claimed that £10 was missing. The participants in this scenario were the truth tellers. Other participants were simply asked to take the money physically out of the wallet and to lie and deny that they had done so. The truthful and lying participants were also provided with a scenario of the events which the truthful participants had participated in. So the truth tellers actually participated in all of the events, whereas the liars did not do so – although they knew about the events. Both truth tellers and liars were interviewed, using a standard protocol. They were promised a cash reward if they convinced the interviewer that they were telling the truth, but an additional chore if they did not do so. The instructions were slightly different for some participants in order to increase their cognitive load. They were required to recall the events in reverse order of their actual occurrence. This is, of course, quite a hard task.

The interviews were videotaped and transcribed. The videos were coded for visual cues to lying and the transcriptions were coded for verbal cues to lying. The coding was done by persons unaware of the nature of the hypotheses underlying the study. Other features were also coded, such as the time delay between the question being asked and the start of their account of the events; the number of errors of speech; the number of pauses; the use of illustrators (hand gestures which emphasise or illustrate the point being made); hand and finger movements; and the number of seconds of gaze aversion. The data analysis showed very clearly that the interviews with the liars showed more cues to deceit than those with the truth tellers with the reversed presentation. However, this in itself does not mean that a police officer actually could identify which interviewees were lying. So, using these same videos, the researchers also had a group of British police officers make judgements about the person in the video relevant to an assessment of their truthfulness. The reverse order – the high cognitive load – interviews proved easier for the officers to detect truth or lies in than the forward order interviews.

Of course, asking someone to provide their evidence in reverse order is totally opposite to our normal way of giving narrative accounts. Although it is part of the cognitive interview (see Chapter 11), this reverse order tactic is often avoided by police interviewers. So it would be helpful if there was some way of checking the effectiveness of obtaining evidence in reverse without actually having to make such an unusual request. Vrij, Leal, Mann and Fisher (2012) created a novel situation for doing so. They asked people the route between two places – in one case going there and in the other case coming back (the reverse order). Thus reverse order was introduced naturally. The credibility of the study was enhanced by using police officers and human intelligence personnel from the Ministry of Defence in the UK. Participants were asked to get ready for 'a mission'. They were given a map of the town, which gave a location where they would be given a package, together with the route that they had to follow back to their present location. They needed to prepare themselves to lie about details of their mission if necessary. When the mission had been completed, they were met by one friendly and one hostile 'agent', who interviewed the participants separately. An identical set of questions was used for all of the interviews. The questions concerned route details such as how they would get from one location to the other and, the reverse, how they would get from the second location to the first. Liars could not use their actual routes and so had to fabricate the sequence of steps they had taken, while presenting them in reverse order sometimes. They could rely on their actual experiences, though these had to be transformed in some way. The interviews were videoed and then transcribed. It was found that observers reading transcripts of the interviews could discriminate between truth tellers and liars better in the reverse order condition. Significantly fewer details were provided in the reverse order condition by liars than by those in the truth telling condition. Contradictions between the information provided in the truth versus the lying condition were greater in the reverse order condition than the chronological order condition.

Vrij, Mann and Fisher (2006) provide further evidence that the style of interviewing that the police adopt may have a bearing on the extent to which cues to deceit are present in the interview and, consequently, the likelihood that the interview will reveal cues to deceit. Three different interview styles were used: 1) information-gathering; 2) accusatory; and 3) behaviour analysis:

- The information-gathering style of interview involves the police officer requesting a detailed statement about the suspect's activities – such as what they did on the day that the crime was committed. This is an open-ended form of questioning in order to elicit as much information as possible and generally it is reasonably successful in this regard.
- In the accusatory style of interview, the police officer is much more confrontational ('What are you trying to hide from me?'). Perhaps not surprisingly, accusatory interviewing styles tend to produce cryptic denials of

such accusations ('Nothing!'). Of course, the more the suspect says, the greater the possibility that the cues to deception will be revealed.

- The third type of interview studied was the Behaviour Analysis Interview as proposed by Inbau *et al.* (2001). This form of interview begins with exploratory open-ended questions – much like the information-gathering interview – but then introduces a standard, predetermined list of 15 questions. The theory underlying the Behaviour Analysis Interview includes the idea that those suspects who are innocent expect to be eventually seen as innocent and, as a consequence, they are more likely to try to be helpful to the police. So, for example, the suspect is asked to answer questions about who would seem to be the person who had the opportunity of committing the crime – truth tellers are more likely to suggest names. However, there is some doubt whether this assumption is adequate (Vrij, Mann, Kristen and Fisher, 2007).

As might be expected, the different types of interview differed in terms of: 1) the numbers of cues to deception that were available to the interviewers; and 2) the extent to which incorrect judgements of guilt were made on the basis of these cues. The accusatory interview fared the least well in this regard, although the rates of positive detections of lying did not differ significantly between the three types of interview. By avoiding fabrication in favour of reporting experienced events, presumably the lies in both studies predominantly required relatively few cognitive resources. To the extent that real crimes allow suspects' accounts of familiar events to feature in interviews, the more difficult it is for the lie detector to identify liars.

What offenders say about lying

Overall, there is good evidence that the cognitive load approach to structuring police interviews is effective. However, there are reasons to think that there are limits to this effectiveness based on what offenders say about their strategies when dealing with the demands of being interviewed as a suspect. Stromwall and Willen (2011) studied these lie-telling strategies in a sample of convicted criminals in prison. Basically, the interviewer was seeking 'advice' from the offenders about how to lie successfully. The recordings of the interviews were transcribed and studied by two coders, who developed coding schemes independently. The two schemes were very similar and they were integrated by discussion. There were 13 main strategies that coders could identify, which could be grouped under the headings of 'general verbal strategies', 'general nonverbal strategies' and 'specific interview strategies'. The most frequent strategies involved:

- sticking close to true things which happened but applying them to the topic of the questioning, which cuts down the memory problems of having to remember what has been said already in the police interview;
- not giving away any information at all; which means that they do not reveal self-incriminating information;
- eye-contact behaviours such as not averting the gaze;
- not having a strategy.

According to Stromwall and Willen, strategies like not giving away information at all in interviews suggest a sophisticated understanding of the true nature of police interviews, which is that the police essentially need evidence rather than the suspect having to prove their innocence. Some offenders were aware that an account richer in detail tends to indicate truth telling. Keeping things simple was another strategy and one which suggests that the offender was trying to avoid cognitive overload. This research points to one important conclusion: liars tend to report versions of their actual experiences rather than fabricate accounts of events that they have never experienced.

Rather similar findings have been found for the lying strategies of people more generally. Research by Leins, Fisher and Ross (2013) had students at a US university explain their strategies for lying. The students first of all described a truthful story from their life which provided a salient event. They then had to lie about the event. Following this they were interviewed about the strategies that they had used when lying. Entirely fabricating things for inclusion was not an important technique. Liars, for the most part, described a truthful story which they had experienced but attributed to the time period that the interview was about. Two-thirds adopted such a strategy. One could describe the events they reported as being ordinary and common; they also tended to have happened recently.

Strategic questioning

The *strategic-questioning approach* (Vrij, Granhag, Mann and Leal, 2011) basically encourages interviewers to formulate their questions in ways which actively encourage cues to lying to emerge. The strategy is to intensify or amplify the manifested cues to deceit. One basic assumption is that liars generally will come to the interview having prepared their answers to some extent. Such planning makes deception easier. Such preparation will only pay off to the extent that the questions that the suspect has planned for are actually asked in the interview itself. By asking unexpected questions, the interviewer can add to the cognitive load on the suspect. Counterstrategies such as evasive answers ('I don't know' or 'I can't remember') would be regarded as suspicious when applied to matters central to the investigation. Vrij, Fisher, Mann and Leal (2009) demonstrated this technique in a study in which the participants had either eaten together or had to pretend that they had eaten together in order to cover up a 'crime'. Some of the questions asked in the interviews that followed could readily be anticipated, but others could not. A question like 'What did you do at the restaurant?' is obvious. But questions about spatial details at the restaurant, such as which other diners were sitting nearest to them, would be harder to anticipate and plan an answer to. Similarly, the request to draw a sketch of the layout of the restaurant may come as a surprise. The research findings were supportive of the strategic use of questions to facilitate lie detection. Liars could be spotted when unexpected questions were introduced, but they could not where the questions more readily anticipated.

Another way of asking questions strategically lies in the timing of the introduction of new information into the investigative interview. Such information could all be incorporated towards the start of the interview, it could all be incorporated towards the end of the interview, or it could be gradually introduced throughout the interview. Of course, the interviewer expects the suspect to come up with an explanation of how the new information fits in with the underlying story that the suspect has been telling up to this point. A liar might be expected to have more problems where new information is gradually introduced. This is because the liar is constantly having to re-think their story to accommodate the new information entering the interview. A truth teller would have little problem with this. Introducing new information in a block all at the beginning or the end is not so difficult since the re-thinking only has to be done once. One might conceive the problem as being a cognitive load issue but it is also possible that the serial introduction of new material also enhances the likelihood that the suspect will simply trip themselves up in the telling of their story – such as by introducing slips or inconsistencies. Dando, Bull, Ormerod and Sandhams (2015) carried out a study to test these ideas. They videoed interviews which used the style and structure of the British police interview. Then they had lay-persons watch the interviews and decide whether the suspect was lying or not. They found that these observer judges were the most accurate where information was gradually revealed rather than revealed *en masse*. In addition, they also were by confident about their decision in this condition. The researcher's also collected information from the 'suspects' who took part in the video. They indicated that they found the gradual reveal of information by the interviewer was cognitively rather more challenging for them than either the early or late conditions. Of these two, the late condition tended to produce better lying deception results. Just in case it is thought that the cognitive load explanation comes out best in this study, another study should be mentioned. McDougall and Bull (2015) found evidence that inconsistency between the statements made by the 'suspect' and the new information may be responsible for decisions about the suspect's veracity. Of course, both could have an influence.

The Strategic Use of Evidence (SUE) technique

So we are beginning to see how a more optimistic view of improving lie detection was achieved. The Strategic Use of Evidence (SUE) technique of Granhag, Strömwal and Hartwig (2007) contributed to revising ideas about lie detection. It is a technique which has some things in common with the timing of the revelation of information within an interview which was discussed in the previous section. The essence of their approach depends on the findings of various research studies which suggest that innocent suspects may volunteer information which might incriminate themselves. In contrast, guilty suspects employ strategies of trying to avoid confrontation with incriminating information or otherwise try to escape the situation. Granhag *et al.* report that guilty suspects are more likely to have a strategy to deal with an interrogative interview than innocent suspects. Innocent people tend to believe that the truth will prevail ultimately. As a consequence, innocent suspects, if they have any strategy in the interview at all, are likely to simply 'tell it like it is' on the assumption that the truth will shine through. The guilty suspect, though, needs a strategy by which they can avoid referring to incriminating information if at all possible. However, if the guilty suspect is 'cornered' in the interview, they deny that they are in possession of the incriminating evidence.

The SUE technique is based on these ideas. The interviewer plans the interview very carefully in the light of any potentially incriminating information. For much of the interview, the suspect remains unaware of the fact that the interviewer has this information. So, for example, a fingerprint belonging to a suspect might be found on a bag in a room from which something was stolen. If the suspect does not mention visiting the room or seeing a bag when asked about their activities on the day of the crime, this suggests that they are avoiding revealing potentially incriminating evidence. There may be innocent reasons why the fingerprint is on the bag, of course. The interviewer needs to carefully check with the suspect any statements that the suspect may make relevant to the potentially incriminating evidence. Towards the end of the interview, the interviewer may ask the suspect to account for discrepancies in their evidence and for the potentially incriminating evidence. Revealing a strong suit towards the end of the interviewing means that the guilty lie teller is faced with facts incompatible with what they have previously claimed in the interview. This may add to the cognitive burden on the lie teller and result in them revealing more cues to their deception. Lying but guilty suspects use aversive counterstrategies to deal with the new information, compared to innocent suspects who tend to be more forthcoming in their responses. This technique, when used with a guilty suspect, is likely to produce elements of the statement which is at variance with the known incriminating evidence. When used with an innocent suspect, the technique produces statements which are consistent with the known incriminating evidence.

To expand a little, the SUE technique involves 1) the strategic level and 2) the tactical level. The strategic level involves the broad general principles of SUE such as the claim that guilty suspects employ aversive verbal strategies for dealing with questioning whereas innocent individuals are more forthcoming in their responses to the interview. The tactical level is about dealing with a specific criminal case. It involves evidence tactics, question tactics and disclosure tactics. The evidence tactics are largely about evaluating the available evidence when the interviewer is planning the interview. The question tactics rigorously consider the various ways that the suspect could account for the evidence which suggest their innocence. The disclosure tactics are the best ways to introduce the evidence to maximise the police's ability to come to conclusions about the veracity of the suspect. Two aspects of the evidence need to be considered in terms of disclosure tactics. One involves the dimension of the strength of the evidence' source. The source might be a relatively weak one such as when the evidence is just hearsay but would be strong if the police had good CCTV of the criminal incident. The other main aspect of disclosure tactics is the precision of the evidence. For example, low precision might be evidence that the suspect had been seen in London on the day in question, but high precision might be that the suspect was seen in the art gallery that the stolen painting, say, had been hanging in. These two aspects of disclosure tactics can be considered independent dimensions so precision may be high but the strength of the source may be weak. Generally speaking, the strongest evidence is introduced later if the interview is to help the police.

There is research evidence on the effectiveness of SUE. Hartwig. Granhag, Stromwell, and Kronvist (2006) used two groups of Swedish police, one of which received training in the SUE method and the other did not. The suspects were either guilty or innocent of stealing a wallet from a campus bookstall, though both the guilty and innocent suspects had been to the bookstall. The officers participating in the study had a file containing such incriminating evidence as the suspects' fingerprints being found on the briefcase. So an officer using the SUE technique would perhaps encourage the suspect to talk about what they had done that day to see if any mention of the bookstall was made or if they had seen a briefcase. The outcome of the study was that the accuracy of the trained officers in detecting the guilty and innocent was 85 per cent, compared with only 56 per cent for the officer untrained in the SUE technique. Once again, using the right approach to interviewing, it can be seen that police officers can recognise liars effectively.

Jordan, Hartwig, Wallace, Dawson and Xhihani (2012) took research on the SUE strategic strategy a little further. In their study, guilty participants (US students) had to 'steal' a wallet from a room, whereas innocent participants went to the room to look for a book by Freud which was ostensibly in a briefcase (which contained a wallet) which was placed on a crate. When interviewed by fresh researchers about the events, participants were given the evidence against them either early or late in the interview. This evidence was: 1) CCTV footage to show that they were outside the room in question at about the time of the wallet theft; 2) that a witness saw them in the room; and 3) that their fingerprints were on the briefcase. In some cases, the key evidence was disclosed earlier, in others it was disclosed late in the interview. Smaller amounts of evidence were provided by guilty participants in the late disclosure condition and they made proportionately fewer statements consistent with the key evidence introduced by the interviewer. In this study, however, both guilty and innocent interviewees confessed at the same rate in the late disclosure condition. Nevertheless, observers viewing videotapes of the interviews could identify reasonably well who was guilty and who was innocent. Confronted with the late evidence, some innocent participants actually fabricated false alibis!

More recently, variations of the SUE method have been tried to clarify when and how the police should introduce the additional information. Just what is the optimum strategy for deploying this information? Studies of real police interviews have shown that often there are some initial disclosures of information by the interviewing police officer. Such disclosure of the police's evidence may happen at any stage of the interview. Granhag, Stromwall, Willen and Hartig (2013) sought to assess the effectiveness of early disclosure versus two versions of the SUE technique:

- SUE-B refers to the basic version of SUE where the evidence is disclosed towards the end of the interview as above;
- SUE-I stands for the incremental version of SUE in which information is disclosed stepwise at various points of the interview.

The *evidence framing matrix* refers to a way in which evidence can be introduced in which the weakest and least precise evidence is introduced first and the strongest and most specific evidence is introduced last. According to Granhag (2010) the dimensions of evidence strength and its degree of precision (or specificity) are important in determining the order of disclosure. The strength dimension (strong–weak) can be illustrated be the difference between 'We have reason to believe that you were in Dewsbury that night' (weak) and 'We have CCTV images of you in Dewsbury that night' (strong). The precision or specificity dimension can be illustrated by 'You were seen going to a DIY store' (low) and 'You were seen buying inflammable liquids at Johnson's DIY shop' (high). The two dimensions allow four different quadrants to be identified: 1) weak source, low precision; 2) strong source, low precision; 3) weak source, high precision; and (4) strong source, high precision. It follows from the logic of SUE that the order of disclosure should be in the same order as the above quadrants. Of course, the second and third quadrants can be reversed. It might be expected that each increment of evidence forces the guilty suspect to consider changing their story in some way.

A variety of participants were used, including students and people recruited from the community. The guilty suspects were asked to go to a bookstore and steal a book, whereas the innocent suspects merely went in and asked the price of a book. (It was explained to them that the bookstore owner was aware of what was happening in the study.) The guilty group was told that they should deny having stolen the book and that they would receive an incentive of movie tickets if they successfully misled the investigtors into believing them to be innocent. The three strategies were: 1) disclosure initially; 2) disclosure at the end, as in SUE-B; and 3) incremental stepwise disclosure, as in SUE-I. The participants were then interviewed. The interviews were transcribed for two measures of inconsistency – statement-evidence inconsistency and within-statement consistency. The strongest cues to deception were found for SUE-I and especially the statement-evidence consistency measure.

Verifiability approach to lie detection

An obvious way in which an offender can avoid detection is simply by not giving information which could be checked or verified by the police. So the verifiability approach argues that liars provide details to the investigator which cannot be checked. The police investigator who is aware of this has a better chance of detecting lies. The verifiability approach has two assumptions: 1) truth tellers are more likely to include more detail into their accounts compared with liars and 2) liars avoid giving too much detail for fear that this detail will be checked out by the investigator and their lie revealed. All of this leads to a clear dilemma for the liar. They realise that they need to appear to be honest which involves including many details in their accounts. At the same time, they are motivated to avoid providing details which would lead to them being caught. So they provide non-verifiable information. For example, the suspect might claim to have seen a red van in a particular street which is information that the police would have difficulty verifying. On the other hand, if they claim to have phoned a particular friend that morning then this claim can be checked. The friend could be asked to confirm that the phone call happened or mobile phone records could be obtained.

In other to test the value of the verifiability approach, Nahari, Vrij, and Fisher (2014a) carried out a study involving a mock crime. This involved some participants stealing a copy of a statistics exam which had been left in a professor's mailbox. These mock criminals were told where to find the key to the box. They were instructed to photocopy the examination and return the original to the professor's mail box. They were instructed to make sure that no one else witnessed the 'crime'. The non-criminals (truth tellers) were instructed to carry out their normal business for half an hour doing as many things as possible in the time. On returning to the laboratory, all participants were informed that a 'crime' had occurred and that they were a suspect. They were informed that the innocent party had spent their time carrying out as many activities as possible. They were told that they would be interviewed and asked to make a statement about what they had been doing at the time of the theft. Some participants were told that the veracity of the details provided would be checked. This would include telephone calls, being in places with closed-circuit television, and activities involving (or observed) by a third party all of which could be checked. It was explained that previous research suggests that liars avoid giving details that can be verified whereas truth tellers provide details that can be verified. The other (uninformed) individuals were told nothing of this.

A little later, the participants were asked to write a statement about what they had been doing. Two independent coders blind to the research condition coded the statements in terms of perceptual details (what the suspect saw, heard, felt or smelt), spatial details (locations or spatial arrangements of people or objects) and temporal details (such as when the even occurred or a description of the sequence of events) which could potentially be verified. Verifiable details were documented activities, things done together with another identified person, and things witnessed by another identified person. The number of verifiable and unverifiable activities were counted. Verifiable details include meeting identified people, being in the presence of CCTV, and withdrawing funds from a bank, for example. Unverifiable details included reading a book outside on a seat, smoking alone, and using the stairs. The conclusion of the study was clearly in support of the verification approach since truth tellers provided more detail which was verifiable than the liars did. Giving the participants the information that liars provide less detail did not affect the liars in the study. However, truth tellers increased the amount of information given in the mock police interviews if told about what liars normally do.

Nahari, Vrij and Fisher (2014b) carried out another study of whether the verifiability approach is vulnerable to countermeasures as a consequence of the offender's knowledge of the low verifiability of offender's statement. Their study used a fairly realistic research paradigm to examine the vulnerability of the verifiability approach to countermeasures. The researcher collected written statements from mock criminals (liars) and innocents (truth tellers). Half were told in advance of writing the statements that the verifiability of their statement would be checked. As a consequence, it was found that truth tellers provided more verifiable details whereas the liars did not. Furthermore, the investigator's ability to detect the lies was considerably improved. In other words, informing suspects about the mechanism underlying the verifiability approach improved lie detection.

Nahari and Vrij (2014) extended the applicability of the verifiability approach to alibi witnesses. In this experiment, they two studied two types of alibi pairs. One alibi pair consisted of two truth tellers who carried a range of non-criminal activities. These activities included verifiable and non-verifiable activities. So examples of verifiable activities included borrowing a book from the social sciences library and to ask a particular question in the university bookshop. Examples of non-verifiable activities were to count the number of bars in a square and to check course information on a university website. The other alibi pairs consisted of one person who did the same variety of non-criminal activities as just mentioned but carried out the activities alone whereas the other person carried out a criminal activity involving doing surveillance of a biology laboratory with the intent of stealing goods from it at some time in the future. However, both members of this pair had to lie by saying that both of them had been together at the time of the criminal offence and that both had carried out the non-criminal tasks. The expectation was that the truth tellers would be motivated to provide honest information including about the alibi. On the other hand, the lying offender would be motivated to come up with honest appearing detail but risking information that could be checked. Both members of the lying pair would avoid associating themselves with each as this could reveal information that could be checked. The behaviours relevant to the various hypotheses were coded and frequencies summated for the truth telling and the lying pairs. For example, 60 per cent of the truth tellers but only 20 per cent of the liars mentioned witnesses and evidence. Sixteen of truth tellers described witnesses whereas none of the lying-pairs did. Among the range of strategies employed by the liars was to suggest that the other member (the alibi) had gone to the toilet or phoned someone during those activities which were verifiable. Nahari and Vrij suggest that applied to these data the verifiability principles correctly classified 88 per cent into the lying and truth telling alibi pairs.

Conclusion

Probably the most important focus for researchers into the assessment of lying and truth telling must be on high-stake lies researched in natural conditions. As we have seen, this sort of research simply has not been available in adequate quantities until now. Porter and ten Brinke (2010) reviewed progress and presented a cautiously optimistic view of the future. They argue that it is important that practitioners are realistic about what is possible and understand the likely limitations of current lie detection knowledge. There is unlikely to be a Pinocchio's-nose indicator of lying, but that does not mean that important progress has not or cannot be made. Porter and ten Brinke (2010), in their review of the field, suggest that changes from baseline measurements for facial expression/information, verbal behaviour and nonverbal behaviour/body language can be useful indicators of lying. Among the specific indicators which may help guide the lie detector are:

- facial cues, especially involving the top or bottom of the face;
- increased delays before answering a question;
- increased or decreased use of illustrators;
- involuntary, fleeting emotional expressions of the face;
- little contextual embedding and reproduced conversation where the incident involves more than one person;
- more frequent and longer pauses in speech;
- reductions in the rate of blinking;
- repetition of details;
- slowing down of the rate of speech;
- vagueness of descriptions given;
- verbal slips such as tense changes (they give the example of speaking of the missing person in the past tense).

Some of these are better supported by research than others, but they do serve to focus attention in potentially profitable directions. There have been developments, they point out, in terms of brain scanning approaches but, whatever the promise of these, they are far from properly validated and far from being practicable as yet for day-to-day police work. We should also be careful to note the concentration of veracity researchers on detecting actual liars. There is clearly a lot of opportunity for extraneous factors to influence judgements about whether another person is truth telling without considering the accuracy of these judgements at all. For example, Douglass, Ray, Hasel and Donnelly (2016) that a flat demeanour on the part of the suspect led to more adverse judgements than an emotional demeanour.

Main points

- There is no simple way of detecting a liar. There is considerable evidence to suggest that for the most part, such groups as the police and psychologists do little better than chance when assessing the truthfulness of those they interview. Nevertheless, given appropriate circumstances, it is possible to improve on this. Most methods of detecting lies rely on detecting the emotions that may go along with lying. By concentrating on this, rather than relying on unproven ideas of the signs of lying, a better hit-rate may be achieved. There is reason to think that observers at an interview do better than the interviewer at detecting lies – presumably because they are faced with a simpler task and can concentrate more on the hard-to-detect indicators of lying.
- Increasingly, researchers have focused on procedures which increase the cognitive load on the suspect during interviews. This increase in cognitive load has an important effect of making some of the cues to deception more apparent and, thus improves the hit rate of anyone who focuses on valid cues to deception.
- Research involving high-stakes situations resembles the typical situation in a police interview and should increasingly be the focus of researchers' efforts. Changes such as these to the way in which research is done are partly responsible for some of the radical revisions in dominant views about the ability of professionals to detect lies.

Further reading

Cooper, B.S., Griesel, D. and Ternes, M. (eds) (2013) *Applied Issues in Investigative Interviewing, Eyewitness Memory, and Credibility Assessment* New York: Springer.

Granhag, P.A., Vrij, A., and Verschuere, B. (eds) (2015) *Detecting Deception: Current Challenges and Cognitive Approaches* Chichester: John Wiley.

Raskin, D.C., Honts, C.R. and Kircher, J.C. (eds) (2014) *Credibility Assessment: Scientific Research and Applications* Amsterdam: Academic Press.

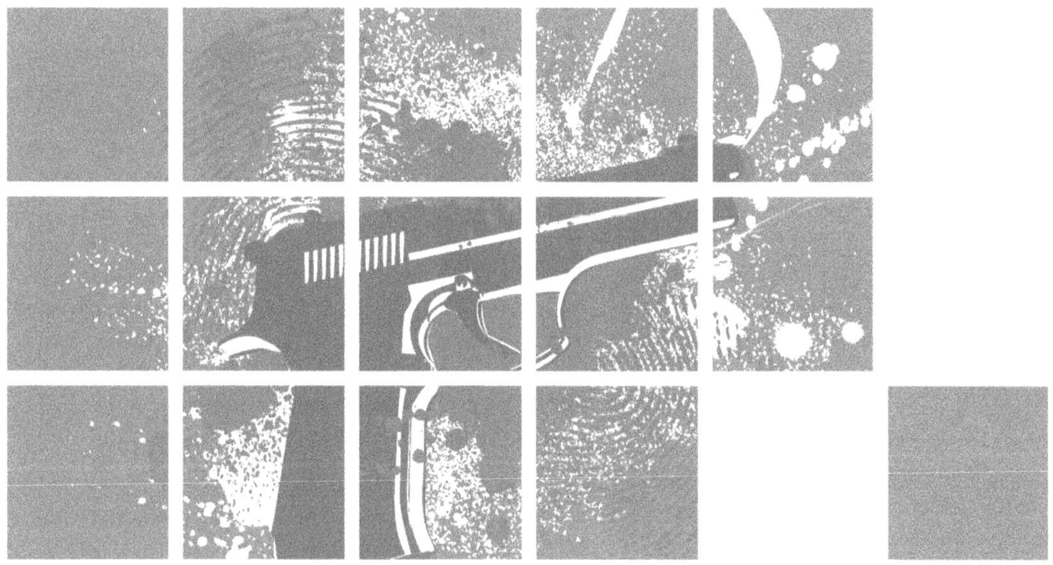

Chapter 19

Lies, lie detecting and credibility 2: the polygraph test and statement validity analysis

Overview

- The lie detector or polygraph test and statement validity analysis are both somewhat controversial.
- The polygraph test depends on the physiological response to the fear of being caught lying. Many believe that its error rate is unacceptably high.
- The usual forensic application of the polygraph is the controlled question technique (CQT). This involves using questions controversially assumed to cause a strong physiological response in the guilty individual and a 'neutral' control question unlikely to produce a response in them.
- Polygraph testing involves far more than the physiological instrument. In particular, it should be noted that the polygraph examiner knows a great deal about the case generally and is not unaware of the strength of the other evidence against the suspect.
- The validity of the normal police polygraph test is difficult to assess and laboratory studies are not particularly pertinent. The accuracy of the polygraph varies widely from study to study and there is still a need for further research studies to clarify issues.
- The use of the polygraph has been extended to the post-conviction management of sex offenders even in countries which do not allow it in court.
- European psychologists have developed statement validity analysis as a way of assessing the credibility of a witness's testimony. It consists of criterion-based content analysis and the lesser-used validity checklist.
- Criterion-based content analysis is based on the working assumption that the way we present memories of real events is different from that for fictitious events.

Introduction

This chapter turns its attention to two techniques for evaluating veracity:

- The polygraph test, which can be used to assess the physiological arousal patterns manifested by a person anxious about the risk of being identified as a liar. In recent years this has been applied in new contexts within the criminal justice system. It has been suggested that the use of the polygraph test has increased worldwide despite frequent criticisms (Meijer and Verschuere, 2010).
- Statement validity analysis, which takes a broad view of the differences between memories for real events and lies. This approach attracted enormous attention from researchers and practitioners in the 1990s and before. The debate surrounding its use has waned somewhat in recent years.

The two are not regarded equally favourably by most psychologists. The polygraph test is well known to most people but the evidence of its worth is rather scarce. Generally it is seen by psychologists as lacking in sufficient validity. Despite this, it is used in court in some jurisdictions – such as parts of the US. Some places allow its use in investigations but not in court.

Statement validity analysis is far less widely known outside of the field of forensic psychology. It consists of methods designed primarily to assess the credibility of the evidence of children. The intellectual roots of statement validity analysis are very different from those of most of the tests and measures with which psychologists are familiar. It is of continental European origins. It is a more holistic procedure than psychologists' usually employ which makes typically issues concerning reliability, validity and item analysis somewhat difficult or impossible to apply. Nevertheless, this did not stop some researchers from putting statement validity analysis under the same scrutiny that psychometrically inclined researchers would apply to their measures.

The polygraph process

> The lie detector is as much a soft or social technology of human management as it is a collection of physical instruments mechanically rendering the body's physiological changes.
>
> (Pettit, 2013, p. 105)

The polygraph, or lie detector, works because of offenders' fear of being found to be lying. The Federal Bureau of Investigation in the United States once maintained a website (now unavailable) where it was claimed that the polygraph could identify guilty people, eliminate innocent suspects from an investigation, save money by shortening investigations, and increase conviction rates by encouraging confession by suspects who previously had lied. This would seem to be a remarkable achievement for a device that does little more than measure some autonomic responses of a person's body when answering questions.

The polygraph is a surprisingly elderly piece of equipment. Its foundations lay in attempts around 1914 to assess lying using the pneumograph – a device that measured breathing patterns. The work of Larson (1922) and Keeler (1934) resulted in the polygraph machine, which is essentially what is used today. Sensors are attached to various parts of the body to detect various responses:

- Blood pressure variations reflecting cardiovascular (heart and veins) changes. These are measured using a version of the blood pressure cuff commonly used by nurses and doctors to measure our blood pressure.
- Respiration rates and amplitude are measured by changes in pressure on inflated tubes placed strategically around the individual's torso.
- Sweating in the palms of the hand. This is part of the galvanic skin response.

The word polygraph merely means 'many drawings' – several 'pens' draw lines on a moving paper chart in the technique. These pens move under electrical control determined by a variety of physiological responses of the body. Physiological changes produce wave patterns that may become more frequent (e.g. the suspect breathes more rapidly) or increase in amplitude (e.g. the suspect breathes more deeply). Nowadays, the apparatus is small enough to be stored in an attaché case. Furthermore, advancing technology has meant that computers may be connected to the polygraph. In this way, complex waves may be broken down into their component parts for easier interpretation. Increases in the physiological responses to a question, as measured by the polygraph, are held to be indicators of lie telling. The commonest procedure is the controlled question technique (CQT) in which two questions are posed. One question is regarded as being likely to evoke a physiological response in the guilty offender (e.g. 'Did you steal the money?'), whereas the other question is thought to be unlikely to produce a physiological response in them (e.g. 'Is it Monday tomorrow?'). The assumptions underlying this are frequently questioned and the idea that innocent people will not be affected by the critical question compared to the control question doubted by critics (e.g. Meijer and Verschuere, 2010).

Figure 19.1 gives the phases in the FBI interview using the polygraph. Note the following points:

- The test itself, Phase 2, is just one component of the procedure using the polygraph or lie detector test.

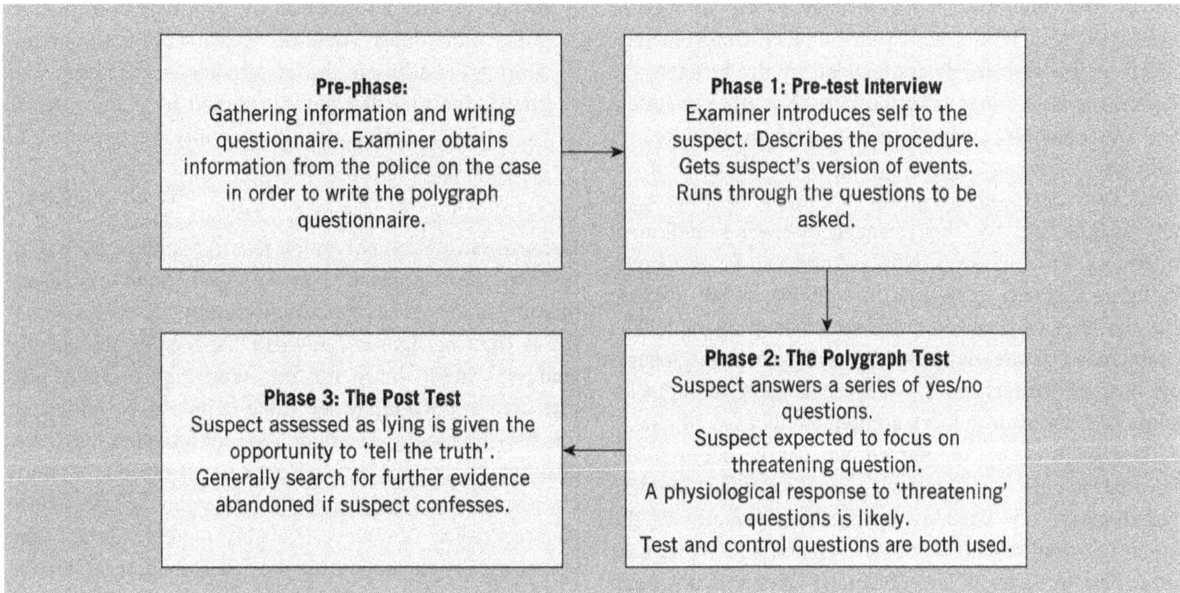

Figure 19.1 The phases of the FBI polygraph process

- The examiner develops the list of questions to be used in a particular application in a pre-phase, partly in collaboration with the investigating officers.
- The process involves rapport building with the suspect. In particular, the questions to be asked are not entirely unknown to the suspect before the polygraph test. It is the threatening nature of certain questions that is mainly the focus since these are the ones that make the suspect fear that they will be caught lying by the machine.
- Most importantly of all, the polygraph examiner does not merely make an assessment of the truth telling of the suspect: the examiner (or the police officers involved) may confront the suspect with evidence that they were lying on the test. At this stage, they are encouraged to tell the truth in various ways.
- Suspects who are deemed to be innocent by the test are unlikely to receive any further questioning.

Thus rather than speaking of 'the polygraph test' it is more appropriate to describe it as 'the polygraph process'.

Few would argue that the polygraph is anything but controversial. Although used in court in some parts of the US, the use of polygraph testing in terms of the selection of employees has been subject to legislation. So, although many thousands of polygraph tests are still given each year, in the United States the *Employee Polygraph Protection Act 1988* essentially reduced pre-employment polygraphs to a trickle of 15 per cent of their use prior to the Act. There are at least 70 countries in the world where the polygraph test is used extensively (Grubin and Madsen, 2005). It should not be thought, though, that the polygraph has been welcomed without reservation even in these places. Commonly, courts in the US have expressed their disapproval of evidence stemming from the polygraph. This can be seen since early in the history of the polygraph following the *Frye* v. *United States* (1923) decision that expert evidence should be based on scientific methods which are reliable in the view of the scientific community. According to Faigman, Kaye, Saks, Sanders and Chen (2010) this cautious attitude persists.

Nevertheless, before concluding that the polygraph is a good thing, a number of issues concerning its use should be considered. One of the problems of risk assessment (see Chapter 27) is that some of the information used comes from what the offender tells the psychologist or other practitioner; for example, it is well established that the extent of previous offending is a predictor of future offending. The question is just where the information about previous offences should come from. Obviously, the information on file for a particular offender might be a good starting point. This information would be obtained from previous disclosures at interview and conviction records, among other sources. For any number of reasons, this information might be partially incomplete. Research studies have demonstrated that polygraphy can be used to increase the amount of information available – for example, it can lead to a several-fold increase in the number of known offences on record. There is evidence that polygraphy can increase the number of crossovers reported by sex offenders (crossovers refer to the variety of sexes, ages and relationships involved in a perpetrator's offending). Crucially, it is known that offences against a wide variety of victims increase the risk level posed by the offender. Unfortunately, much of this research is confounded by the fact that the typical research design takes place in relation to treatment and offenders are given immunity from prosecution for additional offences that they reveal. This raises the possibility that factors other than the polygraph itself are actually responsible for the offender disclosing additional offending. In many ways, what is known so far is encouraging as it seems to suggest that offenders will disclose further offences under the influence of the polygraph. The problem is that it is not known 1) whether those disclosures are factually correct and 2) whether this increase in disclosures actually leads to more accurate predictions of risk.

It perhaps should be pointed out that the polygraph is not used exclusively to test suspects. Sometimes in some jurisdictions it is used to evaluate the veracity of the claims of victims and witnesses. Ginton (2013) regards these uses as particularly problematic given that it is not a pleasant experience to undergo polygraphy.

Problems with the polygraph

There is little doubt that those who use the polygraph are convinced of its value. There is quite clearly a value in the technique, even though it might be incapable of distinguishing between lies and the truth. People, in general, believe that it can detect lies and, more to the point, so do some offenders. Consequently, to tell a suspect that he or she has failed the lie detector test may induce confession in the guilty and false confession in the innocent. Iacono (2008) put it this way:

> a polygraph test could have no better than chance accuracy and still have utility. If one used a 'lie detector' that was no more accurate than a coin toss to adjudicate guilt, half of all guilty individuals would be accurately identified as liars. Confronted with the results of this lie detector by a skilled interrogator, guilty individuals would on occasion confess, demonstrating the utility of the lie detector. In the absence of knowledge that this device worked by chance, those using this technique could naturally be expected to come to believe in its validity.
>
> (p. 231)

Because failing the polygraph test may induce such confessions, the examiners who use the polygraph may regard this as clear evidence of its validity – they decide that someone is showing signs of lying and that person subsequently confesses. In this sense, it is not surprising that police officers used to polygraphy see value in its use. Nevertheless, this may be merely an example of confirmation bias – the disproportionate emphasis we put on evidence that supports our point of view and the relative underplaying of evidence that contradicts our view. Probably more important, and systematically excluded from the FBI-style process, are the individuals who are 'cleared' by the polygraph process. Does this group consist solely of the innocent? If not, just what proportion of this group is, in fact, telling lies? What is known as the 'ground truth' (objective reality) cannot ever be known, of course. Without examining the shortcomings of polygraph evidence, we may confuse ground truth with what the operator decides is the truth.

The basic polygraph equation is given in Figure 19.2 together with some of the issues raised by the equation. The most serious of the problems are (partly based on Iacono and Lykken, 1997; Iacono and Patrick, 1997) as follows:

- In the normal polygraph process, the adequacy of the control questions is vital and it may be difficult to get them right. So, for example, the question 'Have you ever thought of taking revenge against someone who has done you a wrong?' is intended to encourage a lie in everyone, including the innocent. Most of us have thought things like this, although we do not care to admit it. On the other hand, some may answer 'No' to this question – not because they are wilfully lying but because they had forgotten the occasions when they had.

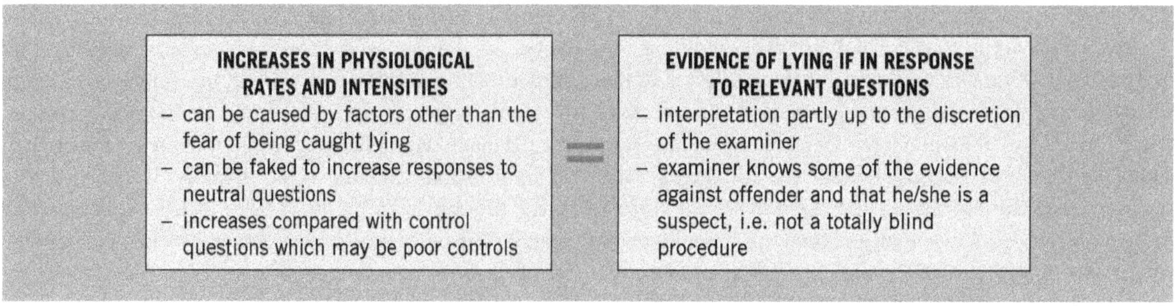

INCREASES IN PHYSIOLOGICAL RATES AND INTENSITIES	=	EVIDENCE OF LYING IF IN RESPONSE TO RELEVANT QUESTIONS
– can be caused by factors other than the fear of being caught lying – can be faked to increase responses to neutral questions – increases compared with control questions which may be poor controls		– interpretation partly up to the discretion of the examiner – examiner knows some of the evidence against offender and that he/she is a suspect, i.e. not a totally blind procedure

Figure 19.2 The basic polygraph equation

- To be accused during the course of polygraphy of, say, murdering one's wife may be emotive for both the guilty and innocent. In these circumstances, the polygraph may fail to differentiate between lying and 'honest denial' (Iacono and Patrick, 1997).
- The control questions may disturb the guilty more than the innocent. For example, if asked in the context of a homicide, 'Have you ever stolen anything?' the guilty might remember a series of armed robberies they had committed. Thus they show the same emotional signs to the control question as they do to the relevant question since, for them, the control question is also a relevant question.
- Faking and countermeasures are possible in response to a polygraph test. Indeed, some experts advertise on the Internet their claims to be able to teach their clients to deceive the lie detector in half an hour. The essential theory of this is simple: manifest the same physiological response to the control questions as the relevant questions. Thus practical advice might be to press down hard with one's toes to the control questions or to engage in a complex task such as mental arithmetic, which might produce a similar physiological response. Another simple technique is to bite one's tongue in response to the control questions.
- In its practical application, the polygraph test is not subjected to 'fair test' procedures. The operator normally does not operate 'blind' to other information about the suspect coming from interview and from police sources. Furthermore, it is known that the suspect is a suspect, so it is likely that there is other evidence against him/her. In normal practice, the polygraph is not tested against groups of known innocent people. Elaad, Ginton and Ben-Shakhar (1994) found in an experimental study that a polygraph examiner's evaluations of lying could be affected by their expectations about the suspect. However, this was only true to the extent that there was no strong indication of lying or truth telling on the polygraph record.
- Even the basic theory of the polygraph may be challenged since it has not been established that the only way that the body responds to fear of detection in lying is increases in the physiological measures assessed by the polygraph.

In the defence of polygraphy, the following points are worth considering:

- The polygraph questionnaire normally consists of several sets of questions. Inadequacies in any question may be compensated for by the other questions.
- There is a distinction to be drawn between the practical utility of the polygraph and its scientific adequacy. If polygraphy encouraged more guilty individuals to tell the truth then this could be seen as an advantage. But this has nothing to do with the validity of the polygraph to detect the fear its advocates claim is the basis of its success. Actually, to play the devil's advocate, it could be argued that it would be more useful if all suspects were adjudged liars by the polygraph. Then all suspects could be confronted with the evidence of their guilt and encouraged to confess. Provided that one is prepared to accept the consequences in terms of increased numbers of false confessions – and it is anyone's guess how many this would be – then one would maximise police success.

The criticisms of present practice do not mean that the concept of polygraphy is worthless – there are other approaches to polygraphy, such as the *guilty knowledge test* (i.e. the concealed information test), that have yet to be generally adopted.

Studies of the validity of polygraphy

There have been several surveys of psychologists regarding the validity of polygraphy. Members of a society devoted to psychological physiological research fairly consistently rejected its sole use in the absence of other information. Nevertheless, they considered it a useful diagnostic tool when used in conjunction with other evidence. In the 1980s and 1990s as many as 60 per cent of the psychologists surveyed considered it useful in those circumstances. Virtually no one considered it totally worthless. Attitudes change and a more recent survey specifically mentioned the different types of polygraph test (Iacono and Lykken, 1997). The common *control question technique* (relevant versus control questions) was seen by only about a third of two separate groups of psychologists to be based on sound psychological principles. Only about a quarter were in favour of the use of the polygraph in courts of law. On average, the psychologists thought that the control question technique was 63 per cent accurate with innocent suspects and 60 per cent accurate with guilty suspects. These figures would indicate a high proportion of errors.

There are a number of laboratory studies that have investigated the validity of the polygraph when the control question technique is employed. Essentially, the procedure is to inculpate some participants in the research, for example in a 'mock crime', and not others, the control group. The polygraph examination is then used to assess which group each participant is in. This seems a reasonable procedure although there are a number of problems:

- In real life, failing the polygraph test may have very serious consequences. Failing the laboratory set-up's polygraph test simply does not carry the same implications about punishment. There is no obvious strong motivation to pass the test. Indeed, the motivation may be to fail the test if you are in the guilty group as it is fairly obvious that the researchers are interested in the validity of the test.

- Because there is no cost of failing the test, it is possible that the control questions are relatively more intrusive and anxiety-provoking. For example, as the experiment is possibly seen as play-acting, the participant may be more concerned about questions that bring into question their integrity and morality. So a question such as 'Have you ever told a lie?' might produce a more physiological response than 'Did you take part in the (mock) crime?'
- Iacono and Patrick (1997) were critical of the so-called friendly polygraph test organised by the defence. Failure on the test would not be publicised, whereas passing the test would be lauded as evidence of innocence. Furthermore, in the friendly test, the examinee has nothing to fear from detection. Remember that the polygraph works using the fear of detection.

One obvious major advantage of the laboratory experiment is that the 'ground truth' (whether the suspect was actually involved in the crime) is easily established – indeed, it is imposed by the researchers. Field studies of real-life polygraph examinations have severe problems in establishing ground truth. The normal criterion of confession is hardly adequate, for reasons already mentioned. Primarily, the confession is a response to the outcome of the polygraph test, so it could hardly fail to support the validity of the polygraph test. The failure to examine the 'cleared' suspects any further is a less obvious problem but nevertheless crucial. If we look at Figure 19.3, only the true positives and the false positives are encouraged to confess. The false negatives and true negatives are essentially ignored. All of this contributes to a spurious enhancement of the apparent validity of the polygraph.

It would obviously be very useful to examine the guilt and innocence of those excluded by the polygraph test – those whom we have classified as true negatives and false negatives. Ideally, then, field studies of the validity of polygraphy should do the following:

- Explore the group of individuals who passed the test as innocent for later evidence of guilt or innocence, e.g. later confession to the crime.
- Independently re-score the polygraph charts blind to the original examiner's conclusions and other information that might have influenced the examiner to decide that the suspect was guilty.

Few studies have met these requirements. Patrick and Iacono's (1991) study involved finding all of the cases from a large Canadian metropolitan area which had involved polygraph testing over a five-year time period. Ignoring the outcomes of these polygraph tests, the researchers scoured police records in order to find evidence that someone had later confessed to the crimes and also cases where it was later found that a crime had not actually occurred (e.g. putative stolen property had really been misplaced). In this way, the results of the polygraph test were not confounded with the confession, for example. They found that the blind polygraph reassessment correctly classified individuals as innocent in only 57 per cent of cases, which is scarcely different from the chance level of 50 per cent. The researchers also identified instances where the suspect failed the initial polygraph test and then confessed. In these circumstances there was a 98 per cent success rate for identifying the 'guilty' individuals. This may be because the criterion of guilt and the initial polygraph findings are confounded since those who were found guilty by the polygraph would have had good reason for confessing. In other words, the innocent are very poorly identified as such by the polygraph test.

These findings are similar in some ways to earlier studies where ground truth was based on confessions that may

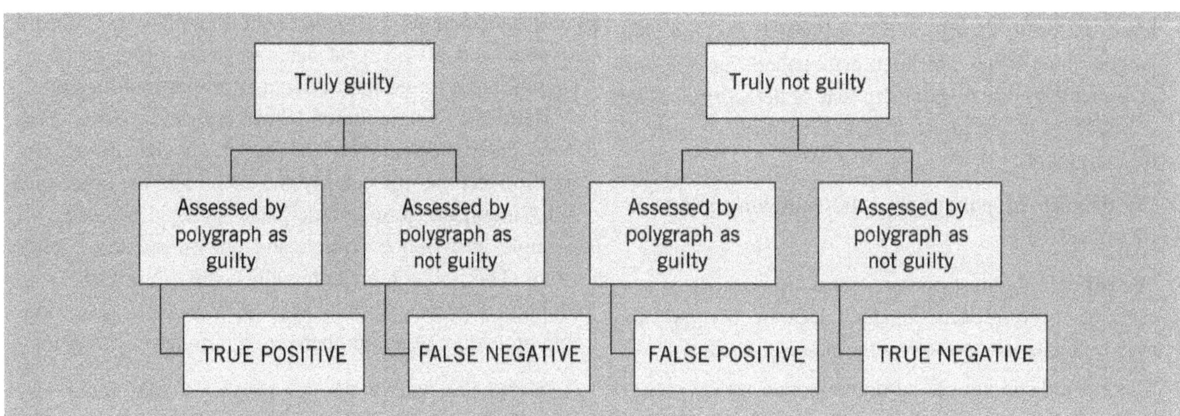

Figure 19.3 Possible outcomes of the polygraph test

Table 19.1 The different types of polygraph test question

	Guilty knowledge test (concealed information test)	Relevant/irrelevant question technique	Directed lie test	Control question technique
Type of questions used	'If you killed your wife, then you will know the sort of weapon. Was it a craft knife . . . a kitchen knife . . . a chisel . . . a Bowie knife . . . a hatchet?'	**Irrelevant question:** 'Is today Friday?' **Relevant question:** 'Did you kill your wife?'	**Control questions**, such as 'Before age 27, did you ever break even one rule or regulation?' Instructed to answer 'No'. **Other questions** relevant to crime.	**Control question:** (emotive question for most people): 'Have you ever plotted revenge on an enemy?' **Relevant question:** 'Did you kill your wife?'
Evidence of its validity		None		
Basis of interpretation	Does not detect lying as much as being aware of information which is normally only available to the offender and the police.	Truth is indicated by similar physiological response to relevant and irrelevant questions. The examiner questions the suspect in order to ascertain whether the suspect has an appropriate demeanour and explanation.	Innocent persons will be more concerned about lying in response to the control questions than to questions relevant to the crime.	Guilty will show more response to the relevant question, innocent will show more response to the control question.
Limitations	Needs careful knowledge of the crime scene to write questions. Not all crimes are amenable to the construction of guilty knowledge questions.	Confounds lying and emotive questions – many people would feel troubled by being asked if they had murdered their wife.		
Popularity	Rare.			Common in forensic applications.

have been influenced by the polygraph outcome. These, of course, do not involve the search for later, non-polygraph-influenced confessions. The best of these studies showed 76 per cent (Kleinmuntz and Szucko, 1984) and 77 per cent (Horvath, 1977) of the guilty were correctly classified, while 63 per cent (Kleinmuntz and Szucko, 1984) and 51 per cent (Horvath, 1977) of the innocent were correctly classified. These trends are true of studies involving the control question test which is the typical situation in forensic settings. But this is not the only form of polygraphy. Table 19.1 gives some information on the different types of polygraph test which are based on different questioning techniques. A British Psychological Society report (British Psychological Society Working Party, 2004) gives a detailed comparison of these techniques, together with the directed lie test (Raskin and Honts, 2002) in which the suspect liar is told to answer 'No' to questions to which everyone should say 'Yes'. There are other questions that are more pertinent to the 'crime' in question. The idea is that innocent people should be more concerned about the first sort of question than those questions about the 'crime'. Unfortunately, as the control question technique is almost exclusively the one used in forensic settings, the research on the other techniques is of lesser forensic interest. Fiedler, Schmid and Stahl (2002) provide an evaluation of the scientific validity of the polygraph employing the control question technique. Their review led the German Supreme Court to stop using the technique in relation to penal matters.

Meijer and Verschuere (2010) in their review of control question technique (CQT) polygraphy express surprise that polygraphy is still claimed to be accurate – just as it was nearly 100 years ago. Many of us will be familiar with the TV shows in which the host acts as if their lie detector test is infallible, despite a great deal of evidence to the contrary. Meijer and Verschuere summarise accuracy data

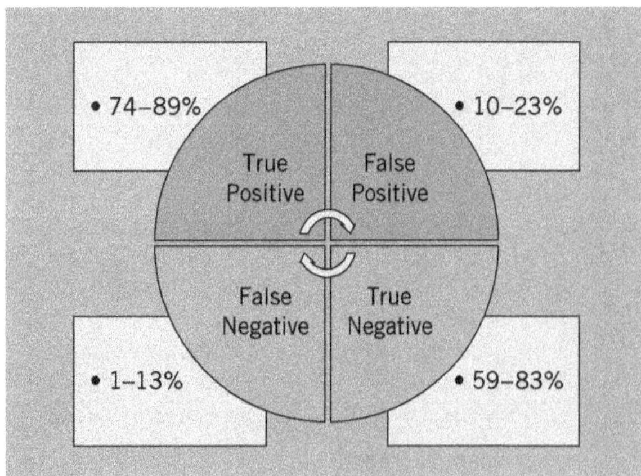

Figure 19.4 The accuracy of the CQT polygraph technique based on past studies

from a large range of studies. Some of this is illustrated in Figure 19.4. The hits on the guilty individual are as high as 89 per cent, which would mean that in polygraph picks out the guilty suspect on nearly nine out of ten occasions. The polygraph also does nearly as well at picking out the innocent person correctly – as many as four out of five innocent suspects were correctly identified, according to the best estimate. But look at the figures for picking out an innocent person as guilty – in the highest estimate nearly a quarter of innocent parties were identified by the test as being guilty. Guilty suspects were judged to be innocent less often, but nevertheless on as many as 13 per cent of occasions a guilty individual was classified as innocent. One way of summarising these figures is to suggest that if a suspect is guilty then they are highly likely to be judged as guilty. But the polygraph seems to hand out a rather more unfair treatment to innocent suspects. Accuracy at judging these innocent is rather poorer. It is more likely that the guilty person will be assessed as guilty than the innocent person will be assessed as innocent. These are cherry-picked figures, of course, but they give some idea of the risks of the polygraph assessment, especially for the innocent individual. In their measured conclusions, Meijer and Verschuere argue the following:

- The CQT polygraph is accurate at better than the chance level.
- The CQT polygraph error rate can be quite substantial according to some studies.
- The CQT polygraph is very susceptible to false-positive outcomes.

Relying on the CQT polygraph findings alone could be especially risky for the scenario where the suspect is innocent. The argument that we can expect anyone who is sent for a polygraph examination by the police to be likely to be guilty is not helpful. We do not know the ground truth anyway and it does not alter the possibility that an innocent person may fail the CQT test. It would merely mean that fewer innocent people are assessed using the polygraph so fewer will be wrongly accused. This is cold comfort if one is innocent and sent for a polygraph assessment.

One final approach to assessing the accuracy of the polygraph warrants mentioning. This took a substantially different approach which Ginton (2013) claims circumvents the problem of ground truth – that is, it is not necessary to know if the suspect is telling the truth or lying in order to estimate the accuracy of the polygraph. The approach involves a somewhat novel situation in polygraph testing and some statistical calculations. The study employed polygraphy cases where *two* people were tested and these people were giving contradictory evidence concerning the same event. An example of this would be a hit-and-run accident in which two people accepted that they were in a car but they disagreed as to who was the driver and who was the passenger when the collision occurred. In these circumstances, if both denied driving and there was no possible third party then one of them would have to be lying. It is possible to calculate the accuracy of the polygraph over the pairs of tests because it is known that one of the examinees is lying. The research involved searching the records of two major polygraph units of the Israeli national police looking for cases where two individuals gave opposite versions of the incident in question. There needed to be one liar and one truth teller, though it is not known for certain which is which. Cases where difference in perspective might explain the two different accounts were excluded. That is, the incidents selected for further study could not conceivably be seen as the consequence of different viewpoints. Just over 60 cases of these pairs of polygraph assessments were found in the records. The control questions technique was employed in all of the polygraph assessments. The polygraph data came from the original police records and various examiners were involved in scoring the test. Based on his calculations, Ginton concluded that the accuracy rate for the polygraph assessment was 80 per cent, with a 20 per cent error rate. The accuracy was higher if polygraph records which are considered to marginal are eliminated, though it is a matter of judgement whether this figure is more appropriate. Of course, while in theory the procedure employed would seem to be a good idea, polygraph assessments are not carried out without considerable additional information being provided to the polygraph examiner by the police. Evidence on this was not available in this study, so it could be that the polygraph examiner was influenced by this additional information when carrying out the tests. And this could be the case whether one or two examiners were involved in a particular case. That is, the testing could have been compromised by the additional information available. So whether the results show the accuracy of the polygraph or artefacts of the social system involved in polygraphy may be considered an open question.

In contrast, research into the accuracy of the guilty knowledge test (more recently known as the concealed information test) tends to demonstrate exactly the reverse trend. Elaad (1990) and Elaad, Ginton and Jungman (1992) found that the guilty knowledge test was extremely accurate in identifying the innocent – over 90 per cent were correctly classified. The guilty, on the other hand, were correctly identified in only 42 per cent of cases in the first study and in 76 per cent of cases in the second.

One should consider the influence of polygraph test evidence and the judgements made by jurors in courts of law having heard this evidence. Myers, Latter and Abdollalhi-Arena (2006) carried out new research and reviewed past research on this topic. There was little support for the idea that jurors uncritically accept poly graph evidence. Instead they are quite sceptical about it.

Polygraphy and the post-conviction sex offender

Even in countries where the polygraph test cannot be used as evidence of guilt in courts of law, it may have alternative uses. A few years ago, the British government initiated trials into the post-conviction use of the polygraph in the supervision and management of convicted sex offenders in the community. In the UK the scope of its use is much more limited than, say, in the United States, where it is used in a majority of states as a condition of probation and parole. Post-conviction sex offender polygraphy is largely about the management of sex offenders following conviction rather than finding evidence for further prosecutions. Polygraphy used in this way is far from new since it dates back to the 1970s in the United States (Grubin and Madsen, 2005). In the US, half of state probation and parole service providers regularly use polygraph testing in the management of sex offenders (English, Jones, Pasini-Hill, Patrick and Cooley-Towell, 2000). Furthermore, the use of polygraph testing for this purpose is required in over 30 states in the USA. Its uses include assessing the truthfulness of what paedophiles say to probation workers about their day-to-day activities. So denials by paedophiles that they are targeting playgrounds in public parks may be evaluated against their responses on the polygraph. It is claimed that the use of the polygraph in this sort of way has prevented the sexual abuse of a number of children and led to the reimprisonment of some offenders (BBC News, 2005). However, the validity of the polygraph in this context is largely unresearched compared to the extensive research base in criminal investigations. One of the problems in dealing with sex offenders is their denial and avoidance of confronting their offending behaviour (see Chapter 10). Proponents of the use of post-conviction sex offender polygraphy argue that 1) it can be used to ensure more reliable information from offenders about their activities, and 2) it can motivate offenders to avoid high-risk situations that might lead to reoffending against children (or other targets). For example, if an offender carries on masturbating to sexual fantasies about children, the belief is that they are much more likely to carry out that fantasy in real life. Without polygraphy, it is harder to assess behaviours like this – though, of course, not impossible in a conversation between the offender and their probation worker. Similarly, it is hard to know just by asking whether an offender gravitates towards children's play areas, which may increase his risk of reoffending. Thus there are alternatives to the polygraph – though they may not be so effective, given what we know about denial and avoidance in sex offenders.

There are four types of use of the post-conviction sex offender polygraph test according to Grubin (2008):

- To help obtain a more complete disclosure of the sex offender's history. The offender will be questioned under polygraphy about aspects of his sex offending history. Having more information inevitably enables better assessments of the offender's risk and also contributes to setting relevant and appropriate treatment targets.
- To help with the maintenance of the offender during treatment and supervision. Maintenance will involve a number of requirements set between the offender and his supervising probation worker or therapist. Regular polygraph testing can help check that these requirements are being adhered to. Grubin (2008) suggests that maintenance polygraph testing is to prevent reoffending rather than detect that it has happened.
- To help overcome denial. This involves testing to obtain a more complete account of the index offence for which the sex offender has been convicted. The aim is to obtain a more complete account of the nature of that offence. This sort of polygraph testing may help overcome behaviours such as the offender's denial or minimisation of their offending. Again the outcome of the polygraph testing may be useful during treatment and management of the sex offender.
- Specific issue testing or monitoring examinations concentrate on a particular matter of concern in relation to a particular offender. One example, mentioned by Grubin, would be the issue of whether the offender might have contacted his victim while under supervision.

Some sex-offender participants in a study (Grubin, Madsen, Parsons, Sosnowki and Warberg, 2004; Madsen,

Parsons and Grubin, 2004) were told that they would retake a polygraph test after three months whereas the other offenders were not told this. At the polygraph reassessment they were asked questions like 'Have you done anything over the last three months that would concern your probation officer?' Out of the men who took the second polygraph test, the vast majority (97 per cent) admitted engaging in this sort of high risk of reoffending behaviour. This means that only one man did not admit any high-risk behaviours – and he failed the test anyway. One way of looking at all of this is that, where the offender wishes to reduce their risk of reoffending, the polygraph can be helpful in helping them maintain a reduced risk of reoffending lifestyle. There was evidence of a great deal of resistance to taking part in the polygraph testing on the part of some offenders and significant numbers of failures to turn up for the second polygraph test. The researchers suggest that these involve individuals with little or no motivation to change their offending behaviour. In contrast, those motivated to change seem to have found it helpful in avoiding risky situations and reoffending.

Despite its long-established use in the United States, post-conviction polygraphy for sex offenders remains somewhat controversial elsewhere. A good example is Ben-Shakhar's (2008) critique. His argument is largely redolent of the criticisms of the use of the controlled question polygraphy technique in police investigations. He is particularly concerned with false positive and false negative outcomes. The post-conviction sex offender who beats the lie detector and appears to be behaving appropriately, he argues, may be an increased risk to children and women because his denials have been reinforced. Grubin (2008), in defence of post-conviction polygraphy, first of all points to the major uses of polygraphy in criminal investigation settings as well as security vetting and, even, in pre-employment vetting. The question in these settings is whether the individual passes or fails the lie detector test. The consequences of failure can be significant, just as the rewards for passing can also be considerable. In these circumstances, issues such as the error rate (false positives and false negatives) become important. Post-conviction sex offender testing, however, is rather different and does not depend on passing or failing for its effectiveness. Instead, it may be evaluated in terms of the extent to which the offender is encouraged to disclose information which otherwise might not be available. This information may be helpful in the supervision and management of the sex offender as well as his treatment. Grubin compares sex offender polygraphy with an investigative interrogation which is essentially confrontational in nature. Grubin suggests that the post-conviction sex offender polygraph test is rather less extreme in its style and consequences. He argues that disclosures made during testing are therapeutically helpful and that they result in rewards for the offender rather than punishment. The sex offender who is open and discloses can be seen to be making progress in treatment and given positive feedback. Apparently, indications of lying on the polygraph test are not acted upon – it is the additional information that is provided that is important, claims Grubin. For this reason, if the polygraph is 80 per cent effective in encouraging disclosure then this is good enough to inform the treatment and management of the sex offender.

The accuracy of these sorts of polygraph testing results is not an entirely meaningful concept to apply. How does one validate statements about whether or not the offender has masturbated to deviant fantasy, for example? Grubin suggests that quite high error rates are not really critical in this context, whereas they would be in the crime investigation context. The polygraph test is merely part of a range of information available to those involved in the treatment and management of the sex offender. As such, Grubin regards the outcome of the polygraph test as largely benign, though it is impossible to know whether all post-offence sex offender polygraph tests are evaluated in such a balanced context. Falsely confessing to offending or behaviours merely to please their probation supervisor or therapist is a risk but Grubin indicates that only about 10 per cent of offenders admit in any anonymous survey to doing this (Grubin and Madsen, 2005). Grubin adopts a generally pragmatic approach to sex offender polygraph testing. So on the issue of whether a sex offender can fool the polygraph test, he writes that this is a possibility but indicates that they may fool their therapists and supervisors equally well or better.

There is some controversy concerning the use of post-conviction polygraphy. One critical review of the field is Rosky (2012). He questions the strength of the evidence in favour of post-conviction polygraphy. There are three main claims made about the value of polygraphy in the supervision and treatment of offenders:

- Polygraphy can be used to encourage offenders to report previously undisclosed offences. This increases the range of types of crime known to have been committed by the offender and identifies a larger number of victims.
- Polygraphy improves therapeutic progress, including the identification of important risk factors.
- Fear of being detected by the polygraph deters the offender from violating supervision requirements and committing new offences.

Rosky accepts that disclosure of past offences may be increased and that the number of treatment/supervisions may be reduced by polygraphy. What is in doubt is that polygraphy is particularly effective in these respects. The deterrent effect of polygraphy is far from proven. His view is that research supporting post-conviction polygraphy is weak. It is not surprising to find that this form of polygraphy is beset with many of the problems which affect pre-conviction polygraphy. That is, just how should we interpret the changes in blood pressures, heart rate and perspiration that occur during a polygraph examination? It is too easy to accept conventional wisdom that they measure deception. Viable alternatives to this include that they measure anxiety, fear or anger, for example. According to Rosky, this issue is neglected in the literature supportive of post-conviction polygraph testing. He reiterates the argument that polygraphy is better than chance at lie detection but that how much better than chance is a moot point. What are the consequences of a false positive for the post-conviction offender? Basically, they are left between a rock and a hard place. Their therapeutic progress becomes in doubt and they are under various pressures to confess to things that they may not have done simply to demonstrate their cooperativeness. Rosky points out that the National Research Ccouncil (2003) review of polygraphy found no scientific credibility in estimates of the validity of the polygraph in screening procedures – such as the post-conviction polygraph.

It is, of course, difficult to establish the ground truth of post-conviction polygraphy (just as for any other form of polygraphy). One method used post-conviction is simply to survey offenders about the accuracy of the truth/deception decisions for the polygraph assessment that they have just undergone. Kokish *et al.* (2003) found that almost 95 per cent of offenders said that the test had correctly identified that they were being deceptive. On the other hand, Grubin and Madsen's (2005 research showed that only about 50 per cent of offenders were correctly identified as deceptive. Not many of the offenders actually claimed to have beaten the polygraph – less than 10 per cent made such a claim. In the totality of the context of post-conviction polygraph tests, one might wonder, would offenders see it as being in their personal interest to admit that they had got away with things on the lie detector? It hardly needs pointing out that the assumption that the offender is honest in the survey may be incongruent with the belief that they were lying on the polygraph. If we assume that the polygraph is correct when it identifies deception, we do not know what it was they were being deceptive about. For example, it might be a new sexual felony offence or it might have been a technical violation of the terms of their supervision or treatment. If nearly 10 per cent get away with being deceptive for new sexual offences then this would be a decisive blow against post-offending polygraphy.

One might argue that false positives have no public safety implications as false positive offenders would be regarded by the system as being problematic offenders who need to be prevented from being public dangers. On the other hand, false positives for deception inevitably put additional costs on the criminal justice system since the offender who is believed to be lying is likely to be treated as a retrenched/recalcitrant offender needing longer incarceration, extra supervision, extra treatment, and extra monitoring. Quite simply, the false positive and the true positive may both place extra financial burdens on the criminal justice system – the false positives unnecessarily so.

What of the deterrent effect of polygraph testing on new crimes? This can only work for the proportion of offenders who are likely to reoffend. Some research such as Kokish *et al.* (2003) showed that 90 per cent of offenders in their sample thought that polygraph testing was helpful in that it reduced their criminogenic behaviours. But one might say that they would say that, wouldn't they? What is needed is evidence that post-conviction polygraphy reduces recidivism rates. Remarkably, Rosky (2012 could only find three studies dealing with this and only one of these was methodologically promising. This study was by McGrath, Cumming, Hoke and Bonn-Miller (2007). Included in their methodological refinements were that the polygraph group and the controls were matched in terms of type of treatment and supervision. No differences were found between the two groups for things like risk level and educational attainment. The researches then obtained five-year rates for the following:

- new sex convictions;
- new violent but non-sexual convictions;
- new non-violent convictions;
- violations in the community;
- recalls to prison.

With one exception, there were no statistically significant differences between the polygraphy and the control group on any of these measures of deterrent effects. The exception was for violent (non-sexual) convictions. The polygraphy group included 3 per cent with new violent convictions and the non-polygraphy group 12 per cent! Overall recidivism was not different between the two groups. Interestingly, the offenders in the polygraphy group were more likely to be returned to prison than those in the control group. These results are in the wrong direction to support the use of post-conviction polygraphy. All of this amounts to a need to be cautious about the claims made for post-conviction polygraphy.

Alternatives to the polygraph

If we imagine the polygraph had been invented this year, would its use be accepted by the criminal justice system? Would the available evidence convince the world that it was a good idea? However, the polygraph lie detector is now about 100 years old and has survived remarkably well, despite consistent criticism by the academic community, law professionals and others. A perfectly reasonable question is what alternative technologies might replace the polygraph. Langleben and Moriarty (2013) discuss functional magnetic resonance imaging (fMRI) as one technology that might be somewhere near the breakthrough into becoming a viable lie detector system. Some US litigants have already tried to introduce into court evidence obtained through the use of it – albeit rather unsuccessfully. One of the things that has changed since the early days of the polygraph is the standards for the use of expert scientific evidence in court. The *Daubert* criteria (discussed in Box 1.1) include the important matter of *known error rate*. Unless research can provide clear evidence of the extent of errors then techniques such as fMRI may not be acceptable in court. Given that it is not yet clear what the known error rate is for polygraphy after 100 years, considerable effort and resources would be needed to establish this for fMRI or any other technique. Several of the stalwarts of forensic science have been called into question in the last two decades, including handwriting, fingerprint comparison and evidence from bitemarks (*National Research Council of the National Academies*' report (NRC Report, 2009), *Strengthening Forensic Science in the United States: A Path Forward)*. Langleben and Moriarty, however, doubt whether the courts will rapidly abandon such sources of evidence since, once accepted into courts of law, it is difficult to eradicate them from the system as they become rooted. Mastroberardino and Santangelo (2009) similarly reviewed evidence relevant to EEGs and functional magnetic resonance imaging (fMRI) in relation to lying. They point out the difficulty in finding within these a good specific indicator of lying.

Statement validity analysis: criterion-based content analysis and the validity checklist

Since lying is a verbal process, the use of physiological techniques would appear to be indirect compared with examining language itself for lies. The difficulty, though, should be obvious by now from the previous chapter – most of us are fairly bad at recognising lies without special training. In continental Europe, research interest has focused on a group of techniques known as *statement validity analysis*. This derives largely from the pioneering work of German psychologists, especially Udo Undeutsch (1992), as well as Swedish psychologists. Statement validity analysis is accepted in a number of European legal systems, including the Netherlands, Germany and Sweden, and also in some American states (Vrij, 2005). Researchers speak of the Undeutsch hypothesis as being fundamental to the method. The hypothesis essentially states that witnesses' descriptions of experienced and fictitious events are different in a number of ways. Truthful narratives are not the same in form and structure as untruthful ones. These differences are potential indicators differentiating truthful accounts from falsehoods.

Statement validity analysis is especially important in sexual abuse assessment because sexual abuse can rarely be determined on the basis of physical evidence. Despite popular beliefs about the nature of the sexual abuse of children, much of it leaves few or no physical signs. Thus touching and stroking, for example, show no physical evidence such as semen for DNA testing or injury to the anus or genitals. So it is often necessary to depend on the victim's testimony. This may be contaminated in a number of ways. Adults may suggest events that never occurred to the child or sometimes there may be a deliberate lie by the child who is, say, angry with an adult for some reason. These matters were discussed in Chapter 16 in more detail.

Statement validity analysis consists of the two major components shown in Figure 19.5:

- Criterion-based content analysis involves an analysis of the content of a statement about the crime to see which of about 19 different criteria of 'truthfulness' are present.
- The validity checklist is much more of an in-depth psychological assessment of the possible victim for motivations for giving a false statement. It may incorporate wider knowledge from other sources about the crime.

Of the two major components of statement validity analysis, research has concentrated on criterion-based content analysis with the validity checklist largely ignored.

Statement validity analysis should not be evaluated in terms of traditional North American assessment techniques. It does not provide a numerical score that can be judged against normative data of statement validity. Thus it is not possible to say that if a witness statement has 14 of the characteristics of a truly experienced account then they are telling the truth. It is impossible to use the method to differentiate truth from fiction in a simplistic way. Instead, the psychologist must gather information about the child's general competence in narrating memories of events to compare with the specific statement that is forensically of interest (Greuel, Brietzke and Stadle, 1999). There are several stages in statement validity analysis which help assess whether a witness is probably credible. To concentrate on individual components of statement validity analysis such as criterion-based content analysis is to misunderstand the method's intent and fundamental strategy. A child can be judged a competent witness only

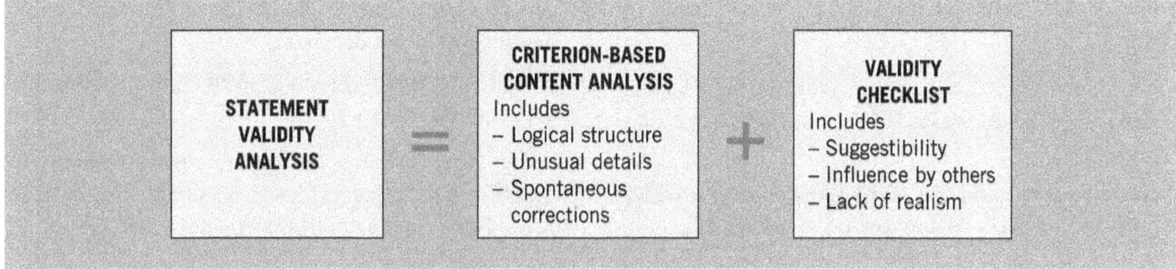

Figure 19.5 The components of a statement validity analysis

by reference to a number of features. The concept of credibility refers to a cluster of three essential components: 1) the individual's competence to testify in court; 2) the quality of the witness's statement; and 3) the reliability of the statement. The process of assessing credibility is illustrated by the flowchart in Figure 19.6.

What differentiates credible from fictitious testimony? These are usually classified into: general characteristics; specific contents; peculiarities of content; motivation-related content; and offence-specific elements (e.g. Bekerian and Dennett, 1992). The major features of statements based on experience are presented diagrammatically

Individual competency to testify

Baseline of individual's general competence at telling about experiences such as life events using similar questioning methods to criterion-based content analysis.

Does the individual have the cognitive competence (verbal skill, autobiographical memory, perceptual skill) to give a reliable report?

yes

no

No need to proceed further as witness not credible.

Does the individual have the cognitive competence to give a false report about the forensic issue?

Statement quality

Criterion-based content analysis used to assess quality of statement about the crime.

Compared with other statements made by witness at other times, e.g. police statements.

Does the statement contain features consistent with statements based on experience rather than fabricated, i.e. criterion-based content analysis?

Statement of reliability

Are there factors about the individual that might lead to unintended distortions?

Are there factors such as suggestions from others, e.g. police officers and other interviewers, that might have led the witness unintentionally to distort the statement?

Criterion-based content analysis cannot differentiate suggested statements from experienced statements. The greater the suggestion, the less use is criterion-based content analysis.

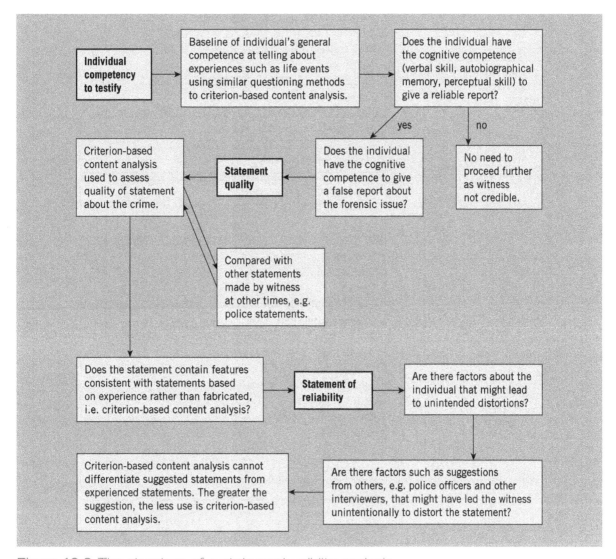

Figure 19.6 The structure of a statement validity analysis

in Figure 19.7. Generally speaking, truthful accounts are ones that:

- contain evidence that the witness regards their account as possibly flawed because of poor/incomplete memory for events;
- contain a greater amount of detail of context, conversations and interactions relevant to the narrative;
- contain a greater amount of irrelevant detail in describing the events that occurred;
- describe logically feasible events in a somewhat unstructured or disorganised fashion.

Criterion-based content analysis uses these features, in conjunction with other evidence, in order to assess the likelihood that the witness's account is credible as an

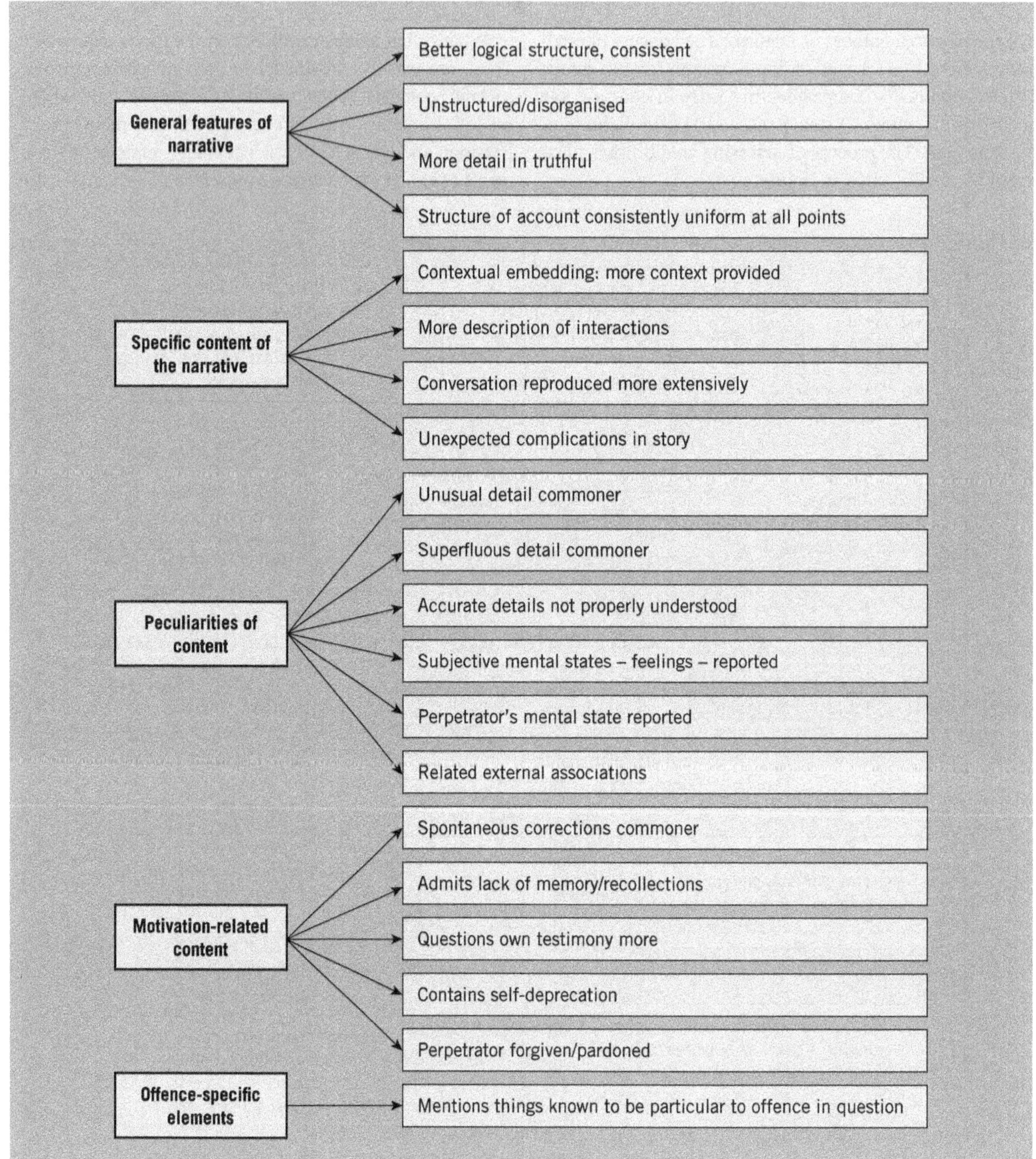

Figure 19.7 Criterion-based content analysis: some aspects of truthful narratives

account of experienced events. Most of these criteria seem to be reasonably valid since many of them are based on empirical evidence from cognitive psychology. Psychologists using the method tend not to write of lies and truth but to refer to credibility instead. A child influenced by an adult into making allegations of abuse is not lying by the criterion of a deliberate intention to deceive. On the other hand, that child is not giving an accurate account of events that they experienced.

Comparison with *other* people is not a feature of statement validity analysis as it would be in a typical psychological test. In statement validity analysis comparisons are made but they are with other data collected about the child in question. There are numerous reasons why it is necessary to compare individuals with themselves rather than others. For example, some credible witnesses will be extremely good at telling narratives about their experiences, whereas other credible witnesses will be less good at telling narratives about their experiences. Some witnesses will have a good memory for detail, for example, whereas others will have a poor memory for detail. As you can see in Figure 19.6, some of the criteria of credible statements are partly dependent on good memory. Thus you would expect a credible witness statement about a crime coming from an individual with a good memory to have high memory content, whereas a credible witness statement about a crime from a witness with a relatively poor memory will start at a lower baseline. The three major stages in a statement validity analysis are as follows:

- *Stage 1: witness competence to testify.* Returning to Figure 19.6, you will see that the initial stage of statement validity analysis is to assess the competence of a witness to testify. There is little point in proceeding any further with a non-competent witness. There are a number of reasons for non-competence. A witness who shows poor ability at giving narrative accounts of recent events in their lives may have a brain disease, for example, which makes their statements suspect. Another witness may give the impression of being unable to tell the truth about anything. On the other hand, yet other witnesses may give the impression of being unable to give a false account about anything. In addition to this sort of assessment, this initial stage provides the opportunity to obtain baseline indications of the ability of the witness to give good narrative accounts of their experiences as well as gathering an impression of the characteristics of their narratives.
- *Stage 2: statement quality.* This involves the assessment of statement quality. This is essentially criterion-based content analysis. This is done in two ways: a) internally to the statement collected from the witness (known as the immanent view) or b) comparatively between that statement and ones obtained in other circumstances, such as in court or during the police interview. This means, firstly, that it is possible to assess the extent to which the statement contains criteria indicative of experience-based statements relative to the psychologist's expectations of the individual in question. Secondly, it is also possible to assess whether these criteria are stable in all accounts of the events provided by the witness.
- *Stage 3: statement reliability.* Witnesses may unintentionally provide testimony that departs materially from the credible. This may be the result of the witnesses' personal characteristics. Distinctive styles of attribution, perceptual styles or motivations may be involved. Childhood victims of sexual abuse, for example, sometimes have distorted perceptions of who was responsible for initiating the abuse and blame themselves rather than the adult who perpetrated the crime. Other victims may consistently embellish or dramatise the truth.

A major part of assessing statement reliability involves the issue of suggestibility. This might be the tendency of the witness to be influenced by distortions due to leading or suggestive questioning by other people, such as police officers, social workers or others. However, more important is whether or not the previous interviews and interrogations involved suggestion. So, for example, is there evidence of a suggestive interviewing style in the transcripts of previous interviews? Does the narrative provided by the witness change markedly following an earlier interview? The answers to these questions have an important bearing on how the criterion-based content analysis from the previous stage is to be interpreted. There may be no evidence at all of suggestion being involved in the statement. For example, there may have been no previous interrogations and so no opportunity for suggestion to have an influence. In these circumstances, criterion-based content analysis can be directly interpreted according to what criteria it contains, together with the psychologically based expectations of that individual developed in Stage 1 – competence assessment. If there is evidence of suggestion then caution is necessary. Criterion-based content analysis cannot distinguish suggestion-based narratives from experientially based ones. The greater the suggestion, the less can be said on the basis of the content analysis.

The forensic use of statement validity analysis has largely been confined to certain parts of Continental Europe and Germany in particular, although research on it has been much more international.

There has been an intriguing analysis of eyewitness evidence surrounding the claims that a UFO (unidentified flying object) crashed near Roswell, New Mexico, USA (Houran and Porter, 2005). An investigation by the military claimed that the fragments found were those of a weather balloon, not a flying saucer. Jim Ragsdale provided a deathbed 'eyewitness' account of the crash and the contents of this flying saucer. He was with a woman who was later killed in a car crash. Ragsdale provided two accounts – one of 600 words and the other an affidavit of 1000 words – which he published in 1996. The delay between 'witnessing' the events and his description was 48 years. This is the sort of material that might be assessed using statement validity analysis for its veracity as a product of human memory. Part of Ragsdale's testimony was as follows:

> Since it was the Fourth of July weekend, I had several days off work. I was working driving a truck, transporting heavy equipment for a gas line. My girlfriend was from Las Cruces, and I lived in Carlsbad. We decided to go to the perfect place near Boy Scout Mountain in a campsite where we could have some solitude. We went up Pine Lodge Road and turned onto a gravel road heading toward the campsite. We went where there is a picnic ground and we had access to water. I parked my pickup behind a clump of trees, got the quilts out and put them in the back of my pickup, and we started drinking and making-out. We were lying in the back of my pickup truck, buck naked, drinking beer, and having a good ole time when about 11:30 the night of July 4, 1947, all hell broke loose. From the northwest, there was a big flash, an intense, bright explosion, and then, shortly thereafter, with a noise like thunder, this thing came plowing through the trees, sheering off the tops, and then stopped between two huge rocks. It was propped up against one rock. It was about twenty feet around. As it was approaching, huge streams like fire were coming out from behind. After the impact, silence. There was a hole in one side about four feet wide and two feet high. There was junk scattered around the disc, and we picked some of it up. I looked inside the hole, and inside, there was a chair that looked like a throne. It looked like it was made of rubies and diamonds. There were other little chairs – four or five and a lot of instruments on a panel. There were also the little people, four of them. They looked like midgets, about four feet long. Their skin, if it was skin, was sort of gray and when I touched one of them, it felt like a wet snake.
>
> (pp. 68–9)

Houran and Porter (2005) suggest that the following were missing among other features of truthful accounts, though the accounts were, for example, coherent and also showed a degree of contextual embedding, such as the detail of the couple's activities in the back of the truck:

- Description of interaction: although the events prior to the explosion do contain detail of the interaction between the couple, the description following these events contains nothing of contact or interaction that the couple may have had.
- Reproduction of conversation: no conversation between the couple is described in Ragsdale's account.
- Spontaneous corrections: Ragsdale corrected his memories on no occasion during the two reports.
- Admitting lack of memory: Ragsdale did not question his ability to recall the events in any way during his account.

Other criteria of truthful accounts were also missing, as can be seen. Thus the analyst concluded that the accounts were not characteristic of memories of real events since very few indicators of truthful accounts according to statement validity analysis were present.

The validity of statement validity analysis

Forensic validity

The origins of statement validity analysis were in practical forensic applications of psychological research, especially in child sexual abuse cases. As such, the forensic rather than the laboratory validity of the approach is important. Udo Undeutsch made great claims about the effectiveness of the methods as he employed them within the German court system. For example, he suggested that of the cases assessed by him in order to provide evidence of the guilt of the suspect, no instances emerged to indicate that statement validity analysis was wrong. Acquittals on appeal after new evidence has emerged of the innocence of the accused would indicate that statement validity analysis was leading to false convictions. But there was no evidence of acquittals on appeal. As Undeutsch was involved in thousands of cases, this appears to be strong evidence of the validity of the method. However, Undeutsch's, and similar, assertions have not been extensively or adequately documented (Bekerian and Dennett, 1992). Basically, the claim is that statement validity analysis is effective and leads to no false convictions but there are a number of considerations that reduce the impact of the claim:

- It is unclear what aspects of statement validity analysis led Undeutsch to his conclusions. Statement validity analysis can draw evidence from a wide variety of sources, as we have seen. Could it be that Undeutsch was more influenced by other forensic evidence than, say, criterion-based content analysis?
- It is not known what numbers of false negatives the method produces. If Undeutsch decided that the allegation was not very credible, this might result in a decision not to prosecute, despite there being other evidence

of guilt – leaving a guilty individual unpunished. The potentially more risky prosecutions are thereby excluded from trial, which obviously minimises the potential for appeals.

- It could be that the decision to obtain a statement validity analysis from Undeutsch was only made if the evidence was strong enough to make a conviction likely, Undeutsch's support being requested merely to strengthen an already strong case. In these circumstances, later reversals of the conviction would be unlikely.
- The evidence is that false allegations of child abuse possibly amount to no more than about 10 per cent of allegations (Howitt, 1992). Thus an allegation is a good sign of guilt and reversals of a conviction are only likely in this small percentage of cases.

These are conjectures that merely serve to reinforce the view that statement validity analysis needs more evaluation in its practical application. For example, Lamers-Winkelman and Buffing (1996) provide evidence from the Netherlands that certain of the components of statement validity analysis show age trends so that if the child's age is not taken into account, the validity of the method is reduced. This is a finding that has been replicated by others such as Pezdek, Morrow, Blandon-Gitlin *et al.* (2005) who also found that statements concerning frequently occurring events in the individual's life are more likely to be judged true by CBCA than events that are rare in a child's life. The latter finding was replicated by Blandon-Gitlin, Pezdek, Rogers and Brodie (2005). Of course, this would make a CBCA analysis harder.

Laboratory validity

The ideal study of the validity of statement validity analysis is impossible. It would probably involve psychologists, well experienced in the method, making judgements of the credibility of witnesses to apparently the same event – one witness telling the truth, the other lying. Using statement validity analysis, the psychologists would decide which was the credible witness. Of course, this sort of situation does not normally occur. Furthermore, unless the 'witnesses' were randomly allocated to truth-telling or lie-telling conditions, even this would not be fully capable of providing evidence of the value of statement validity analysis. Perhaps naturally honest people would choose to tell the truth and dishonest people would choose to lie. In these circumstances, it may be that the psychologists pick the truthful account from the angelic faces of the honest people and the fictitious account from the scowling demeanour of the naturally dishonest person. Clearly, certain issues can be resolved only by using random allocation in controlled experiments. Unfortunately, this does not work very well in other respects. One of the major difficulties is that laboratory experiments cannot involve the serious crimes perpetrated against the witnesses in non-laboratory settings. Another difficulty is the desire of the researchers to simplify the procedures as much as possible by concentrating on the criterion-based content analysis and ignoring the validity checklist. As we have seen, this is to do an injustice to the assumptions of statement validity analysis. Consequently, the laboratory studies can often be criticised as failing to employ the full potential of statement validity analysis. In other words, we should not be surprised that statement validity analysis appears only moderately effective if we rely on research that does fundamental disservice to the approach. Others have noted that the quality of forensic interviews with children may be so poor as to mask the worth of the method to a degree (Lamb, Sternberg, Esplin, Hershkowitz and Orbach, 1997).

Nevertheless, it is unlikely that the North American tradition of psychological testing will readily yield to the requirements of this European approach. For example, Lamb *et al.* (1997) argue that trained assessors using criterion-based content analysis fail to show satisfactory levels of inter-rater reliability on many of the dimensions of the technique (see Figure 19.5). Some should be dropped as of no value and others need to be more carefully defined. Criterion-based content analysis dimensions that were not useful in differentiating truthful from false accounts included logical structure; complications; superfluous details; misunderstood details; external references; subjective feelings; perpetrator feelings; and spontaneous corrections.

However, the following criterion-based content analysis dimensions were helpful in differentiating between allegations believed to be true, according to independent judgements, and the false allegations:

- unstructured production;
- quantity of details;
- contextual embedding;
- interactions;
- conversations;
- unusual details.

All of these were more common in the plausible accounts.

In this context, some American research findings may be even more positive than it at first appears. Porter and Yuille (1996) studied a range of verbal indicators of deception in interrogations. The verbal indicators were partly taken from criterion-based content analysis or one of three other approaches to differentiating truth from lies (such as reality monitoring, and a training programme in detecting lying). The participants in the research were required to give accounts of events that were either truthful or deceptive. Of a substantial list of verbal indicators of lying, only those of quantity of details, coherence (that is, what others call logical structure) and admission of lack of memory were effective. These are all from criterion-based content analysis. The other three methods failed to distinguish truthful from false accounts.

Evidence of the validity of the validity checklist is much less common, perhaps rare. Lamers-Winkelman (1997) is one of the very few researchers to have studied this aspect of statement validity analysis. His Dutch team studied over 100 possible sexual abuse victims in the two- to twelve-year-old-age range. While we might assume that the vast majority of these allegations are truthful, a small percentage are likely to be false allegations, the researcher suggests. Because the normal medical practice in the Netherlands is not to physically examine child victims of sexual abuse, no independent evidence of abuse exists. Of course, physical signs of abuse are not common. By the usual criteria of psychological assessment, there was good agreement between different raters, both in terms of criterion-based content analysis and the validity checklist. Both of these had inter-rater reliabilities of over 0.8, indicating good consistency between raters. It should be stressed that the interviewers were trained by the leading experts in the method (Udo Undeutsch and Max Steller). We might expect that this led to greater reliability. A number of validity checklist items were explored in these interviews:

- *Age appropriateness of language in general:* a child who uses language more advanced than his or her chronological age may be reporting under the influence of older people. Generally speaking, in this sample there was no evidence of age-inappropriate language.
- *Age appropriateness of sexual knowledge:* sexual knowledge too advanced for the child's chronological age and level of development might be an indication that sexual abuse had taken place. Age inappropriateness was common among all of the age range. Thus, the minimum at any age level was 50 per cent but with younger children the figures went much higher: for example, 95 per cent of the four- to five-year-olds had knowledge too advanced for their age and level of development. These high figures might be expected in a group of sexually abused children; it is difficult to judge without the benefit of interviews with a group of non-abused children. There was a further problem. The interviewers found it difficult to decide what was sexually appropriate knowledge for the older age groups. Boys in the nine- to eleven-year-old age group are mentioned as a particularly difficult group. Be cautious about these figures. Remember that in Chapter 16, it is pointed out that some sexual behaviours such as public masturbation do not differentiate sexually abused children from other children very effectively.
- *Resistance to suggestive questioning:* as part of the validity analysis, the children are examined to see whether they are susceptible to the interviewer's 'planting' ideas in their mind. A child who is susceptible to leading or suggestive questioning may be a child who has previously been led by another adult to make the allegations of abuse falsely. From quite an early age – four years – the children demonstrated high levels of resistance to suggestive questions. Younger children than these were more influenced by such questions: 29 per cent of children under four years failed to resist suggestive questions.
- *Appropriateness of affect:* the emotional signs accompanying descriptions of abuse should be appropriate to the abuse and general signs of emotionality may be present. In the study, about half of the children supported their descriptions of abusive events with gestures signalling emotion.

The performance of children when assessed using criterion-based content analysis varies according to the age of the child. The characteristics of the testimony of two-year-olds and fourteen-year-olds are different. Criterion-based content analysis has no specific way of dealing with age trends of this sort. Buck, Warren, Betman and Brigham (2002) obtained transcripts of real-life child sexual abuse interviews and had them rated using criterion-based content analysis. The reliability between different raters was modest. Use of most of the criteria of criterion-based content analysis correlated with age. So older children, for example, demonstrated greater logical structure, quantity of details and contextual embedding. Only criteria such as the amount of unusual detail, references to the offender's mental state, doubting their own testimony, self-deprecation and pardoning the perpetrator showed no overall correlation with age. So, in general, indicators of truthfulness were commoner in the older age groups. Some of the criteria of truthfulness simply did not appear for some ages of children. For example, comments doubting their own testimony did not appear until the twelve- to fourteen-years-of-age group and pardoning the perpetrator only appeared in nine- to eleven-year-olds. This, of course, raises the question of precisely how to deal with age when assessing children's accounts. The temptation might be to assume that older children are simply more honest in their reports but there is no evidence on this one way or the other. They may simply have a different style of reporting events which corresponds better with the criteria of truthfulness. (This is a complex issue – see Chapters 16 and 20 for more on children's age and testimony.) One should also be aware that the interviews subjected to analysis in this study were not the sort that criterion-based content analysis usually employs – they were standard child sexual abuse interviews instead. Thus the comments actually only apply to standard child sexual abuse interviews.

It should be mentioned that some researchers have used statement validity analysis and criterion-based content analysis in attempts to detect deception in adults. One particularly important study made use of London police interviews with rape victims. Some of these interviews contained demonstrably false claims since, for example, the 'victim' freely acknowledged that their allegations were false; there was evidence of the falsity of the claims from eyewitnesses or medical evidence and so forth. The interviews were studied using relatively structured scoring sheets. Correct identifications of true rape victim statements were high, based on criterion-based content analysis (88 per cent correct) and the validity checklist (100 per cent correct). The figures for interviews correctly identifying false statements as being false were 92 per cent for criterion-based content analysis and 58 per cent for the validity checklist. Combining criterion-based content analysis with the validity checklist led to a 100 per cent correct identification for true statements and a 92 per cent correct identification for false statements. False statements tended to be much more organised in style, whereas true statements tended to present a mixed range of emotions and unstructured delivery of the account. There is a lack of confusion in a false account. The validity criteria that differentiated the two types of interview included 'inconsistencies within physical evidence', incongruous affect during interview and 'inconsistent statements'. The researchers also had experienced detectives evaluate the interviews. They concluded that the police officers demonstrated 'little consistency' (p. 249) in their decisions about the truth or otherwise of the statements. Statement validity analysis did better at identifying false statements than any of the individual officers or the group of officers as a whole.

The basic theoretical assumptions of criterion-based content analysis are the idea that lying is mentally more demanding than telling the truth and that liars have greater interest in the effect they have on other people than truth tellers, according to Vrij and Mann (2005). They tested these out experimentally on a groups of liars and truth telling undergraduate students. A questionnaire measure of cognitive load and another of the tendency to exercise control on speech formed the test of the two basic principles. The findings supported these basic principles of criterion-based content analysis.

The status of criterion-based content analysis

The current standing of criterion-based content analysis after several decades of research requires an evaluation. That this categorical based system is admitted in European courts such as those of Germany, Holland, Spain and Sweden as well as certain states of the United States does not, in itself, establish the validity of the method. If it did, then the many other countries which do not admit such evidence in court (such as the UK and Canada) would argue for its lack of value. In Spain, Novo and Seijo (2010) found that where systems such as statement validity analysis suggested that testimony was credible, it was found that it was 93 per cent certain that the accused would be convicted. Where the testimony was judged not credible then there was a zero rate of conviction. This makes the findings of a meta-analysis (see Box 4.1) by Amado, Arce and Farina (2015) all the more important. It also provides a way of summarising the current 'state of the art' of CBCA. They did an extensive keyword search using criterion-based content analysis and a range of other possibly relevant keywords in order to find empirical studies of CBCA. Inclusion criteria included studies with child witnesses between the age of two and eighteen years, the child's statement had to be obtained through an interview, the research should have been published in a scientific peer-reviewed journal, and so forth. This left twenty pertinent studies which met the researchers' requirements for inclusion. The findings for the overall CBCA total scores showed a very substantial effect size supporting the Undeutsch hypothesis that features of a statement can help differentiate true from non-credible testimony. The size of the effect for distinguishing the two was substantial and convincing by the usual criteria. The meta-analysis had included both field studies and experimental studies. Looking at these separately, it was clear that the effect size for the field studies was substantially greater than that for the experimental or laboratory studies. This goes some way to explaining why some experimentalists have tended to be somewhat dismissive of CBCA. Actually, there were no effect sizes for any of the studies which provided negative evidence of the value of CBCA. Each of the 19 individual criteria used in CBCA was shown to provide evidence in favour of the Undeutsch hypothesis though there was some variation in the size of the effect.

Scientific content analysis

There are other verbally based methods of evaluating witness/suspect statements for credibility. Scientific content analysis (SCAN) is one of these, though it has no standardised scoring method and the criteria that it uses are by no means well-defined. It was developed during the 1980s by Avinoam Sapire, a former polygraph examiner in Israel. It has been used in investigations in a number of countries, including Canada, the Netherlands, the United Kingdom and the United States according to Vrij (2008). The witness/suspect writes down their version of the events, including everything that happened, without the involvement of police officers. This version of events is matched against criteria, including gaps found in the chronological sequence and the avoidance of the use of pronouns. The end point of the analysis is to make a judgement about the veracity of the witness/suspect account and it also may help in subsequent interviews. There are overlaps between SCAN criteria and those of criterion-based content analysis (Bogaard, Meijer, Vrij, Broers and Mercklbach, 2013). So, in SCAN, emotion in the statement is indicative of truthfulness if it occurs after the climax of the story, but it is indicative of lying if it occurs before the climax of the story. In contrast, in criterion-based content analysis, the presence of emotion in the statement is indicative of authenticity and its placement is irrelevant. Spontaneous corrections are regarded as evidence of lying in SCAN, but of truth telling in criterion-based content analysis. There is some evidence that the criteria used in criterion-based content analysis can be found in truthful statements but there is no adequate evidence that the SCAN criteria are reflected in truthful statements (Nahari, Vrij and Fisher, 2011).

BOX 19.1 Controversy

Statement validity analysis in forensic settings

Statement validity analysis was used by European forensic psychologists long before its validity in research terms was assessed. In an important and thought-provoking review, Vrij (2005) asks some very searching and demanding questions about the method. He reviewed 37 studies into the 'accuracy' of statement validity analysis. The 'ground truth' of whether a child's evidence is truthful or not really needs to be known before the validity of statement validity analysis can be assessed but obviously obtaining information about this is far from easy. Evidence of the 'ground truth' of witness statements has included: 1) the confession of the accused person; 2) that the accused was convicted by the court; and 3) whether a polygraph examination confirms the guilt of the accused. Unfortunately, none of these is independent of the information which statement validity analysis also depends upon. For example, if the child's evidence appears to be very strong or if the statement validity analysis expert feels that the child's evidence is true then the accused may feel under pressure to confess simply in order to obtain a possible reduction in sentence.

Vrij identifies much subtler problems. For instance, how do we classify the situation in which a child's evidence is overwhelmingly accurate but the wrong person is identified as the perpetrator by the child? It is a false accusation but only in terms of the offender's identity since the rest of the detail may be very accurate. Laboratory experiments into the efficacy of statement validity analysis, of course, do not have problems in establishing the ground truth simply because the researchers have manipulated the situation so that who is telling the truth and who is lying is built into the research design. Unfortunately, the artificial nature of such laboratory experiments is also built into the experiment's design. Despite there being many inherent problems in the way in which the accuracy of child witness statements is assessed, research evidence is fairly consistent in showing that the criteria used in statement validity analysis generally tend to effectively distinguish truth from fiction.

So how powerful is statement validity analysis and, in particular, criteria-based content analysis, at identifying truth tellers and liars? The evidence is that criteria-based content analysis employed by trained persons is better at identifying truth telling than such assessment made by untrained individuals. But the problem is that often the training given to people in the use of criteria-based content analysis in many of the studies appears to be fairly minimal compared with the complexity of the task. The lowest period of training given in any of the studies surveyed was 45 minutes! Remarkably, most field studies of statement validity analysis fail to provide useful information of the accuracy of the procedure. Consequently, Vrij had to turn to the findings of laboratory studies where the ground truth of guilt versus innocence is known. Virtually all laboratory studies gave overall accuracy rates between 65 per cent and 90 per cent for criteria-based content analysis. In finer detail, the accuracy rate for detecting lies was between 60 per cent and 90 per cent, according to Vrij (2005), and that for detecting truth was between 53 per cent and 89 per cent, though the average accuracy was hardly different at 73 per cent accuracy for truth and 72 per cent accuracy for lies.

Finally, Vrij raises the question of the legal implications of the research findings that he reviewed in relation to the American *Daubert* criteria (see Box 1.1) concerning guidelines for the permissibility of expert scientific evidence in court. One of the *Daubert* criteria is whether there is a known error rate for the assessment methods used. Vrij doubts whether this criterion is met by statement validity analysis research as there is no satisfactory research in field settings which would supply forensically valid error rates. But if we use the findings of laboratory studies we get an error rate of 30 per cent or so. This may be accurate or not as an estimate of the error rate in forensic settings. Assuming that it is, this implies a big risk of the expert getting it wrong. Statement validity analysis assessment simply fails to meet reasonable criteria of being error-free. Another *Daubert* criterion is that scientists accept the theory underlying the technique. Statement validity analysis theory has been seriously questioned by some researchers, so this form of analysis may not meet this second *Daubert* criterion. Vrij suggests that, although the method may not be adequate for use in courts, it may still be useful to the police in their work.

Of course, this perspective itself is not without its limitations.

- The error rate of statement validity analysis may not be the same as the risk that the expert's conclusions will be accepted by a court of law. The court may use other information over and above that supplied by the statement validity analyst, which reduces the impact of the big error rate.
- Other legal jurisdictions outside the United States may not accept the *Daubert* criteria. So different criteria must apply to these countries.
- Vrij's argument might be seen by some as more of a condemnation of the use of laboratory studies for forensic research than a decisive verdict on statement validity analysis.

Main points

- The polygraph test may become a more common feature in jurisdictions that do not allow it in court. There is increasing interest in its use in the monitoring of sex and other offenders while out in the community. There are several different ways of asking questions in the polygraph examination and they do not necessarily generate the same outcomes. Not all of the methods are used in practice by professional polygraph operators. The polygraph is more than a piece of physiological apparatus and is better seen as a process in practice. The operator usually has rather more information about the case and the suspect than a totally 'blind' procedure would require. The polygraph can be effective at generating a confession, irrespective of the validity of the technique. The major problem with the polygraph is its error rate, which in polygraph assessment tends to produce more false positives in that a proportion of innocent individuals are judged guilty by the polygraph operator.
- Statement validity analysis is a set of techniques which attempt to establish the credibility of witness evidence and is especially pertinent to the evidence of children in sexual abuse cases. It consists of a mixture of various matters to consider in relation to the testimony. Central to the approach is the idea that memory for events that were truly experienced is different from that for imaginary events. In addition to features of the situation such as the child's apparent resistance to suggestive questioning, the appropriateness of the language used to the child's age group may indicate adult influences on the child. There is evidence of the effectiveness of the approach and there are examples of its use with adult victims of rape in which statement validity analysis seemed able to distinguish 'known' false witness statements from true ones.

Further reading

A report on the status of polygraphy produced by the British Psychological Society can be found at: http://www.bps.org.uk/sites/default/files/documents/polygraphic_deception_detection_-_a_review_of_the_current_scientific_status_and_fields_of_application.pdf

Laws, D.R. and Donohue, W. (eds) (2016) *Treatment of Sex Offenders: Strengths and Weaknesses in Assessment and Intervention* Springer: London.

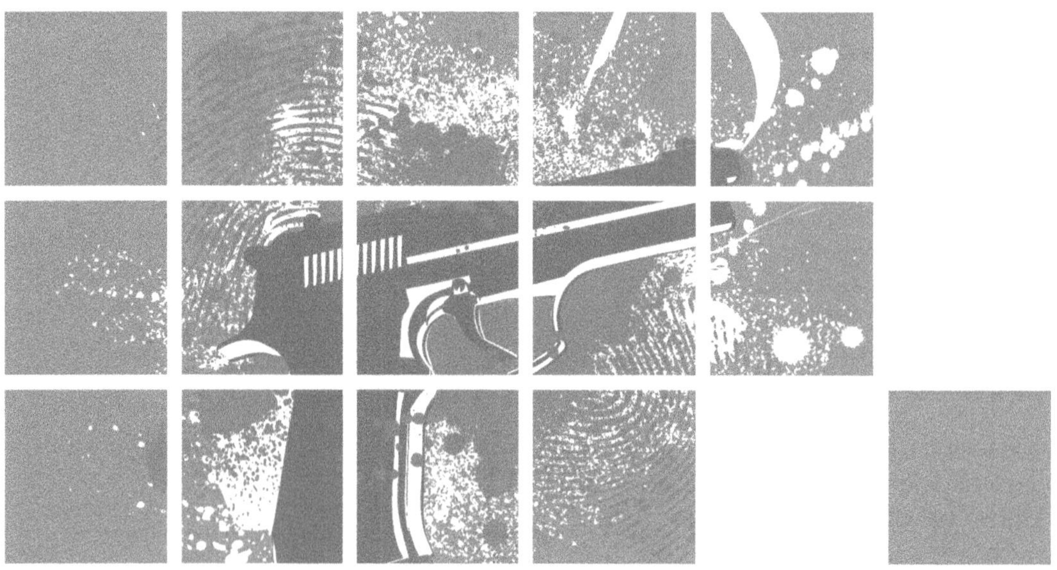

Chapter 20

Children as witnesses

Overview

- Perceptions of children as witnesses have changed markedly in the past century or so. Once they were regarded as dangerously unreliable witnesses, whereas the modern view is that, given appropriate interviewing and support, they can supply good-quality evidence. Nevertheless, countries differ markedly in their presumptions of the competence of children as witnesses.
- Bad interviews with abused children can undermine the value of the evidence produced. Certain characteristics of children can make them problematic witnesses, but equally the interviewer may create problems by not using an appropriate questioning style.
- Anatomically correct dolls can have a place in forensic interviews with children for a number of reasons to do with the enhancement of communications. They allow discussion of topics. Sexual play with such dolls is not a risk indicator of child sexual abuse and it is not appropriate to use the dolls to make such assessments.
- There are numerous improvements to the work of professionals with children that ensure that they provide good-quality information. Generally speaking, open-ended questioning produces the best-quality information for child witnesses. However, the structure of the question only partially determines whether questioning is leading. Despite criticisms, leading questions have a role to play.
- There is evidence that lawyers in the courtroom fail to adapt their questioning appropriately for the age of the child witness. Typical problems include overly complex language, the use of legal terms that the child may not know or fully understand, and dwelling on concepts of time and distance which are not fully developed in early childhood.
- Further material pertinent to this chapter may be found in Chapter 19 (statement validity analysis) and Chapter 16 (false allegations).

Introduction

In the nineteenth century, children were construed as dangerous witnesses who could not be relied on, or worse (Baartman, 1992; Myers, Dietrich, Lee and Fincher, 1999). Generally speaking, in the past courts lacked any recognition of the special requirements of children in such an adult environment. This may have reflected the hostility with which the testimony of children was regarded. In some states of America, for example, the judge would instruct jurors to consider the evidence of children with special care. In a remarkable change, towards the end of the twentieth century it became a common view among professionals that children never lie (Silas, 1985; Driver, 1989). Public disquiet about child abuse and child sexual abuse in the 1970s and 1980s respectively led to needs of child witnesses in the courtroom becoming a prime focus for research and reform of the system. Without the evidence of children, much sexual abuse could not be prosecuted. Numerous changes have been made in many countries in recent years as far as the evidence of children is concerned. The Crown Prosecution Service (2017b) describes what is done in England and Wales but similar changes have taken place elsewhere (Myers, 1996; Robinson, 2015) but not everywhere. Change has been harder to achieve in legal systems based on common law (United States, United Kingdom, Australia, New Zealand, Canada, South Africa and the republic of Ireland) given the adversarial nature of court proceedings. In the United States, for example, the right to have witnesses cross-examined is incorporated into the constitution. Legal systems based on civil law such as those in France and Germany are not hindered in such ways.

Children may not have the ability to cope with what may be fairly oppressive cross-examinations. Special arrangements may have to be applied to child witnesses. One or both of the following are to be found in some jurisdictions:

- *Preparation for court:* youngsters can be given professional help to understand court procedures, to deal with stress and anxiety about court as well as their abuse, and to testify competently in court. They may also be provided with an official advocate who works on their behalf with agencies. Sattar and Bull (1996) surveyed professionals working with children in a legal context in the United Kingdom. These professionals were well aware of the problems for child witnesses, including the children's fears and anxieties. The provision of support for children in this context included special child witness preparation provided by agencies.
- *Children's hearsay statements:* usually hearsay (essentially second-hand evidence) is disallowed in adversarial systems, except in exceptional circumstances. Some states of the United States, England and Wales and Scotland now allow hearsay in proceedings for the protection of children.

Competence to testify and give the oath is a key issue with child witnesses. A child witness is required to meet certain standards of cognitive and moral ability if they are to testify. Three different arrangements seem to apply:

- Some jurisdictions impose a presumptive incompetent criterion. This means that, under a certain age (say ten years but it does depend on location), the child has to be examined on competence to testify. If they meet these criteria, they can give evidence.
- In other jurisdictions, everyone is accepted as competent, irrespective of their age. Should an individual's competence become an issue, then it can be evaluated.
- Still other jurisdictions judge all victims of abuse as competent, although they may not be assumed competent in other circumstances. In some jurisdictions (e.g. Canada, United Kingdom, France and Germany), the child does not have to be sworn in before they can provide evidence.

Other changes involve, for example, methods of altering the court physically to be rid of the intimidating, over powerful aura of traditional courtrooms. For example, expecting lawyers to remain seated when examining child witnesses can make the courtroom seem less daunting. The court may allow the use of leading questions with young children. The court may sit in a simpler, more comfortable and relaxed environment for the child. Other changes may include the following:

- Closing the court to the public/press.
- Video testimony: interviews with the police or social workers as part of the investigation process may be shown via video. In England and Wales, interviews with police or social workers may be used as a substitute for the child's in-court evidence. This has been adopted by, for example, some American states; video may be used to present either live or pre-recorded testimony from the child. Many countries allow closed-circuit television to help the giving of evidence by children. This was first developed in the United States in 1983, but New Zealand, followed suit, as did Britain and Australia, among others. Not only is there evidence that children are happier using the video links, but the quality of their evidence seems better (Davies and Noon, 1993).

In the UK, there is an automatic eligibility for alternative methods of giving testimony for children under 18 years of age but this is not the case everywhere (Hanna, Davies, Crothers and Henderson, 2012). Some have argued for the recording of a child's main evidence (evidence in chief) prior to the court hearing as a further improvement (Hanna *et al.*, 2012).

The system in England and Wales is since 1999 has been to give child witnesses or victims attending criminal court a *witness care officer*. This officer helps the child through the court process. Additionally, they attend court with the child. They can indicate directly to the judge whether a particular question is inappropriate for the child but they cannot give evidence on behalf of the child. In contrast, Robinson (2015) argues that the history of child witnesses in US courts has been 'troubled'.

What is difficult about forensic interviews with children?

It has been known for quite some time that there are techniques which an interviewer can use to instil suggestions into a child's mind unintentionally. These can have calamitous consequences as in the notorious McMartin Pre-School case of 1987 in the US. Howe and Knott (2015) cite the texts of flawed interviews from this which show the adverse effect of the following: 1) repetition of the question which suggests to the child that their previous response was in some way inadequate or unacceptable; 2) providing information from co-witnesses such as other children which provides social proof which the child will feel under pressure to respond to; 3) inviting speculation about whether something could have happened; 4) introducing new information which was not consistent with the account given by the child; and 5) reinforcement which consists of given praise to the child for something they said or could say which the interviewer would be pleased by (positive reinforcement) or when a child is subject to criticism or disagreed with (negative reinforcement).

Children's voices need to be heard in courts of law. The voices of children and those expert in dealing with them has formed the basis of a number of reports and studies. There is an extensive discussion of this in research published by the European Union Agency for Fundamental Rights (2015). Westcott (1995) studied a small group of children and young people, each of whom had experienced sexual abuse investigation interviews. For the most part, these children had disclosed their abuse. Issues the children mentioned included:

- *Language and questioning styles:* complex words and sentences. In addition the interviewer talking extensively and interrupting the child.
- *Cognitive issues:* sometimes the children and young people had problems with the amount of detail about their abuse for which they were being asked although it had occurred many years earlier. One of the sample mentioned being asked about the frequencies and dates of their abuse!
- *Personal issues:* discussing the detail of what happened in the abuse can be embarrassing.
- *Motivational issues:* who was present at the interview may influence the victim's willingness to talk. Neglect of the child's feelings by the interviewer who might appear to be mainly interested in the punishment of the abuser was perceived by some of the children.
- *Social characteristics:* some interviewers were disliked for reasons such as: 'made it feel unimportant', 'disbelieving', 'bored', and 'treated me younger than I am'.

It should be stressed that the issues discussed in this chapter are not simply ones involving forensic professionals. A great deal may have happened to the child before any involvement with professionals (Hobbs and Goodman, 2014). In particular, abuse may be first reported by the child to their parents. Korkman, Juusola, and Santatila (2014) point out the importance of understanding that parents may have suspected that their child had been abused before any official investigation. Korkman *et al.* studied 19 conversations that Finnish parents had recorded between the parents and children for the purposes of providing evidence to the police. About a half of the instances were associated with parental child custody disputes. They found that the procedures used by the parents were in themselves very leading. New information in the interviews was mostly provided by the parents who, nevertheless, saw the interviews as being a record of their child's account of abuse. This was the case in two-thirds of the interviews. It is naturally very difficult to obtain data on disclosures to parents. As a way of circumventing some of the problems, Korkman, Laajasalo, Juusola, Uusivuori and Santtila (2015) had parents listen to acted versions of a mother–daughter conversation concerning child sexual abuse based on the interviews mentioned earlier in this paragraph. The parents then reported what the child had told the mother. It was found that most of the information that the mother in the conversation brought into the conversation was attributed to the child. Despite this, when asked to identify the source of the information it was attributed to the correct source.

So with these points in mind, we can turn to some of the research-based ideas about the nature of children's testimony. Lamb, Sternberg and Orbach (1999) suggested that the following factors may have an influence on the quality of children's evidence:

- *Fantasy:* some believe that children are especially prone to fantasise events and report them as fact. However, by the age of six years children are probably little different from adults in terms of their ability to distinguish reality from fantasy (Woolley, 1997). If an interviewer asks a child to imagine or pretend, the child will respond appropriately by being imaginative and pretending. Similarly, sometimes it is argued that the presence of dolls and toys encourages fantasy behaviour (Box 20.1). Forensic interviews should be planned to exclude these possibilities. However, Lamb. Sternberg and Orbach (1999) indicated that the children who have a tendency to fantasise are no more likely to make false reports or fabrications when giving evidence.

- *Language:* children's accounts of events tend to be short and lacking in much detail. Their speech can be difficult to follow because of their inconsistencies in enunciation and sometimes they use words which they do not understand the use of properly. These can be quite simple words such as 'yesterday' or 'before', which are readily understood by adults.
- *Interviewers:* it is too easy for adults to pose questions in ways that are difficult for even adolescents to understand. The consequences are obvious. Children do not always correct an adult who has failed to understand what the child is saying. So, with support from the research literature, it can be recommended that children should NOT be expected to:
  - have a complete mastery of adult vocabulary;
  - confirm complex summaries of the information that the child has provided;
  - reverse negative statements by adults ('Is it not true that you stole the apples?');
  - understand passive wording ('Was the apple taken by her?') as opposed to active wording ('Did she take the apple?').

  There is evidence also that using indirect speech acts involving questions such as 'Do you know what she did?' can lead to underestimations of a child's abilities. This is because such a question might be answered with a 'yes' by the child who does not understand that it also involves an indirect question about what was done. Not realising this may result in a single syllable 'yes' answer with no elaboration (Evans, Stolzenberg, Lees and Lyon, 2014). Different forms of complex questions confuse children and young adults greatly. There is evidence that about one-third of questions asked by lawyers in court were not understood by six- to fifteen year-old children (e.g. Brennan and Brennan, 1988). Furthermore, Davies and Seymour (1998) suggested that their use by lawyers may be deliberate to confuse the child. This may explain why defence lawyers in sexual abuse cases ask more leading questions than prosecution lawyers in Stolzenberg and Lyon's (2014) study of court transcripts. It was also notably the case that the preponderance of questions asked by lawyers simply require a 'yes' or 'no' answer rather than an extended reply.
- *Memory:* the brevity of young children's accounts does not mean that their memories are bad. In fact, their memory is quite good. There is a distinction to be made between memory performance and memory capacity. Thus a young child may appear not to have a good memory capacity simply because they provide only a brief account of events. This may really be an issue of memory performance – they have poorer vocabularies, they lack motivation to provide the account, and they are less capable of using analogy to elaborate their descriptions.
- *Suggestibility:* in some settings even three- and four-year-olds are very resistant to leading questions that were irrelevant to the actual events. Questions such as 'Did he kiss you?' and 'Did he keep his clothes on?' failed to lead the children.
- *Interviewer characteristics:* the characteristics of the interviewer – such as how friendly or how accusatory they are – do not appear consistently over studies to influence the suggestibility of the children they interview.

BOX 20.1 Controversy

Anatomical dolls and the diagnosis of abuse

It is an obvious idea to use toys as an aid when interviewing children. Anatomical dolls have been used extensively in child sexual abuse assessment. Quite simply, they are dolls with 'extra' anatomical details – genitals, anuses, mouths. According to the *American Professional Society on the Abuse of Children* Practice Guidelines (APSAC, 1996), research shows that the use of such dolls does not increase sexualised behaviour in non-abused children and their use does not seem to encourage suggestibility and error in recall. The doll is almost invariably clothed apart from exceptional circumstances in which the child has previously said that sexual abuse had taken place with naked individuals.

BOX 20.1 (continued)

Anatomical dolls should only be used by skilled interviewers. 'Sexual' play with dolls such as inserting another doll's penis into a doll's mouth, anus or vagina is *not* diagnostic of sexual abuse. While such behaviour may be more common among sexually abused children, the risk of misdiagnosis is too great to interpret it as such (see Chapter 16 on diagnosticity of signs). Four-year-old boys from low social class families are the group most likely to display such behaviour. Exploration of a doll's genitals or anus with the finger is not infrequent among young children. However, the interviewer should be sensitive to other possible indications of abuse. In short, it would be a mistake to attempt to diagnose sexual abuse on the basis of play with anatomical dolls in the absence of other supportive evidence.

The use of the dolls should not be presented as pretend or play. Instead, the interviewer should encourage the child to talk about 'things that really happened'. Putting pairs of dolls in sexual positions and asking whether this had ever happened to the child is tantamount to a leading question and should not be done. On the other hand, anatomical dolls help communication and promote better recall of events, though drawings or ordinary non-anatomical dolls may be equally effective:

- The dolls can be used as an *icebreaker*, allowing the child to talk about sexual issues that might be taboo to the child normally.
- The dolls can be used as an *anatomical model* to find out the names used by the child for the different parts of the body and what they know about their functions.
- The interviewer might also use the dolls to make clear just what it is the child has said about the acts of abuse (i.e. as a *demonstration aid*).
- The doll may also be used in a non-threatening setting to gain insight into the child's sexual interest and knowledge (i.e. as a *screening tool*). After a period of free play, the interviewer may add questions to elaborate on what had been observed. The guidelines suggest that spontaneous 'suspicious' comments by the child should be followed up. For example, 'Daddy's pee-pee gets big sometimes'.

According to Everson and Boat (2002), anatomical dolls may also be used as a *memory stimulus*. Seeing the doll's sexual characteristics (genitals and breasts) may help the child remember sexual episodes in which they were involved – for example, as victims of sexual abuse.

The Guidelines suggest that other matters of good practice when using anatomical dolls need to be considered, including the following:

- The interviewer should recognise that children of less than four years may be unable to re-enact scenes well.
- Interviewers using anatomical dolls should be trained in their use and regularly updated on new research findings relevant to the use of the dolls.
- Videotaping interviews using anatomical dolls is a wise precaution as it is with other aspects of forensic investigation.

There is a substantial body of research on the usefulness of anatomical dolls and similar props (such as drawings) in sexual abuse interviews with young children. Everson and Boat (2002) address two critical issues concerning anatomical dolls which have arisen in research: 1) anatomical dolls are so suggestive that sexual fantasy and sexual play will be encouraged by the dolls in a way that some interviewers will interpret as indicating sexual abuse in children who have not been abused; and 2) evidence that the use of the dolls facilitates disclosure of abuse is required:

- *Suggestibility of dolls for non-abused children:* Everson and Boat (2002) mention 11 studies concerning the behaviour of non-sexually-abused children (two- to eight-year-olds) when playing with anatomical dolls. Some interest in the doll's genitals was fairly common; explicit play involving sexual intercourse with the doll or oral sex was fairly rare. Only 4 per cent of children in all of the studies combined demonstrated such heavily sexualised behaviours. Furthermore, there may be other sources of sexual knowledge even where the child displayed sexualised behaviours of this sort. These sources would include pornography or observing sexual activity at home, for example. This could account for the majority of instances of such sexual knowledge in non-sexually-abused children.
- *Efficacy of the use of anatomical dolls:* the better research relevant to this tends to use real medical examinations/procedures which would necessitate the medic to touch the child's genitals or anus, for example. In other words, a situation which is realistic and pertinent in that it involves what in other circumstances would constitute sexually abusive acts.

Children can be interviewed some time after the medical procedure in order to see whether they reveal the genital or anal touching. Whether interviews using anatomical dolls are more successful at identifying the touching can be assessed. Steward and Steward (1996) carried out a study along these lines. About a quarter of the children revealed the touching without the anatomical dolls. This figure more than doubled to three-fifths of children in interviews using anatomical dolls. It increased to nearly three-quarters when the children were interviewed with the anatomical dolls and the interviewer asked direct and suggestive questions. False reports were not very common. No false reports were made in the simple verbal interview. This increased to 3 per cent in the anatomical doll interview and 5 per cent where the anatomical doll interview included the direct and suggestive questioning.

Dickinson, Poole and Bruck (2005) have five concerns about the use of anatomical dolls:

- *Young children do not necessarily have the cognitive sophistication to use anatomical dolls reliably:* In particular, they mean that young children lack the representational insight to understand that anatomical dolls are objects which are being used to symbolise their own body. They need to be able to concentrate on the symbolic function of the doll and avoid engaging in unrelated play behaviours, for example, in the interview. Research questions whether young children have this ability. DeLoache (1995) found that children of around three years have problems understanding the relationship between a model of a room filled with furniture and the full-sized version of the same room. They could watch a researcher hide a model toy in a piece of furniture but could not use this information to find a real toy in the equivalent furniture in the full-sized room.
- *Dolls can elicit irrelevant behaviour:* Collectively research findings indicate that non-abused children rarely use dolls to play in a sexually explicit manner. Nevertheless, it is not unusual for them to touch or play in some other way with a doll's genitals. Sometimes they may also put the dolls in a sexually suggestive position. Children who can use the dolls representatively can also show explorative play behaviour which has the potential to be misinterpreted. In other words, the children lose the representational focus in favour of exploratory play using the anatomical doll.
- *The use of anatomical dolls may not improve interviews:* The volume of information produced with the anatomical dolls may not be enhanced. For example, the children may choose to play with the doll and so become less talkative (Lamb, Herkowitz, Sternberg, Boat and Everson, 1996).
- *Anatomical dolls give interviewers additional suggestive techniques:* Research has shown, for example, that when using anatomical dolls, interviewers speak more (Santtila *et al.*, 2004). This can be seen as the control of the interview moving further away from the child to the interviewer. It can also be seen as giving the child permission to stop speaking in favour of the adult.
- *Interview bias/memory distortion influences their interpretation of children's doll interaction:* There is no completely objective way of knowing just what the meaning is of a child putting their finger into a doll's genitals. There are no validated standards for this judgement call apart from the interviewer's interpretation. Suspecting abuse, the interviewer may interpret such behaviours in sexual terms rather than in terms of exploratory play.

Some topics in forensic and criminal psychology have been controversial and continue to be controversial. This is manifestly the case with research on anatomical dolls. The problems in evaluating the field are substantial. One problem is, of course, that practices change and improve in response to research. So what may have been the case in the past no longer applies. Equally, research may fail to mimic practice accurately enough and if poor simulations of current practice are used then research has little to offer practitioners. Hlavka, Olinger and Lashley (2010) dismiss the negative criticism of the use of anatomical dolls on the basis that research has failed to keep up with how anatomical dolls are actually used. They suggest that past research simply looked for increases in the information provided by children following the introduction of anatomical dolls into the interview. However, Hlavka *et al.* find in their research that forensic interviewers at an urban Midwestern children's advocacy centre in the US used the dolls for a much wider set of purposes and found them useful. In this study, actual child abuse interviews were recorded on video. At the end of the session, the interviewer was given a copy of the interview and also answered questions about what was happening in the interview. About 500 separate interviews were involved. It is important to note that anatomical dolls were NOT used in the child abuse

BOX 20.1 (continued)

interviews until after the child had disclosed his or her abuse. At which point, the chest containing a range of anatomical dolls could be opened and appropriate dolls selected jointly by the child and the interviewer. In other words, the dolls were not used to find initial evidence of abuse. Broadly speaking, the practitioners indicated that the dolls were more useful in child abuse interviews than merely as a way of eliciting more details. Among the uses identified by the practitioners in the context of their actual child protection interviews were:

- *Clarification:* To help clarify things that the children had said (82 per cent mentioned this in relation to specific interviews). For example, the interviewer may use the dolls to establish a common language to use for the different body parts. Or the child may have said that the man pinched its wee-wee and the interviewer wished to clarify just what this meant – i.e. what did pinching mean?
- *Consistency:* To look for consistency between what children say and their demonstrations with the dolls (77 per cent mentioned this). So the child may have indicated that they were touched on their bottom and the interviewer can use the doll to check that the child is consistent in what they indicate.
- *Distancing:* To help the child distance their account from their own bodies. That is, to avoid situations in which the child attempts to use their own body to show what had happened in their abuse (67 per cent mentioned this). This would not be appropriate.
- *Communication:* This is enhanced sometimes by the use of the doll. The child may have limited verbal ability, for example, or they may be embarrassed when talking about sexual matters. The doll help the interviewer communicate better with the child (61 per cent mentioned this).

Overwhelmingly, the evidence seemed to be that anatomical dolls were seen as more valuable for use with school age children.

The use of anatomically correct dolls is not the only problem area when assessing children for sexual abuse. The use of diagrams of body parts as an aid to communication is also somewhat questionable on the basis of available evidence. Bruck, Kelley, and Poole (2016) studied the reports of children about what parts of their bodies had been touched in an earlier legitimate medical examination. Some of the children's examinations involved touching the genitals and anuses by the medic. The locations of the medical touching were recorded onto the medical record and provided objective evidence of what had happened. So the list would include forehead, nose, tongue, chest, stomach, and knees etc. as well as anus and genitals. Those children who experienced both touching of the anus and genitals were attending a sexual abuse clinic when the examination happened. The children who experienced anal touching were attending gastrointestinal clinics. The children who experienced neither of these forms of touching were also attending a gastrointestinal clinic but with no anal or genital examination. A memory interview was given about seven days later. The children were firstly allowed to describe the medical examination in free recall – everything that happened they were told. Then some children were interviewed with the body diagram and others without. The questioning included simple recognition questions about touches to different parts of the body as well as cued-recall questions about touching. The interviewer asked in the cued-recall where the child had been touched in the medical examination. In the cued-recall with body diagrams the child was asked to point on the diagrams to the parts of the body that the doctor had touched. They were also asked about the body parts that had been touched by the interviewer naming them or pointing to them on the diagram with the child replying yes or no to indicate whether or not touch had occurred.

The number of correct reports by the child was increased by the use of body diagrams. This was true for the questions about the anus and genitals. So in that sense the use of body diagrams was advantageous because the information gathered was more accurate. The problem was that for the youngest age group in the study (the three- to five-year-olds) there was a greater risk of false sexual touching reports as well. The rates of these errors were high with as many as 50 per cent of the three-year-olds making a false report although this figure declined with age. This was not the case for the six- to eight-year-old age group. In other words, the use of body diagrams can have problems not dissimilar from those affecting the use of anatomically complete dolls in the assessment of sexual abuse.

It has been said that the failure to identify cases of the sexual abuse of children is a major public health issue and perhaps more serious than the risk of falsely convicting someone for sexual abuse (Olafson, 2012). Finding that interview aids tend to produce more false information may imply that they do more to deal with the former problem than the latter.

The ground rules for interviews

As might be expected, over the years there have been specific guidelines laid-down for forensic interviews involving children. Such guidelines have been offered by the Crown Prosecution Service (2011) in England and Wales though others have been produced elsewhere. These explain what the child interviewee should be made aware of about interviews. According to Krahenbuhl, Blades and Cherryman (2015) such ground rules should be implemented from the beginning of the interview to make sure that the evidence is obtained in an appropriate legal way and to ensure that the child understands the interview process. Over 50 police investigative interviews with children victims of sexual or physical abuse were studied by Krahenbuhl *et al.* in terms of adherence to the guidelines. These recommendations recommend that interviews should follow the structure: 1) a *rapport* phase; 2) a *free narrative* phase during which the child is allowed to describe the witnessed events in the absence of significant interruption by the interviewers; 3) a *questioning* phase in which the interviewer requests more information, and 4) *closure* at which point the interviewer summarises what has been said and terminates the interview. The rapport phase should consist of four distinct ground rules plus an additional requirement. These are:

- The interviewer should explain that they did not themselves see what happened and so the interviewer is dependent entirely on what the child has to say.
- The child should say 'don't understand' if they fail to understand.
- The child should say 'don't know' if they do not know the answer to the question.
- If the child thinks that the interviewer has got something wrong they should correct the interviewer.
- There should be a discussion and exploration of the child's understanding of the difference between truth and lies. The importance of being truthful throughout the interview is also stressed.

The guidelines stress the importance of using concrete instance of the various ground rules and giving the child practice on the implementation of the ground rules. It is suggested that the ground rules are covered again in the third phase (questioning) of the interview. Krahenbuhl *et al.* found that the mean number of ground rules followed in the intervals was about three out of five. The ground rule of correcting the interviewer occurred in one-third of the interviews whereas truth and lies was almost universal. Rarely were the children given an opportunity to practise using the ground rules or given examples except for truth and lies where more opportunities were given. Rarely were ground rules repeated later in the interview. Fundamentally, interviews did not completely accord with the Crown Prosecution Service guidelines and for some aspects fell well short of requirements.

Warren, Woodhall, Hunt and Perry (1996) investigated the adherence of interviewers to similar good practice guidelines. They obtained transcripts of child protection workers' videotaped interviews with children. Typically, the interviews were conducted by a single interviewer but in some cases more than one additional person was present. The following are some of the more important findings:

- Establishing rapport in order to relax the child and make them feel comfortable: most (71 per cent) of the interviews studied included an attempt to establish rapport. However, rather than encouraging the child to talk, the interviewer would do something like three times the amount of talking during the rapport stage. Equally important is the fact that in nearly one-third of interviews no attempt was made at all to build rapport with the child.
- Establishing interview ground rules: only a minority of the interviewers (29 per cent) made any reference to the sort of ground rules that establish in the mind of the child just what is expected by the interviewer. Children erroneously assume that they have to give an answer to every question, that there is a right and wrong answer to every question, that the interviewer knows exactly what happened and so the child defers to the 'superior' knowledge of the interviewer where the interviewer seems to differ from the child, and that it is inappropriate to ask for clarification or say that they do not know in response to a question. In various ways, the interviewer can indicate that such assumptions may be wrong. But they rarely did. In only 29 per cent of the interviews were the children told to tell the truth, in 14 per cent of interviews was it explained to the child that it was appropriate to say 'Don't know' in answer to a question, and in only 7 per cent of cases was the child told to tell the interviewer that they didn't understand a question. Other ground rules were never or rarely mentioned.

It is not fully understood why those interviewing children do not follow the detailed requirements of ground rules. Carson and La Rooy (2015) describe their analysis of the views of police officers (mostly the most junior rank) working in family protection units who had been trained using the Scottish Executive *Guidance on Interviewing Child Witnesses and Victims in Scotland* (2003). Like many others, Carson and La Rooy consider that personal experiences about child development and memory have no place when interviewing children. Psychology has developed to an advanced stage in terms of understanding of these things and amount to a professional consensus concerning how children should be interviewed. For example, it is widely accepted that children should be interviewed using open-prompts which elicit memory through free recall. Although the guidelines are evidence based, it became clear that police officers fail to follow them in many instances. The topics included rapport building, open-ended questioning, the telling of the truth, and similar. The views of the officers were characterised in terms of lay beliefs or common-sense psychology underlying their failure to follow the guidelines. For example, the responses of the police officers were full of lay psychological ideas rather than the psychological science relevant to the guidelines. One quote:

> 'As I've said before every child is different and it depends on the individual child on how you respond/act with them.'

The implication of this comment, and many similar ones, is to reject the psychological principles underlying the Scottish guidelines. It provides a reason for not following standard procedures. These lay psychological ideas appear to be held unproblematically as if they were accurate, useful, and relevant.

Collins, Doherty-Sneddon, and Doherty (2014) carried out a qualitative investigation of police officer's and social workers views of rapport building in Scotland. The three main themes which emerged dealt with things which could facilitate the interview process. The first theme was the use of rapport in order to assess the child. The age difference between the interviewer and the child results in communicative differences. During the rapport phase there are likely to be indications of what these differences may be. The participants in the research tended to believe that this stage is especially beneficial for five- to nine-year-olds. Because they have anxiety, for example, the rapport stage can help deal with that. The second theme concerned allowing the adjustment of the approach used in the light of what occurred in the rapport stage. For example, the way in which the interviewer interacts during the rapport stage, say, by the use of open questions can indicate to the child the level of information expected in the main part of the interview. Gaining the attention of the child is another thing which can be done through the rapport stage. Talking about things such as television which is of interest to children is one way of doing this. The third theme of the strategy for the rapport stage was to produce a psychological outcome which benefits communication with the child such as making the child more relaxed and less anxious. The comments of the interviewers broadly met recommendations for best practice. But there were things said which did not meet this test nor have research backing which is indicative of non-compliance.

There is another way in which interviewers disregard the expectations for ground rules. Earhart, La Rooy, Brubachers, and Lamb (2014) studied the use of the *don't know* rule in investigative interviews for child abuse. The interviewers did not all introduce the rule but this seemed to make no difference in terms of the rates of use of 'don't know' as a reply to questions. Intriguingly, on 30 per cent of occasions when the child said 'don't know' the interviewer simply ignored this and the rule and proceeded to ask more questions about the same topic such as risky question styles such as leading questions or gave encouragement to guess.

So it would seem that the use of formal ground rules is somewhat spasmodic and incomplete. That is one obstacle. A second issue is whether children actually understand the use of ground rules. Dickinson, Brubacher and Poole (2015) studied children's comprehension of ground rules designed to deal with the expectations of children unused to being questioned by adults in a forensic interview. They carried out the first study to systematically understand children's ability with ground rule instructions. Five hundred children between four and twelve years of age were studied when responding to five ground rule practice questions. For example, the interviewer might ask 'What is my dog's name?' to which a correct answer would be 'I don't know' according to the 'don't guess answers' rule. The child would be asked 'How do you like being (wrong age) years old?' to test the child on the 'tell me if I say something wrong rule'. The 'don't guess' and 'tell the truth rules' were the easiest for the children to understand. Generally speaking, the children performed well on nearly all of the ground rules especially if they had more than one attempt. So, for example, over 90 per cent could say what was true and what was a lie after practice. However, it was more common that a child had difficulty with at least one of the ground rules. Dickinson *et al.* recommend giving children practice in some depth if they initially fail on understanding a ground rule.

Huffman, Warren and Larson (2001) carried out research with young children into the effectiveness of warnings not to lie. They point out that this idea is far from easy with the youngest children. They report the following exchange between an interviewer (I) and a child (C):

> I: Now, C., do you know the difference between the truth and a lie?
> C: [Nods]
> I: If I told you that – that you were standing on your head right now, what would I be telling you?
> C: Old McDonald said that at the police station.
> I: Uh-huh. At the police station?
> C: You've got to take his shirt off. [Referring to small boy doll]
>
> (p. 10)

Problems similar to these can even emerge when trying to establish interview ground rules with older children.

Huffman *et al.* obtained a substantial sample of transcripts of interviews with children, largely of pre-school age. A small majority (56 per cent) of these interviews actually contained a discussion between the interviewer and child about the difference between the truth and a lie. Not only this, but this analysis provided information about the standard procedures used by interviewers in this context. Consequently, a further study actually investigated the effectiveness of the discussion about lies on the quality of the information supplied by the child. Two procedures were employed:

- *The standard protocol:* this was based mainly on the transcripts which contained a discussion with the child about truth and lies. So one question was included which asked the child if they understood what is different between lies and truths. Then they would have to answer a real example such as 'If I said that you were a boy, would that be a truth or a lie?' Finally, the interviewer would ask the child only to give truthful answers.
- *The elaborated protocol:* this was much more open-ended in terms of questioning and focused on the concept of a lie by the use of examples of lies and definitions of lies. The researchers believe that the concept of truth is too abstract to communicate. The children were given three different scenarios involving possible lies and they had to judge them. The following is an example:

> One day Jane/Jim and his/her mother were at home and the phone rang. Jim/Jane's mother did not want to talk on the phone and asked Jim/Jane to answer the phone but say she was not at home. When Jim/Jane answered the phone and the person asked for Jim/Jane's mother, Jim/Jane said, 'My mother is not at home.' Did Jim/Jane tell the truth, a lie, or something else? Why is that a ____? Was it okay for Jim/Jane to say his/her mother was not at home? Why/Why not?

It was found that the value of the children's evidence was enhanced by the elaborated protocol. There was little difference between using the standard approach and not having any discussion of the difference between truth and lies.

Improving forensic questioning of children

According to researchers, open-ended questions produce the most accurate answers from children. This is partly because open-ended questions encourage children to give as much detail as they can in their replies. They act as recall probes. In contrast, focused or closed questions, directive questions or leading questions involve the child in a recognition task that can be answered completely with merely a yes or no. That is, leading and similar questions act as recognition probes about the things on which the interviewer wishes to focus. As such, they may pressure the child into a response even though the child does not know what that response should be. Figure 20.1 illustrates the differences between the two different forms of questioning.

Most lawyers and psychologists are familiar with the concept of leading questions. These are questions that encourage a particular reply. Myers, Saywitz and Goodman (1996) argue that there is a continuum of suggestiveness in questioning:

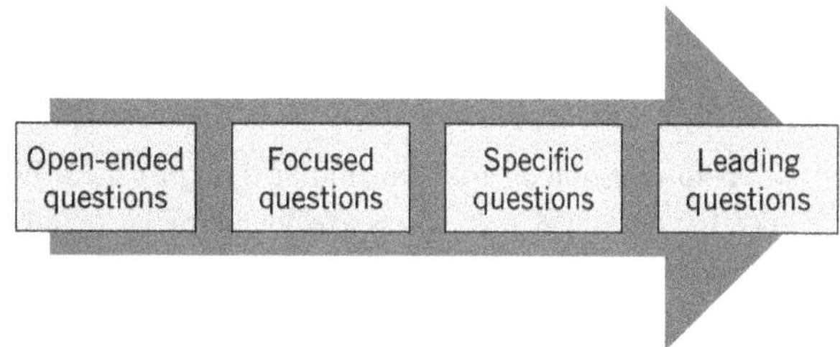

This is very important since there is a tendency to concentrate on the two question types – open-ended and leading. This, to a degree, misrepresents the situation in interviews.

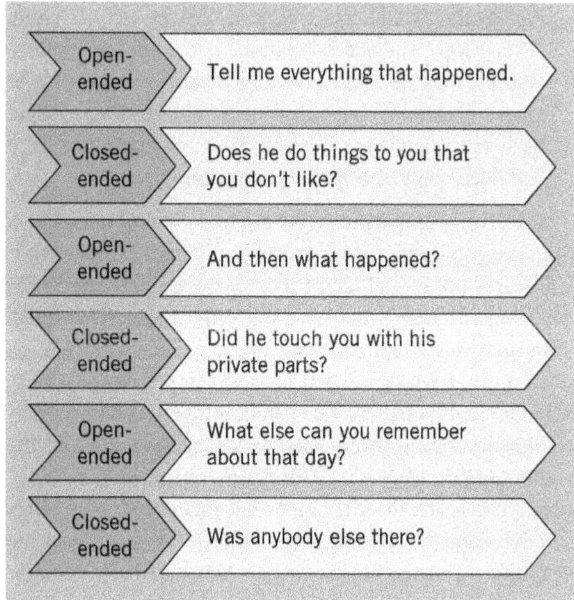

Figure 20.1 Open-ended versus focused/closed questions as they might appear in a child sexual abuse interview

Source: Based on Lamb, M.E., Sternberg, K.J. and Orbach, Y. (1999) 'Forensic interviews of children' in A. Memon and R. Bull (eds) *Handbook of the Psychology of Interviewing.* © 1999 John Wiley & Sons, Ltd

By considering more types of question, we begin to appreciate how structuring can take a number of different forms. The underlying order is from the least to most suggestive questioning style:

- An open-ended question is a fairly general question which is little other than a request for the interviewee to speak as in 'Did anything happen?' or 'Tell me about that'.
- A focused question brings a child's attention to a particular issue such as a location or a person. So a question such as 'Shall we talk about school?' brings a child around to the topic of school without suggesting anything about the sorts of information that the interviewer wants. Questions such as 'where' or 'who' and 'when' are other examples.

There is no rigid dividing line between focused and the next level of specific questioning.

- Specific questioning may be similar though generally specific questions call for a greater level of detail. Questions in this category include 'What is her name?' or 'What colour dress did she have on?'
- A leading question is one that implies that the interviewer is expecting a particular answer. Leading questions are often statements of fact to which the interviewee is expected to agree. So 'You felt very angry, didn't you?' makes it very clear what answer is expected. This is a continuum of suggestiveness since each level has increasing likelihood to suggest answers to the child. Even the open-ended question, according to circumstances, may be suggestive. For example, a parent who asks a child what happened in school yesterday might be suggesting the sort of reply if, for example, the child had been caught cheating in an exam.

It is overly simplistic, some argue, to regard open questions as good and closed questions as bad. Professionals who carry out sexual abuse interviews are presented with a serious dilemma: that is, using only open-ended questions may well fail to obtain the necessary information from a child who has been abused (Myers *et al.*, 1996). Unfortunately, there may be a trade-off between the poorer disclosure coming from open-ended questioning and the contamination of evidence emerging out of leading questions. The issue, then, is somewhat intangible. Is it better to have some false allegations in order to maximise the detection of actual abuse, or is it better to have no false allegations but fail to maximise the detection of abuse? The answer depends, in part, on one's perspective. Is it more important to have abuse disclosed or is it more important to be able to prosecute abusers successfully in court? This dilemma cannot be addressed by research evidence on different questioning styles. It is a moral, ethical and political issue.

Following from this, it is useful to note the findings of research into the sequencing of interviewer questions and the replies given in sexual abuse interviews. What sort of question asked by the interviewer is productive in terms of the child's reply? What sort of reply by the child leads to what sort of next question by the interviewer? Wolfman, Brown and Jose (2016) obtained a sample of over 100 child sexual abuse interviews in New Zealand. The children involved were from six to sixteen years of age. The questions asked by the interviewer were coded into a number of different types. These were: 1) open-ended questions or invitations like 'Tell me what happened'; 2) cued open-ended questions or invitations like 'Tell me what happened in the shop'; 3) closed or direct questions like 'What time was this?'; 4) option posing questions like 'Was it your brother or sister that went to the kitchen?'; 5) suggestive or leading questions in which seem to indicate what the interviewer believes to be the answer like 'You stole the money, didn't you?'; and 6) summaries which are not really questions since they involve the interviewer repeating back exactly what the child had said. By far the most common category was closed or direct questions (55 per cent), followed by cued open questions or invitations (20 per cent), then open questions or invitations (12 per cent), then summaries (6 per cent), and leading or suggestive questions which were uncommon at under 1 per cent. The replies of the children were classified as reply or non-reply. Although much of the time the children responded to the interviewer's question, sometimes they made a non-response. Non-responses were more likely following an open-ended (invitation) question than for other types of questions. One can see, then, that the use of open-questioning because it was not rewarded with an answer by the child so frequently made the interview more difficult. There was more response to more structured questions (the authors call this scaffolding) than to the less structured ones. Irrespective of the child's response, there tended to be consistency in the questioning style the interviewers used. Similarly, the children tended to respond in a consistent way irrespective of the questioning approached adopted by the interviewer. Wolman *et al.* describe there being two parallel processes in the interviews in which the interviewer consistently did whatever she did in terms of questioning and the child consistently responding in a particular sort of way without a great deal of impact on one another. They discuss this as the interviewer and child 'talking past each other'.

Interviewing very young children

There are problems in interviewing child witnesses which are greater the younger the child involved. However, this does not mean that children under the age of five years, for example, cannot be interviewed; it merely means that the skills of the interviewer and the assumptions made about the language ability of the child have to be borne in mind. Shepherd (2007) gives a great deal of advice on this. For example, among the information that might surprise some adults are the following (p. 272):

- Children know that adults want children to reply since they understand that when a powerful adult stops speaking then it is the child's turn to speak.
- It is only older children, in general, who will tell the adult in some way that they don't understand what is being said to them.
- It is the responsibility of the interviewer that the child understands what is being said to them.
- Rather than say nothing, a child will prefer to say something, no matter what it is.
- Simply asking a child whether he/she understands is a poor way of checking comprehension. Instead, Shepherd suggests that the interviewer asks the child what the child thinks the interviewer means. This has to be repeatedly checked throughout the interview.
- While it is often the case that a child does not understand what an adult is saying to them, children do not know that they don't understand.

Saywitz (1994) also had a number of practical guidelines for interviewing very young children under the age of seven years. Nevertheless, they also contain lessons for interviewing older children:

- Avoid complex grammatical constructions such as double negatives (e.g. 'You're not saying you didn't steal the apple, are you?').
- Avoid questions requiring counting ability if the child is too young to be able to count. Similarly, time, linear measurements and similar concepts may be beyond the child's cognitive ability.
- Avoid using personal pronouns (him, her, they, she) in favour of proper names (such as Darren or Sue). Personal pronouns can cause confusion about what they actually indicate during speech.
- Children may appear to be uncooperative and uninformative because of their emotional and psychiatric states. Social withdrawal, as a consequence of abuse, should not be confused with uncooperativeness, for example.
- Concrete terms are better than abstract ones (e.g. 'gun' is better than 'weapon').
- Jargon words should not be used (e.g. legalese such as 'sentence' and 'charge' which also have more obvious meanings).
- Make it absolutely clear to what you are referring (e.g. 'When did your mother go to work?' is better than 'When did that happen?').
- The passive voice should be avoided (e.g. the active voice 'Did Adam steal the money?' is clearer than the passive voice 'Was the money stolen by Adam?').
- Use short sentences. Break down compound or overloaded questions into several simple questions.
- Use short words rather than longer ones (e.g. 'mend' rather than 'repair').
- Use simple verb constructions. Avoid complex verb structures (e.g. 'Do you think it possibly could have been?').
- With younger children, concrete, imaginable and observable things are better than abstract things.

The problem of non-compliance with good questioning

We have already seen evidence that practitioners often fail to follow recommendations concerning explaining to children the rules of the interview. This sort of failure has also been demonstrated in terms of how to ask questions. The following study generally supports the conclusion that open-ended questioning tends to produce superior evidence from children. However, more importantly, it reveals some of the problems in encouraging practitioners to use this form of questioning. The research took place in Israel and the United States and involved coding recordings of real-life interviews with children (Sternberg *et al.*, 1997). The interviewers' utterances were classified into a number of categories:

- invitations to open-ended responses;
- facilitators such as 'okay', feedback of the child's previous statement, and general encouraging comments;
- directive utterances – directing the child towards certain aspects of the events already mentioned by the child;
- leading utterances – directing the child towards things not already mentioned by the child;
- suggestive utterances which could indicate strongly to the child what reply is expected by the interviewer or include references to details that have not previously been mentioned by the child.

The children's answers were coded in terms of the number of new details supplied by the child. These details would include such matters as identifying and describing individuals, objects, events and actions relevant to the incident under investigation. Irrespective of the age of the child being interviewed, the findings showed that open-ended questions encouraged the child to give longer replies (that is, up to four times longer), containing about three times the amount of new detail.

Despite the superiority of open-ended styles of questioning in this regard, experienced interviewers generally used the least productive, closed interview techniques. The majority (over four-fifths) of the interviewers' dialogue consisted of focused or closed prompts. Only 6 per cent were invitational (open) questions and statements. The researchers attempted to improve interviewing technique during intensive interviewing workshops over the period of a week. In these workshops children's memory capacity was explained, the factors that might encourage suggestibility were discussed and advantages of open-ended questioning explained. Unfortunately, this made little or no difference as the interviewers carried on using their focused questioning style!

In an attempt to find a solution to this problem of the non-compliance of interviewers with best practice, Sternberg *et al.* (1997) provided introductory scripts to the interviewers. Some of the scripts were open-ended whereas the others were closed-ended. This led, irrespective of the questioning style adopted by the interviewer later in the interview, to lengthier narratives from the children in the open-ended condition. In other words, once the children had begun to respond to questions in detail, they then continued to do so, irrespective of the nature of the later questioning. When the introductory script was used, the children on average provided 91 details, compared with the five or six details obtained when the script was not used.

Questioning styles are not the only way in which interviewers can adversely affect the information obtained. Poole and Lindsay (2002) explain that sometimes an interviewer can produce ambiguity in ways that are very different from leading the child. Young children drift readily off topic and fail to appreciate what is actually being discussed, so they can be difficult to interview. Poole and Lindsay (p. 358) highlight the following excerpt of transcript of an interview with a child originally reported by Warren, Nunez, Keeney, Buck and Smith. (2002):

Interviewer:	Is it good or bad to tell a lie?
Child:	G.A. touched me.
Interviewer:	Jesus loves me? Is that what you said?
Child:	Yeah.

This is clearly a situation in which the difficulty of interviewing the child led the interviewer to offer the child an interpretation which amounted to a suggestion. However, there was no intent to produce that outcome. In this case, what appears to be a claim of abuse was essentially turned into something very different.

The trade-off of accuracy against completeness

There is an obvious but extremely important distinction to be made between:

- the amount of accurate information collected in an interview;
- the amount of inaccurate information collected in an interview.

Unfortunately, in real life, it is often more or less impossible to know what is accurate information and what is inaccurate information. Nevertheless, the distinction means that there is an important choice between the risk of incorrect information and the risk of incomplete information. There seems to be little doubt that general, non-directive questions encourage children to give testimony that is accurate and low on inaccuracy. Unfortunately, this is at the expense of answers that are complete. The question is which is to be accepted – inaccuracy or incompleteness? Both reflect adversely on the quality of the evidence of child witnesses. Hutcheson *et al.* (1995) accept that there is such a dilemma when questioning young children. They found that the age of the child makes a considerable difference to the effect of questioning. The researchers found that interviewers who tended to ask a high proportion of focused or specific questions obtained success according to the age of the child:

- Focused and specific questions addressed to five- and six-year-olds produced more inaccurate answers. There was no benefit of increasing the completeness of the answers.
- Interviewers who asked eight- and nine-year-olds a high proportion of focused questions obtained more complete answers. In this case accuracy was not affected.

It should be noted that not all researchers see a simple contrast between open and closed questions, one being good and the other being not so good.

What do we know about interviewing children?

It is not possible to summarise everything that is known about interviewing children in a short space. However, Buck, Warren, Bruck and Kuehnle (2014) provide a list of ideas about interviewing children which they evaluate using the available research evidence. For our purposes these have been turned into a series of statements which are either true or false. Read through them and decide what you think is true and what false:

1. Playing sexually with anatomically correct dolls indicates that the child has been abused sexually.
2. Young children who falsely allege abuse are inconsistent in what they say over time.
3. An interviewer's notes made during the interview with a child accurately report what question was asked by the interviewer and what the child replied.
4. Interviewers can report accurately whether a child made claims of abuse as a consequence of particular leading questions or whether it was spontaneous.
5. It is alright for an interviewer to use suggestive questioning once the child has revealed that they were abused.
6. It is alright for an interviewer to use suggestive questioning if they believe that the child has suffered abuse.
7. It is alright for the interviewer to say things like 'Don't be afraid to tell me what the man did to you' when asking questions about sexual abuse.
8. It is ok for an interviewer to ask a child about things that *might* have happened if the child has not remembered much.
9. It is ok for the interviewer to keep questioning a child until the child discloses abuse if the interviewer believes the child has been abused.
10. More accurate information is reported by the child if the interview uses anatomically correct dolls.
11. Using anatomically correct dolls with young children increases the amount of false information that the child supplies.
12. Young children need to be asked leading questions so that they disclose abuse. Otherwise they are too afraid or embarrassed to say.
13. Young children's answers to open-ended questions are generally as accurate as those of adults.
14. Young children's answers to strongly leading questioning are generally as accurate as those of adults.

Only statements 11 and 13 are correct according to the research literature.

Is the research base complete?

Sometimes one is surprised by the lack of research into some commonly held ideas. One example of this comes from the idea that rapport between the interviewer and the child interviewee is essential for a good interview in a forensic context. Since clinicians and forensic practitioners seem to consider rapport essential, one question is whether this belief is supported by the research evidence. Rapport was introduced as a concept in Freud's psychoanalytic writings (Freud, 1913). Interviews with children occur in a range of legal contexts including adoption, delinquency, custody in divorce, and immigration. There has been some controversy over the value of rapport despite it being commonly recommended in discussions of interviewing children. It has been suggested that the process of providing rapport can lead to an increase in the suggestibility on the part of the child so as not to disappoint the interview or experience rejection by the interview (Hershkowitz, 2011). Furthermore, since rapport is commonly held to be built up prior to the interview proper, it has been wondered whether this load on the attention capacity of the child in unproductive in terms of how children perform in the later interview. The consequence of this is to lower the child's accuracy. One problem is the weakness of available definitions of rapport. Saywitz, Larson, Hobbs, and Wells (2015) mention that the strategies to elicit rapport include giving attention, sensitivity, smiling, open arms, open-ended questioning, supportiveness, warmth, empathy and tact. The researcher searched the relevant literature for potentially relevant studies. Although they identified nearly three thousand examples nearly all of them were excluded by the researchers' exclusion criteria. Experimental studies amounted to three in the previous twenty five years! That is, studies testing the independent contribution of rapport are rare. In all three cases, the rapport building came at the beginning of the interview and was not part of all stages of the interview. Not surprisingly, given the research journey that they went through, Saywitz *et al.* do not draw conclusions based on the studies. Instead, they concluded that the scientific basis of the available research into rapport is weak. The research agenda is clearly in need of amendment.

BOX 20.2 Controversy

Communicative competence in the courtroom and those working with children

Adult language can be complex, especially when sophisticated users of language such as lawyers and forensic psychologists are involved. There is good reason to believe that the language of the courtroom is

BOX 20.2 (continued)

inappropriate for many children. Some of the following issues have been raised in connection with other forms of interviewing, but they bear repetition because they are drawn from courtroom experience:

- *Linguistic complexity:* the following question in a court transcript: 'On the evening of January third, you did, didn't you, visit your grandmother's sister's house and didn't you see the defendant leave the house at 7:30, after which you stayed the night?' (Myers *et al.*, 1996). The child expected to answer this was four years of age!
- *Children may not understand legal terms:* Myers *et al.* (1996) point out that quite young children of five or six years do understand some terms, so they know words such as 'lie', 'police' and 'promise'. This does not mean that they have full understanding of the terms. So a child may have an idea of what the police do but will certainly not know the full ramifications of the job. Other words are beyond the understanding of even teenagers in the forensic setting. There is a potential for misunderstanding legal terms such as 'court' (which is a place where tennis is played), 'charges' (which are to do with money), 'hearing' (which is listening), 'party' (which is a social gathering) and 'swear' (which is to say a rude word).
- *Time, date and distance:* these are concepts built up gradually in the school years. It is pointless, for example, to ask a seven-year-old child the time that something happened because they do not have sufficient knowledge of the concept.
- *Comprehension:* monitoring is being able to assess how well we understand things that are said to us. Children are not particularly good at this and they may believe that they understand questions which, in fact, they do not. Furthermore, children rarely ask for clarification about the meaning of a question.

Lawyers' use of language in their dealings with victims in child abuse cases may be seen as oppressive and abusive from some perspectives. Zajac, Gross and Hayne (2003) found that defence lawyers in New Zealand asked a greater proportion of problematic questions to children than did prosecution ones. Brennan (1994) lists 13 different verbal tactics that are difficult or impossible for young witnesses to deal with effectively because they stretch their linguistic competence. For example, the following is an example of a multi-faceted question: 'And did your mother ever say to you that if somebody asks you the questions I am asking you, you should say that we didn't say what was going to be said?' (p. 213). It should be stressed that this is a question addressed in court to a ten-year-old. A good illustration of the problem is reported in Carter, Bottom and Levine (1996). Children were asked two versions of a question. One version was in legalese: 'To the best of your knowledge, X, in fact, kissed you, didn't she?' and the other version was simpler: 'X kissed you didn't she?' The version in legalese was much more likely to produce inaccurate replies in five- to seven-year-olds than the simpler wording. Actually, even this version of questioning introduces a feature that may be problematic – the tag – as in a question like 'Amy touched your bottom, didn't she?' as opposed to the direct version which is 'Did Amy touch your bottom?' With questions such as these, the child's answer is vital in that a case of abuse could rest on it. Krackow and Lynn (2003) investigated this very tag question and others in a sample of 48- to 70-month-old children. They set up a situation (actually an innocuous game) that included either innocuous bodily touch or no such touch. All that happened actually was that half of the children were touched on their hands, arms, calves or feet by an assistant whereas the others were not touched at all. A week later the children were interviewed about the events using tag and direct questioning techniques. 'Did Amy touch your bottom?' produced fewer erroneous 'Yes' answers than the corresponding tag-question version 'Amy touched your bottom, didn't she?' It did not matter whether there had been any touch at all during the play session with Amy. In fact, the children who answered the direct question were almost always accurate in their answer; those answering the tag question seemed to be responding almost at random since nearly 50 per cent falsely agreed that their bottom had been touched when none of the children's bottoms had actually been touched.

While it may be easy to understand why some lawyers may not be good at communicating effectively with children, there is considerable evidence that those whose professional lives involve working with children may not be very much better. Korkman, Santtila, Drzewiecki and Sandnabba (2008) studied the investigative interviews which Finnish mental health professionals conducted with children concerning suspected child sexual abuse. These children were in the age range of three to eight years and the question was whether these key mental health professionals were using age-appropriate language with the children. One would expect that they would make fewer demands on the language ability of young children than the older ones. The researchers obtained interviews from child sexual abuse investigations. Nearly all of them had been video-recorded. Generally, the researchers found that the interviewers failed to use age-appropriate language. For example, children of this age group have generally poor concepts of time. The researchers noted that, when dealing with the issue of time, the interviewers had a tendency to give the child a string of unproductive options, as in the following interview involving a five-year-old:

> Interviewer: Do you remember when this happened?
> Child: [no response]
> I: Do you? Was it in the summer or in the winter?
> C: [no response]
> I: Was it long ago or a short time ago?
> C: [no response]
>
> (p. 53)

Overall, the researchers found that about a fifth of the utterances of the interviewers included some form of unsuitable language structure: for example, sentences using complicated, multiple and long questions or unclear material about people or places. The interviews tended to be somewhat unstructured, with a lack of consistent focus on topic. There are a number of possible explanations for this. Sexual matters are sensitive and the interviewers might not feel confident in talking about them, irrespective of the age of the interviewee. Furthermore, this is an emotive area and the emotional reactions raised in the interviewer may detrimentally affect their cognitive processes. As a consequence, they may fail to apply the knowledge they have about interviewing children appropriately. Whatever the reason, this is an area where there is still a substantial amount of work to be done to ensure good quality interviews with children.

Children and lying

Research on children and lying goes back to the early years of the twentieth century. Talwar and Crossman (2012) provide a very useful account of children's lie telling ability. They slant their review towards children's lying in the context of court hearings. Lying develops at a very young age but it has to be borne in mind that children's ability to lie closely parallels their moral development in that they know that lie-telling is morally wrong. They do not condone many types of lie, such as malicious ones intended to hurt or harm other people. Among the many points made by Talwar and Crossman based on the extensive research literature are the following:

- As with adults, objectively it is difficult to tell that a child is lying; this applies even to very young children.
- Lying begins in the pre-school years. But children also begin to understand that it is wrong to lie when they are about two to three years of age.
- Children's ability to lie develops with age and increased levels of cognitive sophistication. Nevertheless, they cannot be regarded as being skilled at lying until they are at school.
- Early lying is motivated by the wish to avoid negative consequences for themselves. Lying for other reasons comes later.
- Lies for another person's benefit can be coached in children but these come later in life than self-protection motivated lies.
- The lies told by children tend not to be elaborate. Compared with adults, they cannot sustain their lies under questioning so well.

Talwar and Crossmany discuss the relevance of research on children's lying to children's testimony in courts of law. Much of the research on children's lying deals with ethically acceptable situations involving lying. This needs to be differentiated from, say, physical and sexual abuse or being coached by an adult to falsely make allegations about child abuse. However, some of the implications from research on children's lying relevant to forensic applications include:

- There is no doubt that children can recognise self-serving and hurtful lies for what they are – lies. They also see most lies negatively and as morally unacceptable. This level of conceptual understanding about lies, however, is nothing to do with desistance from lying. This makes some courtroom procedures for assessing the credibility of child witnesses suspect. That is, courts questioning children to see whether they understand the difference between truth and lies is unlikely to indicate whether they are willing or able to be truthful in court, say Talwar and Crossman.
- There is a risk in testing children's knowledge of truth and lies. What happens if the child does not convince the judge etc. that they understand the difference between the two? One possible consequence might be that the child is not allowed to present their perfectly sound evidence in court.

- Depending on what questions are asked, competency questions may not always be developmentally appropriate to a particular child. So asking a very young child about the intentions of hypothetical honest or deceptive individuals may simply confuse the child. But that child may nevertheless provide honest evidence in court.

Talwar and Crossman suggest that, rather than test a child's conceptual understanding of truth and lies, it might be more diagnostic to understand their motives for lying in particular circumstances. They suggest that a simple approach to facilitate truth telling would involve reassuring the child that it would be best for them to tell the truth. But simply asking children to promise to tell the truth is a soundly based method of ensuring truthful testimony.

Errors of omission and commission

There is a basic difference between two major types of error in recall – errors of omission versus errors of commission. Much of the work on children's evidence has concentrated on errors of commission, where the child recalls things or events which did not actually happen. In contrast, errors of omission are when the child fails to recall something which did happen. Otgaar, Camdel, Smeets and Merckelbach (2009) argue that errors of omission are especially relevant to some child sex abuse cases. In particular, they mention those cases where the child is told by their abuser or even their parents that the abuse did not happen. The researchers used an intriguing methodology to encourage errors of omission and commission. Basically, their research involved children in two age groups – one group was around four years of age and the other group was around nine years of age. They were introduced to an 80-cm doll named Lucy dressed in a variety of pink items of clothing such as a hat, jacket, pants, shoes and skirt. The children's task was to take off *three* of the items of Lucy's clothing. Immediately afterwards, the children's recollection of what items they had removed was virtually perfect – 95 per cent of children correctly recalled the three removed items accurately. In half of the cases the children were next led to believe that they had taken off just two pieces of clothing and the other children were led to believe that they had removed four items. That is, in a separate room they were asked about the items of clothing removed. In the omission condition, they were told that it was impossible that they had removed that many pieces of clothing. Furthermore, they were taken to the other room, where they were shown the doll, Lucy, but one of the items of clothing that had previously been removed by the child had been replaced by the researchers. In the other condition – the commission condition – the children were told that they had forgotten one item of Lucy's clothing and taken to see the puppet to 'prove' it. That is to say, the researchers had removed an item of clothing in addition to the three that the child had.

Then each child was interviewed by a female interviewer on three occasions at one-week intervals. This, of course, emulated the repeated questioning that a child victim would experience in real cases. The children were asked to name the items of clothing that they had to take off. Both errors of omission and commission decreased over time – though the authors say that errors of commission tended to be persistent. Forty-five per cent of children in the omission suggestion condition failed to report taking off items of clothing which in fact they had removed. This tendency became less strong over time. Age made no difference in the likelihood of making omission errors but commission errors were substantially more typical of younger children. Errors of commission were also more likely to occur as a result of the experimental manipulation. This study therefore demonstrates the creation of errors of omission and commission in children, using misinformation techniques.

In another study of both errors of omission and commission, Horowitz (2009) looked at three styles of questioning – direct (closed) questions, open-ended questions and mixed questions including cued invitations. The meaning of each of these is illustrated in Figure 20.2. The mixed-question format has not been mentioned so far in this chapter and so it warrants explanation. A mixed question consists of both a direct question and an opportunity to say more or explain just how things happened. So a mixed question might be: 'Did you see the policeman's hat blow off? Tell me more about what happened.' One particular type of mixed question is termed a cued invitation. In this the child is reminded of something that they had said earlier and then invited to say more. An example might be: 'You told me earlier that you laughed when the policeman's hat blew away. What happened?' There is an alternative version of the mixed question in which the first direct part of the question is based on something that the child has already mentioned which the researcher reminds them of before asking them to say more about it.

Are the different forms of questioning in Figure 20.2 equally good at eliciting accurate information? In order to answer this question, Horowitz (2009) obtained samples of children in the six-year-old (approximately) and the eleven-year-old (approximately) categories. The basic design was as follows:

- In the first week of the study, the children were shown a series of pictures of animals engaged in various activities. Collectively, these pictures told a story.

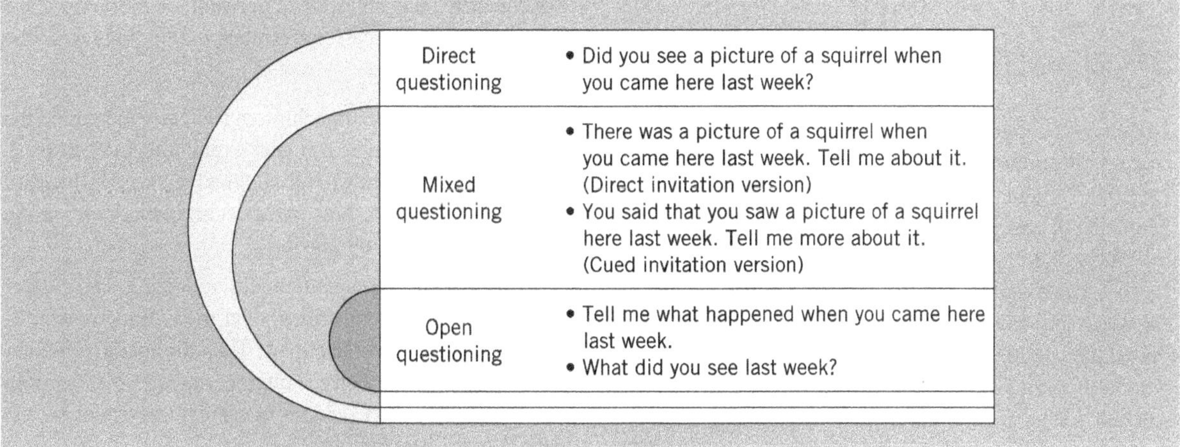

Figure 20.2 Types of question

- One week later, the child was sat down with an interviewer. The interviewer first of all built up rapport and generally got the child used to the interview setting. An interview then began which used the three different styles of questioning (direct, mixed and open) in a counterbalanced design.
- The direct questions were like 'Were you shown a picture of a kangaroo?'
- The mixed questions were like 'Was there [or 'You mentioned'] a picture of a kangaroo? Tell me more about that.'
- The open questions were like 'Tell me about the pictures you saw.'

The interviews were videoed and later transcribed. Where there was an incorrect answer it was classified as being either an error of omission or commission. In order to do this, the researcher created an arbitrary list of items of information, some of which were part of the direct questioning while the rest were not part of the direct questioning though they had happened in the first week. This strategy made the researcher's task manageable.

As had been found in many studies before, direct questions resulted in shorter answers and open questions resulted in longer answers in terms of the number of words. Mixed questioning produced answers of an in-between length. The children in the older age group tended to say more when giving their answers, though this was only statistically significant when open-ended questions are considered. The following were among the main findings:

- Remember that some of the events had been mentioned when the children were prompted using direct questioning. In these circumstances, if the direct questioning came before the open-ended questioning then there was an increased number of errors of commission in the open-ended answers. Cued invitations which used the replies to the direct questions as part of the mixed questions led to fewer errors of omission but did not increase the number of errors of commission.
- For the details which were *not* prompted by the direct questions, the direct questioning produced more errors of omission followed by the mixed questions followed by the open-ended questions. Younger children tended to make more errors of omission except for the direct questions. Direct and mixed questions generated more errors of commission than open questions.

Considering these and other findings, Horowitz (2009) argued for what he describes as an inverted pyramid approach to questioning. This is illustrated in Figure 20.3. The interviewer should begin with open-ended questions but if the outcome from this is unsatisfactory then mixed questions may be used, followed by direct questions if the required information is still not obtained.

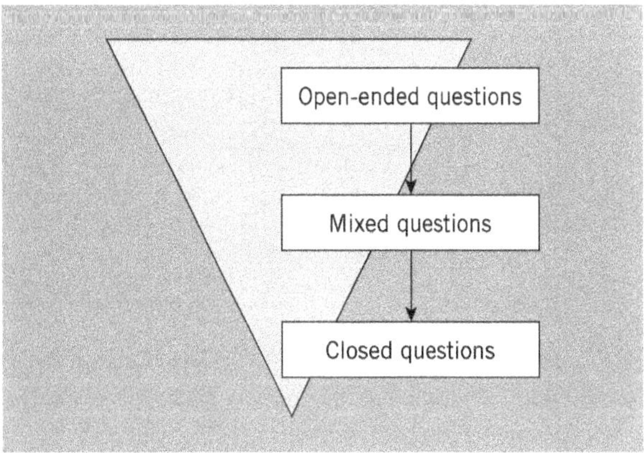

Figure 20.3 The inverted pyramid of questioning

Long-term influences of questioning

It is clearly important to understand the long-term influence of questioning on children's memory for events. A study by London, Bruck and Melnyk (2009) investigated the effects of post-event information given by interviewers on young children's memory for events. Their research design is a little complicated so it is summarised in Figure 20.4. The most important aspect of this study is that it investigated the children' memories over a period of about 15 months. Children of four to six years living in Montreal watched a standardised magic show containing a number of target events including such things as the magician tripping over her shoelaces, falling over and then requesting assistance from the child. Memory for these things would be tested 15 months later. Sometime later (see Figure 20.4), the children were subjected to two sessions of suggestive interviewing. This was done by using in the questions true and false reminders of what happened at the magic show. So the child might be asked about the boots they wore at the show, using correct or incorrect detail. This incorrect detail was the post-event information. Subsequently, the children underwent memory tests for the events on two occasions. Among the findings were the following:

- In free recall where the children basically recounted the magic show events, the post-event information (suggestive interviewing) initially had clearly influenced what was recalled. This trend declined markedly at the 15-month follow-up session.
- Correct spontaneous utterances reflecting the correct detail given earlier declined over the two memory testing sessions 15 months apart. They dropped from 29 to 4 per cent of the correct utterances. This was entirely responsible for the decline in correct utterances by the child over the 15-month period.
- For incorrect spontaneous utterances during free recall, there was no significant decline over the 15-month period. However, incorrect spontaneous utterances were initially 75 per cent, based on the misleading questioning at the first memory testing stage, but then declined to absolutely none of the incorrect recollections 15 months later! That is to say, the children made incorrect statements when tested more than a year later which were generated by other memory phenomena

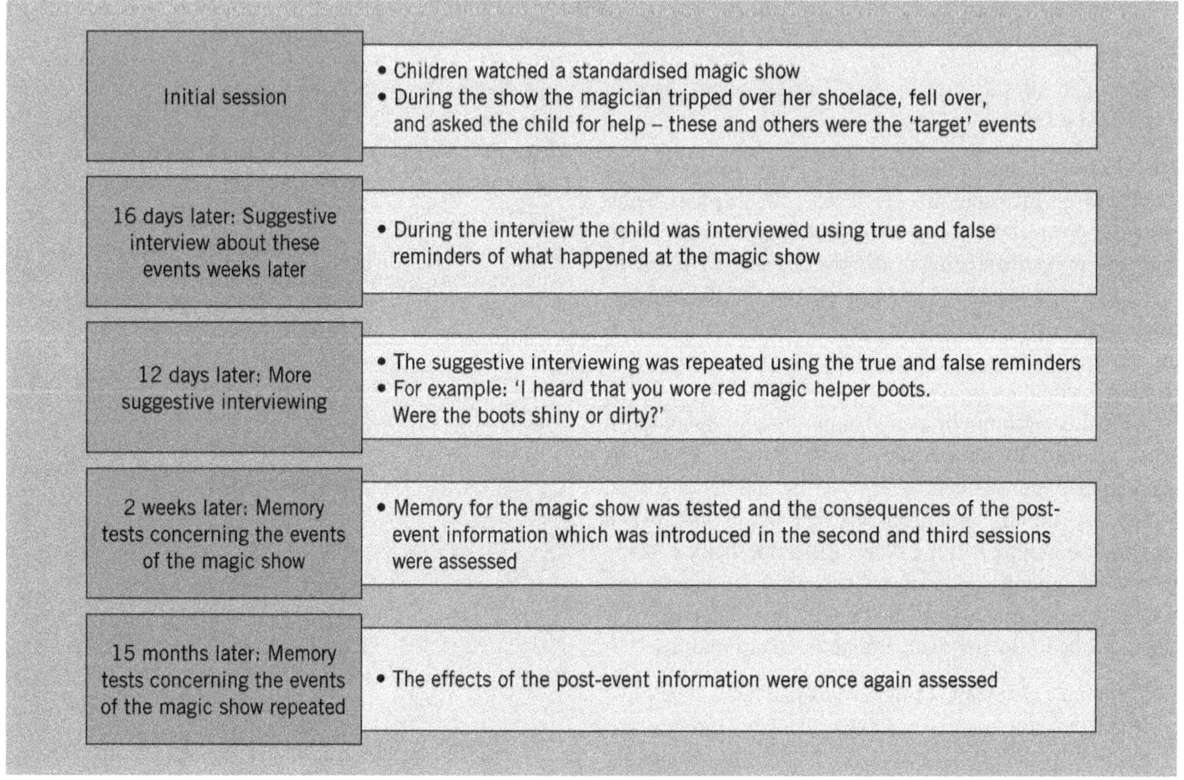

Figure 20.4 The design of London, Bruck and Melnyk's (2009) study of the long-term effects of suggestive interviewing

and not the influence of misinformation provided in the two interview stages.

- For correct reminder items assessed using yes/no questions, there was a decrease in correct answers over the 15-month period. However, there was no decline in the accuracy for correct items which had not been subject to the correct reminders at the interview stages.
- For false reminder (misinformation) items assessed using yes/no questions, there was evidence that the misinformation affected the accuracy of recall at both memory assessment stages although there was evidence that the effect of the interviewer's misinformation was less at 15 months than earlier.

Thus it is fairly clear that misinformation effects in interviews following events tend to decline with a longer interval between the interview and the recollection stage. Nevertheless, the data is fairly complex. London, Bruck and Melnyk (2009) argue that, forensically, it is better to rely on spontaneous recollection of events by children. Questioning based on 'yes/no' answers to questions (closed questioning), they suggest, is better reserved for situations where additional information is needed. All of the time, however, the interviewer needs to be aware of the possibility that previous interviews had been suggestive. Of course, this is an issue where we need to await further research findings.

Children and line-up identifications

Research has demonstrated quite frequently that children make more false identifications – guess more – than adults do faced with the same circumstances (see Chapter 13). The question of just why they do this is addressed in the research of Lowenstein, Blank and Sauer (2010). They investigated and found that in the United Kingdom, police officers sometimes dress formally in uniform and sometimes they wear more informal, civilian clothing. Does wearing of a uniform act as a sort of cue concerning authority which adversely affects the quality of children's eyewitness evidence? The problem is that children tend to assume that they must provide an answer or make an identification. The consequence is that they make risky, error-prone decisions because of their assumption that adults are requiring them to make an identification. To explore this further, Lowenstein *et al.* staged a theft in front of nine- to ten-year-old participants in which a computer monitor was stolen before their very eyes. However, none of the children mentioned to the researcher that this had happened at the time. About one week later they were asked to identify the culprit from an array of black and white photographs – i.e. a simultaneous line-up/identification parade (see Chapter 13). Some of the line-ups included the offender's photo and others did not. The children were asked to say which was the offender if he was present but otherwise to say that he was not present. In some cases the parade was conducted by a uniformed 'police officer', in other cases by the same individual but more casually dressed. More choices were made in the presence of the uniform. Most importantly, children made more errors for the target-absent parades than the target-present parades. Children seem to be uncertain in the target-absent situation but do not express this uncertainty in the presence of the authority of a uniform. In the target-absent condition, the children took much longer to reach a decision and they were less confident in the decision they made than in the target-present condition. Where there was no uniform, there was a relationship between the identification time, confidence and accuracy, but this was not the case where the officer was in a uniform. Less time is needed in a target-present line-up because the search can end as soon as the offender is recognised. The children's task seems to have been become more complex with the uniform present and they seemed to want to find a culprit, irrespective of what their memories told them. Clearly, there is a case for not using uniformed officers in line-ups/identity parades involving child witnesses and possibly the same applies to child interviews in general.

It is worthwhile mentioning the suggestive evidence from a 'laboratory' study which compared how mock student jurors evaluated evidence presented as if it were that of a child with how they evaluated the same evidence but presented as hearsay evidence from an expert interviewer of children (Warren *et al.*, 2002). Although the evidence was not perfectly consistent, there were some indications that the jurors tended to regard the evidence of the interviewer as more believable – but largely in a condition where they only presented the gist of the child's evidence rather than the detail. In other words, interviewer testimony may be effective, so care must be needed over the degradation of that testimony compared with that of the child's original interview.

In general, the research on children and line-ups/identification parades is clear-cut and consistent in its conclusions. When they are over five years of age, they can be just as good at identifying the correct suspect in a line-up/identity parade as adults – but only when the target is actually present in the line-up. When the correct target is not present in the line-up then children continue to make choices but in error (Havard, 2013). In other words, children guess when guessing is inappropriate. This would mean that an innocent person has been identified as the suspect. This is not a problem when the child's choice is known to be innocent because they are a police foil. However, in other circumstances, it could be a wrongful identification of an innocent suspect. The main difficulty for children is that they find it difficult to resist the social pressure to make a choice. The potential solutions to the problem include sequential line-ups, elimination line-ups, practice line-ups and the availability of an additional response such as 'don't know'. However, they do not work equally well. The sequential line-up in which the line-up participants are presented one at a time in sequence does not work well with children who use relative judgement to choose a suspect similar to the guilty individual. The elimination line-up involves the children making a relative judgement of the person in the line-up who looked the most similar to the offender. Once they have done that, they have to decide whether it was that person or not. In a study by Pozzulo and Lindsay (1999), this was shown to reduce false identifications. The additional choice is favoured by Havard. In this, for example, the line-up can include a picture of a tree that the true target might be hiding behind. This provides an alternative to picking out a person erroneously and has proven effective. An alternative is to have a card with a big question mark.

Facial fit construction

Although children may be not as good as adults at all forensic relevant tasks, their contributions may nevertheless be of some value. What about facial composites? We know that facial composites produced by adult witnesses are less than perfect (see Chapter 13) yet may be helpful in police investigations. A degree of imperfection does not necessarily preclude children as eyewitnesses. Payne, Lonsway and Fitzgerald (2008) investigated whether children under the age of ten years could produce worthwhile facial composites using modern computer-based facial composite creation techniques (E-FIT). Previous research had shown that children could perform reasonably well when older methods of facial composite construction were used. Paine *et al.* argued that children's composite building might be affected by vocabulary limitations. So they developed a technique for using visual prompts to help the communication between the child and the composite-maker. So, for example, take the matter of the distance between the eyes of the facial composite target. Verbal prompts might ask how wide the eyes were apart, which then means that the child has to be able to respond appropriately verbally. In the visual prompts condition the children were presented with stylised pictures of faces with the eyes different distances apart. Their task in these circumstances was simply to pick the picture which best represented the face that they were reconstructing. Although the evidence suggested that indeed younger children's composites were not as good as those of older children and adults, they were nevertheless able to help create a facial composite of an unfamiliar face. Indeed, in some cases, children produced facial composites which were better than those of some adults. The authors indicate that although the police use 10 years and below as the cut-off point below which facial composites are not attempted, there is reason to think that this is unduly cautious.

The role of the interviewer in child witness testimony

Children are only part of the equation in terms of child testimony. The process of obtaining evidence is interactive and interdependent. As such, it is also very difficult to study. There is a body of research on the role of the interviewer/investigator in the production of children's testimony, though this is fairly patchy and lacks the depth and coherence that research into child testimony has. It is also an area which can spark controversy, as we shall see, given its potential for criticism of the work of professionals, especially in the field of child protection. It is often assumed that the main problems when interviewing children are to do with the characteristics of children and the way in which questions are posed. Researchers are beginning to question whether cognitive factors such as these, alone, provide us with a full account of the difficulties associated with child interviews. In other words, the cognitive approach dominates research in this area and is too focused on helping the child's memory, say, while ignoring the organisational and interpersonal characteristics of child interviewing which impinge on the quality of the evidence that the child provides. For example, Almerigogna, Ost, Akehurst, and Fluck (2008b) found that children in the eight- to ten-year-old range perceived interviewers more positively when they were smiling and more negatively when they fidgeted. Building on this finding, the researchers had children of this age engage in an educational activity concerning vocal cords. The children were interviewed a week later but the interviewer either adopted a supportive (they smiled and avoided fidgeting) or non-supportive (they fidgeted such as tapping their hands and feet and avoided smiling) style of behaviour during the interview. The supportive interviewer yielded better-quality information from the children. The supportive interviewer obtained more accurate information from the children, who were also less likely to give the false information that they had been touched in the educational activity ('Where on your body did the lady touch you to feel the vibrations'). None of the children had been touched. Children interviewed by the supportive interviewer also gave proportionately nearly four times the number of 'don't know' answers to questions. In another study, Almerigogna *et al.* (2008a) found that the children who were characteristically anxious (trait anxiety) and those who showed higher levels of anxiety following the interview (state anxiety) tended to give more wrong answers when interviewed using misleading questions. It is important to note that non-supportive interviewers could produce higher levels of state anxiety in children.

Children are interviewed for particular purposes and the interviewer often will need to report the contents of the interview to others – perhaps in a court of law. Evidence based on what the child says in interview, when discussed in court is 'hearsay', since it is passed on by a third party and not the child's direct evidence. So a crucial question is that of how accurate are professionals carrying out interviews with children? Warren and Woodhall (1999) studied this question by asking a group of mainly child protection workers with between four and 21 years of experience to conduct interviews with three- to five-year-olds. The children were to be questioned about a magic show (which involved a disappearing book and lights pulled out of the magician's ears, among other things) and a silly doctor session in which the child played with Dr Tracy who took their blood pressure, checked their ears, tested their knee jerk response, and measured the child's muscles, among other things. The interviews took place a month after these experiences. The interview started with a cue question such as 'Tell me about the time you went with Tracy to play silly doctor' (p. 360). The task for the interviewer was to find out as much as possible about the events that the child had experienced. The interviews were recorded. The interviewers were asked to give a written account from their memory of the interview, its contents and sequence as accurately as they could. They were to use as accurate wording as possible.

Each interview was transcribed and broken down into 'units' which were the number of aspects of the events that the child recounted in the interview. So, for example, mentioning the lights being pulled out of the magician's ear would be one unit. Each unit was broken down into more specific subunits involving greater detail of things that happened when the magician pulled the lights out of their ears. The interviewer's recollections of what had been said were good. They recalled 83 per cent of the major units of the events and 65 per cent of the detail. They also recalled 60 per cent of the errors made by children when they recalled the events, such as claims that the magician had a magic wand – which he did not have. So, according to Warren and Woodhall, there is some degradation of the child's testimony such that some of the important detail is omitted in the 'hearsay' evidence supplied by the interviewer.

Prosecutions for child sexual abuse are low. The usual explanation of this reflects the absence of corroborating evidence such as DNA evidence or even photographs of the abuse. Another possibility is that poor-quality child sexual abuse interviews make prosecution difficult and so less likely. Hagborg, Stromwall and Tidefors (2012) studied the quality of interviews at a children's advocacy centre in Sweden. They used transcripts of investigative interviews involving three- to sixteen-year-old children reporting sexual abuse. Ninety per cent of the children in the interviews were girls. For the most part, the offence was rape. They coded the transcripts for a number of features of interview quality. One of two female police officers conducted the videotaped interviews. These officers had been trained in how to interview children. The features of the interviews used to assess quality were:

- how clearly ground rules are established (e.g. it is alright to say 'don't know' in answer to a question and the same question might be asked more than once);
- rapport with the child on the part of the interviewer;
- the extent to which the interviewer uses closed-end or open-ended questions;
- how well the interviewer refrains from interrupting the child telling the story;
- the extent to which the child seems tormented during the interview;
- the extent to which the interview consists of short questions and long answers;
- the general quality of the interview.

These are mostly features stipulated in the cognitive interview (see Chapter 11). The results provided no evidence that better-quality interviews by these criteria led more frequently to prosecution. There was no correlation, either, between interview quality and the children's age. Furthermore, the closeness of the relationship (biological/non-biological) between the alleged offender and the victim did not relate to prosecution. However, generally speaking, the interviews with older children were of a higher quality in terms of the above criteria. There was a low rate of prosecution, with only a quarter of the allegations leading to prosecution. Of these, only half led to a conviction.

More vocal criticisms have been made concerning the value of child protection interviews. Notably, Herman (2009) compared hard, scientific evidence (such as photographs and DNA) of child sexual abuse with the psychosocial or 'soft' evidence, which is often the only evidence available. The softer evidence requires professional judgement in order to evaluate its credibility. Apparently more damaging is his assertion that child protection interviews which involve clinical or professional judgement have been shown by a number of studies to be unreliable. His estimate is that reliability for child abuse assessments is about 75 per cent. This is the percentage of occasions when two different assessors faced with the same information would agree. This means that on 25 per cent of occasions they would disagree. Hence, based on this, forensic evaluators will be wrong in a quarter of cases. Herman bases his argument on seven published studies. What the studies relevant to this have in common is that they ask professionals to decide whether a child sexual abuse allegation is true based on a set of facts to do with abuse cases. This means professional judgement is reliable to the extent that different professionals agree about each allegation. It is the extent to which they agree with the 'correct' decision that determines whether they are judged reliable or not. So it would seem settled that professional judgement can be badly wrong too often. Unfortunately, according to Everson, Sandoval, Berson, Crowson and Robinson (2012), there are a number of problems with Herman's thinking:

- The ecological validity of the seven 'critical' studies is not clear since the case information only poorly represents the range of information that child abuse investigators would consider. The CFE model (the American Professional Society on the Abuse of Children, 2002) is commonly used in the USA and can be regarded as a reasonable standard of professional practice. It requires that investigators search for supporting/refuting evidence for the sexual abuse allegation by using a wide range of information sources and evaluating the evidence in terms of the amount of independent corroboration. Alternative hypotheses need to be tested. So, according to Everson *et al.*, the sorts of evidence that one would expect the forensic evaluators to use in reaching their decision would be: medical records; background history and the specific case history; history of the child's behaviour symptoms; earlier statements by the child; and interviews with the suspected offender. In stark contrast, five of the seven critical studies used a one- to two-page case summary; a transcript of the interview with the child; or an interview involving an anatomical doll. The other studies were from a previous era and probably had nothing to do with modern practice. So there would be no opportunity, to question, check, probe, or any of the things possible in a real life child protection interview.
- The professionals used as participants in the majority of the studies do not seem to have adequate training in child protection interviewing. Some of the studies included teachers and day care workers among their forensic professionals! Only three of the studies had professionals trained in forensic child protection interviewing.
- Reliability is not a fixed characteristic of interviews or research studies. So to suggest that a quarter of child protection interviews are erroneous is rather misleading. The likelihood of disagreement between professionals will change as a function of the strength of the evidence. If a researcher provides weak or ambiguous evidence for the child protection professional to judge then the reliability of their decision making will also be low. If the evidence is stronger then the reliability will be better. For example, even the soft, psychosocial evidence does not seem so weak when we consider examples such as 1) records of earlier unproven allegations against the suspect by other children and 2) the child's school independently recorded behaviour changes in the child, accompanied by sexual acting out. In a study demonstrating this, Everson, Sandoval, Berson, Crowson and Robinson (2012) found agreements ranging from 49 per cent to 100 per cent.
- In nearly all of the studies, the decisions being made on the basis of the case evidence were ones for the purposes of a research exercise and not as part of real-life child protection decision making. Hence we might expect that these decisions were made rather less cautiously and perhaps more riskily for these purposes. The participants could have, if they had so chosen, refused to make a decision, given the very limited nature of the case information before them.

Of course, all of this amounts to a need for better research evidence involving ecologically more valid situations more relevant to actual professional practice and, perhaps, rather less convenient for researchers.

Blanket condemnations of child protection interviews are not very constructive. It might be better to try to understand the factors which influence professional decision making in the child protection area. Quite clearly, there are many possibilities but Everson and Sandoval (2011) thought it important to understand child protection workers' attitudes. They had over 100 relevant professionals

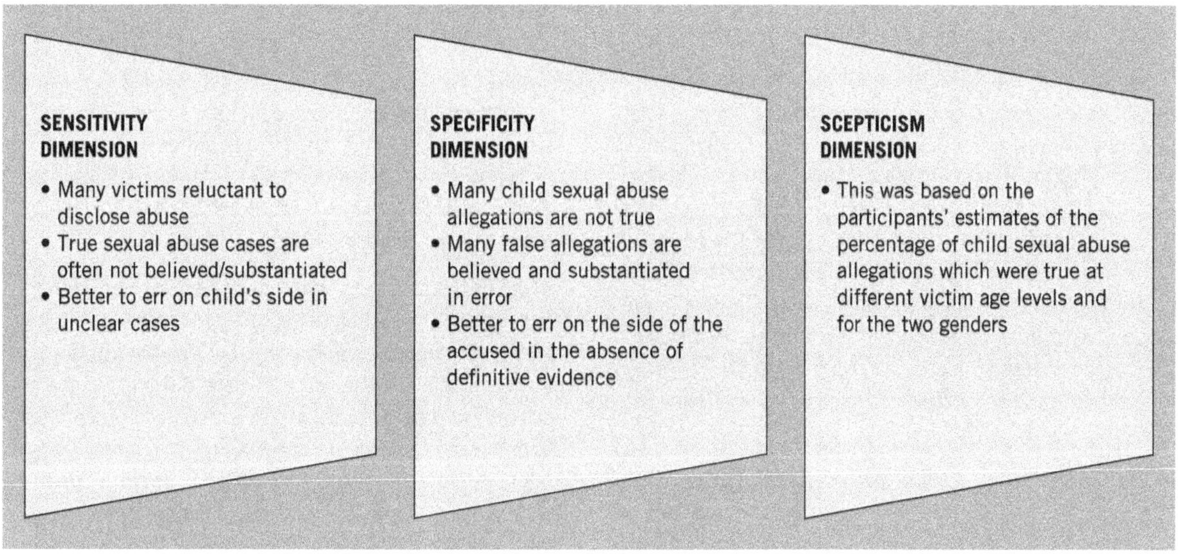

SENSITIVITY DIMENSION

- Many victims reluctant to disclose abuse
- True sexual abuse cases are often not believed/substantiated
- Better to err on child's side in unclear cases

SPECIFICITY DIMENSION

- Many child sexual abuse allegations are not true
- Many false allegations are believed and substantiated in error
- Better to err on the side of the accused in the absence of definitive evidence

SCEPTICISM DIMENSION

- This was based on the participants' estimates of the percentage of child sexual abuse allegations which were true at different victim age levels and for the two genders

Figure 20.5 The proposed underlying dimensions of professional attitudes to child protection decisions

working in the child maltreatment complete the *Child Forensic Attitude Scales* (SFAS). This consists of 28 items concerning things which possibly influence professional child sexual abuse judgements. It measures three broad categories of attitudes which are illustrated in Figure 20.5. This figure also gives some of the features of each category (i.e. factors):

- *Emphasis on sensitivity:* This refers to the diagnosticity (epidemiological) concept of sensitivity, which is a measure of the extent to which guilty individuals are diagnosed as guilty. In other words, it is a concept which prioritises making sure that the guilty are found to be guilty. The assumption would be that professionals high on the sensitivity attitude would tend to be more accepting of the allegation as justice for the child is primary.
- *Emphasis on specificity:* This is another diagnosticity (epidemiological) concept, which measures the extent to which the innocent accused person is found to be innocent. A person high on the specificity attitude would tend to be more doubting of a child's allegation.
- *Scepticism towards child and adolescent reports alleging sexual abuse:* This is simply a rating of the percentage of child abuse allegations which are actually true. The rating is repeated for different age group and different gender combinations.

This was the expectation but empirically things emerged slightly differently, according to Everson and Sandoval's statistical analysis. The sensitivity dimension actually split into two factors in the analysis. Items like 'failing to believe true case is common' and 'over 50 per cent of child victims are too traumatised to disclose' were on a separate factor from items like 'Better to err on the side of child' and 'More harmful to miss true cases than to substantiate false cases'. The researchers used this scale in relation to a number of decision making exercises involving child protection professionals. There were three separate decision exercises which varied quite considerably. They involved various cases which had extensive detail in one of the exercises. All of these exercises had featured in previous research. The important finding is that the decisions about the credibility of the allegations were predictable from the attitudes of the participants. So those who were high on sensitivity tended to accept the credibility of the child's allegation, whereas those high on specificity were less inclined to see the allegation as credible. Scepticism about child abuse was associated with less belief in the credibility of the available evidence. There were slight variations but the analyses for the different exercises were reasonably consistent. Furthermore, there were surprising findings concerning the child protection service professionals compared to some of the other professional groups in the criminal justice system. They were the group most likely to score highly on specificity and scepticism. In other words, they seemed to have a predilection towards thinking that child abuse allegations are false and erring towards protecting the suspect from the risk of false allegations. These findings were somewhat unexpected and the researchers wondered whether they represent a sea-change in the beliefs of child protection service professionals.

Main points

- In order for child victims to gain justice under the law it is necessary for them to provide evidence that is credible in a specific case. There are a number of procedures that have been adopted which may reduce some of the stress of appearing in court – a very adult environment normally. In some jurisdictions, video links of either the children giving testimony live or pre-recorded links may reduce the stress, as does making the court less formal by allowing lawyers to be seated when they ask the child questions.
- Experienced interviewers of children may employ closed questions a lot, despite the research evidence which suggests that this tends to generate a much smaller amount of material from the children involved. It may be advantageous to use scripted introductions to interviews, which use open-ended questioning, as once children are freely answering, they tend to carry on in the same way, no matter the type of questioning style used. It should not be forgotten that children at different stages of childhood may have very different communication skills. Some types of question – tag questions for example – may cause inaccurate testimony.
- Many of the problems in interviewing children are not ones of the child's competence and accuracy but matters to do with the interviewer. For example, there is evidence that lawyers in court have difficulty in consistently phrasing questions in a manner appropriate to the child's developmental stage. Furthermore, when interviewers were asked to recall the detail of interviews with children they are less than perfectly accurate, despite the importance of being able to do so. The way in which the interviewer raises issues of truth and lying can have an influence on the accuracy of the child's testimony.

Further reading

The following cover the field of interviewing especially child witnesses thoroughly, taken collectively:

Bull, R., Valentine, T. and Williamson, T. (eds) (2009) *Handbook of Psychology of Investigative Interviewing: Current Developments and Future Directions* Chichester: Wiley-Blackwell.

Milne, R. and Bull, R. (eds) (2015) *Investigative Interviewing: Psychology and Practice* (2nd edn) Chichester: Wiley.

Poole, D.A. (2016) *Interviewing Children: The Science of Conversation in Forensic Contexts* Washington: American Psychological Association.

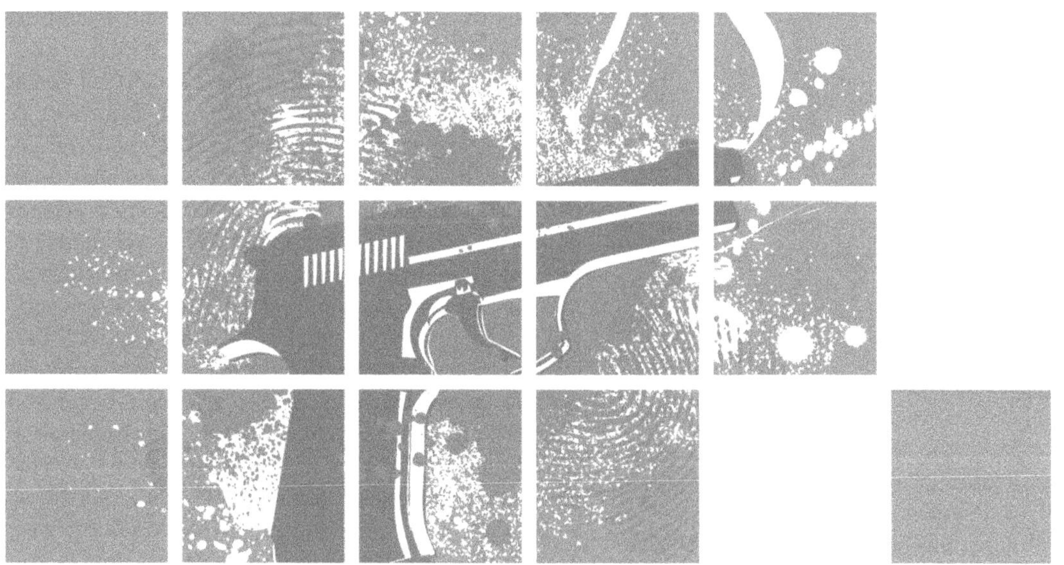

Chapter 21

Mental disorders and crime

Overview

- In popular culture, mental illness is frequently portrayed as being linked to crime. The media selectively exaggerate the violence and extreme nature of crimes perpetrated by the mentally ill. However, the evidence of major mental illness in a substantial minority of killers is quite strong.
- Several factors cloud the evidence on the link between mental illness and crime: 1) the mentally ill tend to be of lower socio-economic status, which means that they may live in more violent communities; 2) psychiatric categories of mental illness tend to involve violence in their definition, consequently, the mentally ill are violent because they are required to be if they are so categorised; and 3) the public may be more alarmed by a given level of violent behaviour if that person shows signs of mental illness and so are more likely to report it to the police.
- Surveys involving general population samples and objective measures of psychiatric illness are a way of avoiding the biasing effects of using clinical/hospital/prison samples. These studies show that mental illness does increase the risk of violent crime, but other factors, such as substance abuse, have a disproportionately greater influence.
- Mentally ill people are themselves more likely to be victims of violence. Nevertheless, reoffending by those with a criminal history and who have spent time confined in high-security special hospitals is quite frequent after release from the hospital.
- Other pertinent material may also be found in Chapter 22 on mental problems in court and Chapter 27 on risk and dangerousness.

Introduction

The professions of law and psychology share little in terms of how they conceptualise their subject matter – people. The causes and motivations of behaviour are central to both, yet there is conceptual divide. Even the concept 'mental illness' means different things in the law and in psychology. Thus a definition of mental illness, for example, from clinical psychology or psychiatric textbooks may tell one little about the legal meaning of the term. Under English law, for instance, mental illness is not a technical phrase. It means what it means in ordinary language to ordinary people. It is for the jury or court to decide whether the term applies to a particular defendant (Pilgrim, 2000). Belief in a link between mental illness and violent crime has a long history (Howitt, 1998b). As long ago as 1857, Dr John Gray suggested that serious mental illness is associated with attempted or actual homicide. This theme became common in the mass media. As early as 1909, *The Maniac Cook* movie had the mentally ill as homicidal maniacs. Modern cinema continues exactly the same themes in films such as *Psycho* (1960); *Silence of the Lambs* (1991); *Black Swan* (2010); *Shutter Island* (2010); *Silver Linings Playbook* (2012) *True Story* (2015); and many others. The dominant characteristic of media portrayals of the mentally ill are dangerousness and unpredictability (Day and Page, 1986; Wahl and Roth, 1982). Furthermore, public opinion surveys indicate that mentally ill people (especially those with schizophrenia) are perceived as violent and dangerous. Even potential jury members do not properly differentiate the psychopath from the psychotic. For example, they frequently attributed delusions to the archetypal psychopath (Smith, Edens, Clark, and Rulseh (2014)).

Not surprisingly then, research indicates that the media may shape the public's beliefs about the dangerousness of the mentally ill. A German study concentrated on the way in which daily newspapers portray the mentally ill (Angermeyer and Schulze, 2001). A German tabloid newspaper (*Bild-Zeitung*) with daily sales of 11 million copies was analysed in terms of its coverage of mental illness in relation to crime. The largest proportions of stories about the mentally ill (68 per cent) concerned murder; multiple murder; physical injury/grievous bodily harm; attempted murder; rape/sexual abuse; multiple infanticide; and infanticide. Indeed, 49 per cent involved some form of homicide. The researchers also showed that individual news events in which public figures were violently attacked by mentally ill people seemed to affect the public's attitudes to mentally ill people in general. The public's attitudes to the mentally ill became more negative after highly publicised violent incidents involving the mentally ill, such as the knife attack on court against the tennis star Monica Seles in 1993.

There is little doubt that people with mental health issues are over-represented in the criminal justice system. The criminal justice system (the police, courts, prison, probation services) is only one aspect of a complex structure dealing with mental illness. Medical services such as hospitals clearly have a part to play, as do voluntary services, say, dealing with mental health issues or homelessness. Furthermore, we should not forget that the community and family also have a central role and that some individuals with mental disturbances never seek or receive psychiatric or psychological help. The relationship between different parts of the system is dynamic and changing and there is an interplay between the medical system and the criminal justice system: that is, problematic individuals will be diverted into one or other system according to what capacity there is in the medical system. It has been shown, for example, that British mental hospital admissions correlate negatively with rates of prison imprisonment (Weller and Weller, 1988). The prisons were apparently receiving cases who previously would have entered psychiatric institutions. In this context, one should note the findings of Robertson, Pearson and Gibb (1996) concerning people detained at London police stations. About 1 per cent of detainees were acutely mentally ill. They tended to get diverted to other services and not to go through the criminal justice system. Violence at the time of arrest tended to lead to processing through the criminal justice system.

To get matters into proportion, it is useful to quote a few statistical findings. Based on data from 500 homicide cases in England and Wales in 1996–7 for whom psychiatric reports could be obtained, the levels of mental disorder were (Shaw *et al.*, 1999):

- 44 per cent had a record of mental disorder at some time in their life;
- 14 per cent had symptoms of mental illness at the time of the offence;
- 8 per cent had had contact with mental health services in the year before the offence.

Only in a small proportion of homicides did the offender show signs of mental illness at the time of the offence. According to Hodgins and Cote (1993), studies using 'unbiased' samples of killers find rates of major mental illness among them from about a fifth to over a half. One should bear in mind when assessing these trends that mental disorder is very common in the general population. Relatively frequent problems include depression.

In passing, it should be noted that the terms 'mental illness' and 'mental disorder' are not synonymous. 'Mental disorder' incorporates the mental illnesses which are regarded as treatable and changing but includes, in

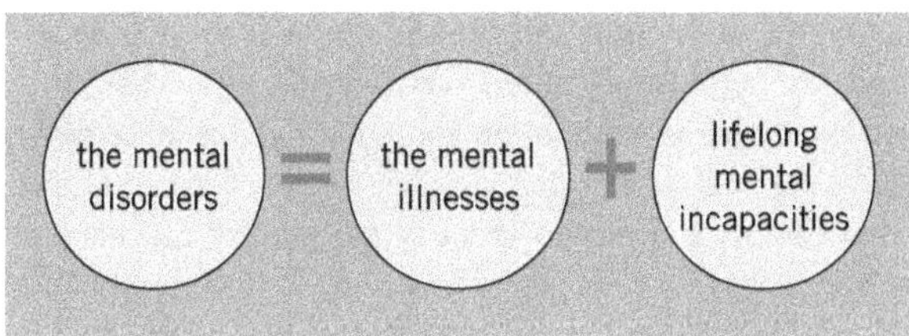

Figure 21.1 How the concept of mental disorder includes mental illness and mental incapacities

addition, long-term and unchangeable conditions such as learning disorders. Figure 21.1 illustrates this. So one might say that mental illness involves an interruption of mental functioning. This has the implication that the individual functioned normally at some stage and may function normally in the future. 'Mental disorder' is a general term for various problems in mental functioning, including lifelong problems like learning difficulties as well as familiar mental illnesses such as cyclical disorder and depression. Much of the research and theory described in this chapter is specifically about mental illness.

The question 'What is the relationship between mental illness and crime?' is relatively simple to answer compared with the methodological and conceptual difficulties inherent in the question 'Does mental illness cause violent crime?' (Arboleda-Florez, Holley and Crisanti, 1996). There are a number of other difficulties that need to be resolved.

Controlling for confounding factors

No matter what the statistical association between mental illness and violent crime (positive, negative or none), there remains the possibility that the apparent relationship is an artefact of the influence of third variables or confounding factors. So, to give a somewhat unlikely example, it is possible that the mentally ill appear to be more violent because they respond to taunts about their behaviour. Without these taunts, there might be no violent response. There are other possibilities:

- Some variables cannot be considered to be alternative causal variables. Mental illness cannot cause a person's age or sex, for example. This is not to say that mental illness does not correlate with age or sex. Schizophrenia was originally called *dementia praecox* because it was seen as an illness of young people. It is a common observation that, for whatever reason, women appear more frequently than men among the statistics on rates of mental illness. Such variables as gender can be appropriately partialled-out or controlled using common statistical techniques.
- Other factors that initially appear to be appropriately dealt with by statistical methods may actually be somewhat problematic. What is considered to be a confounding factor is a complex matter. Social class is a case in point. It is known that there is downward social drift among the seriously mentally ill (Hudson, 2005; Monahan, 1993). A company director who becomes mentally ill may be launched into a downward spiral because of being unable to keep a job, perhaps because they can no longer cope with the stresses of a managerial career. Their consequent income drop may cause them to lose their home and any work they obtain will be poorly paid. Once their socio-economic status has dropped markedly, they may find themselves in contact with violent subcultures (e.g. from living on the streets if they become homeless). The net effect of the downward spiral is that the mentally ill will tend to be disproportionately of lower socio-economic status. In this sense, mental illness can cause their social class. Removing socio-economic status from the association between mental illness and violent crime statistically would distort the findings in this case.
- Things can be even more complicated than this implies since such downward drift does not always happen and may be caused by factors other than mental illness anyway. For example, what if mental illness is sometimes the consequence of stress caused by bad housing or financial difficulties? In these circumstances, there is potentially a need to control for socio-economic status since it is part of the chain of factors causing mental illness.

Neither of the preceding points of view is wrong. Nevertheless, they lead to very different approaches to statistical control in the data. Of course, if both approaches lead to the same broad conclusion, then interpretation is easy.

The research on the relationship between psychosis and criminal violence is, inevitably, largely epidemiological in nature. Nederlof, Muris and Hovens (2013) carried out a systematic review of such studies from 1980. The schizophrenia-related disorders were schizo-affective disorder, delusional disorder, and psychotic disorder (not otherwise specified). They found initially nearly 6000 articles on the link but they filtered this down to just 26 which met their selection criteria. These requirements were a minimum sample size of 500 general population participants (not prisoners or in psychiatric hospitals), all of whom had to be 16 years of age or older. (It is generally thought that psychotic disorders cannot be reliably diagnosed before this age.) The studies included:

- birth cohort studies which followed through a group of the general population over a number of years;

- cross-sectional community studies which took a sample of community members at a particular point in time;
- clinical/criminal record studies which examine the link retrospectively.

This just about covers the range of possibilities but excludes those where offenders or psychiatric patients are the focus of the sampling. The researchers found that there was good evidence that schizophrenia and other psychotic disorders are associated with violent behaviour. (The odds ratio varied between 2 and 28. This essentially means the odds of criminal violence in a person with psychosis compared with the odds of criminal violence in a person without psychosis. So an odds ratio of 2 in this context means that it is twice as likely that a person with psychosis will commit criminal violence as a person without psychosis.) However, despite the relative methodological sophistication of the studies that they used, Nederlof *et al.* were still wary of concluding that schizophrenia and the other conditions lead to the individual being violent. The reason is that there are many risk factors which are associated with violence which may also be associated with schizophrenia etc. but do not constitute the psychosis in themselves. Risk factors that they mention include: living circumstances; family history of violence; problems in childhood; genetic vulnerability; gene environmental interactions; and impulsivity. Furthermore, the studies tend to overlook comorbid conditions such as substance use, mood disorders and anxiety disorders. Each and every one of these things could be related to violence and they could be related to psychosis.

The big problem is, of course, the sheer number of possible confounding variables that need to be taken into account. Many are taken into account in the individual studies, but this is never a complete list in Nederlof *et al.*'s opinion. A related problem is that of just what variables are related to psychosis etc. but are not psychosis and just what variables actually are involved directly with psychosis? The bottom line, of course, is that if a person has, say, schizophrenia then they are more likely to commit violent crimes. But this may be because of uncontrolled factors which are related to schizophrenia but do not constitute schizophrenia. In other words, schizophrenia is a risk factor for criminal violence but whether schizophrenia itself in some way causes criminal violence is the complicating issue. We do know that controlling for these confounding variables weakens the relationship between schizophrenia and violence but does not eliminate the relationship. So Nederlof *et al.* regard psychosis of various sorts as a risk factor in violence but its contribution to the variation in violence is relatively modest (i.e. 5 per cent to 40 per cent of the variation in violent crime can be attributed to the psychosis). But in the end, homelessness; living in group shelters; living in socially disorganised communities with multiple economic disadvantages; and family fragmentation also play their role and it may be possible to do something about these more easily than about the mental state. They recommend that future research needs to identify the precise mechanism by which psychoses lead to violence. Are there specific psychotic symptoms which are involved in violence? Are emotions such as anger and anxiety processed in different ways? Are distorted cognitions involved in some way? This would involve very different research methods from the ones which have dominated the field to date.

Violence in the mentally ill and national trends

The question of whether schizophrenia contributes a fixed quantity of homicides relative to the national figures at first sight seems to be little to do with the question of the role of mental illness in violence. But it is actually at the root of the problem since it contextualises the issue into a complex social situation and questions whether violence in the mentally ill can be seen independently of social trends. So country to country, region to region, is the contribution of schizophrenia to violent crime like homicide constant? According to Large, Smith and Nielssen (2009) this question has not been systematically tested, despite it being traditionally assumed that the contribution of schizophrenia to homicide is fixed. This goes back to the early 1970s with the work of Schipkownsky (1973), but Coid (1983) stated it as an epidemiological law:

> the higher the rate of homicide in a population, the lower the percentage of offenders who are found to be mentally abnormal
>
> (p. 857)

and Large *et al.* (2009) point out that:

> Constant rates of homicide by the mentally ill between regions and over time could be regarded as evidence that most of these homicides are due to aspects of the illness itself.
>
> (p. 123)

If it is the case that the contribution of schizophrenia is fixed, then this might suggest that there is something at the core of schizophrenia which leads to violent behaviour, almost as if schizophrenia contributed a fixed violence package. Large, Smith and Nielssen (2009) systematically reviewed the relevant research literature and also provide a meta-analysis (see Box 4.1) based on statistics of trends overall in the studies. Their research survey identified 25 relevant studies, conducted in economically well-off countries, which included homicide rates by the seriously mentally ill, of which 18 dealt specifically with schizophrenia. Throughout all of the studies and across regions, homicides by those diagnosed as schizophrenic were approximately 6–7 per cent of the total of homicides. Overall there was a very large correlation between the rates of homicide by those diagnosed as schizophrenic and the total rates of homicides across countries. The correlation was almost r = 0.9. That is, the correspondence between schizophrenic homicide rates and general homicide rates is almost as perfect as such relationships are likely to be! Both forms of homicide (in the mentally ill and in the general population), according to Large *et al.*, share some common aetiological factors such as substance abuse and how accessible weapons are in the region. So work to reduce the risk factors of homicide in general may well work to reduce schizophrenia-related homicides. Control of schizophrenic symptoms may further reduce schizophrenia-related homicides. It would seem that the mentally ill are just as vulnerable to societal factors leading to homicide as any other sector of the community.

Confounding by overlapping definitions

Mental illnesses are largely defined in terms of a number of diagnostic categories. Imagine that among those diagnostic features is violence itself. One possible consequence is that there will be an association between mental illness and violent crime. People who are violent then have a greater chance of also being defined as mentally ill since they show one of the symptoms of mental illness – violence. For many of the psychiatric disorders described and defined in the *Diagnostic and Statistical Manual* of the American Psychiatric Association, the 'bible' of psychiatric classification, violence is listed as a key diagnostic feature. Illnesses such as *antisocial personality disorder* and *borderline personality disorder* are partly defined in terms of violence. For other disorders, such as schizophrenia, violence is mentioned as an associated feature, although not a diagnostic characteristic (see Box 21.1 and Chapter 22):

- A study of *DSM-I* (published 1952) showed that only 2 per cent of the listed disorders characteristically involved violence. In *DSM-II* (published 1968), this percentage increased slightly to just 13 per cent of disorders. Things changed markedly with the issue of *DSM-III* in 1980. This time, 47 per cent of the psychiatric categories listed violence as a characteristic (Harry, 1985).
- These changes in definition coincided with changes in research findings. Prior to this time, research studies tended to show *no* relationship between mental illness and violent crime. After that time a relationship was more often shown (Link, Andrews and Cullen, 1992).

The confounding effects of medication

Psychiatric drugs are often prescribed to the mentally ill to control the symptoms of their illness. These drugs may have side effects leading to violent behaviour. For example, it is known that certain tranquillising drugs with neuroleptic effects can make users more aggressive. In other words, the drugs that the mentally ill take to alleviate undesirable symptoms are the actual cause of their aggressiveness, not the mental illness as such. Thus aggression in this case is not a direct effect of mental illness.

The clinical sample problem

Imagine that there is no relationship between mental illness and violence. It would still be possible to produce an association by selecting one's sample of mentally ill people in such a way that the mentally ill who are also violent have a better chance of being sampled. One way in which this might happen is to draw one's samples from mental hospitals. These people may be in hospital because they drew attention to themselves in the community – perhaps they were violent and so were arrested. In reality, violence may be no more common in the mentally ill than in the general population. Any selection method that favours the violent mentally ill may be responsible for a spurious association.

Misclassification of the mentally ill and violence

The use of hospital and crime records to classify people as mentally ill and violent may depend on a flawed classification system. For example, the general public may be more likely to report violence or threats of violence by people who show signs of mental illness. This is because their psychiatric symptoms make their violence appear to be more disturbing. As a consequence, the relationship between mental illness and violent crime would strengthen.

Effects of general social trends

It is possible that the apparent relationship between mental illness and violent crime will vary with major changes in social policy. In many countries there has been a policy known as deinstitutionalisation, the beginnings of which can be seen in the US as early as the 1960s. This policy involves retaining fewer of the mentally ill in mental institutions in favour of supporting them in the community. According to Markowitz (2011), in the US there were more than 300 beds per 100,000 of the population in psychiatric hospitals. By the 1990s, this figure had dropped to around 40 beds per 100,000 population and in 2005 the figure was 17 beds per 100,000. Since the early 1980s there has been a policy of retaining fewer of the mentally ill in mental institutions in favour of supporting them within the community (Bachrach, 1984, 1989; Shadish, 1984). Among the factors which allowed this change were (Markowitz, 2011):

- Much better drugs had been developed, allowing for the control of some of the most debilitating mental disorders.
- Ideas and ideologies surrounding the treatment of the mentally ill were beginning to change in ways which demanded a more liberal position on the confinement of the mentally ill. This in its turn led to a decline in the frequency of involuntary commitments for the mentally ill.
- Financing of the care of the mentally ill moved from individual states to the US federal government and budget cuts and underfunding resulted in the long run.

The net effect was that more of the mentally ill were being managed in the community, but also that the mentally ill became a big proportion of the homeless. This, combined with their other vulnerabilities, put them at risk of incarceration. Markowitz says that about a third of the homeless in the US satisfy the diagnostic criteria for major mental illnesses. If substance-related disorders are added to this figure then something like three-quarters of the homeless are mentally ill. There is a shortage of support facilities, which increases the risk. Vagrancy, drunkenness and disorderly conduct, as well as more serious crimes, put this group of individuals in contact with the police and the criminal justice system. Mental illness and homelessness is a criminogenic combination.

In the UK the process of deinstitutionalisation began later, around the 1980s. It is notable that, prior to the 1980s, researchers tended to conclude that the mentally ill were, if anything, less violent than people were in general. This could have been an artefact of the likelihood that the violent mentally ill were kept institutionalised and not allowed to return to the community. Since then, the view has been that mental illness has a tendency to be associated with violence. Drawing conclusions about the relationship between mental illness and crime based on their review of the literature, Lurigio and Harris (2009) suggest that the best studies have consistently found a small relationship between the two. Family members are more likely to suffer the violence of the mentally ill than are strangers. It is not possible to say that the violence of the mentally ill has trivial effects since there may be severe consequences in those cases in which it occurs.

BOX 21.1 Controversy

Psychiatric diagnosis

Forensic and criminal psychologists associate professionally with a variety of other professions – the law, social work, policing, prison administrators, prison officers and psychiatrists. This means, inevitably, that forensic and criminal psychologists should be able to communicate effectively across professional boundaries. This poses special problems in relation to psychiatry. Psychiatry overlaps with psychology in seeking to understand and explain human behaviour, including criminal activity, while at the same time the two disciplines are very different in their practical and theoretical basis. One particularly problematic area is that of psychiatric diagnosis, in which individuals are classified as manifesting the characteristics of particular mental illnesses, for example, or not. This is much the same as diagnosing physical diseases such as typhoid, carcinoma and the like.

Psychiatrists have mainly worked with diagnostic schemes based on the work of Emil Kraepelin in nineteenth-century Germany. For Kraepelin, each psychiatric disorder should demonstrate a cluster of symptoms that invariably tend to occur together. The prognoses of people classified as having the same 'mental disease' should be similar since the same pathological root is shared by all of them. Kraepelin

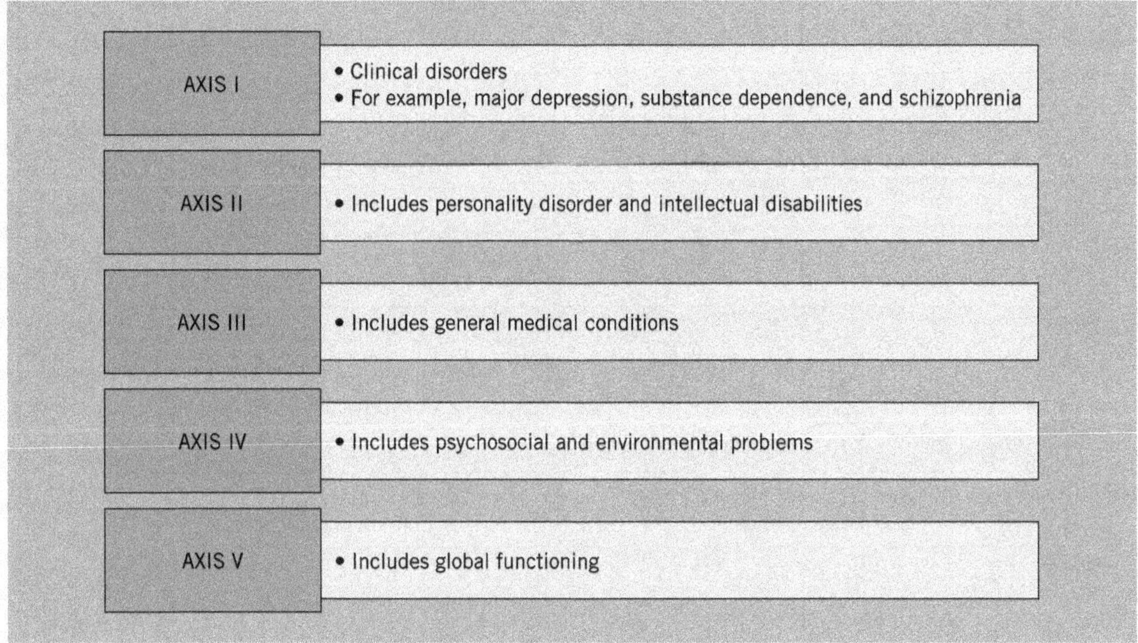

AXIS I
• Clinical disorders
• For example, major depression, substance dependence, and schizophrenia
AXIS II
• Includes personality disorder and intellectual disabilities
AXIS III
• Includes general medical conditions
AXIS IV
• Includes psychosocial and environmental problems
AXIS V
• Includes global functioning

Figure 21.2 The five axes of the Diagnostic and Statistical Manual

believed that there were three major types of psychosis:

- dementia praecox or schizophrenia – hallucinations and delusions;
- manic depression – extremes of mood, including depression and mania;
- paranoia – delusions of a persecutory or grandiose nature.

Given the origins and rationale of this psychiatric classification, it is hardly surprising that many psychologists regard it as the epitome of the medical model of *mental illness*. According to Eastman (2000), any conception of mental illness in terms of diseases such as lesions or disturbances of the function of a part of the personality are indicative of the underlying acceptance of the medical approach. His term for this is the *psychiatric phenomenological approach*. Control of symptoms is an important part of the 'treatment' of such conditions and one may seek a 'cure'. In contrast, what he terms the *psycho-understanding approach* sees psychological content as valid and enlightening (rather than the outcome of a fault in the system, as it is in the medical model).

Currently, there are two standard diagnostic systems. The most famous is the *Diagnostic and Statistical Manual of the American Psychiatric Association* (*DSM-I* to *DSM-V* have been published to date but *DSM-V* was first made available in 2014 and so is only beginning to have an impact on the research discussed in this edition) and the *International Classification of Diseases* (World Health Organization, 2011). The rapid growth of forensic and criminological psychology occurred contemporaneously with the publication of *DSM-IV*. Consequently, it is probably the most important version for our purposes. *DSM-IV* employed a system of classification involving five broad aspects of psychiatric diagnoses, which are labelled from Axis I to Axis V. These are shown in Figure 21.2. The various categories of mental illness are defined by various characteristics. So, for example, *schizophrenia* would be defined by the demonstration of the following things:

- Two or more symptoms from the following shown over a month:
  - delusions;
  - disorganised speech;
  - grossly disorganised or catatonic behaviour;
  - hallucinations;
  - negative symptoms such as flattened emotions.
- Social and/or occupational dysfunctions.

BOX 21.1 (continued)

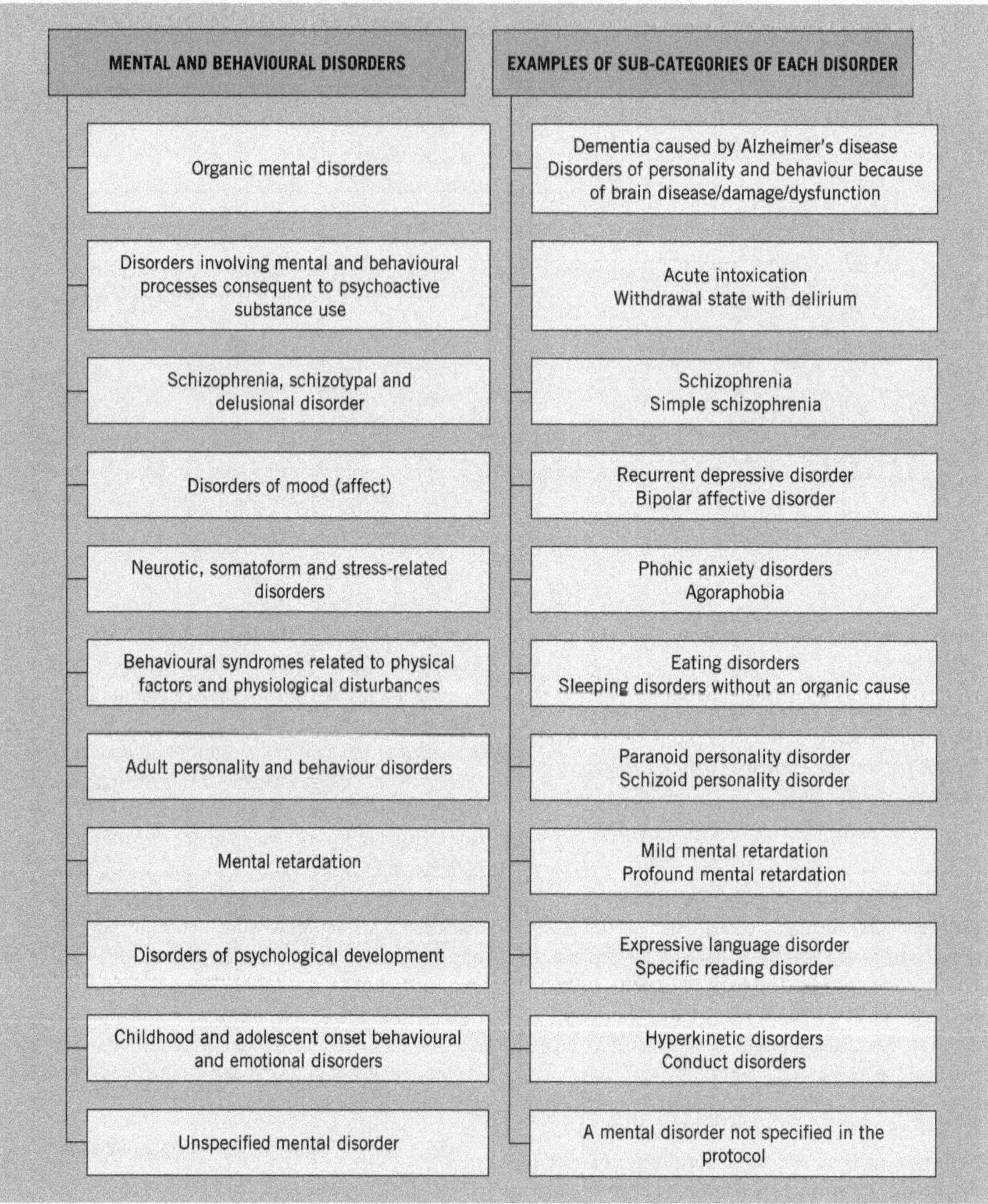

MENTAL AND BEHAVIOURAL DISORDERS
EXAMPLES OF SUB-CATEGORIES OF EACH DISORDER
Organic mental disorders
Dementia caused by Alzheimer's disease
Disorders of personality and behaviour because of brain disease/damage/dysfunction
Disorders involving mental and behavioural processes consequent to psychoactive substance use
Acute intoxication
Withdrawal state with delirium
Schizophrenia, schizotypal and delusional disorder
Schizophrenia
Simple schizophrenia
Disorders of mood (affect)
Recurrent depressive disorder
Bipolar affective disorder
Neurotic, somatoform and stress-related disorders
Phohic anxiety disorders
Agoraphobia
Behavioural syndromes related to physical factors and physiological disturbances
Eating disorders
Sleeping disorders without an organic cause
Adult personality and behaviour disorders
Paranoid personality disorder
Schizoid personality disorder
Mental retardation
Mild mental retardation
Profound mental retardation
Disorders of psychological development
Expressive language disorder
Specific reading disorder
Childhood and adolescent onset behavioural and emotional disorders
Hyperkinetic disorders
Conduct disorders
Unspecified mental disorder
A mental disorder not specified in the protocol

Figure 21.3 The World Health Organization's system for classifying mental and related disorders

The World Health Organization's (2011) system is briefly summarised in Figure 21.3. The system contains a greater description of the characteristics of each of the subcategories of each of the diagnostic categories. The system contains a wide range of medical conditions, although Figure 21.3 concentrates on those related to mental illness etc.

The problems for a psychologist using these diagnostic manuals include the following (Pilgrim, 2000):

- Diagnostic categories are created by psychiatrists and others. Consequently, they may change, be abandoned, subdivided and so forth largely on the basis of expert opinion rather than scientific utility.
- Unlike many diagnoses of physical illness, even for major psychiatric classifications of illness such as schizophrenia, the utilitarian value of the diagnosis is unclear. For example, the bodily causes of schizophrenia have not been clearly identified, despite years of research. This is quite different from the situation with physical illnesses such as typhoid and carcinoma for which the physical mechanisms are known.
- There are major difficulties when the user tries to differentiate one diagnostic category from another. Different diagnosticians may put the same patient in very different categories. Similarly, simply diagnosing people as normal or abnormal is far from an objective process, with different clinicians reaching different conclusions.
- Some would argue that these diagnostic systems have nothing extra to offer than does ordinary language. So to suggest people are mad, bad, sad or afraid may be to effectively offer the equivalent of diagnoses such as schizophrenia, antisocial personality disorder, depression or phobia. Pilgrim (2000) suggests that the psychiatric diagnoses tend to stigmatise people more than ordinary language does. The descriptions of ordinary language tend to be associated with relatively subtle explanations of why a person is a particular way and often a variety of notions about what can be done to help the person with the problem.
- The diagnoses may merely present technical terms that fulfil no other function than to enhance the technical reputation of diagnosticians. The ordinary person in the street understands the violent, often repetitive and antisocial nature of rape, so what extra is gained by diagnosing such a person as a psychopath?
- There is circularity in the definition of mental illness. A person is classified as mentally ill on the basis of their behaviour, then this diagnosis is used to explain their behaviour. This circularity is illustrated below. Notice that things are different in medical diagnosis since, although the disease is often defined by its symptoms, there is frequently an independent test to determine the correctness of the diagnosis. Interestingly, Pickel (1998) found evidence that simulated jurors tended to make judgements about the insanity of defendants accused of homicide if there were unusual features about how the crime was committed, e.g. that the body was covered with strange designs done with yellow mustard.

To these we should add a very important point of great relevance to forensic practitioners: the way in which people with mental disorders are conceived psychologically and psychiatrically is simply not the same as the legal categories used in relation to the same people. That is, legal definitions are not simply the application of psychological concepts or psychiatric classifications. In brief, there is no common language between psychiatry or psychology and the law on these matters. The law is made by legislators and can reflect profound ideological changes in the way in which mental disorders are understood (Forrester, Ozdural, Muthukumaraswamy and Carroll, 2008).

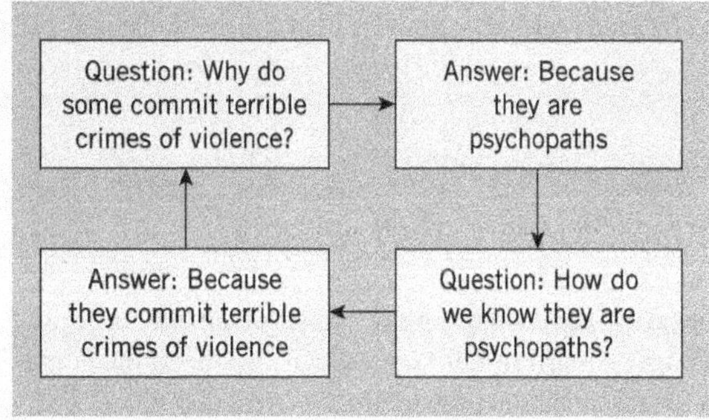

Mental illness and violent crime in community samples

Two important studies have been carried out involving substantial samples from the community (as opposed to, say, prisons or mental hospitals). Using community samples removes some potential artefacts (McNeil, 1997) and may be regarded as the ideal type of study to answer the question of whether mental illness is linked to crime:

- Link, *Andrews and Cullen* (1992) studied representative samples of 500 never-treated community residents in New York City, together with a mental patient sample. As might be expected, mental patients had the highest levels of a variety of official and self-report measures of violent and illegal behaviour. Statistical control for socio-demographic and community context variables still left the mental patient group more violent and more criminal. The researchers employed the *Psychiatric Epidemiology Research Interview* with both samples. This assesses the extent of mental illness symptoms independently of the mental health system. There was a relationship between having psychotic symptoms and violence. Despite this, the presence of psychotic symptoms was a weaker predictor of violence than other variables such as age, education level and gender.

- Swanson, *Holzer, Ganju and Jono's* (1990) study was similar in that psychiatric symptoms were assessed using the *Diagnostic Interview Schedule*. They obtained a sample from the communities of Baltimore, Raleigh-Durham and Los Angeles in the United States. Socio-demographic variables including age and sex were statistically controlled.

Following this, it was clear that schizophrenia and major affective disorders were associated with an approximately fourfold increase in the likelihood of violence in the year following assessment. These findings need to be set against the 14-fold increase in the likelihood of violence associated with substance abuse. The presence of mental disorder and substance abuse together increased the likelihood of violence to 17-fold. Mental disorders differ in their relationship with violence. Psychotic illness (i.e. schizophrenia and similar) resulted in higher levels of violence than affective or anxiety disorders. Nevertheless, serious mental illness is rare compared with, for example, substance abuse. Consequently, the relative risk is far greater from substance abusers than the mentally ill.

Post-traumatic stress disorder and crime

Concerns about the levels of involvement in crime amongst American military veterans has been the stimulus for research into post-traumatic stress disorder (PTSD) and crime. Crimes of violence are especially implicated. According to Corry, Kulka, Fairbank and Schlenger (2016), a wide range of studies on the prevalence of PTSD in Vietnam War veterans yield consistent findings. Current PTSD prevalence is estimated to be approximately 10–15 per cent. This includes veterans who have manifested PTSD from when first diagnosed, those who manifested PTSD initially but no longer, and those who did not manifest PTSD initially but in whom it has developed since. There is plenty of evidence implicating PTSD in some criminal behaviour. The literature contains graphic instances of the effects of PTSD on troops. Silva, Derecho, Leong, Weinstock and Ferrari (2001) give the case of a man who, while experiencing a flashback, saw in the face of his victim the face of the enemy. Such cases as these clearly raise questions about criminal responsibility, although PTSD is not a psychosis. (A psychosis is an abnormal condition of the mind which involve a loosened grip on reality and deficient reality testing. Hallucinations, delusions and similar thought disturbances impair thinking. Psychotic conditions affect the individual's ability to function effectively in society.)

There has been a steady output of research into the military and PTSD (e.g. Freeman, and Roca, 2001; Taft, Vogt, Marshall, Panuzio and Niles, 2007). A typical example of such studies is Begic and Begic (2001) though there are numerous others yielding similar findings. In Begic and Begic's study, over two-thirds of the war veterans they sampled had been diagnosed with PTSD. Violent behaviour was virtually universal in those diagnosed with PTSD and it was three times more common in PTSD sufferers than the others. Furthermore, the annual average number of violent acts per PTSD sufferer was 18, as opposed to three for the non-PTSD group. The analysis suggested that being exposed to trauma alone was not in itself responsible for the violence but that it was the PTSD which often followed the trauma that was to blame.

Later research tends to paint a rather more subtle picture of the relationship between PTSD and crime. Elbogen *et al.* (2012) hypothesised veterans with PTSD who report anger and irritability symptoms would have higher rates of criminal arrest following release from the forces. They used data from a national survey of nearly 1400 Iraq and Afghanistan war veterans, both men and women. For the most part, the veterans completed an online version of the survey though about a fifth of the sample filled in a written survey. The basic figure for arrest following release from the military was 9 per cent. However, for the most part these arrests were for minor, non-violent offences which resulted in imprisonment for under two weeks. Exposure to combat in itself did not have a significant influence on the risk of arrest but those who had higher (more frequent) levels of combat exposure were more likely to be arrested for crime. Arrest was most likely for veterans who had PTSD associated with anger and irritability symptoms. But there were other factors such as being young, male, having a prior arrest history, alcohol and drug abuse and witnessing their parents fight which were also associated with criminal behavior. Substance abuse and criminal history were more important predictors of criminal arrest in veterans than PTSD.

Research in cultures other than the US paints a slightly or somewhat different picture. MacManus *et al.* (2013) carried out a major study of veterans of the Iraq and Afghanistan conflicts. Of course, one would expect that those most at risk of PTSD are personnel who have been in active combat and service in the forces, in itself, does not mean that the individual has been deployed to a war zone let alone active combat. So MacManus *et al.* took this into account. Also, they incorporated into their design pre-existing risk factors for violent crime which pre-dated entry into the military. Although some studies use self-reports of crime, this study used criminal records taken from the UK National Computer database. The full sample consisted of nearly 14,000 randomly selected serving/ex-serving UK military personnel. The study also made extensive use of additional data derived from self-completion questionnaires.

Evidence that the military are crime-prone was not found. It was found that only 17 per cent of military personnel had a criminal record of some sort at the time of the study compared with 28 per cent of men in the equivalent age range in the United Kingdom general population of men. Eleven per cent of the military personnel had records for violent offences. The chances of a military person having served a custodial sentence in prison was just 1.7 per cent compared with 7 per cent of the comparable general population. In a sense, military service tends to occur at an age when men, in general, are most at risk of committing crimes. So, in that sense, perhaps being in the military is protective from crime. Interestingly, younger military personnel were far more likely to have a record for violence than older men. This might suggest that troublesome men leave the service younger. Those deployed to a combat role had a 6.3 per cent risk of violent offending but for those deployed to a non-combat role the figure was 2.4 per cent. Of course, PTSD is associated with traumatic events. Self-reported aggressive behavior and alcohol misuse were the strongest risk factors which may warrant intervention. Those who engaged in alcohol misuse post-deployment to a war zone increased the likelihood of violent offending to 9.0 per cent compared to 2.3 per cent of those who did not misuse alcohol. Similarly, Taft, Pless and Stalans *et al.* (2005) identify the comorbidity of alcohol and/or substance abuse with PTSD as the mechanism. They found evidence that alcohol misuse actually mediates the relationship of PTSD and violence.

What about the role of PTSD? The authors describe there being a strong link between PTSD and offending in the deployed group. PTSD mediated between traumatic events and violent offending. Exposure to larger number of traumatic events in the combat increased the risk of violent offending. The more symptoms of PTSD the greater the risk of violent offending. Those who showed symptoms of PTSD had an 8.6 per cent risk of violent offending as opposed to 3.0 per cent for those without symptoms. Those who showed more of the arousal (hyper-arousal) cluster of symptoms of PTSD were more likely to offend violently. This would include symptoms such as irritability and constant monitoring the environment for possible threats. This might be an alternative mechanism by which PTSD links to crime.

In the US and the UK, military conscripts are volunteers. In contrast, in Israel military service involves conscription and every young person is eligible to be called up. This may have a big effect on the sort of person who enters the military in the different countries and, as a consequence, on the propensity to crime. Sherman, Fostick and Zohar (2014) studied Israeli veterans who had diagnoses of PTSD and compared them with a matched control sample of veterans without this diagnosis. Data on the offending behavior of these veterans was obtained from the Israeli Police criminal records database. In keeping with previous research, the Israeli veterans with PTSD were more likely to have a criminal record than veterans without PTSD. However, the trend was quite small and did not apply to all crimes. Violence and crimes against the public order and legal authorities were a little more common in the PTSD veterans but other crimes like sex crimes, drug crimes and property crimes showed no differences. While there is no theoretical reason why PTSD should lead to sex crimes and property crimes, the lack of association with drug crimes is surprising since it suggests that drugs did not mediate between PTSD in this Israeli sample. Perhaps the fact that Israeli veterans come from relatively high socioeconomic backgrounds may be part of the reason. Factors such as this may be responsible for the difference between this Israeli study and the American studies.

Clinical aspects of violence

There are other factors in mental illness that affect the likelihood of violence (McNeil, 1997). Mental illnesses, as we have seen, are not all associated with violence or in the same way. Furthermore, mental illness is not an invariant feature of a person's life. It changes in intensity and form over time. Consequently, studies of patients in the acute phase of a mental illness may find higher levels of violence. Studies of patients in remission (the non-acute phase) may find lower levels of violence. In particular, people with schizophrenia in stages of frequent and intense symptoms (i.e. during acute exacerbation) are more violent than groups of patients with a different psychiatric classification. In the case of mania (manic depression/bipolar disorder), the manic phase may show the highest levels of violence.

Mental disorders can be the consequence of traumatic injuries or physical disease. Head injuries tend to elevate the risk of violence – in particular, damage to the temporal or frontal lobes may encourage aggressive behaviours.

Other factors need to be taken into account. *Command hallucinations* (the hearing of voices instructing the patient to commit violence or other harm against a third party) seem to heighten the risk of violence. The famous case of the Yorkshire Ripper who, in the 1970s, murdered at least 13 women, generally prostitutes, featured such hallucinations. It was claimed at Peter Sutcliffe's trial that he was instructed by the voice of God to carry out the murders. This may have been a failed attempt to be pronounced mentally ill by the court (Ainsworth, 2000a). However, a study of schizophrenic men detained under the UK Mental Health Act of 1983 for serious sexual offences against women and considered by the courts to be a special risk to the public, found a poor relationship between their delusions and their sexual offending. Ninety-four per cent had some sort of delusions and hallucinations at the time of the offence but did the contents of these have any relationship to the offence? For 51 per cent of these offenders, the delusions were just coincidental and had no bearing on the attack. Another 25 per cent had delusions that were of a sexual or persecutory nature but which did not reflect the characteristics of the sexual assault. Eighteen per cent had delusions that appeared to be directly related to the sexual attack (Smith and Taylor, 1999). O'Kane and Bentall (2000) concentrate on severe psychotic disorders, which they see as characteristically involving hallucinations, delusions and apparent loss of contact with reality. They discuss the symptom approach to violence in the mentally ill in which the search is for the symptoms associated with violence (as opposed to the diagnosis approach, which concentrates on the psychiatric diagnoses associated with violence). The sorts of symptoms they implicate in violence are already partly familiar:

- delusions and passivity delusions with paranormal influences;
- psychotic individuals with organised delusions are especially likely to commit either lethal or near-lethal acts;
- paranoid symptoms are associated with violent behaviour;
- command hallucinations often involve aggression and self-punishment – they have also been implicated in sexual offences.

Among the most interesting of these symptoms are command hallucinations. Auditory hallucinations of various sorts are a main symptom of psychotic disorders in general. Command hallucination is merely one particular type of auditory hallucination and involves a voice commanding the person to do a particular thing. Other voice hallucinations may involve the comments of the 'voice' but what is said lacks directions. Research suggests that the prevalence of command hallucinations depends on the particular type of sample being studied. The figure is in excess of 50 per cent for those who experience auditory hallucinations of any sort (e.g. Mackinnon, Copolov and Trauer 2004). However, perhaps surprisingly, the rates of command hallucinations are no different in forensic and non-forensic populations. Command hallucinations can be categorised as belonging to three different types:

- benign commands involving no harm to oneself or others;
- other-harm commands instructing the hearer to do something harmful to another person;
- self-harm commands instructing the hearer to do something damaging to themselves.

But just what leads to a command being carried out? There is some evidence to suggest that this is partly dependent on the individual's beliefs about the voice that they hear and not the particular content of the instruction. The voice may be perceived as powerful compared to the vulnerable self. Such circumstances have been found to relate to compliance to the instruction of the command hallucination and particularly so where the instruction is to inflict harm on others (Fox, Gray and Lewis, 2004). Those who obey other-harm commands tend to perceive the voice as all-powerful and controlling. One possibility is that if the hearer regards themselves as being of low social power then they will be more inclined to implement self-harm commands than other-harm commands. The hearer who regards themselves as being higher in social power is more likely to obey other-harm commands.

Reynolds and Scragg (2010) researched two groups of men who heard command hallucinations. One group were compliers with the commands and the other group resisted commands. All the men were recruited from a variety of types of forensic location. The researchers were interested in three aspects:

- the hearer's perceptions of the perceived power of the voice;
- the hearer's perceptions of the social rank of the voice compared to their own;
- the hearer's perceptions of their own social rank compared with that of others.

The focus of the research was solely on the other-harm command. The men were interviewed and a number of psychiatric tests administered. These included the *Voice Power Differential Scale*, which includes the aspects of ability to inflict harm, confidence, knowledge, respect, strength, and superiority, and the *Social Comparison Scale*, which assesses the individual's perceived social rank relative to others. It was found that compliance with voices did not depend on the severity of an individual's psychiatric symptoms or psychopathy. However, compliers with the voices saw the voice as more powerful than did resisters and compliers saw the voice as being of a higher social rank compared with themselves. These findings were as the researchers predicted. Nevertheless, the expectation that the individuals who complied with the command of the voices would perceive themselves as of higher social rank compared with other people was not supported.

McNeil (1997) believes that the following should be considered when trying to understand the violence of individuals with psychiatric difficulties:

- A previous history of violence is the best single predictor of future violence in both clinical and non-clinical populations.
- Among the mentally ill, homelessness is associated with violent behaviour.
- Being victimised by child abuse or observing adults being violent to each other at home increases the risk of acting violently.
- Care-givers and nurses are at the greatest risk of violence from the mentally ill.
- Gender is a poor predictor of violence. Violence by male psychiatric patients may be perceived as more fear-provoking because they are more likely to threaten and damage property. Nevertheless, women psychiatric patients would appear to commit more assaults. Studies of people *living in the community* who attend psychiatric emergency facilities generally suggest that the genders are comparable in violence levels.
- Poor social networks are associated with violence.
- Race, ethnicity and culture are inconsistent and so worthless predictors of violence in the mentally ill. This is the case after social class and similar variables have been taken into account.
- Some environments are actually threatening, which may encourage violence.
- The availability of weapons increases risk.

While some forms of mental illness carry an increased risk of violence to others, the meaning of this needs to be clarified. The rates of serious mental illness are small compared with people manifesting other risk factors for violence (e.g. substance abuse, youth). In other words, the likelihood of an individual being assaulted by someone with a serious mental illness is less than that of being assaulted by someone with a different risk factor.

So what are the characteristics of the offending associated with different types of mental illness? One area of particular interest is homicide. In Finland, Häkkänen and Laajasalo (2006) obtained samples of forensic psychiatric statements for four different *DSM-III-R* diagnostic groups – schizophrenics, abusers of alcohol or drugs, offenders with personality disorder, and offenders with no diagnosis or a relatively minor disorder. There were some characteristics particularly associated with these different groups:

- *Alcoholics:* they were all drunk when committing the homicide; they were the group most likely to use a weapon present at the crime scene; they were most likely to kill following an argument; they were the most likely to give themselves up; they were very unlikely to use a handgun.
- *Drug addicts:* these stole more frequently from their victims and they killed in the context of another crime more frequently; surprisingly, they showed some of the same patterns as schizophrenics since their choice of weapons was very similar and the killings of both of these groups seem not to be the consequence of external events such as quarrels.
- *Personality disorder:* guns and blunt and sharp weapons were associated with this group, as was kicking and hitting; there were few other characteristics, which may reflect the tenuous nature of this classification.
- *Schizophrenics:* sharp and blunt weapons are used more often than guns – perhaps because their crimes are more impulsive; they injured their victim's face more frequently than the other groups of mentally ill offenders – possibly because the face is symbolically the essence of a person or because they find facial expressions threatening; their attacks were less likely to follow arguments; mostly they suffered from hallucinations/delusions at the time of the attack; their victims were frequently relatives.

BOX 21.2 Controversy

Does research on violence and psychosis need a change of direction?

Do we know enough about the mechanisms which link psychosis to violence? Taylor (2005) argues that research showing that the risk of violence in society attributable to people with schizophrenia is very low at 4 per cent of violent incidents. This does not help us clinically when it comes to the risk presented by a

BOX 21.2 (continued)

particular individual with schizophrenia. She suggests that we need to look at the symptoms which increase the risk of physical violence. However, studies of such symptoms are beset with the sort of methodological difficulties which characterise studies of the relationship between psychosis and violence in general. Taylor's view is that there is too much emphasis on the statistical correlation between violence and psychosis, which may reflect that researchers have been concentrating on the wrong question. Evidence suggests that violence is generally an interplay between the individual and the social context. For example, we need to understand what sort of person becomes the target of the violence of psychotic persons.

What is it about some individuals with psychosis which makes it more likely that they will exhibit violence whereas others do not act violently? Taylor makes three main points about this:

- Persecutory delusions and passivity delusions are known to be associated with violence, but we need to know whether there are different factors which result in these different delusions resulting in violence.
- Some offenders reoffend many times violently whereas others reoffend just once but extremely seriously – so are these very different patterns of violence to be understood in very different ways?
- Very little is known chronologically about the changes in factors such as family environment and peer relationships which may lead to later violence.

In other words, there is a great deal yet to be learnt about why a small proportion of people with psychosis actually act violently.

Who among the mentally ill is violent?

The origins of criminals with major mental disorders (schizophrenia, major depression, bipolar disorder, other non-toxic psychoses) are not uniform. There are two clearly definable groups (Hodgins, 1997; Hodgins, Cote and Toupin, 1998):

- Early starters have a stable history of antisocial behaviour from childhood and throughout their lives. Interestingly, within the criminal justice system, they are not usually identified as mentally disordered. When they are in the acute stages of mental illness, they show no pattern of antisocial behaviour, so they are not seen by the psychiatric services as criminal or antisocial.
- Late starters do not have the early history of criminal and antisocial behaviour. Such behaviours emerge only at about the same time as symptoms of the mental disorder appear. The late starters are more likely to be positively helped by treatment of the mental disorder.
- Laajasalo and Häkkänen (2004) studied the schizophrenics in their sample by subdividing them into those whose criminal convictions started by the age of 18 years (early starters) and those whose criminal convictions began after that age (late starters). Early-start offenders, compared with the late-start offenders, were more likely to have killed following an argument, were less likely to kill an acquaintance, and were more likely to kill their victims by strangulation using some object. Overall, however, despite these differences, the use of crime scene characteristics was only modestly successful in predicting the age of onset of their criminal career.

It is possible that at least some of the violence of the mentally ill has not been included in the analysis of the relationship between violence and mental illness. If we concentrate our attention on the sort of violence that is measured by criminal convictions and recidivism, we probably underestimate the violence of the mentally ill. The violence of the mentally ill when inpatients in clinics and hospitals is unlikely to lead to prosecution and conviction. It probably leads to prosecution only when it is very extreme. Inpatient violence ranges from 3 per cent for hospitalised patients to 45 per cent for outpatients to 62 per cent for committed individuals (Dernevik, Johansson and Grann, 2000). Obviously, this is a clearer issue in relationship to violence in an institution or prison than out in the community. For instance, Dernevik *et al.* (2000) found some evidence of the effectiveness of risk management on violent incidents. High-risk management was the amount of time spent on a high-security ward with no community access. Medium-risk management was an amount of time spent living in the hospital but with some access to occupational and recreational activities in the community. Low-risk management was time spent in a less secure living arrangement and having access to the community while still being regularly monitored. While a standard risk assessment measure predicted violence in the final two risk situations well, it was a poor predictor within the high-security arrangement.

Mental illness and crime in general

While the threat of violence by the mentally ill has been a major issue, there is a more general question of the general criminality of those suffering from a major mental illness. According to Hodgins (1997), three different types of evidence support the association between major mental illness and criminality:

- Major long-term studies of people born in a particular time period which show that those who develop a major mental illness also tend to have higher levels of criminality.
- Studies that compare the criminality of those suffering a major mental disorder on release into the community with members of that same community with no mental disorder.
- Studies showing the higher levels of mental illness in convicted offenders.

A good example of the relevant research is a study of the 15,000 people born in Stockholm during 1953 (Hodgins, 1992). This was an unselected sample except in so far as people no longer living in Stockholm ten years later were excluded. The figures varied somewhat by gender, but there was an association between the development of a major mental disorder and having committed a criminal offence by the age of 30. For men, 32 per cent with no mental disorder (or mental retardation) became criminal, but 50 per cent of those with a major mental disorder did so. For women, 6 per cent of the non-mentally-ill compared with 19 per cent of the mentally ill became criminal. The risks were somewhat greater for violent than non-violent crime. This and other research (Hodgins, Mednick, Brennan, Schulsinger and Engberg 1996) suggests that many of the mentally ill commit their initial crime at the age of 30 plus. About a third of the mentally ill men and two-thirds of the mentally ill women demonstrated this pattern.

Why should there be greater criminality among the mentally ill?

The question of why criminality should be commoner among those with a major mental disorder needs to be addressed. There are a number of explanations (Hodgins, 1997):

- The police easily detect mentally ill offenders because they tend to offend in public, do not flee the crime scene too readily and are more likely to confess their crimes. Research evidence on this is equivocal.
- The comorbidity of major mental disorders with alcoholism and drug abuse. In other words, alcoholism and drug abuse in combination encourages criminality. These conditions seem to exist in high proportions among offenders with a major mental disorder.
- Treatment delivery is more problematic with deinstitutionalisation and care in the community. This may be made worse by the greater rights of patients to refuse treatment.

Violent victimisation of the mentally ill

One intriguing possible explanation of the link between mental illness and violent crime emerges out of the observation that the mentally ill are actually proportionately more likely to be victims of crime than members of the general public. Hiday, Swanson, Swartz, Borum and Wagner (2001) interviewed severely mentally ill patients (e.g. schizophrenic or another psychotic disorder) who had been involuntarily admitted to a psychiatric unit. Some of them had substance abuse histories. In the four months prior to the interview, over a quarter (27 per cent) had been the victim of some sort of crime, 8 per cent had been a victim of a violent crime and 22 per cent had been a victim of a non-violent crime. However, half of the sample was known to have acted violently in the same time period. Thus it cannot be said that these violent acts were simply fights involving a mentally ill person rather than attacks on a mentally ill person, for example. Compared with the general population, the rates of non-violent victimisation of the mentally ill were average in this study, though this is not the usual finding of research (see below). On the other hand, the mentally ill were rather more likely to be victims of violent crime than were members of the general population. This was still the case when demographic variables were controlled in the analysis. Consequently, it seems unlikely that the relationship between mental illness and being a victim of violent crime is a spurious one. However, since this was a cross-sectional study, one should be cautious about inferring exactly what the causal relationship is. Nevertheless, the findings of this study are consistent with the view that a mentally ill person may be violent because of their earlier violent victimisation.

Maniglio (2009) searched major research databases and found nine studies published between 1966 and 2007 concerning the prevalence of crime victimisation among the severely mentally ill. His search keywords included 'depression', 'mental illness', 'psychiatric/mental disorders', 'psychosis', and 'schizophrenia'. The retrieved studies involved research on 5000 different patients. The mentally ill faced a high risk of victimisation by others. Prevalence rates for violent criminal victimisation based on self-reports were found to be 4–35 per cent according to the study and non-violent victimisation ranged from 8 to 28 per cent, unlike the findings of Hiday *et al.* above. It is not easy to find explanations of the considerable variation in prevalence estimates from study to study. Possibilities include the at-risk period of time which was used for victimisation and whether an urban or rural location was involved. Remarkably, criminal victimisation was between 2 and 140 times higher than figures for the general population. There was evidence that a number of factors such as alcohol and or illicit drug use, homelessness, more extreme symptoms and involvement in a criminal lifestyle were associated with increased levels of victimisation.

Just why should the mentally ill be prone to suffer from violent victimisation? One possibility is that an intervening factor in the relationship is stress – the mentally ill tend to be more susceptible to violent when they are under stress. Stress may make the mentally ill deplete in resources to deal effectively with inter-personal relationships. They might 'fly off the handle' more easily when stressed which leads to inter-personal conflict and friction. Teasdale (2009) tested this possibility in the US but found no evidence to support the idea that violent victimisation increased at times of stress in a simple, direct fashion among the mentally ill. However, some other possible mechanisms linking mental illness and victimisation were investigated:

- Stress and gender interact in ways which leads to different patterns of response to stress in men and women. Men tend to adopt flight or fight strategies during stress but women, in contrast, use coping strategies involving tending and befriending. Thus stress should increase male victimisation but decrease female victimisation.
- Violent victimisation of the mentally ill increases when things happen or they do things which decrease the guardianship (the watchful eye) that others have over them. So mentally ill people are better protected from violent victimisation if they are married or working. This is because their partner and their supervisor, for example, provide a certain amount of guardianship.
- Increased levels of symptoms may indicate to others the vulnerability of the mentally ill person, which makes them more exposed to victimisation. Furthermore, they may not be able to look after themselves effectively. Another alternative is that their symptoms may involve their becoming more socially conflictful or failing to engage in normal social protocols.

The research was based on data from the MacArthur Violence Risk Assessment Study, which was a longitudinal study of people released from psychiatric hospitals. The researchers found support for all three of the mechanisms listed above.

Although these research studies constitute progress, a great deal more work will be needed before this area of victim research is well understood.

The special issue of psychopaths and crime

There is no doubt that some psychopaths engage in criminal behaviour. There is also no doubt that there are many psychopaths in prison. However, this leads to the important issue of just what it is about psychopathy which leads to crime. Is criminal behaviour a symptom of psychopathy or is criminal behaviour a consequence of the abnormal personality characteristics which define psychopathy? One can see, for example, that since psychopaths are impulsive and irresponsible this may lead to them getting in trouble with the law. The concepts of the psychopath and psychopathy have been among the most researched topics in recent years in forensic and criminal psychology. Nevertheless, they have slowly developed over a long period of time, starting from the beginning of the nineteenth century (Forrester, Ozdural, Muthukumaraswamy and Carroll, 2008). Pinel (1809) formulated a condition which he termed *manie sans délire*. This was primarily a disorder of the emotions rather than thinking and, as such, was an important breakthrough in the way psychiatric disorders were conceived, since it extended conceptions from mental conditions to emotional conditions. Various monomanias were proposed by Esquirol (1838) – one of which included *lesions of the will* which allowed the individual to carry out bad acts which were based neither on reason nor emotion. These developments gradually led to the concept of the psychopath. Partridge (1930) was responsible for developing the closely related concept of sociopathy, which had all sorts of social maladjustment as a defining essential feature. Most important of all, Cleckley in *The Mask of Sanity* (1941) provided clear criteria for the diagnosis of psychopathy. These describe psychopathy in terms of deceitfulness; egocentricity; failure to follow a life plan; grandiose interpersonal style; inability to experience anxiety; inability to love; manipulativeness; shallowness and superficial charm. Criminality was not particularly germane to Cleckley's defining features of psychopathy.

It was Cleckley's conceptualisation which Robert Hare turned to when developing his highly influential *Psychopathy Checklist (PCL)* and the *Psychopathy Checklist Revised (PCL-R)* (see Chapter 27). It is fair to suggest that these measures have dominated in research into psychopathy and the checklists have been referred to as the gold standard for assessing psychopathy. There is good evidence of its power as a predictor of violent recidivism (see Chapter 27). Despite acknowledging Cleckley's influence on his work, Hare elevates criminality to a more central position into his conceptualisation than Cleckley had. For example, Hare's PCL and PCL-R questionnaires include items referring to aspects of antisocial and criminal behaviour.

This has led to a debate among researchers which is of considerable importance. Skeem and Cooke (2010) argue that the massive amounts of research generated by the PCL and PCL-R have largely concentrated on its predictive power in relation to criminal recidivism. They believe that Hare's concentration on criminality in relation to psychopathy has been the basis of substantial conceptual confusions. In particular, they say, there is a risk of equating the theoretical construct of psychopathy with the means of measuring that construct (usually the PCL-R). For them, the question is whether criminal behaviour is at the core of psychopathy or what they refer to as merely a 'downstream correlate' of psychopathy. This is ultimately not a matter that can be resolved by statistical analyses of the PCL-R since these can only inform us about the nature of the PCL-R – the more fundamental question of what psychopathy is cannot be dealt with in this way. To stress an important point, the construct of the psychopath was to be found in the clinical and research literature long before the PCL was created. In the early writings on psychopathy, it was not discussed in tandem with criminality. Instead the focus was on trying to understand the interpersonal and affective characteristics of the psychopath – what might be termed the psychopath's emotional detachment. Provocatively, Skeem and Cooke argue that a person with all of the characteristics of psychopathy as defined, say, by Cleckley is nevertheless unlikely to be diagnosed as a psychopath. In addition, they need a history of violent and criminal behaviour.

Despite this fundamental argument, Cooke and others have debated the use of the PCL-R with Hare. Essentially, Cooke argues that items related to criminality should not be part of the measurement of psychopathy. Leaving these out means that the PCL-R corresponds more closely to Cleckley's conceptualisation of psychopathy. Cooke and others (e.g. Cooke and Michie, 2001) simply deleted items to do with criminality from the PCL-R. They found that this revision led to there being three different components or factors underlying the measure. These correspond to the first three factors of the model shown in Figure 21.4. Hare (2003) then more or less reinstated the criminality items, which resulted in all of the four factors shown in Figure 21.4. The difference is that Cook's

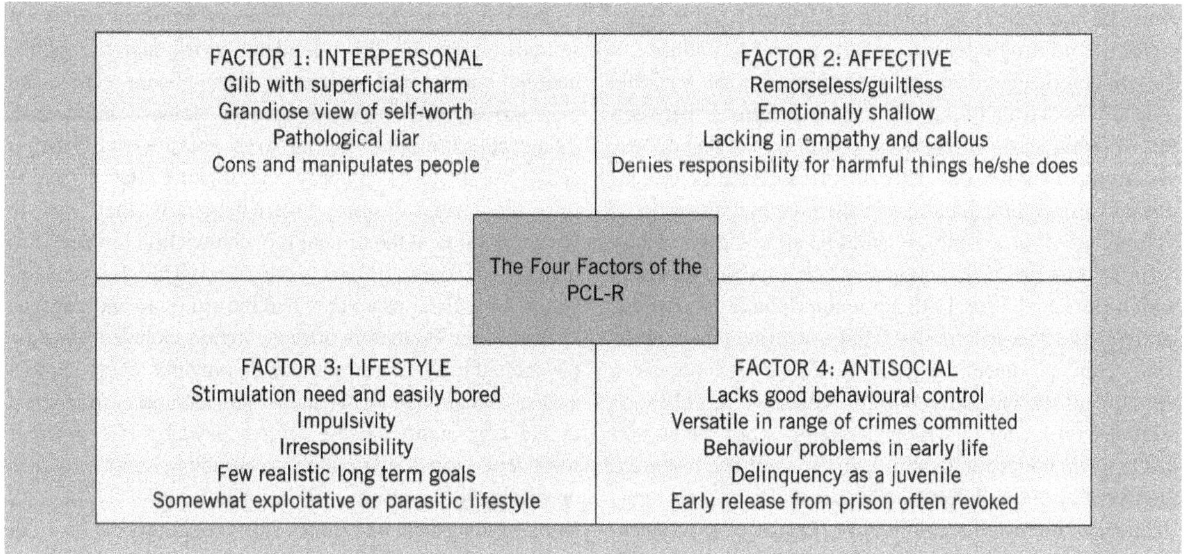

Figure 21.4 The Four Factors underlying the PCL-R Measure of Psychopathy

three-factor model concentrates on psychopathy in terms of personality pathology and personal dispositions, whereas Hare's four-factor model involves social behaviours (including criminality) as well. Of course, this highlights the issue of what the concept of psychopathy is and what its relation to crime is. Take a look at Factor 4 in Figure 21.4 and you will see that it is measured, in part, using items about delinquency and offence versatility. So it is not surprising that psychopathy as measured by the PCL-R predicts criminality – the relationship is a tautology in this sense.

Perhaps a little futilely, given Skeem and Cooke's insistence that the conceptualisation of psychopathy is a theoretical issue rather than an empirical one, Roberts and Coid (2007) chose to address some of the issues empirically. Their study was based on a major national sample of prisoners in England and Wales. The final sample included almost 500 male and female prisoners. They were interviewed extensively and assessed for psychopathy using Hare's PCL-R. The relationships between the overall PCL-R score, scores on Hare's four factors of psychopathy and criminal offences were explored using multiple regression. Briefly, the researchers looked at the relationships between the total score on the PCL-R and lifetime offending and controlled for the influence on the relationship of Factors 1 to 3 as well as the additional variables of age, ethnicity, alcohol problems and drug problems. So is there any relationship between the PCL-R Factor 4 when the influence of the other three (undisputed) PCL-R factors is removed? The researchers found that even after all of these controls had been applied, total scores on the PCL-R were correlated with many offending categories such as robbery/blackmail, burglary and theft, violence and so forth, with the exceptions of murder and manslaughter, sex offences and drug offences. A further analysis adding in the disputed Factor 4 as a further control variable resulted in virtually all of the associations between PCL-R total score and the various criminal behaviours becoming insignificant. This, to the authors, is indicative of the need for Factor 4 in the conceptualisation of psychopathy but, equally, it could be argued that the key defining features of psychopathy (the first three factors which Hare and Cook both agree upon) have no particular relevance to criminality. However, there is a problem. That is, Factor 3 (which Cooke accepts as a measure of psychopathy purely defined) is highly correlated with Factor 4 (which Cooke does not see as part of the basic conceptualisation). In terms of the research, the two were very difficult to separate. This is, perhaps, stronger evidence that criminality (Factor 4) is a necessary part of the construct of psychopathy. Of course, this is a matter of the underlying theory of psychopathy; it does not undermine the value of the PCL-R as a predictive measure in the field of forensic and criminal psychology.

Reconviction and mental illness

Of particular public concern are those groups of offenders who commit serious offences but are found to have a major mental disorder. There have been a number of high-profile cases in which it would appear that offenders seek to use provisions for dealing with offenders with such problems to avoid prison. In England, many such offenders would be detained in high-security special hospitals such as Broadmoor and Rampton. Among the criteria for such admissions would be that the offender has one of the major psychiatric classifications according to *DSM-IV* (see Box 21.1) and is an immediate danger to the public. The majority in such hospitals have a psychotic illness; a smaller proportion have personality disorders (e.g. borderline personality disorder, antisocial personality disorder, schizoid and paranoid); and a very small proportion have general learning disability. Jamieson and Taylor (2004) studied a complete cohort of patients discharged from special hospitals in a single year (1984). A 12-year follow-up period was possible and the releases were after the implementation of important legislation in the Mental Health Act of 1983. Some would have been discharged to another type of hospital, some would be returned to a prison following hospitalisation in the special hospital because of a major crisis in their behaviour in prison or returned to court for sentencing, and others would be discharged into the community.

Reconviction data were obtained from a variety of sources, including the offenders' index and the police national computer. A quarter of patients were reconvicted of a serious offence (e.g. homicide, violence and sexual, though the commonest by far were grievous bodily harm/actual bodily harm, robbery and assault) after discharge from the special hospital. Overwhelmingly, they were in the community at the time of the reconviction (86 per cent) though, of course, others were reconvicted for offences which took place when they had moved on to another type of institution. Predictors of reconviction included having a psychopathic disorder; number of previous court appearances; younger age on discharge; and amount of time spent in the community. Those with a psychopathic disorder were seven times more likely to commit a serious offence on discharge than those with a mental illness. Those with mental impairment and those with a psychopathic disorder were equally likely to be reconvicted.

In the United States, Gagliardi, Lovell, Peterson and Jemella (2004) studied recidivism in a sample of mentally ill offenders who had been released from Washington prisons in 1996–7. These prisoners were defined as mentally ill on the basis of having at least two of the following: 1) a diagnosis of a major mental illness recorded; 2) a prescription for indicative psychotropic medications; and 3) spending over 30 days on a residential mental health treatment programme while in prison. Quite clearly, this is a different sort of mentally ill sample from the one used in the special hospitals study just described. Presumably, the members of the US sample were regarded as less dangerous. Also, the follow-up period in the US study was only 27–55 months. Nevertheless, after release, the mentally ill offenders demonstrated high levels of arrest or charge for crime. Over three-quarters (77 per cent) came to the attention of the police in this way. Forty-one per cent of the entire sample were found guilty of a new crime, which is much the same as the 38 per cent of a similar sample of offenders who were not mentally ill. The figures for violent crimes are particularly relevant – 10 per cent of the mentally ill committed a violent felony offence – exactly the same percentage as the comparison sample of non-mentally ill offenders. Felonies are grave – that is, serious – offences.

The police and mental illness

One important but so far undeveloped theme runs through this chapter – the role of the police. How the police deal with the mentally ill is fundamental to their treatment in the criminal justice system.

There is some research with the mentally ill about how they have been treated by the police. For example, in Vancouver, researchers found a general satisfaction among the mentally ill who had been in contact with police in that they were treated fairly and appropriately. Nevertheless, there was considerable evidence that such contacts could also be negative experiences (Livingston, Desmarais, Verdun-Jones, Parent, Michalak and Brink, 2014). Furthermore, the mentally ill did not have such a positive attitude towards the police as the general population. They did not have the same degree of confidence in the police and did not see themselves as being as fairly treated by the police (Livingston *et al.*, 2014). However, there is more objective evidence concerning police interactions with mentally ill people.

One basic question concerns the adequacy of the police's ability to recognise mental illness. Baksheev, Ogloff and Thomas (2012) researched police practices involved in the identification of mentally ill arrestees in police custody. A sample of people detained at two police stations in Melbourne was studied. They were assessed using the structured clinical interview for *DSM-IV-TR* as well as two screening tools:

- the Brief Jail Mental Health Screen (BJMHS)
- Jail Screening Assessment Tool (JSAT).

The police procedure misidentified mentally ill individuals as normal quite frequently. That is, there was a high frequency of false negatives. The police system in Australia is based on the prisoner information record, which is a file located at the police station and contains police documentation. It contains the custody risk assessment form which is usually completed by the custody sergeant when the suspect is taken into custody. The questions include 'Depressed or suicidal?' and 'Mentally ill or been diagnosed with any mental illness?'. The two screening tools were relatively better at identifying the mentally ill using the *DSM-IV-TR* as the 'gold standard' for the diagnosis.

Kesic, Thomas and Ogloff (2013) introduce a further factor into the situation – the use of force by police officers against the mentally disordered. Their study found that, of the individuals against whom the Australian police used force, over 7 per cent appeared to be mentally ill. In terms of the police record, those who appeared to the police to have a mental disorder were over four times more likely to be seen as irrational and unstable by officers. These were the police's own assessments based on what they observed at the time of the incidents. However, perceptions of alcohol involvement were lower for the mentally disordered than incidents in general. Half of the mentally disordered were recorded as manifesting violent behaviour at the scene of the incident and a third used abusive language. It needs to be added that this group also threaten with weapons more and use violence against the police. In terms of actual injuries, these incidents involving the mentally disordered did not lead to especially serious consequences. Almost half of the mentally disordered suffered some sort of injury when force was used, but their injuries were mild. These incidents were most likely to occur at residential premises and, in many cases, the police knew that they were being sent to a mental-health-related incident. Despite this, usually the police knew nothing of the previous violent history of the mentally ill person. The police were twice as likely to use pepper spray in the mental disorder incidents and this was the case after controlling for situational and other characteristics. This is in agreement with other studies. The police mainly threatened or used weaponless contact overwhelmingly and the perceived mentally disordered followed this pattern too. However, the police threatening the use of firearms occurred in less than 4 per cent of times and none of the mentally disordered had a firearm in any of the incidents.

Main points

- There seems to be little doubt that some forms of mental illness and certain patterns of symptoms elevate the likelihood of violent crime and crime in general. A major difficulty is in identifying exactly what the pattern of risk is and who among the mentally ill is the most likely to be violent and criminal. It is also difficult to form a clear impression of the risk posed by the mentally ill. Other factors, such as drug or alcohol abuse, seem to have much greater effects relative to mental illness simply because there are proportionately fewer mentally ill people. So, the relationship between mental illness and crime is relatively small and, in general, the public is at greater risk from, for example, young men and substance abusers than from schizophrenics. The latter are relatively rare in the population.
- Exactly why mental illness is associated with violence is equally difficult to explain. It is a little too simplistic to suggest that mental illness is a cause of violence. There are many reasons for this. For example, some of the drugs used to treat mental illness are known to cause aggression. Furthermore, the extent of the relationship between mental illness and violence can change with changes in social policy dealing with the mentally ill. With the use of care in the community, the risk to the public may increase.
- The risk factors that predict the likelihood that a mentally ill person will commit a violent offence are increasingly understood. Factors which affect the pattern, apart from type of diagnosis, include whether antisocial behaviour began in childhood or much later, and hallucinations and delusions. The mentally ill may have an elevated risk of being victims of violence, though whether this is the consequence of their aggressive behaviour is not known.

Further reading

McMurran, M., Khalifa, N. and Gibbon, S. (2009) *Forensic Mental Health* Cullompton: Willan.

Shug, R.A., and Fradella, H.G. (2014) *Mental Illness and Crime*. London: Sage.

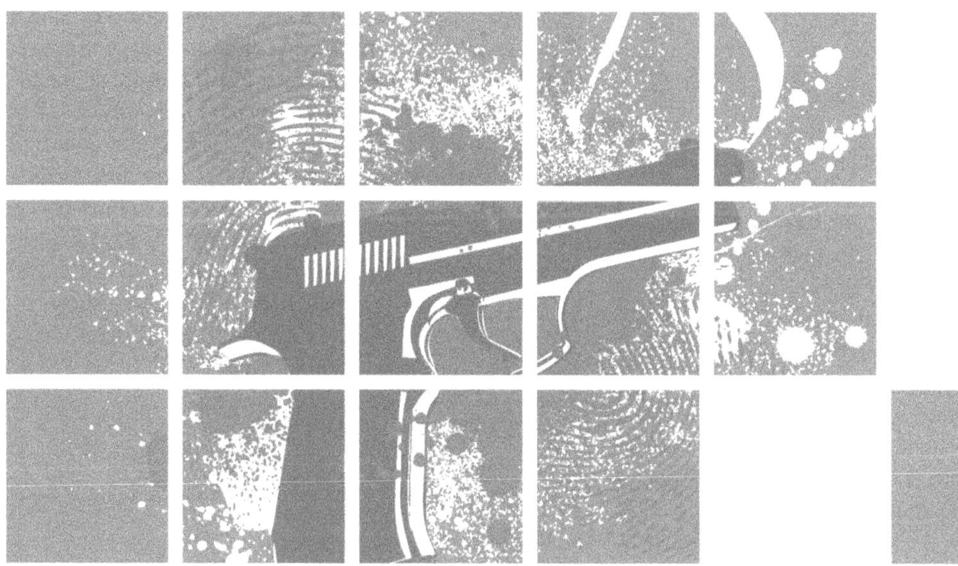

Chapter 22

Mental, personality and intellectual problems in court

Overview

- The psychological and intellectual states of some individuals determine what happens to them in law courts. Competency to stand trial refers to mental state at the time of trial whereas the psychological state of the defendant at the time of the crime may, for example, provide mitigating circumstances relevant to sentencing (e.g. diminished responsibility/capacity and insanity pleas).
- Defendants have to be competent at the time of their trial. The definition of this depends on the legal jurisdiction in question. Typically, a fundamental requirement is that defendants should be able to participate in their defence (with the aid of a lawyer) and understand the court procedure. Substantial minorities of juvenile offenders fail the competency requirement when assessed by a standardised test of competency.
- The MacArthur Competence Assessment Tool for Criminal Adjudication deals with the American standard of competence. Nevertheless, clinicians such as psychiatrists and psychologists are more likely to make such assessments. There is evidence that a psychotic illness diagnosis, non-psychotic diagnosis and being unemployed are predictive of an incompetence assessment by the clinician. Other research suggests that, generally, psychiatrists are unaffected by legally irrelevant factors when coming to their decisions. For example, having had a spell of time in a psychiatric hospital is not relevant to current competency to stand trial.
- Individuals with a learning disability are often vulnerable and may be subject to various forms of sexual abuse, for example. As such, their testimony may be essential for justice to be done. They can supply good-quality evidence and can make legally competent witnesses. However, the style of questioning adopted with them should be open-ended, as closed or leading questioning can lead to poor-quality evidence from them.
- Psychopaths do not always manifest the criminality which is frequently used to characterise them. Since the condition may be adaptive, it is difficult to equate it with the idea of a dysfunctional mental disease. The *McNaughten* rule suggests that a person is not criminally responsible if at the time of the crime they did not know the nature and quality of the act they did. Despite this, some experts believe that psychopathy is a reason for more punishment, not less. Others argue that psychopaths do not pass through crucial stages of moral development, which leaves them incapable of knowing right from wrong; thus punishment is inappropriate since they cannot learn from it.

Introduction

There are a number of circumstances in which a defendant's psychological state may be taken into account in court. These do not necessarily apply at the same stages of a trial. For example, competence to stand trial needs to be considered prior to the start of the trial as this decision determines what happens next. The reasons for judging a person incompetent to stand trial have to do with poor cognitive functioning or mental illness. Competence to stand trial has nothing to do with the reason why an individual committed a criminal act; it refers solely to a person's situation at the time of their trial. If someone is judged incompetent to stand trial, it does not mean that they will go free but merely that they will be processed differently – for example, they might be sent to a psychiatric facility. Sentencing decisions may be influenced by psychological factors which were present at the time of the offence. That is, there are some psychological factors which might work in mitigation of the sentence. Of course, simply because an individual has a psychological condition is not necessarily a reason for more lenient punishment. Courts of law are not psychologists' consulting rooms; arguments appropriate in court are not necessarily ones that would be appropriate in a psychology lecture. Consequently, there are controversies, as we shall see, about the standing of diagnoses such as psychopathy as a mitigating factor. Indeed, some argue that psychopathy is an aggravating factor and may warrant greater punishment.

There are additional points in the criminal justice system where the individual's mental state may be considered (Gunn and Buchanan, 2006):

- during the police investigation;
- when making the plea of guilt or otherwise;
- during the trial;
- when deciding the sentence.

Figure 22.1 summarises Gunn and Buchanan's argument about differences between the UK and the US.

ENGLAND AND WALES	USA (E.G. CONNECTICUT)
Police investigation: If the person appears to be or if there is good reason to think the suspect is mentally ill then they are to be treated as such and an appropriate adult may be appointed and they may be diverted into the psychiatric system.	**Police investigation:** The individuals protected by exercising their Miranda rights but this is made less likely by their mental condition and they may well waive their rights putting them at risk.
Plea: The individual may be judged unfit to plead by virtue of factors such as not understanding the difference between a guilty and a not guilty plea or being unable to understand the evidence against them.	**Plea:** There is a much greater likelihood that an individual will be assessed as unfit to plead and they may be sent to a unit to restore competence.
Trial: The judge may decide that it is undesirable that an individual gives evidence. A court may remand a person to a hospital for treatment rather than to custody.	**Trial:** The individual may be returned to the court for trial if their competency is restored within a reasonable period of time.
Sentence: Especially if they plead guilty and substantial psychiatric evidence provided in mitigation, the most common outcome is a hospital order but prison and treatment in the community are alternatives.	**Sentence:** There is no equivalent of hospital orders in the USA. The psychiatric condition is not regarded as pertinent to the sentence although it is frequently introduced in mitigation. The most common outcome is that the individual will be sent to prison and receive psychiatric treatment there.

Figure 22.1 Possible relevance of mental health considerations at the various stages of the criminal justice system

Competence/capacity to stand trial

Many different criminal justice systems require that defendants should be able to contribute effectively to their own defence (Hollin and Swaffer, 1995). Competency requirements to assist in one's own defence during legal proceedings date back to the fourteenth century and possibly earlier. Historically, common law courts refused to try those who were incompetent because of mental illness or mental defects (Otto, 2006). Ultimately, it is the accused and not their lawyers who makes the decisions relevant to the trial. The requirement of competence is necessary in adversarial systems of justice. In these, winning in court is the key objective of the court appearance. As such, the opposing sides of prosecution and defence line up against each other, much as in a battle. Should the defendant be a hapless individual incapable of understanding and coping with this affray, then is it possible for him or her to have a fair trial? It is clearly important for the public credibility of the legal system that: 1) trials are fair; 2) that the legal process is dignified and demonstrates integrity; and 3) that the defendant understands the reason why they are being punished (Zapf and Roesch, 2001). A 'reasonable and legitimate' justice process would be severely compromised without the requirement of competence to stand trial. In contrast, the inquisitorial systems employed in many parts of Continental Europe and elsewhere involve much more of a guided search for the 'truth' by the inquiring judge. So, in the inquisitorial court system, the issue of fitness is not so important as it is in the adversarial system. It is noteworthy, then, that the inquisitorial legal systems of Austria and Denmark, for example, have no 'fitness to stand trial' criteria. As might be expected, psychiatric reports may be called for if there appear to be any problems with the mental state of the accused that may help inform the judgement of the court.

The issue of competence is more frequently raised in some jurisdictions than in others. Competence is a commoner issue in the United States than in the United Kingdom, for example (Hollin and Swaffer, 1995). In England and Wales, the annual numbers of defendants judged unfit to stand trial is very small – around 30 cases per year – which carries the implication that there are numbers of defendants who stand trial who should not. Some do not stand trial because they are taken out of the justice system at an earlier stage under mental health legislation. In other countries, such as the United States, the competence to stand trial decision is much more common. For example, Bonnie and Grisso (2000) estimate that there are about 60,000 competency evaluations in the United States annually. Sometimes competence to stand trial is referred to as capacity to stand trial.

The following case from the United States demonstrates graphically some of the problems associated with the issue of competence:

> Andy was just 11 when he started hanging around with the teenage gang members in his neighborhood. They used him as a lookout when they sold drugs . . . until one drug deal turned violent and two people were shot. That's how Andy ended up facing a charge of murder. The prosecutor offered a deal: Andy could admit he was there, testify against the others, and face a few years in juvenile detention. Otherwise he would be transferred to adult court and, if found guilty, spend a much longer time in detention and prison. Andy had just a few minutes to make a decision that would determine the rest of his life. He chose to take the risk: he would go to trial.
>
> (Steinberg, 2003)

The psychologist who assessed Andy's competence to stand trial asked him whether he understood what would happen if he was found guilty of the crime. 'I'll go to prison for a long, long time,' was his reply. He was assessed a few weeks later by another person and asked the identical question. Andy gave much the same reply, but he was then asked to explain what he had said. His reply was that 'It's like when you do something bad and your mother sends you to your room for the whole weekend.' Andy seems not to understand the nature of the process of which he was part, since his conception of imprisonment is inadequate. This is not an exceptional circumstance. Steinberg (2003) reports the findings of a study of the competence of young Americans to stand trial using a standardised competence assessment procedure. Thirty per cent of 11- to 13-year-olds were not competent to stand trial, as were 19 per cent of 14- and 15-year-olds and 12 per cent of later adolescents and young adults. This is of major importance in a country such as the United States where increasingly young people have been tried in adult rather than juvenile courts.

There is a concept in English law that dates back to the fourteenth century and is also found in Australian law, for example. *Doli incapax* refers to the assumption that children below a certain age are incapable of being evil, which may be equated with an incapability of committing a crime because they do not know the difference between right and wrong. *Doli incapax* is a presumption and it does not mean that children cannot be tried for crimes; however, it has to be established that they did know what they were doing when they committed the offence. Without using the *doli incapax* terminology, other countries may have ages below which children may not be tried in an adult court. This varies substantially from legislature to legislature.

The United Kingdom

The court, prior to the commencement of the trial proper, assesses competence. The criteria vary according to jurisdiction. The criteria in the United Kingdom determining whether a defendant is fit to stand trial include the abilities to:

- comprehend the details of the evidence;
- follow court proceedings;
- instruct lawyers effectively;
- understand that jurors may be challenged (objected to);
- understand the meaning and implications of the charges (Grubin, 1996a).

A number of matters are important (Grubin, 1996a):

- Competence is judged by the jury in the United Kingdom (elsewhere it may be an issue for the judge solely).
- The consequences of being found unfit to stand trial are drastic. In the United Kingdom, the defendant may be compulsorily detained in some sort of hospital for indeterminate periods of time. Given this serious outcome, the issue of fitness to stand trial or competence is far more frequent for trials of extremely serious offences. In the United Kingdom, modern legislation requires the following. After the decision that the defendant is not competent to stand trial, a hearing is held to determine whether it is likely that the defendant committed the offence. If unlikely or disproved, then the accused will be discharged. This ensures that the judgement of incompetence for the innocent is not followed by extremely serious consequences.
- White, Meares and Batchelor (2014) carried out a systematic review of studies and dissertations on the role of cognition in fitness to stand trial. In addition to intelligence, the decision that an individual is fit to stand trial tended to be associated with better cognitive skills. They tended to have better verbal memory and memory generally, faster processing speed, and better visuo-perceptual skills. So cognition is important in fitness to stand trial assessments. Poor mental functioning, however, is not the main reason for classifying an offender as unfit to stand trial. British evidence (Grubin, 1996b) indicates that the majority are classified as having schizophrenia.

The United States and Canada

Court rulings in Canada and the United States have established that decisions to waive counsel, decisions to confess and decisions to plead guilty all require a certain and invariant level of competency, which is unaffected by particular circumstances (Coles, 2004). In some parts of the United States, expert witnesses can only advise the court about an individual's abilities relevant to their competency – not on the matter of their competency to stand trial directly. In the United States, competence to stand trial, according to the US Supreme Court, is whether (the defendant) has 'sufficient present ability to consult with his lawyer with a reasonable degree of rational understanding' – and whether he has a 'rational as well as factual understanding of the proceedings' against him. This standard was established in the Supreme Court ruling of *Dusky* v. *United States* (1960) (Heilbrun, Hawk and Tate 1996). In practical terms, competence to stand trial requires that the accused can comprehend the charges against them and understand what the judge, jury and lawyers do. Variants of this definition of competence are used by most states, though in these no mental conditions are defined as limiting this capacity. The courts may take the advice of professionals in the field but ultimately it is a decision of the courts and not experts. Furthermore, a defendant may be competent to be tried on one charge but incompetent to be tried on another. For example, drunken driving might need a lower competence level than a complex case of fraud (Otto, 2006). However, in Canada, there is a different competency that does not include the criterion of rationality. The Canadian standard only requires the defendant to be able to communicate with and understand their lawyer (Zapf and Roesch, 2001).

Assessing competence is a specialist skill and there is a risk that different practitioners would not agree on an individual's competence to stand trial. There are, of course, guidelines to help establish common standards in the United States (e.g. Baker, Lichtenberg and Moye, 1998). However, one important development in the United States is the *MacArthur Competence Assessment Tool for Criminal Adjudication*. This is a standardised instrument to assess fitness to participate in legal proceedings within the US legal system (Otto *et al.*, 1998). There are other MacArthur competence measures (e.g. for competence to agree to medical treatment). The MacArthur charity funded the MacArthur Research Network on Mental Health and the Law, which developed this competence measure. The assessor using the competence assessment tool presents a short description of a crime and consequent events. The administrator then asks a series of questions concerning court procedures, the roles of various people (e.g. the jury), and the reasoning processes underlying the decisions made in court.

Strictly speaking, the MacArthur Competence Assessment Tool for Criminal Adjudication is applicable only to the United States. It may assess people incompetent to stand trial who would be competent in other jurisdictions. Zapf and Roesch (2001) compared the *Fitness Interview Test (FIT)* with the *MacArthur Competence Assessment Tool*. The FIT measures competence in terms of Canadian legal definitions, whereas the MacArthur tool measures competence in

American terms. Both measures were given to a sample of males remanded in a forensic psychiatry institute. Although the two measures correlated moderately well, it was clear that the MacArthur measure was more likely to classify individuals as unfit to plead than the measure based on the Canadian standard of competence. This confirms that the American criteria for competence are stricter than the Canadian. This is a reminder, if a further one is needed, that forensic and criminal psychologists must be aware of the legal codes and practices of the jurisdiction in which they operate.

Any clinical assessment will be to some extent subjective. However, what sort of agreement might one expect between different competency assessors? Clinical assessments of competence to stand trial and court decisions concerning competency concur highly. Of course, a high degree of overlap may simply reflect that clinicians and courts share the same biases. Cooper and Zapf (2003) looked at the question of how competency decisions are made by clinicians by using a variety of demographic, clinical and criminological measures extracted from files on over 400 individuals assessed for competency. Only about a fifth of those assessed had been previously classified as unfit to stand trial. Those with a psychotic disorder (e.g. schizophrenia) or with a major non-psychotic disorder were much more likely to be classified as unfit to stand trial. However, those who had an alcohol or a drug-related disorder were less likely to be deemed 'unfit to stand trial'. Four variables were strong predictors of the classification as incompetent when the researchers tried to develop a statistical model of the decisions. These were psychotic diagnosis, non-psychotic major diagnosis and non-psychotic minor illness diagnosis – all clinical dimensions – together with unemployment. Based on this model, it was possible to predict the actual classification of 89 per cent of the competent cases and 47 per cent of the incompetent cases. Thus prediction was substantially superior for the competent cases. The authors argue that because the clinical variables are so important in the decision-making model, there is no evidence of bias in the judgements. This, however, assumes that there are no biases in these clinical assessments in the first place. Furthermore, there are a lot of instances where these seemingly rational judgements fail to apply – for example, 53 per cent of the incompetent cases could not be predicted on the basis of the clinical variables plus unemployment.

Some research provides a more reserved interpretation. Plotnick, Porter and Bagby (1998) used an experimental design. Psychiatrists rated a number of vignettes relevant to fitness evaluations. In some conditions, the vignettes actually contained legally irrelevant information which should not be considered as part of the evaluation of fitness to plead. These potentially biasing but legally irrelevant variables were a previous psychiatric hospitalisation (or not); the nature of the current crime (violent versus petty larceny); and prior legal involvement (six prior arrests versus no prior arrests). In addition, there were several conditions that were legally pertinent to fitness evaluations. For example, the unfit condition involved the defendant having psychotic symptoms in abundance and being incapable of communicating with their lawyer. The research findings suggested that, overwhelmingly, the fit and unfit categories were correctly used. Over 70 per cent of both the fit and unfit vignettes were correctly classified. Nevertheless, for the legally fit vignettes, sometimes legally irrelevant factors affected the psychiatrists' judgements. The psychiatrists tended to misclassify legally fit individuals if they had been charged with a violent crime and had a lot of previous psychiatric admissions to hospital but no previous arrests. In other words, classification as fit or unfit to plead could be affected by legally irrelevant information but, nevertheless, the psychiatrists tended to make correct classifications in general.

For anyone wishing to understand the similarities and differences between the British and US systems, Gunn and Buchanan (2006) describe how a fictitious case would be treated in the two countries.

There are circumstances in which an offender believes that it is in their interest to feign incompetence to stand trial. Such a claim has the advantage that it delays the criminal conviction and means that the offender lives in hospital rather than prison. In the US, when a suspect is judged to be incompetent to stand trial they are usually sent for competence reinstatement treatment in hospital. Only in a minority of cases will this treatment fail. Remember that competence to stand trial refers to the trial and not to the offence. So competence reinstatement allows the trial to go ahead although it is delayed. Paradis, Solomon, Owen and Brooker (2013) prefer not to use the term 'malingering' and refer to 'suboptimal effort' instead. The accused were asked to rate their memory ability by the researchers. Claims of memory problems were regarded as indicative of possible cognitive malingering. Actually, rather few made claims of memory problems – just 15 per cent of a sample of nearly 170 individuals. The suspected cognitive malingerers underwent the assessment using two tests:

- *The Rey Fifteen-Item Test (RFT):* This test is quick to administer. A page featuring items grouped in threes in five rows are shown (Roman numbers, Arabic numbers, capital letters, small letters, and a square, circle and triangle). The task is for the offender to draw as many items as they can recall.
- *The Test of Memory Malingering (TOMM):* This test consists of 50 items assessing recognition. Offenders are given two learning trials in which 50 line drawings of common objects are shown. Then they are shown pairs of items – one new item and one of the 50 line drawings shown earlier. They have to say which they have previously seen

The suspected malingerer group had higher rates of affective disorders and lower rates of psychosis. About half of the suspected malingerers failed both of the tests. Two-thirds failed at least one of the two. Among the suspected malingerers with psychotic disorders nearly all of them failed both of the malingering tests. As there is no ground truth or gold standard to identify malingering, these findings are useful evidence that the tests may be potential indicators of malingering in this forensic setting. Nevertheless, we do not know for certain quite how good they are at spotting malingering. Paradis *et al.* caution there are sometimes other reasons why the accused may fail the malingering test. Some of those who failed seemed to have limited intellectual ability and so could not cope with even these simple memory tests. Others showed evidence of depression, which may have lowered motivation.

BOX 22.1 Forensic psychology in action

Insanity in court

Mental illness is common among non-convicted and convicted prisoners. Indeed, there may be more persons with serious mental illnesses in prisons than in mental hospitals (Blaauw, Roesch and Kerkhof, 2000). Furthermore, current prevalence rates for any psychiatric disorder for those in European prison systems have been estimated as anywhere between 37 per cent and 89 per cent, according to the study in question. Not surprisingly, then, mental conditions may have a significant bearing on a lot of trials. Issues related to mental illness and limited cognitive functioning may influence the course of a trial. This can be both in terms of the requirements of proof and mitigation of punishment. Under British law, two Latin phrases cover the requirements of proof in a criminal trial: 1) *actus reus* and 2) *mens rea*. These are not universal in all legal systems, of course, but they are important concepts in their own right:

- *Actus reus:* this is the requirement in some jurisdictions that the prosecution needs to show that a crime has indeed been committed and, further, that the accused was the person who committed that crime. This may be a matter for psychologists since forensic practitioners may be asked, for example, to evaluate the confession evidence that implicated the accused. A self-confession may have been obtained unfairly or from a person incapable of understanding the police caution, for example.
- *Mens rea:* this is the legal requirement in some jurisdictions that the accused actually understood that what they did was wrong or that they had behaved recklessly. Intentionality or recklessness is the important factor. Actually, this requirement does not apply to all crimes. Some offences are *strict liability* to which matters of recklessness or intentionality are inapplicable. Road traffic offences are often strict liability offences (see Ward, 1997). Lack of criminal intent can be used in strict liability cases, but only in mitigation.

Diminished responsibility (*diminished capacity* in the United States) is an excuse offered by the defence that, although the defendant broke the law, they are not criminally liable since their mental functioning was impaired in some way. An obvious situation in which diminished responsibility might apply is where the defendant is intellectually very challenged. There are other defences such as *insanity* that may be very similar. However, the choice between diminished responsibility and insanity defences may depend on the jurisdiction in question. Beck (1995) points out that in the United Kingdom, the defence of insanity had hardly been used. This was because disposal after a decision of 'not guilty by reason of insanity' meant indefinite diversion into a mental hospital until new legislation was enacted in 1991. Legislation changed things to allow commitment to a mental hospital for a limited time or, even, release back to the community, given certain provisions. Diminished responsibility is used as a defence only in murder trials since, if accepted, murder becomes the less serious crime of manslaughter. The only sentence for murder is a mandatory life sentence. There are a variety of options for manslaughter – probation, prison or hospital. In the United States, the use of the insanity defence is also rare and where used is rarely successful. So less than 1 per cent of felony charges would meet with an insanity defence and acquittals on the grounds of insanity occurred in about 1 in 400 felony cases (Lymburner and Roesch, 1999).

Defences of insanity and diminished responsibility/capacity (among others) may be supported by psychiatric or psychological evidence of mental disorder in the accused. This is true also of the crime of infanticide, which is a lesser form of homicide. The distinction between insanity and diminished responsibility, according to a survey of psychiatrists (Mitchell, 1997), is not something that causes difficulties for the majority of practitioners. It is also worthwhile noting that there is some question as to whether psychiatric assessment that an individual demonstrated diminished responsibility actually is acted on by courts when sentencing. Ribeaud and Manzoni (2004) suggest that, taking into account the legal seriousness of the crime, psychiatric assessment of diminished responsibility slightly *increases* the likely sentence in the Swiss cases they studied. This is clearly an issue about which more research is needed.

In the UK (as in other countries such as the United States), an offender may be placed on probation subject to the condition that they undergo psychiatric treatment. Treatment is voluntary and those who refuse it will be disposed of otherwise by the criminal justice system. In different countries, different standards apply about the involuntary treatment of the mentally ill. The UK system allows the mentally ill (and mental illness is not defined by law or regulation) to be identified solely by psychiatric opinion. Forced medication for up to three months is also allowed. This is different from the United States where substantial legislation surrounds any attempt by the authorities to deny citizens their liberty (Beck, 1995).

In the United Kingdom, recent legal provisions limit the 'right to silence' which means that a jury may interpret the silence of a witness in whatever way it wishes (Criminal Justice and Public Order Act, 1994). If it appears that the mental or physical condition of the accused means that if they do not give evidence, then the court may not make such an inference (Grubin, 1996a). This is clearly an area in which forensic experts may be expected to provide evidence on the mental condition of the accused.

Temporary psychiatric states are particularly problematic in court. For example, 'dissociation' is the term for the experience in which the individual ceases to be fully aware of themselves, time or the external environment. Dissociation may be a fairly normal everyday experience, such as when the individual becomes lost in a television programme so that the sense of the passage of time is lost and with it a sense of the surroundings. Dissociation may be a feature of post-traumatic stress disorder, for example (see Chapter 4). Bert Stone murdered his wife in Canada in 1993. Part of his account of the murder is as follows:

> I sat there with my head down while she's still yelling at me that I'm nothing but a piece of shit and that when she had talked to the police, that she had told them lies, that I was abusing her, and that they were getting all the paperwork ready to have me arrested, and that all she had to do was phone them, and once they had me arrested, that she was going to get a court order so that I wouldn't be allowed back onto our property and that I would have to go and live with my mother and run my business from there, that she was going to quit working and she was just going to stay in the house with her children and that I would have to pay her alimony and child support . . . Well, she just continued on and she just said that she couldn't stand to listen to me whistle, that every time I touched her, she felt sick, that I was a lousy fuck and that I had a little penis and that she's never going to fuck me again, and I'm just sitting there with my head down; and by this time, she's kneeling on the seat and she's yelling this in my face.
>
> (McSherry, 2004, p. 447)

His wife was killed by 47 stab wounds to her body. Stone was unaware of the moments during which he stabbed his wife repeatedly. Bert Stone describes how his wife's voice faded away and a 'whooshing' sensation enveloped him. The defence argued that under extreme provocation, Stone demonstrated a degree of loss of self-control 'and the dissociation which resulted in automatism was the result of extreme levels of external stress'. The jury decided that Stone was provoked, which led to a partial loss of self-control, though they did not accept that he was experiencing dissociation, which would have made his actions involuntary.

The evaluation of criminal responsibility has grave conseqences. In these circumstances it is appropriate to ask how different experts evaluate sanity – are they consistent? Just how reliable are insanity evaluations made by experts? This in psychological terms would be a basic question of any measurement or rating. Do clinicians, then, who independently assess a particular defendant's sanity, come to the same conclusions? This question is difficult to assess in a normal forensic setting because often – or usually – courts will depend on the evaluation of just one expert, which means that reliability cannot be assessed. However, the legal requirements in the state of Hawaii do provide circumstances which amount to a natural laboratory to test the reliability of legal sanity assessment. In Hawaii,

BOX 22.1 (continued)

it is required that two psychiatrists acting as independent practitioners make the assessment. Both of these have to be psychiatrists. But there is a third independent assessor, who may either be a third psychiatrist or a psychologist. It is another legal requirement that there is no communication whatsoever between the assessors. As a result of this arrangement, it is possible to compare the three assessments in order to see how frequently the same conclusion is reached. Gowensmith, Murrie and Boccaccini (2012) carried out a study involving 165 criminal defendants and multiple sanity assessment reports. The assessors reviewed relevant files and other records; they interviewed the accused; they carried out whatever psychological testing they saw fit; and finally the submitted their assessment directly to the court. In 59 per cent of the assessments the decision was that the defendant was sane. The headline finding was that the evaluators reached unanimous agreement in just 55 per cent of the cases. There was no evidence that particular assessors tended to be out of line with the other assessors and there were no obvious characteristics such as the assessors' discipline or what organisation employed them that explained the disagreements. It was found, however, the there was more disagreement about sanity when the suspect was under the influence of drugs or alcohol when the offence was committed. Furthermore, there was greater agreement when the diagnosis of psychotic disorder was being considered and when the defendant had been hospitalised for a psychiatric condition prior to the offence. The judge at the trials followed the majority opinion in 91 per cent of the cases. But when the judge disagreed with the majority, the decision was that the defendant was legally sane. Also taking advantage of the possibility of multiple examiners in Hawaii, Acklin, Fuger and Gowensmith (2015) found an average agreement between pairs of examiners assessing not guilty by reason of insanity of about 63 per cent.

In Poland, it is possible for the court to request additional assessments if it thinks appropriate. Kacperska, Heitzmana, Bak, Lesco and Opio (2016) obtained a number of sanity assessments. Nearly a half were multiple-assessments of the same individual – up to five assessments. In nearly a half of these, there was a change in the initial sanity assessment with the introduction of a new sanity assessment. In other words, the reliability of the legal sanity assessments was not high.

Psychopaths and mental illness

Criminal jurisdictions commonly employ rules in order to protect some offenders suffering from insanity. Psychopaths make an interesting topic in relation to this. The question of whether psychopaths are bad or mad it central to this. The *M'Naghten* (or *McNaughten*) case of 1843 led to a rule to protect such individuals in the United Kingdom. The *McNaughten* rule indicates that a person is not criminally responsible if:

> at the time of the committing of the act, the party accused was labouring under such a defect of reason from disease of the mind, as not to know the nature and quality of the act he was doing; or if he did know it, he did not know he was doing what was wrong.

This is a difficult rule for psychologists because it promulgates a nineteenth-century view of mental illness as a disease and a defect. Not all, perhaps not many, psychologists subscribe to this medical view of mental illness. The American Law Institute proposed a different rule to accommodate the mentally ill offender in the 1960s:

> a person is not responsible for criminal conduct if at the time of such conduct as a result of mental disease or defect he lacks substantial capacity to appreciate the criminality of his conduct or to conform his conduct to the requirements of law.

This 'rule' also causes problems since it promotes the idea that the bad can be excused as mad. To offset this, the American Psychiatric Association offered the Bonnie rule in 1983 which identifies a person as mentally ill if:

> as a result of mental disease or defect he was unable to appreciate the wrongfulness of his conduct at the time of the offence.

This seems to hark back to the original *McNaughten* rule.

The question of 'mad or bad?' is particularly difficult in relation to the concept of psychopathy. Just what is a psychopath? The answer to this question has changed constantly over the years. Hodgins (1997) suggests that there are a number of reliable research findings concerning psychopaths. In particular, there is physiological evidence to suggest that, when threatened with a noxious/unpleasant stimulus, the psychopath shows little or no physiological response. Thus the indicators of emotional arousal (e.g. skin conductivity or heart rate) hardly or do not change. Psychopaths generally fail to anticipate emotional noxious events. So they might learn to avoid touching a hot stove through experience of touching one; they do not learn to avoid criminal activity through anticipating the aversive consequences of being arrested and imprisoned.

According to Hare (1998):

- psychopaths readily engage in predatory, dispassionate and instrumental violence (p. 104);
- the violence of psychopaths is remorseless, frequently motivated by vengeance, greed, anger, money and retribution;
- psychopaths tend to attack strangers;
- psychopaths are responsible for half of the deaths of police personnel who die on duty;
- probably 1 per cent of the general population is a psychopath;
- psychopaths are much more frequent than this in prison populations.

Some have proposed that psychopathy is not a mental disorder but a cheating lifestyle that has evolved over history (Rice, 1997). The characteristics of psychopaths suggest that they should make excellent cheats – things such as glibness and charm, pathological lying and so forth. The idea is that psychopathy is adaptive and facilitative in many environments. So some highly successful business people are psychopaths and not involved in the violence of the typical psychopath (Pardue, Robinson and Arrigo, 2013a, 2013b). Perhaps a violent and hostile upbringing leads some psychopaths down the violent route.

It has been argued by Hare (1998) that psychopathy is the most important clinical psychological concept relevant to the criminal justice system. He also claims to be able to assess it with a high degree of certainty. Hence the ironic quote from one prisoner talking to Hare: 'So what if 80% of criminals with a high score on your psycho test, or whatever the hell it's called, get nabbed for a violent crime when they get out. What about the other 20% who don't screw up? You're flushing *our* lives down the drain' (p. 101). Hare's conception of the term *psychopath* is relatively exact and so his measure cannot be used to assess psychopathy in terms of any other conceptualisation (Hare, 1998). This is very important in connection with any forensic use of the scale Hare constructed to measure it – the *Psychopathy Checklist*. For example, in one case, a forensic psychiatrist claimed a very high score on Hare's *Psychopathy Checklist Revised (PCL-R)* for a particular offender, using the psychiatrist's own personal understanding of the term. A proper examination by trained personnel found the man to have a very much lower score. The judge directed the dismissal of the psychiatrist's evidence in this case. The PCL-R has been used in court cases in the US with increasing frequency. How is it dealt with in court? Two publications by DeMatteo and Edens with others, cover the USA cases in which the Psychopathy Chceklist-Revised (2003) had been introduced in court between 1991 and 2011 (DeMatteo and Edens, 2006; DeMatteo and Edens *et al.*, 2014). Generally speaking, the PCL-R was introduced into court by the prosecution (67 per cent of the time) and so can be seen as being a tool of the prosecution rather than the defence. The defence introduced it only 19 per cent of the time. It was mainly used for risk assessment purposes such that high PCL-R scores were seen as predictive of violent recidivism. Indeed, DeMatteo and Edens *et al.* suggest that a PCL-R score is treated as if it were a measure of recidivism. However, the strength of the relationship was generally overstated compared to the strength established through meta-analysis. Rarely did the defence challenge the admissibility of this evidence and, where there was such a challenge, it was unlikely to be successful.

Antisocial personality disorder and psychopathy are sometimes confused, even in professional writings. The confusion is understandable and not fully revolved. Antisocial personality disorder is part of the personality disorders to be found listed in the *Diagnostic and Statistical Manual* of the American Psychiatric Association including the most recent version *DSM-V*. The diagnostic criteria for antisocial personality disorder given in *DSM-V* can be summarised as including significant impairments in self-functioning and interpersonal functioning. For example, setting of goals on the basis of personal gratification or a failure to conform to legal or culturally normative ethical standards. Interpersonally they lack empathy for others and they lack remorse if they transgress against others. Intimate relations with others are replaced by deceit, dominance, intimidation, and coercion. Their personality traits include callousness, hostility, irresponsibility, impulsivity, manipulativeness, and risk taking. Other personality disorders in *DSM-V* include borderline personality disorder and obsessive-compulsive personality disorder. Psychopathy is not given as a diagnostic category in the *Diagnostic and Statistical Manual*. According to Fine and Kennett (2004), antisocial personality disorder is very common in prison populations at somewhere between 50–80 per cent of prisoners. In contrast, psychopathy is present in 30 per cent of the forensic population. The antisocial lifestyle is only part of the diagnosis of psychopathy, but it is the defining feature of antisocial personality disorder. Hare's ideas about the nature of psychopathy are discussed more extensively in Chapter 27. The vast majority of the research on psychopaths has been carried out on offender populations (as opposed to clinical populations, for example) so it is not surprising to find that the concept of psychopath is associated with antisocial behaviours.

Despite the concept of *antisocial personality disorder* being listed in the *DSM-V*, is it only possible to recognise the disorder by the antisocial and criminal behaviours that its victims possess? If so, then how can one differentiate between the different causes of those behaviours: ASPD, unemployment, poor parenting and so forth? According to Blackburn (1995a), the English Mental Health Act category of psychopathic disorder is similar. The only way in which psychopathic disorder can be defined is using the symptoms of serious antisocial conduct that are also the consequence of having psychopathic disorder. Blackburn, in his research, noted that legally defined psychopaths are a varied (heterogeneous) selection of individuals. This observation strengthens the view that the antisocial behaviour of legally defined psychopaths is not dependent on any single psychological state. Furthermore, there appears to be a great difference between:

- legally defined psychopaths confined to special hospitals;
- psychopaths defined psychologically by the Hare Psychopathy Checklist.

The latter includes characteristics such as superficial charm, unreliability, lack of remorse and egocentricity. Blackburn suggests that no more than a quarter of the psychopaths studied by him would also be defined as psychopaths, using Hare's Psychopathy Checklist.

For Blackburn, the ultimate question appears to be whether or not a disorder of personality, such as psychopathy, as is apparent in terms of modern psychological research, can also be regarded as a mental disorder. The *Diagnostic and Statistical Manual* of the American Psychiatric Association (*DSM-V*) defines a mental disorder as a syndrome 'characterised by clinically significant disturbance in an individual's cognition, emotion regulation, or behavior that reflects a dysfunction in the psychological, biological, or developmental processes underlying mental functioning . . . Socially deviant behavior (e.g., political, religious, or sexual) and conflicts that are primarily between the individual and society are not mental disorders unless the deviance or conflict results from a dysfunction in the individual'. One could then take the view that psychopathy should not be a mitigating factor in court but, instead, should be treated as an aggravating factor, perhaps deserving of greater levels of punishment. In this way, diagnostic categories such as psychopathy and anti-social personality disorder seem to lack any mitigating aspects (Fine and Kennett, 2004). However, Fine and Kennett take the view that there is considerable evidence that psychopaths do not pass through crucial stages in normal moral development and perhaps can be considered as not criminally responsible in the sense that they have not got a proper understanding that what they do is wrong or immoral. This does not mean that they go free; it merely means that to punish them is wrong as they cannot respond to punishment. Nevertheless, detaining psychopaths proven to have committed serious crimes serves as self-defence for society.

The concepts of *psychopathic personality* and *antisocial personality disorder* have been dominant aspects to consider when trying to decide who are dangerous offenders. However, use of the terms has been inconsistent and Blackburn (2007) described the situation as 'confusing'. Sometimes the two concepts appear to be interchangeable, but the development of Axis II classification in the APA diagnostic manual has resulted in a clearer separation. As stated in Box 21.1, in *DSM-IV* the psychiatric diagnoses are sorted into five different levels, known as axes. Axis I refers to clinical disorders and includes mental disorders, such as depression, schizophrenia, bipolar disorder and anxiety disorders. Axis II refers to pervasive or personality conditions such as borderline personality disorder, antisocial personality disorder and mild intellectual disabilities. *Antisocial personality disorder* is more relevant to the mental health system whereas *psychopathy* is more relevant to the criminal literature.

Although *psychopathy* literally means 'psychologically damaged', its usage refers to someone who is antisocial or socially damaging (Blackburn, 2007). *DSM-V* criteria for *antisocial personality disorder* are lists of 'socially undesirable activities' rather than personality characteristics of the sort that the PCL-R deals with. Blackburn suggests 'Defining a disorder of personality in terms of social deviance confounds the dependent with the independent variable and precludes any understanding of the relationship' (p. 10).

Ogloff, Campbell and Shepherd (2016) set themselves the task of understanding the relationship between psychopathy and antisocial personality disorder using a sample of mentally disordered offenders in a secure forensic facility in Australia. They measured psychopathy in the sample using the Psychopathy Checklist-Revised (PCL-R) and the Psychopathy Checklist Screening Version (PCL:SV). Separately they assessed all members of the sample using the diagnostic criteria for antisocial personality disorder based on the diagnostic criteria in *DSM-IV*. These criteria include impulsivity, irresponsibility, remorselessness, and disregard for the safety of others. *DSM-V* indicates that the antisocial personality disorder classification has been described as psychopathy. This implies a complete overlap between the two conditions. What was the actual degree of overlap between psychopathy and antisocial personality disorder? Of those classified as having antisocial personality disorder, only 6 per cent were high on psychopathy. Of those classified as being high on psychopathic traits, 65 per cent were diagnosed with antisocial personality disorder. That is, the majority of psychopaths meet the diagnostic criteria of antisocial personality disorder also but very few of those with antisocial personality disorder can be classified as psychopaths. The main difference between the two conditions is that the psychopath shows weak affect and poor empathy over and above antisocial behaviours. Related to this, Khalifa and Howard (2015) showed that psychopathy was related to various aspects of the personality disorders including antisocial personality disorder.

Blackburn (1995a) suggested that the question of whether psychopaths are bad or mad is nonsensical. Psychopaths can be both mad and bad, or just mad or just bad. Mad and bad are not opposites; they are different. Reduced to its elements, the real question for the forensic psychologist is whether the presence of a personality disorder including psychopathy should affect the eventual disposal of the offender. The essential problem, for forensic and criminal psychology, is that the concept of psychopath brings together a personality concept with deviant and criminal activities. This fails to differentiate between the following two distinct things:

- the medical/psychiatric state of psychopathy;
- the behaviour which amounts to its symptoms.

Of course, psychopathy is not the only psychological condition which presents difficult questions when brought to court. For example, Freckelton and List (2009) discuss some of the arguments about the criminal culpability of those with Asperger's Disorder. This condition only entered the *Diagnostic and Statistical Manual* in the 1990s – very little time for it to have developed a significant case law different from that for related conditions. Similarly, Eme (2015) considers the arguments surrounding whether to allow Attention Deficit Hyperactivity Disorder (ADHD) in mitigation of criminal responsibility. ADHD's characteristic symptom is impulsivity without considering prior consequences or ignoring them.

Post-traumatic stress disorder as a defence

Post-traumatic stress disorder (PTSD) has been used as a part of the US defence of 'not guilty by reason of insanity' but also as a mitigating factor at the time of sentencing. We discussed PTSD in Chapter 4 in relation to victims. Members of the military exposed to traumatising situations are an important group suffering from PTSD. The trauma they experienced may be involved in the violent crime they commit in civilian life. The role of PTSD in military life and its role in civilian life have been alternating foci of interest for many years (Miller, L. 2012). As long ago as 1678, the Swiss army surgeon Johannes Hoffer was of the opinion that the abnormally vivid images formed in the overexcitement of battle resulted in the mental and physical decline of soldiers – a condition that he termed nostalgia. Throughout military history, medical personnel have been expected to provide diagnosis and treatment for conditions related to trauma. The purpose of this is to get active frontline personnel back to the frontline as quickly as is feasible. When peace returns, the focus returns to the ordinary accidents and violent incidents which lead to pain, trauma, and stress. The industrial revolution in the eighteenth and nineteenth centuries brought heavy machinery, with its potential for inflicting traumatic injury. With industrialisation came the increasingly industrialised methods of military destruction. The First World War involved the incapacitation of individuals both emotionally and intellectually. This became known as 'shell shock'. Originally, it was seen as the consequence of the brain being concussed by exploding weaponry. The Second World War introduced a change of terminology and 'shell shock' became known as 'combat or battle fatigue'. Discharge from the forces because of combat fatigue was far commoner than it had been in the First World War.

The consequences of shell shock, combat fatigue or PTSD on its victim are wide-ranging. Among the possible outcomes are violence and aggression. In an early case in the US, lawyers for a former solder claimed that his offence of child molestation was the consequence of insanity ensuing from shell shock (*People* v. *Gilberg*, 1925). More generally, commentators were beginning to identify upsurges of violent crime after periods of war or other forms of unrest. Gradually, the trauma of war and its psychological consequences were being used as a legal defence for ex-military personnel. Diagnoses such as *shell shock* and *combat fatigue* though did not refer to recognised medical/psychiatric diagnoses. Most insanity standards in the US involved the criterion of the presence of a mental disease or defect. The situation changed when in 1980 the *Diagnostic and Statistical Manual of Mental Disorders* (*DSM-III*) introduced post-traumatic stress disorder as a diagnostic category. More and more military and civilian offenders invoked PTSD as a defence or in mitigation in criminal trials in the 1980s. There were abuses, not surprisingly, and quite a few military claimed PTSD though they had never been in combat.

According to Miller (2012), the indicators of PTSD are:

- A precipitating stressor exposes the individual to death or injury, accompanied by high levels of horror, fear and the feeling of hopelessness. The threat may be to oneself or to other people. PTSD shares symptoms such as anxiety, depression and agitation with other conditions so they are not sufficiently diagnostic in themselves – hence the requirement for a specific precipitating traumatic event.
- The traumatic event is replayed in memory, in dreams, in flashback and through over-responsiveness to things similar to the traumatic event.

- The individual stays away from any situation which would serve as a reminder of the traumatic event. Hence their social activity becomes restricted. Some individuals become psychologically unresponsive to stimuli redolent of the traumatic situation. They are therefore seen as emotionally/interpersonally unresponsive.
- Symptoms of persistent arousal: many descriptors may be used to describe this such as high anxiety, irritability, anger, excessive startle responses, sleep problems, concentration and memory problems.

There are a number of mechanisms by which PTSD has been linked to violent crime (Silva *et al.*, 2001; Wilson and Zigelbaum, 1983):

- Violence may be the result of flashbacks or dissociation. In this the offender seemingly acts in self-defence. However, the events really relate to a delusional re-experience of the traumatic stressor.
- Another suggested mechanism is combat addiction or sensation-seeking syndrome. The individual becomes dependent on the 'high' that was involved in combat. By engaging in violent or dangerous behaviours, this high is recreated.
- Mood disorder-associated violence, which may be extreme manic agitation and suicidal depression, among other things.
- Sleep disorder related violence – for example, sleep-walking or a lower violence threshold because of insomnia.

In other words, in the US the insanity defence is employed or diminished capacity used in mitigation of sentence. The insanity and diminished capacity defences were discussed earlier. Of course, the barriers to using the insanity defence are set high and it is used in only about 1 per cent of felony cases and then mostly it will not be accepted (Slobogin, 2006). Miller (2012) argues that only somnambulistic sleepwalking involving dissociative flashback episodes in which a crime occurs might meet either the *McNaughten* or American Law Institute guidelines.

BOX 22.2 Forensic psychology in action

Victims and learning disability

The level of intellectual functioning of those with learning disability can be extremely low. Three-quarters of learning disability individuals in Texas replied 'Yes' when they were asked 'Does it snow here in summer?' Despite the fact that none of them was Chinese, 44 per cent said that they were Chinese when asked 'Are you Chinese?' (Siegelman, Budd, Spanhel and Schoenrock 1981).

Individuals who suffer mental or intellectual disabilities (we use the term *intellectual disability* despite the original studies using the older, pejorative term *mental retardation*) amount to 1 per cent of Western populations. Competence to stand trial may be separated conceptually from competence in terms of giving evidence. Some countries allow evidence from people with limited intellectual ability without requiring them to swear an oath (Kebbell and Hatton, 1999). Nevertheless, the full picture suggests that there is a serious risk that people with limited intellectual powers will be served extremely poorly by the criminal justice system. See Figure 22.2 for more information about different types of mental disability. Willner (2011) claims that people with intellectual disabilities who had experience in the criminal justice system found it poorly adapted to their needs. Courts of law and other parts of the criminal justice system are the worst organisations in terms of integrating those with intellectual disabilities. Those with intellectual disabilities are also victimised by crime in ways more extreme than other people:

- People with intellectual disabilities are a high-risk group and are more likely to become victims by a factor of two and possibly as much as ten times. In particular, they have a greater risk of suffering personal crimes such as assault and robbery. They often have little property, which may account for them having a much smaller greater relative risk of suffering property crimes.
- The crime which people with intellectual disabilities suffer is rather less likely to be reported to the police than that against people in general. The likelihood of reporting is lower for those with greater intellectual disabilities. The figures for non-reporting of sexual assaults may be as high as 97 per cent.
- They are also systematically excluded from the criminal justice system, even when crimes against them have been reported. The probable reason for this is that they are assumed to lack competency to act as reliable witnesses.

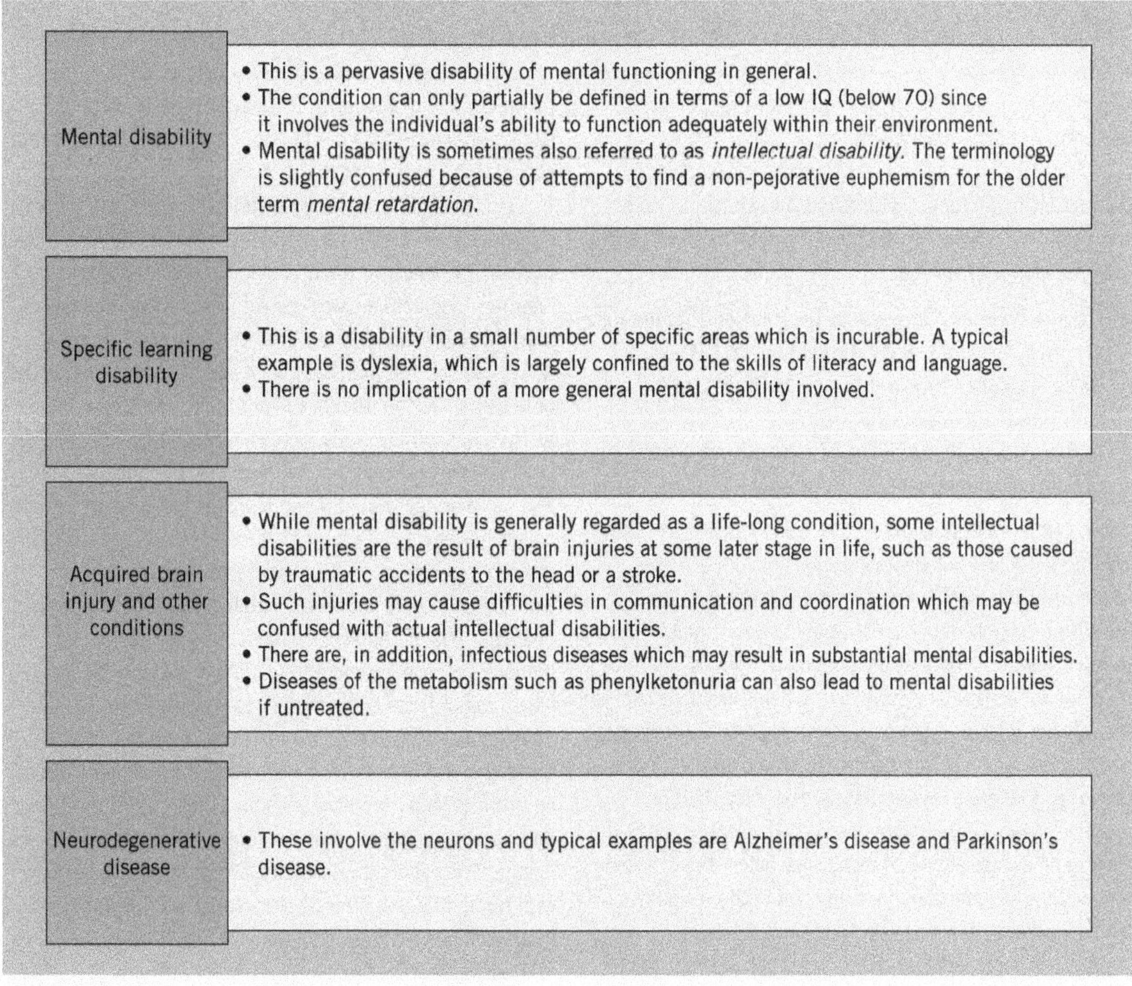

Mental disability
• This is a pervasive disability of mental functioning in general.
• The condition can only partially be defined in terms of a low IQ (below 70) since it involves the individual's ability to function adequately within their environment.
• Mental disability is sometimes also referred to as intellectual disability. The terminology is slightly confused because of attempts to find a non-pejorative euphemism for the older term mental retardation.
Specific learning disability
• This is a disability in a small number of specific areas which is incurable. A typical example is dyslexia, which is largely confined to the skills of literacy and language.
• There is no implication of a more general mental disability involved.
Acquired brain injury and other conditions
• While mental disability is generally regarded as a life-long condition, some intellectual disabilities are the result of brain injuries at some later stage in life, such as those caused by traumatic accidents to the head or a stroke.
• Such injuries may cause difficulties in communication and coordination which may be confused with actual intellectual disabilities.
• There are, in addition, infectious diseases which may result in substantial mental disabilities.
• Diseases of the metabolism such as phenylketonuria can also lead to mental disabilities if untreated.
Neurodegenerative disease
• These involve the neurons and typical examples are Alzheimer's disease and Parkinson's disease.

Figure 22.2 Varieties of intellectual disability

Things have improved in general, though. For example, in the United Kingdom vulnerable adults can give evidence using closed-circuit video systems and there are clear guidelines for the investigation of allegations of abuse against them. Nevertheless, substantial disadvantages persist (Willner, 2011).

There are other reasons why people with an intellectual disability may witness more crime than people in general. The practice of deinstitutionalisation, which ensures that many of them live in poor neighbourhoods, puts them at increased risk of being victimised by others in the community. Sexual assaults on people with a mental impairment can often only be prosecuted if they can provide evidence in court or in interview (Kebbell and Hatton, 1999). The quality of witness evidence from people with mental impairment varies, but nevertheless may be valuable. Gudjonsson, Murphy and Clare (2000) assessed approximately 50 men and women residents at two private residential homes. These were clients incapable of surviving independently. There were allegations of ill treatment by members of the staff. These allegations were eventually proven in court. As part of the assessment the following were administered:

- the Wechsler Adult Intelligence Scale;
- the Gudjonsson Suggestibility Scale, which measures memory, suggestibility and confabulation;
- a measure of acquiescence specially developed for the purpose.

Pairs of incompatible statements were given and the resident replied whether each was true or false. For example:

- I am happy most of the time.
- I am sad most of the time.

BOX 22.2 (continued)

A 'Yes' to both statements was scored as acquiescence. Acquiescence is the tendency to agree, irrespective of the content of the statement.

Under British case law, a witness is classed as competent if the judge is satisfied on two main issues for which the advice of psychologists and psychiatrists may be sought. They are:

- Does the witness understand the oath and its implied sanction, i.e. 'I swear by Almighty God, that the evidence I shall give will be the truth, the whole truth, and nothing but the truth?'
- Is the witness capable of giving an accurate account of what they have seen?

The potential witnesses among the residents were assessed. The highest IQ for 'intellectual disabilities' is 70. Many of the residents assessed could not complete the IQ test because they lacked the verbal ability to do so. More than a third of them were right at the bottom of the IQ scale since they did not achieve any score on the items or subtests of the intelligence scale. Similarly, they generally showed poor ability to recall either immediately or on a delayed basis a story read to them by the assessing psychologists. For example, over a quarter were unable to remember any of the story in an immediate recall test. Delay before being asked to recall the story resulted in nearly half of the residents being unable to remember anything from the story.

The residents were asked to say what the standard oath, as given above, meant. Some were capable of doing this and said things like:

> You swear on the Bible to tell the truth. You must tell the truth. The whole truth means you give a complete picture of what happened.
>
> A lie is when you are not telling the truth.

About a fifth could explain the oath to the satisfaction of the psychologists' standards. Almost without exception these had an IQ score of 60 or over. Of course, some of the clients had difficulty answering the question, so they were presented with alternative questions:

- 'If I said your name was (the client's actual name given) would that be true or a lie?'
- 'If I said your name was Fred (or the female equivalent) Bloggs would that be true or a lie?'

A resident who could answer these questions was considered to have some understanding of the concepts of lies and truth. This may be considered as part of understanding the oath entirely. Another fifth of the residents could answer at this level. Almost without exception, those who could explain a lie in this concrete situation had an IQ of 50 or more.

According to Kebbell and Hatton (1999), the style of questioning used with people with mental limitations may have an influence on the quality of the testimony elicited. The most accurate answers by witnesses with intellectual disabilities are open-ended free-recall ones: for example, 'What can you tell me about what you saw?' Accuracy may be regarded as the ratio of correct to incorrect information. As the question becomes increasingly specific, the answers become less accurate. So, for example, the question 'What was he wearing?' would produce better results than 'What colour jacket was he wearing?' Similar trends are found in the general population, but the trends are a little more extreme for people with intellectual disabilities. Another characteristic of people with mental impairment is their tendency to respond more to leading questions. This is only a minor trend since many people with limited intelligence can be accurate even with such leading questions. The reason for their greater suggestibility might lie in their poorer memory capacity. These individuals may only be suggestible on matters about which they are unsure. They also have less intellectual resources to cope with unfamiliar and stressful tasks such as those involved in providing eyewitness testimony.

People who are classified as having intellectual disabilities are often able to provide accurate enough testimony (Kebbell and Hatton, 1999). Lawyers' tactics as employed in examination and cross-examination interfere with the quality of the information obtained. The use of complex questions, such as those involving double negatives, is especially problematic. People in general tend to reply 'don't know' to such questions but will reply accurately to similar but simply expressed questions. The language used by the criminal justice system is complex for even intellectually able people:

- An IQ of 111 (substantially above average) is needed to understand the rights notice used to inform detained suspects of their legal rights (such as the Miranda in the United States).
- People with mental disability understood only about a tenth of the sentences in some of the rights notices.
- The closed questions used in cross-examination are a strain for verbally fluent, well-educated and trained expert witnesses to deal with effectively.

Milne, Clare and Bull (1999) describe research which suggests that the cognitive interview (see Chapter 11) may be helpful in obtaining information in adults with mild learning disabilities.

This is an area in which great care is needed – the risk is always that witnesses with a mental disability are regarded as potentially unreliable. With this in mind, it is worthwhile to consider a case study reported by Willner (2011). This describes 'Joan' who was a 38-year-old victim of a theft against her by a person she knew. A clinical psychology unit assessed her in terms of her capacity to testify should it be necessary. This involved the use of a number of psychometric tests together with formal clinical interviews. Her intellectual ability was assessed to be in the lower range of 'mild learning disability'. This means that she was likely to be able to take the oath. She understood the concept of truth and the requirement to tell the truth in court, and the solemnity of the proceedings of a court of law. She also understood that there was a possibility that the accused might be acquitted in a court of law and she demonstrated that she would be able to cope with this. These are the positive signs. However, there were doubts about her ability to withstand the cross-examination of a lawyer for the defence so special arrangements would be needed for her evidence. She also performed badly on the Gudjonnson Suggestibility Scale (see Box 16.2) which involves a practical test of being influenced by leading questions and other pressures. That is, like many others with an intellectual disability, she was very suggestible. This might have been sufficient for the authorities to decide that she would not make a reliable witness. In this test, a story is read which basically has to be memorised and then the suggestive pressures are applied to this. So memory is involved. The clinical psychologists, however, tried another approach. Joan had provided a lot of information about her own life during the course of the interviews. The psychologists applied similar suggestive pressures to this information. It was found that Joan was very resistant to suggestion when important facts in her life were involved. On the basis of this, it was recommended that the trial go ahead. The thief pleaded guilty in court in this case.

Of course, false confession under, say, police pressure, is a risk with such a vulnerable group. The law will vary under different jurisdictions: in the United Kingdom, three criteria were set out to help deal with this situation. In the case of confessions, the judge should consider the following:

- Does the prosecution case solely depend upon the confession?
- Does the defendant exhibit a significant degree of mental handicap?
- Is the confession unconvincing? Would a properly directed jury be unable to convict because of these inadequacies?

In these circumstances, the judge's responsibility is to withdraw the case from trial by the jury (Torpy, 1994).

This brings us to the question of how people with learning deficiencies are dealt with as witnesses in court. Are their needs accommodated by judges and lawyers? As we have seen, in appropriate circumstances, people with intellectual deficiencies give accurate information, though this is highly dependent on the way in which they are interviewed or questioned. The accuracy of their testimony is best when they were asked open-ended free-recall questions such as 'What happened?' Requests that are very specific ('Tell me about the shirt the man was wearing') produce poorer-quality information. They may produce more details with the latter form of question but the information is more likely to be inaccurate. Kebbell, Hatton and Johnson (2004) located transcripts of British trials, half of which contained evidence provided by a person with intellectual disability. These witnesses were matched as closely as possible with witnesses who were not intellectually impaired in terms of type of crime and the type of court. A high proportion were trials for rape and sexual assault but some were for assault. The researchers coded the types of questions asked of the witnesses, including: open questions ('What was Mr Jones wearing?'); closed questions ('And what was he wearing on top?'); 'yes/no' questions ('And your keyworker does the shopping for you?'); either/or questions ('And when you lived at St Anne's, did you have your own bedroom or did you share a bedroom?'); leading questions ('I suggest that on this occasion Kate did not come into the flat at all, that you left before Kate had come home?'); negative questions ('Did you not think it might be important to tell somebody?'); double-negatives ('Now, did you say that you did not say that it was something that you did not like?'); multiple questions (two plus questions without allowing a chance for the reply to be given before the next question is asked); and repeated questions (when the same question is asked more than once). There was virtually nothing to differentiate the questions asked of witnesses with intellectual limitations and those asked of members of the general population. In other words, lawyers were making no adjustments in their questioning style in order to meet the special needs of those with low intellectual abilities. However, fewer leading questions

BOX 22.2 (continued)

were asked of people with intellectual limitations but they tended to have questions repeated more often. The most disturbing feature of Kebbell *et al.*'s findings was that those with intellectual limitations were the most likely to agree with the implied direction of the leading in response to leading questions and were less likely to provide additional information.

In a further analysis of the same data, O'Kelly, Kebbell, Hatton and Johnson (2003) studied the judge's interventions in the court hearings by coding the transcripts of the hearings into three broad categories: interactions with witnesses; interactions with lawyers; and interactions with the jury. The most frequent interventions with those with learning disabilities were clarifying issues with witnesses, calling breaks and asking additional questions about issues not raised by the lawyers. Overall, there were actually fewer such interventions with witnesses with learning disabilities, though this was not statistically significant. The same is true of interventions directed towards the lawyers, though, once again, this was not statistically significant. Probably most important among the findings was that the judge did not intervene more with people with learning difficulties to simplify the questions or to stop oppressive questioning.

Main points

- Legal concepts such as competency/capacity to stand trial and diminished responsibility are not simple to equate with psychological variables and are not exactly the same in different jurisdictions. In practice, such concepts will largely be assessed on the basis of clinical judgement and although more objective psychological measures are gradually becoming available, clinical judgement probably remains the main method. A person may be incompetent to stand trial for reasons of low intellectual functioning or as a consequence of suffering certain psychiatric conditions, both of which make it difficult to be a party to one's own defence and to understand the procedures of the court. Only factors relevant to the individual's psychological state at the time of trial should be part of the assessment of competency.
- The extent to which practitioners who assess competence are objective in their judgement is clearly an important question. Doubts have been cast on the validity of clinical assessment in other contexts. The evidence that practitioners use psychiatric variables in making their assessment rather than other information such as criminal background is indicative of the objectivity of these assessments. There are many decisions that are poorly predicted by these psychiatric variables so we do not know the basis of the decision. There is evidence that practitioners can be influenced by inappropriate factors from experimental studies but generally factors irrelevant to the assessment of competence are ignored.
- Psychological and intellectual problems can affect the likelihood of obtaining justice. Victims of crime who have limited intellectual resources may be further victimised by police and court procedures. As with many issues in forensic and criminal psychology, it is not possible to state absolutely that such individuals do or do not provide good evidence. If interviewed appropriately, especially using open-ended questioning, the quality of the evidence provided may be perfectly satisfactory. Nevertheless, there is emerging evidence that judges and lawyers in court do not always behave appropriately towards people with intellectual limitations. The questioning style of lawyers tends to be too complex and lacks adaptation to the needs of the witness, and judges tend not to intervene in these cases in support of the witness's needs.

Further reading

McMurran, M., Khalifa, N. and Gibbon, S. (2009) *Forensic Mental Health* Cullompton: Willan Publishing.

Rogers, T.P., Blackwood, N.J., Farnham, F., Pickup, G.J. and Watts, M.J. (2008) 'Fitness to plead and competence to stand trial: a systematic review of the constructs and their application' *Journal of Forensic Psychiatry and Psychology* **19** (4), 576–96.

Crown Prosecution Service: 'Special measures': http://www.cps.gov.uk/legal/s_to_u/special_measures/

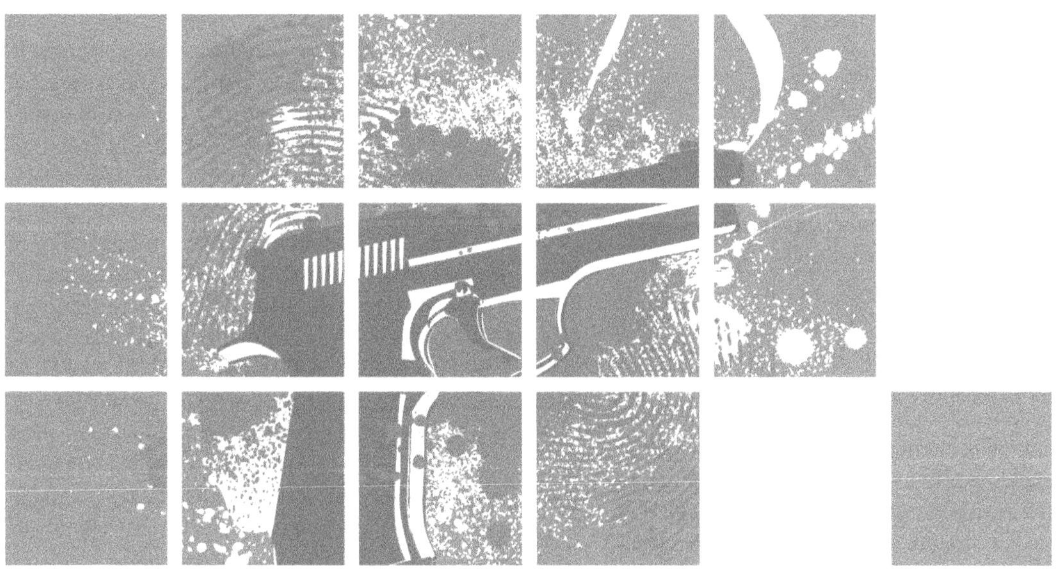

Chapter 23

Judges and lawyers

Overview

- Public opinion about the courts and justice system is mixed. In the UK, a considerable minority believe that some accused persons are treated unfairly and do not have their rights respected by courts of law. A majority feel that the system does not bring criminals to justice.
- Substantial numbers of the public have attended court in some capacity – one in ten of the British public have been accused of committing a crime.
- The roles of judges and lawyers in the Anglo-American adversarial system are different from those of the inquisitorial systems where a prosecution and defence are not in battle. The differences between adversarial and inquisitorial systems result in different relative strengths of the two types of court. Outcomes of trials do not seem to be materially affected overall by the type of system.
- The outcomes of trials are only modestly predictable from a range of relevant variables. However, many people consult a lawyer in the hope that he or she will be able to accurately assess the outcome of a particular legal situation they face. Lawyers' assessments of likely outcomes follow the principles of the psychology of decision making under conditions of uncertainty.
- How evidence can be more effectively presented in court has received considerable attention. There is advice that is based on general psychological developments in understanding effective communications, although their adequacy in the legal context needs to be assessed more thoroughly. For example, powerful speech styles in which directness, assertiveness and rationality are characteristic tend to be perceived as delivering a more credible message.
- Many researchers have pointed to the importance of studying the effectiveness of narrative when trying to understand legal arguments. The effectiveness of evidence depends on the narrative context it is placed in, rather than its 'factual value'. The more the narrative is based in commonsense notions, the more positive the outcome.
- Various models have been proposed to account for judges' decision making. To a degree these utilise extra-legal considerations, just as is the case for jury decision making.

Introduction

Public confidence in the justice system and courts varies across the world. It is highest in Asia where 65 per cent claim to be confident in it, and lowest in former soviet Russia (28 per cent). The figures for Europe are 47 per cent and the US 45 per cent (Rochelle and Loschky (2014). According to the British Crime Survey (Home Office, 2001), a third of British adults have been to court as a witness, spectator or juror at some time. Ten per cent of the population have been to court accused of a crime. About two-thirds of British people believe that the criminal justice system respects the rights of and treats fairly people accused of committing a crime. The figure is slightly lower for those who have been in trouble with the law but, nevertheless, as a group, even they remained very satisfied with the criminal justice system. However, only about 40 per cent of the population believe that the criminal justice system brings people who commit crime to justice. Hough, Bradford and Jackson (2013) report findings from the 2010/11 Crime Survey for England and Wales and UK data from the European Crime Survey. The majority of participants regarded the courts as passing too lenient sentences. But at the same time, the public's awareness of current sentencing practices of courts was inaccurate and did not reflect properly the true severity of sentencing. Despite this, people were lenient when suggesting sentences for a specific hypothetical case. They seemed more inclined to believe in the fairness than the effectiveness of the criminal justice system. There is an obvious need to understand better what happens in courts of law. Nevertheless, one must be realistic about the direct impact of courts on much crime. In the majority of cases, questions of guilt have been already settled by the admission of the accused. In some jurisdictions something like 90 per cent of cases are settled by a plea of guilty (Williams, 1995). Of course, in the United States, this may involve plea bargaining – that is, prosecution and defence agreeing a guilty plea to a less serious charge than the prosecution originally intended (Colvin, 1993). This encourages more guilty pleas.

The adversarial and inquisitorial types of trial

The Anglo-American adversarial system can be described as 'lawyers arguing, judges refereeing, and juries deciding the outcome. Litigation is a form of combat, and good lawyers excel at combat' (Dabbs, Alford and Fielden, 1998, p. 84). Trial lawyers work in a place where concrete demands are made on their services rather than with abstract concepts involved in, for example, giving advice that does not demand delivery of results. They have to achieve and this requires knowledge and skills not taught in law school. Dabbs *et al.* considered the possibility that trial lawyers would show higher levels of the hormone testosterone. This has been linked to heightened interpersonal dominance as well as sexual activity. Trial lawyers of both sexes were studied by Dabbs *et al.* (1998) as well as other lawyers who had not been trial lawyers for a period of at least five years. Saliva samples were analysed for testosterone. It was found that in all the cases studied, irrespective of gender, the trial lawyers had higher testosterone levels than non-trial lawyers. In another study, they compared trial lawyers and appeal court lawyers with similar outcomes.

The institution of the jury has a history that goes back to Socrates but, more importantly, the Norman (French) law of trial by jury (Arce, Farina, Vila and Santiago, 1996). The jury is associated with British and US developments and other countries the legal systems of which derive from these roots. History took rather different routes in Continental Europe. There, legal experts working with lay people decided on matters such as guilt. (The mixed jury is different since in this, lay people working as a group reach the verdict but the judge(s) also contributes in terms of sentencing.) The inquisitorial or *escabinato* system first developed in Germany and refers to legal systems in which qualified legal experts and lay people make decisions jointly. However, today, in Germany, the system deals mainly with rather minor offences. In France and Italy the development of *escabinatos* was associated with Fascism in the first half of the twentieth century.

Naturally, one of the questions is whether the legal professional has undue power over the other members in such a 'jury'. Arce *et al.* carried out research into the *escabinato* system using a real rape case that was video recorded and edited down to 75 minutes of tape. The *escabinato* juries were composed of five lay persons together with a judge. The results showed that the judge's initial verdict was usually very persuasive for the lay persons. No lay member changed their position to be against the judge. Given the two-thirds majority rule for the verdict applied in this study, the groups overall tended to adopt the judge's stance.

It is believed that the adversarial system of England was a response to the historical shortcomings of the European inquisitorial system. Torture was employed sometimes in some secular judicial proceedings using the inquisitorial model (McEwan, 1995). The contrast between the Continental European inquisitorial legal system and those based on the British adversarial system is marked (see Figure 23.1). The latter is common to other parts of the world, including the United States and judicial systems emerging out of British colonialism. The adversarial system can be seen to have the following characteristics:

- The judge's role is minimised as far as deciding the question of guilt is involved.

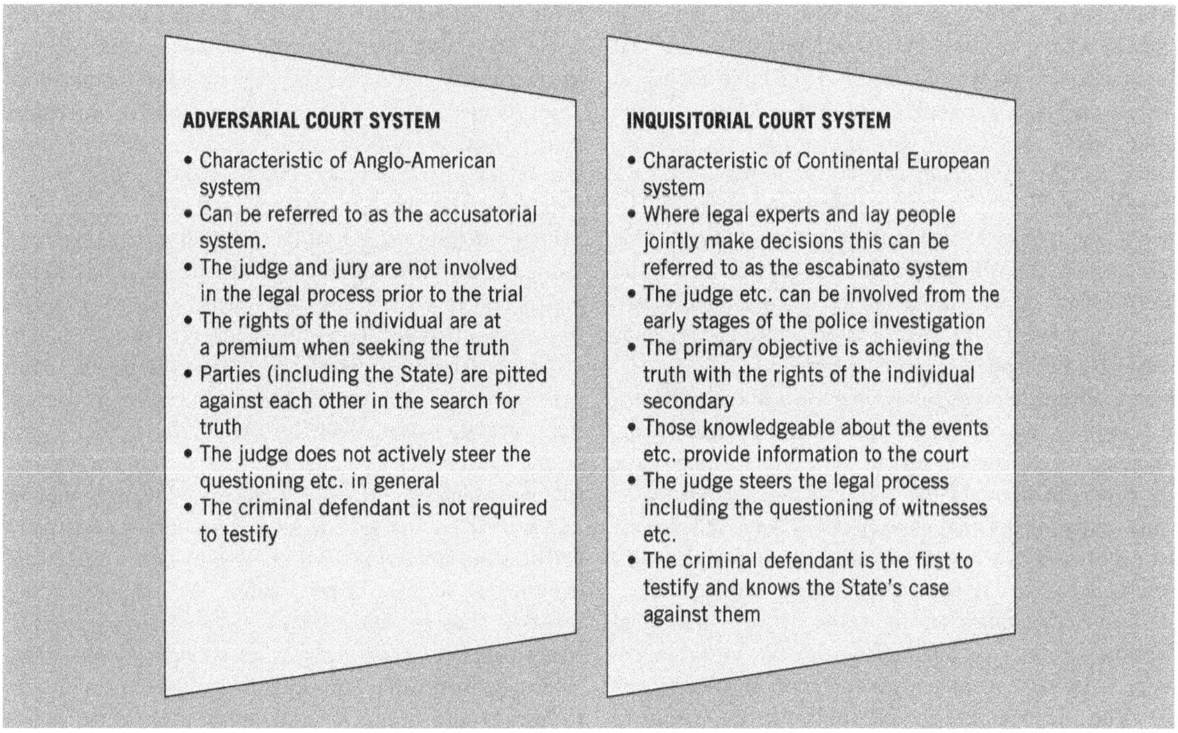

ADVERSARIAL COURT SYSTEM

- Characteristic of Anglo-American system
- Can be referred to as the accusatorial system.
- The judge and jury are not involved in the legal process prior to the trial
- The rights of the individual are at a premium when seeking the truth
- Parties (including the State) are pitted against each other in the search for truth
- The judge does not actively steer the questioning etc. in general
- The criminal defendant is not required to testify

INQUISITORIAL COURT SYSTEM

- Characteristic of Continental European system
- Where legal experts and lay people jointly make decisions this can be referred to as the escabinato system
- The judge etc. can be involved from the early stages of the police investigation
- The primary objective is achieving the truth with the rights of the individual secondary
- Those knowledgeable about the events etc. provide information to the court
- The judge steers the legal process including the questioning of witnesses etc.
- The criminal defendant is the first to testify and knows the State's case against them

Figure 23.1 Adversarial versus inquisitorial trial systems

- The lawyers or advocates are partisan and act for opposed parties.
- The jury is commonly employed, although it is not strictly a requirement of the adversarial system.
- Evidence is presented orally rather than as written evidence or submissions.

Nevertheless, the two systems are not quite so distinct as they might appear. Sometimes the two systems are employed within the same jurisdiction. For example, in the United Kingdom proceedings concerning the care of children are often closer to the inquisitorial model than the adversarial model. Coroner's courts, which deal with matters of the causes of death (and treasure trove) in England, employ something closer to the inquisitorial approach. Similarly, in France and other countries there is no pure inquisitorial system since a large proportion of cases do not go through the examination by the investigating magistrate. In the inquisitorial system, the police may be called on to investigate matters pertinent to the defence and not just the prosecution.

There are two broad types of jury:

- The lay person jury consisting only of lay persons. This often has 12 people but the number can vary and we will see in Chapter 24 that some jurisdictions use juries as small as six persons. It is 15 in Scotland.
- The *escabinato* jury which has a mixture of lay persons and legal experts. For example, there may be one legal expert and two lay persons. This is the system used in Germany (Arce, 1998).

Of course, it is an obvious question to ask whether adversarial and inquisitorial systems differ markedly in terms of their merits such as how they are experienced by offenders etc. Thibaut and Walker (1975) argued that the two different systems have different underlying objectives. They suggested that the adversarial system is best suited to situations in which there is a conflict of interest between the parties. The adversarial system is good at producing justice in that it allows for the effective distribution of resources among the litigants. The system allows for the introduction of information by the representatives of the litigants which allows the decision maker to distribute resources appropriately. In contrast, the inquisitorial system is better for dealing with issues which are full of cognitive conflict. This requires that the correct factual answer is found. The inquisitorial system is good at achieving this end. It relies on disinterested third parties to seek the facts without the influence of vested interests. There have been a number of studies comparing the inquisitorial and adversarial systems. Among the more recent ones were two by Sevier (2014) into what they term the truth-justice tradeoff. The first of his studies provided some evidence that the adversarial system produces more justice than truth whereas the inquisitorial system produces more truth than justice as perceived by the participants. This research involved 'potential litigants' reading material which dealt with an adversarial trial or similar material which involved the procedures of inquisitorial system. The focus was on disputed scientific evidence. The second study was similar except the outcomes of the 'trials' were given – these may or may not have been the ones which the participants would have liked. In the case of the inquisitorial system, the outcome made no difference to the ratings of truth and of justice obtained. This was not the case with the adversarial system. Truth and justice ratings went up if one got the outcome one wanted but down if one got the undesired outcome. These trends were generally modest rather than large.

Not all research is as favourable towards the adversarial system as the early work by Thibaut and Walker, for example, suggested. The inquisitorial system may have advantages in terms of the well-being of the victim of crime according to Laxminarayan (2014) which the adversarial system does not. She is critical of some of the early work which tended to conclude in favour of the adversarial system. Laxminarayan argues that victims may gain psychologically from interaction with the judge in the inquisitorial system and presence in court may be beneficial. The judge in the inquisitorial system is actively involved in the evidence gathering process whereas in the adversarial system the judge generally takes a more passive role. The victim in the inquisitorial system may be freer to tell their story fully and in a narrative form. The prosecuting and defending lawyers will not interrupt this to any great extent. Improperly obtained evidence is less likely to be excluded than in in the adversarial system. The victim may thus find the judge more helpful than in the adversarial system and that evidence was presented in full. Victims of serious crimes were studied in New South Wales, Australia, which has a version of the adversarial system, and in Holland which has a version of the inquisitorial system. The crime victims were asked about the influence of the criminal proceedings on their ability to cope with the crime, their self-esteem, their trust in the legal system, and belief in a just world. They were also asked about whether or not they attended court and whether or not they had had contact with the judge. Although not the case with the Australian sample, the evidence for the Dutch sample was that contact with the judge produced beneficial effects on Dutch victims who were protected from part of the negative effects of the criminal justice system on victims. In the Australian data no significant effect was found due to involvement in court and with the judge.

Chapter 24 is devoted to the Anglo-American type of jury.

UK and US trial procedures are different, despite both being based on the broad adversarial strategy (Collett and Kovera, 2003). There are many differences between the two. For example, in the UK system, the lawyers are confined and are not free to roam around the courtroom while presenting their case; the opening statement from the defence is given after the other side has presented its case and not right at the beginning of the trial; objections from lawyers are not dealt with in the presence of the jury; UK judges are more active in the general flow of evidence during the trial than US judges, who may be described as being more reserved. All of this led Collett and Kovera to the view that these differences in the demeanour of both judges and lawyers in the two systems may have consequences for how the proceedings affect the jury.

One possibility is that the process of persuasion in the two systems is different. Theories of persuasion suggest that there are two methods by which information is processed (Petty and Cacioppo, 1981). One is the central route in which people actively process all the information that is pertinent to their situation. Since this is a relatively cerebral and rational process, the quality of the arguments determines the level of persuasion. The peripheral route involves considerably less effort since it involves relatively simple decision-making rules or procedures when coming to a decision. For example, in the peripheral route to persuasion, aspects such as the status of the person making the argument affect acceptance of that argument. Distractive US courtroom environments would encourage the peripheral route to be more influential, say on the jury, than the more orderly UK system, which would favour the more central route to persuasion. On the other hand, the greater level of involvement of the UK judges may mean that jurors are more influenced by their non-verbal cues concerning the case than would be a jury with a US judge.

In an experiment testing this possibility, Collett and Kovera (2003) set up mock trials, some of which followed the UK ways outlined above while others followed the US way. All other things were standard to all of the trials. The amount of non-verbal behaviour expressed by the judge was varied as well as the strength of the evidence in the trials. Those who were subject to the UK-style trials could remember the evidence presented in the trial better than those who experienced the US-style trial. However, there was no evidence that the UK-style trial allowed the jurors to be more influenced by the stronger evidence than did the US-style trial. The non-verbal cues given by the judge were clearly emphasised by the UK-style procedures since participants rated the judge's non-verbal cues as more salient. There was also evidence that the UK-style trial resulted in the jury being more confident in their verdicts. However, the study did not demonstrate that the two systems affected the trial outcomes differently. The study did not show the superiority of one system over the other. The strengths of the UK system in terms of allowing the jury to focus unfettered on the evidence are offset by the apparently greater risk that non-verbal signals from the judge will affect the jury.

Are trial outcomes predictable?

If the court process is capable of being studied and analysed effectively, one might assume that the outcomes of trials are predictable. Fitzmaurice, Rogers and Stanley (1996) studied how accurately sentencing could be predicted for a sample of 4000 cases in England. The possible sentences included community service order, custody, discharge, fine, fully suspended sentence, partially suspended sentence and probation order. Over 30 variables were assessed for each case. Different combinations of predictor variables predicted different types of sentence most effectively. In general, the predictions were not particularly good. Thus the percentage of correctly predicted sentences (i.e. the sentence matched that predicted by the measures) could be as low as 20 per cent and no higher than 60 per cent. The correlation between the prediction and the actual sentence similarly could be lower than 0.2 and no higher than 0.5.

Another study into the predictability of sentencing was that of Cauffman, Piquero, Kimonis, Steinberg, Chassin and Fagan (2007). This investigated factors predicting the disposal of serious juvenile offenders by juvenile courts. There are two main models which might account for this: 1) The protection of the public from further criminal activity by the offender; and 2) attention to the criminogenic needs of the individual youngster. Are demographic, psychological, contextual and legal factors equally involved in decisions to award a custodial sentence rather than probation? The researchers obtained a large US sample of over 1300 juvenile offenders in the age range 14–18 years. Both genders were included and the youngsters had committed serious offences (felony offences against persons and property, or a misdemeanor offence involving weapons, or sexual assault). The following were amongst the data collected by the researchers:

- sentence received (disposition) – either probation or confinement (i.e. prison/secure unit);
- demographic characteristics such as age, gender, parents' education level and race;
- legal considerations – current and past involvement with the criminal justice system, including whether the most serious crime involved violence, the number of court referrals they had ever had, and whether previous disposition was probation or not;
- individual factors – psychosocial maturity and mental health problems as well as gang involvement; psychosocial maturity (self-reliance, identity, and work orientation) and IQ; resistance to peer pressure; perspective taking; control over one's impulses; environmental matters to do with school and family.

The participants were interviewed about 37 days after the sentencing on average. Those taking part were mainly from the lower socio-economic status groups. The findings indicated that legal factors were the most important in determining whether a prison sentence or probation was awarded. The more previous court referrals the offender had, the more likely they were to be confined in a prison. Gender was a factor in disposal since males were more likely to receive a prison sentence though there was no evidence that race was related to the disposal method used. However, previous experience of probation increased the likelihood of a probation disposition. Individual factors such as developmental maturity were poor predictors of disposal.

Despite these relatively modest sentencing predictions, one of the most important functions that lawyers have is making predictions about the most likely outcome of taking a case to court or appealing a court decision. Clients go to lawyers partly for advice on what the law is, but also for an assessment of the consequences of legal processes. So, a client who wishes to sue another person for damages needs to know from their lawyer some sort of forecast of the likelihood of success. The advice offered by lawyers can be extremely influential on whether a case goes to court. So lawyers' advice needs to be understood. As yet, not a great deal is known about this. There are a small number of exceptions to this: Fox and Rirke (2002) argued that the task facing a lawyer when making predictions about the outcome of a trial is analogous to any other decision-making process under conditions of uncertainty. Supporting theory is built on the research into such judgements. This theory assumes that probabilities are attached to descriptions of events (or hypotheses) rather than the events as such. Since descriptions of what constitutes a set of events are different from each other, the probabilities assigned to what is otherwise the same event will also differ.

Imagine that the client wants to know whether seeking damages would be successful in court. The lawyer has to judge the probability of outcome A (damages awarded) versus the probability of outcome B (no damages awarded). The theory assumes that the lawyer's estimate of the probability of outcome A plus the probability of outcome B should equal 1, just as it would in statistical probability theory where the probability of a head or a tail when tossing a coin sums to 1. That is simple. However, the theory suggests that, where the possible outcomes are more finely subdivided, the principle of sub-additivity should apply. For example, imagine the lawyer decides that the probability of winning the damages cases is 0.6 (that is, that the client would win in six out of every ten cases like this). What would happen if the probability of winning damages were calculated for two subdivisions of damages – for example, where the damages are more than €10,000 and where the damages are less than €10,000? What happens is that the two probabilities actually sum to more than the 0.6 that they should in theory. The lawyer might assess the probability of getting over €10,000 at 0.4 and the probability of getting under €10,000 at 0.5. Adding these together, this amounts to a probability of 0.9, which is bigger than the rational outcome of 0.6. The more subdivisions of a category, the more the sum of the probabilities of the individual categories would be. There is a further idea – that of implicit sub-additivity. This basically says that the more subdivisions of a category that are listed, the greater the probability that will be assigned. So, for example, if a lawyer is asked the probability that a case will end in a guilty verdict and the defendant put on probation, fined or sent to prison then the probability given will be greater than for when a lawyer is asked simply what the probability is of the case ending in a guilty verdict.

In one study, lawyers were asked to give an estimate of the probability of one or other of a variety of trial outcomes. So one set of lawyers was asked to make some judgements about the outcome of an antitrust case involving Microsoft in the United States. Some estimated the probability that the case would go directly to the Supreme Court. The average probability assigned to this was 0.33. However, when the other group was asked to assess the probability that the case would go directly to the high court and be affirmed, reversed or modified then the probability was judged to be 0.40. This difference supports the principle of implicit sub-additivity. Of course, there is a great deal more that needs to be known but even this one study points in the direction of improving decision making in relevant legal situations by compensating for the biases in lawyers' judgements.

It might be useful here to point out that there is a variety of evidence about the impact of particular lawyers on trials. Williams (1995) reviewed the evidence on this matter and found that the lawyer did not matter much or at all in the majority of studies. His own research was on appeal-level courts. Whether the lawyer was privately employed or a counsel supplied by the public defender made no difference overall. Private attorneys, then, were not more likely to win the appeal. One of the reasons for this may be that many criminal appeals (these were in Florida) are seen as hopeless, frivolous or routine, i.e. unlikely to be affected even by the most brilliant of courtroom performers.

Kulik, Perry and Pepper (2003) asked whether personal characteristics of judges such as their age, gender, political affiliation, and race had an influence on the outcomes of US federal cases of sexual harassment over and above case characteristics such as how serious the harassment was. The research involved a search for suitable cases and obtaining information about the characteristics of the judge. Especially important was the control of case characteristics since these can confound the relationship between judge characteristics and case outcomes. Only in 16 per cent of older judges favoured the plaintiff whereas 45 per cent of younger judges favoured the plaintiff. Other judge characteristics such as their race and gender did not, in this study, impact decision making to a measurable extent. Research has shown that the political affiliation of the judge can have an important effect on case outcomes. Republican appointed judges would be expected to be less socially liberal. This was much as Kulik *et al.* found. As few as 18 per cent of Republican appointed judges made decisions favouring the plaintiff. On the other hand, 46 per cent of the democratic appointed judges did so.

Decision making may be affected by the nature of the offence involved so, in that sense, can sometimes be subjective. Beattey, Matsuura and Jeglic (2014) studied the bail bond setting behaviours of judges in the US. Bail decisions are frequently made speedily by the US courts and there is little by way of standardisation in bail decisions. They found evidence that certain types of crime attracted higher bail amounts than others. Specifically they found that bail for sex offenders was substantially higher than for non-sex offenders. This remained true when the statutory serious-ness of the offence was taken into account. It cannot be explained on the basis of sex offenders being more likely to reoffend when on bail as the evidence does not support this.

The presentation of evidence in court

It is not possible to present just any evidence in court. Structural constraints are defined which essentially prescribe how, what, where and when evidence may be provided. The precise nature of these constraints varies according to jurisdiction, as well as who and what is being tried. There are usually constraints on the *order* in which evidence may be presented in court (Bartlett and Memon, 1995). For example, the accepted structure may involve one-way questioning by lawyers and judges exclusively. The answer may also have an accepted form. Replies such as 'I would say so, wouldn't you?' violate such principles. There are other requirements:

- In adversarial systems, restrictions on the use of information about previous offences are common. Such evidence may be admissible only in circumstances where there are common features between the present charge and the past offences. Even in these circumstances there are constraints. The pre-judicial effect of the information should not exceed the benefits of its provision.
- Furthermore, again commonly in adversarial systems, the accused may only be cross-examined about their past convictions if the character of prosecution witnesses is contested or if the defence concerns evidence of the good character of the defendant (McEwan, 1995).

The procedure is for the prosecution to give its case first, which is then followed by the defence evidence. Many psychologists will be reminded of the research on the effectiveness of different orders of presenting opposing persuasive communications. It has been demonstrated that arguments presented first differ in their persuasive impact from arguments presented second. This is known as the primacy-recency effect. The findings of different studies reveal a complex picture and it is difficult to say that the first argument has greatest impact. Similarly, with court evidence, the research does not result in a simple formula such as the case presented first always has the advantage. The longer the trial, the greater the advantage to the more recent case; the shorter the trial, the greater the advantage of the case presented first (Lind and Ke, 1985).

Bartlett and Memon (1995) suggest a number of strategies that may help a lawyer to persuade jurors and judges of the strength of their case. The first few can be regarded as means of increasing persuasiveness in the argument:

- *Vivid language* enhances the impact of important testimony. Thus they regard 'He came towards me' as bland, whereas 'He lunged at me with flashing eyes and a contorted grimace. . .' (p. 546) might have more effect on the listener.
- *Repetition* of particularly important pieces of information may be an effective strategy.
- *Loaded questions* such as 'Did you see the broken window?' (p. 546) contain an implication that the unwary might accept – that indeed the window was broken. The question 'Did you see the window in question?' contains no such implication.
- *Subtle shifts in wording* may profoundly influence what meaning is chosen for a sequence of events. For example, the phrases 'to sit with you' and 'to sit near you' can have rather different meanings. Nevertheless, despite this, an unwary witness might accept either.

The following strategies concern the manipulation of the credibility of the witness:

- *Powerful speech* styles are characterised by directness, assertiveness and rationality. In contrast, powerless speech contains a high density of 'intensifiers' such as 'so', 'well' and 'surely' together with many words dealing with hesitations such as 'you know' and 'well'. It is also characterised by polite words such as 'please' and 'thank you very much'. According to Bartlett and Memon (1995), the powerful typifies male speech and the powerless typifies female speech. Generally speaking, males using powerful speech were regarded as more credible and much the same was true for female speakers.
- *Making witnesses appear incompetent* by providing, say, expert testimony that casts serious doubt on whether they could possibly have seen what they claim to have seen. For example, it might be impossible to see a face at a given distance in the dim lighting at the time.

Underlying narrative of legal arguments

Many of the major advances in understanding powerful legal arguments have come from trying to understand the narratives that underlie lawyers' cases. Decision making in a legal context is an example of a top-down process (Van Koppen, 1995). One can consider the hypothesis presented in court (the allegation of a crime) as preceding the fact-finding to support or reject that hypothesis. There is not a body of facts that is sifted through and then the most likely person to accuse selected on the basis of the facts. Quite the reverse: someone is thought to be responsible for a crime and then the facts sought that explain the accused's responsibility for the crime. The evidence verifies the charge rather than the charge verifying the evidence. The evidence, as such, is not the key, however. The important thing is the story that links the evidence together. Take the following instance from legal writing that begins with the observation that in car accidents the facts are interpretable in more than one way:

> The fact that the driver did not see the pedestrian is at once an explanation of the collision in terms of accident rather than recklessness, and also a suggestion that he was not keeping a proper lookout.
>
> (Abrahams, 1954, p. 28)

Research evidence has demonstrated that the quality of the narrative is vital in making judgements. In a classic study, Bennett and Feldman (1981) adopted a very simple methodology. They asked students to tell a story to other students – half of them had to tell a true story and the other half were told to invent a story. As might be expected from what we know about lie detection (Chapter 18), listeners could not differentiate between the true story and the invented story at better than the chance level. But, of course, they believed some stories but not others. So here was an opportunity to study the features of stories that made them appear truthful. Believable stories contained what might be termed 'a readily identifiable central action'. This provides a reasonable context for the actions of the participants. Pennington and Hastie (1981, 1986) found that the following were crucial to a good narrative:

- goals of the participants;
- physical conditions;
- psychological conditions.

Bennett and Feldman (1981) give the following story as an example of one which listeners saw as being invented. It involves a birthday party:

> Ummm – last night I was invited to a birthday party for a friend her name's Peggy Sweeney it was her twenty-fourth birthday. At the party we had this just super spaghetti dinner – you know – just great big hunks of meat and mushrooms and what not – a nice salad. And then for dessert we had a um cherry and blueberry um cheesecake. It was really good.
>
> (p. 75)

The researchers argued that this story can be broken down into a number of structural elements: the connections between them being ambiguous. The two elements – I was invited to a birthday party and last night – are joined together as a meaningful connection. Others are not:

> I was invited to a birthday party – At the party we had this just super spaghetti dinner.

The significance of the phrase *At the party we had this just super spaghetti dinner* does not lie in the context of the birthday party. The spaghetti dinner is ambiguous in terms of its relevance to the birthday party story. Similarly, what is the relevance of the phrase 'her name's Peggy Sweeney' to the spaghetti meal? Why mention it? Unless the hearer knows who Peggy Sweeney is, her mention just complicates the picture. If the hearer thought that Peggy Sweeney was an expert in fine food then the ambiguity might be resolved.

> It is not clear what facts, logic, norms, or the like, would yield a clear inference about the relationship between these story elements.
>
> (Bennett and Feldman, 1981, p. 78)

Story ambiguities can be of three distinct types:

- There may be no obvious interpretative rule (fact, language category, norm, etc.) to provide a meaningful link between two elements of the story.
- The listener can see many possible links between the two elements but the rest of the story fails to provide the information to support any of these plausible links.
- The listener can make sensible, that is unambiguous, connection between the story elements but then realises that it is inconsistent with the most obvious connections among the other elements of the story.

Bennett and Feldman suggest that the number of ambiguous linkages of this sort (what they term 'structural ambiguities') partly determines and undermines the credibility or perceived truthfulness of the story. Indeed, they studied a number of predictors of story credibility. Of these, only structural ambiguity showed a substantial relationship with the credibility of the story. The length of the story, the number of actions performed in the story, the number of pauses in the story, and the length of the pauses each had no bearing on story credibility. The structural properties of the story far outweigh factors such as witness credibility, lawyer histrionics and so forth in perceptions of its truthfulness, claim Bennett and Feldman.

The birthday party story, by the way, was true, despite being perceived otherwise. Bennett and Feldman's argument then suggests that the following areas are employed by lawyers in the courtroom when constructing plausible accounts of reality:

- *Definitional tactics:* the language used by witnesses (elicited by lawyers) to define pieces of evidence. Bennett and Feldman give the example of a drunk driving case in which the prosecution lawyer tried to establish the number of beers the defendant had had prior to the offence. The defence tactic was to stress the extended period of time in which drinking had taken place:

Prosecution:	How much did you have to drink that evening prior to being stopped by these police officers? (Objection by the defense)
Prosecution:	Answer the question, Mr. H_____
Defendant:	Well, now, I was working (at) my locker the whole day on Fisherman's Wharf. I have a locker there.
Prosecution:	How much did you have to drink?
Defense:	May he be permitted to answer the question, be responsive. Your Honor? He started to . . . .
The Court:	Go ahead. Let him explain.
Defendant:	Well, it will have to all come into this now, what I am going to say.
Prosecution:	Fine.
Defendant:	I left Fisherman's Wharf . . . .

  (Bennett and Feldman, 1981, p. 119)

  Notice how the defence lawyer shaped the defendant's testimony despite not actually asking the questions. Furthermore, the definition of the drinking behaviour was extended to provide a different picture from the negative impression that would have been created by a simple tally of the number of beers drunk.

- *Establishing and disrupting connections in stories: inferential tactics.* The structural location of a piece of evidence is made in relation to the remaining elements of the story. Bennett and Feldman give the example of a woman prosecuted for robbery. One of the salient facts was that the defendant gave her shoulder bag to a friend before committing the robbery so that she would be able to carry out a better robbery without this encumbrance. Under questioning, she explains that the bag kept slipping because of the leather coat she was wearing, the implication being that this was the reason for handing the bag over:

Q: You could ball the strap in your hand like a leash, couldn't you?
A: Yes.
Q: Isn't it true, Miss V_____, the reason you gave the purse to D_____ was because you wouldn't be burdened down with it when you ran?

(Bennett and Feldman, 1981, p. 126)

In other words, the lawyer made explicit the connection between handing over the bag and the crime.

- *Establishing the credibility of evidence: validational tactics.* Can (a) and (b) be validated by other information and explanations, or can they be invalidated by showing plausible alternative definitions and connections between the elements of the story? An example of this is the use of objections. These serve three purposes: one is to stop prejudicial evidence being presented, a second is to build up a catalogue of errors on which to base an appeal, and the third is really to address the jury:

Prosecution: Isn't it true that in February of 1964 you were convicted of manslaughter and sentenced to twenty years in the state penitentiary?
Defendant: Well, yeah.
Defense: We object to that for the record.
The Court: Overruled.

(Bennett and Feldman, 1981, p. 133)

The prosecution lawyer was acting properly in terms of the location of the court studied. By objecting 'for the record' the impression is deliberately created that such questioning is on the margins of acceptability and that, as such, it should not be given too much weight for fear of inadvertently prejudicing the case.

Anchored narratives are also based on narrative theory that emerges out of cognitive psychology. This argues that evidence is meaningless without being placed into a narrative context. The story is decided upon, not the evidence. The story may have gaps but these are filled automatically by the listener. Wagenaar, van Koppen and Crombag (1993) point to some of the gap-filling in the following:

> Margie was holding tightly to the string of her beautiful new balloon. Suddenly, a gust of wind caught it. The wind carried it into a tree. The balloon hit a branch and burst. Margie cried and cried.
>
> (p. 33)

Now this you probably took to be the equivalent of the following:

> Margie, *a little girl*, was holding tightly to the string of her beautiful new balloon. *The wind was so strong that* suddenly a gust of wind caught it. The wind carried it into a tree. The balloon hit a branch and burst *on a sharp twig. The loss of her balloon made* Margie cry and cry.

But, equally, the story that fits the facts could have been:

> Margie, *a young mother*, was holding tightly to the string of her beautiful new balloon. *Forgetfully, she let go of the balloon*. Suddenly a gust of wind caught it. The wind carried it into a tree. The balloon hit a branch and burst *when a boy managed to hit it with a stone from a catapult*. Margie cried and cried *when the boy turned the catapult on her*.

The story context determines the meaning of the central factors of the story. As a consequence, it is possible to find two radically different stories in which to set the facts to different effects. This is, after all, what prosecution and defence lawyers do to try to achieve opposite ends.

Wagenaar *et al.* (1993), working within the context of earlier 'good story' theories of evidence, suggest that good stories are 'anchored' into a system of general rules which are valid most of the time. This knowledge of the world helps determine the truth-value of the evidence to the listener. Evidence, in itself, does not have this truth-value in the absence of these rules. For example, suppose that the evidence from DNA testing says that X's semen was found in the victim's vagina. This does not prove, in itself, that X murdered the woman. It does not even prove that the pair had intercourse, forcibly or not. The victim might have been a lesbian wanting a child who obtained the sperm from her friend X. She might have inserted the semen using a spatula as she could not bring herself to have sex with a man.

Among the commonsense or legal rules that firmly anchor some stories as true are the following:

- Drug addicts are thieves.
- If a witness has a good sighting of the perpetrator then they will accurately identify the offender.
- Once a thief, always a thief.
- Police officers are the best witnesses.
- Prosecutors usually do not take innocent individuals to trial.
- The associates of criminals are criminals themselves.
- Witnesses rarely lie under oath in court.

These rules need not have any factual basis at all in order to be effective.

There is another way of construing lawyers' activities. From a social-psychological perspective they could be regarded as attempting to manipulate guilt attribution. So the job of the lawyer for the defence is to present his or her client's behaviour in a way that minimises guilt attribution. Schmid and Fiedler (1998) suggest that the social-psychological notion of the peripheral route to persuasion (as opposed to the central route) is appropriate to lawyers' arguments. The central route presents the substantial arguments that are listened to and evaluated. The hearer would normally be critical in their evaluation of these arguments. In the case of the peripheral route, influence is achieved far less directly in a way that does not arouse this critical evaluation. Subtle cues of an evaluative nature, which suggest the response hoped for by the lawyer, become the basis for persuasion. Schmid and Fiedler argue that most listeners in court will be skilled language users who recognise the sorts of strategy for peripheral persuasion employed by the lawyers. If too positive, the risk is that the hearers will simply discount the argument the lawyer is making. The researchers videotaped the closing speeches of lawyers in training. Listeners (jurors, had this been real life) responded to the arguments in terms of a composite of blame attributed to the defendant, the competence of the lawyers, the fairness of the lawyer and so forth. Severity of punishment for the offences was, predictably, dependent on the seriousness of the crime involved. But there was evidence that subtle language strategies also played a role:

- *Intentionality of negative behaviour:* this is defined in terms of the internal attribution of the negative behaviour to the offender. The focus of the cause of the offence is on the offender rather than the victim. This corresponds to different language characteristics. For example, more punishment was suggested when the lawyer used more negative interpretative action verbs (such as *hurt*, as opposed to *help*) to the offender and less to the victim.
- *Dispositionality of negative behaviour:* language characteristics that brought about higher punishment recommendations included descriptive action verbs (such as push and shout).

Do not assume that good narrative accounts of the evidence which favour one side are the only requirements of a good legal case. Spiecker and Worthington (2003) studied the influence of what they call the lawyers' organisational strategies on decisions made in simulated civil courts in the United States. The organisational strategies are the ways in which the lawyer chooses to organise the evidence. Two broad structures were identified – the narrative structure and the legal-expository structure. The narrative organisational structure emphasises such matters as describing the setting of events, describing the series of events in a meaningful and interrelated way, describing the important people in the narrative and organising the narrative in a meaningful temporal fashion. The legal-expository structure emphasises the legal requirements of the decision to be taken. These legal elements may include a description of the relevant law to the case, the nature of the burden of proof required for such cases, and the identification of the legal elements needed in order to establish the case. Each side may take a different view as to whether or not the case in question meets the requirements of proof. Of course, lawyers have more than one opportunity to make their argument. For example, they make opening statements and closing statements. So it is possible to mix the organisational strategies within a case – the opening statement could be narrative and the closing statement legal-expository. In the study in question, various possible combinations of strategies by both sides of the case were studied in terms of their effects on the jury. Broadly, it was found that both sides benefit from having the closing statement centred around a legal-expository format. That is, the lawyer should identify the legal aspects that should govern the case and offer an interpretation as to how well the evidence in a particular case meets these requirements. In terms of the overall strategy, this study showed that using a narrative opening and a legal-expository closing was more effective for the plaintiff's side than using the narrative approach for both. In contrast, the defence fared better with mixed strategy or a legal-expository approach throughout. In other words, the situation is not simply one of the narrative approach being best; it is one in which ignoring other strategies can lead to poor outcomes – strictly narrative approaches were not in the interest of the defence in this case.

Other lawyer tactics

Research has just begun to shed light on some of the tactics used by lawyers in court. The role of the expert witness in the adversarial system requires countermeasures from lawyers of the opposite side. This could be simply using an expert with views contrary to those of the opposition. However, in some locations at least, a more direct line of attack has been tried. Expert witnesses can be targets of various forms of discrediting strategy from the other side's lawyers. For example, should the expert witness be a psychologist then their training and educational background might be criticised, their evidence discredited by questioning psychology's scientific status, and more finely tuned matters such as the controversies associated with the diagnosis of mental illness emphasised. Larson and Brodsky (2010) point out that some of the strategies used in the US involve more personal attacks on expert witnesses. These personal attacks highlight the expert witness's shortcomings. Quite scurrilously, the expert might be asked about their personal substance abuse problems or the circumstances of their divorce. Apparently this style of questioning tends to be reserved more for females acting as expert witnesses. Larson and Brodsky (2010) evaluated the effectiveness of such tactics. In their study, US university students were shown a videoed summary of a murder trial, including part of the cross-examination stage. It concerned a multiple murder in which a father was tried for killing his son, niece, and wife and attempting to kill his daughter. A psychologist acted as an expert witness, assessing the father's state of mind at the time of the killings. The gender of the psychologist was varied across the different conditions of the research design, as was the presence or absence of intrusive personal questioning. Examples of this sort of question included: 'To your knowledge, Dr Jeffries, has your own husband/wife cheated on you, or have you ever cheated on your own husband/wife?' and 'Isn't it true that you psychologists often have sexual feelings toward your clients?' In the transcripts presented to participants of the research, Dr Jeffries essentially rebuts the questioner. The mock jurors tended to rate the female expert witness as less trustworthy, reliable, believable and credible than male ones. However, the gender-intrusive questioning was counterproductive to the lawyer's apparent intent. Experts subjected to this sort of questioning were seen as being more credible, trustworthy and believable than those who were treated more fairly. Apparently, the jurors developed a negative impression of the prosecuting lawyer when his case included these personal attacks.

Another tactic employed by lawyers in the US is to use abstract language when examining child witnesses (see Chapter 20). Generally, previous research has shown that the abstract nature of some lawyer language affects the accuracy of the testimony provided by a child. Typically, defence lawyers ask more complex questions than prosecution lawyers. Such a strategy potentially may lead to less favourable juror perceptions of the accuracy of the child witness. But none of this research has focused on whether the complexity of the questions predicted the outcome of the trial. Evans, Lee and Lyon (2009) addressed the issue of whether the outcome of a trial is predictable from the complexity of the questions asked, using a novel, innovative method involving a computer program which automatically carries out a linguistic analysis of text. The researchers studied the transcripts of 46 Californian child sexual abuse trials. Half of the trials ended in conviction and half ended in acquittal. The average ages of the child witnesses were also equalised across conditions.

The Connexor Functional Dependancy Grammar (FDG) program was used to obtain measures of the complexity and wordiness measures for both the prosecution and defence lawyers in each of the trials. This software provided an in-depth analysis of the syntactical relationships between words in the transcripts. Each question is broken down into noun and verb phrases, using a visual tree diagram output, and then each of these phrases is broken down into tokens (i.e. words). Every time a sentence is broken down, a new layer of the tree diagram is produced. This number of layers was used as the measure of question complexity. The relatively simple sentence 'Do you recall testifying in April and saying that your mother cleaned up after you threw up?' has four layers. In contrast, a similar but more complex sentence 'Do you recall telling us that your mother had cleaned up after you throwing up back in April when you testified?' has six layers.

The trial verdict could be predicted accurately in 83 per cent of cases from the complexity of the defence lawyers' questioning. However, contrary to expectations, complex questions characterised convictions and not acquittals. The defence lawyer's complex questions were related to the verdict through the response that the child makes. If a complex question leads to an answer such as 'I don't know' or no expansion in the response, a conviction was more likely to occur. Simply responding 'Yes' or 'No' to complex questions did not relate to conviction. Replying with 'No' and expanding the response was related to a conviction. Possibly the 'I don't know' answer is seen as an indicator of the child's competency by the jury since they have coped with a complex question with an appropriate response as they have not let the question confuse them.

Naturally, the question which follows from this is whether there are ways of countering a possibly damaging cross-examination by the opposing lawyer. One straightforward tactic is to deal with witness unfamiliarity with the court process by preparing them for the style of question that they may face during the cross-examination. The task facing the witness in court goes beyond the need to speak in public. They also have to cope with potentially unsympathetic questioning by the lawyer for the other side. For witnesses who otherwise might be overawed by the practices of the courtroom, some general training or familiarisation with what to expect may be a positive thing. This does not imply coaching the witness in precisely what to say in court – this would be unacceptable. Nevertheless, sensible trial preparation might help reduce the disadvantages that ignorance can bring. In the UK, the Court of Appeal was content with such familiarisation training in the case of *R* v. *Momodou* (2005). The structure of the examination/cross-examination process is illustrated in Figure 23.2. This questioning, as we have seen, can often involve difficult question formats which in the best of circumstances many may find difficult to cope with – as is only to be expected. 'Lawyerese' questioning is more tactical than clumsy and is not intended to be easily coped with. Leading questions may be posed during cross-examination, though they would be disallowed at other stages in the hearing. The cross-examination process allows for a constructed account of the events to be

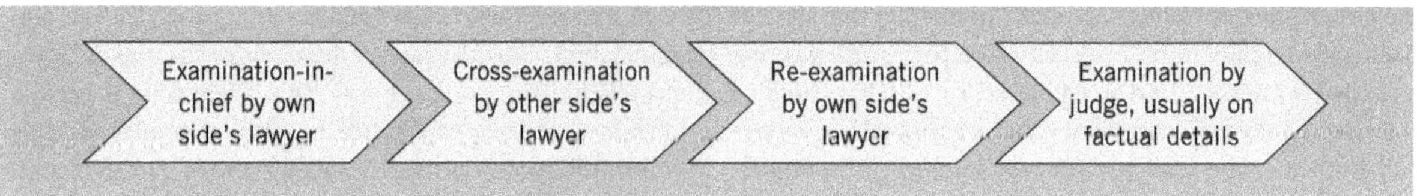

Figure 23.2 The stages of examination and cross examination

presented by the lawyer which counters what the witness has said. So the questioning can be very suppositional in its nature and reinterpretive in intention. Wheatcroft and Ellison (2012) studied a simple method of witness preparation which employed an informative booklet. The research design involved the 'witnesses' watching a crime event. The video was an eyewitness perspective film of a young woman (complainant) standing at a bus stop where she is approached by the two defendants. One of the men brandishes a gun during a brief struggle. The woman is manhandled into the back of a car, which is then driven away at speed by a third but unidentified man. The witnesses were told that they were to be cross-examined on the video. Crucially, some of the witnesses were given the leaflet *A Guide to Cross-Examination*. In this the purpose of the cross-examination was explained – that is, it is an opportunity to test the witness and to obtain information that might support the case that the cross examiner wishes to make. The leaflet included the following in addition:

- Advice to:
  - listen carefully to all of the questions;
  - ask for clarification if you don't understand a question;
  - answer truthfully;
  - only agree with questions/suggestions if they are accurate
- An explanation and examples of leading and multi-part questions.

The other half of the witnesses did not receive the booklet and so were not prepared in the same way for the cross-examiner's questions. Each 'witness' was later cross-examined by a practising barrister in a moot courtroom context. The barrister used either a completely scripted 'lawyerese' cross-examination or a rather simpler scripted version of the cross-examination:

- *The 'lawyerese' scripted cross-examination:* Here the questioning involved complex sentence structures including leading questions, multi-part questions and double negatives, for example 'The shorter defendant was wearing sunglasses and a hat, wasn't he?' The questions also might include incorrect information as well as correct information, such as this three-part question, any part of which might be true without the other parts necessarily being so: 'It would be correct to say that the taller of the two men then placed the woman's suitcase in the boot of the car while the woman herself got into the car and sat in the passenger seat?' (p. 828)
- *Simply phrased cross-examination:* This still included leading and multi-part questions but the language employed was simpler and avoided double negatives. So an example of a simply worded question would be: 'Turning to the weather conditions that afternoon – it would not be inaccurate to say that this was a dry afternoon – would you agree?' whereas the same basic question asked in the lawyerese style might be: 'Turning to the weather conditions that afternoon – it would not be inaccurate to say that this was not a seasonally dry afternoon – would you agree?' (p. 829)

The type of questioning had no effect on accuracy. Perhaps it is not surprising that the simple questioning approach still contained leading questions and multi-part questions. However, the important finding was that those who had been given the guidance booklet were not only more accurate in their answers when being cross-examined but also made rather fewer errors. The number of requests for clarification also increased after the booklet had been read. Multi-part questions were answered as if they were single-part ones, which implies that they remained difficult to deal with even after preparation. When the witness was not cognitively stressed by the need to understand what was happening in the cross-examination, they could retrieve information about the crime events from their memory better.

Another strategy involved in lawyers' work is the advice that they give to their clients about whether or not to agree to a plea bargain. In plea bargaining thee lawyer's client agrees to plead guilty, usually to a lesser charge, in return for a lesser punishment. This is a common practice in the US. Of course, most crimes end with a guilty plea, though the extent to which this is encouraged by plea bargaining agreements is not known. Similar decisions would be necessary in countries where there is an automatic reduction in the punishment tariff if the accused admits guilt at the start of a trial. One implication of this is that jury trials are actually relatively uncommon ways in which to deal with a case. The 'in the shadow of the trial' model of plea bargaining (Mnookin and Kornhauser, 1979) assumes that plea bargaining decisions are based on the strength of evidence in the case and the expected sentence for the crime. This model has come to dominate the literature, though there is good reason to think that it lacks something in sophistication and completeness. Bibas (2004) identified a whole range of influences on plea bargaining over and above evidence strength and expected sentence, including:

- Lawyers on a flat fee may prefer a plea bargain because it means that they can get the job done without spending more time in court.
- Sentencing guidelines strongly push towards plea bargaining in cases like this.
- The defence may be keen to use plea bargaining as a way of encouraging good relations with the judge and the prosecuting lawyers.
- The judge may be keen as a workload-reducing procedure.
- The prosecution may strongly push for a plea bargain because it can reduce time pressures and the like.

Kramer, Wolbranksy and Heilbrun (2007) studied lawyers' decision making when advising a client about plea bargaining. The research extended the situation by having the defence lawyer's client already express a preference concerning plea bargaining. The participants were US attorneys, including private criminal defence lawyers and lawyers working for the public defender's office. They were presented with one of eight versions of the experimental conditions created by the variables 1) high or low likelihood of conviction (i.e. strong or weak evidence); 2) the preference of the client for possible plea bargaining or not; and 3) high likely sentence versus low likely sentence. The sentences were ten years or three years if convicted, which reduced to five years or 18 months with plea bargaining respectively. Attorneys rated the likelihood of recommending a plea on a five-point scale from very likely to very unlikely. Where the evidence was strong, where the likely sentence was long and where the defendant had a preference to go to trial then the lawyers were most likely to recommend plea bargaining. Not surprisingly, when the evidence was weak but the likely sentence, if convicted, long and the defendant had a preference to go to trial then there was a low likelihood of the lawyer recommending a plea bargain deal.

There have been high-profile cases in which the defendant did not appear in the witness box to give evidence in their own defence. The decision by a lawyer not to expose their client to questioning in court is another way in which a lawyer can try to influence the outcome of a trial. Defendants are not required to give evidence in many jurisdictions, including the US, UK and elsewhere. There is clearly potential for the jury to be suspicious of the reasons why the defendant does not take the witness stand, despite it being a right not to do so. At the same time, if the defendant chooses to go into the witness stand to give evidence, then the court may admit into evidence their criminal record (if it is pertinent to the evidence). So there is a risk either way of making things worse for the defendant. It has been commonly and consistently found in research studies that a defendant with a criminal record is perceived more negatively – as lacking somewhat in trustworthiness and credibility. Where any previous offences revealed in court are similar to the current charge then the effects are even stronger. The purpose of introducing the criminal history is to discredit their evidence, but the jury takes things beyond this and makes more general assumptions concerning the character of the defendant. That is, they assume that because a defendant has previously committed a crime then they are likely to have committed the current one also. Thus they attribute the crime to dispositional factors, not situational ones. A whole series of studies by Shaffer (Shaffer, 1985; Shaffer and Case, 1982; Shaffer and Sadowski, 1979) showed that defendants who do not take the stand are more likely to be judged negatively. However, simply taking the stand to claim one's innocence is equally risky (Shaffer and Sadowski, 1979). The jury members may feel that this is merely self-serving rhetoric which is readily discounted.

Jones and Harrison (2009) designed a study to examine the consequences of a defence lawyer's decision to take the witness stand. There were a total of four different conditions in their study (see Figure 23.3) since not all possibilities are legally possible or meaningful (e.g. not going on the witness stand but, nevertheless, a criminal record being revealed). The study involved US students serving as a mock jury in a fictitious case. Two men had got involved in a fight in a bar and one was charged with

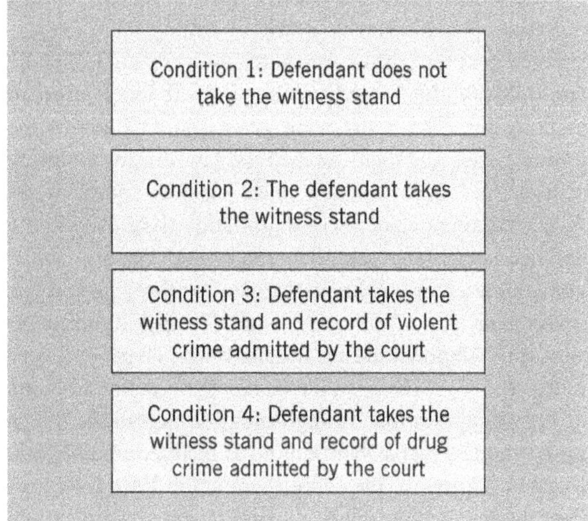

Figure 23.3 The four conditions of Jones and Harrison's (2009) study

assault and battery against the other. A short transcript of the court hearing was provided. The evidence was ambiguous about which of the two men started the fight. The four conditions of the study were:

- The accused did not take the stand.
- The defendant took the stand and said that the victim had started the fight and that he, personally, had acted in self-defence.
- The defendant took the witness stand and the evidence that he had a previous record for similar crimes was introduced.
- The defendant took the witness stand and his previous record for a drugs-related crime was introduced.

There was evidence that jurors who thought the defendant was guilty could be influenced by their failure to take the witness stand. They were also more likely to see the offender as guilty if they perceived him as aggressive, less trustworthy and less credible as a witness. These findings were not dependent on the research manipulations in any way. The jurors were suspicious of the defendants, irrespective of them having a criminal record or taking the witness stand. In other words, the study gave no general indication either way of whether it is best to go on the witness stand or to remain silent as a defendant. However, the trial transcripts did not, in this study, include any instructions from the judge to the jurors about disregarding any implications they might draw from the failure to take the witness stand. This may have affected the outcome somewhat since it is known from past research that such warnings, perversely, merely make jurors more suspicious about the defendant who does not testify (Diamond, Casper and Ostergren, 1989; Wissler and Saks, 1985).

One final possible tactic for lawyers is to employ ingratiation to the jury as a way of getting them favourable towards the lawyer and on the lawyer's side. Ziemke and Brodsky (2015) used a mock trial with mock jurors to explore this. The jurors were given some details of the criminal case and then watched the lawyers for the prosecution and defence make their closing argument on video. Different amounts of ingratiation were used in the defence lawyer's presentation. An example of an ingratiating comment was 'I know that you're all caring and fair individuals, and I know that when you make your decision you will do the caring and fair thing. Thank you very much. (p. 63)'. There was evidence that greater amounts of ingratiation in the closing statements led to the jurors rating the lawyers as being more attractive, credible and likeable. However, the more ingratiation the less confident the lawyer was rated as being. There was no simple relationship between ratings of the lawyer and ratings of the guilt of the person accused of perpetrating the crime. With greater levels of lawyer ingratiation the jurors' ratings of lawyer confidence decreased. Alongside this decrease in rating of lawyer confidence so did the guilt rating of the defendant increase. In summary of this, although ingratiation may be seen as a favourable lawyer tactic, it is likely to work for in the lawyer's favour only if the lawyer can create the impression of confidence at the same time.

Is expert evidence understood in court?

Expert evidence has an important role in court and none more so than forensic evidence. Although some forensic evidence can be absolute in nature, as in the case of DNA evidence, much forensic evidence is at best statistical and probabilistic. Increasingly, forensic scientists use the statistical concept of likelihood ratio when trying to give the diagnostic implications of their investigations. This is known as the *logically correct approach*. The standards of the Association of Forensic Science Providers (2009) actually encourage this to be done in numerical form or using verbal equivalents. Do criminal judges and defence lawyers understand expert testimony given to them in this form? This is the question that de Keijser and Elffers (2012) investigated. In Holland, they have changed to using likelihood ratios in forensic evidence in court. De Keijser and Elffers created fictitious forensic reports which used the likelihood ratio when the forensic expert gave their conclusions. They found that proper understanding of likelihood ratios by the judges and lawyers was actually poor. They also included a group of forensic scientists who did understand likelihood ratios somewhat better, but even they also made some mistakes. The main error made was the prosecutor's fallacy. Just what is this? I am accused of a crime. A bloodstain is found at the crime scene which is the same as mine. If I am the perpetrator of the crime then it is highly likely that I left the bloodstain. The prosecutor would seize on this to press for conviction. But what if I am not the perpetrator of the crime? Because many people have the same blood group as mine then there are many other people who might have perpetrated the crime. The likelihood ratio is the likelihood that I left the blood if I were guilty divided by the likelihood that anyone in general might have left the blood stain if I were innocent. If my blood group occurs in 25 per cent of the population then the likelihood ratio would be 1 (the likelihood of a blood group match if I commit the crime – that is, a certainty) divided by .25 which is the likelihood that a random person from the population left the blood. So in this case the likelihood ratio is 1/.25 = 4. Of course, if my blood group was so rare that just one person in a thousand had it then the likelihood ratio would be 1 divided by .001, which is a likelihood ratio of 1000. This is much stronger evidence that I am guilty of the crime. Despite their poor showing in the study, the judges and lawyers generally believed that they understood the meaning of likelihood ratios. (The older way of expressing the forensic science was to put in words the likelihood of me being the source, given the evidence. This is the logically incorrect way.)

Martire, Kemp, Watkin, Sayle and Newell (2013) provide evidence which is perhaps even more concerning than the relative inability of people to understand forensic evidence presented to them in the form of a likelihood ratio. The weak evidence effect is a familiar finding in cognitive psychology. It refers to the research finding that when evidence provided by experts is little in favour of guilt it is perceived as evidence of guilt. Two very similar experiments were carried out in Australia. Participants read a vignette dealing with a larceny trial in which the strength of the evidence was varied at random from low to moderate to high depending, on the condition in the first study. The information was either presented numerically or verbally. One important finding was the evidence in favour of the weak evidence effect – that is, when the expert evidence was only weakly in favour of guilt, those exposed to the expert opinion tended to believe that the offender was guilty. This is of course the very reverse of what the expert forensic opinion implied. This effect was stronger for the verbally presented forensic evidence. The second study was similar, except that the forensic expert evidence was either pointing towards guilt or towards innocence and only low- and high-strength levels were included. The weak evidence effect was found again, but only for the inculpatory evidence and not for the exculpatory. Of course, these are counterintuitive finding but ones which have regularly been found in non-forensic contexts. The figures are substantial for the numbers responding incongruently with the expert's evidence in the weak condition with the verbal presentation. About 62 per cent responded counterintuitively in these circumstances. However, the other groups only had 13 per cent on average who responded counterintuitively.

In the US, Thompson and Newman (2015) investigated understanding of forensic statistics including likelihood ratios, random match probabilities in which the probability of things occurring by chance is given, and verbal equivalents as explained by an expert. This was done for a DNA comparison and a shoeprint comparison. 'Verdicts' were affected by the strength of the DNA comparison irrespective of the way the expert explained it. But this was not the case for the shoeprint comparison where only the random match probabilities approach produced the appropriate variation in the verdict.

Judgements

Courts of law work through the rather formal language of legal experts, including judges and lawyers. Inevitably, then, this specialized use of language must be a primary focus of research. Harris (1994) argued that the language of the law is basically and effectively highly ideological. So she regards concepts such as equality before the law and impartiality of judgement as the meat of ideological conflicts in courtroom exchanges. She suggests that the magistrates in the courts she studied use propositions that are inevitably ideological in that they are not verifiable for their truth. They reinforce power and domination relationships, and are effectively presented as common sense. However, this is expressed in complex ways. Feminist writers have noted that the higher courts, especially, have great power to define the parameters of a range of important topics. Williams (1991) describes the role of the US Supreme Court in relation to gender equality. She suggests that legal cases are a 'focal point' where the issue and meaning of equality may be argued.

If judges do ideological work then just how is this achieved? The lack of a repertoire of discourse appropriate to certain crimes may result in them being interpreted through other inappropriate frameworks (Coates, Bavelas and Gibson, 1994). These authors mention a Canadian trial judgement concerning a man who went into a room and put his penis in the mouth of a sleeping woman. How one describes these events may vary according to perspective, but the trial judge described this as 'the act of offering his penis' (p. 189). Now this is a rather strange use of the verb 'to offer'. Had the woman been sexually attacked in the street it is inconceivable that a judge would use a phrase such as 'the accused offered the victim his penis' if he had put his penis in her mouth or told her to fellate him. That is, in terms of our usual discourse about stranger rape, the phrase 'to offer' has no meaning. It implies choice on the part of the woman. The language might be more appropriate if the events are interpreted using the discourse repertoire of erotic/affectionate relationships. In the context of a long-standing relationship, it is just about possible to understand the use of the verb 'to offer'. That is, it was a direct and forthright sexual invitation in a relationship in which the partners had previously established a mutually acceptable robust approach to sex and the man was 'offering' sexual intercourse. The authors surveyed a number of relevant judgements and suggested five 'anomalous' themes in similar trials:

- *Appropriate resistance:* this is the idea that victims have certain obligations to prevent or resist the attack on them. Physical struggling is part of the appropriate actions of a victim, it would appear from the judges' comments. In one of the judgements, the victim is described as eventually acquiescing to her own rape once she ceased struggling: 'She testified that after the first bout of intercourse she stopped struggling and that she acquiesced in the second bout, although the inter course was still without her consent' (p. 195). Ehrlich (1999), dealing with a university disciplinary hearing, describes related linguistic devices. One woman was questioned in the following way: 'You never make an attempt to put him on the floor or when he leaves the room, to close the door behind him or you know you have several occasions to lock the door. You only have to cross the room. Or move him to the floor, but these things are offensive to you?' (p. 244). Ehrlich suggests that this actually contains forceful illocutory assertions rather than questions. In other words, 'You should have put him on the floor; you should have closed the door; you should have locked the door' (p. 244).

- *Avoidance of agency for assault:* the actions involved in the sexual violence were frequently ascribed to the events themselves rather than to the offender, in phrases such as 'the struggle got into the bedroom' and 'there was advantage taken of a situation which presented itself' (p. 196). The acts seem to be doing themselves rather than being done by the offender.
- *Erotic/affectionate characterisation:* judges described sexual crimes in terms of a man carrying out an offence against women or children as for the man's sexual gratification. This is to minimise or deny that the crime is an assault and also to suggest that it is sexual in nature rather than violent. Similarly, the language used to describe the attacks carries very different implications from what had actually happened. For example, forced oral contact was described as 'attempted unsuccessfully to kiss'. Forced oral/genital contacts were described as 'acts of oral sex'. Forced vaginal penetration was described as a 'bout of intercourse' (p. 192).
- *Offender's character:* the judges often described the man's character in very positive terms. For example, a man who raped a woman on two occasions was described as being of 'impeccable character' (p. 196).
- *Sexual assault distinct from violence:* especially from a feminist viewpoint, to describe a sexual assault as non-violent is to undermine the notion that sexual assault is a violent act: for example, 'there was no violence and no physical force' (p. 194).

In a similar vein, Cederborg (1999) showed how, in the context of child abuse trials, Swedish judges construct children's credibility as witnesses. Overwhelmingly, the judgements encouraged the view that the children were credible. Such children, according to Cederborg, were perceived as credible because they fitted the judge's commonsense theory of what behaviour is normal. For example, 'Nancy told her story calmly and clearly and with no contradictory details. Her stories at the main hearing agreed well with her previous statements' (p. 151). The material in the judgement relevant to Nancy's character included 'It must be regarded as out of the question that at the age of 11 Nancy would have been sexually interested in him and should have even suggested that they have intercourse' (p. 151). Nancy's case was one of the majority in which the accused was convicted. In cases in which there was not a conviction, the judgement almost always lacked any assessment of the character of the child. An instance of the sorts of terminology and style used by the judges in these cases is the following: '. . . despite the efforts of the interrogating officer, this questioning does not give any clear impression that Hilda F actually experienced the events about which she answered questions' (p. 153). The judge's assessment of the child cannot be validated by any existing test so the interpretation becomes a subjective reality.

Decision making in court

Legal decision making is governed by a variety of formal aspects such as the use of case law, precedents, guidelines and so forth. So any discussion of the psychology of legal decision making needs to be considered in this wider context. In other words, the work of judges in courts of law is highly structured, which may limit the potential influence of psychological factors. Even so, the psychological research literature concerning how judges reach decisions is not extensive. Of course, judges are a hard-to-reach research population and the opportunities to study them directly are limited for obvious reasons. Consequently, sometimes the research literature concerning legal decision making by judges elides into that on how jurors make decisions in courts of law. It is far from clear that there are distinct psychological approaches to juror and judge decision making. Often similar theoretical ideas could apply equally to the two. Nevertheless, there are occasions when researchers obtain access to judges as participants in their research. Such examples are particularly to be welcomed, though their scarcity value exceeds their impact as a body of knowledge.

One example of this rare sort of research concerned the influence of the label 'psychopathy' on the judgements of young offenders (Jones and Cauffman, 2008). The concept of psychopath refers to a glib, charming, callous, self-centred, irresponsible and amoral cluster of personality characteristics. This is discussed elsewhere in Chapters 21 and 27. As a concept applied to young offenders it is controversial and debated with an unusual degree of passion on each side. One issue is that the term 'psychopath' serves as a label which may steer the way that the individual is treated by the criminal justice system into their adult lives. The study by Jones and Cauffman showed that the label of psychopathy changed perceptions of amenability to treatment and dangerousness, together with recommendations for placement made by US judges. The study involved 100 well-experienced judges working in juvenile and adult courts in south-eastern USA. Judges from adult courts would be involved in judgements where a young person has been sent to adult court for trial by a juvenile court. Various scenario cases were distributed at random to the judges, who read them and then responded to a series of questions. The basic scenario was an aggravated assault between two 15-year-old male youngsters involving a mutual assault. There is considerable legal discretion in the disposal (sentencing, etc.) of aggravated assault. This discretion makes aggravated assault ideal to show extra-legal factors in the decision making of judges. The manipulation of psychopathy appeared in information concerning a mental health expert's testimony. Of the four scenarios, one contained no mental health information; the second indicated that the defendant was a psychopath; the third was attributed the characteristics of psychopathy (such as manipulativeness, pathological lying, lack of emotion or remorse, refusal to accept responsibility for their own actions, difficulties in controlling anger, etc.); and the fourth condition included both the attribution of these traits and the label of 'psychopath'. The judges rated the youngster on four characteristics – culpability, restrictiveness, amenability and dangerousness. Young people labelled as psychopaths and those who had psychopathic traits applied to them were seen as less amenable to treatment and were recommended for a disposal which involved restrictive placements. However, judgements about their culpability were NOT influenced by such ratings. When perceptions of dangerousness were controlled, this relationship was no longer significant. This suggests that psychopathy is equated with dangerousness in the minds of these judges.

Ideally, one would like and expect professionals within the criminal justice system to be open to the possibility that the suspect identified by the police is innocent. But we know from well-established psychological research findings that there is a tendency or bias towards confirming our beliefs rather than disconfirming them. This is known as the *confirmation bias* and was first demonstrated in a classic, early study by Wason (1968) which had nothing at all to do with crime. Participants in the study were given a set of four cards and asked to decide whether the set fitted a rule supplied by the researcher. They were told that each of the four cards had a letter on one face and a number on the other, hidden, face. The rule for their consideration was that if one face showed a vowel then the other face had to show an even number. Imagine that the participant is shown four

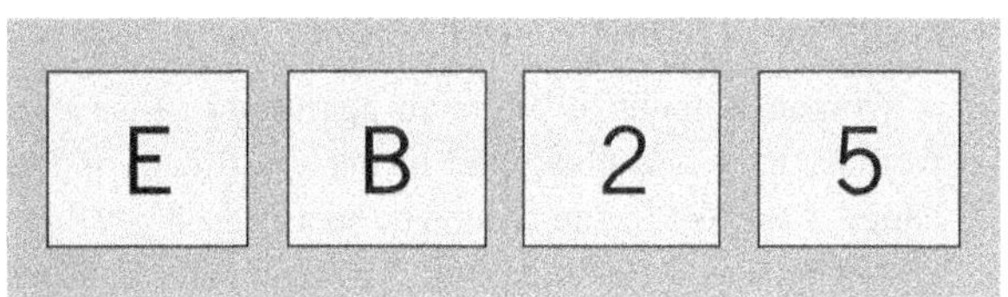

Figure 23.4 What cards need to be turned over to test the rule that if there was a vowel on one side there is an even number on the other?

cards with the following on the visible faces – E, B, 2 and 5 (see Figure 23.4). The task for the participant is to turn over as few cards as possible to determine whether the vowel–even number rule is true. The most effective strategy would be to turn over just two of the four cards – the one showing the vowel (E) and the one showing the odd number (5). The other two cards logically have nothing to do with testing the rule. The findings indicated that most people basically make choices which confirm the rule. So they tend to turn over cards which at best can only confirm the rule – they ignore the important cards which could disconfirm the rule. Thus they do not usually turn over the card with the odd number (5) despite the fact that if there is a vowel on the hidden side then the rule is disproven.

Evidence over the years has supported the idea of confirmation bias in people's thinking. That is, they do not seek the evidence to disconfirm what they think. They have a preference for the evidence which supports what they think. Hence the importance of understanding the role of the confirmation bias in the criminal justice system. Ask and Granhag's (2005) study of police officers found that they were not affected by the knowledge of an alternative suspect when judging the incriminating power of the rest of the evidence available to them. This is discussed in Chapter 11. Rassin (2010) carried out two studies related to this, the first of which replicated Ask and Granhag's study with a sample which included judges and district attorneys as well as police officers as in the original study. Participants were given one of two alternative vignettes describing a crime. The first was called the motive version and was as follows:

> A woman is found dead in an apartment. A second woman, Eva, is encountered in the apartment, and is hence a suspect in the case. The victim is a psychiatrist who was acquainted with Eva and who had her office in the apartment. Eva's partner was a client of the victim, and hence (the partner and the victim) had regular contact. According to the victim's assistant, Eva had expressed suspicion about a sexual relationship between the victim and Eva's partner and was deeply jealous. The following observations have been made thus far in the investigation . . .
>
> (pp. 155–6)

The 'alternative suspect' version read:

> A woman is found dead in an apartment. A second woman, Eva, is encountered in the apartment, and is hence a suspect in the case. The victim is a psychiatrist who was acquainted with Eva and who had her office in the apartment. The victim had recently received several phone calls from an anonymous man who each time threatened to kill her with a knife. These phone calls are known to the police from before. The victim had told the police that she thought the man must be a patient or a former patient. The following observations have been made thus far in the investigation. . .

The vignettes then went on to list some facts about the crime such as:

- it happened at lunchtime;
- when she returned back to work after lunch, the victim's assistant found the apartment door was locked from the inside;
- worried, the assistant phoned for police assistance;
- the police banged on the door, which was eventually opened by the suspect, etc.

Twenty items of information like the above were rated separately on a scale from exonerating to incriminating by participants. They then rated the guilt of the suspect and whether they would convict the suspect. All of the professional groups studied gave much the same evaluations of the incriminating power of the known evidence. Most importantly, judgements about the incriminating power of the evidence were not affected by the suggestion that there was another suspect. That is to say, this is evidence of the confirmation bias in operation. Quite clearly, confirmation bias has to be regarded as worthy of inclusion in explanations of judicial decision making.

As mentioned earlier, the opportunities of researchers to study actual judges are somewhat limited. So any evidence, no matter how preliminary, warrants consideration. De Keijser and van Koppen (2007) proposed two possible psychological mechanisms which may affect the decisions judges make about guilt or innocence and the appropriate punishment for a particular crime:

- *The conviction paradox:* according to de Keijser and van Koppen, the conviction paradox suggests that, for very serious cases, judges adopt a lower standard of proof than they ordinarily would for less serious offences. De Keijser and van Koppen relate this suggestion to signal detection theory (see Figure 23.5). Signal detection assumes that there are two kinds of stimuli – the signal and the non-signal. The decision maker has to decide between each of these two. However, the problem is that there is a background of noise and that most signals are continuous and not discrete so signal detection is prone to errors. Two types of error are possible – a false positive, where a non-signal is detected as being a signal, and a false negative, where a signal is detected as being a non-signal. In judicial decision making there is a choice between guilty and not guilty. The characteristics of the guilty and the not-guilty overlap quite considerably. This requires decision criteria of guilt to be established. There is a trade-off between the risks inherent in a false not guilty decision and a false guilty decision. Legal rhetoric has it that it is 'better to acquit ten guilty persons than to convict a single innocent'. There is evidence from research that jurors tend to go for a guilty decision where the charge is more serious, all other

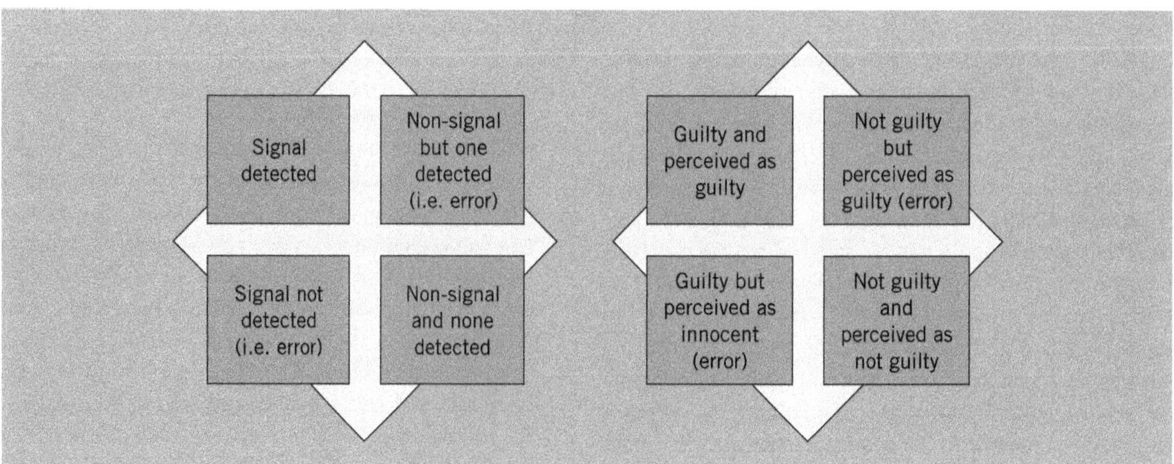

Figure 23.5 The basic signal detection problem applied to judicial judgements

things being equal. Although one would tend to think that judges are more stringent in serious cases where the punishments can be expected to be large, the risks of letting a terrorist go free are much greater than letting a shoplifter go free. So criteria become less stringent, not more stringent, where the crime is serious and the risks of acquittal for the public greater.

- *Compensatory punishment mechanism:* this suggests that, where the evidence is relatively weak, judges who decide on a guilty verdict will tend to compensate for their initial doubts by giving lesser punishments. The authors indicate that psychological research has demonstrated the influence of anticipated regret for the possible outcomes. Generally speaking, the judge goes for the safe option in their decision making. This means that the judge, when choosing a punishment, will opt for a more lenient sentence in the case of a serious crime. There is evidence of this from studies of negligence cases but none for criminal cases.

De Keijser and van Koppen's study involved Dutch judges and justices serving in criminal courts. They were supplied with fictitious but very realistic dossiers on criminal cases. The crimes involved were aggravated assault, simple assault and burglary. The strength of the evidence was manipulated, with some versions involving strong evidence and others minimal evidence but legally sufficient to allow a conviction. Where the evidence was strong, a guilty decision was given, no matter whether it was a serious case or not. There were no differences in the pattern of decisions made for the cases where the evidence was weak, whether or not the offence was serious. There was no support for either of the proposed mechanisms in de Keijser and van Koppen's research. This may be disappointing theoretically, but given that the data were from real judges makes the findings of some importance.

Judges (and jurors too) need to evaluate accurately all kinds of witnesses, including defendants. There are, however, doubts as to their ability to do that. Why should it be so difficult? According to Porter and ten Brinke (2009), part of the explanation may be found in dangerous decision theory (DDT), which may help us understand just how injustices occur in the courtroom (see Figure 23.6). The problem lies in the initial interpretation of information gleaned from the face of the defendant or their expressions of emotion. For many reasons judgements made in this way are risky since, for example, there are no perfect indicators of honesty and many misleading indicators (as discussed in Chapter 18). Research has shown that judges, when sentencing, are influenced by pragmatic ways of thinking based on their previous

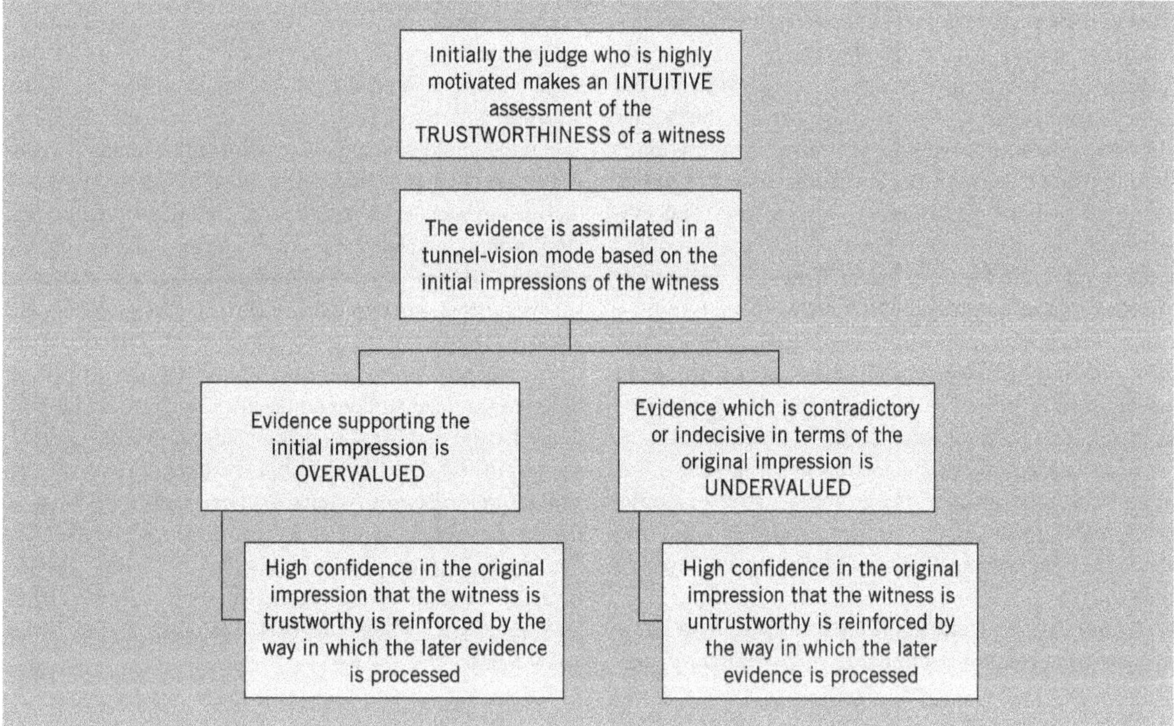

Figure 23.6 The dangerous decisions theory of how assessments of credibility are used in the courtroom

experiences in court. Judges are highly influenced by initial impressions. Motivation will lead to close scrutiny of evidence but initial impressions colour the entire decision-making process.

Witness demeanour and the 'face of deceit' may well be involved. If judges concentrate on the face and demeanour and incorrectly understand them as indicating lying then errors may dominate in their decision making. Such impressions are risky, but they nevertheless initiate a whole sequence of dangerous decisions about credibility. Although these initial judgements are highly influential, they are perceived as being intuitive and not, for example, based on prejudices or biases. An informal survey of judges in Canada about the characteristics indicative of deception found virtually a complete lack of consensus about what such indicators are, though things like body movements, fidgeting and eye contact were mentioned (Porter, Woodworth and Birt, 2000). Nevertheless, the judges expressed a high level of confidence in their own ability to detect deception. Judges commonly self-report using strategies which seek the ring of truth in the testimony. This is relying on intuition or gut instinct, according to the authors of the research. Porter *et al.* found that self-reported reliance on intuition was inversely correlated with judges' accuracy at identifying deception! The initial judgement – whatever it is and however accurate it is – tends to persist and influence the interpretation and assimilation of subsequent evidence about the defendant. These later interpretations of the evidence are irrational but appear rational because each judge has their own schemas concerning people's trustworthiness or schemas about trustworthiness and methods (or heuristics) for deciding whether the behaviour of a witness is deceptive. The judge is highly motivated to reach a decision or conclusion. A sort of tunnel vision (or perhaps confirmation bias) ensures that evidence supporting the initial perception is preferred and so takes a hold. In contrast, disconfirming or ambiguous information is underplayed. The outcome is that, right or wrong, the initial impression influences later evaluations. Relying on stereotypical beliefs about deceptive behaviour may introduce biases in the decisions made about different cultural groups. Social science research (Vrij, 2000) suggests that detection of lying across different cultural groups is difficult. For example, Aboriginals in Canada tend to suppress their emotions, which may undermine their credibility in the eyes of some judges.

Although there is little evidence that judges and jurors can assess the credibility of people at all accurately, they make credibility judgements quite frequently. Sometimes they do so on the basis of minimal information such as facial expression only. We can make very rapid assessments of an individual merely from their facial expressions. These impressions can be treated almost as if they were facts – though they are probably incorrect. One study found that we can evaluate the trustworthiness of faces in about a tenth of a second and that the judgement does not change with longer exposures (Willis and Todorov, 2006). Extra time merely increases confidence in that judgement. In a demonstration of dangerous decision theory, Porter, ten Brink and Gustow (2010) used early impressions based on facial expressions and showed that they profoundly biased the interpretation of subsequent information about individuals. Porter *et al.* used hypothetical criminal cases which had their basis in true cases. These included a robbery/murder; a sexually motivated murder; a car theft; and a fraud. The first two were the serious crimes and the final two the more petty crimes. Participants in the study were randomly allocated to either the serious or the petty crime conditions. A photograph of the 'defendant' was attached to the vignette. The photo could either be of someone who independent third parties had rated as highly trustworthy in appearance or of someone who looked untrustworthy. The two types of photograph balanced across the crimes. There was a set of evidence for each crime which began with ambiguous items, then went on to inculpatory items and then to an exonerating item. The participant read the evidence until they were certain beyond reasonable doubt that the accused was guilty or innocent. At this stage, they indicated the culpability or otherwise of the accused and rated their confidence in their decision. When the photo was of an untrustworthy-looking person, it took less evidence in order to reach a guilty verdict and the verdict was decided with more confidence in the decision compared with the trustworthy-looking photo. Actually, things were even more intriguing than this since participants would decide on the guilt of the untrustworthy-looking person based solely on the ambiguous evidence. When the person looked trustworthy then they would need to hear some of the incriminating evidence before making a decision. This was for the serious crimes; they did not need more incriminating evidence to convict the trustworthy-looking defendant in the case of the minor crimes. In other words, in support of dangerous decision theory, initial invalid credibility assessments based on facial expression led to a decision making process which was biased strongly by the initial assessment.

Main points

- Courts of law provide procedures for the presentation of evidence and the making of judgements. The two broad approaches to justice are 1) the adversarial system employed in Anglo-American countries in which opposing sides do battle against each other and 2) the inquisitorial system, which is largely led by the judge/magistrate, who may be involved at an early stage of police work. Nevertheless, even within a particular system, there are many procedural and other variations.
- A great deal is known about persuasive communications from the psychology of communications and attitude change, for example. However, the emphasis in forensic psychology has been on the importance of narrative structures rather than, for example, peripheral factors such as the authority of the lawyers involved. A good narrative structure is one that unites the individual components of evidence into a coherent story which supports one's own side in the case. Anchored narrative theory goes one step further by suggesting that notions which are grounded in commonsense notions of what is true, for example, will tend to be more effective. Dangerous decision theory and other evidence draw attention to the problematic nature of legal judgements.
- From a feminist perspective, judges seem to do a great deal of ideological work when faced with cases involving women victims. So commentaries made about particular events tend to present the evidence in terms favourable to the man's point of view. For example, a man who had a history of raping women might be described as having 'an impeccable character'. These tendencies can be contrasted with the idea that decision making in court follows a hypothesis-testing model in which probabilities are calculated mentally about each stage of the evidence. There is no reason to believe that such a model applies in court.

Further reading

Posey, A.J. and Wrightsman, L.S. (2005) *Trial Consulting* Oxford: Oxford University Press.

Wiener, R.L. and Bornstein, B.H. (2011) *Handbook of Trial Consulting* New York: Springer.

Carson, D. and Bull, R. (2003) *Handbook of Psychology in Legal Contexts* (2nd edn) Chichester: John Wiley. (section 3)

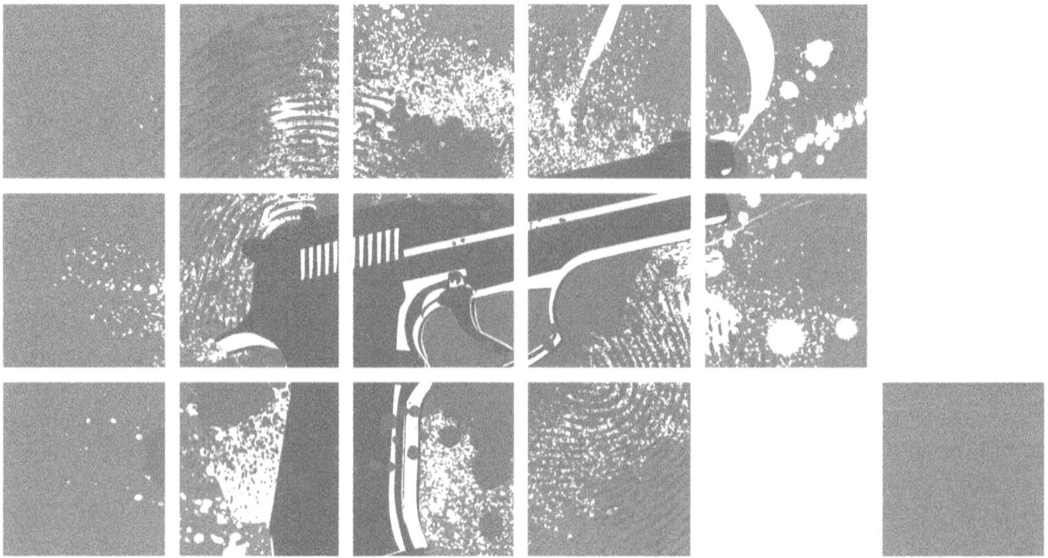

Chapter 24

Juries and decision making

Overview

- Only a small percentage of criminal cases are heard before a jury. Trials with juries reduce the importance of the judge in decisions of guilt or innocence. Evidence is presented orally in jury trials so there is less reliance on written documentation than in inquisitorial systems.
- In the US legal system some scope exists for lawyers to influence the jury's make-up by peremptory challenges of some jurors. Research on improving the effectiveness of these challenges has used surveys to identify the sorts of juror who are sympathetic to, say, the defence. This is known as scientific decision making, though the evidence in its favour is not compelling.
- Simple changes can help alleviate some of the problems which jurors face. For example, permitting note-taking by jurors and allowing them to ask questions in court.
- Jury decision making is governed by rules determining permissible jury sizes and the size of the majority on which a guilty verdict can be reached. The larger the jury, the longer the decision time. Where a majority decision as to guilt is required, the jury makes more effort to try to reach a verdict.
- Simulated jury research is inevitably the norm given the lack of access of researchers to real juries and jurors. Important questions arise about the applicability of such research.
- Pre-trial publicity can influence potential jurors. However, in law, prejudice is not conceived in the same way as it would be in a psychological study. In the United States prejudice would involve a resistance to change one's mind in the light of new information.

Introduction

Trial by jury became part of English law in the twelfth century as an alternative to trial by ordeals such as walking on hot coals. In England and Wales about 95 per cent of criminal cases are tried in a magistrates' court before three lay magistrates supported by expert legal advice. Only about 5 per cent are tried in a higher court with the possibility of a trial by jury (Crown Prosecution Service, 2011a). Thus the role of the jury trial should not be overstated, although the figures may be different in other jurisdictions. Everyone is familiar with well-publicised instances of juries acquitting defendants who seemed to be guilty beyond any question of doubt. Inevitably, such cases lead to questioning of the jury system. Nevertheless, we can all appreciate the complex task of jurors and the pressure that they can sometimes be under. Is there anything that can be done to aid jurors in these circumstances? Very simple procedural changes, such as allowing jurors to take notes or perhaps to ask questions, might be advantageous.

As in many other forensic issues, there is considerable doubt about the worth of laboratory experiments for addressing research questions such as these. It matters little if psychologists are happy with such procedures if those responsible for policy will not accept the findings of their research. The procedures are easily defined as artificial since real juries are not involved. Field studies, because they usually lack random allocation to experimental and control conditions, are similarly beset with problems in terms of interpretation. This chapter will range widely into the limited research into the jury and, especially, how juries reach decisions. Wherever possible, we will concentrate on research that involves real juries, but this is quite rare. There is a great deal more research involving mock jurors of various sorts. There is no single type of mock jury and the term can refer to individuals making judgements in isolation in a psychological laboratory as much as to a fairly realistic representation of a typical jury deliberating in a research setting which is very close to the situation in a real court of law. Anything which is not a real jury in a real court with real evidence making decisions which affect the future of individuals is a mock jury. Care is needed to evaluate how convincing a particular sort of mock jury is (see Box 24.1).

In addition to discussing how juries make decisions, we will also consider what can be done to enhance the likelihood that the evidence of one side of the case will prevail.

Scientific jury selection and litigation consultation

Trial or litigation consultancy involves the work of psychologists and other social scientists helping to influence a trial in favour of one of the sides. It is now possible to study it in US universities (Cramer and Brodsky, 2014). It also has a professional body the *American Society of Trial Consultants* (ASTC). In the legal world there is a vast amount of advice to lawyers written by prominent lawyers about juries and jurors (Fulero and Penrod, 1990). This advice alludes to many 'theories' about what sorts of people make 'good' jurors for the prosecution or defence. Take, for example, the following advice taken by Fulero and Penrod from a number of texts about female jurors which may appear arcane if not bizarre to you as it did all those years ago:

- Avoid women as they are unpredictable and influenced by their husbands.
- Old women wearing too much make-up are unstable and bad for state prosecutors.
- Women are not good for the defence of attractive females.
- Women are sympathetic and extraordinarily conscientious jurors.
- Women's libbers may be antagonistic to male defendants.

It should be taken for granted that none of this advice is based on empirical research.

In the US, a plethora of advice and support for lawyers preparing court cases is commercially available as a quick search of the Internet will show. This tradition is very different from most psychological research on jury decision making since the objective is to gain advantage for one side in the courtroom rather than improve the overall fairness of jury trials. Scientific jury selection is something of an outmoded term and outside of academia the phrase 'trial consultant' is more likely to be used. The original work on scientific jury selection concentrated on the jurors' demographic characteristics which related to how they voted in the jury room. Nowadays the focus is more on developing an overriding 'theory' to help the development of the case by the lawyers (Seltzer, 2010). Predicting the outcome of the trial is seen now as a somewhat futile and irrelevant task, given the complexity of the trials involved. So the preference now is not to use surveys to collect data on basic correlates of decision making but to use focus groups and trial simulations. The focus is on generating an overriding theory of the development of the case for use by the lawyers. Trial consultants are concerned with predicting potential jurors' likely attitudes to the case. The sort of group averages obtained from telephone surveys are seen as too blunt an instrument to be useful. These group averages are poor at predicting the thinking of an individual and, hence, hopeless for predicting how juries will deliberate. Jury research, though, can help develop the trial strategy, including a profile of favourable and unfavourable individuals which can help guide peremptory challenges to jurors. Trial consultants attempt to predict attitudes towards a case and not the verdict. Selzer advises that very particular characteristics of a particular juror may be far more influential in some cases than any of the factors explored in the data. Such characteristics are impossible to identify in surveys. So the trial consultant and lawyers should be willing to abandon the research evidence in these circumstances.

Finkelman (2010) lists some of the main activities carried out by litigation consultants in their quest to develop persuasive themes to present to the jury or otherwise tip the balance:

- *Change of venue surveys:* Trial venues may seemingly be unfair because of factors such as adverse pre-trial publicity in the community or it being in some way a community with attitudes unfavourable to one side. Surveys may be conducted to assess whether the venue is unduly unfavourable to the defence. However, adverse pre-trial publicity may not be sufficient reason to get the venue shifted.
- *Coaching and counselling:* Litigation work is stressful and demanding. There may be informal counselling support provided by the litigation consultant in support of the lawyers. This is probably an informal role rather than a specific brief.
- *Jury selection:* The task here is to work out how the beliefs and attitudes of the individual juror in the jury deliberation will come to favour their side. An important issue is whether the juror is likely to become a leader during the deliberations. Gut instinct may be used but so is the use of research evidence. So the results of attitude surveys and other measurement scales would be appropriate. But such broad-based information needs to be adapted to the needs of a particular case. General demographic tendencies may not be sufficiently precise.
- *Mock trials:* In this a complete 'mock' trial is staged. But, of course, the financial cost of these is high, particularly as the validity of the mock trial needs to be as great as possible. Often the staged trial takes place in the location of the trial, using people eligible for jury service. The jury deliberation is videotaped and may be viewed by interested parties, who may raise issues to be discussed with the jury. All stages of the trial are involved, including opening statements for each side, witness evidence, examinations and cross examinations, expert witnesses, etc. These staged juries provide meaningful data by which to evaluate the themes to be developed by the lawyers. The likely financial costs of losing the case may also be calculated.
- *Opening and closing argument testing:* There is reason to believe that over 80 per cent of jurors have come to their final verdict by the end of the opening statements. It is obviously desirable to make these statements as effective as possible as they influence how the rest of the hearing is perceived. Memorable themes or psychological anchors are an important contribution to the power of the statement. The opening remarks may be tested on a sample as similar to the actual jury as possible, preferably using the actual lawyer to make the presentation as his or her style may affect how the statements are perceived. This may be a mock jury or a focus group.
- *Post-trial juror interviews:* If it is permitted, attorneys and jurors may talk after the trial is over. The feedback may be in the interests of the long-term performance of both lawyers and trial consultants.
- *Shadow juries:* One way of doing this is to recruit a sample of potential jurors who sit in as visitors to the court and listen to and observe what is going on. At the end of each court session, the shadow jury meets with the trial consultant away from the court to address a number of issues about the day in court. Usually, the consultant requires the shadow jury members to indicate their likely verdict at the end of each day. The whole point is that all of this information may be used to adjust strategies where necessary or otherwise repair any damage that happened during the day.
- *Voir dire research:* This is the preliminary assessment of prospective jurors to see whether they are qualified and suitable for the task. The voir dire in the US may involve questioning by the judge or the lawyers. The intention of the lawyer during the voir dire is to maximise the number of jurors favourable to their case and minimise the numbers likely to be antagonistic or punitive to one's side. Obviously, the lawyer does not wish to expose their strategy to the other side's lawyers, so trial consultants provide, if they can, pre-researched questions which identify the right sort of juror while not making it obvious what their intent is.
- *Witness preparation:* There are a variety of types of witnesses involved in trials, including expert witnesses, defendants, plaintiffs as well as witnesses to the facts. Presentational skills are clearly helpful to each of these types of witness, though Finkelman points out that it

can be difficult to coach a fact witness in presentational skills without compromising their evidence in some way. Furthermore, witnesses may have to say in court that they have taken part in coaching. The training may involve recording and playing back simulations of the witness testimony. Witnesses who perform poorly during coaching may not be used in court.

The initial stimulus to the development of trial consultation was what is known as scientific jury selection, though this is at best a minor part of this sort of work. Scientific jury selection depends on there being an opportunity (the voir dire) for the lawyer to influence the final composition of the jury in order to avoid the jurors less favourable to that lawyer's side. Formally, the voir dire (which is a French phrase meaning 'to speak the truth') is the stage at the beginning of a trial at which judges (and lawyers according to the jurisdiction) seek to identify biases or prejudices among potential jurors. It is often described as a 'trial within a trial'. It is the stage at which judges and lawyers sort out legal matters between themselves, including who should be excluded from the jury There is no common systematic way of assessing bias, so different questions may be asked of each potential juror on the venire (the list from which the jury is selected). Lawyers are more concerned about prejudice that might adversely affect their side rather than a just outcome, no matter what that is. Scientific jury selection is built on the voir dire and the wish to gain advantage for a particular side. In areas of the US system, the lawyer makes a challenge for cause when it is felt that there is overt prejudice on the part of the potential juror or for some other reason. Nevertheless, it is for the judge to decide whether the challenge is accepted and the judge may choose to ask the potential juror if they can put their prejudice aside. Peremptory challenges require no stated reason and lead to the dismissal of the potential juror (Kovera, Dickinson and Cutler, 2002). Scientific jury selection uses research evidence on the sorts of juror who are likely to favour a particular side. Figure 24.1 illustrates the steps.

Turning to research, the first major account of scientific jury selection comes from the group of social scientists, in the United States, who helped the defence of the Harrisburg Seven for conspiracy. The accused included priests and ex-priests, nuns and ex-nuns! The trial took place in 1972 against the backdrop of America's war in Vietnam. Philip Berrigan and others were accused of various plots against the state – for example, they were accused of planning to bomb heating tunnels in Washington and to kidnap Henry Kissinger, Assistant to the President for National Security Affairs. The central problem for the defence lawyer was that the trial was taking place in an area that was fundamentally conservative (and generally pro the war) but the defendants were anti-war activists.

The researchers became actively involved in the case because they were unhappy that informers and *agents provocateurs* were being used against the accused. They believed that the location of the trial in Harrisburg, Pennsylvania, was favourable to the prosecution. A survey was carried out around Harrisburg using a sample matched to be similar to the panel from which the jury was to be selected (Schulman, Shaver, Colman, Emrich and Christie, 1973). So factors such as age, occupation, education and race were taken into account. Over 1200 individuals were obtained by random sampling from similar voters on the voting list.

The questionnaire was detailed and covered a range of issues – including the matter of the influence of the media.

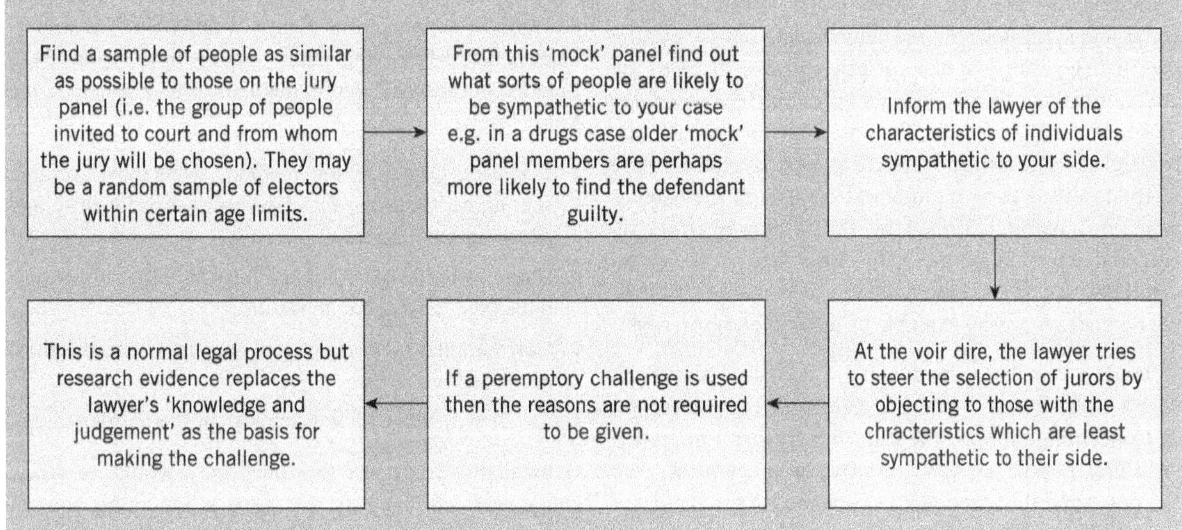

Figure 24.1 Scientific jury selection

The participants' choice of media to use, their knowledge of the defendants, and their knowledge of their case were measured and the following covered:

- the acceptability of certain anti-war activities and other political indicators;
- the ages and activities of their children;
- the organisations to which they belonged and so forth;
- their degree of trust in government;
- their religious attitude and commitment;
- their spare-time activities;
- who they saw as the greatest Americans during the previous 10 to 15 years so that their social values might be assessed.

Religious attitudes had a bearing on trial-relevant predispositions. Religions bad for the defendants were Episcopalians, Presbyterians, Methodists and fundamentalists; religions better for the defence included Catholics. Other trends included the following:

- Overwhelmingly, the public in Harrisburg agreed with the statement that the right to private property is sacred.
- Nearly two-thirds thought that a citizen should support his/her country even when it was wrong.
- Four-fifths believed that the police should use violence to maintain order.
- Although sex and political party were weak predictors of attitudes, Democrats and women were more liberal on certain questions. Education and contact with metropolitan newspapers in this area were associated with conservatism/republicanism.

The researchers considered that the ideal juror for the defence should have the following characteristics: female; Democrat; no religion; a white-collar job/skilled blue-collar job; sympathy with the defendants' views regarding the Vietnam war; tolerance of peaceful resistance to the government's policies; and would presume the defendants innocent until proven guilty. Based on this profile, the researchers and lawyers selected prospective jurors who were closest to these requirements, although the choices were also partly informed by the responses made by potential jurors in court. Of the final jury of 12, seven could be rated as good prospects from the point of view of the defence. A typical example of these good jurors was:

> Pauline Protzline, a housewife in her late 40s or early 50s, whose son-in-law had been killed in Vietnam. Concerning the war, she had said: 'I wasn't too much at first, but the last few years I've been against it.' We considered this statement to be a good sign. She listed no church affiliation.
>
> (Schulman *et al.*, 1973, p. 25)

The researchers re-interviewed a sample of the original survey chosen as being a match to the real 12-person jury. Of the three-quarters who were prepared to give further opinions, the following were found:

- Just over half presumed the defendants to be guilty. The others were classified as having only low to moderate presumptions of the guilt of the defendants.
- Age and political preference made little difference to presumptions of guilt.
- Only 37 per cent of women thought the defendants guilty on all or most counts. For men, the figure was 57 per cent.
- Of the respondents with high-school education and the preferred religious stance favouring the defence, only about a fifth had a strong presumption of guilt.

At the trial, the defence chose to offer no defence and the defendants, consequently, did not provide any evidence supporting their case. For the minor charges, the jury found the accused guilty of smuggling letters out of a federal prison. They could not agree a verdict on the conspiracy charge. Of the jury, ten were against conviction. This is not particularly impressive evidence in favour of scientific jury selection. Nevertheless, the surveys certainly picked up on the ambiguity of the jury's position.

Whether or not this is the best way in which lawyers can help their clients is also in some doubt. There is not a lot of research into the effectiveness of scientific jury selection, which is surprising since it appears to be big business (Strier, 1999). Lloyd-Bostock (1996) pointed out that research on over 2000 cases in the United Kingdom found that the use of peremptory challenge did not lead to more acquittals.

Horowitz (1980) is an important exception to the general lack of convincing evidence in this field. The important details of Horowitz's study are given in Figure 24.2. In terms of the two different methods of jury selection, the following were found:

- Scientific jury selection methods were most accurate (i.e. agreed with the real lawyers' view) for drug and courts martial crimes.
- These were the cases studied for which the survey produced the most accurate results.
- Conventional methods of jury selection were the most accurate for murder.
- The survey was of low accuracy for the murder case.

Generalising from just this one study would be risky. Other research suggests that experts are often poor at identifying biased potential jurors. One study had groups of potential jurors who had been challenged in court as

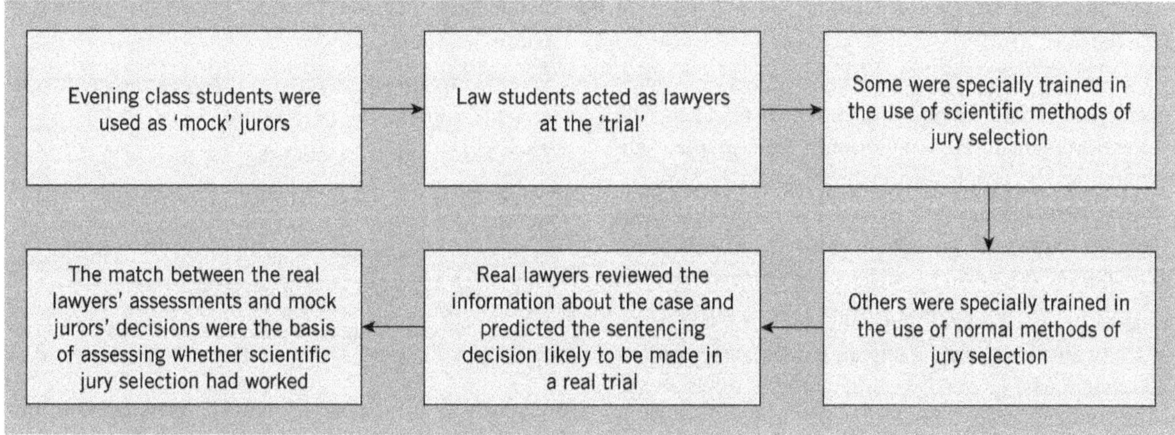

Figure 24.2 The key features of Horowitz's design to investigate scientific jury selection

biased for a trial and compared their verdicts with those of the actual jurors who had not been challenged (Zeisel and Diamond, 1978). Essentially, there was no difference between the verdicts of the 'actual' and the 'biased' juries, thus indicating that scientific jury selection was ineffective in these examples. This may not be surprising given that lawyers use little more than stereotypes in making their challenges.

As ever, due regard should be exercised for the fact that jurisdictions differ in terms of procedures used. The peremptory challenge in which no reason is given for wishing to reject a potential juror is a feature of the US legal system. Peremptory challenges are not possible in some other jurisdictions. In England and Wales, the right to make peremptory challenges was abolished in 1988 (Lloyd-Bostock, 1996). This means that the US style of scientific jury selection is not possible for the defence in the UK. Commenting on the US situation, Van Wallendael and Cutler (2004) express some reservations about the general efficacy of scientific jury selection methods in the United States. One issue they mention is that very little is known about the activities of lawyers in voir dire situations. For example, it is not known whether lawyers actually effectively assess trial-relevant attitudes during the voir dire process. Furthermore, there are many situations in which the lawyer has little influence on the process of jury selection: courts in some states do not allow lawyers to assess the attitudes of members of the venire panel (the pool of potential jurors).

It is hard to evaluate the effectiveness of scientific jury selection (Lieberman, 2011). Scientific jury selection is so expensive that is can only used in cases where the client can afford the very best lawyers as well as litigation consultants. As a consequence, it is difficult to separate the contribution of high-quality legal representation from that of the trial consultant. Similarly, a client who can afford the best can also afford the best and most distinguished expert witnesses. Additionally, it is very difficult to define what success is in such trials. Is achieving a hung jury a success, for example? It may well be seen as a good outcome compared with a guilty verdict. Similarly, is a life sentence a victory or failure when the alternative is the death penalty? Or if a mock trial suggests that a client will lose £100,000 and so the client decides to settle out of court?

Research on jury decision making seems to place a distinct limit on what might be achieved by the use of scientific jury selection. It has been an overriding finding from jury research that the best predictor of the outcome of a case is the strength of evidence presented to the jury. For example, Visher (1987) studied jurors who had participated in a substantial number of sexual assault trials. She measured the jurors' demographic variables and attitudes such as being tough on crime and attitudes towards the defendant. Furthermore she assessed the available evidence, including physical evidence, eyewitness testimony and the use of weapons, amongst other things. The findings were that the strength of the evidence accounted for the most variation in verdicts (34 per cent). The characteristics of jurors accounted for only 2 per cent of the variation in verdicts. And juror characteristics, of course, are what scientific jury selection tries to manipulate. In other words, changing the characteristics of a jury only has limited potential for affecting the outcome of a trial. Nevertheless, in finely balanced trials, a client may feel that even a small contribution favouring their defence is a sound financial investment.

A number of ethical issues have been raised about the use of scientific jury selection by Saks (1987):

- The researchers need to explain to respondents just what purposes the survey is to be used for. It is not appropriate to say that the information is for research purposes when, in fact, the intention is to use it to help the defence.

- A further ethical issue concerns the fact that most defendants could not afford to employ researchers (the interviewers in the Harrisburg study, for example, were volunteers). Consequently, in the long run, the prosecution is normally much more likely to benefit from this sort of research. They are the side most capable of funding the research.

Furthermore, Lecci, Snowden and Morris (2004) argue that trial consultants are largely an unregulated group of practitioners who have not been required to establish the validity of their procedures. They should be required to employ standardised measures to assess juror bias.

Simple improvements to aid jurors

Research into jury decision processes has been based almost exclusively on simulations of trial (mock trials). These simulations are unrealistic to varying degrees. Perhaps the most realistic mock jury is shadow jury. Shadow juries sit in on the court proceedings at the request of the researcher, so they hear exactly the same evidence delivered in the same manner as the real jury, and then retire to reach a verdict. Nevertheless, there is evidence of considerable inconsistency between the real jury verdict and that of shadow juries. The difference is that the latter can be studied by researchers, whereas normally researchers do not have access to real juries.

Jurors face a number of problems in modern trials. The evidence may simply be rather too complex or confusing but some cases can be extraordinarily demanding. Generally speaking, taking notes is a permitted activity of the juror almost everywhere. This does not prevent concerns about note taking distracting the juror from the trial or the best note taker dominating the jury. Heuer and Penrod (1988) found little empirical support for these concerns. With the complexity of modern legal evidence, one can imagine that note-taking is a tempting option. Penrod and Heuer (1997) review the evidence coming from field experiments involving a fairly large number of different judges, trials, lawyers and jurors. In one national study, judges gave the jurors permission to take notes as soon as was practicable in the trial. The majority of jurors took up the option, although as many as a third chose not to in some instances. On average, taking into account the civil and criminal trials, just over half a page of notes was taken each hour of the trial. While studies do not show a spectacular effect of note-taking, some of Penrod and Heuer's conclusions are of particular interest:

- Note-takers consider all of the evidence and not just that in their notes.
- Note-taking does not interfere with the juror's ability to keep up with the trial proceedings.
- Note-taking jurors are not more satisfied with the trial, the judge or the verdict than those who do not take notes.
- Note-taking seems to be neutral in regard to the prosecution and defence cases in terms of its effects.
- The notes taken tend to be accurate records as far as they go.

Note taking is at the discretion of the jury member and takes an unstructured, blank sheet of paper, format. Developments in the use of note taking in trials include the use of a trial-ordered notebook for the jurors as demonstrated by Hope, Eales and Mirashi (2014) and others. They had members of the public watch a video of a murder trial. Participants were allocated at random to a no-notes condition, an unstructured notes condition, or a trial-ordered notebook condition. Just what is a trial-ordered notebook? In this case it was a printed questionnaire structured to structure notes of thing like the accused's name, the opening statement by the prosecuting lawyer and the opening statement by the defending lawyer, and notes for each witness and their names. They found that the use of such a notebook was better than unstructured or freestyle note taking. Those who used the structured trial-ordered notebook remembered more legally relevant detail than those who took unstructured notes or no notes at all. There was no relationship between the three different note taking conditions and their verdict which was overwhelmingly not guilty.

Research into the effectiveness of allowing jurors to ask questions using much the same sort of methods led Penrod and Heuer (1997) to the following conclusions:

- Jurors do understand the facts and issues better if they ask questions.
- Allowing questions seems to make no difference to the jurors', judge's and lawyers' satisfaction with the trial and verdict.
- If a juror asks an inappropriate question, lawyers will object and the jury does not draw inappropriate conclusions from this. However, generally speaking, the jurors ask perfectly appropriate questions.

In other words, research of this sort tends to demonstrate few or no negative consequences of the potential innovations of note-taking and juror questions, and modest, at best, improvements. Of course, the more research of this sort, the better will be our understanding of the difficulties facing jurors.

BOX 24.1 Controversy

Mock jury studies

The basic facts are clear. The use of mock juries of one sort or another and student samples dominates jury research in psychology. The problems resulting from this are obvious. Currently, it seems almost obligatory that researchers draw attention to the limitations that follow from their use in journal publications. Despite this, simulated juries using student jurors remain the norm. The general unavailability of real juries to researchers makes the use of simulated juries inevitable. Even if they were available, controlled experiments would scarcely be possible for the most part. But are things this simple? Mock juries vary tremendously in the extent to which they appear to map onto real juries. Sometimes the 'jury' is nothing other than a group of isolated and non-interacting individuals who at no point deliberate as a group in the way that real juries do. Why do researchers not create more mock jury research in which jurors do interact when reaching their decision and have been taken through a realistic facsimile of court proceedings (e.g. opening and closing statements, examinations of witnesses, including the accused, and realistic direction by a judge)? Of course, even in realistic simulations, nobody actually goes to prison or ends up on death row. Perhaps psychologists are simply stuck with the limitations imposed by their chosen subject matter in this case – as is common in research. But then, one might point out, even given this, the use of students as mock jurors is not forced on researchers by their subject matter. Their use is merely a matter of convenience. Real juries are drawn much more generally from the community. Are students sufficiently representative of the ways in which the general population makes judgements? Is there something about being young, intelligent and educated which means that they represent most jurors adequately? In the case of *Lockhart* v. *McCree*, 476 US 162 (1986) the defence wished to use the findings of jury studies. However, the United States Supreme Court decided that the studies were insufficient to reverse a death sentence (Caprathe, 2011). Increasingly, researchers have begun to make challenging arguments about the use of mock juries and the associated emphasis on students as jurors.

Wiener, Krauss and Lieberman (2011) explain the basic problems with mock jury research in the context of the framework of Campbell and Stanley (1963) and Cook and Campbell (1979). This framework is one of the classic formulations of psychological research methods. Most pertinent in the present context are the concepts of *construct* and *external validity*. Construct validity reflects the extent to which aspects of the research, such as the measures taken and the manipulations of variables, generalise to the real-life courtroom situation. Wiener *et al.* then pose the question of the extent to which jury studies involve the essentials of the legal system which would allow us to make claims about how real juries are likely to make decisions. Many of the choices that researchers make in mock jury research inevitably tax the construct validity of their methods. These choices include the lack of deliberation and the use of pre-test measures (which have no corollaries in court). Not surprisingly, some researchers (e.g. Vidmar, 2008) are sceptical that the legal system may be disassembled and then reconstructed in the psychology laboratory. How can the findings from this enterprise then be assembled to tell us about what is likely to happen in court? The problem for researchers is that any attempt to increase the construct validity of their studies (i.e. to sample the important features of real criminal cases) will tend to reduce the internal validity of the study by making randomisation, pre-testing, and other procedures which allow them to make causal inferences difficult or impossible to implement. This is the age-old debate in psychological methods which sets experimental control of variables at odds with relevance to the real world. That is, increased internal validity leads to reduced external validity.

Not surprisingly, then, some have called for a 'two-stage' or 'two-tier' approach in which research ideas are initially tested using relatively unrealistic mock jury simulations and, then, if the findings encourage further investigation, the ideas can be tested in more realistic and legally relevant situations. Whether this is sensible perhaps depends on one's viewpoint. After all, it assumes that the initial testing of ideas provides the most generous test of the hypothesis. Ideas which stand no hope of being supported in more valid research settings are filtered out – or so the argument goes. Unfortunately, there is no way of knowing this with any

BOX 24.1 (continued)

certainty without a body of research which seeks to address the issue. Wiener *et al.* regard such a two-stage research process as efficient, though they do not explain precisely what they mean by this. One might, instead, argue that the two-stage process merely allows for the creation of red herrings which waste research resources by failing to concentrate on realistic simulations of trial processes in the first place. This begs the question of just what is a realistic simulation of trial processes? What has to be included in order to make it realistic? It is a long time since Weiten and Diamond (1979) suggested various threats to the relevance of jury studies to the real world. These included lack of jury deliberation, the very different roles implied by mock jurors versus real jurors whose decisions have real consequences as opposed to being merely a tick on a questionnaire, and failures to include in mock trials the sorts of procedures and precautions which characterise real trials.

The debate repeatedly returns to the use of student samples in mock jury research. Imagine that in the real world juries consisted solely of students, would the findings from mock jury trials generalise to the real world? If they did then the mock jury study would show external validity – that is, the findings from the mock study would map closely to what happens in real life. This is, of course, an impossible hypothetical situation. Unfortunately, the research literature appears to neglect the question of the extent to which studies using students generate findings which are robust under conditions of increasing fidelity to real life. If this evidence was available then it would be favourable to the use of mock juries. It would not be, however, evidence that findings involving student juries (mock or real) are in any way predictive of what would happen with regular juries consisting of members of the community.

The crux of the matter is whether university students have attitudes and beliefs which in some way alter how they perceive legal concepts and procedures in ways which are different from how community members would respond. Things like what defines a particular sort of crime, what 'beyond reasonable doubt' means, what 'criminal intent' is, and what 'burden of proof' is come to mind in this context, but there are obviously other more arcane examples. The possible characteristics of university students that might be relevant here include their information-processing capacities. Young students, for example, might have higher memory capacity and they may be able to process more strands of information than the run-of-the-mill jury-eligible member of the community. Even these basic characteristics might result in differences in decisions made by students compared to community samples.

Legal decision making (including mock juries) involves a great deal in terms of knowledge, background and understanding and can be affected by things such as the elements of law involved and the quality of any simulation. Given that higher education can generate improved reasoning and arguing skills, one can imagine many more reasons why student jurors might make decisions differently from jury-eligible members of the public. Not surprisingly there is research which compares student and community member decision making, but the consistency of this appears not to be great (Wiener, Krauss and Lieberman, 2011). It would be a big step forward if we could model the characteristics of a mock jury trial which interact with sample characteristics. As a psychologist would put it: just what characteristics of mock jury trials interact with the type of jury (student versus community) to produce different sorts of trial outcome? Perhaps such a question requires a more comprehensive programme of research than is feasible. Bornstein (1999) is often quoted as a study in which findings for student juries were compared with those for community juries. He listed 26 mock jury studies which made such a comparison. He concluded that jury researchers may take comfort in his findings. There was not much evidence that student and community jurors behaved differently when making decisions in mock jury trials. Only six out of the total of 26 studies found differences according to the type of 'jury' member and even fewer provided any evidence that participant type interacted with any other feature of the mock trial. Superficially, this may seem to answer a basic question but it fails to deal systematically with the features of trials which may interact with sample type (e.g. sort of charge; burden of proof; judges' instructions; and the like). More research seems to be called for.

Keller and Wiener (2011) provide an example of the sort of research needed in order to address some of the many validity issues surrounding mock juries. They further the debate by assessing the extent to which student and community samples are different in the way they think about two different types of charge – sexual assault and homicide. They used various measures known to be effective in past studies, including: the Attitudes toward Rape (ATR) scale (Kovera, 2002); the Attitudes toward Sexual Abuse (ATSA) scale (Briere, Hehschel and Smiljanich, 1992); and the Juror Bias Scale (JBS) (Kassin and Wrightsman, 1983). The fundamental question for the research was whether the type of juror sample moderated the relationships between attitudes as measured by these instruments and mock jury decisions about the culpability of the accused. In other words, are very different correlations found between attitudes and jury decisions for student juries compared to community juries? Their findings showed substantial differences between the relationships between attitudes to sexual assault and homicide cases and external validity factors such as type of participant. Attitude factors also interact with construct validity factors such as the specific charges. There were some differences between student and community mock jurors in general and especially so for culpability judgements (which includes guilt likelihood; convincingness of each side's arguments; and the defendant's criminal intentions). Student mock jurors were not so severe as community jurors when assigning guilt in the homicide cases, for example.

For Nunez, McCrea and Culbane(2011), to concentrate criticisms on the use of student samples is to mistake the mouse in the room for an elephant. The real elephant in the room is not properly acknowledged by most critics of mock juries. What is the elephant? According to Nunez and McCrea, the greatest threat to the validity of jury decision making is that the process of jury deliberation is ignored. A great deal of the research purporting to be on juries is actually on decision making individuals who come to their decisions essentially in isolation. Real juries are required to interact and discuss in order to reach a verdict. Nunez and McCrea suggest that, had the unit of analysis in research been the jury rather than isolated decision makers, conclusions from research might have been different. Unfortunately, there is no research which bears directly on this. But the important issue of the neglect of jury deliberation cannot be avoided.

There has been research into what researchers see as acceptable practices in jury decision making research. That is, what standards should be applied to the field. One US judge suggested that limitations in method could render some studies of little interest to the courts: 'mock jury studies comprising only students would not likely be given a great deal of weight in the absence of scientific proof that the results apply to actual juries.' (Caprathe, 2011, p. 330). However, it is not certain that psychologists actually share this view. Nevertheless, there is evidence of a rather rapid decline in the numbers of jury-related studies in the important empirical journal *Law and Human Behavior* (Bornstein, 1999). Jury studies made up 30 per cent of the published journal articles in 1995/6 but only 6 per cent in 2011/2. Lieberman, Krauss, Heen and Sakiyama (2016) were well-aware of the great variety of procedures used in jury research. They surveyed individuals who were actively engaged in such research. The participants completed a questionnaire which was designed to identify what practices the research sample would find acceptable and essential or unacceptable. Interestingly, the sample considered that internal validity (i.e. a carefully controlled experiment) to be rather more important than ecological validity. That is, they did not think that the jury set-up needed to be a close parallel of a real jury. They thought that the experimental design was more crucial than the realism of the study. The single most important trial element that the sample thought should be included was the use of instructions to the jury paralleling the instructions that in a real court the judge would give to the jurors.

To conclude about the use of mock juries is to strike at some of the roots of psychological research methods. It is both hard to dismiss mock jury studies as irrelevant, given the difficulty of studying juries in any other way, but it is also difficult to say exactly what we can draw from the many mock jury studies over the last 40 years. Probably it is as much the quest to identify the factors which lead to particular jury verdicts that is at fault. The problems in predicting any real-life trial outcome on the basis of mock jury study findings are legion. It is probably a task best not contemplated. Yet in the absence of any other sources of knowledge, psychologists must be tempted to at least speculate that the findings from mock jury research may be our best estimate of what influences a trial's outcome. At the same time, the focus on the determinants of trial outcomes based on mock jury studies has tended to dominate the research that has been carried out. Other questions, such as the broad psychological patterns in the weighing of evidence tend to be overlooked – issues like confirmation bias as it applies to legal evidence, for example.

The effect of jury size and decision rules

Jury decision rules are the formal constraints applied to jury decision making, including the size of the majority required to reach a verdict and the required size of the jury itself. Interest in the influence of jury size on the verdict was partly the result of the trial of *Williams* v. *Florida* (1970). In this case, the US Supreme Court decided that 6-person juries were as good as 12-person juries. Factors considered included the quality of deliberation; the reliability of the jury's fact finding; the verdict ratio; the ability of dissenters to resist majority pressure; and the capacity of the jury to involve a fair cross-section of the community.

So a jury may vary in terms of its size but also in terms of the proportion of the jurors who must agree in order to decide on the guilt of the accused. These rules may vary according to the jurisdiction involved but may also vary within a jurisdiction (Arce *et al.*, 1998):

- In the United Kingdom there is sometimes a combined decision rule. Unanimity may be required at first, followed by a 10 out of 12 majority after a period of deliberation.
- In Spain, a qualified majority decision rule has been used. A not guilty verdict requires a simple majority of 5 out of 9, but a guilty verdict needs 7 out of 9.

Other jurisdictions employ different rules.

An important question is whether factors such as the size of the jury and the decision rule in force make a substantial difference to deliberations and outcomes. Zeisel (1971) suggested the greater the size of the jury, the greater the risk of a hung jury. A hung jury is one in which cannot reach a verdict. There is some evidence that the requirement of unanimity in the decision increases the likelihood that the jury will be hung. Similarly, it is possible that complex cases are more likely to result in failure to reach a decision. In research to test these ideas (Arce *et al.*, 1998), participants eligible for Spanish jury service were selected at random from the electoral register. Gender was equalised in the juries. Participants viewed the re-enactment of a real-life rape trial, including the testimony of eyewitness and forensic experts, opening and closing defence and prosecution arguments, and the judge's definition of the legal terms involved and the decision rule. The participants were randomly assigned to one of a number of juries that were then studied through the use of questionnaires. Among the findings were the following:

- Hung juries deliberated longer.
- Hung juries report perceptions of intransigence, lack of dialogue and irrelevant deliberations.
- Hung juries tended to manifest more simultaneous interruptions.
- Hung juries tended to use less of the trial evidence.
- Hung jury members employed more assertions in their communications with each other.

One way of summarising the wide range of findings about the effects of jury size on verdicts and other matters is a meta-analysis (see Box 4.1) by Saks and Marti (1997) which brought together findings of 17 studies. The following trends were found over the various research studies:

- Deliberation time is longer for larger juries.
- For civil cases, smaller juries tend to award more to the injured party.
- Guilty verdicts are not more common in large juries.
- Hung verdicts are commoner for larger juries. This is a finding that is really only true for studies that used a mock jury. In studies involving real juries, hung verdicts were rare – they occurred in only about 1 per cent of instances.

These findings emerged for studies that have a unanimous decision rule (that is, all of the jurors must agree for a guilty verdict). There is evidence to suggest that such juries tend to be evidence-driven. For example, they make more references to the evidence, establish more connections between the evidence and legal issues, examine the evidence in detail, and their deliberations are more exhaustive and detailed. Juries operating with a majority decision rule are more driven to reach a verdict. So majority verdict juries are more likely to begin their deliberations with a vote. For example, Arce *et al.* (1998) compared six- and twelve-person juries that used unanimous decision criteria. The smaller juries made rather fewer references to the evidence and seemed to make fewer pro-defendant arguments.

A related aspect of jury rules is the range of different verdicts available. Generally, researchers have concentrated on guilty versus not-guilty choices but there are others, such as the *not proven* verdict. A study by Smithson, Deady and Cracik (2007) investigated the impact of having this *not proven* alternative, which is probably most familiar from the legal system in Scotland. One possibility is that the *not proven* category might be used as an alternative to the guilty verdict where it is available. The researchers employed a counterbalanced design with different ranges of alternative verdict options for the different conditions. Participants were students and public servants eligible for jury service at two Australian universities. The research findings suggested that, contrary to expectations, the *not proven* choice replaced some not guilty decisions. It did not replace the guilty decision. That it is to say, there were just as many guilty decisions when there was the additional *not proven* alternative as when there were just guilty and not guilty choices. There were also indications from the study that jurors found the *not proven* verdict somewhat more difficult to choose than any of the other verdicts.

How real juries make decisions

Relatively little is known about the psychological processes that happen in real juries, as opposed to the mock juries of the psychological experiment (McCabe and Purves, 1974). There are a few rare instances in which courts have allowed access to recordings of jury deliberations, but these are very much exceptions. For the most part, researchers have had to find approximations to real juries. Figure 24.3 illustrates some of the main alternatives. All of these suffer from a degree of artificiality – the extent of which depends on the study in question. Sometimes the mock jury will merely consist of individuals making individual decisions in isolation – sometimes a group of interacting persons will be used. No matter what, the mock jury is always a pale reflection of real juries. For example, often the mock juror will merely read a scenario of a crime and trial rather than experience the full spectacle of a court of law in session.

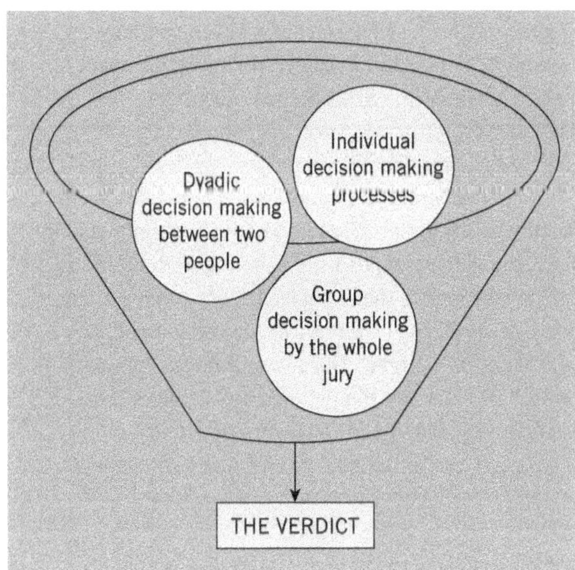

Figure 24.3 Different levels of jury deliberation in psychological research

Myers (1979) chose a somewhat circuitous approach to investigating the features of trials that increase the likelihood of a guilty verdict. She did not have access to the jury room and so obtained her data in other ways. Her research involved the cases of about a thousand defendants on felony charges in Indiana. Two-thirds of the cases involved trials by jury. Myers obtained qualitative data from a variety of sources:

- file folders of the assistant prosecutor;
- police arrest records;
- telephone interviews to obtain any necessary supplementary data.

She was on the prosecutor's staff at the time so was also able to conduct informal discussions with prosecutors and court personnel. It emerged that the following factors influenced the jury's decision of guilt:

- a weapon was recovered;
- a large number of witnesses were specified;
- the defendant or an accomplice made a statement either concerning involvement in crime or lack of involvement in crime;
- the defendant had large numbers of previous convictions (admissible evidence there);
- the defendant was not employed;
- the victim was young;
- it was a less serious rather than a more serious crime.

Juries were not dependent on the following in their decisions:

- eyewitness identification of the defendant;
- expert testimony;
- recovery of stolen property;
- victim's prior criminality and relationship with the defendant;
- past conduct of the victim perhaps warranting the injury.

Interesting as these findings may be, they tend to provide a view of the jury which is rather different from that to be found in the general run of psychological jury research. For example, the lack of influence of things such as eyewitness identification and expert testimony is incongruous, considering the great emphasis that researchers have placed on both of these. Furthermore, psychological research into the jury has raised the role of extra-legal or extra-evidential factors on jury decision making – for example, where the defendant is physically attractive or where the racial characteristics of the accused lead to greater or lesser leniency.

BOX 24.2 Forensic psychology in action

Pre-trial publicity

O.J. Simpson was tried for the murder of his wife and a male companion. Shortly after the murders, the sportsman/actor was seen on national television apparently speeding along American freeways trying to avoid arrest. Consequently, the effects of pre-trial prejudicial events in the media was an issue Does pre-trial publicity prejudice the result of a trial?

- Different countries/jurisdictions have different practices about media coverage of crime. In the United States, the constitutional guarantee of freedom of speech effectively reduces controls over media coverage, as also does courtroom television. In other countries, restrictions are in place. So, for example, in the United Kingdom, media coverage is limited once a suspect has been charged. Offending media may be charged with contempt of court and the criminal trial of the suspect abandoned. Civil trials are not subject to pre-trial publicity restrictions.
- Factors limiting the influence of pre-trial publicity include the facts that: 1) most suspects plead guilty at trial anyway and these cases cannot be influenced by prejudicial publicity and 2) very few trials receive any coverage in the national press. In the United States, the figure may be as low as 1 per cent (Simon and Eimermann, 1971). There is five times the likelihood that the trial will be covered by the local press. A trial tried by jury has at least twice the baseline probability of being reported.
- Prejudice, in legal terms, should not be seen in social-scientific terms which would suggest that prejudice leads to biasing the outcome of the trial (Howitt, 1998b). In the United States, the Supreme Court has ruled that prejudice involves both 1) a preconceived notion of the defendant's guilt and 2) this opinion being fixed and resistant to change (Moran and Cutler, 1991). In other words, what is prejudicial to a psychologist may not be prejudice in the eyes of a US judge.

Research into the effects of media on verdicts goes back to the origins of forensic psychology in nineteenth-century Germany. More intensive research began in the 1960s. Some of the research is problematic as it was based on 'mock' juries assembled solely for research purposes. Obviously, this has the inevitable ecological validity problem – just how representative are the verdicts of mock juries of the verdicts of real juries? Some research involved exposing the participants to a fictitious news story and then obtaining their views about the guilt of the accused and so forth without even allowing jury discussion.

Studebaker and Penrod (1997) point out how complex the modern media environment is and how voracious the demand for news. This means that often there is nowhere the trial could be held where the jurors are unaware of the publicity given to the crime. However, some venues may be less prejudiced than others. One suggestion is that researchers could help by investigating factors in pre-trial publicity that may lead to prejudice in laboratory studies and then seeking evidence that this sort of publicity is especially common in the area where the case would normally be tried (Studebaker, Robbennolt, Pathak-Sharma and Penrod, 2000). They undertook research relevant to a hearing for a change of venue for the trial of those accused of the Oklahoma City bombing (Timothy McVeigh and Terry Nichols). Newspapers in the Oklahoma City area were analysed, as were those for a number of possible alternative locations for the trial. The researchers coded the contents of these newspapers along a number of dimensions known to be relevant to pre-trial publicity effects from experiments. These aspects were: 1) measures of the general amount of publicity given to the crime; 2) negative characterisations of the defendants; 3) information about the emotional suffering of those involved as victims of the crime; 4) information about putative confessions; 5) suggestions about the defendants' motives for the crime; and 6) information about eyewitness identifications.

Compared with *The Denver Post*, newspapers in the Oklahoma City area had more negative pre-trial publicity about the defendants and the suffering of the victims.

The researchers then compared their content analysis findings with those of surveys of the general public carried out at the time. There were parallels between the content analysis and the findings of the survey. For example, respondents in Oklahoma were much more likely to believe in the guilt of one of the defendants, McVeigh. Respondents in Denver, away from the possible venues for the hearing in Oklahoma, were relatively unlikely to claim that they were absolutely confident of McVeigh's guilt – less than 20 per cent did so. In contrast, about 50 per cent of the Oklahoma respondents were absolutely confident of his guilt. They were also more likely to follow the news of the crime and trial carefully and they knew a great deal more about the events. The findings are indicative of the value of the content analysis approach to venue selection according to Studebaker *et al.* (2000).

However, researchers do not always have an easy time in court when they argue that, based on their data, the venue of the trial should or should not change. Posey and Dahl (2002) describe some of the problems, including the likelihood that a judge will ask the researcher why questions were not included in the survey which asked respondents the extent to which they could be impartial. Research suggests little value in such questions, although they are the sort of questions asked in court during a voir dire examination. There is no relationship between a potential juror's claims to be impartial and how much they know about the case and how strong they believe the evidence against the accused to be.

What happens behind jury room doors? Gastil, Burkhalter and Black's (2007) study is unusual in that the researchers had co-operation from a Seattle court which allowed them to study accounts by jurors of 60 trials, albeit for relatively trivial offences. The researchers were particularly interested in satisfaction with the deliberation process and the outcome of their deliberations. The court typically used six-person juries plus or minus one juror. The gender mix of jurors was about equal, though the majority were white. Deliberations generally lasted for about two hours. Data were collected from the juries both before the actual trial and afterwards. Antecedents to the deliberations were measured using a measure called *trust in the jury system*, which included the extent of their confidence in the jury system and the extent to which the criminal jury system is a fair way to determine guilt and innocence. Other data were also collected at this stage. Having provided these initial data, the jurors participated in a trial and deliberated in the jury room. After the trial, their experiences were measured using five-point scales assessing the extent to which they discussed the relevant facts related to the trials; discussed the judge's instructions thoroughly; listened to each respectfully during the jury's discussions; and the extent to which they were satisfied with the final verdict and the quality of the jury's deliberations. The findings showed that:

- Jurors felt that their jury operated at a 'remarkably' high level of competence.
- The vast majority of jurors rated their experience of jury deliberation as being of a 'remarkably' high quality overall. Very few suggested less than that.
- Almost no juries included a juror who disagreed with the view that the jury listened respectfully to each other, that the relevant facts of the trial were discussed, and that they discussed the judge's instructions.
- Nearly all (98 per cent) indicated that they had an adequate opportunity to express themselves within the jury room.
- However, relationships between the characteristics of the jurors and the characteristics of the deliberation tended to show fairly complex patterns. It was clear that jurors who had the greatest faith in the jury system were more likely to experience the jury deliberations as mutually respectful; the more the juror was self-confident and interested in the trial, the more they were likely to feel that they had adequate opportunities to speak, the more likely they were to engage in careful analysis during the deliberations, and the more likely they were to perceived the deliberations as mutually respectful. Nevertheless, there was a direct relationship between how satisfied the jury was and the perceived quality of the deliberation.

Quite clearly, all of this is a meta-perspective on jury deliberation processes. It is about how the jury members perceived the deliberation process. As such, it is not truly an investigation of the process of deliberation itself.

The nature of interaction in juries

Just what are the processes involved in jury deliberation? How do these relate to psychological theory? Underlying some models of jury decision making is an assumption that a jury consists of people with different arguing and reasoning styles which impact on the deliberations and may, ultimately, influence the verdict. Kuhn, Weinstock and Flaton (1994) suggested that the evidence co-ordination is the responsibility of each member of the jury (Figure 24.4). They need to construct alternative accounts (or story-verdict constellations) concerning what happened at the scene of the crime which are then evaluated against the available evidence. These accounts may be those supplied by the defence and prosecution lawyers, as discussed in Chapter 23. They have to decide between the account which is most consistent with the evidence and the account which is inconsistent with much of the evidence. As can be seen in

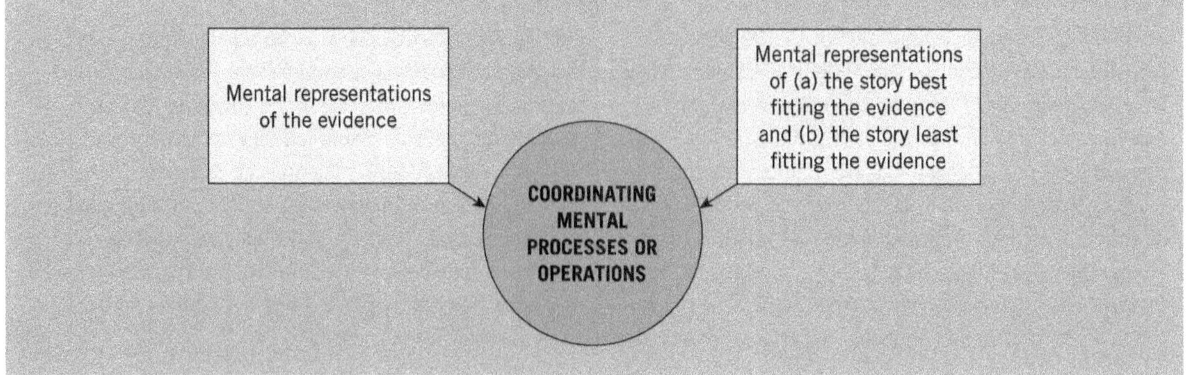

Figure 24.4 Kuhn, Weinstock and Flaton's 1994 theory of juror decision making

Figure 24.4, the model involves three components: 1) mental representations of the evidence; 2) representations of each of the accounts or verdict definitions; and 3) a set of mental operations co-ordinating these. Previous research has shown that people whose thinking is the most advanced epistemologically believe that absolute certainty is not possible. These tend to be more highly educated individuals and so are more likely to select moderate verdicts than extreme ones. Skilful performances by jury members during a deliberation tended to involve arguing skills such as discounting, counter-argumentation, and justifying alternative verdicts.

Along similar lines, Warren, Kuhn and Weinstock (2010) suggest that there are three different types of reasoning reflecting different epistemological styles:

- *Absolutists:* These would tend to say that only one account of the events can be correct and that the other must be wrong. That is, they believe that the absolute and objective truth can be determined.
- *Multiplists:* Would tend to think that both points of view are accurate from the point of view of the historian involved. They would recognise that accounts of history change at different time periods. That is, they recognise that interpretations are subjective, as are judgements, and this is given first priority in their thinking.
- *Evaluativists:* Would also see that both historians are likely to be highly accurate from their own point of view. They would tend to believe that, by combining a variety of viewpoints, some consensus on what had happened is achievable. That is, they also recognise the subjectivity of viewpoints, though they accept that these can be evaluated and one viewpoint preferred.

It is possible to classify people into the above three thinking styles using the Livia task, which involves two different historians' accounts of a war. The task is to answer various questions about what can be known based on these two different viewpoints. In terms of the analysis, the multiplists and the evaluativists were very similar and so they were combined into a single group. Warren and Kuhn (2010) used pairs of about-to-be jurors waiting in a court to be assigned to jury service. They listened to 20-minute, shortened versions of a real homicide trial on audiotape which included many features of the full trial such as the examination, cross-examination and opening and closing statements. There were four alternative verdicts from which the 'juror' could choose – first-degree murder, second-degree murder, manslaughter and self-defence. The judge in the 'trial' explained the criteria for reaching these different verdicts. Having heard the recording, the juror had to make a verdict choice and justify it. Following this was an interactive phase in which each 'juror' was paired with another juror, who had made a different verdict choice. Seventy-eight per cent of the jurors managed to reach a joint verdict within the 30 minutes that the researchers allowed them. Their 'deliberations' were then systematically coded by the researchers into units which consisted of either a question or a claim accompanied by supporting justification). Each deliberation included an average of 119 of these units. Generally speaking, each of the jury members contributed substantially – the range of units per member varying within the relatively restricted range of about 40–60 per cent per individual. The 'jurors' made frequent references to the evidence (8 per cent) and nearly as often to the verdict categories (7 per cent), though they rarely mentioned the criteria distinguishing the various verdicts. Jurors were more likely to add to the other juror's statements (9 per cent) than to challenge them (6 per cent). Frequent meta-level statements were made about their own thinking or the other's contribution (18 per cent).

There were some very clear differences between the multiplists/evaluativists (combined) group and the absolutists in terms of how they behaved in the 'jury' deliberations. The multiplists/evaluativists tended to be more persuasive than their partners in the juror dyad and were much more likely to:

- discuss the meta-processes in their deliberation – i.e. talk about aspects of their thinking processes;
- critique what the other jury member had said or counter it in some way;
- dominate the discussion/deliberation;
- refer to the judge's verdict criteria.

In general, criticism of the other juror's arguments was relatively less common than to add to the other juror's contribution in ways that did nothing to challenge that contribution. Of course, it remains to be seen the extent to which larger juries would show similar trends.

Jurors and the facts of eyewitness evidence

How knowledgeable are jurors about the problems of eyewitness evidence? In some jurisdictions, expert witnesses may provide information about issues related to eyewitness evidence. For example, Loftus (2010) discusses in detail the simple factor of the distance between an eyewitness and something that they believe that they have seen. It is a psychological fact and common sense that the bigger the distance, the less detail can be seen, all other things being equal. So imagine an eye-witness claims to have seen a car with a spoiler at the back from a distance of a quarter of a mile (0.4 kilometres). Is it possible to discern a car's spoiler from this distance? This cannot be answered on the basis of common sense since a specific question of what can be discerned at such a distance is involved. We can make out an aircraft at a much greater height than this but, of course, aircraft are much bigger than cars. So common sense begins to let us down. Loftus explains that it is possible to digitally manipulate (blur) an image to show just how it would appear at different distances. A photo of a car can be made to appear as it would at a quarter-mile distance so that the jury can judge for itself whether a spoiler may indeed be seen at this distance. Just in case you are wondering, this very example was at the centre of an actual Californian road rage case. It is clear that the expert witness can add something over and above what common sense supplies in circumstances like these. Loftus mentions a number of actual examples of such visual eyewitness issues where the clarity of the view is reduced by distance.

However, many of the issues to do with eyewitness evidence are not so clear cut, as we saw in Chapter 13. One question is the extent to which the lay knowledge of jurors about eyewitness evidence is as good as that of expert witnesses. Research suggests that jurors are often poor in terms of their knowledge of factors affecting the quality of eyewitness testimony and, most certainly, their knowledge is somewhat variable and uneven. It can be somewhat frustrating to the psychological profession when judges and prominent lawyers claim that the findings from psychological research into eyewitness testimony are little more than common sense and decisions concerning eyewitness testimony can consequently be left to jurors. Given the problems that researchers have had reaching any sort of consensus about the factors which lead to good eyewitness evidence, the ability of jurors to deal effectively with eyewitness evidence has to be in some doubt. Researchers have some matters on which they agree – these might be termed the important 'facts' of eyewitness testimony. To what extent do jurors agree with the facts as researchers themselves agree on them?

Kassin, Tubb, Hosch and Memon (2001) generated a list of eyewitness testimony 'facts' by carrying out a survey of expert psychologists to identify the research findings which tend to be agreed on by all psychologists. As perfect consensus is rare among researchers, Kassin *et al.* adopted the criterion for a 'fact' that 80 per cent of psychologists agreed that it was true. They divided the research into system variables and estimator variables:

- System variables are things which are in the power of the criminal justice system to alter such as the way in which the line-up is run. Things agreed by 80 per cent of psychologists were:
  - confidence malleability;
  - line-up instructions;
  - mugshot-induced bias;
  - question wording.
- Estimator variables are characteristics of the witness and witnessing situation which the criminal justice system cannot alter, such as how drunk the witness was at the time of the crime. These would have to be estimated using whatever methods are possible.
  - accuracy and confidence;
  - attitudes and expectations;
  - child suggestibility;
  - cross-race bias;
  - exposure time;
  - hypnotic suggestibility;
  - post-event information;
  - unconscious transference;
  - weapon focus.

There are doubts about the validity of some of these based on recent developments in eyewitness testimony research (see Chapter 13). Nevertheless they do provide a useful baseline of expert opinion.

To what extent do jurors agree with these 'facts' of eyewitness testimony? Desmarais and Read (2011) carried out a meta-analysis (see Box 4.1) of 23 studies into the public's knowledge of the 'facts' of eyewitness testimony. The majority of the studies were Canadian and used samples of community volunteers (the general public) but student samples were also well represented. Nearly 5000 participants in total took part in the research. Using the criterion of 80 per cent consensus which was applied to researchers, there were very few aspects of eyewitness testimony which the lay public agreed on. These exceptions were:

- alcohol intoxication;
- attitudes and expectations;
- question wording.

Of course, less stringent criteria for agreement produce greater levels of consensus. Nevertheless, since 80 per cent agreement had been accepted as appropriate for experts then the same criterion is reasonable if the assumption that expert evidence is little more than the common sense that the general public can provide in equal measure were true! It is important to emphasise that this creates a somewhat misleading impression that the general public is substantially inferior to experts about the 'facts' of eyewitness testimony, whereas they did agree with the 'correct' answer based on expert opinion on about two-thirds of occasions. Of course, the extent to which the correct answers are based on knowledge of research findings rather than being the result of a reasoned 'guess' cannot be assessed. Desmarais and Read (2011) believe that their findings indicate that the lay public seem to be increasingly knowledgeable since more recent studies in their meta-analysis tended to produce higher levels of correctness. They take the view that this increased level of awareness can be, in part, attributed to the efforts of researchers in promoting research findings from eye-witness research.

Assessing credibility in court

The process of forming judgements about other people and their behaviour is complex and not less so for jurors. One particularly relevant aspect of this in the forensic context is the tendency for some people to hold crime victims responsible for their misfortune. So the woman who walks home late at night alone is blamed for the sexual assault perpetrated against her or the man who carries large amounts of money in his wallet is blamed when it is stolen from him. Of course, such victim blaming is unjustified but nevertheless it happens – and it is especially important when it happens in court. Van den Bos and Maas (2009) explain the thought processes behind this tendency on the basis of *The Just World Theory* (Lerner and Goldberg, 1999). According to the just world theory, people see the world as a fair, just and equitable place in which we deserve whatever happens to us, whether this is a good thing or a bad thing. The idea that people are the architects of their own fortune is built into us through the process of socialisation – for example, we are taught that if we work well at school then we will get a well-paid job. Applied to the victims of crime, this theory encourages the view that the victim is a deserving victim. Closely associated with the just world theory is Epstein's *Cognitive Experiential Self Theory* (Epstein, 1985, 1994; Epstein and Pacini, 1999). This argues that thinking involves two alternative pathways, two sorts of mindset which need to be considered in relation to our decision-making processes. These mindsets operate in parallel to each other, as seen in Figure 24.5. They are:

- The rational pathway, which is a conscious analytic system. It is based on analysis, logic and facts. It requires a lot of cognitive effort to execute rational analyses. The rationalistic mindset is reasoning and based on logic. As such, it is very slow and deliberative in nature, with judgements being rational.
- The intuitive-experiential pathway, which is preconscious and intuitive. It essentially depends on what feels good. Little effort is required since it involves emotion and stereotypical thinking based on previous experiences. The processes involved cannot be put into words and it is not amenable to logical analysis. The intuitive-experiential mindset is a quick, straightforward and effortless way of understanding the world.

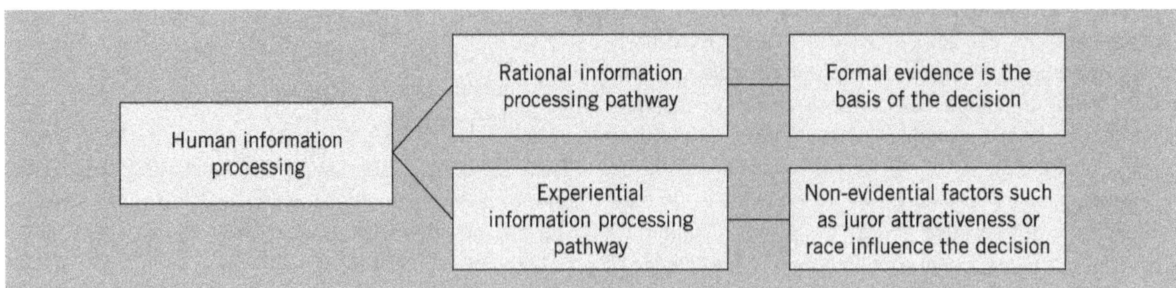

Figure 24.5 When extra-legal or legally irrelevant information may affect jury decisions

Bos and Maas use Epstein's Cognitive Experiential Self Theory in order to understand the acceptance and application of the just world theory to forensic contexts. If a person bases their judgements of other people on the assumption that the world is a just place, then the logical conclusion is that the victim of a crime deserved what happened to them – for example, they were asking for trouble by dressing provocatively. It is difficult for those who believe in a just world to accept that a victim can be innocent. People who do not have this belief will find less difficulty with the idea of an innocent victim since it is not incongruent with their beliefs. Now Bos and Maas argue that individuals who believe in a just world and adopt the rationalistic way of thinking of Epstein's theory are the most likely to blame the victim for their victimisation. This prediction was supported by two studies carried out by Bos and Maas.

Non-evidential factors and jury decisions

To describe the research literature on the non-evidential characteristics of jurors and defendants as substantial is something of an understatement. Of course, the idea that legally irrelevant factors have an influence on judgements of the guilt of the defendant promotes feelings of injustice. Such studies are often cited in psychology textbooks – such as those which suggest that attractive defendants are treated differently or that defendants of another race received harsher treatment. Devine and Caughlin (2014) chose to carry out a meta-analysis (see Box 4.1) of nearly 300 published and unpublished studies on this topic. Nearly 500 relationships were found in these. Studies were included if they involved an experimental design, measured or manipulated participant characteristics, measured the individual juror's judgement about sentence or punishment. Real-trials were not studied because measurements are readily confounded in non-experimental studies. The meta-analysis concentrated on 11 juror and defendant characteristics. The juror characteristics included authoritarianism, gender, jury experience, race, legal system trust, and need for cognition; the defendant characteristics were attractiveness, gender, information given about prior criminal record, race, and socio-economic status.

The underlying hypothesis was that jury members would be more likely to convict the defendant when they were high on legal system trust, high on authoritarianism, where the defendant was of a different race, and where they had a low need for cognition. People with a low need for cognition do not enjoy thinking about things and issues or do not spend time deliberating about things. The strongest relationships were found the socio economic status of the defendant (negative relationship), the jurors trust in the justice system, the authoritarianism of the juror, and the defendant's criminal record but most variables showed relationships. However, there was a lot of evidence that other variables moderated nearly all of these relationships. In other words, the relationship between the defendant's criminal record, for example, and sentencing recommendations by the jurors in the study could vary substantially according to the study characteristics on other variables.

Epstein's Cognitive Experiential Self Theory (Epstein, 2003) discussed above and summarised in Figure 24.6 has been applied to other aspects of the activities of jury members. One of the classic findings of jury research is that physically attractive defendants are treated differently by jurors compared to unattractive ones. Studies do not universally reach this conclusion but, nevertheless, it is important to know just how non-evidential (peripheral) factors can affect jury decision making. The range of studies into defendant attractiveness is enormous and there is reasonably clear evidence that physically attractive defendants are treated leniently (the relevant studies go back as far as Efran (1974) and Sigall and Ostrove (1975)).

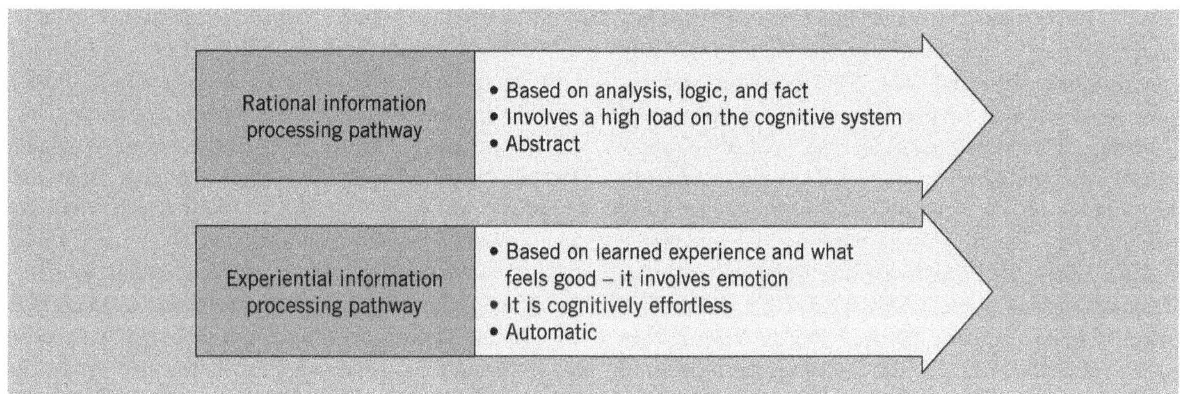

Figure 24.6 Epstein's Cognitive Experiential Self Theory

Epstein's Cognitive Experiential Self Theory is relevant to jury decision making because it helps us understand some of the circumstances in which such extra-evidential (non-legal) factors as defendant attractiveness may be influential. One suggestion is that legal evidence presented in court will largely be processed through the rational information-processing pathway. The more intuitive and emotion-based extra-evidential information such as the attractiveness of the defendant (and perhaps also the race of the defendant) will be processed through the experiential information-processing pathway which lacks a rational focus. This is the basis of Gunnell and Ceci's (2010) study in which the individual's tendency to use one pathway rather than the other was measured using the Rational Experiential Inventory (REI) (Epstein *et al.*, 1996; Pacini and Epstein, 1999). The basic framework of Gunnell and Ceci's argument is presented in Figure 24.5. Participants in Gunnell and Ceci's research read a criminal trial transcript, a defendant profile and then decided their verdict and appropriate sentencing. Different groups were given different pictures of the defendant – either a more attractive or a less attractive person. Experiential thinkers made more decisions to convict the defendant than did rational thinkers. The findings were a little more complex than expected:

- If the defendant was attractive then the type of thinking made no difference to conviction. That is, experiential and rational thinkers were equally likely to convict.
- If the defendant was unattractive, then the trend was for the experiential thinkers to convict more often than the rational thinkers. Experiential thinkers convicted the unattractive offender in 89 per cent of cases whereas rational thinkers convicted on only 67 per cent of occasions.

This is despite the relevant evidence being the same in all cases. Experiential processers were more likely to say that extra-legal factors would influence their verdict.

The credibility of rape victims is, of course, assessed at different levels during a court's proceedings. A study by Lievore (2004) found that Australian Crown Prosecutors unanimously saw the issue of victim credibility as being important in sexual assault trials. They believed that credibility was revealed by the demeanour of the victim. Systematic evidence suggests that rape victims who show high levels of emotionality are viewed as the most credible. Nevertheless, the assumptions of the person assessing credibility may alter the way in which cues are interpreted in such contexts. Heuristic processing is the way in which particular cues are employed when assessing whether the person is lying or telling the truth. Such heuristics are forms of mental shortcut which speed up the process of making decisions. The heuristics may work fine in many instances but they may result in incorrect judgements in other circumstances because heuristics encourage the individual to neglect important information. In the heuristic-systematic model, the assumption is that the least mental effort is applied and that short-cut methods are generally used unless there are good reasons not to use them. Expectance violation theory (Jussim, Coleman and Lerch, 1987) assumes that expectations about another person's behaviour will influence perceptions of their behaviour. So if the expectation is that a rape victim is likely to be highly emotional but the rape victim shows a lack of emotional behaviour that will lead to judgements that the victim lacks credibility. An experiment by Hackett, Day and Mohr (2008) involved participants watching a video of a rape victim reporting the offence committed against her. The emotional expressiveness of the victim when making this report was varied in terms of 1) non-verbal characteristics such as eye contact and crying and 2) paralinguistic features such as tone of voice. A semi-professional actress played the rape victim in three separate videos in which:

- The victim speaks in a matter-of-fact style looking straight ahead.
- The victim is emotionally numbed, nervous and timid.
- The victim is portrayed crying several times, with choked, trembling speech.

The offence involved the victim's rape by a neighbour. The 'jurors' rated the woman's credibility on a 24-item credibility scale which including items such as 'Do you believe the woman's story?' Overall, the emotionality of the woman had no effect. Where it did make a difference was when the 'juror' believed that certain emotional behaviours were characteristic of rape victims. In this case, the emotional victim tended to be believed and the unemotional victim tended to be disbelieved.

Perhaps the most contentious of topics in research on juries is the question of racial biases in jury decision making (as well as sentencing). This is not simply a factual question of how the race of the defendant affects jury decisions. It extends much more widely to the idea that black people are treated unfairly by the criminal justice system. This is basically the idea behind the term *anticipatory injustice* – or the belief or expectation that the legal system is basically biased against certain groups of people and will treat them in a biased or prejudicial way. Woolard, Harvell and Graham (2008) employed data from the *McArthur Juvenile Competence Study* which involved nearly 1400 adolescents/young adults. The research took place in a variety of settings in the USA and involved the young people answering questions about judicial fairness. An example of the sort of question tapping anticipatory injustice would be: 'Compared to other people in trouble with the law, are you more likely, less likely, or just as likely to be treated fairly by the legal system?' (Woolard,

Harvell and Graham, 2008, p. 213). Approximately 40 per cent of the young people agreed with at least one of four items asking about anticipatory injustice. Those with greater experience of the legal system and African Americans and Latinos were the most likely to expect unfair treatment by the justice system. The influence of these beliefs ran deep since they were associated with a reduced willingness to confess; incomplete disclosure to their own lawyer; and a reduced likelihood of entering a plea bargaining agreement. These relationships held after other important variables were controlled for, such as prior experience of the criminal justice system.

General processes in juror decision making

There has been some debate about very broad psychological processes in jury decision making. We are not referring here to the sorts of factors which may influence decision making but to broad cognitive strategies that may be involved in how jurors reach decisions. Some aspects may generally be seen as being detrimental to decision making, including 1) confirmation bias and 2) the feature positive effect (Eerland and Rassin, 2012). The *confirmation bias* in criminal justice is that decision makers will tend to favour incriminating over exonerating evidence (see Chapter 11 also) and the *feature positive effect* is that decision makers will give more emphasis to the finding of evidence about events than the failure to secure any evidence. (The feature positive effect was first noted in relation to animal conditioning. Pigeons learn more quickly if they refer to two stimuli than if the learning involves the presence of one stimulus and the absence of any other. This has been extended to humans and it has been shown that the absence of a symbol makes it harder to learn what the rule is than would the presence of the symbol.)

Eerland and Rassin carried out a study in which the evidence was manipulated in order to assess the influence of these two biases on guilt estimation and conviction rates. In the study, undergraduate law students read a lengthy case study which involved experimental manipulation. It concerned a man suspected of physically attacking another man. Participants were provided with the police report; interview reports; a report of a photo line-up; and testimonies from a number of eyewitnesses. For participants in the control condition, this was all the information provided. However, in the four experimental conditions, additional information was given. In two of these conditions, the extra information that was provided incriminated the suspect (e.g. clothing had been checked for fingerprints of the suspect; the victim had been shown pictures of the suspect; a search for further witnesses). In the remaining two experimental conditions, very similar additional sorts of information were provided, but this time it was exonerating in nature rather than incriminating. In part, the findings identified both sorts of biases. When participants were fairly convinced of the guilt of a suspect, adding further incriminating evidence increased the guilt ratings more than adding further exonerating evidence decreased the guilt rate. This is evidence for the confirmation bias in this setting. Furthermore, there was another important difference in terms of the influence of finding compared with not finding evidence. Finding evidence had more effect on guilt estimates than did not finding that evidence. Eerlands and Rassin compare this with the police finding fingerprints from the suspect at the crime scene, which is considered incriminating much more than not finding them is seen as exonerating. Not all their measures showed this trend – conviction rates were not affected but the trends applied to guilt estimates. A rational theory of decision making would be that individuals use information in an unbiased way and so reach a balanced and fair conclusion. Unfortunately, factors such as confirmation bias and the feature positive effect help bias decision making.

We also need to examine two models of decision making which may have relevance to decision making by professionals in the legal system. However, there is a case for seeing whether they are also features of the thinking of lay people. The *story model* of jury decision making involves the juror creating a chronological narrative (i.e. mental construction or story of what happened) as the basis for explaining their choice of verdict. Pennington and Hastie (1986) in their narrative or story model suggest that jurors rely on narrative-type mental models which provide an account of the evidence in story form. The implications of the narrative form the basis of their decision. The narrative provides a form of explanation of what happened in the sequence of events which led to the crime which are usually linked over time. The story underlying the 'crime' provides a sequence of events which relate causally to each other over time. The narrative can include such things as actions, intentions, motivations and states of mind, each of which can help the narrative. Conviction should follow if the narrative favours guilt; acquittal should follow if the narrative favours innocence. But an explicit justification for the choice of verdict could also be in the form of a relational or *knowledge-transforming* argument structure that incorporates various pieces of evidence which are not chronologically related as they would be in a story (Anderson, Schum and Twining, 2005). In the jury, knowledge-transforming jurors would also have the goal of constructing an account of what actually happened, but their method of doing so would involve relating the variety of elements of evidence together in order to solve problems which occur in the account. A simple example can illustrate the knowledge-transforming approach. The defence argument is that the victim drew a knife first. A witness also says that the victim drew a knife first. Hence the decision-making process in the case has to involve an evaluation of the question of whether there was provocation by the witness. This does not involve the telling of a narrative to describe the events but a reference to what is known and how it relates to the decision. That is, the task involves deciding what problems have to be solved and understanding how the various pieces of evidence relate and contribute to solving the problems.

Weinstock (2011) studied people's use of story-telling or knowledge-transforming approaches in relation to legal decision making. An important subsidiary issue is whether narrative-based decision making or knowledge-transforming decision making is related to argumentative skills and understanding the nature of knowledge. A sample of people on jury duty reached verdict decisions for two shortened cases. They listened to shortened re-enactments of two actual murder cases, which included opening and closing arguments by the lawyers; examination and cross-examination of witnesses; and the judges' instructions to the jury among other more realistic trial features. The jurors came to their decisions, which they then had to explain or justify to the researchers, with supporting arguments. The tendency was for the same argument structure to be used across cases. Those using knowledge-transforming structures were better in the juror argument skills task and were higher on epistemic understanding. Epistemic understanding essentially refers to the difference between those who consider that knowledge is absolute and certain – either right or wrong. Thus there is no need to justify knowledge. At the other extreme are evaluativists, who accept that knowledge has both subjective and objective features. Thus, for the evaluativist, any claims must be justified. Educational level is strongly related to this.

Non-evidential evidence

Finally, a classic study in social psychology is Erving Goffman's *The Presentation of Self in Everyday Life* (1959). This contains a framework which can help us to understand the way in which jurors focus on information which is not part of the formal evidence at a trial. This can be referred to as *offstage observation*. Jurors are influenced by the evidence and the formal case presented but, in addition to that, other information obtained by watching people in the courtroom who are not actually part of the evidence presentation or argument. Especially when these people are unaware that they are being observed, they may do things which the juror may regard as informative to the trial. Unusually, Rose, Diamond and Baker (2010) had access to recordings of 50 real jury discussions and deliberations in US civil proceedings largely concerned with motoring offences. During the trials, prior to the jury discussions, the judge explained to the jury that their decisions should be based on the legal instructions and the evidence, including testimony, exhibits or other things which they have been instructed to accept. In Goffman's terms, these formal matters take place *frontstage*. However, in a courtroom there are few physical boundaries to separate those performing their roles frontstage and the rest of the people around. Goffman points out that social observers of a social situation – such as the juror is – take an interest in what people on the periphery of the main social action are doing as well as those more central to the action. One could say that the courtroom is rather like a theatre in the round in which all sorts of people are in full view of the jury: the parties in the action; attorneys and their assistants; those watching in the public gallery of the courtroom; and so forth. Cues from the responses of the secondary parties may well appear to be particularly informative about what is going on in court. Of course, impression management will generally characterise the demeanour of professionals working in court as well as others, but this façade may slip at times.

In their study, Rose, Diamond and Baker (2010) coded any reference to things in the jury deliberations which had not happened frontstage in the court. So anything involving members of the public would be offstage, as would be anything involving an attorney when they were not directly involved in the formal business of the trial. Some of the behaviours coded as offstage occurred in the courthouse but not in the courtroom. In 80 per cent of trials, jurors made at least one offstage remark. The majority of offstage remarks involved courtroom behaviours (74 per cent) and the rest in hallways, elevators or outside the courthouse. The most common observation concerned the plaintiff and the second most common concerned non-witness audience members at the trial. Of course, given the nature of the trials, matters related to the physical health of the plaintiff were common. This included expressions of surprise at how physically mobile the plaintiff was, given the nature of their injuries, for example. About half of the comments were positive or negative towards one of the parties in the case. There was evidence that more negative offstage observations were made about the plaintiff during deliberations. However, in this study there was no evidence that this was associated with outcomes (verdicts) favouring the defence. Only one instance was found in which offstage observations related directly to decision making. This particular instance concerned the amount of damages that the plaintiff ought to receive. No factors were found that distinguished jurors making offstage comments from those who did not in terms of demographic factors. Of course, in this study, the offstage observations had to be articulated in the jury room before they were registered by the researchers, so it may be possible that the exchanges between the jurors negated the impact of the observations, whatever their effect on the individual making the offstage observation.

Main points

- Research on juries is considerably affected by legal constraints on studying real juries making real decisions. As a consequence, a great deal of research has simulated trial procedures in psychological laboratories as an alternative means of studying the jury. Sometimes the simulation involves individuals reacting in isolation rather than in interaction as in a real jury. There have been attempts to improve the validity of jury research by using shadow juries which sit and listen to the evidence in court and then 'sit' in parallel to the real jury. Quite clearly, great care is needed when generalising from the findings of such 'laboratory' juries to real-life juries.
- Juries differ in many ways, which may have a detrimental effect on the quality of the decision making. For example, in some countries juries are larger and in others they are smaller. The research evidence, such as it is, finds relatively small differences between large and small juries in terms of decisions made but they do not operate identically. The rules that govern how the jury must reach a decision (e.g. is a majority verdict allowed) can affect how the jury operates.
- Psychologists have been involved in providing expert guidance to lawyers about how best to conduct a trial, which potential jurors to reject if possible, and arguments about the effect of pre-trial publicity. Virtually all of the research in this field has been conducted in the United States rather than in other jurisdictions which, for example, may not allow lawyers to challenge jurors in this way. Nevertheless, if there were better evidence available on scientific jury selection and other related activity, it would inform us about some aspects of jury decision making.

Further reading

Devine, D.J. (2012) *Jury Decision Making* New York University Press.

Kovera, M.B. (2016) *The Psychology of Juries* Washington DC: American Psychological Society.

Martin, A.M. and Kaplan, M.F. (eds) (2006) *Understanding World Jury Systems Through Social Psychological Research* Hove: Psychology Press.

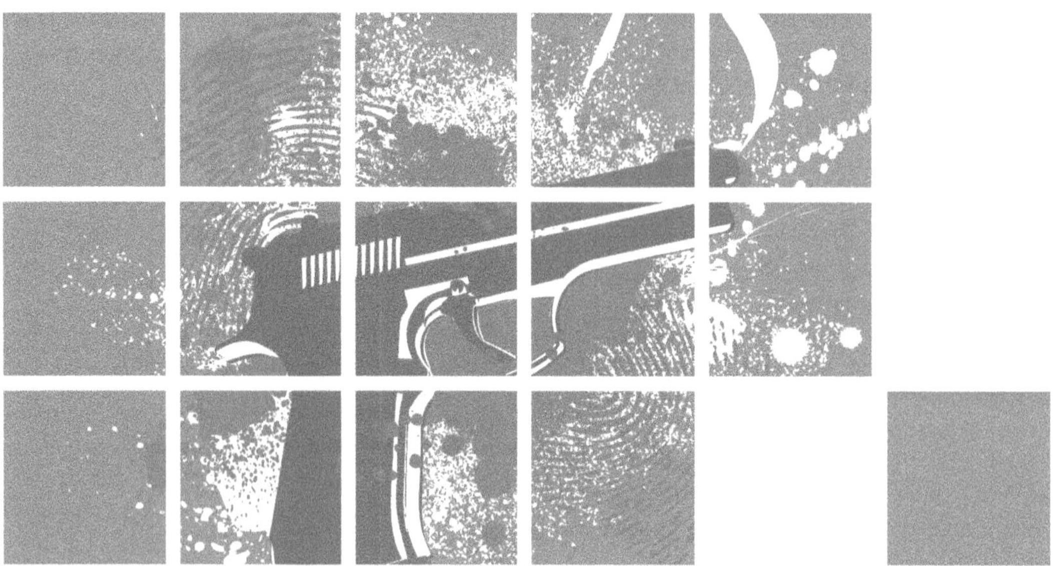

Chapter 25

Effective prison

Overview

- There are a number of ideologies that are concerned with what prison is for: retribution holds that prison is for punishment; utilitarianism suggests that prison should produce changes that reduce the risk of reoffending; and humanitarianism suggests that the role of prison should be the rehabilitation of casualties of social deprivation and victimisation.
- Models for the treatment of prisoners vary with the presumed origins of crime. For example, if one believes that there are too many rewards for crime and too little punishment, then the appropriate treatment for prisoners may be harsh and severe in order to make prison a deterrent to reoffending.
- Prisoners are a population at risk. This includes the risk of violence from other prisoners, though prison homicides are relatively infrequent.
- Evidence suggests that prison increases the riskof prisoners committing suicide. However, prisoners (largely young males) tend to be a high-risk group for suicide in the general community. The period spent in prison before trial is associated with the greatest risk of suicide and is higher then than during any other time spent in prison.
- There is substantial evidence that prison and other forms of sentence have some, if limited, effectiveness in terms of criteria such as the reduction of recidivism. Educational programmes for prisoners within prison seem to be the most effective aspect of the prison experience in this regard.
- 'Nothing works' was a dominant view of prison until relatively recently. Increasingly, it is accepted that a lot of the work done within the prison service pays off in terms of reducing future reoffending. In recent years, there have been consistent attempts to provide effective treatment programmes to prisoners. Cognitive behavioural therapies are commonly used by psychologists in prisons for the treatment of various sorts of offender, especially sex offenders such as paedophiles and rapists and violent offenders. These are multi-faceted strategies based on group work to provide knowledge and insight into the offending process.

Introduction

Well, we have finally got to prison. Although it may seem like the end of the criminal justice system process, it is actually the start of a new one. For some, prison will contribute something to their rehabilitation and, perhaps, change of lifestyle. For others, prison will be the end of the road – they may spend the rest of their lives there. Others will pass through and return again several times. There is no consensus about the purpose of prison but there is a wide range of different viewpoints. What we do know is that it is estimated that there are ten million people in prisons around the world (Walmsley, 2009). Hollin (2002), along with many others, regards imprisonment as the focus of a moral debate which has long historical roots. The major views in the debate about prison are as follows:

- *Retributionists* regard the purpose of prison as being to deliver punishments.
- *Utilitarians* see prison as part of a process of bringing about changes which reduce the probability of reoffending.
- *Humanitarians* see that prisoners often come from backgrounds of deprivation and victimisation, so are deserving of rehabilitation.

This is a complex debate that goes far beyond the work of psychologists in the prison service. It hardly needs pointing out that crime and punishment are at the forefront of the political agenda in many countries. Hollin suggests that sex offenders are a good example where confusion can reign because 'moral beliefs, principles and utility, and effectiveness become fused and can lead to confusion in policies and procedures within the criminal justice system' (Hollin, 2002, pp. 1–2). The repugnance that many feel for sex offenders might encourage lengthy prison sentences in order to make the punishment proportionate to the heinousness of the crime. However, the utilitarian might argue that this in itself has little point unless it reduces the chances of others being victimised in the future and so more than imprisonment is required. The humanitarian might suggest that sex offenders in many instances have been victims of sexual assault themselves, such that harsh punishment alone is inappropriate. Humane treatment is required in order to meet the needs of the offender and in order to stop the endless cycle of abuse in which victims become future offenders. The various 'ideologies' associated with imprisonment (*retributionism, utilitarianism* and *humanism*) tend to coexist in varying proportions within the criminal justice system. Pure retribution, for example, may be relatively uncommon.

There are many different types of punishment available within the criminal justice system apart from imprisonment. In some systems, such as the United Kingdom, relatively minor offences committed by minor offenders might be dealt with by admonitions in the form of a police caution. Generally speaking, monetary fines are the commonest punishment. Sometimes one will find direct compensation of the victim or community associated with the crime. This may involve financial compensation or service to the community through a work programme. Suspended prison sentences are a step up in seriousness. Prison sentences are regarded as being suitable for the most serious offences and more committed or persistent offenders, though it is far from certain that prison is reserved for the worst offenders. For example, those who default on fines may well receive prison sentences eventually.

The utilitarian approach assumes that penalties of all sorts should increase the likelihood that the offender (and others seeing the possible outcome of the risk they are taking) will stop offending in the future. The effectiveness of the penal system in reducing crime may be evaluated in various ways. Recidivism in the form of further crimes is very common. There are many offenders who repeatedly offend, despite being punished repeatedly. Depending on a large number of factors, about half of criminals reoffend after punishment. These could be regarded in two ways:

- as depressing statistics on the persistence of crime;
- as evidence of the large numbers who do not reoffend after punishment.

Punishment and rehabilitation are not the only ways in which justice can proceed. For example, there is the concept of restorative justice which is discussed in Chapter 4. A central theme in restorative justice is the righting of the wrong done to victims by helping them to return to their former self as a survivor. The process encourages the offender to reflect upon their harmful behaviours and to accept responsibility for their offending. Restorative justice utilises the methods of reconciliation and mediation in meeting its ends. Sometimes the process operates in parallel with the criminal justice system. (See Table 25.1 for further indications of the functions of prison.)

Some of the more severe consequences of prison can be seen in the evidence of suicide and other forms of death in prison. These are also matters which the prison service is actively expected to prevent.

Prison as a therapeutic community

The therapeutic community aims to provide offenders with an institutional environment which encourages their development as members of an effective community. In this way, it is hoped that they will be more effective

Table 25.1 Treatment strategies associated with criminality

Model of criminogenesis	Treatment model
Insufficient deterrent to crime: the rewards for crime are greater than the costs of punishment.	Harsher prison regimes, 'boot camps' for offenders possibly in exchange for reductions in offending.
Emotional distress: deep-seated emotional problems are expressed in criminal behaviour.	Psychodynamic treatments such as psychoanalysis.
Crime is thus seen as a consequence of pathological aspects of the individual.	Client-centred counselling.
Educational deficit: failure to complete schooling leaves the individual with important skill deficits which exclude them from society's mainstream in many instances.	Education programmes such as reading, mathematics, etc. Training in practical job skills.
Learning of criminal behaviour: criminal conduct is learnt.	Institutions organised as token economies in which members are rewarded in tangible ways for improvements and changes in standards of conduct.
Social interaction skills: offenders have difficulty in interacting with others effectively in a social context.	Cognitive behavioural intervention in which the offender's deficits in cognitive and interaction skills are examined and regular group sessions are held, involving such things as interpersonal cognitive problem solving and social skills training.
Social/institutional balance: possibly because of early experience of institutions such as children's homes, offenders do not learn a healthy and balanced approach to life and may resolve difficulties inappropriately through the use of violence.	Creating a healthy institutional environment by reducing rigid controls and sanctions, giving the task of controlling the inmates' behaviour to the whole of the community and having forums to discuss problems arising in the institutions.
Labelling individuals as deviant ensures that it is difficult for them to operate effectively in normal contexts, thus forcing them into deviant social systems and crime.	Divert individuals such as young offenders from the prison system into probation, mediation, reparation, community supervision, etc.

Source: Based on Redondo, S., Sanchez-Meca, J. and Garrido, V. (2002) *Offender Rehabilitation and Treatment: Effective Programmes and Policies to Reduce Re-offending*. © John Wiley & Sons, Ltd

participants in the wider community after their release from prison. Perhaps the therapeutic community-based prison provides the greatest contrast to our everyday expectations of what a prison should be like. Furthermore, it probably exhibits some of the more humanitarian features that we have already referred to. A therapeutic institution has the following characteristics (Woodward, 1999):

- ongoing evaluation;
- ongoing monitoring;
- responsivity to residents' needs;
- skills-oriented;
- sufficient 'dosage' or amounts of treatment;
- targeted on criminogenic factors;
- thorough care.

One of the best known examples of the therapeutic community prison is Grendon Prison in the United Kingdom. The antecedents of Grendon lie in the democratic therapeutic communities which developed after the Second World War as a model for the rehabilitation and treatment of war-traumatised service personnel. The term *therapeutic community* came from the psychiatrist Tom Main in 1946. He wished to facilitate the incorporation of the involvement of patients within a community. In more modern terminology, he sought to empower patients. The therapeutic community is built upon the proven therapeutic value of socially supportive (affirmative) environments in therapy. As it is not based on research findings or established clinical methods, it can be seen as an ideologically-based model. In other words, therapeutic communities are ideologically driven (Shuker, 2010). In this regard, the therapeutic community has roots in the Quaker movement, which stressed humane and moral treatments of offenders. The core of therapeutic communities is that responsibility is handed to prisoners and other members of the prison community in general. Responsibility extends throughout much of the structure of the organisation. So responsibility is shared in terms of domestic issues, interpersonal relationships, and the treatment aspects of the community. There is openness in communication is important between members of staff and inmates and the staff and inmates share in matters such as the management of conflict within the community setting.

Rapoport (1960) provided the following list of features which are the basis of therapeutic prisons:

- All aspects of decision making are democratised and include prisoner involvement.
- There is a general permissiveness towards pathological behaviours which might be a problem in other contexts.
- Day-to-day living of the institution is as a community.
- Development, progress, and change are driven by the interpersonal forces within the community.

Grendon Prison in Buckinghamshire, UK, was the first prison based on therapeutic community values. It opened early in the 1960s as an experimental approach to dealing with prisoners. One of its innovations was that it was headed by a medical superintendent rather than the traditional prison governor. This followed the recommendations of East and Hubert (1939) including experimentation within the penal service and a special kind of institution which followed primarily a medical model of treatment. This tradition of a medical superintendent came to an end in the 1980s when symbolically a prison governor was deemed the appropriate figure to lead the prison. The prison's function in the prison service also changed in response to a number of pressures. What was new was that serious violent and sexual offenders became the core inmates. Previously, the emphasis had been on recidivistic property offenders. In the past, therapeutic communities have been criticised for the lack of evidence base in their work and their neglect of what was important in terms of recidivism reduction and risk factors.

Although there is a belief that therapeutic communities are influenced by psychoanalytical principles, this is not very apparent. One indication of this is that therapeutic communities are not based on the one-to-one client–therapist model that is familiar from the work of Freud and others in that tradition. Instead, it is worthwhile listing the main areas of practice in therapeutic communities identified by Shine and Morris (2000). These are: 1) attachments (childhood memories); 2) scripts or schemas formed during crucial periods of early life; 3) offending history; and 4) behaviour within the therapeutic community, such as interpersonal style and antisocial characteristics. The current emphasis is on psychotherapy, group-based therapies, and skill acquisition. All of this operates in a climate where group processes are harnessed to the therapeutic aims.

One current criterion for the effectiveness of prison treatments is the reduction of recidivism. Unfortunately, research in this area is particularly problematic for reasons such as the difficulty of deciding on appropriate control groups. However, it is notable that suicide and self-harm are relatively infrequent relative to other prisons dealing with the same category of offender (Rivlin, 2007). This is more remarkable because 50 per cent of the prisoners going to Grendon report suicide/self-harm attempts prior to entering the therapeutic community. A similar story applies to forms of institutional misdemeanour, such as violence. Again, it is hard to put this down to prisoners at Grendon having a better history of non-violence. One way of summarising this is that therapeutic communities may be better at containing particularly difficult and violent prisoners than at the reduction of recidivism. Generally, the evidence is that they improve mental health and reduce psychological and emotional distress as well as personality disorder (e.g. Bateman and Fonagy, 1999). See Shuker (2010) for a detailed account of the development of the therapeutic community prison.

It hardly needs saying that the experience facing most prisoners is very different from that at therapeutic community-based prisons such as Grendon. There are a number of significant issues which are the focus of prison policy as well as research. In particular, the problems of violence and suicide in prison are immense. Prisoners are not to be subject to degrading treatment but an ambience of risk inevitably raises questions about the way the prison system is managed.

Violence in prison

Murder is rare in prison in the United Kingdom. For the years 2006–2016, the number of deaths from homicide in prison per year averaged less than 3 for England and Wales (Inquest, 2017). The yearly prison suicide rate over the same period was 75. The rate in the United States is about ten times higher (Gordon, Oyebode and Minne, 1997). Nearly 16 per cent of prison officers in the US have been the victims of assault by an inmate(s) (Duhart, 2001) and 21 per cent of prisoners in the US report being victimised by violence in prison (Wolff, Blitz, Shi, Siegel and Bachman (2007)).

According to Lahm (2008) there are two main theories about violence in the prison context. One is deprivation theory and the other is importation theory. Both of these are illustrated in Figure 25.1:

- *Deprivation theory:* Although difficult to attribute to specific authors, deprivation theory assumes that prison violence is the consequence of degrading and stigmatising prison conditions (Goffman, 1961; Sykes, 1958). That is, prison violence is the result of the bad prison environment. Some prisoners respond to these oppressive conditions by acting out violently. That is, they are

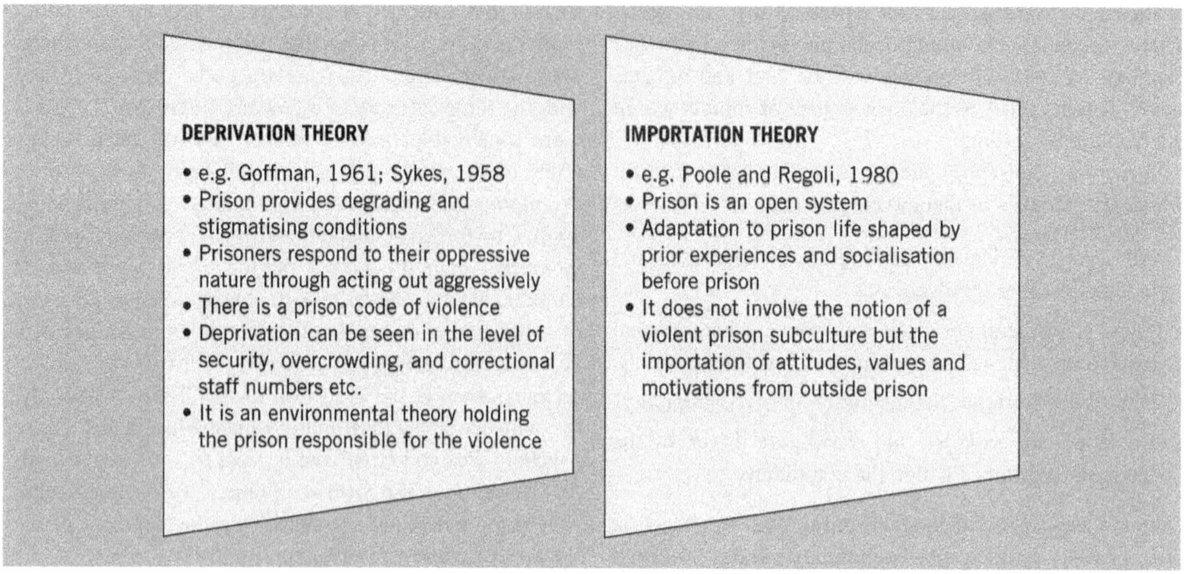

DEPRIVATION THEORY

- e.g. Goffman, 1961; Sykes, 1958
- Prison provides degrading and stigmatising conditions
- Prisoners respond to their oppressive nature through acting out aggressively
- There is a prison code of violence
- Deprivation can be seen in the level of security, overcrowding, and correctional staff numbers etc.
- It is an environmental theory holding the prison responsible for the violence

IMPORTATION THEORY

- e.g. Poole and Regoli, 1980
- Prison is an open system
- Adaptation to prison life shaped by prior experiences and socialisation before prison
- It does not involve the notion of a violent prison subculture but the importation of attitudes, values and motivations from outside prison

Figure 25.1 A comparison of deprivation theory and importation theory as explanations of prison violence

not violent by disposition. In these circumstances, they adapt to the brutality of the 'prison code'. This is a purely environmental explanation. It can be considered that there are macro and micro prison-related variables. A micro prison-related variable concerns each individual prisoner, such as the length of their prison sentence and the number of outside visits. These are associated with violent behaviour in prison – though negatively in the case of outside visits, which are associated with less violence. There are also macro-level variables, which have been relatively much less researched in the past than those concerned with the individual inmate. Examples of these include the level of security to be found in each prison, the amount of crowding, and the number of correctional staff to be found.

- *Importation theory:* (e.g. Poole and Regoli, 1980) In contrast this regards prison as an open system in which adaptation to prison life is shaped by the prisoner's experiences and socialisation prior to imprisonment. What is imported into prison has its origins in attitudes, values and motivations held prior to imprisonment. Thus subcultural values about violent behaviour are brought to the prison from outside. So measures such as prior offence types, previous escapes, previous incarceration, and previous violence are all associated with the importation model.

Which of the two theories is best supported by the evidence? Lahm (2008) surveyed inmates at 30 prisons in Kentucky, Ohio and Tennessee. Self-report measures were employed primarily since a lot of prison violence does not get recorded or staff are unaware of it. Serious or deadly assaultive behaviour was somewhat rare in these self-reports and so Lahm excluded it from the study. Thus the violent acts studied were not the most extreme possible. Participants had to have been in the facility for a minimum of six months, to give them a chance to acclimatise to that particular regime. Seventeen per cent had committed at least one assault on another prisoner in the previous year. Being younger and having a higher level of violence in their past were associated with higher levels of involvement in inmate-on-inmate assault. These constitute good evidence in favour of the importation model. However, beliefs and similar violence-related variables did not predict violence in prison. Evidence also emerged supporting the deprivation theory. So, among the micro-level variables, length of time served in prison and sentence length predicted assaultive behaviour in prison, as did having fewer prison visitors. In addition, some macro-level variables were predictive of prison violence:

- *The proportions of non-white prisoners:* Lahm suggests that white prisoners in predominantly non-white prisons may feel that the conditions are more deprived, hence more likely to be violent according to deprivation theory.
- *The size of the prison population:* Lahm suggests that larger prisons may have more contact places and places to be violent than small prisons. Monitoring by prison staff may also be less effective.

In summary, then, both prison and pre-prison variables contributed to prison violence, giving support to both the deprivation and the importation theories. There is no reason to see importation and deprivation as mutually exclusive.

In a review of research on the individual social and psychological characteristics of those who are violent in prison, Schenk and Fremouw (2012) found a range of expected findings together with a few unexpected ones. Particularly unexpected (and/or difficult to explain) is that prisoners convicted of non-violent crimes and who received a short sentence, are more likely to be involved in violent infractions in the prison context. This is quite the opposite to the idea of the stir-crazy thug having nothing to lose by hitting out in prison. Schenck and Fremouw (p. 440) provide what they describe as the prototype of the prisoner who is violent in prison, citing inmates with psychological aggressive tendencies, symptoms of confusion, high self-esteem but little social support. Major mental illness was also associated with prison violence.

They provide a more concrete example:

> Inmate #13471 is a 20-year-old minority male convicted of burglary. He was sentenced to 5–10 years and this term is his second time being incarcerated. He previously was incarcerated for one year for aggravated assault and he has an extensive arrest history including violent and non-violent offenses. He has affiliated with a recognized gang since he dropped out of school in the ninth grade. At intake, it was documented that Inmate #13471 has a history of major mental illness, specifically a delusional disorder. He scored high in aggression and unstable self-esteem and lacks positive social support in the community, as his friends and family also are associated with the gang.
>
> (p. 440)

We know that relationships outside of prison provide a level of psychological and social protection which allows for more successful rehabilitation into the community, together with less risk of recidivism (Mauer, 2006). Much less interest has been devoted to the relationship between prison experiences and the quality of adjustment to life outside of prison. One exception to this is the interest in the US in the consequences of rape and other non-consensual sexual activity and violence more generally during incarceration in prison. How do prisoners react to their prison experiences? Do they affect their longer-term prospects? Do bad experiences like these influence behaviour on leaving prison? There is little doubt that violent and sexual victimisation can be traumatic and life-changing. However, the majority of this research involves young victims of abuse rather than the population in general. Haden and Scarpa (2008) list the following as consequences of being victimised violently or repeatedly witnessing such episodes:

- interpersonal problems;
- depression;
- aggression;
- post-traumatic stress disorder.

Boxer, Middlemass and DeLorenzo (2009) studied ex-prisoners from state prison or county jail. On average they had spent 30 months outside of prison and they mostly lived in a very urban metropolitan part of the North East of the United States. Thirty per cent of the sample had violent criminal histories according to their own self-reports and available records. A history of murder, robbery, rape or assault was required for classification into the violent group. There was 87 per cent agreement between the records and self-reports. The remainder of the sample were classified as non-violent. The measure of exposure to violent crime used was based on questions asking about lifetime experiences as observers and victims of violent crime. This was turned into two indicators:

- Incarcerated experience of violent crime based on the following scale: 0 = no witnessing of violence or victimisation by violent crime in prison; 1 = witnessing but no victimisation; and 2 = both witnessing and victimisation.
- Community experience of violent crime used exactly the same scale but applied to the experiences outside of prison.

Psychological and social adjustment variables were measured using a battery of measures. The findings from the research demonstrated that prison exposure to violence was correlated with measures of adjustment on leaving prison. Once indicators of exposure to violence outside of prison as well as demographic variables had been controlled, it was found that those who encountered violence in prison were significantly more likely to be aggressive and to show anti-social tendencies.

A quick fix for prison aggression?

Quick fixes to any problem have an appeal. One of the most intriguing of these is the belief in the prison system that a particular shade of pink has the effect of subduing aggressive inmates. The particular shade of pink in question is known a Baker-Miller pink. The underlying idea is that this colour reduces strength and consequently aggression. The story began in 1979 when Schauss reported that prisoners calmed down more when they were put in cells painted this particular pink colour compared with cells painted white. The assumption is that Baker-Miller pink affects neurological and endocrime processes which leads to a lowering of physical strength and a concomitant reduction in aggression. The strength of this theory may be suspect but this was insufficient to prevent the spread of pink cells. Prison cells in countries including the UK, US, Canada, Germany, Poland, Austria, and Switzerland. Obviously the earliest studies were quite influential but may be subject to various experimental biases. For example, Schauss (1979), following a pre-test, showed individuals a coloured card (pink) and their strength measured by the researcher pressing down on their outstretched arms. They were told to resist this. Then their strength was measured again having been shown a blue card. They had less resistance (less strength) when they had been exposed to a pink card. There are obvious problems with this study – in particular the experimenter was not blind to the condition being run (i.e. the colour of card that had been shown). There was another problem of lack of counterbalancing in running the colours. In general the effects were rather weak anyway. There were some studies supporting the value of pink cells but other studies failed to find significant differences. So it is worth considering much more recent research by Genschow, Noll, Wänke and Gersbach (2015). This research took place in a Swiss prison. Prisoners who got in trouble for violating prison rules such as assaulting other prisoners or using alcohol were randomly assigned to several days of attention to a pink versus a white detention cell. Aggression on the part of the prisoners was assessed using a questionnaire which would be completed by the guards. Although aggressiveness declined with time in the detention cell, prisoners in the pink cells compared to those in the white cells showed no greater level of aggression reduction. Although Genschow *et al.* argue that their study was methodologically superior to earlier ones, there is still potential for experimenter effects to be having an effect in their study as it was based on the subjective ratings of prison guards who were aware that some prisoners were being put in a white cell whereas others were being put in a pink cell.

Suicide in prison

On an international basis, the main cause of death in prisons is suicide (World Health Organization, 2007). Something between one third and a half of custody deaths are suicide (Fazel and Benning, 2006) in the UK and US. Prison rates are disproportionately high compared to the general population. There are between three and six times more suicides in prison than in the community (Fazel, Grann, King, and Hawton, 2011). In general, completed suicides are relatively uncommon compared to suicide attempts and suicidal thoughts. There are 22 times more suicide attempts and thoughts of suicide among prisoners than actual suicides (Tartaro and Ruddell, 2006). McHugh (1999) suggested that, while not frequent, suicide is a significant issue in the prison context. This is not a surprise since the offenders entering prison have heightened risk due to other risk factors such as low socio-economic status, coming from dysfunctional families and having an involvement with drugs (McHugh, 1998). The extra factors of prison build on these. Suicide rates are higher among prisoners with mental health problems (Towl and Crighton, 1996, 2000). Women prisoners are proportionately more common among prison suicide completers (Snow, Paton, Oram and Teers, 2002). Suicide is more likely in prisons housing those on short sentences, the first parts of a long sentence and prisoners awaiting trial. Such prisons are characterised by a rather rapid turnover of inmates. We should not ignore the fact that there is a great deal of non-suicidal self-harm in prisons in which inmates inflict harm to their bodies without any clear suicidal intent (Marzano, Adler, and Ciclitira (2015).

The *importation model* would suggest that suicide is due to characteristics of the individual which are brought into the prison. The *deprivation model* suggests that suicide and related things are the consequence of the deprivations of prison. *Combined models* stress an interaction between the prison environment and pre-prison characteristics. Rivlin, Fazel, Marzano and Hawton (2013) interviewed male prisoners who had nearly succeeded in their near-lethal (medically serious) suicide attempt. The researchers wanted to know about the nature of the offenders' psychological problems culminating in the suicide attempt. Prisons were monitored for suitable cases and the men were interviewed within about four weeks of the attempt. Aversive events such as the death of a family member or friend and the break-up of a relationship often preceded the suicidal events. Factors to do with the criminal justice system might also play a part, such as the offender's worries to do with their sentence. Depression, anxiety, and the consequences of drug withdrawal were among the psychological reasons involved. For the most part, prisoners made these suicide attempts with the intention of killing themselves. Nevertheless, a substantial minority (40 per cent) described the act as impulsive. Visual ideation concerning suicide was reported by 82 per cent at some stage prior to the suicide event. These images concerned things such as what might happen to them if they died or were about making the plans to harm or kill themselves. In deciding the method of the suicide attempt, the prisoners considered factors such as speed and painlessness. The method of suicide chosen was hanging/ligature in 67 per cent of cases. However, the methods available were constrained by the activities of the prison service to prevent suicide. Things such as tablets, needles, and ligature material are hard to obtain in prison now and so less certain alternatives had to be considered. Bedding that can readily be torn into strips was an obvious source of ligature. There were patterns in the location where the suicide attempts took place. Nearly always it was in the offender's cell in a general part of the prison and not in segregated locations such as the prison hospital. Many had no special reason for their timing of the suicide attempt but when they did they chose a time when the cell was unlikely to be inspected by prison officers. Overall, suicide can be regarded as the result of a complex mixture of background factors; mental/psychological health problems; adverse life events; and cognitive processes, according to Rivlin *et al.* (2013).

The small numbers of women prisoners masks the fact that they attempt suicide at a greater rate than male prisoners. In comparison to the general population, female prisoners have higher relative rates of suicide than male prisoners. In the United Kingdom, Marzano, Fazel, Rivlin and Hawton (2011) studied near-lethal self-harm acts in 60 women prisoners. Mostly, these attempts involved ligature and hanging. About half could be described as impulsive. But the background of long-term suicidality and multiple suicide attempts was very common. Feelings of hopelessness and past trauma were characteristic of the women. Triggers were usually events in prison, such as interpersonal problems and mental health issues. Sometimes news from outside was the triggering factor. Flash forward ideation of images of a future suicide attempt also occurred.

Dye and Aday (2013) studied women serving life sentences in US prisons. This involved a convenience sample drawn from three women's prisons in the southern US. Most (93 per cent) had been convicted of murder. It is not uncommon for women to enter prison exhibiting the very vulnerabilities which put them at risk of suicide. During the demanding process of adjustment to prison, thoughts of suicide (suicide ideation) are common. In comparison to their male counterparts, women in prison were more likely to have a psychiatric disorder, to have suffered abuse (84 per cent), and to have attempted suicide prior to imprisonment. Over 45 per cent of the women said that they had contemplated suicide prior to imprisonment. Nearly as many (44 per cent) said that they had attempted suicide. About 38 per cent had thought about suicide during the previous two weeks. There was a near absolute overlap between suicide ideation and attempted suicide. Some had pre-prison suicide ideation but not when in prison and others had prison suicide ideation but not prior to prison. Pre-prison ideation was significantly related to histories of abuse as well as prior mental health treatment.

Suicide sometimes follows quickly after a serious crime, which possibly explains some of the suicides in prison among prisoners on remand awaiting trial. However, it has to be stressed that such offence-related suicides are comparatively rare and small in comparison to suicides among prisoners in general. According to Flynn *et al.* (2009), there are only about 30 suicides a year following homicides in England and Wales (these figures exclude suicides after conviction for the killing). Over the nine-year period, 1996–2005, just over 203 cases of suicide following homicide were identified by Flynn *et al.* in their review. Eighty-six per cent were men. The average age of the offender involved was 41, although the range includes virtually all of the adult lifespan. There were a number of notable trends:

- The suicidal men usually killed their spouse or partner whereas women were more likely to kill their children.
- A wide range of methods of suicide were employed. Sharp instruments were the most common method of homicide but these amounted to only 23 per cent.
- Forty-two per cent died the same day as the homicide and 75 per cent killed themselves within three days.
- Criminal histories were relatively uncommon, as were instances of contact with mental health services – only 10 per cent had such histories.

These findings suggest that prison, in itself, is not the primary stimulus to suicide. Nevertheless, it is a potential location for suicide and, consequently, this is an important matter for the prison service to address.

It may be tempting to explain prison suicides by suggesting that the overcrowding of prisoners – the population density – is responsible. There is plenty of evidence to show that human beings have preferred space requirements and that crowding, at least in some circumstances, is distressing. Nevertheless, one should not jump to conclusions. For example, in the United States it has been noted that about half of prison suicides occur during the first day of confinement. This cannot be explained in terms of the stress of population density. According to Cox, Paulus and McCain (1984), as prison populations increase, there is a tendency for rates of death from all causes to increase disproportionately to population increase. Of particular relevance is the finding that single-occupied cells (where clearly crowding is less of an issue) were associated with very few deaths, whereas death was much more common in multi-occupied cells (Ruback and Innes, 1988). Nevertheless, prison is a safe place and the overall risk of death in prison is less than in the outside world. Of course, the proper comparison between prison and the outside world needs to compare like with like. Prisoners tend to be younger and disproportionately from a racial minority compared with the general population. Adjusting for these trends, this leaves the following:

- Deaths due to illness and homicide were significantly *lower* in prison.
- Deaths due to suicide were significantly *higher* in prison.

One can overstate the dangers, since the rate of prison suicide in the United States was 29 per 100,000 of the prison population as opposed to 20 per 100,000 in similar non-prisoner populations. Prisoners, of course, are not a sample of the general population but different on a range of factors.

The possibility of suicide is not an easy one for prison authorities and psychologists working in a prison context to manage effectively. One obvious strategy is to classify prisoners as either suicidal or not at risk. According to Towl (1996), this has its own dangers. If a prisoner has been classified as non-suicidal then this may be a signal for prison officers to lessen their vigilance over them: that is, a great weight is placed on the classifying system, which may be rather less than perfect. There are a number of high-risk-of-suicide situations that may encourage greater vigilance. These include the period immediately after admission; significant clinical improvement and the achievement of some insight; and periods of leave for offenders in medium secure units for psychiatric difficulties (James, 1996). Towl (1996) suggests a number of strategies that may be helpful in dealing with the potential problem of suicide:

- Reduce the numbers of remand prisoners and those with mental illness.
- Try to avoid the negative consequences for prisoners who report suicidal thoughts to staff. The consequences may be extremely unpleasant, such as routine strip searches and the like, which may deter reporting.
- Enable staff to identify and assist prisoners with suicidal feelings.

For a time, beginning in 1991, the UK prison service's policy on suicide prevention and risk management was referred to within the service as the F2052SH system. This was the reference number of the document recording that the prisoner had been assessed as being at risk of suicide. Historically, the management of suicidal prisoners had been the responsibility of a prison's medical staff. The new policy changed this and gave the responsibility for the management of suicidal prisoners to all members of a prison's staff. Any staff member could initiate the process of assessing whether a prisoner was a suicide risk – a decision which involved both medical and other prison staff. If assessed as at risk, then the prisoner had to be observed three times a day, contacts between staff and that prisoner recorded and the case had to be reviewed every two weeks. The records were available to all staff to consult, unlike medical records, which would be confidential. If the review meeting felt that the prisoner was no longer a suicide risk then the monitoring etc. would be discontinued. This system was replaced by a system known as ACCT (i.e. Assessment, Care in Custody, and Teamwork), which kept the multidisciplinarity which was introduced in F2052SH but introduced new roles of assessor and case manager to ensure accountability in delivering the care plan.

Senior *et al.* (2007) carried out a study of the F2052SH system at four local units housing prisoners – one for adult male prisoners, two for male young offenders, and one for both young and adult female offenders. The researchers compared the prisoners identified as at risk under the system with prisoners in general. Stratified random samples of prisoners were used so that prisoners from all parts of the prison were included (i.e. medical wings, vulnerable prisoner units, remand wings, and sentenced prisoner wings). Each prisoner was interviewed and a number of psychological measures taken. Prisoners in general have significant problems according to the various measures (see Figure 25.2), such as previous suicide attempts; suicidal thoughts; suicide plans; and having the necessary requirements to complete their suicide. This was true of the prisoners assessed as being suicide risks. Remember that these were identified by members of the prison staff. Eighty-one per cent had previously attempted suicide, 53 per cent had levels of suicidal ideation necessitating further clinical assessment, 21 per cent had made a specific suicide plan, and 26 per cent felt that they had the necessary requirements to complete their suicide.

Slade and Forrester (2015) point out the trend in UK prisons that the number of suicides declined between 1999 and 2012. Their study examined an unusually sustained reduction in suicide rates at a particular local London prison during the three year period 2008–2011. This corresponded to a period when centralised suicide and self-harm management systems were introduced much as already described, for example, the introduction of suicide prevention training for staff. In addition, locating responsibility for the management of suicide firmly with both prison managers and health care services within the prison was an important change. The particular success of this prison reducing suicide encouraged Slade and Forrester to explore the reasons for this in the light of the broader institutional changes. They developed a questionnaire based on the organisational changes that had occurred at the time and collected qualitative data in addition. They broadly concluded that changes in the organisational culture impacted on institutional safety outcomes. These were associated with positive changes in the attitudes of staff and their behaviour. The senior management team had prioritised suicide reduction and integrated it into their strategic decision making.

Finally, it is worthwhile pointing out that death from causes other than suicide can be a significant factor in deaths in prison. For example, Kullgren, Tengstrom and

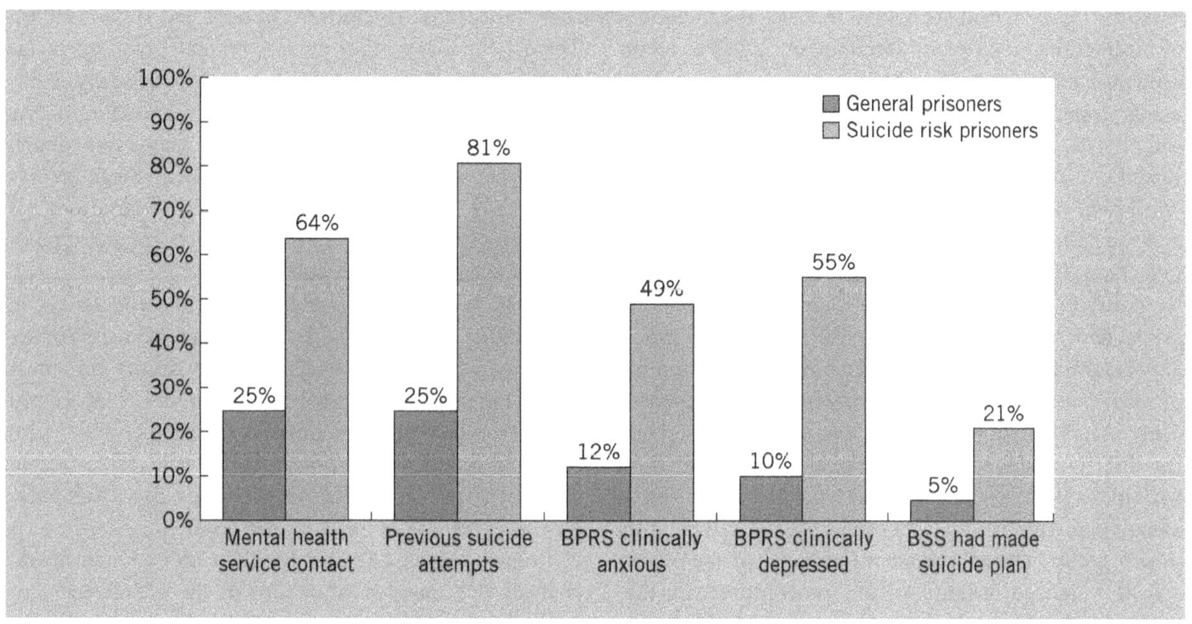

Figure 25.2 Prisoners in general compared with those identified as being a suicide risk on some clinical indicators

Gran (1998) found that 7 per cent of Swedish offenders who had been subject to a major forensic psychiatric examination died within a follow-up period of no more than eight years. Less than 3 per cent of these were from suicide in general, although it constituted 6 per cent for those with personality disorders. This is a similar finding to that found in other mentally disordered offender populations.

The effectiveness of prison

This aim of rehabilitation is explicit to the penal systems of many countries. Examples include the Netherlands, Spain and Germany in Europe. This aim is not explicitly stated in some systems, such as France and England and Wales. Nevertheless, rehabilitation may still be seen as an appropriate activity within the latter systems. There are many reasons why rehabilitation might not be a priority in some prison systems. Lack of the needed financial resources to pay for prison psychological, psychiatric, social and educational services might be exacerbated by rapidly expanding prison populations. The growth of offending might lead to a political climate that sees society as soft on crime. Consequently, tougher penalties are needed, not the easy option of training and therapy. Furthermore, only in recent years have effective treatments for, say, sex offenders been developed.

According to Redondo, Sanchez-Meca and Garrido (2002) criminology has demonstrated that punishment may not be effective for all offenders. Crime is not altogether dependent on rationality so sometimes will not be affected by punishment. There are many factors that contribute to crime. Redondo *et al.* list many of the factors already identified in earlier chapters of this book. These should include, among others, social factors such as school failure; ineffective child-rearing; unemployment; illegal drug trafficking; strains between social groups; criminal subcultures and individual psychological factors such as low educational level; aggressive tendencies; occupational incompetence; drug addiction; frustration; beliefs and criminal values; egocentrism; impulsiveness; and lack of social perspective. Punishment, as such, is unlikely to have much influence on such criminogenic factors. However, they might be amenable to influence through educational programmes and psychotherapeutic programmes, either in the community or in prison. One would expect psychology to contribute effectively to these.

Experiments into the effect of imprisonment on offending could be designed but are very difficult to carry out in practice. This probably explains the extremely small number of such studies that are to be found in the research literature. Bergman (1976) compared the outcomes for offenders who were randomly given prison sentences or placed in a probabation program. Similarly, Killias, Aebi, and Ribeaud (2000) studied the effect of being randomly placed in prison or on a community based programme. The outcomes were similar. Imprisonment seemed to increase the likelihood of reoffending. Jolliffe and Hedderman (2015) as a consequence adopted a different approach to the question using propensity score matching. They used a very large sample of over 5000 male offenders in the United Kingdom. Basically they used two groups of offenders – one group had been imprisoned for their index offence and the other group had been given community orders involving supervision. However, all of the offenders were involved with the probation service – but one group had been to prison prior to this. As you would expect, these two groups differed substantially in terms of their characteristics. To deal with this, propensity score matching was used to achieve a situation in which the final two groups were 'identical' in terms of these variables. Relevant background variables are used to calculate the probability that each prisoner will be in the prison group. The consequence being that if the offenders are balanced in terms of this probability then they will be matched on all relevant covariates. A large number of covariates were used to do this which included demographic, familial, legal, mental health, psychological, psychosocial and substance abuse variables. With these adjustments in place, it was found that the offenders who had been imprisoned were more likely to commit another confirmed offence within one year of release. Fifty-three per cent of the imprisoned group re-offended but only 33 per cent of the probation only group reoffended. They were also more likely to be re-imprisoned for this new offence. This study confirmed the trend of other relevant research which is that imprisonment has the effect of slightly increasing the likelihood of future offending.

'Nothing works'

As you now know, 'nothing works' is the idea that interventions to prevent reoffending, especially those of a social or psychological nature, are ineffective. This idea has a long history. It largely developed out of concerns that psychodynamic therapies were ineffective. They simply did not change the behaviour of offenders in relevant ways (Martinson, 1974). Since that time, ideas about how psychological therapy should be conducted have substantially changed. This was a result of the introduction of behaviour therapies around the 1960s but, more importantly, the introduction of cognitive behavioural therapies in the last two decades of the twentieth century. There have been a number of influential analyses of the research into interventions aimed at preventing reoffending. These include, in North America, such reviews as those of Andrews, Bonta and Hoge, (1990). These, and many other similar reviews, employ meta-analysis (see Box 4.1). This involves statistically amalgamating the findings from as many as possible of the relevant studies. The analysis can be refined to examine the effects in subcategories of studies, e.g. those involving say sex offenders, or those involving a particular age group of offender, or those involving a particular type of cognitive behavioural treatment.

It has to be said that, at first sight, the effect sizes in such studies appear small. A correlation (effect size) of 0.1 or 0.2 between treatment and outcome seems unimpressive. This can be translated into the numbers of treated offenders who will not reoffend. A correlation (effect size) of 0.1 indicates a reduction in recidivism in the treated group of 10 per cent of the rate of recidivism without treatment (i.e. the rate in the control group).

Redondo *et al.* (2002) carried out an important meta-analysis of a number of studies of the effectiveness of prison and community treatment programmes in Europe between 1980 and 1998. The same authors had previously published a related study in which they found a global effect size of 0.1, which equates to a reduction in recidivism of 10 per cent (Redondo, Sanchez-Meca and Garrido, 1999). They confined their newer investigation to the prevalence of recidivism involving study designs that included a non-treated control group. Of the studies in their meta-analysis, about two-fifths were British, one-fifth were German and a sixth were Dutch. They found an effect size (correlation) of 0.2 between treatment and outcome. The differential in reoffending was 22 per cent between the treated and untreated offenders. The best outcomes (largest effect sizes) were for educational programmes (r = 0.49), followed by cognitive behaviour therapy (r = 0.3). Therapeutic communities and diversion programmes were not so effective (effect size = 0.1). Programmes in the community had the greatest effects. Sex offending had bigger effect sizes than other crimes (such as drug trafficking).

Of course, all of this is evidence that aspects of prison work; it does not indicate that imprisonment, in itself, is a good thing. As might be expected, there has been quite a lot of research into the effects of punishments such as imprisonment and community sanctions on recidivism. Among the most thorough reviews is the work of Smith, Goggin and Gendreau (2002), who reviewed over a hundred research studies from the last 40 or so years of the twentieth century into the relationship between 1) the length of prison sentences and 2) receiving a prison sentence rather than a community-based sanction (including greater surveillance and electronic tagging). Meta-analysis (see Box 4.1) was used to assess this plethora of data into the effects of sanctions. Their main findings, which summarise the findings of many different studies, included:

- Recidivism was *not* lower when prison terms were given or when longer prison terms were served.
- This lack of an impact of prison on recidivism applies to juveniles, women and minority groups just as much as men.
- There is a little evidence to suggest that longer periods of incarceration may be associated with small increases in the amount of recidivism.

The researchers suggest that prison sentences should not be assumed to have any influence on criminal recidivism. Gendreau, Goggin and Fulton (2000) found that the only moderator effect obtained in a large data set was in the case of community sanctions where a small reduction of 10 per cent in recidivism was associated with treatment services.

Research studies suggest much the same lack of influence of prison on recidivism. The relationship between incarceration and recidivism was studied by Nunes, Firestone, Wexler, Jensen and Bradford (2007), using a sample of 627 adult male sex offenders. The majority were child abusers, either inside or outside of the family. Recidivism was based on information gathered from the Canadian Police Information Centre and the researchers concentrated on the first reoffence. Incarceration for a sexual index offence was not related to recidivism for a sexual or violent crime. This was true irrespective of whether a dichotomy of incarcerated versus not or a continuous variable based on length of time in prison was used. Risk was assessed using a modification of the Rapid Risk Assessment for Sexual Offense Recidivism (RRASOR) (Hanson, 1997). The lack of relationship between incarceration and recidivism was unaffected by risk as measured by RRASOR or the length of that incarceration. The authors suggest that incarceration appears to have little or no impact on violent or sexual recidivism following release. Like sexual recidivism, violent recidivism was not associated with being incarcerated or the length of that incarceration. However RRASOR was correlated with violent recidivism. The researchers suggest that their findings support seeking alternatives to prison for sex offenders whose offending behaviour falls below a certain level of risk.

There is a simple answer to the question of what works according to MacKenzie and Farrington (2015) although their argument is based on a wide range of randomised controlled trials (random experiments), systematic reviews and meta-analyses carried out in the twenty-first century. Attempts at reducing reoffending based on control, deterrence, discipline, and surveillance simply do not work. Interventions based on restorative methods or skills training work.

Prison work works

One of the characteristics of prisons is the availability of simple, paid work. There are a number of reasons for this but an important one is that the skills picked up doing even the most menial of job may help in the search for work post-prison. In addition, there may be training courses available which help orientate the offender towards productive work after release. There are a number of important things to bear in mind in connection with work in prison and the reintegration of prisoners in society (Bushway, 2003):

- Prior to entering prison, many offenders have a poor relationship with the world of legitimate work. They may have poor educational achievements and little by way of vocational work. High proportions have a history of unemployment.
- It has been highly expensive to provide prisoners with resources to improve their employability as there is limited evidence of the effectiveness of such initiatives. The transition from ex-offender to worker is a difficult one. Work-related skills programmes are helpful in this regard but many ex-prisoners return to much the same environment and social ties which they had prior to prison. Reintegration needs more than a job but attention being paid to other things such as housing, medical care, and emotional ties.
- There is some suggestion that abandoning crime depends on the motivation of the offender. However, motivation alone is not sufficient and the offender will need to develop new skills such as those of a worker. So it is wasteful to spend resources on offenders lacking the motivation to change.
- It is difficult for ex-prisoners to hold on to a job for a lengthy period of time. Irrespective of any professional qualifications and experience they may have, the work that they obtain is generally among the worst paid and least desirable. The experience can be one of failure.
- The role of work training in prisons is not best seen in terms of eventual rehabilitation. More importantly it occupies and structures their time in prison and provides them with a modest income to buy treats. Nevertheless, rehabilitation may be a secondary benefit. They learn punctuality, self-discipline, and responsibility among other things which contribute to their rehabilitation into the world of work.

Alós, Esteban, Jódar, and Miguélez (2015) studied a large sample of discharged prisoners in the Catalan area of Spain. Forty-four percent had been on a prison work programme and 17 per cent had undergone vocational training while in prison. Several data bases were used to provide a wide variety of information about each of the offenders including that from social security computers. It was possible to identify three types of ex-prisoners: 1) those with a job, 2) those without a job, and 3) those who reoffend after discharge from prison. The best situation is ex-prisoners with a job who do not recidivate. Non-recidivists who do not have a job are in an intermediate position in relation to work. About 23 per cent had reoffended in the study period but 44 per cent had obtained work at some stage though many lost their jobs. Older ex-prisoners were the group who found it hardest to obtain work. In brief, despite a substantial proportion obtaining work this was not stable work and was frequently temporary work precipitating the offender back into unemployment. So the background in terms of employability was somewhat grim due to the wider economic difficulties of Spain. However, in terms of the role of prison work on the employability of ex-prisoners, it was better that the ex-prisoner had engaged in prison work than not. It was not so clear that engaging in vocational training had a positive effect.

BOX 25.1 Controversy

What research designs work?

Modern governments frequently engage researchers to carry out evaluation studies relevant to government policy and academics enjoy the benefits of such funding for their research. This is also the case in forensic research where government departments and agencies fund substantial amounts of research into the efficacy of programmes designed to reduce offending. Of course, research findings which support government policy are more likely to be welcomed than those which in some way challenge it. Crime is a major issue on the political agenda and, not surprisingly, the findings of research studies are themselves politically sensitive (e.g. Howitt, 1994). Government departments have research management teams which are actively involved from the start of the commissioning process in decisions about whether research will be publicised. Hollin (2008) reports that the Home Office in the United Kingdom has been reluctant to publish the findings of some research on the effectiveness of certain offending behaviour programmes. Raynor (2008) refers to this as 'sunsetting' which is a graphic way of describing the process by which some research findings disappear into the 'sunset' without being published.

One of the ways in which the impact of some studies is reduced is by evaluating the research against 'gold standard' criteria which stress the scientific worth of some forms of research method and also indicate the diminished scientific value of other forms of research. Indeed, the UK government has used a 'Scientific Methods Scale' (see Hollin, 2008) which gives lower credibility to research that involves merely establishing a correlation between taking part in some crime prevention programme and measures of criminal activity. On the other hand, studies that involve random assignment of participants to experimental and control groups are seen as meeting the necessary criteria of scientifically acceptable evaluation research. This sort of study is often referred to as a randomised control trial (RCT). Anyone familiar with psychological research will know that, historically, this type of research was regarded by many psychologists as the ideal. It is often suggested that such randomised control trials have internal validity, which means that strong inferences about causality (what caused the differences between the experimental and control groups) can be made on the basis of the study findings. Unfortunately, often the price of good internal validity is poor external validity in that the study reflects real life very poorly, just as laboratory experiments can be very different from real life.

The lack of external validity that is associated with RCTs has meant that many researchers are not totally convinced by claims of the RCTs' scientific superiority in the forensic field. Some researchers see advantages in good-quality quasi-experiments in which the participants in the treatment and no-treatment groups are matched (statistically or otherwise) to be as similar as possible on important variables before the treatment is undergone. However, random assignment does not take place in the quasi-experiment.

Do RCTs produce very different findings or better findings than these quasi-experiments?

- One problem with RCTs in forensic research is that they would require random sentencing to either the treatment or the control conditions. It is easy to see that there might be problems with this. For example, if the sentencing involves a new treatment for paedophilia which seems to work well, then to allocate an offender to the control condition (no treatment) may result in that offender further offending against children in the future. Consequently, the sentencer may be disinclined to allocate a man to the untreated control group. Furthermore, it may be that not participating in treatment results in the offender being classified as a serious risk and so retained in a high-security prison which itself may have an influence on some outcome measures. Alternatively, an offender who is allocated to the treatment condition but who drops out of treatment may be regarded as a bigger risk because of this non-compliance with treatment and so, once again, may appear different on outcome measures.

- Is there a difference in the findings which are obtained from RCTs and non-randomised studies? Meta-analyses (see Box 4.1) have been used to address this question and consistent results have emerged in a variety of areas of psychological research between good-quality RCTs and good-quality non-randomised studies (quasi-experiments) (e.g. Heinsman and Shadish, 1996; Lipsey, Chapman and Landenberger, 2001). Such comparability emerges when 1) participants are restricted in their ability to self-select in which condition of the study they partake; 2) there are no major differences between the experimental groups on important variables prior to the treatment programme; and 3) attrition from the different conditions of the study is minimised, such as by reducing the number of dropouts from the study.

One overriding danger is that policy-related decisions about how to present the research findings can radically influence just how effective interventions seem to be. For example, if those undergoing the intervention or treatment are presented together as a single group to compare with the control group then this means that those who fail to complete the treatment dilute the data from the treatment completers. That is to say, they reduce the differences between the treatment and non-treatment groups, thus adding to the impression that the intervention did not work – exemplified in the phrase 'nothing works'. This can be justified on the grounds that, by combining completers and non-completers, this represents the effectiveness overall of the intervention. However, it completely overlooks the possibility that the problem of non-completion could be targeted and maybe reduced, thus increasing the overall effectiveness of the programme.

The many dimensions of psychology in prison

The potential roles for forensic and criminal psychologists in prisons vary widely. By way of illustration of the variety, simply in terms of the work of psychologists with life prisoners in the United Kingdom, the following types of activity have been indicated (Willmot, 1999):

- *Risk assessment:* a prisoner's time in prison needs to be planned and targets set. For example, at what stage may the offender be moved to a less secure environment? When should home leave be permitted and when should the offender be released on licence?
- *Initial risk assessment:* this is dependent on the past history of the offender, including an assessment of the factors that led to their offending. Progress in dealing with these contributory factors needs to be assessed when making future decisions about particular offenders.
- *Individual clinical work:* this might include any of the following – anger and stress management; cognitive behavioural treatments for anxiety or depression; and interpersonal skills.
- *Decisions to progress through the prison system possibly to final release:* this is a corporate task rather than for the psychologist alone, although the contribution of the psychologist to the decision may be substantial. Considerations would include attitudes to the offence; insight into offence-related behavioural problems; behaviour in prison; and other factors indicating suitability for progression.
- *Discretionary life panels:* in the United Kingdom, once a lifer has completed their basic tariff, a parole board reviews the case every two years. This may include evidence or assessments from psychologists, who may be cross-examined by lawyers for the lifer.

These tasks clearly involve an estimate of the likely future behaviour of the offender. The next chapter considers some of the more objective ways of assessing the potential future risk of offenders.

Main points

- There is little or no role for psychology in the punishment of prisoners. On the other hand, the utilitarian and humanitarian functions of prison can utilise the skills of psychologists effectively in order to produce changes in prisoners that may reduce their likelihood of reoffending in many cases. Psychologists have a part to play in many aspects of prison life, from the training of officers to decisions about the release of prisoners. Such activities are rarely carried out by psychologists working alone or as part of teams of psychologists only; it is much more likely that psychologists work with other professional groups as part of these activities.
- The range of psychological techniques employed within the prison service is wide. It stretches from assessment using psychological instruments such as intelligence tests to the delivery of therapy to individual prisoners or, more likely, groups of prisoners. There is every reason to believe that prison, so long as appropriate services are provided, can have a limited but significant impact on future crime. The evidence that prison, as opposed to the services provided in prison, prevents recidivism is weak. It is wrong to believe that this is the consequence of the work of psychologists alone since they are only part of the total package. Meta-analyses seem to suggest that educational services are the most important in terms of allowing prisoners to return to a crime-free life in society. Furthermore, we should not neglect the fact that what happens on release from prison may have an important bearing on an offender's ability not to reoffend. Such services include various forms of supervision as well as housing and employment. The key to all of this is not being too optimistic and not too pessimistic about the value of psychological work within prison.

Further reading

Craig, L.A., Gannon, T.A. and Dixon, L. (eds) (2013) *What Works in Offender Rehabilitation: An Evidence-Based Approach to Assessment and Treatment* Wiley-Blackwell: Chichester.

Shuker, R. and Sullivan, E. (2010) *Grendon and the Emergence of Forensic Therapeutic Communities* Chichester, West Sussex: Wiley-Blackwell.

Towl, G. and Crighton, D. (eds) (2008) *Psychology in Prisons* (2nd edn) Chichester, West Sussex: Wiley-Blackwell.

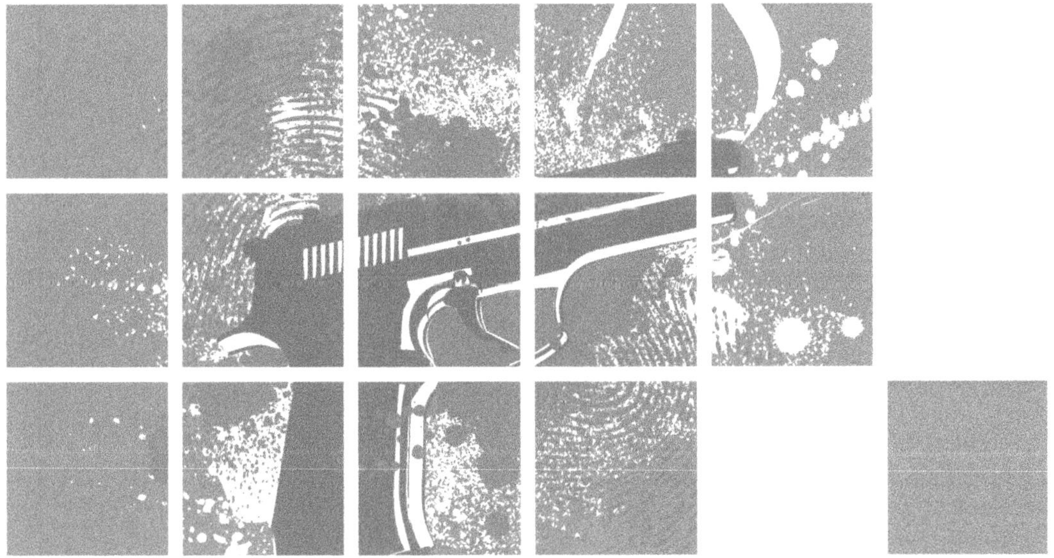

Chapter 26

Psychological treatments for prisoners and other offenders

Overview

- Psychological treatments for sex offending and violent offending have become increasingly common over the last 30 years. Variants of cognitive behavioural therapy tend to dominate.
- Modern sex offender treatment programmes are generally based on structured group work. Individual therapy is far less common due to expense though it may be available. Relapse prevention can be an integral part of the work to discourage reoffending.
- Quite how effective evaluation studies have shown them to be is not entirely clear but many accept that there are worthwhile but modest reductions in reoffending in treated individuals compared to controls.
- RNR (risk-need-responsivity) principles seem to lead to more effective treatment for sex offenders. In this, offenders who pose the greatest risks are assessed in order to understand their criminogenic needs. Whatever needs to be done to improve their responsiveness to treatment is implemented.
- Programmes are available for violent prisoners, such as anger management courses. However, there are important questions about whether anger is fundamental to violent crime.
- The effectiveness of treatment varies according to setting. By ensuring that all therapists understand the rationale of the treatment and adopt appropriate therapeutic strategies, manualisation ensures that the consistency of treatment delivery is improved as well as the overall effectiveness of treatment. It also allows for less qualified personnel to be employed.
- In recent years, the focus has been on treating high-risk offenders, including psychopaths. These are regarded as a very difficult client group and it is probably premature to evaluate the effectiveness of recent treatment innovations for them.

Introduction

Worldwide, crime is a political issue. Currently tough approaches to crime dominate social policy. The numbers in prison reflect the modern political agenda. The financial cost of imprisoning so many offenders is enormous. There is some optimism that prison can contribute to crime reduction for some offenders. Reducing recidivism is one way of reducing the pressure of crime on the public purse. Psychological treatments can be cost-effective to the extent that they demonstrably reduce the risk of reoffending. Although there are arguments over this, generally modern psychological treatments reduce reoffending by about 10 per cent or more. But this depends on where one puts the bar in terms of methodological rigour. Random assignment to treatment and non-treatment groups is a somewhat rare feature of research in this area. It is generally accepted that among the most effective programmes in terms of reducing recidivism are those based on the psychological principles of cognitive behavioural therapy (Blud, 1999). Arguably, these treatment programmes are effective because they work to correct a number of cognitive deficits exhibited by offenders. The sorts of cognitive deficits that offenders may demonstrate include:

- *Cognitive style:* lack of empathy with abstract social concepts. Such offenders may be rigid and inflexible in their thinking. They may be poor at tolerating ambiguity, which results in what may be described as rather simplistic, dogmatic thought processes.
- *Critical reasoning:* their thinking is often irrational and illogical. Self-analysis is avoided. They justify what they do by blaming others and, consequently, do not see themselves as to blame.
- *Interpersonal problem solving:* offenders are often socially handicapped without recognising the fact. They are sometimes unaware of the other courses of action available to them. They rarely examine the likely consequences of their actions.
- *Self-control:* to correct impulsiveness and action.
- *Social perspective taking:* prisoners are often egocentric. They fail to understand why they should consider other people. They may lack the skill involved in seeing matters from the perspective of other people. They tend to interpret the actions of others purely from their own perspective and misinterpret the actions of others as a consequence.
- *Values:* their moral reasoning skills are poor. They do not recognise the incongruity between their actions and their beliefs.

In the United Kingdom, for example, the prison service has an accreditation system for therapeutic programmes. This has a commitment to research-based therapy. The criteria for evaluation may include:

- the range of therapeutic targets addressed;
- a structured living environment;
- an aim to change the behaviour of the residents;
- clear and research-based model of change;
- consenting participation in the programme expected from those involved;
- control of behaviour by authorities is not the sole means of changing behaviour;
- effective methods.

Sex offender therapy in prison

The effective treatment of sex offenders originated in the behavioural therapies of the 1960s. Before that time, Sigmund Freud's belief that sex offenders were untreatable using psychodynamic methods dominated thinking. Not surprisingly, given the ubiquity of this view, sex offender treatment was a low priority. In the UK in the 1980s increasing numbers of sex offenders received custodial sentences (Fisher and Beech, 1999) – there was a 50 per cent increase in a decade. This was not matched by a commensurate determination to reduce reoffending. This came in the 1990s. The dominant approach to sex offender treatment is cognitive behavioural therapy. According to Jennings and Deming (2013), this is in a sense a misnomer since most cognitive behavioural therapy is dominated by the cognitive rather than the behaviour. They provide a number of ways in which the behaviourally observable aspects of the group could be used to improve self-disclosure, empathy and the management of deviant thoughts. For example, the therapist can pre-organize the physical setting of the therapy in ways which can reinforce pro-social behaviour. To illustrate, the physical comfort of the room depends on the therapist ensuring that the temperature should be acceptable. The room should be clean, neat, and quiet which encourages the offenders to be alert and ready for learning. The room should not be accessible to others who interrupt the group processes and disrespect the treatment ethos. Seating should be in a circle with everyone equidistant and nobody in a position of communicative power from which they can dominate the group.

There are numerous accounts of the use of cognitive behavioural therapies in the treatment of sex offenders – both those in prison and those in the community (e.g. Craissati and McClurg, 1997). It is useful to concentrate on a concrete example of what may be typical within the prison service context. As ever, the precise details will differ somewhat from jurisdiction to jurisdiction. The case of the UK prison service is well documented and, as it was far from the first of such programmes to be developed, it adapted features from other programmes. As such, it should be of fairly general interest. It is known as the Sex Offender Treatment Programme (SOTP) (Beech, Fisher and Beckett, 1998). After nearly 30 years, the Government announced that the treatment programme was discontinued. New research evidence had suggested that sex offenders who took the treatment were a little more likely to reoffend than those who did not (BBC News, 2017). Despite this, the Sex Offender Treatment Programme illustrates such treatments very well.

Fundamental to a treatment programme is a set of decisions about how, when, where, to and by whom therapy is to be delivered. The basic decisions for the prison SOTP included the following:

- *Where:* in a limited number of prison establishments which could be resourced appropriately to deliver the treatment.
- *Who:* priority is given to offenders at the greatest risk of reoffending according to a formal risk-assessment procedure. Some characteristics, such as mental illness, lack of English, very low IQ, suicide risk and severe personality disorder, effectively debar the individual from the programme.
- *When:* at an appropriate stage in a sentence of two or more years, provided that time is available to complete the programme.
- *By whom:* the approach is multidisciplinary. That is, all sorts of staff besides psychologists may be involved, such as prison officers, teachers and chaplains. Of course, they are given appropriate training in terms of knowledge of cognitive behavioural treatments and relevant skills in working with others in groups.

The therapeutic procedure is based on structured group work. A group consists of eight offenders and two tutors/therapists. The treatment manual contains a structured series of cognitive behavioural activities and exercises that are explained and described in detail. It concentrates on the thought processes involved in offending as well as attempting to place limits on the behaviour of the offender. The core programme is designed to work on the motivation of the offender to avoid reoffending and to develop personal skills that enable this. These latter skills are collectively known as relapse prevention. According to Beech, Fisher and Beckett (1999), the programme consists of 20 blocks (treatment sessions) that cover a number of areas. For the purposes of this description, these may be classified as cognitive modification and relapse prevention. The methods employed in group treatment of this sort are a mixture of methods familiar to those who have engaged in any type of group work, and matters much more specific to sex offending. Some of the techniques involved include the following:

- *Brainstorming and group discussion:* topics discussed by the group are often written down as a list on a board or flip chart. An individual often responds to this collection of ideas in terms of his experiences.
- *Focus on the individual:* the work of one individual is subject to scrutiny and evaluation by the rest of the group.
- *Homework:* activities such as keeping a diary are carried out by members outside the group meeting itself. This is almost always written work.
- *Role-playing:* members of the group (and this may include the tutors or facilitators) may play out a situation. The rest of the group observe and respond to the role-play. The actual participants may also analyse their experiences.
- *Smaller or buzz groups:* some activities are carried out by a pair of offenders, perhaps three or four. This sort of activity helps the offender develop communicative skills with others, assertiveness and a degree of empathy. The experience with the small group can then be combined with that of other groups in a 'plenary' session.
- *Videos:* film is available which deals with various aspects of sex offending. In particular, there may be video available about the experiences of victims. Viewing this is then followed by individual response and group discussion.

The above are the main treatment methods employed. Substantial areas are covered using these methods, including the following:

- *Describing the offence:* it is known that sex offenders tend to describe their offences in ways that are self-exculpatory. Often the offender will present himself almost as if he were the victim. Vagueness and being non-committal is characteristic of their responses. The following is a short extract from an interview with an offender (Howitt, 1995a, p. 95):

  Interviewer: Did you kiss her on the breast?
  Bennie: Maybe I did maybe I didn't . . . [when you are arrested] they try to use psychology on you, they make you say you did . . . so I am going to say I did.
  Interviewer: . . . that's no use to me . . . I don't want to know what they say, I want to know what it is.
  Bennie: . . . maybe I probably did . . .

  At the end of the exchange, the reader may feel that they still do not know whether or not Bennie accepts that he kissed the girl's breasts sexually despite a clear challenge from the interviewer. Nevertheless, despite this, Bennie uses the phrase 'maybe I probably did . . .' which leaves him free psychologically to maintain his position that he said things because he, in fact, was the victim of pressure from other people. Therapists may describe this as a 'passive account' since it does not truly describe what the offender did. An active account would be much more direct. For example, in the above example, the offender might have said 'I encouraged the girl to roll about in front of the television with me. We were pretending to play at being animals. I pulled up her clothes and played at biting her stomach. Then I took it further and sucked her breast for a couple of minutes.' In order to encourage the active account, it is necessary for the offender to provide information about the following: 1) the process of planning the actual offence by the offender since it did not just happen; 2) the extent and nature of the offender's sexual or emotional preoccupation with the victim; 3) how the offender was responsible for initiating all of the aspects of the abuse; and 4) the measures he took to prevent the victim from disclosing the abuse to others.

- *Challenging distorted thinking:* aspects of the distorted thinking that each offender has about his own offending will be familiar after a while to members of the group. This may be distorted thinking about children's sexual motivations and interest in adults or the adult rape victim's secret desire to be sexually violated, for example. The distorted thinking may be challenged by asking for evidence to support the offender's assumptions that may then be criticised by other members of the group. It has to be stressed that this may occur at any stage of the treatment and not simply during the sessions specifically devoted to distorted thinking.
- *Victim empathy work:* showing a video of victims of abuse talking about the consequences or having outside speakers come and describe these experiences are ways of increasing empathy for the victim. Given that many offenders will themselves have been victims (see Chapters 6 and 10), this may profoundly influence their response. Their own experiences of vulnerability and being unable to disclose their abuse at the time may contribute to the lessons learnt by the group. Eventually, the offenders will role-play the position of victim in their own offences.
- *Fantasy modification:* it is widely accepted that there is a relationship between sex offending and fantasy (see Box 9.2). Some believe that masturbation to sexual fantasy is the basis for its development through a process of conditioning. *Irrespective* of the actual role of fantasy in sex offending, there would seem to be a compelling case to reduce this fantasy as part of the treatment programme. Normally, this is not included in the work of the therapy group except at the broad level of the role of fantasy in offending behaviour. Otherwise trying to modify sexual fantasy would usually be carried out using one of four or so main behaviour modification techniques on an individual basis with a psychologist:
  - *aversive therapy* – the fantasy would be associated with some negative *consequence*;
  - *masturbatory reconditioning* – new and socially more acceptable fantasies would be associated with masturbation (in other words, the offender masturbates and switches to the new fantasy at the point of orgasm; this is repeated until the new fantasy becomes sexually arousing);
  - *satiation* – the offender repeatedly masturbates to the fantasy until the fantasy is incapable of causing sexual arousal.
- *Covert sensitisation:* the fantasy is extended to the negative consequences. So a fantasy of raping a woman is associated with the negative consequences of arrest, trial and imprisonment, for example.
- *Social skills, assertiveness and anger control:* while a lack of social skills is not a *universal* feature of sex offenders, by any means, the inability to form relationships with adults may be a contributing factor to the offending of some. Anger control problems have to be seen as an issue with rapists, for whom issues of anger are common. Social skills, including those of knowing how to deal with situations without aggression, can contribute to a potentially more social prisoner at the time of release. Issues such as body language, the meaning of social cues and the range of behavioural alternatives available for dealing with situations may be dealt with through analysis and role-play, for example.
- *Relapse prevention:* relapse prevention (e.g. Marshall, Hudson and Ward, 1992; Pithers *et al.*, 1988) prepares the offender to deal with the feelings and experiences that he will have on release which are known to be progenitors of offending behaviour. These may be regarded as warning signs that must not go unheeded. It is known, for example, that sex offending patterns in some offenders are preceded by a negative mood state. Thus depression and anxiety might serve as danger signals for imminent offending. Similarly, the return of deviant fantasies may serve a similar function. There are other aspects of offending that a relapse prevention strategy would signal as dangerous: for example, moving into a job involving children, moving to a neighbourhood where there is a school nearby or just offering to babysit for a neighbour. For most people, these may be innocuous life-events; for the paedophile or child molester, they may be a precursor to the offending process.

There are many similarities between the contents of this programme and the activities in a medium security unit of the New Zealand prison system (Hudson, Marshall, Ward, Johnson and Jones, 1995). Indeed, dissimilarities are few in number. For example:

- The men who volunteer for this treatment are required to undergo phallometric assessment (see Box 9.1) in order to gain information about any potentiality they may have for sexual arousal in response to deviant sexual stimuli.
- One therapist is used with a group of ten offenders compared with the two tutors used in the UK prison service programme.
- The group meets four times a week – rather more frequently than in the United Kingdom – for about the same length of time (24 weeks in New Zealand).

Many of the components of this cognitive behavioural programme were much the same as those of any cognitive behavioural programme. Hughes, Hogue, Hollin and Champion (1997) found evidence of improvements in personality disordered offenders in a high-security setting. They indicate that the cognitive programme in the context of a supportive ward environment (though not a therapeutic community) produced changes in a global measure of various aspects of change, which included reduced impulsivity, reduced macho attitudes and better social problem solving.

Particularly pertinent to therapy given in prisons is the question of whether this reduces reoffending. Although evaluation research has been carried out into the cognitive behavioural programme described above, this could be criticised as stopping short of the question of recidivism. Instead, the evaluation concentrated on measures of things such as cognitive distortion, the reduction of which is only a step towards decreasing recidivism (Beech *et al.*, 1998).

Before moving on, it might be helpful to point out that almost all therapy for sex offenders occurs in a prison setting or in the community after conviction. This begs the question of the extent to which alternatives to these are neglected. Some potential paedophiles are aware of their potential risk to children. The question is how these men can be found and helped before they begin offending and before a child has been harmed. The Berlin Prevention Project Dunkelfeld (PPD) targeted men who freely seek help (Beier *et al.*, 2009). A media campaign was the starting point of recruitment. Those who phoned in were screened over the telephone for 18 months. Of 286 participants who completed the screening (60 per cent completed it), most were interviewed by a clinician; 58 per cent expressed a sexual interest in prepubescent minors and pubescent minors (28 per cent). Eleven per cent had a sexual preference for mature adults. The rest were uncategorisable. The majority (70 per cent) had strong or very strong feelings of distress. Many of them (about a half) had previously sought professional help and a similar number had sought helps from their friends, etc. The media primarily involved a poster placed into print media but also on billboards in the city. There was a TV spot which was used on various German television stations and in cinemas. Of course, the big problem with such initiatives is that any offences reported to the therapist would have to be passed over to the police.

Does treatment work?

In a critical article on government policy and sex offender treatment and rehabilitation, Towl and Crighton (2016) argue that penal policy in recent years has favoured the use of harsher sentencing in order to minimize the likelihood of future sex offending. Managers within the prison service increasingly manage contracts for the delivery of treatment services rather than managing the delivery of service itself. There has been a move towards the use of a less skilled and less expensive workforce for the delivery of treatment. Consequently, the treatment services provided are not geared to the specific individual needs of a particular sex offender but standard, one-size-fits-all, services are the order of the day. The effectiveness of more severe sentencing is not at all clear and the effectiveness of the treatments delivered to rehabilitate offenders are equally unclear. The available research has tended to show modest benefits from treatment but the research is beset with methodological inadequacies. Very little of the available research employs gold standard methods such as randomised control trials according to reviews (Dennis, Khan, Ferriter, Huband, Powney and Duggan, 2012). The reviewers found only ten studies of adequate quality for inclusion in their review. Only half of these involved cognitive behavioural therapy. In the largest of the studies, there was no evidence that treatment actually reduced recidivism. However, many of the included studies did not measure recidivisim. The need for more research was the paramount conclusion. The question is whether things are as bleak as Towl and Crighton suggest.

Craissati, South and Bierer (2009) describe the difficulties which can be had when trying to evaluate the effects of community-based treatment on recidivism. Designing and implementing such research is far from easy. There is, of course, one fundamental dilemma which severely limits research – is it ethical to release non-treated sex offenders back into the community? There would doubtless be considerable public disquiet if it became known that this was happening. Yet the logic of the randomised treatment study would demand that this is done. Otherwise one would not have an appropriate treated group to compare with an untreated group. The only way of avoiding this problem is to carry out the randomised experiment within the prison setting. They could be assessed using, say, a recidivism predictive measure. So some research on the effectiveness of prison therapies resorts to using changes relevant to the therapeutic objectives of the programme (e.g. changes in measures of victim empathy) or measures predictive of risk are sometimes used instead. This sort of variability in the use of outcome variables makes it important to take care when assessing the research into the effectiveness of therapy. But this is not a measure of recidivism itself. Of course, the untreated group would undergo treatment before they are returned to the community for public relations reasons. An alternative is to compare completers of therapy with non-completers. This is not completely satisfactory since there non-completion is not a random thing but may reflect systematic differences between completers and non-completers. Otherwise one is left with the general conclusion of meta-analytic studies that most treatment effectiveness studies are methodologically unsound (Koehler, Lösel, Akoensi and Humphreys, 2013)

Meta-analytic studies

There is a great deal of evidence to suggest that certain types of treatment reduce reoffending (recidivism). Meta-analytic studies are among the most effective ways of understanding recidivism risk changes following sex offender therapy. These systematically review the findings of available studies addressing the question of the effectiveness of treatment. (See Box 4.1 for an explanation of meta-analysis.) In an early meta-analysis, Hall (1995) reviewed 12 studies of recidivism involving a total of over 1300 offenders. The tremendous range of outcomes found in the studies is remarkable. For example, a few found no differences between the treated and untreated groups (or even slight negative relationships), whereas others showed a treatment versus comparison group correlation (effect size) of 0.55. The latter, in one instance, corresponded to a recidivism rate of 15 per cent for the treated group but 68 per cent for the untreated comparison group. The overall recidivism was 19 per cent for all of the treated groups versus 27 per cent for all of the untreated groups. Treatment was not confined to cognitive behavioural methods – behavioural methods and hormonal treatments were also included. There was no statistical difference between the cognitive behavioural treatments and hormonal treatments in terms of their effectiveness. Behavioural modification seems to have a negative effect – that is, it makes matters worse if given alone compared with no treatment at all. A little later, Hanson *et al.* (2002) reviewed the findings of over 30 studies into sex offender reconviction in treated and untreated groups. On average, 17 per cent of non-treated offenders reoffended sexually compared with only 12 per cent of treated offenders. Much the same pattern applied to general recidivism for any type of crime in these two groups.

Duwe and Goldman (2009) suggest that based on meta-analytic studies that there is more or less a consensus that reoffending rates are between 5 and 10 percentage points lower in treated sex offender groups than untreated controls. Furthermore, the indications are that cognitive behavioural therapy involving aspects of relapse prevention is the most effective. Although these positive findings are important, there is always the caveat that the quality of a meta-analysis depends substantially on the quality of the studies included.

The randomised control trial or true experiment

We need to introduce another consideration – the extent to which the studies used involved experiments or randomised control trials in which participants are randomly allocated to the treatment and non-treatment groups. So in Lösel and Schmucker's (2005) meta-analysis only 7 per cent of studies employed random allocation to the experimental and control groups. The vast majority of studies (84 per cent) did not use random assignment or matching techniques to equate treated and untreated control groups. In other words, it is a distinct possibility that the treatment and no-treatment groups differed in important characteristics which are confused with the effects of treatment. This lack of random allocation in studies of the effectiveness of therapy has been responsible for some arguing that we cannot confidently assume that therapy works (Hanson, Bourgon, Helmus and Hodgson, 2009). Kenworthy, Adams, Brooks-Gordon and Fenton (2004), questioned whether it was ethical to devote resources to the treatment of sex offenders when studies involving random allocation produced limited evidence of the success of treatment. However, this study involved a range of different types of therapy and the authors suggest that cognitive behaviour therapies may be superior to, for example, psychodynamic approaches.

Research lacking a control group

A good example of the problematic nature of research into the effectiveness of sex offender programmes also relates to the UK Sex Offender Treatment Programme. This was not a randomised control study with a treatment group and control group. Wakeling, Beech and Freemantle (2013) studied changes on psychometric measures over the course of treatment for sex offending and asked the question of whether these changes were related to recidivism. Theirs was a large sample of nearly 4000 sex offenders who had completed their sex offender treatment in prison in the United Kingdom – the sample consisted of all sex offenders who had undergone treatment over a ten-year period and had been released. Two-thirds of the offenders were child molesters and a quarter rapists. Most had served over four years in prison. On average, the men were followed up for 1500 days for possible recidivism.

The researchers used the 'clinically significant change' approach (Kazdin, 2003). This focuses on the situation where the offender moves into the normal range for non-offenders on the measures used. That is, where the individual has moved from the dysfunctional to the functional position on the measure. They also included those who start off in the functional range. The analysis concentrated on offenders who had changed overall on at least three of the four risk domains: 1) sexual interests; 2) pro-offending attitudes; 3) socio-affective problems; and 4) self-regulation problems. Offenders could be classified into one of five treatment change categories on the basis of the measures taken:

- *Deteriorated:* The individual's scores changed reliably but in the negative direction.
- *Unchanged:* The individual showed no reliable change in terms of their scores.
- *Improved:* The individual showed reliable change but not sufficiently so to put them in the normal functioning range.
- *Recovered:* The individual improved reliably into the normal functioning range.
- *Already okay:* The individual was already in the desirable range both at pre-test and post-test.

To be clear, this research compared offenders who were 'therapeutic successes' on the treatment programme with those who were failures, so it cannot accurately be described as a study of the effectiveness of the sexual offender treatment programme. The reconviction rates of those who had been released for at least two years was 12 per cent for all offending (general reconviction rate). However, the sexual offending reconviction rate was very low at 1.7 per cent and 4.4 per cent for the sexual and violent reconviction rate combined. It is the last measure of reconviction that the researchers used in their analysis. These low reconviction rates may reflect the system's success at dealing with sex offenders in general. However, we are interested in the outcomes from sexual offender therapy here so we need to concentrate on the difference between the therapeutic successes and the therapeutic failures. Men whose scores were in the 'normal range' both before and after treatment were less likely to reoffend than those whose scores did not change in these areas after treatment into the normal zone of the various psychometric measures. Participants who had changed overall on three of the four risk domains were reconvicted less often than those who had not changed in these areas. But overall the findings were not too impressive. The researchers suggest that their findings provided no more than limited support for the use of change in risk factors in order to predict future recidivism. Most of the individual instruments they used related only weakly to recidivism. And it did not matter much whether the pre-test, post-test, or the average of the two was considered. These are somewhat uncomfortable findings, though some comfort might be taken in the low recidivism rates found in the study. Wakeling *et al.* suggest that, where resources are scarce, treatment might not be offered to offenders whose scores are in the normal range.

What works with sex offenders?

Ho and Ross's (2012) article serves as a salutary lesson to anyone regarding the case for sex offender treatment programmes as decisive. They simply questioned the claims made by the UK's National Offender Management Service (2010) publication *What Works With Sex Offenders?* NOMS is the government agency that deals with prisons and probation services. The Sex Offender Treatment Programme (SOTP) began in 1991 (see p. 1) and treats about 1000 prisoners each year in the UK – mainly child sex abusers. Ho and Ross point out numerous examples of possible overstatements about the effectiveness of sex offender treatment programmes. So one claim was that 'Large scale research indicates that sex offenders who receive treatment, in both prison and community settings, have a lower sexual reconviction rate than those who do not receive treatment' (p. 1). This is based on the study by Hanson *et al.* (2002) who found that reconviction rates for treated sex offenders were 12.3 per cent, compared to 16.8 per cent for untreated sex offenders. The interpretation of these recidivism rates needs to be tempered by the fact that the designs of the studies involved non-comparable treatment and control groups. The non-treated control groups, for example, contained high-risk offenders who are known to be more likely to refuse treatment than lower-risk offenders (Rice and Harris, 2003).

Another claim from the NOMS document is: 'Cognitive behavioural treatment is the most effective, especially if paired with pharmacological treatment (e.g. hormonal drugs that reduce sexual drive)' (p. 1). There is no citation of the source of this assertion. Ho and Ross state that, to their knowledge, there is only one methodologically sound study of the effectiveness of combined medical/psychotherapeutic treatment available. This found that psychotherapy alone (CBT) did not prevent the return of sexual fantasies, masturbation and sexual deviancy compared to combined treatment. However, this in itself only shows that combined treatment is better than CBT alone. What NOMS claim may be correct on this basis, but the only certain thing is that CBT on its own is not sufficiently effective. All of the therapeutic gains actually might have come from the medical treatment alone. This is a case of the available evidence being insufficient to support NOMS' claims. That is, where is the evidence? Of course, the effective treatment of sex offenders is a political issue and so interpretations of research evidence should be treated with due caution. For Ho and Harris, whether the Sex Offender Treatment Programme is effective remains to be 'convincingly demonstrated' (p. 5). The UK Government, as we have seen, came to share these doubts when it abandoned the programme.

Can therapy cause harm?

It is glib to suggest that even if it does no good, it is unlikely to do harm either. There is the possibility that treatment may be harmful to certain sorts of offender despite being effective with others. Welsh and Rocque (2014) discuss some of the criminological interventions such as boot camp which have had adverse effects on the recipients. A case in point is the psychopathic personality. There is evidence which claims that certain sorts of therapy with this group may be harmful (Rice, 1997; Rice, Harris and Cormier, 1992). They studied treatment outcomes for men who had undergone treatment for two or more years in a Canadian therapeutic community, compared to a control group of men who had spent time in prison but had not received therapy. Most had been admitted to a psychiatric hospital for assessment following a violent offence. The offenders in the treatment and the prison groups were matched man-to-man in terms of age, type of offence and extent of criminal history, though this matching turned out to be poor in many respects (Reidy, Kearns and DeGuea, 2013). The outcome in terms of recidivism after an average of ten years at risk was unimpressive. Some of the recidivism was common assault but there were also cases of multiple homicides and sexual assaults. The men in the treatment programme fared little differently from those sent to prison.

The treatment programme had appeared to be especially suited to the needs of psychopaths (see Chapter 21). Consequently, the researchers studied the outcome of the treatment programme for psychopaths (as assessed by the Hare Psychopathy Checklist) and non-psychopaths separately. The findings were opposite to those expected. In terms of their violent recidivism, 40 per cent higher rates were found for treated psychopaths than non-treated psychopaths. For the non-psychopaths in the study, however, the treatment seemed to reduce recidivism. That is, recidivism was about 50 per cent lower in the treated than the untreated group! This demonstrates, along with other research on psychopaths in therapeutic communities, that psychopaths may well be a totally different subgroup of offenders for whom treatment is ineffective or even counterproductive. Speculatively, it could be that treatment raised self-esteem in psychopaths, which resulted in a greater willingness to use aggression. Alternatively, most prisoners may learn to be empathic with others in treatment whereas the psychopath learns how to appear empathic and generally to manipulate the system. This, though, is a somewhat controversial issue which lacks, as yet, a definitive answer and Rice *et al.*'s much-cited study is increasingly being seen as controversial. Reidy, Kearns and DeGuea (2013), for example, take issue with the usual interpretation of their findings. If we ignore methodological problems in matching the treatment and control groups for this study, then the treatment regime at the time (1968–78) seems somewhat unacceptable compared to modern procedures. Possibly problematic features of the treatment included (Harris, Rice and Cormier, 1994):

- treatment was peer-led with minimal professional involvement on a day-to-day basis;
- treatment involved high-dosage group therapy for up to eight hours a week – which would equate to 11 hours of group therapy per day;
- treatment involved nude encounter groups;
- LSD and other drugs were sometimes part of the treatment programme;
- no part of the treatment programme sought to alter criminal attitudes and behaviours; unlike what modern thinking would expect.

At best, it could be said, that these features might mean than only the most cooperative offenders might gain from this sort of therapy.

Nevertheless, the possibility that treatment can do harm is an important consideration when evaluating treatment. Jones (2007) discusses the concept of *iatrogenic treatment* responses, which refers to the fact that some treatments, for some clients, can have an undesirable effect. The concept is more readily applied to medical interventions (e.g. adverse effects of medicines) than psychological ones. The word literally means 'outcomes which are the consequence of the healer', but it has come to mean adverse consequences due to treatment. Therapies with offenders diagnosed as having personality disorders have long been known to be unsuccessful. Iatrogenic outcomes are difficult to identify from research which concentrates on the success of a treatment in terms of the overall numbers who improve. Such an approach tends to disguise the negative effects if a positive outcome is more likely overall. However, in research where different groups of participants are involved, it may be possible to see that perhaps certain groups tend to respond well to treatment while others seem to worsen.

There are a number of potentially harmful outcomes of therapeutic interventions for offenders, according to Jones. It is possible that a treatment may have an impact on an offender's capacity and skills to offend in the future:

- Increased likelihood of reoffending possibly because the offender wishes to demonstrate that they beat the therapy which they felt forced to engage in.

- Increased skills for accessing victims so improved social skills might allow psychopaths to manipulate other people to a greater degree of effectiveness.
- Increased triggering salience, as in the case of the sadistic offender who is taught empathy for other people but this greater empathy merely increases the ability of the offender to become aroused by the distress of his victim.
- Increased skills at evading detection which, for example, might emerge as a consequence of hearing how other offenders in the therapy group went about committing their crimes.

While the research in support of most of these processes is fairly fragmentary, the evidence that some types of offenders might become greater risks following therapy should encourage a more systematic approach to researching iatrogenic outcomes.

Non-completers of treatment

Another important issue in the effectiveness of treatment is the issue of the offender who does not complete treatment. There is evidence that non-completion of treatment is very high. About a quarter of offenders fail to complete their treatment programme (McMurran and Theodosi, 2007). Non-completion is much commoner for offenders being treated in the community than those treated in prison. It is important to note that non-completion of treatment can be for a number of different reasons, not all of which indicate non-cooperation from the offender. The reasons, according to Wormith and Oliver (2002), include: 1) administrative matters such as where an offender is released from prison or is transferred to another one during treatment; 2) agency-initiated removal from treatment by staff because the offender is unruly or fails to keep to the rules of the treatment; and 3) offender-initiated cessation of treatment.

There are numerous studies which consider the fate of those who do not complete treatment compared with those who do. For example, Dutton, Bodnarchuk, Kropp and Hart (1997) studied a group of wife-assaulters in Vancouver, Canada. The typical treatment was anger management. The men could be divided into several groups:

- men who did not show up for the assaultive husbands treatment programme;
- men who were assessed but deemed unsuitable for treatment;
- men who were assessed as suitable but did not complete the treatment programme;
- men who completed the treatment programme.

In terms of recidivism ratios (which are the total number of repeat assaults by the group divided by that group's sample size) there were differences. This measure is a better estimate of the amount of recidivism than is the incidence of recidivism:

- no-shows recidivism ratio = 9 per cent;
- unsuitable for treatment = 20 per cent;
- dropouts = 11 per cent;
- completers = 6 per cent.

While these seem small differences, for 1000 completers this would amount to a total of 320 crimes, whereas 1000 people in the unsuitable for treatment category would generate 810 crimes (these are for all acts of violence). Non-completers would generate 550 and no-shows would generate 400. For violence against women, dropouts would commit 500, no-shows 230, rejects 290 and completers 230. Thus treatment is associated with fewer offences.

Studer and Reddon (1998) in Alberta, Canada, found that treatment may affect risk prediction for sex offenders. This study looked only at those who completed treatment versus those who failed to complete treatment. The treatment programme included educational components on human sexuality and substance abuse among other things, such as relapse therapy. The initial treatment period was up to 12 months followed by a further up to 8 months of out-patient treatment. Prior sexual offences were used as their predictor of recidivism prior sexual offences. For men who dropped out of the treatment programme, the relationship between prior sexual offences and recidivism was statistically significant and positive. That is, previous sex offences predicted recidivism for those who did not complete their treatment. On the other hand, there was virtually a zero correlation between previous offences and recidivism for the men who completed the full treatment. That is, the treatment broke the link between previous offence rates and recidivism. This was true despite the fact that prior recidivism in the two groups was at identical levels. More generally, non-completion of treatment is a good predictor of reoffending (Hanson and Bussière, 1998).

There are problems in terms of how to interpret the common finding from research that those who fail to complete treatment programmes are at greater risk of reoffending than treatment completers. Non-completers may be different in terms of risk of recidivism prior to treatment so that their elevated risk merely reflects this pre-treatment difference. There is growing evidence that this is the case. This raises the question of whether failure to complete treatment actually makes matters worse than not starting treatment at all. McMurran and Theodosi (2007) reviewed research on cognitive behavioural therapy programmes as these are believed to be the most effective at reducing the risk of reoffending. Among the requirements for inclusion in the analysis was that either: 1) treatment versus non-treatment was randomly assigned so that there was no systematic bias in the selection process; or 2) the treatment versus non-treatment groups were matched by the researchers to be equal on their assessed level of risk prior to treatment. Not many studies existed which met these requirements but data were found for 17 samples. Some of the research was based on prison samples and some on samples living in the community.

There was a small negative relationship between treatment completion and recidivism, which led McMurran and Theodosi to the conclusion that failing to complete cognitive behavioural treatment has an adverse effect. This adverse effect was stronger for the community samples than the prison samples. One reason why failure to complete treatment may be associated with greater risk of reoffending is that an offender who is removed from treatment by staff may feel aggrieved and develop more anti-authority and antisocial attitudes.

The importance of the quality of treatment in evaluating its worth is not easily addressed and is obviously pertinent to the question of whether treatment is effective. One way of assessing quality of treatment is to look at the extent to which the treatment meets the offender's criminogenic needs. This may be rephrased as the question of whether the RNR (risk-need-responsivity) principles are being successfully applied. RNR is a famous approach to the assessment and treatment of offenders (Andrews, Bonta and Hodge, 1990). The basic criteria of RNR are:

- *Risk principle:* the greater the offender's risk of reoffending, the greater should be the services to try to prevent this.
- *Need principle:* the individual's needs which contributed to their criminal behaviour should be assessed and then targeted during treatment.
- *Responsivity principle:* consideration should be given to ways in which the offender's learning from an intervention or treatment is maximised. These considerations include learning style, motivation and strengths and abilities of each offender as well as issues to do with the way in which treatment is delivered.

One might expect that these principles would facilitate the effects of treatments for sex offenders. The study by Hanson, Bourgon, Helmus and Hodgson (2009) was a meta-analysis of 23 recidivism outcome studies using the criteria implied by the RNR approach. The treatments involved were coded in terms of the extent to which their aims/objectives addressed a list of criminogenic needs related to sex offence recidivism, such as attitudes tolerant of sexual crime, deviant sexual interests, intimacy deficits, and sexual preoccupation. Each of the treatment programmes was assessed in terms of how many of the above three RNR (risk, need and responsivity) principles were applied. To be included in the meta-analysis, a study had to involve at a minimum a sex offender treatment group and a sex offender non-treated group. Over all of the studies, the recidivism rate for the treated sex offenders was 11 per cent, whereas that for the controls was 19 per cent for sexual recidivism, but substantially higher at 32 per cent and 48 per cent for any recidivism in the treated and untreated groups respectively. The RNR-compliant treatments were more likely to be effective. The more recent the study, the more effective RNR-compliant treatments were likely to be, suggesting that RNR principles have been more effectively applied in recent years. Effects were stronger in the weaker designs compared to the stronger designs, which is a concern for the validity of the findings. Effects were highest when all three RNR principles were met. Effects were low where no RNR principles were adhered to.

Summarising the research of the effectiveness of treatments for sex offending is far from easy given the somewhat indecisive state of research in the area. There is little doubt that anyone wishing to claim that sex offender treatment does not work merely has to point to the lack of randomised control trials of sufficient quality. This is especially true where sexual recidivism reduction is used as the criterion of success. Yet, almost stubbornly, meta-analyses of research of an adequate quality generally suggests some success of treatment on recidivism especially when studies using matching of a control sample on the characteristics of the treated sample is employed. Inevitably, though, such studies cannot remove the final doubt that matching has not been complete. This makes it all the more interesting when Schmucker and Lösel (2015) carry out a major meta-analysis of studies of sound quality – that is, a meta-analysis of the best evaluative work in the field – and find an overall reduction in sexual recidivism of only 3.6% in the treated groups compared to the control groups. Whether such a small effect is worth the investment is a nuanced decision to make. Schmucker and Lösel suggest that too much effort has been invested into trying to address the broad-brush controversy of whether sex offender treatment works. They suggest that attention should be directed at the question of what treatment works with what sorts of offenders, in what context it works, under what conditions, and for what outcomes.

To put all of this into what may be an uncomfortable context for some psychologists is worthwhile. Kim, Benekos and Merlo (2016) reviewed a number of meta-analytic studies and were gratified to find that all of them suggested that sex offender therapy reduced recidivism. They suggest that the effectiveness of sex offender treatment could, at best, be described as proven and, at worst, promising. However, they found better outcomes for treatments such as chemical and surgical castration than for psychological ones!

Treating violent criminals

The need for methods of reducing the violent behaviour of some criminals is self-evident. For many years, the commonest help for violent criminals were anger management courses. Recently, the value of anger management has been questioned and newer, more broadly based methods of treatment have been developed. There are many similarities between the different approaches, which makes it difficult to differentiate them based merely on descriptions of the procedures involved.

Anger management

Anger management is a classic form of treatment which is employed in a variety of contexts, including prison services. Howells (1998) suggests a variety of strategies which can be used in intervention strategies in anger management. These include improving the client's general understanding of their aggression and violence, identifying and modifying their triggers to violence, dealing with contextual stressors, widening their range of coping responses, stopping the escalation of maladaptive social behaviours, and strengthening their commitment to change. In the United Kingdom, the prison service developed a National Anger Management Package (Towl, 1995) which is used with prisoners with temper-control difficulties. It is based on group work with two facilitators present and a group of six to eight prisoners over, typically, eight sessions. Its main aims are to heighten awareness of the process of becoming angry in the individual; to increase awareness of self-monitoring of one's own behaviour; to learn the benefits of controlling anger; and to enhance participants' knowledge and skill at managing their anger (Keen, 2000). The components are illustrated in Figure 26.1.

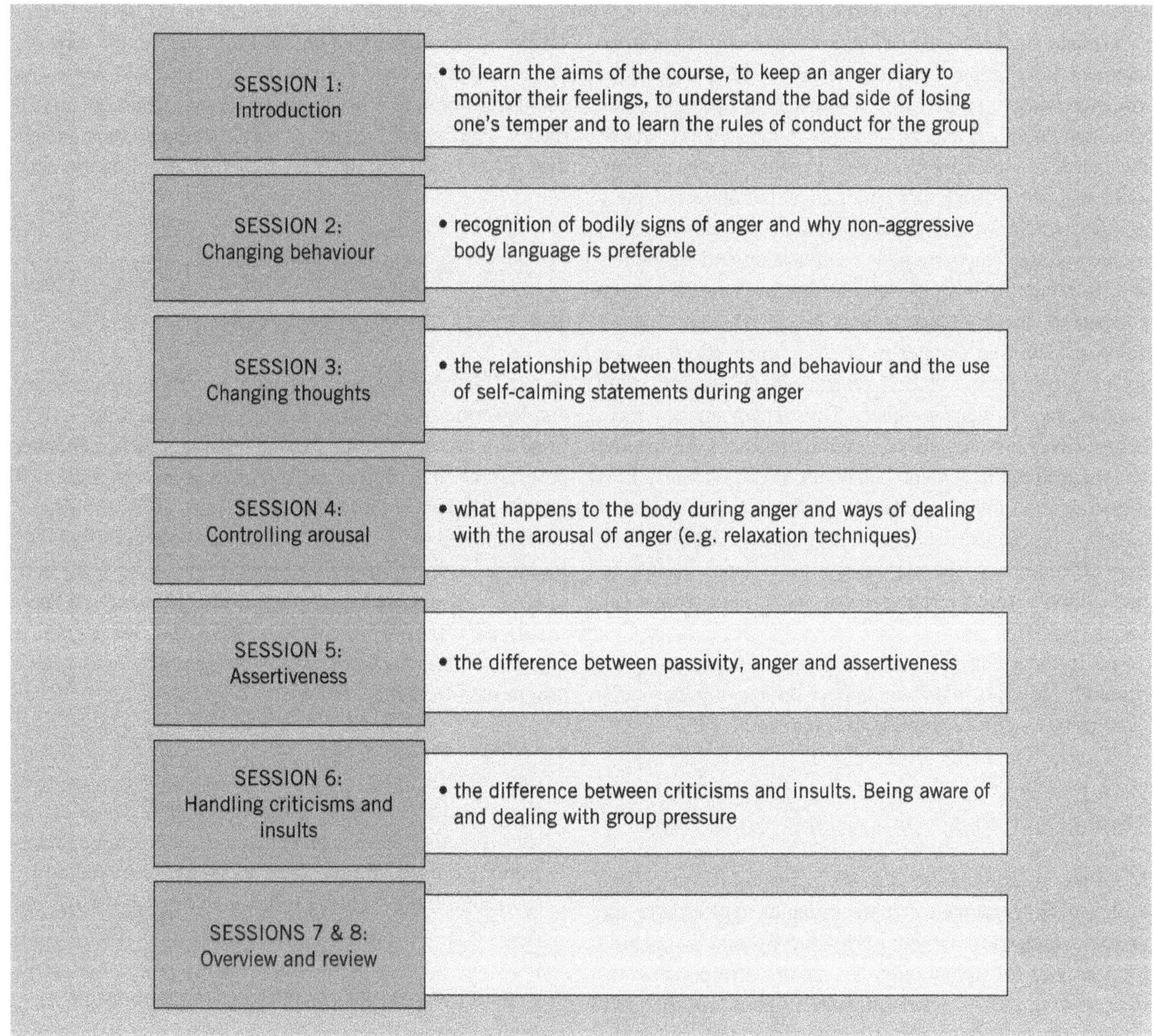

SESSION 1:
Introduction
• to learn the aims of the course, to keep an anger diary to monitor their feelings, to understand the bad side of losing one's temper and to learn the rules of conduct for the group
SESSION 2:
Changing behaviour
• recognition of bodily signs of anger and why non-aggressive body language is preferable
SESSION 3:
Changing thoughts
• the relationship between thoughts and behaviour and the use of self-calming statements during anger
SESSION 4:
Controlling arousal
• what happens to the body during anger and ways of dealing with the arousal of anger (e.g. relaxation techniques)
SESSION 5:
Assertiveness
• the difference between passivity, anger and assertiveness
SESSION 6:
Handling criticisms and insults
• the difference between criticisms and insults. Being aware of and dealing with group pressure
SESSIONS 7 & 8:
Overview and review

Figure 26.1 Components of the National Anger Management Package

Theoretically, the emphasis of such programmes is on cognitive components of anger and, in particular, the process of appraisal (Howells, Watt, Hall and Baldwin, 1997). The event is appraised and an emotional response is the consequence:

For anger to emerge, the individual must be displeased about the related undesirable event and disapprove of someone's blameworthy action. So, if you hit your finger with a hammer, you are unlikely to feel anger. On the other hand, if you hit your finger with a hammer at the moment someone begins talking to you unexpectedly, you may well get angry. There is thus an aversive event and a blamable individual. Of course, anger is an inappropriate emotion in these circumstances since the other person almost certainly did not wish to cause harm to you.

Despite the name *anger management*, many anger management programmes recruit offenders with problems of violence without reference to whether their problem is the management of anger. The difficulty is the sheer variety of the causes of violence individuals: 1) some may be psychopaths who act violently *not* out of anger but dispassionately in order to achieve their particular goals – perhaps to obtain money; and 2) others may lack self-esteem and be vulnerable to taunts by other people. In the first case, a general package of anger reduction may be of no advantage. It could possibly be counter-productive since efforts to get such a person to control their temper may fail to understand the origins of their violence. Thus anger management courses have been criticised for failing to assess the specific factors leading to violent behaviour in individuals. It is therefore a mistake to assume that violence in the context of a theft, say, cannot be helped with anger management – it may or it may not. The reasons for the violence need to be understood before the relevance of anger management can be addressed.

As to the efficacy of anger management programmes, research indicates that their impact on anger is not sufficient to be of clinical significance (Howells, 1998).

Violent offender programmes

More recent attempts to develop programmes to reduce violence have adopted a more in-depth approach to the factors which cause violent behaviour. Special therapeutic programmes for violent offenders are not common in comparison with those for sex offenders. According to Attrill (1999), three findings about violent offenders are at the root of treatment:

- Violence is learned behaviour that is adopted as a way of coping with difficult life experiences. Violence, then, works effectively and reliably for them and serves to reinforce their sense of their own power and self-efficiency.
- Patterns of criminal behaviour include a diversity of criminal acts and are rarely confined to violent behaviour. Studies suggest that reoffending by, say, those convicted of crimes against property may well involve violence rather than another property crime.
- Patterns of violent and criminal behaviour are entwined with ways of thinking that support those acts.

Offenders show a sort of antisocial logic, which makes violence seem acceptable and normal, necessary, justified. Attrill indicates that if an offender sees themselves as one of society's victims they may regard this as sufficient justification to behave just as they want. Anyone who interferes with this is being unfair and further victimising the offender. So a prison sentence would be seen as justifying further offending because it was unfair. Furthermore, the offender believes that they are entitled to do what they please and should not be told what to do by others. Consequently, if their violent acts in support of these beliefs go unpunished, they further reinforce the offender's feelings of entitlement.

The Aggression Training Programme (ART)

In the UK, Her Majesty's Prison and Probation Service employs the Aggression Replacement Training (ART) programme to deal with violent offenders. It is a broader programme than typical anger management courses. ART was developed by Goldstein (Goldstein, 2004; Goldstein, Glick and Gibbs, 1998) for work with younger offenders. Its basic assumption is that aggression results from both internal and external *multiple* causes. The internal (personal) factors are threefold. These are listed below together with indications of how they are used in the ART programme to reduce violence:

- *General deficit of skills of a personal, interpersonal and social-cognitive nature:* Skills acquisition exposes the offenders to opportunities to identify, develop, and then practise pro-social skills. Social learning procedures are used and the core social skills modelled by the group leader. This is followed by group discussion, role-play, and feedback on performance. The participants are encouraged to apply their newly learnt skills to their lives beyond the treatment environment.
- *Low levels of anger control accompanied by frequent impulsive and aggressive behaviours:* Anger control

training essentially follows the founding work of Novaco (1975) – that is anger management training. It seeks to help the individual develop self-control to deal with their anger and aggression. During these sessions, the triggers to violence and aggression for a particular individual are identified, together with an understanding of the probable consequences of anger and aggression if triggered. The offender's consequent improved self-awareness is employed to develop alternative coping strategies to situations. Typical strategies include avoidance of situations which lead to anger and methods of negotiating with others.

- *Moral reasoning deficits:* Moral reasoning training tackles the very concrete and egocentric thinking typical of those who commit violent crimes. Moral reasoning training seeks to enhance the offender's moral reasoning skills in pro-social ways.

Hatcher, Palmer, McGuire, Housome, Bilby and Hollin (2010) used a quasi-experimental design to investigate the effectiveness of this programme,. The treated group had been allocated to the treatment by probation staff, whereas the comparison group were also convicted of a violent offence and had received a community sentence. The two groups were matched by the researchers using the Offender Group Reoffending Scale Version 2 (OGRS2) risk score (National Offender Management Service, 2010). This score is calculated from information on the Offenders Index (a national database of convictions for all offenders in England and Wales), including static offender variables such as gender; custody and breaches of custody; number of previous convictions; offence type; and age amongst other things. Its normal use is to predict the likelihood of reconviction in two years, but in this study it was used to ensure that the treated and untreated groups did not differ initially in terms of risk. The findings suggested that the treated group showed a 13 per cent decrease in reconviction compared to their matched controls. The treatment completers were less likely to reoffend than non-completers.

Other treatments for violent offending

Gilbert and Daffern (2010) review some of the treatments employed for violent offenders within prison services around the world. Most of them claim to be based on social cognition – though the extent of this is often far from fully apparent according to Gilbert and Daffern, who are also critical of the lack of theoretical guidance involved. Nevertheless, they suggest that many of the social-psychological models of aggression tend to be too broadly conceptualised (that is, too abstract or open-ended for them to be used in comprehensive violence-correction programmes). Among those they discuss are *cognitive skills and cognitive self-change programmes* and *multi-faceted programmes*:

Cognitive skills and cognitive self-change programmes

These focus on the cognitions of violent offenders. Their underlying strategy is to help offenders enhance their thinking capacity to solving their interpersonal problems in particular. The belief is that social skills deficits leave the individual at an increased risk of acting aggressively because they simply do not have adequate knowledge about how to deal with situations non-violently. The training involves a variety of social skills such as conflict-resolution; critical thinking; impulse control and management; interpersonal skills; and problem solving.

The British prison service has piloted the Cognitive Self-Change Programme, which is aimed at reducing the risk of reoffending in men with a record for violent offending. It concentrates on specifically criminogenic types of thinking, which are replaced through treatment by an ability on the part of the offenders to recognise and change their criminogenic thought processes. Such criminogenic thought processes include attitudes, assumptions and beliefs which lead to and maintain violent behaviour patterns. The programme assumes that violence is usually intended, so offenders need to do various things to change that behaviour. They need to take control of their lives by becoming motivated to skilfully control their thoughts and feelings.

The programme is divided into six blocks, each of which consists of sessions totalling 100 hours or so. Group treatment averages four sessions per week:

- Skills are taught which allow offenders to observe and report their thoughts, feelings, attitudes and beliefs.
- Thinking patterns are identified which have resulted and will result in their offending and violent behaviour in general.
- Offenders try to identify new ways of thinking and ways of stopping these violence supporting thought patterns.
- A relapse prevention plan is prepared and the strategies are practised.
- The offenders practise the relapse prevention plan in prison.
- The final block has the offender back in the community with structured support and supervision.

Gilbert and Daffern argue that this and similar programmes are based on the social-psychological literature on aggression. Unfortunately they are not tied specifically to particular offenders' well entrenched aggressive patterns. Nevertheless, there is evidence that they reduce all sorts of criminal behaviour – not just violence (Polaschek and Collie, 2004).

Multi-faceted interventions

Recent innovations in programmes for violent offenders have been much more intense than the original anger management programmes, for example. The cognitive behavioural treatment may involve in excess of 300 hours of group and individual sessions over a 28-week period, as in the case of the Violence Prevention Program in New Zealand (Polaschek *et al.*, 2004). Considerable assessment of the offenders is involved, such as their social and personal histories, how they are likely to respond to group situations, and details of their offending and its processes in the past and present. The programme consists of different modules such as:

- cognitive restructuring of thinking leading to offending;
- communication/interpersonal skills;
- emotion regulation;
- moral reasoning;
- offence chain identification;
- problem solving;
- planning for relapse prevention;
- victim empathy.

Research findings suggest that over a two-year follow-up period, twice the number of men in an untreated control group than in the treated group were reconvicted for a violent offence. In contrast to other violence-reduction methods, there seemed to be no difference in terms of non-violent offences (Polaschek *et al.*, 2004).

Polaschek, Yesberg, Bell, Casey and Dickson (2016) carried out a quasi-experimental study into the outcome of intensive psychological treatment for high risk violent offenders who had a predicted risk of reoffending of over 70 per cent. The study group underwent highly intensive psychological treatment in one of four high risk special treatment units in New Zealand prisons and the control group was a matched sample of offenders who had not undergone this treatment though they may have undertaken treatment at some stage. It was found the treated groups were significantly better in terms of parole violations, new convictions of any sort, new convictions for violence, and sentences to reimprisonment.

Anger and violence

Anger is not an essential feature of violence. The evidence that anger is not an essential component of violence can be seen in the observation that, although men and women may feel anger equally, men are more violent than woman (Archer, 2004). Similarly, violent rapists, non-violent rapists and non-rapist offenders showed no differences in anger (Loza and Loza-Fanous, 1999). Walker and Bright (2009) systematically explore the role of anger in violent crime. They identify humiliation as a missing factor in anger management, though it features in psychoanalytic traditions. They point to the low level of self-esteem which is apparent in many violent offenders. This makes them susceptible to feeling humiliated when they interact with other people. Consequently, they act violently. Violence is seen as a justified retaliation which allows the offender to both express and discharge the negative feelings associated with the threat. Furthermore, the violent act of assaulting and injuring the victim serves the social function of restoring a degree of personal pride for the offender.

Walker and Bright refer to three layers of thought which can contribute to violence:

- *Layer one: Negative automatic thoughts.* These are closely associated with emotions and are fleeting, such that they may go unnoticed. Offenders must learn in therapy to be aware of and monitor such thoughts.
- *Layer two: Dysfunctional assumptions.* These are the rules which the individual plays by or applies to their lives. They can be found by simply asking offenders to say what rules they employ in given situations, though they may not know their dysfunctional nature. These dysfunctional assumptions relate to core beliefs which are deeply held and not consciously accessible.
- *Layer three: Cognitive beliefs or schemas.* This is the deepest cognitive level and consists of beliefs about the self, the world, and the future. They are normally somewhat extreme, such as 'I am worthless'. The therapist may have to identify these beliefs and schemas in order to understand how they relate to a person's psychological state.

Three things are important for Walker and Bright in therapy for violence and aggression:

- Understanding the cognitive components specific to a particular individual's violent behaviour and how these impact their behaviour.
- It is the responsibility of the therapist to identify the dysfunctional thoughts which play a role in the individual's violence.

- The modification of the cognitive elements which need to change during therapy and that the individual acknowledges the changes to be their own and their responsibility to maintain.

Manualisation

Despite there being some dissenting voices, there seems to be sufficient evidence from a variety of sources to suggest that treatment programmes work. But there seems to be some inconsistency in outcomes and this variability suggests that the quality of the programme's implementation is vital to its effectiveness. Different therapists do differ in terms of their effectiveness, of course, but there is more to it than that. McMurran and Duggan (2005) are among those forensic and criminal psychologists who suggest that effective treatment is 'driven' by theory and is based on research evidence. Adherence to the principles derived from these is termed 'treatment integrity'. A treatment programme that has a high degree of treatment integrity in practice will conform closely to the programme's underlying theory and design. Therapists in programmes demonstrating good treatment integrity will keep on the course determined by the principles of the treatment programme and will not drift away from these. Treatment integrity is dependent on a number of things of which the careful ongoing training of personnel is an important component, as is their continual monitoring.

Inexperienced therapists, especially, benefit from the use of highly structured materials that provide clear descriptions of the techniques and processes to be used in therapy (Crits-Cristoph *et al.*, 1991). In the search to reduce costs, many of the treatments described in this chapter would be delegated to prison officers, nurses, and any other suitable personnel. The provision of highly structured materials is simply the instruction manuals for the treatment programme. Hence, there is a concept – manualisation – which simply means that the structure of the therapeutic programme is enshrined in a formal manual describing the practice of the therapy rather than leaving the programme to the whims of the therapists. Manuals vary in their style. Some are best described as prescriptive in the detail of how and what is to be done. Others stress the concepts underlying the treatment programme and leave more to the individual therapist's discretion in terms of how those principles are implemented. Manualisation is quite simply the process of turning the basic principles of the treatment programme into a detailed, systematic manual describing what must be done in practice.

Manualisation, taken at face value, may seem a simple, practical step in increasing the effectiveness of therapeutic programmes. However, it actually reverses many of the traditional principles that underlie psychological therapies. Hollin (2002) suggests that the following are among the major criticisms of manualisation, although he does not share all of them:

- *Negation of theoretical principles:* rather than tailor cognitive behavioural treatments to the individual needs of offenders, manualisation encourages 'off the peg' treatment which is the same for all. This is particularly evident in the stress of cognitive behavioural programmes on working with groups of offenders rather than individuals. Rapists and child molesters go through identical treatment programmes.
- *Lack of individual case formulation:* the thorough assessment of the individual prior to treatment is a given in traditional cognitive behavioural treatment. So an individually tailored treatment plan would be integral to treatment. Assessment in cognitive behavioural programmes tends to be confined to excluding those unsuitable for cognitive behaviour therapy by virtue, say, of their low levels of intelligence.
- *Lack of clinical artistry:* the clinician's insights, personal qualities, skill in decision making and judgements in relation to an individual client are seen by some as being integral to good therapy. Treatment is an unfolding process, the precise detail of which is dependent on the therapist's use of these skills. The use of a manual diminishes the opportunity for using such skills. However, it is these very processes in which the therapist makes continuing adjustments on the basis of their clinical skills that actually threaten the integrity of treatment programmes.
- *Emphasis on single schools of therapy:* a treatment manual will almost certainly feature a single theoretical approach to psychotherapeutic intervention. This, most commonly, will be the cognitive behavioural approach. Inevitably, then, this squeezes out eclectic approaches where features of different schools of therapy are used by the therapist, depending on circumstances. One consequence of the monopoly of one school of therapy in a treatment programme is that it may stifle the development of new approaches to therapy as it prevents new things from being tried out.

One consequence of manualisation is that less-qualified personnel may be used to deliver therapy than would be possible if the system allowed therapeutic discretion, for example.

The high-risk offender problem

High-risk offenders may show many of the following characteristics: aggression; anger; egocentricity; failings at school; irritability; negative attitudes to schooling;

neuropsychological deficiencies; non-compliance; non-persistence when the treatment tasks become too hard; self-control deficiencies; lack of commitment to change; untrustworthiness; verbal ability deficiencies; and victimisation feelings. This sounds like a checklist for a difficult client on a treatment programme and it is. They may have difficulties interacting with others, concentrating, and studying – all of which are requirements of modern cognitive behaviour-based treatments. High-risk offenders, as a consequence, may languish in the prison system for many years. Their treatment places demands on the system. It is fairly clear that these treatment programmes are different from those described earlier in this chapter because of the intensity and pervasiveness in the lives of the offenders.

Irrespective of what is happening to crime rates, there has been a rapid rise in the numbers of prisoners in many countries in the Western world. This is partly the result of policies aimed at getting tough on crime. Prisons are expensive necessities. Politicians offer themselves for judgement in terms of the success of their penal policies. When a particularly horrific crime catches the public's attention then people expect something to be done. In 1999, for example, the British government instigated the Dangerous and Severe Personality Disorder (DSPD) initiative, which came into being in 2001. This was in the aftermath of a crime which had outraged the public. Michael Stone had murdered in a particularly brutal fashion. In the incident, Stone tied up Lin Russell and her two daughters and beat them brutally in a robbery attempt. One of the daughters survived, but he left dead the mother, one daughter and their dog. The background to this killing is fairly complex but Stone was known to the psychiatric services as being a risk to others. According to the law as it stood at the time, he could not be detained since psychiatrists regarded him as being untreatable. The Mental Health Act 1983 meant that personality-disordered individuals could be detained only if treatment was likely to lead to an alleviation of their condition or prevent its deterioration. The law has been since modified to merely require that a suitable treatment is available. The Dangerous and Severe Personality (DSPD) services were consequently established at Her Majesty's Prison Whitemore, Rampton Hospital, Broadmoor Hospital, and Her Majesty's Prison Frankland. This DSPD initiative has been scaled back and is now discontinued.

BOX 26.1 Forensic psychology in action

A high-risk offender treatment programme

Among the internationally well-known high-risk offender treatment programmes is the Clearwater Sex Offender Treatment Programme in Saskatoon, Canada. This is one of the longest-established of these programmes, having begun in the 1980s. Olver and Wong (2013) provide a detailed description of the work of this unit and important features of the programme can be extracted from this:

Background

- Priority for treatment is given to high-risk offenders.
- It consists of a 48-bed in-patient unit located in a mental health facility.
- From its inception, it has been consistent in its use of cognitive behavioural therapy in treatment.
- Updated to meet the RNR model.

Induction

- On arriving in the unit, the offender is assessed using risk assessment procedures and psychological measures.
- The individual's criminogenic needs to be prioritised during treatment are assessed. Furthermore, responsivity issues such as the individual's intellectual ability and cultural specificities are assessed.

Offender characteristics

- Extensive sexual and non-sexual criminal histories characterise the offenders who may have been sentenced to long-term imprisonment.
- The offenders are medium- to high-risk on the Static-99 test.
- In terms of psychiatric diagnosis, about half had been diagnosed with substance abuse disorder, half had been diagnosed with antisocial personality disorder or had related traits, but only a small percentage had a major Axis-1 psychiatric disorder.
- About 40 per cent are aboriginal Canadians.
- Recently the focus has moved to sex offenders with special needs, including brain injury, learning disability, and serious mental illness. This is the

consequence of treatment for most sex offenders being carried out within the corrections service. This involves additional responsivity requirements to deal with these special features.

Basic programme facts

- Daily programme modules are involved.
- Fifteen therapy contact hours are the minimum per week.
- The usual treatment length is eight months.
- Currently the Clearwater Programme is organised into two groups of 24 patients which run simultaneously. Latecomers to treatment can join part way through and catch up at a later appropriate stage in the treatment process.
- 'Old hands' in treatment therapeutically mentor the newcomers, giving them help and support with the system.
- Those with good intellectual ability may receive information at an accelerated rate.
- Treatment can be lengthened if necessary.

The treatment team

- The treatment team includes Aboriginal elders, correctional/parole staff, occupational therapists, psychiatric nurses, psychiatrists and psychologists.

Treatment delivery

- Each client is allocated a primary therapist who helps train the client to develop cognitive and behavioural skills on an individual basis during day-to-day business. The techniques include modelling, role play, written assignments and groups for specific skill building.
- Treatment delivery is individual and group format.
- Treatment modules include attitudes and cognitions, developing health relationships and sexuality, intimacy skills deficiencies, and so forth.
- Treatment modules are delivered to groups of 10 and 12 offenders.
- For each group there is a facilitator and co-facilitator.
- The facilitators are able to alter how the programme is paced and the number of sessions is flexible according to response from group members.
- Didactic instruction to give the basic framework followed by group discussion is supplemented by paper and pencil exercises and audio/video media.
- Cognitive, affective and behavioural change is treated as a skill acquisition process designed to be relevant to particular treatment targets.
- Offenders learn from the modelling by the therapists of appropriate interpersonal skills and problem-solving techniques.
- The expectation is that they will also learn from other offenders.

Specific groups

- The disclosure group is conducted twice weekly for two hours throughout the treatment process and covers personal autobiography preparation and the offence cycle, including the cognitive, affective, and behavioural dynamics for current/previous sexual offences. It also includes the development of a relapse-prevention plan.
- The antisocial attitudes and cognitions groups helps identify, confront and challenge distorted cognitions linked to the offender's sexual offending.
- The regulation of emotion group focuses on anger and its negative consequences.
- The social skills group focuses on assertiveness and strategies to respond prosocially to interpersonal issues.
- The intimacy and relationships group involves coping skills for the control of jealousy, rejection and loneliness.
- The empathy and victim awareness group provides the offender with the chance of addressing their own victimisation and to understand more the impact of their offending on their own victim.
- There are other groups such as alcoholics anonymous, narcotics anonymous, independent work skills and the like.

When treatment is complete

- There is a final treatment report which indicates the client's progress towards addressing their dynamic risk factors and, consequently, their risk of recidivism. The psychologist's opinion about the offender's manageability in the community is also included together with what is required to manage the individual's risk. The treatment team liaises with community agencies etc. about the offender's aftercare in the community.

Many of the features of high-risk offender treatment programmes can be seen in the Clearwater programme. For example, the high-dosage approach is self-evident, as is the focus on the individual's criminogenic needs. The tailoring of the treatment to the individual characteristics of the offender can perhaps be best seen in terms of the use of the Aboriginal elder as part of the treatment team.

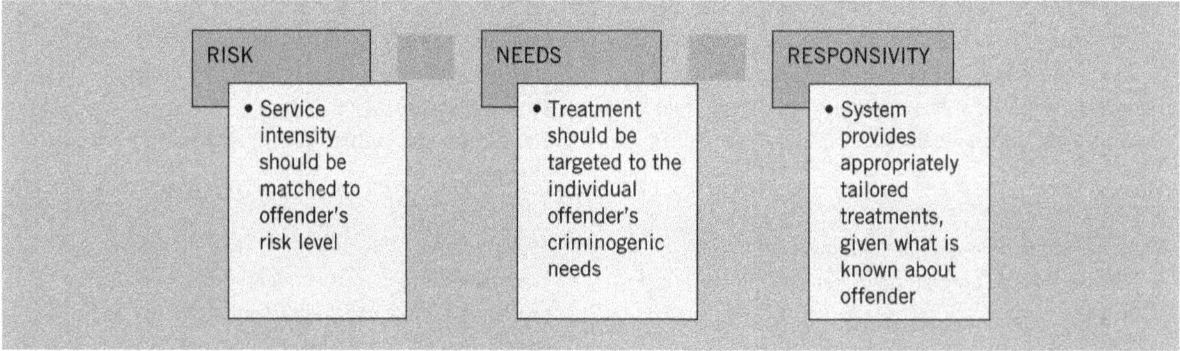

Figure 26.2 A summary of the RNR principles

Currently, then, there has been a shift in focus to the treatment of high-risk offenders. At the same time, there is trepidation about whether we have effective treatment methods to deal with them and whether convincing research studies are available which evaluate properly the effectiveness of these treatments. So this section can only describe what the situation is without drawing really firm conclusions. The need to prioritise the treatment of high-risk offenders would follow directly from Andrews and Bonta's (2010) RNR principles. These have guided a lot of penal policy. Essentially they require the targeting of resources on those offenders whose criminogenic needs are the greatest in ways which are most likely to be effective. The basics of the RNR approach are summarised in Figure 26.2 in the light of the offender's known characteristics. Acceptance of RNR principles means that high-risk offenders ought to be prioritised for treatment and that this treatment should concentrate on alleviating the factors which put the offender at risk of reoffending but in a way which takes into account things like the personal motivation of the offender; their intellectual abilities; their cultural background and so forth. This contrasts with older ideas such as concentrating resources on easy cases where treatment is more guaranteed to be effective.

'One-size-fits-all' summarises a major criticism of many offender treatment programmes. That is, in the past the tendency has been to adopt a standard treatment package which is delivered to any offenders for whom it might be appropriate. But this means, for example, that an exhibitionist who is unlikely to re-offend is regarded as having much the same treatment needs as a psychopathic violent sex offender – a somewhat unworkable idea. Some offenders are difficult in treatment, difficult to treat, and deeply antagonistic to treatment. According to Polaschek (2011) the formula should be 'many sizes fit all' instead. Differential treatment or 'What works for whom?' is the basis for current thinking, she suggests. That is, the provision of offender treatment needs to be flexible, varied, but most of all tailored to the needs of the individual offender if the high-risk sex offender is to be successfully treated. Polaschek proposes that there is a need for theoretical approaches to treatment programme design. She divides treatment programmes into three risk levels (low, medium and high) – these may be called *basic-level treatment programmes*, *mid-level multifactorial treatment programmes*, and *high-level comprehensive therapy programmes*. These different levels of treatment vary on a number of dimensions. Figure 26.3 is a schematic representation of much of what she has to say. The characteristics of each of the different categories of treatment programme are shown. Comparisons are then made between the three in terms of:

- policy-related issues;
- programme responses to offender characteristics;
- assumptions about the offender.

Examples of each of these are given in the figure. Another way of conceiving Figure 26.3 is that it indicates the main characteristics of treatment programmes appropriate to the different levels of offender risk.

It should be obvious that the low-risk programmes are substantially cheaper to run than the high-risk programmes. For instance, they can successfully employ staff, such as prison officers, who have only basic therapy skills. Since this level of clientele are not difficult, the facilitator can work from a standard manual. Treatment is relatively low-dosage, requiring a relatively small number of sessions. Some programme characteristics, such as monitoring treatment and payments to facilitators, are decidedly managerial, of course. Of course, high, medium and low risk are difficult to define labels. They are judgement calls in practice, so how could a rigorous definition be developed? One approach is to use scores on risk assessment instruments in order to establish cut-off points for each level of risk. Even then, just what should be called high, medium and low risk? Is high risk a 30 per cent chance of reoffending within five years of release from prison? Or should one simply rely on the labels given by the risk instrument's developers? Or should the seriousness of the likely reoffence be part of the criteria? Generally, commentators on this matter seem content to accept that the definition of risk is inherently problematic, no matter what approach is adopted.

BASIC-LEVEL REHABILITATION PROGRAMME	MID-LEVEL MULTIFACTORIAL TREATMENT PROGRAMME	HIGH-LEVEL COMPREHENSIVE FORENSIC THERAPY PROGRAMME
POLICY-RELATED ISSUES • Treatment integrity: Monitored in terms of adherence to manual. Delivery closely scrutinised. • Therapist skills; limited training/ dual role • Manualisation: Highly prescribed procedures	POLICY-RELATED ISSUES • Treatment integrity: Monitored by staff self-reflection and peer review • Therapist skills: Some professional training • Manualisation: More discretion for the training facilitator	POLICY-RELATED ISSUES • Treatment integrity: Monitored by skilled, theoretical sophisticated supervisor, Extensive supervision by peers and group, etc. • Therapist skills: Highly trained in skills • Manualisation: Manual guides choices but decision relevant to needs are facilitator's
PROGRAMME REPONSES TO CLIENT CHARACTERISTICS • Treatment readiness: This is assumed and only treatment-ready offenders included • Learning application: Lot of available time spent on teaching skills and knowledge • Fit between client and programme: Largely client-determined	PROGRAMME RESPONSES TO CLIENT CHARACTERISTICS • Treatment readiness: This is not assumed and offender's readiness for programme developed. • Learning application: More time devoted to application rather than merely learning skills • Fit between client and programme: Client- and programme-determined	PROGRAMME RESPONSES TO CLIENT CHARACTERISTICS • Treatment readiness: Treatment-resistant group; needs constant work during treatment • Learning application: Much of time devoted to the application of skills and feedback • Fit between client and programme: Programme-determined and formulation-driven
ASSUMPTIONS ABOUT CLIENT • Treatment needs: Few problem areas to deal with • Change process: Conscious skills and knowledge by didactic teaching and limited practice	ASSUMPTIONS ABOUT CLIENT • Treatment needs: Rather more, often entrenched. Offender has strengths • Change process: Offender needs more learning help/active methods	ASSUMPTIONS ABOUT CLIENT • Treatment needs: Many needs are deeply entrenched • Change process: Offender finds learning difficult; much support needed

Figure 26.3 Features of treatment programmes aimed at different offender risk levels

However, there are two additional issues which tend to be associated with the concept of high risk:

- Some offenders manifest little motivation for treatment and display difficult and disruptive behaviour during treatment sessions.
- Psychopathy and high risk are not identical, but they are substantially interrelated. Research evidence indicates that high-risk offenders tend to have higher scores on measures of psychopathy.

Both of these not only influence risk but they bring the responsivity issue to the fore. Responsivity (according to Bonta and Andrews, 2007) is to do with the socio-biological-personality factors which can interfere with treatment. Treatment-readiness is a composite of those characteristics of the individual and the therapeutic situation which encourage engagement in therapy and thus enhance the likelihood of therapeutic change. It is an idea which is based on an interplay between the readiness of the client and the intervention's capacity to respond to the client.

There are many problems in evaluating the effectiveness of high-intensity treatment programmes for high-risk offenders. Fundamentally, these are not necessarily the group of individuals most amenable to or ready for treatment. Their scores on 'risk assessment' instruments such as the Psychopathy Checklist Revised (PCL-R) and Level of Service Inventory Revised (LSI-R) tend to be high, which is also indicative of the level of problems they are likely to present. Amongst them will be some offenders who fail to complete treatment, some who do not complete treatment particularly well, and some will be 'seat-warmers' who sit through the programme but benefit in no way therapeutically from their experience. Some will show a pattern of sporadic and inconsistent progress. This means that therapeutic change and risk reduction may be the most appropriate measures of effectiveness rather than the more difficult issue of recidivism reduction. Olver and Wong (2013) reviewed the research on four internationally renowned high-intensity sex offender treatment programmes:

- Sex Offender Treatment Evaluation Project (SOTEP) – California, USA;
- Custody-Based Intensive Treatment (CUBIT) Program – New South Wales, Australia;
- Regional Treatment Centre's Sex Offender Program (RTCSOP) – Kingston Ontario, Canada;
- Clearwater Program – Correctional Service of Canada's Prairie Region.

Olver and Wong reached the following conclusions:

- There is some support for the conclusion that high-risk sex offender treatment can substantially change offenders' measured risk and improve important areas of psychological functioning.
- Caution has to be exercised about the above conclusion because, even following these improvements, many of the sex offenders fail to reach healthy or adaptive functioning levels in these areas.
- There may be improvements within treatment to psychological health variables but these may not necessarily be related to reductions in the offender's level of risk. This includes measures such as acceptance of responsibility, cognitive distortions, intimacy, loneliness, and self-esteem.

But even within these programmes, higher-risk sex offenders have a substantially greater risk of dropping out of treatment and, not surprisingly, also have a higher risk of reoffending. Olver and Wong describe the question of what to do about such offenders as a 'therapeutic and public safety conundrum' (Hanson and Thornton, 1999; Wong, Olver, Nicholaichuk and Gordon, 2003).

Many different things lead to such failures to complete treatment – offenders may simply drop out; they may cease to be motivated to participate in treatment; they may get discharged from the institution; they may be refused further treatment; or they may simply move if they are being treated in the community. Those who fail to complete treatment may be the highest-risk offenders. This group includes violent, domestic, and sex offenders, together with those suffering from psychopathy. Olver and Wong (2011) sought the predictors of sex offender treatment dropout among a sample of over 150 incarcerated sex offenders. These men were on a high-intensity sex offender treatment programme – the Clearwater Sex Offender Treatment Program in Canada. Almost half were rapists of 14-year olds and older, about a sixth were child molesters, and about a fifth were mixed sex-offence offenders. High percentages met the criteria for antisocial personality disorder or substance abuse disorder. The researchers collected a range of demographic, criminal history, mental health and treatment-related information, together with the outcomes of a number of risk assessment measures, including the following:

- Static 99 (Hanson and Thornton, 1999): This is an actuarial sex offender risk assessment scale. It covers matters like sexual offence history, non-sexual offence history, victim characteristics, and offender demographics.
- Violence Risk Scale – Sexual Offender Version (VRS-SO) (Wong, Olver, Nicholaichuk and Gordon, 2003): This mixes static and dynamic risk factors (those that cannot and those that can be changed by treatment). It is intended for both risk assessment purposes and for treatment planning purposes.
- Psychopathy Checklist-Revised (PCL-R) (Hare, 2003). This well-established measure of psychopathy has two dimensions: the first involves the affective/interpersonal aspects of psychopathy and the second involves antisocial/behavioural aspects.

Fifteen per cent of the participants on the programme withdrew or were discharged prematurely from the programme and their participation deemed unsuccessful when the programme was complete. Among the reasons for their dropping out were: lack of motivation or effort (30 per cent); disruptive behaviours such as aggressiveness/abusiveness (35 per cent); personal requests such as frustration with the treatment programme or not being willing to change, etc. (26 per cent); and administrative reasons such as early release (22 per cent). Nevertheless, the completers/non-completers were indistinguishable on the basis of variables like age, length of sentence, mental illness, paraphilia, prior nonviolent convictions, prior sexual offences, prior violent offences, sex offence type, and substance abuse disorder. This 15 per cent could be fairly effectively predicted using just two variables. Drop out from treatment could be predicted with 70 per cent accuracy using just Factor 1 (the emotional factor) of the psychopathy checklist and that the offender had never been married. This does not mean that the other psychometric measures were not predictive, merely that the best prediction required only the two variables mentioned. Again these findings should not be used to argue that such offenders ought to be denied treatment. Instead, they should be regarded as identifying a 'responsivity' issue to be addressed by finding the most effective ways of dealing better with these offenders' criminogenic need.

This brings us to the question of whether psychopaths are treatable. Psychopathy is a pathology of the personality which makes it more likely that the individual will be involved in chronic severe violence throughout their lives. Their violent crimes are a substantial drain on the resources of the public health system and criminal justice systems throughout the world. Despite considerable developments in our understanding of psychopathy, what we should do about psychopathic traits such as meanness and disinhibition in therapy is far from clear. Perhaps they are not an issue for treatment or maybe they should receive direct attention. More generally, it is hard to say which psychopathic traits, if any, should be addressed during therapy. We are a long way from knowing whether psychopaths need special treatments or whether any programme specialising in difficult clients would work. Reidy, Kearns, and DeGuea (2013) reviewed the published research. They argue that, despite more than 70 years of research and debate about psychopathy, we have made little progress in terms of understanding just how to treat the condition. The findings of research on the effectiveness of therapy of forensic populations of psychopaths are not fully coherent and they are very limited in scope. In the past and still now, there have been numerous claims about the unsuitability of psychopaths for treatment. Nevertheless, Reidy *et al.* argue that interventions tailored to the needs of the psychopathic individual may be effective. In such treatment, they argue, it is important to pay attention to the individual's unique behavioural conditioning and personal predispositions which possibly may be used in attempts to reduce their violence.

There is a minority of research which allows for what Reidy *et al.* describe as 'the most optimistic interpretation'. This is that intense, rigorous interventions may reduce psychopathic violence (Caldwell, 2011; Caldwell, Skeem, Salekin and Van Rybroek, 2006). Very similar conclusions were reached in Polaschek and Daly's (2013) review of the treatment potential of psychopaths. They also argue that there are some recent good-quality studies suggestive of the treatability of psychopaths. Polaschek and Daly claim that psychopaths show similar reductions in criminal risk to other participants on treatment targets, though whether this is reflected in lowered rates of recidivism awaits research attention. They describe the successful treatment of psychopaths as a mere fledgling idea, though there is tentative encouraging evidence. Psychopathy should not be seen as a disorder that leads to criminality, they argue. Instead it should be seen as a disorder which has various dimensions, but it is unclear how they lead to criminality or desistance from crime. However, for the moment, the inescapable bottom line is that psychopaths as a group are treatment-resistant. Treatment programmes consequently need to be very skilfully constructed if counterproductive outcomes are to be avoided. The treatment of high-risk offenders is in its infancy and treatment programmes and evaluation studies need to be viewed cautiously for the moment.

Main points

- Modern prison services are likely to have tailored cognitive behavioural programmes for the treatment of sex offenders and some violent offenders in particular. The important thing is that the demand that such programmes be evaluated for effectiveness has resulted in a number of studies which demonstrate beyond question that such programmes not only produce the changes they intend in some prisoners but that recidivism is also reduced as a consequence. One should not overestimate the effectiveness of such programmes, but neither is pessimism appropriate. We have gone a long way from the time when 'Nothing works' was the overriding view to today when 'Why does it work?' and 'How can we make it work better?' are the more common views. Increasingly, therapeutic and research attention is focusing on the high-risk offender who was previously regarded as being too difficult or impossible to treat. Clear evidence of the effectiveness of treatment with this group has to be a research objective of the future. Manualisation refers to the standardisation of treatment such that therapy is effectively used in all locations, irrespective of the experience and skills of the particular personnel involved. There are a number of problems in evaluating any programme and the choice of outcome measures (e.g. psychometric tests versus recidivism rates) is crucial.
- Programmes for sexual offenders tend to be very widely based and tackle a wide variety of aspects of the offender, the offence, and cognitions about the offence. It is not always the case that treatment involves aspects which have been demonstrated empirically to be associated with sexual offending. It would appear that programmes which are based on the RNR principles of risk, need, and responsivity tend to be the most effective.
- The treatment of violent offenders has often involved the methods of anger management. The difficulty with this is the lack of certainty that a great deal of violent offending is due to anger problems. Indeed, there is good reason to believe that it is not. Violence treatment programmes have a more sophisticated theoretical basis and there is some evidence that they are effective. Increasingly the issue of the treatability of high-risk offenders, including psychopaths, has been put on the research agenda. Definitive conclusions, though, are inappropriate, given the present state of our knowledge.

Further reading

Craig, L.A., Gannon, T.A. and Dixon, L. (eds) (2013) *What Works in Offender Rehabilitation: An Evidence-Based Approach to Assessment and Treatment* Chichester, West Sussex: Wiley Blackwell.

Harrison, K. and Rainey, B. (2013) *The Wiley-Blackwell Handbook of Legal and Ethical Aspects of Sex Offender Treatment and Management* Chichester, West Sussex: Wiley-Blackwell.

Marshall, W.L., Fernandez, Y., Marshall, L. and Serran, G. (eds) (2005) *Sexual Offender Treatment: Controversial Issues* Chichester, West Sussex: John Wiley.

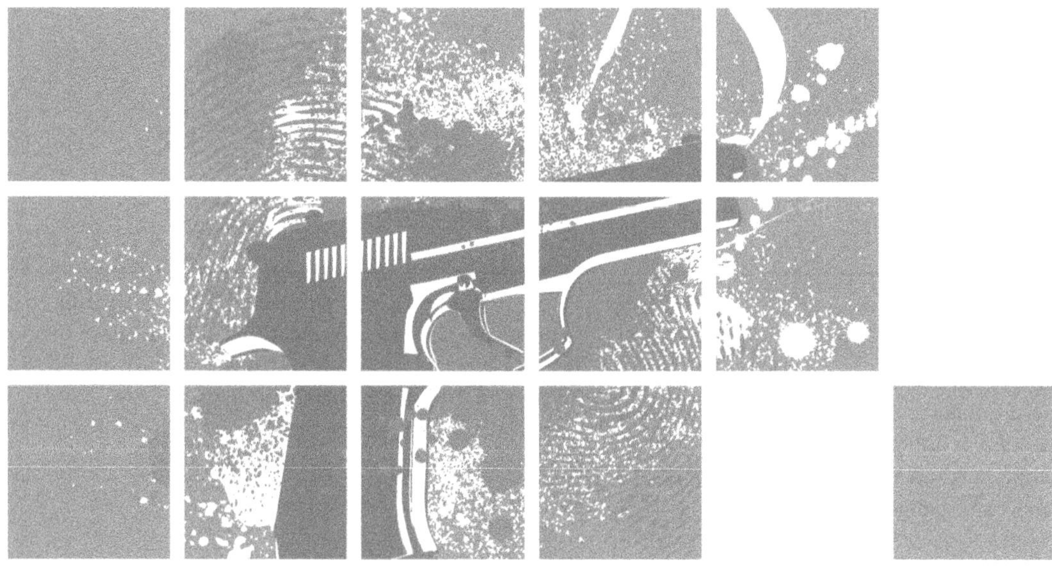

Chapter 27

Assessment of risk, dangerousness and recidivism

Overview

- Psychological practitioners have an ethical responsibility and duty of care in relation to those who can be affected by the decisions they make. Their decisions about the disposal (e.g. early release, to live in the community) of offenders may result in the public becoming victims.
- Risk and dangerousness assessment refers to a variety of methods developed to limit the levels of risk and danger to the public while allowing offenders liberty. The *Tarasoff* decision in the United States imposed legal requirements pertinent to this.
- Risk assessment is different from risk management. Risk management is the various techniques that minimise the risk to other people – keeping the potential offender in prison is a form of risk management.
- Risk assessment is not a precise science though there are some useful predictors. These include historical factors such as a background of violent offending and age. These are often referred to as static factors because they cannot be changed in therapy. Dynamic risk factors can be changed by treatment, for example. Changes in them are sometimes used as indicators of the success of therapy.
- Although most risk assessment is carried out using psychological measures, there is some interest in using within-institution behaviour to assess the likelihood of similar behaviours on release.
- The factors which need to be taken into account when assessing risk and dangerousness may be, to some extent, different for a sexual offender than for a violent offender. These, in turn, may be very different from the predictors of suicide by the offender. Different contexts will influence the risk posed by the offender. Risk factors are those that predict recidivism, and are different from causal factors that caused the individual to be dangerous to others in the first place.
- Clinical judgement of risk is different from statistical assessment of risk, which is based on empirically established relationships. There are many reasons why clinical judgement may fail, including the lack of available feedback about whether a decision was correct. Structured clinical methods have been developed which involve a degree of clinical judgement but provide a systematic checklist of decisions which need to be taken. The Psychopathy Checklist Revised (PCL-R) is a very successful example of this approach.
- Prediction of dangerousness refers to the likely level of, say, violence if it happens.

- It is harder to predict rare events than common events. False negatives are the offenders who are declared safe but actually reoffend. False positives are those who are declared a risk but do not reoffend.
- The Good Lives Model provides an alternative approach to offender rehabilitation to the risk management approach which dominates this chapter.

Introduction

A British forensic psychiatrist once said: 'I could let free half of my patients – if I knew which half' (Gretenkord, 1991). The German banker Hermann Josef Abs pointed out: 'Prognoses are a difficult matter, especially when regarding future events' (Gretenkord, 1993). The assessment of the risks and dangers posed by offenders is a very serious matter, however. It is of concern to all in forensic work.

There are a number of responsibilities inherent in decision making in forensic work. These include protecting the general public, institutional staff and other institutional inmates from dangerous individuals and dangerous individuals from themselves. These duties include an element of prediction. Individuals within the criminal justice system pass through a number of stages for which assessment of the consequences of particular decisions is required. For example, if a prisoner is to be transferred from a maximum security prison to one more open and free, then this decision implies that some consideration is given to their likely future behaviour: they should be unlikely to abscond from their new prison and constitute little or no danger to the general public, for example. The search for ways of predicting which offender is likely to reoffend on a future occasion has involved a wide search for indicators. These have included demographics; criminal history; psychological traits; institutional behaviour; clinical judgements; factors related to therapeutic change; the presence of positive characteristics; and others. New possibilities emerge from time to time – for example, the investigation of offenders' social networks as an indicator of recidivism (Pomp, Spreen, Bogaerts and Volker, 2010).

Risk and dangerousness assessments are subject to political pressures of many sorts. Equally, the management of risk and dangerousness is not solely in the hands of the primary decision makers, including psychologists. In terms of the work of the British Parole Boards, McGeorge (1996) suggested that there is a relationship between the political climate regarding crime and decisions to allow parole. His index of political influence is the number of life sentence prisoners to whom the Home Secretary (the government minister then responsible for law and order matters) refused parole out of those recommended by the Parole Board. As the number rejected increased, so the number recommended for release by the Parole Board decreased. This suggests that the parole recommendations were influenced by the toughness of the Home Secretary. (The Minister of Justice would be responsible for such matters nowadays.)

The *Tarasoff* and other US legal decisions

Research into the prediction of dangerousness was spurred on in the 1970s by important cases in American law courts. The most famous of these was the *Tarasoff* decision which arose out of a Californian court case of the early 1970s. The outcome was basically that psychologists and other clinicians began to be under a greater duty to protect the general public from their clients. The basic facts are as follows. Tatiana Tarasoff was a young student at the University of California in the late 1960s and early 1970s. Another student, Prosenjit Poddar, told a student health therapist that he intended to kill Tatiana. These basic facts were reported to the medical authorities at the campus and their response was to get Poddar checked out by the campus police. Apart from this, no other action was taken. Shortly afterwards, Tatiana was killed by Poddar. Tatiana Tarasoff had not been informed about the threat to her life at any stage before her death. Her parents pursued the matter through the Californian legal system.

In a watershed case, *Vitaly Tarasoff* v. *the Regents of the University of California*, her father won in 1974 a legal ruling that therapists were legally obliged by duty to inform such potential victims of the threat to their safety made by clients of the therapist. This was a duty to inform.

The judgement was reviewed in 1976 in the light of a number of practical difficulties raised by professional bodies. The 1976 judgement obliged therapists to use reasonable care in order to ensure the public's safety from the therapists' clients. The difficulties inherent in this led to a second judgement in 1976 which revised the obligation to that of using reasonable care to protect potential victims. This is a duty to protect. The new obligation on the therapist involved managing the dangerous individual better, say, with medication, institutionalisation or by whatever means.

One difficulty with the *Tarasoff* decision is that the named potential victim may not be the actual victim: that is, the violence may be against individuals whom the client has not directly threatened. A client who threatens to harm members of his or her own family may actually end up violently assaulting staff supervising him in a psychiatric facility. The threat needs to be evaluated in terms of the potential for attack, which may involve many others apart from those mentioned directly in the threat (McNeil, 1997).

Of course, a Californian legal judgement is not US law, let alone international law. There were a number of lawsuits in the United States during the 1960s and 1970s concerning the civil rights of offenders diverted into institutions for the criminally insane. Two court cases, in addition to the *Tarasoff* ones, also led to a new research effort into the prediction of dangerousness starting in the 1970s (Cooper, Griesel and Yuille, 2008).

The *Baxstrom* v. *Herold* (1966) case involved Johnny Baxstrom, who had been sentenced in 1958 to up to three years in prison for a second-degree assault. However, in 1961 he was judged to be mentally ill and was relocated from prison into a psychiatric unit and detained there after his original three-year sentence had been completed. A law permitted the detention of mentally ill individuals after their sentence expired. The legal outcome was that the court decided that Johnny's detention beyond his original sentence was not just. This led to about a thousand patients being transferred from maximum security mental hospitals (i.e. hospitals for the criminally insane) to regular psychiatric hospitals for the mentally ill. Some were later released into the community. Psychiatrists had decided implicitly that these patients were dangerous – that, after all, was the reason for them being detained. Researchers realised the need to research thoroughly the adequacy of these psychiatric assessments. Few behavioural problems emerged and the patients were no more violent than any other patients after they had been transferred to the regular hospital. The psychiatrists had simply grossly overestimated the levels of dangerousness of offenders like Johnny Baxstrom (Steadman and Cocozza, 1974).

Much the same situation arose in the case of *Dixon* v. *Attorney General of the Commonwealth of Pennsylvania* (1971) which involved a similar law allowing involuntary and indeterminate commitment based on the opinion of two physicians. A number of patients were detained after the expiry of their sentences for criminal behaviour. No review was required concerning the internment. The legal outcome of this case changed things entirely. Once again, research into these inmates-turned-patients after release revealed that the psychiatrists' assessments of dangerousness were woefully over-pessimistic.

To summarise the current position, two points are important (Glover, 1999):

- From the 1980s onwards, the ideology had changed to one in which the majority of the mentally ill should be cared for in the community. Institutional care was seen as a temporary respite for use only in acute circumstances when there was no realistic alternative.
- The modern situation balances the right of individuals to their liberty with the inevitability that, in some instances, the general public and other third parties require protection.

Risk assessment

Gannon, Beech and Ward (2008) schematically considered risk assessment as being made up of three distinct components: functional assessments, actuarial assessment and dynamic risk assessment:

- Functional assessments are based on interviews with the offender about the events associated with their offending. The interview may help identify acute dynamic risk factors which led to the offence. So the interview considers the offender's cognitions, feelings, decisions and actions which led to the heightened risk of offending. The clinician may use this information to help the offender understand his or her offending.
- Actuarial assessments explore the statistical relationship between the characteristics of the offender, such as previous offences, criminality and so forth and the probability of reconviction. Much of this information is readily available on file, so is easy to obtain and use. There are problems with such measures, especially as they are dependent on official recidivism data which may be an underestimate of offenders' true rates of reoffending. It also needs noting that instruments designed to give these actuarial assessments tend to rely on static or unchanging factors, which may not be very helpful to those interested in understanding the influence of therapy on the likelihood of reoffending.
- Dynamic risk assessments use risk factors which can change as a result of, say, therapy or the experience of prison. It is believed that changes in dynamic risk factors are related to changes in the risk of recidivism. Deviant sexual interests and offence-supportive attitudes may be risk factors for future offending but they are also matters which may change as a result of the offender's experiences. Dynamic factors such as situational and psychological factors may change. A paedophile who lives close to a school may be less at risk of offending if they move to a child-free location. The introduction of dynamic risk factors was the result of the work of Andrews and Bonta beginning early in the 1980s. They defined dynamic risk factors in terms of dynamic characteristics of offenders and their environments which, when changed, results in alterations in

the likelihood of reoffending (Andrews, Bonta and Hoge, 1990, p. 31).

Schwalbe (2007) divides the history of risk assessment into three historical phases, though they overlap markedly:

- First-generation risk assessment was based on the impressions or subjective judgements of professionals within the criminal justice system. No structured assessment instruments were involved.
- Second-generation risk assessment was dependent on the statistical relationship between a risk assessment instrument and subsequent offending. The emphasis was on classifying the risk level and predicting reoffending. So long as the assessment method produced the required associations, that was good enough. The content of the assessment was secondary in importance. The risk factors tended to be static in nature, such as the number of previous offences for a particular category of crime, etc. (A static predictor is one which is fixed and normally cannot be changed by therapy or another type of intervention.) Schwalbe (2007) describes the actuarial/statistical approach as being the gold standard for risk assessment.
- Third-generation risk assessment was similarly devoted to the basic statistical association between the predictor instrument and recidivism but introduced dynamic risk factors such as drug use or school problems which may be subject to change through treatment or some other sort of intervention.

The study of recidivism dates back to the early twentieth century when researchers used official records or files that held information about the demographic and criminal history of offenders. The work of Burgess (1928) seems to be the earliest use of statistically based methods of risk assessment. Conceptually, there is an obvious distinction to be made between the statistical risk of the occurrence of an event in the future and the dangerousness of that event. For example, the likelihood of an offender reoffending in the future by shoplifting may be very high. In terms of the consequences of this reoffending, it poses fairly small consequences for the individual victim (Clark, 1999). That is, there is a distinction to be made between the assessment of risk and the assessment of dangerousness.

The prediction of dangerousness seems to refer to two distinct professional activities (Hodgins, 1997):

- Deciding which patients or clients or offenders will behave violently or aggressively or criminally in a particularly dangerous way;
- Identifying the particular conditions in which a specific individual is likely to behave violently, aggressively or criminally.

These are very different activities, although clearly interrelated. By knowing more about the conditions encouraging violence, say, in a particular individual, we may be in a position to make more accurate predictions of their dangerousness. If, for example, we know that a particular man is prone to violence only when under stress and challenged by a woman, we are likely to see him as of little danger to other male prisoners in a male-only prison environment. There are no universal predictors of future behaviours and the factors predicting different types of behaviour are different. For example, the predictors of rape are not the same as the predictors of non-violent criminality.

For criminal and other behaviours, a number of effective but simple predictor variables have been established. These are largely associated with the age of the offender (youthful offenders are more likely to reoffend) and criminal history (those with the most criminal offences are the most likely to reoffend). Such indicators are readily measured and are prime aspects in predicting future behaviour (Clark, 1999). One difficulty is the non-dynamic nature of these predictions. They would give a prisoner the same likelihood of reoffending at the start of a term of imprisonment as when it finishes. Thus if the prisoner has received therapy within the prison context, there perhaps should be some adjustment to the prediction (i.e. successful therapy might reduce reoffending), but much of the data available is not sophisticated enough to allow that to be done.

Care should be taken to distinguish between:

- those factors that predict dangerousness in an individual;
- the factors that caused that particular individual to be a danger to others (Hodgins, 1997).

The distinction between predictors and causes is important. The predictors of dangerousness are often very simple things such as age and previous history of crime. The causes of crime are multiple and complexly interrelated. For example, assume that studies of twins have established that genetics plays a role in the aetiology of the violence of some offenders. This means that genetic characteristics caused the offending. Just because we know that the cause is genetic does not mean that we have the technology to identify precisely what genes are involved – that is, we have no genetic test. Nevertheless, we may still be able to predict risk, though not through a genetic test. Research may show that a long history of crime is strongly correlated with future violence. This history of violent crime cannot be said to be the cause of future violent crime – genes are the cause in this example. In these circumstances, we can use history of crime as an indicator of likely future violence but not the explanation of it. Some predictors may turn out to be causes of violence but this is not a requirement.

Risk and dangerousness prediction is at the moment not exact and we are unlikely ever to have perfect predictors. In particular, currently we do not know how stable risk factors are across different forensic populations (types of offender, locations of offenders). This sort of uncertainty led Monahan (1993) in the USA to argue that *all* organisations dealing therapeutically or otherwise with potentially dangerous client populations (including all forensic settings) should adopt the following principles:

- Experts in assessing client dangerousness should be employed.
- All therapists should collect data on the risk demonstrated by their client pool as part of an effort to extend knowledge in the field.
- Data on risk and dangerousness are potentially of value to all practitioners. Consequently, it is incumbent on practitioners to communicate their findings to other practitioners/decision makers working with potentially dangerous client populations.

Some authors stress the positive aspects of risk assessment (e.g. Glover, 1999). If risk had only negative outcomes (such as the general public suffering violent assaults) then there would be no reason to take that risk: just leave the offender behind bars, which reduces the risk to the general public to the very minimum. It is because we want the positive benefits of taking the risk that we take that risk. For example, we may feel it more humane to release prisoners into the community wherever possible or we may seek the economic benefit of not having to pay the high financial costs of keeping an offender in prison.

Box 27.1 Key concept

Risk management

Risk management can be considered to be all of the actions that can be employed by professionals to prevent the risk that they assess to be present in an offender, client or situation materialising. Many of the techniques are not intended to have a lasting effect but merely an immediate one. According to Harris and Rice (1997) these include the following:

- *Static controls* include video monitoring, locked wards and so forth.
- *Situational controls* might include, for example, the exclusion of violent partners from the family home or reducing the availability of guns and access to them.
- *Pharmacological controls* are common. They involve the use of sedatives and other drugs to reduce aggressive behaviour, for example.
- *Interpersonal controls* include encouraging talking with others as a means of reducing or circumventing the arousal of emotions such as anger. There are procedures available for the use of counselling or therapy in increasing self-control, such as anger management programmes.
- *Risk management* involves the practices and procedures that minimise the risk of clients to others (Monahan, 1993). It is not necessary to know the actual levels of risk posed by a particular individual before they are deployed:
  - Hospitalisation or imprisonment may incapacitate (make less risky) potentially dangerous clients effectively compared with, say, releasing them on parole.
  - Second opinions from experts in dangerousness are essential in all cases of potentially dangerous clients. A practitioner's sole opinion is insufficient.
  - Non-compliance with treatment should not simply be regarded as a stumbling block to effective treatment. It is a major risk indicator for dangerousness and should be responded to in that light.

The effectiveness of dynamic risk factors

The distinction between static and dynamic risk factors is a common one in discussions of risk assessment. As we have seen, the key difference is that static risk factors such as gender and previous history of criminality are unchangeable by treatment, for example. They can be regarded as essentially fixed. For now, we can identify the characteristics of dynamic risk factors as including the following:

- They change in their nature or severity over time.
- They relate to changes in the likelihood of offending.

Despite a lot of discussion, there does not seem to be convincing evidence of the superiority of dynamic risk factors over static risk factors in risk assessment. It has been proposed that dynamic risk factors which change as a consequence of therapy should be called 'causal risk factors' (Kraemer *et al.*, 1997), though this has not been generally adopted for reasons which the next section will help clarify. Nevertheless, to the extent that dynamic risk factors are indicative of therapeutic success then changes in them should be therapeutic markers in therapy. There are at least two ways of studying dynamic risk factors. The first would be to take a cross-sectional approach and study the relationship between changes in dynamic risk factors and recidivism for a particular snapshot in time. The alternative is to look at changes in dynamic risk factors and offending behaviour over a period of time to see if there is a close interplay between changes in the dynamic risk factor and changes in criminal behaviour. The latter is relatively uncommon.

Barnett, Wakeling, Mandeville-Norden and Rakestrow (2013) asked about the relationship between a variety of psychometric test score changes over the course of treatment and sexual/violent reoffending. Their study involved over 3000 convicted sex offenders undergoing community-based sexual offender treatment provided by the UK probation service. There were four separate treatment programmes involved in different parts of the country. Participants completed psychometric tests of various sorts, both prior to beginning treatment and after treatment.

Reoffending information was obtained from the Police National Computer (PNC) for all of the participants in the research. The average length of the follow-up period for monitoring new offending was three years. Reoffending was not at all common – only just over 5 per cent had been reconvicted for a sexual offence and less than 2 per cent had been reconvicted for a violent offence. These are low baselines so the researchers based their outcome measure on reconvictions for either a sexual or a violent offence, which included about 7 per cent of the total sample. The analysis showed that the improvements in scores following treatment on any of the measures were not related to reconviction for violent or sexual offences. These psychological measures included self-esteem, locus of control, emotional loneliness, personal distress, under-assertiveness, victim empathy distortions, cognitive distortions and emotional congruence with children. Most of these would be considered dynamic risk factors.

The researchers looked at the change scores on their predictor variables for participants who were not originally in the functional range on the measures involved (that is, outside of the range of scores obtained by normally functioning people). None of the relationships between reconviction and change on the psychological tests were statistically significant. Not only this, the researchers carried out a similar analysis of those whose scores on the measures were in the functional range. The outcome was just the same – no relationships. The researchers then adopted a different approach to the analysis. They divided the participants into two groups:

- Those whose scores on socio-affective functioning (an amalgamated measure of offence-supportive attitudes, self-management and socio-affective functioning) changed to be within the functional range.
- Those whose scores did not change to be in the functional range.

This time, it was found that those whose socio-affective functioning scores had changed to be in the functional range were less likely to reoffend than those whose scores did not change to be in the normal functioning range. This is an intriguing outcome as it implies that only treatment-induced changes which bring the offender into the functional range for the dynamic risk factor will produce the change which lessens the risk of offending. This is a novel finding and no doubt warrants further research attention. However, it should also be remembered that the researchers in this case were trying to predict a very low incidence of reoffending, which is less than optimal from the point of view of risk assessment.

Other research has adopted a more dynamic sort of research design in which a series of changes in dynamic risk factors were compared with variations in violent behaviour within an institution rather than after release. Wilson, Desmarais, Nicholls, Hart and Brink (2013) studied a sample of 30 male forensic psychiatric inpatients at a Canadian forensic hospital. These were men who had exhibited violence in the institution. The researchers defined institutional violence in terms of physical harm to another person – whether real, attempted or threated – and intimidation and other fear-inducing behaviours were also included. There was a control group of case-by-case matched non-violent inmates of the institution. The researchers measured static and dynamic risk factors every three months, using standard scales of measurement. They also measured violent behaviour. In more detail, the measures employed were:

- Static risk factors: HCR-20 (the Historical Clinical Risk Management for violence) is a structured professional judgement scale developed by Webster, Douglas, Eaves and Hart (1997). It involves a number of static risk factors of a historical nature though it includes additional risk factors which are more dynamic in nature. However, the historic risk factors can be seen as a measure of static risk factors.
- Dynamic risk factors: START (the Short-term Assessment of Risk and Treatability) is another structured professional judgement scale. It consists of a number of items related to risk of various types, though only risk of violence to others items were used in the present study.

- Violent behaviour: the Overt Aggression Scale (Yudofsky, Silver, Jackson, Endicott and Williams, 1986).

There was strong evidence found of the predictive validity of dynamic risk factors in this context. The dynamic risk factors predicted institutional violence, as did changes in the dynamic risk factors. This remained the case when static risk factors were taken into account. The dynamic risk factors varied over time and these changes actually predicted future aggression. Including dynamic risk factors improved predictions of aggression over and above what could have been achieved using static risk factors on their own. When predicting institutional violence, it was found that dynamic factors alone were the best predictors of institutional violence in the short term. Static risk factors did not add to the prediction in these circumstances. This, however, was not true in the case of long-term predictions of violence. Here the static risk factors were important. One way of conceptualising this is that dynamic risk factors fluctuate over time. Consequently, they are less successful at predicting violence in the longer term than in the short term.

Just what are dynamic risk factors?

There is a degree of confusion if not downright disagreement between researchers in terms of how dynamic risk factors should be conceived – and the extent to which they can improve prediction. The range of opinions seems to be from the view that dynamic risk factors are simply predictive constructs with little sound theoretical basis (e.g. Ward, 2016) to the view that dynamic risk factors will lead to stronger theories of offending and can be considered, alongside protective factors, to give useful theoretical accounts of reoffending. One advantage of dynamic risk factors is that they appear to offer to the public a means of reducing recidivism and to the offender are more positive outcome in the form of more fulfilling lives. To reiterate, the idea of dynamic risk factors originated in the early 1980s out of the work of Andrews and Bonta (2010). This is known as the Risk-Need-Responsivity approach. The basic assumption is that any social and psychological factors which are theoretically known or can be empirically shown to be related to offending are legitimate targets for treatment. Andrews and Bonta defined dynamic risk factors as risk factors which can change and that these changes are associated with changes in recidivism risk. Dynamic risk factors are 'dynamic attributes of offenders and their circumstances that, when changed, are associated with changes in the chances of recidivism' (Andrews, Bonta and Hoge, 1990, p. 31). They are also termed 'criminogenic needs'. A dynamic risk factor may be traits of the offender or characteristics of the offender's environment or both. The main or big four risk factors predictive of reoffending are a history of antisocial behaviour and showing an antisocial personality, antisocial thinking patterns, and having antisocial associates (Andrews and Bonta (2010). Serin, Chadwick and Lloyd (2016) identify a number of dynamic risk factors which include employment motivation and history, hostility, impulsivity, interpersonal problems, negative peer group influences and sensitivity to provocation. Risk factors at the beginning of an offending career may be different from those later on in the criminal career which contribute to the maintenance of offending.

There are a number of problems associated with dynamic risk factors. The relationship of risk factors to recidivism is important since recidivism is legally defined which makes the associated dynamic risk factors also dependent on legal norms for their definition (Ward, 2016). So there is no straightforward way in which dynamic risk factors are causative since we have to refer back to the social, political and legal institutions which lead to the thing we call recidivism. A second problem, according to Ward, is the assumption inherent in Andrews and Bonta's definition that measures of dynamic risk factors are valid. That is, dynamic risk factors appear to refer to particular psychological processes of individuals which are involved in their interactions with the world. The third major weakness of Andrews and Bonta's definition is that it basically is one of risk predictors which are not in themselves causal factors. They put a ragbag of different variables within the same domain but mostly these are only weakly correlated. This works fine if one is in the business of making predictions but they work badly if the idea is to have theoretically coherent ways of explaining criminal behaviour. Making predictions is best when predictor variables are used all of which correlate with the thing which is being predicted but prediction is bad if the things being measured are highly correlated with each other. Dynamic risk factors are described by Andrews and Bonta as being vulnerabilities without describing their relationship to the causes of offending. For example, Andrews and Bonta include in their list of dynamic risk factors the notion of antisocial personality but this is made up of many different forms of personality traits, behaviours and attitudes. Other authors defining dynamic risk factors also tend to provide a list of weakly associated aspects which may even be mutually exclusive – that is, they do not occur at the same time in the same person.

Ward argues that dynamic risk factors are not particularly well or consistently defined by researchers. There is also little clarity as to whether dynamic risk factors should be regarded as causal processes in offending or simply as a means of making predictions. Furthermore, there is a lack of clarity among practitioners as to how dynamic risk factors should be used in clinical assessments and treatment. Given the name, dynamic risk factors, it is notable that Serin, Chadwick and Lloyd (2016) mention that rarely are dynamic risk factors studied at two or more different points in time. Consequently, one could claim that dynamic risk factors are effectively being treated as if they are static risk factors. In other words, research has failed to capture the dynamic features of dynamic risk factors. These and other arguments all lead to the same conclusion according to Ward. That is, dynamic risk factors do not provide sound explanations of offending and should not be regarded as doing so. They are simply best regarded as predictive constructs which are of no more value than static risk factors. Researchers need to refrain from using dynamic risk factors as the basis for theories of offending. He suggests that postulating dynamic risk factors and placing offenders on programmes believed to treat these dynamic risk factors is not likely to work well. The problem is that this is to ignore key psychological features of each individual offender's situation. It replaces sound psychological interventions based on good knowledge of causal mechanisms with behavioural control strategies.

So what are the advantages of dynamic risk factors? One of the ways in which they are quite commonly used is to act as a substitute for recidivism measures in research on the effectiveness of treatment. Dynamic risk factors correlate with recidivism. So the research procedure is to look for changes in the dynamic risk factors as a consequence of treatment instead of changes in offending as a consequence of treatment. The extent to which this is convincing as a research methodology perhaps depends upon one's point of view but it does allow research on the effects of treatment without the high expense of carrying out a follow up to investigate differences in recidivism.

It is a not unreasonable assumption to think that dynamic risk factors add something on top of static risk factors when making predictions about reoffending. There is evidence that there is a relationship between sexual recidivism and dynamic risk factors according to Casey (2016). Dynamic risk factors include things like sexual preoccupation, any deviant sexual interest, offence supportive attitudes, emotional congruence with children and so forth (Casey, 2016). Such dynamic risk factors can be used as targets to be achieved in treatment despite it not being clear how they causally affect reoffending (Mann, Hanson and Thornton, 2010). Klepfisz, Daffern and Day (2016) argue that there is a lack of evidence to suggest that changes in the dynamic risk factors for violence are associated with reductions in recidivism violently. They argue that very few dynamic risk factors for violence that have been identified are truly dynamic. Actuarial risk assessment instruments based on static risk variables are thought to be effective in predicting recidivism by some because the static risk variables they employ actually map onto dynamic risk assessment variables – that is, the static variables are markers for dynamic risk variables (Beech and Ward, 2004). But how much is gained through the use of dynamic risk variables in addition to that attributable to static variables? The increase in variance explained by any additional dynamic risk factors is comparatively small or negligible according to some meta-analytic studies. Whether or not this matters depends on one's point of view. Durrant (2016) argues that there is evidence for the effectiveness of both static risk assessment measures and dynamic risk assessment measures. Different risk assessment tools seem to be more or less equally effective in predicting violent recidivism (Yang, Wong and Coid (2010). Furthermore, the evidence seems to suggest that risk assessment measures based on static risk assessment variables (including age, gender and criminal history) are at least as effective in predicting recidivism than those based on dynamic risk assessment variables and possibly better. Olver, Wong, Nicholaichuk and Gordon (2007) suggest that there is no point in trying to establish some incremental validity due to dynamic risk factors over static risk factors. They see the point of the dynamic risk factor as lying in helping the clinician plan the treatment for the offender. Just because all of the variance is taken up by static risk factors is irrelevant in this formulation. It is the informative nature of dynamic risk factors which is their contribution. If one adopts Ward and Beech's (2015) aetiological model then the joint aetiology of static and dynamic risk factors means that they share the same sources of variance anyway.

Some researchers are rather more optimistic about the potential of dynamic risk factors to develop sound theoretical accounts of offending. Thornton (2016), for example, argues that the *Propensities Model* is the dominant way of seeing dynamic risk factors in sexual offenders and that this model may be developed into well-founded theory. The Propensities Model basically regards dynamic risk factors as enduring propensities towards reoffending. The setting and events which occur determine whether or not the propensity will be activated. Offending is more likely to happen if relevant propensities are currently active and the environment permits them to influence reoffending. The model has drawbacks including: 1) that it assumes that the propensities are directly causal on reoffending though the evidence for this not discussed; 2) it omits from consideration the role of human agency in human action; and 3) it has no account of how propensities develop. The Propensities Model suggests that static risk indicators have predictive power since they reflect risk related propensities. That is to say, static risk indicators find their expression in dynamic risk indicators. This implies that in a study involving both static and dynamic indicators that controlling statistically for dynamic indicators should result in the static indicators losing their predictive power. The available research does not support this. Thornton argues that the

Propensities Model would be improved by incorporating elements from the *Good Lives Model* (see Box 27.4). For example, human agency could be included by understanding the individual's sources of motivation in terms of what they want and the nature of their decision making in terms of pursuit of these goals. This could incorporate the Good Lives Model which considers valued sources of motivation in terms of ways of achieving those ends when for some reason legitimate ways of achieving them are blocked. The sources of motivation or primary goods as they are described in the Good Lives Model include excellence at work and in play, inner peace, friendship, creativity, happiness, and community among others. How these are pursued is partly down to maladaptive ways of living one's life encouraged by things such as adverse childhood happenings, genetics, or the continuation of ways of doing things which may have been adaptive in childhood but are distinctly counterproductive in adulthood. Helping the offender see and utilize pro-social ways of achieving their goals provides them with a greater variety of resources to deal with life and their needs.

Perhaps more extreme in terms of the theoretical potential of dynamic risk factors is Polaschek's (2016) argument that there is an important connection between the ideas of dynamic risk factors and desistance from crime. His view is that reductions in dynamic risk may be associated with psychological aspects of desistance from crime. Desistance from crime is involved with protective factors against crime. There are three different definitions of protective factors. The first is in terms of being the reverse of a dynamic risk factors. Virtually all research has focused on this sort of definition although clearly this is not the entire picture. The second is that they are independent desistance promoting factors which does not have a linear relationship with offending. An example of this sort of protective factor is a high involvement in church. Others protective factors are things like emotional support, employment, intelligence, positive attitudes towards authority, social support, structured leisure, and stable living circumstances. The third is that a dynamic protective factor is a buffer – a factor that may not predict crime but which changes the relationship between risk factors and reoffending. Polaschek does not entirely explain how his ideas would work in practice. The most important thing to bear in mind, though, is the belief in dynamic risk factors relating to theory rather merely being useful ways of predicting recidivism.

Clinical judgement versus statistical assessment

There is a common consensus that there are two types of risk and dangerousness assessment. The first, perhaps the traditional form, as we saw earlier, is based on *clinical judgement*. It is generally held not to be successful. The second type is *statistical or actuarial assessment* and is held to be more successful by modern psychologists. The debate follows the pattern of Meehle's (1954) critique of the efficacy of purely clinical methods such as the interview. One needs to review the evidence with care before any final conclusions can be drawn on the best form of risk and dangerousness assessment. Figure 27.1 is a chart illustrating the complexity of risk and dangerousness assessment. Many factors need to be taken into account. The clear lesson is that the context and intentions of the assessment are a vital consideration in planning that assessment.

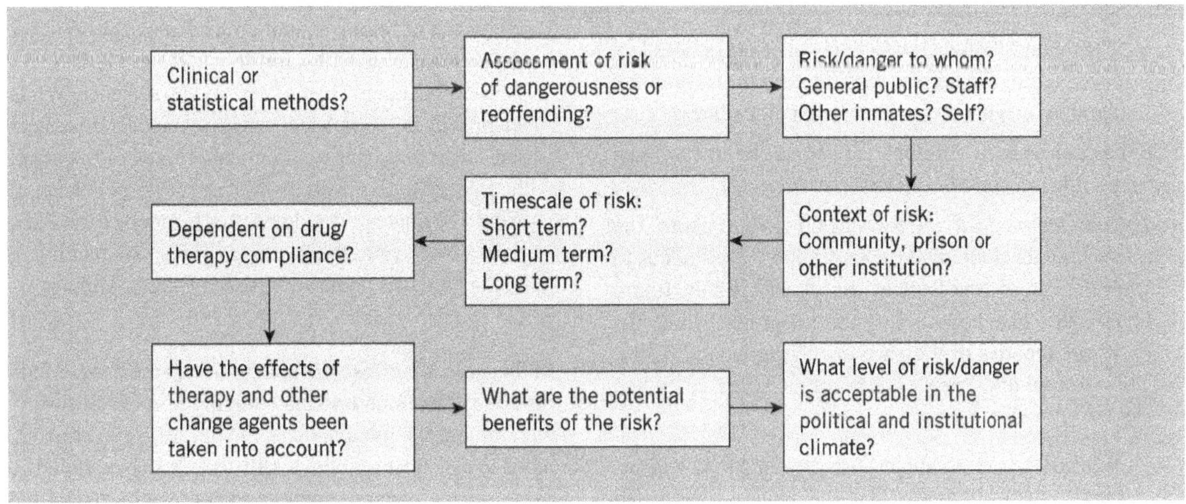

Figure 27.1 Aspects of the assessment of dangerousness

Clinical approaches in risk and dangerousness assessment

There have been a number of distinct clinical approaches to the assessment of risk and dangerousness (Limbandari and Sheridan, 1995). While they may not be frequently used by forensic psychologists it is helpful to be aware of these alternative approaches to assessment as recent work in the area of risk and dangerousness assessment has been largely psychometric in nature, employing structured assessment methods. The following more clinical approaches differ in terms of their tactics and scope as much as anything. Some of these approaches are described as clinically based prediction models. This means that they rely on the experience and skilled judgement of the psychiatrist, psychologist or therapist involved rather than empirical evidence favouring the prediction:

- *Linear model*: this is the simplest sort of model. It is based on a limited number of decision choices that can be represented as a flow diagram or a decision tree. The simplicity means that relatively inexpert personnel may use it. An example of this comes from the work of Gross, Southard, Lamb and Weinberger (1987). In the event of a threat to the safety of other persons made by the client, the therapist or other decision maker should go through the steps of the decision tree to decide the appropriate action or whether action is appropriate. One route through the decision tree under consideration would be:
  - Is there a clear (as opposed to a vague) threat?
  - Is there serious danger (as opposed to marginal danger)?
  - Is there a specific victim (as opposed to a non-identifiable victim)?
  - Is there an imminent danger (as opposed to no imminent danger)?
  - Is the threat to a public official (as opposed to family member/acquaintances or other person)?
  - The therapist should contact the police (as opposed to, say, warning the person, warning the family, or going through involuntary hospitalisation procedures).

Had the choices been different, then some clients might be recommended for family therapy.

- *Hypothetico-deductive model*: knowledge about the previous behaviour of the client allows a clinician to formulate hypotheses about the client's likely future behaviour. The hypotheses are integrated with, for example, theories of violence or other relevant theory. This inferential process becomes clearer when expressed with a concrete example:

  > While tightly clenching his fists, a young man tells his high school counselor that his grades plummeted because his girlfriend, whom he refers to in sexually derogatory terms, broke off their relationship. The counselor knows that this student has a history of frequent alcohol abuse and fighting on school grounds. The young man's father is in the Navy on an extended overseas assignment. The mother reports that her son refuses to accept her authority and that he has become difficult to manage in the absence of the father.
  >
  > (Gross *et al.*, 1987, p. 7)

  In this method, the clinician initially focuses on cues to the individual's behaviour to be found in the case history. Such possible clues include anger, rage, rejection and alcohol abuse. The combination of clinical theory and experience of similar clients might lead to the hypothesis that the client is depressed, full of feelings associated with being abandoned and out of control. Other important factors might include the observation that the location of the school is in an area noted for its high levels of violence. Say if this were confirmed by complaints by other students at the school, the indications are that there is a systematic problem with violence in the community which may lead to extra risk of the client's acting violently. In this example, the counsellor recommended:
  - the therapeutic confrontation of the young man's anger;
  - that the boy is not to take the same lessons or classes as the individuals against whom he had previously aggressed in order to minimise the risk of contact;
  - a counsellor–client contract in which the young man would agree to stay away from the girl and not to harm her in any way.

- *Risk assessment model*. This model (Gottfredson and Gottfredson, 1988) accepts the multi-dimensional nature of violence. Thus it is regarded not solely as a characteristic of the personality of an individual but also as the product of certain social and political climates. The following case study illustrates this approach:

  > convicted of felony assault on his former girlfriend, a 28-year-old male with a history of alcoholism is up for parole after serving half of a 12-month sentence. While in prison, he completed extensive alcohol treatment and anger management programs. On release from jail he intends to live with his mother. As the clinician, it would be imperative to know that his mother lives less than a block from the former girlfriend and that living in the mother's home are several alcoholic siblings.
  >
  > (p. 8)

- In this case, to release the man to live in the home of his mother is tantamount to encouraging him back towards alcohol and its attendant risks. After all, several of his alcohol-dependent siblings still live at home. Equally, the former girlfriend's residence is close to that of his mother, so enhancing the likelihood of future violence.

There is a general consensus in the literature that clinical inference based on case files and interviews is not a very powerful tool for assessing the probability of reoffending or the level of risk. Clark (1999) and Blackburn (1984) reviewed studies of this sort and suggest that clinical prediction is at best weak, and at worst totally ineffective. Particularly important is the research that found that even experienced clinicians failed to predict future violence in cases which would have readily been predicted from simple indicators such as previous recidivism. Not all evidence against clinical methods constitutes a fair test. In particular, studies requiring clinicians to predict outside of their domain of expertise (i.e. clinical matters) are unfair. For example, we should not expect a clinician to be able to predict educational achievement accurately since this stretches beyond their normal clinical experience.

Some structured clinical methods

Clinical assessments are not necessarily confined to the sorts of subjective impression implied by the critics. Blackburn (2000) stressed that the provision of guidelines to focus the clinician on crucial aspects of prediction can improve decisions. The apparent success of actuarial or statistical methods of prediction and the apparent failure of clinical prediction may mean several things (Hollin and Palmer, 1995; Palmer, 2001). One possibility is that we need better clinical measures of clinical variables to equal those of the statistical approaches. If clinical variables do not matter then this suggests that there are no individual differences among offenders that might affect their likelihood of reoffending. This seems most unlikely. Furthermore, it is difficult to believe that situational factors such as stress are not important in predicting violence in specific circumstances and that these are not easily incorporated into future predictions. The distinction is between the role of clinical variables and clinical judgement.

The following are some of the main predictive tools (see Figure 27.2).

Static-99 and Static-2002

Static-99 is a well-regarded, short, ten-item assessment tool which is simple to score and is cost-effective. It essentially combined two earlier scales – RRASOR and Structured Anchored Clinical Judgement (SACJ – min). Its ten items involve static, historical factors such as age and prior offences which are not generally alterable or manipulable or changed by therapy, for example. An improved version of this is Static-2002 (and Static-2002R) (Hanson and Thornton, 2003) which consists of 14 items organised into five subscales:

- age at time of release;
- persistence of sexual offending (e.g. measured by things such as number of occasions sentenced for sexual offences);
- relationship to victims (e.g. any stranger victims);

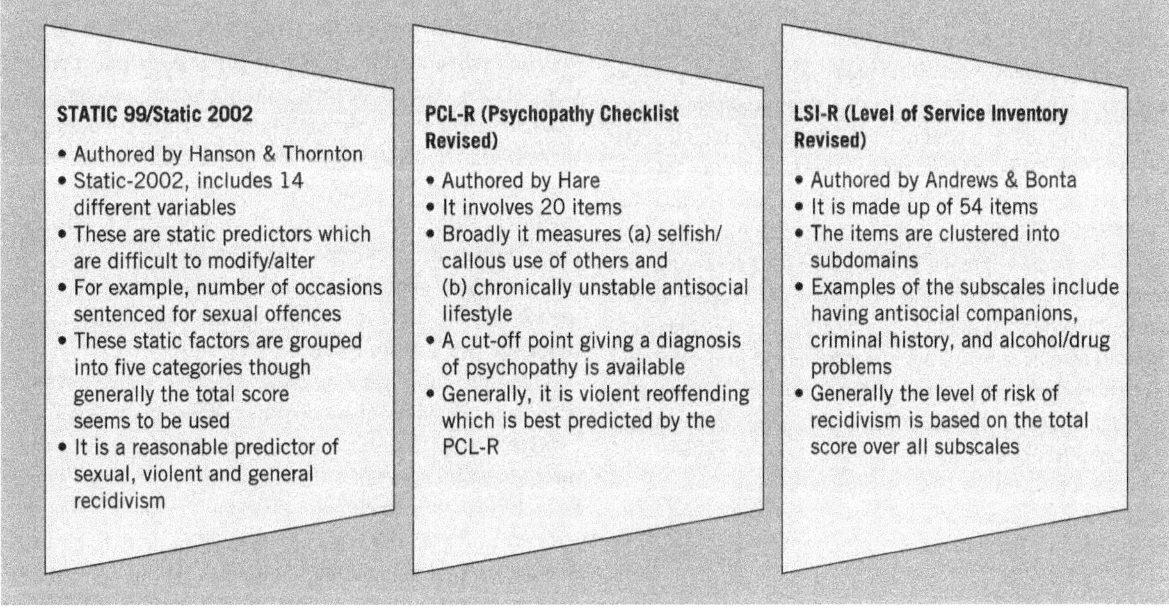

STATIC 99/Static 2002
• Authored by Hanson & Thornton
• Static-2002, includes 14 different variables
• These are static predictors which are difficult to modify/alter
• For example, number of occasions sentenced for sexual offences
• These static factors are grouped into five categories though generally the total score seems to be used
• It is a reasonable predictor of sexual, violent and general recidivism
PCL-R (Psychopathy Checklist Revised)
• Authored by Hare
• It involves 20 items
• Broadly it measures (a) selfish/callous use of others and (b) chronically unstable antisocial lifestyle
• A cut-off point giving a diagnosis of psychopathy is available
• Generally, it is violent reoffending which is best predicted by the PCL-R
LSI-R (Level of Service Inventory Revised)
• Authored by Andrews & Bonta
• It is made up of 54 items
• The items are clustered into subdomains
• Examples of the subscales include having antisocial companions, criminal history, and alcohol/drug problems
• Generally the level of risk of recidivism is based on the total score over all subscales

Figure 27.2 Some well-known structured risk assessment methods

- deviant sexual interests (e.g. any male victim, any young victim);
- general criminality (e.g. any prior involvement with the criminal justice system).

Based on the total score on the full 14 items, offenders are placed into five categories of risk ranging from low, through low-moderate, to moderate, to moderate-high, and high. Hanson, Helmus and Thornton (2010) present an analysis of the data from a range of studies into the validity of Static-2002 as a predictor of five- and ten-year recidivism rates. It was found that Static-2002 was successful at predicting sexual, violent and any recidivism. These predictions were marginally better than those based on Static-99. However, it was not possible to predict absolutely the level of risk from a Static-2002 score. Different samples varied in the scores needed to predict recidivism.

Psychopathy Checklist PCL-R

Good clinical measures seem capable of predicting reoffending: for example, the Psychopathy Checklist (PCL and PCL-R) (Hare, 1980, 1991) consists of 20 items. These include a component that may be described as 'selfish, callous and remorseless use of others'. Items reflecting this tap aspects such as superficial charm or glibness; grandiose sense of self-worth; pathological lying; manipulativeness; and failure to accept responsibility for one's actions. These characteristics reflect the psychopath – a type of offender known to be highly involved in persistent offending and reoffending. The other dimension is of a 'chronically unstable and antisocial lifestyle' which includes a need for stimulation; a parasitic lifestyle; poor behavioural controls; early behaviour problems; impulsivity; and juvenile delinquency. The Psychopathy Checklist is a good predictor of recidivistic tendencies in some areas. It may be as good as many purely actuarial measures of risk at predicting recidivism (Palmer, 2001), which is not surprising given that the checklist measures a wide range of criminogenic factors. There is a range of studies demonstrating that the Psychopathy Checklist is a robust indicator of recidivism. Sloore, Rossi and Hauben (2004), for example, found that 36 per cent of their sample of Belgian recidivists had a score which defined them as psychopaths on this measure. It should also be stressed that the clinician requires training before they can use it effectively. Generally the Psychopathy Checklist is used in the prediction of violence, for which it has a good track record.

Level of Service Inventory (LSI)

The Level of Service Inventory Revised (LSI–R) consists of 54 items in ten categories. Its purpose is both to help understand and predict criminality (Andrews, 1982; Andrews and Bonta, 1995, 2006). LSI-R assesses rule violation or deviant behaviours in an everyday context. The ten categories or subscales are:

- (antisocial) companions;
- attitude/orientations;
- accommodation;
- alcohol/drug problems;
- criminal history;
- education/employment;
- emotional/personal problems;
- finance;
- family/marital;
- leisure/recreation.

Not only are there individual subscales as defined by the above categories but they are combined into a total score which is relevant to the level of risk of recidivism. According to Andrews and Bonta, it is not possible to understand deviant behaviour unless one considers it alongside common, routine everyday behaviours. It has become clear that this inventory has the capacity to identify the heterogeneous patterns of specific needs for particular groups of offender. The different components of the LSI-R score are due to the offenders' special characteristics and the characteristics of the penal setting in question. Useful research findings on LSI-R come from research by Hsu, Caputi and Byrne (2009) involving a sample of nearly 80,000 Australian (New South Wales) offenders. Overall scores on the inventory were not related to gender, but the scores of females exceeded those of males on average for the finance subscale and the family/marital subscale of the inventory. The total score on the inventory was predictive of reoffending, though the largest correlation was for custodial female offenders and was only 0.2. Subscales such as criminal history, education/employment, and antisocial companions were predictive of reoffending for males whereas for female offenders the important subscales were education/employment, alcohol/drug problems, accommodation, antisocial companions and attitudes/orientations. It has to be pointed out, as the authors do, in fact, that these correlations indicate very moderate predictive power.

One intriguing question is the extent to which psychiatrists and psychologists can use their knowledge and expertise to compensate for any shortcomings that structured questionnaires like these may have. In other words, can clinical judgement complement the more objective strengths of structured questionnaires? Elkovitch, Viljoen, Scalora and Ullman (2008) studied this issue in terms of the judgements of graduate psychologists of the likelihood of reoffending by young offenders built on the data from structured risk assessment instruments. In this case, the SAVRY (Structured Assessment of Violence Risk in Youth) and J-SOAP-II (Junior Sex Offender Assessment Protocol) scales were completed by young offenders. The graduate raters who made the assessments of risk tended to agree strongly in their assessments. The male adolescent offenders who took part in the study were followed up for a minimum of 250 days in order to see whether they reoffended. Eighty per cent of them had sexually offended against another young person three years younger than themselves. Their recidivism was measured in terms of charges rather than convictions against them. The clinical judgements drawing on the assessment instruments were not predictive of sexual recidivism but neither were the structured questionnaires themselves. The measuring instruments did predict non-sexually violent offending but the clinical assessment based on these did not! Whatever clinical judgement was adding to the structured measures did not compensate in any way for their inadequacy at predicting sexual violence. Clinical judgement undermined the scales when predicting non-sexual violent recidivism. Even the confidence of the clinical assessor did not predict more accurate instrument-informed clinical judgements of risk.

Predictors may be specific rather than general

It is important to stress that predictors that are good for one sort of offence may be relatively poor at predicting recidivism for another sort of offence or using a different sort of prisoner group. Sjostedt and Langstrom (2000) carried out a study of *two* well-established measures associated with recidivism (the *Psychopathy Checklist Revised* and the *Violence Risk Appraisal Guide*). Their sample was a group of Swedish rapists diagnosed as having personality disorders. Follow-up was for an average of 92 months after release or discharge from prison or forensic treatment:

- The Psychopathy Checklist Revised (PCL-R), as we have seen, is highly regarded in predicting violent recidivism, and performed moderately well at predicting violent recidivism (of a non-sexual nature) in this sample. It predicted sexual recidivism badly. Similarly, the Violence Risk Appraisal Guide (VRAG) could predict violent recidivism (of a non-sexual nature). The VRAG includes additional assessment on a number of factors, such as: alcohol abuse history; evidence on record at the time of the index offence of schizophrenia or personality disorder; female victim of the index offence; maladjustment at elementary school; non-violent criminal offences before the index offence; previous failures of conditional release; separation from either parent under age 16 (except through death); and victim injury on a scale from no injury to death with mutilation.
- On the other hand, the PCL-R and the VRAG measures (see Harris, Rice and Quinsey, 1993; Rice and Harris, 1997) both failed to predict sexual reoffending. It was possible to predict sexual reoffending from another measure – the *Rapid Risk Assessment for Sexual Offender Recidivism* (RRASOR) (on which Static-2002 is partly based). This consists of just four variables:
  - any male victim of a sex offence;
  - extrafamilial victim of a sex offence;
  - offender is under 25 years old.
  - previous sexual offences.

The more of these characteristics the offender possesses, the greater the risk of sexual reoffending. Despite being good at predicting sexual reoffending, this measure fared poorly at predicting violent recidivism of a sexual nature.

Statistical or actuarial prediction

The statistical prediction of recidivism and dangerousness attempts to replace the subjectivity of clinical methods with empirically based prediction methods. The essential feature of this method is the availability of a database demonstrating the relationship between predictor variables and reoffending variables in a large group of offenders. To this ought to be added the use of a validation sample for use after the scale has been fine-tuned (see Figure 27.3). These predictor characteristics would include demographic variables such as age, criminal history, personality and similar factors. Reoffending would involve appropriate measures of recidivism, such as reconviction for a similar offence in a five-year period on release. The stronger the relationship between these predictor variables and recidivism, the more useful the predictor variables would be for predicting reoffending. The theory is fairly simple but, in practice, things are a little more complicated.

Basically, statistical prediction is founded on the assumption that a particular offender can be understood in the light of how other, similar offenders behaved. In this sense, the approach can deal only with the characteristics of recidivists that are common to a number of, if not all, offenders. It does not take into account totally individual factors which might lead to recidivism in an individual case. Table 27.1 gives a breakdown, which should help. It is similar to Table 16.1, the diagnosticity table. In predicting recidivism, particular signs are being used to identify

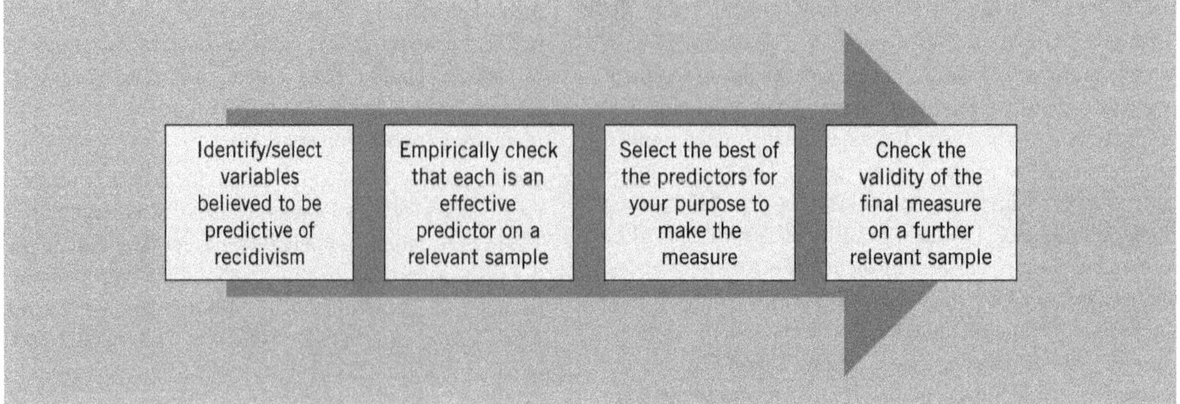

Figure 27.3 The key stages in constructing a recidivism prediction instrument

the recidivists. So in terms of Table 27.1, the assessment of recidivism should maximise true positives (accurate predictions of recidivism) and minimise false positives (inaccurate predictions of recidivism). The best predictions of (say) recidivism occur when that behaviour is to be found in half (50 per cent) of the group in question (Milner and Campbell, 1995).

This can be elaborated. Imagine that a researcher has developed a test of recidivism that is very accurate – say that it correctly classifies 90 per cent of recidivists as recidivists and 90 per cent of non-recidivists as non-recidivists. Imagine also that half of the sample of 400 offenders is recidivist:

- Then the recidivism test will correctly classify 90 per cent of the 200 recidivists (i.e. it will find 180 recidivists).
- By the same token, it will also classify 10 per cent of the non-recidivists as recidivists (i.e. 20 of the non-recidivists).

In other words, 180 of the recidivists are correctly identified at the cost of 20 of the non-recidivists being wrongly identified as recidivists (see Table 27.2). This is an impressive 'hit' rate.

But what, say, if recidivism were much less – 10 per cent rather than 50 per cent?

- The test remains 90 per cent accurate but because there are only 40 reoffenders then it will classify 36 of them as reoffenders and 4 of them as non-recidivists.
- It is just as accurate with the non-recidivists. Out of the 360 non-recidivists the test will select 36 as recidivists and 324 as non-recidivists.

In this case, the ratio of true positives to false positives is much poorer than in the previous example where the criterion of recidivism was to be found in half of the participants. In fact, as many non-recidivists as recidivists are identified as recidivists in these circumstances (Table 27.3).

Thus, unless recidivism is common, even the best tests are likely to make many mistakes. The general principle is that it is easier to predict relatively frequent events than uncommon events. Thus one is more likely to be able to predict cases of domestic violence than murder simply because the rates of domestic violence are nearer the optimum 50 per cent for accurate prediction.

Table 27.1 Predicting recidivism

	Reoffends	Does not reoffend
Shows predictive characteristics	True positive	False positive
Does not show predictive characteristics	False negative	True negative

Table 27.2 Theoretical accuracy in a sample of 200 recidivists and 200 non-recidivists using a 90 per cent accurate test

	Reoffends $N = 200$	Does not reoffend $N = 200$
Shows predictive characteristics	True positive 180	False positive 20
Does not show predictive characteristics	False negative 20	True negative 180

Table 27.3 Theoretical accuracy in a sample of 40 recidivists and 360 non-recidivists using a 90 per cent accurate test

	Reoffends $N = 40$	**Does not reoffend** $N = 360$
Shows predictive characteristics	True positive 36	False positive 36
Does not show predictive characteristics	False negative 4	True negative 324

BOX 27.2 Controversy

Why is clinical judgement bad at risk assessment?

The first major critique of clinical judgement in the prediction of behaviour was Meehle's (1954) examination of clinical versus statistical prediction methods. Assuming for the moment that this is the case, just why are clinicians so poor when making judgements? Dernevik, Johannson and Grann (2000) list some of the reasons:

- The diagnostic categories on which much clinical judgement is based (e.g. schizophrenia, affective disorder) are extremely broad. So allocating offenders to these categories does not say too much about their likely behaviour since, for example, schizophrenics are such a heterogeneous group.
- The ecological validity of the clinical judgement is important. One would not expect clinicians to make an accurate judgement of violent behaviours about which their experience and training have little to say. For example, they might be better at making predictions about the mentally ill (the usual location of psychiatry and clinical psychology) than the run of the mill offender with no particular or marked psychiatric characteristics.
- Human information processing, because of the limited capacity of short-term memory, means that we process information serially rather than in parallel. Thus very simple cues may be dwelt upon when we form our judgements.
- Biases: when making judgements we tend to stick with our initial assessments and do not make full use of new information. Furthermore, there is the issue of illusory correlation in which we assume that there is a correlation between two things if they appear to coexist. Thus, if we notice that children who are sexually abused turn up early for school, we may assume a relationship between the two which comparison with other children who have not been abused would also show.
- The sheer amount of information available for clinicians to review when making their judgements may be counterproductive.
- Experience does not necessarily increase the validity of clinical predictions. For example, the true positives in risk prediction may never come to the attention of the clinician again. Their feedback is more likely from the false negatives who are released but reoffend. In other words, the feedback loop is poor, with no certainty of useful information coming to the clinician's attention.

Of course, one has to consider the costs involved. From the point of view of an offender, the possibility that he or she will not be put on parole is a major cost; from the point of view of the public, the issue may only be keeping behind bars those likely to reoffend. If some prisoners are not given parole as a consequence then this is not a problem from this perspective.

Gretenkord (2000) demonstrates some of the advantages of preparing simple tables for assessing the likely rates of recidivism in a study of mentally disordered offenders. He carried out a study of men hospitalised in a forensic unit. Using complex statistical techniques (logistic regression) he was able to reduce his original list of predictors down to just four predictors of recidivism with a violent offence. These were:

- personality disorder (yes or no);
- violent pre-offence not included in the crime leading to present institutionalisation (yes or no);
- physical aggression during stay at the forensic hospital at least two times (yes or no);
- age at the time of discharge in years.

The worst prognosis by these criteria was for: the younger inmates – the group in their 20s; who also manifested a personality disorder; who had a violent previous offence in

Table 27.4 A simple prediction table based on Gretenkord's data

	Pattern of predictor variables							
	Has personality disorder				Does not have personality disorder			
	Violent pre-offence		No violent pre-offence		Violent pre-offence		No violent pre-offence	
	Aggression during treatment	No aggression during treatment	Aggression during treatment	No aggression during treatment	Aggression during treatment	No aggression during treatment	Aggression during treatment	No aggression during treatment
20 years	65%	36	39	16	37	15	17	6
30 years	52	25	27	10	25	9	11	4
40 years	38	16	18	6	16	6	6	2
50 years	27	19	11	4	10	3	4	1
60 years	17	6	7	2	6	2	2	1

Source: from Gretenkord, L. (2000) 'How to use empirical findings for the prognosis of mentally disordered offenders'. Paper presented at the Tenth European Conference of Psychology and Law, Limassol, Cyprus.

their records; and who manifested physical aggression during the course of their treatment in the institution.

Sixty-five per cent of these reoffended violently after release. In contrast, the likelihood of reoffending for a 60-year-old who did not have a personality disorder, did not have a violent pre-offence and did not show physical aggression during treatment was only 1 per cent. Gretenkord argues for simple contingency tables that allow the clinician access to data on probabilities. (See Table 27.4.) So, given the four contingencies known to predict violent reoffending, it is possible to predict the likelihood of recidivism for offenders showing every combination of the four predictors.

It should be noted that even Gretenkord's simple approach leaves a considerable margin for discretion (i.e. further decisions). It tells us only what groups are likely to reoffend, not which inmates should be released and which should not. That is a further matter for our judgement. Very rarely do researchers actually stipulate scores on predictors that can be used as cut-off points for decisions of this sort.

Predictive factors

It is important to note that the more precise the question asked, the more likely is statistical prediction to be effective. Consider the following:

- There may be better prediction if the type of offence is taken into account. For example, predictions of domestic violence against adults based on previous violence against adults may be better than predictions of domestic violence against children based on previous violence against adults.
- The time period of a prediction may affect its accuracy. For example, certain factors may predict the short-term or acute dangers posed by an individual but have little validity for predicting longer-term or chronic risks.
- The predictive factors for any sort of criminal activity will vary according to the crime in question, the precise circumstances and numerous other factors.
- The best predictors of a crime such as domestic violence have been broadly established.

They tend to be relatively mundane for the most part (Milner and Campbell, 1995):

- Mental illness is associated with domestic violence.
- Previous history: a person with a track record for domestic violence is more likely to act violently in the future.
- Substance abuse (drugs and/or alcohol) is predictive.

Similar lists may be possible for predictors of other types of recidivism. Furthermore, it is important to realise that even long-established predictors may only be moderately powerful. For example, Dowden and Brown (2002) surveyed 45 studies into the relationship between substance abuse and general recidivism – that is recidivism for any type of crime. Studies were included in their meta-analysis (see Box 4.1) if substance abuse was measured prior to the recidivism. This cuts down the risk that offenders will blame their recidivism on substance abuse as an easy excuse. In this study, general recidivism included things such as reconvictions, new charges and violations, say, of suspended sentence such that the offender has to serve his or her sentence as a consequence. Studies focusing on violent recidivism separately were excluded from this meta-analysis. The analysis showed that various substance abuse indicators correlated (had an effect size of) between 0.1 and 0.2 in general. Alcohol abuse had the lowest effect size, whereas a combined category which essentially assessed whether the offender had abused drugs or alcohol or both produced the largest effect size.

The use of a wider variety of predictors may increase the accuracy of predictions. Gresnigt *et al.* (2000) studied predictors of violent crime recidivism among Dutch prison inmates who were also drug users. The addiction severity index, cultural origin, level of education, duration of detention, diagnostic interval schedule and *DSM-III* classification were among the predictors. Classification as to the likelihood of future violent convictions was 82 per cent accurate using cultural origin, history of violent offences and property offences. It increased very moderately to 85 per cent when the diagnostic interview schedule was added. It reached 93 per cent when all these factors plus the addiction severity index were added in.

BOX 27.3 Forensic psychology in action

Convicted sex offenders back in the community

In many countries, a conviction for a sex offence can have long-term consequences for the offender after release from prison. Sex offenders are subject to a range of further controls on their return to the community – sex offender registration being just one example. Megan's Law (and similar initiatives outside the United States such as Sarah's Law in the United Kingdom) is founded on the belief that sexual offenders are dangerous and highly likely to reoffend. Megan Kanka was a seven-year-old who was abducted and murdered in 1994 by a convicted sex offender living near Megan's home in New Jersey. Megan's Law is US legislation about providing local communities with information about any sex offenders who may be living in the community. In the United States, sex offenders might have their home address, home telephone number, work address, vehicle description and licence plate number released to the community.

There are numerous studies identifying the characteristics of sex offenders who are the most likely to reoffend. In their meta-analysis (Box 4.1) of the relevant studies, Hanson and Morton-Bourgon (2005) found 82 relevant studies which involved sex offender recidivism after release from prison. Sex offenders sometimes reoffend with sexual offences but they also reoffend more generally. This was discussed in Chapters 9 and 10. The meta-analysis revealed that the major predictors of sexual recidivism over all of these studies were deviant sexual preferences and antisocial orientations. Antisocial orientation includes things such as antisocial personality, impulsivity, substance abuse, unemployment and a history of violating rules. Antisocial orientation was also the major predictor of violent recidivism and general recidivism. Some of the good and bad predictors of sexual recidivism are shown in Figure 27.4. As the bottom of the figure is reached, the predictors such as general psychological problems and clinical presentation have very small effect sizes (indicated by *d*). An effect size of 0.2 is often described as small, an effect size of 0.5 is medium, and an effect size of 0.8 is large. At best, the worthwhile predictors are small to medium. Importantly, many variables which

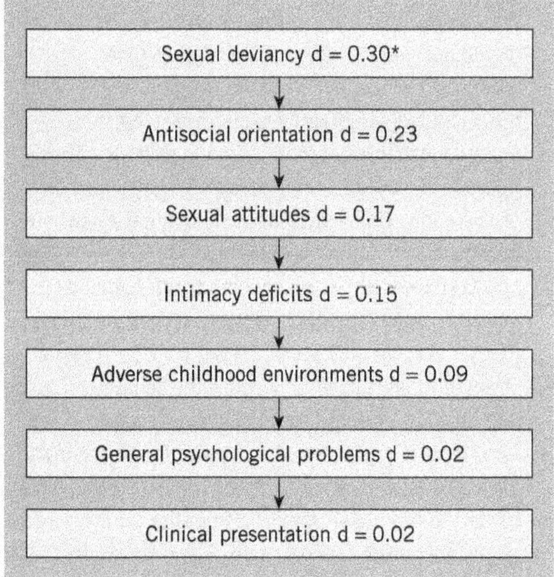

Figure 27.4 Some of the good predictors of sexual recidivism and some of the poorer ones

*A value of d = 0.2 is usually regarded as a small-sized effect and a value 0.4 a medium-sized effect

BOX 27.3 (continued)

are commonly focused on in treatment for sex offenders, such as denial of sex crime, victim empathy, motivation for treatment and psychological distress, show no useful association with sexual and violent recidivism. These characteristics are often regarded by clinicians as indicators of a poor prognosis. Freeman, Palk and Davey (2010) chose to investigate the attitudes of forensic psychologists to the effect of denial on risk assessment. A sample of 31 practising Australian psychologists varied considerably about whether denial should affect the assessment of risk for reoffending and whether it should affect suitability for supervised release into the community. That is to say, some forensic psychologists believe that denial is predictive of future behaviour whereas research seems to suggest that it is not.

Research on sex offenders highlights many of the issues when attempting to predict dangerousness and recidivism. Good examples of this are to be found in the work of Firestone *et al.* on Canadian sex offenders:

- Firestone, Bradford, McCoy, Greenberg, Curry and Larose (1998b) carried out a study of convicted rapists who were followed up for up to 12 years, with an average of 7.6 years.
- About half of these offenders had reoffended by the time they had been out of prison for five years.
- What crimes did they reoffend with? Only 16 per cent reoffended with a sexual crime. Rather more reoffended with a violent crime (26 per cent), though this included sexual crimes, and over a half reoffended with any sort of crime (e.g. theft). These figures are fairly typical in research in different parts of the world. This sort of figure is familiar elsewhere in the world for other sex offenders. In Germany, Egg (1999) carried out a ten-year study of recidivism in child molesters. About a half were reconvicted within that period, but only about 20 per cent for a sexual offence. Interestingly, only about the same percentage had previous convictions for sexual offences.
- According to Firestone *et al.*, prediction of recidivism for a sexual offence was not good. Sexual recidivists tended to have been removed from the family home under the age of 16 compared to non-recidivists. The use of phallometry (see Box 9.1) was not effective in determining the recidivists.

For a group of child molesters who committed their assaults outside the family, the reoffending figures were slightly lower, but with a similar overall pattern. The prediction of sexual recidivism in this group was weak. Only men who rated themselves higher on alcohol abuse, men rated higher on guilt and men who were sexually aroused by assaultive rather than consenting sex stimuli involving children (i.e. the paedophile assault index) showed a greater likelihood of reoffending.

- Incestuous-only (family abuse) offenders showed a different pattern still. They reoffended in any category much less than extrafamily offenders or rapists. Only 6 per cent had reoffended sexually at the end of the up-to-12-year period.
- Finally, Firestone, Bradford, Greenberg, Larose and Curry (1998a) attempted to differentiate homicidal (actual or attempted) child molesters from non-homicidal ones. Intrafamilial offenders were excluded. In Canada, sexual murders constitute only 3 per cent of killings and of these only 8 per cent involve the deaths of children. In other words, only about a quarter of 1 per cent of murders involve the sexual killing of children. These are rare events not particularly conducive to prediction. Many factors failed to differentiate between the homicidal and the non-homicidal offenders. Homicidal offenders tended to abuse complete strangers, whereas non-homicidal ones rarely did. Homicidal offenders rated themselves as having a more extreme history of violence and having had contact with a forensic psychiatrist. They tended to have higher sexual arousal on the phallometric assault index. The murderers had more extreme sexual involvement with children than the kissing and fondling that was more typical of the non-homicidal offenders.

One of the common criticisms of recidivism statistics is that they deal with reconviction rather than reoffending. That is, offenders may commit crimes which are simply not reported to the criminal justice system, hence the low recidivism. Falshaw, Friendship and Bates (2003) studied 173 offenders' records at a community-based sex offender treatment programme in the United Kingdom. The period at risk of reoffending covered by the study was a minimum of nearly four years. Two different national information sources were examined for data for each of the offenders: the Offender Index had information about reconviction for only about a third of the men for whom the Police National Computer had information. So recidivism rates may appear low simply because of problems in recording information on the databases. Another source of recidivism data was the therapy records of the programme's clientele which was collected in the course of the work of the programme itself. If this information is combined with the national information, then reoffending occurred in the at-risk period in 12 per cent of the clientele. Additional information was available from the project's records about known instances of the sorts of behaviours known to encourage reoffending – for example, waiting around a school gate as children were leaving for home. If this information is added into the measure of recidivism, then 21 per cent exhibited some form of recidivistic behaviour. This figure is between two and seven times higher than the information on the recidivism data on the national databases. Of course, whether these figures apply to offenders leaving prison is unknown.

It might be assumed that men diagnosed as paedophiles might be particularly prone to reoffending sexually. One particularly challenging and thought-provoking study (Moulden, Firestone, Kingston and Bradford, 2009) asked the superficially simple question of just how a diagnosis of paedophilia relates to the prediction of recidivism for a child molestation offence. However, just how does one define paedophilia for these purposes? Moulden *et al.* suggested four somewhat different ways of defining paedophilia in practice:

- The formal criteria for a diagnosis of paedophilia to be found in the psychiatric diagnosis manual *DSM-IV*. Moulden *et al.* used a psychiatrist's diagnoses based on this. In their study, each patient was interviewed by a psychiatrist who offered a *DSM* diagnosis of some sort. Of course, additional information was available to the psychiatrist about the criminal and psycho-social history of the offender.
- Phallometry can be used to identify a deviant sexual arousal profile (see Chapter 9). In this case, the measure was based on the degree of change in the offender's penis size when presented with sexually deviant stimuli auditorily. Among the sexual stimuli included were (a) child-initiated sexual activity; (b) child–adult mutual sexual activity; (c) non-physical coercion of child into sexual activity; (d) physical coercion of child into sexual activity; (e) violent sex with child; (f) non-sexual assault of child; (g) consenting sex with female adult; and (h) sex with female child relative (incest). Of course, phallometry may not be routinely available for clinicians to use.
- Moulden *et al.* used the non-standard approach of combining the above two measures. That is, one of their measures of paedophilia was a combination of the psychiatrist's diagnosis and a deviant phallometric result. The offender was therefore categorized as paedophilic if both the *DSM-IV* diagnosis was paedophilia and the phallometric assessment was in the top half of the distribution.
- Use of a scale designed to assess sexual interest in children. One notable scale of this sort is the *Screening Scale for Pedophilic Interest* (Seto and Lalumière, 2001) and this was employed by Moulden *et al.*

Participants were a sample of just over 200 adult male Canadians convicted of a contact sexual offence against a non-related child under 16 years of age. Recidivism rates were 23 per cent for sexual crime; 34 per cent for violent crime; and 46 per cent for any crime. Generally speaking, the prediction of recidivism controlling for the time at risk was unimpressive. Only the measure based on phallometry had reasonable predictive power for recidivism. This is supported by other studies (Hanson and Bussière, 1998; Hanson and Morton-Bourgon, 2004).

One might expect that, where sex offenders are monitored and controlled on release from prison, recidivism would be less likely. There is little point monitoring and controlling them otherwise. The idea that sex offenders should not live in close proximity to schools and nurseries is part of relapse prevention programmes, but also increasingly part of legal requirements in various parts of the world. Zandbergen, Levenson and Hart (2010) used a matched sample of recidivists and non-recidivists in Florida over a two-year period. The research question was simply whether offenders who lived close to schools and daycare centres/nurseries are more likely to reoffend than those who live further away. Proximity with other risk factors taken into account does not seem to contribute to sexual recidivism. According to the authors, a minimum of 30 states and many municipalities in the USA require registered sex offenders to live more than certain minimum distances from schools, parks, daycare centres, bus stops and similar places where children are commonly to be found. Sex offenders may intentionally live close to such locations but the financial circumstances of sex offenders due to unemployment means that they are more likely to live in densely populated parts of town where accommodation is cheaper, which also means that schools and other

BOX 27.3 (continued)

facilities are close together. In Florida, registered sex offenders on probation may be prohibited from living less than 1000 feet from schools and similar locations. Recidivism in this study was defined in terms of an offender having one conviction for a sex offence and who was rearrested for a new sex offence during the entirety of one year. The offender files were used to obtain a sample of non-recidivists. A number of variables such as age; race; marital status; number of prior offences; number of prior sex offences; victim's age category (or previous victims were used in the case of recidivists); predator/offender status; and residential address were recoded into simple categories which could be used for matching. Only for schools was a recidivist/non-recidivist difference found in terms of numbers of schools within a 1000-ft buffer zone. There was no difference for the other types of location where children are commonly found.

Release of prisoners imprisoned for serious violent and/or sexual crimes is problematic. Traditional risk-assessment methods may not accurately predict those who will go on to reoffend. There are likely to be available packages of monitoring and support which, to some extent, are geared to the individual offender's level of risk. Arrangements will be different from country to country, but in the UK the statutory procedures for this are referred to as MAPPA (Multi-Agency Public Protection Arrangements). These are managed by the police and prison/probation authorities but involve additional support from other services, such as social, housing, education, and health. The aim is to mitigate risk of reoffending as far as is possible by dealing with criminogenic needs while at the same time looking for signs of problems which may need intervention. Among the categories of offender who are included in the MAPPA supervision process are all registered sex offenders; violent offenders with mental health problems; and offenders at imminent risk of reoffending because they make threats to kill or kidnap, for example. The aim, of course, is to minimise reoffending. Those with higher risks of reoffending are reviewed very regularly as part of this system. An important part of the system is offender registration, which is a long-term – if not life-long – requirement. The British statutory arrangements did not involve a 'Megan's Law' style element of compulsory notification of communities where there were sex offenders in their midst. After many years of resistance, Sarah's Law arrangements came into force, allowing community notification. Sex offender registration requires sex offenders to keep the police informed about their current address and places severe limits on their foreign travel, for example. The available evidence seems to suggest that these are effective since UK figures indicate that 93 per cent of offenders register their whereabouts (Expert Law, 2003). Rates of serious sexual or violent offences for offenders on a MAPPA programme seem low. In a year in which there were 25,000 offenders on the register, only 26 committed a serious sexual or violent offence (*Daily Telegraph*, 2004). However, this does not mean that every system of this sort is equally effective.

Much of the available research on sex offender registration and community notification is from the USA. The first sex offender registration law there was passed in California in 1947. Since then, similar legislation has been enacted in many states and countries though the form may vary, as we have already seen. The initial thinking was largely that offenders might be deterred from offending if they knew that they could readily be tracked down by the police because they had registered their whereabouts. Thinking has changed since then and informing the public about sexual offenders living in the community became an alternative strategy. In other words, it is important to distinguish between 1) sex offender registration laws and 2) sex offender notification laws. They are not necessarily the same thing though, of course, both can operate in any given locality. Much of the initiative came in the 1990s after a number of high-profile cases and campaigns resulted in a flurry of new legislation. In 1989 Jacob Wetterling was kidnapped by a suspected sex offender while biking with his brother and a friend. This led, in the US, to legislation actively monitoring released sex offenders.

So, given the number of high-profile sex offence cases which fill our newspapers, just what is the effectiveness of sex offender registration and other legal initiatives? Is the UK success matched elsewhere? This involves a slightly complex answer and a number of research strategies. Maurelli and Ronan (2013) carried out a time series analysis of the influence of sex offender notification laws on the pattern of forcible rapes across all states in the USA over the period 1960–2008. The different states enacted legislation at different times and in slightly different forms. This provided the opportunity to see what happened to the level of sex offences following the introduction of new legislation. The data on forcible rape came from the FBI's Uniform Crime Reports. The researchers compared the rates of forcible rape prior to sex offender registration laws with the rates afterwards in each state. The findings were that 17 states showed reductions in these offences following the introduction of sex offender registration, but 32 of the states showed no measurable change. Thus the trend is for reductions in sex offending overall but no change is actually the dominant pattern. Part of the reason for the failure of some states to show benefits from registration is that there are a range of different notification practices, registration procedures and so forth. Furthermore, changes in legislation may happen at the same time as other changes in terms of policy. For example, if introducing registration is accompanied by a move to make sex offender treatment more available then this may partly explain the apparent effects of registration legislation. And, of course, the impact of increasingly punitive sentencing may also be part of the total equation.

In a rare study of *offenders'* responses to community notification laws in the United States where community notification is common, it was found that over two-thirds of offenders believed that this was an incentive for them not to reoffend (Elbogen, Patry and Scalora, 2003). So, in a sense, modern criminal justice system practices will change the meaning of recidivism statistics for the simple reason that sex offenders are not simply released back into the community with little by way of support. Instead, their situation is addressed by a variety of agencies and their activities monitored for signs of possible recidivism.

The basic question is whether sex offender registration actually affects sex offender recidivism. There is a secondary question of whether the other procedures for monitoring sex offenders are effective. As we have just seen, the answer to the second question is quite positive as far as the situation in the United Kingdom is concerned. It is not clear that registration in itself necessarily reduces offending. The accuracy of offender registers can be fairly poor in the US and studies have shown that as few as half of registered offenders have their current address accurately recorded. Furthermore, different states have differing rules on whether a sex offender is required to go on a sex offender register and courts have varying amounts of discretion about whether it is required in a particular case. Levenson, D'Amora and Hern (2007) surveyed 239 sex offenders in Connecticut and Indiana about the negative consequences of sex offender registration. They were invited to complete a survey about the influence of sex offender policies on their reintegration into the community. Amongst the findings were:

- 10 per cent said they experienced physical assaults;
- 46 per cent said that they were afraid for their own safety because of Megan's Law;
- 50 per cent said they had lost friends or a close relationship because of Megan's Law;
- 54 per cent said that they felt alone and isolated because of Megan's Law;
- 58 per cent said that the shame and embarrassment due to Megan's Law stops them from engaging in activities;
- 62 per cent said that recovery was more difficult because Megan's Law causes stress in their lives.

According to Levenson *et al.*, research suggests that job loss, threats and harassment, property damage, and the suffering of other household members were the commonest negative outcomes identified in this sort of research. Fewer experienced housing problems and physical violence as a consequence of community notification. However, there is generally no difference between sex offenders on the register and sex offenders not on the register in terms of sexual recidivism. In other words, there is a lack of clear evidence that sex offender registration works.

In Minnesota, failure to register as a predatory offender is the most common form of recidivism for a sexual offence! Duwe and Donnay (2010) studied offenders released from Minnesota prisons between 2000 and 2004 when the first 'failure to register' prisoners were beginning to be released. They concentrated on whether a 'failure to register' offence (or a history of 'failure to register' offences) was predictive of sexual, general and 'failure to register' (or FTR) recidivism. A quasi-experimental design was used, in which offenders with and without a previous 'failure to register' conviction were compared. The follow-up period for recidivism was a minimum of three years.

'Failure to register' offenders were different from other non-FTR offenders in a number of ways, including: 1) longer criminal histories; 2) less likely to have had had treatment in prison; 3) less well educated; 4) less likely to have used force; and 5) less likely to have victims from a variety of age groups. The researchers controlled for a number of factors such as prior criminal history, time at risk of recidivism, and so forth. It was found that, with such control variables taken into account, a current or prior 'failure to register' conviction

BOX 27.3 (continued)

was *not* predictive of sexual recidivism. In this particular study, neither was there any evidence that failure to register was associated with other, non-sexual recidivism. However, there was an elevated risk of a further 'failure to register' offence in offenders with a current or past 'failure to register' offence.

Juvenile sex offenders are increasingly included in legislation dealing with sex offender registration. In some jurisdictions which have sex offender registration legislation, there is some discretion over whether or not an offender goes on the register. Caldwell and Dickinson (2009) took a group of registered and another group of unregistered juvenile sex offenders. Registered youth had lower risk scores on standard measures but registered and unregistered youth were charged with new crimes at much the same rates. Some have suggested that registration could be criminogenic by creating barriers to employment and community reintegration, leading to offenders having unstructured time on their hands and possibly new offending. Caldwell and Dickinson (2009) concluded that sex offender registration for juvenile offenders is ineffective as a means of reducing recidivism.

Much the same outcome was found in Letourneau, Bandyopadhyay, Armstrong and Singha's (2010) study, despite adopting a very different type of methodology. They studied sexual offence registration and juvenile sex crime in South Carolina. They subjected juvenile sex crime data to a trend analysis over the period 1991–2004. Juvenile sex crime registration was introduced in 1995 and online registration was allowed in 1999. Superficially, the data seemed to suggest that the policy was having a deterrent effect on first-time juvenile sex crime. However, it emerged that exactly the same trend was appearing for first-time robbery, which, of course, does not result in sex offender registration. The researchers interpreted the data as being the result of changes in 1995 which moved the court location for 16-year-old offenders to the adult courts meaning that fewer went through juvenile court. These researchers also concluded that sex offender registration for juveniles has no deterrent effect. They suggest that in order for a deterrent effect to happen, juvenile offenders would have to go through several stages in their reasoning, as shown in Figure 27.5. These stages seem very unlikely.

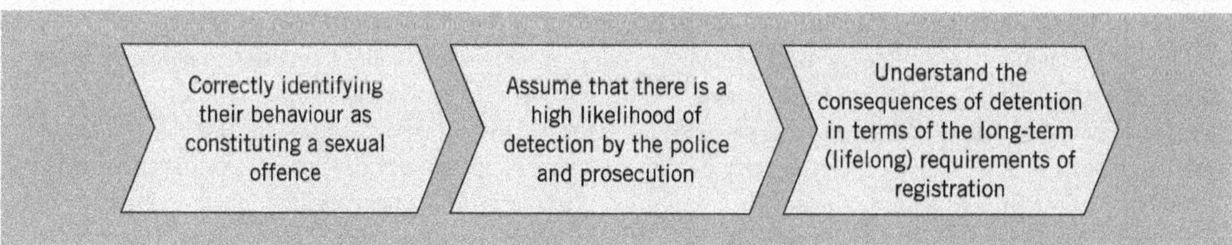

Figure 27.5 The unlikely steps in a juvenile sex offender's thinking which would lead to a deterrent effect of sex offender registration and notification laws

Issues in the assessment of risk and dangerousness

There are a number of issues associated with the assessment of risk and dangerousness that should be highlighted, some of which have already briefly been mentioned (Clark, 1999; Monahan and Steadman, 1994):

- The assessment of risk is different from the assessment of dangerousness. The assessment of risk (of occurrence) involves predicting how likely it is that the individual will commit another crime in the future. Dangerousness is more about the level of the danger or adverse consequences to the victim of such a crime. Thus an offender might be adjudged to be greatly at risk of reoffending, but that offence is likely to be no more than getting involved in a modest brawl. On the other hand, a person may have a low risk of reoffending but, if they do, very serious consequences are expected for the victim.
- Along with the assessment of risk and dangerousness should go planning to safeguard others in the light of the level of risk and dangerousness. For example, if there is no option but to release an offender from prison, what is the point of a careful risk and dangerousness assessment? On the other hand, while the individual remains in prison, risk and dangerousness

may be helped, say, by placing the offender on an anger management programme.

- Risk and dangerousness are not fixed parameters but will change with context and the passage of time and they should be regarded as such in any assessment.
- There is no single risk factor and consequent likelihood of risk. There are many possible risk factors that need to be understood. Information is also needed on the extent to which these can be found in different contexts of risk. So, for example, a prisoner may be much more at risk of offending violently in prison if sharing his cell with a violent fellow prisoner than if, on release, he goes to live with his mother in isolation.
- Different risk factors have different proven levels of influence on the future behaviour of an offender. Well-established risk factors such as previous recidivism should be given greater weight in decision making than a speculative factor such as that the man has taken up a new hobby or interest.
- There is no evidence that it is possible to predict serious criminal violence by individuals who have not already committed a violent act (Harris and Rice, 1994): in other words, the very group of individuals one needs predictions about the most.
- The criterion to be predicted needs careful consideration, as many variants are possible. Gretenkord (2000) illustrates the importance for the rates of reoffending of the criteria for deciding what is reoffending. His was a sample of mentally disordered males in a German forensic hospital who had largely committed violent physical or sexual crimes against other people. After discharge from this hospital for the average period of eight years, 44 per cent had reappeared on the German crime register. This included minor offences, such as riding on a bus without paying the fare. Thirty per cent had to return to prison or a forensic hospital. Thirteen per cent committed a violent or sexual offence. Quite clearly, the rate of reoffending is substantially determined by the criteria employed.

Quite good predictions of reoffending can be obtained from relatively straightforward indicators. A good example of this is the British study that involved a ten-year follow-up of a representative sample of men convicted of sexual offences and sentenced to at least four years in prison (Clark, 1999). This classified higher-risk offenders as the men who had any of these characteristics: a current or previous conviction for a non-sexual violent assault, four or more previous convictions for any offence, or a previous conviction for a sexual offence. Lower-risk men were those who showed none of these four features. The high-risk groups showed considerable recidivism in the 10 years after release. A quarter were reconvicted for a sexual offence (but only 1 in 20 of the low-risk group) and nearly a half for a sexual or violent offence (but only 1 in 8 of the low-risk group).

Sometimes offenders approach forensic services about the risk that they will sexually offend against children, despite having no history of such offending. Are current risk assessment methods appropriate to evaluate such individuals? Duff and Willis (2006) present a single case study of a man in his early twenties without a previous criminal record who was referred by the probation service which was dealing with him because of a charge of domestic violence. His partner was younger than him and was only 15 years of age when their relationship started – though he denied that there was sexual intercourse before she was 16. Although he had never actually offended against a child, he described sexual fantasies involving children, did a certain amount of grooming, identified locations suitable for offending, and manifested a distrust of women. He also thought that he might sexually offend against a child in the future, though he indicated that, as soon as he got to know a young child his sexual interest in them declined. He had a collection of children's television videos and pictures from catalogues. Most forensic risk assessments are based on the assumption that there is a relevant offence history. This leaves us with the unanswerable question of just what risk this man posed.

See Box 27.4 for a discussion of an approach to offender rehabilitation which goes beyond the management of risk.

Box 27.4 Key concept

The Good Lives Model of offender rehabilitation

Offender rehabilitation is generally conceived largely in terms of risk management. But there are other ways of looking at it. The Good Lives Model (GLM) provides one such alternative approach to offender rehabilitation which is basically a holistic approach to enabling the offender to achieve their life goals in a prosocial rather than criminal way. By building on the strengths and capabilities of the offender, it is possible to reduce their risk of reoffending. The risk management approach, in contrast, seeks to counter the risks the offender poses. The Good Lives Model was

BOX 27.4 (continued)

developed in a series of papers by Ward (e.g. Fortune and Ward, 2013; Ward and Fortune, 2013; Ward, 2002; Ward and Brown, 2004; Ward and Marshall, 2004; Ward, Gannon, and Mann, 2007). The GLM approach is basically a theory of what all people do in their lives. It sees people as agents in achieving what for them are valued outcomes in life. Our upbringings involve our parents, teachers, and the community in general helping to provide us with the means by which we can achieve successfully lived lives. All people share basic needs and inclinations in life; they are predisposed towards certain life goals which the GLM refers to as *primary goods*. This is true for criminally inclined individuals as much as the rest of society. The difference is that criminally inclined individuals commit crime in the process of trying to achieve their goals (i.e. primary goods). The offender has personal and environmental deficits/weaknesses which mean that their valued outcomes in life are sought in harmful, antisocial ways. For example, achieving a sense of being part of the community – a very human desire – by being a gang member with a violent, aggressive persona represents a very human goal achieved in ways unacceptable to society. In other words, the criminally inclined individual uses maladaptive ways of achieving things which other people can achieve prosocially.

So interventions must do more than manage or remove problems by restricting behaviour: they must enhance the offender's personal functioning. This can be done by providing them with the repertoire of strengths and personal skills as well as opportunities which allow them to live their lives in the way they plan and to achieve their valued life-goals. The GLM approach to rehabilitation works with the characteristic of the offender which may be enhanced to result in a crime-free life – it embraces the offender's aspirations and abilities.

An individual's way of living and their life plans may manifest clear problems. Rehabilitation needs to be tailored to the individual with their own particular skills, preferences, capacities and opportunities. The aim would be to enable the offender to achieve their most important primary goods in socially acceptable ways. This involves a focus on both the internal factors such as the individual's values and priorities in life and the external resources and opportunities which are needed. The basic ideas underpinning the Good Lives Model are those of human dignity and human rights. Humans are seen as the agents of their own actions – that is, we all have agency – we act in a purposive way to achieve things. We put together plans and actively implement them. Our goals are desired because they enhance our personal sense of well being when we achieve them. They are, therefore, intrinsically rewarding and desirable for their own sake. These goals include states of mind (e.g. peace of mind, pleasure) and personal characteristics (e.g. excellence at work and in leisure/play) which Ward and Brown (2004) and Ward and Marshall (2004) call primary goods. We can add the sense of agency; the sense of relatedness to other people (such as romantic, family, community); being well-informed; and spirituality. Each of us would weight these different primary goods differently. There are three clusters of goods – body, self, and social life. We all fulfil a range of roles in life, including parent and child; our work role defined by our job; and our leisure roles defined primarily by our recreational pursuits. Quite clearly, these different roles provide different opportunities in terms of achieving valued goals.

In order to reach an outcome or goal, we need means of doing so. Primary goods are achieved through instrumental or secondary goods. Obtaining a university degree, for example, is one way of achieving knowledge goods. Joining a football team is part of the process of achieving excellence in sport, but it also may help achieve the sense of belonging to the community. It should be obvious that these instrumental or secondary goods are examples of activities which are not risk factors for crime and, furthermore, are basically incompatible with dynamic risk factors for crime. They are more like protective factors. The more deficiencies that the individual and their environment have, the more likely it is that a barrier is formed preventing the individual achieving their primary goods – their way of life as they would like it to be. In other words, criminogenic needs amount to deficiencies in the individual or their environment. Because of the barriers they create, the individual cannot convert their personal strengths and abilities into primary goods, so they attempt to achieve them through illegal or deviant means. Thus an individual with a poor capacity to regulate their emotions may be unable to achieve inner peace.

The GLM model claims that there are number of ways in which problems arise of the individual's life plan. Remember that the individual's lifestyle actually reflects aspects of their values. They may be living their life in a way which does not reflect their ideal. These problems can be classified into four categories – capacity, coherence, means and scope:

- *Capacity*: These may be internal to the person or external to the person. Internal capacities are things such as skills and the ability to secure primary goods. Support needs to focus on acquiring or enhancing the necessary skills. There may be any of a number of barriers such as the lack of knowledge or intellectual ability or a psychological lack of self-belief. External capacity includes things like the availability of employment opportunities, the quality of the individual's social support network, and the availability of training and education. There are numerous barriers created externally. For example, there may be a lack of social support in the family or community for knowledge goods – for example, a generally negative response to attending college and university. Professional encouragement may reduce the impact of such barriers.

- *Coherence*: Primary goods need to exhibit a harmonious pattern and interrelate coherently. Otherwise difficulties can arise. These may be described as problems of horizontal coherence between the primary goods. A good example is where the primary goal of agency potentially conflicts with other primary goals. The individual who wants always to do things their own way may have problems working with others in work and other environments. In such environments the individual needs to accommodate to the wishes of other people. Failure to do so may, in some circumstances, block the individual from achieving excellence in work. For example, it may result in conflict with others or even more direct harm to others – such as when the individual ignores the instructions of their manager. However, the same individual may function well in self-employment. Goals not only have to be compatible but they also need to be prioritised. That is, there is a vertical dimension to coherence which needs to work effectively. We need to understand what is most important to us and behave accordingly. For example, if excellence at work and romantic relationships are seen to be equally important then problems may arise. One or other may suffer and result in a range of difficulties. Turning to alcohol, for example, as a way of coping may result in all sorts of ill-judged behaviours which may result include criminal ones.
- *Means*: Primary goods are normally achieved through any number of appropriate means. However, some may use inappropriate means of achieving their primary goals. These may make it impossible to achieve the goods or truly benefit from the goals. Take, for example, an individual who wishes to secure promotion or get chosen at an interview for an important job. There are appropriate ways of achieving the sense of excellence in the work environment, such as adding to one's work qualifications or building up a wide portfolio of working in a variety of capacities. But there are also inappropriate ways of doing so. Fraudulently claiming to have qualifications which one has not achieved is one such inappropriate means.
- *Scope*: The GLM assumes that everyone will strive for all of the primary goals at some level. Failure to do so indicates a lack of scope. This may manifest itself in a number of ways, such as physiological disfunctions, psychological distress, or social maladjustment leading to unhappiness. One reason for the lack of scope is the lack of capacity in some form. For example, someone who lacks interpersonal skills may have difficulties in achieving excellence in primary goals such as relatedness to others and the community. They may also have problems in achieving work excellence or play excellence where they involve interaction with others. The result may be unhappiness and poor psychological functioning.

It should be fairly evident that professional support needs to be built upon a thorough and detailed knowledge of the individual's valued activities and experiences in their day-to-day life. This knowledge is obtained through extensive and careful questioning. In other words, the first stage is to understand just how the offender construes what a good life would be like for them. The question then is just how their goals and values were manifested in the happenings which led to the offence. The secondary goods which provide means for socially acceptable ways of achieving the primary goods need to be explored. This is done in collaboration with the offender. The intervention may involve building on the individual's capacities and skills and also on the available environmental resources. Criminogenic needs which are blocking the achievement of primary goods also need to be addressed.

Offence paralleling behaviour

Of course, there are always concerns about the adequacy of risk assessments. This has led to the search for other methods of assessing risk which involve a more complete criminal justice system approach to risk assessment in which all of the information available can be incorporated into risk assessment. Behaviour within the institution is an example of this sort of additional information. The term *offence paralleling behaviour* is becoming increasingly familiar in clinical recidivism assessment – especially in decisions about release. Release from an institution is usually dependent on the following:

- the results of a structured or similar risk assessment measure;
- the results of a clinical assessment of progress in therapy and other forms of treatment;
- the individual's behaviour within the institution.

Certain changes in the offender's behaviour – such as improvements in prosocial behaviours and attitudes – are considered positive signs in favour of release. These are regarded as reducing the likelihood of future violent behaviour. On the other hand, aggressive and violent behaviours against members of staff would be negative signs. Increasingly, it is being accepted that if institutional behaviour patterns are similar to the offender's main offences in the past then this indicates a higher risk of reoffending (Jones, 2004). These matched patterns inside and outside of the institution are called *offence paralleling behaviour* (OPB). The basic problem is, of course, just how one decides that institutional and pre-institutional behaviours parallel each other. This would require a minimum of two things:

- Criteria to be used to describe the institutional and pre-institutional behaviours;
- Ways of saying just what the similarity is between the pre-institutional behaviour (i.e. major offences) and institutional behaviour.

Daffern, Howells, Mannion and Tonki (2009) believe that the criteria of similarity should reflect their functional similarity rather than superficial resemblances. That is, the acts should serve similar purposes. So simple characteristics such as the gender of the target of the pre-institutional and institutional behaviours are probably not useful since, for example, violent/aggressive behaviour is most common between males. Using superficial criteria such as these means that common aspects of violence and aggression are likely to manifest themselves in the institutional setting – and they are unlikely to change. But, despite this, the functions of violent/aggressive behaviour for the individual may have been changed quite considerably under the influence of therapy, for example. So it is questionable whether the study by Mooney and Daffern (2015) would meet the requirements of offence paralleling behaviour. They merely tried to predict violent recidivism outside of prison from the number of violent disciplinary offences a sample of violent offenders committed in prison. There was a relationship in that offenders with multiple offences in prison were more likely to offend violently outside prison. However, no investigation was made of the functional similarity between the violent events.

Among the characteristics of the pre-institutional and institutional behaviours that Daffern *et al.* (2009) consider important in a functional analysis of an offender's behaviour are the following:

- cognitive antecedents to the events, such as the belief that one's emotional needs will never be met and the expectation that one will be abused or mistreated by others;
- distal and proximal environmental triggers for the violence;
- function of the violent behaviour (e.g. social distance reduction, to observe suffering etc.);
- psycho-physiological activation such as calm–tense/irritable, passive/tired and active/energetic;
- type of weapon used;
- victim characteristics (e.g. was victim an acquaintance, friend, intimate or stranger).

All of these and others are part of the structured aggressive behaviour analysis schedule (SABAS) which the researchers developed to assess functionally the behaviours of the offender outside and inside the institution.

The structured aggressive behaviour analysis schedule provides the criteria by which functional similarity of behaviours could be recorded. So how is this turned into measures of similarity between pre-institutional and institutional behaviours? Daffern *et al.* used several approaches to the data they had collected concerning men in a high-security personality disorder service unit in the UK who were high-risk violent and sexual offenders. These approaches included:

- A clinical psychologist rated the functional similarity measures in terms of their similarity (from 'not similar', through 'some similarity', to 'very similar'). Using this, 50 per cent of incidents involving the men in the unit were rated as not at all similar to the pre-institutionalisation index offence; 38 per cent were rated as similar; and 11 per cent were rated as very similar.
- A count of the similarity of features between the index offence and the institutional pattern in terms of the SABAS schedule. The two were considered similar if a certain number of features (four) were found to be shared. Sixty-five per cent of the pairs of SABAS schedules met this criterion of similarity.

What is one to make of these findings? Irrespective of the method used to assess similarity, the essential trend seems to be for there to be some association between institutional aggression patterns and pre-institutional (index offence). At the same time, there were some individuals for whom there was a fairly strong relationship and others for whom the relationship was weak or imperceptible. The implication may be that the offence paralleling behaviour may only be relevant to those cases where it is possible to establish that offence characteristics and characteristics shown within the institution are very similar. In these circumstances, a change in pattern may be of considerable clinical importance. For individuals who fail to show stability in their patterns, then the application of offending paralleling behaviour approaches could be very misleading.

Although not couched in the framework of offence paralleling behaviour, the research of Heil, Harrison, English and Ahlmeyer (2009) is of more than passing interest in this context. Is it possible, they asked, to predict future sex offending in the community and violent behaviour more generally on the basis of sex offences committed in prison? The researchers formed four groups of male sex offenders from offenders sentenced in Colorado: 1) offenders with community sex crime convictions; 2) community sex offenders convicted under non-sex-crime charges where somewhere on record was information about sex crimes; 3) offenders known only to commit sexually abusive misconduct in prison; and 4) offenders with both community and prison sex offences. Prison sex offenders generally produced the greatest evidence for recidivism a year and five years after release. They were particularly prone to violent offences but also to sexual offences. The prison plus community sex offenders had the highest rates of hands-on sex offences after release. Prison sex offenders were more likely to be arrested for violent offences on release. Their level of risk was much the same as that for convicted sex offenders in terms of arrests for sex offences but their average time before getting arrested was shorter. After five years from release, the prison-only group still showed the highest levels of violent recidivism (see Figure 27.6).

The ADViSOR project was set up in the United Kingdom in order to better appreciate the potential of prison behaviour monitoring for improving monitoring and supervision in the community. The study by McDougall, Pearson, Willoughby and Bowles (2013) evaluated this project. One particular prison was the focus of the work, which involved a group of prisoners who would be released into the MAPPA system the next year being monitored by prison officers in terms of behaviours which might be associated with problems after release into the community. (MAPPA is discussed in more detail in Box 27.3.) They were to be released into two adjacent probation trust areas. These will be referred to as the ADViSOR group of offenders. This group was followed up in the community for a period of a year. There were also comparison groups of offenders who simply went through the standard MAPPA procedures prior to release from prison. These men were released into the same two probation areas but not necessarily from the prison in question. These we can refer to the MAPPA-only group. Technically, we cannot refer to the behaviours being monitored as offence paralleling behaviours because this refers to behaviours that occur in the institution which reflect the index crime for which the offender was sentenced. The ADViSOR system uses prison behaviours as predictors for post-release offending – and there are more behaviours which 'ring warning bells' in prison than reflect the offender's index offence. So all negative behaviours 'causing concern' in prison were of interest in this study. Examples of good, positive behaviours which were incompatible with planning to reoffend when released into the community were also of interest. The prison staff recorded any such behaviours for the ADViSOR researchers as part of their daily supervision activities. These included low-level concerns as well as more serious ones.

The researchers found that there was a close correspondence or similarity between each prisoner's prison behaviours of concern to the prison officers and the negative

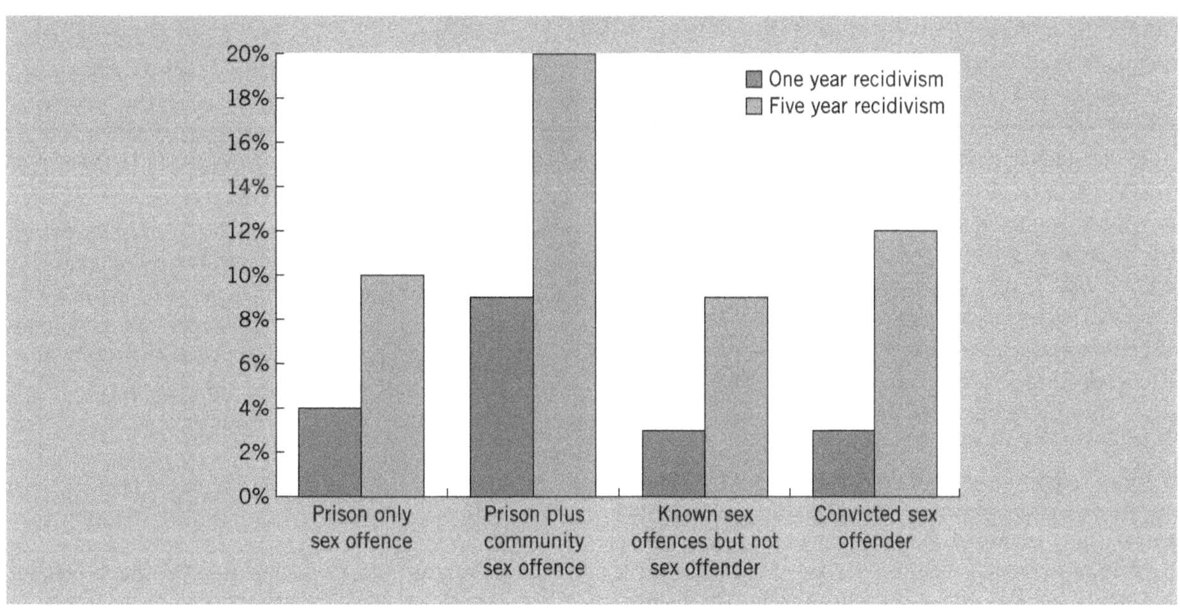

Figure 27.6 One-year and five-year recidivism for sexual offences

behaviours that they committed in the community. Random pairings of prison behaviours and community behaviours showed a much lower level of correspondence. For example, take McDougall *et al.*'s example of the prisoner who got into debt with other prisoners and wanted to change his prison wing to avoid any consequent problems. This man also got into debt in the community, owing a quite a large sum of money, and then absconded from his hostel. The similarities between these two behaviours are obvious – debt and avoiding the ensuing difficulties he faced. Another example is the prisoner noted by female staff at the prison for staring at them inappropriately. This man was recalled to prison by the Justice Ministry for staring at a woman and her child when very drunk in the community. There was a correlation between the level of negative behaviour a prisoner in the ADViSOR group showed in prison and their negative behaviours in the community. But the reverse was the case for the positive behaviours in prison as these correlated with little or no negative behaviour in the community. Finally, the frequency of negative behaviours assessed by the ADViSOR approach predicted with over 90 per cent accuracy which of the offenders would reoffend again in the community or be recalled to prison by the Ministry of Justice under the terms of the parole licence.

Although offence-related behaviours and the more general approach taken by the ADViSOR project clearly hold promise, they are unlikely to be problem-free. One of the obvious difficulties is that prison officers, etc. are the suppliers of information and there may be problems in delivering this. Obtaining their full cooperation is obviously essential but this takes a lot of time, care and skill to be optimally successful. Atkinson and Mann (2012) see prison officers as being an extremely valuable source of relevant information. They organised focus groups with prison officers to discuss offence paralleling behaviours. It was clear that prison staff make potentially useful observations of the prisoners that they supervise. The sorts of things mentioned included anti-authority behaviours and associating with antisocial prisoners. However, there emerged a number of reasons which might result in relevant behaviours going unrecorded. One is the normalisation of certain behaviours. So certain negative behaviours would be perceived as normal within the culture of a prison or normal for the individual in question. Procedural factors reducing reporting can include things like staff not seeing such observations as part of their role. Being less involved by management in risk assessment may distance the officers from the process. A final reason would be the perception that nothing happens when things are reported anyway. In other words, the practical application of these methods depends on a complex variety of organisational, managerial and interpersonal factors which may work to reduce the effectiveness of the procedures. New initiatives and research involvement may be highly motivating but the longer-term problems of maintaining 'enthusiasm' and interest in a work task may be more challenging.

Gradually there seems to be emerging evidence of the moderate gains to be made by studying offence paralleling behaviour. The difficulty of establishing just what behaviours parallel other behaviours is no easy obstacle to overcome. Recent research has suggested ways of dealing with this difficulty (Kadra, Daffern and Campbell, 2014).

Protective factors in risk assessment

Although the idea of protective factors is familiar in forensic and criminal psychology (see Chapter 6 and earlier in the present chapter), the idea has only recently been introduced into risk assessment. Using protective factors seems to improve the validity of the risk assessment. A protective factor is a personal characteristic or an aspect of the individual's environment or situation which reduces the risk of violent behaviour in the future. De Vries Robbě, de Vogel and Douglas (2013) use protective factors as the basis for their work. They studied nearly 200 forensic patients in Holland with histories of violent or sexual offending. Each of them had been given a TBS order by the Dutch Criminal Court System. TBS is an acronym for *terbeschikkingstelling* which is a court order requiring the mandatory treatment of seriously violent offenders. Because of their extreme levels of psychopathology, these offenders are deemed not to be fully responsible for their crime. Similar arrangements apply in many other countries. The typical psychiatric diagnosis was of an Axis 2 disorder (see Box 21.1) and only about 15 per cent were diagnosed with a psychotic condition such as schizophrenia. Comorbidity with substance abuse problems was present in over 70 per cent of the men. The participants all underwent cognitive behaviour therapy and relapse prevention therapy in the hospital. On average, each offender spent between five and six years in the hospital before release. Most of the patients had a history of general violent offending but not sexual offending and the rest had been involved in sexually violent offences although they possibly had previous convictions for violence of a non-sexual nature too. The risk and protective factors were clinically assessed from the details contained in each offender's file:

- The risk factors were measured using the HCR-20 (discussed above).
- The protective factors were measured by the Structured Assessment of Protective Factors for Violence Risk (SAPROF). This is a new structured professional

judgement measure which seeks to assess the protective factors for violence risk. Some risk factors on the scale seem to be the reverse of some familiar risk factors such as self-control as opposed to impulsivity or coping as opposed to stress. However, SAPROF also involves protective factors which stand alone without being in comparison to risk factors. These include taking medication; having leisure activities; being under professional care; and being in an intimate relationship.

Recidivism statistics for each of the men were obtained from the Dutch Ministry of Justice. The definition used was any new conviction following release from the hospital for a sexual or non-sexual violent offence. The follow-up period after discharge was a minimum of three years but the average was 11 years.

The combination of risk and protective factors predicted violent recidivism following treatment. Good predictions of desistance from violence were associated with the use of the dynamic factors from both assessment instruments. There was also evidence of what is called the *incremental validity* of the protective factors over the risk factors alone. That is to say, when the prediction based on the risk factors has been taken into account, adding in protective factors increased predictive accuracy above and beyond that based on risk factors alone. But this only applied to the long-term follow-up. The predictive ability of protective and risk factors together was very good indeed for short-term follow-up into the community. Their performance was a little poorer for long-term follow-ups.

Main points

- The assessment of risk and dangerousness had its impetus from US legislation requiring practitioners to deal with the risk to the public posed by their clients. In part this is achieved by managing the risk in various ways such as keeping the offender physically away from the public and others at risk. However, the decision about how likely an individual is to harm another (risk) and the assessment of how serious the risk is (dangerousness) is a complex one and is a characteristic of the situation as much as the offender in question.
- Risk assessment is an area of psychology in which clinical judgement and empirical research both have a role to play. There is reason to think that it is profitable to use the two methods together in ways that combine the advantages of each. Empirical methods can demonstrate the broad relationship between risk factors and risk but cannot effectively deal with individual instances, which need a careful evaluation within the parameters set by research. As a consequence, measures such as the Psychopathy Checklist Revised have shown themselves to be effective in identifying factors that are strongly predictive of recidivism.
- When we attempt to predict recidivism, we do so with less than perfect predictors, which means that there is always an amount of error. The amount of error that can be tolerated depends on the risk in question. One difficulty with predictions of this sort is that they tend to be the most accurate when the behaviour in question occurs in 50 per cent of the population in question. So predictions of things such as sex offences for which the recidivism rate is actually quite small are likely to be poor. Similarly, predicting which violent mentally ill offenders will kill in future is likely to be fraught with problems simply for statistical reasons.

Further reading

Conroy, M.A. and Murrie, D.C. (2007) *Forensic Assessment of Violence Risk: A Guide for Risk Assessment and Risk Management* Chichester: John Wiley.

Otto, R.K. and Douglas, K.S. (2010) *Handbook of Violence Risk Assessment* Abingdon: Routledge/

Singh, J.P., Bjorkly, S. and Fazel, S. (2016) *International Perspectives on Violence Risk Assessment* Oxford: Oxford University Press.

Glossary

A

Absolute judgement: Postulated process by which eyewitness judgements in an identity parade are made by reference to the original sighting of the offender and are not dependent on the characteristics of the members of the line-up.

Absolute liability offences: Offences for which defences of lack of criminal intent are not allowed statutorily.

Accused: The individual(s) charged with an offence or who it has been alleged has/have committed the offence.

Acquisitive crime: A crime primarily for the gaining of property or money.

Active listening skills: Methods of being a better listener, especially in hostage negotiation. The main aim is to increase the flow of communication with the hostage taker.

Actuarial assessment: Assessment of clients, etc. based on accumulated statistical information.

Actuarial profiling: Criminal profiling methods based on aggregated statistical data.

Actuary: Someone who is expert with statistical or aggregated information.

***Actus reus*:** The guilty act – the offence which the accused has allegedly committed.

Ad hoc: Decisions or arrangements made to deal with the demands of a particular situation.

Adaptive behaviour: This refers to behaviours aimed at adjusting to a new situation or environment.

Addiction to crime: The theory that criminal behaviour is rather like an addiction and shares many of the characteristics of addiction to drugs.

Admissible evidence: Evidence which conforms to the rules governing the sorts of evidence which may be used in courts of law.

Adolescence: The period from after puberty to adulthood.

Adolescence-limited offender: An offender who offends as an adolescent but at no other stage.

Adoption study: In this context, a study investigating criminality in siblings (especially twins) brought up in a different family.

Adversarial system: The Anglo-American system of court procedure in which two opposing sides take turns to question the accused and witnesses.

Adversarial: Involving conflict or opposition such as cross-examination techniques where the prosecution and defence take turns to question the defendant or a witness.

Advocate: A lawyer representing an individual(s) in court. In the UK this may be a barrister or a solicitor.

Aetiology: The knowledge we have about the causes of phenomena (such as mental illness) and the way that they develop.

Affidavit: A written statement made in evidence which is confirmed as truthful in front of an authorised person.

Age of criminal responsibility: The lowest age at which a person can be held to be capable of committing a crime and, hence, charged with that crime. This varies internationally and in terms of the nature of the crime.

Algorithm: A step-by-step procedure for carrying out a mathematical calculation.

***Amicus curiae*:** An independent or neutral individual who provides the court with an independent point of view. The *amicus curiae* does not represent any party in the case.

Amnesia: Memory loss or disturbance.

Anatomical dolls/anatomically correct dolls/anatomically detailed dolls: Toy dolls which have genitals and secondary sexual characteristics, sometimes used in sexual abuse interviews with children.

Anchored narratives: 'Stories' linking together a series of events using generally accepted commonsense notions which are held to be correct.

Anchors: Commonsense assumptions or ideas which are regarded as if they are fact. They underlie our judgements of events. For example, the belief that the police make infallible eyewitnesses.

Anger management: A form of counselling which helps individuals deal with anger in a constructive way rather than through aggression.

Antisocial behaviour orders (ASBOs): In the UK, a court order which is tailored to deal with the antisocial behaviour patterns of individuals, such as vandalism and graffiti.

Antisocial personality disorder (ADP): A mental disorder appearing in the APA's *Diagnostic and Statistical Manual* which is characterised by persistent disregard for the rights of others and violations of those rights. Sufferers are considered deceitful and manipulative. The term is not applied to persons under 18 years of age.

Appeal: A request or application to a higher court, etc. that the decision of a lower court be reviewed and reversed.

Appellant: A person making an appeal to a higher court.

Arson: Firesetting or maliciously setting fire to property.

Assertiveness: Assertiveness is strongly differentiated from aggressiveness. It is a manner of communication in which wishes are made clear in a respectful manner. Hostility is not involved.

Atavism theory: A long-abandoned theory which claimed that criminals are genetically throwbacks to an earlier stage and their criminal acts simply match those of ancient ancestors.

Attachment theory: The developmental theory which stresses the role of disruptions to children's early relationships with the mother in developing interpersonal relationship problems later in life.

Attention deficit hyperactive disorder (ADHD): A psychological state where a child shows inappropriate levels of hyperactivity and impulsivity combined with a failure to attend appropriately.

Autistic Spectrum Disorders: This includes conditions such as Asperger's syndrome and autism. These conditions influence the interaction of the individual with other people.

Automatism: This is an unconscious act which may be criminal, such as a murder when sleepwalking.

Availability heuristic: A cognitive strategy in which assessments and decisions are based on the knowledge that is readily available to the individual. It does not involve examining alternative possibilities or the procedures through which the judgement is made.

Aversion therapy: A form of conditioning therapy in which the 'undesired' behaviour is paired with a punishment (unpleasant experience) in order to reduce its incidence.

B

Bail: When the accused is released from custody until their next court appearance. Sometimes a financial arrangement has to be involved as security and certain conditions may have to be met.

Baker-Miller pink: a paint shade which has been claimed to reduce aggressiveness.

Barrister: This is a member of the bar, a lawyer, who is qualified to represent clients in a court of law.

Behaviour analysis interview: This is an interrogation technique developed by Fred Inbau and others. It encourages different responses from liars and truth tellers. This method has been commonly employed by the police in the USA/British Crime Survey.

Behavioural intervention: Any treatment/therapy which is intended to directly change behaviour.

Behavioural therapy: *See* Cognitive behavioural therapy.

Biological determinism: This is the assumption that criminality can be directly inherited in families prone to crime or indirectly inherited in a family the members of which experience insanity or alcoholism.

Biology: The scientific study of living organisms.

Biosocial theory: This assumes that crime is the product of an interaction between biological and social factors.

Bipolar disorder (formerly manic depression): A group of disorders of mood characterised by the presence of one or more periods of abnormally elevated positive mood. This is likely to be followed by a normal mood and then a depressive episode.

Blank line-up: An identification parade in which the suspect is not present.

Blended memories: Memories which are a mixture of what was initially memorised and events that happened later. For example, the original memory of the crime plus suggestions that emerged during a later police interview.

Blind procedure: In eyewitness testimony, this would be a line-up or identity parade in which the identity of the person suspected by the police of committing the crime is unknown to the person conducting the parade, for example.

Bonnie rule: An American test of diminished responsibility.

Borderline personality disorder: A psychiatric term describing a long-standing disturbance of the functioning of personality. Instability and chaos in mood, interpersonal relations, behaviour and sense of identity are among the associated characteristics.

British Crime Survey: A survey of the experiences of victims of crime.

Burglary: Entering a property with the intention of committing theft or damage or to do physical harm to a person.

C

Canteen culture: A term referring to the conservative beliefs and discriminatory attitudes held to characterise the lower ranks of the police.

Catatonic behaviour: This is not a mental disorder in itself but is found in mental disorders such as schizophrenia. The motor skills of the sufferer decline to a significant extent or they may show continuous hyperactive movement.

CCTV: Closed-circuit television.

Change order: One of the procedures of the cognitive interview in which events are recalled in a different order from that in which they were experienced.

Change perspective: A procedure in the cognitive interview in which experienced events are described from the perspective of another witness in a different location.

Chartered Forensic Psychologist: A professional qualification at the highest level awarded by the British Psychological Society.

Chemical restraints: 'Chemical straightjackets' or anti-psychotic drugs which are used to treat some violent individuals.

Chicago School: An important movement in criminology which moved the explanation of crime to environment and situational factors.

Child molester: A term used to describe someone who has sexually abused a child. The use of the term avoids the psychological implications of the use of the term *paedophile*.

Civil: These are legal matters which concern the rights of private individuals and are different from crimes which are offences against the state. Examples include unpaid debts, enforcement of contracts, and so forth. Family matters and employment, for example, are not matters of the civil law in the UK.

Claimant (previously plaintiff in UK law): A person who issues a claim against another person.

Classical conditioning: The conditioning of reflex responses – most famously Pavlov's dogs which learnt to associate a bell with food and salivated to the sound of the bell.

Clear-up rates: The rates of known crimes which lead to prosecution, although they may include offences dealt with by other means, such as where an offender admits further offences.

Clinical judgement: Judgements based on the assessment of practitioners in a clinical setting rather than systematic research.

Clinical prediction: Predictions of, for example, recidivism based on clinical judgement.

Clinical psychology: That aspect of the practice of psychology which deals with psychologically based distress or dysfunction.

Clinical samples: Samples of participants obtained from a medical setting.

Closed question: A question worded in such a way that little is required by way of answer other than a yes or no or some other simple, unelaborated response.

Coerced-compliant (false) confession: A confession produced under some form of pressure or coercion but which is not actually believed by the person who confesses.

Coerced-internalised (false) confession: As for coerced-compliant confession, but the confessor believes that they actually carried out the act confessed.

Cognitive: To do with knowing and perceiving rather than emotion and action.

Cognitive behavioural therapy: Form of psychological therapy directed to altering both behaviour and thoughts, usually using procedures based on modifying the way the offender thinks about their behaviours.

Cognitive dissonance: The negative state when there are inconsistencies between an individual's attitudes and their behaviour. It may motivate a change in the individual's cognitions.

Cognitive distortions: A very loose term to describe the unusual, offence-supportive beliefs, attitudes and other cognitions which are conducive to offending behaviour, especially sex offending against children.

Cognitive interview and enhanced cognitive interview: Procedures for conducting interviews based on the findings of cognitive psychology and, in the case of the enhanced cognitive interview, communications psychology.

Cognitive skills training/programmes: Techniques for the improvement of problem solving relevant, especially, to social interaction.

Cognitive-behavioural: Approaches based on behaviourism and cognitive psychology, especially the relationship between the two.

Combat fatigue: Shell shock – the mental and bodily disturbances that result from prolonged involvement in combat. It should be considered in relation to post-traumatic stress syndrome.

Command hallucinations: A hallucination in which voices instruct the person to do a certain act (possibly a crime).

Common law: The branch of law which is based on precedents such as previous judicial decisions and arrangements well established within the community.

Community sentence: A sentence for a crime based on making direct amends to the community by carrying out relatively menial tasks within that community.

Comorbidity: The presence of a disease or condition additional to the one of primary interest and the resulting combined effect. For example, alcoholism and schizophrenia may be comorbid.

Competence to stand trial: (in the USA) Ability of a defendant to meet the criteria regarded as sufficient to establish that they can participate in their own defence. (*See also* Fitness to plead, which is the UK equivalent).

Compliance: Yielding to the wishes or commands of another person.

Compos mentis: (of a person) of sound mind and legally capable, for example, of being involved in their defence in court.

Conditioning: The learning of behaviour (actions). Includes classical and operant conditioning.

Conduct disorder: A psychological state characterised by repeated, extreme antisocial activities.

Confession culture: The idea that police officers obtain confessions as their primary objective rather than obtain evidence.

Confidence, eyewitness: An eyewitness's belief in the accuracy of their memories and testimony.

Confirmatory factor analysis: A statistical technique which allows the researcher to test the adequacy of a factor structure or a model against new data.

Conformity: Compliance with the behaviours of others.

Confounding factors: Factors which confuse the interpretation of statistical relationships which the researcher may be unaware of.

Context reinstatement: In the cognitive interview, thinking of the context of the original events as part of the process of recall.

Control question test: A way of asking questions in a polygraph test.

Conversation management approach: Procedures for conducting interviews which concentrate on managing the flow of the police interview, using both verbal and non-verbal techniques.

Correctional psychologist: A psychologist working in a prison or some other organisation devoted to the correction of criminal behaviour.

Correlation coefficient: An index of the degree of association between two variables in which +1 indicates a perfect positive relationship, +0.5 indicates a moderate positive relationship, 0 indicates no relationship and a negative sign (–) indicates a negative relationship.

Corroboration: Supportive information from a second source.

Counselling: The process which takes place between client and counsellor in which a difficulty experienced by the client is explored.

Counselling psychologist: A psychologist who works primarily using counselling techniques in the treatment of clients.

County court: In the UK, these deal with civil law matters, especially those with a financial aspect.

Covert sensitisation: An approach in behaviour modification (conditioning) where an undesired behaviour is associated with a negative image so as to reduce the likelihood of the behaviour reoccurring.

Credible: Believable.

Crime: Actions punishable by the law.

Crime linkage: A procedure for establishing whether two or more separate crimes may have been perpetrated by the same individual(s).

Crime mapping: Research which seeks to place crime in its precise geographical context. It can help identify crime hot spots.

Crime profiling: Usually, but not always, a description of the sorts of person who engage in a particular sort of crime, and their characteristics.

Crime reconstruction: Attempts to reproduce the sequence of events which took place during a crime, based on the evidence left at the scene.

Crime scene classification: The classification of crime scenes usually into *organised* and *disorganised* types.

Criminal behaviour profiling: One of a variety of virtually synonymous terms for offender profiling. It is an investigative method which uses information from the crime scene and more to develop a social, behavioural and, possibly, physical description of the offender.

Criminal cases: Cases which are regarded in law as against society (as opposed to the rights of individuals).

Criminal justice system: The governmental organisations and practices which serve to both control crime and maintain control on the population. The criminal justice system includes punishments for violations of the law.

Criminality: This is a personal characteristic or trait of an individual, whereas a crime is a particular sort of event.

Criminally insane: To be convicted of a crime the offender has to understand that they were doing wrong at the time of the offence. The mental defects of the criminally insane prevented their understanding that what they were doing was wrong.

Criminogenic: Causing or resulting in crime.

Criminogenic needs: Needs which, unless satisfied, may lead to or encourage criminal behaviour.

Criminology: The science of crime. It is broader than either forensic or criminal psychology and could be regarded as embracing both of them.

Criterion-based content analysis (CBCA): Part of statement validity analysis. It is a way of examining, primarily, children's statements for content which is characteristic of truthfulness.

Cross-examination: The questioning of a witness by the other side (e.g. prosecution or defence) in a court hearing.

Cross-race identification: Eyewitness identification of other races.

Crown Court: This deals with criminal cases sent to it by a magistrates' court. A judge and a jury are involved. It also deals with certain civil and family issues.

Cycles of abuse: The idea that abuse in one generation leads to abuse by later generations.

D

Dangerous and severe personality disorder: This is a neither a legal nor a psychiatric category but one developed by government. It may be regarded, in the absence of a better definition, as an extreme variant of antisocial personality disorder. It is part of an attempt to protect the public from a small but extremely harmful minority of mentally disordered individuals.

Danish experiment: The liberation of pornography by the Danish government in the late 1960s.

***Daubert* guidelines:** In the US, rules defining when an expert witness is appropriate.

De facto: In fact.

De jure: Rightful – a matter of right.

Decision rule: The broad principles by which juries reach a verdict – for example, the size of the majority needed.

Deficit model: An explanation based on the lack of certain characteristics.

Deinstitutionalisation: The process by which the mentally ill were transferred to care in the community from care in mental hospitals.

Delusion: A false belief which is relatively fixed or constant.

Dementia praecox: *See* schizophrenia.

Denial: In forensic psychology the refusal to accept aspects of one's offending, such as its extent or seriousness.

Desistance: The process of resisting criminal activity in those with a criminogenic profile.

Deviancy amplification: The process of bringing into focus a particular issue to do with criminal activity by continual reference to it by the media.

***Diagnostic and Statistical Manual* (*DSM*):** The key published source for definitions of mental illness such as bipolar disorder, schizophrenia, etc.

Diagnostic Interview Schedule: A questionnaire for assessing the presence of various mental illnesses.

Diagnosticity of signs: The extent to which a sign is accurate as an indication of some characteristic. For example, how accurate previous convictions are as a predictor of future offending.

Differential association theory: The idea that criminal ideas are learned through social interaction with others.

Diminished responsibility: Mental and other incapacities which limit the offender's responsibility for a crime and may make them less liable to punishment.

Directed lie test: A way of questioning used for the polygraph.

Disclosure: The requirement in UK law that the sides involved in a civil case must show the other side documentation that they will rely on in court as evidence.

Disinhibition: The removal of factors which inhibit an individual from a course of action. Commonly used as an explanation of sex offending.

Disorganised crime scene: A crime scene which is characterised by chaos. This type of crime scene is seen in some forms of profiling as being associated with offenders with disorganised lifestyles.

Dissociation: The loss of connections between emotions, thoughts, memories, etc. as a defensive reaction to extreme stress.

Distal factors: Things that are more distant (usually in time in psychology) such as early childhood factors in criminality. Opposite = proximal.

Distorted thinking: Patterns of thought which are distortions of reality. Often used to describe the thinking which leads to sex offending.

Divisional court: Courts which have the right to hear appeals from lower courts, etc. They also have their own jurisdiction.

DNA: Deoxyribonucleic acid. This carries a pattern of genetic information unique to each individual.

DNA testing: The process of comparing a suspect's DNA with a sample of DNA from another source to assess whether the two match.

Doli incapax: The incapability of committing a crime because of youth.

Downward comparison process: The idea that we make judgements about ourselves by comparison with those less fortunate than ourselves in some regard.

Drift theory: The idea that criminal activity is the product of the activities of people who drift between a deviant and a non-deviant lifestyle at will.

Drug dependency units: Treatment units for abusers.

***DSM*:** *See Diagnostic and Statistical Manual.*

Dynamic risk predictor: A variable which can change over time which is used in risk prediction.

Dynamic variables: Variables which may be altered by practitioners or researchers, as opposed to static variables such as gender, which are largely fixed.

E

Early onset: The process by which a criminal career starts early in life (childhood), which leads to persistent crime.

Ecological validity: This is the extent to which behaviours, etc. observed in a research study accurately reflect what occurs in natural settings.

Ectomorphs: Persons with a lean and delicate body build.

EEG activity: Electrical activity of the brain, as measured by the electroencephalogram.

Effect size: A term in statistics for something which indicates the size of the influence of the independent variable in a standardised form which allows comparison of studies. Common examples of effect size measures are Pearson's correlation coefficient and Cohen's *d*.

E-FIT: A method of facial image reconstruction.

Emotional dysregulation: A failure to deal effectively with one's emotions. May result in dysfunctional coping methods.

Encoding: The process by which information is changed into different forms. In psychology, it is the initial process in memory in which the stimulus is transferred into memory.

Endomorph: A body type which is soft and rounded – according to Sheldon's theory.

Enhanced cognitive interview: Interview techniques based on the research findings from memory research and communications psychology.

Erotomania: The deluded belief that another person, e.g. a film or television personality, is in love with one.

Escabinato: A system in which a judge sits with lay persons during a trial, as opposed to a jury system where a judge conducts the trial and a jury reaches a verdict.

Estimator variable: In eyewitness testimony, an estimator variable is something which affects the accuracy of the eyewitness but is not within the powers of the criminal justice system to influence. So, for example, an estimator variable might be the age of the eyewitness or how close they were to the offender at the crime scene. These are different from system variables, which can be controlled by the criminal justice system as they involve the characteristics of the line-up or identity parade, etc.

Evolutionary theory of rape: This argues that males have a propensity to rape because of natural selection – rape is a means by which inadequate males can transmit their genes.

Excitation transfer theory: A theory of aggression which suggests that a person in a state of arousal is more likely to act aggressively, irrespective of the source of that arousal.

Exhibitionism: The act of publicly exposing one's genitals for the purpose of personal sexual excitement.

Expert witness: A person qualified in a specific area, or otherwise having expertise, who is employed to give evidence in court.

Extraversion: A characteristic of personality describing someone who is outgoing and gregarious. According to Hans Eysenck's theory of crime, extroverts condition relatively poorly and consequently do not learn social rules quickly, which leaves them more likely to be criminal.

Eyewitness testimony: Evidence provided to a court by a witness who saw the events in question.

F

Facet theory: This is a theory proposed by Louis Guttman which sets out methods of defining observations for multivariate investigations. It has entered forensic psychology through its adoption by David Canter in his approach to criminal profiling.

Facial composites: Representations of faces built up from a set of standard elements.

False allegation: An accusation of committing a crime which the accused party did not commit.

False confession: A confession to a crime which the confessor did not actually commit.

False memory: A memory of something which did not occur or a very distorted memory which is substantially false. *See also* Recovered memories.

False memory induction: The process of developing a false memory of events. It is claimed that this may be the result of the influence of therapists.

False memory syndrome: A description of a state in which an individual has memories which are regarded as being fantasy and this is a central focus of their lives. The term usually refers to memories which emerged during or as a consequence of therapy.

Familicide: The killing of one's spouse and children.

Fantasy: Fanciful thoughts and ideas which have little or no basis in real experience.

FBI profiling: The form of crime-scene offender profiling based on largely clinical approaches which was developed by the FBI at their Quantico academy.

Fear of crime: Being afraid of becoming a victim of crime – there is usually a disproportionality in that these fears are not in keeping with the actual risk of victimisation for the particular sort of person in question.

Fear–victimisation paradox: The finding from research that the most likely victims of crime tend not to be afraid of the risk of victimisation and vice versa.

Felony: (in the USA) A significant offence that can lead to one or more years in a state prison.

Feminist movement: A variety of social movements, theories and philosophies which critique gender differences and promote gender equality of women with men.

Feminist theory: Theory which critiques gender differences.

Fetishism: A sexual pathology in which a person is aroused by objects or parts of the body which do not normally serve a sexual function.

Field dependence: The idea that some people are very dependent on peripheral factors in terms of their perceptions and judgements.

Firesetting: *See* Arson.

FIRO: Fundamental Interpersonal Relations Orientation, which is William Schutz's theory of interpersonal relationships. FIRO-B is a measuring instrument to assess components of this theory.

Fitness to plead: In the United Kingdom, to stand trial an accused must be capable of understanding the proceedings. *See also* Competence to stand trial, which is the US equivalent.

Fixated offenders: A sex offender against children whose psychosexual development is held to have been arrested in childhood.

Flashbacks: Intrusive and vivid memories of traumatic episodes.

Flashbulb memory: The photographically detailed memories which occur in response to emotionally and personally significant events.

Flesch index: A measure of the readability of text.

Foils: The non-suspected persons in an identity parade or line-up.

Folie a deux: The co-occurrence of psychosis in two closely associated persons.

Forensic hypnosis: Hypnosis used in the interviewing of witnesses.

Forensic linguistics: Linguistics applied to a forensic setting.

Forensic psychology: Strictly, psychology applied to courts of law but generally used to refer to the forms of psychology used within the criminal justice system.

Forensic validity: The extent to which research findings can be generalised to aspects of the work of courts of law (and the criminal justice system).

Frottage: A perverse sexual act involving obtaining sexual arousal from physical contact with another person in a crowded situation.

Fundamental Interpersonal Relations Orientation: *See* FIRO.

G

Galvanic skin response (GSR): The electrical activity of the skin (electrical resistance) fluctuates over time. Variation in emotional arousal is associated with variations in skin resistance, hence GSR is used in lie detection, for example.

General strain theory (GST): The theory that strain created on the individual by a variety of life's pressures combines with the emotionality of the individual in a way that results in criminality.

Genetic fingerprinting: *See* DNA testing.

Genetic: To do with genes – the basic components of inheritance.

Good Lives Model (GLM): An approach to offender rehabilitation based in what people in general need to live a satisfactory, rewarding life.

Grooming: The processes by which paedophiles and other sexual offenders against children initiate and maintain social and personal relationships with potential victims prior to offending against them.

Ground truth: The absolute or underlying 'truth' concerning a set of events, which may or may not be known to researchers or practitioners.

Guardian: A person who looks after the affairs and interests of a child or someone suffering mental disability.

Guardians (capable): People such as neighbours and the police who act as a deterrent to crime simply because of their presence in the area.

Guilty Knowledge Test: A form of asking questions in a polygraph examination.

H

***Habeas corpus*:** A written instruction or command (writ) which instructs that someone held in custody should be brought before the court.

Hallucination: A perception of something which appears to be real and present but is not.

Halo effect: The process by which a person is perceived to be entirely good on the basis of a small number of positive characteristics.

Hate crime: Usually a violent crime based on prejudices against a group, as in homophobia.

Hearsay: Evidence that is anything other than the statement by a witness about things that they witnessed. The rules are complex and varied. For example, evidence confirming that certain things were said out-of-court is not hearsay.

Hedonistic (serial) killer: Someone whose primary motive is some sort of pleasure associated with the killing of another person.

Heuristic: Procedures which reach a solution by a process akin to trial and error in which each stage better approximates the best solution.

Hidden crime: Crime which does not manifest itself in official statistics.

High court: In the UK this is a civil court which has three divisions dealing with civil disputes, family matters and property (such as fraud and bankruptcy).

High-stake lies: A lie to cover up something which would have serious consequences if found out.

Homicide: A killing of another human being, though this is not always an illegal act.

Hostile witness: A non-cooperative witness.

Hung jury: A jury which fails to reach a clear verdict on the basis of legal rules about decision making.

Hypnosis: A trance-like or sleep-like state where the individual responds only to the suggestions of the hypnotist.

Hypothetico-deductive model: A way of proceeding in research whereby the research deduces hypotheses from a theory which are then tested empirically by the researcher.

I

Iatrogenic: Caused by the medical or psychological treatment being given to the individual.

Identification parade: People in a group containing the suspect for a crime who are shown to the witness to see whether the suspect is correctly identified by the witness. Also called identity parade and line-up.

Identikit: A procedure for producing facial composites of suspects based on a set of drawings of different varieties of facial characteristics such as nose shape.

Identity parade: *See* Identification parade.

Imitation: The process of learning by observing another person carry out a task.

Implicit memory: Memories dependent on learning of which the individual is not aware.

In camera: This literally means in the chamber/room. It is a hearing which takes place in private rather than publicly. The facts of the case are not made public.

In curia: This refers to a hearing in a court open to the public.

Inadmissible evidence: Evidence which cannot be presented in court because it violates some rule governing evidence.

Incestuous offenders: Sex offenders against children within the biological family and/or the more general social family in some formulations.

Incidence: (From medicine) The number of people who have a condition on an annual basis.

Index offence: The most serious of the criminal offences an individual is accused of at any one time in court. Sometimes refers to the crime used to classify the offender for research purposes.

Indirect aggression: Forms of aggression which do not involve physical attack but verbal attacks and so forth instead.

Individualist culture: A culture in which the individual is the primary unit and in which ties with the family and community are very restricted.

Information-processing theories: Theories of cognition and cognitive development which propose that thought involves strategies which may become more effective with experience or training. The mind has a limited information-processing capacity.

Innocence Project: An American organisation which uses evidence from DNA testing technology to seek to deal with cases of wrongful conviction.

Inquisitorial system: The legal system common in Europe and elsewhere where trials are conducted by a judge (and others) seeking to establish the truth of a case. This contrasts with the adversarial Anglo-American system in which opposing sides in the case present their evidence and arguments and a judge – or often a jury – attempts to determine the truth of the case.

Insanity: In legal settings, insanity is the lack of ability of the accused to know that what they did was wrong during the offence. This is a legal judgement and not judged as such by mental health professionals.

Intellectual disability: A general substantial impairment of cognitive functioning including intelligence.

Intelligence: A general term to describe a variety of abilities such as problem solving, ability to learn, abstract thinking, comprehension and so forth.

Intentionality: A complex concept with a complex history – however, in a forensic psychology context it generally means purposefulness.

International Classification of Diseases: A systematic categorisation of diseases, including mental health problems.

Interpersonal skills training: Training to improve an individual's ability to interact with others.

Interrogation manuals: Instruction books purportedly giving instruction in how to interview offenders effectively.

Interrogation: Questioning – but in a somewhat forceful way which may result in the disclosure of significant information.

Interviewer bias: The process by which the predetermined views of an interviewer may influence the interviewee to answer in ways consistent with that predetermined view.

Intimate partner violence: Violence (physical, sexual, emotional) perpetrated against an individual's wife, husband or partner.

Intimacy deficits: The idea that sex offenders lack the ability to form close sexual relationships with other adults.

Intra vires: Within the power or jurisdiction of a court.

Investigative interviewing: The interviewing process used by the police during the course of a criminal investigation. The term could also be applied, for example, to similar work carried out by psychologists or social workers.

Investigative psychology: A term used by David Canter to describe the application of scientific psychology to the analysis and investigation of crimes.

Irrelevant question technique: A method of questioning in the polygraph lie detector test.

Isomorphism hypothesis: The suggestion that there are marked parallels between the offending behaviour of paedophiles and the sexually abusive/sexualisation experiences of the offender as a child.

J

Joyriding: Taking a vehicle for the enjoyment or thrill of driving it – as opposed to, for example, taking a vehicle for monetary gain.

Judge: An administrator of the law who may hear and try cases in court.

Jurisdiction: The geographical area and the issues over which a court has authority in law.

Jurisprudence: The theory and philosophy of the law and legal systems.

Jury: The group of lay persons sworn to reach an impartial verdict on legal issues presented to them – usually a guilty or not guilty verdict based on the evidence put before them.

Just world: A theoretical notion referring to the tendency of some people to regard life as being based on principles of fairness and justice.

Justice of the Peace (JP): In the UK, a lay magistrate in a magistrates' court. Sometimes found in a Crown Court sitting with professional judges in cases of appeals and certain other matters.

K

Kleptomania: A psychiatric term referring to a persistent urge to steal property.

Klinefelter's syndrome: A term used to describe the behaviours, etc. of a person with an XXY-chromosome configuration.

L

Labelling: The idea that being labelled as deviant locks an individual or group of individuals into deviancy.

Larceny: Theft which does not involve violence, threat, or breaking into another person's property.

Law Lords: The highest-level judges in the House of Lords in the UK. They are known as the Lords of Appeal.

Law: A system of rules established by the highest legislature (parliament in the UK) and by custom, which encourages or prohibits certain actions.

Lawyer: A member of the legal profession. In the UK there are barristers who largely operate in the highest courts and solicitors who operate in the lower courts.

Lay person jury: The usual jury in the Anglo-American legal system.

Leading question: A question framed in such a way that it implies a particular answer.

Leakages: This is a term used in lie-detection and refers to behavioural, etc. manifestations of underlying emotions which are aroused by lying.

Learning disabilities: A broad label for various conditions which cause substantial difficulties in skills such as listening, speaking, writing and mathematics. These are generally seen as being the consequence of an underlying neurological dysfunction.

Legal psychology: Theoretical and empirical psychology into aspects of the criminal justice system.

Legalese: The jargon of members of the legal profession.

Level of Service Inventory – Revised (LSI-R): A questionnaire for the assessment of criminogenic needs.

Lie detector test: Usually refers to the polygraph.

Line-up: *See* Identification parade.

Live links: Video links between a witness and a law court which reduce some of the negative aspects of giving evidence in court.

Lone-wolf terrorism: Terrorist acts carried out or planned by an isolated individual with no contacts with other terrorists or terrorist groups.

Long-term memory: Memory after the stage of encoding by the working memory (aka short-term memory). Confusingly, long-term memory may be short-lasting or long-lasting in the sense that it may last, say, hours or decades.

Low-stakes lies: Untruths which have only minor consequences if detected.

LSI-R: *See* Level of Service Inventory – Revised.

M

MacArthur Competence Assessment Tool: An assessment procedure dealing with the issue of competence (fitness) to stand trial in North America.

Mad versus bad: A phrase used to capture the difference between psychological and moral explanations of extreme forms of crime.

Madness: *See* Insanity.

Magistrates' court: A lower-level court where criminal prosecutions commence. The offence may be dealt with by the magistrates (Justices of the Peace) or sent to a higher court. Some civil matters are also dealt with at the magistrates' court.

Magnetic resonance imaging (MRI): A non-invasive medical technique used in the diagnosis of many diseases, including cancer.

Male rape: Forced/unwanted anal or oral penetration of a male by another male's penis.

Manic depression: *See* Bipolar disorder.

Manslaughter: The killing of another human in a way that is legally less culpable than murder. The intention to kill may not be present, though there may be an element of recklessness.

Manualisation: Defining precisely the procedures which should be employed in psychotherapies: adherence to the theory is known to lead to improved outcomes from therapy.

MAPPA: *See* Multi-agency public protection arrangements.

Masturbatory reconditioning: Techniques used to redirect masturbation to a legal sexual object from an illegal one such as a child (i.e. to substitute fantasies of a legal sex object for fantasies of an illegal one).

Maximisation: A style of questioning in which the strength of the police's evidence is exaggerated in the hope that the suspect will confess.

McNaughten Rule: British rules for determining whether someone is criminally insane and so not legally responsible for the crime.

Megan's law: A US act which enables the disclosure of information concerning the whereabouts of sex offenders in the community.

***Mens rea*:** Many crimes require that the offender knowingly breaks the law in that they know the law but proceed to ignore it. Thus *mens rea* is criminal intent or a guilty mind.

Mental illness: A variety of psychological conditions in which there is a characteristic disabling and distressing impairment in some aspect of the psychological functioning of the individual.

Mesomorph: A compact and muscular body type. Appears in Eysenck's Theory of Crime.

Meta-analysis: Statistical methods of synthesising the findings from a variety of different studies on a topic. It is the analysis of analyses.

Methadone: A synthetic version of opium which is used in treatment for addiction.

Microexpressions: These are brief and partial expressions of the face which occur extremely soon after, say, a particular question is put. They are then actively concealed. They might be regarded as informative by the interrogator.

Minimisation: A style of questioning in which the seriousness of an act is underplayed by an interviewer or it is 'justified' in some way. The intention is to encourage a confession.

Minnesota Multiphasic Personality Inventory (MMPI): A long-established personality measure which assesses several aspects of personality.

Miranda rights: US rules governing arrest in which the suspect's legal rights to remain silent, etc. are explained to them.

Miscarriages of justice: This is a failure of the legal system to give the accused a trial which is fair based on the evidence presented to the court. It is not the same thing as wrongful conviction but they do overlap.

Mitigation: Submitted prior to sentencing, mitigation is the reasons submitted on behalf of the accused to provide excuses for the offence in the hope of reducing the sentence awarded.

Mixed crime scene: A crime scene which involves both organised and disorganised characteristics. It may occur, for example, because there are two or more offenders.

MMPI: *See* Minnesota Multiphasic Personality Inventory.

Mock crime: An imitation or pretend crime set up for research purposes.

Mock jury: An imitation or pretend staged jury set up for research purposes.

Monozygotic twins: Twins from the same fertilised egg, hence identical.

Moral panic: A criminological theory describing situations in which heightened public interest is expressed about groups, people or events which fundamentally challenge dominant values.

Multi-agency public protection arrangements (MAPPA): UK procedures for monitoring sexual and violent offenders in the community.

Multiple killing: Killing several people at the same time.

Munchausen's syndrome by proxy: The condition in which a primary caregiver exaggerates, fabricates, or causes illness or symptoms of illness in a child. The existence of this condition is controversial.

N

Necrophilia: Sexual activity with a dead person.

Neuropsychology: The study of how the structure and functions of the brain relate to behaviour and psychological processes.

Neuroticism: Emotional instability in the sense that neurotic people readily experience negative emotional states and so are vulnerable to anger and depression.

Neutralisation: Mental acts which help protect the criminal from responsibility for their actions.

Next friend: *See* Guardian.

Non compos mentis: Not of a sound mind. That is, the person is unfit to conduct or defend legal proceedings.

Norms: Rules describing how members of a group or wider community should behave and should not behave.

Notary public: A person with the authority to perform certain legal procedures – i.e. the swearing of oaths.

Nothing works: The outmoded view that interventions and treatments to reduce offending and reoffending are largely unsuccessful.

O

Offence paralleling behaviour: Behaviours in institution which reflect the individual's offending behaviours outside of the institution.

Offender profiling: *See* Profile analysis.

Open-ended questioning: Questions designed to get the interviewee to respond extensively rather than using a small number of fixed alternatives (such as yes and no).

Operant behaviour (modification): The process of increasing/decreasing the frequency of naturally occurring behaviours through the use of reinforcements or rewards when the targeted behaviour is exhibited.

Optimal foraging theory: An idea from animal ecology which suggests that creatures use foraging strategies which maximise the food they obtain while minimising the risks involved in foraging. Applied to crime, optimal foraging theory suggests that offenders maximise the rewards of burglary while minimising the negative consequences such as getting caught.

Organised crime scene: A crime scene that seems to exhibit methodological rather than chaotic offender behaviours when committing the crime. It is said to reflect certain characteristics of the offender.

Organised crime: Crime committed by organised criminal groups.

Overkill: Violence beyond what is necessary for an offender to achieve their ends.

P

PACE: *See* Police and Criminal Evidence Act.

Paedophile: An adult with a sexual interest in children though the term is often used to refer to adults with a sexual interest in young people in general.

Paranoia: An extreme or exaggerated distrust of other people who, often, are seen as persecutors.

Parole: The process by which a prisoner may be let out of prison on a temporary basis subject to certain requirements.

Pathways model of sexual abuse: A theory accounting for the development of sex offending against children which suggests that there are four major routes to offending behaviour.

PCL-R: *See* Psychopathy Checklist–Revised.

PEACE: In the UK this is the best practice approach to investigative interviewing. It is an acronym for preparation and planning, engaging and explaining, accounting, closure and evaluation.

Penology: The study of the management of prisons and punishment for crime.

Peremptory challenge: The process by which potential jury members may be objected to (at the voir dire phase of the trial) without the requirement to give a valid legal reason for that challenge.

Peripheral route: The form of persuasion which involves little cognitive processing. So things such as the credibility of the source of the persuasive message influence attitude change rather than careful cognitive elaboration.

Personality disorder: A mental disorder which involves inflexible thought and behaviour patterns which are somewhat enduring.

Phallometry: *See* Plethysmography.

Phobia: An intense and lasting fear of certain activities, persons, situations and so forth. Phobias are regarded as irrational and are typified by behaviours involving the avoidance of the thing that one is afraid of.

Photofit: A way of constructing a facial composite of a suspect from photographs of different varieties of parts of the face.

Photo-spread: A sort of identification parade or line-up which is based on photographs rather than actual people.

Plaintiff: The person who initiates a case against a defendant in a court of law.

Plethysmography: Measurement of the erection or tumescence of the penis based on its circumference or volume. Regarded by some as an indication of sexual arousal.

Police and Criminal Evidence Act (PACE): An important piece of UK legislation regulating the powers of the police in matters such as interviewing, stopping and searching, arrest.

Police caution: A formal situation in which an offender is addressed by a senior police officer. It is a stern warning about any future misconduct. Sometimes it is treated as the same as a conviction for statistical purposes.

Polygraph: The lie detector which measures physiological responses to certain types of questioning.

Post-event information: Pertinent information which becomes available to the individual at some time after they witnessed a crime.

Post-traumatic anger: One of the possible outcomes of post-traumatic stress.

Post-traumatic stress disorder (PTSD): The psychological defence/coping mechanism which may follow extreme stress.

Power killers: People who kill for the sense of power that this instils in them.

Powerful speech: The type of speech which characterises powerful individuals.

Powerless speech: The type of speech which would be used by powerless individuals.

Preconditions model: A theory (by David Finkelstein) of sex offenders against children which suggests that a number of things must occur or be present before a person will offend sexually against children.

Prejudice: A bias or preconceived view without consideration of whether it is fair.

Pre-trial publicity: Publicity given to a crime or offender from the point of a charge being made.

Prevalence: (From medicine) The number of people who have a particular condition at a particular point in time. *See also* Incidence.

Prima facie: Means first sight and there must be prima facie evidence for a case to be answered and, in itself, is sufficient proof unless disproved at the trial.

Primacy-recency effect: Items at certain serial positions in a list of things to be remembered are more likely to be remembered than those at other positions. Usually items in the middle are the least well remembered.

Probative: Providing proof or evidence.

Profile analysis: One of a number of terms for offender profiling in which elements found at the crime scene are identified and linked with the likely characteristics of the culprit. However, sometimes the term is used to describe research which merely gives the typical characteristics of offenders who commit a particular type of crime.

Profile generation: The process of creating a description of the characteristics of the likely offender from the characteristics of the crime scene.

PRO-fit: A way of generating facial composites based on computer techniques.

Prospective study: A research design which involves the assessment of changes over time.

Protective factors: Factors which, if present, tend to protect an otherwise vulnerable person from engaging in a crime.

Proximal factors: Factors which are close (usually in time in psychology), such as peer pressure as a cause of adolescent offending.

Psychiatric disorders: A variety of maladaptive behaviours and psychological functioning problems. They may also be referred to as *emotional* or *mental illness.*

Psychiatry: The branch of medical science which deals with mental and emotional conditions.

Psychoanalysis: An approach which treats mental and emotional problems by revealing the unconscious basis for the condition.

Psychodynamic: Relating to the interrelations between different aspects of the personality.

Psychological profiling: *See* Crime profiling, Profile analysis.

Psychology: The scientific study of the human mind and behaviour.

Psychopath: A person demonstrating chronic amorality and antisocial behaviours.

Psychopathic disorder (psychopathy): A term describing continual long-term problems associated with lack of morality and antisocial tendencies.

Psychopathy Checklist Revised (PCL-R): A checklist for assessing for psychopathy. It is completed by a psychologist or a psychiatrist.

Psychosis: Mental states which involve some degree of loss of contact with reality, such as hallucinations or delusional beliefs.

Psychosocial: Relating to the way an individual develops through an interaction between the individual's psychology and the social environment.

Psychotherapy: Any form of treatment of mental conditions using psychological techniques.

Psychotic: Relating to various mental states which feature a loss of grasp on reality.

Psychoticism: The state of being psychotic.

PTSD: *See* Post-traumatic stress disorder.

Pyromania: A psychological impulse to set fire to things as a way of relieving tension, which often leads to a sense of relief and euphoria afterwards. It is thus clearly different from arson, although it involves arson.

Q

Quadripartite model: A theory of sex offending against children.

Queen's/King's Counsel: Barristers with a minimum of 10 years' experience can apply for this title. They take on important work.

R

Rape trauma syndrome: The broadly characteristic psychological response to rape and attempted rape (such as shock and denial) which is accompanied by a characteristic accommodation process over a lengthy period of time.

Rape: The precise definition of rape varies from jurisdiction to jurisdiction but is often nowadays defined in terms of the forcible/non-consenting penetration of another person's vagina, anus or mouth by the penis. As such, it is no longer a gender-specific crime.

Rape-Myth Acceptance Scale: A measure of the acceptance of rape myths such as that a woman deserves to be raped if she dresses provocatively.

Rapport: Comfortable and harmonious communications or interactions between, usually, an interviewer and interviewee.

Reality monitoring: The process by which people distinguish memories of real events from any other memories.

Recall: The process of memory by which things come back into one's mind. Recall is different from recognition, which occurs when the remembered thing is represented.

Recidivism: Future reoffending by an offender. Usually measured in terms of reconviction rates or survival rates (the proportions having not reoffended after a particular number of years).

Recovered memories: Memories of traumatic incidents (especially child sexual abuse) which re-emerge in adulthood.

Regressed offenders: Sexual offenders against children who, putatively, in response to stress move their sexual interest from adults to children.

Rehabilitation: The process by which a person is returned to a normal lifestyle.

Relapse prevention: Therapeutic methods for sex offenders that teach ways of avoiding situations and thoughts which will lead to reoffending.

Relative judgement theory: The idea that in identity parades or line-ups the witness tends to choose someone similar to the suspect if the suspect is missing from that line-up.

Relevant question technique: A technique of questioning in a polygraph examination.

Remand prisoners: Prisoners awaiting trial who have not been convicted.

Remand: To order an accused person to be kept in custody or placed on bail pending further court appearance.

Reparation: Attempts to make good the damage caused to a victim of a crime.

Repressed memory: A memory (usually of child sexual abuse) which is not available at a particular time to conscious experience.

Researcher-practitioners: The term used to indicate that practitioners (e.g. forensic and clinical psychologists) should be active researchers in order that their field may develop in an evidence-based fashion.

Restorative justice: Procedures which, through a mediator, bring offender and victim into direct or indirect contact. The victim may get answers to questions important to them and the offender may learn more about the impact of their offending behaviour and perhaps offer reparation.

Retribution: The idea that the harm done to society by an offender should be counterbalanced by proportionate punishment being given to the offender.

Risk assessment: The methods and procedures by which a judgement is formed about the likely extent of the negative outcomes of a course of action such as releasing a sex offender from prison.

Risk factor: Any variable which is predictive of a risk such as the risk of reoffending or the risk of an attempted escape.

Risk management: The procedures and practices employed to limit or prevent the risk materialising that has been perceived to be posed by an offender or client. Incarceration may be one such procedure.

Routine activity theory: A criminological theory which describes offending behaviour in terms of the everyday activities of offenders.

RRASOR (Rapid Risk Assessment for Sexual Offender Recidivism): A questionnaire measure of the likelihood of future recidivism by sex offenders.

Rules of evidence: This refers to the principles governing the presentation of evidence in court – for example, the rules concerning the use of hearsay evidence or previous convictions.

S

Sarah's law: The UK equivalent of Megan's law – that is, the community notification of registered sex offenders in the community.

SCAN: Scientific Content Analysis – one of several procedures which seek to differentiate truthful and untruthful statements. The method is based on the assumption that truthful and dishonest statements differ in a number of structural and content features.

Schizophrenia: A complex mental illness in which the sufferer has problems differentiating real experiences from unreal experiences, has problems in thinking logically about issues, and behaving as others do in social situations. No decisive differentiating feature exists and diagnosis calls for a thorough understanding of the condition and other conditions which may have some similar symptoms.

Scientific Content Analysis: *See* SCAN.

Scientific jury selection: The use of survey and other evidence to identify the characteristics of jurors likely to be sympathetic with one side of a trial, which may be used in juror selection.

Scientist-practitioner: A term used to describe the situation in which practitioners (including forensic psychologists) are expected to also be active researchers. *See also* Researcher-practitioner.

Script: Essentially, a typical or expected sequence of actions which integrates individual actions in a way which may be regarded as meaningful.

Secondary victimisation: The consequences of being the victim of crime for those who were not directly victimised. Thus the family of a victim of violence may experience secondary victimisation because of the loss of family income while the direct victim is hospitalised.

Sequential line-up/identification parade: A line-up where the eyewitness sees the suspect and the other members of the line-up one at a time.

Serial killer: A killer who kills three or more people with a clear separation between each of the crimes.

Sexual offender register: A legally required list of most sex offenders who must register many of their movements within defined limits.

Sexual scripts: Much social behaviour follows broad patterns which can be likened to an actor's script. However, the detail of the performance is left to the act. Sexual scripts are the idea that sexual behaviour is similarly broadly structured.

Sexualisation model of paedophilia: The theory that early sexual experiences in childhood in certain circumstances can lead to paedophilia later in life.

Sexually violent predator (SVP) laws: US laws dealing with serious repeat sexual offenders.

Signature: Characteristics of a crime scene which are typical of a particular offender but which have no particular relevance to the crime's perpetration itself.

Simultaneous line-up/identification parade: Where the eyewitness sees the suspect and the other members of the line-up all at the same time.

Smallest space analysis (SSA): A form of complex statistical analysis used to identify underlying patterns in characteristics of a crime scene.

Social learning theory: The idea that much human socialisation takes place through a process of social observation.

Solicitor: A lawyer in the UK who primarily advises clients and may represent clients in some courts.

Somatypes: Body shape types in Sheldon's theory.

Special hospitals: High-security units in which mentally disordered offenders are treated.

SSA: *See* Smallest space analysis.

Staging: Altering a crime scene in a way which the offender thinks will divert investigative attention away from them.

Stalking: Various behaviours which have the consequence of harassing the victim, leading to fear and anxiety. It takes many forms but involves unwelcome/malicious attention from another person such as a former partner or complete stranger.

Stare decisis: The principle of using previous legal decisions as the standard for making later decisions.

Statement validity (or reality) analysis: A variety of procedures which generate hypotheses about the likely truthfulness or accuracy of a person's (usually a child's) evidence. The procedures also allow for the testing of the hypotheses generated.

Static risk predictor: A variable such as gender which does not vary for an individual over time used to predict risk of reoffending, etc.

Statistical profiling: Those forms of offender profiling particularly dependent on aggregated statistical data.

Statute of limitations: The amount of time that the state has in order to bring a prosecution for a crime.

Statutory rape: Sexual intercourse with a person too young to legally give consent.

Statutory: Related to laws produced by the legislature – as opposed to common law, for example.

Strain theory: A criminological theory in which it is assumed that social structures may be responsible for crime.

Strategic use of evidence (SUE) technique: A technique for investigative interviewing.

Strict liability: Offences for which there is no requirement of criminal intent (*mens rea*).

Structural equation modelling: A statistical technique which seeks to test different models of the relationships between a number of variables. As such, it can be used in theory development.

Structured interview: A way of describing the typical police interview with a witness (as opposed to the cognitive interview).

Structured trauma writing: *See* Trauma writing.

Sub judice: The matter is under judicial consideration and may not be discussed publicly.

Suggestibility: The characteristic of a person who is easily swayed or influenced by another person such as an interviewer.

Summary offence: In the UK, an offence that can be tried in the lowest courts, i.e. magistrates' courts.

Suicide ideation: Thoughts about committing suicide or a preoccupation with suicide.

Survival rates: One way of presenting reconviction, recidivism or other data which changes over time. Survival is the rate of persons *not* showing the characteristic in question. So survival rate from reconviction is the number *not* being reconvicted at each point in time.

System variables: Variables over which a researcher or practitioner has control.

T

***Tarasoff* decision:** An American court decision requiring therapists to deal with threats and risks to third parties from the therapist's clients.

Testosterone: The most common male sex hormone but it is also to be found in females.

Theory of mind: This refers to our ability to understand that other people have mental states as well as we do.

Therapeutic community: An organisation for the treatment of mental illness and drug addiction in which the policies and practices of the organisation and the general social atmosphere are part of the curative process.

Tort: This is the law concerned with wrongs and damages caused by one person against another, such as libel, slander, negligence and so forth.

Tranquilliser: A drug which has a calming or quietening effect on anxiety.

Trauma: The extreme emotional shock which is the consequence of stressful events.

Trauma writing: Writing about one's own trauma, which tends to have therapeutic benefits in itself.

Treatment integrity: This is the extent to which a therapeutic intervention is implemented closely to the original intention or plan.

Trophies: Body parts of or property of a victim sometimes taken by serial killers and others.

U

Ultra vires: The matter is not within a particular court's jurisdiction.

Undeutsch hypothesis: The idea that language which describes actual experiences has characteristics which are different from those which are imagined. It is the basis for statement validity analysis.

Upward comparison process: The process of making judgements about oneself or one's circumstances by comparison with those more advantaged than oneself.

Validity checklist: One of the two components of statement validity analysis.

Validity: Whether something measures what it purports to measure.

Vicarious learning/reinforcement: Learning by observation or imitation of others.

Victim surveys: Surveys of the general population to assess how many have been a victim of crime.

Victimisation: The process of being made a victim.

Victimless crime: A crime with no obvious victims that is more generally perpetrated against society. This might include drug use and graffiti.

Victimology: The branch of criminology devoted to the study of victims.

Video identification: A form of identification parade/line-up in which the witness views video clips of the suspect and others rather than people face to face.

Visionary (serial) killers: Those who kill in response to verbal commands or visions.

Voir dire: In the Anglo-American system, the process of asking questions which help in the decision as to whether the person is suitable to be a member of a jury. The process may be conducted by the judge or by the lawyers or by both in different systems.

Voluntary false confession: A false confession made without outside pressures such as the influence of the interviewer.

Voyeurism: The process by which an individual obtains sexual pleasure from observing another person naked, semi-naked or participating in a sexual act.

Vulnerable witness: This refers to a child or any other person suffering a mental, social, intellectual or similar disability which may reduce the quality of their evidence or make the presentation of evidence in court difficult.

Weapons effect: In this, an eyewitness focuses disproportionately on the weapons used in a crime in a way which is detrimental to the quality of their memory for other aspects of the crime scene.

Wechsler Adult Intelligence Scale: A well-established measure of intelligence. It is administered to a single person at a time and includes both verbal and non-verbal scales.

White-collar crime: Crimes held to be characteristic of middle-class (white-collar) workers, for example, using the firm's telephone for private calls.

Working memory: A theoretical notion to describe the parts of memory which are actively involved in the processing and putting into storage of things which may pass into long-term memory.

XYY chromosome: The outmoded idea that some criminals have an additional male chromosome in their genetic make-up which is partly responsible for their criminality.

Youth subculture: The idea that there are groups of youngsters who have a somewhat distinct culture which contributes to delinquency.

Zero tolerance: The policing strategy which requires arrest whenever a crime is committed, no matter how trivial an instance it is.

References

A

Aamodt, M.G. (2008) 'Reducing misconceptions and false beliefs in police and criminal psychology' *Criminal Justice and Behavior* **35**, 1231–40.

Aamodt, M.G. and Custer, H. (2006) 'Who can best catch a liar? A meta-analysis of individual differences in detecting deception' *Forensic Examiner* **15** (1), 6–11.

Abdel-Khalek, A. (2004) 'Neither altruistic suicide, nor terrorism but martyrdom: a Muslim perspective' *Archives of Suicide Research* **8**, 99–113.

Abel, G.G., Barlow, D.H., Blanchard, E.B. and Guild, D. (1977) 'The components of rapists' sexual arousal' *Archives of General Psychiatry* **34**, 895–903.

Abel, G.G., Becker, J.V. and Cunningham-Rathner, J. (1984) 'Complications, consent, and cognitions in sex between children and adults' *International Journal of Law and Psychiatry* **7**, 89–103.

Abel, G.G., Becker, J.V., Mittelman, M.S., Cunningham-Rathner, J., Rouleau, J.L. and Murphy, W.D. (1987) 'Self-reported sex crimes of non-incarcerated paraphiliacs' *Journal of Interpersonal Violence* **2**, 3–25.

Abel, G.G., Mittelman, M., Becker, J.V., Cunningham-Rathner, M.S. and Lucas, L. (1983) 'Characteristics of men who molest young children' Paper presented at the World Congress of Behavior Therapy, Washington, DC.

Abrahams, G. (1954) *The Legal Mind: An Approach to the Dynamics of Advocacy* London: H.F.L. Publishers.

Abramsky, L., and Chapple, J. (1997) '47, XXY (Klinefelter Syndrome) and 47, XYY: estimated rates of and indication for postnatal diagnosis with implications for prenatal counselling' *Prenatal Diagnosis*, **17**, pp. 363–368.

Abramson, L.Y., Seligman, M.E.P. and Teasdale, I. (1978) 'Learned helplessness in humans: Critique and reformulation' *Journal of Abnormal Psychology* **87**, 49–59.

Acklin, M.W., Fuger, K. and Gowensmith, W. (2015) 'Examiner agreement and judicial consensus in forensic mental health evaluations' *Journal of Forensic Psychology Practice* **15** (4), 318–343.

Addiction Hope (2013) 'Kleptomania causes, statistics, addiction signs, symptoms and side effects' https://www.addictionhope.com/mood-disorder/kleptomania/

Adorjan, M., Christensen, T., Kelly, B. and Pawluch, D. (2012) 'Stockholm syndrome as vernacular resource' *Sociological Quarterly* **53** (3), 454–74.

Agnew, R. (1992) 'Foundation for a general strain theory of crime and delinquency' *Criminology* **30**, 47–87.

Agnew, R. (1997) 'Stability and change in crime over the life course: A strain theory explanation' in T.P. Thornberry (ed.), *Developmental Theories of Crime* Brunswick, NJ: Transaction.

Agnew, R. (2001) 'Building on the foundation of general strain theory: Specifying the types of strain most likely to lead to crime and delinquency' *Journal of Research in Crime and Delinquency* **38**, 319–61.

Agnew, R. (2016) 'A theory of crime resistance and susceptibility' *Criminology* **54** (2), 181–211.

Ainsworth, P.B. (1981) 'Incident perception by British police officers' *Law and Human Behavior* **5**, 331–6.

Ainsworth, P.B. (1995) *Psychology and Policing in a Changing World* Chichester: John Wiley.

Ainsworth, P.B. (1998) *Psychology, Law and Eyewitness Testimony.* Chichester: Wiley.

Ainsworth, P.B. (2000) *Psychology and Crime: Myths and Reality* Harlow: Longman.

Ainsworth, P.B. and Moss, K. (2000) 'Perceptions and misperceptions of crime amongst a sample of British students' Paper presented at the conference of the European Association of Psychology and Law, Limassol, Cyprus.

Alexy, E., Burgess, A.W., Baker, T. and Smoyak, S. (2005) 'Perceptions of cyberstalking among college students' *Brief Treatment and Crisis Intervention* **5**, 279–89.

Alison, L., Goodwill, A., Almond, L., van den Heuvel, C. and Winter, J. (2010) 'Pragmatic solutions to offender profiling and behavioural investigative advice' *Legal and Criminological Psychology* **15**, 115–132.

Alison, L., Smith, M.D. and Morgan, K. (2003) 'Interpreting the accuracy of offender profiles' *Psychology, Crime and Law* **9** (2), 185–95.

Alison, L., Smith, M.D., Eastman, O. and Rainbow, L. (2003) 'Toulmin's philosophy of argument and its relevance to offender profiling' *Psychology, Crime and Law* **9** (2), 173–83.

Allen, J. (2004) 'Worry about crime' in S. Nicholas and A. Walker (eds) *Crime in England and Wales 2002/2003: Supplementary Vol. 2: Crime, Disorder and the Criminal Justice System – Public Attitudes and Perceptions* London: Home Office, pp. 41–54: http://webarchive.nationalarchives.gov.uk/20110220105210/http://rds.homeoffice.gov.uk/rds/pdfs2/hosb0204.pdf

Almerigogna, J., Ost, J., Bull, R. and Akehurst, L. (2008a) 'A state of high anxiety: how non-supportive interviewers can increase the suggestibility of child witnesses' *Applied Cognitive Psychology* **21** (7), 963–74.

Almerigogna, J., Ost, J., Akehurst, L. and Fluck, M. (2008b) 'How interviewers' nonverbal behaviors can affect children's perceptions and susceptibility' *Journal of Experimental Child Psychology* **100** (1), 17–39.

Almond, L., Duggan, L., Shine, J. and Canter, D. (2005) 'Test of the arson action system model in an incarcerated population' *Psychology, Crime and Law* **11** (1), 1–15.

Almond, L., McManus, M.A., Worsley, J., and Gregory, P. (2015) 'Cold case reviews of serious sexual offenders: an exploration of pre- and post-index offending patterns' *Journal of Forensic Psychology Practice*, **15** (3), 205–225.

Alós, R., Esteban, F., Jódar, P. and Miguélez, F. (2015) 'Effects of prison work programmes on the employability of ex-prisoners' *European Journal of Criminology* **12** (1), 35–50.

Amado, B.G., Arce, R. and Farina, F. (2015) 'Undeutsch hypothesis and criteria based content analysis: a meta-analytic review' *European Journal of Psychology Applied to Legal Context* 7, 3–12.

American Professional Society on the Abuse of Children (2002) *Investigative interviewing in cases of alleged child abuse* Chicago: Author.

American Psychiatric Association (2000) *Diagnostic and Statistical Manual of Mental Disorders (DSM-IV)* Washington, DC: APA.

American Psychiatric Association (2013) *Diagnostic and Statistical Manual of Mental Disorders (DSM-V)* Arlington, VA: American Psychiatric Publishing.

American Psychological Association (2017) (http://www.apa.org/practice/guidelines/forensic-psychology.aspx, accessed 1 June 2017)

Anderson, R. J., Goddard, L. and Powell, J. H. (2010) 'Reduced specificity of autobiographical memory as a moderator of the relationship between daily hassles and depression' *Cognition and Emotion* **24**, 702–709.

Anderson, T., Schum, D. and Twining, W. (2005) *Analysis of Evidence* (2nd edn) Cambridge, Cambridge University Press.

Andrews, B., and Brewin, C.R. (2017) 'False memories and free speech: is scientific debate being suppressed?' *Applied Cognitive Psychology* **31**, 45–49.

Andrews, D. A., Bonta, J. and Hoge, R. D. (1990) 'Classification for effective rehabilitation: rediscovering psychology' *Criminal Justice and Behavior* **17**, 19–52.

Andrews, D.A. (1982) *The Level of Supervisory Inventory (LSI): The first follow-up* Toronto: Ontario Ministry of Correctional Services.

Andrews, D.A. and Bonta, J. (1995) *The Level of Service Inventory–Revised* Toronto: Multi-Health Systems Inc.

Andrews, D.A. and Bonta, J. (2006) *The Psychology of Criminal Conduct* (4th edn) Cincinnati, OH: Anderson Publishing Co.

Andrews, D.A. and Bonta, J. (2010) *The Psychology of Criminal Conduct* (5th edn) New Providence, NJ: Matthew Bender.

Andrews, D.A., Zinger, I., Hoge, R.D., Bonta, J., Gendreau, P. and Cullen, F.T. (1990) 'Does correctional treatment work? A clinically relevant and psychologically informed meta-analysis' *Criminology* **28**, 369–404.

Angermeyer, M.C. and Schulze, B. (2001) 'Reinforcing stereotypes: how the focus on forensic cases in news reporting may influence public attitudes towards the mentally ill' *International Journal of Law and Psychiatry* **24**, 469–86.

APA (2013) 'Statement of the American Psychological Association regarding pedophilia and the *Diagnostic and Statistical Manual of Mental Disorders (DSM-5)*' http://www.apa.org/news/press/releases/2013/10/pedophilia-mental.aspx

Appel, A.E. and Holden, G.W. (1998) 'The co-occurrence of spouse and physical child abuse: a review and appraisal' *Journal of Family Psychology* **12** (4), 578–99.

Appleby, S. C., Hasel, L. E. and Kassin, S. M. (2013) 'Police-induced confessions: An empirical analysis of their content and impact' *Psychology, Crime and Law* **9**, 111–128.

APSAC (1996) 'Practice guidelines: use of anatomical dolls in child sexual abuse assessment' *Pacific Law Review* **28** (1), 78–128.

Araji, S. and Finkelhor, D. (1985) 'Explanations of pedophilia: review of empirical research' *Bulletin of the American Academy of Psychiatry and the Law* **13** (1), 17–37.

Arboleda-Florez, J., Holley, H.L. and Crisanti, A. (1996) *Mental Health and Violence: Proof or Stereotype?* Health Promotion and Programs Branch, Health Canada. http://hwcweb.hwc.ca/hppb/mentalhealth/pubs/mental_illness/index.htm

Arce, R. (1998) 'Empirical studies on jury size' *Expert Evidence* **6**, 227–41.

Arce, R., Farina, F., Novo, M. and Seijo, D. (1998) 'In search of causes of hung juries' *Expert Evidence* **6**, 1–18.

Arce, R., Farina, F., Vila, C. and Santiago, R. (1996) 'Empirical assessment of the escabinato jury system' *Psychology, Crime and Law* **2**, 175–83.

Arce, R., Seijo, D., Farina, F. and Novo, M. (2004) 'Family interaction factor: analysing the effects on personal, social and school inadaptability and delinquent behaviour' Krakow, European Association of Psychology and Law (EAPL) Conference.

Archer, J. (2004) 'Sex differences in aggression in real-world settings: A meta-analytic review' *Review of General Psychology* **8**, 291–321.

Arkowitz, S. and Vess, J. (2003) 'An evaluation of the Bumby RAPE and MOLEST scales as measures of cognitive distortions with civilly committed sexual offenders' *Sexual Abuse: A Journal of Research and Treatment* **15** (4), 237–49.

Arndorfer, A., Malloy, L.C. and Cauffman, E. (2015) 'Interrogations, confessions, and adolescent offenders' perceptions of the legal system' *Law and Human Behavior* **39** (5), 503–513.

Arson Prevention Forum (2014) 'Arson: a call to action. A 'State of the Nation' report' http://stoparsonuk.org/documents/resources/DS2014-1156ArsonReportandappendix.pdf

Artz, S. (1998) 'Where have all the school girls gone? Violent girls in the school yard' *Child and Youth Care Forum* **27** (2), 77–109.

Ashcroft, Lord (2011) 'Crime, punishment and the people: Public opinion and the criminal justice debate' http://lordashcroftpolls.com/wp-content/uploads/2011/12/crime-punishment-and-the-people.pdf

Ask, K. and Granhag, P.A. (2005) 'Motivational sources of confirmation bias in criminal investigations: the need for cognitive closure' *Journal of Investigative Psychology and Offender Profiling* **2**, 43–63.

Association of Forensic Science Providers (2009) 'Standards for the formulation of evaluative forensic science expert opinion' *Science and Justice* **49**, 161–4.

Atkinson, D.F. and Mann, R.E. (2012) 'Prison officers as observers of offence paralleling behaviours: an untapped resource?' *The Journal of Forensic Psychiatry and Psychology* **23** (2), 139–55.

Atran, S. (2003) 'Genesis of suicide terrorism' *Science* **299**, 1534–9.

Attrill, G. (1999) 'Violent offender programmes' in G. Towl and C. McDougal (eds), *Issues in Forensic Psychology 1: What do Forensic Psychologists do? Current and Future Directions in the Prison and Probation Services* Leicester: British Psychological Society, pp. 58–61.

Australian Psychological Society (2017) (http://www.psychology.org.au/community/specialist/forensic, accessed 1 June 2017)

Averduk, M., van Galder, J.-L., Eisner, M., and Ribeaud, D. (2016) 'Violence begets violence . . . but how?: a decision making perspective on the victim-offender overlap' *Criminology* 54 (2), 282–306.

Avery, D.R., McKay, P.F. and Hunter, E.M. (2012) 'Demography and disappearing merchandise: How older workforces influence retail shrinkage' *Journal of Organizational Behavior* **33** (1), 105–20.

Avery-Clark, C.A. and Laws, D.R. (1984) 'Differential erection response patterns of sexual child abusers to stimuli describing activities with children' *Behavior Therapy* **15**, 71–83.

B

Blacks, S. (2012) 'Frequently Cited Journals in Forensic Psychology' *Psychological Reports* **110** (1), 276–82.

Browne, D. (1999) 'From the frying pan to the fire: exploring the role of foster care in the development of criminal behaviour'. Paper presented to the Joint International Conference, Dublin.

Browne, D. (2000) 'Foster care and forensic psychology' *Forensic Update* **61**, 11–14.

Baartman, H.E.M. (1992) 'The credibility of children as witnesses and the social denial of the incestuous abuse of children' in F. Lösel, D. Bender and T. Bliesner (eds) *Psychology and Law: International Perspectives* Berlin: Walter de Gruyter, pp. 345–51.

Babchishin, K.M., Hanson, R.K., and Van Zuylen, H. (2015) 'Online child pornography offenders are different: a meta-analysis of the characteristics of online and offline sex offenders against children' *Archives of Sexual Behavior* **44**, 45–66.

Bachrach, L.L. (1984) 'Deinstitutionalization and women: assessing the consequences of public policy' *American Psychologist* **39** (10), 1187–92.

Bachrach, L.L. (1989) 'Deinstitutionalization: a semantic analysis' *Journal of Social Issues* **45** (3), 161–72.

Bailey, A.K., Tolnay, S.E., Beck, E.M., Roberts, R., and Wong, N.H. (2008) 'Personalizing lynch victims: a new database to support the study of southern mob violence' *Historical Methods* **41**, 47–61.

Bailey, A.K., Tolnay, S.E., Beck. E.M., and Laird, J.D. (2011) 'Targeting lynch victims: social marginality or status transgressions?' *American Sociological Review* **76** (3) 412–436.

Baker, R.R., Lichtenberg, P.A. and Moye, J. (1998) 'A practice guideline for assessment of competence and capacity of the older adult' *Professional Psychology: Research and Practice* **29** (2), 149–54.

Baksheev, G., Ogloff, J.R. and Thomas, S.D.M. (2012) 'Identification of mental illness in police cells: a comparison of police processes, the Brief Jail Mental Health Screen and the Jail Screening Assessment Tool' *Psychology, Crime and Law* **18** (6), 529–42.

Balemba, S., Beauregard, E. and Mieczkowski, T. (2012) 'To resist or not to resist? The effect of context and crime characteristics on sex offenders' reaction to victim resistance' *Crime and Delinquency* **58**, 588–611.

Ballard, M.E. and Wiest, J.R. (1996) 'Mortal Kombat™: the effects of violent videogame play on males' hostility and cardiovascular responding' *Journal of Applied Social Psychology* **26** (8), 717–30.

Bandura, A. (1973) *Aggression: A Social Learning Analysis* Englewood Cliffs, NJ: Prentice Hall.

Bandura, A. (1977) *Social Learning Theory* Englewood Cliffs, NJ: Prentice Hall.

Bandura, A. (1983) 'Psychological mechanisms of aggression' in R.G. Green and C.I. Donnerstein (eds) *Aggression, Theoretical and Empirical Reviews Vol. 1: Theoretical and Methodological Issues* New York: Academic Press, pp. 1–40.

Bandura, A. (1990) 'Mechanisms of moral disengagement' in W. Reich (ed.) *Origins of Terrorism: Psychologies, Ideologies, Theologies, States of Mind* New York: Cambridge University Press, pp. 161–91.

Bandura, A. (1991) 'Social cognitive theory of moral thought and action' in W. M. Kurtines and J. L.Gewirtz (Eds.), *Handbook of Moral Behavior and Development: Theory,Research and Application*. Hillside, NJ: Lawrence Erlbaum, pp. 71–129.

Bandura, A. and Huston, A.C. (1961) 'Identification as a process of incidental learning' *Journal of Abnormal and Social Psychology* **63**, 311–18.

Bandura, A., Barbaranelli, C., Caprara, G.V., and Pastorelli, C. (1996) 'Mechanisms of moral disengagement in the exercise of moral agency' *Journal of Personality and Social Psychology* **71**, 364–374.

Bandura, A., Barbaranelli, C., Caprara, G.V., Pastorelli, C. and Regalia, C. (2001) 'Sociocognitive self-regulatory mechanisms governing transgressive behavior' *Journal of Personality and Social Psychology* **80**, 125–135.

Bandura, A., Ross, D. and Ross, S.A. (1961) 'Transmission of aggression through imitation of aggressive models' *Journal of Abnormal and Social Psychology* 63575–82.

Bandura, A., Ross, D. and Ross, S.A. (1963) 'Imitation of film-mediated aggressive models' *Journal of Abnormal and Social Psychology* **66**, 3–11.

Barbaree, H.E. (1998) 'Denial and minimization among sex offenders: assessment and treatment outcome' *Sex Offender Programming* **3** (4), 1–7.

Barclay, G., Tavares, C. and Siddique, A. (2001) *International Comparisons of Criminal Justice Statistics 1999* London: Home Office Research, Development and Statistics Directorate.

Barkworth, J.M., and Murphy, K. (2015) 'Procedural justice policing and citizen compliance behaviour: the importance of emotion' *Psychology, Crime and Law*, **21**(3), 254–273.

Barnes, G. M., Welte, J. W., Hoffman, J. H. and Dintcheff, B. A. (2005) 'Shared predictors of youthful gambling, substance use and delinquency' *Psychology of Addictive Behaviours* **19**, 165–174.

Barnett, G.D., Wakeling, H., Mandeville-Norden, R. and Rakestrow, J. (2013) 'Does change in psychometric test scores tell us anything about risk of reconviction in sexual offenders?' *Psychology, Crime and Law* **19** (1), 85–110.

Baron, L. and Straus, M. (1984) 'Sexual stratification, pornography and rape in the United States' in N.M. Malamuth and E. Donnerstein (eds) *Pornography and Sexual Aggression* New York: Academic Press, pp. 185–209.

Baron, L. and Straus, M. (1989) *Four Theories of Rape: A State Level Analysis* New Haven, CT: Yale University Press.

Bartels, J.M., Ryan, J.J., Urban, L.S. and Glass, L.A. (2010) 'Correlations between estimates of state IQ and FBI crime statistics' *Personality and Individual Differences* **48**, 579–83.

Bartlett, D. and Memon, A. (1995) 'Advocacy' in R. Bull and D. Carson (eds) *Handbook of Psychology in Legal Contexts* Chichester: John Wiley, pp. 543–54.

Bartol, C.R. and Bartol, A.M. (1999) 'History of forensic psychology' in A.K. Hess and I.B. Weiner (eds) *Handbook of Forensic Psychology* (2nd edn) London: John Wiley & Sons, pp. 3–23.

Barton, J., Vrij, A. and Bull, R. (2000a) 'High speed driving: police use of lethal force during simulated incidents' *Legal and Criminological Psychology* **5**, 107–21.

Barton, J., Vrij, A. and Bull, R. (2000b) 'The influence of field dependence on excitation transfer by police officers during armed confrontation' in A. Czerederecka, T. Jaskiewicz-Obdzinska and J. Wojcikiewicz (eds) *Forensic Psychology and Law: Traditional Questions and New Ideas* Krakow: Institute of Forensic Research Publishers, pp. 282–6.

Barrett-Lennard, G.T. 'The empathy cycle: refinement of a nuclear concept' *Journal of Counseling Psychology* **28** (2), 91–100.

Bateman, A.L. and Salfati, C.G. (2007) 'An examination of behavioral consistency using individual behaviors or groups of behaviors in serial homicide' *Behavioral Sciences and the Law* **25** (4), 527–44.

Bateman, A.W. and Fonagy, P. (1999) 'Effectiveness of partial hospitalization in the treatment of borderline personality disorder: a randomized controlled trial' *American Journal of Psychiatry* **156** (10), 1563–9.

Bates, A. (1996) 'The origins, development and effect on subsequent behaviour of deviant sexual fantasies in sexually violent adult men' Unpublished manuscript, Thames Valley Project, 17 Park Road, Didcot, OX11 8QL, UK.

Baumeister, R.F. Bratslavsky, El., Muraven, M. and Tice, D.M. (1998)

'Ego depletion: Is the active self a limited resource?' *Journal of Personality and Social Psychology* **74** (5), 1252 –65.

Baxter, D.J., Barbaree, H.E. and Marshall, W.L. (1986) 'Sexual responses to consenting and forced sex in a large sample of rapists and non-rapists' *Behavioral Research and Therapy* **24**, 513–20.

Baxter, D.J., Marshall, W.L., Barbaree, H.E., Davidson, P.R. and Malcolm, P.B. (1984) 'Deviant sexual behaviour' *Criminal Justice and Behavior* **11**, 477–501.

Baxter, J.S. and Bain, S.A. (2002) 'Faking interrogative suggestibility: the truth machine' *Legal and Criminological Psychology* **7** (2), 219–25.

Bazargan, M. (1994) 'The effects of health, environment, and sociopsychological variables on fear of crime and its consequences among urban black elderly individuals' *International Journal of Ageing and Human Development* **38** (2), 99–115.

BBC News (2005) 'Sex offenders may face lie detector tests', http://news.bbc.co.uk/1/hi/uk/2208779.stm

BBC News (2017) 'Sex offender treatment in prison led to more offending' http://www.bbc.co.uk/news/uk-40460637

Beattey, R.A., Matsuura, T. and Jeglic, E.L. (2014) 'Judicial bond-setting behavior: the perceived nature of the crime may matter more than how serious it is' *Psychology, Public Policy, and Law* **20** (4), 411–420.

Beaumont, G. (2000) 'Clinical neuropsychology in practice' *The Psychologist* **13** (1), 16–17.

Beauregard, E. and Mieczkowski, T. (2012) 'Risk estimations of the conjunction of victim and crime event characteristics on the lethal outcome of sexual assaults' *Violence and Victims* **27**, 470–86.

Beaver, K.M., and Wright, J.P. (2011) 'The association between county-level IQ and county-level crime rates' *Intelligence* **39**, 22–26.

Beaver, K.M., DeLisi, M., Vaughn, M.G. and Wright, J.P. (2010) 'The intersection of genes and neuropsychological deficits in the prediction of adolescent delinquency and low self-control' *International Journal of Offender Therapy and Comparative Criminology* **54** (1), 22–42.

Beck, A.T. (2002) 'Prisoners of hate' *Behavior Research and Therapy* **40** (3), 209–16.

Beck, J.C. (1995) 'Forensic psychiatry in Britain' *Bulletin of the American Academy of Psychiatry and the Law* **23** (2), 249–60.

Becker, G. (1968) 'Crime and punishment: an economic analysis' *Journal of Political Economy* **78**,169–217.

Becker, H. (1963) *Outsiders: Studies in the Sociology of Deviance* New York: The Free Press.

Becker-Blease, K., and Freyd, J.J. (2017) 'Additional questions about the applicability of "false memory" research' *Applied Cognitive Psychology* **31**, 34–36.

Beech, A. R., and Ward, T. (2004) 'The integration of etiology and risk in sexual offenders: A theoretical framework' *Aggression and Violent Behavior* **10**, 31–63.

Beech, A., Fisher, D. and Beckett, R. (1998) 'Step 3: An Evaluation of the Prison Sex Offender Treatment Programme' London: Home Office.

Beech, A., Fisher, D. and Beckett, R. (1999) *STEP 3: An Evaluation of the Prison Sex Offender Treatment Programme.* A report for the Home Office by the STEP team, November 1998. London: Home Office Information Publications Group, Research Development Statistics Directorate.

Beech, A.R. and Chauhan, J. (2013) 'Evaluating the effectiveness of the Supporting Offenders through Restoration Inside (SORI) Programme delivered in seven prisons in England and Wales' *Legal and Criminological Psychology* **18**, 229–39.

Begic, D. and Begic, N.J. (2001) 'Aggressive behaviour in combat veterans with posttraumatic stress disorder' *Military Medicine* **166**, 671–6.

Bègue, L. and Roche, S. (2005) 'Birth order and youth delinquent behaviour testing the differential parental control hypothesis in a French representative sample' *Psychology, Crime & Law* **11** (1), 75–85.

Behrman, B.W. and Davey, S.L. (2001) 'Eyewitness identification in actual criminal cases: An archival analysis' *Law and Human Behavior* **25** (5), 475–91.

Beier, K.M., Ahlers, C.J., Goecker, D., Neutze, J., Mundt, I.A., Hupp, E. and Schaefer, G.A. (2009) 'Can pedophiles be reached for primary prevention of child sexual abuse? First results of the Berlin Prevention Project Dunkelfeld' *Journal of Forensic Psychiatry & Psychology* **20** (6), 851–67.

Bekerian, D. and Dennett, J.L. (1992) 'The truth in content analyses of a child's testimony' in F. Lösel, D. Bender and T. Bliesner (eds) *Psychology and Law: International Perspectives* Berlin: Walter de Gruyter, pp. 335–44.

Bender, D. and Lösel F. (2011) 'Bullying at school as a predictor of delinquency, violence and other anti-social behaviour in adulthood' *Criminal Behaviour and Mental Health* **21**, 99–106.

Bender, D., Bliesener, T. and Lösel, F. (1996) 'Deviance or resilience? A longitudinal study of adolescents in residential care' in G. Davies, S. Lloyd-Bostock, M. McMurran and C. Wilson (eds) *Psychology, Law and Criminal Justice: International Developments in Research and Practice* Berlin: Walter de Gruyter, pp. 409–23.

Bennell, C. and Canter, D.V. (2002) 'Linking commercial burglaries by *modus operandi*: tests using regression and ROC analysis' *Science & Justice* **42**, 153–64.

Bennell, C. and Jones, N. (2005) 'Between a ROC and a hard place: a method for linking serial burglaries by *modus operandi*' *Journal of Investigative Psychology and Offender Profiling* **2**, 23–41.

Bennett, T., Holloway, K. and Farrington, D. (2008) 'The statistical association between drug misuse and crime: A meta-analysis' *Aggression and Violent Behavior* **13** (2), 107–18.

Bennett, W.L. and Feldman, M.S. (1981) *Reconstructing Reality in the Courtroom* London: Tavistock Publications.

Bennett, T, and Wright, R. (1984) *Burglars on Burglary* Farnham, Surrey: Gower

Ben-Shakhar, G. (2008) 'The case against the use of polygraph examinations to monitor post-conviction sex offenders' *Legal and Criminological Psychology* **13**, 191–207.

Benton, T.R., Ross, D.F., Bradshaw, E., Thomas, W.N. and Bradshaw, G.S. (2006) 'Eyewitness memory is still not common sense: comparing jurors, judges and law enforcement to eyewitness experts' *Applied Cognitive Psychology* **20**, 115–29.

Berger, M.A. (2008) 'Eyewitness testimony and false confession' in *Beyond Common Sense: Psychological Science in the Courtroom* Oxford: Blackwell, 315–26.

Bergman, G. R. (1976) 'The evaluation of an experimental program designed to reduce recidivism among second felony criminal offenders' (Unpublished doctoral dissertation) Department of Measurement and Evaluation, Wayne State University, Detroit, MI.

Berkowitz, L. (1989) 'The frustration-aggression hypothesis: An examination and reformulation' *Psychological Bulletin* **106**, 59–73.

Berkowitz, L. and Rawlings, E. (1963) 'Effects of film violence on inhibitions against subsequent aggression' *Journal of Abnormal and Social Psychology* **66**, 405–12.

Berkowitz, L., Corwin, R. and Heironimus, M. (1963) 'Film violence and subsequent aggressive tendencies' *Public Opinion Quarterly* **27**, 217–29.

Berliner, L. and Conte, J.R. (1993) 'Sexual abuse evaluations: conceptual and empirical obstacles' *Child Abuse and Neglect* **17**, 111–25.

Bernasco, W. (2006) 'Co-offending and the choice of target areas in burglary' *Journal of Investigative Psychology and Offender Profiling* **3**, 139–55.

Bernet, W. (1997) 'Case study: allegations of abuse created in a single interview' *Journal of the American Academy of Child and Adolescent Psychiatry* **36** (7), 966–70.

Berry, M.J., Robinson, C.A. and Bailey, J. (1999) 'The use of hypnosis to recover evidence from convicted offenders: issues and implications' Paper presented at International Psychology and Law Conference, University College, Dublin, 6–9 July.

Besemer, S. (2014) 'The impact of timing and frequency of parental criminal behaviour and risk factors on offspring offending' *Psychology, Crime and Law* **20**, 78–99.

Bessmer, S. (1984) *The Laws of Rape* New York, NY: Praeger.

Bibas, S. (2004) 'Plea bargaining outside the shadow of a trial' *Harvard Law Review* **117** (8), 2464–546.

Bickman, L. (1979) 'Interpersonal influence and the reporting of a crime' *Personality and Social Psychology Bulletin* **5**, 32–35.

Biro, M., Vuckovic, N. and Duric, V. (1992) 'Towards a typology of homicides on the basis of personality' *British Journal of Criminology* **32** (3) 361–71.

Bisogno, E., Dawson-Faber. J. and Jandl, M. (2015) 'The international classification of crime for statistical purposes: a new instrument to improve comparative criminological research' *European Journal of Criminology* 12(5), 535–550.

Bjorkqvist, K. (1994) 'Sex differences in physical, verbal, and indirect aggression: a review of recent research' *Sex Roles* **30** (3/4), 177–88.

Bjorkqvist, K. (1997) 'Learning aggression from models: from a social learning toward a cognitive theory of modeling' in S. Feshbach and J. Zagodzka (eds) *Aggression: Biological, Developmental, and Social Perspectives* New York: Plenum, pp. 69–81.

Bjorkqvist, K. and Niemela, P. (1992) 'New trends in the study of female aggression' in K. Bjorkqvist and P. Niemela (eds) *Of Mice and Women: Aspects of Female Aggression* San Diego: Academic Press, pp. 3–17.

Bjorkqvist, K., Osterman, K. and Kaukiainen, A. (1992) 'The development of direct and indirect aggressive strategies in males and females' in K. Bjorkqvist and P. Niemela (eds) *Of Mice and Women: Aspects of Female Aggression* San Diego: Academic Press, pp. 51–64.

Blaauw, E., Roesch, R. and Kerkhof, A. (2000) 'Mental disorders in European prison systems' *International Journal of Law and Psychiatry* **23** (5–6), 649–63.

Black, S. (2012) 'Frequently Cited Journals in Forensic Psychology' *Psychological Reports* **110** (1), 276–82.

Blackburn, R. (1971) 'Personality types among abnormal homicides' *British Journal of Criminology* **11**, 14–31.

Blackburn, R. (1984) 'The person and dangerousness' in D.J. Muller, D.E. Blackman and A.J. Chapman (eds) *Psychology and Law* Chichester: John Wiley, pp. 101–11.

Blackburn, R. (1993) *The Psychology of Criminal Conduct* Chichester: John Wiley.

Blackburn, R. (1995a) 'Psychopaths: are they bad or mad?' in N.K. Clark and G.M. Stephenson (eds) *Issues in Criminological and Legal Psychology 22: Criminal Behaviour: Perceptions, Attributions, and Rationality* Leicester: British Psychological Society, pp. 97–103.

Blackburn, R. (1995b) 'Violence' in R. Bull and D. Carson (eds) *Handbook of Psychology in Legal Contexts* Chichester: John Wiley, pp. 357–73.

Blackburn, R. (1996) 'What is forensic psychology?' *Legal and Criminological Psychology* **1** (1), 3–16.

Blackburn, R. (2000) 'Risk assessment and prediction' in J. McGuire, T. Mason and A. O'Kane (eds) *Behaviour, Crime and Legal Processes: A Guide for Forensic Practitioners* Chichester: John Wiley, pp. 177–204.

Blackburn, R. (2007) 'Personality disorder and psychopathy: conceptual and empirical integration' *Psychology, Crime and Law* **13** (1), 7–18.

Blacks, S. (2012) 'Frequently cited journals in forensic psychology' *Psychological Reports* **110** (1), 276–82.

Blagden, N., Winder, B., Thorne, K. and Gregson, M. (2011) '"No-one in the world would ever wanna speak to me again": an interpretative phenomenological analysis into convicted sexual offenders' accounts and experiences of maintaining and leaving denial' *Psychology, Crime and Law* **17** (7), 563–86.

Blaine, B. and Crocker, J. (1993) 'Self-esteem and self-serving biases in reactions to positive and negative events: An integrative review' In R. E Baumeister (ed.), *Self-esteem: The Puzzle of Low Self-regard* (pp. 55–85). New York: Plenum Press.

Blanchard, R., Kuban, M. E., Blak, T., Cantor, J. M., Klassen, P., and Dickey, R. (2006) 'Phallometric comparison of pedophilic interest in nonadmitting sexual offenders against stepdaughters, biological daughters, other biologically related girls, and unrelated girls' *Sexual Abuse: A Journal of Research and Treatment*, **18**, 1–14.

Blandon-Gitlin, I., Pezdek, K., Rogers, M. and Brodie, L. (2005) 'Detecting deception in children: an experimental study of the effect of event familiarity on CBCA ratings' *Law and Human Behavior* **29** (2), 187–197.

Blasi, A. (1980) 'Bridging moral cognition and action: A critical review of the literature' *Psychological Bulletin* **88**, 1–45.

Blasi, A. (1983) 'Moral cognition and moral action: a theoretic perspective' *Developmental Review* **3**, 179–210.

Blau, J.R. and Blau, P.M. (1982) 'The cost of inequality: Metropolitan structure and violent crime' *American Sociological Review* **47**, 114–129.

Blau, T.H. (1994) *Psychological Services for Law Enforcement* New York: John Wiley.

Bliesener, T. and Lösel, F. (1992) 'Resilience in juveniles with high risk of delinquency' in F. Lösel, D. Bender and T. Bliesener (eds) *Psychology and the Law: International Perspectives* Berlin: Walter de Gruyter, pp. 62–75.

Blud, L. (1999) 'Cognitive skills programmes' *Issues in Forensic Psychology* **1**, 49–52.

Blumenthal, S., Gudjonsson, G. and Burns, J. (1999) 'Cognitive distortions and blame attribution in sex offenders against adults and children' *Child Abuse and Neglect* **23**, 129–48.

Boden, J.M., Fergusson, D.M. and Horwood, L.J. (2012) 'Alcohol misuse and violent behavior: Findings from a 30-year longitudinal study' *Drug and Alcohol Dependence* **122**, 135–41.

Bogaard, G., Meiher, E.H., Vrij, A., Broers, N.J. and Merckelbach, H. (2013) 'SCAN is largely driven by 12 criteria: results from sexual abuse statements' *Psychology, Crime and Law* **20** (5), 440–49.

Bojahr, L.S. and van Emmerik, A.A. (2016) 'Traumatic events and trauma-related psychopathology in former drug cartel soldiers in Rio de Janeiro: A pilot study' *Psychological Trauma* **8** (1), 34–40.

Bolton, M.J. (2012) 'Execution, castration, imprisonment, treatment, rehabilitation: America's ever-shifting sex crime policies' *Public Administration Review* **72** (5), 766–8.

Bond, G.D. (2008) 'Deception Detection Expertise' *Law and Human Behavior* **32**, 339–51.

Bongiorno, R., McKimmie, B.M. and Masser, B.M. (2016) 'The selective use of rape-victim stereotypes to protect culturally similar perpetrators' *Psychology of Women Quarterly*, **40** (3), 1–11.

Bonnie, R.J. and Grisso, T. (2000) 'Adjudicative competence and youthful offenders' in R.G. Schwartz and T. Grisso (eds) *Youth on Trial: A Developmental Perspective on Juvenile Justice* Chicago, IL: University of Chicago Press, pp. 73–103.

Bonta, J. and Andrews, D. A. (2007) *Risk-Need-Responsivity Model for Offender Assessment and Rehabilitation.* Ottowa: Public Safety Canada

Boon, J. and Baxter, J.S. (2004) 'Minimising extraneous interviewer based interrogative suggestibility' *Legal and Criminological Psychology* **9** (2), 229–38.

Borg, I. and Shye, S. (1995) *Facet Theory: Form and Content* Thousand Oaks, CA: Sage.

Bornstein, B. (in press) 'Jury simulation research: Pros, cons, trends, and alternatives' in Kovera, M. (ed) *The Psychology of Juries: Current Knowledge and a Research Agenda for the Future.* Washington, DC: American Psychological Association.

Bornstein, B.H. (1999) 'The ecological validity of jury simulations: Is the jury still out?' *Law and Human Behavior* **23** (1), 75–9.

Bornstein, B.H., Liebel, L.M. and Scarberry, N.C. (1998) 'Repeating testing in eyewitness memory: A means to improve recall of a negative emotional event' *Applied Cognitive Psychology* **12**, 119–31.

Borrowcliffe, E.R., and Gannon, T.A. (2015) 'The characteristics of un apprehended firesetters living in the UK Community' *Psychology, Crime and Law* **21** (9), 836–853.

Borum, R. (2004) *Psychology of Terrorism* Tampa: University of South Florida.

Borum, R. (2014) 'Psychological vulnerabilities and propensities for involvement in violent extremism' *Behavioral Sciences and the Law* **32**, 286–305.

Bosco, D., Zappala, A. and Pekka, S. (2010) 'The admissibility of offender profiling in courtroom: A review of legal issues and court opinions' *International Journal of Law and Psychiatry* **33**, 184–191.

Bothwell, R.K., Deffenbacher, K.A. and Brigham, J.C. (1987) 'Correlation of eyewitness accuracy and confidence: optimality hypothesis revisited' *Journal of Applied Psychology* **72**, 691–5.

Bouhana, N., Johnson, S.D. and Porter, M. (2016) 'Consistency and specificity in burglars who commit prolific residential burglary: testing the core assumptions underpinning behavioural crime linkage' *Legal and Criminological Psychology* **21**, 77–94.

Boutwell, B. B., and Beaver, K. M. (2008) 'A biosocial explanation of delinquency abstention' *Criminal Behaviour and Mental Health* **18**, 59–74.

Bowlby, J. (1944) 'Forty-four juvenile thieves: their characteristics and home-life' *International Journal of Psychoanalysis* **25**, 19–53.

Bowlby, J. (1951) *Maternal Care and Mental Health* Geneva: World Health Organization.

Bowlby, J. (1973) *Attachment and Loss: II. Separation Anxiety and Anger* London: Hogarth Press.

Bowlby, J. (1980) *Attachment and Loss: III. Loss, Sadness and Depression* New York: Basic Books.

Box, S. (1981) *Deviance, Reality, and Society* New York: Holt, Rinehart and Winston.

Boxer, P., Middlemass, K. and Delorenzo, T. (2009) 'Exposure to violent crime during incarceration: Effects on psychological adjustment following release' *Criminal Justice and Behavior* **36** (8), 793–807.

Brace, C., Scully, M., Clark, B. and Oxley, J. (2010) 'The relationship between crime and road safety' Report number 284, Monash University Accident Research Centre. http://www.monash.edu/__data/assets/pdf_file/0005/216698/muarc284.pdf

Brace, N.A., Pike, G.E., Allen, P. and Kemp, R.I. (2006) 'Identifying composites of famous faces: investigating memory, language and system issues' *Psychology, Crime and Law* **12** (4), 351–66.

Brace, N.A., Pike, G.E., Kemp, R.I. and Turner, J. (2009) 'Eye-witness identification procedures and stress: a comparison of live and video identification parades' *International Journal of Police Science and Management* **11** (2), 183–92.

Bradley, A.R. and Wood, J.N. (1996) 'How do children tell? The disclosure process in child sexual abuse' *Child Abuse and Neglect* **9**, 881–91.

Braithwaite, A. (2013) 'The logic of public fear in terrorism and counter-terrorism' *Journal of Police and Criminal Psychology*, 28, 95–101.

Braithwaite, J. (1989) *Crime, Shame and Reintegration* New York, NY: Cambridge University Press.

Brand, S. and Price, R. (2001) 'The social and economic cost of crime' Home Office Research Study 217, http://www.sadas.org.uk/uploads/The_economic_and_social_costs_of_crime.pdf

Brauser, D. (2013) 'DSM-5 typo: pedophilia described as 'sexual orientation' Medscape http://www.medscape.com/viewarticle/813669

Brennan, M. (1994) 'Cross-examining children in criminal courts: child welfare under attack' in J. Gibbons (ed.) *Language and the Law* London: Longman, pp. 199–216.

Brennan, M. and Brennan, R. (1988) *Stranger Language* Wagga Wagga, New South Wales, Australia: Riverina Murry Institute of Higher Education.

Brewer, N. and Palmer, M.A. (2010) 'Eyewitness identification tests' *Legal and Criminological Psychology* **15**, 77–96.

Brewin, C. R., and Andrews, B. (2017) 'Creating memories for false autobiographical events in childhood: a systematic review' *Applied Cognitive Psychology* **31**, 2–23.

Brewin, C.R. and Holmes, E.A. (2003) 'Psychological theories of post-traumatic stress disorder' *Clinical Psychology Review* **23**, 339–76.

Brewin, C.R., Andrews, B. and Rose, S. (2000) 'Fear, helplessness and horror in post-traumatic stress disorder: investigating DSM-IV criterion A2 in victims of violent crime' *Journal of Traumatic Stress* **13** (3), 499–509.

Brewin, C.R., Andrews, B. and Valentine, J.D. (2000) 'Meta-analysis of risk factors for post-traumatic stress disorder in trauma-exposed adults' *Journal of Consulting and Clinical Psychology* **68** (5), 748–66.

Brewin, C.R., Dalgleish, T. and Joseph, S. (1996) 'A dual representation theory of post-traumatic stress disorder' *Psychological Review* **103** (4), 670–86.

Brezina, T., and Piquero, A. R. (2007) 'Moral beliefs, isolation from peers, and abstention from delinquency' *Deviant Behavior* **28**, 433–465.

Briere, J., Henschel, D. and Smiljanich, K. (1992) 'Attitudes toward sexual abuse: Sex differences and construct validity' *Journal of Research in Personality* **26**, 398–406.

British Psychological Society (2007/8) *Diploma in Forensic Psychology: Candidates Handbook*. http://www.bps.org.uk/downloadfile.cfm?file_uuid=984CD7F0-1143-DFD0-7E65-2850080DE7AF&ext=pdf. Accessed 21 April 2011.

British Psychological Society (2011) *Qualification in Forensic Psychology (Stage 2) Candidate Handbook* http://www.bps.org.uk/careers-education-training/society-qualifications/forensic-psychology/qfp-2011-documents/qualification

British Psychological Society (2015). *Psychologists as Expert Witnesses: Guidelines and Procedures for England, Wales and Northern Ireland* (4th edn). Leicester: British Psychological Society, http://www.bps.org.uk/system/files/Public%20files/inf129_april_2015_web_expert_witness_guidance.pdf

British Psychological society (2017) http://www.bps.org.uk/psychology-public/psychological-terms/psychological-terms (accessed 1 June 2017)

British Psychological Society Working Party (2004) 'A review of the current scientific status and fields of application of polygraphic deception detection: final report' (6 October 2004) Leicester: British Psychological Society.

Broken Spirits Network (2004) 'Post-traumatic stress disorder', http://www.brokenspirits.com/information/ptsd.asp

Brookes, D. (2003) 'Investigating child abuse online: the interactive approach' in A. MacVean and P. Spindler (eds) *Policing Paedophiles on the Internet*

Bristol: New Police Bookshop, pp. 49–60.

Brown, B. (1995) *CCTV in Town Centres: Three Case Studies* Crime Detection and Prevention Series Paper 68. London: Home Office.

Brown, C.M., Traverso, G. and Fedoroff, J.P. (1996) 'Masturbation prohibition in sex offenders: a crossover study' *Archives of Sexual Behavior* **25** (4), 397–408.

Brown, R. and Kulik, J. (1977) 'Flashbulb memories' *Cognition* **5**, 73–99.

Brown, S. (1999) 'Public attitudes to the treatment of sex offenders' *Legal and Criminological Psychology* **4** (2), 239–5.

Browne, K.D. (1999) 'From the frying pan to the fire: exploring the role of foster care in the development of criminal behaviour'. Paper presented to the Joint International Conference, Dublin.

Browne, K.D. (1999) 'Violence in the media causes crime: myth or reality?' Unpublished inaugural lecture, University of Birmingham, 3 June 1999.

Browne, K.D. and Pennell, A.E. (1998) *The Effects of Video Violence on Young Offenders*. Home Office Research and Statistics Directorate, Research Findings No. 65. London: Home Office.

Brownmiller, S. (1975) *Against Our Will: Men, Women, and Rape* London: Secker and Warburg.

Bruck, M. and Ceci, S.J. (1997) 'The suggestibility of young children' *Current Directions in Psychological Science* **6** (3), 75–9.

Bruck, M., Ceci, S.K., Francoeur, E. and Barr, R. (1995) '"I hardly cried when I got shot!" Influencing children's reports about a visit to their pediatrician' *Child Development* **66**, 193–208.

Bruck, M., Kelley, K. and Poole, D.A. (2016) 'Children's reports of body touching in medical examinations: the benefits and risks of using body diagrams' *Public Policy, and Law* **22** (1), 1–11

Brugman, D. and Aleva, E. (2004) 'Developmental delay or regression in moral reasoning by juvenile delinquents?' *Journal of Moral Education* **33**, 321–38.

Brusten, C., Stams, G.S. and Gibbs, J.C. (2007) 'Commentary: Missing the mark' *British Journal of Developmental Psychology* **25**, 185–9.

Brym, R.J. and Araj, B. (2012) 'Are Suicide Bombers Suicidal?' *Studies in Conflict and Terrorism* **35** (6), 432–443.

Buck, J.A., Warren, A.R., Betman, S.I. and Brigham, J.C. (2002) 'Age differences in criterion-based content analysis scores in typical child sexual abuse interview' *Applied Developmental Psychology* **23**, 267–83.

Buck, J.A., Warren, A.R., Bruck, M. and Kuehnle, K. (2014) 'How common is "common knowledge" about child witnesses among legal professionals? comparing interviewers, public defenders, and forensic psychologists with lay people' *Behavioral Science and the Law* **32**, 867–883.

Budd, T., Sharp, C. and Mayhew, P. (2005) 'Offending in England and Wales: first results from the offending, crime and justice survey' Home Office Research Study 275, London: Home Office.

Budd, T., Sharp, C. and Mayhew, P. (2005) 'Offending in England and Wales: first results from the 2003 Crime and Justice Survey' *Findings 244*, Home Office.

Bull, R. (1984) 'Psychology's contribution to policing' in D. Muller, D. Blackman and A. Chapman (eds) *Psychology and Law* Chichester: Wiley.

Bull, R. and Reid, R.L. (1975) 'Police officers' recall of information' *Journal of Occupational Psychology* **48**, 73–8.

Bumby, K.T. (1996) 'Assessing the cognitive distortions of child molesters and rapists: Development and validation of the MOLEST and RAPE scales' *Sexual Abuse: A Journal of Research and Treatment* **8** (1), 37–54.

Bunn, G.C. (2012) *The Truth Machine: A Social History of the Lie Detector* Baltimore, MD: Johns Hopkins University Press.

Burcar, V. (2013) 'Doing masculinity in narratives about reporting violent crime: young male victims talk about contacting and encountering the police' *Journal of Youth Studies* **16** (2), 172–90.

Bureau of Justice (2001a) 'Characteristics of crime' http://www.ojp.usdoj.gov/bjs/cvict_c.htm#findings/

Bureau of Justice (2001b) 'The odds of being a crime victim' http://nsi.org/Tips/odds.htm

Bureau of Justice (2001c) 'Drug and crime facts, 1994' http://www.ojp.usdoj.gov/bjs/abstract/dcfacts.htm

Bureau of Justice (2001d) 'Intimate homicide' http://www.ojp.usdoj.gov/bjs/homicide/intimates.htm

Bureau of Justice (2004) 'Criminal offenders statistics' http://www.ojp.usdoj.gov/bjs/crimoff.htm#lifetime

Bureau of Justice Statistics (2003) *Reporting Crime to the Police, 1992–2000* Washington, DC: US Department of Justice.

Bureau of Justice Statistics (2011) 'Violent Crime' http://bjs.ojp.usdoj.gov/index.cfm?ty=tp&tid=31 (accessed 21 February 2011).

Bureau of Justice Statistics (2013) 'Drugs and Crime' http://www.bjs.gov/index.cfm?ty=tpandtid=35

Burgess, E.W. (ed.) (1928) 'Factors determining success or failure on parole. Springfield: Illinois State Board of Parole' *Law and Human Behavior* (2007) **31**: 449–62.

Burnam, M. A., Stein, J.A., Golding, J.M., Siegel, J.M., Sorenson, S.B., Forsythe, A.B. and Telles, C.A.(1988) 'Sexual assault and mental disorders in a community population' *Journal of Consulting and Clinical Psychology* **56** (6), 843–850

Burrell, A., Bull, R., Bond, J. and Herrington, G. (2015) 'Testing the impact of group offending on behavioural similarity in serial robbery' *Psychology, Crime and Law* **21** (6), 551–569.

Burt, M. (1980) 'Cultural myths and support for rape' *Journal of Personality and Social Psychology* **38**, 217–30.

Burton, A.M., Wilson, S., Cowan, M. and Bruce, V. (1999) 'Face recognition in poor quality video: evidence from security surveillance' *Psychological Science* **10**, 243–8.

Busey, T.A. and Loftus, G.R. (2007) 'Cognitive science and the law' *Trends in Cognitive Science* **11** (3), 111–17.

Bushway S (2003) 'Employment dimensions of reentry: understanding the nexus between prisoner reentry and work' New York: New York University School.

Butler-Sloss, E. (1988) *Report of the Inquiry into Child Abuse in Cleveland 1987* London: Her Majesty's Stationery Office, Cm 412.

C

Caldwell, M. (2007) 'Sexual offense adjudication and recidivism among juvenile offenders' *Sexual Abuse: A Journal of Research and Treatment* **19**, 107–13.

Caldwell, M. (2011) 'Treatment-related changes in behavioral outcomes of psychopathy facets in adolescent offenders' *Law and Human Behavior* **35**, 275–87.

Caldwell, M.F. and Dickinson, C. (2009) 'Sex offender registration and recidivism risk in juvenile sexual offenders' *Behavioral Sciences and the Law* **27**, 941–56.

Caldwell, M.F., Skeem, J.L., Salekin, R. and Van Rybroek, G. (2006) 'Treatment response of adolescent offenders with psychopathy features: A 2-year follow up' *Criminal Justice and Behavior* **33**, 571–96.

Cale, J., Leclerc, B. and Smallbone, S. (2014) 'The sexual lives of sexual offenders: the link between childhood sexual victimization and non-criminal sexual lifestyles between types of offenders' *Psychology, Crime and Law* **20** (1), 37–60.

Caleb, D., Lloyd, C.D. and Serin, R.C. (2012) 'Agency and outcome expectancies for crime desistance: measuring offenders' personal beliefs about change' *Psychology, Crime and Law* **18** (6), 543–65.

Calof, D.L. (1993) 'A conversation with Pamela Freyd, Ph.D. Co-Founder and Executive Director, False Memory Syndrome Foundation, Inc., Part I' in *Treating Abuse Today*, Vol. III, No. 3. http://idealist.com/facts/v3n3-pfreyd.shtml (accessed 12 July 2001).

Campbell, D. and Stanley, J. (1963) *Experimental and Quasi-experimental Designs for Research* Chicago, IL: Rand-McNally.

Candel, I., Merckelbach, H., Loyen, S. and Reyskens, H. (2005) '"I hit the shift key and then the computer crashed": Children and false admissions' *Personality and Individual Differences* **38**, 1381–7.

Cann, J., Friendship, C. and Gozna, L. (2007) 'Assessing crossover in a sample of sexual offenders with multiple victims' *Legal and Criminological Psychology* **12**, 149–63.

Canter, D., Alison, L., Alison, E. and Wentink, E. (2004) 'The organized/disorganized typology ofserial murder: Myth or model?' *Psychology, Public Policy and the Law* **10**, 293–320.

Canter, D., and Gregory, A. (1994) 'Identifying the residential location of rapists' *Journal of the Forensic Science Society* **34**, 169–175.

Canter, D.V. (1983) 'The potential of facet theory for applied social psychology' *Quality and Quantity* **17**, 35–67.

Canter, D.V. (1994) *Criminal Shadows* London: HarperCollins.

Canter, D.V. (2004) 'Offender profiling and investigative psychology' *Journal of Investigative Psychology and Offender Profiling* **1**, 1–15.

Canter, D.V. and Wentink, N. (2004) 'An empirical test of Holmes and Holmes's serial murder typology' *Criminal Justice and Behavior* **31** (4), 489–515.

Canter, D.V., Alison, L.J., Alison, E. and Wentink, N. (2004) 'The organized/disorganized typology of serial murder: myth or model?' *Psychology, Public Policy, and Law* **10** (3), 293–320.

Canter, D.V., Bennell, C., Alison, L.J. and Reddy, S. (2003) 'Differentiating sex offences: a behaviorally based thematic classification of stranger rapes' *Behavioral Sciences and the Law* **21**, 157–74.

Cantor, J.M., and McPhail, I.V. (2015) 'Sensitivity and specificity of the phallometric test for hebephilia' *Journal of Sexual Medicine*, **12**, 1940–1950.

Caprathe, W. J. (2011) 'Commentary: participant differences and validity of jury studies' *Behavioral Sciences and the Law* **29**, 328–30.

Carlucci, M.E., Compo, N. and Zimmerman, L. (2013) 'Lie detection during high-stakes truths and lies' *Legal and Criminological Psychology* **18**, 314–23.

Carson, D. (2011) 'Investigative psychology and law: towards collaboration by focusing on evidence and inferential reasoning' *Journal of Investigative Psychology and Offender Profiling* **8**, 74–89.

Carson, L. and La Rooy, D. (2015) 'Commonsense psychology' is a barrier to the implementation of best practice child interviewing guidelines: a qualitative analysis of police officers' beliefs in Scotland' *Journal of Police and Criminal Psychology* **30**, 50–62

Carter, C.A., Bottom, B.L. and Levine, M. (1996) 'Linguistic and socioemotional influences on the accuracy of children's reports' *Law and Human Behavior* **20**, 335–58.

Casey, S. (2016) 'Dynamic risk and sexual offending: the conundrum of assessment' *Psychology, Crime and Law* **22** (1–2), 104–123.

Caspi, A., McClay, J., Moffitt, T. E., Mill, J., Martin, J., Craig, I. W., *et al.* (2002) 'Role of genotype in the cycle of violence in maltreated children' *Science*, **297**, 851–854.

Cauffman, E., Piquero, A.R., Kimonis, E., Steinberg, L., Chassin, L. and Fagan, J. (2007) 'Legal, individual, and environmental predictors of court disposition in a sample of serious adolescent offenders' *Law and Human Behavior* **31**, 519–35.

Cavezza, C. and McEwan, T.E. (2014) 'Cyberstalking versus offline stalking in a forensic sample' *Psychology, Crime and Law*, **20**, 955–970.

Ceci, S.J. and Bruck, M. (1993) 'Suggestibility and the child witness: a historical review and synthesis' *Psychological Bulletin* **113** (3), 403–39.

Ceci, S.J., Loftus, E.W., Leichtman, M. and Bruck, M. (1994) 'The role of source misattributions in the creation of false beliefs among preschoolers' *International Journal of Clinical and Experimental Hypnosis* **62**, 304–20.

Cécile, M. and Born, M. (2009) 'Intervention in juvenile delinquency: Danger of iatrogenic effects?' *Children and Youth Services Review* **31** (2009) 1217–221.

Cederborg, A.-C. (1999) 'The construction of children's credibility in judgements of child sexual abuse' *Acta Sociologica* **42**, 147–58.

Centerwall, B.S. (1989) 'Exposure to television as a cause of violence' *Public Communication and Behavior* **2**, 1–58.

Centerwall, B.S. (1993) 'Television and violent crime' *Public Interest* **111**, 56–71.

Cerezo, A. (2013) 'CCTV and crime displacement: a quasi-experimental evaluation' *European Journal of Criminology* **10** (2), 222–236.

Chadee, D., and Ng Ying, N.K.. (2013) 'Predictors of fear of crime: general fear versus perceived risk' *Journal of Applied Social Psychology* **2** (43), 1896–1904.

Chadee, D., Austen, L., and Ditton, J. (2007) 'The relationship between likelihood and fear of criminal victimization: evaluating risk sensitivity as a mediating concept' *British Journal of Criminology*, 47, 133– 153.

Chan, M. (2016) 'Number of U.S. police officers killed on duty rises to 5-year high in 2016' *Time* 29 December 2016.

Chaplin, R., Flatley, J. and Smith, K. (2011) 'Crime in England and Wales 2010/11' Home Office Statistical Bulletin 10/11 London: Home office.

Chapman, R., Flatley, K. and Smith, J. (eds.) (2011) *Crime in England and Wales 2010/11* London: Home Office Statistical Bulletin.

Chen, C.-A. and Howitt, D. (2007) 'Different crime types and moral reasoning development in young offenders compared with non-offender controls' *Psychology, Crime and Law* **13** (4), 405–16.

Chen, X. and Adams, M. (2010) 'Are teen delinquency abstainers social introverts? A test of Moffitt's theory' *Journal of Research in Crime and Delinquency* **47**, 439–468.

Chermak, S.M. (1995) *Victims in the News: Crime and the American News Media* Boulder, CO: Westview.

Cherryman, J., Bull, R. and Vrij, A. (2000) 'How police officers view confessions: is there still a confession culture?' *European Conference on Psychology and Law*, Cyprus, March 2000.

Chifflet, P. (2015) 'Questioning the validity of criminal profiling: an evidence-based approach' *Australian and New Zealand Journal of Criminology* **48** (2), 238–255.

Christensen, J., Schmidt, K. and Henderson, J. (1982) 'The selling of the police: media, ideology and crime control' *Contemporary Crises* **6**, 227–39.

Christianson, S.-A., Karlsson, I. and Persson, L.G.W. (1998) 'Police personnel as eyewitnesses to a violent crime' *Legal and Criminological Psychology* **3**, 59–72.

Chrysanthi S. Leon (2011) *Sex Fiends, Perverts, and Pedophiles: Understanding Sex Crime Policy in America* New York: New York University Press.

Chung, M.C., Xiaohu, D. and Wan, K.H. (2016) 'Past trauma, alexithymia, and posttraumatic stress among perpetrators of violent crime' *Traumatology*, **22**(2), 104–112.

Church, W. T., II, Wakeman, E. E., Miller, S. L., Clements, C. B. and Sun, F. (2008) 'The community attitudes toward sex offenders scale: the development of a psychometric assessment instrument' *Research on Social Work Practice*, **20**, 251–259.

Clancy, S.A., Schacter, D.L., McNally, R.J. and Pitman, R.K. (2000) 'False recognition in women reporting recovered memories of sexual abuse' *Psychological Science* **11**, 26–31.

Clare, J. (2011) 'Examination of systematic variations in burglars' domain-specific perceptual and procedural skills', *Psychology, Crime and Law* **17** (3), 199–214.

Clark, D. (1999) 'Risk assessment in prisons and probation' *Forensic Update* **1**, 15–18.

Clark, J. (2004) 'Crime, fears and phobias' *Psychiatry, Psychology and Law* **11** (1), 87–95.

Clark, S.E. (2012) 'Costs and benefits of eyewitness identification reform: Psychological science and public policy' *Perspectives on Psychological Science* **7** (3), 238–59.

Clark, S.E. (2012) 'Eyewitness identification reform: Data, theory, and due process' *Perspectives on Psychological Science* **7** (3) 279–83.

Clarke, R.V. and Cornish, D.B. (1985) 'Modelling offenders' decisions: a framework for policy and research' in M. Tonry and N. Morris (eds) *Crime and Justice* Vol. 6. Chicago: University of Chicago Press.

Cleary, S. (2004) *Sex Offenders and Self-Control: Explaining Sexual Violence* New York: LFB Scholarly Publishing LLC.

Cleckley, H. (1976) *The Mask of Sanity: An Attempt to Clarify Some Issues About the So Called Psychopathic Personality* (5th edn) London St Louis: Mosby.

Clements, C.B., Brannen, D.N., Kirkley, S.N., Gordon, T.M. and Church, W.T. (2006) 'The measurement of concern about victims. Empathy, victim advocacy and the Victim Concern Scale (VCS)' *Legal and Criminological Psychology* **11**, 283–95.

Clifford, B.R. (1995) 'Psychology's premises, methods and values' in R. Bull and D. Carson (eds) *Handbook of Psychology in Legal Contexts* Chichester: John Wiley, pp. 13–28.

Clifford, B.R. and Richards, V.J. (1977) 'Comparison of recall by policemen and civilians under conditions of long and short durations of exposure' *Perceptual and Motor Skills* **45**, 503–12.

Clifford, S.R. (1976) 'Police as eyewitnesses' *New Society* **22**, 176–7.

Cloninger, C.R., Christiansen, K.O., Reich, T. and Gottesman, I.I. (1978) 'Implications of sex differences in the prevalence of antisocial personality, alcoholism and criminality for familial transmission' *Archives of General Psychiatry* **35**, 941–51.

Cloward, R.A. and Ohlin, L.E. (1960) *Delinquency and Opportunities: A Theory of Delinquent Gangs* Glencoe, IL: Free Press.

Coates, L., Bavelas, J.B. and Gibson, J. (1994) 'Anomalous language in sexual assault trial judgements' *Discourse and Society* **5** (2), 189–206.

Cochran, J.L. and Bromley, M.L.(2003) 'The myth(?) of the police subculture' *Policing: An International Journal of Police Strategies and Management* **26**, 88–117.

Cohen, M., Seghorn, T. and Calmas, W. (1969) 'Sociometric study of the sex offender' *Journal of Abnormal Psychology*, 74, 249–255.

Cohen, S. (1972) *Folk Devils and Moral Panics* London: McGibbon and Kee.

Cohen, S. (1980) *Folk Devils and Moral Panics* Oxford: Basil Blackwell.

Cohn, A.M., Jakupcak, M., Seibert, L.A., Hildebrandt, T.B. and Zeichner, A. (2010) 'The role of emotion dysregulation in the association between men's restrictive emotionality and use of physical aggression' *Psychology of Men and Masculinity* **11** (1), 53–64.

Coid, J. (1983) 'The epidemiology of abnormal homicide and murder followed by suicide' *Psychological Medicine* **13** (4), 855–60.

Cole, S.A. (2009) 'Cultural consequences of miscarriages of justice' *Behavioral Sciences and the Law* **27**, 431–49.

Coleman, C. and Norris, C. (2000) *Introducing Criminology* Cullompton, Devon: Willan Publishing.

Coleman, H. (1997) 'Gaps and silences: the culture and adolescent sex offenders' *Journal of Child and Youth Care* **11** (1), 1–13.

Coles, E.M. (2004) 'Psychological support for the concept of psycholegal competencies' *International Journal of Law and Psychiatry* **27**, 223–32.

Coles, E.M. and Veiel, H.O.F. (2001) 'Expert testimony and pseudoscience: how mental health professionals are taking over the courtroom'. *International Journal of Law and Psychiatry* **24**, 607–25.

Collett, M.E. and Kovera, M.B. (2003) 'The effects of British and American trial procedures on the quality of juror decision-making' *Law and Human Behavior* **27** (4), 403–22.

Collins, J.J. and Bailey, S.L. (1990) 'Traumatic stress disorder and violent behaviour' *Journal of Traumatic Stress* **3** (2), 203–20.

Collins, K., Doherty-Sneddon, G. and Doherty, M.J. (2014) 'Practitioner perspectives on rapport building during child investigative interviews' *Psychology, Crime, and Law* **20** (9), 884–901.

Colvin, M. (1993) *Negotiated Justice: A Closer Look at the Implications of Plea Bargains* London: Justice.

Compo, N.S., Gregory, A.H. and Fisher, R. (2012) 'Interviewing behaviors in police investigators: a field study of a current US sample' *Psychology, Crime and Law* **18** (4), 359–75.

Condron, M.K. and Nutter, D.E. (1988) 'A preliminary examination of the pornography experience of sex offenders, paraphiliac sexual dysfunction and controls' *Journal of Sex and Marital Therapy* **14** (4), 285–98.

Connors, E., Lundregan, T., Miller, N. and McEwen, T. (1996) *Convicted by Juries, Exonerated by Science: Case Studies in the Use of DNA Evidence to Establish Innocence after Trial* Washington, DC: National Institute of Justice Research Study.

Cook, T.D. and Campbell, D.T. (1979) *Quasi-experimentation: Design and analysis issues for field settings* Boston, MA: Houghton Mifflin Company.

Cooke, D.J. and Michie, C. (2001) 'Refining the construct of psychopath: Towards a hierarchical model' *Psychological Assessment* **13** (2), 171–88.

Cooke, D.J. and Philip, L. (1998) 'Comprehending the Scottish caution: do offenders understand their right to remain silent?' *Legal and Criminological Psychology* **3**, 13–27.

Cooper, B.S., Griesel, D. and Yuille, J.C. (2008) 'Clinical-forensic risk assessment: the past and current state of affairs' *Journal of Forensic Psychology Practice* **7** (4), 1–63.

Cooper, B.S., Kennedy, M.A., Herve, H.F. and Yuille, J.C. (2002) 'Weapon focus in sexual assault memories of prostitutes' *International Journal of Law and Psychiatry*, **25**, 181–91.

Cooper, C. and Roe, S. (2012) 'An estimate of youth crime in England and Wales: police recorded crime committed by young people in 2009/10' *Research Report 64*, London: Home Office.

Cooper, S. (2005) 'Modifying sexual fantasies using behaviour therapy: a case study' *Forensic Update* **80**, 17–22.

Cooper, V.G. and Zapf, P.A. (2003) 'Predictor variables in competency to stand trial decisions' *Law and Human Behavior* **27** (4), 423–36.

Corabian, G. and Hogan, N.R. (2015) 'Attitudes towards sex offenders in Canada: further validation of the CATSO-R factor structure' Psychiatry, *Psychology and Law*, **22** (5), 723–730.

Cornish, D. and Clarke, R.V.G. (eds) (1986) *The Reasoning Criminal* New York: Springer-Verlag.

Correll, J., Park, B., Judd, C.M. and Wittenbrink, B.W. (2002) 'The police officers dilemma: using ethnicity to disambiguate potentially threatening individuals' *Journal of Personality and Social Psychology* **83**, 1314–29.

Corry, N.H., Kulka, R., Fairbank, J.A. and Schlenger, W.E. (2016) 'Forty years after the war: how are Vietnam veterans doing today?' *PTSD Research Quarterly* **27** (1), 1–11.

Corwin, D. and Olafson, E. (1997) 'Videotaped discovery of a reportedly unrecallable memory of child sexual abuse: Comparison with a childhood interview videotaped 11 years before' *Child Maltreatment* **2**, 91–112.

Court, J.H. (1977) 'Pornography and sex-crimes: a re-evaluation in the light of recent trends around the world' *International Journal of Criminality and Penology* **5**, 129–57.

Court, J.H. (1984) 'Sex and violence: a ripple effect' in N.M. Malamuth and E. Donnerstein (eds) *Pornography and Sexual Aggression* Orlando, FL: Academic Press, 143–72.

Cox, V.C., Paulus, P.B. and McCain, G. (1984) 'Prison crowding research: The relevance for prison housing standards and a general approach regarding crowding phenomena' *American Psychologist* **39** (100), 1148–60.

Craig, A.R., Franklin, J.A. and Andrews, G. (1984) 'A scale to measure locus of control of behaviour' *British Journal of Medical Psychology* **57**, 173–80.

Craissati, J. and McClurg, G. (1997) 'The Challenge Project: a treatment program evaluation for perpetrators of child sexual abuse' *Child Abuse and Neglect* **21** (7), 637–48.

Craissati, J.,South, R. and Bierer, K. (2009) 'Exploring the effectiveness of community sex offender treatment in relation to risk and re-offending' *Journal of Forensic Psychiatry and Psychology* **20** (6), 769–784,

Cramer, D. and Howitt, D. (1998) 'Romantic love and the psychology of sexual behaviour: open and closed secrets' in V.C. de Munck (ed.) *Romantic Love and Sexual Behaviour: Perspectives from the Social Sciences* Westport, CT: Praeger, pp. 113–32.

Cramer, R.J.,and Brodsky,S.L. (2014) 'Bringing psychology to the courtroom and vice versa: conceptualization and design of a course in trial consulting' *Journal of Forensic Psychology Practice* **14** (2), 145–157.

Crego, J. and Alison, L. (2004) 'Control and legacy as functions of perceived criticality in major incidents' *Journal of Investigative Psychology and Offender Profiling* **1**, 207–25.

Crenshaw, M. (1986) 'The psychology of political terrorism' in M.G. Hermann (ed.) *Political Psychology: Contemporary Problems and Issues* London: Jossey-Bass, pp. 379–413.

Cressey, D.R. (1952) 'Application and Verification of the Differential Association Theory' *Journal of Criminal Law, Criminology, and Police Science* **43**, 43–52.

Crick, N.R. (1997) 'Engagement in gender normative versus non-normative forms of aggression: links to social-psychological adjustment' *Developmental Psychology* **33** (4), 610–17.

Crick, N.R. and Bigbee, M.A. (1998) 'Relational and overt forms of peer victimization: a multi-informant approach' *Journal of Consulting and Clinical Psychology* **66** (2), 337–47.

Crick, N.R., Casas, J.F. and Mosher, M. (1997) 'Relational and overt aggression in preschool' *Developmental Psychology* **33** (4), 579–88.

Criminal Justice Information Service Division (2015) 'Crime in the United States 2014' https://ucr.fbi.gov/crime-in-the-u.s/2014/crime-in-the-u.s.-2014/offenses-known-to-law-enforcement/murder

Crits-Cristoph, P., Carroll, K., Perry, K., Luborsky, L., McLellan, A.T., Woody, G.E., Thompson, L., Gallagher, D. and Zitrin, C. (1991) 'Meta-analysis of therapist effects in psychotherapy outcome studies' *Psychotherapy Research* **1**, 81–91.

Croll, P. (1974) 'The deviant image'. Paper presented at British Sociological Association Mass Communication Study Group.

Crombag, H.F.M., Wagenaar, W.A. and Van Kopen, P.J. (1996) 'Crashing memories and the problem of source monitoring' *Applied Cognitive Psychology* **10**, 95–104.

Crown Prosecution Service (2011a) 'Achieving best evidence in criminal proceedings: guidance' http://www.cps.gov.uk/publications/docs/best_evidence_in_criminal_proceedings.pdf

Crown Prosecution Service (2011b) The Court Case, http://www.cps.gov.uk/victims_witnesses/going_to_court/court_case.html

Crown Prosecution Service (2014) Expert Evidence, http://www.cps.gov.uk/legal/assets/uploads/files/expert_evidence_first_edition_2014.pdf

Crown Prosecution Service (2017a) 'Confessions, unfairly obtained evidence and breaches of PACE', http://www.cps.gov.uk/legal/a_to_c/confession_and_breaches_of_police_and_criminal_evidence_act/

Crown Prosecution Service (2017b) 'Safeguarding children as victims and witnesses', http://www.cps.gov.uk/legal/v_to_z/safeguarding_children_as_victims_and_witnesses/

Crown Prosecution Service. (2011). 'Achieving best evidence in criminal proceedings: guidance on interviewing victims and witnesses, and guidance on using special measures' London: Crown Prosecution Service. http://www.cps.gov.uk/publications/docs/best_evidence_in_criminal_proceedings.pdf

Cullen, F.T., Gendreau, P., Jarjoura, G.R. and Wright, J.P. (1997) 'Crime and the bell curve: lessons from intelligent criminology' *Crime and Delinquency* **3** (4), 387–411.

Cumberbatch, G. and Howitt, D. (1989) *A Measure of Uncertainty* London: Broadcasting Standards Council/John Libbey.

Cundiff, P.R. (2013) 'Ordered delinquency: the 'effects' of birth order on delinquency' *Personality and Social Psychology Bulletin*, **39** (8), 1017–1029.

Curtis, G.C. (1963) 'Violence reeds violence – perhaps?' *American Journal of Psychiatry* **120**, 386.

Custers, K., and Van den Bulck, J. (2013) 'The cultivation of fear of sexual violence in women: processes and moderators of the relationship between television and fear' *Communication Research*, 40, 96–124.

Cutler, B.L. and Penrod, S.D. (1989) 'Forensically relevant moderators of the relation between eyewitness identification accuracy and confidence' *Journal of Applied Psychology* **74**, 650–3.

Czerederecka, A. and Jaskiewicz-Obydzinska, T. (1996) 'The factors neutralizing developmental disorders in children from broken families' in G. Davies, S. Lloyd-Bostock, M. McMurran and C. Wilson (eds) *Psychology, Law and Criminal Justice: International Developments in Research and Practice* Berlin: Walter de Gruyter, pp. 240–7.

D

Daily Telegraph (2004) 'Sex offenders register grows by 15 per cent' 28 July 2004. http://www.telegraph.co.uk/news/main.jhtml?xml=/news/2004/07/28/uoffend.xml&sSheet=/portal/2004/07/28/ixportaltop.html

Dabbs, J.M., Alford, E.C. and Fielden, J.A. (1998) 'Trial lawyers and testosterone: blue-collar talent in a white-collar world' *Journal of Applied Social Psychology* **28** (1), 84–9.

Dabney, D.A., Dugan, L., Topalli, V. and Hollinger, R.C. (2006) 'The impact of implicit stereotyping on offender profiling: unexpected results from an observational study of shoplifting' *Criminal Justice and Behavior* **33** (5), 646–74.

Daffern, M., Howells, K., Mannion, A. and Tonki, M. (2009) 'A test of methodology intended to assist detection of aggressive offence paralleling behaviour within secure settings' *Legal and Criminological Psychology* **14**, 213–26.

Dalby, J.T. (2014) 'Forensic psychology in Canada a century after Münsterberg' *Canadian Psychology* **55** (1), 27–33

Daleiden, E.L., Kaufman, K.L., Hilliker, D.R. and O'Neil, J.N. (1998) 'The sexual histories and fantasies of youthful males: a comparison of sexual offending, nonsexual offending, and nonoffending groups' *Sexual Abuse: A Journal of Research and Treatment* **10** (3), 19–209.

Daly, M. and Wilson, M. (1988) *Homicide* New York: Aldine de Gruyter.

Dando, C., Wilcock, R. and Milne, R. (2008) 'The cognitive interview: Inexperienced police officers' perceptions of their witness/victim interviewing practices' *Legal and Criminological Psychology* **13**, 59–70.

Dando, C.J., Bull, R., Ormerod, T.C. and Sandhams, A.L. (2015) 'Helping to sort the liars from the truth-tellers: the gradual revelation of information during investigative interviews' *Legal and Criminological Psychology* **20**, 114–128.

Darley, J.M. and Latané, B. (1968) 'Bystander intervention in emergencies: Diffusion of responsibility' *Journal of Personality and Social Psychology* **8**, 377–83.

Darwin, C. (1965/1872) *The Expression of the Emotions in Man and Animals* Chicago: University of Chicago.

Daubert v. Merrell Dow Pharmaceuticals, Inc. 509 U.S 579 Supreme Court of U.S.A 1993.

Davies, A. (1997) 'Specific profile analysis: a data-based approach to offender profiling' in J.L. Jackson and D.A. Bekerian (eds) *Offender Profiling* Chichester: Wiley, pp. 191–207.

Davies, E. and Seymour, F.W. (1998) 'Questioning child complainants of sexual abuse: analysis of criminal court transcripts in New Zealand' *Psychiatry, Psychology and Law* **5** (1), 47–61.

Davies, F.J. (1952) 'Crime news in Colorado newspapers' *American Journal of Sociology* **57**, 325–30.

Davies, G. and Noon, E. (1993) 'Video links: their impact on child witness trials' in N.K. Clark and G.M. Stephenson (eds) *Issues in Criminological and Legal Psychology 20: Children, Evidence and Procedure* Leicester: Division of Criminological and Legal Psychology, British Psychological Society, pp. 22–6.

Davies, G. and Thasen, S. (2000) 'Closed-circuit television: how effective an identification aid?' *British Journal of Psychology* **91**, 411–26.

Davies, G.M., Smith, S. and Blincoe, C. (2008) 'A "weapon focus" effect in children' *Psychology, Crime & Law* **14**, 19–28.

Davis, D. and Leo, R.A. (2012) 'Interrogation-Related Regulatory Decline: Ego Depletion, Failures of Self-Regulation, and the Decision to Confess' *Psychology, Public Policy, and Law* **18** (4), 673–704.

Davis, J.P., Lander, K., Evans, R. and Jansari, A. (2016) 'Investigating predictors of superior face recognition ability in police super recognisers' *Applied Cognitive Psychology* **30**, 827–840.

Davis, J.P., Valentine, T., Memon, A. and Roberts, A.J. (2015) 'Identification on the street: a field comparison of police street identifications and video lineups in England' *Psychology, Crime and Law* **21** (1), 9–27

Day, D.M. and Page, S. (1986) 'Portrayal of mental illness in Canadian newspapers' *Canadian Journal of Psychiatry* **31**, 813–16.

DCLP Training Committee (1994) 'The core knowledge and skills of the Chartered Forensic Psychologists' *Forensic Update* **38**, 8–11.

De Fabrique, N., Romano, S.J., Vecchi, G.M. and van Hasselt, V.B. (2007) 'Understanding Stockholm Syndrome' *FBI Law Enforcement Bulletin* **76** (7), 10–15.

de Keijser, J. and Elffers, H. (2012) 'Understanding of forensic expert reports by judges, defense lawyers and forensic professionals' *Psychology, Crime and Law* **18** (2), 191–207.

de Keijser, J.W. and van Koppen, P.J. (2007) 'Paradoxes of proof and punishment: Psychological pitfalls in judicial decision making' *Legal and Criminological Psychology* **12**, 189–205.

DeLoache, J.S. (1995) 'Early symbol understanding and use' in D. Medin (ed) *The Psychology of Learning and Motivation* **33**, 65–114). New York: Academic Press.

De Riviera, J. (1997) 'The construction of false memory syndrome: the experience of retractors' *Psychological Inquiry* **8**, 271–92.

de Vries Robbé, M., de Vogel, V. and Douglas, K.S. (2013) 'Risk factors and protective factors: a two-sided dynamic approach to violence risk assessment' *Journal of Forensic Psychiatry and Psychology* **24** (4), 440–57.

Deese, J. (1959) 'On the prediction of occurrence of particular verbal intrusions in immediate recall' *Journal of Experimental Psychology* **58**, 17–22.

Deffenbacher, K.A. (1980) 'Eyewitness accuracy and confidence: can we infer anything about the relationship?' *Law and Human Behavior* **4**, 243–60.

Degenhardt, L., Conroy, E., Gilmour, S. and Collins, L. (2005) 'The effect of a reduction in heroin supply in Australia upon drug distribution and acquisitive crime' *British Journal of Criminology* **45**, 2–24.

DeMatteo, D., and Edens, J. F. (2006) 'The role and relevance of the psychopathy checklist-revised in court: a case law survey of U.S. courts (1991–2004)' *Psychology, Public Policy, and Law* **12**, 214–241.

DeMatteo, D., Edens, J.F., Galloway, M., Cox, J., Smith, S.T., Kollwer, J.P. and Bersoff. B. (2014) 'Investigating the role of the psychopathy checklist–revised in United States case law' *Psychology, Public Policy, and Law* **20** (1), 96–107.

Dennis, J.A., Khan, O., Ferriter, M., Huband, N., Powney, M.J. and Duggan, C. (2012) 'Psychological interventions for sex offenders or those who have sexually offended or are at risk of offending *Cochrane Review,* http://www.cochrane.org/CD007507/BEHAV_psychological-interventions-for-sex-offenders-or-those-who-have-sexually-offended-or-are-at-risk-of-offending

Dernevik, M., Beck, A., Grann, M., Hogue, T. and McGuire, J. (2009a) 'The use of psychiatric and psychological evidence in the assessment of terrorist offenders' *Journal of Forensic Psychiatry & Psychology* **20** (4), 508–15.

Dernevik, M., Beck, A., Grann, M., Hogue, T. and McGuire, J. (2009b) 'A response to Dr. Gudjonsson's commentary' *Journal of Forensic Psychiatry & Psychology* **20** (4), 520–2.

Dernevik, M., Johansson, S. and Grann, M. (2000) 'Prediction of violent behaviour in mentally disordered offenders in forensic psychiatric care'. Paper presented at European Association of Psychology and Law (EAPL) Conference, Cyprus.

Desmarais, S.L. and Read, J.D. (2011) 'After 30 years, what do we know about what jurors know? A meta-analytic review of lay knowledge regarding eyewitness factors' *Law and Human Behavior* **35** (3), 200–10.

DeValve, E.Q. (2005) 'A qualitative exploration of the effects of crime victimization for victims of personal crime [Electronic Version]' *Applied Psychology in Criminal Justice* **1** (2), 71–89.

Devery, C. (2010) 'Criminal profiling and criminal investigation' *Journal of Contemporary Criminal Justice* **26** (4), 393–409

Devine, D.J. and Caughlin, D.E. (2014) 'Do they matter? A meta-analytic investigation of individual characteristics and guilt judgments' *Psychology, Public Policy, and Law*. **20** (2), 109–134.

Dhami, M.K. and Ayton, P. (2001) 'Bailing and jailing the fast and frugal way' *Journal of Behavioral Decision Making* **14**, 141–68.

Diamond, S.S., Casper, J.D. and Ostergren, L. (1989) 'Blindfolding the jury' *Law and Contemporary Problems* **52**, 247–67.

Dickinson, J.J., Poole, D.A. and Bruck, M. (2005) 'Back to the future: a comment on the use of anatomical dolls in forensic interviews' *Journal of Forensic Psychology Practice* **5** (1), 63–74.

Dickinson,J.J., Brubacher, S.P. and Poole, D.A. (2015) 'Children's performance on ground rules questions: implications for forensic interviewing' *Law and Human Behavior* **39** (1), 87–97.

DiMaggio, C. and Galea, S. (2006) 'The behavioral consequences of terrorism: a meta-analysis' *Academy of Emergency Medicine* **13**, 559–66.

DiMaggio, C., Galea, S. and Richardson, L. (2007) 'Emergency department visits for behavioral and mental health care after a terrorist attack' *Annals of Emergency Medicine* **50** (3), 327–34.

Ditton, J., Chadee, D., Farrall, S., Gilchrist, E. and Bannister, J. (2004) 'From imitation to intimidation: a note on the curious and changing relationship between the media, crime and fear of crime' *British Journal of Criminology* **44**, 595–610.

Dobash, R.P. and Dobash, R.E. (2004) 'Women's violence to men in intimate relationships: working on a puzzle' *British Journal of Criminology* **44**, 324–49.

Docherty, D. (1990) *Violence in Television Fiction* London: Libbey/Broadcasting Standards Council.

Doerner, W.G. and Ho, T.P. (1994) '"Shoot/don't shoot": police use of deadly force under simulated field conditions' *Journal of Crime and Justice* **17** (2), 49–68.

Doley, R. (2003) 'Pyromania: fact or fiction?' *British Journal of Criminology* **43**, 797–807.

Dolnik, A. and Fitzgerald, K.M. (2011) 'Negotiating hostage crises with the new terrorists' *Studies in Conflict and Terrorism* **34** (4), 267–94.

Dombert, B., Schmidt, A.F., Banse, R., Briken, P., Hoyer, J.N. and Osterheider, M. (2016) 'How common is men's self-reported sexual interest in prepubescent children?' *Journal of Sex Research*, **53** (2), 214–223

Doob, A.N. and Kirkenbaum, H.M. (1973) 'Bias in police line-ups – partial remembering' *Journal of Police Science and Administration* **1** (3), 287–93.

Douglas, J.E. and Olshaker, M. (1995) *Mind Hunter: Inside the FBI's Elite Serial Crime Unit* New York: Pocket Books.

Douglas, J.E. and Olshaker, M. (1997) *Journey into Darkness* New York: Pocket Star.

Douglas, J.E., Burgess, A.W., Burgess, A.G. and Ressler, R.K. (1992) *Crime Classification Manual* New York: Lexington.

Douglas, K.S., Cox, D.N. and Webster, C.D. (1999) 'Violence risk assessment: science and practice'. *Legal and Criminological Psychology* **4**, 149–84.

Douglass, A.B., Ray, J.L., Hasel, L.E. and Donnelly, K. (2016) 'Does it matter how you deny it?: the role of demeanour in evaluations of criminal suspects' *Legal and Criminological Psychology* **21**, 141–160.

Dowden, C. and Brown, S.L. (2002) 'The role of substance abuse factors in predicting recidivism: a meta-analysis' *Psychology, Crime and Law* **8** (3), 243–64.

Drake, R.D., Ward, T., Nathan, P. and Lee, J.K.P. (2001) 'Challenging the cognitive distortions of child molesters: an implicit theory approach' *Journal of Sexual Aggression* **7** (1), 25–40.

Driver, E. (1989) 'Introduction' in E. Driver and A. Droisen (eds) *Child Sexual Abuse: Feminist Perspectives* London: Macmillan, pp. 1–44.

Dror, I.E. and Charlton, D. (2006) 'Why experts make errors' *Journal of Forensic Identification* **56** (4), 600–16.

Dror, I.E., Champod, C., Langenburg, G., Charlton, D., Hunt, H. and Rosenthal, R. (2011) 'Cognitive issues in finger print analysis: Inter- and intra-expert consistency and the effect of "target" comparison' *Forensic Science* **208**, 10–17.

Dubourg, R., Hamed, J. and Thoms, J. (2005) 'The economic and social costs of crime against individuals and households' 2003/04. Home Office On-Line Report 30/05: June 2005. http://www.crimereduction.homeoffice.gov.uk/statistics/statistics39.htm. Accessed 21 January 2008.

Ducat, L., McEwan, T.W. and Ogloff, J.R.P. (2015) 'An investigation of firesetting recidivism: factors related to repeat offending' *Legal and Criminological Psychology*, **20**, 1–18.

Ducat, L., Thomas, S. and Blood, W. (2009) 'Sensationalising sex offenders and sexual recidivism: impact of the serious sex offender monitoring ACT 2005 on media reportage' *Australian Psychologist*, **44** (3), 156–165.

Duff, S. and Willis, A. (2006) 'At the precipice: assessing a non-offending client's potential to sexually offend' *Journal of Sexual Aggression* **12** (1), 43–51.

Duhart, D.T. (2001) Violence in the workplace, 1993–99 (Bureau of Justice Statistics Special Report NCJ 190076). Retrieved from the U.S. Department of Justice, Office of Justice Programs, Bureau of Justice Statistics website: http://bjs.ojp.usdoj.gov/content/pub/pdf/vw99.pdf (accessed 4 April, 2014).

Dunning, D. and Stern, L.B. (1994) 'Distinguishing accurate from inaccurate eyewitness identifications via inquiries about decision processes' *Journal of Personality and Social Psychology* **67**, 818–35.

Durrant, R. (2016) 'Putting risk factors in their place: an evolutionary developmental approach to understanding risk' *Psychology, Crime and Law* **22** (1–2), 17–32.

Dutton, D.G., Bodnarchuk, M., Kropp, R. and Hart, S.D. (1997) 'Wife assault treatment and criminal recidivism: an 11-year follow-up' *International Journal of Offender Therapy and Comparative Criminology* **4** (1), 9–23.

Duwe, G. and Donnay, W. (2010) 'The effects of failure to register on sex offender recidivism' *Criminal Justice and Behavior* **37**, 520–36.

Duwe, G. and Goldman, R.A. (2009) 'The impact of prison-based treatment on sex offender recidivism: Evidence from Minnesota' *Sexual Abuse: A Journal of Research and Treatment* **21** (3), 279–307.

Dye, M.H. and Aday, R.H. (2013) '"I Just Wanted to Die": Preprison and Current Suicide Ideation Among Women Serving Life Sentences' *Criminal Justice and Behavior* **40**, 832–49.

Dysart, J.E. and Strange, D. (2012) 'Beliefs about alibis and alibi investigations: a survey of law enforcement' *Psychology, Crime and Law* **18** (1), 11–25.

E

Earhart, B., La Rooy, D.J., Brubachers, S. and Lamb, M.E. (2014) 'An examination of "don't know" responses in forensic interviews with children' *Behavioral Sciences and the Law* **32**, 746–761.

East, W.N. and Huber, W.H. de B. (1939) *Report on the Psychological Treatment of Crime* London: HMSO.

Eastman, N. (2000) 'Psycholegal studies as an interface discipline' in J. McGuire, T. Mason and A. O'Kane (eds) *Behaviour, Crime and Legal Processes: A Guide for Forensic Practitioners* Chichester: John Wiley, pp. 83–110.

Eastwood, C.J. and Snook, B. (2010) 'Comprehending Canadian police cautions: Are the rights to silence and legal counsel understandable?' *Behavioral Science and the Law* **28**, 366–77.

Ebberline, J. (2008) 'Geographical offender profiling obscene phone calls: A case study' *Journal of Investigative Psychology & Offender Profiling* **5** (1), 93–105.

Ebbesen, E.B. and Konecni, V.J. (1997) 'Eyewitness memory research: probative v. prejudicial value' *Expert Evidence* **5** (1 and 2), 2–28.

Ebbinghaus, H. (1913) *Grundzüge der psychologie* Leipzig: Von Veit.

Eck, J.E. (2014) 'If the fox knows many ways to forage, the modeller cannot be a hedgehog: reflections on the use of wildlife foraging models to understand criminal target search' *Legal and Criminological Psychology* **19**, 211–214.

Edwards, D.A. (1969) 'Early androgen stimulation and aggressive behavior in male and female mice' *Physiology and Behavior* **4**, 333–8.

Edwards, D.A. and Herndon, J. (1970) 'Neonatal estrogen stimulation and aggressive behavior in female mice' *Physiology and Behavior* **4**, 993–5.

Edwards, E. (2004) 'An ambiguous participant: the crime victim and criminal justice decision-making'

British Journal of Criminology **44**, 967–82.

Eerland, A. and Rassin. E. (2012) 'Biased evaluation of incriminating and exonerating (non)evidence' *Psychology, Crime and Law* **18** (4), 351–58.

Efran, M.G. (1974) 'The effect of physical appearance on the judgment of guilt, interpersonal attraction, and the severity of recommended punishment in a simulated jury task' *Journal of Research in Personality* **8**, 45–54.

Egan, R. and Wilson, J.C. (2012) 'Rape victims' attitudes to rape myth acceptance' *Psychiatry, Psychology and Law* **19**, 345–57.

Egan, V., and Taylor, D. (2010) 'Shoplifting, unethical consumer behavior, and personality' *Personality and Individual Differences* **48**, 878–883.

Egg, R. (1999) 'Criminal careers of sex offenders'. Paper presented at Psychology and Law International Conference, Dublin, 7 July.

Ehrlich, S. (1999) 'Communities of practice, gender, and the representation of sexual assault' *Language in Society* **28** (2), 239–56.

Eigen, J.P. (2004) 'Delusion's odyssey: charting the course of Victorian forensic psychiatry' *International Journal of Law and Psychiatry* **27**, 395–412.

Eisen, M.L., Goodman, G.S., Qin, J. and Davis, S. (1998) 'Memory and suggestibility in maltreated children: new research relevant to evaluating allegations of abuse' in S.L. Lynn and K. McConkey (eds) *Truth in Memory* New York: Guilford, pp. 163–89.

Eisner M. (2008) 'Modernity strikes back? A historical perspective on the latest increase in interpersonal violence (1960–1990)' *International Journal of Conflict and Violence* **2**: 288–316.

Ekman, P. ([1985] 1992) *Telling Lies: Clues to Deceit in the Marketplace, Politics, and Marriage* New York: Norton.

Ekman, P. (1996) 'Why don't we catch liars?' *Social Research* **63** (3), 801–17.

Ekman, P., O'Sullivan, M. and Frank, M.G. (1999) 'A few can catch a liar' *Psychological Science* **10** (3), 263–5.

Elaad, E. (1990) 'Detection of guilty knowledge in real-life criminal investigations' *Journal of Applied Psychology* **75** (5), 521–9.

Elaad, E., Ginton, A. and Jungman, N. (1992) 'Detection measures in real-life criminal guilty knowledge tests' *Journal of Applied Psychology* **77** (5), 757–67.

Elaad, E., Ginton, A. and Ben-Shakhar, G. (1994) 'The effects of prior expectations and outcome knowledge of polygraph examiners' decisions' *Journal of Behavioral Decision Making* **7**, 279–292.

Elbogen, E.B., Johnson, S.C., Newton, V.M., Straits-Troster, K., Vasterling, J.J., Wagner,H.R., and Beckham, J.C. (2012) 'Criminal justice involvement, trauma, and negative affect in Iraq and Afghanistan War era veterans' *Journal of Consulting and Clinical Psychology*, **80** (6), 1097–1102.

Elbogen, E.B., Patry, M. and Scalora, M.J. (2003) 'The impact of community notification laws on sex offender treatment attitudes' *International Journal of Law and Psychiatry* **26**, 207–19.

Elkovitch, N., Viljoen, J.L., Scalora, M.J. and Ullman, D. (2008) 'Assessing risk of reoffending in adolescents who have committed a sexual offense: the accuracy of clinical judgments after completion of risk assessment instruments' *Behavioral Sciences and the Law* **26**, 511–28.

Elliott, I., Thomas, S.D.M. and Ogloff, J.R.P. (2012) 'Procedural justice in contacts with the police: the perspective of victims of crime' *Police Practice and Research* **13** (5), 437–49.

Ellis, L. (1989) *Theories of Rape: Inquiries into the Causes of Sexual Aggression* New York: Hemisphere.

Eme, R. (2015) 'Attention deficit hyperactivity disorder: a mitigation of criminal responsibility?' *Journal of Forensic Psychology Practice* **14**, 221–236.

Emerson, R.M., Ferris, K.O. and Gardner, C.B. (1998) 'On being stalked' *Social Problems* **45** (3), 289–314.

Engle, J. and O'Donogue, W. (2012) 'Pathways to False Allegations of Sexual Assault' *Journal of Forensic Psychology Practice* **12**, 97–123.

English, K., Jones, L., Patrick, D. and Pasini-Hill, D. (2003) 'Sexual offender containment: Use of the postconviction polygraph' *Annals of the New York Academy of Sciences* **989**, 411–27.

Enzmann, D., Marshall, I.H., Killias, M., Junger-Tas, J., Steketee, M. and Gruszczynska, B. (2010) 'Self-reported youth delinquency in Europe and beyond: First results of the Second International Self-Report Delinquency Study in the context of police and victimization data' *European Journal of Criminology* **7**, 159–83.

Epps, K. (1995) 'Sexually abusive behaviour in an adolescent boy with the 48, XXYY syndrome: a case study' in N.K. Clark and G.M. Stephenson (eds) *Investigative and Forensic Decision Making, Issues in Criminological and Legal Psychology No. 26* Leicester: Division of Criminological and Legal Psychology, British Psychological Society, pp. 3–11.

Epstein, S. (1985) 'The implications of cognitive-experiential self-theory for research in social psychology and personality' *Journal for the Theory of Social Behaviour* **15**, 283–310.

Epstein, S. (1994) 'Integration of the cognitive and the psychodynamic unconscious' *American Psychologist* **49**, 709–24.

Epstein, S. (2003) 'Cognitive-experiential self-theory of personality' in T. Millon and M.J. Lerner (eds) *Handbook of Psychology* Vol. 5 *Personality and Social Psychology* Hoboken, NJ: Wiley, pp. 159–84.

Epstein, S. and Pacini, R. (1999) 'Some basic issues regarding dual-process theories from the perspective of cognitive-experiential self-theory' in S. Chaiken and Y. Trope (eds) *Dual Process Theories in Social Psychology* New York: Guilford, pp. 462–82.

Ergil, D. (2001) 'Suicide terrorism in Turkey: the Workers' Party of

Kurdistan' Herzlia, Israel: Countering Suicide Terrorism, An International Conference, The International Policy Institute for Counter-Terrorism, pp. 105–14, 118–28.

Erikson, M. and Friendship, C. (2002) 'A typology of child abduction events' *Legal and Criminological Psychology* **7**, 115–20.

Eron, L.D. (1963) 'Relationship of TV viewing habits and aggressive behavior in children' *Journal of Abnormal and Social Psychology* **67**, 193–6.

Eron, L.D., Lefkowitz, M.M., Huesmann, L.R. and Walder, L.O. (1972) 'Does television violence cause aggression?' *American Psychologist* **27**, 253–63.

Esquirol, Étienne (1838). Baillière, Jean-Baptiste (and sons), ed. *Des maladies mentales considérées sous les rapports médical, hygiénique et médico-légal* Volume 1 [*Mental illness as considered in medical, hygienic, and medico-legal reports*, Volume 1] (in French). Paris: Chez J.-B. Baillière.

Estrich S (1987) *Real Rape: How the Legal System Victimizes Women Who Say No* Boston: Harvard University Press.

Estrich S. (1987) *Real Rape: How the Legal System Victimizes Women who say No* Boston: Harvard University Press.

European Union Agency for Fundamental Rights (2015) 'Child-friendly justice: perspectives and experiences of professionals on children's participation in civil and criminal judicial proceedings in 10 EU member states' fra.europa.eu/sites/default/files/fra-2015-child-friendly-justice

Evans, A.D., Lee, K. and Lyon, T.D. (2009) 'Complex questions asked by defense lawyers but not prosecutors predicts convictions in child abuse trials' *Law and Human Behavior* **33**, 258–64.

Evans, A.D., Stolzenberg, S.N., Lees, K. and Lyon, T.D, (2014) 'Young children's difficulty with indirect speech acts: implications for questioning child witnesses' *Behavioural Sciences and the Law* **32**, 775–788.

Evans, J.R. and Claycomb, S. (1998) 'Abnormal QEEG patterns associated with dissociation and violence'. Unpublished manuscript, University of South Carolina. Annual Meeting of the Society for the Study of Neuronal Regulation, Austin, TX.

Everson, M.D. and Boat, B.W. (2002) 'The utility of anatomical dolls and drawings in child forensic interviews' in M.L. Eisen, J.A. Quas and G.S. Goodman (eds) *Memory and Suggestibility in the Forensic Interview* Mahwah, NJ: Lawrence Erlbaum, pp. 383–408.

Everson, M.D. and Sandoval, J.M. (2011) 'Forensic child sexual abuse evaluations: Assessing subjectivity and bias in professional judgements' *Child Abuse and Neglect* **35**, 287–98.

Everson, M.D., Sandoval, J.M., Berson, N., Crowson, M. and Robinson, H. (2012) 'Reliability of professional judgments in forensic child sexual abuse evaluations: Unsettled or unsettling science?' *Journal of Child Sexual Abuse* **21** (1), 72–90.

Expert Law (2003) Megan's Law. http://www.expertlaw.com/library/pubarticles/megans_law.html

Eysenck, H.J. (1996) 'Personality and crime: where do we stand?' *Psychology, Crime and Law* **2**, 143–152.

F

Faigman, D.L. (2008) 'The limits of science in the courtroom' *Beyond Common Sense: Psychological Science in the Courtroom* Oxford: Blackwell, pp. 303–14.

Faigman, D.L., Kaye, D.H., Saks, M.J., Sanders, J. and Cheng, E.K. (2010) *Modern Scientific Evidence: The Law and Science of Expert Testimony Eagan* MN: Thomson West.

Falshaw, L., Friendship, C. and Bates, A. (2003) 'Sexual offenders – measuring reconviction, reoffending and recidivism' Findings 183. Home Office, Research, Development and Statistics Directorate. London, http://webarchive.nationalarchives.gov.uk/20110218135832/http://rds.homeoffice.gov.uk/rds/pdfs2/r183.pdf

Farrall, S. and Gadd, D. (2004) 'The frequency of fear of crime' *British Journal of Criminology* **44**, 127–32.

Farrall, S., Jackson, J. and Gray, E. (2007) 'Theorising fear of crime: the cultural and social significance of feelings of insecurity' http://papers.ssrn.com/sol3/papers.cfm?abstract_id=1012393

Farrell, A. (2015) 'Explaining leniency: organizational predictors of the differential treatment of men and women in traffic stops' *Crime and Delinquency* **61** (4) 509–537

Farrell, G. and Bouloukos, A. (2001) 'A cross-national comparative analysis of rates of repeat victimization' in G. Farrell and K. Pease (eds) *Repeat Victimization* Monsey, NY: Criminal Justice Press.

Farrington, D.P. (1979) 'Experiments on deviance with special reference to dishonesty' in L. Berkowitz (ed.) *Advances in Experimental Social Psychology, No. 12* New York: Academic Press, pp. 207–53.

Farrington, D.P. (1987) 'Epidemiology' in H.C. Quay (ed.) *Handbook of Juvenile Delinquency* Chichester: John Wiley, pp. 33–61.

Farrington, D.P. (1990) 'Age, period, cohort, and offending' in D.M. Gottfredson and R.V. Clarke (eds) *Policy and Theory in Criminal Justice: Contributions in Honour of Leslie T. Wilkins* Aldershot: Avebury, pp. 51–75.

Farrington, D.P. (1991) 'Childhood aggression and adult violence: Early precursors and later life outcomes' in D.J. Pepler and K.H. Rubin (eds). *The Development and Treatment of Childhood Aggression*, pp. 5–29, Hillsdale, NJ: Erlbaum.

Farrington, D.P. (1995) 'The psychology of crime: influences and constraints on offending' in R. Bull and D. Carson (eds) *Handbook of Psychology in Legal Contexts* Chichester: John Wiley, pp. 291–314.

Farrington, D.P. (1996) 'Psychosocial influences on the development of antisocial personality' in G. Davies, S. Lloyd-Bostock, M. McMurran and C. Wilson (eds) *Psychology, Law and Criminal Justice: International Developments in Research and Practice* Berlin: Walter de Gruyter, pp. 424–44.

Farrington, D.P. (1998) 'Developmental crime prevention initiatives in 1997' *Forensic Update* **54**, 19–25.

Farrington, D.P. (2001) 'What has been learned from self-reports about criminal careers and the causes of offending?' Home Office Online Report, http://www.crim.cam.ac.uk/people/academic_research/david_farrington/srdrep.pdf

Farrington, D.P. (2011) 'Families and crime' in J.Q. Wilson & J. Petersilia (eds), *Crime and Public Policy* New York: Oxford University Press, pp. 130–57.

Farrington, D.P. and Kidd, R.F. (1977) 'Is financial dishonesty a rational decision?' *British Journal of Social and Clinical Psychology* **16**, 139–46.

Farrington, D.P., Barnes, G.C. and Lambert, S. (1996) 'The concentration of offending in families' *Legal and Criminological Psychology* **1** (1), 47–63.

Farrington, D.P., Langan, P.A. and Tonry, M. (eds) (2004) *Cross-National Studies in Crime and Justice* Washington: US Department of Justice.

Faul, M., Xu, L., Wald, M.M. and Coronado, V.G. (2010) 'Traumatic brain injury in the United States: emergency department visits: hospitalizations and deaths 2002–2006' Atlanta, GA: Centers for Disease Control and Prevention, National Center for Injury Prevention and Control.

Fawcett, J.M., Russell, E.J., Peace, K.A. and Christie, J. (2013) 'Of guns and geese: a meta-analytic review of the "weapon focus" literature', *Psychology, Crime and Law* **19** (1), 35–66.

Fazel, S. and Benning, R. (2006) 'Natural deaths in male prisoners: A 20-year mortality study' *European Journal of Public Health* **16**, 441–44.

Fazel, S., Grann, M., Kling, B. and Hawton, K. (2011) 'Prison suicide in 12 countries: An ecological study of 861 suicides during 2003–2007' *Social Psychiatry and Psychiatric Epidemiology*, **46**, 191–195.

Federal Bureau of Investigation (2004) *Uniform Crime Reporting Handbook* Washington, DC: U.S. Department of Justice.

Feilzer, M.Y. (2015) 'Public knowledge of crime and criminal justice: the neglected role of public narratives', Oxford Handbooks Online, C37Criminology and Criminal Justice, Communities and Crim. http://www.oxfordhandbooks.com/view/10.1093/oxfordhb/9780199935383.001.0001/oxfordhb-9780199935383-e-104

Felson, M. (2014) 'Eight crime foraging contingencies' *Legal and Criminological Psychology* **19**, 215–217.

Felson, R., Savolainen, J., Aaltonen, M. and Moustgaard, H. (2008) 'Is the association between alcohol use and delinquency causal or spurious?' *Criminology* **46** (3), 785–808.

Felson, R.B. (1993) 'Predatory and dispute-related violence: A social interactionist approach' in R.V. Clarke and M. Felson (eds), *Advances in Criminological Theory* (Vol. 5, pp. 189–235) New Brunswick, NJ: Transaction.

Felson, R.B. (1996) 'Mass media effects on violent behavior' *Annual Review of Sociology* **22**, 102–28.

Felson, R.B. and Massoglia, M. (2012) 'When is Violence Planned?' *Journal of Interpersonal Violence* **27**, 753–74.

Fenichel, O. (1933) 'Outline of clinical psychoanalysis' *Psychoanalytic Quarterly* **2**, 562–91.

Ferguson, C.J. (2009) 'Media violence effects: confirmed truth or just another X-file?' *Journal of Forensic Psychology Practice* **9**, 103–26.

Ferguson, C.J. and Dyck, D. (2012) 'Paradigm change in aggression research: The time has come to retire the General Aggression Model' *Aggression and Violent Behavior* **17**, 220–28.

Ferguson, C.J., Rueda, S.M., Cruz, A.M., Ferguson, D.E., Fritz, S. and Smith, S.M. (2008) 'Violent video games and aggression: Causal relationship or byproduct of family violence and intrinsic violence motivation?' *Criminal Justice and Behavior* **35** (3), 311–32.

Ferguson, C.J., White, D.E., Stacey, C., Lorenz, M. and Bhimani, Z. (2003) 'Defining and classifying serial murder in the context of perpetrator motivation' *Journal of Criminal Justice* **31** (3), 287–92.

Ferguson, N. and Kamble, S.V. (2012) 'The role of revenge, denial, and terrorism distress in restoring just world beliefs: the impact of the 2008 Mumbai attacks on British and Indian students' *Journal of Social Psychology* **152** (6), 687–96.

Ferraro, K. F. (1995) 'Fear of crime: Interpreting victimization risk' Albany, NY: SUNYPress. Scherer, K. R. (1988) 'Facets of emotion: recent research' Hillsdale,NJ:Erlbaum.

Fiedler, K., Schmid, J. and Stahl, T. (2002) 'What is the current truth about polygraph lie detection?' *Basic and Applied Social Psychology* **24** (4), 313–24.

Fine, C. and Kennett, J. (2004) 'Mental impairment, moral understanding and criminal responsibility: psychopathy and the purposes of punishment' *International Journal of Law and Psychiatry* **27**, 425–43.

Finkelhor, D. (1984) *Child Sexual Abuse: New Theory and Research* New York: Free Press.

Finkelman, J. (2010) 'Litigation consulting: Expanding beyond jury selection to trial strategy and tactics' *Consulting Psychology Journal: Practice and Research*, **62** (1), 12–20.

Finlayson, L.M. and Koocher, G.P. (1991) 'Professional judgement and child abuse reporting in sexual abuse cases' *Professional Psychology: Research and Practice* **22**, 464–72.

Firestone, P., Bradford, J.M., Greenberg, D.M., Larose, M.R. and Curry, S. (1998a) 'Homicidal and nonhomicidal child molesters:

psychological, phallometric and criminal features' *Sexual Abuse: A Journal of Research and Treatment* **10** (4), 305–23.

Firestone, P., Bradford, J.M., McCoy, M., Greenberg, D.M., Curry, S. and Larose, M.R. (1998b) 'Recidivism in convicted rapists' *Journal of American Academy Psychiatry and Law* **26** (2), 185–200.

Fisher, D. and Beech, A.R. (1999) 'Current practice in Britain with sexual offenders' *Journal of Interpersonal Violence* **14** (3), 240–56.

Fisher, R.P. and Geiselman, R.W. (1992) *Memory Enhancing Techniques for Investigative Interviewing: The Cognitive Interview* Springfield: Charles C. Thomas.

Fisher, R.P., Brennan, K.H. and McCauley, M.R. (2002) 'The cognitive interview method to enhance eyewitness recall' in M.L. Eisen, J.A. Quas and G.S. Goodman (eds) *Memory and Suggestibility in the Forensic Interview* Mahwah, NJ: Lawrence Erlbaum, pp. 265–86.

Fitzgerald, P. and Seeman, M.V. (2002) 'Erotomania in women' in J. Boon and L. Sheridan (eds) *Stalking and Psychosexual Obsession: Psychological Perpsectives for Prevention, Policing and Treatment* Chichester: John Wiley, pp. 165–80.

Fitzgerald, R.J., Oriet, C., and Price, H.L. (2015) 'Suspect-filler similarity in eyewitness lineups: a literature review and a novel methodology' *Law and Human Behavior* **39** (1), 62–74.

Fitzgerald, R.J., Price, H.L., Oriet, C. and Charman, S.D. (2013) 'The effect of foil-suspect similarity on eyewitness identification decisions: A meta analysis' *Psychology, Public Policy and Law* **19**, 151–64.

Fitzmaurice, C., Rogers, D. and Stanley, P. (1996) 'Predicting court sentences: a perilous exercise' in G. Davies, S. Lloyd-Bostock, M. McMurran and C. Wilson (eds) *Psychology, Law and Criminal Justice: International Developments in Research and Practice* Berlin: Walter de Gruyter, pp. 305–13.

Flatley, J., Kershaw, C., Smith, K., Chaplin, R. and Moon, D. (eds) (2010) 'Home Office Statistical Bulletin. Crime in England and Wales 2009/10. Findings from the British Crime Survey and police recorded crime', http://webarchive.nationalarchives.gov.uk/20110218135832/rds.homeoffice.gov.uk/rds/pdfs10/hosb1210.pdf

Flood, J.J. (2003) *A Report of Findings from the Hostage Barricade Database System (HOBAS)* Quantico, VA: Crisis Negotiation Unit, Critical Incident Response Group, FBI Academy.

Flowe, H.D., Mehta, A. and Ebbesen, E.B. (2011) 'The role of eyewitness identification evidence in felony case dispositions' *Psychology, Public Policy, and Law* **17** (1), 140–59.

Flynn, S.M., Swinson, N., While, D., Hunt, I.M., Roscoe, A., Rodway, C., Windfuhr, K., Kapur, N., Appleby, L. and Shaw, J. (2009) 'Homicide followed by suicide: a cross-sectional study' *Journal of Forensic Psychiatry and Psychology* **20** (2), 306–21.

Foa, E.B., Riggs, D.S., Dancu, C.V., and Rothbaum, B.O. (1993) 'Reliability and validity of a brief instrument for assessing post-traumatic stress disorde' *Journal of Traumatic Stress* **6**, 459–473.

Folino, J.O. (2000) 'Sexual homicides and their classification according to motivation: A report from Argentina' *International Journal of Offender Therapy and Comparative Criminology* **44**, 740–50.

Fontaine, R.G., Fida, R., Paciello,M., Tisak, M.S. and Caprara, G.V. (2014) 'The mediating role of moral disengagement in the developmental course from peer rejection in adolescence to crime in early adulthood' *Psychology, Crime and Law* **20** (1), 1–19.

Forrester, A., Ozdural, S., Muthukumaraswamy, A. and Carroll, A. (2008) 'The evolution of mental disorder as a legal category in England and Wales' *Journal of Forensic Psychiatry and Psychology* **19** (4), 543–60.

Fortune, C.A. and Ward, T. (2013) 'The rehabilitation of offenders: Striving for good lives, desistance, and risk reduction' in J. Helfgott (ed.), *Criminal Psychology* New York, NY: Praeger Publishers.

Fowles, J. (1999) *The Case for Television Violence* Thousand Oaks, CA: Sage.

Fox, C. and Rirke, R. (2002) 'Forecasting trial outcomes: lawyers assign higher probability to possibilities that are described in greater detail' *Law and Human Behavior* **26** (2), 159–73.

Fox, J.A. and Zawitz, M.W. (2004) 'Homicide trends in the United States' US Bureau of Justice, http://www.ojp.usdoj.gov/bjs/homicide/homtrnd.htm (no longer available)

Fox, J.R.E., Gray, N.S. and Lewis, H. (2004) 'Factors determining compliance with command hallucinations with violent content: The role of social rank, perceived power of the voice and voice malevolence' *Journal of Forensic Psychiatry & Psychology* **15**, 511–31.

Francis, B. and Soothill, K. (2000) 'Does sex offending lead to homicide?' *Journal of Forensic Psychiatry and Psychology*, Vol. 11, No. 1, April, pp. 49–61.

Freckelton, I., and List, D. (2009) 'Asperger's disorder, criminal responsibility and criminal culpability' *Psychiatry, Psychology and Law* **16** (1), 16–40.

Freeman, J., Palk, G. and Davey, J. (2010) 'Sex offenders in denial: a study into a group of forensic psychologists' attitudes regarding the corresponding impact upon risk assessment calculations and parole eligibility' *The Journal of Forensic Psychiatry and Psychology* **21** (1), 39–51.

Freeman, T.W. and Roca, V. (2001) 'Gun use, attitudes towards violence, and aggression among combat veterans with chronic post traumatic stress disorder' *Journal of Nervous and Mental Disease*, **189** (5), 317–320.

Freud, S. (1913) 'On beginning the treatment' in P. Gray (Ed.), *The Freud Reader* (1995) (pp. 363–377) 'New York: Norton and Company, Inc.

Freud, S. (1916) 'Some character-types met with in psycho-analytic work' *The Standard Edition of the Complete Psychological Works of Sigmund Freud, Volume XIV (1914–1916): On the History of the Psycho-Analytic Movement, Papers on Metapsychology and Other Works*, 309–333.

Freyd, J.J. (1996) *Betrayal Trauma: The Logic of Forgetting Childhood Abuse* Cambridge, MA: Harvard University Press.

Friedrich, W.N. (undated) *Psychological Assessment Resources* PO Box 998, Odessa, Florida FL33556.

Friedrich, W.N., Grambach, P., Damon, L., Hewitt, S.K., Koverola, C., Lang, R.A., Wolfe, V. and Broughton, D. (1992) 'Child sexual behavior inventory: normative and clinical comparisons' *Psychological Assessment* **4** (3), 303–11.

Froggio, G. (2007) 'Strain and juvenile delinquency: a critical review of Agnew's General Strain Theory' *Journal of Loss and Trauma* **12** (4), 383–418.

Frowd, C.D., Carson, D., Ness, H., McQuiston-Surrett, D., Richardson, J., Baldwin, H. and Hancock, P. (2004) 'Contemporary composite techniques: the impact of forensically-relevant target delay'. Paper presented at XIV Conference of the European Association of Psychology and Law (EAPL), Krakow, Poland.

Frowd, C.D., Carson, D., Ness, H., Richardson, J., Morrison, L., McLanaghan, S. and Hancock, P.J.B. (2005) 'A forensically valid comparison of facial composite systems' *Psychology, Crime and Law* **11** (1), 35–52.

Frumkin, B., Lally, S.J. and Sexton, J.E. (2012) 'The Grisso Tests for Assessing Understanding and Appreciation of Miranda Warnings with a Forensic Sample' *Behavioral Sciences and the Law* **30**, 673–692.

Fulero, S.M. and Penrod, S. (1990) 'The myths and realities of attorney jury selection and folklore and scientific jury selection: what works?' *Ohio Northern University Law Review* **17**, 339–53.

Fullerton, R.A. and Punj, G.N. (2004) 'Shoplifting as moral insanity: historical perspectives on kleptomania' *Journal of Macromarketing* **24** (1), 8–16.

Funder, D.C. (1999) *Personality Judgment: A Realistic Approach to Person Perception*. San Diego, CA: Academic Press.

G

Gabbert, F., Hope, L. and Fisher, R.P. (2009) 'Protecting eyewitness evidence: Examining the efficacy of a self-administered interview tool' *Law and Human Behavior* **33**, 298–307.

Gabriel, R., Ferrando, L., Sainz Corton, E., Mingote, C., Garcia-Camba, E., Fernandez-Liria, A.G. and Galea, S. (2007) 'Psychopathological consequences after a terrorist attack: an epidemiological study among victims, police officers, and the general population' *European Psychiatry* **22** (6), 339–46.

Gagliardi, G.J., Lovell, D., Peterson, P.D. and Jemelka, R. (2004) 'Forecasting recidivism in mentally ill offenders released from prison' *Law and Human Behavior* **28** (2), 133–55.

Gakhal, B.K. and Brown, S.J. (2011) 'A comparison of the general public's, forensic professionals' and students' attitudes towards female sex offenders' *Journal of Sexual Aggression* **17** (1), 105–16.

Galen, B.R. and Underwood, M.K. (1997) 'A developmental investigation of social aggression among children' *Developmental Psychology* **33** (4), 589–600.

Gannon, T. A., and Pina, A. (2010) 'Firesetting: psychopathology, theory and treatment' *Aggression and Violent Behaviour*, **15**, 224–238.

Gannon, T.A. (2006) 'Increasing honest responding on cognitive distortions in child molesters: the bogus pipeline procedure' *Journal of Interpersonal Violence* **21**, 358–75.

Gannon, T.A. (2010) 'Female arsonists: Key features, psychopathologies and treatment needs' *Psychiatry: Interpersonal and Biological Processes* **73**, 173–89.

Gannon, T.A. and Polaschek, D. (2005) 'Do child molesters deliberately fake good on cognitive distortion questionnaires? An information processing-based investigation' *Sexual Abuse: A Journal of Research and Treatment* **17**, 183–200.

Gannon, T.A., Beech, A.R. and Ward, T. (2008) 'Does the polygraph lead to better risk prediction for sexual offenders?' *Aggression and Violent Behavior* **13**, 29–44.

Gannon, T.A., Hoare, J.A., Rose, M.R. and Parrett, N. (2012) 'A re-examination of female child molesters' implicit theories: evidence of female specificity?' *Psychology, Crime and Law* **18** (2), 1–16.

Gannon, T.A., Ó Ciardha, C., Doley, R.M. and Alleyne, E. (2012) 'The multi-trajectory theory of adult firesetting (M-TTAF)' *Aggression and Violent Behavior* **17** (2), 107–21.

Garner, R. (2005) 'Police attitudes: the impact of experience after training' *Applied Psychology in Criminal Justice* **1** (1), 56–70.

Garner, R. (2008) 'Police stress: Effects of criticism management training on health' *Applied Psychology in Criminal Justice* **4** (2), 243–59.

Garrett, B. (2011) *Convicting the Innocent: Where Criminal Prosecutions Go Wrong* Cambridge, MA: Harvard University Press.

Garrido, E. and Masip, J. (1999) 'How good are police officers at spotting lies?' *Forensic Update* **58**, 14–20.

Garven, S., Wood, J.M., and Malpass, R.S. (2000) 'Allegations of wrongdoing: the effects of reinforcement on children's mundane and fantastic claims' *Journal of Applied Psychology* **85** (1), 38–49.

Gastil, J., Burkhalter, S. and Black, L.W. (2007) 'Do juries deliberate? A study of deliberation, individual difference, and group member satisfaction at a municipal courthouse' *Small Group Research* **38** (3), 337–59.

Gavin Oxburgh, G., Ost, J. and Cherryman, J. (2012) 'Police

interviews with suspected child sex offenders: does use of empathy and question type influence the amount of investigation relevant information obtained?' *Psychology, Crime and Law* **18** (3), 259–73.

Geberth, V.J. (1996) *Practical Homicide Investigation: Tactics, Procedures and Forensic Techniques* Boca Raton, FL: CRC Press.

Gebhard, P.H., Gagnon, J.H., Pomeroy, W.B. and Christenson, C.V. (1965) *Sex Offenders: An Analysis of Types* New York: Harper & Row.

Geis, G. and Loftus, E.F. (2009) '*Taus* v. *Loftus*: determining the legal ground rules for scholarly inquiry' *Journal of Forensic Psychology Practice* **9** (2), 147–62.

Geiselman, R.E. and Fisher, R.P. (1997) 'Ten years of cognitive interviewing' in D. Payne and F. Conrad (eds) *Intersections in Basic and Applied Memory Research* New York: Lawrence Erlbaum, pp. 291–310.

Geiselman, R.E., Fisher, R.P., Firstenberg, I., Hutton, L.A., Sullivan, S., Avetissian, I. and Prosk, A. (1984) 'Enhancement of eyewitness memory: an empirical evaluation of the cognitive interview' *Journal of Police Science and Administration* **121**, 74–80.

Gelles, R.J. (1979) *Family Violence* Beverly Hills, CA: Sage.

Gelles, R.J. and Cornell, C. (1985) *Intimate Violence in Families* Beverly Hills, CA: Sage.

Gelles, R.J. and Straus, M.A. (1979) 'Determinants of violence: towards a theoretical integration' in W. Burr, R. Hill, I. Nyer and I. Reiss (eds) *Contemporary Theories About the Family* New York: Free Press, pp. 549–81.

Gendreau, P., Goggin, C. and Fulton, B. (2000) 'Intensive supervision in probation and parole' in C.R. Hollin (ed.) *Handbook of Offender Assessment and Treatment* Chichester: John Wiley, pp. 95–204.

Gendreau, P., Goggin, C., Cullen, F.T. and Paparozzi, M. (2002) 'The common sense revolution and correctional policy' in J. Maguire (ed.) *Offender Rehabilitation and Treatment: Effective Programmes and Policies to Reduce Re-offending* Chichester: John Wiley & Sons, pp. 359–86.

General Elec. Co. V. Joiner. 522 U.S. 136. Supreme Court of U.S.A 1997.

Genschow, O., Noll, T., Wänke, M. and Gersbach, R. (2015) 'Does Baker-Miller pink reduce aggression in prison detention cells? a critical empirical examination' *Psychology, Crime and Law* **21** (5), 482–489.

Gentry, C.S. (1991) 'Pornography and rape: an empirical analysis' *Deviant Behaviour* **12** (3), 277–88.

Geraerts, E., Raymaekers, L. and Merckelbach, H. (2008) 'Recovered memories of childhood sexual abuse: Current findings and their legal implications' *Legal and Criminological Psychology* **13**, 165–76.

Gerbner, G. (1972) 'Violence in television drama: trends and symbolic functions' in G.A. Comstock and E.A. Rubenstein (eds) *Television and Social Behaviour, Vol. 1: Media Content and Control* Washington, DC: US Government Printing Office, pp. 28–187.

Gerbner, G., Gross, L., Eley, M.E., Jackson Breek, M., Jeffries-Fox, S. and Signorielli, N. (1977) 'Television violence profile, No. 8' *Journal of Communication* **27**, 171–80.

Gershon, R.M., Barocas, B., Canton, A.N., Li, X. and Vlahov, D. (2009) 'Mental, physical, and behavioral outcomes associated with perceived work stress in police officers' *Criminal Justice and Behavior* **36**, 275–89.

Gibbs, J.C. (2003) *Moral Development and Reality: Beyond the Theories of Kohlberg and Hoffman* Thousand Oaks, CA: Sage Publications.

Gibbs, J.C., Basinger, K.S. and Fuller, D. (1992) *Moral Maturity: Measuring the Development of Sociomoral Reflection* Hillsdale, NJ: Lawrence Erlbaum.

Gierowski, J.F., Jaskiewicz-Obydzinska, T. and Slawik, M. (1998) 'The planning of a criminal act as a fundamental aspect of psychological profiling – its relation to the personality, motivation and modus operandi of a perpetrator' 8th European Conference on Psychology and Law, Krakow, 2–5 September.

Gierowski, J.F., Jaskiewicz-Obydzinska, T. and Slawik, M. (2000) 'The planning of a criminal act as a fundamental aspect of psychological profiling – its relation to the personality, motivation and modus operandi of a perpetrator' in A. Czerederecka, T. Jaskiewicz-Obdzinska and J. Wojcikiewicz (eds) *Forensic Psychology and Law: Traditional Questions and New Ideas* Krakow: Institute of Forensic Research Publishers, pp. 88–94.

Gilbert, F. and Daffern, M. (2010) 'Integrating contemporary aggression theory with violent offender treatment: How thoroughly do interventions target violent behavior?' *Aggression and Violent Behavior* **15**, 167–80.

Gilchrist, E., Bannister, J., Ditton, J. and Farrall, S. (1998) 'Women and the "fear of crime"' *British Journal of Criminology* **38** (2), 283–98.

Gill, M., Little, R., Spriggs, A., Allen, J., Argomaniz, J. and Waples, S. (2005) 'Assessing the impact of CCTV: The Hawkeye case study' (Home Office Online Report 12/05) London: Home Office.

Gilligan, C. (1982) *In a Different Voice: Psychological Theory and Women's Development* Cambridge, MA: Harvard University Press.

Ginton, A. (2013) 'A non-standard method for estimating accuracy of lie detection techniques demonstrated on a self-validating set of field polygraph examinations' *Psychology, Crime and Law* **19** (7), 577–94.

Ginton, A. (2013) 'Decisions to be taken in the use of polygraph examinations for verifying complaints about violence: analysis and,policy recommendations' *Journal of Investigative Psychology and Offender Profiling* 10, 166–181.

Glasser, M., Kolvin, I., Campbell. D., Glasser, A., Leitch, I. and Farrelly. S. (2001) 'Cycle of child sexual abuse: links between being a victim and becoming a perpetrator' *British Journal of Psychiatry* **179**, 482–94.

Gleaves, D.H. and Smith, S.M. (2004) 'False and recovered memories in the laboratory and clinic: a review of experimental and clinical evidence' *Clinical Psychology: Science and Practice* **11**, 3–28.

Glover, N. (1999) *Risk Assessment and Community Care in England and Wales* Liverpool: Faculty of Law, University of Liverpool.

Glueck, S. and Glueck, E. (1950) *Unraveling Juvenile Delinquency* New York: Commonwealth Fund.

Glueck, S. and Glueck, E. (1962) *Family Environment and Delinquency* London: Routledge and Kegan Paul.

Glueck, S. and Glueck, E. (1968) *Delinquents and Nondelinquents in Perspective* Cambridge, MA: Harvard University Press.

Goddard, H. H. (1912) *The Kallikak Family: A Study in the Heredity of Feeble-mindedness* New York: Macmillan.

Goffman, E. (1959) *The Presentation of the Self in Everyday Life* Garden City, New York: Doubleday/Anchor Books.

Goffman, E. (1961) *Asylums* New York: Anchor Books.

Goldstein, A.P. (2004) 'Evaluations of effectiveness' in A.P. Goldstein, R. Nensen, B. Daleflod and M. Kalt (eds) *New Perspectives on Aggression Replacement Training* Chichester: John Wiley & Sons, pp. 230–44.

Goldstein, A.P., Glick, B. and Gibbs, J.C. (1998) *Aggression Replacement Training* (rev. edn) Champaign, IL: Research Press.

Goncalves, R.A. (1998) 'Correctional treatment in Portugal' in J. Boros, I. Munnich and M. Szegedi (eds) *Psychology and Criminal Justice: International Review of Theory and Practice* Berlin: de Gruyter, pp. 327–31.

Goodman, G.S. and Melinder, A. (2007) 'Child witness research and forensic interviews of young children: A review' *Legal and Criminological Psychology* **12**, 1–19.

Goodman-Delahunty, J. and Graham, K. (2011) 'The influence of victim intoxication and victim attire on police responses to sexual assault' *Journal of Investigative Psychology and Offender Profiling* **8**, 22–40.

Goodwill, A.M. and Alison, L.J. (2007) 'When is profiling possible? Offense planning and aggression as moderators in predicting offender age from victim age in stranger rape' *Behavioral Sciences and the Law* **25**, 823–40.

Goodwill, A.M., Alison, L.J. and Beech, A.R. (2009) 'What works in offender profiling? A comparison of typological, thematic, and multivariate models' *Behavioral Sciences and the Law* **27**, 507–29.

Gordon, B.N., Schroeder, C.S. and Abrams, J.M. (1990a) 'Age and social-class differences in children's knowledge of sexuality' *Journal of Clinical Child Psychology* **19**, 33–43.

Gordon, B.N., Schroeder, C.S. and Abrams, J.M. (1990b) 'Children's knowledge of sexuality: a comparison of sexually abused and nonabused children' *American Journal of Orthopsychiatry* **60**, 250–7.

Gordon, H., Oyebode, O. and Minne, C. (1997) 'Death by homicide in special hospitals' *Journal of Forensic Psychiatry* **8** (3), 602–19.

Gossop, M., Marsden, J., Stewart, D. and Kidd, T. (2003) 'The National Treatment Outcome Research Study (NTORS): 4–5 year follow-up results' *Addiction* **98**, 291–303.

Gottfredson, D.M. and Gottfredson, S.D. (1988) 'Stakes and risks in the prediction of violent criminal behavior' *Violence and Victims* **3** (4), 247–62.

Gottfredson, M. and Hirschi, T. (1986) 'The true value of lambda would appear to be zero: an essay on career criminals, criminal careers, selective incapacitation, cohort studies, and related topics' *Criminology* **24**, 213–34.

Gottfredson, M.R. and Hirschi, T. (1990) *A General Theory of Crime* Stanford, CA: Stanford University Press.

Götz, J.M., Johnstone, E. and Ratcliffe, G.S. (1999) 'Criminality and antisocial behaviour in unselected men with sex chromosome abnormalities' *Psychological Medicine* **29**. 953–62.

Gowensmith, W.N., Murrie, D.C. and Boccaccini, M.T. (2013) 'How reliable are forensic evaluations of legal sanity?' *Law and Human Behavior* **37** (2), 98–106.

Graber, D.A. (1980) *Crime News and the Public* New York: Praeger.

Granhag, P. A. (2010) 'The strategic use of evidence (SUE) technique: a scientific perspective. High Value Detainee Interrogation Group (HIG, FBI). HIG Research Symposium: Interrogation in the European Union, Washington, DC.

Granhag, P.A. and Vrij, A. (2010) 'Introduction: What works in investigative psychology?' *Legal and Criminological Psychology* **15**, 1–3.

Granhag, P.A., Andersson, L.O., Stromwall, L.A. and Hartwig, M. (2004) 'Imprisoned knowledge: criminals beliefs about deception' *Legal and Criminological Psychology* **9**, 103–19.

Granhag, P.A., Ask, K., Rebelius, A., Öhman, L. and Giolla, E.M. (2013) '"I saw the man who killed Anna Lindh!" An archival study of witnesses' offender descriptions' *Psychology, Crime and Law* **19** (10), 921–31.

Granhag, P.A., Strömwall, L.A. and Hartwig, M. (2007) 'The SUE technique: the way to interview to detect diction' *Forensic Update* **88**, 25–9.

Granhag, P.A., Stromwall, L.A., Willen, R.M. and Hartwig, M. (2013) 'Eliciting cues to deception by tactical disclosure of evidence: The first test of the Evidence Framing Matrix' *Legal and Criminological Psychology* **18**, 341–55.

Grant, D. and Williams, D. (2011) 'The importance of perceiving social contexts when predicting crime and anti-social behavior in CCTV images' *Legal and Criminological Psychology* **16** (2), 307–22.

Grant, J.E., Odlaug, B.A. and Kim, S.W. (2010) 'Kleptomania: clinical characteristics and relationship to substance use disorders' *The American*

Journal of Drug and Alcohol Abuse **936**) 291–295.

Grant, J.E., Odlaug, B.L., Davis, A.A. and Kim, S.W. (2009) 'Legal consequences of kleptomania' *Psychiatric Quarterly* **80**, 251–9.

Graves, R.B., Openshaw, D.K., Ascione, F.R. and Ericksen, S.L. (1996) 'Demographic and parental characteristics of youthful sexual offenders' *International Journal of Offender Therapy and Comparative Criminology* **40** (4), 300–17.

Green, D.P., Glaser, J. and Rich, A. (1998) 'From lynching to gay bashing: the elusive connection between economic conditions and hate crime' *Journal of Personality and Social Psychology* **75** (1), 82–92.

Green, D.P., Strolovitch, D.Z. and Wong, J.S. (1998) 'Defended neighborhoods, integration and racially motivated crime' *American Journal of Sociology* **104** (2), 372–403.

Greenall, P.V. and Wright, M. (2015) 'Exploring the criminal histories of stranger sexual killers' *Journal of Forensic Psychiatry and Psychology*, **26** (2), 242–259.

Greenberg, D. M., Firestone, P., Nunes, K. L., Bradford, J. M. and Curry, S. (2005) 'Biological fathers and stepfathers who molest their daughters: psychological, phallometric, and criminal features' *Sexual Abuse: A Journal of Research and Treatment*, **17**, 39–46.

Greenberg, M.S. and Beach, S.R. (2001) 'The role of social influence in crime victim's decision to notify the police' in R. Roesch, R.R. Carrado and R. Dempster (eds), *Psychology in the Courts: International Advances in Knowledge*. London/New York: Routledge, pp. 305–16.

Greenberg, M.S. and Beach, S.R. (2004) 'Property crime victims' decision to notify the police: social, cognitive and affective determinants' *Law and Human Behavior* **28** (2), 177–86.

Greene, E., and Evelo, A.J. (2015) 'Cops and robbers (and eyewitnesses): a comparison of lineup administration by robbery detectives in the USA and Canada' *Psychology, Crime & Law*, **21** (3), 297–313

Gregg, V., Gibbs, J.C. and Basinger, K.S. (1994) 'Patterns of developmental delay in moral judgement by male and female delinquents' *Merrill-Palmer Quarterly* **40**, 538–53.

Gresnigt, J.A.M., Breteler, M.H.M., Schippers, G.M. and Van den Hurk, A.A. (2000) 'Predicting violent crime among drugusing inmates: the addiction severity index as a prediction instrument' *Legal and Criminological Psychology* **5**, 85–95.

Gresswell, D.M. and Hollin, C.R. (1994) 'Multiple murder: a review' *British Journal of Criminology* **34**, 1–14.

Gresswell, D.M. and Hollin, C.R. (1997) 'Addictions and multiple murder: a behavioural perspective' in J.E. Hodge, M. McMurran and C.R. Hollin (eds) *Addicted to Crime?* Chichester: John Wiley.

Gretenkord, L. (1991) *Prediction of Illegal Behaviour of Mentally Ill Offenders* Proceedings of the 17th International Congress of the International Academy of Law and Mental Health, Leuven, Belgium, May.

Gretenkord, L. (1993) 'Actuarial versus clinical versus political prediction'. Paper presented at XIX International Congress of the International Academy of Law and Mental Health, Lisbon, Portugal, June.

Gretenkord, L. (2000) 'How to use empirical findings for the prognosis of mentally disordered offenders'. Paper presented at the 10th European Conference of Psychology and Law, Limassol, Cyprus.

Greuel, L., Brietzke, S. and Stadle, M.A. (1999) 'Credibility assessment: new research perspectives'. Joint International Conference on Psychology and Law, Dublin, 6–9 July.

Griffiths, A. and Milne, R. (2006) 'Will it all end in tiers? Police interviews with suspects in Britain' in T. Williamson (Ed.), *Investigative Interviewing: Rights, Research and Regulation* (pp. 167–189)

Grimshaw, R. (2008) 'Young people who sexually abuse: source document' Youth Justice Board: Centre for Crime and Justice Studies, https://www.crimeandjustice.org.uk/publications/young-people-who-sexually-abuse-0

Grisso, T. (1991) 'A developmental history of the American psychology-law society' *Law and Human Behavior* **15** (3), 213–231.

Groscup, J., Penrod, S., Studebaker, C., Huss, M. and O'Neil, K. (2002) 'The effects of *Daubert* v. *Merrell Dow Pharmaceuticals* on the admissibility of expert testimony in state and federal criminal cases'. *Psychology, Public Policy and Law* **8**, 339–72.

Gross, B.H., Southard, M.J., Lamb, R. and Weinberger, L.E. (1987) 'Assessing dangerousness and responding appropriately' *Journal of Clinical Psychiatry* **48** (1), 9–12.

Groth, A.N. and Birnbaum, H.J. (1978) 'Adult sexual orientation and attraction to underage persons' *Archives of Sexual Behavior* **7** (3), 175–81.

Groth, A.N. and Burgess, A.W. (1978) 'Rape: a pseudosexual act' *International Journal of Women's Studies* **1** (2), 207–10.

Groth, A.N., Burgess, A.W. and Holmstrom, L.L. (1977) 'Rape, power, anger and sexuality' *American Journal of Psychiatry* **134**, 1239–48.

Grounds, A. (2004) 'Psychological consequences of wrongful conviction and imprisonment' *Canadian Journal of Criminology and Criminal Justice* **46** (2), 165–82.

Grover, C. and Soothill, K. (1999) 'British serial killing: towards a structural explanation' *British Criminology Conferences: Selected Proceedings*, Vol. 2. http://britsoccrim.org/volume2/008.pdf

Grubb, A. and Turner, E. (2012) 'Attribution of blame in rape cases: A review of the impact of rape myth acceptance, gender role conformity and substance use on victim blaming' *Aggression and Violent Behavior* **17**, 443–52.

Grubin, D. (1994) 'Sexual murder' *The British Journal of Psychiatry* **165**, 624–9.

Grubin, D. (1996a) *Fitness to Plead in England and Wales* Hove: Psychology Press.

Grubin, D. (1996b) 'Silence in court: psychiatry and the Criminal Justice and Public Order Act 1994' *Journal of Forensic Psychiatry* **7** (3), 647–52.

Grubin, D. (2008) 'The case for polygraph testing of sex offenders' *Legal and Criminological Psychology* **13**, 177–89.

Grubin, D. and Madsen, L. (2005) 'Lie detection and the polygraph: a historical review' *British Journal of Forensic Psychiatry and Psychology* **16**, 357–69.

Grubin, D., Madsen, L., Parsons, S., Sosnowki, D. and Warberg, B. (2004) 'A prospective study of the impact of polygraphy on high risk behaviors in adult sex offenders' *Sexual Abuse: A Journal of Research and Treatment* **16**, 209–22.

Grubin, D.H. and Kennedy, H.G. (1991) 'The classification of sexual offenders' *Criminal Behaviour and Mental Health* **1**, 123–9.

Gudjonsson, G., Sigurdsson, J.F. and Sigfusdottir, I.D. (2009) 'False confessions among 15- and 16 year-olds in compulsory education and the relationship with adverse life events' *Journal of Forensic Psychiatry & Psychology* **20** (6), 950–63.

Gudjonsson, G.H. (1984) 'A new scale of interrogative suggestibility' *Personality and Individual Differences* **5**, 303–14.

Gudjonsson, G.H. (1992) *The Psychology of Interrogations, Confessions and Testimony* Chichester: John Wiley.

Gudjonsson, G.H. (2003) *The Psychology of Interrogations and Confessions: A Handbook* Chichester: John Wiley.

Gudjonsson, G.H. (2006) 'Sex offenders and confessions: How to overcome their resistance during questioning' *Journal of Clinical Forensic Medicine* **13**, 203–7.

Gudjonsson, G. (2009) 'The assessment of terrorist offenders: a commentary on the Dernevik et al. article and suggestions for future directions' *Journal of Forensic Psychiatry and Psychology* **20** (4), 516–19.

Gudjonsson, G.H. and Copson, G. (1997) 'The role of the expert in criminal investigation' in J.L. Jackson and D.A. Bekerian (eds) *Offender Profiling: Theory, Research and Practice* Chichester: John Wiley, pp. 61–76.

Gudjonsson, G.H. and Haward, L.R.C. (1998) *Forensic Psychology: A Guide to Practice*. London: Routledge.

Gudjonsson, G.H. and Pearse, J. (2011) 'Suspect Interviews and False Confessions' *Current Directions in Psychological Science* **20** (1), 33–7.

Gudjonsson, G.H. and Sigurdsson, J.F. (1999) 'The Gudjonsson Confession Questionnaire-Revised (GCQ-R): Factor structure and its relationship with personality' *Personality and Individual Differences* **27**, 953–68.

Gudjonsson, G.H., Murphy, G.H. and Clare, I.C.H. (2000) 'Assessing the capacity of people with intellectual disabilities to be witnesses in court' *Psychological Medicine* **30** (2), 307–14.

Gudjonsson, G.H., Sigurdsson, J.F., Asgeirsdottir, B.B. and Sigfusdottir, I.D. (2007) 'Custodial interrogation: What are the background factors associated with claims of false confession to police?' *Journal of Forensic Psychiatry and Psychology* **18** (2), 266–75.

Guerette, R.T. and Santana, S.A. (2010) 'Explaining victim self-protective behavior effects on crime incident outcomes: a test of opportunity theory' *Crime and Delinquency* **56** (2) April, 198–226.

Gunn, J. and Buchanan, A. (2006) 'Paranoia in the Criminal Courts' *Behavioural Sciences and the Law* **24**, 373–83.

Gunnell, J. and Ceci, S.J. (2010) 'When emotionality trumps reason: A study of individual processing style and juror bias' *Behavioral Science and the Law* **28**, 850–77.

Gunter, B. (1987) *Television and the Fear of Crime* London: John Libbey.

Guthrie, R.V. (1998) *Even the Rat was White: A Historical View of Psychology* (2nd edn) Boston: Allyn and Bacon.

H

Haapasalo, J. and Tremblay, R.E. (1994) 'Physically aggressive boys from ages 6 to 12: family background, parenting behavior, and prediction of delinquency' *Journal of Consulting and Clinical Psychology* **62** (5), 104–52.

Haapasalo, J. (1999) 'Sons in prison and their mothers: is there a relationship between childhood histories of physical abuse?' Dublin conference, Dublin, Ireland, 6–9 July.

Haapasalo, J. and Kankkonen, M. (1997) 'Self-reported childhood abuse among sex and violent offenders' *Archives of Sexual Behavior* **26** (4), 421–31.

Haapasalo, J. and Pokela, E. (1999) 'Child-rearing and child abuse antecedents of criminality' *Aggression and Violent Behavior* **4** (1), 107–27.

Haapasalo, J., Puupponen, M. and Crittenden, P.M. (1999) 'Victim to victimizer: the psychology of isomorphism in the case of a recidivist pedophile in Finland' *Journal of Child Sexual Abuse* **7** (3), 97–115.

Haber, R.N., and Haber, L. (2013) 'The culture of science: bias and forensic evidence' *Journal of Applied Research in Memory and Cognition* **2**, 65–67.

Hackett, L., Day, A. and Mohr, P.L. (2008) 'Expectancy violation and perceptions of rape victim credibility' *Legal and Criminological Psychology* **13**, 323–34.

Haden, S.C. and Scarpa, A. (2008) 'Community violence victimization and depressed mood: The moderating effects of coping and social support' *Journal of Interpersonal Violence* **23**, 1213–34.

Hagbor, J.M., Stromwall, L.A. and Tidefors, I. (2012) 'Prosecution Rate and Quality of the Investigative Interview in Child Sexual Abuse Cases' *Journal of Investigative Psychology and Offender Profiling* **9**, 161–73.

Hagell, A. and Newburn, T. (1994) *Young Offenders and the Media: Viewing Habits and Preferences* London: Policy Studies Institute.

Haggård, U., Gumpert, C.H. and Grann, M. (2001) 'Against all odds – A qualitative follow-up study of high risk violent offenders who were not reconvicted' *Journal of Interpersonal Violence* **16** (10), 1048–65.

Haginoya, S. (2014) 'Offender demographics and geographical characteristics by offender means of transportation in serial residential burglaries' *Psychology, Crime and Law* **20** (6), 515–534.

Häkkänen, H. and Laajasalo, T. (2006) 'Homicide crime scene actions in a Finnish sample of mentally ill offenders' *Homicide Studies* **10**, 33–54.

Häkkänen, H., Lindlof, P. and Santtila, P. (2004) 'Crime scene actions and offender characteristics in a sample of Finnish stranger rapes' *Journal of Investigative Psychology and Offender Profiling* **1**, 17–32.

Hales, J., Nevill, C., Pudney, S. and Tipping,S. (2009) 'Longitudinal analysis of the Offending, Crime and Justice Survey 2003–06' *Research Report 19* London: Home Office.

Hall, G.C.N. (1995) 'Sexual offender recidivism revisited: a meta-analysis of recent treatment studies' *Journal of Consulting and Clinical Psychology* **63** (5), 802–9.

Hall, G.C.N. and Barongan, C. (1997) 'Prevention of sexual aggression: sociocultural risk and protective factors' *American Psychologist* **52** (1), 5–14.

Hall, G.C.N. and Hirschman, R. (1991) 'Toward a theory of sexual aggression: a quadripartite model' *Journal of Consulting and Clinical Psychology* **59**, 662–9.

Hall, G.C.N., Hirschman, R. and Oliver, L.L. (1995) 'Sexual arousal and arousability to pedophilic stimuli in a community sample of normal men' *Behavior Therapy* **26**, 681–94.

Hall, G.C.N., Shondrick, D.D. and Hirschman, R. (1993) 'The role of sexual arousal in sexually aggressive behavior: a meta-analysis' *Journal of Consulting and Clinical Psychology* **61** (6), 1091–5.

Hall, J. (2007) 'The emergence of clinical psychology in Britain from 1943 to 1958 Part 1: core tasks and the professionalisation process' *History & Philosophy of Psychology* **9** (1), 29–55.

Hall, S., Crilcher, C., Jefferson, T., Clarke, J. and Roberts, B. (1978) *Policing the Crisis: Mugging, the State and Law and Order* London: Macmillan.

Hall, T.A., Cook, N.E., Berman, G.L. (2010) 'Navigating the Expanding Field of Law and Psychology: A Comprehensive Guide to Graduate Education' *Journal of Forensic Psychology Practice* **10** (2), 69–90.

Haller, J.S. and Haller, R.N. (1974) *The Physician and Sexuality in Victorian America* Urbana, IL: University of Illinois Press.

Halligan, S.L., Michael, T., Clark, D.M., and Ehlers, A. (2003) 'Post-traumatic stress disorder following assault: the role of cognitive processing, trauma memory, and appraisals' *Journal of Consulting and Clinical Psychology* **71**(3), 419–431.

Halloran, J.D., Brown, R.L. and Chaney, D.C. (1970) *Television and Delinquency* Leicester: Leicester University Press.

Hamilton, D.L. and Gifford, R.K. (1976) 'Illusory correlation in interpersonal perception: a cognitive basis of stereotypic judgments' *Journal of Experimental Social Psychology* **12**, 392–407.

Hammond, L. (2014) 'Geographical profiling in a novel context: prioritising the search for New Zealand sex offenders' *Psychology, Crime and Law* **20** (4), 358–371.

Hammond, L., Wagstaff, G.F. and Cole, J. (2006) 'Facilitating eyewitness memory in adults and children with context reinstatement and focused meditation' *Journal of Investigative Psychology and Offender Profiling* **3**, 117–30.

Hanks, H., Hobbs, C. and Wynne, J. (1988) 'Early signs and recognition of sexual abuse in the pre-school child' in K. Browne, C. Davies and P. Stratton (eds) *Early Prediction and Prevention of Child Abuse* Chichester: John Wiley, pp. 139–60.

Hanna, K., Davies, E., Crothers, C. and Henderson. E. (2012) 'Child Witnesses' Access to Alternative Modes of Testifying in New Zealand' *Psychiatry, Psychology and Law* **19** (2), 184–97.

Hanson, R.K. (1997) 'The development of a brief actuarial risk scale for sexual offense recidivism', User Report No. 1997-04. Ottawa: Department of the Solicitor General of Canada.

Hanson, R.K. and Bussière, M.T. (1998) 'Predicting relapse: a meta-analysis of sexual offender recidivism studies' *Journal of Consulting and Clinical Psychology* **66**, 348–64.

Hanson, R.K. and Morton-Bourgon, K. (2004) 'Predictors of sexual recidivism: An updated meta-analysis' *Corrections User Report No.* 2004-02 Public Safety and Emergency Preparedness Ottawa Canada.

Hanson, R.K. and Slater, S. (1988) 'Sexual victimization in the history of sexual abusers: a review' *Annals of Sex Research* **1**, 485–99.

Hanson, R. K. and Thornton, D. (1999) 'Static-99: Improving actuarial risk assessments for sex offenders' User Report 99-02. Ottawa: Department of the Solicitor General of Canada.

Hanson, R. K. and Thornton, D. (2003). 'Notes on the development of the Static-2002 (User Report 2003-01). Ottawa, ON: Solicitor General', Canada. http://www.static99.org/pdfdocs/HansonThornton2003.pdf

Hanson, R.K. and Wallace-Capretta, S. (2000) 'A multi-site study of treatment for abusive men' User Report 2000–05. Ottawa: Department of the Solicitor General of Canada.

Hanson, R.K. and Morton-Bourgon, K. (2005) 'The characteristics of persistent sexual offenders: A meta-analysis of recidivism studies' *Journal of Consulting and Clinical Psychology* **73**, 1154–1163.

Hanson, R.K., Bourgon, G., Helmus, L. and Hodgson, S. (2009) 'The principles of effective correctional treatment also apply to sex offenders: a meta-analysis' *Criminal Justice and Behavior* **36**, 865–91.

Hanson, R.K., Gordon, A., Harris, A.J.R., Marques, J.K., Murphy, W., Quinsey, V.L. and Seto, M.C. (2002) 'First report of the collaborative outcome data project on the effectiveness of psychological treatment for sex offenders' *Sexual Abuse: A Journal of Research and Treatment* **14** (2), 169–94.

Hanson, R.K., Helmus, L. and Thornton, D. (2010) 'Predicting recidivism amongst sexual offenders: a multi-site study of Static-2002' *Law and Human Behavior* **34** (3), 198–211.

Hare, R.D. (1980) 'A research scale for the assessment of psychopathy in criminal populations' *Personality and Individual Differences* **1**, 111–19.

Hare, R.D. (1991) *The Hare Psychopathy Checklist–Revised* Toronto: Multi-Health Systems.

Hare, R.D. (1998) 'The Hare PCL-R: some issues concerning its use and misuse' *Legal and Criminological Psychology* **3**, 99–119.

Hare, R.D. (2003) *Manual for the Revised Psychopathy Checklist* (2nd edn) Toronto, ON: Multi-Health Systems.

Hargreaves, C., and Francis, B. (2014) 'The long-term recidivism risk of young sexual offenders in England and Wales: enduring risk or redemption' *Journal of Criminal Justice*, 42, 164–172

Harris, D.A., Mazerolle, P. and Knight, R.A. (2009) 'Understanding male sexual offending: a comparison of general and specialist theories' *Criminal Justice and Behavior* **36**, 1051–69.

Harris, G.T. and Rice, M.E. (1994) 'The violent patient' in R.T. Ammerman and M. Hersen (eds) *Handbook of Prescriptive Treatments for Adults* New York: Plenum, pp. 463–86.

Harris, G.T. and Rice, M.E. (1997) 'Risk appraisal and management of violent behaviour' *Psychiatric Services* **48** (9), 1168–76.

Harris, G.T., Lalumiere, M.L., Seto, M.C., Rice, M.E. and Chaplin, T.C. (2012) 'Explaining the erectile responses of rapists to rape stories: the contributions of sexual activity, non-consent, and violence with injury' *Archives of Sexual Behavior* **41**, 221–9.

Harris, G.T., Rice, M.E. and Cormer, C.A. (1994) 'Psychopaths: Is a Therapeutic Community Therapeutic?' *Therapeutic Communities* **15**, 283–99.

Harris, G.T., Rice, M.E. and Quinsey, V.L. (1993) 'Violent recidivism of mentally disordered offenders: the development of a statistical prediction instrument' *Criminal Justice and Behavior* **20** (4), 315–35.

Harris , J. (2000) 'An evaluation of the use and effectiveness of the Protection from Harassment Act 1997', Home Office Research Study 203, Research, Development and Statistics Directorate) http://www.homeoffice.gov.uk/rds/pdfs/hors203.pdf (accessed 3 June 2008).

Harris, S. (1994) 'Ideological exchanges in a British magistrates court' in J. Gibbons (ed.) *Language and the Law* London: Longman, pp. 156–70.

Harrower, J. (1998) *Applying Psychology to Crime* London: Hodder and Stoughton.

Harry, B. (1985) 'Violence and official diagnostic nomenclature' *Bulletin of the American Academy of Psychiatry and the Law* **13**, 385–8.

Hartshorne, H. and May, M.A. (1928) *Studies in the Nature of Character* New York: Macmillan.

Hartwig, M. and Bond, C.F. (2011) 'Why do lie-catchers fail? A lens model meta-analysis of human lie judgments' *Psychological Bulletin* **137** (4), 643–59.

Hartwig, M., Granhag, P., Strömwall, L. and Kronkvist, O. (2006) 'Strategic use of evidence during police interviews: when training to detect deception works' *Law and Human Behavior* **30** (5), 603–19.

Hatcher, R.M., Palmer, E.J., McGuire, J., Housome, J.C., Bilby, C.A.L. and Hollin, C.R. (2008) 'Aggression replacement training with adult male offenders within community settings: a reconviction analysis' *Journal of Forensic Psychiatry & Psychology* **19** (4), 517–32.

Hatz, J.L. and Bourgeois, M.J. (2010) 'Anger as a cue to truthfulness' *Journal of Experimental Social Psychology* **46**, 680–3.

Havard, C. (2013) 'Are children less reliable at making visual identifications than adults? A review' *Psychology, Crime and Law* **20** (4), 372–88.

Hayes, B.K. and Delamothe, K. (1997) 'Cognitive interviewing procedures and suggestibility in children's recall' *Journal of Applied Psychology* **82** (4), 562–77.

Hazelwood, R.R. (1987) 'Analyzing the rape and profiling the offender' in R.R. Hazelwood and A.W. Burgess (eds) *Practical Aspects of Rape Investigation: A Multidisciplinary Approach* New York: Elsevier, pp. 16–24.

Hearold, S. (1986) 'A synthesis of 1,043 effects of television on social behaviour' in G. Comstock (ed.) *Public Communications and Behavior* New York: Academic Press, pp. 65–133.

Heath, W.P. (2009) 'Arresting and convicting the innocent: the potential role of an "inappropriate" emotional display in the accused' *Behavioral Science and the Law* **27**, 313–32.

Heil, P., Ahlmeyer, S. and Simons, D. (2003) 'Crossover sexual offenses' *Sexual Abuse: A Journal of Research and Treatment* **15** (4), 221–36.

Heil, P., Harrison, L., English, K. and Ahlmeyer, S. (2009) 'Is prison sexual offending indicative of community risk?' *Criminal Justice and Behavior* **36**, 892–908.

Heilbrun, K. and Brooks, S. (2010) 'Forensic psychology and forensic science: a proposed agenda for the next decade' *Psychology, Public Policy, and Law* **16** (3), 219–53.

Heilbrun, K., Hawk, G. and Tate, D.C. (1996) 'Juvenile competence to stand trial: research issues in practice' *Law and Human Behavior* **20** (5), 573–8.

Heilbrun, K., Leheny, C., Thomas, L. and Huneycutt, D. (1997) 'A national survey of U.S. statutes on juvenile transfer: implications for policy and practice' *Behavioral Sciences and the Law* **15**, 125–49.

Heinsman, D.T. and Shadish, W.R. (1996) 'Assignment methods in experimentation: when do nonrandomised experiments approximate answers from randomized experiments?' *Psychological Methods* **1** (2), 154–69.

Henderson, Z., Bruce, V. and Burton, M. (2000a) 'Effects of prior familiarity on video verification'. Paper presented at the European Association of Psychology and Law (EAPL) Conference, Limassol, Cyprus.

Henderson, Z., Bruce, V. and Burton, M. (2000b) 'Identification of faces from CCTV images'. Paper presented at the European Association of Psychology and Law (EAPL) Conference, Limassol, Cyprus.

Henkel, L.A., Coffman, K.A. and Dailey, E.M. (2008) 'A survey of people's attitudes and beliefs about false confessions' *Behavioral Sciences and the Law* **26**, 555–84.

Hennigan, K.M., Delrosario, M.L., Heath, L., Cook, T.D., Wharton, J.D. and Calder, B.J. (1982) 'Impact of the introduction of television crime in the United States. Empirical findings and theoretical implications' *Journal of Personality and Social Psychology* **42** (3), 461–77.

Herman, S. (2009) 'Forensic child sexual abuse evaluations: Accuracy, ethics and admissibility' in K. Kuehnle and M. Connell (eds) *The Evaluation of Child Sexual Abuse Allegations: A comprehensive guide to assessment and testimony* pp. 247–66. Hoboken, NJ: Wiley.

Herndon, J. S. (2007) 'The image of profiling: media treatment and general impressions' in R. N. Kocsis (Ed.), *Criminal Profiling: International Theory, Research and Practice* (pp. 303–326) Totowa, NJ: Humana Press.

Herrnstein, R.R. and Murray, C. (1994) *The Bell Curve: Intelligence and Class Structure in American Life* New York: Free Press.

Hershkowitz, I. (2011) ''Rapport-building in investigative interviews' in M. E. Lamb, D. J. La Rooy, L. C. Malloy, and C. Katz (Eds.), *Children's Testimony: A Handbook of Psychological Research and Forensic Practice* (pp. 109–128) Chichester, UK: John Wiley and Sons.

Hershkowitz, I., Lamb, M.E. and Katz, C. (2014) 'Allegation rates in forensic child abuse investigations: comparing the revised and standard NICHD protocols' *Psychology, Public Policy, and Law* **20** (3), 336–344.

Heuer, L and Penrod, S.D. (1988) 'Increasing jurors' participation in trials: a field experiment with jury notetaking and question asking' *Law and Human Behavior,* **12**, 231262.

Hewitt, A. and Beauregard, E. (2014) 'Offending patterns of serial sex offenders: escalation, de-escalation, and consistency of sexually intrusive and violent behaviours' *Journal of Investigative Psychology and Offender Profiling* **11**, 57–80.

Hickle, K.E. and Roe-Sepowitz, D.E. (2010) 'Female juvenile arsonists: An exploratory look at characteristics and solo and group arson offences' *Legal and Criminological Psychology* **15** (2), 385–99.

Hiday, V.A., Swanson, J.W., Swartz, M.S., Borum, R. and Wagner, H.R. (2001) 'Victimization: a link between mental illness and violence?' *International Journal of Law and Psychiatry* **24**, 559–72.

Hill, C., Memon, A. and McGeorge, P. (2008) 'The role of confirmation bias in suspect interviews: A systematic evaluation' *Legal and Criminological Psychology* **13**, 357–71.

Hirtenlehnera, H. and Hardie, B. (2016) 'On the conditional relevance of controls: n application of situational action theory to shoplifting' *Deviant Behavior*, **37** (3), 315–331.

Hjelmsater E.R., Stromwall L.A. and Granhag P.A. (2012) 'The self-administered interview: A means of improving children's eyewitness performance?' *Psychology Crime & Law* **18** (10), 897–911.

Hlavka, H.R., Olinger, S.D. and Lashley, J. (2010) 'The use of anatomical dolls as a demonstration aid in child sexual abuse interviews: a study of forensic interviewers' perceptions' *Journal of Child Sexual Abuse* **19** (5), 519–53.

Ho, D.K. and Ross, C.C. (2012) 'Cognitive behaviour therapy for sex offenders. Too good to be true?' *Criminal Behaviour and Mental Health* **22**, 1–6.

Hobbs, S.D., and Goodman, G.S. (2014) 'Child witnesses in the legal system: improving child interviews and understanding juror decisions' *Behavioral Sciences and the Law* **32**, 681–685.

Hochschild, A. (1983) *The Managed Heart: Commercialization of human feeling* Berkeley: University of California Press.

Hodge, J.E., McMurran, M. and Hollin, C.R. (1997) *Addicted to Crime?* Chichester: John Wiley.

Hodgins, S. (1992) 'Mental disorder, intellectual deficiency and crime: evidence from a birth cohort' *Archives of General Psychiatry* **49**, 476–83.

Hodgins, S. (1997) 'An overview of research on the prediction of dangerousness' *Nordic Journal of Psychiatry* **51**, Suppl. 39, 33–8.

Hodgins, S. and Cote, G. (1993) 'The criminality of mentally disordered offenders' *Criminal Justice and Behavior* **20**, 115–29.

Hodgins, S., Cote, G. and Toupin, J. (1998) 'Major mental disorder and crime: an etiological hypothesis' in D.J. Cooke *et al.* (eds) *Psychopathy: Theory, Research and Implications for Society* (NATO ASI Series. Series D, Behavioural and Social Sciences, No. 88) Dordrecht: Kluwer, pp. 231–56.

Hodgins, S., Mednick, S., Brennan, P.A., Schulsinger, F. and Engberg, M. (1996) 'Mental disorder and crime: evidence from a Danish birth cohort' *Archives of General Psychiatry* **53** (6), 489–96.

Hoeve, M., Dubas, J.S., Eichelsheim, V.I., van der Laan, P.H., Smeenk, W. and Gerris, J.R.M. (2009) 'The relationship between parenting and delinquency: a meta-analysis' *Journal of Abnormal Child Psychology* **37** (6), 749–775.

Hohl, K. and Stanko, E.A. (2015) 'Complaints of rape and the criminal justice system: Fresh evidence on the attrition problem in England and Wales', *European Journal of Criminology* **12** (3) 324–341.

Hollin, C.R. (2002) 'An overview of offender rehabilitation: something old, something borrowed, something new' *Australian Psychologist* **37** (3), 1–6.

Hollin, C.R. (2008) 'Evaluating offending behaviour programmes: does only randomization glister?' *Criminology & Criminal Justice* **8** (1), 89–106.

Hollin, C.R. and Palmer, E.J. (1995) *Assessing Prison Regimes: A Review to Inform the Development of Outcome Measures.* Commissioned report for the Planning Group, HM Prison Service.

Hollin, C.R. and Swaffer, T. (1995) 'Mental health: psychology's contribution to diagnosis, assessment and treatment' in R. Bull and D. Carson (eds) *Handbook of Psychology in Legal Contexts* Chichester: John Wiley, pp. 129–44.

Holmberg, U. and Christianson, S. (2002) 'Murderers' and sexual offenders' experience of police interviews and their inclination to admit or deny crimes' *Behavioral Sciences and the Law* **20**, 31–45.

Holmes, J. (2014) *John Bowlby and Attachment Theory* Hove, East Sussex: Routledge.

Holmes, R.M. and Holmes, S.T. (1996) *Profiling Violent Crimes: An Investigative Tool* Thousand Oaks, CA: Sage.

Holmes, R.M. and Holmes, S.T. (1998) *Serial Murder* (2nd edn) Thousand Oaks, CA: Sage.

Homant, R.J. and Kennedy, D.B. (1998) 'Psychological aspects of crime scene profiling' *Criminal Justice and Behavior* **25** (3), 319–43.

Home Office (2001) 'The British Crime Survey 2000', http://tna.europarchive.org/20100413151441/http://www.homeoffice.gov.uk/rds/pdfs/hosb1800.pdf

Home Office (2002) 'Tackling drugs to build a better Britain: The Government's 10-year strategy for tackling drug misuse'. London: HMSO.

Home Office (2003) 'Criminal statistics: England and Wales 2002. Statistics relating to criminal proceedings for the year 2002' London: The Stationery Office.

Home Office (2004) *Reconvictions of prisoners discharged from prison in 1996* Prisons: research development statistics, http://www.homeoffice.gov.uk/rds/prischap9.html (no longer available).

Home Office (2005a) 'Crime Reduction Toolkit: Arson' http://www.community-safety.info/37.html

Home Office (2005b) 'Recorded Crime Statistics 1898–2002/03', http://www.homeoffice.gov.uk/rds/pdfs/100years.xls (no longer available).

Home Office (2007) 'Recorded Crime Statistics 2002/02–2006/7', http://www.homeoffice.gov.uk/rds/recordedcrime1.html (no longer available).

Home Office (2010) 'Crime in England and Wales 2009/2010', https://www.gov.uk/government/uploads/system/uploads/attachment_data/file/116347/hosb1210.pdf

Home Office (2011) 'Revisions made to the multipliers and unit costs of crime used in the integrated offender management value for money toolkit' London: Home Office, https://www.gov.uk/government/uploads/system/uploads/attachment_data/file/97813/IOM-phase2-costs-multipliers.pdf

Home Office (2014). Home Office Counting Rules. https://www.gov.uk/government/uploads/system/uploads/attachment_data/file/299317/count-general-april-2014.pdf (accessed 10 April, 2014).

Home Office (2016a) 'A summary of recorded crime data from year ending Mar 2003 to year ending Mar 2015' https://www.gov.uk/government/statistics/historical-crime-data

Home Office (2016b) 'Deliberate fires attended by fire and rescue services in England, by incident type and fire and rescue authority' https://www.gov.uk/government/statistical-data-sets/fire-statistics-data-tables.

Home Office (2016c) 'Summary of recorded crime data from year ending Mar 2003 to year ending Mar 2015' https://www.gov.uk/government/statistics/historical-crime-data.

Honts, C.R., Kassin, S.M., and Craig, R.A. (2014) ''I'd know a false confession if I saw one': a constructive replication with juveniles' *Psychology, Crime and Law* **20** (7), 695–704.

Hope, L., Blocksidge, D., Gabbert, F., Sauer, J.D., Lewinski, W., Mirashi, A. and Atuk, E. (2016) 'Memory and the operational witness: police officer recall of firearms encounters as a function of active response role' *Law and Human Behavior* **40** (1), 23–35.

Hope, L., Eales, N. and Mirashi, A. (2014) 'Assisting jurors: promoting recall of trial information through the use of a trial-ordered notebook' *Legal and Criminological Psychology* **19**, 316–331.

Hopkins, M. (2002) 'Crimes against business: the way forward for future research' *British Journal of Criminology* **42**, 782–97.

Horgan, J. and Braddock, K. (2010) 'Rehabilitating the terrorists? Challenges in assessing the effectiveness of de-radicalization programs' *Terrorism and Political Violence* **22** (2), 267–91.

Horgan, J. and Taylor, M. (2001) 'The making of a terrorist' *Jane's Intelligence Review* **13** (12), 16–18.

Horley, J. (2000) 'Cognitions supportive of child molestation' *Aggression and Violent Behaviour* **5**, 551–64.

Horley, J. and Bowlby, D.A (2011) 'Theory, research, and intervention with arsonists' *Aggression and Violent Behavior* **16**, 241–49.

Horn, R. and Hollin, C.R. (1997) 'Police beliefs about women who offend' *Legal and Criminological Psychology* **2**, 193–204.

Horner, T.M., Guuyer, M.J. and Kalter, N.M. (1993) 'Clinical expertise and the assessment of child sexual abuse' *Journal of the American Academy of Child and Adolescent Psychiatry* **32**, 925–31.

Horowitz, I.A. (1980) 'Juror selection: a comparison of two methods in several criminal cases' *Journal of Applied Social Psychology* **10** (1), 86–99.

Horowitz, M.J. (1986) *Stress Response Syndromes* (2nd edn) Northvale, NJ: Jason Aronson.

Horowitz, S.W. (2009) 'Direct mixed and open questions in child interviewing: An analog study' *Legal and Criminological Psychology* **14**, 135–47.

Horselenberg, R., Merckelbach, H. and Josephs, S. (2003) 'Individual differences and false confessions: a conceptual replication of Kassin and Kiechel (1996)' *Psychology, Crime and Law* **9** (1), 1–8.

Horselenberg, R., Merckelbach, H., Smeets, T., Franssens, D., Peters, G.-J.Y. and Zeles, G. (2006) 'False confessions in the lab: do plausibility and consequences matter?' *Psychology, Crime & Law* **12** (1), 61–75.

Horvath, F. (1977) 'The effect of selected variables on interpretation of polygraph records' *Journal of Applied Psychology* **62**, 127–36.

Hough, M., Bradford, B., Jackson, J., Roberts, J.V. (2013) *Attitudes to Sentencing and Trust in Justice: Exploring Trends from the Crime Survey for England and Wales* Ministry of Justice Analytical Series, Ministry of Justice, London, UK.

Houran, J. and Porter, S. (2005) 'Statement validity analysis of "The Jim Ragsdale Story": implications for the Roswell incident' *Journal for Scientific Exploration*, **12** (1), Article 2, http://www.scientificexploration.org/journal/jse_12_1_houran.pdf

House, J.C. (1997) 'Towards a practical application of offender profiling: the RNC's criminal suspect prioritization system' in J.L. Jackson and D.A. Bekerian (eds) *Offender Profiling: Theory, Research and Practice* Chichester: John Wiley, pp. 177–90.

Hovdestad, W.E. and Kristiansen, C.M. (1996a) 'A field study of "false memory syndrome": construct validity and incidence' *Journal of Psychiatry and Law* **Summer**, 299 338.

Howe, M.L., and Knott, L.M. (2015) 'The fallibility of memory in judicial processes: lessons from the past and their modern consequences' *Memory* **23** (5), 633–656.

Howells, K. (1998) 'Cognitive behavioural interventions for anger, aggression and violence' in Tarrier, N.,Wells, A. and Haddock, F. *Cognitive Behavioural Therapy for Complex Cases* Chichester: John Wiley and Sons.

Howells, K. (2004) 'Anger and its links to violent offending' *Psychiatry, Psychology and Law*, **11** (2), 189–196

Howells, K., Watt, B., Hall, G. and Baldwin, S. (1997) 'Developing programs for violent offenders' *Legal and Criminological Psychology* **2** (1), 117–28.

Howitt, D. (1991a) 'Britain's "substance abuse policy": realities and regulation in the United Kingdom' *International Journal of the Addictions* **3**, 1087–111.

Howitt, D. (1991b) *Concerning Psychology* Milton Keynes: Open University Press.

Howitt, D. (1992) *Child Abuse Errors* Harlow: Harvester Wheatsheaf.

Howitt, D. (1994) 'Pornography's piggy in the middle' in C. Haslam and A. Bryman (eds) *Social Scientists Meet the Media* London: Routledge, pp. 93–107.

Howitt, D. (1995a) *Paedophiles and Sexual Offences Against Children* Chichester: John Wiley.

Howitt, D. (1995b) 'Pornography and the paedophile: is it criminogenic?' *British Journal of Medical Psychology* **68** (1), 15–27.

Howitt, D. (1998a) 'Are causal theories of paedophilia possible? A reconsideration of sexual abuse cycles' in J. Boros, I. Munnich and M. Szegedi (eds) *Psychology and Criminal Justice: International Review of Theory and Practice* Berlin: de Gruyter, pp. 248–53.

Howitt, D. (1998b) *Crime, the Media and the Law* Chichester: John Wiley.

Howitt, D. (1998c) 'Crime news' Paper presented at the European Association of Psychology and Law (EAPL) Conference, Krakow, Poland.

Howitt, D. (2000) 'Just what is the role of fantasy in sex offending?' Paper presented at the European Association for Psychology and the Law (EAPL) Conference, Limassol, Cyprus, April.

Howitt, D. (2004) 'What is the role of fantasy in sex offending?' *Criminal Behaviour and Mental Health* **14** (3), 182–8.

Howitt, D. (2005) 'Paedophilia prevention and the law' in M. Stevens and K. Moss (eds) *Crime Prevention and the Law* London: Routledge, pp. 113–34.

Howitt, D. (2016) *Introduction to Qualitative Methods in Psychology* (3rd editon) Harlow: Pearson Education.

Howitt, D. and Cramer, D. (2008) *Introduction to Statistics in Psychology* (4th edn) Harlow: Pearson Education.

Howitt, D. and Cramer, D. (2017). *Understanding Statistics in Psychology with SPSS* Harlow: Pearson.

Howitt, D. and Cumberbatch, G. (1975) *Mass Media Violence and Society* London: Elek Science.

Howitt, D. and Cumberbatch, G. (1990) *Pornography: Impacts and Influences* London: Home Office Research and Planning Unit.

Howitt, D. and Owusu-Bempah, J. (1994) *The Racism of Psychology* London: Harvester Wheatsheaf.

Hsu, C-I., Caputi, P. and Byrne, M.K. (2009) 'The Level of Service Inventory-Revised (LSI-R): a useful risk assessment measure for Australian offenders?' *Criminal Justice and Behavior* **36**, 728–40.

Hudson, C.G. (2005) 'Socioeconomic status and mental illness: tests of the social causation and selection hypotheses' *American Journal of Orthopsychiatry* **75** (1), 3–18.

Hudson, R.A. (1999) *The Sociology and Psychology of Terrorism: Who Becomes a Terrorist and Why?* A report prepared under an interagency agreement by the Federal Research Division, Library of Congress.

Hudson, S.M., Marshall, W.L., Ward, T., Johnston, P.W. and Jones, R.L. (1995) 'Kia Marama: a cognitive-behavioural program for incarcerated child molesters' *Behaviour Change* **12** (2), 69–80.

Huesmann, L.R. and Eron, L.D. (eds) (1986) *Television and the Aggressive Child: A Cross-national Comparison* Hillsdale, NJ: Lawrence Erlbaum.

Huesmann, L. R. and Malamuth, N. M. (1986) 'Media violence and antisocial behavior: an overview' *Journal of Social Issues*, **42**, 1–6.

Huffman, M.L., Warren, A.R. and Larson, S.M. (2001) 'Discussing truth and lies in interviews with children: whether, why, and how?' in R. Bull (ed.) *Children and the Law: The Essential Readings* Malden, MA: Blackwell, pp. 225–46.

Hughes, G., Hogue, T., Hollin, C. and Champion, H. (1997) 'First-stage evaluation of a treatment programme for personality disordered offenders' *Journal of Forensic Psychiatry* **8** (3), 515–27.

Hughes, M., Bain, S.A., Gilchrist, E. and Boyle, J. (2013) 'Does providing a written version of the police caution improve comprehension in the general population?' *Psychology, Crime and Law*, **19** (7), 549–64.

Hughes, N., Williams, W.H., Chitsabesan, P., Walesby, R.C., Mounce, L.T.A. and Clasby, B. (2015) 'Prevalence of traumatic brain injury among young offenders in custody: a systematic review' *Head Trauma Rehabilitation* **30** (2), 94–105.

Hutcheson, G.D., Baxter, J.S., Telfer, K. and Warden, D. (1995) 'Child witness statement quality. Question type and errors of omission' *Law and Human Behavior* **19** (6), 631–48. research/hosb1910/hosb1910?view=Binary

I

Iacono, W.G. (2008) 'Polygraph testing' in E. Borgida and S.T. Fiske (eds) *Beyond Common Sense: Psychological Science in the Courtroom* Oxford: Blackwell, pp. 218–35.

Iacono, W.G. and Lykken, D.T. (1997) 'The validity of the lie detector: two surveys of scientific opinion' *Journal of Applied Psychology* **82** (3), 426–33.

Iacono, W.G. and Patrick, C.J. (1997) 'Polygraphy and integrity testing' in R. Rogers (ed.) *Clinical Assessment of Malingering and Deception* New York: Guilford, pp. 252–81.

Inbau, F.E., Reid, J.E. and Buckley, J.P. (1986) *Criminal Interrogation and Confessions* Baltimore, MD: Williams and Wilkins.

Inbau F.E., Reid, J.E., Buckley, J.P. and Jayne, B.P. (2001) *Criminal Interrogations and Confessions* Gaithersburg, MD: Aspen.

Inbau, F.E., Reid, J.E., Buckley, J.P. and Jayne, B.P. (2004) *Criminal Interrogations and Confessions* Gaithersburg, MD: Aspen.

Inbau F.E., Reid, J.E., Buckley, J.P. and Jayne, B.P. (2013) *Criminal Interrogations and Confessions* (5th edition) g, MD: Aspen.

Ingram, J.R., Paoline, E.A. and Terrill,W. (2013) 'A multilevel framework for understanding police culture: the role of the workgroup' *Criminology* **51** (2), 365–397.

Innes, M. (2002) 'The "process structures" of police homicide investigations' *British Journal of Criminology* **42** (4), 669–88.

Innocence Project (2017) 'Eyewitness Misidentification' https://www.innocenceproject.org/causes/eyewitness-misidentification/

Inquest (2017) 'Deaths in prison' http://www.inquest.org.uk/statistics/deaths-in-prison

International Association of Chiefs of Police (2005a) *Investigating sexual assaults: Model policy* Alexandria, VA: International Association of Chiefs of Police.

International Crime Victimisation Survey (2001) http://ruljis.leidenuniv.nl/group/jfcr/www/icvs/Index.htm (no longer available).

Ireland, C.A. and Vecchi, G.M. (2009) 'The Behavioral Influence Stairway Model (BISM): a framework for managing terrorist crisis situations?' *Behavioral Sciences of Terrorism and Political Aggression* **1** (3), 203–18.

Ireland, J.L. (1999) 'Provictim attitudes and empathy in relation to bullying behaviour among prisoners' *Legal and Criminological Psychology* **4** (1), 51–66.

Itzin, C. (ed.) (1992) *Pornography: Women, Violence and Civil Liberties* Oxford: Oxford University Press.

J

Jackson, J. (2009) 'A psychological perspective on vulnerability in the fear of crime' *Psychology, Crime and Law*, **15** (4), 365–390.

Jackson, J.L. and Bekerian, D.A. (1997) 'Does offender profiling have a role to play?' in J.L. Jackson and D.A. Bekerian (eds) *Offender Profiling: Theory, Research and Practice* Chichester: John Wiley, pp. 1–7.

Jakob, R. (1992) 'On the development of psychologically oriented legal thinking in German speaking countries' in F. Losel, D. Bender and T. Bliesener (eds) *Psychology and Law: International Perspectives* Berlin: Walter de Gruyter, pp. 519–25.

James, A. (1996) 'Suicide reduction in medium security' *Journal of Forensic Psychiatry* **7** (2), 406–12.

James, D.V., Mullen, P.E., Meloy, J.R., Pathe, M.T., Preston, L., Darnley, B., Farnham, F.R. and Scalora, M.J. (2010) 'Stalkers and harassers of British royalty: an exploration of proxy behaviours for violence' *Behavioral Sciences and the Law* **29** (1), 64–80.

James, L., Klinger, D., and Vila, B. (2014) 'Racial and ethnic bias in decisions to shoot seen through a stronger lens: experimental results from high-fidelity laboratory simulations' *Journal of Experimental Criminology*, **10**, 323–340.

Jamieson, L. and Taylor, P.J. (2004) 'A reconviction study of special (high security) hospital patients' *British Journal of Criminology* **44**, 783–802.s

Jansson, K. (2007) 'British Crime Survey – measuring crime for 25 Years' http://webarchive.nationalarchives.gov.uk/20110218135832/rds.homeoffice.gov.uk/rds/pdfs07/bcs25.pdf

Jenkins. P. (1994) *Using Murder: The Social Construction of Serial Homicide* New York: Aldine de Gruyter.

Jenkins-Hall, K.D. and Marlatt, G.A. (1989) 'Apparently irrelevant decisions in the relapse process' in D.R. Laws (ed.) *Relapse Prevention with Sex Offenders* New York: Guilford, pp. 47–55.

Jennings, J.L. and Deming, A. (2013) 'Effectively utilizing the "behavioral" in cognitive-behavioral group therapy of sex offenders' *International Journal of Behavioral Consultation and Therapy* **8** (2), 7–13.

Jennings, W.G., Piquero, A.R. and Reingle, J.M. (2012) 'On the overlap between victimization and offending: A review of the literature' *Aggression and Violent Behavior* **17**, 16–26.

Jespersen, A.F., Lalumière, M.L. and Seto, M.C. (2009) 'Sexual abuse history among adult sex offenders and non-sex offenders: A meta-analysis' *Child Abuse and Neglect* **33**, 179–92.

Jhangiani, R. (2010) 'Psychological concomitants of the 11 September 2001 terrorist attacks: A review' *Behavioral Sciences of Terrorism and Political Aggression* **2** (1), 38–69.

Johnson, J.G., Smailes, E., Cohen, P., Kasen, S. and Brook, J.S. (2004) 'Antisocial parental behaviour, problematic parenting and aggressive offspring behaviour during adulthood: a 25-year longitudinal investigation' *British Journal of Criminology* **44**, 915–30.

Johnson, S.D. (2014) 'How do offenders choose where to offend? perspectives from animal foraging' *Legal and Criminological Psychology* **19**, 193–210.

Johnson, S.D. and Bowers, K.J. (2004) 'The stability of space–time clusters of burglary' *British Journal of Criminology* **44**, 55–65.

Jolliffe, D., and Hedderman, C. (2015) 'Investigating the impact of custody on reoffending using propensity score matching' *Crime and Delinquency* **61** (8), 1051–1077.

Jones, J.C. and Barlow, D.H. (1990) 'Self-reported frequency of sexual urges: fantasies and masturbatory fantasies in heterosexual males and females' *Archives of Sexual Behavior* **19**, 269–79.

Jones, L. (2007) 'Iatrogenic interventions with personality disordered offenders' *Psychology, Crime and Law* **13** (1), 69–79.

Jones, L.F. (2004) 'Offence paralleling behaviour (OPB) as a framework for assessment and interventions with offenders' in A. Needs and G. Towl (eds) *Applying Psychology to Forensic Practice* BPS Blackwell: British Psychological Society, pp. 34–63.

Jones, S. (2011) 'Under pressure: Women who plead guilty to crimes they have not committed' *Criminology and Criminal Justice* **11**, 77–90.

Jones, S. and Cauffman, E. (2008) 'Juvenile psychopathy and judicial decision making: an empirical analysis of an ethical dilemma' *Behavioral Science and the Law* **26**, 151–65.

Jones, S. and Harrison, M. (2009) 'To testify or not to testify – that is the question: Comparing the advantages and disadvantages of testifying across situations' [Electronic version]. *Applied Psychology in Criminal Justice* **5** (2), 165–81.

Jordan, S., Hartwig, M., Wallace, B., Dawson, E. and Xhiani, A. (2012) 'Early versus Late Disclosure of Evidence: Effects on Verbal Cues to Deception, Confessions, and Lie Catchers' Accuracy' *Journal of Investigative Psychology and Offender Profiling*, 9, 1–12.

Joyce, D. (1993) 'How comprehensible are the Pace Codes of Practice to the majority of persons who might wish to read them?' in N.K. Clark and G.M. Stephenson (eds) *Issues in Criminological and Legal Psychology 20: Children, Evidence and Procedure* Leicester: Division of Criminological and Legal Psychology, British Psychological Society, pp. 70–4.

Jung, J. (1971) *The Experimenter's Dilemma*. New York: Harper and Row.

Juslin, P., Olsson, N. and Winman, A. (1996) 'Calibration and diagnosticity of confidence in eyewitness identification: comments on what can be inferred from the low confidence-accuracy correlation' *Journal of Experimental Psychology: Learning, Memory, and Cognition* **22**, 1304–1316.

Jussim, L., Coleman, L.M. and Lerch, L. (1987) 'The nature of stereotypes: A comparison and integration of three theories' *Journal of Personality and Social Psychology* **52**, 536–46.

K

Kacperska, I., Heitzmana, J., Bak, T., Leśko, A.W. and Opio, M. (2016) 'Reliability of repeated forensic evaluations of legal sanity' *International Journal of Law and Psychiatry* **44**, 24–29.

Kadra, G., Daffern, M., and Campbell, C. (2014) 'Detecting offence paralleling behaviours in a medium secure psychiatric unit' *Legal and Criminological Psychology* **19**, 147–159.

Kamin, L.J. (1977) *The Science and Politics of IQ* Harmondsworth: Penguin.

Kappeler, V., Blumberg, V. and Potter, G. (2000) *The Mythology of Crime and Justice* Prospect Heights, IL: Waveland.

Karlsson, I. and Christianson, S.-A. (1999) 'Memory for traumatic events among police personnel'. Paper presented at the International Conference of Psychology and the Law, Dublin, 6–9 July.

Karnik, N. S. and Steiner, H. (2007) 'Evidence for interventions for young offenders' *Child & Adolescent Mental Health*, **12** (4), 154159

Kassin, S. and Wrightsman, L. (1983) 'The construction and validation of a juror bias scale' *Journal of Research in Personality*, 17, 423–42.

Kassin, S. M., Dror, I. E. and Kukucka, J. (2013) 'The forensic confirmation bias: problems, perspectives, and proposed solutions' *Journal of Applied Research in Memory and Cognition* **2**, 42–52.

Kassin, S. M., Meissner, C. A. and Norwick, R. J. (2005) ''I'd know a false confession if I saw one': a comparative study of college students and police investigators' *Law and Human Behavior* **29**, 211–227.

Kassin, S.M. (1997b) 'The psychology of confession evidence' *American Psychologist* **52** (3), 221–33.

Kassin, S.M. (1998) 'Eyewitness identification procedures: the fifth rule' *Law and Human Behavior* **22**, 649–53.

Kassin, S.M. (2008) 'Confession evidence: commonsense myths and misconceptions' *Criminal Justice and Behavior* **35** (10), 1309–22.

Kassin, S.M. (2015) 'The social psychology of false confessions' *Social Issues and Policy Review* **9** (1), 25–51.

Kassin, S.M. and Kiechel, K.L. (1996) 'The social psychology of false confessions: compliance, internalization, and confabulation' *Psychological Science* **7** (3), 125–8.

Kassin, S.M. and McNall, K. (1991) 'Police interrogations and confessions: communicating promises and threats by pragmatic implication' *Law and Human Behavior* **15** (3), 233–51.

Kassin, S.M. and Neumann, K. (1997) 'On the power of confession evidence: an experimental test of the fundamental difference hypothesis' *Law and Human Behavior* **21** (5), 469–84.

Kassin, S.M. and Norwick, R.J. (2004) 'Why people waive their Miranda rights: the power of innocence' *Law and Human Behavior* **28** (2), 211–21.

Kassin, S.M. and Sukel, H. (1997) 'Coerced confessions and the jury: an experimental test of the "harmless error" rule' *Law and Human Behavior* **21** (1), 27–45.

Kassin, S.M., Bogart, D. and Kerner, J. (2012) 'Confessions That Corrupt: Evidence From the DNA Exoneration Case Files' *Psychological Science* **23**, 41–45.

Kassin, S.M., Drizin, S.A., Grisso, T., Gudjonsson, G.H., Leo, R.A. and Redlich, A.D. (2010) 'Police-induced confessions: risk factors and recommendations' *Law and Human Behavior* **34**, 3–38.

Kassin, S.M., Tubb, V.A., Hosch, H.M. and Memon, A. (2001) 'On the "general acceptance" of eyewitness testimony research: A new survey of the experts' *American Psychologist* **56** (5) May, 405–16.

Kavanaugh, A.E. (2016) 'A college graduate confesses to a murder he did not commit: a case of a voluntary false confession' *Journal of Forensic Psychology Practice* **16** (2), 94–105.

Kaysen, D.L., Lindgren, K.P., Lee, C.M., Lewis, M.A., Fossos, N. and Atkins, D.C. (2010) 'Alcohol-involved assault and the course of PTSD in female crime victims' *Journal of Traumatic Stress*, **23**(4), 523–527.

Kazdin, A.E. (2003) 'Clinical significance: Measuring whether interventions make a difference' in A.E. Kazdin (ed.) *Methodological issues and strategies in clinical research* (3rd edn) Washington, DC: American Psychological Association, pp. 691–710.

Keane, T.M., Zimering, R.T. and Caddell, R.T. (1985) 'A behavioral formulation of PTSD in Vietnam veterans' *Behavior Therapist* **8**, 9–12.

Kebbell, M.R. and Hatton, C. (1999) 'People with mental retardation as witnesses in court: a review' *Mental Retardation* **37** (3), 179–87.

Kebbell, M.R. and Milne, R. (1998) 'Police officers' perceptions of eyewitness performance in forensic investigations' *Journal of Social Psychology* **138** (3), 323–30.

Kebbell, M.R. and Wagstaff, G.F. (1998) 'Hypnotic interviewing: the best way to interview eyewitnesses?' *Behavioral Sciences and the Law* **16**, 115–29.

Kebbell, M.R., Hatton, C. and Johnson, S.D. (2004) 'Witnesses with intellectual disabilities in court: what questions are asked and what influences do they have?' *Legal and Criminological Psychology* **9**, 23–35.

Kebbell, M.R., Milne, R. and Wagstaff, G.F. (1998) 'The cognitive interview: a survey of its forensic effectiveness' *Psychology, Crime and Law* **5**, 101–15.

Kebbell, M.R., Wagstaff, G.F. and Covey, J.A. (1996) 'The influence of item difficulty on the relationship between eyewitness confidence and accuracy' *British Journal of Psychology* **87**, 653–62.

Keeler, L. (1934) 'Debunking the "lie detector"' *Journal of Civil Law and Criminology* **25**, 153–9.

Keen, J. (2000) 'A practitioner's perspective: anger management work with young offenders' *Forensic Update* **60**, 20–5.

Keenan, C.A. (2007) 'Implicit knowledge of facial growth patterns: Identification of normal vs. abnormal facial growth' Unpublished.

Keller, S.R. and Wiener, R.L. (2011) 'What are we studying? Student jurors, community jurors, and construct validity' *Behavioral Sciences and the Law* 29, 376–94.

Kellett, S. and Gross, H. (2006) 'Addicted to joyriding? An exploration of young offenders' accounts of their car crime' *Psychology, Crime and Law* **12** (1), 39–59.

Kelly, C.E., Miller, J., Kleinman, S.M. and Redlich, A.D. (2013) 'A taxonomy of interrogation methods' *Psychology, Public Policy, and Law* **19** (2), 165–178.

Kelly, L. (1988) *Surviving Sexual Violence* Cambridge: Polity.

Kelly, L. (1989) 'What's in a name? Defining child sexual abuse' *Feminist Review* **28**, 65–73.

Kelly, L., Lovett, J. and Regan, L. (2005)' A gap or chasm? Attrition in reported rape cases' (Home Office Research Study 293) London: Home Office.

Kemp, R., Pike, G., Brace, N. and Badal, P. (2000) 'Caught on camera:

identification from CCTV footage' Paper presented at the European Association of Psychology and Law (EAPL) Conference, Limassol, Cyprus.

Kemp, R., Towell, N. and Pike, G. (1997) 'When seeing should not be believing: photographs, credit cards and fraud' *Applied Cognitive Psychology* **11** (3), 211–22.

Kenworthy, T., Adams, C.E., Brooks-Gordon, B. and Fenton, M. (2004) Psychological interventions for those who have sexually offended or are at risk of offending (CD004858; Cochrane Database of Systematic Reviews, Issue 3) Chichester: John Wiley & Sons.

Keppel, R.D., Weis, J.G. Brown, K.M. and Welch, K. (2005) 'The Jack the Ripper murders: a modus operandi and signature analysis of the 1888–1891 Whitechapel murders' *Journal of Investigative Psychology and Offender Profiling* **2**, 1–21.

Kerby, J. and Rae, J. (1998) 'Moral identity in action: young offenders' reports of encounters with the police' *British Journal of Social Psychology* **37**, 439–56.

Kerr, K.J., Beech, A.R. and Murphy, D. (2013) 'Sexual homicide: Definition, motivation and comparison with other forms of sexual offending' *Aggression and Violent Behavior* **18**, 1–10

Kershaw, C., Nicholas, S. and Walker, A. (2008) 'Crime in England and Wales 2007/08. *Home Office Statistical Bulletin 07/08*. London: Home Office.

Kesic, D., Thomas, S.D.M. and Ogloff, J.R.P.James, R.P. (2013) 'Use of Nonfatal Force on and by Persons With Apparent Mental Disorder in Encounters With Police' *Criminal Justice and Behavior* **40** (3), 321–37.

Khalifa, N, and Howard, R.C. (2015) 'Is PCL-R psychopathy associated with either type or severity of personality disorder?' *Journal of Forensic Psychiatry and Psychology* **26** (6), 862–877.

Killias, M., Aebi, M., and Ribeaud, D. (2000) 'Does community service rehabilitate better than short-term imprisonment? Results of a controlled experiment' *Howard Journal*, **39**, 40–57.

Kilpatrick, R. (1997) 'Joy-riding: an addictive behaviour' in J.E. Hodge, M. McMurran and C.R. Hollin (eds) *Addicted to Crime*? Chichester: John Wiley, pp. 165–90.

Kim, B., Benekos, P.J. and Merlo, A.V. (2016) 'Sex Offender Recidivism Revisited: Review of Recent Meta-analyses on the Effects of Sex Offender Treatment' *Trauma, Violence and Abuse* **17** (1), 105–117.

Kim, H.J. and Gerber, J. (2012) 'The Effectiveness of Reintegrative Shaming and Restorative Justice Conferences: Focusing on Juvenile Offenders' Perceptions in Australian Reintegrative Shaming Experiments International' *Journal of Offender Therapy and Comparative Criminology* **56** (7), 1063–79.

King, L. and Snook, B. (2009) 'Peering inside the Canadian interrogation room: An examination of the Reid model of interrogation, influence tactics, and coercive strategies' *Criminal Justice and Behavior* **36**, 674–94.

Kirkendall, L.A. and McBride, L.G. (1990) 'Pre-adolescent and adolescent imagery and sexual fantasies: beliefs and experiences' in M.E. Perry (ed.) *Handbook of Sexology, Vol. 7: Childhood and Adolescent Sexology* Amsterdam: Elsevier, pp. 263–87.

Kleban, H. and Jeglic, E. (2012) 'Dispelling the myths: Can psychoeducation change public attitudes towards sex offenders?' *Journal of Sexual Aggression*, **18** (2), 179–193

Kleinmuntz, B. and Szucko, J.J. (1984) 'A field study of the fallibility of polygraphic lie detection' *Nature* **308**, 449–550.

Klepfisz, G., Daffern, M. and Day, A. (2016) 'Understanding dynamic risk factors for violence' *Psychology, Crime and Law* **22** (1–2), 124–137.

Kline, M. (1927) 'Criminal tendencies in normal children' *Psychology and Psychotherapy* **7** (2), 177–192.

Kline, M. (1934) 'On criminality' *Psychology and Psychotherapy* **14** (4), 312–315.

Knafo, D. and Jaffe, Y. (1984) 'Sexual fantasizing in males and females' *Journal of Research in Personality* **18**, 451–62.

Knight, R.A. and Prentky, R.A. (1990) 'Classifying sexual offenders: The development and corroboration of taxonomic models' in W.L. Marshall, D.R. Laws and H.E. Barbaree (eds) *Handbook of Sexual Assault: Issues, Theories, and Treatment of the Offender* New York: Plenum, pp. 25–32.

Knight, R.A., Prentky, R.A. and Cerce, D.D. (1994) 'The development, reliability, and validity of an inventory for the multidimensional assessment of sex and aggression' *Criminal Justice and Behavior* **21**, 72–94.

Kocsis, R.N. (2003a) 'Criminal psychological profiling: Validities and abilities?' *International Journal of Offender Therapy and Comparative Criminology* **47** (2), 126–44.

Kocsis, R.N. (2003b) 'An empirical assessment of content of criminal psychological profiles' *International Journal of Offender Therapy and Comparative Criminology* **47**, 37–46.

Kocsis, R.N. (2010) 'Criminal profiling works and everyone agrees' *Journal of Forensic Psychology Practice* **9**, 147–62.

Kocsis, R.N. (2013) 'The criminal profiling reality: what is actually behind the smoke and mirrors?' *Journal of Forensic Psychology Practice* **13** (2), 79–91.

Kocsis, R.N. (2015) 'The name of the rose and criminal profiling: the benefits of ViCAP and ViCLAS' *Journal of Forensic Psychology Practice* **15**, 58–79.

Kocsis, R.N., Middledorp, J. and Karpin, A. (2008) 'Taking stock of accuracy in criminal profiling: the theoretical quandary for investigative psychology' *Journal of Forensic Psychology Practice* **8** (3), 244–61.

Kocsis, R.N., Middledorp, J. and Try, A.C. (2005) 'Cognitive processes in criminal profile construction: A preliminary study' *International Journal of Offender Therapy and Comparative Criminology* **49**, 662–81.

Koehler, J. A., Lösel, F., Akoensi, T. D. and Humphreys, D. K. (2013) 'A systematic review and meta-analysis on the effects of young offender treatment programs in Europe' *Journal of Experimental Criminology* **9**, 19–43.

Kohlberg, L. (1963) 'The development of children's orientations toward a moral order: 1. Sequence in the development of moral thought' *Human Development* **6**, 11–33.

Kohlberg, L. (1984) The Psychology of Moral Development: Essays on Moral Development (Vol. 2) New York: Harper and Row.

Kohnken, G., Milne, R., Memon, A. and Bull, R. (1999) 'The cognitive interview: a meta-analysis' *Psychology, Crime and Law* **5**, 3–27.

Kohnken, G., Thurer, C. and Zoberbeier, D. (1994) 'The cognitive interview: are the interviewers' memories enhanced, too?' *Applied Cognitive Psychology* **8**, 13–24.

Kolton, D.J.C., Boer, A. and Boer, D.P. (2001) 'A revision of the Abel and Becker Cognition Scale for intellectually disabled sexual offenders' *Sexual Abuse: A Journal of Research and Treatment* **13**, 217–19.

Konecni, V.J., Ebbesen, E.B. and Nehrer, E. (2000) 'Retrospective implications for the probative value of psychologists' testimony on eyewitness issues of exonerations by DNA evidence' in A. Czerederecka, T. Jaskiewicz-Obdzinska and J. Wojcikiewicz (eds) *Forensic Psychology and Law: Traditional Questions and New Ideas* Krakow: Institute of Forensic Research Publishers, pp. 41–8.

Korkman, J., Juusola, A. and Santitila, P. (2014) 'Who made the disclosure? Recorded discussions between children and caretakers suspecting child abuse' *Psychology, Crime and Law* **20** (10), 994–1004.

Korkman, J., Laajasalo, T., Juusola, A., Uusivuori, L. and Santtila, P. (2015) 'What did the child tell? the accuracy of parents' reports of a child's statements when suspecting child sexual abuse' *Journal of Forensic Psychology Practice* **15** (2), 93–113.

Korkman, J., Santtila, P., Drzewiecki, T. and Sandnabba, N.K. (2008) 'Failing to keep it simple: language use in child sexual abuse interviews with 3–8 year-old children' *Psychology, Crime & Law* **14** (1), 41–60.

Kovera, M.B. (2002) 'The effects of general pretrial publicity on juror decisions: An examination of moderators and mediating mechanisms' *Law and Human Behavior*, **26**, 43–72.

Kovera, M.B., Dickinson, J. and Cutler, B.L. (2002) '*Voir dire* and jury selection: practical issues, research findings and directions for future research' in A.M. Goldstein (ed.) *Comprehensive Handbook of Psychology, Vol. 11: Forensic Psychology* New York: John Wiley & Sons, pp. 161–75.

Krackow, E. and Lynn, S.J. (2003) 'Is there touch in the game of twister? The effects of innocuous touch and suggestive questions on children's eyewitness memory' *Law and Human Behavior* **27** (6), 589–604.

Kraemer, H.C., Kazdin, A.E., Offord, D.R., Kessler, R.C., Jensen, P.S. and Kupfer, D.J. (1997) 'Coming to terms with the terms of risk' *Archives of General Psychiatry*, **54**, 337–43.

Krahenbuhl, S.J., Blades, M. and Cherryman, J. (2015) 'A qualitative examination of "ground rules" implementation practice in investigative interviews with children' *Psychiatry, Psychology and Law*, **22** (6), 830–841.

Kramer, G.M., Wolbransky, M.S. and Heilbrun, K. (2007) 'Plea bargaining recommendations by criminal defense attorneys: evidence strength, potential sentence, and defendant preference' *Behavioral Sciences and the Law* **25**, 573–85.

Krasnovsky, T. and Lane, R. C. (1998) 'Shoplifting: A review of the literature' *Aggression and Violent Behavior*, **3**, 219–235.

Krill, A. L., Lake, T. M. and Platek, S. M. (2006) 'Do "good genes" predict forced copulation? A test of whether facial symmetry is related to sexual battery' Poster presented at the annual meeting of the Human Behavior and Evolution Society, Philadelphia, PA.

Kristiansen, C.M., Felton, K.A. and Hovdestad, W.E. (1996) 'Recovered memories of child abuse: fact, fantasy or fancy?' *Women and Therapy* **19** (1), 47–59.

Krug, K. (2007) 'The relationship between confidence and accuracy: current thoughts of the literature and a new area of research' *Applied Psychology in Criminal Justice* **3** (1), 7–41.

Kruttschnitt, C., Heath, L. and Ward, D.A. (1986) 'Family violence, television viewing habits, and other adolescent experiences related to violent criminal behaviour' *Criminology* **24** (2), 235–65.

Kuhn, D., Weinstock, M. and Flaton, R. (1994) 'How well do jurors reason? Competence dimensions of individual variation in a juror reasoning task' *Psychological Science* **5**, 289–96.

Kulas, J.T., McInnerney, J.E., DeMuth, R.F. and Jadwinski, V. (2007) 'Employee satisfaction and theft: testing climate perceptions as a mediator' *Journal of Psychology* **141** (4), 389–402.

Kulik, C.T., Perry, E.L. and Pepper, M.B. (2003) 'Here comes the judge: the influence of judge personal characteristics on federal sexual harassment case outcomes' *Law and Human Behavior*, **27** (1), 69–86.

Kullgren, G., Tengstrom, A. and Gran, M. (1998) 'Suicide among personality-disordered offenders: a follow-up study of 1,943 male criminal offenders' *Social Psychiatry and Psychiatric Epidemiology* **33**, 102–6.

Kumho Tire Company, Ltd. V. Carmichael. 526, U.S.137. Supreme Court of U.S.A 1999.

Kunst, M.J.J. (2011) 'Affective personality type, post-traumatic stress disorder symptom severity and post-traumatic growth in victims of violence' *Stress and Health* 27, 42–51

Kury, H. (1998) 'Legal psychology in Europe: results of a survey' in J. Boros, I. Munnich and M. Szegedi (eds) *Psychology and Criminal Justice: International Review of Theory and Practice* Berlin: Walter de Gruyter, pp. 428–35.

Kutchinsky, B. (1970) 'The effect of pornography: a pilot experiment on perception, behavior and attitudes' in *Technical Report of the Commission on Obscenity and Pornography*, Vol. VIII, *Erotica and Social Behavior* Washington, DC: US Government Printing Office, pp. 133–70.

Kutchinsky, B. (1973) 'The effect of easy availability of pornography on the incidence of sex crimes: the Danish experience' *Journal of Social Issues* **29** (3), 163–91.

Kutchinsky, B. (1991) 'Pornography and rape: theory and practice?' *International Journal of Law and Psychiatry* **14** (1/2), 145–51.

L

Langleben, D.D. and Campbell, H. (2013) 'Using Brain Imaging for Lie Detection: Where Science, Law, and Policy Collide' *Psychology, Public Policy and Law* **19** (2), 222–34.

Laajasalo, T. and Häkkänen, H. (2004) 'Background characteristics of mentally ill homicide offenders: a comparison of five diagnostic groups' *Journal of Forensic Psychiatry and Psychology* **15** (3), 451–74.

LaFree, G., Curtis, K., and McDowall, D. (2015) 'How effective are our 'better angels'? Assessing country-level declines in homicide since 1950' *European Journal of Criminology* **12** (4), 482–504.

Lahm, K.F. (2008) 'Inmate-on-inmate assault: a multilevel examination of prison violence' *Criminal Justice and Behavior* **35**, 120–37.

Lamb, M. E., Hershkowitz, I., Sternberg, K. J., Boat, B. and Everson, M. D. (1996) 'Investigative interviews of alleged sexual abuse victims with and without anatomical dolls' *Child Abuse and Neglect* **20** (12), 1251–1259.

Lamb, M.E., Sternberg, K.J. and Orbach, Y. (1999) 'Forensic interviews of children' in A. Memon and R. Bull (eds) *Handbook of the Psychology of Interviewing* Chichester: John Wiley, pp. 253–77.

Lamb, M.E., Sternberg, K.J., Esplin, P.W., Hershkowitz, I. and Orbach, Y. (1997) 'Assessing the credibility of children's allegations of sexual abuse: a survey of recent research' *Learning and Individual Differences* **9** (2), 175–94.

Lambie, I. and Randell, I. (2013) 'The impact of incarceration on juvenile offenders' *Clinical Psychology Review* **33**, 448–59.

Lamers-Winkelman, F. (1997) 'The second part of statement validity analysis'. Paper presented at conference on Responding to Child Maltreatment, San Diego.

Lamers-Winkelman, F. and Buffing, F. (1996) 'Children's testimony in the Netherlands: a study of statement validity analysis' *Criminal Justice and Behavior* **23** (2), 304–21.

Lampinen, J., Arnal, J.D., Adams, J., Courtney, K. and Hicks, J.L. (2012) 'Forensic age progression and the search for missing children', *Psychology, Crime and Law* **18** (4), 405–15.

Lampinen, J.M., Erickson, W.B., Frowd, C. and Mahoney, G. (2015) 'Mighty morphin' age progression: how artist, age range, and morphing influences the similarity of forensic age progressions to target individuals' *Psychology, Crime and Law* **21** (10), 952–967.

Lande, R.G. (1993) 'The video violence debate' *Hospital and Community Psychiatry* **44** (4), 347–51.

Langleben, D.D. and Moriarty, J.C. (2013) 'Using brain imaging for lie detection: where science, law and research policy collide' *Psychology Public Policy and Law* **19** (2), 222–34.

Langos, C. (2015) 'Cyber-bullying: the challenge to define' *Cyberpsychology, Behavior, and Social Networking* **15** (6), 285–89.

Langsdale, A. and Greenberg, M.S. (2006) 'The impact of situational cues and bystander emotion on labeling an event as a robbery' *Applied Psychology in Criminal Justice* **2** (2), 130.

Langstrom, N. (1999) *Young Sex Offenders: Individual Characteristics, Agency Reactions and Criminal Recidivism* Stockholm: Karolinka Institutet, Department of Public Health, Division of Psychosocial Factors and Health, Division of Forensic Psychiatry.

Large, M., Smith, G. and Nielssen, O. (2009) 'The relationship between the rate of homicide by those with schizophrenia and the overall homicide rate: A systematic review and meta-analysis' *Schizophrenia Research* **112**, 123–9.

Larissa, K. Barber, Matthew, Grawitch, J. and Trares, Shawn, T. (2009) 'Service-oriented and force-oriented emotion regulation in police officers' *Applied Psychology in Criminal Justice* **5** (2), 182–202.

Larson, B.A. and Brodsky, S.L. (2010) 'When cross-examination offends: how men and women assess intrusive questioning of male and female expert witnesses' *Journal of Applied Social Psychology* **40** (4), 811–30.

Larson, J.A. (1922) 'The cardio-pneumo psychogram and its use in the study of emotions, with practical applications' *Journal of Experimental Psychology* **5**, 323–8.

Lasky, N., Jacques, S. and Fisher, B.S. (2015) 'Glossing over shoplifting: how thieves act normal, *Deviant Behavior* **36** (4), 293–309

Lassiter, G.D. (2002) 'Illusory causation in the courtroom' *Current Directions in Psychological Science* **11**, 204–8.

Lassiter, G.D., Geers, A.L., Munhall, P.J., Handley, I.M. and Beers, M.J. (2001) 'Videotaped confessions: Is guilt in the eye of the camera?' *Advances in Experimental Social Psychology* **33**, 189–254.

Lassiter, G.D., Ware, L.L., Ratcliff, J.J. and Irvin, C.R. (2009) 'Evidence of the camera perspective bias in authentic videotaped interrogations: Implications for emerging reform in the criminal justice system' *Legal and Criminological Psychology* **14**, 157–70.

Laws, D.R. (1994) 'How dangerous are rapists to children?' *Journal of Sexual Aggression* **1**, 1–14.

Laws, D.R. and Gress, C.L.Z. (2004) 'Seeing things differently: the viewing time alternative to penile plethysmography' *Legal and Criminological Psychology* **9**, 183–96.

Laws, D.R. and Marshall, W.L. (1990) 'A conditioning theory of the etiology and maintenance of deviant sexual preference and behaviour' in W.L. Marshall, D.R. Laws and H.E. Barbaree (eds) *Handbook of Sexual Assault: Issues, Theories and Treatment of the Offender* New York: Plenum, pp. 209–30.

Laxminarayan, M. (2014) 'Psychological effects of criminal proceedings through contact with the judge: the moderating effect of legal system structure' *Psychology, Crime and Law* **20** (8), 781–797.

Lecci, L., Snowden, J. and Morris, D. (2004) 'Using social science research to inform and evaluate the contributions of trial consultants in the *voir dire' Journal of Forensic Psychology Practice* **4**, 67–78.

Leclerc, B., Proulx, J. and McKibben, A. (2005) 'Modus operandi of sexual offenders working or doing voluntary work with children and adolescents' *Journal of Sexual Aggression*, **11**, 187–195.

Lee, A.F., Li, N.-C., Lamade, R., Schuler, A. and Prentky, R.A. (2012) 'Predicting hands-on child sexual offenses among possessors of Internet child pornography' *Psychology, Public Policy, and Law* **8** (4), 644–72.

Leeney, D.G. and Mueller-Johnson, K. (2012) 'Examining the forensic quality of police call-centre interviews' *Psychology, Crime and Law* **18** (7), 669–88.

Lefkowitz, M.M., Eron, L.D., Walder, L.O. and Huesmann, L.R. (1977) *Growing Up to be Violent: A Longitudinal Study of the Development of Aggression* New York: Pergamon.

Leichtman, M.D. and Ceci, S.J. (1995) 'The effects of stereotypes and suggestions on pre-schoolers' reports' *Developmental Psychology* **31**, 568–78.

Leins, D.A., and Charman, S.D. (2016) 'Schema reliance and innocent alibi generation' *Legal and Criminological Psychology*, **21**, 111–126

Leins, D.A., Fisher, R.F. and Ross, S.J. (2013) 'Exploring liars' strategies for creating deceptive reports' *Legal and Criminological Psychology*, **18** (1), 141–51.

Lemert, E.M. (1951) *Social Pathology: Systematic Approaches to the Study of Sociopathic Behavior* New York: McGraw-Hill.

Lemert, E.M. (1967) *Human Deviance, Social Problems, and Social Control* Englewood Cliffs, NJ: Prentice-Hall.

Lens, K.M.E., Pemberton, A., Brans, K., Braeken, K., Bogaerts, S. and Lahlah, E. (2014) 'Delivering a victim impact statement: emotionally effective or counterproductive?' *European Journal of Criminology* **12** (1), 17–34.

Leo, R.A. (1996) 'Miranda's revenge: police interrogation as a confidence game' *Law and Society Review* **30** (2), 259–88.

Leo, R.A. and Liu, B. (2009) 'What do potential jurors know about police interrogation techniques and false confessions?' *Behavioral Sciences and the Law* **27**, 381–99.

Leo, R.A. and Ofshe, R.J. (1998) 'The consequences of false confessions: deprivations of liberty and miscarriages of justice in the age of psychological interrogation' *Journal of Criminal Law and Criminology* **88** (2), 429–96.

Lerner, J.S., and Tiedens, L.Z. (2006) 'Portrait of the angry decision maker: how appraisal tendencies shape anger's influence on cognition' Journal of Behavioral Decision Making 19, 115–37.

Lerner, M.J. (1980) *The Belief in a Just World: A Fundamental Delusion* New York: Plenum Press.

Lerner, M.J. and Goldberg, J.H. (1999) 'When do decent people blame victims? The differing effects of the explicit-rational and implicit-experiential cognitive systems' in S. Chaiken and Y. Trope (eds) *Dual Process Theories in Social Psychology* New York: Guilford Press, pp. 627–40.

Letourneau, E.J., Bandiyioadhyay, K.S., Armstrong, K.S. and Singha, D. (2010) 'Do sex offender registration and notification requirements deter juvenile sex crimes?' *Criminal Justice and Behavior* **37**, 553–69.

Levenson, J. S., Brannon, Y. N., Fortney, T. and Baker, J. (2007) 'Public perceptions about sex offenders and community protection policies' *Analysis of Social Issues and Public Policy*, **7**, 137–161.

Levenson, J.S., D'Amora, D.A. and Hern, A.L. (2007) 'Megan's Law and its impact on community re-entry for sex offenders' *Behavioral Sciences and the Law* **25**, 587–602.

Levi, A.M. (2012) 'Much better than the sequential lineup: a 120-person lineup' *Psychology, Crime and Law* **18** (7), 631–40.

Lewis, N. and Yarnell, H. (1951) 'Pathological Firesetting (Pyromania)' *Nervous and Mental Disease Monographs*, No. 82/437.

Leyton, E. (1986) *Hunting Humans: The Rise of the Modern Multiple Murderer* Toronto: McClelland and Stewart.

Lieberman, J.D. (2011) 'The utility of scientific jury selection: still murky after 30 years' *Current Directions in Psychological Science* **20**, 48.

Lieberman, J.D., Krauss, D.A. and Wiener, R.L. (2011) Preface to 'When does sample matter in juror decision-making research? differences between college student and representative samples of jurors' *Behavioral Sciences and the Law* **29**, 325–7.

Lieberman, J.D., Krauss, D.A., Heen, M. and Sakiyama, M. (2016) 'The good, the bad, and the ugly: professional perceptions of jury decision-making research practices' *Behavioral Sciences and the Law* **34** (4), 475–594.

Lievore, D. (2004) 'Victim credibility in adult sexual assault cases' *Trends & Issues in Crime and Criminal Justice* No 288. Available at http://www.aic.gov.au/media_library/publications/tandi2/tandi288.pdf

Lilienfeld, S.O. and Landfield, K. (2008) 'Science and pseudoscience in law enforcement: a user-friendly primer' *Criminal Justice and Behavior* **35**, 1215–30.

Limbandari, B.J. and Sheridan, D.J. (1995) 'Prediction of intentional interpersonal violence: an introduction' in J.C. Campbell (ed.) *Assessing Dangerousness* Thousand Oaks, CA: Sage, pp. 1–19.

Lind, B., Chen, S., Weatherburn, D. and Mattick, R. (2005) 'The effectiveness of methadone maintenance treatment in controlling crime: an Australian aggregate-level analysis' *British Journal of Criminology* **45**, 201–11.

Lind, J.E. and Ke, G.Y. (1985) 'Opening and closing statements' in S.M. Kassin and L.S. Wrightsman (eds) *The Psychology of Evidence and Trial Procedure* London: Sage, pp. 229–53.

Lindeman, M., Harakka, T. and Keltikangas-Jarvinen, L. (1997) 'Age and gender differences in adolescents' reactions to conflict situations: aggression, prosociality, and withdrawal' *Journal of Youth and Adolescence* **26** (3), 339–51.

Lindholm, T., Christianson, S.-A. and Karlsson, I. (1997) 'Police officers and civilians as witnesses: intergroup biases and memory performance' *Applied Cognitive Psychology* **11**, 431–4.

Lindquist, J. H., and Duke, J. M. (1982) 'The elderly victim at risk: Explaining the fear-victimization paradox' *Criminology*, **20** (1), 115–126.

Link, B.G., Andrews, H. and Cullen, F.T. (1992) 'The violent and illegal behaviour of mental patients reconsidered' *American Sociological Review* **57**, 275–92.

Lipian, M.S., Mills, M.J. and Brantman, A. (2004) 'Assessing the verity of children's allegations of abuse: A psychiatric overview' *International Journal of Law and Psychiatry* **27**, 249–63.

Lipkus, I. (1991) 'The construction and preliminary validation of a global belief in a just world scale and the exploratory analysis of the multidimensional belief in a just world scale' *Personality and Individual Differences* **12**, 1171–78.

Lippert, T., Cross, T.P., Jones, L.M. and Walsh, W. (2010) 'Suspect confession of child sexual abuse to investigators' *Child Maltreatment* **15** (2), 161–70.

Lipsey, M. (2009) 'The primary factors that characterize effective interventions with juvenile offenders: a meta-analytic overview' *Victims and Offenders* 4, 124–47.

Lipsey, M.W., Chapman, G.L. and Landenberger, N.A. (2001) 'Cognitive behavioral programs for offenders' *Annals of the American Academy of Political and Social Science* **578** (1), 144–57.

Lisak, D., Gardinier, L., Nick, S.C. and Cote, A.M. (2010) 'False Allegations of Sexual Assault: An Analysis of Ten Years of Reported Cases' *Violence Against Women* **16** (12), 1318–34.

Liska, A.E. and Baccaglini, W. (1990) 'Feeling safe by comparison: crime in the newspapers' *Social Problems* **37** (3), 360–74.

Littleton, H., and Ullman, S.E. (2013) 'PTSD symptomatology and hazardous drinking as risk factors for sexual assault revictimization: examination in European American and African American women' *Journal of Traumatic Stress* **26**, 345–353.

Littleton, H. and Decker, M. (2016) 'Predictors of resistance self-efficacy among rape victims and association with revictimization risk: a longitudinal study' *Psychology of Violence*. Advance online publication. http://dx.doi.org/10.1037/vio0000066

Livingston, J.D., Desmarais, S.L., Greaves, C.L., Johnson, K.L., Verdun-Jones, S., Parent, R. and Brink, J. (2014) 'Police perceptions and contact among people with mental illnesses: comparisons with a general population survey' *Psychology, Public Policy, and Law* **20** (4), 431–442.

Livingston, J.D., Desmarais, S.L., Verdun-Jones, S., Parent, R., Michalak, E. and Brink, J. (2014) 'Perceptions and experiences of people with mental illness regarding their interactions with police' *International Journal of Law and Psychiatry* **37**, 334–340.

Lloyd, C. and Walmsley, R. (1989) 'Changes in rape offences and sentencing' *Home Office Study No. 105* London: HMSO.

Lloyd-Bostock, S. (1996) 'The jury in the United Kingdom: juries and jury research in context' in G. Davies, S. Lloyd-Bostock, M. McMurran and C. Wilson (eds) *Psychology, Law and Criminal Justice: International Developments in Research and Practice* Berlin: De Gruyter, pp. 349–59.

Löbmann, R., and Verthein, U. (2009) 'Explaining the effectiveness of heroin-assisted treatment on crime reductions' *Law and Human Behavior*, **3**(1), 83–95.

Loftus, B. (2009) *Police Culture in a Changing World* Oxford University Press: Oxford.

Loftus, E. and Palmer, J.C. (1974) 'Reconstructions of automobile destruction: an example of the interaction between language and memory' *Journal of Verbal Learning and Verbal Behavior* **13**, 585–9.

Loftus, E. and Pickrell, J.E. (1995) 'The formation of false memories' *Psychiatric Annals* **25**, 720–5.

Loftus, E., Garry, M. and Hayne, H. (2008) 'Repressed and recovered memories' in E. Borgida and S.T. Fiske (eds) *Beyond Common Sense: Psychological Science in the Courtroom* Oxford: Blackwell, pp. 177–94.

Loftus, E.F. and Guyer, M.J. (2002) 'Who abused Jane Doe?: The hazards of the single case study' *Skeptical Inquirer* **26 (May–June)**, 24–32; ibid., **2** (26) **(July–August)**, 37–40, 44.

Loftus, E.F., Miller, D.G. and Burns, H.J. (1978) 'Semantic integration of verbal information into a visual memory' *Journal of Experimental Psychology, Human Learning and Memory* **4** (1), 19–31.

Loftus, G.R. (2010) 'What can a perception–memory expert tell a jury?' *Psychonomic Bulletin and Review* **17** (2), 143–48.

Lomborg, B. (2008) 'The mechanics of terrorism'NATO Review http://www.nato.int/docu/review/2008/04/AP_COST/EN/index.htm

Lombroso, C. (1911) *Crime, Its Causes and Remedies* Boston, MA: Little, Brown.

London, K., Bruck, M. and Melnyk, L. (2009) 'Post-event information affects children's autobiographical memory after one year' *Law and Human Behavior* **33** (4), 344–55.

Long, M., Alison, L., Tejeiro, R., Hendricks, E., and Giles, S. (2016) 'KIRAT: law enforcement's prioritization tool for investigating indecent image offenders' *Psychology, Public Policy and Law* **22** (1), 12–21.

Looman, J. (1999) 'Mood, conflict and deviant sexual fantasies'. Unpublished manuscript. Ontario: Regional Treatment Centre.

Los, M. and Chamard, S.E. (1997) 'Selling newspapers or educating the public? Sexual violence in the media' *Canadian Journal of Criminology*, **July**, 293–328.

Lösel, F. and Schmucker, M. (2005) 'The effectiveness of treatment for sexual offenders: A comprehensive meta-analysis' *Journal of Experimental Criminology* **1**, 117–46.

Lowenstein, J.A., Blank, H. and Sauer, J.D. (2010) 'Uniforms affect the accuracy of children's eyewitness identification decisions' *Journal of Investigative Psychology and Offender Profiling* **7**, 59–73.

Loza, W. and Loza-Fanous, A. (1999) 'The fallacy of reducing rape and violent recidivism by reducing anger' *International Journal of Offender Therapy and Comparative Criminology* **43**, 492–502.

Luckabaugh, R., Fuqua, H.E., Cangemi, J.P. and Kowalski, C.J. (1997) 'Terrorist behavior and United States foreign policy: who is the enemy? Some psychological and political perspectives' *Psychology* **34** (2), 1–15.

Luna, K. and Martin-Luengo, B. (2010) 'New advances in the study of the confidence–accuracy relationship in the memory for events' *The European Journal of Psychology Applied to Legal Context* **2** (1), 55–71.

Lundi, S., Vrij, A., Mann, S., Hope, L., Hillman, J., Warmelink, L. and Gahr, E. (2013) 'Who should I look at? Eye contact during collective interviewing as a cue to deceit' *Psychology, Crime and Law* **19** (8), 661–71.

Lurigio, A.J., and Harris, A.J. (2009) 'Mental illness, violence, and risk assessment: an evidence-based review' *Victims and Offenders* **4** (4), 341–347.

Lussier, P. and Cale, J. (2013) 'Beyond sexual recidivism: A review of the sexual criminal career parameters of adult sex offenders' *Aggression and Violent Behavior* **18**, 445–57.

Lussier, P., Leclerc, B., Calse, J. and Proulx, J. (2007) 'Developmental pathways of deviance in sexual aggressors' *Criminal Justice and Behavior* **34** (11), 1411–62.

Lussier, P., Leclerc, B., Healey, J., and Proulx, J. (2008) 'Generality of deviance and predation: crime switching and specialization patterns in persistent sexual offenders' in M. Delisi and P. Conis (Eds.) *Violent Offenders: Theory, Public Policy and Practice* (pp. 97–140) 'Boston, MA: Jones and Bartlett Publishers.

Lussier, P., Van Den Berg, C., Bijleveld, C. and Hendriks, J. (2012) 'A developmental taxonomy of juvenile sex offenders for theory, research, and prevention: the adolescent-limited and the high-rate slow desister' *Criminal Justice and Behavior* **39**, 1559–81.

Luus, C.A.E. and Wells, G.L. (1994) 'The malleability of eyewitness confidence: Co-witness and perseverance effects' *Journal of Applied Psychology* **79**, 714–24.

Lymburner, J.A. and Roesch, R. (1999) 'The insanity defence: five years of research (1993–97)' *International Journal of Law and Psychiatry* **22** (3–4), 213–40.

Lynn, S.J., Neuschatz, J. and Fite, R. (2002) 'Hypnosis and memory: implications for the courtroom and psychotherapy' in M.L. Eisen, J.A. Quas and G.S. Goodman (eds) *Memory and Suggestibility in the Forensic Interview* Mahwah, NJ: Lawrence Erlbaum, pp. 287–307.

Lyon, T.D. (1995) 'False allegations and false denials in child sexual abuse' *Psychology, Public Policy, and Law* **1** (2), 429–437.

Lyons, P.M., Anthony, C.M., Davis, K.M., Fernandez, K., Torres, A.N. and Marcus, D.K. (2005) 'Police judgements of culpability and homophobia' *Applied Psychology in Criminal Justice* **1** (1), 1–14.

M

MacCulloch, M.J., Snowden, P.R., Wood, P.J.W. and Mills, H.E. (1983) 'Sadistic fantasy, sadistic behaviours and offending' *British Journal of Psychiatry* **143**, 20–9.

MacKenzie, D.L., and Farrinton, D.P. (2015) 'Preventing future offending of delinquents and offenders: what have we learned from experiments and meta-analyses?' *Journal of Experimental Criminology* **11**, 565–595.

Mackinnon, A., Copolov, D.L. and Trauer, T. (2004) 'Factors associated with compliance and resistance to command hallucinations' *The Journal Nervous and Mental Disease* **192**, 357–62.

MacManus, D., Dean, K., Jones, M., Rona, R.J., Greenberg, N., Hull, L., Fahy, T., Wessely, S., and Fear, N.T. (2013) 'Violent offending by UK military personnel deployed to Iraq and Afghanistan: a data linkage cohort study' *The Lancet* 381, 16 March 2013.

MacMartin, C. and Yarmey, A.D. (1998) 'Repression, dissociation and the recovered memory debate: constructing scientific evidence and expertise' *Expert Evidence* **6**, 203–26.

Madrigal, D.O., Bowman, D.R. and McClain, B.U. (2009) 'Introducing the Four-Phase Model of Hostage Negotiation' *Journal of Police Crisis Negotiations* **9** (2), 119–33.

Madsen, L., Parsons, S. and Grubin, D. (2004) 'A preliminary study of the contribution of periodic polygraph testing to the treatment and supervision of sex offenders' *British Journal of Forensic Psychiatry and Psychology* **15**, 682–95.

Maghan, J. (1998) 'Terrorist mentality' in J. Boros, I. Munnich and M. Szegedi (eds) *Psychology, Law and Criminal Justice: International Review of Theory and Practice* Berlin: Walter de Gruyter, pp. 335–45.

Makowsky, M. D., and Stratmann. T. (2009) 'Political economy at any speed: what determines traffic citations?' *American Economic Review* **99**, 509–52.

Malamuth, N.M. and Ceniti, J. (1986) 'Repeated exposure to violent and non-violent pornography: likelihood of raping ratings and laboratory aggression against women' *Aggressive Behavior* **12**, 129–37.

Malloy, L. C., Shulman, E. P. and Cauffman, E. (2013) 'Interrogations, confessions, and guilty pleas among serious adolescent offenders' *Law and Human Behavior* **38**, 181–193.

Malpass, R. and Devine, P. (1981) 'Guided memory in eyewitness identification' *Journal of Applied Psychology* **66** (3), 343–50.

Mancini, C., and Budd, K.N. (2016) 'Is the public convinced that "nothing works?": predictors of treatment support for sex offenders among Americans' *Crime and Delinquency* **62** (6) 777–799.

Maniglio, R. (2009) 'Severe mental illness and criminal victimization: a systematic review' *Acta Psychiatrica Scandinavica* **119**, 180–91.

Maniglio, R. (2010) 'The role of deviant sexual fantasy in the etiopathogenesis of sexual homicide: A systematic review' *Aggression and Violent Behavior* **15**, 294–302.

Mann, R. E., Hanson, R. K. and Thornton, D. (2010) 'Assessing risk for sexual recidivism: some proposals on the nature of psychologically meaningful risk factors' *Sexual Abuse: A Journal of Research and Treatment* **22** (2), 191–217.

Marenin, O. (2016) 'Cheapening death: danger, police street culture, and the use of deadly force' *Police Quarterly* **19** (4), 461–487.

Marion, S.B., Kukucka, J., Collins, C., Kassin, S.M. and Burke, T.M. (2016) 'Lost proof of innocence: the impact of confessions on alibi witnesses' *Law and Human Behavior* **40** (1), 65–71.

Markowitz, F.E. (2011) 'Mental illness, crime, and violence: Risk, context, and social control' *Aggression and Violent Behavior* **16**, 36–44.

Marsh, H.L. (1991) 'A comparative analysis of crime coverage in newspapers in the United States and other countries from 1960 to 1989: a review of the literature' *Journal of Criminal Justice* **19**, 67–79.

Marshall, B.C. and Alison, L.J. (2006) 'Structural behavioural analysis as a basis for discriminating between genuine and simulated rape allegations' *Journal of Investigative Psychology and Offender Profiling* **3**, 21–34.

Marshall, G.N. and Schell, T.L. (2002) 'Reappraising the link between peritraumatic dissociation and PTSD symptom severity: evidence from a longitudinal study of community violence survivors' *Journal of Abnormal Psychology* **111**(4), 626–636.

Marshall, W.C. (1988) 'The use of sexually explicit stimuli by rapists, child molesters and non-offenders' *Journal of Sex Research* **25** (2), 267–88.

Marshall, W.L., Hudson, S.M. and Ward, T. (1992) 'Sexual deviance' in P.H. Wilson (ed.) *Principles and Practice of Relapse Prevention* New York: Guilford Press, pp. 235–54.

Marshall, W.L., Marshall, L.E. and Kingson, D.A. (2011) 'Are the cognitive distortions of child molesters in need of treatment?' *Journal of Sexual Aggression* **17** (2), 118–29.

Marshall, W.L., Marshall, L.E., Sachdev, S. and Kruger, R. (2003) 'Distorted attitudes and perceptions, and their relationship with self-esteem and coping in child molesters' *Sexual Abuse: A Journal of Research and Treatment* **15**, 171–81.

Marshall, W.L., Serran, G.A., Fernandez, Y.M., Mulloy, R., Mann, R.E. and Thornton, D. (2003) 'Therapist characteristics in the treatment of sexual offenders: Tentative data on their relationship with indices of behaviour change' *Journal of Sexual Aggression* **9**, 25–30.

Marshall, W.L., Smallbone, S. and Marshall, L.E. (2015) 'A critique of current child molester subcategories: a proposal for an alternative approach' *Psychology, Crime and Law* **21** (3), 205–218.

Martinson, R. (1974) 'What works? Questions and answers about prison reform' *Public Interest* **10**, 22–54.

Martire, K. A., Kemp, R.I., Watkins, I., Sayle, M. and Newell, B.R. (2013) 'The expression and interpretation of uncertain forensic science evidence: Verbal equivalence, evidence strength and the weak evidence effect' *Law and Human Behavior* **37**, 197–207.

Maruna, S. and Copes, H. (2005) 'What have we learned in five decades of neutralization research?' *Crime and Justice: A Review of Research* **32**, 221–320.

Maruna, S. and Mann, R. (2006) 'Fundamental attribution errors? Re-thinking cognitive distortions' *Legal and Criminological Psychology* **11**, 155–77.

Marzano, L., Fazel, S., Rivlin, A. and Hawton, K. (2011) 'Near-lethal self-harm in women prisoners: contributing factors and psychological processes' *Journal of Forensic Psychiatry and Psychology* **22** (6), 863–84.

Marzano,L., Adler, J.R., and Ciclitira, K. (2015) 'Responding to repetitive, non-suicidal self-harm in an English male prison: staff experiences, reactions, and concerns' *Legal and Criminological Psychology* **20**, 241–254.

Mastroberardino, S. and Santangelo, V. (2009) 'New perspectives in assessing deception: the evolution of the truth machine' *European Journal of Cognitive Psychology* **21** (7), 1085–1099.

Matjasko, J.L., Vivolo-Kantor, A.M., Massetti, G.M., Holland, K.M., Holt, M.K. and Dela Cruz, J. (2012) 'A systematic meta-review of evaluations of youth violence prevention programs:

Common and divergent findings from 25 years of meta-analyses and systematic reviews' *Aggression and Violent Behavior* **17**, 540–52.

Matte, J.M. (2002) *Forensic Psychophysiology Using the Polygraph* Williamsville, NY: J.A.M.

Mauer, M. (2006) *Race to Incarcerate* (2nd edn) Washington, DC: The Sentencing Project.

Maurelli, K. and Ronan, G. (2013) 'A time-series analysis of the effectiveness of sex offender notification laws in the USA' *Journal of Forensic Psychiatry and Psychology* **24** (1), 128–43.

McAdams, D.P. (1990) 'Unity and purpose in human lives: the emergence of identity as a life story' in A.I. Rabin, R.A. Zucker, R.A. Emmons and S. Frank (eds) *Studying Persons and Lives* New York: Springer, pp. 148–200.

McCabe, M.P. and Wauchope, M. (2005) 'Behavioural characteristics of rapists' *Journal of Sexual Aggression* **11** (2), 235–47.

McCabe, S. and Purves, R. (1974) *The Shadow Jury at Work* Oxford: Blackwell.

McCann, J.T. (1998) 'Broadening the typology of false confessions' *American Psychologist* **March**, 319–20.

McConaghy, N. (1991) 'Validity and ethics of penile circumference measures of sexual arousal: a critical review' *Archives of Sexual Behavior* **19** (4), 357–69.

McConkey, K.M., Roche, S.M. and Sheehan, P.W. (1989) 'Reports of forensic hypnosis: a critical analysis' *Australian Psychologist* **24** (2), 249–72.

McConnaughy, E.A., Prochaska, J.O. and Velicer, W.F. (1983) 'Stages of change in psychotherapy: Measurement and sample profiles' *Psychotherapy: Theory, Research and Practice* **20**, 368–75.

McCord, J. (1979) 'Some child-rearing antecedents of criminal behavior in adult men' *Journal of Personality and Social Psychology* **37** (9), 1477–86.

McCoy, S.P. and Aamodt, M.G. (2010) 'A comparison of law enforcement divorce rates with those of other occupations' *Journal of Police and Criminal Psychology* **25**, 1–16.

McCrory, E., Hickey, N., Farmer, E. and Vizard, E. (2008) 'Early onset sexually harmful behaviour in childhood: a marker for life course persistent antisocial behaviour?' *Journal of Forensic Psychiatry and Psychology* **19**, 382–395

McCuish, E., Lussier, P. and Corrado, R. (2016) 'Criminal careers of juvenile sex and nonsex offenders: evidence from a prospective longitudinal study' *Youth Violence and Juvenile Justice* **14** (3), 199–224.

McDougall, A.J., and Bull, R. (2015) 'Detecting truth in suspect interviews: the effect of use of evidence (early and gradual) and time delay on criteria-based content analysis, reality monitoring and inconsistency within suspect statements' *Psychology,Crime and Law* **21** (6), 514–530.

McDougall, C., Pearson, D.A.S., Willoughby, H. and Bowles, R.A. (2013) 'Evaluation of the ADViSOR project: Cross-situational behaviour monitoring of high-risk offenders in prison and the community' *Legal and Criminological Psychology* **18**, 205–28.

McElvain, J.P. and Kposowa, J. (2008) 'Police officer characteristics and the likelihood of using deadly force' *Criminal Justice and Behavior* **35**, 505–21.

McEwan, J. (1995) 'Adversarial and inquisitorial proceedings' in R. Bull and D. Carson (eds) *Handbook of Psychology in Legal Contexts* Chichester: John Wiley, pp. 495–501.

McEwan, T.E., Mullen, P.E. and MacKenzie, R. (2009) 'A study of the predictors of persistence in stalking situations' *Law and Human Behavior* **33**, 149–58.

McGarrell, E.F. (2001) 'Restorative justice conferences as an early response to young offenders' *Juvenile Justice Bulletin* Washington, DC: U.S. Department of Justice, Office of Justice Programs, Office of Juvenile Justice and Delinquency Prevention.

McGeorge, N. (1996) 'Risk assessment and political decision making' *Forensic Update* **45**, 21–2.

McGrath, R.J., Cumming, G.F., Hoke, S.E. and Bonn-Miller, M.O. (2007) 'Outcomes in a community sex offender treatment program: A comparison between polygraphed and matched non-polygraphed offenders' *Sexual Abuse: A Journal of Research and Treatment* **19**, 381–93.

McGregor, G. and Howells, K. (1997) 'Addiction models of sexual offending' in J.E. Hodge, M. McMurran and C.R. Hollin (eds) *Addicted to Crime?* Chichester: John Wiley, pp. 107–37.

McGuire, J. (1997) '"Irrational" shoplifting and models of addiction' in J.E. Hodge, M. McMurran and C.R. Hollin (eds) *Addicted to Crime?* Chichester: John Wiley, pp. 207–31.

McGuire, J. (2000) 'Explanations of criminal behaviour' in J. McGuire, T. Mason and A. O'Kane (eds) *Behaviour, Crime and Legal Processes: A Guide for Forensic Practitioners* Chichester: John Wiley, pp. 135–59.

McGuire, J. (2004) *Understanding Psychology and Crime: Perspectives on Theory and Action* Maidenhead: Open University Press.

McHugh, M. (1998) 'Strategies for reducing suicides in prison'. Paper presented at Eighth European Conference on Psychology and Law, Krakow, September.

McHugh, M. (1999) 'Suicide and self injury' *Issues in Forensic Psychology* **1**, 23–6.

McIntosh, J., Bloor, M. and Robertson, M. (2007) 'The effect of drug treatment upon the commission of acquisitive crime' *Journal of Substance Use* **12** (5), 375–84.

McIntyre,A.H., Hancock, P.J.B., Frowd, C.D. and Langton, S.R.H, (2016) 'Holistic face processing can inhibit recognition of forensic facial composites' *Law and Human Behavior* **40** (2), 128–135.

McKeon, B., McEwan, T.E. and Luebbers, S. (2015) '"It's not really stalking if you know the person: measuring community attitudes that normalize, justify and minimize stalking' *Psychiatry, Psychology and Law* **22** (2), 291–306.

McKibbin, W.F., Shackelford, T.K., Goetz, A.T. and Starratt, V.G. (2008) 'Why do men rape? an evolutionary psychological perspective' *Review of General Psychology* **12** (1), 86–97.

McMurran, M. and Cusens, B. (2005) 'Alcohol and violent and non-violent acquisitive offending' *Addiction Research and Theory* **13** (5), 439–43.

McMurran, M. and Duggan, C. (2005) 'The manualisation of a treatment programme for personality disorder' *Criminal Behaviour and Mental Health* **15** (1), 17–27.

McMurran, M. and Theodosi, E. (2007) 'Is treatment non-completion associated with increased reconviction over no treatment?' *Psychology, Crime and Law* **13** (4), 33–43.

McMurran, M., Hodge, J.E. and Hollin, C.R. (1997) 'Introduction: current issues in the treatment of addictions and crime' in J.E. Hodge, M. McMurran and C.R. Hollin (eds) *Addicted to Crime?* Chichester: John Wiley, pp. 1–9.

McMurran, M., Hoyte, H. and Jinks, M. (2012) 'Triggers for alcohol-related violence in young male offenders' *Legal and Criminological Psychology* **17**, 307–21.

McMurran, M., Jinks, M., Howells, K. and Howard, R. (2011) 'Investigation of a typology of alcohol related violence defined by ultimate goals' *Legal and Criminological Psychology* **16** (1), 75–89.

McNally, R.J. (2017) 'False memories in the laboratory and in life: commentary on Brewin and Andrews' *Applied Cognitive Psychology* **31**, 40–41.

McNeil, D.E. (1997) 'Correlates of violence in psychotic patients' *Psychiatric Annals* **27** (10), 683–90.

McSherry, B. (2004) 'Criminal responsibility, fleeting states of mental impairment, and the power of self-control' *International Journal of Law and Psychiatry* **27**, 445–57.

Mednick, S.A., Gabrielli, W.F. and Hutchings, B. (1994) 'Genetic influences in criminal convictions' *Science* **224**, 841–94.

Meehle, P.E. (1954) *Clinical Versus Statistical Predictions* Minneapolis: University of Minnesota Press.

Meijer, E.H. and Verschuere, B. (2010) 'The polygraph and the detection of deception', *Journal of Forensic Psychology Practice* **10** (4), 325–38.

Meissner, C.A., Redlich, A.D., Michael, S.W., Evans, J.R., Camilletti, C.R., Bhatt, S. and Brandon, S. (2014) 'Accusatorial and information-gathering interrogation methods and their effects on true and false confessions: a meta-analytic review' *Journal of Experimental Criminology* **10**, 459–486.

Melinder, A., and Magnussen, S. (2015) 'Psychologists and psychiatrists serving as expert witnesses in court: what do they know about eyewitness memory?' *Psychology, Crime and Law* **21** (1), 53–61.

Meloy, M.R. (2002) 'Stalking and violence' in J. Boon and L. Sheridan (eds) *Stalking and Psychosexual Obsession: Psychological Perspectives for Prevention, Policing and Treatment* Chichester: John Wiley, pp. 105–24.

Memon, A. and Young, M. (1997) 'Desperately seeking evidence: the recovered memory debate' *Legal and Criminological Psychology* **2**, 131–54.

Memon, A., Havard, C., Clifford, B., Gabbert, F. and Watt, M. (2011) 'A field evaluation of the VIPER system: a new technique for eliciting eyewitness identification evidence' *Psychology, Crime and Law* **17** (8), 711–29.

Memon, A., Holley, A., Milne, R., Koehnken, G. and Bull, R. (1994) 'Towards understanding the effects of interviewer training in evaluating the cognitive interview' *Applied Cognitive Psychology* **8**, 641–59.

Merari, A. (2007) 'Psychological aspects of suicide terrorism' in B. Bongar, L.M. Brown, L.E. Beutler, J.N. Breckenridge and P.B. Zimbardo (eds) *Psychology of Terrorism* New York: Oxford University Press, pp. 101–15.

Merari, A. (2012) 'Studying suicide bombers: a response to Brym and Araj's critique' *Studies in Conflict and Terrorism* **35** (6), 444–455.

Merari, A., Diamant, I., Bibi, A., Broshi, Y. and Zakin, G. (2010) 'Personality characteristics of 'self martyrs'/'suicide bombers' and organizers of suicide attacks' *Terrorism and Political Violence* **22**, 87–101.

Merdian, H.L., Curtis, C., Thakker, J., Wilson, N. and Boer, D.P. (2014) 'The endorsement of cognitive distortions: comparing child pornography offenders and contact sex offenders' *Psychology, Crime and Law* **20** (10), 971–993.

Merton, R.K. (1968) *Social Theory and Social Structure* New York: Free Press.

Messner, S.F. (1986) 'Television violence and violent crime: an aggregate analysis' *Social Problems* **33** (3), 218–35.

Metropolitan Police Service (2013) 'Surveys in the MPS: Londoners' Views Count' http://www.met.police.uk/about/performance/documents/LVC_Quarter_2_13_14.pdf

Meyer-Lindenberg, A., and Weinberger, D. R. (2006) 'Intermediate phenotypes and genetic mechanisms of psychiatric disorders' *Nature Reviews Neuroscience* **7**, 818–827.

The Michigan Daily (2002) 'Speaker says terrorists are normal people' *The Michigan Daily* **112** (77), 1 + 7.

Miethe, T.D. (1995) 'Fear and withdrawal from urban life' *Annals of the American Association of Political and Social Science* **539**, 14–27.

Milavsky, J.R., Kessler, R.C., Stipp, H.H. and Rubins, W.S. (1982) *Television and Aggression: A Panel Study* New York: Academic Press.

Milgram, S. (1974) *Obedience to Authority: An Experimental View* New York: Harper and Row.

Miller, E. (1999a) 'The neuropsychology of offending' *Psychology, Crime and Law* **5**, 515–36.

Miller, E. (1999b) 'Head injury and offending' *Journal of Forensic Psychiatry* **10** (1), 157–66.

Miller, E. (2012) 'Patterns of onset and decline among terrorist organizations'

Journal of Quantitative Criminology **28**, 77–101.

Miller, L. (2012) 'Posttraumatic stress disorder and criminal violence: Basic concepts and clinical-forensic applications' *Aggression and Violent Behavior* **17**, 354–64.

Miller, M.E., Adya, M., Chamberlain, J. and Jehle, A. (2010) 'The effects of counterfactual thinking on reactions to victimization' *Applied Psychology in Criminal Justice* **6** (1), 17–30.

Miller, N.E. and Dollard, J. (1941) *Social Learning and Imitation* Yale: Yale University Press.

Milne, R. and Bull, R. (1994) 'Improving witness recall: the cognitive interview and the legal profession' *Journal of Child Law* **6** (2), 82–4.

Milne, R. and Bull, R. (1996) 'Interviewing children with mild learning disability with the cognitive interview' in N.K. Clark and G.M. Stephenson (eds) *Issues in Criminological and Legal Psychology 26: Investigative and Forensic Decision Making* Leicester: Division of Criminological and Legal Psychology, British Psychological Society, pp. 44–51.

Milne, R., Bull, R., Koehnken, G. and Memon, A. (1995) 'The cognitive interview and suggestibility' in N.K. Clark and G.M. Stephenson (eds) *Issues in Criminological and Legal Psychology 22: Criminal Behaviour: Perceptions, Attributions and Rationality* Leicester: Division of Criminological and Legal Psychology, British Psychological Society, pp. 21–7.

Milne, R., Clare, I.C.H. and Bull, R. (1999) 'Using the cognitive interview with adults with mild learning disabilities' *Psychology, Crime and Law* **5**, 81–99.

Milner, J.S. and Campbell, J.C. (1995) 'Prediction issues for practitioners' in J.C. Campbell (ed.) *Assessing Dangerousness* Thousand Oaks, CA: Sage, pp. 20–40.

Mimoto, T., and Fukada, N. (1999) 'Renzoku houkahan no kyojuchi suitei no kokoromi: Chiriteki jushin moderu wo mochiita chiri purofairingu [Attempt to residence estimation of serial arsonists: Geographical profiling based on geographical gravity model]' Kagaku Keisatsu Kenkyujo Houkoku (Bouhan Syonen Hen) [Reports of National Research Institute of Police Science: Prevention-Minor],

Miner, M.H. and Dwyer, S.M. (1997) 'The psychological development of sex offenders: differences between exhibitionists, child molesters and incest offenders' *International Journal of Offender Therapy and Comparative Criminology* **41** (1), 36–44.

Ministry of Justice (2016) 'Proven reoffending statistics quarterly bulletin October 2013 to September 2014, England and Wales' https://www.gov.uk/government/uploads/system/uploads/attachment_data/file/541187/proven-reoffending-2014-q3.pdf

Ministry of Justice, Home Office & the Office for National Statistics, Statistics Bulletin.

Ministry of Justice, Home Office and the Office for National Statistics (2013) *An Overview of Sexual Offending in England and Wales.* https://www.gov.uk/government/uploads/system/uploads/attachment_data/file/214970/sexual-offending-overview-jan-2013.pdf (Accessed 11 March, 2014).

Ministry of Justice. (2015) 'Public confidence in the Criminal Justice System – findings from the Crime Survey for England and Wales (2013/14): analytical summary' https://www.gov.uk/government/uploads/system/uploads/attachment_data/file/449444/public-confidence.pdfethan

Mirrlees-Black, C. (2001) 'Confidence in the criminal justice system'. Home Office Research, Development and Statistics Directorate, Research Findings, 137. http://www.homeoffice.gov.uk/rds/pdfs/r137.pdf (no longer available).

Mischel, W. (1999) 'Personality coherence and dispositions in a cognitive-affective personality system (CAPS) approach' in D. Cervone and Y. Shoda (eds) *The Coherence of Personality: Social-cognitive Bases of Consistency, Variability and Organisation* London: Guilford Press, pp. 37–60.

Mitchell, B. (1997) 'Putting diminished responsibility law into practice: a forensic psychiatric perspective' *Journal of Forensic Psychiatry* **8** (3), 620–34.

Mnookin, R.H. and Kornhauser, L. (1979) 'Bargaining in the shadow of the law: the case of divorce' *Yale Law Journal* **88**, 950.

Moffitt, T.E. (1993) 'Adolescence-limited and life-course-persistent antisocial behavior: A developmental taxonomy' *Psychological Review* **100**, 674–701.

Moffitt, T.E., Caspi, A., Harrington, H. and Milne, B.J. (2002) 'Males on the life-course-persistent and adolescence-limited antisocial pathways: Follow-up at age 26 years' *Development & Psychopathology* **14**, 179–220.

Monahan, J. (1993) 'Mental disorder and violence: another look' in S. Hodgins (ed.) *Mental Disorder and Crime* Newbury Park, CA: Sage, pp. 287–302.

Monahan, J. and Steadman, H. (1994) 'Toward the rejuvenation of risk research in J. Monahan and H. Steadman (eds) *Violence and Mental Disorder: Developments in Risk Assessment* Chicago: University of Chicago Press, pp. 1–17.

Mooney, J.L. and Daffern, M. (2015) 'The relationship between aggressive behaviour in prison and violent offending following release' *Psychology, Crime and Law* **21** (4), 314–329.

Moore, P.J., Ebbesen, E.B. and Konecni, V.J. (1994) *What Does Real Eyewitness Testimony Look Like? An Archival Analysis of Witnesses to Adult Felony Crimes.* Technical Report. San Diego, CA: University of California, San Diego, Law and Psychology Program.

Moran, G. and Cutler, B.L. (1991) 'The prejudicial impact of retrial publicity' *Journal of Applied Social Psychology* **21** (5), 345–67.

Morgado, A.M. and Vale Dias, M.L. (2013) 'The antisocial phenomenon in adolescence: What is literature telling us?' *Aggression and Violent Behavior* **18** (4), 436–43.

Morgan, W. and Wells, M. (2016) ''It's deemed unmanly': men's experiences of intimate partner violence (IPV)' *The Journal of Forensic Psychiatry and Psychology*, **27** (3), 404–418.

Mosher, D.L. and Anderson, R.D. (1986) 'Macho personality, sexual aggression and reactions to guided imagery of realistic rape' *Journal of Research in Personality* **20**, 77–94.

Mossman, D. and Kapp, M.B. (1998) '"Courtroom whores"? – or why do attorneys call us? Findings from a survey on attorneys' use of mental health experts'. *Journal of the American Academy of Psychiatry and Law* **26** (1), 27–36.

Motzkau, J.F. (2004) 'Cross-examining suggestibility: memory, childhood, expertise: children's testimony between psychological research and juridical practice'. Paper presented at the 14th European Conference on Psychology and Law, Krakow: Poland.

Moulden, H.M., Firestone, P., Kingston, D. and Bradford, J. (2009) 'Recidivism in pedophiles: an investigation using different diagnostic methods' *Journal of Forensic Psychiatry and Psychology* **20** (5), 680–701.

Mowrer, O.H. (1960) *Learning Theory and Behavior* New York: Wiley.

Mucchielli, L. (2011) 'CCTV: The French controversy' *Crime Prevention and Community Safety* **13**, 294 – 298.

Muir, G. and Macleod, M.D. (2003) 'The demographic and spatial patterns of recorded rape in a large UK metropolitan area' *Psychology, Crime and Law* **9** (4), 345–55.

Mullen, P.E., James, D.V., Meloy, J.R., Pathé, M.T., Farnham, F.R., Preston, L., Darnley, B. and Berman, J. (2009) 'The fixated and the pursuit of public figures' *Journal of Forensic Psychiatry and Psychology* **20** (1), 33–47.

Mulvey, E.P. (2011) *Highlights from pathways to desistance: A longitudinal study of serious adolescent offenders* Washington, DC: Office of Justice Programs, U.S. Department of Justice.

Murphy, C. M., and Hoover, S. A. (1999) 'Measuring emotional abuse in dating relationships as a multifactorial construct' *Violence and Victims* **14**, 39–53.

Murphy, W.D., Haynes, M.R., Stalgaitis, S.J. and Flanagan, B. (1986) 'Differential sexual responding among four groups of sexual offenders against children' *Journal of Psychopathology and Behavioral Assessment* **8** (4), 339–53.

Murray, J., Loeber, R. and Partini, D. (2012) 'Parental involvement in the criminal justice system and the development of youth theft, marijuana use, depression, and poor academic performance' *Criminology* **50** (1), 255–302.

Myers, B., Latter, R., and Abdollahi-Arena, M.K. (2006) 'The court of public opinion: lay perceptions of polygraph testing' *Law and Human Behavior* **30**, 509–523.

Myers, J.E.B. (1996) 'A decade of international legal reform regarding child abuse investigation and litigation: steps toward a child witness code' *Pacific Law Journal* **28** (1), 169–241.

Myers, J.E.B., Diedrich, S., Lee, D. and Fincher, K.M. (1999) 'Professional writing on child sexual abuse from 1900 to 1975: dominant themes and impact on prosecution' *Child Maltreatment* **4** (3), 201–16.

Myers, J.E.B., Saywitz, K.J. and Goodman, G.S. (1996) 'Psychological research on children as witnesses: practical implications for forensic interviews and courtroom testimony' *Pacific Law Review* **28** (1), 3–92.

Myers, M.A. (1979) 'Rule departures and making law: juries and their verdicts' *Law and Society Review* **13**, 781–97.

Myhill, A. and Allen, J. Home Office (2002) 'Findings 159: Rape and Sexual Assault of Women: Findings from the British Crime Survey', Home Office. http://www.wdvf.org.uk/RapeHO.pdf (accessed 11 March 2014).

Myklebust, T. and Bjørklund, R.A. (2006) 'The effect of long-term training on police officers' use of open and closed questions in field investigative interviews of children (FIIC)' *Journal of Investigative Psychology and Offender Profiling* **3**, 165–81.

Mythen, G. and Walklate, S. (2005) 'Criminology and terrorism: which thesis? Risk society or governmentality' *British Journal of Criminology* **46**, 379–98.

N

Nahari, G. (2012) 'Elaborations on credibility judgments by professional lie detectors and laypersons: strategies of judgment and justification' *Psychology, Crime and Law* **18** (6), 567–77.

Nahari, G., and Vrij, A. (2014) 'Can I borrow your alibi? the applicability of the verifiability approach to the case of an alibi witness' *Journal of Applied Research in Memory and Cognition* **3** (2), 89–94.

Nahari, G., Vrij, A. and Fisher, R.P. (2012) 'Does the truth come out in the writing? SCAN as a lie detection tool' *Law and Human Behavior*, **36**, 68–76.

Nahari, G., Vrij, A., and Fisher, R. P. (2014a) 'Exploiting liars' verbal strategies by examining unverifiable details' *Legal and Criminological Psychology* **19**, 227–239.

Nahari, G., Vrij, A., and Fisher, R,P. (2014b) 'The verifiability approach: countermeasures facilitate its ability to discriminate between truths and lies' *Applied Cognitive Psychology* **28**, 122–128.

Narchet, F.M., Meissner, C.A. and Russano, M.B. (2011) 'Modeling the influence of investigator bias on the elicitation of true and false confessions' *Law and Human Behavior* **35**, 452–465.

Nash, C.L. and West, D. (1985) 'Sexual molestation of young girls: a retrospective survey' in D. West (ed.) *Sexual Victimization: Two Recent Researches into Sex Problems and their Social Effects* Aldershot: Gower, pp. 1–92.

Nash, R.A., Wade, K.A., Garry, M., Loftus, E.F. and Ost, J. (2017)

'Misrepresentations and flawed logic about the prevalence of false memories' *Applied Cognitive Psychology* **31**, 31–33.

National Offender Management Service. 2010 Offender Group Reoffending Scale Version 3. http://www.probation.homeoffice.gov.uk/files/pdf/Offender%20Group%20Reconviction%20Scale%20v3%20Guidance%20(Appendix).pdf (no longer available).

National Research Council (2003) *The Polygraph and Lie Detection* Committee to Review the Scientific Evidence on the Polygraph. Washington, DC: The National Academic Press.

National Research Council of the National Academies (2009) *Strengthening Forensic Science in the United States: A Path Forward* Washington DC: National Research Council of the National Academies.

Naughton, M. (2005) 'Redefining miscarriages of justice: a revived human rights approach to unearth subjugated discourses of wrongful criminal conviction' *British Journal of Criminology* **45**, 165–82.

Nederlof, A.F., Muris, P. and Hovens, J.E. (2013) 'The epidemiology of violent behavior in patients with a psychotic disorder: A systematic review of studies since 1980' *Aggression and Violent Behavior* **18**, 183–9.

Nee, C. (2004) 'Research on burglary at the end of the millennium: a grounded approach to understanding crime' *Security Journal* **16** (3), 37–44.

Nee, C. (2015) 'Understanding expertise in burglars: from pre-conscious scanning to action and beyond' *Aggression and Violent Behavior* **20**, 53–61.

Nee, C. and Ellis, T. (2005) 'Treating offending children: what works?' *Legal and Criminological Psychology* **10** (1), 133–48.

Nee, C. and Meenaghan, A. (2006) 'Expert decision making in burglars' *British Journal of Criminology* **46**, 935–49.

Nee, C. and Ward, T. (2015) 'Review of expertise and its general implications for correctional psychology and criminology' *Aggression and Violent Behavior* **20**, 1–9.

Neisser, U. (1982) *Memory Observed: Remembering in Natural Contexts* San Francisco: W.H. Freeman.

Neisser, U. and Winograd, E. (1988) *Remembering Reconsidered: Ecological and Traditional Approaches to the Study of Memory* Cambridge: Cambridge University Press.

Nelson, J.R., Smith, D.J. and Dodd, J. (1990) 'The moral reasoning of juvenile delinquents: a meta-analysis' *Journal of Abnormal Child Psychology* **18**, 231–9.

Nelson, T.O., Gerler, D. and Narens, L. (1984) 'Accuracy of feeling of knowing judgements for predicting perceptual identification and relearning' *Journal of Experimental Psychology: General* **113**, 282–300.

Neutze, J., Grundmann, D., Scherner G. and Beier K.M. (2012) 'Undetected and detected child sexual abuse and child pornography offenders' *International Journal of Law and Psychiatry* **35** (3), 168–75.

Newburn, T. (2015) 'The 2011 England riots in recent historical perspective' *British Journal of Criminology*, **55**, 39–64.

Newson, E. (1994a) 'Video violence and the protection of children' *The Psychologist* **7** (6), 272–4.

Newson, E. (1994b) *Video Violence and the Protection of Children* Report of the Home Affairs Committee London: HMSO, pp. 45–9.

Niebieszczanski, R., Harkins, L., Judson, S., Smith, K., and Dixon, L. (2015) 'The role of moral disengagement in street gang offending' *Psychology, Crime and Law*, **21** (6), 589–605.

Nijboer, H. (1995) 'Expert evidence' in R. Bull and D. Carson (eds) *Handbook of Psychology in Legal Contexts*. Chichester: John Wiley, pp. 555–64.

Noesner, G.W. and Webster, M. (1997) 'Crisis intervention: using active listening skills in negotiations' *FBI Law Enforcement Bulletin*, http://www.fbi.gov/publications/leb/1997/aug974.htm

Nonnemaker, J.M., McNeely, C.A. and Blum, R.W. (2003) 'Public and private domains of religiosity and adolescent health risk behaviors: evidence from the National Longitudinal Study of Adolescent Health, Social Science and Medicine' *Social Science and Medicine* **57** (11), 2049–54.

Nordanger, D., Hysing, M., Posserud, M.-B.1, Johansen Lundervold, A., Jakobsen, R., Olff, M., and Stormark, K.M. (2013) 'Posttraumatic responses to the July 22, 2011 Oslo terror among Norwegian high school students' Journal of Traumatic Stress 26, 679–685.

Norris, C. and Armstrong, G. (1999b) *The Maximum Surveillance Society: The Rise of CCTV* Oxford: Berg.

Norwood, A., and Murphy, C. (2012) 'What forms of abuse correlate with PTSD symptoms in partners of men being treated for intimate partner violence?' *Psychological Trauma: Theory, Research, Practice, and Policy* **4** (6), 596–604.

Novaco, R.W. (1975) *Anger Control: The Development and Evaluation of an Experimental Treatment* Lexington, MA: Lexington Books, D.C. Heath.

Novaco, R.W. (2011) 'Anger dysregulation: driver of violent offending' *The Journal of Forensic Psychiatry and Psychology* **22** (5), 650–68.

Novo, M., and Seijo, D. (2010) 'Judicial judgement-making and legal criteria of testimonial credibility' *European Journal of Psychology Applied to Legal Contex*, **2**, 91–115.

Nowinski, S. N., and Bowen, E. (2012) 'Partner violence against heterosexual and gay men: prevalence and correlates' *Aggression and Violent Behavior*, **17**, 36–52.

Nugent, P.M. and Kroner, D.G. (1996) 'Denial, response styles and admittance of offences among child molesters and rapists' *Journal of Interpersonal Violence* **11** (4), 476–86.

Nunes, K.L. and Jung, S. (2013) 'Are cognitive distortions associated with denial and minimization among sex offenders?' *Sex Abuse* **25** (2), 166–88.

Nunes, K.L., Firestone, P., Wexler, A.F., Jensen, T.L. and Bradford, J.M. (2007a) 'Incarceration and recidivism among sexual offenders' *Law and Human Behavior* **31**, 305–18.

Nunes, K.L., Hanson, K., Firestone, P., Moulden, H.M., Greenberg, D.M. and Bradford, J.M. (2007b) 'Denial predicts recidivism for some sexual offenders' *Sex Abuse* **19**, 91–105.

Nunez, N., McCrea, S.M. and Culhane, S.E. (2011) 'Jury Decision Making Research: Are Researchers Focusing on the Mouse and Not the Elephant in the Room?' *Behavioral Sciences and the Law* **29**, 439–51.

O

Ó Ciardha, C. and Gannon, T. (2011) 'The cognitive distortions of child molesters are in need of treatment' *Journal Of Sexual Aggression*, **17**, 130–141.

Ó Ciardha, C., Barnoux, M. F. L., Alleyne, E. K. A., Tyler, N., Mozova, K. and Gannon, T. A. (2015) 'Multiple factors in the assessment of firesetters' fire interest and attitudes' *Legal and Criminological Psychology*, **20**, 37–47.

O'Connell, M. and Synnott, J. (2009) 'A Position of Influence: Variation in Offender Identification Rates by Location in a Lineup' *Journal of Investigative Psychology and Offender Profiling* **6**, 139–49.

O'Donohue, W. and Bowers, A.H. (2006) 'Pathways to false allegations of sexual harassment' *Journal of Investigative Psychology and Offender Profiling* **3**, 47–74.

O'Kane, A. and Bentall, R. (2000) 'Psychosis and offending' in J. McGuire, T. Mason and A. O'Kane (eds) *Behaviour, Crime and Legal Processes: A Guide for Forensic Practitioners*. Chichester: John Wiley, pp. 161–76.

O'Kelly, C.M.E., Kebbell, M.R., Hatton, C. and Johnson, S.D. (2003) 'Judicial intervention in court cases involving witnesses with and without learning disabilities' *Legal and Criminological Psychology* **8**, 229–40.

O'Sullivan, M. (2008) 'Home runs and humbugs: Comment on Bond and DePaulo' *Psychological Bulletin* **134** (4), 493–7.

O'Sullivan, M. and Ekman, P. (2004) 'The wizards of deception detection' in P.A. Granhag and L. Strömwell (eds) *The Detection of Deception in Forensic Contexts* London: Cambridge University Press.

O'Sullivan, M., Frank, M.G., Hurley, C.M. and Tiwana, J. (2009) 'Police lie detection accuracy: the effect of lie scenario' *Law and Human Behavior* **33**, 530–53.

Odlaugh, B.L. and Grant, J.E. (2010) 'Impulse control disorders in a college sample' *The Primary Care Companion to the Journal of Clinical Psychiatry* **12** (2), 227–9.

Odlaug, B.L., Grant, J.E., and Kim, S.W. (2012) 'Suicide attempts in107 adolescents and adults with kleptomania' *Archives of Suicide Research*, 16(4), 348–359.

Office for National Statistics (2014) 'About this release: focus on violent crime and sexual offences 2012/13' http://www.ons.gov.uk/ons/rel/crime-stats/crime-statistics/focus-on-violent-crime-and-sexual-offences--2012-13/rpt---about-this-release.html

Office for National Statistics (2016b)'Crime in England and Wales: Year Ending December2015' http://www.ons.gov.uk/peoplepopulationandcommunity/crimeandjustice/bulletins/crimeinenglandandwales/yearendingdecember2015

Ofshe, R.J. and Leo, R.A. (1997) 'The decision to confess falsely: rational choice and irrational action' *Denver University Law Review* **74** (4), 979–1122.

Ogloff, J.R.P., Campbell, R.E. and Shepherd, S.M. (2016) 'Disentangling psychopathy from antisocial personality disorder: an Australian analysis' *Journal of Forensic Psychology Practice* **16** (3), 198–215.

Olafson, E. (2012) 'A call for field-relevant research about child forensic interviewing for child protection' *Journal of Child Sexual Abuse* **21** (1), 109–129.

Oleson, J.C., and Chappell, R. (2013) 'Self-reported violent offending among subjects with genius-level IQ scores' *Journal of Family Violence, Youth Violence and Juvenile Justice* **27** (8), 715–730.

Oliver, C.J., Beech, A.R., Fisher, D. and Beckett, R.C. (2007) 'A comparison of rapists and sexual murderers on demographic and selected psychometric measures' in J. Proulx, E. Beauregard, M. Cusson, and A. Nicole (eds), *Sexual Murderers: A Comparative Analysis and New Perspectives* Chichester, UK: Wiley, pp. 70–86.

Olson, E.A. and Charman, S.D. (2012) '"But can you prove it?" examining the quality of innocent suspects' alibis' *Psychology, Crime and Law* **18** (5), 453–71.

Olver, M. E., Wong, S. C. P., Nicholaichuk, T. and Gordon, A. (2007) 'The validity and reliability of the violence risk scale-sexual offender version: assessing sex offender risk and evaluating therapeutic change' *Psychological Assessment* **19**, 318–329.

Olver, M.E. and Wong, S. (2011) 'Predictors of sex offender treatment dropout: psychopathy, sex offender risk, and responsivity implications' *Psychology, Crime and Law* **17** (5), 457–71.

Olver, M.E. and Wong, S.C.P. (2011) 'A comparison of static and dynamic assessment of sexual offender risk and need in a treatment context' *Criminal Justice and Behavior* **38**, 113–26.

Olver, M.E. and Wong, S.C.P. (2013) 'A description and research review of the Clearwater Sex Offender Treatment Programme' *Psychology, Crime and Law* **19** (5–6), 477–92.

Olver, M.E. and Wong, S.C.P. (2013) 'Treatment programs for high risk sexual offenders: Program and offender characteristics, attrition, treatment change and recidivism' *Aggression and Violent Behavior* **18**, 579–91.

Ono, M., Devilly, G.J., and Shum, D.H.K. (2016) 'A meta-analytic review of overgeneral memory: the role of trauma. history, mood, and the presence of posttraumatic stress disorder' *Psychological Trauma: Theory, Research, Practice, and Policy* **8**(2), 157–164.

Orth, U., and Maercker, A. (2009) 'Posttraumatic anger in crime victims: directed at the perpetrator and at the self' *Journal of Traumatic Stress* **22** (2), 158–161.

Orth, U., Cahill, S.P., Foa, E.B. and Maercker, A. (2008) 'Anger and posttraumatic stress disorder symptoms in crime victims: a longitudinal analysis' *Journal of Consulting and Clinical Psychology* **76** (2), 208–18.

Osgood, D.W, Wilson, J.K., O'Malley, P.M. Bachman, J.G. and Johnston, L.D. (1996) 'Routine activities and individual deviant behavior' *American Sociological Review* **61**, 635–55.

Ost, J., Costall, A. and Bull, R. (2002) 'A perfect symmetry? Retractors' experiences of recovering then retracting abuse memories' *Psychology, Crime and the Law* **8** (2), 155–81.

Ost, J., Granhag, P.-A., Udell, J. and Roos af Hjelmsäter, E. (2008) 'Familiarity breeds distortion: the effects of media exposure on false reports concerning media coverage of the terrorist attacks in London on 7 July 2005' *Memory* **1**, 76–85.

Ost, J., Wright, D.B., Easton, S., Hope, L. and French, C.C. (2013) 'Recovered memories, satanic abuse, dissociative identity disorder and false memories in the UK: a survey of clinical psychologists and hypnotherapists' *Psychology, Crime and Law* **19** (1), 1–19.

Osterman, K., Bjorqvist, K. and Lagerspetz, K.M.J. (1998) 'Cross-cultural evidence of female indirect aggression' *Aggressive Behavior* **24**, 1–8.

Ostermann, M. and Matejkowski, J. (2014) 'Estimating the impact of mental health on costs of crimes: a comparison of matched samples' *Criminal Justice and Behavior* **41** (1), 20–40.

Otgaar, H., Candel, I., Smeets, T. and Merckelbach, H. (2009) '"You didn't take Lucy's skirt off": The effect of misleading information on omissions and commissions in children's memory reports' *Legal and Criminological Psychology* **15** (2), 229–41.

Otto, R.K. (2006) 'Competency to stand trial' *Applied Psychology in Criminal Justice* **2** (3), 82–113.

Otto, R.K., Poythress, N.G., Nicholson, R.A., Edens, J.F., Monahan, J., Bonnie, R.J., Hoge, S.K. and Eisenberg, M. (1998) 'Psychometric properties of the MacArthur Competence Assessment Tool – criminal adjudication' *Psychological Assessment* **10** (4), 435–43.

Overholser, J.C. and Beck, S.J. (1988) 'The classification of rapists and child molesters' *Journal of Offender Counseling Services and Rehabilitation* **13**, 1715–25.

Owens, J.G., and Slocum, L.A. (2015) 'Abstainers in adolescence and adulthood: exploring the correlates of abstention using Moffitt's developmental taxonomy *Crime and Delinquency* **61** (5) '690–718.

Oxburgh, G. and Ost, J. (2011) 'The use and efficacy of empathy in police interviews with suspects of sexual offences' *Journal of Investigative Psychology and Offender Profiling* **8** (2), 178–88.

Oxburgh, G., Ost, J. and Cherryman, J. (2012) 'Police interviews with suspected child sex offenders: does question type, empathy, or interviewer training influence the amount of investigation relevant information obtained?' *Psychology, Crime & Law*. **18** (3), 259–273.

Oxburgh, G., Williamson, T. and Ost, J. (2006) 'Police officers' use of emotional language during child sexual abuse investigations' *Journal of Investigative Psychology and Offender Profiling* **3**, 35–45.

P

Pacini, R. and Epstein, S. (1999) 'The relation of rational and experiential information processing styles to personality, basic beliefs, and the ratio-bias phenomenon' *Journal of Personality and Social Psychology* **76** (6), 972–987.

Paik, H. and Comstock, G. (1994) 'The effects of television violence on antisocial behavior: a meta-analysis' *Communication Research* **21** (4), 516–46.

Paine, C.B., Pike, G.E., Brace, N.A. and Westcott, H.L. (2008) 'Children making faces: the effect of age and prompts on children's facial composites of unfamiliar faces' *Applied Cognitive Psychology* **22** (4), 455–74.

Palmer, E.J. (2001) 'Risk assessment: review of psychometric measures' in D.P. Farrington, C.R. Hollin and M. McMurran (eds) *Sex and Violence: The Psychology of Crimes and Risk Assessment* Reading: Harwood Academic Press, pp. 7–22.

Palmer, E.J. (2003) *Offending Behaviour: Moral Reasoning, Criminal Conduct and the Rehabilitation of Offenders* Cullompton: Willan Publishing.

Palmer, E.J. and Hollin, C.R. (1998) 'A comparison of patterns of moral development in young offenders and non-offenders' *Legal and Criminological Psychology* **3**, 225–35.

Palmer, M.A., Brewer, N. and Weber, N. (2012) 'The information gained from witnesses' responses to an initial "blank" lineup' *Law and Human Behavior* **36** (5), 439–47.

Paradis, C.M., Solomon, L.Z., Owen, E. and Brooker, M. (2013) 'Detection of cognitive malingering or suboptimal effort in defendants undergoing competency to stand trial evaluations' *Journal of Forensic Psychology Practice* **13** (3), 245–65.

Pardue, A.D., Robinson, M.B. and Arrigo, B.A. (2013) 'Psychopathy and corporate crime: a preliminary examination, part 1' *Journal of Forensic Psychology Practice* **13** (2), 116–144.

Pardue, A.D., Robinson, M.B. and Arrigo, B.A. (2013) 'Psychopathy and corporate crime: a preliminary examination, part 2' *Journal of Forensic Psychology Practice*, **13** (2), 145–169.

Parker, H. and Kirby, P. (1996) *Methadone Maintenance and Crime Reduction on Merseyside* Home Office Police Research Group. Crime Detection and Prevention Series Paper 72, Home Office Police Policy Directorate Police Research Group.

Partridge, G.E. (1930) 'Current conceptions of psychopathic personality' *American Journal of Psychiatry* **10**, 53–99.

Passer, M.W. and Smith, R.E. (2001) *Psychology: Frontiers and Applications* Boston, MA: McGraw-Hill.

Passini, S. (2012) 'The delinquency–drug relationship: The influence of social reputation and moral disengagement' *Addictive Behaviors* **37** (4), 577–579.

Patrick, C.J. and Iacono, W.G. (1991) 'A comparison of field and laboratory polygraphs in the detection of deception' *Psychophysiology* **28**, 632–8.

Payne, B.K. (2013) *White Collar Crime: The Essentials* Los Angeles: Sage.

Payne, D.L., Lonsway, K.A. and Fitzgerald, L.F. (1999) 'Rape myth acceptance: Exploration of its structure and its measurement using the Illinois Rape Myth Acceptance Scale' *Journal of Research in Personality*, **33**, 27–68.

Payne, J.D., Jackson, E.D., Ryan, L., Hoscheidt, S., Jacobs, W.J. and Nadel, L. (2006) 'The impact of stress on neutral and emotional aspects of episodic memory' *Memory* **14**, 1–16.

Peace, K.A., Porter, S. and Almon, D.F. (2012) 'Sidetracked by emotion: Observers' ability to discriminate genuine and fabricated sexual assault allegations' *Legal and Criminological Psychology* 17, 322–35.

Pearse, J. and Gudjonsson, G.H. (1999) 'Measuring influential police interviewing tactics: a factor analytic approach' *Legal and Criminological Psychology* **4**, 221–38.

Pearse, J., Gudjonsson, G.H., Clare, I.C.H. and Rutters, S. (1998) 'Police interviewing and psychological vulnerabilities: predicting the likelihood of a confession' *Journal of Community and Applied Social Psychology* **8**, 1–21.

Pease, K. (1998) 'Repeat victimization: taking stock' Home Office, London, Crime Detection and Prevention, series 90.

Pease, K. (2001) 'Rational choice theory' in E. McLaughlin and J. Muncie (eds) *The Sage Dictionary of Criminology* London: Sage, pp. 233–4.

Pease, K. (2007) 'Victims and victimization' in S. Shoham, O. Beck and M. Kent (eds) *International Handbook of Penology and Criminal Justice* Abingdon: Taylor and Francis, 587–611.

Pease, K. (2014) 'Voles don't take taxis' *Legal and Criminological Psychology* **19**, 221–223.

Pennebaker, J. (ed.) (1995) *Emotion, Disclosure, and Health* Washington, DC: American Psychological Association.

Pennell, A.E. and Browne, K. (1998a) 'Young offenders' susceptibility to violent media entertainment' *Prison Service Journal* **120**, 23–7.

Pennell, A.E. and Browne, K.D. (1998b) 'Film violence and young offenders' *Aggression and Violent Behavior* **4** (1), 13–28.

Pennington, N. and Hastie, R. (1981) 'Juror decision making models: the generalization gap' *Psychological Bulletin* **89**, 246–87.

Pennington, N. and Hastie, R. (1986) 'Evidence evaluation in complex decision making' *Journal of Personality and Social Psychology* **51**, 242–58.

Pennington, N. and Hastie, R. (1988) 'Explanation-based decision making: the effects of memory structure on judgment' *Journal of Experimental Psychology: Learning, Memory, and Cognition* **14**, 521–33.

Pennington, N. and Hastie, R. (1992) 'Explaining the evidence: tests of the story model for juror decision making' *Journal of Personality and Social Psychology* **62**, 189–206.

Penrod, S.D. and Heuer, L. (1997) 'Tweaking commonsense: assessing aids to jury decision making' *Psychology, Public Policy and Law* **3** (2/3), 259–84.

Perera, A.L., Van Hasselt, V.B., Baker, M.T., Ramano, S.J., Schlessinger, K.M., Zucker, M. and Dragone, R. (2006) 'Crisis (hostage) negotiation training: a preliminary evaluation of program efficacy' *Criminal Justice and Behavior* **33** (1), 56–69.

Perina, K. (2002) 'Suicide terrorism: suicide bombers have distinctive personality traits' *Psychology Today* 2 October.

Perry, C. (1997) 'Admissibility and per se exclusion of hypnotically elicited recall in American courts of law' *International Journal of Clinical and Experimental Hypnosis* **XLV** (3), 266–79.

Pettit, M. (2013) 'Book review: Geoffrey C. Bunn, *The Truth Machine: A Social History of the Lie Detector*, Baltimore, M.D: Johns Hopkins University Press' *Journal of the History of the Behavioral Sciences* 49 (1), 104–5.

Pettit, B., Sykes, B. and Western, B. 'Technical report on revised population estimates and NLSY 79 analysis tables for the Pew Public Safety and Mobility Project', Harvard University, 2009.

Petty, R.E. and Cacioppo, J.T. (1981) *Attitudes and Persuasion: Classic and contemporary Approaches* Dubuque, IL: Wm. C. Brown.

Pezdek, K., Morrow, L.,Blandon-Gitlin, I. *et al.* (2005) 'Detecting deception in children: event familiarity affects criterion-based content analysis ratings' *Law and Human Behavior* **29**, 187–197.

Pezdek,,K., and Bladon-Gitlin, I. (2017) 'It is just harder to construct memories for false autobiographical events' *Applied Cognitive Psychology* **31**, 42–44.

Philbrick, K. (2002) 'Imprisonment: the impact on children' in L. Falshaw (ed.) *Issues in Forensic Psychology 3*

Leicester: British Psychological Society, pp. 72–81.

Piaget, J. (1970) 'Piaget's theory' in P.H. Mussen (ed.) *Carmichael's Manual of Child Psychology* (Vol. 1) New York: Wiley, pp. 703–32.

Pickel, K. (1998) 'The effects of motive information and crime unusualness on jurors' judgments in insanity cases' *Law and Human Behavior* **22** (5), 571–84.

Pickel, K.L., Narter, D.B., Jameson, M.M. and Lenhardt, T.T. (2008) 'The weapon focus effect in child eyewitnesses' *Psychology, Crime & Law* **14**, 61–72.

Pike, G., Brace, N. and Kynan, S. (2002) *The Visual Identification of Suspects: Procedures and Practice* Home Office, Briefing Note 2/02.

Pilgrim, D. (2000) 'Psychiatric diagnosis: more questions than answers' *The Psychologist* **19** (6), 303–5.

Pimental, P.S., Arndorfer, A. and Malloy, L. (2015) 'Taking the blame for someone else's wrongdoing: the effects of age and reciprocity' *Law and Human Behavior* **39** (3), 219–231.

Pinel, P. (1809) *Traité Medico-philosophique sur l'aliénation mentale, ou la manie* (2nd edition) Paris: Brosson.

Pinizzotto, A.J. and Finkel, N.J. (1990) 'Criminal personality profiling: an outcome and process study' *Law and Human Behavior* **14**, 215–33.

Piquero, A.R., Jennings, W.G. and Barnes, J.C. (2012) 'Violence in criminal careers: A review of the literature from a developmental life-course perspective' *Aggression and Violent Behavior* **17**, 171–9.

Pithers, W.D., Kashima, K.M., Cumming, G.F. and Beal, L.S. (1988) 'Relapse prevention: a method of enhancing maintenance of change in sex offenders' in A.C. Salter (ed.) *Treating Child Sex Offenders and Victims: A Practical Guide* Newbury Park, CA: Sage, pp. 131–70.

Plassmann, R. (1994) 'Munchausen syndromes and factitious diseases' *Psychotherapy and Psychosomatic Medicine* **62**, 7–26.

Plotnick, S., Porter, J. and Bagby, M. (1998) 'Is there bias in the evaluation of fitness to stand trial?' *International Journal of Law and Psychiatry* **21** (3), 291–304.

Polaschek, D.L.L. (2011) 'Many sizes fit all: A preliminary framework for conceptualizing the development and provision of cognitive–behavioral rehabilitation programs for offenders' *Aggression and Violent Behavior* **16** 20–35.

Polaschek, D.L.L. (2016) 'Desistance and dynamic risk factors belong together' *Psychology, Crime and Law* **22** (1–2), 171–189.

Polaschek, D.L.L. and Collie, R.M. (2004) 'Rehabilitating serious violent adult offenders: an empirical and theoretical stocktake' *Psychology, Crime & Law* **10** (3), 321–34.

Polaschek, D.L.L. and Daly, T.E. (2013) 'Treatment and psychopathy in forensic settings' *Aggression and Violent Behavior* **18**, 592–603.

Polaschek, D.L.L., Yesberg, J.A., Bell,R.K., Casey, A. and Dickson, S.R. (2016) 'Intensive psychological treatment of high-risk violent offenders: outcomes and pre-release mechanisms' *Psychology, Crime and Law* **22** (4), 344–365.

Pollock, P.H. (1999) 'When the killer suffers: post-traumatic stress reactions following homicide' *Legal and Criminological Psychology* **4**, 185–202.

Pomp, L., Spreen, M., Bogaerts, S. and Volker, B. (2010) 'The Role of Personal Social Networks in Risk Assessment and Management of Forensic Psychiatric Patients' *Journal of Forensic Psychology Practice* **10**, 267–84.

Poole, D.A. and Lindsay, D.S. (1998) 'Assessing the accuracy of young children's reports: lessons from the investigation of child sexual abuse' *Applied and Preventative Psychology* 7, 1–26.

Poole, D.A. and Lindsay, D.S. (2002) 'Children's suggestibility in the forensic context' in M.L. Eisen, J.A. Quas and G.S. Goodman (eds) *Memory and Suggestibility in the Forensic Interview* Mahwah, NJ: Lawrence Erlbaum, pp. 355–81.

Poole, E. and Regoli, R. (1980) 'Race, institutional rule-breaking, and disciplinary response: A study of discretionary decision making in prison' *Law and Society Review* **14**, 931–46.

Pornari, C. D., and Wood, J. (2010) 'Peer and cyber aggression in secondary school students: the role of moral disengagement, hostile attribution bias, and outcome expectancies' *Aggressive Behavior* **36** (2), 81–94.

Porter, S. and ten Brinke, L. (2009) 'A theoretical framework for understanding how judges assess credibility in the courtroom' *Legal and Criminological Psychology* **14**, 119–34.

Porter, S. and ten Brinke, L. (2010) 'The truth about lies: What works in detecting high-stakes deception?' *Legal and Criminological Psychology* **15**, 57–75.

Porter, S. and Yuille, J.C. (1996) 'The language of deceit: an investigation of the verbal clues to deception in the interrogation context' *Law and Human Behavior* **20** (4), 443–58.

Porter, S., ten Brinke, L. and Gustaw, C. (2010) 'Dangerous decisions: the impact of first impressions of trustworthiness on the evaluation of legal evidence and defendant culpability' *Psychology, Crime and Law* **16** (6), 477–91.

Porter, S., Woodworth, M. and Birt, A.R. (2000) 'Truth, lies and videotape: An investigation of the ability of federal parole officers to detect deception' *Law and Human Behavior* **24**, 643–58.

Posey, A.J. and Dahl, L.M. (2002) 'Beyond pre-trial publicity: legal and ethical issues associated with change of venue' *Law and Human Behaviour* **26** (1), 107–25.

Post, J.M., McGinnis, C. and Moody, K. (2014) 'The changing face of terrorism in the 21st Century: the communications revolution and the virtual community of hatred'

Behavioral Sciences and the Law, **32** (3), 306–334

Powell, M.B., Hughes-Scholes, C.H. and Sharman, S.J. (2012) 'Skill in Interviewing Reduces Confirmation Bias' *Journal of Investigative Psychology and Offender Profiling* **9**, 126–34.

Pozgain, I., Mandic, N. and Barkic, J. (1998) 'Homicides in war and peace in Croatia' *Journal of Forensic Sciences* **43** (6), 1124–6.

Pozzulo, J.D. and Lindsay, R.C.L. (1997) 'Increasing correct identifications by children' *Expert Evidence* **5** (4), 126–32.

Pratt T.C. and Godsey T.W. (2003) 'Social support, inequality, and homicide: A cross-national test of an integrated theoretical model' *Criminology* 41: 611–644.

Price, W.H., Strong, J.A., Whatmore, P.B. and McClemont, W.F. (1966) 'Criminal patients with XYY sex-chromosome complement' *The Lancet* **1**, 565–6.

Prison Reform Trust (2009) Bromley Fact File. http://www.prisonreformtrust.org.uk/uploads/documents/june2009factfile.pdf

Putkonen, A., Ryynänen, O.P., Eronen, M. and Tiihonen, J. (2007) 'Transmission of violent offending and crime across three generations' *Social Psychiatry and Psychiatric Epidemiology* **42**, 94–9.

Q

Quinsey, V.L. (2002) 'Evolutionary theory and criminal behaviour' *Legal and Criminological Psychology* **7** (1), 1–13.

Quinsey, V.L. (2009) 'Are we there yet? stasis and progress in forensic psychology' *Canadian Psychology* **50** (1), 15–21.

Quinsey, V.L., Steinman, C.M., Bergersen, S.G. and Holmes, T.F. (1975) 'Penile circumference, skin conductance, and ranking responses of child molesters and "normals" to sexual and nonsexual visual stimuli' *Behavior Therapy* **6**, 213–19.

R

Rade, C.B., Desmarais, S.L. and Mitchell, R..E. (2016) 'A meta-analysis of public attitudes toward ex-offenders' *Criminal Justice and Behavior*, **43** (9), 1260–1280.

Radford, L., Corral, S., Bradley, C., Fisher, H., Bassett, C., Howat, N., and Collishaw, S. (2011) 'Child abuse and neglect in the UK today' London: NSPCC.

Radley, L. (2001) 'Attitudes towards sex offenders' *Forensic Update* **66**, 5–9.

Rafter, N.H. (2006) 'H.J. Eysenck in Fagin's kitchen: the return to biological theory in 20th-century criminology' *History of the Human Sciences* **19**, 37–56.

Rallings, M. (2002) 'The impact of offending on police officers' *Issues in Forensic Psychology* **3**, 20–40.

Ramoutar, K. and Farrington, D. (2006) 'Are the same factors related to participation and frequency of offending by male and female prisoners?' *Psychology, Crime and Law* **12** (5), 557–72.

Rapoport, D. (2004) 'The four waves of modern terrorism' in A. K. Cronin and J. Ludes (Eds.), *Attacking Terrorism: Elements of a Grand Strategy* (46–73) 'Washington, DC: Georgetown University Press.

Rapoport, R. (1960) *Community as Doctor: New Perspectives on a Therapeutic Community* London: Tavistock.

Rappert, B. (2002) 'Constructions of legitimate force: the case of CS sprays' *British Journal of Criminology* **42**, 689–708.

Raskin, D.C. and Honts, C.R. (2002) 'The comparison question test' in M. Klener (ed.) *Handbook of Polygraph Testing* San Diego, CA: Academic Press, pp. 1–47.

Rassin, E. (2010) 'Blindness to alternative scenarios in evidence evaluation' *Journal of Investigative Psychology and Offender Profiling* 7, 153–63.

Ray, J. V., Kimonis, E. R. and Seto, M. C. (2014) 'Correlates and moderators of child pornography consumption in a community sample' *Sexual Abuse: A Journal of Research and Treatment*, **26**, 523–545.

Ray, J.V., Kimonis, E.R. and Seto, M.C. (2014) 'Correlates and moderators of child pornography consumption in a community sample' *Sexual Abuse: A Journal of Research and Treatment* **26** (6) 52332, 306–334.

Raynor, P. (2008) 'Community penalties and Home Office research: on the way back to "nothing works"?' *Criminology & Criminal Justice* **8** (1), 73–97.

Re, L., and Birkhoff, J.M. (2015) 'The 47, XYY syndrome, 50 years of certainties and doubts: a systematic review' *Aggression and Violent Behavior* **22**, 9–17.

Redlich, A.D., Kulish, R. and Steadman, H.J. (2011) 'Comparing true and false confessions among persons with serious mental illness' *Psychology, Public Policy, and Law* **17** (3), 394–418.

Redondo, S., Luque, E. and Funes, J. (1996) 'Social beliefs about recidivism in crime' in G. Davies, S. Lloyd-Bostock, M. McMurran and C. Wilson (eds) *Psychology, Law and Criminal Justice: International Developments in Research and Practice* Berlin: Walter de Gruyter, pp. 394–400.

Redondo, S., Sanchez-Meca, J. and Garrido, V. (1999) 'The influence of treatment programmes on the recidivism of juvenile and adult offenders: a European meta-analytic review' *Psychology, Crime and Law* **5**, 251–78.

Redondo, S., Sanchez-Meca, J. and Garrido, V. (2002) 'Crime treatment in Europe: a final view of the century and future perspectives' in J. McGuire (ed.) *Offender Rehabilitation and Treatment: Effective Programmes and Policies to Reduce Re-offending* Chichester: John Wiley, pp. 131–41.

Reid, A.A,and Andresen, M.A. (2014) 'An evaluation of CCTV in a car park using police and insurance data' *Security Journal* **27** (1), 55–79.

Reidy, D.E., Kearns, M.C. and DeGuea, S. (2013) 'Reducing psychopathic violence: A review of the treatment literature' *Aggression and Violent Behavior* **18**, 527–38.

Reinares, F. (2011) 'Exit From Terrorism: A Qualitative Empirical Study on Disengagement and Deradicalization Among Members of ETA' *Terrorism and Political Violence* **23** (5), 780–803.

Reiner, R. (2010) *The Politics of the Police* Oxford: Oxford University Press.

Ressler, R., Burgess, A. and Douglas, J. (1988) *Sexual Homicide: Patterns and Motives* New York: Free Press.

Ressler, R.K. and Burgess, A.W. (1985) 'Violent crime' *FBI Law Enforcement Bulletin* **August**, 1–322.

Ressler, R.K. and Shachtman, T. (1997) *I Have Lived in the Monster* New York: St Martin's Press.

Ressler, R.K., Burgess, A.W. and Douglas, J.E. (1988) *Sexual Homicide: Patterns and Motives* Lexington, MA: Lexington Books.

Revitch, E. (1965) 'Sex murder and the potential sex murderer' *Diseases of the Nervous System* **26**, 640–48.

Reynolds, N. and Scragg, P. (2010) 'Compliance with command hallucinations: the role of power in relation to the voice, and social rank in relation to the voice and Others' *Journal of Forensic Psychiatry & Psychology* **21** (1), 121–38.

Ribeaud, D. and Manzoni, P. (2004) 'The relationship between defendant's social attributes, psychiatric assessment and sentencing – a case study in Switzerland' *International Journal of Law and Psychiatry* **27**, 375–86.

Rice, M.E. (1997) 'Violent offender research and implications for the criminal justice system' *American Psychologist* **52** (4), 414–23.

Rice, M.E. and Harris, G.T. (1997) 'Cross-validation and extension of the violence risk appraisal guide for child molesters and rapists' *Law and Human Behavior* **21** (2), 231–41.

Rice, M.E. and Harris, G.T. (2003) 'The size and sign of treatment effects in sex offender therapy' *Annals of the New York Academy of Sciences* **989**, 428–40.

Rice, M.E., Harris, G.T. and Cormier, C.A. (1992) 'Evaluation of a maximum security therapeutic community for psychopaths and other mentally disordered offenders' *Law and Human Behavior* **16**, 399–412.

Rice,M.E., and Harris, G.T. (2002) 'Men who molest their sexually immature daughters: Is a special explanation required?' *Journal of Abnormal Psychology*, **111**, 329–339.

Riddle, K. (2010) 'Always on my mind: exploring how frequent, recent, and vivid television portrayals are used in the formation of social reality judgments' *Media Psychology* 13 (2), 155–179.

Riggs, D.S., Dancu, C.V., Gerhuny, B.S., Greenberg, D. and Foa, E.B. (1992) 'Anger and post-traumatic stress disorder in female crime victims' *Journal of Traumatic Stress* **5** (4), 613–25.

Rivlin, A. (2007) 'Self harm and suicide at Grendon therapeutic community prison' *Prison Service Journal* **173**, 34–8.

Rivlin, A., Fazel, S., Marzano, L. and Hawton, K. (2013) 'The suicidal process in male prisoners making near-lethal suicide attempts' *Psychology, Crime and Law* **19** (4), 305–27.

Roach, J. (2010) 'Home is where the heart lies? A study of false address giving to police' *Legal and Criminological Psychology* **15**, 209–20.

Robbins, P. and Darlington, R. (2003) 'The role of industry and the Internet Watch Foundation' in A. MacVean and P. Spindler (eds) *Policing Paedophiles on the Internet* Bristol: New Police Bookshop, pp. 79–87.

Roberton, T., Daffern, M. and Bucks, R.S. (2012) 'Emotion regulation and aggression' *Aggression and Violent Behavior* **17**, 72–82.

Roberton, W., Daffern, M. and Bucks, R.S. (2014) 'Maladaptive emotion regulation and aggression in adult offenders' *Psychology, Crime and Law*, **20** (10), 933–954.

Roberts, A.D.L. and Coid, J.W. (2007) 'Psychopathy and offending behaviour: Findings from the national survey of prisoners in England and Wales' *Journal of Forensic Psychiatry & Psychology* **18** (1), 23–43.

Roberts, J.V., and Erez, E. (2004) 'Communication in sentencing: exploring the expressive function of victim impact statements' *International Review of Victimology***10**, 223–244

Roberts, K.A. (2005) 'Associated characteristics of stalking following the termination of romantic relationships' *Applied Psychology in Criminal Justice* **1** (1), 13–35.

Roberts, K.P. and Blades, M. (1995) 'Do children confuse memories of events seen on television and events witnessed in real life?' in N.K. Clark and G.M. Stephenson (eds) *Investigative and Forensic Decision Making, Issues in Criminological and Legal Psychology No. 26* Leicester: Division of Criminological and Legal Psychology, British Psychological Society, pp. 52–7.

Roberts, L. and Wagstaff, G.F. (1996) 'The effects of beliefs and information about hypnosis on the legal defence of automism through hypnosis' *Psychology, Crime and Law* **2**, 259–68.

Roberts, Y. (1995) 'Is this modern justice?' *Guardian* 7 October, p. 6.

Robertson, G., Gibb, R. and Pearson, R. (1995) 'Drunkenness among police detainees' *Addiction* **90**, 793–803.

Robertson, G., Pearson, R. and Gibb, R. (1996) 'Police interviewing and the use of appropriate adults' *Journal of Forensic Psychiatry* **7** (2), 297–309.

Robertson, K., McNeill, L., Green, J. and Roberts, C. (2012) 'Illegal Downloading, Ethical Concern, and Illegal Behavior' *Journal of Business Ethics* **108**, 215–27.

Robinson, J. (2015) 'The experience of the child witness: legal and psychological issues' *International Journal of Law and Psychiatry* 42–43, 168–176.

Robson, D. (2015) 'The strange expertise of burglars' http://www.bbc.

com/future/story/20150618-the-strange-expertise-of-burglars

Rochelle, S.M and Loschky, J. (2014) 'Confidence in judicial systems varies worldwide' Gallup http://www.gallup.com/poll/178757/confidence-judicial-systems-varies-worldwide.aspx

Rocque, M., Posick, C., Marshall, I.H. and Piquero, A.R. (2015) 'A comparative, cross-cultural criminal career analysis'. *European Journal of Criminology* **12** (4), 400–419.

Roesch, R., Ogloff, J.R.P. and Golding, S.L. (1993) 'Competence to stand trial: legal and clinical issues' *Applied and Preventative Psychology* **2**, 45–51.

Roettger, M.E., Boardman, J.D., Harris, K,M, and Guo, G. (2016) 'The association between the MAOA 2R genotype and delinquency over time among men: the interactive role of parental closeness and parental incarceration' *Criminal Justice and Behaviour* **43** (8), 1076–1094.

Rogers, J. and Bloom, F. (1985) 'Neurotransmitter metabolism and function in the ageing central nervous system' in C.E. Finch, and E.L. Schneider (eds), *Handbook of Biology of Aging* (pp. 645–62). New York: Van Nostrand Reinhold.

Rogers, R., Fiduccia, C. E., Robinson, E. V., Steadham, J. A. and Drogin, E. Y. (2013) 'Investigating the effects of repeated Miranda warnings: Do they perform a curative function on common Miranda misconceptions?' *Behavioral Sciences and the Law* **31** (4), 397–529

Rogers, R., Fiduccia, C.E., Drogin, E.Y., Steadham, J.A., Clark, J.W. and Cramer, R.J. (2013) 'General knowledge and misknowledge of Miranda Rights: are effective Miranda Advisements still necessary?' Psychology, Public Policy, and Law 19 (4), 432–442

Romyn, D. and Kebbell, M. (2013) '"Terrorists" planning of attacks: a simulated "red-team" investigation into decision-making' *Psychology, Crime and Law* **20** (5).

Rose, M.R., Diamond, S.S. and Baker, K.M. (2010) 'Goffman on the Jury: Real Jurors' Attention to the "Offstage" of Trials' *Law and Human Behavior* **34** (4), 310–23.

Rosenthal, R. (1966) *Experimenter Effects in Behavioral Research* New York: Appleton-Century-Crofts.

Roshier, R.J. (1971) 'Crime and the press' *New Society* **468**, 502–6.

Roshier, R.J. (1973) 'The selection of crime news by the press' in S. Cohen and J. Young (eds) *The Manufacture of News* London: Constable, pp. 28–39.

Rosky, J.W. (2012) 'The (f)utility of post conviction polygraph testing' *Sexual Abuse: A Journal of Research and Treatment* **25** (3), 259–81.

Rossmo, D.K. (2000) *Geographic Profiling* Boca Raton, FL: CRC Press.

Rothmund,T., Bender, J., Nauroth, P., and Gollwitzer, M. (2015) 'Public concerns about violent video games are moral concerns—How moral threat can make pacifists susceptible to scientific and political claims against violent video games' *European Journal of Social Psychology*, **45** (6), 769–783.

Royo, J.B. di (1996) 'Legal psychology in Spain: reflections on its short history' in G. Davies, S. Lloyd-Bostock, M. McMurran and C. Wilson (eds) *Psychology, Law and Criminal Justice: International Developments in Research and Practice* Berlin: Walter de Gruyter, pp. 598–601.

Ruback, R.B. and Innes, C.A. (1988) 'The relevance and irrelevance of psychological research' *American Psychologist* **43** (9), 683–93.

Ruby, C.L. (2002) 'The definition of terrorism' *Analyses of Social Issues and Public Policy* **2** (1), 9–14.

Ruchkin, V.V., Eisemann, M. and Cloninger, C.R. (1998a) 'Behaviour/emotional problems in male juvenile delinquents and controls in Russia: the role of personality traits' *Acta Psychiatrica Scandinavica* **98**, 231–6.

Ruchkin, V.V., Eisemann, M. and Hagglof, B. (1998b) 'Aggression in delinquent adolescents versus controls: the role of parental rearing' *Children and Society* **12**, 275–82.

Ruchkin, V.V., Eisemann, M. and Hagglof, B. (1998c) 'Parental rearing and problem behaviours in male delinquent adolescents versus controls in Northern Russia' *Social Psychiatry and Psychiatric Epidemiology* **33**, 477–82.

Rulison, K.L.,Kreager,D.A., and Osgood, D.W. (2014) 'Delinquency and peer acceptance in adolescence: a within-person test of Moffitt's hypotheses' *Developmental Psychology* **50** (11), 2437–2448.

Rushton, J. P., and Templer, D. I. (2009) 'National differences in intelligence, crime, income, and skin color' *Intelligence* **37**, 341–346.

Rushton, J.P. (1990) 'Race differences, r/K theory, and a reply to Flynn' *The Psychologist: Bulletin of the British Psychological Society* **5**, 195–8.

Russano, M.B., Meissner, C.A., Narchet, F.M. and Kassin, S.M. (2005) 'Investigating true and false confessions within a novel experimental paradigm' *Psychological Science* **16** (6), 481–6.

Russell, C.A. and Miller, B.H. (1977) 'Profile of a terrorist' *Terrorism: An International Journal* **1** (1), 17–34.

Russell, D.E.H. (1988) 'Pornography and rape: a causal model' *Journal of Political Psychology* **9** (1), 41–73.

Russell, D.E.H. (1992) 'Pornography and rape: a causal model' in C. Itzin (ed.) *Pornography: Women, Violence and Civil Liberties* Oxford: Oxford University Press, pp. 310–49.

Ryan, N.P., Anderson, V., Godfrey, C., Beauchamp, M.H., Coleman, L., Eren, S., Rosema, S., Taylor, K., and Catroppa, C. (2014) 'Predictors of very long-term sociocognitive function after pediatric traumatic brain injury: evidence for the vulnerability of the immature "social brain"' *Journal of Neurotrauma* **31**. 649–657.

S

Sageman, M. (2004) *Understanding Terror Networks* Philadelphia: University of Pennsylvania Press.

Sakadi, A., Kristiansson, R., Oberklaid, F. and Bremberg, S. (2007) 'Fathers' involvement and children's developmental outcomes: a systematic review of longitudinal studies' *Acta Pædiatrica* **97**, 153–8.

Saks, M.J. (1987) 'Social scientists can't rig juries' in L.S. Wrightsman, S.M. Kassin and C.E. Willis (eds) *In the Jury Box: Controversies in the Courtroom* Thousand Oaks, CA: Sage, pp. 48–61.

Saks, M.J. and Marti, M. (1997) 'A meta-analysis of the effect of jury size' *Law and Human Behavior* **21**, 451–67.

Salerno, J.M., Najdowski, C.J., Stevenson, M.C., Wiley, T.R.A., Bottoms, B.L., Vaca, R. and Pimentel, P.S. (2010) 'Psychological mechanisms underlying support for juvenile sex offender registry laws: prototypes, moral outrage, and perceived threat' *Behavioral Sciences and the Law* **28**, 58–83.

Salfati, C.G. and Canter, D.V. (1998) 'Differentiating stranger murders: profiling offender characteristics from behavioral styles' *Behavioral Sciences and the Law* **17** (3), 391–406.

Salter, A.C. (1988) *Treating Child Sex Offenders and Victims: A Practical Guide* Newbury Park, CA: Sage.

Salter, D., McMillan, D., Richards, M., Talbot, T., Hodges, J., Bentovim, A., Hastings, R., Stevenson, J., Skuse, D. (2003) 'Development of sexually abusive behaviour in sexually victimised males: a longitudinal study' *The Lancet* **361**, 471–476.

Sampson, R.J. and Laub, J.H. (1990) 'Crime and deviance over the life course: The salience of adult social bonds' *American Sociological Review* **55** (5), 609–27.

Santtila, P., Korkman, J. and Sandnabba, N.K. (2004) 'Effects of interview phase, repeated interviewing, presence of a support person, and anatomically detailed dolls on child sexual abuse interviews' *Psychology, Crime and Law* **10**, 21–35.

Sarangi, S. and Alison, L. (2005) 'Life story accounts of left wing terrorists in India' *Journal of Investigative Psychology and Offender Profiling* **2**, 69–86.

Sarasalo, E., Bergman, B. and Toth, J. (1997) 'Kleptomania-like behaviour and psychosocial characteristics among shoplifters' *Legal and Criminological Psychology* **2**, 1–10.

Sattar, G. and Bull, R. (1996) 'Pre-court preparation for child witnesses' in N.K. Clark and G.M. Stephenson (eds) *Issues in Criminological and Legal Psychology 26, Child Witnesses* Leicester: British Psychological Society, Division of Criminological and Legal Psychology, pp. 67–75.

Saunders, R.C. (2012) 'Reconceptualizing false allegations of rape' *British Journal of Criminology* **52**, 1152–71.

Savage, J. and Yancey, C. (2008) 'The effects of media violence exposure on criminal aggression: a meta-analysis' *Criminal Justice and Behavior* **35**, 772–91.

Saywitz, K.J. (1994) 'Children in court: principles of child development for judicial application' in *A Judicial Primer on Child Sexual Abuse* Chicago: American Bar Association Center on Children and the Law.

Saywitz, K.J., Larson, R.P., Hobbs, S.D. and Wells, C.R. (2015) 'Developing rapport with children in forensic interviews: systematic review of experimental research' *Behavioral Sciences and the Law* **33**, 372–389.

Schauss, A. G. (1979) 'Tranquilizing effect of color reduces aggressive behavior and potential violence' *Journal of Orthomolecular Psychiatry* **8**, 218–221.

Scheflin, A.W. (2012) 'How not to conduct a forensic hypnosis interview: a case study' *American Journal of Clinical Hypnosis* **55** (1), 68–84.

Schenk, A.M. and Fremouw, W.J. (2012) 'Individual characteristics related to prison violence: A critical review of the literature' *Aggression and Violent Behavior* **17**, 430–42.

Schiffer, B., Peschel, T., Paul, T., Gizwski, E., Forsting, M., Leygraf, N., Schedlowski, M. and Kruege, H.C. (2007) 'Structural brain abnormalities in the frontostriatal system and cerebellum in pedophilia' *Journal of Psychiatric Research* **41** (9), 753–62.

Schipkowensky, N. (1973) 'Epidemiological aspects of homicide' in Arieta, S. (ed.) *World Biennial of Psychiatry and Psychotherapy* New York: Basic Books.

Schlesinger, P., Tumber, H. and Murdock, G. (1991) 'The media politics of crime and criminal justice' *British Journal of Sociology* **42** (3), 397–420.

Schmid, J. and Fiedler, K. (1998) 'The backbone of closing speeches: the impact of prosecution versus defense language on judicial attributions' *Journal of Applied Social Psychology* **28** (13), 1140–72.

Schmucker, M. and Lösel, F. (2015) 'The effects of sexual offender treatment on recidivism: an international meta-analysis of sound quality evaluations' *Journal of Experimental Criminology* **11**, 597–630.

Schreck, C.J., Fisher, B.S. and Miller, J.M. (2004) 'The social context of violent victimization: a study of the delinquent peer effect' *Justice Quarterly* **21**, 23–48.

Schreck, C.J., Wright, R.A. and Miller, J.M. (2004) 'A study of individual and situational antecedents of violent victimization' *Justice Quarterly* **19** (1), 159–180.

Schulman, J., Shaver, P., Colman, R., Emrich, B. and Christie, R. (1973) 'Recipe for a jury' *Psychology Today* May, 37–44, 77–84.

Schwalbe, C.S. (2007) 'Risk assessment for juvenile justice: a meta-analysis' *Law and Human Behavior* **31** (5), 449–62.

Scott, A. J., Gavin, J., Sleath, E. and Sheridan, L. (2014) 'The attribution of responsibility in cases of stalking' *Psychology, Crime & Law*, **20** (7), 705–721.

Scott, A.J., Rajakaruna, N., and Sheridan.L. (2014) 'Framing and perceptions of stalking: the influence of conduct severity and the perpetrator–target relationship' *Psychology, Crime and Law*, **20** (3), 242–260.

Scott, J.E. and Schwalm, L.A. (1988) 'Pornography and rape: an examination of adult theater rates and rape rates by state' in J.E. Scott and T. Hirschi (eds) *Controversial Issues in Crime and Justice* Beverly Hills: Sage, pp. 40–53.

Scott, N., Higgs, P., Caulkins, J.P., Aitken, C., Cogger, S. and Dietzel, P. (2016) 'The introduction of CCTV and associated changes in heroin purchase and injection settings in Footscray, Victoria, Australia' *Journal of Experimental Criminology* **12**, 265–275.

Scottish Executive (2003) 'Guidance on interviewing child witnesses and victims in Scotland' Scottish Executive, Edinburgh, http://www.scotland.gov.uk/Publications/2003/09/18265/27036

Scullin, M.H., Kanaya, T. and Ceci, S.J. (2002) 'Measurements of individual differences in children's suggestibility across situations' *Journal of Experimental Psychology: Applied* **8** (4), 233–46.

Scully, D. and Marolla, J. (1984) 'Convicted rapists' vocabulary of motives: excuses and justifications' *Social Problems* **31** (5), 530–44.

Sealy, A.P. and Cornish, W.R. (1973) 'Juries and the rules of evidence' *Criminal Law Review* 208–23.

Sear, L. and Williamson, T. (1999) 'British and American interrogation strategies' in D. Canter and L. Alison (eds) *Interviewing and Deception* Dartmouth: Ashgate, pp. 67–81.

Sears, D.O., and Funk, C.L. (1991) 'The role of self-interest in social and political attitudes' in M. Zana (Ed.), *Advances in Experimental Social Psychology* (Vol. 24, pp. 1–91) Orlando, FL: Academic Press.

Security Service: MI5 (2007) 'Counter-terrorism spending increased' (10 October 2007 http://www.mi5.gov.uk/output/Page541.html (accessed 6 December 2007).

Seltzer, R. (2006) 'Scientific jury selection: Does it work?' *Journal of Applied Social Psychology* **36**, 2417–35.

Senior, J., Hayes, A.J., Pratti, D., Thomas, S.D., Fahy, T., Leese, M., Bowen, A., Taylor, G., Lever-Green, G., Graham, T., Pearson, A., Ahmed, M. and Shaw, J.J. (2007) 'The identification and management of suicide risk in local prisons' *Journal of Forensic Psychiatry and Psychology* **3**, 368–80.

Serin, R.C., Chadwick, N. and Lloyd, C.D. (2016) 'Dynamic risk and protective factors' *Psychology, Crime and Law* **22** (1–2), 151–170.

Seto, M.C. (2012) 'Is Pedophilia a Sexual Orientation?' *Archives of Sexual Behavior* **41**, 231–6.

Seto, M.C. and Eke, A.W. (2005) 'The criminal histories and later offending of child pornography offenders' *Sexual Abuse: A Journal of Research and Treatment* **17** (2), 201–10.

Seto, M.C. and Lalumiere, M.L. (2001) 'A brief screening scale to identify pedophilic interests among child molesters' *Sexual Abuse: A Journal of Research and Treatment* **13**, 15–25.

Seto, M.C. and Lalumiere, M.L. (2010) 'What is so special about male adolescent sexual offending? A review and test of explanations through meta-analysis' *Psychological Bulletin* **136** (4), 526–75.

Seto, M.C., Babchishin, K.M., Pullman, L.E. and McPhail, I.V. (2015) 'The puzzle of intrafamilial child sexual abuse: A meta-analysis comparing intrafamilial and extrafamilial offenders with child victims' *Clinical Psychology Review* **39**, 42–57.

Seto, M.C., Lalumière, M.L., Harris, G.T. and Chivers, M.L. (2012) 'The sexual responses of sexual sadists' *Journal of Abnormal Psychology* **121**, 739–53.

Sevier, J. (2014) 'The truth-justice tradeoff: perceptions of decisional accuracy and procedural justice in adversarial and inquisitorial legal systems' *Psychology, Public Policy, and Law* **20** (2), 212–224.

Shackley, M., Weiner, C., Day, A. and Willis, G.M. (2013) 'Assessment of public attitudes towards sex offenders in an Australian population' *Psychology, Crime and Law* 1–20.

Shadish, W.R. (1984) 'Policy research: lessons from the implementation of deinstitutionalization' *American Psychologist* **39** (7), 725–38.

Shaffer, D.R. (1985) 'The defendant's testimony' in S.M. Kassin and L.S. Wrightsman (eds) *The Psychology of Evidence and Trial Procedure* Beverly Hills, CA: Sage, pp. 124–49.

Shaffer, D.R. and Case, T. (1982) 'On the decision to testify in one's own behalf: Effects of withheld evidence, defendant's sexual preferences, and juror dogmatism on juridic decisions' *Journal of Personality and Social Psychology* **42**, 335–46.

Shaffer, D.R. and Sadowski, C. (1979) 'Effects of withheld evidence on juridic decision II: Locus of withholding strategy' *Personality and Social Psychology Bulletin* **5**, 40–3.

Shapiro, P.N. and Penrod, S. (1986) 'Meta-analysis of facial identification studies' *Psychological Bulletin* **100**, 139–56.

Shapland, J., Atkinson, A., Atkinson, H., Dignana, J., Edwards, L., Hibbert, J., Howes, M., Johnstone, J., Robinson, G. and Sorsby, A.L. (2008) *Restorative Justice: Does Restorative Justice affect reconviction? The fourth report from the evaluation of three schemes.* Ministry of Justice Research Series 10/08, http://www.restorativejustice.org.uk/resource/ministry_of_justice_evaluation_does_restorative_justice_affect_reconviction_the_fourth_report_from_the_evaluation_of_three_schemes/

Sharma, L., Markon, K.E., and Clark, L.A. (2014) 'Toward a theory of distinct types of "impulsive" behaviors: a meta-analysis of self-report and behavioral measures' *Psychological Bulletin* **140** (2), 374–408.

Shaw, C.R. and McKay, H.D. (1942) *Juvenile Delinquency in Urban Areas* Chicago: University of Chicago Press.

Shaw, J., Appleby, L., Ames, T., McDonnell, R., Harris, C., McCann, K., Kiernan, K., Davies, S., Biddey, H. and Parsons, R. (1999) 'Mental disorder and clinical care in people convicted of homicide: national clinical survey' *British Medical Journal* **318** (8 May), 1240–4.

Shaw, J., Öhman, L. and van Koppen, P. (2013). 'Psychology and Law: The Past, Present, and Future of the

Discipline' *Psychology, Crime and Law* **19**, 643–7.

Shaw, M. and Pease, K. (2002) 'Minor crimes, trivial incidents: the cumulative impact of offending' *Issues in Forensic Psychology* **3**, 41–8.

Sheehan, P.W. (1997) 'Recovered memories: towards resolution of some issues across experimental and clinical domains'. Unpublished manuscript, University of Queensland, Australia. Plenary address, 14th International Congress of Hypnosis, San Diego, USA, June.

Sheldon, K. (2004) 'A new type of sex offender? Recent findings on Internet sex offenders: a pilot study' *Forensic Update* **79**, 24–31.

Sheldon, K. and Howitt, D. (2007) *Sex Offenders and the Internet* Chichester: John Wiley and Sons.

Sheldon, K. and Howitt, D. (2008) 'Sexual fantasy in paedophile offenders: can any model explain satisfactorily new findings from a study of Internet and contact sexual offenders?' *Legal and Criminological Psychology* **13** (1), 137–58.

Sheldon, W.H. (1940) *The Varieties of Human Physique: An Introduction to Constitutional Psychology* New York: Harper.

Sheldon, W.H. (1942) *The Varieties of Temperament: A Psychology of Constitutional Differences* New York: Harper.

Sheldon, W.H. (1949) *Varieties of Delinquent Youth: An Introduction to Constitutional Psychiatry* New York: Harper.

Shepherd, E. (2007) *Investigative Interviewing: The Conversation Management Approach* Oxford: Oxford University Press.

Shepherd, E. and Milne, R. (1999) 'Full and faithful: ensuring quality practice and integrity of outcome in witness interviews' in A. Heaton-Armstrong, E. Shepherd, D. Wochover and Lord Bingham of Cornhill (eds) *Analysing Eyewitness Testimony: Psychological, Investigative and Evidential Perspectives* London: Blackstone Press, pp. 124–45.

Shepherd, E.W., Mortimer, A.K.O. and Mobaseri, R. (1995) 'The police caution: comprehension and perceptions in the general population' *Expert Evidence* **4**, 60–7.

Sheridan, L. and Davies, G.M. (2001) 'What is stalking? The match between legislation and public perception' *Legal and Criminological Psychology* **6**, 3–17.

Sheridan, L. and Davies, G.M. (2002) 'Stalking: the elusive crime' *Legal and Criminological Psychology* **6**, 133–47.

Sheridan, L., Scott, A.J., and Nixon, K. (2016) 'Police officer perceptions of harassment in England and Scotland' *Legal and Criminological Psychology* **21**, 1–14.

Sheridan, L.P. and Grant, T. (2007) 'Is cyberstalking different?' *Psychology, Crime and Law* **13** (6), 627–40.

Sherman, L. and Strang, H. (2007) *Restorative Justice: The Evidence*, London: Smith Institute.

Sherman, L.W., Gartin, P.R. and Buerger, M.E. (1989) 'Hot spots of predatory crime: Routine activities and the criminology of place' *Criminology* **27**, 27–55.

Sherman, L.W., Strang, H., Angel, C., Woods, D., Barnes, G., Bennett, S., Inkpen, N. and Rossner, M. (2005) 'Effects of face-to-face restorative justice on victims of crime in four randomized, controlled trials' *Journal of Experimental Criminology* **1** (3), 367–95.

Sherman, L.W., Strang, H., Barnes, G., Woods, D.J., Bennett, S., Inkpen, N., Newbury-Birch, D., Rossner, M., Angel, C., Mearns, M., and Slothower, M. (2015) 'Twelve experiments in restorative justice: the Jerry Lee program of randomized trials of restorative justice conferences' *Journal of Experimental Criminology* **11**, 501–540.

Sherman, Ms., Fostick, L. and Zohar, J. (2005) 'Comparison of criminal activity between Israeli veterans with and without PTSD' *Depression and Anxiety*, **31**, 143–149.

Shevlin, M., Hyland, P., and Elklit, A. (2014) 'Different profiles of acute stress disorder differentially predict posttraumatic stress disorder in a large sample of female victims of sexual trauma' *Psychological Assessment* 26 (4), 1155–1131

Shigihara, A.M. (2013) 'It's Only Stealing a Little a Lot: Techniques of Neutralization for Theft Among Restaurant Workers' *Deviant Behavior* **34**, 494–512.

Shine, J. and Morris, M. (2000) 'Addressing criminogenic needs in a prison therapeutic community' *Therapeutic Communities* **21** (3), 197–219.

Shover, N, and Hochstetler, A. (2002) 'Cultural explanation and organizational crime' *Law and Social Change*, **37**, 1–18.

Shrum, L.J. (1996) 'Psychological processes underlying communication effects' *Human Communication Research* **22** (4), 482–509.

Shuker, R. (2010) 'Forensic therapeutic communities: a critique of treatment model and evidence base' *Howard Journal* **49** (5), 463–77.

Shulman, E.P., Cauffman, E., Piquero, A.R., and Fagan, J. (2011) 'Moral disengagement among serious juvenile offenders: a longitudinal study of the relations between morally disengaged attitudes and offending' *Developmental Psychology*, **47** (6), 1619–1632.

Shutz, W. (1994) *The Human Element: Productivity, Self-esteem and the Bottom Line* San Francisco, CA: Jossey-Bass.

Shuy, R.W. (1998) *The Language of Confession, Interrogation and Deception* Thousand Oaks, CA: Sage.

Shye, S. (1985) 'A nonmetric model for behavioral action systems' in D. Canter (ed.) *Facet Theory: Approaches to Social Research* New York: Springer-Verlag, pp. 97–148.

Shye, S. and Elizur, D. (1994) *Introduction to Facet Theory: Content Design and Intrinsic Data Analysis in Behavioural Research* Thousand Oaks, CA: Sage.

Siegelman, C.K., Budd, E.C., Spanhel, C.I. and Schoenrock, C.J. (1981)

'When in doubt say yes: acquiescence in interviews with mentally retarded persons' *Mental Retardation* **19**, 53–8.

Sigall, H. and Ostrove, N. (1975) 'Beautiful but dangerous: Effects of offender attractiveness and nature of the crime on juridic judgment' *Journal of Personality and Social Psychology* **31**, 410–14.

Sigfusdottir, I.D., Gudjonsson, G.H. and Sigurdsson, J.F. (2010) 'Bullying and delinquency: The mediating role of anger' *Personality and Individual Differences* **48**, 391–6.

Signorielli, N. and Gerbner, G. (1988) *Violence and Terror in the Mass Media* New York: Greenwood.

Sigurdsson, J. F., and Gudjonsson, G. H. (1996) 'Illicit drug use among "false confessors": a study among Icelandic prison inmates' *Nordic Journal of Psychiatry* **50**, 325–328.

Sigurdsson, J.F. and Gudjonsson, G.H. (1997) 'The criminal history of "false confessors" and other prison inmates' *Journal of Forensic Psychiatry* **8** (2), 447–55.

Silas, F.A. (1985) 'Would a kid lie?' *Journal of the American Bar Association* **71**, 17.

Silke, A. (1998) 'Cheshire-Catalogic: the recurring theme of terrorist abnormality in psychological research' *Psychology, Crime and Law* **4** (1), 51–69.

Silke, A. (2003) 'Deindividuation, anonymity, and violence: findings from Northern Ireland' *Journal of Social Psychology* **143** (4), 493–9.

Silke, A. (2004) 'Introduction to terrorism research' in A. Silke (ed.) *Research on Terrorism: Trends, Achievements and Failures* London: Frank Cass, pp. 1–29.

Silva, J.A., Derecho, D.V., Leong, G.B., Weinstock, R. and Ferrari, M.M. (2001) 'A classification of psychological factors leading to violent behavior in posttraumatic stress disorder' *Journal of Forensic Sciences* **46** (2), 309–16.

Silvern, L., Karyl, J. and Landis, T. (1995) 'Individual psychotherapy for the traumatized children of abused women' in E. Peled, P. Jaffe and J. Edleson (eds) *Ending the Cycle of Violence: Community Responses to Children of Battered Women* Thousand Oaks, CA: Sage, pp. 43–76.

Simon, L. (2000) 'An examination of the assumptions of specialization, mental disorder, and dangerousness in sex offenders' *Behavioural Sciences and the Law* **18**, 275–308.

Simon, R.R. and Eimermann, T. (1971) 'The jury finds not guilty: another look at media influence on the jury' *Journalism Quarterly* **48**, 343–4.

Sinn, M.P.(2017) 'Think by numbers' https://thinkbynumbers.org/

Sjogren, L.H. (2000) 'Problems and sources of errors when investigating alleged child sexual abuse' in A. Czerederecka, T. Jaskiewicz-Obdzinska and J. Wojcikiewicz (eds) *Forensic Psychology and Law: Traditional Questions and New Ideas* Krakow: Institute of Forensic Research Publishers, pp. 246–9.

Sjostedt, G. and Langstrom, N. (2000) 'Assessment of risk for criminal recidivism among rapists: a comparison of four different measures'. Unpublished manuscript, Karolinska Institutet, Stockholm, Sweden.

Skeem, J.L. and Cooke, D.J. (2010) 'Criminal behavior a central component of psychopathy? Conceptual directions for resolving the debate' *Psychological Assessment* **22** (2), 433–45.

Skett, S. and Dalkin, A. (1999) 'Working with young offenders' *Issues in Forensic Psychology* **1**, 31–5.

Skolnick, J.H. (1966) *Justice Without Trial: Law Enforcement in a Democratic Society* New York: Wiley.

Slade, K., and Forrester, A. (2015) 'Shifting the paradigm of prison suicide prevention through enhanced multi-agency integration and cultural change' *Journal of Forensic Psychiatry and Psychology* **26** (6), 737–758.

Sleath, E., and Woodhams, J. (2014) 'Expectations about victim and offender behaviour during stranger rape' *Psychology, Crime and Law* **20** (8), 798–820.

Slobogin, C. (2006) *Minding Justice: Laws that Deprive People with Mental Disability of Life and Liberty* Cambridge, MA: Harvard University Press.

Sloore, H., Rossi, G. and Hauben, C. (2004) 'Are recidivists psychopaths?' Paper presented at the 14th European Conference of Psychology and Law, Krakow, Poland, July.

Slusser, M.M. (1995) 'Manifestations of sexual abuse in pre-school-aged children' *Issues in Mental Health Nursing* **16**, 481–91.

Smalarz, L., Buck, S., Madon, S., Yang, Y. and Guyll, M. (2016) 'The perfect match: do criminal stereotypes bias forensic evidence analysis?' *Law and Human Behavior* **40** (4), 420–429.

Smallbone, S., Marshall, W.L. and Wortley, R. (2008) *Preventing Child Sexual Abuse: Evidence, Policy and Practice* Cullompton, Devon: Willan Publishing.

Smallbone, S.W. and Wortley, R.K. (2000) *Child Sexual Abuse in Queensland: Offender Characteristics and Modus Operandi* Brisbane: Queensland Crime Commission.

Smeets, T., Merckelbach, H., Jelicic, M., and Otgaar, H. (2017) 'Dangerously neglecting courtroom realities' Applied Cognitive Psychology 31, 26–27.

Smith, A. (1977) 'Exploiting psychology in the name of the law: what benefits, what dangers?' *Science Forum* **57**, 25–7.

Smith, A.D. and Taylor, P.J. (1999) 'Serious sex offending against women by men with schizophrenia' *British Journal of Psychiatry* **174**, 233–7.

Smith, C. and Allen, J. (2004) 'Violent crime in England and Wales. Home Office Online Report 18/04', http://webarchive.nationala'rchives.gov.uk//20110218135832/rds.homeoffice.gov.uk//rds/pdfs04/rdsolr1804.pdf

Smith, J.A. (2008) *Qualitative Psychology: A Practical Guide to Research Methods* (2nd edn) London: Sage.

Smith, K., Taylor, P., and Elkin, M. (2013) *Crimes detected in England and*

Wales 2012/13 (2nd edn) London: National Statistics.

Smith, M.R. and Alpert, G.P. (2007) 'A theory of social conditioning and illusory correlation' *Criminal Justice and Behavior* **34** (10), 1262–83.

Smith, P., Goggin, C. and Gendreau, P. (2002) *The Effects of Prison Sentences and Intermediate Sanctions on Recidivism: General Effects and Individual Differences* Ottawa, ON: Correctional Services of Canada.

Smith, S.T., Edens, J.F., Clark, J. and Rulseh, A. (2014) '"So, what is a psychopath?" venire person perceptions, beliefs, and attitudes about psychopathic personality' *Law and Human Behavior* **38** (5), 490–500.

Smithson, M., Deady, S. and Gracik, L. (2007) 'Guilty, not guilty, or . . .? Multiple options in jury verdict choices' *Journal of Behavioral Decision Making* **20**, 481–98.

Snook, B., Cullen, R.M., Bennell, C., Taylor, P.J. and Gendreau, P. (2008) 'The criminal profiling illusion: What's behind the smoke and mirrors?' *Criminal Justice and Behavior* **35**, 1257–76.

Snook, B., Cullen, R.M., Mokros, A. and Harborts, S. (2005) 'Serial murderers' spatial decisions: factors that influence crime location choice' *Journal of Investigative Psychology and Offender Profiling* **2**, 147–64.

Snook, B., Dhami, M.K. and Kavanagh, J.M. (2011) 'Simply criminal: predicting burglars' occupancy decisions with a simple heuristic' *Law and Human Behavior,* **35**(4), 316–326

Snook, B., Eastwood, J., Gendreau, P. and Bennell, C. (2010) 'The importance of knowledge cumulation and the search for hidden agendas: a reply to Kocsis, Middledorp, and Karpin (2008)' *Journal of Forensic Psychology Practice* **10** (3), 214–23.

Snook, B., Eastwood, J., Gendreau, P., Goggin, C. and Cullen, R.M. (2007) 'Taking stock of criminal profiling: a narrative review and meta-analysis' *Criminal Justice and Behaviour* **34**, 437–53.

Snow, L., Paton, J., Oram, C. and Teers, R. (2002) 'Self-inflicted deaths during 2001: An analysis of trends' *The British Journal of Forensic Practice* **4** (4), 3–17.

Snyder, C.J., Lassiter, G.D., Lindberg, M.J. and Pinegar, S.K. (2009) 'Videotaped interrogations and confessions: does a dual-camera approach yield unbiased and accurate evaluations?' *Behavioral Sciences and the Law* **27**, 451–66.

Soibelman, M. (2004) 'Palestinian suicide bombers' *Journal of Investigative Psychology and Offender Profiling* **1**, 175–90.

Sorochinski, M. and Salfati, C.G. (2010) 'The consistency of inconsistency in serial homicide: Patterns of behavioral change across series' *Journal of Investigative Psychology and Offender Profiling* **7**, 109–36.

Sourander A., Jensen P., Rönning J.A., Niemelä, S., Helenius, H., Sillanmäki, L., Kumpulainen, K., Piha, J., Tamminen, T., Moilanen, I. and Almqvist, F. (2007) 'What is the long-term outcome of boys who steal at age eight? Findings from the Finnish nationwide "From A Boy To A Man" birth cohort study' *Pediatrics* **120** (2), 397–404.

Sparr, L.F. (2015) 'Combat-related PTSD in military court: a diagnosis in search of a defense' *International Journal of Law and Psychiatry* **39**, 23–30

Spiecker, S.C. and Worthington, D.L. (2003) 'The influence of opening statement/closing argument organization strategy on juror verdict and damage awards' *Law and Human Behavior* **27** (4), 437–56.

Sporer, S.L. (1993) 'Eyewitness identification accuracy, confidence, and decision times in simultaneous and sequential lineups' *Journal of Applied Psychology* **78**, 22–33.

Sprott, J.B. (1998) 'Understanding public opposition to a separate youth justice system' *Crime and Delinquency* **44** (3), 399–411.

Spruit, J.E. (1998) 'The penal conceptions of the emperor Marcus Aurelius in respect of lunatics' *International Journal of Law and Psychiatry* **21**, 315–33.

Stalans, L.J. (1996) 'Family harmony or individual protection? Public recommendation about how police can handle domestic violence situations' *American Behavioral Scientist* **39**, 433–48.

Stalenheim, E.G. (1997) *Psychopathy and Biological Markers in a Forensic Psychiatric Population* Uppsala: Acta Universitatis Upsaliensis.

Stams, G.J.M.M., Brugman, D., Dekovic, M., Van Rosmalen, L., Laan, P. van der *et al.* (2006) 'The moral judgment of juvenile delinquents: A meta-analysis' *Journal of Abnormal Child Psychology* **34**, 697–713.

Stanik, J.M. (1992) 'Psychology and law in Poland' in F. Losel, D. Bender and T. Bliesener (eds) *Psychology and Law: International Perspectives* Berlin: Walter de Gruyter, pp. 546–53.

Stanko, E.A. (1995) 'Women, crime, and fear' *Annals of the American Association for Political and Social Science* **539**, 46–58.

Stark, E. (1993) 'The myth of black violence' *Social Work* **38** (4), 485–90.

Staunton, C., and Hammond, S. (2016) 'Investigation of the labial photoplethysmograph (LPG) in the idiographic assessment of female sexual interest: its viability in the forensic context' *The Journal of Forensic Psychiatry and Psychology*, **27** (1), 110–134.

Steadman, H.J. and Cocozza, J.J. (1974) 'Some refinements in the measurement and prediction of dangerous behaviour' *American Journal of Psychiatry* **131** (9), 1012–14.

Steblay, N., Dysart, J., Fulero, S. and Lindsay, R.C.L. (2003) 'Eyewitness accuracy rates in police show-up and line-up presentations: a meta-analytic comparison' *Law and Human Behavior* **27** (5), 523–40.

Steblay, N.K., Dysart, J.E. and Wells, G.L. (2011) 'Seventy-two Tests of the Sequential Lineup Superiority Effect: A Meta-Analysis and Policy

Discussion' *Psychology, Public Policy, and Law* **17** (1), 99–139.

Steblay, N.K., Wells, G.L., and Douglass, A.B. (2014) 'The eyewitness post identification feedback effect 15 years later: theoretical and policy implications' *Psychology, Public Policy, and Law* **20** (1), 1–18.

Steck, P. (1998) 'Deadly ending marital conflicts'. Paper presented at 8th European Conference on Psychology and Law, Krakow, 2–5 September.

Steinberg, L. (2003) 'Juveniles on trial: MacArthur Foundation study calls competency into question' *Criminal Justice Magazine* **Fall 18** (3), http://www.americanbar.org/publications/criminal_justice_magazine_home/crimjust_juvjus_cjmag_18_3ls.html

Steinmetz, K.F. and Tunnel, K.D. (2013) 'Under the pixelated Jolly Roger: a study of on-line pirates' *Deviant Behavior* **34** (1), 53–67.

Steinmetz, S. (1977) 'The battered husband syndrome' *Victimology* **2**, 499–509.

Stekel, W. (1911) 'The sexual root of kleptomania' *Journal of the American Institute of Criminal Law and Criminology* **2** (2), 239–46.

Stephenson, G.M. (1992) *The Psychology of Criminal Justice* Oxford: Blackwell.

Stermac, L.E. and Quinsey, V.L. (1986) 'Social competence among rapists' *Behavioral Assessment* **8**, 171–81.

Stern, W. (1904) 'Die Aussage als geistige Leistung und als Verhörsprodukt' *Beiträge zur Psychologie der Aussage* **3**, 269–415.

Sternberg, K.J., Lamb, M.E., Hershkowitz, L., Orbach, Y., Esplin, P.W. and Hovav, M. (1997) 'Effects of introductory style on children's abilities to describe experiences of sexual abuse' *Child Abuse and Neglect* **21** (11), 1133–46.

Steward, M. and Steward, D. (1996) 'Interviewing young children about body touch and handling' *Monograph Series for the Society for Research in Child Development* **61** (4–5, Serial No. 248).

Steward, M.S. and Steward, D.S. (with L. Farquhar, J.E.B. Myers, M. Reinhart, J.Welker, N. Joye, J. Driskill, and J. Morgan) (1996) 'Interviewing young children about body touching and handling' *Monograph of the Society for Research in Child Development* **61** (4–5, Serial No. 248).

Stockburger, S.J. and Homar, H.A. (2014) 'Firesetting behavior and psychiatric distorder' in H. Omar, C. Bowling and J. Merrick (Eds.) *Playing with Fire* New York: Nova Science Publishers.

Stolzenberg, S.N., and Lyon, T.D. (2014) 'How attorneys question children about the dynamics of sexual abuse and disclosure in criminal trials' *Psychology, Public Policy, and Law* **20** (1), 19–30.

Stone, A.A., Smyth, J.M., Kaell, A. and Hurewitz, A. (2000) 'Structured writing about stressful events: exploring possible psychological mediators of positive health effects' *Health Psychology* **19** (6), 619–24.

Storey, J.E., Hart, S.D., Meloy, J. and Reavis, J.A. (2009) 'Psychopathy and stalking' *Law and Human Behavior* **33**, 237–46.

Straus, M. (1992) 'Sociological research and social policy: the case of family violence' *Sociological Forum* **7** (2), 211–37.

Straus, M., Hamby, S.L., Boney-McCoy, S. and Sugarman, D.B. (1996) 'The Revised Conflict Tactics Scales (CTS2)' *Journal of Family Issues* **76** (3), 283–316.

Strentz, T. (2006) *Psychological Aspects of Crisis Negotiation* Boca Raton, FL: CRC Press.

Strier, F. (1999) 'Whither trial consulting? Issues and projections' *Law and Human Behavior* **23**, 93–115.

Stromwall, L.A. and Granhag, P.A. (2003) 'How to detect deception? Arresting the beliefs of police officers, prosecutors and judges' *Psychology, Crime and Law* **9**, 19–36.

Stromwall, L.A. and Willen, R.M. (2011) 'Inside Criminal Minds: Offenders' Strategies when Lying' *Journal of Investigative Psychology and Offender Profiling* **8**, 271–81.

Stromwall, L.A., Alfredsson, H. and Landstrom, S. (2013) 'Blame attributions and rape: Effects of belief in a just world and relationship level' *Legal and Criminological Psychology* **18**, 254–61.

Studebaker, C.A. and Penrod, S.D. (1997) 'Pre-trial publicity' *Psychology, Public Policy and Law* **3** (2/3), 428–60.

Studebaker, C.A., Robbennolt, J.K., Pathak-Sharma, M.K. and Penrod, S.D. (2000) 'Assessing pre-trial publicity effects: integrating content analytic results' *Law and Human Behavior* **24**, 317–36.

Studer, L.H. and Reddon, J.R. (1998) 'Treatment may change risk prediction for sexual offenders' *Sexual Abuse: A Journal of Research and Treatment* **10** (3), 175–81.

Studer, L.H., Aylwin, A.S., Clelland, S.R., Reddon, J.R. and Frenzel, R.R. (2002) 'Primary erotic preference in a group of child molesters' *International Journal of Law and Psychiatry* **25**, 173–80.

Sullivan, J. and Beech, A. (2003) 'Are collectors of child abuse images a risk to children?' in A. MacVean and P. Spindler (eds) *Policing Paedophiles on the Internet* Bristol: New Police Bookshop, pp. 11–20.

Sutherland, E. (1949) *White Collar Crime* New Haven, CT: Yale University Press.

Sutton, R.M., Robinson, B., and Farrall, S.D. (2011) 'Gender, fear of crime, and self-presentation: an experimental investigation' *Psychology, Crime and Law* **17** (5) '421–433.

Swanson, J.W., Holzer, C.E., Ganju, V.K. and Jono, R.T. (1990) 'Violence and psychiatric disorder in the community: evidence from the epidemiologic catchment area surveys' *Hospital and Community Psychiatry* **41**, 761–70.

Sykes, G. (1958) *The Society of Captives* Princeton, NJ: Princeton University Press.

Sykes, G.M. and Matza, D. (1957) 'Techniques of neutralization: a theory of delinquency' *American Sociological Review* **22**, 664–70.

Szegedi, M. (1998) 'The development of Hungarian forensic psychology' in J. Boros, I. Munnich and M. Szegedi (eds) *Psychology and Criminal Justice: International Review of Theory and Practice* Berlin: Walter de Gruyter, pp. 441–56.

Szumski, J. (1993) 'Fear of crime, social rigorism and mass media in Poland' *International Review of Victimology* **2**, 209–15.

T

Tabor, P.D. (2011). Vicarious traumatization: Concept analysis' *Journal of Forensic Nursing* **7** (4), 203–208.

Taft, C.T., Pless, A.P., Stalans, L.J. *et al.* (2005) 'Risk factors for partner violence among a national sample of combat veterans' *Journal of Consulting and Clinical Psychology*, **73** (1), 151–159.

Taft, C.T., Vogt, D.S., Marshall, A.D., Panuzio, J. and Niles, B.L. (2007) 'Aggression among combat veterans: relationships with combat exposure and symptoms of post traumatic stress disorder, dysphoria, and anxiety' *Journal of Traumatic Stress*, **20** (2), 135–145.

Talwar, V. and Crossman, A.M. (2012) 'Children's lies and their detection: Implications for child witness testimony' *Developmental Review* **32**, 337–59.

Tarry, H. and Emler, N. (2007) 'Attitudes, values and moral reasoning as predictors of delinquency' *British Journal of Developmental Psychology* **25** (2), 169–83.

Tartaro, C. and Ruddell, R. (2006) 'Trouble in Mayberry: A national analysis of suicide attempts in small jails' *American Journal of Criminal Justice* **31**(1), 81–101.

Taylor, D.M. and Louis, W.R. (2004) 'Terrorism and the quest for identity' in F. Moghaddam and A.J. Marsella (eds) *Understanding Terrorism: Psychosocial Roots, Consequences, and Interventions* Washington, DC: APA Press, pp. 169–85.

Taylor, J. (2005) 'The relationship between violence and psychosis: time for a different approach?' *Forensic Update* **82**, 10–14.

Taylor, M. (2010) 'Is terrorism a group phenomenon?' *Aggression and Violent Behavior* **15**, 121–9.

Taylor, M. and Quayle, E. (1994) *Terrorist Lives* London: Brassey's Publishers.

Taylor, M. and Quayle, E. (2003) *Child Pornography: An Internet Crime* Hove: Brunner-Routledge.

Taylor, M. F. (2010) 'Addicted to the risk, recognition and respect that the graffiti lifestyle provides: towards the understanding of the reasons for graffiti engagement' *International Journal of Mental Health and Addiction*, **10**, 54–68.

Taylor, S.E. and Fiske, S.T. (1975) 'Point of view and perception so causality' *Journal of Personality and Social Psychology* **32**, 439–45.

Taylor, S.E. and Fiske, S.T. (1978) 'Salience, attention, and attribution: Top of the head phenomenon' in L. Berkowitz (ed.) *Advances in Experimental Social psychology* Vol. 11 New York: Academic Press, pp. 249–88.

Teasdale, B. (2009) 'Mental disorder and violent victimization' *Criminal Justice and Behavior* **36**, 513–35.

Technical Working Group on Eyewitness Evidence (1999) *Eyewitness Evidence: A Guide for Law Enforcement* Washington, DC: US Department of Justice.

Tedeschi, J. and Felson, R.B. (1994) *Violence, Aggression, and Coercive Actions* Washington, DC: American Psychological Association.

Thaler, R.H. and Sunstein, C.R. (2008) *Nudge: Improving Decisions About Health, Wealth and Happiness* New Haven: Yale University Press.

The Guardian (2015) 'Number of people killed by US police in 2015 at 1,000 after Oakland shooting', 16 November.

The National Federal Courts Rules Committee (2017) 'Federal rules of evidence'. https://www.rulesofevidence.org/article-vi/

Thibaut, J. and Walker, L. (1975) *Procedural Justice: A Psychological Analysis* Hillsdale, NJ: Wiley.

Thompson, B. (1994) *Soft Core: Moral Crusades Against Pornography in Britain and America* London: Cassell.

Thompson, E.R. (2007) 'Development and validation of an internationally reliable short-form of the positive and negative affect schedule (PANAS)' *Journal of Cross-Cultural Psychology*. **38** (2): 227–242

Thompson, W.C. (2010) 'An American psychology–law society scientific review paper on police interrogation and confession' *Law and Human Behavior* **34**, 1–2.

Thompson, W.C., and Newman, E.J. (2015) 'Lay understanding of forensic statistics: evaluation of random match probabilities, likelihood ratios, and verbal equivalents' *Law and Human Behavior* **39** (4), 332–349.

Thornberry, Terence P. (ed.) 1997 *Developmental Theories of Crime and Delinquency* New Brunswick, NJ: Transaction Publishers.

Thornhill, R. and Palmer, T. (2000) *A Natural History of Rape: Biological Bases of Sexual Coercion* Cambridge, MA: MIT Press.

Thornhill, R., and Thornhill, N. (1992) 'The evolutionary psychology of men's coercive sexuality' *Behavioral and Brain Sciences* **15**, 363–375.

Thornton, D. (2016) 'Developing a theory of dynamic risk' *Psychology, Crime and Law* **22** (1–2), 138–150.

Thornton, D., and Knight, R. (2007) 'Is denial always bad?' Presentation at the 26th Annual Research and Treatment Conference of the Association for the Treatment of Sexual Abusers, San Diego, CA.

Thurstone, L.L. (1922) 'The intelligence of policemen' *Journal of Personnel Research* **1**, 67–74.

Tieger, T. (1981) 'Self-rated likelihood of raping and the social perception of rape' *Journal of Research in Personality* **15**, 147–58.

Tisak, M. (1995) 'Domains of social reasoning and beyond' in R. Vasta (ed.) *Annals of Child Development* Vol. 11 London: Jessica Kingsley, pp. 95–130.

Tjaden, P. and Thoennes, N. (1998) *Stalking in America: Findings from the National Violence against Women Survey* Washington, DC: US Department of Justice.

Tjaden, P. and Thoennes, N. (2000) *Full Report of the Prevalence, Incidence, and Consequences of Violence Against Women: Findings from the National Violence Against Women Survey*. Research Report. Washington, DC: National Institute of Justice and the Centers for Disease Control and Prevention.

Tolin, D.F., and Foa, E.B. (2006) 'Sex differences in trauma and posttraumatic stress disorder: a quantitative review of 25 years of research' *Psychological Bulletin* **132**(6), 959–992.

Tonkin, M., Bond, J.W. and Woodhams, J. (2009) 'Fashion conscious burglars? Testing the principles of offender profiling with footwear impressions recovered at domestic burglaries', *Psychology, Crime and Law* **15** (4), 327–45.

Tonks, J., Slater, A., Frampton, I., Wall, S.E., Yates, P., Williams, W.H. (2008) 'The development of emotion and empathy skills after childhood brain injury' *Developmental Medicine and Child Neurology* **51**, 8–16.

Topalli, V., Jacques, S., and Wright, R. (2015) '"It takes skills to take a car": perceptual and procedural expertise in carjacking' *Agression and Violent Behavior* **20**, 19–25.

Torpy, D. (1994) 'You must confess' in N.K. Clark and G.M. Stephenson (eds) *Rights and Risks: The Application of Forensic Psychology* Leicester: British Psychological Society, pp. 21–3.

Torres, A.N., Boccaccini, M.T. and Miller, H.A. (2006) 'Perceptions of the validity and utility of criminal profiling among forensic psychologists and psychiatrists' *Professional Psychology: Research and Practice* **37** (1), 51–8.

Towl, G. (1995) 'Anger management groupwork' in G.J. Towl (ed.) *Groupwork in Prisons. Issues in Criminological and Legal Psychology, No. 23* Leicester: British Psychological Society, pp. 31–5.

Towl, G. (1996) 'Homicide and suicide: assessing risk in prisons' *The Psychologist* **9** (9), 398–400.

Towl, G. and Crighton, D.A. (1996) *The Handbook of Psychology for Forensic Practitioners* London: Routledge.

Towl, G. and Crighton, D. (2000) 'Risk assessment and management' in G. Towl, L. Snow and M. McHugh (eds) *Suicide in prisons* Leicester: British Psychological Society, 66–92.

Towl, G., and Crighton, D. (2016) 'The emperor's new clothes?' *The Psychologist* **29** (3), 188–191..

Townsend, E. (2007) 'Suicide terrorists: Are they suicidal?' *Suicide and Life Threatening Behavior* **37** (1), 35–49.

Tracy, P.E., Wolfgang, M.E. and Figlio, R.M. (1990) *Delinquency Careers in Two Birth Cohorts* New York: Plenum Press.

Travin, S., Bluestone, H., Coleman, E., Cullen, K. and Melella, M.S.W. (1985) 'Pedophile types and treatment perspectives' *Journal of Forensic Science* **31** (2), 614–20.

Tseloni, A., Wittebrood, K., Farrell, G. and Pease, K. (2004) 'Burglary victimisation in England and Wales, the United States and the Netherlands: a cross-national comparative test of routine activities and lifestyle theories' *British Journal of Criminology* **44**, 66–91.

Ttofi, M.M., Farrington, D.P. and Lösel, F. (2012) 'School bullying as a predictor of violence later in life: A systematic review and meta-analysis of prospective longitudinal studies' *Aggression and Violent Behavior* **17**, 405–18.

Tull, M.T., Jakupcak, M., Paulson, A. and Gratz, K.L. (2007) 'The role of emotional inexpressivity and experiential avoidance in the relationship between posttraumatic stress disorder symptom severity and aggressive behavior among men exposed to interpersonal violence' *Anxiety, Stress, and Coping* **20**, 337–51.

Tulving, E. (1974) 'Cue-dependent forgetting' *American Scientist* **62**, 74–8.

Turiel, E. (1983) *The Development of Social Knowledge: Morality and Convention* Cambridge: Cambridge University Press.

Turiel, E. and Nucci, L. (1978) 'Social interactions and the development of social concepts in preschool children' *Child Development* **49**, 400–7.

Tyler, T. and Lind, E.A. (1992) 'A relational model of authority in groups' in M.P. Zanna (ed.) *Advances in Experimental Social Psychology, Vol. 25* San Diego: Academic Press, pp. 115–91.

U

Ullman, S.E. and Peter-Hagene, L. (2014) 'Social reactions to sexual assault disclosure, coping, perceived control, and PTSD symptoms in sexual assault victims' *Journal of Community Psychology* **42**(4), 495–508.

Ullman, S.E.,Townsend, S.M., Fililpas,H.H. and Starzynski, L.L. (2007) 'Structural models of the relations of assault severity, social support, avoidance coping, self-blame, and PTSD among sexual assault survivors' *Psychology of Women Quarterly* **31**, 23–37.

Umanath, S., Sarezky, D. and Finger, S. (2011) 'Sleepwalking through history: medicine, arts, and courts of law' *Journal of the History of the Neurosciences* **20** (4), 253–76.

Undeutsch, U. (1992) 'Highlights of the history of forensic psychology in Germany' in F. Lösel, D. Bender and T. Bliesener (eds) *Psychology and Law: International Perspectives* Berlin: Walter de Gruyter, pp. 509–18.

US Census Bureau (2011) 'The 2011 Statistical Abstract'. http://www.census.gov/compendia/statab/cats/law_

enforcement_courts_prisons//crimes_and_crime_rates.html. Accessed 28 March 2011.

US Department of Commerce, Economics and Statistics Information (1996) *Statistical Abstract of the United States* Washington, DC: US Government Printing Office.

V

Valier, C. (1998) *Psychoanalysis and Crime in Britain During the Interwar Years. The British Criminology Conferences: Selected Proceedings. Volume 1: Emerging Themes in Criminology*, http://britsoccrim.org/volume1/012.pdf

Van den Bos, K. and Lind, E.A. (2002) 'Uncertainty management by means of fairness judgments' in M.P. Zanna (ed.) *Advances in Experimental Social Psychology* Vol. 34, San Diego, CA: Academic Press, pp. 1–60.

Van den Bos, K. and Maas, M. (2009) 'On the psychology of the belief in a just world: exploring experiential and rationalistic paths to victim blaming' *Personality and Social Psychology Bulletin* **35**, 1567–78.

Van Dijk, J., van Kesteren, J. and Smit, P. (2007) 'Criminal Victimisation in International Perspective: Key findings from the 2004–2005 ICVS and EU ICS' Tilburg University: Wetenschappelijk Onderzoeken Documentatiecentrum. http://www.unicri.it/services/library_documentation/publications/icvs/publications/ICVS2004_05report.pdf

van Emmerik, A.P., Kamphuis, J.H., Hulsbosch, A.M. and Emmelkamp, P.M.G. (2002) 'Single session debriefing after psychological trauma: a meta-analysis' *The Lancet* **360**, 766–771.

Van Gelder, J.-L. (2013) 'Beyond rational choice: the hot/cool perspective of criminal decision making' *Psychology, Crime and Law*, **19** (9), 745–763.

van Hasselt, V.B., Romano, S.J. and Vecchi, G.M. (2008) 'Role playing: Applications in hostage and crisis negotiation skills training' *Behavior Modification* **32** (2), 248–63.

Van Koppen, P.J. (1995) 'Judges' decision-making' in R. Bull and D. Carson (eds) *Handbook of Psychology in Legal Contexts* Chichester: John Wiley, pp. 581–610.

Van Koppen, P.J. and Lochun, S.K. (1997) 'Portraying perpetrators: the validity of offender descriptions by witnesses' *Law and Human Behaviour* **21** (6), 661–85.

Van Ness, D. W. and Strong, K. H. (2015) Restoring Justice: *An Introduction to Restorative Justice* London: Routledge.

Van Wallendael, L. and Cutler, B. (2004) 'Limitations to empirical approaches to jury selection' *Journal of Forensic Psychology Practice* **4** (2), 79–86.

Vanderveen, G. (2006) *Interpreting Fear, Crime, Risk and Unsafety* Collumpton, Devon: Willan.

Vandiver, D.M. (2006) 'A prospective analysis of juvenile male sex offenders characteristics and recidivism rates as adults' *Journal of Interpersonal Violence* **21** (5), 673–688.

Vaughn, M.G., DeLisi, M., Beaver, K.M. and Howard, M.O. (2008) 'Toward a quantitative typology of burglars: a latent profile analysis of career offenders' *Journal of Forensic Science* **53** (6), 1387–92.

Vecchi, G.M., Van Hasselt, V.B. and Romano, S.S. (2005) 'Crisis (hostage) negotiation: Current strategies and issues in high-risk conflict resolution' *Aggression and Violent Behaviour* **10**, 533–51.

Vidmar, N. (2008) 'Civil juries in ecological context: Methodological implications for research' in B. H. Bornstein, R. L.Wiener, R.Schopp and S. L.Willborn (eds.) *Civil Juries and Civil Justice: Psychological and Legal Perspectives* (pp. 35–65). New York, NY: Springer Science + Business Media.

Vieraitis, L.M., Copes, H., Powell, Z.A. and Pike, A. (2015) 'A little information goes a long way: expertise and identity theft' *Aggression and Violent Behavior* **20**, 10–18.

Villar, G., Arciuli, J. and Patterson, H. (2013) 'Linguistic Indicators of a False Confession' *Psychiatry, Psychology and Law* **20** (4), 504–18.

Villar, G., Arciuli, J., and Paterson, H.M. (2014) 'Remorse in oral and handwritten false confessions' *Legal and Criminological Psychology* **19**, 255–269.

Visher, C.A. (1987) 'Juror decision making; The importance of evidence' *Law and Human Behavior* **11** (1), 1–17.

Visionmetric Forensic imaging (2017) 'About E-FIT' http://www.visionmetric.com/products/about-e-fit/

Vitacco, M.J., Viljoen, J. and Petrila, J. (2009) 'Introduction to this issue: adolescent sexual offending' *Behavioral Sciences and the Law* **27**, 857–61.

Vitelli, R. and Endler, N.S. (1993) 'Psychological determinants of fear of crime: a comparison of general and situational prediction models' *Personality and Individual Differences* **145** (1), 77–85.

Vizard, E., Hickey, N., French, L. and McCrory, E. (2007) 'Children and adolescents who present with sexually abusive behaviour: A UK descriptive study' *Journal of Forensic Psychiatry and Psychology* **18** (1), 59–73.

Voumvakis, S.E. and Ericson, R.V. (1982) *New Accounts of Attacks on Women: A Comparison of Three Toronto Newspapers* Toronto: University of Toronto, Centre of Criminology.

Vrij, A. (2000) *Detecting Lies and Deceit: The psychology of lying and its implications for professional practice* Chichester: John Wiley and Sons.

Vrij, A. (2004) 'Why professionals fail to catch liars and how they can improve' *Legal and Criminological Psychology* **9**, 159–81.

Vrij, A. (2005) 'Criteria-based content analysis: a qualitative review of the first 37 studies' *Psychology, Public Policy, and Law* **11**, 3–41.

Vrij, A. (2008) 'Beliefs about nonverbal and verbal cues to deception' in A. Vrij (ed.), *Detecting Lies and Deceit* Chichester: Wiley, pp. 115–40.

Vrij, A. and Mann, S. (2001) 'Who killed my relative? Police officers' ability to detect real-life high stake lies' *Psychology, Crime and Law* **7**, 119–32.

Vrij, A. and Mann, S. (2005) 'Criteria-based content analysis: an empirical test of its underlying processes' *Psychology, Crime and Law* **12** (4), 337–349.

Vrij, A., Ennis, E., Farman, S. and Mann, S. (2010) 'People's perceptions of their truthful and deceptive interactions in daily life' *Open Access Journal of Forensic Psychology*, **2**, 6–42.

Vrij, A., Fisher, R., Mann, S. and Leal, S. (2009) 'Increasing cognitive load in interviews to detect deceit' in B. Milne, S. Savage and T. Williamson (eds), *International Developments in Investigative Interviewing* (pp. 176–89). Uffculme, UK: Willan Publishing.

Vrij, A., Granhag, A., Mann, S. and Leal, S. (2011) 'Outsmarting the Liars: Toward a Cognitive Lie Detection Approach' *Current Directions in Psychological Science* **20**, 28–32.

Vrij, A., Leal, S., Mann, S. and Fisher, R. (2012) 'Imposing cognitive load to elicit cues to deceit: inducing the reverse order technique naturally' *Psychology, Crime and Law* **18** (6), 579–94.

Vrij, A., Mann, S. and Fisher, R.P. (2006) 'An empirical test of the Behaviour Analysis Interview' *Law and Human Behavior* **30**, 329–45.

Vrij, A., Mann, S., Kristen, S. and Fisher, R.P. (2007) 'Cues to deception and ability to detect lies as a function of police interview styles' *Law and Human Behavior* **31**, 499–518.

Vrij, A., Mann, S., Fisher, R., Leal, S., Milne, B. and Bull, R. (2008) 'Increasing cognitive load to facilitate lie detection: the benefit of recalling an event in reverse order' *Law and Human Behavior*, **32** (3), 253–265.

W

Wagenaar, W.A., van Koppen, P.J. and Crombag, H.F.N. (1993) *Anchored Narratives: The Psychology of Criminal Evidence* Hemel Hempstead: Harvester Wheatsheaf.

Wagstaff, G.F. (1996) 'Should "hypnotized" witnesses be banned from testifying in court? Hypnosis and the M50 murder case' *Contemporary Hypnosis* **13** (3), 186–90.

Wagstaff, G.F. (1997) 'What is hypnosis?' *Interdisciplinary Science Reviews* **22** (2), 155–63.

Wagstaff, G.F., Green, K. and Somers, E. (1997) 'The effects of the experience of hypnosis, and hypnotic depth, on jurors' decisions regarding the defence of hypnotic automatism' *Legal and Criminological Psychology* **2**, 65–74.

Wagstaff, G.F., Macveigh, J., Boston, R., Scott, L., Brunas-Wagstaff, J. and Cole, J. (2003) 'Can laboratory findings on eyewitness testimony be generalized to the real world? An archival analysis of the influence of violence, weapon presence, and age on eyewitness accuracy' *Journal of Psychology: Interdisciplinary and Applied* **137** (1), 17–28.

Wahl, O.F. and Roth, R. (1982) 'Television images of mental illness: results of a metropolitan Washington media watch' *Journal of Broadcasting* **26**, 599–605.

Waite, D., Keller, A., McGarvey, E.L., Wieckowski, E.W., Pinkerton,R. and Brown, G.R. (2005) 'Juvenile sex offender arrest rates for sexual, violent nonsexual and property crimes: a 10-Year follow-up' *Sexual Abuse: A Journal of Research and Treatment* **17** (3), 313–331.

Wakeling, H., Beech, A.R. and Freemantle, N. (2013) 'Investigating treatment change and its relationship to recidivism in a sample of 3773 sex offenders in the UK' *Psychology, Crime and Law* **19** (3), 233–252.

Walker, J.S. and Bright, J.A. (2009) 'Cognitive therapy for violence: reaching the parts that anger management doesn't reach' *Journal of Forensic Psychiatry and Psychology* **20** (2), April, 174–201.

Walker, J.S. and Bright, J.A. (2009) 'False inflated self-esteem and violence: a systematic review and cognitive model' *Journal of Forensic Psychiatry and Psychology* **1**, 1–32.

Walker, K., Bowen, E. and Brown, S.J. (2013) 'Psychological and Criminological Factors Associated with Desistance from Violence: A Review of the Literature' *Aggression and Violent Behavior* **18** (2), 286–99.

Walker, L.E. and Meloy, J.R. (1998) 'Stalking and domestic violence' in J.R. Meloy (ed.) *The Psychology of Stalking: Clinical and Forensic Perspectives* San Diego: Academic Press, pp. 139–61.

Walmsley, R. (2009) 'World prison population list' London, England: Kings College.

Walmsley, R., Howard, L. and White, S. (1992) *The National Prison Survey 1991* London: Her Majesty's Stationery Office.

Walsh, R.M., and Bruce, S.E. (2014) 'Reporting decisions after sexual assault: the impact of mental health variables' *Psychological Trauma: Theory, Research, Practice, and Policy* **6**(6), 691–699.

Walter, N. (1996) 'Dead women who suit the news agenda' *Guardian* 18 January, p. 15.

Waples, S., Gill, M. and Fisher, P. (2009) 'Does CCTV displace crime?' *Criminology and Criminal Justice* **9** (2), 207–224.

Ward, T. (1997) 'Insanity in summary trials' *Journal of Forensic Psychiatry* **8** (3), 658–61.

Ward, T. (2000) 'Sexual offenders' cognitive distortions as implicit theories' *Aggression and Violent Behavior* **5**, 491–507.

Ward, T. (2002) 'Good lives and the rehabilitation of sexual offenders: Promises and problems' *Aggression and Violent Behavior* **7**, 513–528.

Ward, T. (2016) 'Dynamic risk factors: scientific kinds or predictive constructs' *Psychology, Crime and Law* **22** (1–2), 2–16.

Ward, T. and Beech, A. R. (2015) 'Dynamic risk factors: a theoretical dead-end?' *Psychology, Crime and Law* **21**(2), 100–113.

Ward, T. and Brown, M. (2004) 'The good lives model and conceptual issues in offender rehabilitation' *Psychology, Crime, & Law* **10**, 243–57.

Ward, T. and Fortune, C.A. (2013) 'The Good Lives Model: Aligning risk reduction with promoting offenders' personal goals' *European Journal of Probation* **5**, 29–46.

Ward, T. and Hudson, S.M. (2001) 'Finkelhor's precondition model of child sexual abuse: a critique' *Psychology, Crime and Law* **7**, 291–307.

Ward, T. and Keenan, T. (1999) 'Child molesters' implicit theories' *Journal of Interpersonal Violence* **14**, 821–38.

Ward, T. and Marshall, W.L. (2004) 'Good lives, etiology and the rehabilitation of sex offenders: A bridging theory' *Journal of Sexual Aggression* **10**, 153–69.

Ward, T. and Siegert, R.J. (2002) 'Towards a comprehensive theory of child sexual abuse: a theory knitting perspective' *Psychology, Crime and Law* **8**, 319–51.

Ward, T., Gannon, T. and Mann, R. (2007) 'The Good Lives Model of Offender Rehabilitation: Clinical Implications' *Aggression and Violent Behavior* **12**, 87–107.

Ward, T., Polaschek, D.L.L. and Beech, A.R. (2006) *Theories of Sexual Offending* Chichester: John Wiley.

Ware, J. and Mann, R.E. (2012) 'How should "acceptance of responsibility" be addressed in sexual offending treatment programs?' *Aggression and Violent Behavior* **17**, 279–288.

Ware, J., Marshall, W.L. and Marshall, L.E. (2015) 'Categorical denial in convicted sex offenders: the concept, its meaning, and its implication for risk and treatment' *Aggression and Violent Behavior* **25**, 215–226

Warren, A.R. and Woodhall, C.E. (1999) 'The reliability of hearsay testimony: how well do interviewers recall their interviews with children?' *Psychology, Public Policy and Law* **5** (2), 355–71.

Warren, A.R., Nunez, N., Keeney, J.M., Buck, J.A. and Smith, B. (2002) 'The believability of children and their interviewers' hearsay testimony: when less is more' *Journal of Applied Psychology* **87** (5), 846–57.

Warren, A.R., Woodhall, C.E., Hunt, J.S. and Perry, N.W. (1996) 'It sounds good in theory but . . . : do investigative interviewers follow guidelines based on memory research?' *Child Maltreatment* **1**, 231–45.

Warren, J., Kuhn, D. and Weinstock, M. (2010) 'How do jurors argue with one another?' *Judgment and Decision Making* **5** (1), 64–71.

Wason, P.C. (1968) 'Reasoning about a rule' *Quarterly Journal of Experimental Psychology* **20**, 273–81.

Waterhouse, L., Dobash, R.P. and Carnie, J. (1994) *Child Sexual Abusers* Edinburgh: Central Research Unit.

Weber, N. and Perfect, T.J. (2012) 'Improving Eyewitness Identification Accuracy by Screening Out Those Who Say They Don't Know' *Law and Human Behavior* **36** (1), 28–36.

Weber, N., Brewer, N. and Wells, G.L. (2004) 'Is there a "magical" decision latency that discriminates correct from incorrect eyewitness identifications?' Paper presented at 14th conference of the European European Association of Psychology and Law, Krakow, Poland.

Weber, N., Brewer, N., Wells, G., Semmler, C. and Keast, A. (2004) 'Eyewitness identification accuracy and response latency: the unruly 10–12 second rule' *Journal of Experimental Psychology: Applied* **10** (3), 139–47.

Webster, C.D., Douglas, K.S., Eaves, D. and Hart, S.D. (1997). *HCR-20. Assessing risk of violence. Version 2.* Burnaby: Simon Fraser University and Forensic Psychiatric Services Commission of British Columbia.

Webster, M. (2004) 'Do crisis negotiators practice what they preach?' *Canadian Review of Policing Research* **1**. http://crpr.icaap.org/index.php/crpr/article/view/16/15

Weerman, F.M., Bernasco, W., Bruinsma, G.J.N., and Pauwels, L.J.R. (2015) 'When is spending time with peers related to delinquency? the importance of where, what, and with whom' *Crime and Delinquency* **61** (10), 1386–1413.

Weinberg, M., Gil, S., and Gilbar, O. (2014) 'Forgiveness, coping, and terrorism: do tendency to forgive and coping strategies associate with the level of posttraumatic symptoms of injured victims of terror attacks?' *Journal of Clinical Psychology* **70** (7), 693–703.

Weinstock, N. (2011) 'Knowledge-telling and knowledge-transforming arguments in mock jurors' verdict justifications' *Thinking and Reasoning* **17** (3), 282–314.

Weiss, K.J. and Xuan, Y. (2015) 'You can't do that! Hugo Münsterberg and misapplied psychology' *International Journal of Law and Psychology* 42–43, 1–10.

Weissman, S.H., Busch,K.G., and Schouten, R. (2014) 'Introduction to this issue: the evolution of terrorism from 1914 to 2014' *Behavioral Science and the Law* **32**, 259–262.

Weiten, W. and Diamond, S. S. (1979) 'A critical review of the jury simulation paradigm: The case of defendant characteristics' *Law and Human Behavior* **3**, 71–93.

Weller, M.P. and Weller, B.G. (1988) 'Crime and mental illness' *Medicine, Science, and the Law* **28**, 38–45.

Wells, G.L. (1984) 'The psychology of line-up identifications' *Journal of Applied Social Psychology* **14**, 89–103.

Wells, G.L. (1993) 'What do we know about eyewitness identification?' *American Psychologist* **48**, 553–71.

Wells, G.L. and Quinlivan, D.S. (2009) 'Suggestive eyewitness identification procedures and the Supreme Court's Reliability Test in light of eyewitness science: 30 years later' *Law and Human Behavior* **33**, 1–24.

Wells, G.L., Memon, A. and Penrod, S.D. (2006) 'Eyewitness evidence improving its probative value' *Psychological Science in the Public Interest* **7** (2), 45–75.

Wells, G.L., Small, M., Penrod, S., Malpass, R.S., Fulero, S.M. and Brimacombe, C.A.E. (1998) 'Eyewitness identification procedures: recommendations for line-ups and photospreads' *Law and Human Behavior* **22**, 603–47.

Welsh, B.C. and Farrington, D.P. (2002) 'Crime prevention effects of close circuit television: a systematic review' Home Office, London: Home Office Research Study 252.

Welsh, B.C., and Rocque M. (2014) 'When crime prevention harms: a review of systematic reviews' *Journal of Experimental Criminology* 10, 245–266.

Welsh, B.C., Loerber, R., Stevens, B.R., Stouthamer-Loeber, M., Cohen, M.A. and Farrington, D.P. (2008) 'Costs of juvenile crime in urban areas: a longitudinal perspective' *Youth Violence and Juvenile Justice* **6** (1), 3–27.

Wemmers, J.-A. and Cyr, K. (2006a) 'Victims' perspectives on restorative justice: how much involvement are victims looking for?' *International Review of Victimology* **11** (2–3), 259–74.

Wemmers, J.-A. and Cyr, K. (2006b) 'What fairness means to crime victims: a social psychological perspective on victim-offender mediation' *Applied Psychology in Criminal Justice* **2** (2), 102–28.

Wenzel, M., Okimoto, T.G., Feather, N.T. and Platow, M.J. (2008) 'Retributive and restorative justice' *Law and Human Behavior* **32**, 375–89.

West, D.J. (1982) *Delinquency: Its Roots, Careers and Prospects* London: Heinemann.

Westcott, H.L. (1995) 'Children's views on investigative interviews for suspected sexual abuse' *Issues in Criminological and Legal Psychology* Leicester: Division of Criminological and Legal Psychology, British Psychological Society.

Western, B. and Pettit, B. (2010) 'Incarceration and social inequality' *Daedalus* **139**, 8–19.

Wetmore, S.A., Neuschatz, J.S. and Gronlund, S.D. (2014) 'On the power of secondary confession ,evidence' *Psychology, Crime and Law* **20** (4) 339–357.

Wevodau, A. L., Cramer, R. J., Gemberling, T. M. and Clark, J. W. (2016) 'A psychometric assessment of the Community Attitudes Toward Sex Offenders (CATSO) Scale: implications for public policy, trial, and research' *Psychology, Public Policy, and Law.* Advance on line publication.

Wheatcroft, J.M. and Ellison, L.E. (2012) 'Evidence in Court: Witness Preparation and Cross-Examination Style Effects on Adult Witness Accuracy' *Behavioral Science and the Law* **30**, 821–40.

Whelan, C.W., Wagstaff, G. and Wheatcroft, J.M. (2015) 'High stakes lies: police and non-police accuracy in detecting deception' *Psychology, Crime and Law* **21** (2), 127–138.

White, A.J., Meares, S. and Batchelor, J. (2014) 'The role of cognition in fitness to stand trial: a systematic review' *Journal of Forensic Psychiatry and Psychology* **25** (1), 77–99.

Widom, C.S. and Morris, S. (1997) 'Accuracy of adult re-collections of childhood victimization. Part 2 Childhood sexual abuse' *Psychological Assessment* **9** (1), 34–46.

Wiegman, O., Kuttschreuter, M. and Barda, B. (1992) 'A longitudinal study of television viewing on aggressive and prosocial behaviours' *British Journal of Social Psychology* **31**, 147–64.

Wiener, R.L., Krauss, D.A. and Lieberman, J.D. (2011) 'Mock Jury Research: Where Do We Go from Here?' *Behavioral Sciences and the Law* **29** (3), 467–79.

Wikström, P.-O. H. and Treiber, K. (2007) 'The role of self-control in crime causation. beyond Gottfredson and Hirschi's general theory of crime' *European Journal of Criminology* **4** 237–264.

Wikström, P-O., and Treiber, K. (2016) 'Social disadvantage and crime: a criminological puzzle. American Behavioral Scientist' 60(10), 1232–1259.

Willard, J., Madon, S. and Curran, T. (2015) 'Taking blame for other people's misconduct' *Behavioral Sciences and the Law* **33**, 771–783.

Willard, N.E. (2007) *Cyberbullying and Cyberthreats.* Champaign, Illinois: Research Press.

Williams, D. (2007) 'Effective CCTV and the challenge of constructing legitimate suspicion using remote visual images' *Journal of Investigative Psychology and Offender Profiling* **4**, 97–107.

Williams, J. M. G., and Broadbent, K. (1986) 'Autobiographical memory in suicide attempters' *Journal of Abnormal Psychology* **95**, 144–149.

Williams, J.J. (1995) 'Type of counsel and the outcome of criminal appeals: a research note' *American Journal of Criminal Justice* **9** (2), 275–85.

Williams, K.M., Cooper, B.S., Howell, T.M, Yuille, J.C. and Paulhus, D.L. (2009) 'Inferring sexually deviant behavior from corresponding fantasies: the role of personality and pornography consumption' *Criminal Justice and Behavior* **36**, 198–222.

Williams, L. M., and Finkelhor, D. (1990) 'The characteristics of incestuous fathers: a review of recent studies' in W. L. Marshall, D. R. Laws, and H. E. Barbaree (Eds.), *Handbook of Sexual Assault: Issues, Theories, and Treatment of the Offender* (pp. 231–255) New York, NY: Plenum Press.

Williams, M. (1994) 'Murder in mind' *Division of Criminological and Legal Psychology Newsletter* **36**, 9–11.

Williams, W.H., McAuliffe, K.A., Cohen, M.H., Parsonage, M. and Ramsbottham, D.J. (2015) 'Traumatic brain injury and juvenile offending: complex causal links offer multiple targets to reduce crime' *Head Trauma Rehabilitation* **30** (2), 69–74.

Williams, W.H., McAuliffe, K.A., Cohen, M.H., Parsonage, M. and Ramsbottham, D.J. (2015) 'Traumatic brain injury and juvenile offending: complex causal links offer multiple targets to reduce crime' *Journal Head Trauma Rehabilitation*, 30 (2), 69–74.

Williams, W.W. (1991) 'The equality crisis: some reflections on culture, courts and feminism' in K.T. Bartlett and R. Kennedy (eds) *Feminist Legal Theory: Readings in Law and Gender* Boulder, CO: Westview, pp. 15–34.

Willis, J. and Todorov, A. (2006) 'First Impressions: Making Up Your Mind After a 100-Ms Exposure to a Face' *Psychological Science* **17** (7), 592–8.

Willmot, P. (1999) 'Working with life sentence prisoners' *Issues in Forensic Psychology* **1**, 36–8.

Willner, P. (2011) 'Assessment of capacity to participate in court proceedings: a selective critique and some recommendations' *Psychology, Crime and Law* **17** (2), 117–31.

Wilson, C.M., Desmarais, S.L., Nicholls, T.L., Hart, S.D. and Brink, J. (2013) 'Predictive Validity of Dynamic Factors: Assessing Violence Risk in Forensic Psychiatric Inpatients' *Law and Human Behavior* **37** (6), 377–88.

Wilson, H. (1980) 'Parental supervision: a neglected aspect of delinquency' *British Journal of Criminology* **20** (3), 203–35.

Wilson, H.A. and Hoge, R.D. (2013) 'The Effects of Youth Diversion Programs on Recidivism: A Meta-Analytic Review' *Criminal Justice and Behavior* **40** (5), 497–518.

Wilson, J.P. and Zigelbaum, S.D. (1983) 'The Vietnam Veteran on Trial: the relation of post-traumatic stress disorder to criminal behavior' *Behavioral Sciences and the Law* **1**, 69–83.

Wilson, M. and Smith, A. (2000) 'Rules and roles in terrorist hostage taking' in D. Canter and L. Alison (eds) *The Social Psychology of Crime: Groups, Teams and Networks* Aldershot: Ashgate, pp. 129–51.

Wilson, P., Lincoln, R. and Kocsis, R. (1997) 'Validity, utility and ethics of profiling for serial violent and sexual offenders' *Psychiatry, Psychology and Law* **4** (1), 1–11.

Wimbush, J.C. and Dalton, D.R. (1997) 'Base rate for employee theft: Convergence of multiple methods' *Journal of Applied Psychology* **82**, 756–63.

Wingrove, T., Korpas, A.L. and Weis, B. (2011) 'Why were millions of people not obeying the law? Motivational influences on non-compliance with the law in the case of music piracy' *Psychology, Crime and Law* **17** (3), 261–76.

Winkel, F.W. (1998) 'Fear of crime and criminal victimisation' *British Journal of Criminology* **38** (3), 473–84.

Winkel, F.W. (2007) *Post Traumatic Anger: Missing Link in the Wheel of Misfortune* Tilburg University: Intervict.

Winkel, F.W. and Blaauw, E. (2001) 'Structured trauma writing (STW) as a victim-supportive intervention: examining the efficacy of emotional ventilation and downward writing' in R. Rosesch, R.R. Carrado and R. Dempster (eds) *Psychology in the Courts: International Advances in Knowledge* London/New York: Routledge, pp. 317–29.

Winkel, F.W. and Vrij, A. (1998) 'Who is in need of victim support? The issue of accountable, empirically validated selection and victim referral' *Expert Evidence* **6**, 23–41.

Winter, A. (2013) 'The rise and fall of forensic hypnosis' *Studies in History and Philosophy of Biological and Biomedical Sciences* **44**, 26–35.

Wissler, R.L. and Saks, M.J. (1985) 'On the inefficiency of limiting instructions: When jurors use prior conviction evidence to decide on guilt' *Law and Human Behavior* **9**, 37–48.

Witkin, H.A. and Goodenough, D.R. (1981) 'Cognitive styles: essences and origins, field dependence and field independence' *Psychological Issues Monograph No. 51* New York: International Universities Press.

Witkin, H.A., Mednick, S.A. and Schulsinger, F. (1976) 'Criminality in XY and XYY men' *Science* **193**, 547–55.

Wixted, J. T., Mickes, L., Clark, S. E., Gronlund, S. D. and Roediger, H. L. (2015) 'Initial eyewitness confidence reliably predicts eyewitness identification' *American Psychologist* **70**, 515–526.

Wogalter, M.S., Malpass, R.S. and McQuiston, D.E. (2004) 'A national survey of US police on preparation and conduct of identification line-ups' *Psychology, Crime and Law* **10** (1), 69–82.

Wojcikiewicz, J., Bialek, I., Desynski, K. and Dawidowicz, A.L. (2000) 'Mock witness paradigm in the casework of the Institute of Forensic Research in Cracow'. Paper presented at the 10th European Conference on Psychology and Law, Limassol, Cyprus.

Wolf, R.C., Pujara, M.S., Motzkin, J.C., Newman, J.P., Kiehl, K.A., Decety, J., Kosson, D.S., and Koenigs, M. (2015). 'Interpersonal traits of psychopathy linked to reduced integrity of the uncinate fasciculus' *Human Brain Mapping* **36**, 4202–4209.

Wolff, N., Blitz, C.L., Shi, J., Siegel, J. and Bachman, R. (2007) 'Physical violence inside prisons: Rates of victimization' *Criminal Justice and Behavior* **34** (5), 588–99.

Wolfgang, Marvin E., Figlio, R. and Sellin, T. (1994) 'Delinquency in a birth cohort in Philadelphia, Pennsylvania, 1945–1963' ICPSR07729-v3. Ann Arbor, MI: Inter-university Consortium for Political and Social Research.

Wolfman, M., Brown, D., and Jose, P. (2016) 'Talking past each other: interviewer and child verbal exchanges in forensic interviews' *Law and Human Behavior* **40** (2), 107–117.

Wood, H. (2013)'Internet pornography and paedophilia' *Psychoanalytic Psychotherapy* **27** (4), 319–338.

Wood, J.M. (1996) 'Weighting evidence in sexual abuse evaluations: an introduction to Bayes' theorem' *Child Maltreatment* **1**, 25–36.

Wood, W., Wong, F.Y. and Chachere, J.G. (1991) 'Effects of media violence on viewers' aggression in unconstrained social interaction' *Psychological Bulletin* **109** (3), 371–83.

Wood, W.R. (2015) 'Why restorative justice will not reduce incarceration' *British Journal of Criminology* **55**, 883–900

Woodhams, J., Grant, T.D. and Price, A.R.G. (2007) 'From marine ecology to crime analysis: improving the detection of serial sexual offences using a taxonomic similarity measure' *Journal of Investigative Psychology and Offender Profiling* **4**, 17–27.

Woodhams, J., Hollin, C.R. and Bull, R. (2007) 'The psychology of linking crimes: A review of the evidence' *Legal and Criminological Psychology* **12**, 233–49.

Woodward, R. (1999) 'Therapeutic regimes' *Issues in Forensic Psychology* **1**, 39–43.

Woody, W.D. and Forrest, K.D. (2009) 'Effects of false-evidence ploys and expert testimony on jurors' verdicts, recommended sentences, and perceptions of confession evidence' *Behavioral Sciences and the Law* **27**, 333–60.

Woolard, J.L., Harvell, S. and Graham, S. (2008) 'Behavioral sciences and the law: anticipatory injustice among adolescents: age and racial/ethnic differences in perceived unfairness of the justice system' *Behavioral Sciences and the Law* **26**, 207–26.

Woolley, J.D. (1997) 'Thinking about fantasy: are children fundamentally different thinkers and believers from adults?' *Child Development* **68**, 991–1011.

Wootton, I. and Brown, J. (2000) 'Balancing occupational and personal identities: the experience of lesbian and gay police officers' *Newsletter of the BPS Lesbian and Gay Psychology Section* **4** (March), 6–13.

World Health Organization (2007) 'Preventing suicide in jails and prisons' Geneva: WHO Document Production Services.

World Health Organization (1993) *Composite International Diagnostic Interview (CIDI)* World Health Organization, Geneva, Switzerland.

World Health Organization (2011) International Classification of Diseases. http://www.who.int/classifications/icd/en/. Accessed 21 March 2011.

Worling, J.R. (1995) 'Sexual abuse histories of adolescent male sex offenders: differences on the basis of the age and gender of their victims' *Journal of Abnormal Psychology* **104** (4), 610–13.

Wormith, J.A. (1986) 'Assessing deviant sexual arousal: physiological and cognitive aspects' *Advances in Behaviour Research and Therapy* **8** (3), 101–37.

Wormith, J.S. and Oliver, M.E. (2002) 'Offender treatment attrition and its relationship with risk, responsivity, and recidivism' *Criminal Justice and Behavior* **29**, 447–71.

Wright, A.M. and Alison, L. (2004) 'Questioning sequences in Canadian police interviews: constructing and confirming the course of events?' *Psychology, Crime and Law* **10** (2), 137–54.

Wright, M. (2002) 'The court as last resort: victim-sensitive, community-based responses to crime' *British Journal of Criminology* **42** (3), 657–67.

Wrightsman, L.S. (2001) *Forensic Psychology* Stamford, CT: Wadsworth.

Wurtele, S. K., Simons, D. and Moreno, T. (2014) 'Sexual interest in children among an online sample of men and women: Prevalence and correlates' *Sexual Abuse: A Journal of Research and Treatment*, **26**, 546–568.

Wyatt, G.W. (1985) 'The sexual abuse of Afro-American and white American women in childhood' *Child Abuse and Neglect* **9**, 507–19.

Wyre, R. (1987) *Working with Sex Offenders* Oxford: Perry.

Wyre, R. (1990) 'Why do men sexually abuse children?' in T. Tate (ed.) *Understanding the Paedophile* London: ISTD/The Portman Clinic, pp. 17–23.

Wyre, R. (1992) 'Pornography and sexual violence: working with sex offenders' in C. Itzin (ed.) *Pornography: Women, Violence and Civil Liberties* Oxford: Oxford University Press, pp. 236–47.

Wyre, R. and Tate, T. (1995) *The Murder of Childhood* Harmondsworth: Penguin.

M. Yang, S. C. P. Wong, and J. Coid 'The efficacy of violence prediction: a meta-analytic comparison of nine risk assessment tools'. *Psychological Bulletin* **136** (5), 740–767, 2010.

Yates, P.M. (2009) 'Is sexual offender denial related to sex offence risk and recidivism? a review and treatment implications' *Psychology, Crime and Law* **15** (2–3), 183–199.

Yokota, K., Fujita, G., Watanabe, K., Yoshimoto, K. and Wachi, T. (2007) 'Application of the Behavioral Investigative Support System for Profiling Perpetrators of Serial Sexual Assaults' *Behavioral Science and the Law* **25**, 841–56.

Yokota, K., Iwami, H., Watanabe, K., Fujita, G. and Watanabe, S. (2004) 'High risk factors of hostage barricade incidents in a Japanese sample' *Journal of Investigative Psychology and Offender Profiling* **1**, 139–51.

Yokota, K., Watanabe, K., Wachi, T., Hoshino, A., Sato, A. and Fujita, G. (2007) 'Differentiation of international terrorism: attack as threat, means, and violence' *Journal of Investigative Psychology and Offender Profiling* **4**, 131–45.

Yoshikawa, H. (1995) 'Long-term effects of early childhood programs on social outcomes and delinquency' *The Future of Children* **5** (3), 51–75.

Youngs, D. (2004) 'Personality correlates of offence style' *Journal of Investigative Psychology and Offender Profiling* **1**, 99–119.

Yudofsky, S.C., Silver, J.M., Jackson, W., Endicott, J. and Williams, D.W. (1986) 'The Overt Aggression Scale for the objective rating of verbal and physical aggression' *The American Journal of Psychiatry* **143**, 35–9.

Yuille, J.C. and Cutshall, J.L. (1986) 'A case study of eyewitness memory of a crime' *Journal of Applied Psychology* **71** (2), 291–301.

Yuille, J.C. and Daylen, J. (1998) 'The impact of traumatic events on eyewitness memory' in C. Thompson, D. Hermann, D. Read, D. Payne and M. Toglia (eds) *Eyewitness memory: Theoretical and applied perspectives* Hillsdale, NJ: Lawrence Erlbaum, pp. 155–78.

Yuille, J.C., Ternes, M. and Cooper, B.S. (2010) 'Expert testimony on laboratory witnesses' *Journal of Forensic Psychology Practice* **10** (3), 238–51.

Yun, I., and Lee, J. (2013) 'IQ and delinquency: the differential detection hypothesis revisited' *Youth Violence and Juvenile Justice* **11** (3), 196–211.

Z

Zahn, M.A. (2007) 'The causes of girls' delinquency and their program implications' *Family Court Review* **45** (3), 456–65.

Zajac, R., Gross, J. and Hayne, H. (2003) 'Asked and answered: questioning children in the courtroom' *Psychiatry, Psychology and Law* **10** (1), 199–209.

Zandbergen, P.A., Levenson, J.S. and Hart, T.C. (2010) 'Residential proximity to schools and daycares: an empirical analysis of sex offense recidivism' *Criminal Justice and Behavior* **37**, 482–502.

Zapf, P.A. and Roesch, R. (2001) 'A comparison of American and Canadian conceptualizations of comptence to stand trial' in R. Roesch, R.R. Carrado and R. Dempster (eds) *Psychology in the Courts: International Advances in Knowledge* London: Routledge, pp. 121–32.

Zauberman, R. (2009) 'Self-reported crime and deviance studies in Europe: current state of knowledge and review of use' Brussels: VUB Press.

Zeisel, H. (1971) 'And then there was none: the diminution of federal jury' *University of Chicago Law Review* **35**, 228–41.

Zeisel, H. and Diamond, S.S. (1978) 'The effect of peremptory challenges on jury and verdict: an experiment in a federal district court' *Stanford Law Review* **30**, 491–531.

Zhang, Y., Ming, Q., Wang, X, and Yao, S. (2016) 'The interactive effect of the MAOA-VNTR genotype and childhood abuse on aggressive behaviors in Chinese male adolescents' *Psychiatric Genetics* **26** (3), 117–123.

Ziemke, M.H., and Brodskly, S.L. (2015) 'To flatter the jury: ingratiation during closing arguments' *Psychiatry, Psychology and Law* **22** (5), 688–700.

Zillmann, D. (1979) *Hostility and Aggression* Hillsdale, NJ: Lawrence Erlbaum.

Zillmann, D. (1982) 'Television viewing and arousal' in D. Pearl, L. Bouthilet and J. Law (eds) *Television and Behavior: Ten Years of Scientific Progress and Implications for the Eighties* Washington, DC: US Government Printing Office, pp. 53–65.

Zinzow, H.M., Rheingold, A.A., Byczkiewicz, M., Saunders, B.E., and Kilpatrick, D.G. (2011) 'Examining posttraumatic stress symptoms in a national sample of homicide survivors: prevalence and comparison to other violence victims' *Journal of Traumatic Stress*, 24 (6), 743-746.

Name Index

Subject Index